Services Marketing

**Integrating Customer Focus
Across the Firm**

Fifth Edition

Valarie A. Zeithaml
*University of North Carolina at
Chapel Hill*

Mary Jo Bitner
Arizona State University

Dwayne D. Gremler
Bowling Green State University

Boston   Burr Ridge, IL   Dubuque, IA   Madison, WI   New York   San Francisco   St. Louis
Bangkok   Bogotá   Caracas   Kuala Lumpur   Lisbon   London   Madrid   Mexico City
Milan   Montreal   New Delhi   Santiago   Seoul   Singapore   Sydney   Taipei   Toronto

The McGraw-Hill Companies

SERVICES MARKETING: INTEGRATING CUSTOMER FOCUS ACROSS THE FIRM
International Edition 2009

Exclusive rights by McGraw-Hill Education (Asia), for manufacture and export. This book
cannot be re-exported from the country to which it is sold by McGraw-Hill. This International
Edition is not to be sold or purchased in North America and contains content that is different
from its North American version.

Published by McGraw-Hill/Irwin, a business unit of The McGraw-Hill Companies, Inc., 1221
Avenue of the Americas, New York, NY, 10020. Copyright © 2009, 2006, 2003, 2000, 1996 by
The McGraw-Hill Companies, Inc.. All rights reserved. No part of this publication may be
reproduced or distributed in any form or by any means, or stored in a database or retrieval
system, without the prior written consent of The McGraw-Hill Companies, Inc., including, but
not limited to, in any network or other electronic storage or transmission, or broadcast for
distance learning.

Some ancillaries, including electronic and print components, may not be available to
customers outside the United States.

10 09 08 07 06 05 04 03 02 01
20 09 08
CTF   ANL

When ordering this title, use ISBN: 978-007-126393-1 or MHID: 007-126393-4

Printed in the Singapore

www.mhhe.com

Aan mijn alleriefste, Jan Benedict Steenkamp—husband, colleague, and friend.

—V.A.Z.

In loving memory of my father, Ralph Heuving—immigrant, entrepreneur, writer, and philosopher.

—M.J.B.

To my wife, Candy, for her many years of love, support, and encouragement.

—D.D.G.

About the Authors

Mary Jo Bitner (left), Valarie Zeithaml, and Dwayne Gremler

Valarie A. Zeithaml   *University of North Carolina—Chapel Hill*

VALARIE ZEITHAML is the David S. Van Pelt Professor of Marketing at the Kenan-Flagler Business School of the University of North Carolina at Chapel Hill. Since receiving her MBA and PhD in marketing from the Robert H. Smith School of Business at the University of Maryland, Professor Zeithaml has devoted her career to researching and teaching the topics of service quality and services management. She is the co-author of *Delivering Quality Service: Balancing Customer Perceptions and Expectations* (Free Press, 1990), now in its 17th printing; and *Driving Customer Equity: How Customer Lifetime Value Is Reshaping Corporate Strategy* (with Roland Rust and Katherine Lemon. Free Press, 2000). In 2002, *Driving Customer Equity* won the first Berry–American Marketing Association Book Prize for the best marketing book of the past three years.

In 2008, Professor Zeithaml won the Paul D. Converse Award from the American Marketing Association. The Converse Award, granted every four years to one or more persons, acknowledges enduring contributions to marketing through one or more journal articles, books, or a body of work. She was recognized for her work with colleagues on service quality, specifically for two articles: "A Conceptual Model of Service Quality and Its Implications for Future Research," in the *Journal of Marketing,* and "SERVQUAL: A Multiple-Item Scale for Measuring Service Quality," in the *Journal of Retailing.* In 2004, Professor Zeithaml received both the Innovative Contributor to Marketing Award given by the Marketing Management Association and the Outstanding Marketing Educator Award given by the Academy of Marketing Science. In 2001, she received the American Marketing Association's Career Contributions to the Services Discipline Award.

Professor Zeithaml has won five teaching awards, including the Gerald Barrett Faculty Award from the University of North Carolina and the Fuqua School Outstanding MBA Teaching Award from Duke University. She is also the recipient of numerous research awards, including the Robert Ferber Consumer Research Award from the *Journal of Consumer Research,* the Harold H. Maynard Award from the *Journal of Marketing,* the MSI Paul Root Award from the *Journal of Marketing,* the

Jagdish Sheth Award from the *Journal of the Academy of Marketing Science,* and the William F. O'Dell Award from the *Journal of Marketing Research.* She has consulted with more than 50 service and product companies.

Professor Zeithaml served on the Board of Directors of the American Marketing Association from 2000 to 2003 and was an Academic Trustee of the Marketing Science Institute between 2000 and 2006.

Mary Jo Bitner   *Arizona State University*

MARY JO BITNER is the PetSmart Chair in Services Leadership in the Marketing Department at the W. P. Carey School of Business, Arizona State University. She also serves as Academic Director for the Center for Services Leadership at ASU. Dr. Bitner was a founding faculty member of the Center for Services Leadership and has been a leader in its emergence as a premier university-based center for the study of services marketing and management. At ASU, she led the development of the W. P. Carey MBA Services Marketing and Management specialization. Alumni of this program now work in companies across the United States, leading the implementation of services and customer-focused strategies. Dr. Bitner has published more than 50 articles and has received a number of awards for her research in leading journals, including the *Journal of Marketing, Journal of the Academy of Marketing Science, Journal of Service Research, Journal of Business Research, Journal of Retailing, Business Horizons, International Journal of Service Industry Management,* and *Academy of Management Executive.* She has consulted with and presented seminars and workshops for numerous business, including Yellow Roadway Corporation. Ford Motor Company, CVSCaremark, IBM Global Services, Mayo Clinic, and RR Donnelley. In 2003, Dr. Bitner was honored with the Career Contributions to the Services Discipline award by the American Marketing Association. She was named an IBM Faculty Fellow in 2005 for her leadership in services science.

Dwayne D. Gremler   *Bowling Green State University*

DWAYNE D. GREMLER is Professor of Marketing at Bowling Green State University. He received his MBA and PhD degrees from the W. P. Carey School of Business at Arizona State University. Throughout his academic career, Dr. Gremler has been a passionate advocate for the research and instruction of services marketing issues. He has served as Chair of the American Marketing Association's Services Marketing Special Interest Group and has helped organize services marketing conferences in Australia, The Netherlands, France, and the United States. Dr. Gremler has been invited to conduct seminars and present research on services marketing issues in several countries. Dr. Gremler's research addresses customer loyalty in service businesses, customer-employee interactions in service delivery, service guarantees, and word-of-mouth communication. He has published articles in the *Journal of Marketing, Journal of the Academy of Marketing Science, Journal of Service Research, Journal of Business Research, International Journal of Service Industry Management, Journal of the Academy of Marketing Science,* and *Journal of Marketing Education.* In 2006 Dr. Gremler was a Fulbright Scholar at the University of Maastricht, The Netherlands. He has also been the recipient of several research awards at BGSU, including the College of Business Administration Outstanding Scholar Award and the Robert A. Patton Scholarly Achievement Award. While a professor at the University of Idaho. Dr. Gremler received the First Interstate Bank Student Excellence in Award for teaching, an award determined by students in the College of Business and Economics.

Preface

This text is for students and businesspeople who recognize the vital role that services play in the economy and its future. The advanced economies of the world are now dominated by services, and virtually all companies view service as critical to retaining their customers today and in the future. Even manufacturing companies that, in the past, have depended on their physical products for their livelihood now recognize that service provides one of their few sustainable competitive advantages.

We wrote this book in recognition of the ever-growing importance of services and the unique challenges faced by managers of services.

WHY A SERVICES MARKETING TEXT?

Since the beginning of our academic careers in marketing, we have devoted our research and teaching efforts to topics in services marketing. We strongly believe that services marketing is different from goods marketing in significant ways and that it requires strategies and tactics that traditional marketing texts do not fully reflect. This text is unique in both content and structure, and we hope that you will learn from it as we have in writing and revising it now for almost 15 years. Over this time period we have incorporated major changes and developments in the field, keeping the book up to date with new knowledge, changes in management practice, and the global economic trend toward services.

Content Overview

The foundation of the text is the recognition that services present special challenges that must be identified and addressed. Issues commonly encountered in service organizations—the inability to inventory, difficulty in synchronizing demand and supply, challenges in controlling the performance quality of human interactions, and customer participation as cocreators of value—need to be articulated and tackled by managers. Many of the strategies include information and approaches that are new to managers across industries. We wrote the text to help students and managers understand and address these special challenges of services marketing.

The development of strong customer relationships through quality service (and services) are at the heart of the book's content. The topics covered are equally applicable to organizations whose core product is service (such as banks, transportation companies, hotels, hospitals, educational institutions, professional services, telecommunication) and to organizations that depend on service excellence for competitive advantage (high-technology manufacturers, automotive and industrial products, and so on). Rarely do we repeat material from marketing principles or marketing strategy texts. Instead, we adjust, when necessary, standard content on topics such as distribution, pricing, and promotion to account for service characteristics.

The book's content focuses on knowledge needed to implement service strategies for competitive advantage across industries. Included are frameworks for customer-focused management and strategies for increasing customer satisfaction and retention through service. In addition to standard marketing topics (such as pricing), this text introduces students to entirely new topics that include management and measurement of service quality, service recovery, the linking of customer measurement to performance measurement, service blueprinting, customer coproduction, and cross-functional treatment of issues through integration of marketing with disciplines such as operations and human resources. Each of these topics represents pivotal content for tomorrow's businesses as they structure around process rather than task, engage in one-to-one marketing, mass customize their offerings, cocreate value with their customers, and attempt to build strong relationships with their customers.

Distinguishing Content Features

The distinguishing features of our text and the new features in this edition include the following:

1. Greater emphasis on the topic of service quality than existing marketing and service marketing texts.
2. Increased focus on customer expectations and perceptions and what they imply for marketers.
3. A feature called "Strategy Insight" in each chapter—a feature that focuses on emerging or existing strategic initiatives involving services.
4. Increased coverage of business-to-business service applications.
5. Two original cases written specifically for this textbook, one on JetBlue's service disaster in 2007 and one on Caterpillar's decision to become an integrated solution provider.
6. Increased technology and Internet coverage, including updated "Technology Spotlight" boxes in each chapter.
7. A chapter on service recovery that includes a conceptual framework for understanding the topic.
8. A chapter on the financial and economic impact of service quality.
9. A chapter on customer-defined service standards.
10. Cross-functional treatment of issues through integration of marketing with other disciplines such as operations and human resources management.
11. Consumer-based pricing and value pricing strategies.
12. A chapter on integrated services marketing communications that includes the new media and social networking.
13. Description of a set of tools that must be added to basic marketing techniques when dealing with services rather than goods.
14. Introduction of three service Ps to the traditional marketing mix and increased focus on customer relationships and relationship marketing strategies.
15. An entire chapter that recognizes human resource challenges and human resource strategies for delivering customer-focused services.
16. Coverage of service innovation and design processes and a detailed and complete introduction to service blueprinting—a tool for describing, designing, and positioning services.
17. Coverage of the customer's role in service delivery and strategies for making customers productive partners in service and value creation.
18. A chapter on the role of physical evidence, particularly the physical environment or "servicescape."
19. Global Feature boxes in each chapter and expanded examples of global services marketing.
20. Exercises in each chapter.
21. Updated or new examples throughout the text.

Conceptual and Research Foundations

We synthesized research and conceptual material from many talented academics and practitioners to create this text. We relied on pioneering work of researchers and businesspeople from diverse disciplines such as marketing, human resources, operations, and management. Because the field of services marketing is international in its roots, we also have drawn from work originating around the globe. We have continued this strong conceptual grounding in the fifth edition by integrating new research into every chapter. The framework of the book is managerially focused, with every chapter presenting company examples and strategies for addressing issues in the chapter.

Conceptual Frameworks in Chapters

We developed integrating frameworks in most chapters. For example, we created new frameworks for understanding service recovery strategies, service pricing, integrated marketing communications, customer relationships, customer roles, and internal marketing.

Unique Structure

The text features a structure completely different from the standard 4P (marketing mix) structure of most marketing texts. The text is organized around the gaps model of service quality, which is described fully in Chapter 2. Beginning with Chapter 3, the text is organized into parts around the gaps model. For example, Chapters 3, 4, and 5 each deal with an aspect of the customer gap—customer behavior, expectations, and perceptions, respectively—to form the focus for services marketing strategies. The managerial content in the rest of the chapters is framed by the gaps model using part openers that build the model gap by gap. Each part of the book includes multiple chapters with strategies for understanding and closing these critical gaps.

Fully Integrated Text

In the 1980s and early 1990s, the field of services marketing was so new that insufficient material had been written on the topic to create a traditional text. For that reason, the books used as texts contained cases and readings that had to be interpreted by educators for their students. These early services marketing books were therefore different from standard texts—where the major function is to synthesize and conceptualize the material—and placed a burden on the professor to blend the components. This book contains integrated text materials, thereby removing from professors and students the tremendous burden of synthesis and compilation.

WHAT COURSES AND STUDENTS CAN USE THE TEXT?

In our years of experience teaching services marketing, we have found that a broad cross-section of students is drawn to learning about services marketing. Students with career interests in services industries as well as goods industries with high service components (such as industrial products, high-tech products, and durable products) want and need to understand these topics. Students who wish to become consultants and entrepreneurs want to learn the strategic view of marketing, which involves not just physical goods but also the myriad services that envelop and add value to these goods. Virtually all students—even those who will work for packaged goods firms—will face employers needing to understand the basics of services marketing and management.

Although services marketing courses are usually designated as marketing electives, a large number of enrollees in our classes have been finance students seeking to broaden their knowledge and career opportunities in financial services. Business students with human resource, information technology, accounting, and operations majors also enroll, as do nonbusiness students from such diverse disciplines as health administration, recreation and parks, public and nonprofit administration, law, sports management, and library science.

Students need only a basic marketing course as a prerequisite for a services marketing course and this text. The primary target audience for the text is services marketing classes at the undergraduate (junior or senior elective courses), graduate (both masters and doctoral courses), and executive student levels. Other target audiences are (1) service management classes at both the undergraduate and graduate levels and (2) marketing management classes at the graduate level in which a professor wishes to provide more comprehensive teaching of services than is possible with a standard marketing management text. A subset of chapters would also provide a more concise text for use in a quarter-length or mini-semester course. A further reduced set of chapters may be used to supplement undergraduate and graduate basic marketing courses to enhance the treatment of services.

WHAT CAN WE PROVIDE EDUCATORS TO TEACH SERVICES MARKETING?

As a team, we have accumulated more than 60 years of experience teaching the subject of services marketing. We set out to create a text that represents the approaches we have found most effective. We incorporated all that we have learned in our many years of teaching services marketing—teaching materials, student exercises, case analyses, research, and PowerPoint slides, which you can find online at www.mhhe. com/Zeithaml5e, along with a comprehensive instructor's manual and test bank.

HOW MANY PARTS AND CHAPTERS ARE INCLUDED, AND WHAT DO THEY COVER?

The text material includes 18 chapters divided into seven parts. Part 1 includes an introduction in Chapter 1 and an overview of the gaps model in Chapter 2. Part 2 discusses the focus on the customer. Part 3 focuses on listening to customer requirements, including chapters covering marketing research for services, building customer relationships, and service recovery. Part 4 involves aligning service strategy through design and standards and includes chapters on service innovation and design, customer-defined service standards, and physical evidence and the servicescape. Part 5 concerns the delivery and performance of service and has chapters on employees' and customers' roles in service delivery, conveying service through intermediaries and electronic channels, and managing demand and capacity. Part 6 focuses on managing services promises and includes chapters on integrated services marketing communications and pricing of services. Finally, Part 7 examines the financial and economic effect of service quality.

THE SUPPLEMENTARY MATERIALS

Instructor's Manual

The *Instructor's Manual* includes sample syllabi, suggestions for in-class exercises and projects, teaching notes for each of the cases included in the text, and answers to end-of-chapter discussion questions and exercises. The *Instructor's Manual* uses the "active learning" educational paradigm, which involves students in constructing their own learning experiences and exposes them to the collegial patterns present in work situations. Active learning offers an educational underpinning for the pivotal work-force skills required in business, among them oral and written communication skills, listening skills, and critical thinking and problem solving.

PowerPoint

We have provided PowerPoint slides online for each chapter and case, including fig-ures and tables from the text that are useful for instructors in class. The full-color PowerPoint slides were created to present a coordinated look for course presentation.

Test Bank

We have also provided test bank files and a computerized test bank, which are avail-able on this text's Online Learning Center. Instructors can easily formulate quizzes and tests from this trusted source.

ACKNOWLEDGMENTS

We owe a great deal to the pioneering service researchers and scholars who developed the field of services marketing. They include John Bateson, Leonard Berry, Bernard Booms, David Bowen, Steve Brown, Larry Crosby. John Czepiel, Ray Fisk, William George, Christian Gronroos, Steve Grove, Evert Gummesson, Chuck Lamb, the late Christopher Lovelock, Parsu Parasuraman, Ben Schneider, Lynn Shostack, and Carol Surprenant. We also owe gratitude to the second generation of service researchers who broadened and enriched the services marketing field. When we attempted to compile a list of those researchers, we realized that it was too extensive to include here. The length of that list is testament to the influence of the early pioneers and to the importance that services marketing has achieved both in academia and practice.

We remain indebted to Parsu Parasuraman and Len Berry, who have been research partners of Dr. Zeithaml's since 1982. The gaps model around which the text is structured was developed in collaboration with them, as was the model of customer expectations used in Chapter 4. Much of the research and measurement content in this text was shaped by what the team found in a 15-year program of research on ser-vice quality.

Dr. Zeithaml also expresses special thanks to Dr. William Schopf, her high school English teacher who gave her a passion for writing. For this edition, she is especially grateful to Holger "HoPi" Pietzsch, Jose "Pepe" Brousset, and Anne Warth of the Latin American Division of Caterpillar Inc. Working with them to provide integrated solutions with products and services led to one of the original cases in this textbook. She thanks the staff of the MBA Program at the Kenan-Flagler Business School at University of North Carolina at Chapel Hill for allowing her to see the gaps model in action while she served as MBA Associate Dean. In particular, Mindy Storrie, Michael Stepanek, Sherry Wallace, Anna Millar, Diane Horton, and Meghan Gosk demonstrated how leadership and teamwork could close the gaps in a complex service organization. She also thanks her colleagues, MBA students, and EMBA students at the University of North Carolina. The students' interest in the topic of services mar-keting, their creativity in approaching the papers and assignments, and their continu-ing contact are appreciated. As always, she credits the Marketing Science Institute, of which she was a researcher and academic trustee, for the ongoing inspiration from their many conferences and working papers. She is especially indebted to David Reibstein, Leigh McAllister, and Donald Lehman for their support and talent.

Dr. Bitner expresses special thanks to the W. P. Carey School of Business at Arizona State University, in particular to Steve Brown and the Center for Services Leadership staff as well as Michael Mokwa and the Department of Marketing faculty and staff. Their support and encouragement has been invaluable throughout the multiple editions of this book. Dr. Bitner also acknowledges the many ideas and examples provided by the 45 member companies of the Center for Services Leadership that are committed to service excellence and that she has the opportunity to continually learn from. For this edition, Dr. Bitner wants to especially acknowledge the leadership of the IBM Corporation through its research divisions, in particular James Spohrer and Paul Maglio of IBM's Almaden Research Center, for inspiring academics, government employees and businesspeople around the world to begin focusing on the science of service. She is also grateful to Buck Pei, Associate Dean for Asia Programs at the W. P. Carey School for providing the opportunity to teach a course on service excellence in ASU's China EMBA. The experience has enriched this book and provided tremendous learning. She also acknowledges and thanks her colleague Amy Ostrom for her support and invaluable assistance in sharing examples, new research, and creative teaching innovations. Finally, Dr. Bitner is grateful to the fine group of Arizona State services doctoral students she has worked with who have shaped her thinking and supported the text: Lois Mohr, Bill Faranda, Amy Rodie, Kevin Gwinner, Matt Meuter, Steve Tax, Dwayne Gremler, Lance Bettencourt, Susan Cadwallader, Felicia Morgan, Thomas Hollmann, Andrew Gallan, and Martin Mende.

Dr. Gremler expresses thanks to several people, beginning with his mentor, Steve Brown, for his advice and encouragement. He thanks other Arizona State University faculty who served as role models and encouragers, including John Schlacter, Michael Mokwa, Kenn Rowe, David Altheide, Dave Gourley, and Ken Evans. Dr. Gremler also thanks those colleagues with whom he has worked on service marketing research projects in recent years. including Steve Brown, Mary Jo Bitner, Kevin Gwinner, Thorsten Hennig-Thurau, Markus Groth, Michael Paul, Caroline Wiertz, Gianfranco Walsh, Mike McCollough, David Martin Ruiz, Judy Washburn, Gabi Cepeda Carrión, Jeroen Bleijerveld, Lisa Brüggen, and Bram Foubert. He acknowledges the fellowship with and support of fellow doctoral student colleagues from Arizona State University, particularly Kevin Gwinner, Mark Houston, John Eaton, Lance Bettencourt, Amy Rodie, Matt Meuter, Steve Tax, and Bill Faranda. Dr. Gremler also expresses thanks to colleagues at various universities who have invited him to speak in their countries in recent years and have provided insight into services marketing issues internationally, including Jos Lemmink, Ko de Ruyter, Hans Kasper, Chiara Orsingher, Stefan Michel, Thorsten Hennig-Thurau, Silke Michalski, Brigitte Auriacombe, David Martin Ruiz, Caroline Wiertz, Vince Mitchell, Sina Fichtel, Nina Specht, Kathy Tyler, Bo Edvardsson, Patrik Larsson, Tor Andreassen, Jens Hogreve, Andreas Eggert, Andreas Bausch, and Thomas Fritz. Finally, a special thanks to Candy Gremler for her unending willingness to serve as copy editor, encourager, wife, and friend.

The panel of academics who helped us by completing a survey include Olivia Lee, St. Cloud State University; Julie Guidry, Louisiana State University; John A. Grant, Ohio Dominican University; Michael F. Walsh, West Virginia University; Khaled Kevin Deeb, Barry University; Lisa Wiltsie, University of Southern Indiana; Edward E. Ackerley, University of Arizona; Sandy Becker, Rutgers Business School;

Gary G. Gray, Johnson & Wales University; Jo Ann Duffy, Sam Houston State University; and Julie Messing, Kent State University.

Finally, we would like to acknowledge the professional efforts of the McGraw-Hill/Irwin staff. Our sincere thanks to Brent Gordon, Paul Ducham, Sara Hunter, Laura Hurst Spell, Dean Karampelas, Dana Pauley, Michael McCormick, Joanne Mennemeier, JoAnne Schopler, Lori Kramer, and Suresh Babu.

Valarie A. Zeithaml

Mary Jo Bitner

Dwayne D. Gremler

Brief Contents

Detailed Contents

Chapter 8
Service Recovery 211

PART 4
ALIGNING SERVICE DESIGN AND STANDARDS 247

Chapter 9
Service Innovation and Design 248

List of Boxes

Foundations for Services Marketing

This first part of the text provides you with the foundations needed to begin your study of services marketing. The first chapter identifies up-to-date trends, issues, and opportunities in services as a backdrop for the strategies addressed in remaining chapters. The second chapter introduces the gaps model of service quality, the framework that provides the structure for the text. The remaining parts of the book will include information and strategies to address specific gaps, giving you the tools and knowledge to become a services marketing leader.

Chapter One

Introduction to Services

This chapter's objectives are to

1. Explain what services are and identify important trends in services.
2. Explain the need for special services marketing concepts and practices and why the need has developed and is accelerating.
3. Explore the profound impact of technology on service.
4. Outline the basic differences between goods and services and the resulting challenges and opportunities for service businesses.
5. Introduce the expanded marketing mix for services and the philosophy of customer focus as powerful frameworks and themes that are fundamental to the rest of the text.

"Services are going to move in this decade to being the front edge of the industry."

This quote from IBM's former CEO, Louis V. Gerstner, illustrates the changes sweeping across industry in the 21st century. Many businesses that were once viewed as manufacturing giants are shifting their focus to services. And, in many ways, IBM has led the pack. Actions of current IBM CEO, Sam Palmisano, have reinforced this focus on service. In his tenure, Mr. Palmisano has led IBM in the expansion of its outsourcing businesses and accentuated its focus on client solutions. He also led IBM in its purchase of PriceWaterhouseCoopers to gain broader strategic services consulting expertise and in its focus in service "products" and solutions.

In a company brochure IBM states that it is the largest *service* business in the world. It is the global leader in information technology (IT) services and consulting with approximately 200,000 services professionals around the world. Through its Global Services division, IBM offers product support services, professional consulting services, and network computing services. Many businesses have outsourced entire service functions to IBM, counting on the company to provide the services better than anyone else. The services side of IBM brings in $48 billion, more than half the company's total revenue. The services strategy has been very successful for IBM to date and promises to be the engine of growth into the future (see the "New Wave of Services" graphic).

No one in IBM would suggest that these positive results have been easily achieved. Switching from a manufacturing to a service and customer focus is indeed a challenge.

It requires changes in management mind-set, changes in culture, changes in the ways people work and are rewarded, and new ways of implementing customer solutions. At IBM this change has evolved over decades. It is suggested that Lou Gerstner's legacy at IBM may well be the definitive switch that the company has made from hardware to services and the strategic focus on customers. This switch to service has carried over into IBM's research division as well, where hundreds of researchers currently focus on service science and service innovation.

Many companies (such as Hewlett-Packard, Oracle, and Cisco) have viewed IBM's success and are pushing to make the same transition to services. It is not as easy as it looks. In moving into services, companies discover what service businesses such as hospitality, consulting, health care, financial services, and telecommunications have known for years: services marketing and management are different—not totally unique, but different. Selling and delivering a computer is not the same as selling and delivering a service that solves a customer's problem.[1]

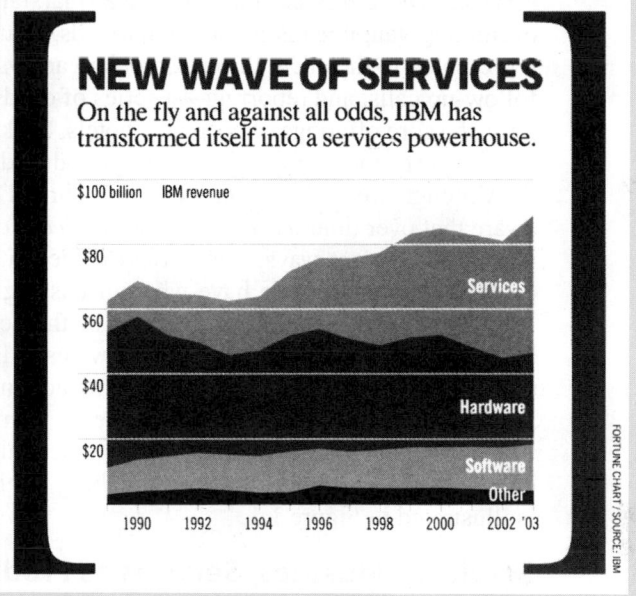

NEW WAVE OF SERVICES

On the fly and against all odds, IBM has transformed itself into a services powerhouse.

As the opening vignette suggests, services are not limited to service industries, services can be very profitable, and services are challenging to manage and market. Services represent a huge and growing percentage of the world economy; yet particularly in the United States, customer perceptions of service are not good.[2] In fact, the University of Michigan's American Customer Satisfaction Index has shown consistently lower scores for services when compared to other products.[3] Given the economic growth in services, their profit and competitive advantage potential, and the overall decline in customer satisfaction with services, it seems that the potential and opportunities for companies who can excel in services marketing, management, and delivery have never been greater.

This text will give you a lens with which to approach the marketing and management of services. What you learn can be applied in a company like IBM with a traditional manufacturing history or in pure service businesses. You will learn tools, strategies, and approaches for developing and delivering profitable services that can provide competitive advantage to firms. At the base of services marketing and management you will find a strong customer focus that extends across all functions of the firm—thus the subtitle of this book, "integrating customer focus across the firm."

WHAT ARE SERVICES?

Put in the most simple terms, *services are deeds, processes, and performances* provided or coproduced by one entity or person for another entity or person. Our opening vignette illustrates what is meant by this definition. The services offered by IBM are not tangible things that can be touched, seen, and felt, but rather are intangible deeds and performances provided and/or coproduced for its customers. To be concrete, IBM offers repair and maintenance service for its equipment, consulting services for IT and e-commerce applications, training services, web design and hosting, and other services. These services may include a final, tangible report, a website, or in the case of training, tangible instructional materials. But for the most part, the entire service is represented to the client through problem analysis activities, meetings with the client, follow-up calls, and reporting—a series of deeds, processes, and performances. Similarly, the core offerings of hospitals, hotels, banks, and utilities are primarily deeds and actions performed for customers, or coproduced with them.

Although we will rely on the simple, broad definition of *services,* you should be aware that over time *services* and the *service sector of the economy* have been defined in subtly different ways. The variety of definitions can often explain the confusion or disagreements people have when discussing services and when describing industries that comprise the service sector of the economy. Compatible with our simple, broad definition is one that defines services to include "all economic activities whose output is not a physical product or construction, is generally consumed at the time it is produced, and provides added value in forms (such as convenience, amusement, timeliness, comfort, or health) that are essentially intangible concerns of its first purchaser."[4] The breadth of industries making up the service sector of the U.S. economy is illustrated in Figure 1.1.

Services Industries, Services as Products, Customer Service, and Derived Service

As we begin our discussion of services marketing and management, it is important to draw distinctions between *service industries and companies, services as products, customer service,* and *derived service.* Sometimes when people think of service, they think only of customer service, but service can be divided into four distinct categories. The tools and strategies you will learn in this text can be applied to any of these categories.

Service industries and companies include those industries and companies typically classified within the service sector whose core product is a service. All of the following companies can be considered pure service companies: Marriott International (lodging), American Airlines (transportation), Charles Schwab (financial services), Mayo Clinic (health care). The total services sector comprises a wide range of service industries, as suggested by Figure 1.1. Companies in these industries sell services as their core offering.

Services as products represent a wide range of intangible product offerings that customers value and pay for in the marketplace. Service products are sold by service

FIGURE 1.1
**Contributions of
Service Industries to
U.S. Gross Domestic
Product, 2006**

Source: *Survey of Current
Business,* May 2007, p. 19,
Table 2.

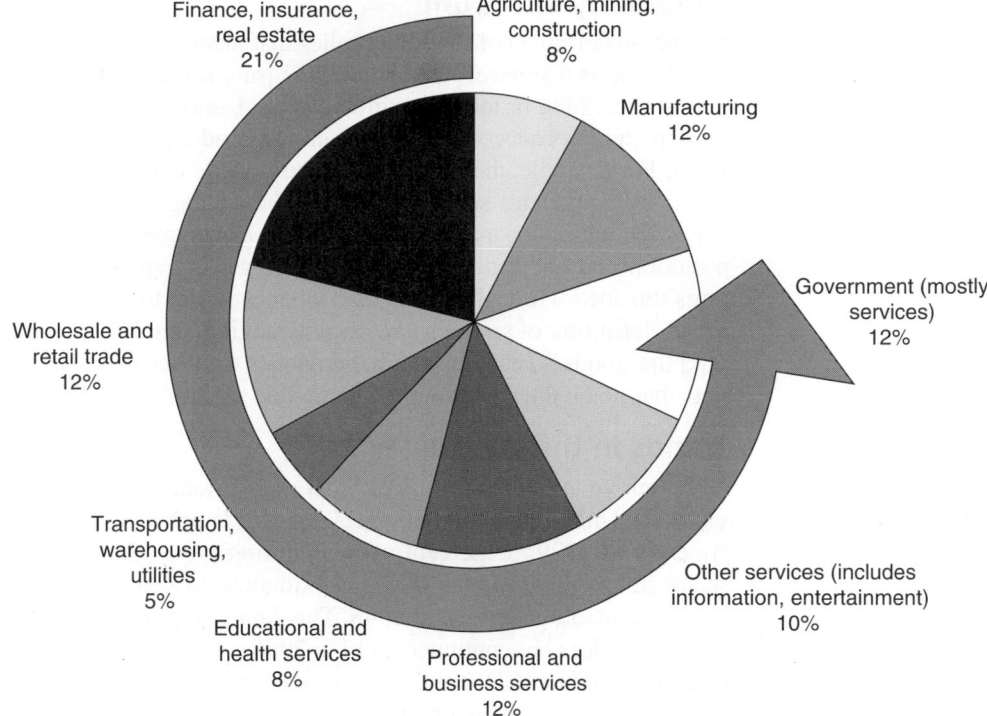

companies and by nonservice companies such as manufacturers and technology companies. For example, IBM and Hewlett-Packard offer information technology consulting services to the marketplace, competing with firms such as EDS and Accenture, which are traditional pure services firms. Other industry examples include department stores, like Macy's that sell services such as gift wrapping and shipping, and pet stores like PetSmart that sell pet grooming and training services.

Customer service is also a critical aspect of what we mean by "service." Customer service is the service provided in support of a company's core products. Companies typically do not charge for customer service. Customer service can occur on-site (as when a retail employee helps a customer find a desired item or answers a question), or it can occur over the phone or via the Internet (e.g., Dell computer provides real-time chat sessions to help customers diagnose hardware problems). Many companies operate customer service call centers, often staffed around the clock. Quality customer service is essential to building customer relationships. It should not, however, be confused with the services provided for sale by the company.

Derived service is yet another way to look at what service means. In an award-winning article in the *Journal of Marketing,* Steve Vargo and Bob Lusch argue for a new dominant logic for marketing that suggests that all products and physical goods are valued for the services they provide.[5] Drawing on the work of respected economists, marketers, and philosophers, the two authors suggest that the value derived from physical goods is really the service provided by the good, not the good itself. For example, they suggest that a pharmaceutical provides medical services, a razor provides barbering services, and computers provide information and data manipulation services. Although this view is somewhat abstract, it suggests an even broader, more inclusive, view of the meaning of *service.*

Tangibility Spectrum

The broad definition of services implies that intangibility is a key determinant of whether an offering is a service. Although this is true, it is also true that very few products are purely intangible or totally tangible. Instead, services tend to be *more intangible* than manufactured products, and manufactured products tend to be *more tangible* than services. For example, the fast-food industry, while classified as a service, also has many tangible components such as the food, the packaging, and so on. Automobiles, while classified within the manufacturing sector, also supply many intangibles, such as transportation and navigation services. The tangibility spectrum shown in Figure 1.2 captures this idea. Throughout this text, when we refer to services we will be assuming the broad definition of services and acknowledging that there are very few "pure services" or "pure goods." The issues and approaches we discuss are directed toward those offerings that lie on the right side, the intangible side, of the spectrum shown in Figure 1.2.

Trends in the Service Sector

Although you often hear and read that many modern economies are dominated by services, the United States and other countries did not become service economies overnight. As early as 1929, 55 percent of the working population was employed in the service sector in the United States, and approximately 54 percent of the gross national product was generated by services in 1948. The data in Figures 1.3 and 1.4 show that the trend toward services has continued, until in 2006 services represented 80 percent of the gross domestic product (GDP) and 82 percent of employment. Note also that these data do not include services provided by manufacturing companies. The number of employees and value of the services they produce would be classified as manufacturing sector data.

WHY SERVICES MARKETING?

Why is it important to learn about services marketing, service quality, and service management? What are the differences in services versus manufactured-goods marketing that have led to the demand for books and courses on services? Many forces have led to the growth of services marketing, and many industries, companies, and individuals have defined the scope of the concepts, frameworks, and strategies that define the field. The field of services marketing and management has evolved as a result of these combined forces.

FIGURE 1.2 **Tangibility Spectrum**

Source: G. Lynn Shostack, "Breaking Free from Product Marketing," *Journal of Marketing* 41 (April 1977), pp. 73–80. Reprinted with permission of the American Marketing Association.

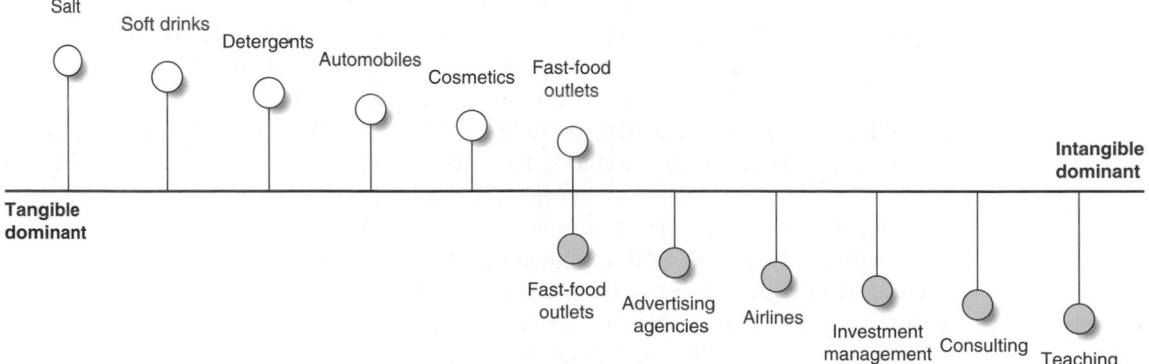

FIGURE 1.3
Percentage of U.S. Labor Force by Industry

Sources: U.S. Department of Labor, Bureau of Labor Statistics, *Industry at a Glance,* May 4, 2007, *Survey of Current Business,* February 2001, Table B.8, July 1988, Table 6.6B, and July 1992, Table 6.4C; E. Ginzberg and G. J. Vojta, "The Service Sector of the U.S. Economy," *Scientific American* 244, no. 3 (1981), pp. 31–39.

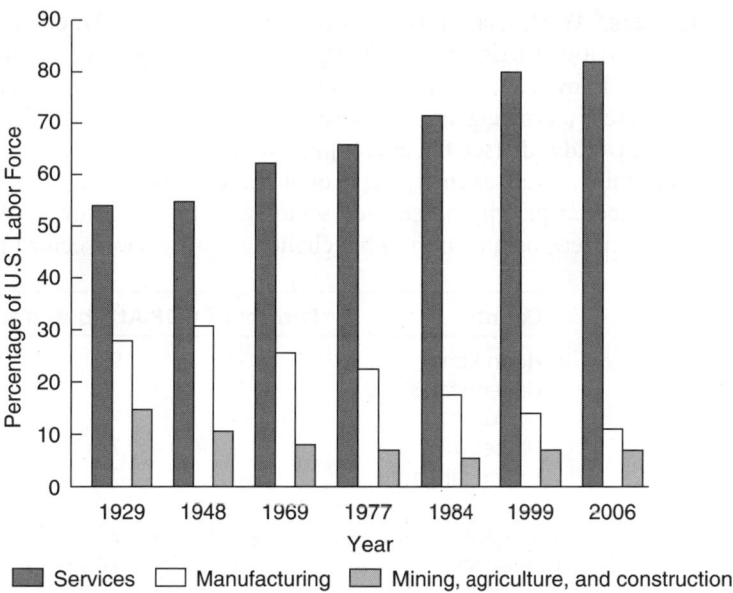

Service-Based Economies

First, services marketing concepts and strategies have developed in response to the tremendous growth of service industries, resulting in their increased importance to the U.S. and world economies. As was noted, in 2006 the service sector represented more than 80 percent of total employment and gross domestic product of the United States. Almost all the absolute growth in numbers of jobs and the fastest growth rates in job formation are in service industries, particularly health care and IT professional services.

Another indicator of the economic importance of services is that trade in services is growing worldwide. In fact, while the U.S. balance of trade in goods remains in the red, in the fourth quarter of 2006 alone there was a $19 billion trade *surplus* in

FIGURE 1.4
Percentage of U.S. Gross Domestic Product by Industry

Sources: *Survey of Current Business,* May 2007, p. 19, Table 2; *Survey of Current Business,* February 2001, Table B.3, and August 1996, Table 11; E. Ginzberg and G. J. Vojta, "The Service Sector of the U.S. Economy," *Scientific American* 244, no. 3 (1981), pp. 31–39.

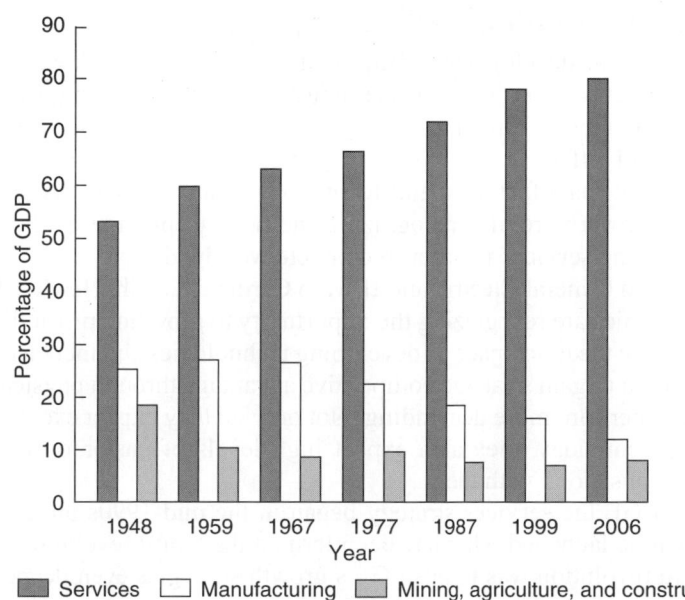

services.[6] World-class providers of services such as American Express, McDonald's, and Marriott Hotels, together with many small service companies, are exporting information, knowledge, creativity, and technology that the world badly needs.

There is a growing market for services and increasing dominance of services in economies worldwide (see the accompanying table). This growth is apparent in established economies as well as emerging economies such as China, where the central government has placed a priority on service sector growth. The growth of the service sector has drawn increasing attention to the challenges of service sector industries worldwide.

Country	Percent of GDP Attributed to Services
Hong Kong	91
United States	79
France	77
Netherlands	74
United Kingdom	73
Japan	73
Sweden	71
Germany	70
Australia	70
Canada	69
New Zealand	69
Spain	68
Finland	67
Singapore	66
India	61
Brazil	54
Thailand	45
China	40

Source: *The World Factbook 2007*, published by the Central Intelligence Agency, www.odci.gov/cia/publications/factbook, country profiles.

Service as a Business Imperative in Manufacturing and Information Technology

Early in the development of the field of services marketing and management, most of the impetus came from service industries such as banking, transportation, and health care. As these traditional service industries evolve and become more competitive, the need for effective services management and marketing strategies continues. Now, however, manufacturing and technology industries such as automobiles, computers, and software are also recognizing the need to provide quality service and revenue-producing services in order to compete worldwide.

From General Electric and IBM to Cardinal Health, Hewlett-Packard, and Siemens, companies are recognizing the opportunity to grow and profit through services.[7] Why? Because the quick pace of developing technologies and increasing competition make it difficult to gain strategic competitive advantage through physical products alone. Plus, customers are more demanding. Not only do they expect excellent, high-quality goods and technology, they also expect high levels of customer service and total service solutions along with them.

At GE the services strategy began in the mid-1990s under then-CEO Jack Welch when he launched what has been termed the "third revolution." A major thrust of the third revolution was to push GE's growth strategies even deeper into services such as after-market and infrastructure services, financial services, broadcasting, management consulting, health care, and utilities. In 2000, GE generated approximately 75 percent of its revenues from services.[8] The move into services has continued with GE's current CEO, Jeffrey Immelt. Under Immelt's initiatives, GE offers a broad range of expertise and services to its customers in an effort to make them more productive and competitive. For GE, the theory behind this broad push is "the more successful our customers are, the more successful we will be."[9]

As manufacturers such as GE and IT companies such as IBM (see the opening vignette and the photo below) transition to become services organizations, the need for special concepts and approaches for managing and marketing services is increasingly apparent.[10]

Services are driving IBM's growth in the 21st century

IBM Global Services

Overview:	IBM Global Services is people. Strategists. Problem solvers. Implementers. Over 100,000 people worldwide who have worked in all kinds of industries. People who understand how technology can solve real business problems, or take advantage of new opportunities. People who help you make sense of technology, who work with you — making sure the solution you want is the solution you get.
Phone:	1 800 IBM 7777, ask for Services
Web:	www.ibm.com/services/info

IBM Global Services

People who think. People who do. People who get it.

*@*business people

IBM.

Deregulated Industries and Professional Service Needs

Specific demand for services marketing concepts has come from deregulated industries and professional services as both these groups have gone through rapid changes in the ways they do business. In the past several decades many very large service industries, including airlines, banking, telecommunications, and trucking, have been deregulated by the U.S. government. Similar deregulatory moves have taken place in many other countries as well. As a result, marketing decisions that used to be tightly controlled by the government are now partially, and in some cases totally, within the control of individual firms.[11] For example, until 1978 all airline fares, routes, and commissions paid to travel agents were determined and monitored by the government. Since that time airlines have been free to set their own pricing structures and determine which routes they will fly. Needless to say, deregulation created turmoil in the airline industry, accelerating the need for more sophisticated, customer-based, and competition-sensitive marketing.

Providers of professional services (such as physicians, lawyers, accountants, engineers, and architects) have also demanded new concepts and approaches for their businesses as these industries have become increasingly competitive and as professional standards have been modified to allow advertising. Whereas traditionally the professions avoided even using the word *marketing,* they are now seeking better ways to understand and segment their customers, to ensure the delivery of quality services, and to strengthen their positions amid a growing number of competitors.

Services Marketing Is Different

As the forces described above coincided and evolved, businesspeople realized that marketing and managing services presented issues and challenges not faced in manufacturing and packaged goods companies. These differences and challenges were captured in a series of interviews by management consultant Gary Knisely in 1979 (see Exhibit 1.1).[12] For example, when a firm's core offering is a deed performed by an employee (such as engineering consulting), how can the firm ensure consistent product quality to the marketplace? As service businesses began to turn to marketing and decided to hire marketing people, they naturally recruited from the best marketers in the world—Procter & Gamble, General Foods, Kodak. People who moved from marketing in packaged goods industries to marketing in health care, banking, and other service industries found that their skills and experiences were not directly transferable. They faced issues and dilemmas in marketing services that their experiences in packaged goods and manufacturing had not prepared them for. These people realized the need for new concepts and approaches for marketing and managing service businesses.

Service marketers responded to these forces and began to work across disciplines and with academics and business practitioners from around the world to develop and document marketing practices for services. As the field evolved, it expanded to address the concerns and needs of *any* business in which service is an integral part of the offering. Frameworks, concepts, and strategies developed to address the fact that "services marketing is different." As the field continues to evolve in the 21st century, new trends will shape the field and accelerate the need for services marketing concepts and tools.

Service Equals Profits

In the final decades of the 20th century, many firms jumped on the service bandwagon, investing in service initiatives and promoting service quality as ways to differentiate themselves and create competitive advantage. Many of these investments were based

In 1979 Gary Knisely, a principal of the consulting firm Johnson Smith & Knisely, asked the title question to practicing services marketers. Specifically, Knisely interviewed several high-ranking marketing executives who had all gone to work in consumer services after extensive experience in the consumer packaged goods industry (known for its marketing prowess).

These executives found differences, all right. Their discoveries came from attempts to apply (with mixed success, it turned out) consumer goods marketing practices directly to services. James L. Schorr of Holiday Inns Inc., formerly with Procter & Gamble, found that he could not overlay a consumer goods firm's marketing system onto a service firm. He, and the other executives interviewed, expressed certain recurring themes. First, more variables exist in the marketing mix for services than for consumer goods. Schorr claimed that in a service business, marketing and operations are more closely linked than in a manufacturing business; thus the service production process is part of the marketing process. Second, customer interface is a major difference between goods marketing and services marketing. Executives from packaged goods companies never had to think in terms of a direct dialogue with their customers. For Schorr, the marketing of hotel rooms boiled down to a "people-on-people" sale. Robert L. Catlin, in relating his experience in the airline industry, stated, "Your people are as much of your product in the consumer's mind as any other attribute of the service." People buy products because they believe they work. But with services, people deal with people they like and they tend to buy services because they believe they will like them. This thought process makes the customer–employee interface a critical component of marketing.

The executives also commented on how the marketing mix variables common to both goods and services have vastly different implications for marketing strategy in the two contexts. In the distribution and selling of services, the firm cannot rely on well-stocked shelves past which the consumer can push a cart and make selections. Consumers' exposure to the full range of need-fulfilling service products may be limited by the salesperson's "mental inventory" of services and how he or she prioritizes them. You could say that the service product manager is competing for the "mental shelf space" of the firm's sales personnel. For Rodney Woods, group marketing officer at United States Trust Co., pricing was the most critical factor in the marketing of services versus products. For Woods, determining the costs associated with service production and delivery proved very difficult, much more of a challenge than he had faced in his earlier career working with such large packaged goods companies as Pillsbury, Procter & Gamble, and Bristol-Myers. Also, the benefits of using price as a promotional weapon were not as apparent. Promotional price cuts tended to erode hard-fought positioning and image.

While scholars debated early on the issue of whether marketing management differs for goods versus services, for top managers with experience in both areas the differences were pronounced in 1979. They still are today. The differences that these early service marketers noted were the impetus for many of the ideas, concepts, and strategies practiced today.

Source: This discussion is based on interviews conducted by Gary Knisely that appeared in *Advertising Age* on January 15, 1979; February 19, 1979; March 19, 1979; and May 14, 1979.

on faith and intuition by managers who believed in serving customers well and who believed in their hearts that quality service made good business sense. Indeed, a dedication to quality service has been the foundation for success for many firms, across industries. In his book *Discovering the Soul of Service,* Leonard Berry describes in detail 14 such companies.[13] The companies featured in his book had been in business an average of 31 years when the book was written. These companies had been profitable in all but 5 of their combined 407 years of existence. Dr. Berry discovered through his research that these successful businesses share devotion to nine common service themes, among them values-driven leadership, commitment to investments in employee success, and trust-based relationships with customers and other partners at the foundation of the organization.

Since the mid-1990s firms have demanded hard evidence of the bottom-line effectiveness of service strategies. And researchers are building a convincing case that service strategies, implemented appropriately, can be very profitable. Work sponsored by the Marketing Science Institute suggests that corporate strategies focused on customer satisfaction, revenue generation, and service quality may actually be more profitable than strategies focused on cost cutting or strategies that attempt to do both simultaneously.[14] Research out of the Harvard Business School builds a case for the "service–profit chain," linking internal service and employee satisfaction to customer value and ultimately to profits.[15] And considerable research shows linkages from customer satisfaction (often driven by service outcomes) to profits.[16] From the University of Michigan American Customer Satisfaction Index (ACSI) comes data suggesting that customer satisfaction is directly linked to shareholder value. Firms in the top 25 percent of the ACSI rankings show significantly higher shareholder value than do firms in the bottom 25 percent. Research based on ACSI data also shows that the top 20 percent of ACSI firms significantly outperform the Standard & Poor's (S&P) 500, NASDAQ, and DowJones Industrial Average.[17]

An important key to these successes is that the right strategies are chosen and that these strategies are implemented appropriately and well. Much of what you learn from this text will guide you in making such correct choices and in providing superior implementation. Throughout the text we will point out the profit implications and tradeoffs to be made with service strategies. See this chapter's Strategy Insight for four ways that firms successfully and profitably compete through service. In Chapter 18 we will come back to this issue by providing integrated coverage of the financial and profit impact of service.

But "Service Stinks"

Despite the importance of service and the bottom-line profit potential for service, consumers perceive that overall the quality of service is declining.[18] We see *BusinessWeek* magazine blatantly condemning service in its cover story "Why Service Stinks."[19] And although there are exceptions in every industry, American Customer Satisfaction Index scores for service industries are generally lower than the average for all industries. Particularly low are ACSI scores in the transportation, communications, and utilities sectors. For example, whereas the national ACSI average across all industries has risen to 75.2, cable and satellite television and most airlines receive ratings in the low to mid 60s.[20]

This condemnation of service is troubling when, at some level, service has never been better. For example, think of just one industry—health care. The ability to prevent and treat diseases has never been greater, resulting in an ever-increasing life expectancy in the United States and in most industrialized countries. Or take the communications industries—communicating quickly, effectively, and cheaply with people all over the world has never been easier. Access to vast quantities of information, entertainment, and music is unbelievable compared to what people had just 10 years ago. So clearly, in some ways and in many industries, services are better than ever.

Despite these obvious improvements, there is hard evidence that consumers perceive a lower quality of service overall and are less satisfied. There are many theories as to why this decline in customer satisfaction with services has occurred, but it is difficult to point precisely to the reason. Plausible theories include these:

- With more companies offering tiered service based on the calculated profitability of different market segments, many customers are in fact getting less service than they have in the past.
- Increasing use by companies of self-service and technology-based service is perceived as less service because no human interaction or human personalization is provided.

Strategy Insight Competing Strategically through Service

Firms can compete profitably through services in a variety of different ways. Through our work with companies across industries and through benchmarking other companies, we see four strategic themes emerge as the primary ways that firms can compete through service. Although firms tend to emphasize one or two of these strategic choices at a given time, it may be possible to do more.

EXEMPLARY OUT-OF-THE-BOX CUSTOMER SERVICE

There are some organizations whose competitive advantage is their reputation for out-of-the-box customer service. Southwest Airlines, Mayo Clinic, Gallery Furniture (a hugely successful furniture store in Texas), and Zanes Cycles (a small bicycle shop in Connecticut) are just a few examples. These organizations focus on going out of their way for customers and providing customer service in unique ways. Special services that these companies provide include

- at Southwest Airlines, a distinctive sense of humor among employees as well as in-flight games and jokes
- at Mayo Clinic, a grand piano in the lobby and doctors who sit physically close to patients, look them in the eye, and truly believe that "the best interest of the patient is the only interest to be considered"
- at Gallery Furniture, free food and day care for children
- at Zanes Cycles, a "flat tire club"

INNOVATIVE, CUTTING-EDGE SERVICES

Other organizations compete through providing innovative and cutting-edge services—being the first and/or best in their industry or being on the forefront of new inventions, technology, or science. Examples here include Amazon.com, the first company to introduce really effective and innovative online retailing. Mayo Clinic falls into this category as well. It is on the leading edge of medicine in the United States and typically only sees patients who have hard-to-diagnose or complex problems. The clinic's research-based, team-oriented, consultative model of medicine keeps it on the forefront.

Being innovative does not necessarily mean that the organization invents something totally new; perhaps its services approach is simply new to that industry. Yellow Transportation (part of YRC Worldwide), an old-line trucking company, reinvented itself as a transportation company by successfully introducing guarantees, express services, and time-definite delivery into this somewhat stodgy industry.

VALUE-ADDED, REVENUE-PRODUCING SERVICES

A major trend in manufacturing, information technology, and other nonservice industries in recent years is the introduction of value-added, revenue-producing services. Firms in these industries have recognized that they cannot compete on the sales and margins produced by their manufactured products alone. Many firms, such as IBM, Hewlett-Packard, Siemens, and General Electric, have integrated services into their mix of offerings. In some cases, as with IBM (see the opening vignette in this chapter), services have actually taken over as the growth engine for the company.

This focus on revenue-producing services also extends to retailers. For example, PetSmart, the largest pet retailer in the United States, has introduced a host of new services in recent years as a way to compete effectively in this relatively low-margin industry. The company targets "pet parents" in its advertising, and its special services include pet training, grooming, and overnight care.

A SERVICE CULTURE THAT DIFFERENTIATES

Finally, a firm can compete by nurturing a service culture that attracts the very best workers in the industry. In attracting the best workers, the company has an advantage over the competition in terms of providing the very best services and thus becoming both the "employer of choice" and the "provider of choice" in its industry. This approach is used, for example, by Southwest Airlines, Mayo Clinic, Disney, and Marriott Hotels. At Marriott, the underlying company philosophy is "take care of your employees and they will take care of your guests." This philosophy permeates all the Marriott brands, from Fairfield Inns to the Ritz Carlton, giving Marriott a worldwide competitive advantage in its industry.

Source: Center for Services Leadership, W. P. Carey School of Business, Arizona State University (www.wpcarey.asu.edu/csl). See also M. J. Bitner and S. Brown, "The Service Imperative," *Business Horizons,* 50th Anniversary Issue, 51 (January–February 2008), pp. 39–46.

- Technology-based services (automated voice systems, Internet-based services, technology kiosks) are hard to implement, with many failures and with poorly designed systems in place.
- Customer expectations are higher because of the excellent service they receive from some companies. Thus, they expect the same from all and are frequently disappointed.
- Organizations have cut costs to the extent that they are too lean and too understaffed to provide quality service.
- The competitive job market results in less-skilled people working in front-line service jobs; talented workers soon get promoted or leave for better opportunities.
- Many companies give lip service to customer focus and service quality, but they fail to provide the training, compensation, and support of employees needed to actually deliver quality service.

These theories as to the causes of declining customer satisfaction can be debated. But for managers, students, and teachers of services marketing and management, the message is clear: there is plenty of work to be done. In this text we will provide many examples of best practices—companies that understand how to get it right and are succeeding with service. We will also delineate many tools, concepts, and strategies that can help to reverse the "service stinks" mind-set.

SERVICE AND TECHNOLOGY

The preceding sections examined the roots of services marketing and the reasons why the field exists. Another major trend—technology, specifically information technology—is currently shaping the field and profoundly influencing the practice of services marketing. In this section we explore trends in technology (positive *and* negative) to set the stage for topics that will be discussed throughout this text. In each chapter you will find a Technology Spotlight box that highlights the influence of technology on issues related to the particular chapter. We will also raise technology and service issues as appropriate throughout the general discussion in the text. Together with globalization, the influence of technology is the most profound trend affecting services marketing today.

Potential for New Service Offerings

Looking to the recent past, it is apparent how technology has been the basic force behind service innovations now taken for granted. Automated voice mail, interactive voice response systems, fax machines, automated teller machines (ATMs), and other common services were possible only because of new technologies. Just think how dramatically different your world would be without these basic technology services.

More recently, people have seen the explosion of the Internet, resulting in a host of new services. Internet-based companies like Amazon and eBay offer services previously unheard of. And established companies find that the Internet provides a way to offer new services as well.[21] For example, *The Wall Street Journal* offers an interactive edition that allows customers to organize the newspaper's content to suit their individual preferences and needs.

Many new technology services are on the horizon. For example, some researchers project that the "connected car" will allow people to access all kinds of existing and new services while on the road. Already many cars are equipped with map and routing software that direct drivers to specific locations. In-car systems also provide recommendations for shopping by informing drivers when they are within a certain number of miles of their preferred retailer. On a road trip, the system may provide weather forecasts and warnings, and when it is time to stop for the night, the car's system could book a room at a nearby hotel, recommend a restaurant, and make dinner reservations. Advances in information technology are also making it possible for whole suites of services, including phone, Internet, video, photography and e-mail, to be available through one device such as Apple's iPhone.[22]

New Ways to Deliver Service

In addition to providing opportunities for new service offerings, technology is providing vehicles for delivering existing services in more accessible, convenient, productive ways. Technology facilitates basic customer service functions (bill paying, questions, checking account records, tracking orders), transactions (both retail and business-to-business), and learning or information seeking. Our Technology Spotlight traces how, through history, evolving technologics have changed one aspect of service, namely, customer service, forever. Companies have moved from face-to-face service to telephone-based service to widespread use of interactive voice response systems to Internet-based customer service and now to wireless service. Interestingly, many companies are coming full circle and now offer human contact as the ultimate form of customer service!

Technology also facilitates transactions by offering a direct vehicle for making purchases and conducting business. In the financial services field, Charles Schwab transformed itself from a traditional broker to an online financial services company that currently conducts more than 70 percent of its customer transactions online. Internet banking is also growing worldwide with the Dutch bank, ING Direct, leading the way with 51 percent of all Internet deposits in the United States. Without a single physical branch, ING regularly attracts deposits away from its much larger competitors.[23] Technology giant Cisco Systems offers virtually all its customer service and ordering functions to its business customers via technology. Almost all of its transactions and follow-up with customers are completed online.

Finally, technology, specifically the Internet, provides an easy way for customers to learn, do research, and collaborate with each other. Access to information has never been easier. For example, more than 20,000 websites currently offer health-related information. Many provide answers to specific disease, drug, and treatment questions. In a study of online health care information usage, the Pew organization found that among Americans with Internet access, 80 percent had looked for health or medical information on the Web.[24]

Enabling Both Customers and Employees

Technology enables both customers and employees to be more effective in getting and providing service.[25] Through self-service technologies, customers can serve themselves more effectively. Via online banking, customers can access their accounts, check balances, apply for loans, shift money among accounts, and take care of just about any banking need they might have—all without the assistance of the bank's employees. Wells Fargo, the first bank to offer online services in the United States, finds that its online customers are its most satisfied customers. These online banking services are just one example of the types of self-service technologies that are proliferating across industries.

Technology Spotlight   The Changing Face of Customer Service

Excellent customer service—the daily, ongoing support of a company's offerings—is critical in creating brand identity and ultimate success. It includes answering questions, taking orders, dealing with billing issues, handling complaints, scheduling appointments, and similar activities. These essential functions can make or break an organization's relationships with its customers. The quality of customer care can significantly impact brand identity for service, manufacturing, and consumer products companies. Because of its importance in creating impressions and sustaining customer relationships, customer service has sometimes been called the "front door" of the organization or its "face."

So how has the "face" of customer service changed with the influx of technology? Long ago all customer service was provided face-to-face through direct personal interaction between employees and customers. To get service you had to visit stores or service providers in person. The telephone changed this, allowing customers to call companies and speak directly with employees, typically Monday–Friday, 8 a.m.–5 p.m. Customer service became less personal, but without a doubt more efficient, through use of the telephone. With the evolution of computer technology, customer service representatives (CSRs)

became even more efficient. Through computer information systems and customer data files, CSRs are able to call up customer records at their workstations to answer questions on the spot.

Over time, because communication and computer technologies allowed it, large organizations began to centralize their customer service functions, consolidating into a few large call centers that could be located anywhere in the country or the world. For example, a large percentage of IBM's customer service calls in North America are handled out of its sales and service center in Toronto, Canada, and calls can be handled 24 hours per day. But still, in these types of call centers, customer service is for the most part an interpersonal event with customers talking directly, one-on-one with an employee.

The advent and rapid proliferation of the efficient, but much maligned, automated voice response systems have changed personal customer service in many organizations into menu-driven, automated exchanges. In almost every industry and any business context, consumers encounter these types of systems, and many are quite frustrating—for example, when a system has a long, confusing set of menu options or when no menu option seems to fit the purpose of the call. Similarly, consumers become angered

For employees, technology can provide tremendous support in making them more effective and efficient in delivering service. Customer relationship management and sales support software are broad categories of technology that can aid frontline employees in providing better service. By having immediate access to information about their product and service offerings as well as about particular customers, employees are better able to serve them. This type of information allows employees to customize services to fit the customer's needs. They can also be much more efficient and timely than in the old days when most customer and product information was in paper files or in the heads of sales and customer service representatives.

Extending the Global Reach of Services

Technology infusion results in the potential for reaching out to customers around the globe in ways not possible before. The Internet itself knows no boundaries, and therefore information, customer service, and transactions can move across countries and across continents, reaching any customer who has access to the Web. Technology also allows employees of international companies to stay in touch easily—to share information, to ask questions, to serve on virtual teams together. All this technology facilitates the global reach as well as the effectiveness of service businesses. Our Global Feature focuses on the migration of service jobs and the ability to produce services almost anywhere.

when they cannot get out of the automated system easily, or when there is no option to speak to a live person.

Some companies have overcome these obstacles, however, and have well-designed automated telephone systems that work well for customers. Charles Schwab provides a notable example. Schwab completes more than 75 percent of its 82 million annual calls through speech and touch-tone automated response systems. Its automated voice response system has been designed to give quick answers with a minimum of navigation beyond the first menu. This efficiency is accomplished through a form of natural-language speech recognition technology that allows customers to easily interact through the telephone in ways that are much like talking to a real person.

Beyond automated telecom systems, explosion of the Internet is also dramatically changing customer service for many companies. Service can now be provided on the Internet via e-mails, website robots, FAQs, and online chats. In these cases there is no direct human interaction, and customers actually perform their own service.

With the relentless proliferation of technology solutions, firms are finding that expectations for customer service have changed. Customers are demanding choices in how they get customer service, whether it be via phone, automated voice system, fax, e-mail, or Internet self-service. Although customers often enjoy technology-based service and even demand it in many cases, they dislike it when it does not work reliably (a common problem), when it does not seem to have any advantages over the interpersonal service alternatives, and when there are no systems in place to recover from failures. Interestingly, when things do not work as they are supposed to on an Internet site or through an automated response system, customers are quick to look for more traditional interpersonal (in person or via telephone) options, coming full circle to where they started. Somewhat ironically, the leading *Internet* bank in Europe and the United States, ING Direct, prides itself on staffing its toll-free customer service phone lines with real *people,* not automated menu systems!

Sources: J. A. Nickell, "To Voice Mail Hell and Back," *Business 2.0,* July 10, 2001, pp. 49–53; M. L. Meuter, A. L. Ostrom, R. I. Roundtree, and M. J. Bitner, "Self-Service Technologies: Understanding Customer Satisfaction with Technology-Based Service Encounters," *Journal of Marketing* 64 (July 2000), pp. 50–64; S. Ali, "If you want to Scream, Press . . . ," *The Wall Street Journal,* October 30, 2006, p. R4; B. Kiviat, "How a Man on a Mission (and a Harley) Reinvented Banking," *Time,* June 25, 2007, pp. 45–46.

The Internet *Is* a Service

An interesting way to look at the influence of technology is to realize that the Internet is just "one big service." All businesses and organizations that operate on the Internet are essentially providing services—whether they are giving information, performing basic customer service functions, or facilitating transactions. Thus all the tools, concepts, and strategies you learn in studying services marketing and management have direct application in an Internet or e-business world. Although technology and the Internet are profoundly changing how people do business and what offerings are possible, it is clear that customers still want basic service. They want what they have always wanted: dependable outcomes, easy access, responsive systems, flexibility, apologies, and compensation when things go wrong. But now they expect these same outcomes from technology-based businesses and from e-commerce solutions.[26] With hindsight it is obvious that many dot-com start-ups suffered and even failed because of lack of basic customer knowledge and failure of implementation, logistics, and service follow-up.[27]

The Paradoxes and Dark Side of Technology and Service

Although there is clearly great potential for technology to support and enhance services, there are potential negative outcomes as well. David Mick and Susan Fournier, well-regarded consumer researchers, have pointed out the many paradoxes

With the ever-growing sophistication of information technology, the global reach of organizations is increasing at a spectacular rate. Activities that used to require close proximity and personal contact can now often be accomplished via the Internet, video, and telecommunication technologies. This advancement means that the jobs that produce and support these activities can be done almost anywhere in the world. The result has been referred to as a "migration of service jobs" out of countries such as the United States and the United Kingdom to countries such as India, Pakistan, the Philippines, Eastern European countries, and, more recently, Columbia and Brazil.

This globalization of services is in many ways inevitable, but it comes with considerable controversy. One clear concern is that some of the highest-paying service jobs are being "lost" to lower-wage countries, and this concern is very real for the individuals whose jobs are lost. However, the numbers are not as large as perhaps imagined. Forrester Research in Cambridge, Massachusetts, estimates that by the year 2015, 3.3 million high-tech and service jobs will move overseas from the United States. Others estimate the member to be much higher. On the other side of this concern are arguments that offshore jobs will spur innovation, job creation in other areas, and increases in productivity that will benefit the consumer and keep companies competitive in the global marketplace. In fact, the Bureau of Labor Statistics estimates that between 2000 and 2010, 22 million new U.S. jobs (mostly in business services, health care, social services, transportation, and communications) will be created. Although the specific outcomes of service job migration are not totally known, it is safe to say that the globalization of services will continue, resulting in further shrinking of the boundaries among people and countries.

Service job migration involves not just call centers and IT help lines, but also services that span industries and levels of skills. Software development, IT consulting, chip design, financial analysis, industrial engineering, analytics, and drug research are just a few examples of services performed in India for global firms. Even medical diagnoses and reading of medical records can be done remotely via video, Internet, and scanning technologies.

Why is service job migration happening now? The root of the acceleration is the rapid development and accessibility of sophisticated information technologies. Services are information intensive, and information can now be shared readily without direct personal contact. For example, at the John F. Welch Technology Center in Bangalore, close to 3,000 Indian researchers and engineers engage in research for General Electric's divisions. Projects span such diverse areas as developing materials

for use in DVDs, boosting productivity of GE plants, and tweaking the designs of turbine engine blades. The design work can be done in India (perhaps even teaming with engineers elsewhere), and the results can be sent instantaneously wherever they are needed. Other examples: more than 20,000 U.S. tax returns annually are prepared and filed by certified public accountants (CPAs) working in India; Indian financial analysts digest the latest disclosures of U.S. companies and file reports the next day; and other workers in India sort through mounds of consumer data provided by non-Indian company clients to determine behavior patterns and develop ideas for marketing. In each of these cases, *where* the work is done is not important or meaningful to the client as long as it is done well and on time.

A major reason that this movement of jobs is possible is that countries outside the developed world are now producing highly skilled, well-educated workforces, particularly in China and India. These workers typically work for far less compensation than their U.S. or U.K. counterparts, allowing global companies to reduce labor costs on the one hand and increase overall productivity on the other. The quality of the work can be very high as well. However, as the growth in offshoring continues and competition for talent increases, firms are zeroing in on cultural and language gaps that can limit quality with some firms, bringing services—particularly call centers—back to their home base.

Sources: U. Karmarkar, "Will You Survive the Services Revolution?" *Harvard Business Review,* 82 (June 2004), pp. 100–107; M. Kripalani and P. Engardio, "The Rise of India," *Business-Week,* December 8, 2003; S. A. Teicher, "A Not So Simple Path," *Christian Science Monitor,* February 23, 2004; M. N. Baily and D. Farrell, "Exploding the Myths of Offshoring," *The McKinsey Quarterly,* online at www.mckinseyquarterly.com, July 2004; S. Ali, "If you want to Scream, Press . . . ," *The Wall Street Journal,* October 30, 2006, R4; A. Vashistha and A. Vashistha, *The Offshore Nation* (NewYork: Mc-Graw Hill, 2006); S. Lohr, "At IBM, a Smarter Way to Outsource," *The New York Times,* July 5, 2007.

of technology products and services for consumers, as shown in Table 1.1.[28] This section highlights some of the general concerns.

Customer concerns about privacy and confidentiality raise major issues for firms as they seek to learn about and interact directly with customers through the Internet. These types of concerns are what have stymied and precluded many efforts to advance technology applications in the health care industry, for example. Nor are all customers equally interested in using technology as a means of interacting with companies. Research exploring "customer technology readiness" suggests that some customers are simply not interested or ready to use technology.[29] Employees can also be reluctant to accept and integrate technology into their work lives—especially when they perceive, rightly or wrongly, that the technology will substitute for human labor and perhaps eliminate their jobs.

With technology infusion comes a loss of human contact, which many people believe is detrimental purely from a quality of life and human relationships perspective. Parents may lament that their children spend hours in front of computer screens, interacting with games, seeking information, and relating to their friends only through instant messaging and MySpace sites without any face-to-face human contact. And workers in organizations become more and more reliant on communicating through technology—even communicating via e-mail or online chat sessions with the person in the next office!

Finally, the payback in technology investments is often uncertain. It may take a long time for an investment to result in productivity or customer satisfaction gains. Sometimes it never happens. For example, McKinsey & Company reports that a firm projected a $40 million savings from moving its billing and service calls to the Web. Instead it suffered a $16 million loss as a result of lower usage by customers than projected, unanticipated follow-up calls and e-mails to the call center from those who had used the Web application initially, and loss of revenue from lack of cross-selling opportunities.[30]

TABLE 1.1   Eight Central Paradoxes of Technological Products

Source: D. G. Mick and S. Fournier, "Paradoxes of Technology: Consumer Cognizance, Emotions, and Coping Strategies," *Journal of Consumer Research* 25 (September 1998), pp. 123–147. Copyright © 1998 University of Chicago Press. Reprinted by permission.

Paradox	Description
Control/chaos	Technology can facilitate regulation or order, and technology can lead to upheaval or disorder.
Freedom/enslavement	Technology can facilitate independence or fewer restrictions, and technology can lead to dependence or more restrictions.
New/obsolete	New technologies provide the user with the most recently developed benefits of scientific knowledge, and new technologies are already or soon to be outmoded as they reach the marketplace.
Competence/incompetence	Technology can facilitate feelings of intelligence or efficacy, and technology can lead to feelings of ignorance or ineptitude.
Efficiency/inefficiency	Technology can facilitate less effort or time spent in certain activities, and technology can lead to more effort or time in certain activities.
Fulfills/creates needs	Technology can facilitate the fulfillment of needs or desires, and technology can lead to the development or awareness of needs or desires previously unrealized.
Assimilation/isolation	Technology can facilitate human togetherness, and technology can lead to human separation.
Engaging/disengaging	Technology can facilitate involvement, flow, or activity, and technology can lead to disconnection, disruption, or passivity.

CHARACTERISTICS OF SERVICES COMPARED TO GOODS

There is general agreement that differences between goods and services exist and that the distinctive characteristics discussed in this section result in challenges (as well as advantages) for managers of services.[31] It is also important to realize that each of these characteristics could be arranged on a continuum similar to the tangibility spectrum shown in Figure 1.1. That is, services tend to be more heterogeneous, more intangible, more difficult to evaluate than goods, but the differences between goods and services are not black and white by any means.[32]

Table 1.2 summarizes the differences between goods and services and the implications of these characteristics. Many of the strategies, tools, and frameworks in this text were developed to address these characteristics, which, until the 1980s, had been largely ignored by marketers. Recently it has been suggested that these distinctive characteristics should not be viewed as unique to services but that they are also relevant to goods, that "all products are services," and that "economic exchange is fundamentally about service provision."[33] Although this view is rather abstract, it does suggest that all types of organizations may be able to gain valuable insights from services marketing frameworks, tools, and strategies.

Intangibility

The most basic distinguishing characteristic of services is intangibility. Because services are performances or actions rather than objects, they cannot be seen, felt, tasted, or touched in the same manner that you can sense tangible goods. For example, health care services are actions (such as surgery, diagnosis, examination, and treatment) performed by providers and directed toward patients and their families. These services cannot actually be seen or touched by the patient, although the patient may be able to see and touch certain tangible components of the service (like the equipment or hospital room). In fact, many services such as health care are difficult for the consumer to

TABLE 1.2 **Comparing Goods and Services**

Source: A. Parasuraman, V. A. Zeithaml, and L. L. Berry, "A Conceptual Model of Service Quality and It's Implications for Future Research." *Journal of Marketing* 49 (Fall 1985) pp. 41–50. Reprinted by permission of the American Marketing Association.

Goods	Services	Resulting Implications
Tangible	Intangible	Services cannot be inventoried. Services cannot be easily patented. Services cannot be readily displayed or communicated. Pricing is difficult.
Standardized	Heterogeneous	Service delivery and customer satisfaction depend on employee and customer actions. Service quality depends on many uncontrollable factors. There is no sure knowledge that the service delivered matches what was planned and promoted.
Production separate from consumption	Simultaneous production and consumption	Customers participate in and affect the transaction. Customers affect each other. Employees affect the service outcome. Decentralization may be essential. Mass production is difficult.
Nonperishable	Perishable	It is difficult to synchronize supply and demand with services. Services cannot be returned or resold.

grasp even mentally. Even after a diagnosis or surgery has been completed the patient may not fully comprehend the service performed, although tangible evidence of the service (e.g., incision, bandaging, pain) may be quite apparent.

Resulting Marketing Implications Intangibility presents several marketing challenges. Services cannot be inventoried, and therefore fluctuations in demand are often difficult to manage. For example, there is tremendous demand for resort accommodations in Phoenix in February, but little demand in July. Yet resort owners have the same number of rooms to sell year-round. Services cannot be easily patented, and new service concepts can therefore easily be copied by competitors. Services cannot be readily displayed or easily communicated to customers, so quality may be difficult for consumers to assess. Decisions about what to include in advertising and other promotional materials are challenging, as is pricing. The actual costs of a "unit of service" are hard to determine, and the price–quality relationship is complex.

Heterogeneity

Because services are performances, frequently produced by humans, no two services will be precisely alike. The employees delivering the service frequently are the service in the customer's eyes, and people may differ in their performance from day to day or even hour to hour. Heterogeneity also results because no two customers are precisely alike; each will have unique demands or experience the service in a unique way. Thus the heterogeneity connected with services is largely the result of human interaction (between and among employees and customers) and all of the vagaries that accompany it. For example, a tax accountant may provide a different service experience to two different customers on the same day depending on their individual needs and personalities and on whether the accountant is interviewing them when he or she is fresh in the morning or tired at the end of a long day of meetings.

Resulting Marketing Implications Because services are heterogeneous across time, organizations, and people, ensuring consistent service quality is challenging. Quality actually depends on many factors that cannot be fully controlled by the service supplier, such as the ability of the consumer to articulate his or her needs, the ability and willingness of personnel to satisfy those needs, the presence (or absence) of other customers, and the level of demand for the service. Because of these complicating factors, the service manager cannot always know for sure that the service is being delivered in a manner consistent with what was originally planned and promoted. Sometimes services may be provided by a third party, further increasing the potential heterogeneity of the offering.

Simultaneous Production and Consumption

Whereas most goods are produced first, then sold and consumed, most services are sold first and then produced and consumed simultaneously. For example, an automobile can be manufactured in Detroit, shipped to San Francisco, sold two months later, and consumed over a period of years. But restaurant services cannot be provided until they have been sold, and the dining experience is essentially produced and consumed at the same time. Frequently this situation also means that customers are present while the service is being produced and thus view and may even take part in the production process as coproducers or cocreators of the service. Simultaneity also means that customers will frequently interact with each other during the service production process and thus may affect each others' experiences. For example, strangers seated next to each other in an airplane may well affect the nature of the service experience for each other. That passengers understand this fact is clearly apparent in the way business travelers will often go to great lengths to be sure they are not seated next to families with small children.

Students in a university class cocreate the service experience with each other and the professor

Another outcome of simultaneous production and consumption is that service producers find themselves playing a role as part of the product itself and as an essential ingredient in the service experience for the consumer. The photo above illustrates a common and complex example of simultaneous cocreation of a service—a university classroom.

Resulting Marketing Implications   Because services often are produced and consumed at the same time, mass production is difficult. The quality of service and customer satisfaction will be highly dependent on what happens in "real time," including actions of employees and the interactions between employees and customers. Clearly the real-time nature of services also results in advantages in terms of opportunities to customize offerings for individual consumers. Simultaneous production and consumption also means that it is not usually possible to gain significant economies of scale through centralization. Often, operations need to be relatively decentralized so that the service can be delivered directly to the consumer in convenient locations, although the growth of technology-delivered services is changing this requirement for many services. Also because of simultaneous production and consumption, the customer is involved in and observes the production process and thus may affect (positively or negatively) the outcome of the service transaction.

Perishability

Perishability refers to the fact that services cannot be saved, stored, resold, or returned. A seat on an airplane or in a restaurant, an hour of a lawyer's time, or telephone line capacity not used or purchased cannot be reclaimed and used or resold at a later time. Perishability is in contrast to goods that can be stored in inventory or resold another day, or even returned if the consumer is unhappy. Would it not be nice if a bad haircut could be returned or resold to another consumer? Perishability makes this action an unlikely possibility for most services.

Resulting Marketing Implications   A primary issue that marketers face in relation to service perishability is the inability to inventory. Demand forecasting and creative planning for capacity utilization are therefore important and challenging decision areas. The fact that services cannot typically be returned or resold also implies a need for strong recovery strategies when things do go wrong. For example, although a bad haircut cannot be returned, the hairdresser can and should have strategies for recovering the customer's goodwill if and when such a problem occurs.

Challenges and Questions for Service Marketers

Because of the basic characteristics of services, marketers of services face some very real and distinctive challenges. Answers to questions such as the ones listed here still elude managers of services:

How can service quality be defined and improved when the product is intangible and nonstandardized?

How can new services be designed and tested effectively when the service is essentially an intangible process?

How can the firm be certain it is communicating a consistent and relevant image when so many elements of the marketing mix communicate to customers and some of these elements are the service providers themselves?

How does the firm accommodate fluctuating demand when capacity is fixed and the service itself is perishable?

How can the firm best motivate and select service employees who, because the service is delivered in real time, become a critical part of the product itself?

How should prices be set when it is difficult to determine actual costs of production and price may be inextricably intertwined with perceptions of quality?

How should the firm be organized so that good strategic and tactical decisions are made when a decision in any of the functional areas of marketing, operations, and human resources may have significant impact on the other two areas?

How can the balance between standardization and personalization be determined to maximize both the efficiency of the organization and the satisfaction of its customers?

How can the organization protect new service concepts from competitors when service processes cannot be readily patented?

How does the firm communicate quality and value to consumers when the offering is intangible and cannot be readily tried or displayed?

How can the organization ensure the delivery of consistent quality service when both the organization's employees and the customers themselves can affect the service outcome?

SERVICES MARKETING MIX

The preceding questions are some of the many raised by managers and marketers of services that will be addressed throughout the text through a variety of tools and strategies. Sometimes these tools are adaptations of traditional marketing tools, as with the services marketing mix presented here. Other times they are new, as in the case of service blueprinting presented in Chapter 9.

Traditional Marketing Mix

One of the most basic concepts in marketing is the *marketing mix,* defined as the elements an organization controls that can be used to satisfy or communicate with customers. The traditional marketing mix is composed of the four Ps: *product, place* (distribution), *promotion,* and price. These elements appear as core decision variables in any marketing text or marketing plan. The notion of a mix implies that all the variables are interrelated and depend on each other to some extent. Further, the marketing mix philosophy implies an optimal mix of the four factors for a given market segment at a given point in time.

Key strategy decision areas for each of the four Ps are captured in the top four groups in Table 1.3. Careful management of product, place, promotion, and price will clearly also be essential to the successful marketing of services. However, the strategies for the four Ps require some modifications when applied to services. For example, traditionally promotion is thought of as involving decisions related to sales, advertising, sales promotions, and publicity. In services these factors are also important, but because services are produced and consumed simultaneously, service delivery people (such as clerks, ticket takers, nurses, and phone personnel) are involved in realtime promotion of the service even if their jobs are typically defined in terms of the operational function they perform.

Expanded Mix for Services

Because services are usually produced and consumed simultaneously, customers are often present in the firm's factory, interact directly with the firm's personnel, and are actually part of the service production process. Also, because services are intangible, customers will often be looking for any tangible cue to help them understand the nature of the service experience. For example, in the hotel industry the design and decor of the hotel as well as the appearance and attitudes of its employees will influence customer perceptions and experiences.

Acknowledgment of the importance of these additional variables has led services marketers to adopt the concept of an *expanded marketing mix* for services shown in the three remaining groups in Table 1.3.[34] In addition to the traditional four Ps, the services marketing mix includes *people, physical evidence,* and *process.*

People   All human actors who play a part in service delivery and thus influence the buyer's perceptions: namely, the firm's personnel, the customer, and other customers in the service environment.

All the human actors participating in the delivery of a service provide cues to the customer regarding the nature of the service itself. Their attitudes and behaviors, how

TABLE 1.3
Expanded Marketing Mix for Services

Product	Place	Promotion	Price
Physical good features	Channel type	Promotion blend	Flexibility
Quality level	Exposure	Salespeople	Price level
Accessories	Intermediaries	Selection	Terms
Packaging	Outlet locations	Training	Differentiation
Warranties	Transportation	Incentives	Discounts
Product lines	Storage	Advertising	Allowances
Branding	Managing channels	Media types	
		Types of ads	
		Sales promotion	
		Publicity	
		Internet/Web strategy	

People	Physical Evidence	Process
Employees	Facility design	Flow of activities
Recruiting	Equipment	Standardized
Training	Signage	Customized
Motivation	Employee dress	Number of steps
Rewards	Other tangibles	Simple
Teamwork	Reports	Complex
Customers	Business cards	Customer
Education	Statements	involvement
Training	Guarantees	

these people are dressed, and their personal appearance, all influence the customer's perceptions of the service. In fact, for some services, such as consulting, counseling, teaching, and other professional relationship-based services, the provider *is* the service. In other cases the contact person may play what appears to be a relatively small part in service delivery—for instance, a telephone installer, an airline baggage handler, or an equipment delivery dispatcher. Yet research suggests that even these providers may be the focal point of service encounters that can prove critical for the organization.

In many service situations, customers themselves can also influence service delivery, thus affecting service quality and their own satisfaction. For example, a client of a consulting company can influence the quality of service received by providing needed and timely information and by implementing recommendations provided by the consultant. Similarly, health care patients greatly affect the quality of service they receive when they either comply or do not comply with health regimens prescribed by the provider.

Customers not only influence their own service outcomes, but they can influence other customers as well. In a theater, at a ballgame, or in a classroom, customers can influence the quality of service received by others—either enhancing or detracting from other customers' experiences.

Physical evidence   The environment in which the service is delivered and where the firm and customer interact, and any tangible components that facilitate performance or communication of the service.

The physical evidence of service includes all the tangible representations of the service such as brochures, letterhead, business cards, reports, signage, and equipment. In some cases it includes the physical facility where the service is offered—the "servicescape"—for example, the retail bank branch facility. In other cases, such as telecommunication services, the physical facility may be irrelevant. In this case other tangibles such as billing statements and appearance of the repair truck may be important indicators of quality. Especially when consumers have little on which to judge the actual quality of service they will rely on these cues, just as they rely on the cues provided by the people and the service process. Physical evidence cues provide excellent opportunities for the firm to send consistent and strong messages regarding the organization's purpose, the intended market segments, and the nature of the service.

Process   The actual procedures, mechanisms, and flow of activities by which the service is delivered—the service delivery and operating systems.

The actual delivery steps that the customer experiences, or the operational flow of the service, also give customers evidence on which to judge the service. Some services are very complex, requiring the customer to follow a complicated and extensive series of actions to complete the process. Highly bureaucratized services frequently follow this pattern, and the logic of the steps involved often escapes the customer. Another distinguishing characteristic of the process that can provide evidence to the customer is whether the service follows a production-line/standardized approach or whether the process is an empowered/customized one. None of these characteristics of the service is inherently better or worse than another. Rather, the point is that these process characteristics are another form of evidence used by the consumer to judge service. For example, two successful airline companies, Southwest and Singapore Airlines, follow extremely different process models. Southwest is a no-frills (no food, no assigned seats), low-priced airline that offers frequent, relatively short domestic flights. All the evidence it provides is consistent with its vision and market position, as illustrated in Exhibit 1.2. Singapore Airlines, on the other hand, focuses on the business traveler

Southwest Airlines occupies a solid position in the minds of U.S. air travelers as a reliable, convenient, fun, low-fare, no-frills airline. Translated, this position means high value—a position reinforced by all elements of Southwest's services marketing mix. It has maintained this position consistently for more than 30 years while making money every year; no other U.S. airline comes close to this record.

Success has come for a number of reasons. One is the airline's low cost structure. It flies only one type of plane (Boeing 737s), which lowers costs because of the fuel efficiency of the aircraft itself combined with the ability to standardize maintenance and operational procedures. The airline also keeps its costs down by not serving meals, having no preassigned seats, and keeping employee turnover very low. Southwest Airlines' Herb Kelleher (president of Southwest from its inception until 2001, and subsequently serving as chairman) is famous for his belief that employees come first, not customers. The Dallas-based carrier has managed to be the low-cost provider and a preferred employer while enjoying high levels of customer satisfaction and strong customer loyalty. Southwest Airlines has the best customer service record in the airline industry and has won the industry's "Triple Crown" for best baggage handling, best on-time performance, and best customer complaint statistics many times.

Observing Southwest Airlines' success, it is clear that all of its marketing mix is aligned around its highly successful market position. The three traditional services marketing mix elements all strongly reinforce the value image of the airline:

- **People** Southwest uses its people and its customers very effectively to communicate its position. Employees are unionized, yet they are trained to have fun, allowed to define what "fun" means, and given authority to do what it takes to make flights light-hearted and enjoyable. People are hired at Southwest for their attitudes; technical skills can be and are trained. And they are the most productive workforce in the U.S. airline industry. Customers also are included in the atmosphere of fun, and many get into the act by joking with the crew and each other and by flooding the airline with letters expressing their satisfaction.

- **Process** The service delivery process at Southwest also reinforces its position. There are no assigned

seats on the aircraft, so passengers line up and are "herded" by assigned groups and numbers onto the plane, where they jockey for seats. With very few exceptions, the airline does not transfer baggage to connecting flights on other airlines. Food is not served in flight. In all, the process is very efficient, standardized, and low-cost, allowing for quick turn-around and low fares. Customers are very much part of the service process, taking on their roles willingly.

- **Physical evidence** All the tangibles associated with Southwest further reinforce the market position. Employees dress casually, wearing shorts in the summer to reinforce the "fun" and further emphasize the airline's commitment to its employees' comfort. No in-flight meal service confirms the low-price image through the absence of tangibles—no food. Because many people joke about airline food, its absence for many is not viewed as a value detractor. Southwest's simple, easy-to-use website is yet another form of consistent, tangible evidence that supports the airline's strong positioning and reinforces its image.

The consistent positioning using the services marketing mix reinforces the unique image in the customer's mind, giving Southwest Airlines its high-value position.

Source: K. Freiberg and J. Freiberg, *Nuts! Southwest Airlines' Crazy Recipe for Business and Personal Success* (Austin, TX: Bard Press, Inc., 1996); K. Labich, "Is Herb Kelleher America's Best CEO?" *Fortune,* May 2, 1994; H. Kelleher and K. Brooker, "The Chairman of the Board Looks Back," *Fortune,* May 28, 2001, pp. 62–76; J. H. Gitell, *The Southwest Airlines Way* (New York: McGraw-Hill, 2003).

and is concerned with meeting individual traveler needs. Thus, its process is highly customized to the individual, and employees are empowered to provide nonstandard service when needed. Both airlines have been very successful.

The three new marketing mix elements (people, physical evidence, and process) are included in the marketing mix as separate elements because they are within the control of the firm *and* because any or all of them may influence the customer's initial decision to purchase a service as well as the customer's level of satisfaction and repurchase decisions. The traditional elements as well as the new marketing mix elements will be explored in depth in future chapters.

STAYING FOCUSED ON THE CUSTOMER

A critical theme running throughout the text is *customer focus*. In fact, the subtitle of the book is "integrating customer focus across the firm." From the firm's point of view, all strategies are developed with an eye on the customer, and all implementations are carried out with an understanding of their impact on the customer. From a practical perspective, decisions regarding new services and communication plans will integrate the customer's point of view; operations and human resource decisions will be considered in terms of their impact on customers. All the tools, strategies, and frameworks included in this text have customers at their foundation. The services marketing mix just described is clearly an important tool that addresses the uniqueness of services, keeping the customer at the center.

In this text, we also view customers as assets to be valued, developed, and retained. The strategies and tools we offer thus focus on customer relationship building and loyalty as opposed to a more transactional focus in which customers are viewed as one-time revenue producers. This text looks at customer relationship management not as a software program but as an entire architecture or business philosophy. Every chapter in the text can be considered a component needed to build a complete customer relationship management approach.

Summary

This chapter has set the stage for further learning about services marketing by presenting information on changes in the world economy and business practice that have driven the focus on service: the fact that services dominate the modern economies of the world; the focus on service as a competitive business imperative; specific needs of the deregulated and professional service industries; the role of new service concepts growing from technological advances; and the realization that the characteristics of services result in unique challenges and opportunities. The chapter presented a broad definition of services as deeds, processes, and performances, and it drew distinctions among pure services, value-added services, customer service, and derived service.

Building on this fundamental understanding of the service economy, the chapter presents the key characteristics of services that underlie the need for distinct strategies and concepts for managing service businesses. These basic characteristics are that services are intangible, heterogeneous, produced and consumed simultaneously, and perishable. Because of these characteristics, service managers face a number of challenges in marketing, including the complex problem of how to deliver quality services consistently.

The chapter ended by describing two themes that provide the foundation for future chapters: the expanded marketing mix for services; and customer focus as a unifying theme. The remainder of the text focuses on exploring the unique opportunities and challenges faced by organizations that sell and deliver services and on developing solutions that will help you become an effective services champion and manager.

Discussion Questions

1. What distinguishes service offerings from customer service? Provide specific examples.
2. How is technology changing the nature of customer service and service offerings?
3. What are the basic characteristics of services compared with goods? What are the implications of these characteristics for IBM Global Service or for Southwest Airlines?
4. One of the underlying frameworks for the text is the services marketing mix. Discuss why each of the three new mix elements (process, people, and physical evidence) is included. How might each of these communicate with or help to satisfy an organization's customers?
5. Think of a service job you have had or currently have. How effective, in your opinion, was or is the organization in managing the elements of the services marketing mix?
6. Again, think of a service job you have had or currently have. How did or does the organization handle relevant challenges listed in Table 1.2?
7. How can quality service be used in a manufacturing context for competitive advantage? Think of your answer to this question in the context of automobiles or computers or some other manufactured product you have actually purchased.

Exercises

1. Roughly calculate your budget for an average month. What percentage of your budget goes for services versus goods? Do the services you purchase have value? In what sense? If you had to cut back on your expenses, what would you cut out?
2. Visit two local retail service providers that you believe are positioned very differently (such as Kmart and Nordstrom, or Burger King and a fine restaurant). From your own observations, compare their strategies on the elements of the services marketing mix.
3. Try a service you have never tried before on the Internet. Analyze the benefits of this service. Was enough information provided to make the service easy to use? How would you compare this service to other methods of obtaining the same benefits?

Notes

1. "Hiding in Plain Sight: Service Innovation, a New Priority for Chief Executives," IBM Corporation, IBM Institute for Business Value, 2006, www.ibm.com/iibv; A. Bednarz, "Customers Applaud IBM Services Face-Lift," *Network World,* October 2, 2006, p. 25; D. Kirkpatrick, "Inside Sam's $100 Billion Growth Machine," *Fortune,* June 14, 2004, pp. 80–98; W. M. Bulkeley, "These Days, Big Blue Is About Big Services Not Just Big Boxes," *The Wall Street Journal,* June 11, 2001, p. A1; A. Radding, "How IBM is Applying Science to the World of Service," *Consulting Magazine,*" May 2006.
2. D. Brady, "Why Service Stinks," *BusinessWeek,* October 23, 2000, pp. 118–128.
3. www.theacsi.org.
4. J. B. Quinn, J. J. Baruch, and P. C. Paquette, "Technology in Services," *Scientific American* 257, no. 6 (December 1987), pp. 50–58.
5. S. L. Vargo and R. F. Lusch, "Evolving to a New Dominant Logic for Marketing," *Journal of Marketing* 68 (January 2004), pp. 1–17; R. F. Lusch and S. L. Vargo, (eds.), *The Service-Dominant Logic of Marketing: Dialog, Debate, and Directions,* (New York: M. E. Sharpe, 2006); *Journal of the Academy of Marketing Science,* Special Issue or the Service-Dominant Logic, Winter 2008.

6. M. J. Argersinger and E. M. Whitaker, "U.S. International Transactions, Fourth Quarter of 2006," *Survey of Current Business,* April 2007, pp. 13–21.

7. M. Sawhney, S. Balasubramanian, and V. V. Krishnan, "Creating Growth with Services," *Sloan Management Review,* 45, (Winter 2004), pp. 34–43.

8. T. Smart, "Jack Welch's Encore," *BusinessWeek,* October 28, 1996, pp. 155–160; and GE company data, 2000.

9. D. Brady, "Will Jeff Immelt's New Push Pay Off for GE?" *BusinessWeek,* October 13, 2003, pp. 94–98.

10. J. A. Alexander and M. W. Hordes, *S-Business: Reinventing the Services Organization* (New York: SelectBooks, 2003); R. Oliva and R. Kallenberg, "Managing the Transition from Products to Services," *International Journal of Service Industry Management* 14, no. 2 (2003), pp. 160–172; W. A. Neu and S. W. Brown, "Forming Successful Business-to-Business Services in Goods-Dominant Firms," *Journal of Service Research,* 8, (August 2005), pp. 3–17.

11. R. H. K. Vietor, *Contrived Competition* (Cambridge, MA: Harvard University Press, 1994).

12. This discussion is based on interviews conducted by Gary Knisely that appeared in *Advertising Age* on January 15, 1979; February 19, 1979; March 19, 1979; and May 14, 1979.

13. L. Berry, *Discovering the Soul of Service* (New York: The Free Press, 1999).

14. R. T. Rust, C. Moorman, and P. R. Dickson, "Getting Return on Quality: Revenue Expansion, Cost Reduction, or Both?" *Journal of Marketing* 66 (October 2002), pp. 7–24.

15. J. L. Heskett, T. O. Jones, G. W. Loveman, W. E. Sasser Jr., and L. A. Schlesinger, "Putting the Service–Profit Chain to Work," *Harvard Business Review,* 72 (March–April 1994), pp. 164–174.

16. E. W. Anderson and V. Mittal, "Strengthening the Satisfaction–Profit Chain," *Journal of Service Research* 3 (November 2000), pp. 107–120.

17. C. Fornell, S. Mithias, F. V. Morgeson III, and M. S. Krishnan, "Customer Satisfaction and Stock Prices; High Returns, Low Risk," *Journal of Marketing,* 70 (January 2006), pp. 3–14; "Economic Indicator," www.theacsi.org, accessed June 29, 2007.

18. C. Fishman, "But Wait, You Promised . . . ," *Fast Company,* April 2001, pp. 116–127.

19. D. Brady, "Why Service Stinks," *BusinessWeek,* October 23, 2000, pp. 116–128.

20. "Improvement in Customer Satisfaction Slows," First Quarter 2007 Commentary and Scores by Industry; www.theacsi.org, accessed June 29, 2007.

21. L. P. Willcocks and R. Plant, "Getting from Bricks to Clicks," *Sloan Management Review,* 42 (Spring 2001), pp. 50–59.

22. W. Mossberg and K. Boehret, "Testing Out the iPhone," *The Wall Street Journal,* June 27, 2007, p. D1.

23. B. Kiviat, "How a Man on a Mission (and a Harley) Reinvented Banking," *Time,* June 25, 2007, pp. 45–46.

24. "Online Health Search, 2006," Pew Internet and American Life Project," www.pewinternet.org, accessed, June 29, 2007.

25. M. J. Bitner, S. W. Brown, and M. L. Meuter, "Technology Infusion in Service Encounters," *Journal of the Academy of Marketing Science* 28 (Winter 2000), pp. 138–149.

26. M. J. Bitner, "Self-Service Technologies: What Do Customers Expect?" *Marketing Management,* 10 (Spring 2001), pp. 10–11.

27. R. Hallowell, "Service in E-Commerce: Findings from Exploratory Research," Harvard Business School, Module Note, N9-800-418, May 31, 2000.

28. D. G. Mick and S. Fournier, "Paradoxes of Technology: Consumer Cognizance, Emotions, and Coping Strategies," *Journal of Consumer Research* 25 (September 1998), pp. 123–147.

29. A. Parasuraman and C. L. Colby, *Techno-Ready Marketing: How and Why Your Customers Adopt Technology* (New York: The Free Press, 2001).

30. "Customer Care in a New World," McKinsey & Company, 2001.

31. Discussion of these issues is found in many services marketing publications. The discussion here is based on V. A. Zeithaml, A. Parasuraman, and L. L. Berry, "Problems and Strategies in Services Marketing," *Journal of Marketing* 49 (Spring 1985), pp. 33–46.

32. For research supporting the idea of goods–services continua, see D. Iacobucci, "An Empirical Examination of Some Basic Tenets in Services: Goods–Services Continua," in *Advances in Services Marketing and Management,* T. A. Swartz, D. E. Bowen, and S. W. Brown ed. (Greenwich, CT: JAI Press, 1992), vol. 1, pp. 23–52.

33. S. L. Vargo and R. F. Lusch, "The Four Service Marketing Myths," *Journal of Service Research* 6 (May 2004), pp. 324–335.

34. B. H. Booms and M. J. Bitner, "Marketing Strategies and Organizational Structures for Service Firms," in *Marketing of Services,* ed. J. H. Donnelly and W. R. George (Chicago: American Marketing Association, 1981), pp. 47–51.

Chapter Two

Conceptual Framework of the Book: The Gaps Model of Service Quality

This chapter's objectives are to

1. Introduce a framework, called the gaps model of service quality, which is used to organize this textbook.
2. Demonstrate that the gaps model is a useful framework for understanding service quality in an organization.
3. Demonstrate that the most critical service quality gap to close is the customer gap, the difference between customer expectations and perceptions.
4. Show that four gaps that occur in companies, which we call provider gaps, are responsible for the customer gap.
5. Identify the factors responsible for each of the four provider gaps.

Service Quality at the Island Hotel, Cedar Key, Florida

For those of you accustomed to staying at hotel chains when you travel, consider your experience with the Island Hotel, a bed-and-breakfast located in Cedar Key, a small barrier reef on the gulf side of the Florida coast. You telephone the inn to reserve a guest room and speak directly to one of the owners, who sounds very happy to take your call. She tells you that the hotel, built in 1859, is on the National Register of Historic Buildings and that each of its 13 guest rooms is uniquely decorated. She discusses each of the available rooms until you find the one that sounds right for you. When you arrive at the Hotel, she and her husband and the inn's famous chef Jahn McCumbers meet you in the lobby and welcome you personally. The husband, not a bellhop, carries your bags to your room, which is charming and has an old-fashioned claw-footed bathtub right in the corner. After you open your bags and freshen up, you go to the restaurant downstairs, renowned as the superior seafood restaurant in Cedar Key and the surrounding area. You choose the house specialties, Crab Bisque and Heart of Palm Salad, and say hello to the chef when she stops by your table to ask if all is OK. You stop in the small bar that has a large mural of King Neptune and his court stretching across the wall and find that the bartender and all the customers welcome you as if you were a regular. When you return to your room, the owner is putting fresh towels on your bed and wishes you a good evening. You make one more stop before you sleep: you step out on the balcony to sit on a large rocking chair and look out over the bay and marina, feeling as if you have just spent a day with a warm, caring family in an impeccable home rather than in a hotel. This feeling is repeated every day of your stay, and when you leave, the owners and chef are in the lobby to personally thank you for coming and send you on your way.

Most of you will agree that the service experience at the Island Hotel is exceptional. The reservation is tailored to you; the employees (in this case, owners and chef and bartender) are concerned and genuinely caring about your comfort; the setting is ideal; the other guests and customers are friendly; the food is superb; and—perhaps most impressive—the whole experience from reservation to stay to checkout is coordinated to make you feel known and special.

Do you typically receive this experience from a stay at the Hilton or Radisson or even the more upscale Hyatt? If not, why not? This chapter will introduce you to some of the ways that organizations fall short in delivering quality service and to the underlying reasons why these gaps occur. You may have guessed that small organizations like the Island Hotel have fewer difficulties than do large organizations in controlling all the factors that influence service delivery. You probably do not yet realize how many different factors must be organized and managed to deliver what the Island Hotel delivers. This chapter will provide that perspective.

Effective services marketing is a complex undertaking that involves many different strategies, skills, and tasks. Executives of service organizations have long been confused about how to approach this complicated topic in an organized manner. This textbook is designed around one approach: viewing services in a structured, integrated way called the *gaps model of service quality*.[1] This model positions the key concepts, strategies, and decisions in services marketing and will be used to guide the structure of the rest of this book; sections of the book are tied to each of the gaps described in this chapter.

THE CUSTOMER GAP

The *customer gap* is the difference between customer expectations and perceptions (see Figure 2.1). Customer expectations are standards or reference points that customers bring into the service experience, whereas customer perceptions are subjective assessments of actual service experiences. Customer expectations often consist of what a customer believes should or will happen. For example, when you visit an expensive restaurant, you expect a high level of service, one that is considerably superior to the level you would expect in a fast-food restaurant. Closing the gap between what customers expect and what they perceive is critical to delivering quality service; it forms the basis for the gaps model.

Because customer satisfaction and customer focus are so critical to competitiveness of firms, any company interested in delivering quality service must begin with a clear

FIGURE 2.1
The Customer Gap

The Customer Gap

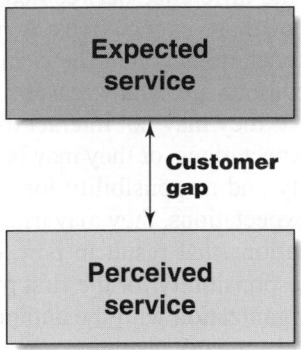

understanding of its customers. This understanding is relatively easy for an organization as small as the Island Hotel but very difficult for a large organization in which managers are not in direct contact with customers. For this reason, we will devote the first section of the textbook to describing the relevant customer concepts so that the focus of everything can relate back to these concepts. Considerable evidence exists that consumer evaluation processes differ for goods and services and that these differences affect the way service providers market their organizations. Unfortunately, much of what is known and written about consumer evaluation processes pertains specifically to goods. The assumption appears to be that services, if not identical to goods, are at least similar enough in the consumer's mind that they are chosen and evaluated in the same manner. We will detail what is known about customer behavior in services in Chapter 3.

The sources of customer expectations are marketer-controlled factors (such as pricing, advertising, sales promises) as well as factors that the marketer has limited ability to affect (innate personal needs, word-of-mouth communications, and competitive offerings). In a perfect world, expectations and perceptions would be identical: customers would perceive that they have received what they thought they would and should. In practice these concepts are often, even usually, separated by some distance. Broadly, it is the goal of services marketing to bridge this distance, and we will devote virtually the entire textbook to describing strategies and practices designed to close this customer gap. We will describe customer expectations in detail in Chapter 4 and customer perceptions in Chapter 5.

THE PROVIDER GAPS

To close the all-important customer gap, the gaps model suggests that four other gaps—the *provider gaps*—need to be closed. These gaps occur within the organization providing the service (hence the term *provider gaps*) and include

Gap 1: The Listening Gap

Gap 2: The Service Design and Standards Gap

Gap 3: The Service Performance Gap

Gap 4: The Communication Gap

The rest of this chapter is devoted to a description of the full gaps model.

Provider Gap 1: The Listening Gap

Provider gap 1, the *listening gap,* is the difference between customer expectations of service and company understanding of those expectations. A primary cause in many firms for not meeting customers' expectations is that the firm lacks accurate understanding of exactly what those expectations are. Many reasons exist for managers not being aware of what customers expect: they may not interact directly with customers, they may be unwilling to ask about expectations, or they may be unprepared to address them. When people with the authority and responsibility for setting priorities do not fully understand customers' service expectations, they may trigger a chain of bad decisions and suboptimal resource allocations that result in perceptions of poor service quality. In this text, we broaden the responsibility for the first provider gap from managers alone to any employee in the organization with the authority to change or influence service policies and procedures. In today's changing organizations, the authority to make adjustments in service delivery is often delegated to empowered teams and frontline people. In business-to-business situations, in particular, account teams make their own decisions about how to address their clients' unique expectations.

Figure 2.2 shows the key factors responsible for provider gap l, the listening gap. An inadequate *marketing research orientation* is one of the critical factors. When management or empowered employees do not acquire accurate information about customers' expectations, this gap is large. Formal and informal methods to capture information about customer expectations must be developed through marketing research. Techniques involving a variety of traditional research approaches—among them customer interviews, survey research, complaint systems, and customer panels—must be used to stay close to the customer. More innovative techniques, such as structured brainstorming and service quality gap analysis, are often needed. This chapter's Global Feature discusses one of these innovative techniques that IKEA and other companies have used to identify customer expectations.

Another key factor that is related to the listening gap is lack of *upward communication.* Frontline employees often know a great deal about customers; if management is not in contact with frontline employees and does not understand what they know, the gap widens.

FIGURE 2.2
Key Factors Leading to Provider Gap l: The Listening Gap

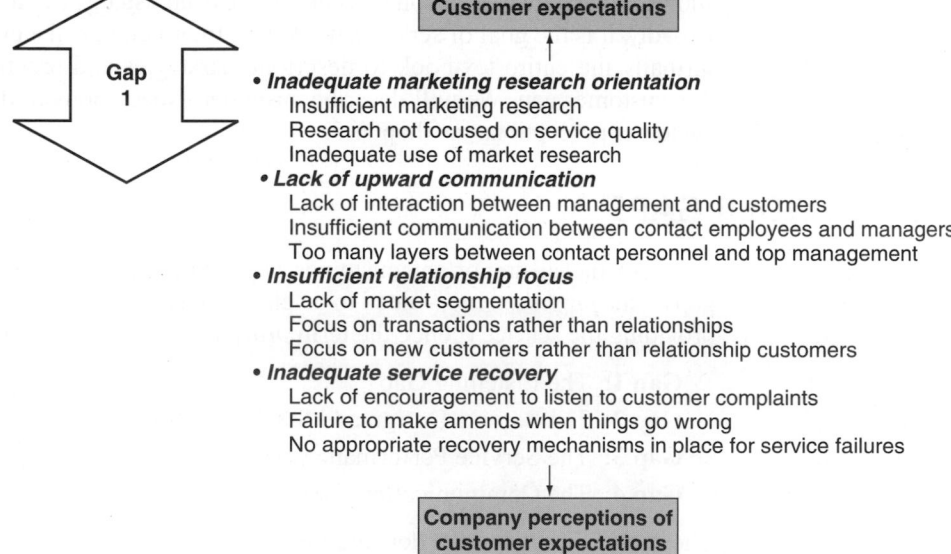

• *Inadequate marketing research orientation*
  Insufficient marketing research
  Research not focused on service quality
  Inadequate use of market research
• *Lack of upward communication*
  Lack of interaction between management and customers
  Insufficient communication between contact employees and managers
  Too many layers between contact personnel and top management
• *Insufficient relationship focus*
  Lack of market segmentation
  Focus on transactions rather than relationships
  Focus on new customers rather than relationship customers
• *Inadequate service recovery*
  Lack of encouragement to listen to customer complaints
  Failure to make amends when things go wrong
  No appropriate recovery mechanisms in place for service failures

Finding out what customers expect is the first step in closing all the gaps in the organization to provide service excellence. In Chapter 6 we will talk about many ways that companies determine customer perceptions, including customer surveys and complaints, but understanding what customers expect can often be more challenging. Putting customers in the "wish mode" is an innovative approach to closing gap 1 that proved successful for IKEA, the world's largest furniture retailer, when it opened its Chicago retail outlet. In this approach, nine groups of a dozen customers each were asked to dream up their ideal IKEA shopping experience. They were told to pretend that all IKEA stores had been destroyed and that new ones had to be designed from scratch. How would the store look? What would the shopping experience be like? Jason Magidson, who helped IKEA create the process, reported that customers responded with statements like the following:

> "I never feel disoriented because I always know exactly where I am in relation to every department."
> "If I am buying one item, all of the other items that go with it are nearby."
> "Shopping is a pleasant, relaxing experience."

Even though they were not technical experts, customers were asked to actually draw up a design for a store that would satisfy their needs.

What is significant about IKEA's approach is not just that the company asked customers what they expected but that they subsequently incorporated these expectations into the service design for the store. Designers created a multistory octagonal building with an atrium in the center that formed a home base for shoppers, addressing their concern about being able to find items easily. In keeping with another customer expectation, items were grouped together with related products. When shoppers were tired or hungry, they could go to the cafeteria-style restaurant on the upper floor that served Swedish food. IKEA's customers were so satisfied with the store (85 percent rated it as "excellent" or "very good") that they returned more and spent about an hour longer than they did in other IKEA stores. These actions close gap 2 because service design was based on customer expectations.

IKEA has done an excellent job of closing all four provider gaps. The company's supplier network is carefully chosen and managed to ensure quality and consistency. Despite the fact that the company has stores in more than 30 countries, it keeps standards, designs, and approaches very consistent everywhere, thereby reducing the service design and standards gap. The company also makes important changes to standards when necessary. In 2006, the company took a major step to address a customer need to reduce long wait times. When company managers realized that wait times were so long that customers were leaving the stores without paying for their items because of congestion at checkout, they implemented a "line busting" initiative using handheld technology. In peak times, extra retail associates now roam the checkout area and invite credit card customers to step out of line and pay with a handheld unit and get a receipt from a mobile printer.

Servicescapes—the indoor and outdoor physical environments—are unique and customer focused, further closing gap 2. IKEA is also well known for its strong employee culture and careful hiring and training—factors that help reduce gap 3. In Chapter 13, we will tell you about another way the company closes gap 3: its innovative service concept that involves customers in the delivery, assembly, and creation of its products. To accomplish this service, the company educates its customers thoroughly with its scriptlike catalogs, thereby helping to close gap 4.

Sources: Jason Magidson and Gregg Brandyberry, "Putting Customers in the 'Wish Mode,'" *Harvard Business Review,* September 2001, pp. 26–27; "Who You Gonna Call?" *Chain Store Age,* January 2006, p. 8.

Also related to the listening gap is a lack of company strategies to retain customers and strengthen relationships with them, an approach called *relationship marketing.* When organizations have strong relationships with existing customers, provider gap 1 is less likely to occur. Relationship marketing is distinct from transactional marketing, the term used to describe the more conventional emphasis on acquiring new customers rather than on retaining them. Relationship marketing has always been a practice of wise business-to-business firms (such as IBM or Boeing) that recognize that clients have the potential to spend more with them if they provide excellent service. Other business-to-business firms, and many companies that sell to end customers, often take a short-term view and see each sale as a transaction. When companies focus too much on attracting new customers, they may fail to understand the changing needs and expectations of their current customers. Technology affords companies the ability to acquire and integrate vast quantities of data on customers that can be used to build relationships. Frequent flyer travel programs conducted by airlines, car rental companies, and hotels are among the most familiar programs of this type.

The final key factor associated with provider gap 1 is lack of *service recovery.* Even the best companies, with the best of intentions and clear understanding of their customers' expectations, sometimes fail. It is critical for an organization to understand the importance of service recovery—why people complain, what they expect when they complain, and how to develop effective service recovery strategies for dealing with inevitable service failures. Such strategies might involve a well-defined complaint-handling procedure and an emphasis on empowering employees to react on the spot, in real time, to fix the failure; other times it involves a service guarantee or ways to compensate the customer for the unfulfilled promise.

To address the factors in the listening gap, this text will cover topics that include how to understand customers through multiple research strategies (Chapter 6), how to build strong relationships and understand customer needs over time (Chapter 7), and how to implement recovery strategies when things go wrong (Chapter 8). Through these strategies, this first gap can be minimized.

Provider Gap 2: The Service Design and Standards Gap

Accurate perceptions of customers' expectations are necessary, but not sufficient, for delivering superior quality service. Another prerequisite is the presence of service designs and performance standards that reflect those accurate perceptions. A recurring theme in service companies is the difficulty experienced in translating customer expectations into service quality specifications that employees can understand and execute. These problems are reflected in provider gap 2, the difference between company understanding of customer expectations and development of customer-driven service designs and standards. Customer-driven standards are different from the conventional performance standards that companies establish for service in that they are based on pivotal customer requirements that are visible to and measured by customers. They are operations standards set to correspond to customer expectations and priorities rather than to company concerns such as productivity or efficiency.

As shown in Figure 2.3, provider gap 2—which we call the *service design and standards gap*—exists in service organizations for a variety of reasons. Those people responsible for setting standards, typically management, sometimes believe that customer expectations are unreasonable or unrealistic. They may also believe that the

FIGURE 2.3
Key Factors Leading to Provider Gap 2: The Service Design and Standards Gap

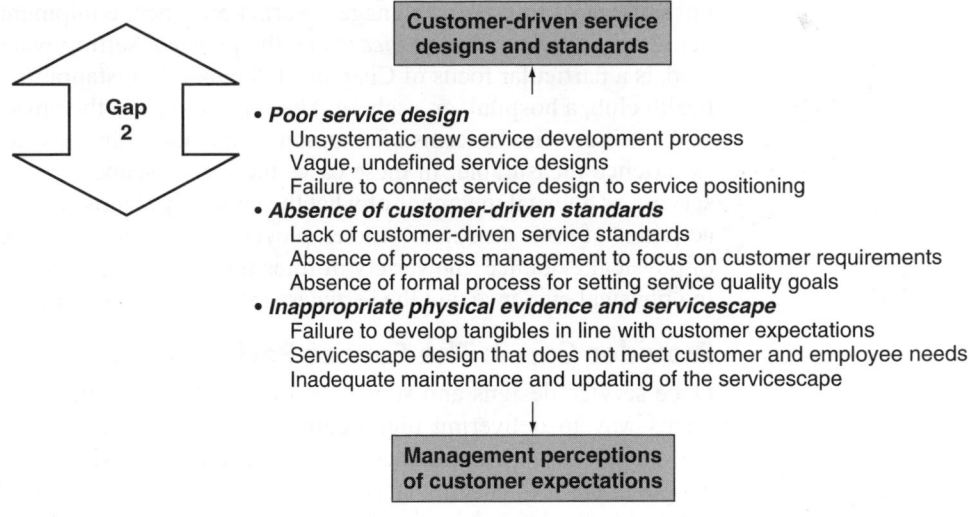

Gap 2

Customer-driven service designs and standards

- *Poor service design*
  Unsystematic new service development process
  Vague, undefined service designs
  Failure to connect service design to service positioning
- *Absence of customer-driven standards*
  Lack of customer-driven service standards
  Absence of process management to focus on customer requirements
  Absence of formal process for setting service quality goals
- *Inappropriate physical evidence and servicescape*
  Failure to develop tangibles in line with customer expectations
  Servicescape design that does not meet customer and employee needs
  Inadequate maintenance and updating of the servicescape

Management perceptions of customer expectations

degree of variability inherent in service defies standardization and therefore that setting standards will not achieve the desired goal. Although some of these assumptions are valid in some situations, they are often only rationalizations of management's reluctance to tackle head-on the difficult challenges of creating service standards to deliver excellent service.

Technology changes and improvements are particularly helpful in closing this gap, as the Technology Spotlight in this chapter describes.

Because services are intangible, they are difficult to describe and communicate. This difficulty becomes especially evident when new services are being developed. It is critical that all people involved (managers, frontline employees, and behind-the-scenes support staff) be working with the same concepts of the new service, based on customer needs and expectations. For a service that already exists, any attempt to improve it will also suffer unless everyone has the same vision of the service and associated issues. One of the most important ways to avoid provider gap 2 is to clearly design services without oversimplification, incompleteness, subjectivity, and bias. To do so, tools are needed to ensure that new and existing services are developed and improved in as careful a manner as possible. Chapter 9 describes the tools that are most effective in *service development and design,* including service blueprinting, a unique tool for services.

The quality of service delivered by customer contact personnel is critically influenced by the standards against which they are evaluated and compensated. Standards signal to contact personnel what management priorities are and which types of performance really count. When service standards are absent or when the standards in place do not reflect customers' expectations, quality of service as perceived by customers is likely to suffer. When standards do reflect what customers expect, perceptions of the quality of service they receive are likely to be enhanced. Chapter 10 discusses the topic of *customer-defined service standards* and shows that if they are developed appropriately they can have a powerful positive impact on closing both provider gap 2 and the customer gap.

In Chapter 11 we focus on the roles of physical evidence in service design and in meeting customer expectations. By *physical evidence,* we mean everything from business cards to reports, signage, Internet presence, equipment, and facilities used to deliver the service. The *servicescape,* the physical setting where the service is delivered, is a particular focus of Chapter 11. Think of a restaurant, a hotel, a theme park, a health club, a hospital, or a school. The servicescape—the physical facility—is critical in these industries in terms of communicating about the service and making the entire experience pleasurable. In these cases the servicescape plays a variety of roles, from serving as a visual metaphor of what the company stands for to actually facilitating the activities of both consumers and employees. In Chapter 11 we explore the importance of physical evidence, the variety of roles it plays, and strategies for effectively designing physical evidence and the servicescape to meet customer expectations.

Provider Gap 3: The Service Performance Gap

Once service designs and standards are in place, it would seem that the firm is well on its way to delivering high-quality services. This assumption is true, but is still not enough to deliver excellent service. The firm must have systems, processes, and people in place to ensure that service delivery actually matches (or is even better than) the designs and standards in place.

Provider gap 3—the *service performance gap*—is the discrepancy between development of customer-driven service standards and actual service performance by company employees. Even when guidelines exist for performing services well and treating customers correctly, high-quality service performance is not a certainty. Standards must be backed by appropriate resources (people, systems, and technology) and also must be enforced to be effective—that is, employees must be measured and compensated on the basis of performance along those standards. Thus, even when standards accurately reflect customers' expectations, if the company fails to provide support for those standards—if it does not facilitate, encourage, and require their achievement—standards do no good. When the level of service delivery falls short of the standards, it falls short of what customers expect as well. Narrowing the performance gap—by ensuring that all the resources needed to achieve the standards are in place—reduces the customer gap.

Research has identified many of the critical inhibitors to closing the *service performance gap* (see Figure 2.4). These factors include *employees* who do not clearly understand the roles they are to play in the company, employees who experience conflict between customers and company management, poor employee selection, inadequate technology, inappropriate compensation and recognition, and lack of empowerment and teamwork. These factors all relate to the company's human resource function and involve internal practices such as recruitment, training, feedback, job design, motivation, and organizational structure. To deliver better service performance, these issues must be addressed across functions (such as marketing and human resources).

Another important variable in provider gap 3 is the *customer.* Even if contact employees and intermediaries are 100 percent consistent in their service delivery, the uncontrollable variables of the customer can introduce variability in service delivery. If customers do not perform their roles appropriately—if, for example, they fail to provide all the information necessary to the provider or neglect to read and follow instructions—service quality is jeopardized. Customers can also negatively influence the quality of service received by others if they are disruptive or take more than their share of a service provider's time. Understanding customer roles and how customers themselves can influence service delivery and outcomes are critical.

FIGURE 2.4
Key Factors Leading to Provider Gap 3: The Service Performance Gap

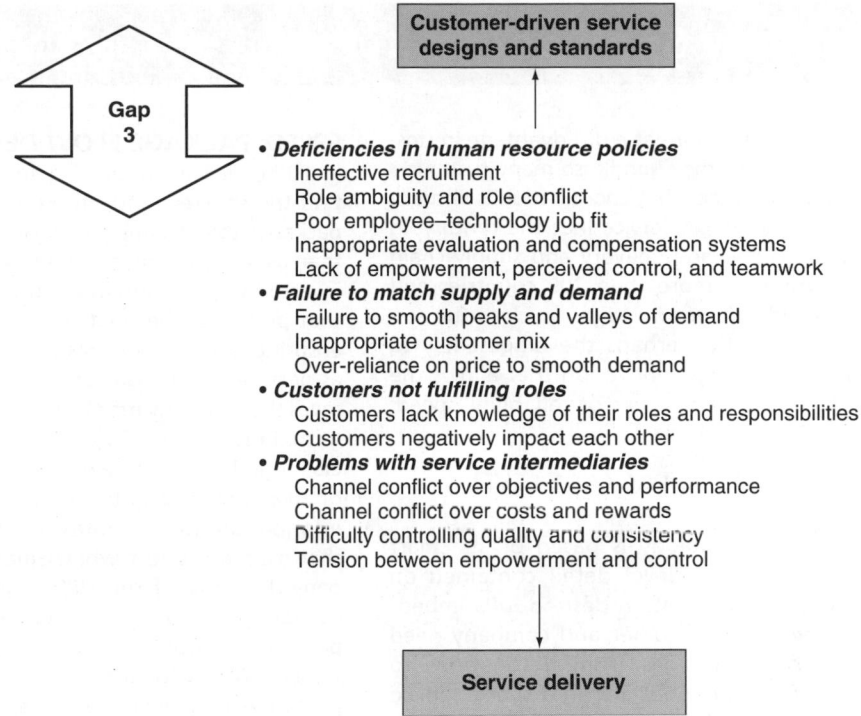

Customer-driven service designs and standards

Gap 3

- *Deficiencies in human resource policies*
  - Ineffective recruitment
  - Role ambiguity and role conflict
  - Poor employee–technology job fit
  - Inappropriate evaluation and compensation systems
  - Lack of empowerment, perceived control, and teamwork
- *Failure to match supply and demand*
  - Failure to smooth peaks and valleys of demand
  - Inappropriate customer mix
  - Over-reliance on price to smooth demand
- *Customers not fulfilling roles*
  - Customers lack knowledge of their roles and responsibilities
  - Customers negatively impact each other
- *Problems with service intermediaries*
  - Channel conflict over objectives and performance
  - Channel conflict over costs and rewards
  - Difficulty controlling quality and consistency
  - Tension between empowerment and control

Service delivery

A third difficulty associated with provider gap 3 involves the challenge in delivering service through such *intermediaries* as retailers, franchisees, agents, and brokers. Because quality in service occurs in the human interaction between customers and service providers, control over the service encounter by the company is crucial, yet it rarely is fully possible. Most service (and many manufacturing) companies face an even more formidable task: attaining service excellence and consistency in the presence of intermediaries who represent them and interact with their customers yet are not under their direct control. Franchisers of services depend on their franchisees to execute service delivery as they have specified it. And it is that execution by the franchisee which the customer uses to evaluate the service quality of the company. With franchises and other types of intermediaries, someone other than the producer is responsible for the fulfillment of quality service. For this reason, a firm must develop ways to either control or motivate these intermediaries to meet company goals.

Another issue in the service performance gap is the need in service firms to *synchronize demand and capacity.* Because services are perishable and cannot be inventoried, service companies frequently face situations of over- or underdemand. Lacking inventories to handle overdemand, companies lose sales when capacity is inadequate to handle customer needs. On the other hand, capacity is frequently underutilized in slow periods. Most service companies rely on operations strategies such as cross-training or varying the size of the employee pool to synchronize supply and demand. Marketing strategies for managing demand—such as price changes, advertising, promotion, and alternative service offerings—can supplement approaches for managing supply.

We will discuss strategies to deal with the roles of employees in Chapter 12, customers in Chapter 13, intermediaries in Chapter 14, and demand and capacity in Chapter 15.

Technology Spotlight   How UPS Closes the Gaps with Technology

Often large companies are at a disadvantage in closing the gaps because they handle so many customers with so many employees that coordination is virtually impossible. United Parcel Service Inc., the century-old global leader in package delivery and supply chain services, operates in more than 200 countries and territories worldwide yet manages to close the service gaps consistently. Perhaps the biggest key to its success is technology innovation that allows the company to address key issues of reliability, speed, and flexibility.

RELIABILITY: THE UPS PACKAGE LEVEL DETAIL

UPS's successful technology is based on its smart label and the package level detail contained on it. To achieve the automation desired, UPS imbeds everything both the customer and company need to know to get packages from destinations to delivery points in bar codes and in a special "maxi code." Information (on addresses, service levels, and billing) appears both in writing and in the bar code, which ensures reliability because it is read by scanners. The label also contains a "1Z" tracking number that allows customers to track packages throughout the supply chain. The 1Z number coordinates the information that the customer has with company databases so that everyone has the same information about the package location at all times.

Another label, called the Pre-Load Assist Label or PAL, also assists with reliability. Printed out on the center of the package, the PAL tells the sorter which conveyor belt to use to get the package to the correct car loading area—and the exact shelf location—for optimum delivery. The value of the PAL can best be understood by recognizing that in the past there were many opportunities for employee error because humans had to remember where they put packages, then arrange and rearrange the packages as they came through to be certain that they were sent to the right location. Now loaders need not shuffle packages, and drivers know exactly in what order to deliver them, thanks to another innovation that will be explained next.

SPEED: PACKAGE FLOW DELIVERY

In 2006, UPS introduced a technology solution to find the shortest and quickest way to get all of its packages to consumers in a geographic area. Rather than using maps and driver knowledge, the company invested $600 million in a route optimization system that plots out the next day's schedules for drivers, ensuring that all packages are delivered as efficiently as possible on the day scheduled. The optimization saves the company money both in the short and long term. In November 2006 alone, the company's drivers logged 3 million fewer miles than they did in all of 2005. In the long term, the software retains vital information about routes, customers, and packing that used to be lost when employees left the company. The task of the UPS driver is complex—both delivering hundreds of packages *and* collecting payments—to both residential and commercial customers. The software creates an optimal dispatch plan for every driver in an area, using current, historical, and forecasted information. The dispatch plan is downloaded each morning into the driver's system, showing exactly what route to follow throughout the day. Without technology, this task could be cumbersome, slow, and variable but instead the software creates consistent and fast service. An extra feature even allows the software to catch driver errors if the truck pulls into the wrong driveway!

FLEXIBILITY: UPS DELIVERY INTERCEPT™

In one of the most innovative updates to package shipping, UPS in 2007 pioneered UPS Delivery Intercept, an automated service that allows shippers to intercept and change the routing of packages before they are delivered. In this first-of-its-kind service, the shipper—using a UPS application such as UPS WorldShip or UPS Internet Shipping—can click on the tracking number and request a reroute on the Web. Once flagged, the shipper can request a return, redirect the package, or hold it until a future date. The service is available 24/7 anywhere in the United States and Puerto Rico, and shippers receive notification of the requested and successful interception. At a mere $10 per intercept, which is charged only if the intercept is achieved, UPS suggests that shippers

can avoid problem scenarios when the wrong material is sent to a client and needs to be recalled. For example, a manufacturer shipping out an order may realize that the wrong products have been shipped only after the order has gone out. In this and other cases, the shipping manager at UPS can intercept the packages, return them to the sender, and then mail out the correct shipment. Being able to change delivery instructions immediately, recall mistakes, and adapt to up-to-the-minute order changes offers customers the assurance that their shipments will be accurate even when they are not.

CUSTOMER CONTROL AND KNOWLEDGE: FLEX GLOBAL VIEW

UPS now offers its shippers a technology that allows them a single Web page on which they can track air, ocean, and ground freight in addition to small package shipments, thereby viewing their entire supply chain in one place. Customers who worked with UPS in all these different ways now can view and react to this integrated shipment information easily. All carriers and global operating organizations can update the system, making the information in the Flex Global View current enough to make real-time decisions. In addition to an integrated screen of information, Flex Global View also offers (1) flexible searches where shippers can locate air, ocean, and surface shipments, inventory, and billing information; (2) proactive e-mail alerts about changes, delays, or problems; (3) standard and customized reports; and (4) advanced analytics.

These examples illustrate why UPS is known for delivering excellent service. According to Kurt Kuehn, senior vice president, Worldwide Sales and Marketing, "Innovations like Package Flow Technology and services like UPS Delivery Intercept are key components of UPS's drive to treat each of our millions of customers as if they're our only customer," adding, "We're constantly working on new and innovative ways to harness technology to help our customers meet their unique needs.

Sources: Kuehn, M., "Marketer of the Year: Kurt Kuehn," *B to B* 91, no. 14 (October 23, 2006), "UPS Changes the Delivery Game with Intercept Service," UPS Pressroom, March 26, 2007, www.ups.com; www.ups.com.; Dean Foust, "How Technology Delivers for UPS," *BusinessWeek,* March 5, 2007, p. 60.

Provider Gap 4: The Communication Gap

Provider gap 4, the *communication gap,* illustrates the difference between service delivery and the service provider's external communications. Promises made by a service company through its media advertising, sales force, and other communications may potentially raise customer expectations, the standards against which customers assess service quality. The discrepancy between actual and promised service therefore can widen the customer gap. Broken promises can occur for many reasons: overpromising in advertising or personal selling, inadequate coordination between operations and marketing, and differences in policies and procedures across service outlets. Figure 2.5 shows the key factors that lead to the communications gap.

In addition to unduly elevating expectations through exaggerated claims, there are other, less obvious ways in which external communications influence customers' service quality assessments. Service companies frequently fail to capitalize on opportunities to educate customers to use services appropriately. They also neglect to manage customer expectations of what will be delivered in service transactions and relationships.

One of the major difficulties associated with provider gap 4 is that communications to consumers involve issues that cross organizational boundaries. Because service advertising promises what people do, and because what people do cannot be controlled like machines that produce physical goods can be controlled, this type of communication involves functions other than the marketing department. This type of marketing is what we call *interactive marketing*—the marketing between contact people and customers—and it must be coordinated with the conventional types of *external marketing* used in product and service firms. When employees who promote the service do not fully understand the reality of service delivery, they are likely to make exaggerated promises or fail to communicate to customers aspects of the service intended to

FIGURE 2.5
Key Factors
Leading to Provider
Gap 4: The
Communications
Gap

Service delivery

• *Lack of integrated services marketing communications*
    Tendency to view each external communication as independent
    Not including interactive marketing in communications plan
    Absence of strong internal marketing program
• *Ineffective management of customer expectations*
    Not managing customer expectation through all forms of communication
    Not adequately educating customers
• *Overpromising*
    Overpromising in advertising
    Overpromising in personal selling
    Overpromising through physical evidence cues
• *Inadequate horizontal communications*
    Insufficient communication between sales and operations
    Insufficient communication between advertising and operations
    Differences in policies and procedures across branches or units
• *Inappropriate Pricing*
    High prices that raise customer expectations
    Prices that are not tied to customer perceptions of value

External communications
to customers

serve them well. The result is poor service quality perceptions. Effectively coordinating actual service delivery with external communications, therefore, narrows the communications gap and favorably affects the customer gap as well.

Another issue in provider gap 4 is associated with the pricing of services. In packaged goods (and even in durable goods), customers possess enough price knowledge before purchase to be able to judge whether a price is fair or in line with competition. With services, customers often have no internal reference points for prices before purchase and consumption. Pricing strategies such as discounting, "everyday prices," and couponing obviously need to be different in service situations in which the customer has no initial sense of prices. Techniques for developing prices for services are more complicated than those for pricing tangible goods.

In summary, external communications—whether from marketing communications or pricing—can create a larger customer gap by raising expectations about service delivery. In addition to improving service delivery, companies must also manage all communications to customers so that inflated promises do not lead to higher expectations. Chapter 16 will discuss integrated services marketing communications, and Chapter 17 will cover pricing to accomplish these objectives.

PUTTING IT ALL TOGETHER: CLOSING THE GAPS

The full conceptual model shown in Figure 2.6, below, conveys a clear message to managers wishing to improve their quality of service: The key to closing the customer gap is to close provider gaps 1 through 4 and keep them closed. To the extent that one or more of provider gaps 1 through 4 exist, customers perceive service quality shortfalls. The gaps model of service quality serves as a framework for service organizations attempting to improve quality service and services marketing. The Strategy Insight provides a *service quality gaps audit* based on the model.

The model begins where the process of improving service quality begins: with an understanding of the nature and extent of the customer gap. Given the service organization's need to focus on the customer and to use knowledge about the customer to drive business strategy, we believe that this foundation of emphasis is warranted.

FIGURE 2.6
Gaps Model of Service Quality

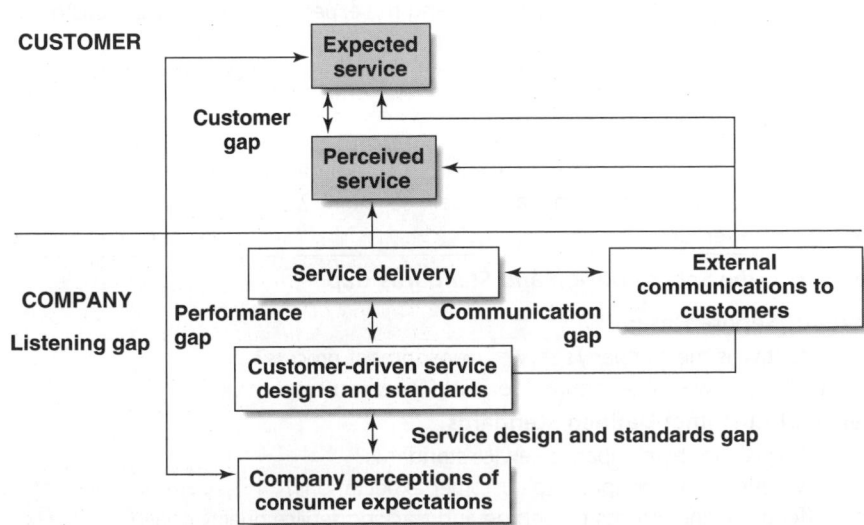

Strategy Insight   Using the Gaps Model to Assess an Organization's Service Strategy

The gaps model featured in this chapter and used as a framework for this textbook is a useful way to audit the service performance and capabilities of an organization. The model has been used by many companies as an assessment or service audit tool because it is comprehensive and offers a way for companies to examine all the factors that influence service quality. To use the tool, a company documents what it knows about each gap and the factors that affect the size of the gap. Although you will learn much more about each of these gaps throughout the book, we provide here a basic gaps audit. In Exercise 1 at the end of the chapter, we propose that you use this audit with a company to determine its service quality gaps. As practice, you could evaluate the Island Hotel, the inn featured in the opening vignette, to see how its approaches work to close each of the gaps.

Service Quality Gaps Model Audit

For each of the following factors in the gaps, indicate the effectiveness of the organization on that factor. Use a 1 to 10 scale where l is "poor" and 10 is "excellent."

Customer Gap	1 = Poor 10 = Excellent
1. How well does the company understand customer expectations of service quality? 2. How well does the company understand customer perceptions of service?	
Provider Gap I, the Listening Gap	
1. Market Research Orientation • Is the amount and type of market research adequate to understand customer expectations of service? • Does the company use this information in decisions about service provision?	
2. Upward Communication • Do managers and customers interact enough for management to know what customers expect? • Do contact people tell management what customers expect?	
3. Relationship Focus • To what extent does the company understand the expectations of different customer segments? • To what extent does the company focus on relationships with customers rather than transactions?	
4. Service Recovery • How effective are the service recovery efforts of the organization? • How well does the organization plan for service failures?	
Score for Provider Gap 1	
Provider Gap 2, the Service Design and Standards Gap	
5. Systematic Service Design • How effective is the company's service development process? • How well are new services defined for customers and employees?	
6. Presence of Customer-Defined Standards • How effective are the company's service standards? • Are they defined to correspond to customer expectations? • How effective is the process for setting and tracking service quality goals?	

	Poor (1) to Excellent (10)
7. Appropriate Physical Evidence and Servicescape • Are the company's physical facilities, equipment, and other tangibles appropriate to the service offering? • Are the company's physical facilities, equipment, and other tangibles attractive and effective? **Score for Provider Gap 2**	
Provider Gap 3, the Service Performance Gap	
8. Effective Human Resource Policies • How effectively does the company recruit, hire, train, compensate, and empower employees? • Is service quality delivery consistent across employees, teams, units, and branches? **9. Effective Role Fulfillment by Customers** • Do customers understand their roles and responsibilities? • Does the company manage customers to fulfill their roles, especially customers that are incompatible? **10. Effective Alignment with Service Intermediaries** • How well are service intermediaries aligned with the company? • Is there conflict over objectives and performance, costs and rewards? • Is service quality delivery consistent across the outlets? **11. Alignment of Demand and Capacity** • How well is the company able to match supply with demand fluctuations? **Score for Provider Gap 3**	
Provider Gap 4, the Communication Gap	
12. Integrated Services Marketing Communications • How well do all company communications—including the interactions between company employees and customers—express the same message and level of service quality? • How well does the company communicate to customers about what will be provided to them? • Does the company avoid overpromising and overselling? • How well do different parts of the organization communicate with each other so that service quality equals what is promised? **13. Pricing** • Is the company careful not to price so high that customer expectations are raised? • Does the company price in line with customer perceptions of value? **Score for Provider Gap 4**	

The score for each gap should be compared to the maximum score possible. Are particular gaps weaker than others? Which areas in each gap need attention?

As you go through the rest of the book, we will provide more detail about how to improve the factors in each of the gaps.

Summary

This chapter presented the integrated gaps model of service quality (shown in Figure 2.6), a framework for understanding and improving service delivery. The entire text will be organized around this model of service quality, which focuses on five pivotal gaps in delivering and marketing service:

The customer gap: Difference between customer expectations and perceptions
Provider gap 1: The Listening Gap
Provider gap 2: The Service Design and Standards Gap
Provider gap 3: The Service Performance Gap
Provider gap 4: The Communication Gap

The gaps model positions the key concepts, strategies, and decisions in services marketing in a manner that begins with the customer and builds the organization's tasks around what is needed to close the gap between customer expectations and perceptions. The final chapter in the book, Chapter 18, discusses the financial implications of service quality, reviewing the research and company data that indicates linkages between service quality and financial performance.

Discussion Questions

1. Think about a service you receive. Is there a gap between your expectations and perceptions of that service? What do you expect that you do not receive?
2. Consider the "wish mode" discussion about IKEA. Think about a service that you receive regularly and put yourself in the wish mode. How would you change the service and the way it is provided?
3. If you were the manager of a service organization and wanted to apply the gaps model to improve service, which gap would you start with? Why? In what order would you proceed to close the gaps?
4. Can provider gap 4, the communication gap, be closed prior to closing any of the other three provider gaps? How?
5. Which of the four provider gaps do you believe is hardest to close? Why?

Exercises

1. Choose an organization to interview, and use the integrated gaps model of service quality as a framework. Ask the manager whether the organization suffers from any of the factors listed in the figures in this chapter. Which factor in each of Figures 2.2 through 2.5 does the manager consider the most troublesome? What does the company do to try to address the problems?
2. Use the Internet to locate the website of Disney, Marriott, Ritz-Carlton, or any other well-known, high-quality service organization. Which provider gaps has the company closed? How can you tell?
3. Interview a nonprofit or public sector organization in your area (it could be some part of your school if it is a state school). Find out if the integrated gaps model of service quality framework makes sense in the context of its organization.

Notes

1. The gaps model of service quality that provides the structure for this text was developed by and is fully presented in Valarie A. Zeithaml, A. Parasuraman, and Leonard L. Berry, *Delivering Quality Service: Balancing Customer Perceptions and Expectations* (New York: The Free Press, 1990).

Focus on the Customer

THE CUSTOMER GAP

The figure shows a pair of boxes from the gaps model of service quality that correspond to two concepts—*customer expectations* and *customer perceptions*—that play a major role in services marketing. Customer expectations are the standards of performance or reference points for performance against which service experiences are compared, and are often formulated in terms of what a customer believes should or will happen. Customer perceptions are subjective assessments of actual service experiences.

The Customer Gap

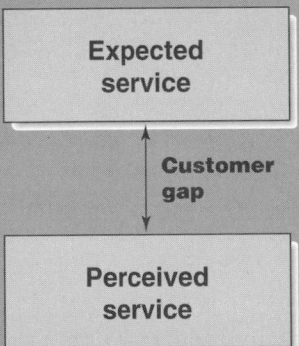

We devote the second part of the textbook to describing this gap and other relevant customer concepts because excellent services marketing requires a focus on the customer. We detail what is known about customer behavior relative to services in Chapter 3, customer expectations in Chapter 4, and customer perceptions in Chapter 5. Knowing what customers want and how they assess what they receive is the foundation for designing effective services.

Chapter Three

Consumer Behavior in Services

The chapter's objectives are to

1. Enhance understanding of how consumers choose, experience, and evaluate services.
2. Describe how consumers judge goods versus services in terms of search, experience, and credence criteria.
3. Develop the elements of consumer behavior that a services marketer must understand: choice behavior, consumer experiences, and postexperience evaluation.

Life Stages: Services for the Generations

In this chapter we focus on consumer behavior in services; that is, how consumers seek, choose, purchase, experience, and evaluate services. As you will see, many influences affect this process, two of the most important being the consumer's life stage and the generation into which he or she was born. As consumers pass through life stages from childhood to retirement, their needs and preferences for services change. Because the ways they choose to experience services also change, the types of services that appeal to them differ. While consumers of most generations and life stages want and need to stay fit, for example, the way they do so varies and the types of services that will be most successful will vary as well.

Different generations of consumers have personalities shaped by events, history, and people that, to some extent, drive their needs for different types of services as well as how they want to live and be treated at work.[1] For example, in the United States, the *traditionalists* (born between 1900 and 1945) were dramatically influenced by the two major World Wars, the Roaring Twenties, and the Great Depression and are characterized by labels such as loyalty, hard work, and patriotism. Most people in this very large group have retired from their careers, and services that focus on age-appropriate leisure, travel, volunteer opportunities, and increasing needs for specialized health care are targeted at them. While there are certainly differences among consumers within a generation, and thus the labels are oversimplified, understanding these generational and life-stage differences provides a lens for understanding aspects of consumer behavior and service innovations that will appeal to each group.

Currently, the largest demographic group in U.S. history, the *baby boomers,* is approaching retirement age. According to those who study generational differences, this huge group (born between 1946 and 1964) is characterized by optimism resulting from their post–World War II birth, competitiveness due to their large numbers, and idealism that the wrongs of the world can be fixed (think women's rights, civil rights, and the ecology movement). As the baby boom surges toward retirement, some of the service innovations developing for this group include:

- Retirement advice and support services [e.g., private 401(k) coaches, long-term health care insurance], made especially necessary given the skepticism surrounding Social Security and Medicare.
- Services for their aging parents (e.g., IBM's "wired home" concept, where technology can remotely monitor vital signs and health of its inhabitants).
- Lifestyle-based living communities and services, such as health clubs for older adults.

At the same time, many of their children (born between 1981 and 1999)—known as *Generation Y* or *the Millenials*—are also demanding services to fulfill their needs. This group is characterized quite differently from their parents as craving connection and authenticity in their lives and meaning in their work. They are also technology savvy and technology dependent, including around-the-clock connection to the ubiquitous Internet. Their technology-integrated lifestyle has resulted in a certain impatience and desire for constant stimulation and a 24/7 culture, where all things are available at all times. Service innovations are also prevalent for this group, including:

- Advanced communication and connection services including MySpace, FaceBook, iPods, iPhone, instant messaging, text messaging, You Tube, and BlackBerries (see photo, next page).
- Wellness, exercise, and healthy living services that capitalize on their desire for social connections.
- Interactive games, simulations, and multisensory entertainment experiences.

A common desire of boomers and millenials alike is exercising and staying fit. Yet very different services have developed to meet this similar need across the two generations. Boomers grew up in the early era of physical fitness and remain avid about exercise. But health clubs that appeal to a younger generation do not work for them. They simply are not comfortable with the young, noisy, and frenetic pace of most health clubs and gyms. Thus, "Nifty after Fifty," "Club 50," and similar concepts were born—places where boomers are comfortable exercising with people the same age. These facilities play softer music and use pressure-driven equipment rather than traditional metal weights, and no one wears belly-bearing tank tops—in fact, they are probably not allowed! Classes such as "gentle yoga" and beginner's pilates may be offered to appeal to less limber members.

Contrast this with a typical gym that caters to the millenials. Lifetime Fitness, an award-winning gym, offers everything from the standard modern exercise equipment (each piece labeled with instructions) to athletic leagues and salsa-dancing lessons. There is a LifeCafe, where healthy, full meals are served along with free Wi-Fi to read e-mail. A lounge provides a space to watch ESPN while relaxing. This is a place geared for young people and their children. According to one member, "Everything makes you want to spend time there. It's like a healthy casino."

Of course, within these generations there are significant differences in needs, depending on individual lifestyle and preferences, but some common patterns are apparent within each generation, creating demand for new and emerging services. For service marketers, a keen understanding of generational differences can help in identifying new services and in shaping the character of existing services.

Tech-savy millennials value services that keep them connected

The primary objectives of services producers and marketers are to develop and provide offerings that satisfy consumer needs and expectations, thereby ensuring their own economic survival. To achieve these objectives, service providers need to understand how consumers choose, experience, and evaluate their service offerings. Our opening vignette suggests generational differences and life stages can influence consumer needs and preferences for services. Much of what is known about consumer evaluation processes pertains specifically to goods. The assumption appears to be that services, if not identical to goods, are at least similar enough in the consumer's mind that they are chosen, experienced, and evaluated in the same manner.

This chapter challenges that assumption and shows that services' characteristics result in some differences in consumer choice and evaluation processes compared with those used in assessing goods. Recognizing these differences and thoroughly understanding consumer evaluation processes are critical for the customer focus on which effective services marketing is based. Because the premise of this text is that the customer is the heart of effective services marketing, we begin with the customer and maintain this focus throughout the text.

SEARCH, EXPERIENCE, AND CREDENCE PROPERTIES

One framework for isolating differences in evaluation processes between goods and services is a classification of properties of offerings proposed by economists.[2] Economists first distinguished between two categories of properties of consumer products: *search qualities,* attributes that a consumer can determine before purchasing a product; and *experience qualities,* attributes that can be discerned only after purchase or during consumption. Search qualities include color, style, price, fit, feel, hardness, and smell; experience qualities include taste and wearability. Products such as automobiles, clothing, furniture, and jewelry are high in search qualities because their attributes can be almost completely determined and evaluated before purchase. Products such as vacations and restaurant meals are high in experience qualities because their attributes cannot be fully known or assessed until they have been purchased and are being consumed. A third category, *credence qualities,* includes characteristics that the consumer may find impossible to evaluate even after purchase and consumption.[3] Examples of offerings high in credence qualities are appendix operations and brake relinings on automobiles. Few consumers possess medical or mechanical skills sufficient to evaluate whether these services are necessary or are performed properly, even after they have been prescribed and produced by the provider.

Figure 3.1 arrays products high in search, experience, or credence qualities along a continuum of evaluation ranging from easy to evaluate to difficult to evaluate. Products high in search qualities are the easiest to evaluate (left end of the continuum). Products high in experience qualities are more difficult to evaluate because they must be purchased and consumed before assessment is possible (center of continuum). Products high in credence qualities are the most difficult to evaluate because the consumer may

FIGURE 3.1
Continuum of
Evaluation for
Different Types
of Products

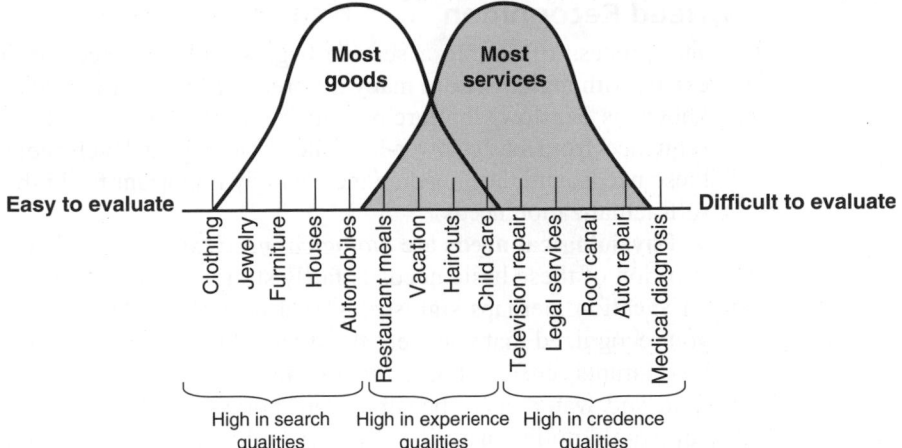

be unaware of or may lack sufficient knowledge to appraise whether the offerings satisfy given wants or needs even after consumption (right end of the continuum). The major premise of this chapter is that most goods fall to the left of the continuum, whereas most services fall to the right because of the distinguishing characteristics described in Chapter 1. These characteristics make services more difficult to evaluate than goods, particularly in advance of purchase. Difficulty in evaluation, in turn, forces consumers to rely on different cues and processes when deciding upon and assessing services.

The next sections of this chapter build from these basic differences to explore the stages of consumer decision making and evaluation for services. This discussion is organized around three broad stages of consumer behavior, as shown in Figure 3.2: consumer choice, consumer experience, and postexperience evaluation. Within each of these stages, you will see similarities and differences between goods and services.

CONSUMER CHOICE

The first important area of consumer behavior that marketers are concerned with is how customers choose and make decisions and the steps that lead to the purchase of a particular service. This process is similar to that used for goods in some ways and different in others. Customers follow a logical sequence, including need recognition, information search, evaluation of alternatives, and purchase. The following sections discuss this sequence, particularly focusing on the ways in which services decision making is different from goods decision making.

FIGURE 3.2 **Stages in Consumer Decision Making and Evaluation of Services**

Need Recognition

The process of buying a service begins with the recognition that a need or want exists. Although there are many different ways to characterize needs, the most widely known is Maslow's hierarchy, which specifies five need categories arranged in a sequence from basic lower-level needs to higher-level needs. Services can fill all these needs, and they become increasingly important for higher-level social, ego, and self-actualization needs.

Physiological needs are *biological needs such as food, water, and sleep.* The recognition of these basic needs is fairly straightforward. Recall the last time you were on vacation, perhaps sightseeing in a new place. At some point around lunchtime, you recognized that you were thirsty and hungry and needed to stop and have lunch. Restaurants, coffee shops, bistros, and other service establishments that provided food and water likely became more noticeable. If you were sightseeing in Tokyo, you would notice that virtually every other street contains a large vending machine with ice cold drinks to quench the thirst of citizens and visitors suffering from the intense heat.

Safety and security needs include *shelter, protection, and security.* Consumers seek to provide for their own and their loved ones' shelter, safety, and security through many types of services. Parents are particularly focused on services that provide for their children's security (e.g., quality child care, medical care, education), and later in life these same people are often faced with needing services that will provide for their own aging parents. As we progress through life, our safety and security needs change and sometimes are heightened by circumstances. For example, immediately following the terrorist attacks on New York and Washington, consumers began to recognize their vulnerability and sought ways to increase their safety and security. Instead of purchasing vacations and making business trips, consumers switched service purchases to bus tickets, movie rentals, insurance, and other services to satisfy their needs for safety and security.

Social needs are for *affection, friendship, and acceptance.* Social needs are critical to all cultures but are particularly important in the East. In countries like Japan and China, consumers place a great deal of value on social and belonging needs. They spend more time with their families and work colleagues than do Westerners and therefore consume more services that can be shared. The Japanese spend more annually per capita in restaurants, for example, than any other country. Consumers in all cultures use many types of services to address social needs, including health clubs, dance clubs, and vacation destinations like Club Med, in which socializing is encouraged. Many of the Internet services that focus on social connections among people (e.g., MySpace.com, Internet dating services, and some blogs) satisfy these basic human social needs.

Ego needs are for *prestige, success, accomplishment, and self-esteem.* Food, safety, and social belonging are not enough for many consumers. Individuals also seek to look good to others and to feel good about themselves because of what they have accomplished. Needs to improve oneself and achieve success are responsible for the growth of education, training, and other services that increase the skills and prestige of consumers. Personal services such as spa services, plastic surgery, teeth whitening, and some forms of physical training and weight-loss also satisfy these needs.

Self-actualization involves *self-fulfillment and enriching experiences.* Consumers desire to live up to their full potential and enjoy themselves. Some consumers purchase experiences such as skydiving, jungle safaris, and bungee jumping for the pure thrill

Teeth whitening is a growing service that is driven by consumers' ego needs

of the experience, a need quite different from the others in Maslow's hierarchy. Other people self-actualize through classes in oil painting or poetry writing, thereby expressing feelings and meanings that are unrelated to the basic needs of day-to-day living.

The hierarchical nature of Maslow's need categorization has been disputed, and evidence exists that people with unfilled basic needs can be motivated to self-actualize. We are not concerned with the hierarchical nature in this section; we use it only as a way to discuss different drives that lead customers to the next stages of consumer behavior in services.

Information Search

Once they recognize a need, consumers obtain information about goods and services that might satisfy this need. Seeking information may be an extensive, formalized process if the service or good is important to the consumer or it represents a major investment (e.g., a European vacation package or a professional landscape service). In other cases, the information search may be quick and relatively automatic (e.g., a restaurant for a quick lunch, or a station for gasoline fill-up). Consumers use both personal sources (such as friends or experts) and nonpersonal sources (such as mass or selective media and websites) to gain information about goods and services. Seeking information is a way of reducing risk, helping consumers feel more confident about their choices.

Personal and Nonpersonal Sources

When purchasing goods, consumers make use of both personal and nonpersonal sources because both effectively convey information about search qualities. However, when purchasing services, consumers seek and rely to a greater extent on personal sources for several reasons.

First, mass and selective media can convey information about search qualities but can communicate far less about experience qualities. By asking friends or experts about services, however, the consumer can obtain information vicariously about experience qualities. A second reason for greater use of personal sources of information for services is that many types of nonpersonal sources of information are not as readily available for services. Many service providers are local, independent merchants with neither the experience nor the funds to advertise, although websites are now expected

Consumers seek and rely on personal sources in purchasing experience goods and services

and common for even small service providers. And, because professional associations banned advertising for so long, both professionals and consumers tend to resist its use even though it is now permitted. Finally, because consumers can assess few attributes before purchase of a service, they may feel greater risk in selecting a little-known alternative. Personal influence becomes pivotal as product complexity increases and when objective standards by which to evaluate a product decrease (i.e., when experience qualities are high). Managers in service industries clearly recognize the strong influence of personal communication.

Interestingly, consumers are now able through the Internet to seek more nonpersonal information about services in the form of visuals, photographs, detailed information, and virtual tours.[4] In addition to these tangible representations of the service experience, consumers can also seek the personal opinions of others via the Web through chat rooms, online ratings, and consumer complaint websites. Some consumer complaint websites even target a specific firm's current and prospective customers, offering unsolicited information.[5]

Perceived Risk

Although some degree of *perceived risk* probably accompanies all purchase transactions, more risk appears to be involved in the purchase of services than in the purchase of goods because services are typically more intangible, variable, and perishable. Risk can come in the form of financial risk, time risk, performance risk, social risk, or psychological risk, any of which may be greater for services.

The intangible nature of services and their high level of experience qualities imply that services generally must be selected on the basis of less prepurchase information than is the case for goods. There is clear evidence that greater intangibility (whether for goods or services) increases perceptions of risk.[6] And because services are non-standardized, the consumer will feel some uncertainty about the outcome and consequences each time a service is purchased. In addition, services purchases may involve more perceived risk than other purchases because services are often not accompanied by warranties or guarantees. Dissatisfied customers can rarely "return" a service; they have already consumed it by the time they realize their dissatisfaction. Finally, many services are so technical or specialized that consumers possess neither the knowledge nor the experience to evaluate whether they are satisfied, even after they have consumed the service.

The increase in perceived risk in purchasing services suggests the use of strategies to reduce risk. Risk reduction can be accomplished through tactics that reduce risk directly (e.g., guarantees) or by addressing the factors that contribute to the perception of risk (e.g., making the service more tangible).[7] For example, UPS and FedEx provide tracking numbers for customers so they can follow their shipments online and know exactly where a package is. This system helps reduce the risk for consumers. Offering a free or reduced-cost trial period for a service is another means to reduce risk. For example, child care centers often encourage a free trial day for prospective clients and their children to reduce the sense of risk in this important decision. To the extent possible, service providers should emphasize employee training and other procedures to standardize their offerings so that consumers learn to expect a given level of quality, again reducing perceived risk.

Evaluation of Service Alternatives

The *evoked set* of alternatives—that set of products that a consumer considers acceptable in a given product category—is likely to be smaller with services than with goods. One reason involves differences in retailing between goods and services. To purchase goods, consumers generally shop in retail stores that display competing products in close proximity, clearly demonstrating the possible alternatives. To purchase services, on the other hand, the consumer visits an establishment (such as a bank, a dry cleaner, or a hair salon) that almost always offers only a single "brand" for sale. A second reason for the smaller evoked set is that consumers are unlikely to find more than one or two businesses providing the same services in a given geographic area, whereas they may find numerous retail stores carrying the identical manufacturer's product. A third reason for a smaller evoked set is the relative difficulty of obtaining adequate prepurchase information about services.

Faced with the task of collecting and evaluating experience qualities, consumers may simply select the first acceptable alternative rather than searching many alternatives. The Internet has the potential to widen the set of alternatives and already has done so in some industries. This trend is most notable in airlines and hotels where comparable information is available through providers such as Travelocity, Orbitz, and Expedia.

For nonprofessional services, consumers' decisions often entail the choice between performing the services for themselves or hiring someone to perform them.[8] Working people may choose between cleaning their own homes or hiring housekeepers, between altering their families' clothes or taking them to a tailor, even between staying home to take care of their children or engaging a day care center to provide child care. Consumers may consider themselves as sources of supply for many services, including lawn care, tax preparation, and preparing meals. Thus, the customer's evoked set frequently includes self-provision of the service. Self-service via technology is also a viable alternative for many services, as the Technology Spotlight demonstrates.

Service Purchase

Following consideration of alternatives (whether an extensive process or more automatic), consumers make the decision to purchase a particular service or to do it themselves. One

Technology Spotlight Self-Service Technologies: How Much Do Customers Like Providing Their Own Services?

One of the major changes in consumer behavior is the growing tendency for consumers to interact with technology to create services instead of interacting with a live service firm employee. *Self-service technologies (SSTs)* are technological interfaces that allow customers to produce services independent of direct service employee involvement. Examples of SSTs that you are probably very familiar with are automated teller machines, pay-at-the-pump terminals at gas stations, and automated hotel checkout and check-in. All forms of services over the Internet are also SSTs, many of which are very innovative. In some states, for example, users can file for divorce or evict a tenant using an automated kiosk rather than go through the traditional court system. Electronic self-ordering is being developed at fast-food chains, and self-scanning at grocery stores is common.

The chart in this box shows a comprehensive set of categories and examples of SSTs in use today. The columns of the matrix represent the types of technologies that companies are using to interface with customers in self-service encounters, and the rows show purposes of the technologies from the customer perspective. As you can see, customers use the technologies to provide customer service (deal with questions about accounts, bill paying, and delivery tracking), to conduct transactions (order, buy, and exchange resources with companies without direct interaction), and for education and self-help (learn, receive information, train themselves, and provide their own services).

A study asked customers across a wide range of industries and applications what they think of SSTs and found that customers have very strong feelings about them. They both love and hate SSTs depending on a few key conditions. Customers love them when:

- *SSTs bail them out of difficult situations.* A single parent with a sleeping child in the car needs to get gas and money for work the following morning. Using a pay-at-the-pump gas station and drive-up ATM allows the parent to accomplish these tasks without leaving the sleeping child.

- *SSTs are better than the interpersonal alternative.* SSTs have the potential to save customers time, money, and psychological costs. The Internet, in particular, allows customers to shop at any time and complete transactions more quickly than they could in person. Internet loans and mortgages also allow customers to avoid the anxiety of meeting a banker in person and feeling judged.

- *SSTs work.* When SSTs work as they are supposed to, customers are impressed. Many of you have had the experience of using one-click ordering at Amazon.com. When these transactions work smoothly, as they usually do after the proper setup, the transactions are satisfying.

On the other hand, customers hate SSTs when the following problems occur:

- *SSTs fail.* The researchers found that 60 percent of the negative stories they heard stemmed from failures of SSTs. Broken machines, failed PIN numbers, websites that were down, and items not shipped as promised all frustrate consumers.

- *SSTs are poorly designed.* Poorly designed technologies that are difficult to use or understand create hassles for customers, making them feel as

of the most interesting differences between goods and services is that most goods are fully produced (at the factory) prior to being purchased by consumers. Thus, consumers, prior to making their final purchase decision, can see and frequently try the exact object that they will buy. For services, much is still unknown at the point of purchase. In many cases, the service is purchased, produced, experienced, and evaluated almost simultaneously—as with a restaurant meal or live entertainment. In other cases, consumers pay all or part of the purchase price up-front for a service they will not fully experience until it is produced for them much later. This situation arises with services such as vacation tours or home remodeling, or ongoing services such as health club memberships or university

though the SST is not worth using. Websites that are difficult to maneuver are particularly troublesome. If customers cannot reach information they need within a few clicks (some researchers say that two clicks are all that customers will tolerate), then customers shun the website.

- *The customer messes up.* Customers dislike using technologies that they feel they cannot perform adequately. Even though they feel partial responsibility, they will avoid using them in the future. A common frustration today is having various user names and passwords for different websites. When confronted with a screen requiring this information—and not recalling it accurately—many customers will give up and go elsewhere.

- *There is no service recovery.* When the process or technology fails, SSTs rarely provide ways to recover on the spot. In these cases customers must then call or visit the company, precisely what they were trying to avoid by using the self-service technology.

It is in evident that these technological innovations are a critical component of customer–firm interactions. To succeed, the researchers contend, they must become more reliable, be better than the interpersonal alternatives, and have recovery systems in place when they fail.

Sources: M. L. Meuter, A. L. Ostom, R. I. Roundtree, and M. J. Bitner, "Self-Service Technologies: Understanding Customer Satisfaction with Technology-Based Service Encounters," *Journal of Marketing* 64 (July 2000), pp. 50–64; A. L. Ostom and M. L. Meuter, "Implementing Successful Self-Service Technologies," *Academy of Management Executive* 16 (November 2002), pp. 96–109.

Purpose \ Interface	**Categories and Examples of SSTs in Use**			
	Telephone/Interactive Voice Response	**Online/Internet**	**Interactive Kiosks**	**Video/DVD/ Web Cam**
Customer Service	• Telephone banking • Flight information • Order status	• Package tracking • Account information	• ATMs • Hotel checkout	• Service preview • Monitor service conditions (e.g., traffic)
Transactions	• Telephone banking • Prescription refills	• Retail purchasing • Financial transactions	• Pay at the pump • Hotel checkout • Car rental	
Education & Self-Help	• Information telephone lines	• Internet information search • Distance learning • Training web casts	• Blood pressure machines • Tourist information	• Tax preparation software • Television/DVD-based training

education. In business-to-business situations, long-term contracts for services (such as payroll, network integration, consulting, or landscaping) may be signed prior to anything being produced at all.

Because of the inherent risk in the purchase decision for services, some providers offer "free" (or "deeply discounted") initial trials or extensive tours of their facilities (e.g., prospective student and parent tours at universities) to reduce risk in the final purchase decision. In business-to-business situations, trust in the provider is paramount when customers sign long-term service contracts, and frequently the contracts themselves spell out in detail the service level agreements and penalties for nonperformance.

Strategy Insight   Consumer Experiences as Corporate Strategy

Customer experiences and experience management have become the foundations for important corporate strategies. According to Bernd Schmitt at Columbia University, customer *experience management* can be defined as the process of strategically managing customers' entire experience with a product—from how they learn about it, to how they consume it, to how they relate to the company that produces it. Firms across industries from health care to airlines and cosmetics to automobiles are developing strategies around providing meaningful customer experiences. Although experience management applies to goods and services, it is particularly relevant for services, given their process nature. Services *are* experiences. Whether they are managed strategically or not is a choice to be made.

Here are just a few companies that have recognized the value of strategically creating distinctive experiences for their customers. For these companies, "the experience is the marketing," as noted authors James Gilmore and Joseph Pine have said.

NASCAR

NASCAR race enthusiasts are among the most loyal sports fans anywhere, and their loyalty stems in large part from the strong emotional ties they have to the sport and to the drivers themselves as a result of their experiences. There are also a lot of these fans—75 million and growing! *Fast Company* magazine awarded NASCAR one of its top "Customer's First" awards in 2006, and it is easy to see why. For those who experience a race firsthand at Dover International Speedway—with 40,000 fellow fans— the atmosphere is charged with excitement, the food is plentiful, and a kaleidoscope of paraphernalia is available for sale. Before a race NASCAR drivers chat with fans and sign autographs. Such opportunities are uncommon in most sports, where stars are typically reluctant to rub shoulders with the crowd, particularly in advance of the event. (Throughout the year, NASCAR drivers appear in stores, auto dealerships, and other locations to meet with fans and show their appreciation, further building connections and loyalty.) Then, of course, there is the race itself with its thundering noise, blurring visuals of cars, and edge-of-the chair anticipation for the eventual winners. As if this live experience were not enough, NASCAR provides many opportunities for fans to enhance their experiences through technology. Live video feeds from inside several of the vehicles allow spectators to listen on their laptops to radio chatter among drivers and crews, see the view from the cockpit of these cars, and even observe mishaps and accidents close up via video. In addition, the corporation proves an online service with more than 300,000 subscribers that provides real-time race information online and a cable service that lets fans watch the race from the perspective of an individual driver. For NASCAR, the real, live experience of the race and all that goes with it, combined with technology-delivered service enhancements and personal interactions with the drivers and other fans combine to create unique connections with the sport, resulting in extreme customer loyalty.

KAISER PERMANENTE

Kaiser Permanente is the largest health maintenance organization in the United States. When IDEO, a strategic consulting firm out of Palo Alto, California, began working with Kaiser to develop a plan to increase Kaiser's long-term growth, the results were not predictable to most of the company's managers. Many assumed they would need to build new medical offices or invest in new hospital facilities. But what Kaiser managers learned through IDEO's innovative consumer research was that the customer experience itself needed a major overhaul. Patients were not happy. Kaiser needed to offer more comfortable waiting rooms and a lobby with clear instructions on where to go. The company needed to enlarge the size of its examining rooms to fit three or more people, with curtains for privacy. The registration and check-in process also needed to be improved. Kaiser learned that it is in the human experience business—not the building design business. What Kaiser and other health care clients of IDEO have learned is that whereas health care providers have traditionally focused on technology and medicines, their patients are concerned with service and information. In health care, patients want positive, informative, supportive, nonstressful experiences for themselves and their family members. Organizations that can design those types of experiences and deliver them consistently have a competitive advantage.

Pike Place Market

PIKE PLACE FISH MARKET

With the distinctive salt sea smells, the constant chatter and auctioneer-like shouts of fish mongers, colorful sights, and the brisk fresh air, customers truly have an experience at the Pike Place Fish Market in Seattle. Many people are familiar with the Pike Place Fish Market because of the popularity of the *Fish!* books and training videos. What is not as well known is that the entire market itself is nearly 100 years old, drawing crowds year-round. Tourists and natives of the area all flock to the Pike Place Market because of the unique experience it affords. Abundant fresh flowers, fruit and vegetable displays, unique restaurants, and all kinds of arts, crafts, and tourist mementos line the narrow walkways of the market, which sits on a hill looking out over Puget Sound. The foghorns of 450-foot commuter ferries are audible, often through the fog and mist that

blanket the Sound. On a clear day, kites fly overhead in the adjacent park. Deep within the market scene is the Pike Place Fish Market. Fish flying through the air, bantering employees, and fresh crab the size of small cats all provide elements of the experience that has made the place famous. Clearly patrons of the Pike Place Fish Market come for the experience—not just the outstanding fresh fish!

BUSINESS-TO-BUSINESS CUSTOMER EXPERIENCES

Although the previous examples have all been consumer companies, business-to-business firms are also recognizing the value of creating experiences. Executive briefing centers, for example, are corporate venues designed to enhance the otherwise mundane customer visit experience for business customers. Customer visits allow business-to-business customers to get to know their suppliers better through personal contact and information provided at the supplier's place of business. To create a memorable experience for its customers, Johnson Controls' flagship center in Milwaukee simulates for its customers inky, cold darkness on the one hand and arid heat on the other to demonstrate how its technologies can help customers avoid these conditions. And Nortel Networks provides guests with smart cards to activate and guide their experience with Nortel technology at its Executive Briefing Center in North Carolina. At IBM's T. J. Watson Research Center, the company's brand image is reinforced when clients experience its innovation center and get a sense of award-winning as well as futuristic new technology applications and service inventions. The design of the customer experience can be a distinctive corporate advantage and asset for organizations that use it strategically.

Sources: B. Nussbaum, "The Power of Design," *Business-Week* cover story, May 17, 2004, pp. 86–94; J. H. Gilmore and B. J. Pine II, "The Experience Is the Marketing," 2002, Strategic Horizons, LLP; B. H. Schmitt, *Customer Experience Management,* Hoboken, NJ: John Wiley & Sons, 2003; M. A. Prospero, "NASCAR," *Fast Company,* "Customer First Awards," September 2006, p. 52 (also at http://www.fastcompany.com/customer/).

CONSUMER EXPERIENCE

Because the choice process for services is inherently risky with many unknowns, the experience itself often dominates the evaluation process. As noted, services are high in experience and credence qualities relative to goods; thus, how consumers evaluate the actual experience of the service is critical in their evaluation process and their decision to repurchase later. In fact, noted customer experience experts have stated that "the experience is the marketing."[9]

Much has been written recently about customer experiences and their important role in influencing consumer behavior. Goods and services companies alike are being admonished to create "memorable experiences for their customers."[10] Our Strategy Insight on page 58, illustrates the prominent role that experiences have assumed in corporate strategy.

In this section we describe elements of consumer behavior that are relevant to understanding service experiences and how customers evaluate them. We do not limit our discussion to fun, exciting, or memorable experiences only. Instead, we use the term *customer experience* to encompass service processes that span the mundane to the spectacular. Customers purchasing building maintenance and dry cleaning services still have experiences, albeit less exciting ones than customers of entertainment or travel services. All services *are* experiences—some are long in duration and some are short; some are complex and others are simple; some are mundane, whereas others are exciting and unique. Creating and managing effective processes and experiences are essential management tasks for service organizations. Many subsequent chapters in this book will provide you with tools and approaches for managing specific elements of the customer experience—the heart of services marketing and management.

Services as Processes

Because services are actions or performances done for and with customers, they typically involve a sequence of steps, actions, and activities. Consider medical services. Some of the steps in medical care involve customers interacting with providers (e.g., patients interacting with their physician), other steps may be carried out by the customers themselves (e.g., "following the doctor's orders," taking medications), and other steps may involve third parties (e.g., going to a lab for blood work). The combination of these steps, and many others along the way, constitute a process, a service experience that is evaluated by the consumer. In many cases, the customer's experience comprises interactions with multiple, interconnected organizations, as in the case of medical services, automobile insurance, or home buying. Diverse sets of experiences across the network of firms (e.g., a doctor's office, medical laboratory, hospital, and physical therapy clinic) will likely influence consumers' overall impressions of their experience.[11] Whether or not the provider acknowledges it or seeks to control this experience in a particular way, it is inevitable that the customer will have an experience—good, bad, or indifferent.

Service Provision as Drama

The metaphor of a theater is a useful framework for describing and analyzing service performances. Both the theater and service organizations aim to create and maintain a desirable impression before an audience and recognize that the way to accomplish this is by carefully managing the actors and the physical setting of their behavior.[12]

The service marketer must play many drama-related roles—including director, choreographer, and writer—to be sure the performances of the actors are pleasing to the audience. The Walt Disney Company explicitly considers its service provision a "performance," even using show business terms such as *cast member, onstage,* and *show* to describe the operations at Disneyland and Walt Disney World.[13]

The skill of the service *actors* in performing their routines, the way they appear, and their commitment to the "show" are all essential to service delivery. Although service actors are present in most service performances, their importance increases in three conditions. First, service actors are critical when the degree of direct personal contact is high. Consider the difference between a visit to Denny's and a trip to a Japanese restaurant like Benihana. In many cases customers go to Japanese steak-houses as much for the show as for the food, and they eagerly anticipate the performance of the real-time chef who twirls knives, jokes with the guests, and even flips shrimp into his hat or onto guests' plates. (It is interesting to note that in Japan the chef is not the focus of attention in this type of restaurant and prepares the food with quiet dignity.) The second condition in which service actors' skills are critical is when the services involve repeat contact. Nurses in hospitals, favorite waiters or tennis pros in resorts, or captains on cruises are essential characters in service theater, and their individual performances can make or break the success of the services. The third condition in which contact personnel are critical is when they have discretion in determining the nature of the service and how it is delivered. When you consider the quality of the education you are receiving in college, you are certain to focus much of your evaluation on your professors' delivery of classes. In education, as in other services such as medical and legal services, the professional is the key actor in the performance.[14]

Ray Fisk and Steve Grove, two experts in the area of service dramaturgy, point out that service actors' performances can be characterized as sincere or cynical.[15] A sincere performance occurs when an actor becomes one with the role that she is playing, whereas a cynical performance occurs when an actor views a performance only as a means to an end, such as getting paid for doing the job. When a service employee takes the time to listen and help, the performance is sincere and often noteworthy. Unfortunately, too many examples of cynical performances exist in which front-line "actors" seem to care little about the "audience" of customers. As Grove and Fisk point out, a single employee can ruin the service experience by ridiculing other cast members' efforts, failing to perform his role correctly, or projecting the wrong image.

The *physical setting* of the service can be likened to the staging of a theatrical production, including scenery, props, and other physical cues to create desired impressions. Among a setting's features that may influence the character of a service are the colors or brightness of the service's surroundings; the volume and pitch of sounds in the setting; the smells, movement, freshness, and temperature of the air; the use of space; the style and comfort of the furnishings; and the setting's design and cleanliness.[16] As an example, the service provided by a cruise ship features its layout (broad and open), decor and comfort (large, cushioned deck chairs), furnishings (lots of polished wood and brass), and cleanliness ("shipshape"). The setting increases in importance when the environment distinguishes the service. Consider how critical the setting is for a downtown law firm, which must appear professional, capable, even imposing. In essence, the delivery of service can be conceived as drama, where service personnel are the actors, service customers are the audience, physical evidence of the service is the setting, and the process of service assembly is the performance.[17]

The drama metaphor offers a useful way to improve service performances. Selection of personnel can be viewed as auditioning the actors. An actor's personal appearance, manner, facial expression, gestures, personality, and demographic profile can be determined in large part in the interview or audition. Training of personnel can become rehearsing. Clearly defining the role can be seen as scripting the performance. Creation of the service environment involves setting the stage. Finally, deciding which aspects of the service should be performed in the presence of the customer (onstage) and which should be performed in the back room (backstage) helps define the performances the customer experiences.[18]

Service Roles and Scripts

Roles are combinations of social cues that guide and direct behavior in a given setting.[19] Just as there are roles in dramatic performances, there are roles in service delivery. For example, the role of a hostess in a restaurant is to acknowledge and greet customers, find out how many people are in their group, and then lead them to a table where they will eat. The success of any service performance depends in part on how well the role is performed by the service actor and how well the team of players—the "role set" of both service employees and customers—act out their roles.[20] Service employees need to perform their roles according to the expectations of the customer; if they do not, the customer may be frustrated and disappointed. If customers are informed and educated about their roles and if they cooperate with the provider in following the script, successful service provision is likely.

One factor that influences the effectiveness of role performance is the *script*—the logical sequence of events expected by the customer, involving her as either a *participant or an observer.*[21] *Service scripts* consist of sequences of actions associated with actors and objects that, through repeated involvement, define what the customer expects.[22] Receiving a dental checkup is a service experience for which a well-defined script exists. For a checkup the consumer expects the following sequence: Enter the reception area, greet a receptionist, sit in a waiting room, follow the dental hygienist to a separate room, recline in a chair while teeth are cleaned by the hygienist, be examined by the dentist, then pay for the services. When the service conforms to this script, the customer has a feeling of confirmed expectations and satisfaction. Deviations from the service script lead to confusion and dissatisfaction. Suppose, on moving to a new town, you went to a dentist who had no receptionist and no waiting area, only a doorbell in a cubicle. Suppose, on answering the doorbell, an employee in shorts took you to a large room where all patients were in a dental chairs facing each other. These actions and objects are certainly not in the traditional service script for dentistry and might create considerable uncertainty and doubt in patients.

Some services are more scripted than others. Customers would expect very expensive, customized services such as spa vacations to be less scripted than mass-produced services such as movie theaters and airline travel. Even within the same industry, the service process and script can be very different, resulting in unique experiences as with fine dining compared with fast food.

The Compatibility of Service Customers

We have just discussed the roles of employees and customers receiving service. We now want to focus on the role of *other customers* receiving service at the same time. Consider how central the mere presence of other customers is in churches, restaurants,

The service process and script are very different for a fine dining and a fast-food restaurant

dances, bars, clubs, and spectator sports: If no one else shows up, customers will not get to socialize with others, one of the primary expectations in these types of services. However, if customers become so dense that crowding occurs, customers may also be dissatisfied.[23] The way other customers behave with many services—such as airlines, education, clubs, and social organizations—also exerts a major influence on a customer's experience. In general, the presence, behavior, and similarity of other customers receiving services has a strong impact on the satisfaction and dissatisfaction of any given customer.[24]

Customers can be incompatible for many reasons—differences in beliefs, values, experiences, abilities to pay, appearance, age, and health, to name just a few. The service marketer must anticipate, acknowledge, and deal with heterogeneous consumers who have the potential to be incompatible. The service marketer can also bring homogeneous customers together and solidify relationships between them, which increases the cost to the customer of switching service providers.[25] Customer compatibility is a factor that influences customer satisfaction, particularly in high-contact services.

Customer Coproduction

In addition to being audience members, as suggested by the drama metaphor, service customers also play a coproduction role that can have profound influence on the service experience.[26] For example, counseling, personal training, or educational services have little value without the full participation of the client, who will most likely have extensive work to do between sessions. In this sense, the client coproduces or cocreates the service. In business-to-business contexts such as consulting, architecture, accounting, and almost any outsourced service, customers also coproduce the service.[27] It has been suggested that customers therefore need to understand their roles and be "trained" in ways that are similar to the training of service employees, so that they will have the motivation, ability, and role clarity to perform.[28] The customer coproduction role is particularly relevant in self-service situations, as noted in this chapter's Technology Spotlight.

The idea of customers as "partners" in the cocreation of products is gaining ground across all industries, not just services.[29] Postmodern consumer behavior experts propose an even broader interpretation of this idea. They suggest that a fundamental characteristic of the postmodern era is consumers' assertiveness as active participants in creating their world—often evidenced in their demands to adjust, change, and use products in customized ways.[30]

Emotion and Mood

Emotion and mood are feeling states that influence people's (and therefore customers') perceptions and evaluations of their experiences. Moods are distinguished from emotions in that *moods* are transient feeling states that occur at specific times and in specific situations, whereas *emotions* are more intense, stable, and pervasive.[31]

Because services are experiences, moods and emotions are critical factors that shape their evaluation. If a service customer is in a bad mood when she enters a service establishment, service provision will likely be interpreted more negatively than if she were in a buoyant, positive mood. Similarly, if a service provider is irritable or sullen, his interaction with customers will likely be colored by that mood. Furthermore, when other customers in a service establishment are cranky or frustrated, whether from problems with the service or from existing emotions unrelated to the service, their mood affects the provision of service for all customers who sense the negative mood. In sum, any service characterized by human interaction is strongly dependent on the moods and emotions of the service provider, the service customer, and other customers receiving the service at the same time.

In what specific ways can mood affect the behavior of service customers? First, positive moods can make customers more obliging and willing to participate in behaviors that help service encounters succeed.[32] Customers in a good emotional state are probably more willing to follow an exercise regimen prescribed by a physical therapist, bus their own dishes at a fast-food restaurant, and overlook delays in service. Customers in a negative mood may be less likely to engage in behaviors essential to the effectiveness of the service.

A second way that moods and emotions influence service customers is to bias the way they judge service encounters and providers consistent with their mood. Mood and emotions enhance and amplify experiences, making them either more positive or more negative than they might seem in the absence of the moods and emotions.[33] After losing a big account, a saleswoman catching an airline flight will be more incensed with delays and crowding than she might be on a day when business went well. Conversely, the positive mood of services customers at a dance or sporting event will heighten the experience, leading to positive evaluations of the service.

Finally, moods and emotions affect the way information about service is absorbed and retrieved in memory. As memories about a service are encoded by a consumer, the feelings associated with the encounter become an inseparable part of the memory. If travelers fall in love during a vacation in the Bahamas, they may hold favorable assessments of the destination due more to their emotional state than to the destination itself. Conversely, if a customer first becomes aware of his poor level of fitness when on a guest pass in a health club, the negative feelings may be encoded and retrieved every time he thinks of the health club or, for that matter, any health club.

Positive moods of customers at a sporting event heighten their service experiences

Because emotions and moods play such important roles in influencing customer experiences, "organizations must manage the emotional component of experiences with the same rigor they bring to the management of product and service functionality."[34] Organizations may observe customers' emotional responses and attempt to create places, processes, and interactions to enhance certain emotions. Research has shown that consumers' emotional responses may be the best predictors of their ultimate loyalty in both consumer and business-to-business markets.[35] Thus, many companies are now beginning to measure emotional responses and connections as well—going beyond traditional measures of satisfaction and behavioral loyalty.

POSTEXPERIENCE EVALUATION

Following the service experience, customers form an evaluation that determines to a large degree whether they will return or continue to patronize the service organization. Historically within the field of marketing, much more attention has been paid to prepurchase evaluations and consumer choice. Yet, postpurchase and postexperience evaluations are typically most important in predicting subsequent consumer behaviors and repurchase, particularly for services.

Postexperience evaluation is captured by companies in measures of satisfaction, service quality, loyalty, and sometimes emotional engagement. We devote an entire chapter (Chapter 5) to exploring the specifics of customer satisfaction and service quality. Another chapter (Chapter 7) will examine the topic of relationships and loyalty.

Word-of-Mouth Communication

Postexperience evaluations will significantly impact what consumers tell others about the service. Because service consumers are strongly influenced by the personal opinions of others, understanding and controlling word-of-mouth communication becomes even more important for service companies. New media in the form of social connection websites, blogs, consumer "hate sites" directed at specific companies, and other forms of individually driven mass communication suggest that controlling and shaping word-of-mouth communication is more important and challenging now than ever before (see Chapter 16 for further discussion of these phenomena). The best way to get positive word of mouth is, of course, to create memorable and positive service experiences. When service is dissatisfactory, it is

It is difficult to imagine a more iconic American brand than Disney, a brand born in the 1920s. Over the decades the company's products, retail outlets, movies, TV shows, and theme parks have been staples for children growing up in the United States. Children living near its Los Angeles and Orlando resorts boast season passes to the parks, and others who can afford the trip (millions a year) take frequent pilgrimages to enjoy the Disney experience. For children in the United States, visiting Disneyland or Disney World is somewhat a badge of honor and rite of passage. Even older children and adults flock to Disneyland and Disney World for vacations.

Yet, as the company has expanded globally over the last several decades, the culture-specific appeal of Disney movies, TV shows, and theme parks is increasingly evident. In 2006, more than 25 percent of the company's revenues and operating income came from outside the United States, with expectations for continued significant growth. Its primary targets for growth are India, China, Russia, Latin America, and South Korea. In each of these areas, the company must understand local consumer behavior and preferences and adjust its service approach to be successful.

HONG KONG DISNEY

Although it suffered a few bumps in its first year of operations, Hong Kong Disney currently is one of the top three attractions in Hong Kong, receiving more than 5 million visitors in its first year of operations after the opening of the park in September 2005. The opening followed six years of careful planning, recognizing cultural differences in an attempt to please the Chinese

market. In designing the park, Disney consulted a feng shui master to help with the park's placement, orientation, and design. This involved such things as rotating the front gate, repositioning cash registers, and locating boulders in key locations to ensure prosperity based on Chinese culture and feng shui traditions. And none of the park's hotels have a designated fourth floor since the number four is considered unlucky in China. Opening on the date September 12 was also by design since the Chinese Almanac indicated that date was an auspicious one for starting a business. Another bow to cultural differences came in the form of diversity in the cast members and the variety of languages spoken as well as signs, messages, and rides—such as the Jungle Cruise—being offered in English, Mandarin, or Cantonese. A wide variety of food offerings also cater to tastes ranging from American to Chinese and Indian. Recognizing the Asian desire to capture everything in photos, Hong Kong Disney includes a garden designed specifically for photo taking, where guests can pose with Mickey, Minnie, and other popular characters.

Despite some of these adaptations, the park was not a great success with Chinese and Hong Kong tourists at the beginning. The Chinese have not grown up with Disney, and thus many of the transplanted rides, characters, and stories did not make sense to them immediately. Many did not know what to expect and found the park confusing. To help guests with these issues, Disney developed a printed introduction to the park that educates them about Disney history, stories, and what to expect. They also offer "one-day trip guides" in Chinese to explain in clear terms how to enjoy Disneyland. Advertising and promotion have also been

critical to have an effective service recovery strategy (see Chapter 8) to curb negative word of mouth.

Attribution of Dissatisfaction

When consumers are disappointed with purchases—because the products do not fulfill the intended needs, do not perform satisfactorily, or are not worth the price—they may attribute their dissatisfaction to a number of different sources, among them the producers, the retailers, or themselves. Because consumers participate to a greater extent in the definition and production of services, they may feel more responsible for their dissatisfaction when they purchase services than when they purchase goods. As an example, consider a consumer purchasing a haircut; receiving the cut she desires

revised to be more informative, and signs and guides in the park are now offered in multiple languages. Other elements of "guestology" (Disney's term for guest operations) also needed to be adapted. Disney quickly found out that Chinese guests take an average of 10 minutes longer to eat than Americans, so they expanded the number of seats provided in dining areas. They also learned that simple things like providing better explanatory signage could make a big difference. Many Chinese had no idea that "Space Mountain" was a roller coaster and thus were extremely surprised (some becoming ill) after waiting in line and getting on the ride for the first time! The company has also adjusted the way it works with Chinese travel agents because most mainland Chinese visitors still take their vacations through package tours rather than arranging their own travel.

DISNEY PRODUCTIONS IN INDIA AND RUSSIA

In its TV and movie production businesses, Disney is rewriting the script for how it does business globally. Rather than simply force-feeding American productions, the company is now seeking to partner with groups in other countries to produce culturally customized shows and movies. The Indian population under 14 years of age is larger than the entire U.S. population, so the opportunities are immense, particularly as incomes in India continue to grow. There, Disney is focusing on TV shows (in part due to India's very strong and vibrant movie production industry), capitalizing on the near-obsessive focus on family of the Indian middle class. In 2004, the company launched the Disney Channel and Toon Disney in India. Disney is also involved in local TV productions and pilot shows with purely Indian themes and actors. In Russia, Disney's strategic focus is on movies where classic and new American Disney films are very popular. However, as in India, the company is also focusing on adapting to the culture with films based on traditional Russian stories using Russian-speaking actors.

Sources: M. Marr, "Disney Rewrites Script to Win Fans in India," *The Wall Street Journal,* June 11, 2007, p. R1; M. Marr and G.A. Fowler, "Disneyland in Hong Kong," *The Wall Street Journal,* June 12, 2006, p. B1; P. M. Miller, "Disneyland in Hong Kong," *China Business Review* (chinabusinessreview.com), January–February 2007, pp. 1, 31, 34; J. Bush, "Mouse Ears over Moscow," *BusinessWeek,* June 11, 2007, p. 42; P. Wiseman, "Ocean Park Takes on Hong Kong Disneyland," *USA Today,* June 15, 2007.

depends in part on her clear specifications of her needs to the stylist. If disappointed, she may blame either the stylist (for lack of skill) or herself (for choosing the wrong stylist or for not communicating her own needs clearly).

The quality of many services depends on the information the customer brings to the service encounter: A doctor's accurate diagnosis requires a conscientious case history and a clear articulation of symptoms; a dry cleaner's success in removing a spot depends on the consumer's knowledge of its cause; and a tax preparer's satisfactory performance relies on the receipts saved by the consumer. Failure to obtain satisfaction with any of these services may not be blamed completely on the retailer or producer, because consumers must adequately perform their part in the production process also.

With many goods, on the other hand, a consumer's main form of participation is the act of purchase. The consumer may attribute failure to receive satisfaction to her own decision-making error, but she holds the producer responsible for product performance. Goods usually carry warranties or guarantees with purchase, emphasizing that the producer believes that if something goes wrong, it is not the fault of the consumer. With services, consumers attribute some of their dissatisfaction to their own inability to specify or perform their part of the service. They also may complain less frequently about services than about goods because of their belief that they themselves are partly responsible for their dissatisfaction.

Positive or Negative Biases

There is a long history of research in psychology and consumer behavior that suggests that people remember negative events and occurrences more than positive ones and are more influenced by negative information than by positive information. Research and personal observation suggest that it is easier for consumers to remember the negative service experiences they have than to think of the many routine, or even positive, experiences. Yet some very interesting and recent research suggests "positivity bias" for services.[36] The research showed that consumers tend to infer positive qualities for the firm and its employees if they have a good experience with one service employee. When individual service providers are regarded positively, customers' positive perceptions of other service providers in the company are also raised. On the other hand, customers who have a negative experience with one employee are less likely to draw a negative inference about all employees or the firm. That is, customers are more likely to attribute that negative experience to the individual provider, not the entire firm. Although this study is just one piece of research, the results and implications are very intriguing.

Brand Loyalty

The degree to which consumers are committed to particular brands of goods or services depends on a number of factors: the cost of changing brands (switching cost), the availability of substitutes, social ties to the company, the perceived risk associated with the purchase, and the satisfaction obtained in the past. Because it may be more costly to change brands of services, because awareness of substitutes is limited, and because higher risks may accompany services, consumers are more likely to remain loyal to service brands when compared with goods producers. The difficulty of obtaining information about services means that consumers may be unaware of alternatives or substitutes for their brands, or they may be uncertain about the ability of alternatives to increase satisfaction over present brands. Monetary fees may accompany brand switching in many services: physicians often require complete physicals on the initial visit; dentists sometimes demand new X rays; and health clubs frequently charge "membership fees" at the outset to obtain long-term commitments from customers. A final reason that consumers may be more brand loyal with services is the recognition of the need for repeated patronage in order to obtain optimum satisfaction from the seller. Becoming a "regular customer" allows the seller to gain knowledge of the customer's tastes and preferences, ensures better treatment, and encourages more interest in the consumer's satisfaction. Thus a consumer may exhibit brand loyalty to cultivate a satisfying relationship with the seller.

However, brand loyalty has two sides. The fact that a service provider's own customers are loyal is, of course, desirable. The fact that the loyal customers of the provider's competition are difficult to capture, however, creates special challenges. The marketer may need to directly communicate with the customers of competitors, emphasizing attributes and strengths that his firm possesses and the competitor lacks. Marketers can also facilitate switching from competitors' services by reducing switching costs.

GLOBAL DIFFERENCES: THE ROLE OF CULTURE

Culture represents the common values, norms, and behaviors of a particular group and is often identified with nations or ethnicity. Culture is learned, shared, multidimensional, and transmitted from one generation to the next. Understanding cultural differences is important in services marketing because of its effects on the ways that customers evaluate and use services. Culture also influences how companies and their service employees interact with customers. Culture is important in global services marketing—taking services from one country and offering them in others—but it is also critical within countries. More and more, individual countries are becoming multicultural, and organizations need to understand how this factor affects evaluation, purchase, and use of services even within countries.

Research provides considerable evidence that there are differences in how consumers perceive services across cultures. For example, a study of service quality perceptions in Taiwan revealed that much greater emphasis is placed on the interpersonal dimensions of service than is generally true in studies of U.S. consumers.[37] Another study showed notable differences in how fast-food and grocery consumers in eight different countries (Australia, China, Germany, India, Morocco, the Netherlands, Sweden, and the United States) evaluate these services.[38] Research also recommends that firms carefully consider global differences in the ways they measure service quality in order to make valid comparisons across cultures.[39] Because of the importance of the global dimensions of business and cultural differences among consumers, we include a Global Feature in every chapter of the text to illustrate how global differences affect services management as well as consumer behavior. Our Global Feature on page 66 in this chapter illustrates differences in how one company (Disney) has adapted its service strategy around the world.

Summary

The intent of this chapter was to provide understanding for how consumers choose, experience, and evaluate services. Services possess high levels of experience and credence properties, which in turn make them challenging to evaluate, particularly prior to purchase. The chapter isolated and discussed three stages of consumer behavior for services, and it looked at how experience and credence properties result in challenges and opportunities in all three stages. The three stages are consumer choice (including need recognition, information search, evaluation of alternatives, and service purchase); consumer experience; and postexperience evaluation. Consumer behavior theories, current research, and insights for managers were highlighted in each of these sections. The chapter concluded with a recognition that global differences and culture are important influences an consumer behavior in services. The Global Feature an Disney provides an illustration of one company's attempts to adapt.

Discussion Questions

1. Based on the chapter, which aspects of consumer behavior are similar and which are different for services versus goods?

2. Where does a college education fit on the continuum of evaluation for different types of products? Where does computer software fit? Consulting? Retailing? Fast food? What are the implications for consumer behavior?

3. What are examples (other than those given in the chapter) of services that are high in credence properties? How do high credence properties affect consumer behavior for these services?

4. For what types of services might consumers depend on mass communication (nonpersonal sources of information, including the Internet) in the purchase decision?

5. Which of the aspects discussed in the chapter describe your behavior when it comes to purchasing services? Does your behavior differ for different types of services?

6. Why are consumer experiences so important in the evaluation process for services?

7. Using the service drama metaphor, describe the services provided by a health club, a fine restaurant, or a vacation cruise line.

Exercises

1. Choose a particular end-consumer services industry and one type of service provided in that industry (such as the financial services industry for mortgage loans, the legal services industry for wills, or the travel industry for a vacation package). Talk to five customers who have purchased that service and determine to what extent the information in this chapter described their behavior in terms of consumer choice, consumer experience, and postexperience evaluation for that service.

2. Choose a particular business-to-business service industry and one type of service provided in that industry (such as the information services industry for computer maintenance services or the consulting industry for management consulting). Talk to five customers in that industry and determine to what extent the information in this chapter described their behavior in terms of consumer choice, consumer experience, and postexperience evaluation for that service.

3. Visit a service provider of your choice. Experience the service firsthand if possible and observe other customers for a period of time. Describe the consumer (service) experience in detail in terms of what happened throughout the process and how customers, including yourself, felt about it. How could the service experience be improved?

Notes

1. L. C. Lancaster and D. Stillman, *When Generations Collide* (New York: Harper Collins, 2002); M. Read, "Boomers Get Pumped Up," *Mesa Tribune,* June 20, 2007; D. Lidsky, "Life Time Fitness," *Fast Company Magazine* Customer's First Awards, September 2006, p. 60; N. A. Hira, "You Raised Them, Now Manage Them," *Fortune,* May 28, 2007, pp. 38–46.

2. P. Nelson, "Information and Consumer Behavior," *Journal of Political Economy* 78, no. 20 (1970), pp. 311–329.

3. M. R. Darby and E. Karni, "Free Competition and the Optimal Amount of Fraud," *Journal of Law and Economics* 16 (April 1973), pp. 67–86.

4. P. Berthon, L. Pitt, C. S. Katsikeas, and J. P. Berthon, "Virtual Services Go International: International Services in the Marketspace," *Journal of International Marketing* 7, no. 3 (1999), pp. 84–105.

5. J. C. Ward and A. L. Ostrom, "Complaining to the Masses: The Role of Protest Framing in Customer-Created Complaint Web Sites," *Journal of Consumer Research,* 33 (September 2006), pp. 220–230.

6. M. Laroche, G. H. G. McDougall, J. Bergeron, and Z. Yang, "Exploring How Intangibility Affects Perceived Risk," *Journal of Service Research* 6, (May 2004), pp. 373–389; K. B. Murray and J. L. Schlacter, "The Impact of Services versus Goods on Consumers' Assessment of Perceived Risk and Variability," *Journal of the Academy of Marketing Science* 18 (Winter 1990), pp. 51–65; M. Laroche, J. Bergeron, and C. Goutaland, "How Intangibility Affects Perceived Risk: The Moderating Role of Knowledge and Involvement," *Journal of Services Marketing* 17, no. 2 (2003), pp. 122–140.

7. M. Laroche et al., "Exploring How Intangibility Affects Perceived Risk."

8. R. F. Lusch, S. W. Brown, and G. J. Brunswick, "A General Framework for Explaining Internal vs. External Exchange," *Journal of the Academy of Marketing Science* 10 (Spring 1992), pp. 119–134; Dorsch, Grove, and Darden, "Consumer Intentions to Use a Service Category."

9. J. H. Gilmore and B. J. Pine II, "The Experience Is the Marketing," report from Strategic Horizons LLP, 2002.

10. See, for example, B. J. Pine II and J. H. Gilmore, *The Experience Economy* (Boston: Harvard Business School Press, 1999); B. H. Schmitt, *Experiential Marketing* (New York: The Free Press, 1999); B. H. Schmitt, *Customer Experience Management* (Hoboken, NJ: John Wiley & Sons, 2003); C. Meyer and A. Schwager, "Understanding Customer Experience," *Harvard Business Review,* 85 (February 2007), pp. 117–126.

11. S. S. Tax and F. N. Morgan, "Toward a Theory of Service Delivery Networks," working paper, W. P. Carey School of Business, Arizona State University, 2004.

12. S. J. Grove and R. P. Fisk, "Service Theater: An Analytical Framework for Services Marketing," in *Services Marketing,* 4th ed., ed. Christopher Lovelock (Englewood Cliffs, NJ: Prentice Hall, 2001), pp. 83–92; F. I. Stuart, "Designing and Executing Memorable Service Experiences: Lights, Camera, Experiment, Integrate, Action," *Business Horizons* 49 (2006), pp. 149–159.

13. S. J. Grove, R. P. Fisk, and M. J. Bitner, "Dramatizing the Service Experience: A Managerial Approach," in *Advances in Services Marketing and Management,* vol. 1, ed. T. A. Swartz, D. E. Bowen, and S. W. Brown (Greenwich, CT: JAI Press, 1992), pp. 91–121.

14. Grove, Fisk, and Bitner, "Dramatizing the Service Experience."

15. Grove and Fisk, "Service Theater."

16. Grove, Fisk, and Bitner, "Dramatizing the Service Experience."

17. Ibid.

18. Stuart, "Designing and Executing Memorable Service Experiences."

19. M. R. Solomon, C. Surprenant, J. A. Czepiel, and E. G. Gutman, "A Role Theory Perspective on Dyadic Interactions: The Service Encounter," *Journal of Marketing* 49 (Winter 1985), pp. 99–111.

20. Ibid.

21. R. F. Abelson, "Script Processing in Attitude Formation and Decision Making," in *Cognition and Social Behavior,* ed. J. S. Carroll and J. S. Payne (Hillsdale, NJ: Erlbaum, 1976).

22. R. A. Smith and M. J. Houston, "Script-Based Evaluations of Satisfaction with Services," in *Emerging Perspectives on Services Marketing,* ed. L. Berry, G. L. Shostack, and G. Upah (Chicago: American Marketing Association, 1982), pp. 59–62.

23. J. E. G. Bateson and M. K. M. Hui, "Crowding in the Service Environment," in *Creativity in Services Marketing: What's New, What Works, What's Developing,* ed. M. Venkatesan, D. M. Schmalensee, and C. Marshall (Chicago: American Marketing Association, 1986), pp. 85–88.

24. C. L. Martin and C. A. Pranter, "Compatibility Management: Customer-to-Customer Relationships in Service Environments," *Journal of Services Marketing* 3 (Summer 1989), pp. 5–15

25. Ibid.

26. N. Bendapudi and R. P. Leone, "Psychological Implications of Customer Participation in Co-Production," *Journal of Marketing* 67 (January 2003), pp. 14–28.

27. L. A. Bettencourt, A. L. Ostrom, S. W. Brown, and R. I. Roundtree, "Client Co-Production in Knowledge-Intensive Business Services," *California Management Review* 44 (Summer 2002), pp. 100–128.

28. S. Dellande, M. C. Gilly, and J. L. Graham, "Gaining Compliance and Losing Weight: The Role of the Service Provider in Health Care Services," *Journal of Marketing* 68 (July 2004), pp. 78–91; M. L. Meuter, M. J. Bitner, A. L. Ostrom, and S. W. Brown, "Choosing among Alternative Service Delivery Modes: An Investigation of Customer Trial of Self-Service Technologies," *Journal of Marketing* 69 (April 2005), pp. 61–83.

29. C. K. Prahalad and V. Ramaswamy, "The New Frontier of Experience Innovation," *Sloan Management Review* 44 (Summer 2003), pp. 12–18.

30. A. F. Firat and A. Venkatesh, "Liberatory Postmodernism and the Reenchantment of Consumption," *Journal of Consumer Research* 22 (December 1995), pp. 239–267.

31. M. P. Gardner, "Mood States and Consumer Behavior: A Critical Review," *Journal of Consumer Research* 12 (December 1985), pp. 281–300.

32. Ibid., p. 288.

33. S. S. Tomkins, "Affect as Amplification: Some Modifications in Theory," in *Emotion: Theory, Research, and Experience,* ed. R. Plutchik and H. Kellerman (New York: Academic Press, 1980), pp. 141–164.

34. L. L. Berry, L. P. Carbone, and S. H. Haeckel, "Managing the Total Customer Experience," *Sloan Management Review* (Spring 2002), pp. 85–89.

35. L. A. Crosby and S. L. Johnson, "Experience Required," *Marketing Management,* 16 (July–August 2007), pp. 20–28.

36. V. S. Folkes and V. M. Patrick, "The Positivity Effect in Perceptions of Services: Seen One, Seen Them All?" *Journal of Consumer Research* 30 (June 2003), pp. 125–137.

37. B. Imrie, J. W. Cadogan, and R. McNaughton, "The Service Quality Construct on a Global Stage," *Managing Service Quality* 12, no. 1 (2002), pp. 10–18.

38. B. D. Keillor, G. T. M. Hult, D. Kandemir, "A Study of the Service Encounter in Eight Countries," *Journal of International Marketing* 12, no. 1 (2004), pp. 9–35.

39. A. M. Smith and N. L. Reynolds, "Measuring Cross-Cultural Service Quality: A Framework for Assessment," *International Marketing Review* 19, no. 5 (2001), pp. 450–481.

Chapter Four

Customer Expectations of Service

This chapter's objectives are to

1. Recognize that customers hold different types of expectations for service performance.
2. Discuss the sources of customer expectations of service, including those that are controllable and uncontrollable by marketers.
3. Acknowledge that the types and sources of expectations are similar for end consumers and business customers, for pure service and product-related service, for experienced customers and inexperienced customers.
4. Delineate the most important current issues surrounding customer expectations.

Undoubtedly, the greatest gap between customer expectations and service delivery exists when customers travel from one country to another. For example, in Japan the customer is supreme. At the morning opening of large department stores in Tokyo, sales personnel line up to welcome patrons and bow as they enter! When one of us—who could speak no Japanese—visited Tokyo a couple of years ago, as many as eight salespeople willingly tried to help me find a calligraphy pen. Although the pen was a very low-priced item, several attendants rushed from counter to counter to find someone to translate, several others spread out to find pens that might serve as the perfect gift, and still others searched for maps to other stores where the perfect pen could be found.

Because of the wonderful treatment Japanese customers are used to in their home country, they often have service expectations that exceed service delivery even when shopping in "civilized" countries such as Great Britain: "Hideo Majima, 57, a Japanese tourist, looked puzzled and annoyed. He was standing in a London department store while two shop assistants conversed instead of serving him. He left without buying anything."[1] His annoyance is understandable when you realize the standard of service treatment in Japan.

Expectations of hotel service may also differ from one country to another. In the United States, a "two-star" designation for a hotel is generally interpreted to mean customers can expect guest rooms to be clean; beds to be comfortable; rooms to be sparsely decorated and equipped with some modern conveniences such as microwave oven, refrigerator, color television, sofa bed, telephone, and coffee maker;

Tokyo sales personnel provide excellent customer service.

as well as to have daily maid service. For such hotels the customer is not expecting (and does not want to pay for) luxury, extra service, beautiful spacious lobbies, or room service availability but still wants to have a fairly decent, clean, and safe place to stay. Often the hotel might also include a work desk, voicemail, and high-speed Internet access in the room. However, experienced travelers to Great Britain would be very surprised to find this level of service at a two-star hotel in London.

In fact, another one of us had firsthand experience with differing customer expectations with hotel service in London. In particular, a four-night hotel stay was booked for a family of four (including two children) at what was promised by a travel agent to be a two-star hotel. However, this London hotel did not meet our expectations of a two-star hotel. Instead, the hotel had rooms for a maximum of two people, slanting floors (and, therefore, beds), 24-inch wide showers stalls, room entry doors that did not fully latch, hallways with no lights, and a huge hole in the wall behind one toilet with insects coming and going as they pleased. In addition, the daily "maid service" consisted of simply emptying the trash cans in the rooms and leaving the door to one of the rooms unlatched. No new towels or sheets were provided, and no cleaning of any kind was done in the room. Clearly the level of service did not match our expectations, although seasoned European travelers were not surprised when we told them of our service experience. Obviously not all two-star London hotels have such "features." However, we were surprised to find that many of our European friends did not find our service experience to be extremely unusual for a two-star hotel in a large, expensive city like London. Their expectations of service are quite different from ours. Imagine how our friend Majima-san would have felt about this service experience!

Customer expectations are beliefs about service delivery that serve as standards or reference points against which performance is judged. Because customers compare their perceptions of performance with these reference points when evaluating service quality, thorough knowledge about customer expectations is critical to services marketers. Knowing what the customer expects is the first and possibly most critical step in delivering quality service. Being wrong about what customers want can mean losing a customer's business when another company hits the target exactly. Being wrong can also mean expending money, time, and other resources on things that do not count to the customer. Being wrong can even mean not surviving in a fiercely competitive market.

Among the aspects of expectations that need to be explored and understood for successful services marketing are the following: What types of expectation standards do customers hold about services? What factors most influence the formation of these expectations? What role do these factors play in changing expectations? How can a service company meet or exceed customer expectations?

In this chapter we provide a framework for thinking about customer expectations.[2] The chapter is divided into three main sections: (1) the meaning and types of expected service, (2) factors that influence customer expectations of service, and (3) current issues involving customer service expectations.

MEANING AND TYPES OF SERVICE EXPECTATIONS

To say that expectations are reference points against which service delivery is compared is only a beginning. The level of expectation can vary widely depending on the reference point the customer holds. Although most everyone has an intuitive sense of what expectations are, service marketers need a far more thorough and clear definition of expectations in order to comprehend, measure, and manage them.

Imagine that you are planning to go to a restaurant. Figure 4.1 shows a continuum along which different possible types of service expectations can be arrayed from low to high. On the left of the continuum are different types or levels of expectations, ranging from high (top) to low (bottom). At each point we give a name to the type of expectation and illustrate what it might mean in terms of a restaurant you are considering. Note how important the expectation you held will be to your eventual assessment of the restaurant's performance. Suppose you went into the restaurant for which you held the minimum tolerable expectation, paid very little money, and were served immediately with good food. Next, suppose that you went to the restaurant for which you had the highest (ideal) expectations, paid a lot of money, and were served good (but not fantastic) food. Which restaurant experience would you judge to be best? The answer is likely to depend a great deal on the reference point that you brought to the experience.

Because the idea of customer expectations is so critical to evaluation of service, we start this chapter by talking about the levels of expectations.

FIGURE 4.1
Possible Levels of Customer Expectations

Source: R. K. Teas, "Expectations, Performance Evaluation and Consumers' Perceptions of Quality," *Journal of Marketing,* October 1993, pp. 18–34. Reprinted by Permission of the American Marketing Association.

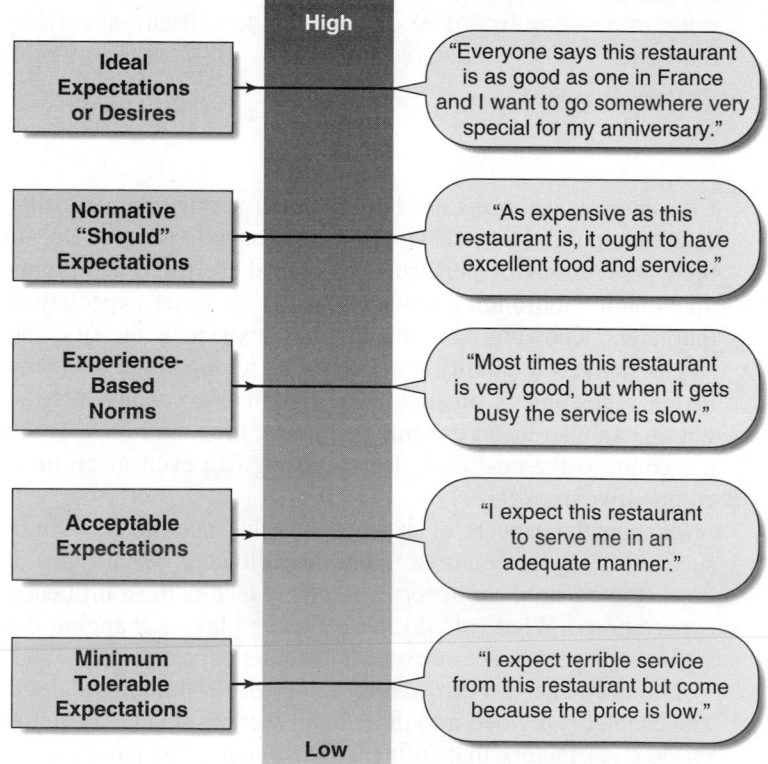

Expected Service: Levels of Expectations

As we showed in Figure 4.1, customers hold different types of expectations about service. For purposes of our discussion in the rest of this chapter, we focus on two types. The highest can be termed *desired service:* the level of service the customer hopes to receive—the "wished for" level of performance. Desired service is a blend of what the customer believes "can be" and "should be."[3] For example, consumers who sign up for a computer dating service expect to find compatible, attractive, interesting people to date and perhaps even someone to marry. The expectation reflects the hopes and wishes of these consumers; without these hopes and wishes and the belief that they may be fulfilled, consumers would probably not purchase the dating service. In a similar way, you will engage the services of your college's placement office when you are ready to graduate. What are your expectations of the service? In all likelihood you want the office to find you a job—the right job in the right place for the right salary—because that is what you hope and wish for.

However, you probably also see that the economy may constrain the availability of ideal job openings in companies. And not all companies you may be interested in have a relationship with your placement office. In this situation and in general, customers hope to achieve their service desires but recognize that this is not always possible. We call the threshold level of acceptable service *adequate service*—the level of service the customer will accept.[4] In the economic slowdown following the World Trade Center disaster, many college graduates who were trained for high-skilled jobs accepted entry-level positions at fast-food restaurants or internships for no pay. Their hopes and desires were still high, but they recognized that they could not attain those desires in the market that existed at the time. Their standard of adequate service from the placement office was much lower than their desired service. Some graduates accepted any job for which they could earn a salary, and others agreed to nonpaying, short-term positions as interns to gain experience. Adequate service represents the "minimum tolerable expectation,"[5] the bottom level of performance acceptable to the customer.

Figure 4.2 shows these two expectation standards as the upper and lower boundaries for customer expectations. This figure portrays the idea that customers assess service performance on the basis of two standard boundaries: what they desire and what they deem acceptable.

Among the intriguing questions about service expectations is whether customers hold the same or different expectation levels for service firms in the same industry.

FIGURE 4.2
Dual Customer Expectation Levels

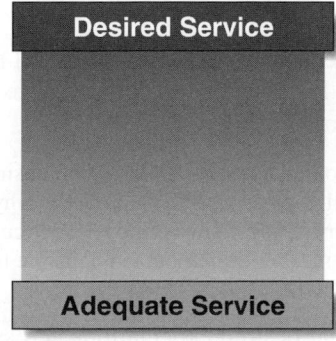

Desired Service

Adequate Service

The characteristics of services often make it difficult for customers to know what to expect from a service provider. Imagine the difficulty of knowing what to expect if you were to "outsource" many of the day-to-day tasks you perform to someone whom you (1) never meet in person and (2) lives in a foreign country. Many families face this situation when they select a service provider located overseas.

OFFSHORING OF PERSONAL CONSUMER SERVICES

As indicated in Chapter 1, many U.S. companies are involved in offshore outsourcing of services. More than $20 billion is spent annually on services provided outside of the United States. A growing percentage of U.S. families are now using service providers in foreign countries to complete personal tasks for them. Thanks to the technology available to many households today, including instant messaging, computer scanners, and e-mail attachments, services that can be completed without requiring face-to-face interaction have the potential to be done overseas. Some of the services that can be outsourced to foreign countries include interior design, word processing, legal services, mural painting, wedding planning, personal website design, and landscape design. To illustrate:

- One customer wanted to create a short, but professional looking, video to show at his sister's wedding. He found a graphic artist in Romania who created a two-minute video with a space theme set to the music of Star Wars that was a hit at the wedding. The cost for everything? Only $59.

- A man was looking for a graphic artist to illustrate a children's book his mother had written for her grandchildren about her early childhood experiences in New York City. Rather than search for a graphic artist

through a local telephone directory, he described his project on the guru.com website. Within a week he received 80 bids from artists in countries like Malaysia, Ukraine, and Lebanon. He ended up hiring a woman from the Philippines who offered to do 25 drawings for $300.

- One family hired an online tutor for their daughter. After obtaining quotes around $40/hour for local tutoring services, they found an online tutor from India who charged $99/month for two-hour, five-day-per-week sessions. The lessons simply required the family to have a digital tablet, instant messaging, and a headset for communication.

EXPECTATIONS OF SERVICE

Outsourcing services at the consumer level raises some issues. As discussed in this chapter, desired service expectations are influenced by explicit service promises, implicit service promises, word-of-mouth communication, and past experience. However, when outsourcing personal services in the manner listed earlier, many of these factors may not be present. For example, in many cases communication may be conducted via e-mail—providing a limited amount of cues upon which promises are based—word-of-mouth recommendations may be restricted to Internet sources, and customers may have no experience with such services. To further complicate the matter for customers, many may have limited exposure to having *any* previous work done for them through the Internet, and most are likely to have never hired a foreign service provider.

In such settings, customers may attempt to communicate their expectations of service, but face obstacles in doing so. If the service provider's native language is not English, there is a good chance for misunderstanding.

For example, are desired service expectations the same for all restaurants? Or just for all fast-food restaurants? Do the levels of adequate service expectations vary across restaurants? Consider the following quotation:

> Levels of expectation are why two organizations in the same business can offer far different levels of service and still keep customers happy. It is why McDonald's can extend excellent industrialized service with few employees per customer and why an expensive restaurant with many tuxedoed waiters may be unable to do as well from the customer's point of view.[6]

Customers typically hold similar desired expectations across categories of service, but these categories are not as broad as whole industries. Among subcategories of

For example, one customer had a language issue with an outsourcer based in Egypt. The outsourcer put together a personal website for the customer—but drafts included several misspelled words. Not surprisingly, e-mails with instructions and explanations were labored because of the language gap. Thus, customers looking to outsource services to foreign providers may anticipate having to put significant energy and effort into communicating expectations.

Wall Street Journal reporter Ellen Gamerman asked an India-based outsourcer to design a change-of-address card for someone who was moving from New York to Arizona. Although he did a good job with the design, there were a couple of communication miscues: (1) he initially put evergreens in the desert background and (2) he had the car in the card driving west to east initially, not east to west. When the instructions were initially given, she did not spell out exactly what she wanted—she gave him a general idea of the theme of the card, and then asked him to be creative. Although he was happy to make changes to correct these issues, the price went up to cover the changes.

Using a foreign service provider may require customers to reset their expectations. One customer decided to use outsourcing for his personal income taxes. After he e-mailed his earnings and scanned receipts, his tax return was completed in two days at a cost of $50—about one-third of what a U.S. firm like H&R Block charges. However, he had to file his return as "self-prepared" since it was not prepared by a U.S. accountant.

Another issue customers may face is one of trust: how willing are customers to entrust a worker thousands of miles away—and in a foreign country—with projects of a personal nature? To provide some information about the quality of service a customer might expect from a service provider, services on auction sites like guru.com provide a ratings system similar to that provided on eBay. Some vendors post short videos of themselves and their offices on the Internet to help shape customers' expectations and gain their trust.

Sources: Ellen Gamerman, "Outsourcing Your Life," *The Wall Street Journal,* June 2, 2007, pp. P1, P4; Alan Blinder, "Offshoring: The Next Industrial Revolution?" *Foreign Affairs* 85 (March/April 2006), pp. 113–118; Ellen Gamerman, e-mail communication, July 30, 2007.

restaurants are expensive restaurants, ethnic restaurants, fast-food restaurants, and airport restaurants. A customer's desired service expectation for fast-food restaurants is quick, convenient, tasty food in a clean setting. The desired service expectation for an expensive restaurant, on the other hand, usually involves elegant surroundings, gracious employees, candlelights, and fine food. In essence, desired service expectations seem to be the same for service providers within industry categories or subcategories that are viewed as similar by customers.

The adequate service expectation level, on the other hand, may vary for different firms within a category or subcategory. Within fast-food restaurants, a customer may hold a higher expectation for McDonald's than for Burger King, having experienced consistent service at McDonald's over time and somewhat inconsistent service at Burger King. It is possible, therefore, that a customer can be more disappointed with service from McDonald's than from Burger King, even though the actual level of service at McDonald's is higher than the level at Burger King. This chapter's Global Feature illustrates some of the challenges firms face in understanding what customers' expectations are, particularly when delivering service to customers in another country.

The Zone of Tolerance

As we discussed in earlier chapters of this textbook, services are heterogeneous in that performance may vary across providers, across employees from the same provider, and even with the same service employee. The extent to which customers recognize and are willing to accept this variation is called the *zone of tolerance* and is shown in Figure 4.3. If service drops below adequate service—the minimum level considered acceptable—customers will be frustrated and most likely dissatisfied with the company. If service performance is above the zone of tolerance at the top end—where performance exceeds desired service—customers will be very pleased and probably quite surprised as well. You might consider the zone of tolerance as the range or window in which customers do not particularly notice service performance. When it falls outside the range (either very low or very high), the service gets the customer's attention in either a positive or negative way. As an example, consider the service at a checkout line in a grocery store. Most customers hold a range of acceptable times for this service encounter—probably somewhere between 5 and 10 minutes. If service consumes that period of time, customers probably do not pay much attention to the wait. If a customer enters the line and find a sufficient number of checkout personnel to serve her in the first 2 or 3 minutes, she may notice the service and judge it as excellent. On the other hand, if a customer has to wait in line for 15 minutes, he may begin to grumble and look at his watch. The longer the wait is below the zone of tolerance (10 minutes in this example), the more frustrated he becomes.

Customers' service expectations are characterized by a range of levels (like those shown in Figure 4.2), bounded by desired and adequate service, rather than a single level. This tolerance zone, representing the difference between desired service and the level of service considered adequate, can expand and contract for a given customer. An airline customer's zone of tolerance will narrow when she is running late and is concerned about making her plane. A minute's delay for anything that occurs prior to boarding the plane seems much longer, and her adequate service level increases. On the other hand, a customer who arrives at the airport early may have a larger tolerance zone, making the wait in line far less noticeable than when he is pressed for time. This example shows that the marketer must understand not just the size and boundary levels for the zone of tolerance but also when and how the tolerance zone fluctuates for a given customer.

Different Customers Possess Different Zones of Tolerance

Another aspect of variability in the range of reasonable services is that different customers possess different tolerance zones. Some customers have narrow zones of tolerance, requiring a tighter range of service from providers, whereas other customers allow a greater range of service. For example, very busy customers would likely always be pressed for time, desire short wait times in general, and also hold a constrained range

FIGURE 4.3
The Zone of
Tolerance

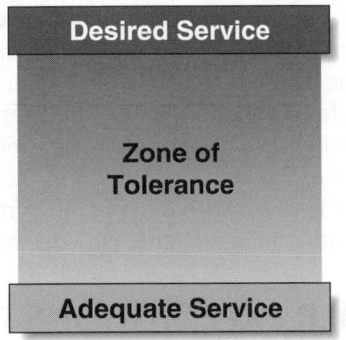

for the length of acceptable wait times. When it comes to meeting plumbers or repair personnel at their homes for appliance problems, customers who work outside the home have a more restricted window of acceptable time duration for that appointment than do customers who work in their homes or do not work at all.

An individual customer's zone of tolerance increases or decreases depending on a number of factors, including company-controlled factors such as price. When prices increase, customers tend to be less tolerant of poor service. In this case, the zone of tolerance decreases because the adequate service level shifts upward. Later in this chapter we will describe many different factors, some company controlled and others customer controlled, that lead to the narrowing or widening of the tolerance zone.

Zones of Tolerance Vary for Service Dimensions

Customers' tolerance zones also vary for different service attributes or dimensions. The more important the factor, the narrower the zone of tolerance is likely to be. In general, customers are likely to be less tolerant about unreliable service (broken promises or service errors) than other service deficiencies, which means that they have higher expectations for this factor. In addition to higher expectations for the most important service dimensions and attributes, customers are likely to be less willing to relax these expectations than those for less important factors, making the zone of tolerance for the most important service dimension smaller and the desired and adequate service levels higher.[7] Figure 4.4 portrays the likely difference in tolerance zones for the most important and the least important factors.[8]

FIGURE 4.4
Zones of Tolerance for Different Service Dimensions

Source: L. L. Berry, A. Parasuraman, and V. A. Zeithaml, "Ten Lessons for Improving Service Quality," *Marketing Science Institute,* Report No. 93–104 (May 1993).

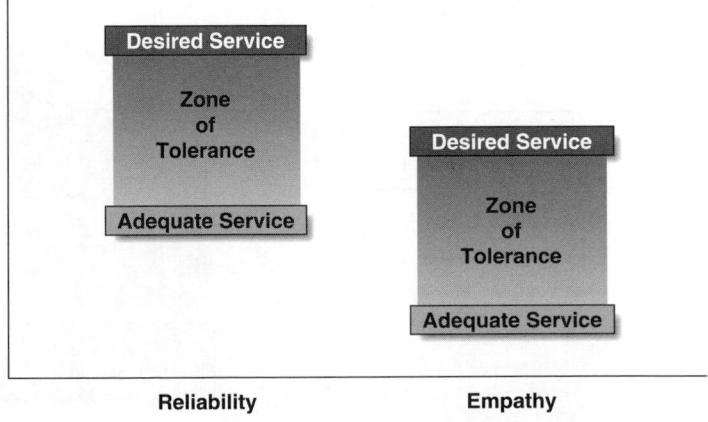

The fluctuation in the individual customer's zone of tolerance is more a function of changes in the adequate service level, which moves readily up and down because of situational circumstances, than in the desired service level, which tends to move upward incrementally because of accumulated experiences. Desired service is relatively idiosyncratic and stable compared with adequate service, which moves up and down and in response to competition and other factors. Fluctuation in the zone of tolerance can be likened to an accordion's movement, but with most of the gyration coming from one side (the adequate service level) rather than the other (the desired service level).

FACTORS THAT INFLUENCE CUSTOMER EXPECTATIONS OF SERVICE

Because expectations play such a critical role in customer evaluation of services, marketers need and want to understand the factors that shape them. Marketers would also like to have control over these factors as well, but many of the forces that influence customer expectations are uncontrollable. In this section of the chapter we describe the many influences on customer expectations.

Sources of Desired Service Expectations

As shown in Figure 4.5, there are two major influences on desired service level. The first, *personal needs,* are those states or conditions essential to the physical or psychological well-being of the customer and are pivotal factors that shape what customers desire in service. Personal needs can fall into many categories, including physical, social, psychological, and functional. A fan who regularly goes to baseball games right from work, and is therefore thirsty and hungry, hopes and desires that the food and drink vendors will pass by his section frequently, whereas a fan who regularly has dinner elsewhere has a low level of desired service from the vendors. A customer with high social and dependency needs may have relatively high expectations for a hotel's ancillary services, hoping, for example, that the hotel has a bar with live music and dancing. The effect of personal needs on desired service is illustrated by the different expectations held by two business insurance customers:

> I expect [an insurance] broker to do a great deal of my work because I don't have the staff . . . I expect the broker to know a great deal about my business and communicate that knowledge to the underwriter.

FIGURE 4.5
Factors That Influence Desired Service

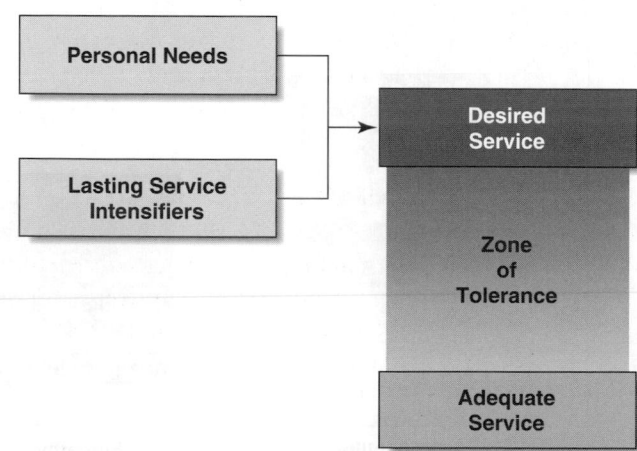

My expectations are different . . . I do have a staff to do our certificates, etc., and use the broker minimally.[9]

The second major influence on desired service expectations are *lasting service intensifiers*—individual, stable factors that lead the customer to a heightened sensitivity to service. One of the most important of these factors is called *derived service expectations,* which occur when customer expectations are driven by another person or group of people. A niece from a big family who is planning a 90th birthday party for a favorite aunt is representing the entire family in selecting a restaurant for a successful celebration. Her needs are driven in part by expectations derived from the other family members. A parent choosing a vacation for the family, a spouse selecting a home-cleaning service, an employee choosing an office for the firm—all these customers' individual expectations are intensified because they represent and must answer to other parties who will receive the service. In the context of business-to-business service, customer expectations are driven by the expectations of their own customers. The head of an information technology department in an insurance company, who is the business customer of a large computer vendor, has expectations based on those of the insurance customers she serves: when the computer equipment is down, her customers complain. Her need to keep the system up and running is not just her own desire but is derived from the pressure of customers.

Business-to-business customers may also derive their expectations from their managers and supervisors. Employees of a marketing research department may speed up project cycles (increase their expectations for speed of delivery) when pressured by their management to deliver the study results. Purchasing agents may increase demands for faster delivery at lower costs when company management is emphasizing cost reduction in the company.

Another lasting service intensifier is *personal service philosophy*—the customer's underlying generic attitude about the meaning of service and the proper conduct of service providers. If you have ever been employed as a waitperson in a restaurant, you are likely to have standards for restaurant service that were shaped by your training and experience in that role. You might, for example, believe that waiters should not keep customers waiting longer than 15 minutes to take their orders. Knowing the way a kitchen operates, you may be less tolerant of lukewarm food or errors in the order than customers who have not held the role of waitperson. In general, customers who are themselves in service businesses or have worked for them in the past seem to have especially strong service philosophies.

To the extent that customers have personal philosophies about service provision, their expectations of service providers will be intensified. Personal service philosophies and derived service expectations can elevate the level of desired service.

Sources of Adequate Service Expectations

A different set of determinants affects adequate service, the level of service the customer finds acceptable. In general, these influences are short-term and tend to fluctuate more than the factors that influence desired service. In this section we explain the five factors shown in Figure 4.6 that influence adequate service: (1) temporary service intensifiers, (2) perceived service alternatives, (3) customer self-perceived service role, (4) situational factors, and (5) predicted service.

FIGURE 4.6
Factors That Influence Adequate Service

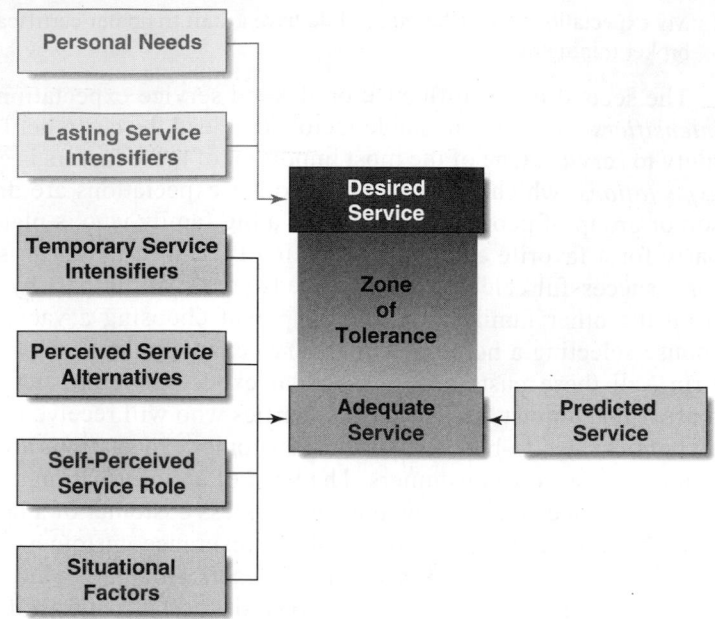

The first set of elements, *temporary service intensifiers,* consists of short-term, individual factors that make a customer more aware of the need for service. Personal emergency situations in which service is urgently needed (such as an accident and the need for automobile insurance or a breakdown in office equipment during a busy period) raise the level of adequate service expectations, particularly in terms of the level of responsiveness required and considered acceptable. A mail-order company that depends on toll-free phone lines for receiving all customer orders will tend to be more demanding of its telephone service provider during peak periods of the week, month, and year. Any system breakdown or lack of clarity on the lines will be tolerated less during these intense periods than at other times. The impact of temporary service intensifiers is evident in these comments by two participants in a research study conducted by one of us:

> An automobile insurance customer: The nature of my problem influences my expectations, for example, a broken window versus a DWI accident requiring brain surgery.

> A business equipment repair customer: I had calibration problems with the X-ray equipment. They should have come out and fixed it in a matter of hours because of the urgency.[10]

Problems with the initial service can also lead to heightened expectations. Performing a service right the first time is very important because customers value service reliability above all other dimensions. If the service fails in the recovery phase, fixing it right the second time (i.e., being reliable in service recovery) is even more critical than it was the first time. Automobile repair service provides a case in point. If a problem with your automobile's brakes sends you to a car repair provider, you expect the company to fix the brakes. If you experience further problems with the brakes after the repair, the level of service which you consider to be adequate will increase. In these and other situations where temporary service intensifiers are present, the level of adequate service will increase and the zone of tolerance will narrow.

Perceived service alternatives are other providers from whom the customer can obtain service. If customers believe they have multiple service providers to choose from, or if they can provide the service for themselves (such as lawn care or personal grooming), their levels of adequate service are higher than those of customers who believe it is not possible to get better service elsewhere. An airline customer who lives in a small town with a tiny airport, for example, has a reduced set of options in airline travel. This customer will be more tolerant of the service performance of the carriers in the town because few alternatives exist. She will accept the limited schedule of flights and lower levels of service more than the customer in a big city who has myriad flights and airlines to choose from. The customer's perception that service alternatives exist raises the level of adequate service and narrows the zone of tolerance.

It is important that service marketers fully understand the complete set of options that customers view as perceived alternatives. In the small town–small airport example just discussed, the set of alternatives from the customer's point of view is likely to include more than just other airlines: limousine service to a nearby large city, rail service, or driving. In general, service marketers must discover the alternatives that the customer views as comparable rather than those in the company's competitive set. For example, airline companies must fully understand customer views of new service technologies (see our Technology Spotlight).

A third factor affecting the level of adequate service is the *customer's self-perceived service role*. We define this as customer perceptions of the degree to which customers exert an influence on the level of service they receive. In other words, customers' expectations are partly shaped by how well they believe they are performing their own roles in service delivery. One role of the customer is to specify the level of service expected. A customer who is very explicit with a waiter about how rare he wants his steak cooked in a restaurant will probably be more dissatisfied if the meat comes to the table overcooked than a customer who does not articulate the degree of doneness expected. The customer's active participation in the service also affects this factor. A customer who does not show up for many of her allergy shots will probably be more lenient with the allergist when she experiences symptoms than one who conscientiously shows up for every shot.

Customers' zones of tolerance seem to expand—that is, the level of service considered to be adequate lowers—when they sense they are not fulfilling their roles. When, on the other hand, customers believe they are doing their part in delivery, their expectations of adequate service are heightened and the zone of tolerance contracts. The comment of an automobile repair customer illustrates: "Service writers [*those who write up what needs to be done*] are not competent. I prepare my own itemized list of problems, take it to the service writer, and tell him or her, 'Fix these.' " This customer will expect more than one who did not prepare as well to receive the service.

Levels of adequate service are also influenced by *situational factors,* defined as service performance conditions that customers view as beyond the control of the service provider. For example, where personal emergencies such as serious automobile accidents would likely intensify customers' service expectations of insurance companies (because they are temporary service intensifiers), catastrophes that affect a large number of people at one time (tornadoes or earthquakes) may lower service expectations because customers recognize that insurers are inundated with demands for their services. During the days following the Hurricane Katrina disaster, telephone and Internet service was poor because so many people were trying to get in touch with friends

Technology Spotlight Customer Expectations of New Technology Services at the Airport

One of the most difficult tasks that marketers face is understanding what customers expect from completely new services, and nowhere is this problem more evident than when these new services involve technology. Customers almost always resist new technology initially—perhaps because they do not understand it, perhaps because they fear change—even when the technology leads to improved service. Technology that makes obtaining service easier and faster is springing up all over, even in airports around the country. Customers are accepting some new service technologies and resisting others. Here we discuss two innovations that are meeting different fates.

One new service technology that has been accepted by customers is automatic airline check-in: customers walk up to computer screens, slide credit cards, and use touch pads to retrieve their boarding passes and receipts. Unless the flight is international, customers can check luggage automatically as well, and an attendant takes their luggage from them before they go to their gates. The service generally takes less time than working with an attendant, and most airlines have added more computers than they previously had lines for attendants, saving customers considerable time. When these computer screens were first installed, customers were not sure what to expect and did not know how to use them. Airlines that supplied extra employees to stand and help customers use the computers found success in converting customers from the human handling to the technology. Today, most customers prefer the computers because of their speed and ease.

Another airport technology that has been accepted more slowly by customers is called Exit Express and is a technology substitute for toll booths as customers leave airport parking areas. It works like this: before customers exit the airport, they use a machine (similar to a subway token machine) to pay their parking fees in advance. They insert their parking ticket, then their credit card or cash, and receive back their stamped parking ticket. When they exit the parking lot, they use one of the many Exit Express lanes, insert their paid tickets, and leave. Airports typically still retain a small number of lanes that use live employees and operate in the traditional way. Surprisingly, many airports are finding that customers do not use Exit Express technology as much as expected. One of us, who loves the new technology and always uses it, typically finds herself alone in the Exit Express lanes while other customers line up in the live employee lane.

Why are many customers resisting the Exit Express technology that clearly meets or exceeds their expectations of getting out of the airport quickly? One possible reason is that they do not understand how the system works, even though a loudspeaker in the parking lots trumpets the new system continuously. They also may not clearly see the benefits being provided, possibly because the airport does not communicate them well enough, leading customers to believe that the old system with toll booths is quick enough. Another reason is that most airports have not stationed employees near the technology to familiarize customers with it and to deal with service failures, as the airlines did with automatic check-in. Customers may also fear that if something goes wrong, they would be embarrassed and not know how to resolve the situation. A final compelling reason is that many customers distrust the technology the way they used to distrust automated teller machine (ATM) technology when it was first introduced.

If new services created by technology are to meet the expectations of customers, they must be trusted, understood, and introduced as valuable to customers. Otherwise, the promise of meeting or exceeding customer expectations will not be realized despite large investments.

Source: M. L. Meuter, M. J. Bitner, A. L. Ostrom, and S. W. Brown, "Choosing among Alternative Service Delivery Modes: An Investigation of Customer Trial of Self-Service Technologies," *Journal of Marketing* 69 (April 2005), pp. 61–83.

and relatives. Similarly, guests at the Ritz-Carlton, Omni, and Marriott hotels in New Orleans quickly realized that they should not expect the level of service to which they had become accustomed. These customers were forgiving because they understood the source of the problem. Customers who recognize that situational factors are not the fault of the service company may accept lower levels of adequate service given the context. In general, situational factors temporarily lower the level of adequate service, widening the zone of tolerance.

The final factor that influences adequate service is *predicted service* (Figure 4.7), the level of service that customers believe they are likely to get. This type of service expectation can be viewed as predictions made by customers about what is likely to happen during an impending transaction or exchange. Predicted service performance implies some objective calculation of the probability of performance or estimate of anticipated service performance level. If customers predict good service, their levels of adequate service are likely to be higher than if they predict poor service. For example, full-time residents in a college town usually predict faster restaurant service during the summer months when students are not on campus. This prediction will probably lead them to have higher standards for adequate service in restaurants during the summer than during school months. On the other hand, customers of telephone companies, cable service providers, and utilities know that installation service from these firms will be difficult to obtain during the first few weeks of school when myriad students are setting up their apartments for the year. In this case, levels of adequate service decrease and zones of tolerance widen.

Predicted service is typically an estimate or calculation of the service that a customer will receive in an individual transaction rather than in the overall relationship with a service provider. Whereas desired and adequate service expectations are global assessments comprising many individual service transactions, predicted service is

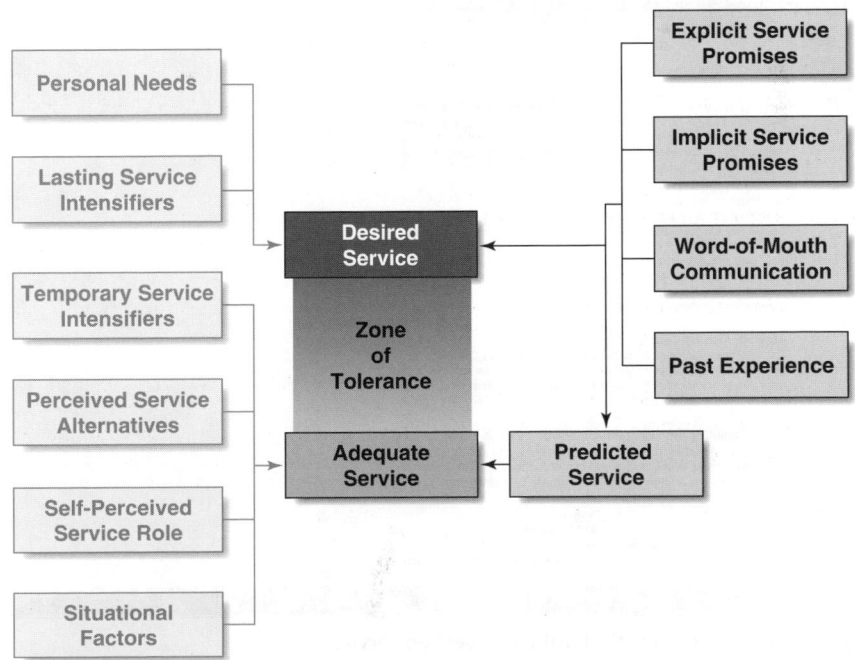

FIGURE 4.7
Factors That Influence Desired and Predicted Service

almost always an estimate of what will happen in the next service encounter or transaction that the customer experiences. For this reason, predicted service is viewed in this model as an influencer of adequate service.

Because predictions are about individual service encounters, they are likely to be more concrete and specific than the types of expectation levels customers hold for adequate service or desired service. For example, your predicted service expectations about the length of time you will spend in the waiting room the next time you visit your doctor will likely be expressed in terms of the number of minutes or hours you have spent in the waiting room this time.

Sources of Both Desired and Predicted Service Expectations

When consumers are interested in purchasing services, they are likely to seek or take in information from several different sources. For example, they may call a store, ask a friend, or deliberately track newspaper advertisements to find the needed service at the lowest price. They may also receive service information by watching television, surfing the Internet, or hearing an unsolicited comment from a colleague about a service that was performed well. In addition to these active and passive types of external search for information, consumers may conduct an internal search by reviewing the information held in memory about the service. This section discusses one internal and three external factors that influence both desired service and predicted service expectations: (1) explicit service promises, (2) implicit service promises, (3) word-of-mouth communications, and (4) past experience.

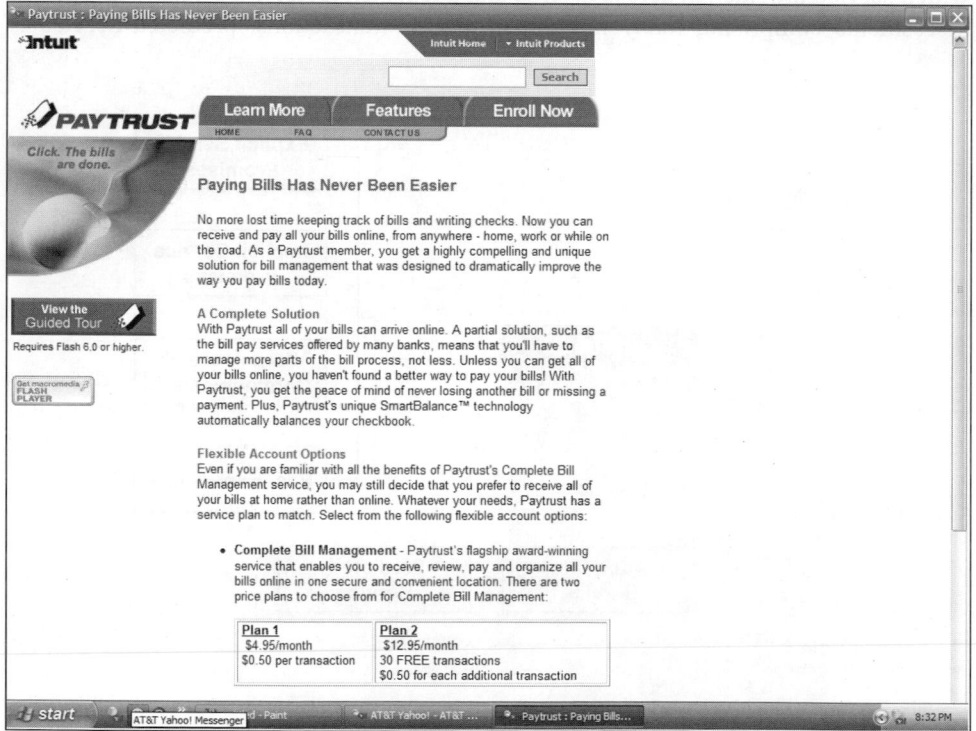

Paytrust's explicit service promises that influence desired service

Explicit service promises are personal and nonpersonal statements about the service made by the organization to customers. The statements are personal when they are communicated by salespeople or service or repair personnel; they are nonpersonal when they come from web pages, advertising, brochures, and other written publications. The web page depicted on the previous page displays the promises made on the Internet by Paytrust, an online bill-paying service offered by the Intuit Corporation. On this web page Paytrust influences customers' expectations by indicating that *all* bills can be received and paid online and that checkbooks can automatically be balanced. Explicit service promises are one of the few influences on expectations that are completely within the control of the service provider.

Promising exactly what will ultimately be delivered would seem a logical and appropriate way to manage customer expectations and ensure that reality fits the promises. However, companies and the personnel who represent them often deliberately overpromise to obtain business or inadvertently overpromise by stating their best estimates about delivery of a service in the future. In addition to overpromising, company representatives simply do not always know the appropriate promises to make because services are often customized and therefore not easily defined and repeated; the representative may not know when or in what final form the service will be delivered.

All types of explicit service promises have a direct effect on desired service expectation. If a bank manager portrays a banking service as available 24 hours a day, the customer's desires for that service (as well as the service of competitors) will be shaped by this promise. A hotel customer describes the impact of explicit promises on expectations: "They get you real pumped up with the beautiful ad. When you go in you expect the bells and whistles to go off. Usually they don't." A business equipment repair customer states, "When you buy a piece of equipment you expect to get a competitive advantage from it. Service is promised with the sale of the equipment." A particularly dangerous promise that many companies today make to their business customers is to provide a "total solution" to their business needs. This promise is very difficult to deliver.

Explicit service promises influence the levels of both desired service and predicted service. They shape what customers desire in general as well as what they predict will happen in the next service encounter from a particular service provider or in a certain service encounter.

Implicit service promises are service-related cues other than explicit promises that lead to inferences about what the service should and will be like. These quality cues are dominated by price and the tangibles associated with the service. In general, the higher the price and the more impressive the tangibles, the more a customer will expect from the service. Consider a customer who shops for insurance, finding two firms charging radically different prices. She may infer that the firm with the higher price should and will provide higher-quality service and better coverage. Similarly, a customer who stays at a posh hotel is likely to desire and predict a higher standard of service than from a hotel with less impressive facilities.

The importance of *word-of-mouth communication* in shaping expectations of service is well documented.[11] These personal and sometimes nonpersonal statements made by parties other than the organization convey to customers what the service will be like and influence both predicted and desired service. Word-of-mouth communication carries particular weight as an information source because it is perceived as unbiased. Word-of-mouth communication tends to be very important in services that are difficult to evaluate before purchase and before direct experience of them. Experts (including

A service firm with a "posh" interior is likely to lead to greater customer expectations.

Consumer Reports, friends, and family) and Internet forums are also word-of-mouth sources that can affect the levels of desired and predicted service.

Past experience, the customer's previous exposure to service that is relevant to the focal service, is another force in shaping predictions and desires. For example, you probably compare each stay in a particular hotel with all previous stays in that hotel. But past experience with the focal hotel is likely to be a very limited view of your past experience. You may also compare each stay with your experiences in other hotels and hotel chains. Customers also compare across industries: hospital patients, for example, compare hospital stays against the standard of hotel visits. Cable service customers tend to compare cable service with the standards set by telephone service, one reason cable service is often judged to be poor. Past experience may incorporate previous experience with the focal service provider, typical performance of similar service offerings, and experience with the last service purchased.[12]

The different sources vary in terms of their credibility as well as their potential to be influenced by the marketer. Our Strategy Insight shows the breakdown of various factors and how services marketers can influence them. Chapter 16 will detail these and other strategies that services marketers can use to match delivery to promises and thereby manage expectations.

ISSUES INVOLVING CUSTOMERS' SERVICE EXPECTATIONS

The following issues represent current topics of particular interest to services marketers about customer expectations. In this section we discuss five of the most frequently asked questions about customer expectations:

1. What does a service marketer do if customer expectations are "unrealistic"?
2. Should a company try to delight the customer?
3. How does a company exceed customers' service expectations?
4. Do customers' service expectations continually escalate?
5. How does a service company stay ahead of competition in meeting customer expectations?

What Does a Services Marketer Do if Customer Expectations Are "Unrealistic"?

One inhibitor to learning about customer expectations is management's and employees' fear of asking. This apprehension often stems from the belief that customer expectations will be extravagant and unrealistic and that by asking about them a company will set itself up for even loftier expectation levels (that is, "unrealistic" levels). Compelling evidence, shown in Exhibit 4.1, suggests that customers' main expectations of service are quite simple and basic: "Simply put, customers expect service companies to do what they are supposed to do. They expect fundamentals, not fanciness; performance, not empty promises."[13] Customers want service to be delivered as promised. They want planes to take off on time, hotel rooms to be clean, food to be hot, and service providers

Strategy Insight   How Services Marketers Can Influence Factors

How might a manager of a service organization use the information we have developed in this chapter to create, improve, or market services? First, managers need to know the pertinent expectation sources and their relative importance for a customer population, a customer segment, and perhaps even a particular customer. They need to know, for instance, the relative weight of word-of-mouth communication, explicit service promises, and implicit service promises in shaping desired service and predicted service. Some of these sources are more stable and permanent in their influence (such as lasting service intensifiers and personal needs) than the others, which fluctuate considerably over time (like perceived service alternatives and situational factors). We provide here some ways that customer expectations might be influenced.

Factor	Possible Influence Strategies
Explicit service promises	• Make realistic and accurate promises that reflect the service actually delivered rather than an idealized version of the service. • Ask contact people for feedback on the accuracy of promises made in advertising and personal selling. • Avoid engaging in price or advertising wars with competitors because they take the focus off customers and escalate promises beyond the level at which they can be met. • Formalize service promises through a service guarantee that focuses company employees on the promise and that provides feedback on the number of times promises are not fulfilled.
Implicit service promises	• Ensure that service tangibles accurately reflect the type and level of service provided. • Ensure that price premiums can be justified by higher levels of performance by the company on important customer attributes.
Lasting service intensifiers	• Use market research to determine sources of derived service expectations and their requirements. Then, focus advertising and marketing strategy on ways the service allows the focal customer to satisfy the requirements of the influencing customer. • Use market research to profile personal service philosophies of customers and use this information in designing and delivering services.
Personal needs Temporary service intensifiers Perceived service alternatives	• Educate customers on ways the service addresses their needs. • Increase service delivery capacity during peak periods or in emergencies. • Be fully aware of competitive offerings, and where possible and appropriate, match them.
Self-perceived service role Word-of-mouth communications	• Educate customers to understand their roles and perform them better. • Simulate word of mouth in advertising by using testimonials and opinion leaders. • Identify influencers and opinion leaders for the service and concentrate marketing efforts on them. • Use incentives with existing customers to encourage them to say positive things about the service.
Past experience	• Use marketing research to profile customers' previous experience with similar services.
Situational factors	• Use service guarantees to assure customers about service recovery regardless of the situational factors that occur.
Predicted service	• Tell customers when service provision is higher than what can normally be expected so that predictions of future service encounters will not be inflated.

Exhibit 4.1 Service Customers Want the Basics

Type of Service	Type of Customer	Principal Expectations
Automobile repair	Consumers	• Be competent. ("Fix it right the first time.") • Explain things. ("Explain why I need the suggested repairs—provide an itemized list.") • Be respectful. ("Don't treat me like a dumb female.")
Automobile insurance	Consumers	• Keep me informed. ("I shouldn't have to learn about insurance law changes from the newspaper.") • Be on my side. ("I don't want them to treat me like a criminal just because I have a claim.") • Play fair. ("Don't drop me when something goes wrong.") • Protect me from catastrophe. ("Make sure my estate is covered in the event of a major accident.") • Provide prompt service. ("I want fast settlement of claims.")
Hotel	Consumers	• Provide a clean room. ("Don't have a deep-pile carpet that can't be completely cleaned . . . you can literally see germs down there.") • Provide a secure room. ("Good bolts and peephole on door.") • Treat me like a guest. ("It is almost like they're looking you over to decide whether they're going to let you have a room.") • Keep your promise. ("They said the room would be ready, but it wasn't at the promised time.")
Property and casualty insurance	Business customers	• Fulfill obligations. ("Pay up.") • Learn my business and work with me. ("I expect them to know me and my company.") • Protect me from catastrophe. ("They should cover my risk exposure so there is no single big loss.") • Provide prompt service. ("Fast claim service.")
Equipment repair	Business customers	• Share my sense of urgency. ("Speed of response. One time I had to buy a second piece of equipment because of the huge downtime with the first piece.") • Be competent. ("Sometimes you are quoting stuff from their instruction manuals to their own people and they don't even know what it means.") • Be prepared. ("Have all the parts ready.")
Truck and tractor rental/leasing	Business customers	• Keep the equipment running. ("Need to have equipment working all of the time—that is the key.") • Be flexible. ("The leasing company should have the flexibility to rent us equipment when we need it.") • Provide full service. ("Get rid of all the paperwork and headaches.")

Source: Reprinted from "Understanding Customer Expectations of Service" by A. Parasuraman, L. L. Berry, and V. A. Zeithaml, *Sloan Management Review* 32 (Spring 1991), pp. 39–48, by permission of publisher. Copyright © 1991 by Massachusetts Institute of Technology. All rights reserved.

to show up when scheduled. Unfortunately, many service customers are disappointed and let down by companies' inability to meet these basic service expectations.

Asking customers about their expectations does not so much raise the levels of the expectations themselves but rather heightens the belief that the company will do something with the information that surfaces. Arguably the worst thing a company can do is show a strong interest in understanding what customers expect and then never act on the information. At a minimum, a company should acknowledge to customers that it has received and heard their input and that it will expend effort trying to address their issues. The company may not be able to—and indeed does not always have to—deliver to expressed expectations. An alternative and appropriate response would be to let customers know the reasons that desired service is not being provided at the present time and describe the efforts planned to address them. Another approach could be a campaign to educate customers about ways to use and improve the service they currently receive. Giving customers progress updates as service is improved to address their needs and desires is sensible because it allows the company to get credit for incremental efforts to improve service.

Some observers recommend deliberately underpromising the service to increase the likelihood of meeting or exceeding customer expectations.[14] While underpromising makes service expectations more realistic, thereby narrowing the gap between expectations and perceptions, it also may reduce the competitive appeal of the offer. Also, some research has indicated that underpromising may have the inadvertent effect of lowering customer *perceptions* of service, particularly in situations in which customers have little experience with a service.[15] In these situations customer expectations may be self-fulfilling; that is, if the customer goes into the service experience expecting good service, she will focus on the aspects of service provision that are positive, but if she expects poor service she may focus on the negative. Thus a salesperson who pitches a customer with a realistic promise may lose the sale to another who inflates the offering. In Chapter 16 we describe various techniques for controlling a firm's promises, but for now consider two options. First, if the salesperson knows that no competitor can meet an inflated sales promise in an industry, he could point that fact out to the customer, thereby refuting the promise made by competitive salespeople.

The second option is for the provider to follow a sale with a "reality check" about service delivery. One of us bought a new house from a builder. Typical sales promises were made about the quality of the home, some less than accurate, in order to make the sale. Before closing on the house, the builder conducted a final check on the house. At the front door, the builder pointed out that each new home has between 3,000 and 5,000 individual elements and that in his experience the typical new home had 100 to 150 defects. Armed with this reality check, the 32 defects found in the house then seemed relatively minor.

Should a Company Try to Delight the Customer?

Some management consultants urge service companies to "delight" customers to gain a competitive edge. The *delight* that they refer to is a profoundly positive emotional state that results from having one's expectations exceeded to a surprising degree.[16] One author describes the type of service that results in delight as "positively outrageous service"— that which is unexpected, random, extraordinary, and disproportionately positive.[17]

A way that managers can conceive of delight is to consider product and service features in terms of concentric rings.[18] The innermost bull's-eye refers to attributes that are central to the basic function of the product or service, called *musts*. Their provision is not particularly noticeable, but their absence would be. Around the musts is a ring called *satisfiers:* features that have the potential to further satisfaction beyond the basic function of the product. At the next and final outer level are *delights,* or product features that are unexpected and surprisingly enjoyable. These features are things that consumers would not expect to find and are therefore highly surprised and sometimes excited when they receive them. For example, in your classes the musts consist of professors, rooms, syllabi, and class meetings. Satisfiers might include professors who are entertaining or friendly, interesting lectures, and good audiovisual aids. A delight might include a free textbook for students signing up for the course.

Delighting customers may seem like a good idea, and can lead to repeat purchasing and customer loyalty,[19] but this level of service provision comes with extra effort and cost to the firm. Therefore, the benefits of providing delight must be weighed. Among the considerations are the staying power and competitive implications of delight.

Staying power involves the question of how long a company can expect an experience of delight to maintain the consumer's attention. If it is fleeting and the customer forgets it immediately, it may not be worth the cost. Alternatively, if the customer remembers the delight and adjusts her level of expectation upward accordingly, it will cost the company more just to satisfy, effectively raising the bar for the future. Research indicates that delighting customers does in fact raise expectations and make it more difficult for a company to satisfy customers in the future.[20]

A delighted customer who has received "positively outrageous service."

The competitive implication of delight relates to its impact on expectations of other firms in the same industry. If a competitor in the same industry is unable to copy the delight strategy, it will be disadvantaged by the consumer's increased expectations. If you were offered that free textbook in one of your classes, you might then expect to receive one in each of your classes. Those classes not offering the free textbook might not have high enrollment levels compared to the delighting class. If a competitor can easily copy the delight strategy, however, neither firm benefits (although the consumer does!), and all firms may be hurt because their costs increase and profits erode. The implication is that if companies choose to delight, they should do so in areas that cannot be copied by other firms.

How Does a Company Exceed Customer Service Expectations?

Many companies today talk about exceeding customer expectations—delighting and surprising them by giving more than they expect. One such example is Pebble Beach Resort, located along the Pacific coast of northern California. The golf resort not only talks about exceeding customer expectations, it actually prints the following phrase on the back side of employee business cards: "Exceed the expectations of every guest, by providing a once in a lifetime experience, every time." This philosophy raises the question, Should a service provider try simply to meet customer expectations or to exceed them?

First, it is essential to recognize that exceeding customer expectations of the basics is virtually impossible. Honoring promises—having the reserved room available, meeting deadlines, showing up for meetings, delivering the core service—is what the company is supposed to do. Companies are *supposed* to be accurate and dependable and provide the service they promised to provide.[21] As you examine the examples of basic expectations of customers in Exhibit 4.1, ask yourself if a provider doing any of these things would delight you. The conclusion you should reach is that it is very difficult to surprise or delight customers consistently by delivering reliable service.

How, then, does a company delight its customers and exceed their expectations? In virtually any service, developing a customer relationship is one approach for exceeding service expectations. The United States Automobile Association (USAA), a provider of insurance to military personnel and their dependents, illustrates how a large company that seldom has face-to-face interactions with its customers can surprise and delight them with its personalization of service and knowledge of the customer. Using a state-of-the-art imaging system, all USAA employees can access any customer's entire information file in seconds, giving them full knowledge of the customer's history and requirements and the status of the customer's recent interactions with the company. Expecting a lower level of personalization from an insurance company and from most any service interaction on the telephone, USAA's customers are surprised and impressed with the care and concern that employees demonstrate.

Using a similar type of information technology, Ritz-Carlton Hotels, a two-time recipient of the Malcolm Baldrige Quality Award, provides highly personalized attention to its customers. The company trains each of its employees to note guest likes and dislikes and to record these into a computerized guest history profile. The company has information on the preferences of several hundred thousand repeat Ritz-Carlton guests, resulting in more personalized service. The aim is not simply to meet expectations of guests but to provide them with a "memorable visit." The company uses the guest history information to exceed customers' expectations of the way they will be treated. When a repeat customer calls the hotel's central reservations number to book accommodations, the reservation agent can call up the individual's preference information. The agent then sends this information electronically to the particular hotel at which the reservation is made. The hotel puts the data in a daily guest recognition and preference report circulated to employees. Employees then greet the repeat guest personally at check-in and ensure that the guest's needs/preferences are anticipated and met.[22]

How well does this approach work? Quite well. According to an independent survey of luxury hotels conducted by J. D. Power and Associates, the Ritz-Carlton was the top-rated hotel in terms of customer satisfaction in 2007.[23]

Another way to exceed expectations is to deliberately underpromise the service to increase the likelihood of exceeding customer expectations. The strategy is to underpromise and overdeliver. If every service promise is less than what will eventually happen, customers can be delighted frequently. Although this reasoning sounds logical, a firm should weigh two potential problems before using this strategy. First, customers with whom a company interacts regularly are likely to notice the underpromising and adjust their expectations accordingly, negating the desired benefit of delight. Customers will recognize the pattern of underpromising when time after time a firm promises one delivery time (we cannot get that to you before 5 p.m. tomorrow) yet constantly exceeds it (by delivering at noon). Second, underpromising in a sales situation potentially reduces the competitive appeal of an offering and must be tempered by what competition is offering. When competitive pressures are high, presenting a cohesive and honest portrayal of the service both explicitly (through advertising and personal selling) and implicitly (such as through the appearance of service facilities and the price of the service) may be wiser. Controlling the firm's promises, making them consistent with the deliverable service, may be a better approach.

A final way to exceed expectations without raising them in the future is to position unusual service as unique rather than the standard. On a flight between Raleigh-Durham and Charlotte, North Carolina, one of us experienced an example of this strategy. The flight is extremely short, less than half an hour, and typically too brief for beverage service. On the night in question, a crew member announced over the intercom that an unusually ambitious crew wanted to try to serve beverages anyway. He warned passengers that the crew may not get to all of them and positioned the service as unique by imploring passengers not to expect beverage service on other flights. In this scenario, passengers seemed delighted but their expectations for regular service were not heightened by the action. (To this day, we have never received beverage service on that route, but are really not expecting it!)

Do Customers' Service Expectations Continually Escalate?

As we illustrated in the beginning of this chapter, customers' service expectations are dynamic. In the credit card industry, as in many competitive service industries, battling companies seek to best each other and thereby raise the level of service above that of competing companies. Service expectations—in this case, adequate service expectations—rise as quickly as service delivery or promises rise. In a highly competitive and rapidly changing industry, expectations can thus rise quickly. For this reason companies need to monitor adequate service expectations continually—the more turbulent the industry, the more frequent the monitoring needed.

Desired service expectations, on the other hand, are far more stable. Because they are driven by more enduring factors, such as personal needs and lasting service intensifiers, they tend to be high to begin with and remain high.

How Does a Service Company Stay Ahead of Competition in Meeting Customer Expectations?

All else being equal, a company's goal is to meet customer expectations better than its competitors. Given the fact that adequate service expectations change rapidly in a turbulent environment, how can a company ensure that it stays ahead of competition?

The adequate service level reflects the minimum performance level expected by customers after they consider a variety of personal and external factors (Figure 4.7), including the availability of service options from other providers. Companies whose service performance falls short of this level are clearly at a competitive disadvantage, with the disadvantage escalating as the gap widens. These companies' customers may well be "reluctant" customers, ready to take their business elsewhere the moment they perceive an acceptable alternative exists.

If they are to use service quality for competitive advantage, companies must perform above the adequate service level. This level, however, may signal only a temporary advantage. Customers' adequate service levels, which are less stable than desired service levels, will rise rapidly when competitors promise and deliver a higher level of service. If a company's level of service is barely above the adequate service level to begin with, a competitor can quickly erode that advantage. To develop a true customer franchise—immutable customer loyalty—companies must not only consistently exceed the adequate service level but also reach the desired service level. Exceptional service can intensify customers' loyalty to a point at which they are impervious to competitive options.

Summary

Using a conceptual framework of the nature and determinants of customer expectations of service, we showed in this chapter that customers hold two types of service expectations: desired service, which reflects what customers want and adequate service, or the minimum level of service customers are willing to accept. The desired service level is less subject to change than the adequate service level. A zone of tolerance separates these two levels of expectations. This zone of tolerance varies across customers can expand or contract with the same customer.

Customer expectations are influenced by a variety of factors. Desired service expectations are influenced by personal needs, lasting service intensifiers, explicit service promises, implicit service promises, word-of-mouth communication, and the customer's past experience. Adequate service expectations are influenced by temporary service intensifiers, perceived service alternatives, the customer's self-perceived service role, and situational factors—many of which are not under the control of the service provider. These sources of expectations are the same for end consumers and business customers, for pure service and product-related service, and for experienced customers and inexperienced customers.

Discussion Questions

1. What is the difference between desired service and adequate service? Why would a services marketer need to understand both types of service expectations?

2. Consider a recent service purchase that you have made. Which of the factors influencing expectations were the most important in your decision? Why?

3. Why are desired service expectations more stable than adequate service expectations?

4. How do the technology changes discussed in the Technology Spotlight in this chapter influence customer expectations?

5. Describe several instances in which a service company's explicit service promises were inflated and led you to be disappointed with the service outcome.

6. Consider a small business preparing to buy a computer system. Which of the influences on customer expectations do you believe will be pivotal? Which factors will have the most influence? Which factors will have the least importance in this decision?

7. What strategies can you add to the Strategy Insight in this chapter for influencing the factors?

8. Do you believe that any of your service expectations are unrealistic? Which ones? Should a service marketer try to address unrealistic customer expectations?

9. In your opinion, what service companies have effectively built customer franchises (immutable customer loyalty)?

10. Intuitively, it would seem that managers would want their customers to have wide tolerance zones for service. But if customers do have these wide zones of tolerance for service, is it more difficult for firms with superior service to earn customer loyalty? Would superior service firms be better off to attempt to narrow customers' tolerance zones to reduce the competitive appeal of mediocre providers?

11. Should service marketers delight their customers?

Exercises

1. What factors influenced your expectations of this course? Which were the most important factors? How would your expectations change if this were a required course? (Alternatively, if this course *is* required, would your expectations change if this were an optional course?)

2. Keep a service journal for a day and document your use of services. Ask yourself before each service encounter to indicate your predicted service of that encounter. After the encounter, note whether your expectations were met or exceeded. How does the answer to this question relate to your desire to do business with that service firm again?

3. List five incidents in which a service company has exceeded your expectations. How did you react to the service? Did these incidents change the way you viewed subsequent interactions with each of the companies? In what way?

Notes

1. "Japanese Put Tourism on a Higher Plane," *International Herald Tribune,* February 3, 1992, p. 8.

2. The model on which this chapter is based is taken from V. A. Zeithaml, L. L. Berry, and A. Parasuraman, "The Nature and Determinants of Customer Expectations of Service," *Journal of the Academy of Marketing Science* 21 (Winter 1993), pp. 1–12.

3. See sources such as C. Gronroos, *Strategic Management and Marketing in the Service Sector* (Helsingfors, Sweden: Swedish School of Economics and Business Administration, 1982); R. K. Teas and T. E. DeCarlo, "An Examination and Extension of the Zone-of-Tolerance Model: A Comparison to Performance-Based Models of Perceived Quality," *Journal of Service Research* 6 (February 2004), pp. 272–286; K. B. Yap and J. C. Sweeney, "Zone-of-Tolerance Moderates the Service Quality-Outcome Relationship," *Journal of Services Marketing* 21, no. 2 (2007), pp. 137–148.

4. R. B. Woodruff, E. R. Cadotte, and R. L. Jenkins, "Expectations and Norms in Models of Consumer Satisfaction," *Journal of Marketing Research* 24 (August 1987), pp. 305–314.

5. J. A. Miller, "Studying Satisfaction, Modifying Models, Eliciting Expectations, Posing Problems, and Making Meaningful Measurements," in *Conceptualization and Measurement of Consumer Satisfaction and Dissatisfaction,* ed. H. K. Hunt (Bloomington, IN: Indiana University School of Business, 1977), pp. 72–91.

6. J. E. Martin, *Command Performance: The Art of Delivering Quality Service* (Boston, MA: Harvard Business School Press, 1994), p. 35.

7. A. Parasuraman, L. L. Berry, and V. A. Zeithaml, "Understanding Customer Expectations of Service," *Sloan Management Review* 32 (Spring 1991), p. 42.

8. L. L. Berry, A. Parasuraman, and V. A. Zeithaml, "Ten Lessons for Improving Service Quality," *Marketing Science Institute,* Report No. 93–104 (May 1993).

9. Zeithaml, Berry, and Parasuraman, "Customer Expectations of Service," p. 7.

10. Ibid., p. 8.

11. D. L. Davis, J. G. Guiltinan, and W. H. Jones, "Service Characteristics, Consumer Research, and the Classification of Retail Services," *Journal of Retailing* 55 (Fall 1979), pp. 3–21; W. R. George and L. L. Berry, "Guidelines for the Advertising of Services," *Business Horizons* 24 (May–June 1981), pp. 52–56; F. v. Wangenheim and T. Bayón, "The Effect of Word-of-Mouth on Services Switching: Measurement and Moderating Variables," *European Journal of Marketing* 38 no. 9–10 (2004), pp. 1173–85; T. J. Brown, T. E. Barry, P. A. Dacin, and R. F. Gunst, "Spreading the Word: Investigating Antecedents of Consumers' Positive Word-of-Mouth Intentions and Behaviors in a Retailing Context," *Journal of the Academy of Marketing Science* 33 (Spring 2005), pp. 123–138.

12. Discussions of the role of past experience in shaping customer expectations of service are included in L. L. Berry, "Cultivating Service Brand Equity," *Journal of the Academy of Marketing Science* 28 (Winter 2000), pp. 128–137; and R. L. Hess Jr., S. Ganesan, and N. M. Klein, "Interactional Service Failures in a Psuedorelationship: The Role of Organizational Attributions," *Journal of Retailing* 83 (January 2007), pp. 79–95.

13. Parasuraman, Berry, and Zeithaml, "Understanding Customer Expectations," p. 40.

14. W. H. Davidow and B. Uttal, "Service Companies: Focus or Falter," *Harvard Business Review* 67 (July–August), pp. 77–85.

15. W. Boulding, A. Kalra, R. Staelin, and V. A. Zeithaml, "A Dynamic Process Model of Service Quality: From Expectations to Behavioral Intentions," *Journal of Marketing Research* 30 (February 1993), pp. 7–27.

16. R. T. Rust and R. L. Oliver, "Should We Delight the Customer?" *Journal of the Academy of Marketing Science* 28 (Winter 2000), pp. 86–94.

17. T. S. Gross, *Positively Outrageous Service* (New York: Warner Books, 1994).

18. J. Clemmer, "The Three Rings of Perceived Value," *Canadian Manager* 15 (Summer 1990), pp. 12–15.

19. T. Keiningham and T. Vavra, *The Customer Delight Principle: Exceeding Customers' Expectations For Bottom-Line Success* (New York: Mcgraw-Hill, 2001).

20. Rust and Oliver, "Should We Delight the Customer?"

21. Parasuraman, Berry, and Zeithaml, "Understanding Customer Expectations," p. 41.

22. "How the Ritz-Carlton Hotel Company Delivers 'Memorable' Service to Customers," *Executive Report on Customer Satisfaction* 6, no. 5 (March 15, 1993), pp. 1–4.

23. J. D. Power and Associates, http://www.jdpower.com/corporate/news/releases/pressrelease.aspx?ID=2007116, accessed July 30, 2007.

Chapter Five

Customer Perceptions of Service

This chapter's objectives are to

1. Provide a solid basis for understanding what influences customer perceptions of service and the relationships among customer satisfaction, service quality, and individual service encounters.
2. Demonstrate the importance of customer satisfaction—what it is, the factors that influence it, and the significant outcomes resulting from it.
3. Develop critical knowledge of service quality and its five key dimensions: reliability, responsiveness, empathy, assurance, and tangibles.
4. Show that service encounters or the "moments of truth" are the essential building blocks from which customers form their perceptions.

Zane's Cycles: Service as a Strategic Differentiator

For Zane's Cycles In Branford, Connecticut, service has been the company's key to success and what truly differentiates it from competing bike stores.[1] Chris Zane, its forty-something chief executive office (CEO), has owned the business since he was 16 years old, when he convinced his grandfather to loan him $20,000 to buy the store from its original owner. As a young man he built the business on basic principles such as "unparalleled service," "one-to-one marketing," "customer relationships," and "employee respect and empowerment." Since then, the business has grown to more than $10 million in annual sales (including retail and corporate sales), and Zane's has eliminated all but a small handful of the original 16 competitors. Moreover, the company has developed highly successful ways to compete with the likes of Wal-Mart and has built a whole new business providing bicycles to corporations for incentive gifts to their employees. So how does Zane's compete? What are some of the things that Chris Zane has done to provide exemplary, out-of-the-box service—service that has driven his competitors out of business? Here are a few examples of the company's exemplary service strategies:

- *Lifetime free service.* Zane's provides "lifetime free service" on the bikes it sells, because they are in the service business, not just the bike business. Of course, lifetime free service (free service for as long as the customer owns the bike) is also a good way to get customers to return to the shop, providing an opportunity to build a lasting relationship.

- *Lifetime parts warranty.* Following the lifetime free service strategy, Zane's soon realized that it should also offer a lifetime warranty on parts as well. He is able to do this by having a small number of vendor partners and holding them accountable for their products.

- *90-day price protection.* To quell possible rumors and beliefs that Zane's is high priced (to cover the lifetime guarantees), the company instituted a 90-day price protection guarantee so that customers can come back within 90 days to receive a cash rebate, plus 10 percent, if they find the same bike elsewhere for less money. Because Zane's is truly in the relationship business, few customers shop the competitors or meticulously compare prices, so the plan results in very few refunds. And, when they do give a refund, the customer frequently spends the cash right on the spot, in the store!

- *Flat Insurance.* For those first-time bike purchasers or less experienced bikers, the idea of a flat tire seems daunting. So, Zane's offers "flat insurance" for a nominal annual fee. Although few tires are ever fixed under the policy, those bikers that do come back to the store to use their flat insurance are treated like royalty. Everything stops, the bike is taken to the back where it the tire is changed and the bike is cleaned up—all in record time with much fanfare. Again, the customer (and anyone in the store) is treated to an unexpected, delightful experience, and relationships are strengthened, all at little cost to Zane's—especially given the amount of the flat insurance that is sold and never used!

- *Less than $1 giveaways.* Another way that Zane's delights customers is by giving away small, but essential parts that cost less than $1. He figures these giveaways result in additional purchases (at the same time or on another visit) far beyond the few cents it costs to provide them.

- *Kids' play area.* The kids' play area in Zane's is a popular place for youngsters to play and remain entertained while their parents shop. Some are even able to purchase the infamous "Christmas Bike" right under the noses of their preoccupied children!

- *Coffee and snapple bar, with free coffee.* To provide a social context and also a place for folks to wait when the store is busy, Chris Zane built a mahogany coffee bar, modeled after a similar cozy coffee bar he had seen in a bike shop on a trip to Switzerland. Here, coffee and other drinks are offered, and customers can watch bike repairs going on through a huge glass window. And, because the cost of a cup of coffee is less than $1, of course there is no charge!

- *Kids bike upgrades.* One of the most innovative service strategies at Zane's is one that helps them compete head on with Wal-Mart. This is the trade-in policy that allows parents to buy a child's bike and then trade it in for full price, credited toward a larger bike. Like many of their service plans, this one is retroactive. When they first started it, Zane's sent postcards to everyone who had bought a small bicycle within the past few years, letting them know about the upgrade plan.

You might wonder how all of these seemingly "too good to be true" service offers can be provided without draining profits. the fact is that relatively few customers take advantage of many of the service offerings. Zane's has found that most customers ask very little, but they are inordinately pleased when the offer is made, and those who do take advantage are customers for life. Further, customers learn over time that Zane's is authentic, trustworthy, and that they can count on the bikes they buy there to be of high quality and fairly priced. All of the strategies make financial sense in the end and all serve to build strong and lasting customer relationships. No wonder Zane's was one of Fast Company magazine's "Local Heroes" in its 2006 Customer First Awards.

Quality bikes, excellent service quality, lots of little extras, and the unexpected attention of Zane's team members all add up to customer satisfaction for customers of Zane's cycles. The same is true for other landmark service companies such as Lands' End, IBM Global Services, Amazon.com, and Ritz-Carlton Hotels to name just a few. In all of these companies, the quality of the core product and exemplary customer service result in high customer satisfaction ratings.

CUSTOMER PERCEPTIONS

How customers perceive services, how they assess whether they have experienced quality service, and whether they are satisfied are the subjects of this chapter. We will be focusing on the *perceived service* box in the gaps model. As we move through this chapter, keep in mind that perceptions are always considered relative to expectations. Because expectations are dynamic, evaluations may also shift over time—from person to person and from culture to culture. What is considered quality service or the things that satisfy customers today may be different tomorrow. Also keep in mind that the entire discussion of quality and satisfaction is based on *customers' perceptions of the service*—not some predetermined objective criteria of what service is or should be.

FIGURE 5.1
Customer Perceptions of Quality and Customer Satisfaction

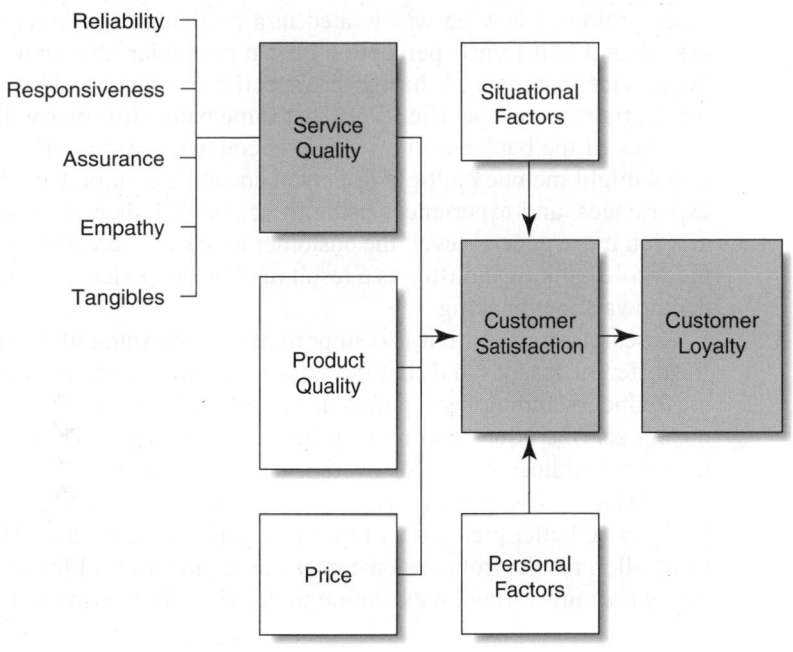

Satisfaction versus Service Quality

Practitioners and writers in the popular press tend to use the terms *satisfaction* and *quality* interchangeably, but researchers have attempted to be more precise about the meanings and measurement of the two concepts, resulting in considerable debate.[2] Consensus is that the two concepts are fundamentally different in terms of their underlying causes and outcomes.[3] Although they have certain things in common, *satisfaction* is generally viewed as a broader concept, whereas *service quality* focuses specifically on dimensions of service. Based on this view, *perceived service quality* is a component of customer satisfaction. Figure 5.1 graphically illustrates the relationships between the two concepts.

As shown in Figure 5.1, service quality is a focused evaluation that reflects the customer's perception of reliability, assurance, responsiveness, empathy, and tangibles.[4] Satisfaction, on the other hand, is more inclusive: it is influenced by perceptions of service quality, product quality, and price, as well as situational factors and personal factors. For example, service quality of a health club is judged on attributes such as whether equipment is available and in working order when needed, how responsive the staff are to customer needs, how skilled the trainers are, and whether the facility is well maintained. Customer satisfaction with the health club is a broader concept that will certainly be influenced by perceptions of service quality but that will also include perceptions of product quality (such as quality of products sold in the pro shop), price of membership,[5] personal factors such as the consumer's emotional state, and even uncontrollable situational factors such as weather conditions and experiences driving to and from the health club.[6]

Transaction versus Cumulative Perceptions

In considering perceptions, it is also important to recognize that customers will have perceptions of single, transaction-specific encounters as well as overall perceptions of a company based on all their experiences.[7] For example, a bank customer will have a perception of how he was treated in a particular encounter with an employee at a branch and will form a perception of that particular transaction based on elements of the service experienced during that specific transaction. That perception is at a very micro, transaction-specific level. That same bank customer will also have overall perceptions of the bank based on all his encounters over a period of time. These experiences might include multiple in-person encounters at the bank branch, online banking experiences, and experiences using the bank's ATMs across many different cities. At an even more general level, the customer may have perceptions of banking services or the whole banking industry as a result of all his experiences with banks and everything he knows about banking.

Research suggests that it is important to understand all these types of perceptions for different reasons and that the viewpoints are complementary rather than competing.[8] Understanding perceptions at the transaction-specific level is critical for diagnosing service issues and making immediate changes. These isolated encounters are also the building blocks for overall, cumulative experience evaluations, as you will learn later in this chapter. On the other hand, cumulative experience evaluations are likely to be better predictors of overall loyalty to a company. That is, customer loyalty most often results from the customer's assessment of all his experiences, not just one single encounter. (For an exception to this rule, look ahead to Exhibit 5.2).

CUSTOMER SATISFACTION

What Is Customer Satisfaction?

"Everyone knows what satisfaction is, until asked to give a definition. Then, it seems, nobody knows."[9] This quote from Richard Oliver, respected expert and long-time writer and researcher on the topic of customer satisfaction, expresses the challenge of defining this most basic of customer concepts. Building from previous definitions, Oliver offers his own formal definition (p. 13):

> Satisfaction is the consumer's fulfillment response. It is a judgment that a product or service feature, or the product or service itself, provides a pleasurable level of consumption-related fulfillment.

In less technical terms, we interpret this definition to mean that *satisfaction* is the customer's evaluation of a product or service in terms of whether that product or service has met the customer's needs and expectations. Failure to meet needs and expectations is assumed to result in *dissatisfaction* with the product or service.

In addition to a sense of *fulfillment* in the knowledge that one's needs have been met, satisfaction can also be related to other types of feelings, depending on the particular context or type of service.[10] For example, satisfaction can be viewed as *contentment*—more of a passive response that consumers may associate with services they do not think a lot about or services that they receive routinely over time. Satisfaction may also be associated with feelings of *pleasure* for services that make the consumer feel good or are associated with a sense of happiness. For those services that really surprise the consumer in a positive way, satisfaction may mean *delight*. In some situations, where the removal of a negative leads to satisfaction, the consumer may associate a sense of *relief* with satisfaction. Finally, satisfaction may be associated with feelings of *ambivalence* when there is a mix of positive and negative experiences associated with the product or service.

Although consumer satisfaction tends to be measured at a particular point in time as if it were static, satisfaction is a dynamic, moving target that may evolve over time, influenced by a variety of factors.[11] Particularly when product usage or the service experience takes place over time, satisfaction may be highly variable, depending on which point in the usage or experience cycle one is focusing on. Similarly, in the case of very new services or a service not previously experienced, customer expectations may be barely forming at the point of initial purchase; these expectations will solidify as the process unfolds and the consumer begins to form his or her perceptions. Through the service cycle the consumer may have a variety of different experiences—some good, some not good—and each will ultimately impact satisfaction.

What Determines Customer Satisfaction?

As shown in Figure 5.1, customer satisfaction is influenced by specific product or service features, perceptions of product and service quality, and price. In addition, personal factors such as the customer's mood or emotional state and situational factors such as family member opinions will also influence satisfaction.

Product and Service Features

Customer satisfaction with a product or service is influenced significantly by the customer's evaluation of product or service features.[12] For a service such as a resort hotel, important features might include the pool area, access to golf facilities, restaurants, room comfort and privacy, helpfulness and courtesy of staff, room price, and so forth. In conducting satisfaction studies, most firms will determine through some means (often focus groups) what the important features and attributes are for their service and then measure perceptions of those features as well as overall service satisfaction. Research has shown that customers of services will make trade-offs among different service features (e.g., price level versus quality versus friendliness of personnel versus level of customization), depending on the type of service being evaluated and the criticality of the service.[13]

Consumer Emotions

Customers' emotions can also affect their perceptions of satisfaction with products and services.[14] These emotions can be stable, preexisting emotions—for example, mood state or life satisfaction. Think of times when you are at a very happy stage in your life (such as when you are on vacation), and your good, happy mood and positive frame of mind have influenced how you feel about the services you experience. Alternatively, when you are in a bad mood, your negative feelings may carry over into how you respond to services, causing you to overreact or respond negatively to any little problem.

Specific emotions may also be induced by the consumption experience itself, influencing a consumer's satisfaction with the service. Research done in a river-rafting context showed that the river guides had a strong effect on their customers' emotional responses to the trip and that those feelings (both positive and negative) were linked to overall trip satisfaction.[15] Positive emotions such as happiness, pleasure, elation, and a sense of warm-heartedness enhanced customers' satisfaction with the rafting trip. In turn, negative emotions such as sadness, sorrow, regret, and anger led to diminished customer satisfaction. Overall, in the rafting context, positive emotions had a stronger effect than negative ones. (These positive emotions are apparent in the photo shown below.) In a different context, drawing on emotional contagion theory, researchers found that the authenticity of employees' emotional display directly affected customers' emotions in a video retail and consulting service.[16] Similar effects of emotions on satisfaction were found in a Finnish study that looked at consumers' satisfaction with a government labor bureau service.[17] In that study, negative emotions including anger, depression, guilt, and humiliation had a strong effect on customers' dissatisfaction ratings.

River rafters experience many positive emotions, increasing their satisfaction with the service.

Attributions for Service Success or Failure

Attributions—the perceived causes of events—influence perceptions of satisfaction as well.[18] When they have been surprised by an outcome (the service is either much better or much worse than expected), consumers tend to look for the reasons, and their assessments of the reasons can influence their satisfaction. For example, if a customer of a weight-loss organization fails to lose weight as hoped for, she will likely search for the causes—was it something she did, was the diet plan ineffective, or did circumstances simply not allow her to follow the diet regimen—before determining her level of satisfaction or dissatisfaction with the weight-loss company.[19] For many services, customers take at least partial responsibility for how things turn out.

Even when customers do not take responsibility for the outcome, customer satisfaction may be influenced by other kinds of attributions. For example, research done in a travel agency context found that customers were less dissatisfied with a pricing error made by the agent if they felt that the reason was outside the agent's control or if they felt that it was a rare mistake, unlikely to occur again.[20]

Perceptions of Equity or Fairness

Customer satisfaction is also influenced by perceptions of equity and fairness.[21] Customers ask themselves: Have I been treated fairly compared with other customers? Did other customers get better treatment, better prices, or better quality service? Did I pay a fair price for the service? Was I treated well in exchange for what I paid and the effort I expended? Notions of fairness are central to customers' perceptions of satisfaction with products and services, particularly in service recovery situations. As you will learn in Chapter 8, satisfaction with a service provider following a service failure is largely determined by perceptions of fair treatment. The example of Sears Auto Centers division illustrates consumers' strong reactions to unfair treatment.[22] Over a decade ago the division was charged with defrauding customers in 44 states by performing unnecessary repairs. Sears employee rewards had been based on the quantity of repairs sold, resulting in substantial unnecessary charges to customers. The $27 million that Sears paid to settle complaints and the additional loss of business all resulted from extreme dissatisfaction of its customers over the unfair treatment.

Other Consumers, Family Members, and Coworkers

In addition to product and service features and one's own individual feelings and beliefs, consumer satisfaction is often influenced by other people.[23] For example, satisfaction with a family vacation trip is a dynamic phenomenon, influenced by the reactions and emotions of individual family members over the duration of the vacation. Later, what family members express in terms of satisfaction or dissatisfaction with the trip will be influenced by stories that are retold among the family and selective memories of the events. Similarly, the satisfaction of the rafters in the photo is certainly influenced by individual perceptions, but it is also influenced greatly by the experiences, behavior, and views of the other rafters. In a business setting, satisfaction with a new service or technology—for example, a new customer relationship management software service—will be influenced not only by individuals' personal experiences with the software itself but also by what others say about it in the company, how others use it and feel about it, and how widely it is adopted in the organization.

National Customer Satisfaction Indexes

Because of the importance of customer satisfaction to firms and overall quality of life, many countries have a national index that measures and tracks customer satisfaction at a macro level.[24] Many public policymakers believe that these measures could and should be used as tools for evaluating the health of the nation's economy, along with traditional measures of productivity and price. Customer satisfaction indexes begin to get at the *quality* of economic output, whereas more traditional economic indicators tend to focus only on *quantity.* The first such measure was the Swedish Customer Satisfaction Barometer introduced in 1989.[25] Throughout the 1990s similar indexes were introduced in Germany (Deutsche Kundenbarometer, or DK, in 1992), the United States (American Customer Satisfaction Index, ACSI, in 1994), and Switzerland (Swiss Index of Customer Satisfaction, SWICS, in 1998).[26]

The American Customer Satisfaction Index

The American Customer Satisfaction Index (ACSI),[27] developed by researchers at the National Quality Research Center at the University of Michigan, is a measure of satisfaction with goods and services. The measure tracks, on a quarterly basis, customer perceptions across 200 firms representing all major economic sectors, including government agencies. Within each industry group, major industry segments are included, and within each industry, the largest companies in that industry are selected to participate. For each company approximately 250 interviews are conducted with current customers. Each company receives an ACSI score computed from its customers' perceptions of quality, value, satisfaction, expectations, complaints, and future loyalty.[28]

The 2006 ACSI results by industry are shown in Table 5.1.[29] The table shows that, overall, consumers tend to be most satisfied with nondurables (like soft drinks and personal care products), a bit less satisfied with durables (such as cars, household appliances, and electronics), and the least satisfied with services (like airlines and telephone wireless and cable services). With the exception of Internet retailers, which ranked near the top, other online services ranked near the middle. The observation

TABLE 5.1
American Customer Satisfaction Index— Ratings by Industry

Source: "American Customer Satisfaction Index—Ratings by Industry, ACSI website, www.theacsi.org. Reprinted by permission of American Customer Satisfaction Index, www.theascsi.org.

Industry	2006 ACSI Score	Percent Change in ACSI Score from Previous Year
Personal care and cleaning Products	84	1.2
Soft drinks	84	1.2
Express delivery	83	2.5
Food manufacturing	83	1.2
Internet retail	83	2.5
Pet food	83	1.2
Breweries	82	0.0
Automobiles and light vehicles	81	1.3
Major appliances	81	1.3
Apparel	80	−1.2
Electronics (TV/VCR/DVD)	80	−1.2
Internet search engines	79	−1.3
Life insurance	79	5.3
Cigarettes	78	−1.3
Health and personal care stores	78	2.6
Internet auctions	78	0.0
Internet brokerage	78	2.6
Property and casualty insurance	78	0.0
Banks	77	2.7
Limited service restaurants	77	1.3
Personal computers	77	4.1
Athletic shoes	76	−1.3
Internet portals	76	1.3
Internet travel	76	−1.3
Hotels	75	2.7
Specialty retail stores	75	1.4
Supermarkets	75	1.4
Computer software	74	N/A
Department and discount stores	74	−1.3
Hospitals	74	4.2
Internet news and information	73	−2.7
Motion pictures	73	2.8
Energy utilities	72	−1.4
Health insurance	72	5.9
Gasoline stations	71	2.9
U.S. Postal Service	71	−2.7
Cellular telephones	70	1.4
Fixed line telephone service	70	0.0
Broadcasting TV news	69	1.5
Wireless telephone service	66	4.8
Airlines	65	−1.5
Cable and satellite TV	63	3.3
Newspapers	63	0.0

that services tend to rank lower in the ACSI rankings than do durable and nondurable products is a trend observed across the ACSI's history. It is important to point out, however, that these rankings are industry averages. Almost every industry has some strong performers in terms of customer satisfaction. For example, in 2007 scores for airlines ranged from 56 (United Airlines) to 76 (Southwest Airlines).

We can only conjecture about the reasons for lower satisfaction with services in general. Perhaps it is because downsizing and right-sizing in service businesses has resulted in stressed and overworked frontline service providers who are unable to provide the level of service demanded. Perhaps it is due to the inherent heterogeneity of services discussed in Chapter 1; in other words, because services are difficult to standardize, and each customer has his or her own unique expectations, the result may be greater variability and potentially lower overall satisfaction. Perhaps it is due to difficulty finding qualified frontline service providers for consumer service businesses. Perhaps it is due to rising customer expectations rather than any real or absolute decline in actual service. Whatever the reason, there is much room for improvement in customer satisfaction ratings across service industries.

Outcomes of Customer Satisfaction

Why all this attention to customer satisfaction? As mentioned in the previous section, some public policymakers believe that customer satisfaction is an important indicator of national economic health. They believe that it is not enough to track economic efficiency and pricing statistics. Satisfaction, they believe, is also an important indicator of quality of life. Further, many believe that customer satisfaction is correlated with other measures of economic health such as corporate earnings and stock value. Through the ACSI data, researchers at the University of Michigan have been able to document a clear relationship between ACSI scores and market value added (MVA) which measures the firm's success in creating wealth for shareholders. This relationship is depicted in Figure 5.2, which shows MVA Averages for the top 25 percent of ACSI firms and the bottom 25 percent.[30]

Beyond these macroeconomic implications, however, individual firms have discovered that increasing levels of customer satisfaction can be linked to customer loyalty and profits.[31] Research also shows that firms that invest in service and excel in customer satisfaction offer excess returns to their shareholders. One study found that firms that do better than their competition in terms of satisfying customers (as measured by the ACSI) generated superior returns at a lower systematic risk.[32] Another study found that retailer announcements of customer service strategies resulted in a significant abnormal return for these firms and increased market value of 1.09 percent on average.[33]

FIGURE 5.2
ACSI and Market Value Added

Source: ACSI website, www.theacsi.org, About ACSI, "Economic Indicator," accessed August 18, 2007. Reprinted by permission of American Customer Satisfaction Index, www.theacsi.org.

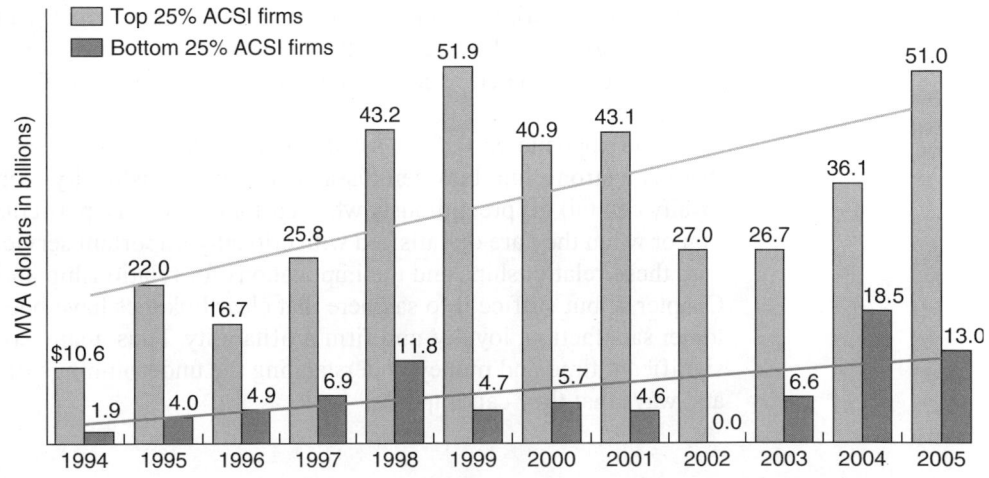

FIGURE 5.3
Relationship between Customer Satisfaction and Loyalty in Competitive Industries

Source: J. L. Heskett, W. E. Sasser Jr., and L. A. Schlesinger, *The Service Profit Chain: How Leading Companies Link Profit and Growth to Loyalty, Satisfaction, and Value* (New York: The Free Press, 1997), p. 83. Copyright © 1997 by J. L. Heskett, W. E. Sasser, Jr., and L. A. Schlesinger. Reprinted with the permission of The Free Press, a Division of Simon & Schuster, Inc.

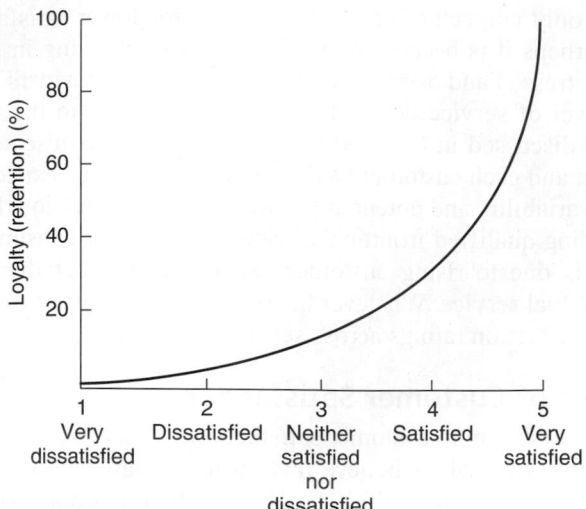

As shown in Figure 5.3, there is an important relationship between customer satisfaction and customer loyalty. This relationship is particularly strong when customers are very satisfied. Thus firms that simply aim to satisfy customers may not be doing enough to engender loyalty—they must instead aim to more than satisfy or even delight their customers. Xerox Corporation was one of the first, if not the first, companies to pinpoint this relationship. In the 1980s Xerox discovered through its extensive customer research that customers giving Xerox a 5 (very satisfied) on a satisfaction scale were six times more likely to repurchase Xerox equipment than were those giving the company a 4 (somewhat satisfied).[34] As another example, Enterprise Rent-A-Car learned through its research that customers who gave the highest rating to their rental experience were three times more likely to rent again than were those who gave the company the second-highest rating.[35] Many other companies have drawn similar conclusions. Information provided by TARP Worldwide Inc.—based on data from 10 studies, including 8,000 customers worldwide from across industries—drew similar conclusions. TARP found that 96 percent of those customers who are "very satisfied" say they will "definitely repurchase" from the same company. The number drops precipitously to only 52 percent for those customers who are "somewhat satisfied." Only 7 percent of customers who are "neutral or very dissatisfied" say they will definitely repurchase.[36]

At the opposite end of the satisfaction spectrum, researchers have also found that there is a strong link between dissatisfaction and disloyalty—or defection. Customer loyalty can fall off precipitously when customers reach a particular level of dissatisfaction or when they are dissatisfied with critically important service attributes.[37] We discuss these relationships and the implications for relationship and loyalty marketing in Chapter 7, but suffice it to say here that clear linkages have been drawn between customer satisfaction, loyalty, and firm profitability. Thus, many companies are spending significant time and money understanding the underpinnings of customer satisfaction and ways that they can improve.

SERVICE QUALITY

We now turn to *service quality,* a critical element of customer perceptions. In the case of pure services (e.g., health care, financial services, education), service quality will be the dominant element in customers' evaluations. In cases in which customer service or services are offered in combination with a physical product (e.g., IT services, auto services), service quality may also be very critical in determining customer satisfaction. Figure 5.1 highlighted these relationships. We will focus here on the left side of Figure 5.1, examining the underlying factors that form perceptions of service quality. First we discuss *what* customers evaluate; then we look specifically at the five dimensions of service that customers rely on in forming their judgments.

Outcome, Interaction, and Physical Environment Quality

What is it that consumers evaluate when judging service quality? Over the years, services researchers have suggested that consumers judge the quality of services based on their perceptions of the technical outcome provided, the process by which that outcome was delivered, and the quality of the physical surroundings where the service is delivered.[38] For example, in the case of a lawsuit, a legal services client will judge the quality of the technical outcome, or how the court case was resolved, and also the quality of the interaction. Interaction quality would include such factors as the lawyer's timeliness in returning phone calls, his empathy for the client, and his courtesy and listening skills. Similarly, a restaurant customer will judge the service on her perceptions of the meal (technical outcome quality) and on how the meal was served and how the employees interacted with her (interaction quality). The decor and surroundings (physical environment quality) of both the law firm and the restaurant will also affect the customer's perceptions of overall service quality. This depiction of service quality as outcome quality, interaction quality, and physical environment quality is captured by Michael Brady and Joseph Cronin in their empirical research.[39] Other researchers have defined similar aspects of service in their examinations of service quality.[40]

Service Quality Dimensions

Research suggests that customers do not perceive quality in a unidimensional way but rather judge quality based on multiple factors relevant to the context. The dimensions of service quality have been identified through the pioneering research of Parsu Parasuraman, Valarie Zeithaml, and Leonard Berry. Their research identified five specific dimensions of service quality that apply across a variety of service contexts.[41] The five dimensions defined here are shown in Figure 5.1 as drivers of service quality. These five dimensions appear again in Chapter 6, along with the scale developed to measure them, SERVQUAL.

- *Reliability:* ability to perform the promised service dependably and accurately.
- *Responsiveness:* willingness to help customers and provide prompt service.
- *Assurance:* employees' knowledge and courtesy and their ability to inspire trust and confidence.
- *Empathy:* caring, individualized attention given to customers.
- *Tangibles:* appearance of physical facilities, equipment, personnel, and written materials.

The development of the service quality dimensions of reliability, responsiveness, assurance, empathy, and tangibles was based on research conducted across multiple contexts within the United States. As a general rule, reliability comes through as the most important dimension of service quality in the United States, with responsiveness also being relatively important when compared with the remaining three dimensions. But what happens when we look across cultures? Are the service quality dimensions still important? Which ones are most important? Answers to these questions can be extremely valuable for companies delivering services across cultures or in multicultural environments.

Researchers have used Geert Hofstede's well-established cultural dimensions to assess whether service quality importance would vary across different cultural orientations. For example, *power distance* refers to the extent to which status differences are expected and accepted within a culture. Research has suggested that most Asian countries are characterized by high power distance, whereas many Western countries score lower on power distance measures. Broadly speaking, *individualism* reflects a self-orientation that is characteristic of Western culture whereas its opposite, *collectivism,* is more typical of the East. Similar comparisons across cultures have been made for the other dimensions: *masculinity, uncertainty avoidance,* and *long-term orientation.* The question is whether these types of cultural differences may affect the importance consumers place on the service quality dimensions.

The figure shown here suggests strong differences in the importance of service quality dimensions across clusters of customers defined by different cultural dimensions. The cultural profile of the clusters is described as:

Followers: Large power distance, high collectivism, high masculinity, neutral uncertainty avoidance, and short-term orientation.

Balance seekers: Small power distance, high collectivism, neutral masculinity, high uncertainty avoidance, and medium-term orientation.

Self-confidents: Small power distance, high individualism, medium femininity, low uncertainty avoidance, and long-term orientation.

Sensory seekers: Large power distance, medium individualism, high masculinity, low uncertainty avoidance, and short-term orientation.

Functional analyzers: Small power distance, medium individualism, high femininity, high uncertainty avoidance, and long-term orientation.

From this figure it is clear that the service quality dimensions are important across cultures, but their relative importance varies depending on cultural value orientation. For example, small power distance cultures with high to medium individualism and long-term

These dimensions represent how consumers organize information about service quality in their minds. On the basis of exploratory and quantitative research, these five dimensions were found relevant for banking, insurance, appliance repair and maintenance, securities brokerage, long-distance telephone service, automobile repair service, and others. The dimensions are also applicable to retail and business services, and logic suggests they would be relevant for internal services as well. Sometimes customers will use all the dimensions to determine service quality perceptions, at other times not. For example, for an ATM, empathy is not likely to be a relevant dimension. And in a phone encounter to schedule a repair, tangibles will not be relevant.

Research suggests that cultural differences will also affect the relative importance placed on the five dimensions, as discussed in our Global Feature. Interesting differences in service quality dimensions themselves also emerge in country-specific studies. For example, research in Pakistan that builds upon the original service quality dimensions revealed the following dimensions of service quality: tangibles, reliability, assurance, sincerity, personalization, and formality.[42] This study also illustrated that cultural differences may cause the original dimensions to be interpreted slightly

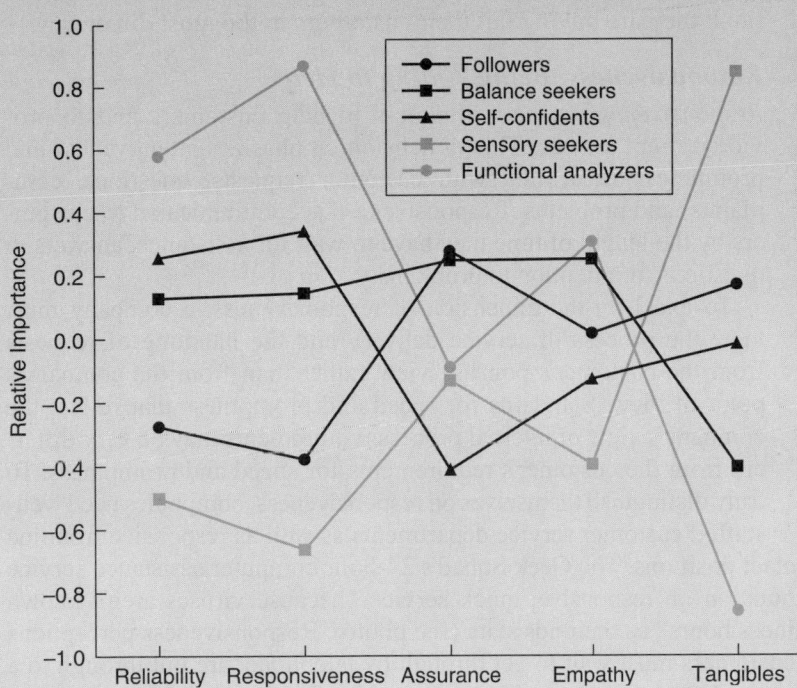

Sources: G. Hofstede, *Cultures and Organizations: Software of the Mind* (New York, McGraw-Hill, 1991); O. Furrer, B. Shaw-Ching Liu, and D. Sudharshan, "The Relationships between Culture and Service Quality Perceptions," *Journal of Service Research* 2 (May 2000), pp. 355–371; www.geert-hofstede.com.

rate these same dimensions as less important. The tangibles dimension shows the widest variation, with sensory seekers rating it most important and functional analyzers rating it least important.

The researchers in this study suggest a number of implications for companies serving multiple cultures. For example, if the target market has a follower cultural profile, service providers may want to emphasize training their employees to have professional knowledge and be trustworthy to gain the trust of these customers, combined with tangibles and empathy to convey service quality. On the other hand, to serve self-confidents, providers should emphasize equipping and empowering the employees so they are capable of providing reliable, responsive service.

orientation (self-confidents and functional analyzers) rate reliability and responsiveness as most important. On the other hand, cultures with large power distance and high masculinity (followers and sensory seekers)

differently as well. In Pakistan, "reliability" was not as absolute in its meaning, but rather was interpreted as "promises are mostly kept," "minimum errors are made on reports or statements," and "service is usually available when needed."

In the following pages we expand on each of the five original SERVQUAL dimensions and provide illustrations of how customers judge them.

Reliability: Delivering on Promises

Of the five dimensions, reliability has been consistently shown to be the most important determinant of perceptions of service quality among U.S. customers.[43] *Reliability* is defined as the ability to perform the promised service dependably and accurately. In its broadest sense, reliability means that the company delivers on its promises—promises about delivery, service provision, problem resolution, and pricing. Customers want to do business with companies that keep their promises, particularly their promises about the service outcomes and core service attributes.

One company that effectively communicates and delivers on the reliability dimension is Federal Express (FedEx). The reliability message of FedEx—when it "absolutely, positively has to get there"—reflects the company's service positioning. But

The Geek Squad emphasize the service quality dimension of *responsiveness* in its service positioning.

even when firms do not choose to position themselves explicitly on reliability, as FedEx has, this dimension is extremely important to consumers. All firms need to be aware of customer expectations of reliability. Firms that do not provide the core service that customers think they are buying fail their customers in the most direct way.

Responsiveness: Being Willing to Help

Responsiveness is the willingness to help customers and to provide prompt service. This dimension emphasizes attentiveness and promptness in dealing with customer requests, questions, complaints, and problems. Responsiveness is communicated to customers by the length of time they have to wait for assistance, answers to questions, or attention to problems.

To excel on the dimension of responsiveness, a company must view the process of service delivery and the handling of requests from the customer's point of view rather than from the company's point of view. Standards for speed and promptness that reflect the company's view of internal process requirements may be very different from the customer's requirements for speed and promptness. To truly distinguish themselves on responsiveness, companies need well-staffed customer service departments as well as responsive frontline people in all contact positions. The Geek Squad's 24-hour computer assistance service was built its reputation on responsive, quick service "because viruses aren't known for keeping business hours" as their ads state (see photo). Responsiveness perceptions diminish when customers must wait to get through by telephone, are put through to a complex voice mail system, or have trouble accessing the firm's website.

Assurance: Inspiring Trust and Confidence

Assurance is defined as employees' knowledge and courtesy and the ability of the firm and its employees to inspire customer trust and confidence. This dimension is likely to be particularly important for services that customers perceive as high risk or for services of which they feel uncertain about their ability to evaluate outcomes—for example, banking, insurance, brokerage, medical, and legal services.

Trust and confidence may be embodied in the person who links the customer to the company, such as securities brokers, insurance agents, lawyers, or counselors. In such service contexts the company seeks to build trust and loyalty between key contact people and individual customers. The "personal banker" concept captures this idea: customers are assigned to a banker who will get to know them individually and who will coordinate all their banking services.

In other situations, trust and confidence are embodied in the organization itself. Insurance companies such as Allstate ("You're in good hands with Allstate") and Prudential ("Own a piece of the rock") illustrate efforts to create trusting relationships between customers and the company as a whole. A recent ad campaign by FedEx uses the tag line "Relax, it's FedEx," going beyond its traditional reliability message to focus on assurance and trust.

Empathy: Treating Customers as Individuals

Empathy is defined as the caring, individualized attention that the firm provides its customers. The essence of empathy is conveying, through personalized or customized service, that customers are unique and special and that their needs are understood. Customers want to feel understood by and important to firms that provide service to them. Personnel at small service firms often know customers by name and build relationships that reflect their personal knowledge of customer requirements and preferences. When such a small firm competes with larger firms, the ability to be empathetic may give the small firm a clear advantage.

In business-to-business services, customers want supplier firms to understand their industries and issues. Many small computer consulting firms successfully compete with large vendors by positioning themselves as specialists in particular industries. Even though larger firms have superior resources, the small firms are perceived as more knowledgeable about customers' specific issues and needs and are able to offer more customized services.

Tangibles: Representing the Service Physically

Tangibles are defined as the appearance of physical facilities, equipment, personnel, and communication materials. Tangibles provide physical representations or images of the service that customers, particularly new customers, will use to evaluate quality. Service industries that emphasize tangibles in their strategies include services in which the customer visits the establishment to receive the service, such as restaurants and hotels, retail stores, and entertainment companies.

Although tangibles are often used by service companies to enhance their image, provide continuity, and signal quality to customers, most companies combine tangibles with another dimension to create a service quality strategy for the firm. For example, Jiffy Lube emphasizes both responsiveness and tangibles—providing fast, efficient service and a comfortable, clean waiting area. In contrast, firms that do not pay attention to the tangibles dimension of the service strategy can confuse and even destroy an otherwise good strategy.

Table 5.2 provides examples of how customers judge each of the five dimensions of service quality across a variety of service contexts including both consumer and business services.

E-Service Quality

The growth of e-tailing and e-services has led many companies to wonder how consumers evaluate service quality on the Web and whether the criteria are different from those used to judge the quality of non-Internet services.[44] Some commercial groups, such as BizRate.com and Gomez.com, capture customer perceptions of specific sites. A more systematic study, sponsored by the Marketing Science Institute, has been conducted to understand how consumers judge e-service quality.[45] In that study, *E-S-QUAL* is defined as the extent to which a website facilitates efficient and effective shopping, purchasing, and delivery. Through exploratory focus groups and two phases of empirical data collection and analysis, this research identified seven dimensions that are critical for core service evaluation (four dimensions) and service recovery evaluation (three dimensions).

The four core dimensions that customers use to judge websites at which they experience no questions or problems are as follows:[46]

Efficiency: The ease and speed of accessing and using the site.

Fulfillment: The extent to which the site's promises about order delivery and item availability are fulfilled.

TABLE 5.2   Examples of How Customers Judge the Five Dimensions of Service Quality

Industry	Reliability	Responsiveness	Assurance	Empathy	Tangibles
Car repair (consumer)	Problem fixed the first time and ready when promised	Accessible; no waiting; responds to requests	Knowledgeable mechanics	Acknowledges customer by name; remembers previous problems and preferences	Repair facility; waiting area; uniforms; equipment
Airline (consumer)	Flights to promised destinations depart and arrive on schedule	Prompt and speedy system for ticketing, in-flight baggage handling	Trusted name; good safety record; competent employees	Understands special individual needs; anticipates customer needs	Aircraft; ticketing counters; baggage area; uniforms
Medical care (consumer)	Appointments are kept on schedule; diagnoses prove accurate	Accessible; no waiting; willingness to listen	Knowledge; skills; credentials; reputation	Acknowledges patient as a person; remembers previous problems; listens well; has patience	Waiting room; exam room; equipment; written materials
Architecture (business)	Delivers plans when promised and within budget	Returns phone calls; adapts to changes	Credentials; reputation; name in the community; knowledge and skills	Understands client's industry; acknowledges and adapts to specific client needs; gets to know the client	Office area; reports; plans themselves; billing statements; dress of employees
Information processing (internal)	Provides needed information when requested	Prompt response to requests; not "bureaucratic"; deals with problems promptly	Knowledgeable staff; well trained; credentials	Knows internal customers as individuals; understands individual and departmental needs	Internal reports; office area; dress of employees
Internet brokerage (consumer and business)	Provides correct information and executes customer requests accurately	Quick website with easy access and no down time	Credible information sources on the site; brand recognition; credentials apparent on site	Responds with human interaction as needed	Appearance of the website as well as flyers, brochures, and other print materials

System availability: The correct technical functioning of the site.

Privacy: The degree to which the site is safe and protects customer information.

The study also revealed three dimensions that customers use to judge recovery service when they have problems or questions:

Responsiveness: The effective handling of prolems and returns through the site.

Compensation: The degree to which the site compensates customers for problems.

Contact: The availability of assistance through telephone or online representatives.

L.L.Bean's Internet website, shown in the photo below, exhibits all of the qualities of an excellent e-tailer. The company excels on the core dimensions of e-service quality, and they also offer excellent and easy to understand recovery through their service guarantee.

L.L.Bean excels on E-S-QUAL

In comparing the dimensions of traditional service quality and e-service quality, we can make several observations. First, the traditional dimensions can and should be considered for e-tailing and Internet-based services, as illustrated by the Internet brokerage example in Table 5.2. However, both similar and different dimensions emerge in the research on e-tailing. Reliability (in terms of "system availability") and responsiveness are shared dimensions, but new Internet-specific dimensions appear to be critical in that context. Efficiency and fulfillment are the most important core dimensions in e-service quality, and both share some elements of the traditional reliability and responsiveness dimensions. The personal (i.e., friendly, empathetic, and understanding) flavor of perceived service quality's empathy dimension is not required on the Internet except as it makes transactions more efficient or in nonroutine or problem situations. While not emerging as a dimension of e-service quality, tangibles are clearly relevant given that the entire service is delivered through technology. The tangible, visual elements of the site will be critical to efficiency as well as to overall perceptions of the firm and the brand. A psychometric assessment of the E-S-QUAL scale concludes that the scale is an excellent and reliable instrument for measuring the quality of e-retailing sites, although modest adjustments may be required for specific contexts.[47]

Strategy Insight Customer Satisfaction, Loyalty, and Service as Corporate Strategies

CEOs of many highly successful, growth-oriented companies are preoccupied with customer satisfaction, loyalty, and service. They see these corporate objectives as critical challenges but also as the keys to their companies' continued profitable growth. In fact, a survey of CEOs by The Conference Board in 2002 identified "customer loyalty and retention" as the leading management issue, ahead of many other critical issues including reducing costs, developing leaders, and increasing innovation. In many firms, these customer goals drive corporate strategies. Measures of improvement in satisfaction and loyalty often are a basis for managers' and employees' incentive compensation, stock performance, growth predictions, and service improvement strategies. Take three specific examples:

- At Enterprise Rent-A-Car, branch managers must meet or exceed corporate customer satisfaction and loyalty averages based on the ESQi (Enterprise Service Quality index) to be eligible for promotion. Clearly this requirement motivates them to develop cross-functional approaches and strategies that will improve satisfaction in their branches. This and other strategies have led to success for Enterprise, a privately held company, that is widely regarded as the largest and most prosperous rental car company in the United States.

- Led by CEO Gary Loveman, Harrah's Entertainment developed a strategy to link frontline employee rewards directly to customer satisfaction. Each and every employee—from slot attendants to valets, from receptionists to chefs—was told: "If your service can persuade one customer to make one more visit a year with us, you've had a good shift. If you can persuade three, you've had a great

shift." The company also implemented a bonus plan to reward hourly workers with extra cash for achieving improved customer satisfaction scores.

- General Electric, recognized every year as the world's largest or second largest business, uses customer satisfaction and loyalty to guide corporate strategy in its business units. For example, at GE Healthcare Financial Services, key findings from its loyalty scores and related surveys have allowed the company to develop programs designed to improve customer relationships and efficiency. Analysis of the data also showed that GE HealthCare Financial Services' scores moved in the same direction as its sister business, GE Healthcare, suggesting a strategic need for the two businesses to work closely together.

As these examples show, customer satisfaction, loyalty, and service quality are used to predict growth and reward performance; thus, measuring them appropriately and using the measures wisely are critical. A multitude of ways to measure customer satisfaction, loyalty, and quality exist, and all are not equally useful. Some are too complex, others are too simple, and yet others measure the wrong things. Some are better for predicting outcomes such as growth and performance, while other types of satisfaction and quality measures are needed for diagnosing underlying problems and making improvements.

One measurement approach, "Net Promoter," was developed by loyalty expert Frederick Reichheld based on business case studies conducted by his firm. Net Promoter has gained tremendous popularity across industries in a very short time. The research promotes *one* customer loyalty question as the best for most industries in terms of predicting repeat

SERVICE ENCOUNTERS: THE BUILDING BLOCKS FOR CUSTOMER PERCEPTIONS

We have just finished a discussion of customer perceptions, specifically customer satisfaction and service quality. As discussed in our Strategy Insight, companies today recognize that they can compete more effectively by distinguishing themselves with respect to service quality, satisfaction and loyalty. Next we turn to what have been termed the building blocks for customer perceptions—service encounters, or

customer purchases, growth, or referrals. The question is "How likely is it that you would recommend [company X] to a friend or colleague?" Based on this question many firms now use Reichheld's "Net Promoter" metric (the proportional difference between a firm's "promoters" and "detractors" based on this one question) to predict growth and loyalty. While the measure enjoys tremendous popularity, there is continuing controversy as to its superiority as a predictor. Academic researcher Timothy Keiningham and colleagues have concluded that it is no better at predicting growth than other measures such as the ACSI (American Customer Satisfaction Index).

Although tools such as Net Promoter or the ACSI index help firms determine where they stand with their customers and predict loyalty, these global measures do not provide the detail that companies need to diagnose underlying causes or to make improvements. Additional, deeper, and more detailed assessment (as discussed in this chapter and Chapter 6) can help firms evaluate potential issues and what improvements may be needed. Improving service and satisfaction most often involves a series of strategic and tactical actions related to employees, service operations, and customers. A successful corporatewide customer satisfaction, loyalty, or service strategy will involve all functional areas that can influence it. It is clearly much more than a marketing, market research, or customer research program. As it does for Enterprise, Harrah's, and GE, this type of corporate strategy can provide a means to tie all functions together around the customer.

Enterprise focuses strategically on customer satisfaction in all its branches

Sources: T. Keiningham, B. Cooil, T. W. Andreassen, and L. Aksoy, "A Longitudinal Examination of Net Promoter and Firm Revenue Growth," *Journal of Marketing,* 71 (July 2007), pp. 39–51; F. F. Reichheld, *The Ultimate Question: Driving Good Profits and True Growth* (Boston: Harvard Business School Press, 2006); N. Kumar, *Marketing as Strategy: Understanding the CEO's Agenda for Driving Growth and Innovation* (Boston, MA: Harvard Business School Press, 2004); M. D. Johnson and A. Gustafsson, *Improving Customer Satisfaction, Loyalty, and Profit* (San Francisco: Jossey-Bass, 2000); F. F. Reichheld, "The One Number You Need to Grow," *Harvard Business Review* December 2003, pp. 46–53; G. Loveman, "Diamonds in the Data Mine," *Harvard Business Review* May 2003, pp. 109–13; C. J. Loomis, "The Big Surprise Is Enterprise," *Fortune* July 24, 2006, pp. 141–150; J. McGregor, "Will You Recommend Us?" *BusinessWeek,* January 30, 2006, pp. 94–95; GE 2007 Customer Citizenship Report, GE website.

"moments of truth." Service encounters are where promises are kept or broken and where the proverbial rubber meets the road—sometimes called "real-time marketing." It is from these service encounters that customers build their perceptions.

Service Encounters or Moments of Truth

From the customer's point of view, the most vivid impression of service occurs in the *service encounter* or *moment of truth,* when the customer interacts with the service firm. For example, among the service encounters that a hotel customer experiences are checking

FIGURE 5.4
A Service Encounter Cascade for a Hotel Visit

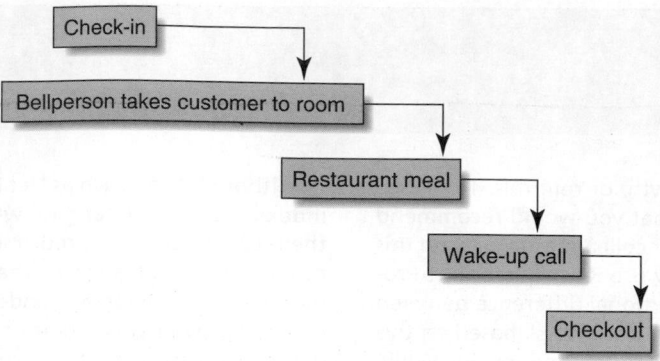

into the hotel, being taken to a room by a bellperson, eating a restaurant meal, requesting a wake-up call, and checking out. You could think of the linking of these moments of truth as a service encounter cascade (see Figure 5.4). It is in these encounters that customers receive a snapshot of the organization's service quality, and each encounter contributes to the customer's overall satisfaction and willingness to do business with the organization again. From the organization's point of view, each encounter thus presents an opportunity to prove its potential as a quality service provider and to increase customer loyalty, as suggested by the ad for Doubletree Hotels shown on the next page.

Some services have few service encounters, and others have many. The Disney Corporation estimates that each of its amusement park customers experiences about 74 service encounters and that a negative experience in any one of them can lead to a negative overall evaluation. Mistakes or problems that occur in the early stages of the service cascade may be particularly critical. Marriott Hotels learned this through their extensive customer research to determine what service elements contribute most to customer loyalty. They found that four of the top five factors come into play in the first 10 minutes of the guest's stay.[48]

The Importance of Encounters

Although early events in the encounter cascade are likely to be especially important, *any* encounter can potentially be critical in determining customer satisfaction and loyalty. If a customer is interacting with a firm for the first time, that initial encounter will create a first impression of the organization. In these first encounter situations, the customer frequently has no other basis for judging the organization, and the initial phone contact or face-to-face experience with a representative of the firm can take on significant importance in the customer's perceptions of quality. A customer calling for repair service on a household appliance may well hang up and call a different company if he is treated rudely by a customer service representative, put on hold for a lengthy period, or told that two weeks is the soonest someone can be sent out to make the repair. Even if the technical quality of the firm's repair service is superior, the firm may not get the chance to demonstrate it if the initial telephone encounter drives the customer away.

Even when the customer has had multiple interactions with a firm, each individual encounter is important in creating a composite image of the firm in the customer's memory. Many positive experiences add up to a composite image of high quality, whereas many negative interactions will have the opposite effect. On the other hand, a combination of positive and negative interactions will leave the customer feeling unsure of the firm's quality, doubtful of its consistency in service delivery, and vulnerable to the appeals of competitors. For example, a large corporate customer of an

Every service encounter is an opportunity to build satisfaction and quality.

institutional food provider that provides food service in all its company dining rooms and cafeterias could have a series of positive encounters with the account manager or salesperson who handles the account. These experiences could be followed by positive encounters with the operations staff who actually set up the food service facilities. However, even with these positive encounters, later negative experiences with the staff who serve the food or the accounting department that administers the billing procedures can result in a mixture of overall quality impressions. This variation in experiences could result in the corporate customer wondering about the quality of the organization and unsure of what to expect in the future. Each encounter with different people and departments representing the food service provider adds to or detracts from the potential for a continuing relationship.

Exhibit 5.1   One Critical Encounter Destroys 30-Year Relationship

"If you have $1 in a bank or $1 million, I think they owe you the courtesy of stamping your parking ticket," said John Barrier. One day Mr. Barrier paid a visit to his bank in Spokane, Washington. He was wearing his usual shabby clothes and pulled up in his pickup truck, parking in the lot next to the bank. After cashing a check, he went outside to drive away and was stopped by a parking attendant who told him there was a 60-cent fee, but that he could get his parking slip validated in the bank and park for free. No problem, Barrier thought, and he went back into the bank (where, by the way, he had been banking for 30 years). The teller looked him up and down and refused to stamp his slip, telling him that the bank validated parking only for people who have transactions with the bank and that cashing a check wasn't a transaction. Mr. Barrier then asked to see the bank manager, who also looked him up and down, stood back, and "gave me one of those kinds of looks," also refusing to validate the parking bill. Mr. Barrier then said, "Fine. You don't need me, and I don't need you." He withdrew all his money and took it down the street to a competing bank, where the first check he deposited was for $1,000,000.

Source: "Shabby Millionaire Closes Account, Gives Bank Lesson about Snobbery." Reprinted with permission of United Press International from *The Arizona Republic* issue of February 21, 1989, p. A3.

Logic suggests that not all encounters are equally important in building relationships. For every organization, certain encounters are probably key to customer satisfaction. For Marriott Hotels, as noted, the early encounters are most important. In a hospital context, a study of patients revealed that encounters with nursing staff were more important in predicting satisfaction than were encounters with meal service or patient discharge personnel.[49] And research at GTE Laboratories documented that small business customers' relationships with GTE depended on specific installation, repair, and sales encounters.[50]

In addition to these key encounters, there are some momentous encounters that, like the proverbial "one bad apple," simply ruin the rest and drive the customer away no matter how many or what type of encounters have occurred in the past. These momentous encounters can occur in connection with very important events (such as the failure to deliver an essential piece of equipment before a critical deadline), or they may seem inconsequential, as in the story of the bank customer described in Exhibit 5.1. Similarly, momentous positive encounters can sometimes bind a customer to an organization for life. Research in a call center context concludes that while the average quality of the individual events in a service encounter sequence will be important, satisfaction can be enhanced by providing a positive peak experience within the sequence.[51] This and other research suggests that "not all events in an experience sequence are created equal" and that in fact there are benefits to be gained by creating truly delightful (or "peak") experiences at pre-determined points in the sequence.

Types of Service Encounters

A service encounter occurs every time a customer interacts with the service organization. There are three general types of service encounters: *remote encounters, phone encounters,* and *face-to-face encounters.*[52] A customer may experience any of these types of encounters, or a combination of all three, in his or her interactions with a service firm.

First, encounters can occur without any direct human contact *(remote encounters),* such as when a customer interacts with a bank through the ATM system, with a retailer through its Internet website, or with a mail-order service through automated touch-tone phone ordering. Remote encounters also occur when the firm sends its billing statements or communicates other types of information to customers by mail. Although there is no direct human contact in these remote encounters, each represents an opportunity for the firm to reinforce or establish quality perceptions in the customer. In remote encounters the tangible evidence of the service and the quality of the technical processes and systems become the primary bases for judging quality.

More and more services are being delivered through technology, particularly with the advent of Internet applications. Retail purchases, airline ticketing, repair and maintenance troubleshooting, and package and shipment tracking are just a few examples of services available via the Internet. All these types of service encounters can be considered remote encounters (see our Technology Spotlight).

In many organizations (such as insurance companies, utilities, and telecommunications), the most frequent type of encounter between an end customer and the firm occurs over the telephone *(phone encounters)*. Almost all firms (whether goods manufacturers or service businesses) rely on telephone encounters to some extent for customer service, general inquiry, or order-taking functions. The judgment of quality in phone encounters is different from remote encounters because there is greater potential variability in the interaction.[53] Tone of voice, employee knowledge, and effectiveness/efficiency in handling customer issues become important criteria for judging quality in these encounters.

A third type of encounter is the one that occurs between an employee and a customer in direct contact *(face-to-face encounters)*. At Mayo Clinic, face-to-face encounters occur between patients and reception staff, nurses, doctors, lab technicians, food service workers, pharmacy staff, and others. For a company such as IBM, in a business-to-business setting direct encounters occur between the business customer and salespeople, delivery personnel, maintenance representatives, and professional consultants. Determining and understanding service quality issues in face-to-face contexts is the most complex of all. Both verbal and nonverbal behaviors are important determinants of quality, as are tangible cues such as employee dress and other symbols of service (equipment, informational brochures, physical setting). In face-to-face encounters the customer also plays a role in creating quality service for herself through her own behavior during the interaction.

Sources of Pleasure and Displeasure in Service Encounters

Because of the importance of service encounters in building perceptions, researchers have extensively analyzed service encounters in many contexts to determine the sources of customers' favorable and unfavorable impressions. The research uses the critical incident technique to get customers and employees to provide verbatim stories about satisfying and dissatisfying service encounters they have experienced (see Chapter 6 for a detailed description and references for this research technique.)

On the basis of thousands of service encounter stories, four common themes—recovery (after failure), adaptability, spontaneity, and coping—have been identified as the sources of customer satisfaction/dissatisfaction in memorable service encounters.[54] Each of the themes is discussed here, and sample stories of both satisfying and dissatisfying incidents for each theme are given in Exhibit 5.2. The themes encompass service behaviors in encounters spanning a wide variety of industries.

Recovery—Employee Response to Service Delivery System Failures

The first theme includes all incidents in which there has been a failure of the service delivery system and an employee is required to respond in some way to consumer complaints and disappointments. The failure may be, for example, a hotel room that is not available, an airplane flight that is delayed six hours, an incorrect item sent from a

Technology Spotlight   Customers Love Amazon

Jeff Bezos, CEO of Amazon, whose name has become a household word worldwide, believes that his customers come first. Although the company was hit hard like all other Internet-based businesses in 2000–2001, it has rebounded and has shown tremendous growth in both revenues and profits. Since 2001 Amazon stock has gained more than 800 percent. With a continued focus on customers, relationships, value, and the brand itself, Bezos and others believe that sales (an estimated $14 billion for 2007) and profits will continue to grow. The 2007 American Customer Satisfaction Index reflected a rating of 87 for Amazon—one of the highest ratings of any company in any industry, and certainly much higher than the 75 average rating for all e-business endeavors and the 63–75 ratings for many other service businesses. According to Bezos, "Customers come first. If you focus on what customers want and build a relationship, they will allow you to make money."

Few would deny that Amazon is a master of technology and technology-based services for consumers. In fact, other companies, such as Target and Office Depot, have sought a technology partnership with Amazon to benefit from the company's experience and success with customers. Amazon now provides Internet retail services for both these companies, and it also provides web services, fulfillment, and technology infrastructure services to other companies.

In its core business, online book sales, Amazon has taken a historically interpersonally dominated transaction and successfully transformed it to a web-based service experience. Let us take a closer look at what the company is doing and why customers love it so much. Since its inception in July 1995, Amazon has grown to the point where it offers more book titles than any bricks-and-mortar bookstore could ever hope to stock. So selection and availability of titles are one key to its popularity with customers. But that is just the beginning.

In addition to a wide selection, Amazon has invested significant effort to simulate the feel of a neighborhood bookstore, where a patron can mingle with other customers, discuss books, and get recommendations from bookstore employees. Amazon allows customers to find related books on virtually any topic by simply typing key words and initiating a search of its massive database. Its one-to-one marketing system allows the company to track what individual consumers buy and let them know of additional titles that might interest them. This marketing is done while the customer is shopping as well as through periodic direct e-mail that identifies books specifically related to the customer's past purchase patterns and interests.

Currently, customers can buy much more than books from Amazon. In fact, Bezos hopes that they can buy just about anything they want through the Amazon website. His goal from the beginning was "to create the world's most customer-centric company, the place where you can find and buy anything you want online." Bezos continues to take risks that are combined with a long-term view of success, and to reflect all new ideas against a customer-focused filter. Small-scale experiments in 2007 with online ordering and grocery delivery services aim to truly understand the market before expanding beyond a limited geographic range in Seattle. Larger scale expansions such as its partnership with Joyo.com in China also maintain a strong customer focus. Joyo.com will provide similar services to Amazon's core

mail-order company, or a critical error on an internal document. The content or form of the employee's response is what causes the customer to remember the event either favorably or unfavorably.

Adaptability—Employee Response to Customer Needs and Requests

A second theme underlying satisfaction/dissatisfaction in service encounters is how adaptable the service delivery system is when the customer has special needs or requests that place demands on the process. In these cases, customers judge service encounter quality in terms of the flexibility of the employees and the system. Incidents categorized within this theme all contain an implicit or explicit request for customization of

Amazons offers personalized gift-giving & organizing services.

service, tailored to the Chinese marketplace. Bezos intends to avoid mistakes of others in China by working with its partner to understand Chinese customers and keep their interests central.

As Amazon stays on the forefront of technology-delivered service, few doubters of its long-term success remain. The philosophy of keeping the customer central to the firm's strategy seems by all accounts to have paid off.

Sources: ACSI results at www.theacsi.org 2007; A. Deutschman, "Inside the Mind of Jeff Bezos," *Fast Company,* August 2004, pp. 52–58; J. Authors, "An Amazing 10-year Amazonian adventure LONG VIEW," *Financial Times,* April 28, 2007, p. 24; J. Dean, "Bezos Says Amazon Will Boost Investment in China, *The Wall Street Journal,* June 6, 2007, p. A-12; V. Vara, "Amazon Is Taking Small Steps toward Grocery-Delivery Service," *The Wall Street Journal,* August 3, 2007, p. B4; D. DeFotis, "New Amazon, Same Old Questions," *Barrons,* July 30, 2007, p. 20.

the service to meet a need. Much of what customers see as special needs or requests may actually be rather routine from the employee's point of view; what is important is that the customer perceives that something special is being done for her based on her own individual needs. External customers and internal customers alike are pleased when the service provider puts forth the effort to accommodate and adjust the system to meet their requirements. On the flip side, they are angered and frustrated by an unwillingness to try to accommodate and by promises that are never followed through. Contact employees also see their abilities to adapt the system as being a prominent source of customer satisfaction, and often they are equally frustrated by constraints that keep them from being flexible.

Exhibit 5.2 Service Encounter Themes

THEME 1: RECOVERY

Satisfactory	Dissatisfactory
They lost my room reservation but the manager gave me the V.P. suite for the same price. Even though I did not make any complaint about the hour-and-a-half wait, the waitress kept apologizing and said the bill was on the house.	We had made advance reservations at the hotel. When we arrived we found we had no room—no explanation, no apologies, and no assistance in finding another hotel. One of my suitcases was all dented up and looked like it had been dropped from 30,000 feet. When I tried to make a claim for my damaged luggage, the employee insinuated that I was lying and trying to cheat them.

THEME 2: ADAPTABILITY

Satisfactory	Dissatisfactory
I did not have an appointment to see a doctor; however, my allergy nurse spoke to a practitioner's assistant and worked me into the schedule. I received treatment after a 10-minute wait. I was very satisfied with the special treatment I received, the short wait, and the quality of the service. It was snowing outside—my car broke down. I checked 10 hotels and there were no rooms. Finally, one understood my situation and offered to rent me a bed and set it up in a small banquet room.	My young son, flying alone, was to be assisted by the flight attendant from start to finish. At the Albany airport she left him alone in the airport with no one to escort him to his connecting flight. Despite our repeated requests, the hotel staff would not deal with the noisy people partying in the hall at 3 a.m.

THEME 3: SPONTANEITY

Satisfactory	Dissatisfactory
We always travel with our teddy bears. When we got back to our room at the hotel we saw that the cleaning person had arranged our bears very comfortably in a chair. The bears were holding hands. The anesthesiologist took extra time to explain exactly what I would be aware of and promised to take special care in making sure I did not wake up during surgery. It impressed me that the anesthesiologist came to settle my nerves and explain the medicine I was getting because of my cold.	The lady at the front desk acted as if we were bothering her. She was watching TV and paying more attention to the TV than to the hotel guests. I needed a few more minutes to decide on a dinner. The waitress said, "If you would read the menu and not the road map, you would know what you want to order."

THEME 4: COPING

Satisfactory	Dissatisfactory
A person who became intoxicated on a flight started speaking loudly, annoying the other passengers. The flight attendant asked the passenger if he would be driving when the plane landed and offered him coffee. He accepted the coffee and became quieter and friendlier.	An intoxicated man began pinching the female flight attendants. One attendant told him to stop, but he continued and then hit another passenger. The copilot was called and asked the man to sit down and leave the others alone, but the passenger refused. The copilot then "decked" the man, knocking him into his seat.

Spontaneity—Unprompted and Unsolicited Employee Actions

Even when there is no system failure and no special request or need, customers can still remember service encounters as being very satisfying or very dissatisfying. Employee spontaneity in delivering memorably good or poor service is the third theme. Satisfying incidents in this group represent very pleasant surprises for the customer (special attention, being treated like royalty, receiving something nice but not requested), whereas dissatisfying incidents in this group represent negative and unacceptable employee behaviors (rudeness, stealing, discrimination, ignoring the customer).

Coping—Employee Response to Problem Customers

The incidents categorized in this group came to light when employees were asked to describe service encounter incidents in which customers were either very satisfied or dissatisfied. In addition to describing incidents of the types outlined under the first three themes, employees described many incidents in which customers were the cause of their own dissatisfaction. Such customers were basically uncooperative—that is, unwilling to cooperate with the service provider, other customers, industry regulations, and/or laws. In these cases nothing the employee could do would result in the customer feeling pleased about the encounter. The term *coping* is used to describe these incidents because coping is the behavior generally required of employees to handle problem customer encounters. Rarely are such encounters satisfying from the customers' point of view.[55] Also of interest is that customers themselves did not relate any "problem customer" incidents. That is, customers either do not see, or choose not to remember or retell, stories of the times when they themselves were unreasonable to the point of causing their own dissatisfactory service encounter.

Table 5.3 summarizes the specific employee behaviors that cause satisfaction and dissatisfaction in service encounters according to the four themes just presented: recovery, adaptability, spontaneity, and coping. The left side of the table suggests what employees do that results in positive encounters, whereas the right side summarizes negative behaviors within each theme.

Technology-Based Service Encounters

All the research on service encounters described thus far and the resulting themes underlying service encounter evaluations are based on interpersonal services—that is, face-to-face encounters between customers and employees of service organizations. Recently researchers have begun to look at the sources of pleasure and displeasure in technology-based service encounters.[56] These types of encounters involve customers interacting with Internet-based services, automated phone services, kiosk services, and services delivered via DVD or video technology. Often these systems are referred to as *self-service technologies* (SSTs) because the customer essentially provides his or her own service.

The research on SSTs reveals some different themes in terms of what drives customer satisfaction and dissatisfaction. The following themes were identified from analysis of hundreds of critical incident stories across a wide range of contexts, including Internet retailing, Internet-based services, ATMs, automated phone systems, and others:

For Satisfying SSTs

> *Solved an intensified need.* Customers in this category were thrilled that the technology could bail them out of a difficult situation—for example, a cash machine that came to the rescue, allowing the customer to get cash to pay a cab driver and get to work on time when a car had broken down.

TABLE 5.3 **General Service Behaviors Based on Service Encounter Themes—Dos and Don'ts**

Theme	Do	Don't
Recovery	Acknowledge problem Explain causes Apologize Compensate/upgrade Lay out options Take responsibility	Ignore customer Blame customer Leave customer to fend for himself or herself Downgrade Act as if nothing is wrong "Pass the buck"
Adaptability	Recognize the seriousness of the need Acknowledge Anticipate Attempt to accommodate Adjust the system Explain rules/policies Take responsibility	Ignore Promise, but fail to follow through Show unwillingness to try Embarrass the customer Laugh at the customer Avoid responsibility "Pass the buck"
Spontaneity	Take time Be attentive Anticipate needs Listen Provide information Show empathy	Exhibit impatience Ignore Yell/laugh/swear Steal from customers Discriminate
Coping	Listen Try to accommodate Explain Let go of the customer	Take customer's dissatisfaction personally Let customer's dissatisfaction affect others

Better than the alternative. Many SST stories related to how the technology-based service was in some way better than the alternative—easy to use, saved time, available when and where the customer needed it, saved money.

Did its job. Because there are so many failures of technology, many customers are simply thrilled when the SST works as it should!

For Dissatisfying SSTs

Technology failure. Many dissatisfying SST stories relate to the technology simply not working as promised—it is not available when needed, PIN numbers do not work, or systems are offline.

Process failure. Often the technology seems to work, but later the customer discovers that a back-office or follow-up process, which the customer assumed was connected, does not work. For example, a product order seems to be placed successfully, but it never arrives or the wrong product is delivered.

Poor design. Many stories relate to the customer's dissatisfaction with how the technology is designed, in terms of either the technical process (technology is confusing, menu options are unclear) or the actual service design (delivery takes too long, service is inflexible).

Customer-driven failure. In some cases, the customers told stories of their own inabilities or failures to use the technology properly. These types of stories are (of course) much less common than stories blaming the technology or the company.

FIGURE 5.5
The Evidence of Service (from the Customer's Point of View)

Source: From "Managing the Evidence of Service" by M. J. Bitner from *The Service Quality Handbook,* ed. E. E. Scheuing and W. F. Christopher, 1993; Reprinted by permission of the American Marketing Association.

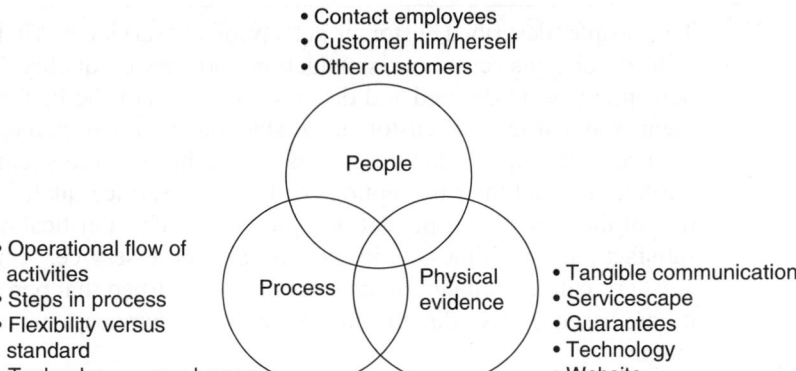

• Contact employees
• Customer him/herself
• Other customers

People

• Operational flow of
  activities
• Steps in process
• Flexibility versus
  standard
• Technology versus human

Process

Physical
evidence

• Tangible communication
• Servicescape
• Guarantees
• Technology
• Website

For all of the dissatisfying SST stories, there is clearly an element of service failure. Interestingly, the research revealed little attempt in these technology-based encounters to recover from the failure—unlike the interpersonal service encounters described earlier, where excellent service recovery can be a foundation for retaining and even producing very satisfied customers. As companies progress further with SSTs and become better at delivering service this way, we expect that growing numbers will be able to deliver superior service via technology. Many are doing it already, as our Technology Spotlight on Amazon.com illustrated. In the future we believe that many firms will be able to deliver highly reliable, responsive, customized services via technology and will offer easy and effective means for service recovery when failure does occur.[57]

The Evidence of Service

Because services are intangible, customers are searching for evidence of service in every interaction they have with an organization.[58] Figure 5.5 depicts the three major categories of evidence as experienced by the customer: people, process, and physical evidence. These categories together represent the service and provide the evidence that makes the offering tangible. Note the parallels between the elements of evidence of service and the new marketing mix elements presented in Chapter 1. The new mix elements essentially *are* the evidence of service in each moment of truth.

All these elements of service evidence, or a subset of them, are present in every service encounter a customer has with a service firm and are critically important in managing service encounter quality and creating customer satisfaction. For example, when a patient has an appointment with a doctor in a health clinic, the first encounter of the visit is frequently with a receptionist in a clinic waiting area. The quality of that encounter will be judged by how the appointment registration *process* works (Is there a line? How long is the wait? Is the registration system computerized and accurate?), the actions and attitude of the *people* (Is the receptionist courteous, helpful, knowledgeable? Does he treat the patient as an individual? Does he handle inquiries fairly and efficiently?), and the *physical evidence* of the service (Is the waiting area clean and comfortable? Is the signage clear?). The three elements of evidence may be differentially important depending on the type of service encounter (remote, phone, face-to-face). All three elements will operate in face-to-face service encounters like the one just described.

Summary

This chapter described customer perceptions of service by first introducing you to two critical concepts: customer satisfaction and service quality. These critical customer perceptions were defined and discussed in terms of the factors that influence each of them. You learned that customer satisfaction is a broad perception influenced by features and attributes of the product as well as by customers' emotional responses, their attributions, and their perceptions of fairness. Service quality, the customer's perception of the service component of a product, is also a critical determinant of customer satisfaction. Sometimes, as in the case of a pure service, service quality may be the *most* critical determinant of satisfaction. You learned that perceptions of service quality are based on five dimensions: reliability, assurance, empathy, responsiveness, and tangibles.

Another major purpose of the chapter was to introduce the idea of service encounters, or "moments of truth," as the building blocks for both satisfaction and quality. You learned that every service encounter (whether remote, over the telephone, or in person) is an opportunity to build customer perceptions of quality and satisfaction. The underlying themes of pleasure and displeasure in service encounters were also described. The importance of managing the evidence of service in each and every encounter was discussed.

Chapters 3, 4, and 5 have provided you with a grounding in customer issues relevant to services. The three chapters together are intended to give you a solid understanding of customer behavior issues and of service expectations and perceptions. Through the rest of the book, we illustrate strategies that firms can use to close the gap between customer expectations and perceptions.

Discussion Questions

1. What is customer satisfaction, and why is it so important? Discuss how customer satisfaction can be influenced by each of the following: product attributes and features, customer emotions, attributions for success or failure, perceptions of fairness, and family members or other customers.

2. What is the ACSI? Do you believe that such national indicators of customer satisfaction should be included as benchmarks of national economic well-being similar to gross domestic product (GDP), price indicators, and productivity measures?

3. Why do service companies generally receive lower satisfaction ratings in the ACSI than nondurable and durable product companies?

4. Discuss the differences between perceptions of service quality and customer satisfaction.

5. List and define the five dimensions of service quality. Describe the services provided by a firm you do business with (your bank, your doctor, your favorite restaurant) on each of the dimensions. In your mind, has this organization distinguished itself from its competitors on any particular service quality dimension?

6. Describe a remote encounter, a phone encounter, and a face-to-face encounter that you have had recently. How did you evaluate the encounter, and what were the most important factors determining your satisfaction/dissatisfaction in each case?

7. Describe an "encounter cascade" for an airplane flight. In your opinion, what are the most important encounters in this cascade for determining your overall impression of the quality of the airline?

8. Why did the gentleman described in Exhibit 5.1 leave his bank after 30 years? What were the underlying causes of his dissatisfaction in that instance, and why would that cause him to leave the bank?

9. Assume that you are a manager of a health club. Discuss general strategies you might use to maximize customers' positive perceptions of your club. How would you know if you were successful?

Exercises

1. Keep a journal of your service encounters with different organizations (at least five) during the week. For each journal entry, ask yourself the following questions: What circumstances led up to this encounter? What did the employee say or do? How did you evaluate this encounter? What exactly made you evaluate the encounter that way? What should the organization have done differently (if anything)? Categorize your encounters according to the four themes of service encounter satisfaction/dissatisfaction (recovery, adaptability, spontaneity, coping).

2. Interview someone with a non-U.S. cultural background. Ask the person about service quality, whether the five dimensions of quality are relevant, and which are most important in determining quality of banking services (or some other type of service) in the person's country.

3. Think of an important service experience you have had in the last several weeks. Analyze the encounter according to the evidence of service provided (see Figure 5.5). Which of the three evidence components was (or were) most important for you in evaluating the experience, and why?

4. Interview an employee of a local service business. Ask the person to discuss each of the five dimensions of service quality with you as it relates to the person's company. Which dimensions are most important? Are any dimensions *not* relevant in this context? Which dimensions does the company do best? Why? Which dimensions could benefit from improvement? Why?

5. Interview a manager, owner, or president of a business. Discuss with this person the strategies he or she uses to ensure customer satisfaction. How does service quality enter into the strategies, or does it? Find out how this person measures customer satisfaction and/or service quality.

6. Visit Amazon.com's website. Visit a traditional bookstore. How would you compare the two experiences? Compare and contrast the factors that most influenced your satisfaction and perceptions of service quality in the two different situations. When would you choose to use one versus the other?

Notes

1. A. Danigelis, "Local Hero: Zane's Cycles," *Fast Company,* (September 2006), p. 60; D. Fenn, *Alpha Dogs: How Your Small Business Can Become a Leader of the Pack* (New York: Collins, 2003); Chris Zane presentation at "Compete Through Service" Symposium, November 2003, Center for Services Leadership, Arizona State University.

2. For more discussion of the debate on the distinctions between quality and satisfaction, see A. Parasuraman, V. A. Zeithaml, and L. L. Berry, "Reassessment of Expectations as a Comparison Standard in Measuring Service Quality: Implications for Future Research," *Journal of Marketing* 58 (January 1994), pp. 111–124; R. L. Oliver, "A Conceptual Model of Service Quality and Service Satisfaction: Compatible Goals, Different Concepts," in *Advances in Services Marketing and Management,* vol. 2, ed. T. A. Swartz, D. E. Bowen, and S. W. Brown (Greenwich, CT: JAI

Press, 1994), pp. 65–85; M. J. Bitner and A. R. Hubbert, "Encounter Satisfaction vs. Overall Satisfaction vs. Quality: The Customer's Voice," in *Service Quality: New Directions in Theory and Practice,* ed. R. T. Rust and R. L. Oliver (Newbury Park, CA: Sage, 1993), pp. 71–93; D. Iacobucci et al., "The Calculus of Service Quality and Customer Satisfaction: Theory and Empirical Differentiation and Integration," in *Advances in Services Marketing and Management,* vol. 3, ed. T. A. Swartz, D. E. Bowen, and S. W. Brown (Greenwich, CT: JAI Press, 1994), pp. 1–67; P. A. Dabholkar, C. D. Shepherd, and D. I. Thorpe, "A Comprehensive Framework For Service Quality: An Investigation of Critical Conceptual and Measurement Issues through a Longitudinal Study," *Journal of Retailing* 7 (Summer 2000), pp. 139–173; J. J. Cronin Jr., M. K. Brady, and G. T. M. Hult, "Assessing the Effects of Quality, Value, and Customer Satisfaction on Consumer Behavioral Intentions in Service Environments," *Journal of Retailing* 76 (Summer 2000), pp. 193–218.

3. See in particular, Parasuraman, Zeithaml, and Berry, "Reassessment of Expectations"; Oliver, "A Conceptual Model of Service Quality"; and M. K. Brady and J. J. Cronin Jr., "Some New Thoughts on Conceptualizing Perceived Service Quality: A Hierarchical Approach," *Journal of Marketing* 65 (July 2001), pp. 34–49.

4. A. Parasuraman, V. A. Zeithaml, and L. L. Berry, "SERVQUAL: A Multiple-Item Scale for Measuring Consumer Perceptions of Service Quality," *Journal of Retailing* 64 (Spring 1988), pp. 12–40.

5. Parasuraman, Zeithaml, and Berry, "Reassessment of Expectations.

6. Oliver, "A Conceptual Model of Service Quality."

7. See V. Mittal, P. Kumar, and M. Tsiros, "Attribute-Level Performance, Satisfaction, and Behavioral Intentions Over Time," *Journal of Marketing* 63 (April 1999), pp. 88–101; L. L. Olsen and M. D. Johnson, "Service Equity, Satisfaction, and Loyalty: From Transaction-Specific to Cumulative Evaluations," *Journal of Service Research* 5 (February 2003), pp. 184–195; P. C. Verhoef, G. Antonides, and A. N. De Hoog, "Service Encounters as a Sequence of Events: The Importance of Peak Experiences," *Journal of Service Research* 7 (August 2004), pp. 53–64.

8. Olsen and Johnson, "Service Equity, Satisfaction, and Loyalty."

9. R. L. Oliver, *Satisfaction: A Behavioral Perspective on the Consumer* (New York: Mcgraw-Hill, 1997).

10. For a more detailed discussion of the different types of satisfaction, see E. Arnould, L. Price, and G. Zinkhan, *Consumers,* 2nd ed. (New York: Mcgraw-Hill, 2004), pp. 754–96.

11. S. Fournier and D. G. Mick, "Rediscovering Satisfaction," *Journal of Marketing* 63 (October 1999), pp. 5–23; Verhoef et al., "Service Encounters as a Sequence of Events."

12. Oliver, *Satisfaction,* chap. 2.

13. A. Ostrom and D. Iacobucci, "Consumer Trade-Offs and the Evaluation of Services," *Journal of Marketing* 59 (January 1995), pp. 17–28.

14. For more on emotions and satisfaction, see Oliver, *Satisfaction,* chap. 11; L. L. Price, E. J. Arnould, and S. L. Deibler, "Consumers' Emotional Responses to Service Encounters," *International Journal of Service Industry Management* 6, no. 3 (1995), pp. 34–63.

15. L. L. Price, E. J. Arnould, and P. Tierney, "Going to Extremes: Managing Service Encounters and Assessing Provider Performance," *Journal of Marketing* 59 (April 1995), pp. 83–97.

16. T. Hennig-Thurau, M. Groth, M. Paul, and D. D. Gremler, "Are All Smiles Created Equal? How Emotional Contagion and Emotional Labor Affect Service Relationships," *Journal of Marketing* 70 (July 2006), pp. 58–73.

17. V. Liljander and T. Strandvik, "Emotions in Service Satisfaction," *International Journal of Service Industry Management* 8, no. 2 (1997), pp. 148–169.

18. For more on attributions and satisfaction, see V. S. Folkes, "Recent Attribution Research in Consumer Behavior: A Review and New Directions," *Journal of Consumer Research* 14 (March 1988), pp. 548–565; and Oliver, *Satisfaction,* chap. 10.

19. A. R. Hubbert, "Customer Co-Creation of Service Outcomes: Effects of Locus of Causality Attributions," doctoral dissertation, Arizona State University, Tempe, Arizona, 1995.

20. M. J. Bitner, "Evaluating Service Encounters: The Effects of Physical Surroundings and Employee Responses," *Journal of Marketing* 54 (April 1990), pp. 69–82.

21. For more on fairness and satisfaction, see E. C. Clemmer and B. Schneider, "Fair Service," in *Advances in Services Marketing and Management,* vol. 5, ed. T. A. Swartz, D. E. Bowen, and S. W. Brown (Greenwich, CT: JAI Press, 1996), pp. 109–126; Oliver, *Satisfaction,* chap. 7; and Olsen and Johnson, "Service Equity, Satisfaction, and Loyalty."

22. As described in K. Seiders and L. L. Berry, "Service Fairness: What It Is and Why It Matters," *Academy of Management Executive* 12 (May 1998), pp. 8–20.

23. Fournier and Mick, "Rediscovering Satisfaction."

24. C. Fornell, M. D. Johnson, E. W. Anderson, J. Cha, and B. E. Bryant, "The American Customer Satisfaction Index: Nature, Purpose, and Findings," *Journal of Marketing* 60 (October 1996), pp. 7–18; *ACSI 10-Year Report Analysis (1994–2004),* University of Michigan, National Quality Research Center, 2005.

25. E. W. Anderson, C. Fornell, and D. R. Lehmann, "Customer Satisfaction, Market Share, and Profitability: Findings from Sweden," *Journal of Marketing* 58 (July 1994), pp. 53–66.

26. M. Bruhn and M. A. Grund, "Theory, Development and Implementation of National Customer Satisfaction Indices: The Swiss Index of Customer Satisfaction (SWICS)," *Total Quality Management* 11, no. 7 (2000), pp. S1017–S1028; A. Meyer and F. Dornach, "The German Customer Barometer," http://www.servicebarometer.de.or.

27. Fornell et al., "The American Customer Satisfaction Index;" *ACSI 10-Year Report Analysis.*

28. For a listing of companies and their scores, go to the ACSI website at www.theacsi.org.

29. ACSI website, www.theacsi.org.

30. Ibid, "About ACSI," "Economic Indicator," website accessed August 18, 2007.

31. J. L. Heskett, W. E. Sasser Jr., and L. A. Schlesinger, *The Service Profit Chain* (New York: Free Press, 1997).

32. C. Fornell, S. Mithas, F. V. Morgeson III, and M.S. Krishnan, "Customer Satisfaction and Stock Prices: High Returns, Low Risk," *Journal of Marketing* 70 (January 2006), pp. 3–14.

33. M. A. Wiles, "The Effect of Customer Service on Retailers' Shareholder Wealth: The Role of Availability and Reputation Cues," *Journal of Retailing,* Special Issue on Service Excellence 83 (January 2007), pp. 19–32.

34. M. A. J. Menezes and J. Serbin, *Xerox Corporation: The Customer Satisfaction Program,* case no. 591-055 (Boston: Harvard Business School, 1991).

35. F. F. Reichheld, "The One Number You Need to Grow," *Harvard Business Review,* December 2003, pp. 47–54.

36. Information provided by TARP Worldwide, Inc., August 2007.

37. E. W. Anderson and V. Mittal, "Strengthening the Satisfaction–Profit Chain," *Journal of Service Research* 3 (November 2000), pp. 107–120; B. Hindo, "Satisfaction Not Guaranteed," *BusinessWeek,* June 19, 2006, pp. 32–36.

38. Brady and Cronin, "Some New Thoughts on Conceptualizing Perceived Service Quality."

39. Ibid.

40. See C. Gronroos, "A Service Quality Model and its Marketing Implications," *European Journal of Marketing* 18, no. 4 (1984), pp. 36–44; R. T. Rust and R. L. Oliver, "Service Quality Insights and Managerial Implications from the Frontier," in *Service Quality: New Directions in Theory and Practice,* ed. R. T. Rust and R. L. Oliver (Thousand Oaks, CA: Sage, 1994), pp. 1–19; M. J. Bitner, "Managing the Evidence of Service," in *The Service Quality Handbook,* ed. E. E. Scheuing and W. F. Christopher (New York, AMACOM, 1993), pp. 358–370.

41. Parasuraman, Zeithaml, and Berry, "SERVQUAL: A Multiple-Item Scale." Details on the SERVQUAL Scale and the actual items used to assess the dimensions are provided in Chapter 6.

42. N. Raajpoot, "Reconceptualizing Service Encounter Quality in a Non-Western Context," *Journal of Service Research* 7 (Novemer 2004), pp. 181–201.

43. Parasuraman, Zeithaml, and Berry, "SERVQUAL: A Multiple-Item Scale."

44. For a review of what is known about service quality delivery via the Web see, V. A. Zeithaml, A. Parasuraman, and A. Malhotra, "Service Quality Delivery through Web Sites: A Critical Review of Extant Knowledge," *Journal of the Academy of Marketing Science* 30 (Fall 2002), pp. 362–375.

45. A. Parasuraman, V. A. Zeithaml, and A. Malhotra, "E-S-QUAL: A Multiple-Item Scale for Assessing Electronic Service Quality," *Journal of Service Research* 7 (February 2005), pp. 213–233.

46. Ibid.

47. C. Boshoff, "A Psychometric Assessment of E-S-QUAL: A Scale to Measure Electronic Service Quality," *Journal of Electronic Commerce Research* 8 (January, 2007), pp. 101–114.

48. "How Marriott Makes a Great First Impression," *The Service Edge* 6, no. 5 (May 1993), p. 5.

49. A. G. Woodside, L. L. Frey, and R. T. Daly, "Linking Service Quality, Customer Satisfaction, and Behavioral Intention," *Journal of Health Care Marketing* 9 (December 1989), pp. 5–17.

50. R. N. Bolton and J. H. Drew, "Mitigating the Effect of Service Encounters," *Marketing Letters* 3, no. 1 (1992), pp. 57–70.

51. Verhoef et al., "Service Encounters as a Sequence of Events."

52. G. L. Shostack, "Planning the Service Encounter," in *The Service Encounter,* ed. J. A. Czepiel, M. R. Solomon, and C. F. Surprenant (Lexington, MA: Lexington Books, 1985), pp. 243–254.

53. Ibid.

54. For a complete discussion of the research on which this section is based, see M. J. Bitner, B. H. Booms, and M. S. Tetreault, "The Service Encounter: Diagnosing Favorable and Unfavorable Incidents," *Journal of Marketing* 54 (January 1990), pp. 71–84; M. J. Bitner, B. H. Booms, and L. A. Mohr, "Critical Service Encounters: The Employee's View," *Journal of Marketing* 58 (October 1994), pp. 95–106; D. Gremler and M. J. Bitner, "Classifying Service Encounter Satisfaction Across Industries," in *Marketing Theory and Applications,* ed. C. T. Allen et al. (Chicago: American Marketing Association, 1992), pp. 111–118; D. Gremler, M. J. Bitner, and K. R. Evans, "The Internal Service Encounter," *Journal of Service Industry Management* 5, no. 2 (1994), pp. 34–56.

55. Bitner, Booms, and Mohr, "Critical Service Encounters."

56. This Discussion is based on research and results presented in M. L. Meuter, A. L. Ostrom, R. I. Roundtree, and M. J. Bitner, "Self-Service Technologies: Understanding Customer Satisfaction with Technology-Based Service Encounters," *Journal of Marketing* 64 (July 2000), pp. 50–64.

57. M. J. Bitner, S. W. Brown, and M. L. Meuter, "Technology Infusion in Service Encounters," *Journal of the Academy of Marketing Science* 28 (Winter 2000), pp. 138–149; Parasuraman, Zeithaml, and Malhotra, "E-S-QUAL: A Multiple-Item Scale."

58. Bitner, "Managing the Evidence of Service."

Understanding Customer Requirements

THE LISTENING GAP

Not knowing what customers expect is one of the root causes of not delivering to customer expectations. Provider gap 1, the listening gap, is the difference between customer expectations of service and company understanding of those expectations. Note that in the accompanying figure we created a link between the customer and the company, showing customer expectations above the line that dissects the model, and provider perceptions of those expectations below the line. This alignment signifies that what customers expect is not always the same as what companies believe they expect.

Provider Gap 1

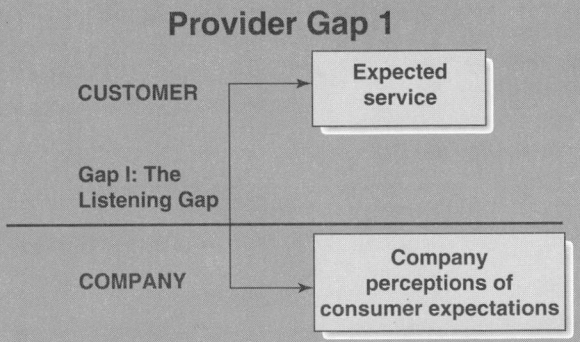

Part 3 describes three ways to close provider gap 1. In Chapter 6, we detail ways that companies listen to customers through research. Both formal and informal methods of customer research are described, including surveys, critical incident studies, and complaint solicitation. Upward communication from frontline employees to managers, another key factor in listening to customers, is also discussed.

Chapter 7 covers company strategies to retain customers and strengthen relationships with them, an approach called relationship marketing. Relationship marketing is distinct from transactional marketing, the more conventional approach that tends to focus on acquiring new customers rather than retaining them. When organizations have strong relationships with existing customers, opportunities for in-depth listening increase over time, and the listening gap is less likely to occur. A variety of strategies, including the creation of switching barriers and the development of relationship bonds, are suggested as a means of relationship development and, ultimately, the cultivation of customer loyalty.

Chapter 8 describes service recovery, the other major strategy needed to close provider gap 1. Service recovery involves understanding why customers complain, what they expect when they complain, and how to deal with service failures. Firms engaged in service recovery must, along with other approaches, create a complaint-handling procedure, empower employees to react in real time to fix failures, and guarantee service. Excellent service recovery strategies seek to gain insight from service failures, allowing firms to better understand customers and their expectations.

Chapter Six

Listening to Customers through Research

This chapter's objectives are to

1. Present the types of and guidelines for marketing research in services.
2. Show how marketing research information can and should be used for services.
3. Describe the strategies by which companies can facilitate interaction and communication between management and customers.
4. Present ways that companies can and do facilitate interaction between contact people and management.

Wachovia Excels at Marketing Research in Services

Wachovia, a megabank originally located in North Carolina but now national, has the best customer satisfaction scores of all banks in the American Customer Satisfaction Index, *Consumer Reports,* and J.D. Power and Associates. Its satisfaction, quality, and loyalty scores have improved steadily since 1999, even during a merger with First Union Bank. A large part of Wachovia's success in delivering excellent service and customer satisfaction is attributable to its strong marketing research program.

Wachovia's service measurement program ensures that delivery in its financial centers and phone centers meets customer expectations. First, the company determined through focus group research the most important aspects of service delivery (such as "makes it easy to do business," "provides unmatched service and advice"), then it created a questionnaire. Every month, Wachovia surveys more than 25,000 customers who have been in the bank within the previous 24 hours. Although the bank has more than 13 million households and businesses who hold accounts at the bank, 25,000 surveys is a significant number no matter what the customer base.[1]

Working with Gallup, Wachovia asks these customers about the key service attributes, and every two weeks, the results are shared directly with the frontline employees who provided the service. Based on the survey results, coaching is offered to the employees in need of improvement. When the bank began its research, it aspired to achieve scores of 6 on the 7-point scale for the service attributes. Now Wachovia regularly achieves scores that exceed 6.65 on all the attributes that matter to customers.

On the same survey, the company also tracks overall customer satisfaction, likelihood to continue to use Wachovia, loyalty, and likelihood to recommend the bank to others. Because it knows that wait times are critical to customer satisfaction, it also measures and tracks the percent of teller wait times that are three minutes or less, aiming for a goal of 85 percent.

This service research is but one of Wachovia's many marketing research studies to listen to customers. The company conducted a major segmentation study to understand precise differences among its customer groups so that offerings and advertising messages can be more targeted. Based on other research, Wachovia changed its online banking website to make it easier to use. Each month the company also collects information to track brand perceptions in all parts of the country, a research study that has been very important in setting bank strategy through the company's merger, logo, and color changes. Other studies gather information about wholesale customers and corporate customers. The company possesses an admirable portfolio of customer research that allows it to listen to and understand its customers clearly.

Despite a genuine interest in meeting customer expectations, many companies miss the mark by thinking inside out—they believe they know what customers *should* want and deliver that, rather than finding out what they *do* want. When this happens, companies provide services that do not match customer expectations: important features are left out, and the levels of performance on features that are provided are inadequate. Because services have few clearly defined and tangible cues, this difficulty may be considerably larger than it is in manufacturing firms. A far better approach involves thinking *outside in*—determining customer expectations and then delivering to them. Thinking outside in uses marketing research to understand customers and their requirements fully. Marketing research, the subject of this chapter, involves far more than conventional surveys. It consists of a portfolio of listening strategies that allow companies to deliver service to customer expectations.

USING MARKETING RESEARCH TO UNDERSTAND CUSTOMER EXPECTATIONS

Finding out what customers expect is essential to providing service quality, and marketing research is a key vehicle for understanding customer expectations and perceptions of services. In services, as with any offering, a firm that does no marketing research at all is unlikely to understand its customers. A firm that does marketing research, but not on the topic of customer expectations, may also fail to know what is needed to stay in tune with changing customer requirements. Marketing research must focus on service issues such as what features are most important to customers, what levels of these features customers expect, and what customers think the company can and should do when problems occur in service delivery. Even when a service firm is small and has limited resources to conduct research, avenues are open to explore what customers expect.

In this section we discuss the elements of services marketing research programs that help companies identify customer expectations and perceptions. In the sections that follow, we will discuss ways in which the tactics of general marketing research may need to be adjusted to maximize its effectiveness in services.

Research Objectives for Services

The first step in designing services marketing research is without doubt the most critical: defining the problem and research objectives. This is where the services marketer poses the questions to be answered or problems to be solved with research. Does the company want to know how customers view the service provided by the company, what customer requirements are, how customers will respond to a new service introduction, or what customers will want from the company five years from now? Each of these research questions requires a different research strategy. Thus, it is essential to devote time and resources to define the problem thoroughly and accurately. In spite of the importance of this first stage, many marketing research studies are initiated without adequate attention to objectives.

Research objectives translate into action questions. While many different questions are likely to be part of a marketing research program, the following are the most common research objectives in services:

- To discover customer requirements or expectations for service.
- To monitor and track service performance.
- To assess overall company performance compared with that of competition.
- To assess gaps between customer expectations and perceptions.
- To identify dissatisfied customers so that service recovery can be attempted.
- To gauge effectiveness of changes in service delivery.
- To appraise the service performance of individuals and teams for evaluation, recognition, and rewards.
- To determine customer expectations for a new service.
- To monitor changing customer expectations in an industry.
- To forecast future expectations of customers.

These research objectives are similar in many ways to the research conducted for physical products: both aim to assess customer requirements, dissatisfaction, and demand. Services research, however, incorporates additional elements that require specific attention.

First, services research must continually monitor and track service performance because performance is subject to human variability and heterogeneity. Conducting performance research at a single point in time, as might be done for a physical product such as an automobile, would be insufficient in services. A major focus of services research involves capturing human performance—at the level of individual employee, team, branch, organization as a whole, and competition. Another focus of services research involves documenting the process by which service is performed. Even when service employees are performing well, a service provider must continue to track performance because the potential for variation in service delivery always exists.

A second distinction in services research is the need to consider and monitor the gap between expectations and perceptions. This gap is dynamic because both perceptions and expectations fluctuate. Does the gap exist because performance is declining, because performance varies with demand and supply level, or because expectations are escalating?

FIGURE 6.1
Criteria for an
Effective Services
Research Program

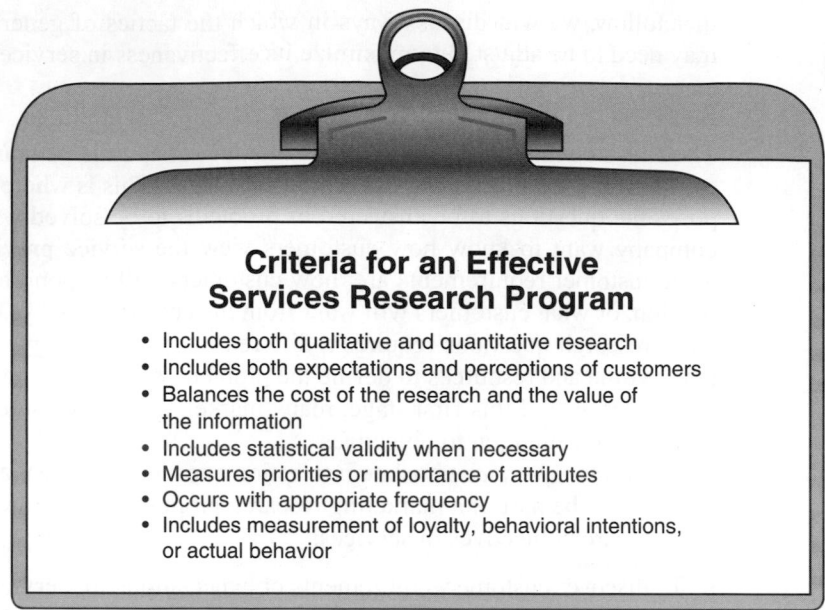

Criteria for an Effective Services Research Program

- Includes both qualitative and quantitative research
- Includes both expectations and perceptions of customers
- Balances the cost of the research and the value of the information
- Includes statistical validity when necessary
- Measures priorities or importance of attributes
- Occurs with appropriate frequency
- Includes measurement of loyalty, behavioral intentions, or actual behavior

Exhibit 6.1 lists a number of services research objectives. Once objectives such as these have been identified, they will point the way to decisions about the most appropriate type of research, methods of data collection, and ways to use the information. The additional columns in this table are described in sections of this chapter.

Criteria for an Effective Services Research Program

A *services research program* can be defined as the composite of separate research studies and types needed to address research objectives and execute an overall measurement strategy. Many types of research could be considered in a research program. Understanding the criteria for an effective services research program (see Figure 6.1) will help a company evaluate different types of research and choose the ones most appropriate for its research objectives. In this section we discuss these criteria.

Includes Qualitative and Quantitative Research

Marketing research is not limited to surveys and statistics. Some forms of research, called *qualitative research,* are exploratory and preliminary and are conducted to clarify problem definition, prepare for more formal research, or gain insight when more formal research is not necessary. Trader Joe's, the specialty food retailer that sells mostly private-label products, listens closely to customers using informal, qualitative research. This research is not done through focus groups or contact centers, and the company has neither a toll-free number nor a customer care e-mail address. The company finds out what customers want by talking to them—managers ("captains") spend most of the day on the floor, where there are always multiple product samplings taking place, and anyone on the sales staff ("crew members") can directly e-mail a buyer to tell them what people are liking or not.[2] Insights gained through one-on-one conversations like those at Trader Joe's, customer focus groups, critical incidents research (described in Chapter 5 and discussed more fully later in this chapter), and direct observation of service transactions show the marketer the right questions to ask of consumers. Because the results of qualitative research play a major role in designing quantitative research, it is often the first type of research done. Qualitative research can also be conducted after quantitative research to make the numbers in computer printouts meaningful by giving managers the perspective and sensitivity that are critical in interpreting data and initiating improvement efforts.[3]

Quantitative research in marketing is designed to describe the nature, attitudes, or behaviors of customers empirically and to test specific hypotheses that a services marketer wants to examine. These studies are key for quantifying the customers' satisfaction, the importance of service attributes, the extent of service quality gaps, and perceptions of value. Such studies also provide managers with yardsticks for evaluating competitors. Finally, results from quantitative studies can highlight specific service deficiencies that can be more deeply probed through follow-up qualitative research.

Includes Both Perceptions and Expectations of Customers

As we discussed in Chapter 4, expectations serve as standards or reference points for customers. In evaluating service quality, customers compare what they perceive they get in a service encounter with their expectations of that encounter. For this reason, a measurement program that captures only perceptions of service is missing a critical part of the service quality equation. Companies need also to incorporate measures of customer expectations.

Measurement of expectations can be included in a research program in multiple ways. First, basic research that relates to customers' requirements—that identifies the service features or attributes that matter to customers—can be considered expectation research. In this form, the *content* of customer expectations is captured, initially in some form of qualitative research such as focus group interviews. Research on the *levels* of customer expectations also is needed. This type of research quantitatively assesses the levels of customer expectations and compares these with perception levels, usually by calculating the gap between expectations and perceptions.

Balances the Cost of the Research and the Value of the Information

An assessment of the cost of research compared with its benefits or value to the company is another key criterion. One cost is monetary, including direct costs to marketing research companies, payments to respondents, and internal company costs incurred by employees collecting the information. Time costs are also important, including the time commitment needed internally by employees to administer the research and the interval between data collection and availability for use by the firm. These and other costs must be weighed against the gains to the company in improved decision making, retained customers, and successful new product launches. As in many other marketing decisions, costs are easier to estimate than the value of the information. For this reason, we include only costs, not value, in Exhibit 6.1. In later chapters we describe approaches to estimating the value of customers to a company, approaches that are useful as input to the trade-off analysis needed to address this criterion.

Includes Statistical Validity When Necessary

We have already shown that research has multiple and diverse objectives. These objectives determine the appropriate type of research and methodology. To illustrate, some research is used by companies not so much to measure as to build relationships with customers—to allow contact employees to find out what customers desire, to diagnose the strengths and weaknesses of their and the firm's efforts to address the desires, to prepare a plan to meet requirements, and to confirm after a period of time

Exhibit 6.1 Elements in an Effective Marketing Research Program for Services

Type of Research	Primary Research Objectives	Qualitative/ Quantitative	Costs of Information		
			Monetary	Time	Frequency
Complaint solicitation	To identify/attend to dissatisfied customers	Qualitative	Low	Low	Continuous
	To identify common service failure points				
Critical incident studies	To identify "best practices" at transaction level	Qualitative	Low	Moderate	Periodic
	To identify customer requirements as input for quantitative studies				
	To identify common service failure points				
	To identify systemic strengths and weaknesses in customer-contact services				
Requirements research	To identify customer requirements as input for quantitative research	Qualitative	Moderate	Moderate	Periodic
Relationship surveys and SERVQUAL surveys	To monitor and track service performance	Quantitative	Moderate	Moderate	Annual
	To assess overall company performance compared with that of competition				
	To determine links between satisfaction and behavioral intentions				
	To assess gaps between customer expectations and perceptions				
Trailer calls or posttransaction surveys	To obtain immediate feedback on performance of service transactions	Quantitative	Low	Low	Continuous
	To measure effectiveness of changes in service delivery				
	To assess service performance of individuals and teams				
	To use as input for process improvements				
	To identify common service failure points				

(usually one year) that the company has executed the plan. The underlying objective of this type of research is to allow contact people to identify specific action items that will gain the maximum return in customer satisfaction for individual customers. This type of research does not need sophisticated quantitative analysis, anonymity of customers, careful control of sampling, or strong statistical controls.

Service expectation meetings and reviews	To create dialogue with important customers	Qualitative	Moderate	Moderate	Annual
	To identify what individual large customers expect and then to ensure that it is delivered				
	To close the loop with important customers				
Process checkpoint evaluations	To determine customer perceptions of long-term professional services during service provision	Quantitative	Moderate	Moderate	Periodic
	To identify service problems and solve them early in the service relationship				
Market-oriented ethnography	To research customers in natural settings	Qualitative	Moderate	High	Periodic
	To study customers from cultures other than America in an unbiased way				
Mystery shopping	To measure individual employee performance for evaluation, or recognition, and rewards	Quantitative Qualitative	Low	Low	Quarterly
	To identify systemic strengths and weaknesses in customer-contact services				
Customer panels	To monitor changing customer expectations	Qualitative	Moderate	Moderate	Continuous
	To provide a forum for customers to suggest and evaluate new service ideas				
Lost customer research	To identify reasons for customer defection	Qualitative	Low	Low	Continuous
	To assess gaps between customer expectations and perceptions				
Future expectations research	To forecast future expectations of customers	Qualitative	High	High	Periodic
	To develop and test new service ideas				
Database marketing research	To identify the individual requirements of customers using information technology and database information	Quantitative	High	High	Continuous

On the other hand, research used to track overall service quality that will be used for bonuses and salary increases of salespeople must be carefully controlled for sampling bias and statistical validity. One of us worked with a company that paid salespeople on the basis of customers' satisfaction scores while allowing the salespeople to control the customers sampled. Obviously, the salespeople quickly learned that they could have surveys sent only to satisfied customers, artificially inflating the scores and—of course—undermining the confidence in the measurement system.

Not all forms of research have statistical validity, and not all forms need it. Most forms of qualitative research, for example, do not possess statistical validity.

Measures Priorities or Importance

Customers have many service requirements, but not all are equally important. One of the most common mistakes managers make in trying to improve service is spending resources on the wrong initiatives, only to become discouraged because customer perceptions of the firm's service does not improve! Measuring the relative importance of service dimensions and attributes helps managers to channel resources effectively; therefore, research must document the priorities of the customer. Prioritization can be accomplished in multiple ways. *Direct importance measures* ask customers to prioritize items or dimensions of service. Several alternatives are available for measuring importance directly, among them asking respondents to rank-order service dimensions or attributes, or to rate them on a scale from "not at all important" to "extremely important." Another effective approach involves asking respondents to allocate a total of 100 points across the various service dimensions. *Indirect importance measures* are estimated using the statistical procedures of correlation and regression analysis, which show the relative contribution of questionnaire items or requirements to overall service quality. Both indirect and direct importance measures provide evidence of customer priorities, and the technique that is chosen depends on the nature of the study and the number of dimensions or attributes that are being evaluated.

Occurs with Appropriate Frequency

Because customer expectations and perceptions are dynamic, companies need to institute a service quality research process, not just do isolated studies. A single study of service provides only a "snapshot" view of one moment in time. For full understanding of the marketplace's acceptance of a company's service, marketing research must be ongoing. Without a pattern of studies repeated with appropriate frequency, managers cannot tell whether the firm is moving forward or falling back and which of their service improvement initiatives are working. Just what does "ongoing research" mean in terms of frequency? The answer is specific to the type of service and to the purpose and method of each type of service research a company might do. As we discuss the different types in the following section, you will see the frequency with which each type of research could be conducted.

Includes Measures of Loyalty, Behavioral Intentions, or Behavior

An important trend in services research involves measuring the positive and negative consequences of service quality along with overall satisfaction or service quality scores. Among the most important generic *behavioral intentions* are willingness to recommend the service to others and repurchase intent. These behavioral intentions can be viewed as positive and negative consequences of service quality. Positive behavioral intentions include saying positive things about the company, recommending the company to others, remaining loyal, spending more with the company, and paying a price premium. Negative behavioral intentions include saying negative things to others, doing less business with the company, switching to another company, and complaining to outside organizations such as the Better Business Bureau. Other more specific behaviors differ by service; for example, behaviors related to medical care include following instructions from the doctor, taking medications, and returning for follow-up. Tracking these areas can help a company estimate the relative value of service improvements to the company and can also identify customers who are in danger of defecting.

ELEMENTS IN AN EFFECTIVE SERVICES MARKETING RESEARCH PROGRAM

A good services marketing research program includes multiple types of research studies. The composite of studies and types of research will differ by company because the range of uses for service quality research—from employee performance assessment to advertising campaign development to strategic planning—requires a rich, multifaceted flow of information. If a company were to engage in virtually all types of service research, the portfolio would look like Exhibit 6.1, but few companies do all types of research. The particular portfolio for any company will match company resources and address the key areas needed to understand the customers of the business. So that it will be easier for you to identify the appropriate type of research for different research objectives, we list the objectives in column 2 of Exhibit 6.1. In the following sections we describe each major type of research and show the way each type addresses the criteria associated with it. The Technology Spotlight discusses research conducted online.

Complaint Solicitation

Many of you have complained to employees of service organizations, only to find that nothing happens with your complaint. No one rushes to solve it, and the next time you experience the service the same problem is present. How frustrating! Good service organizations take complaints seriously. Not only do they listen to complaints—they also employ *complaint solicitation* as a way of communicating about what can be done

Participants in a focus group discuss services using the critical incident technique.

to improve their service and their service employees. Vail Resorts, which owns the Vail, Breckenridge, Heavenly, Keystone, and Beaver Creek resorts, has an innovative way to capture complaints and comments of its customers. The resort hires researchers to ride the lifts with skiers and ask and record into handheld computer devices customers' responses to questions about their perceptions of the resorts. Then the researchers ski down the mountain and ride up again with other customers. At the end of the day, the researchers download the results into a computer at the base. The researchers survey 200 skiers per week, looking for patterns of customer comments and complaints. For example, if the researchers receive a number of complaints about certain lift lines or service in one of the restaurants, they will alert managers in those areas so the problems can be resolved quickly. At the end of the week, the data are collected and reported at weekly meetings.

Firms that use complaints as research collect and document them, then use the information to identify dissatisfied customers, correct individual problems

Technology Spotlight Conducting Marketing Research on the Web

One of the most intriguing applications of the Internet is online research, replacing comment cards and intrusive telephone calls with cyber-surveys that are challenging and fun for consumers. The application is growing rapidly. In 2005, companies spent more than $1.1 billion on online market research, a 16 percent increase over 2004. Annual spending is expected to reach $26 billion by 2010. The reasons are obvious—Internet research has many benefits to marketers besides more willing respondents, including the following:

- *Speed.* Rather than three to four months required to collect data through mail questionnaires, or six to eight weeks needed to train interviewers and obtain data from telephone questionnaires, online surveys can be prepared and executed quickly. A sample of 300 to 400, large enough for many studies, can be completed in a weekend and the results made available for viewing by clients on a secure website the following week. One market research firm reportedly completed 1,000 customer satisfaction surveys in only two hours.

- *Equivalent quality.* Deutskens and colleagues found that the quality of the data when using an online method is comparable: "in the context of a large business-to-business service quality assessment, an analysis of the accuracy and completeness of respondent answers to both open and closed questions suggests that online and mail surveys produce equivalent results."[4]

- *Ability to target hard-to-reach populations.* One of the traditional difficulties in research, particularly segmentation research, is to identify and access respondents who fit a particular lifestyle

or interest profile. The hard-to-reach, business-to-business market accounts for about a quarter of all marketing research studies conducted by U.S. research firms. Doctors, lawyers, professionals, and working mothers are all valuable but difficult-to-access groups of customers. These people might read special interest magazines (such as professional or hobby publications) that are expensive to advertise in. They could be reached in surveys only by having the service company purchase at great cost the mailing list of that magazine. However, online sites for special interests are quite simple to identify, access, and insert survey banners in.

- *Ability to target customers with money.* Online research allows service companies to reach customers who have higher incomes, higher education levels, and greater willingness to spend. Consumers with computers who use online services regularly tend to be in these demographic target groups, and they can be effectively surveyed with online research. Compared with the sample that would be obtained from traditional research using all telephone subscribers, the sample of online users is often far better in terms of marketing potential.

- *Opportunity to use multimedia to present video and audio.* Telephone surveys are limited to voice alone, whereas mail surveys are constrained to two-dimensional visuals. In the past, to present the full range of audio and video needed to give respondents the true sense of a service being researched, surveys had to be conducted in person and were, therefore, very expensive ($30 to $150 per person, depending on the topic and sample). Online research offers broader stimuli potential through all multimedia possibilities at a fraction of the cost.

where possible, and identify common service failure points. Although this research is used for both goods and services, it has a critical real-time purpose in services—to improve failure points and to improve or correct the performance of contact personnel. Research on complaints is one of the easiest types of research for firms to conduct, leading many companies to depend solely on complaints to stay in touch with customers. Unfortunately, there is evidence suggesting that customer complaints alone are a woefully inadequate source of information. As discussed in Chapter 8, only a small percentage of customers with problems actually complain to the company; the rest will stay dissatisfied, telling other people about their dissatisfaction.

To be effective, complaint solicitation requires rigorous recording of numbers and types of complaints through many channels and then working to eliminate the most frequent problems. Complaint channels include employees at the front line, intermediary

- *No interviewers*—and therefore no interviewer errors or interviewer bias. Bias occurs when the interviewer is in a bad mood, tired, impatient, or not objective. These problems occur with human interviews but not cyber-interviews.

- *Control over data quality,* which can eliminate contradictory or nonsensical answers. With traditional surveys, researchers need a step called "data cleaning and editing" in which all data are checked for such problems; electronic checks can be built into online surveys that take care of this problem as it occurs.

- *Inexpensive research.* Data collection costs can be the most expensive part of a study, and the most expensive part of data collection can be paying subjects to participate. Online marketing research, astonishingly, is 10 to 80 percent less expensive than other approaches. The Internet also eliminates postage, phone, labor, and printing costs that are typical with other survey approaches. Respondents also seem to complete Web-based surveys in half the time it would take an interviewer to conduct the survey, perhaps contributing to the lack of need for incentives.

One additional, but to date undersubstantiated, benefit is higher response rate—reportedly as high as 70 percent—possibly stemming from the fact that the interactive nature of cyber-research can make answering surveys fun for respondents. While it is getting more difficult to get consumers to answer traditional surveys, the entertainment value of cyber-surveys makes it easier to recruit participants. One study shows that consumers are five times more likely to complete an electronic survey as they are to

do the same survey with written materials and that researchers obtain the following three additional benefits: (1) consumers "play" an e-survey longer, answering more questions than in a traditional survey; (2) people tend to concentrate more fully on their answers; and (3) the entertainment value of an e-survey actually lowers the respondent's perceived time to complete the survey.

The advantages of online research likely far outnumber the disadvantages. However, marketers need to be aware that there are also drawbacks. Perhaps the major problem is the composition of the sample. Unlike the process used with most telephone and mail surveys, the population of responders is not usually selected but is a matter of convenience, consisting of whomever responds to the survey. This is a particular problem when respondents are recruited from other websites and click through to the survey. In these cases, marketers may not even know who the responders are and whether they are in fact the right profile for answering the survey. To address this problem, companies are prequalifying respondents by telephone or e-mail, then asking for enough demographic information to ensure that the respondents meet the desired requirements. They can also ask qualifying questions early in the web survey to screen respondents.

Sources: R. Weible and J. Wallace, "Cyber Research: The Impact of the Internet on Data Collection," *Marketing Research,* Fall 1998, pp. 19–24; R. Nadilo, "On-Line Research Taps Consumers Who Spend," *Marketing News,* June 8, 1998, p. 12; A. Hogg, "Online Research Overview," MarketingPower.com, updated 2004; R. Kottler, "Eight Tips Offer Best Practices for Online Market Research, *Marketing News,* April I, 2005; C. Li and S. Van Boskirk, "U.S. Online Marketing Forecast: 2005–2010," forrester.com, May 2, 2005.

organizations like retailers who deliver service, managers, and complaints to third parties such as customer advocate groups. Companies must both solve individual customer problems and identify overall patterns to eliminate failure points. More sophisticated forms of complaint resolution define "complaint" broadly to include all comments—both negative and positive—as well as questions from customers. Firms should build depositories for this information and report results frequently, perhaps weekly or monthly.

Critical Incidents Studies

The *critical incident technique (CIT),* a qualitative interview procedure in which customers are asked to provide verbatim stories about satisfying and dissatisfying service encounters they have experienced. According to a recent summary of the use of the technique in services, CIT has been to study satisfaction in hotels, restaurants, airlines, amusement parks, automotive repair, retailing, banking, cable television, public transportation, and education.[5] The studies have explored a wide range of service topics: consumer evaluation of services, service failure and recovery, employees, customer participation in service delivery, and service experience.[6] With this technique, customers (either internal or external) are asked the following questions:

Think of a time when, as a customer, you had a particularly *satisfying* (or *dissatisfying*) interaction.

When did the incident happen?

What specific circumstances led up to this situation?

Exactly what did the employee (or firm member) say or do?

What resulted that made you feel the interaction was *satisfying* (or *dissatisfying*)?

What could or should have been done differently?

Sometimes contact employees are asked to put themselves in the shoes of a customer and answer the same questions: "Put yourself in the shoes of *customers* of your firm. In other words, try to see your firm through your customers' eyes. Now think of a recent time when a customer of your firm had a particularly *satisfying/unsatisfying* interaction with you or a fellow employee." The stories are then analyzed to determine common themes of satisfaction/dissatisfaction underlying the events. In Chapter 5, we described the four common themes—recovery (after failure), adaptability, spontaneity, and coping—that have been identified through research. Individual companies conduct these studies to identify specific satisfying and dissatisfying about their firms or industries.

CIT has many benefits. First, data are collected from the respondent's perspective and are usually vivid because they are expressed in consumers' own words and reflect the way they think. Second, the method provides concrete information about the way the company and its employees behave and react, thereby making the research easy to translate into action. Third, like most qualitative methods, the research is particularly useful when the topic or service is new and very little other information exists. Finally, the method is well suited for assessing perceptions of customers from different cultures because it allows respondents to share their perceptions rather than answer researcher-defined questions.[7]

Requirements Research

Requirements research involves identifying the benefits and attributes that customers expect in a service. This type of research is very basic and essential because it determines the type of questions that will be asked in surveys and ultimately the improvements that will be attempted by the firm. Because these studies are so foundational, qualitative techniques are appropriate to begin them. Quantitative techniques may follow, usually during a pretest stage of survey development. Unfortunately, many companies do inadequate requirements research, often developing surveys on the basis of intuition or company direction rather than thorough customer probing.

An example of requirements research is *structured brainstorming,* a technique developed by researchers in IBM's Advanced Business Systems unit.[8] In this technique a sample of customers and potential customers is assembled. A facilitator leads the group through a series of exercises on creativity and then has the customers describe the ideal provider of the service—what they would want if they could have their ideal service. The facilitator asks "what" customers want (to elicit fundamental requirements), "why" they want it (to elicit the underlying need or benefit sought), and "how" they will know when they receive it (to elicit specific service features).

Another approach to requirements research that has been effective in services industries is to examine existing research about customer requirements in similar service industries. The five dimensions of quality service are generalizable across industries, and sometimes the way these dimensions are manifest is also remarkably similar. Hospital patients and customers of hotels, for example, expect many of the same features when using these two services. Besides expert medical care, patients in hospitals expect comfortable rooms, courteous staff, and food that tastes good—the same features that are salient to hotel customers. In these and other industries that share common customer expectations, managers may find it helpful to seek knowledge from existing research in the related service industry. Because hotels have used marketing and marketing research longer than hospitals have, insights about hotel guests' expectations can inform about patients' expectations. Hospital administrators at Albert Einstein Medical Center in Philadelphia, for example, asked a group of nine local hotel executives for advice in understanding and handling patients. Many improvements resulted, including better food, easier-to-read name tags, more prominent information desks, and radios in many rooms.[9]

Relationship and SERVQUAL Surveys

One category of surveys could appropriately be named *relationship surveys* because they pose questions about all elements in the customer's relationship with the company (including service, product, and price). This comprehensive approach can help a company diagnose its relationship strengths and weaknesses. For example, Federal Express conducts a number of different customer satisfaction studies to assess satisfaction, identify reasons for dissatisfaction, and monitor satisfaction over time. They conduct 2,400 telephone interviews per quarter, measuring 17 domestic service attributes, 22 export service attributes, 8 drop-box attributes, and 8 service center attributes. They also conduct 10 targeted satisfaction studies on specialized business functions.

Relationship surveys typically monitor and track service performance annually, with an initial survey providing a baseline. Relationship surveys are also effective in comparing company performance with that of competitors, often focusing on the best competitor's performance as a benchmark. When used for this purpose, the sponsor of the survey is not identified, and questions are asked about both the focal company and one or more competitors.

A sound measure of service quality is necessary for identifying the aspects of service needing performance improvement, assessing how much improvement is needed on each aspect, and evaluating the impact of improvement efforts. Unlike goods quality, which can be measured objectively by such indicators as durability and number of defects, service quality is abstract and is best captured by surveys that measure customer evaluations of service. One of the first measures to be developed specifically to measure service quality was the *SERVQUAL survey.*

The SERVQUAL scale involves a survey containing 21 service attributes, grouped into the five service quality dimensions (discussed in Chapter 5) of reliability, responsiveness, assurance, empathy, and tangibles. The survey sometimes asks customers to provide two different ratings on each attribute—one reflecting the level of service they would expect from excellent companies in a sector and the other reflecting their perception of the service delivered by a specific company within that sector. The difference between the expectation and perception ratings constitutes a quantified measure of service quality. Exhibit 6.2 shows the items on the basic SERVQUAL scale as well

The SERVQUAL scale was first published in 1988 and has undergone numerous improvements and revisions since then. The scale currently contains 21 perception items that are distributed throughout the five service quality dimensions. The scale also contains expectation items.

Although many different formats of the SERVQUAL scale are now in use, we show here the basic 21 perception items as well as a sampling of ways the expectation items have been posed.

PERCEPTIONS

Perceptions Statements in the Reliability Dimension

	Strongly disagree						Strongly agree
1. When XYZ Company promises to do something by a certain time, it does so.	1	2	3	4	5	6	7
2. When you have a problem, XYZ Company shows a sincere interest in solving it.	1	2	3	4	5	6	7
3. XYZ Company performs the service right the first time.	1	2	3	4	5	6	7
4. XYZ Company provides its services at the time it promises to do so.	1	2	3	4	5	6	7
5. XYZ Company insists on error-free records.	1	2	3	4	5	6	7

Statements in the Responsiveness Dimension

1. XYZ Company keeps customers informed about when services will be performed.	1	2	3	4	5	6	7
2. Employees in XYZ Company give you prompt service.	1	2	3	4	5	6	7
3. Employees in XYZ Company are always willing to help you.	1	2	3	4	5	6	7
4. Employees in XYZ Company are never too busy to respond to your request.	1	2	3	4	5	6	7

Statements in the Assurance Dimension

1. The behavior of employees in XYZ Company instills confidence in you.	1	2	3	4	5	6	7
2. You feel safe in your transactions with XYZ Company.	1	2	3	4	5	6	7
3. Employees in XYZ Company are consistently courteous with you.	1	2	3	4	5	6	7
4. Employees in XYZ Company have the knowledge to answer your questions.	1	2	3	4	5	6	7

Statements in the Empathy Dimension

1. XYZ Company gives you individual attention.	1	2	3	4	5	6	7
2. XYZ Company has employees who give you personal attention.	1	2	3	4	5	6	7
3. XYZ Company has your best interests at heart.	1	2	3	4	5	6	7
4. Employees of XYZ Company understand your specific needs.	1	2	3	4	5	6	7
5. XYZ Company has operating hours that are convenient to all its customers.	1	2	3	4	5	6	7

Statements in the Tangibles Dimension	Strongly disagree						Strongly agree
1. XYZ Company has modern-looking equipment.	1	2	3	4	5	6	7
2. XYZ Company's physical facilities are visually appealing.	1	2	3	4	5	6	7
3. XYZ Company's employees appear neat.	1	2	3	4	5	6	7
4. Materials associated with the service (such as pamphlets or statements) are visually appealing at XYZ Company.	1	2	3	4	5	6	7

EXPECTATIONS: Several Formats for Measuring Customer Expectations Using Versions of SERVQUAL

There are a number of different ways that expectations can be asked in surveys. We present four of these types below: (l) matching expectations statements, (2) referent expectations formats, (3) statements that combine both expectations and perceptions, and (4) statements that cover different types of expectations.

Matching Expectations Statements (Paired with the Previous Perception Statements)

	Strongly disagree						Strongly agree
When customers have a problem, excellent firms will show a sincere interest in solving it.	1	2	3	4	5	6	7

Referent Expectations Formats

1. Considering a "world-class" company to be a "7," how would you rate XYZ Company's performance on the following service features?

	Low						High
Sincere, interested employees	1	2	3	4	5	6	7
Service delivered right the first time	1	2	3	4	5	6	7

2. Compared with the level of service you expect from an excellent company, how would you rate XYZ Company's performance on the following?

	Low						High
Sincere, interested employees	1	2	3	4	5	6	7
Service delivered right the first time	1	2	3	4	5	6	7

Combined Expectations/Perceptions Statements

For each of the following statements, circle the number that indicates how XYZ Company's service compares with the level you expect:

	Lower than my desired service level			The same as my desired service level			Higher than my desired service level		
1. Prompt service	1	2	3	4	5	6	7	8	9
2. Courteous employees	1	2	3	4	5	6	7	8	9

(continued)

Exhibit 6.2   (concluded)

Expectations Distinguishing between Desired Service and Adequate Service

For each of the following statements, circle the number that indicates how XYZ Company's performance compares with your *minimum service level* and with your *desired service level*.

When it comes to ...	Compared with my *minimum* service level XYZ's service performance is:									Compared with my *desired* service level XYZ's service performance is:								
	Lower				Same				Higher	Lower				Same				Higher
1. Prompt service	1	2	3	4	5	6	7	8	9	1	2	3	4	5	6	7	8	9
2. Employees who are consistently courteous	1	2	3	4	5	6	7	8	9	1	2	3	4	5	6	7	8	9

Source: A. Parasuraman, V. A. Zeithaml, and L. L. Berry, "SERVQUAL: A Multiple-Item Scale for Measuring Consumer Perceptions of Service Quality," *Journal of Retailing* 64, no. 1 (Spring 1988). Reprinted by permission of C. Samuel Craig.

as the phrasing of the expectations and perceptions portions of the scale.[10] Data gathered through a SERVQUAL survey can be used for a variety of purposes:

- To determine the average gap score (between customers' perceptions and expectations) for each service attribute.
- To assess a company's service quality along each of the five SERVQUAL dimensions.
- To track customers' expectations and perceptions (on individual service attributes and/or on the SERVQUAL dimensions) over time.
- To compare a company's SERVQUAL scores against those of competitors.
- To identify and examine customer segments that differ significantly in their assessments of a company's service performance.
- To assess internal service quality (that is, the quality of service rendered by one department or division of a company to others within the same company).

This instrument spawned many studies focusing on service quality assessment and is used all over the world in service industries. Published studies have used SERVQUAL and adaptations of it in a variety of contexts: real estate brokers, physicians in private practice, public recreation programs, dental schools, business school placement centers, tire stores, motor carrier companies, accounting firms, discount and department stores, gas and electric utility companies, hospitals, banking, pest control, dry cleaning, fast food, and higher education.

Trailer Calls or Posttransaction Surveys

Whereas the purpose of SERVQUAL and relationship surveys is usually to gauge the overall relationship with the customer, the purpose of transaction surveys is to capture information about key service encounters with the customer. In this method, customers are asked a short list of questions immediately after a particular transaction (hence the name *trailer calls*) about their satisfaction with the transaction and contact personnel with whom they interacted. Because the surveys are administered continuously to a broad spectrum of customers, they are more effective than complaint solicitation (where the information comes only from dissatisfied customers).

At checkout, immediately after staying at Fairfield Inns, customers are asked to use a computer terminal to answer four or five questions about their stay in the hotel. This novel approach has obvious benefits over the ubiquitous comment cards left in rooms—the response rate is far higher because the process engages customers and takes only a few minutes. In other companies, transaction surveys are administered by telephone within a couple of days after a transaction such as installation of durable goods or claims adjustment in insurance. Because they are timed to occur close to service transactions, these surveys are useful in identifying sources of dissatisfaction and satisfaction. For example, Enterprise Rent-A-Car often calls customers a day after a car has been rented (and is still in the customer's possession) to ensure that customers are satisfied with the rental. If the customer has problems with the car (a broken window, a nonworking radio), a new car is provided at no charge to the customer.

A strong benefit of this type of research is that it often appears to customers that the call is following up to ensure that they are satisfied; consequently the call does double duty as a market research tool and as customer service. This type of research is simple and fresh and provides management with continuous information about interactions with customers. Further, the research allows management to associate service quality performance with individual contact personnel so that high performance can be rewarded and low performance corrected. It also serves as an incentive for employees to provide better service because they understand how and when they are being evaluated. One posttransaction study that you may be familiar with is the BizRate. com study that follows online purchases. When a consumer makes a purchase at one of BizRate's online partners (which include many major companies), a message automatically pops up on the site and invites consumers to fill out a survey. Consumers who agree are asked questions about ease of ordering, product selection, website navigation, and customer support.

Service Expectation Meetings and Reviews

In business-to-business situations when large accounts are involved, a form of customer research that is highly effective involves eliciting the expectations of the client at a specified time of the year and then following up later (usually after a year) to determine whether the expectations were fulfilled. Even when the company produces a physical product, the meetings deal almost completely with the service expected and provided by an account or sales team assigned to the client. Unlike other forms of research we have discussed, these meetings are not conducted by objective and unbiased researchers but are instead initiated and facilitated by senior members of the account team so that they can listen carefully to the client's expectations. You may be surprised to find that such interaction does not come naturally to sales teams who are used to talking *to* clients rather than listening carefully to their needs. Consequently, teams have to be carefully trained not to defend or explain but instead to comprehend. One company found that the only way it could teach its salespeople not to talk on these interviews was to take a marketing researcher along to gently kick the salesperson under the table whenever he or she strayed from the format!

The format, when appropriate, consists of (1) asking clients what they expect in terms of 8 to 10 basic requirements determined from focus group research, (2) inquiring what particular aspects of these requirements the account team performed well in the past as well as what aspects need improvement, and (3) requesting that the client rank the relative importance of the requirements. After getting the input, senior account members go back to their teams and plan their goals for the year around client requirements. The next step is verifying with the client that the account plan will satisfy requirements or, when it will not, managing expectations to let the client know what cannot be accomplished. After executing the plan for the year, the senior account personnel then return to the client, determine whether the plan has been successfully executed and expectations met, then establish a new set of expectations for the coming year.

Process Checkpoint Evaluations

With professional services such as consulting, construction, and architecture, services are provided over a long period, and there are no obvious ways or times to collect customer information. Waiting until the entire project is complete—which could last years—is undesirable because myriad unresolvable problems could have occurred by then. But discrete service encounters to calibrate customer perceptions are also not usually available. In these situations, the smart service provider defines a process for delivering the services and then structures the feedback around the process, checking in at frequent points to ensure that the client's expectations are being met. For example, a management consulting firm might establish the following process for delivering its services to clients: (1) collect information, (2) diagnose problems, (3) recommend alternative solutions, (4) select alternatives, and (5) implement solutions. Next, it could agree with the client up front that it will communicate at major *process checkpoints*—after diagnosing the problem, before selecting the alternative, and so on—to make certain that the job is progressing as planned.

Market-Oriented Ethnography

Many of the types of research we discuss in this section are particularly relevant for the United States and cultures similar to it. Structured questionnaires, for example, make key assumptions about what people are conscious of or can recall about their behavior and what they are willing to explain to researchers about their opinions. These assumptions are based on American culture. Even focus group interviews are inherently culture based because they depend on norms of participation, or what people are willing to say in front of others and to researchers. To fully understand how customers of other cultures assess and use services, it may be necessary and effective to use other approaches, such as *market-oriented ethnography*. This set of approaches allows researchers to observe consumption behavior in natural settings. The goal is to enter the consumer's world as much as possible—observing how and when a service is used in an actual home environment or consumption environment, such as watching consumers eat in restaurants or attend concerts. Among the techniques used are observation, interviews, documents, and examination of material possessions such as artifacts. Observation involves entering the experience as a participant observer and watching what occurs rather than asking questions about it. One-on-one interviews, particularly with key informants in the culture

In professional services, evaluations are made at important checkpoints in the process.

rather than consumers themselves, can provide compelling insights about culture-based behavior. Studying existing documents and cultural artifacts can also provide valuable insights, especially about lifestyles and usage patterns.[11]

Best Western International used this technique to better understand its senior market. Rather than bringing participants into focus group facilities and asking them questions, the company paid 25 over-55 couples to videotape themselves on cross-country journeys. The firm was able to listen to how couples actually made decisions rather than the way they reported them. The insights they gained from this research were decidedly different from what they would have learned otherwise. Most noteworthy was the finding that seniors who talked hotel clerks into better deals on rooms did not need the lower price to afford staying at the hotel—they were simply after the thrill of the deal, as illustrated in this description:

> The 60-ish woman caught on the grainy videotape is sitting on her hotel bed, addressing her husband after a long day spent on the road. "Good job!" she exults. "We beat the s—t out of the front desk and got a terrific room."[12]

These customers then spent their discount money on better dinners elsewhere, contributing nothing to Best Western. "The degree of discount clearly isn't what it used to be in importance—and we got that right out of the research," claimed the manager of programs for Best Western.[13] This finding would be highly unlikely using traditional research and asking customers directly, for few customers would admit to being willing to pay a higher price for a service!

Mystery Shopping

In this form of research, which is unique to services,[14] companies hire outside research organizations to send people into service establishments and experience the service as if they were customers. These *mystery shoppers* are trained in the criteria important to customers of the establishment. They deliver objective assessments about service performance by completing questionnaires about service standards or, in other cases, open-ended questions that have a qualitative feel to them. Questionnaires contain items that represent important quality or service issues to customers. Au Bon Pain, for example, sends mystery shoppers to its stores to buy meals and then complete questionnaires about the servers, the restaurant, and the food. Servers are evaluated on standards that include the following:

> Acknowledged within three seconds after reaching first place in line.
>
> Acknowledged pleasantly.
>
> Server suggested additional items.
>
> Server requested payment prior to delivering order.
>
> Received receipt.
>
> Received correct change.
>
> Correct order received.

Au Bon Pain motivates workers to perform to service standards by using the mystery shopper program as a key element in its compensation and reward system. Individual workers who receive positive scores have their names posted on the store's bulletin board and receive letters of congratulations as well as bonuses. Managers whose stores earn high scores can receive on-the-spot bonuses of "Club Excellence" dollars that can be traded like green stamps for items in a company catalog. Perhaps more important, the overall scores received by shift and district managers qualify them for monthly profit-sharing cash bonuses. A score lower than 78 percent removes them from consideration for a bonus, whereas high numbers lead to good bonuses.

Mystery shopping keeps workers on their toes because they know they may be evaluated at any time. They know they are being judged on the company's service standards and therefore carry out the standards more consistently than if they were not going to be judged. Mystery shopping can be a very effective way of reinforcing service standards.

Customer Panels

Customer panels are groups of customers assembled to provide attitudes and perceptions about a service over time. They offer company regular and timely customer information—virtually a pulse on the market. Firms can use customer panels to represent large segments of end customers.

Customer panels are used in the entertainment industry to screen movies before they are released to the public. After a rough cut of a film has been created, the movie is viewed by a panel of consumers that matches the demographic target. In the most basic of these panels, consumers participate in postscreening interviews or focus groups in which they report on their responses to the movie. They may be asked questions as general as their reactions to the ending of the movie and as specific as whether they understood different aspects of the plot line. Based on these panels, movies are revised and edited to ensure that they are communicating the desired message and that they will succeed in the marketplace. In extreme situations, entire endings of movies have been changed to be more consistent with customer attitudes. In some of the most sophisticated consumer panel research on movies (also used for television shows and commercials), consumers have digital devices in their seats through which they indicate their responses as they watch films. This instantaneous response allows the producers, directors, and editors to make changes at the appropriate places in the film to ensure that the story line, characters, and scenery are "tracking."

Lost Customer Research

This type of research involves deliberately seeking customers who have dropped the company's service to inquire about their reasons for leaving. Some *lost customer research* is similar to exit interviews with employees in that it asks open-ended, in-depth questions to expose the reasons for defection and the particular events that led to dissatisfaction. It is also possible to use more standard surveys on lost customers. For example, a Midwestern manufacturer used a mail survey to ask former customers about its performance during different stages of the customer–vendor relationship. The survey also sought specific reasons for customers' defections and asked customers to describe problems that triggered their decreases in purchases.[15]

One benefit of this type of research is that it identifies failure points and common problems in the service and can help establish an early-warning system for future defectors. Another benefit is that the research can be used to calculate the cost of lost customers.

Future Expectations Research

Customer expectations are dynamic and can change very rapidly in markets that are highly competitive and volatile. As competition increases, as tastes change, and as consumers become more knowledgeable, companies must continue to update their information and strategies. In dynamic market situations, companies want to understand

FIGURE 6.2
Tracking of Customer Expectations and Perceptions of Service Reliability

Source: E. Sivadas, "Europeans Have a Different Take on CS [Customer Satisfaction] Programs," *Marketing News,* October 26, 1998, p. 39. Reprinted by permission of the American Marketing Association.

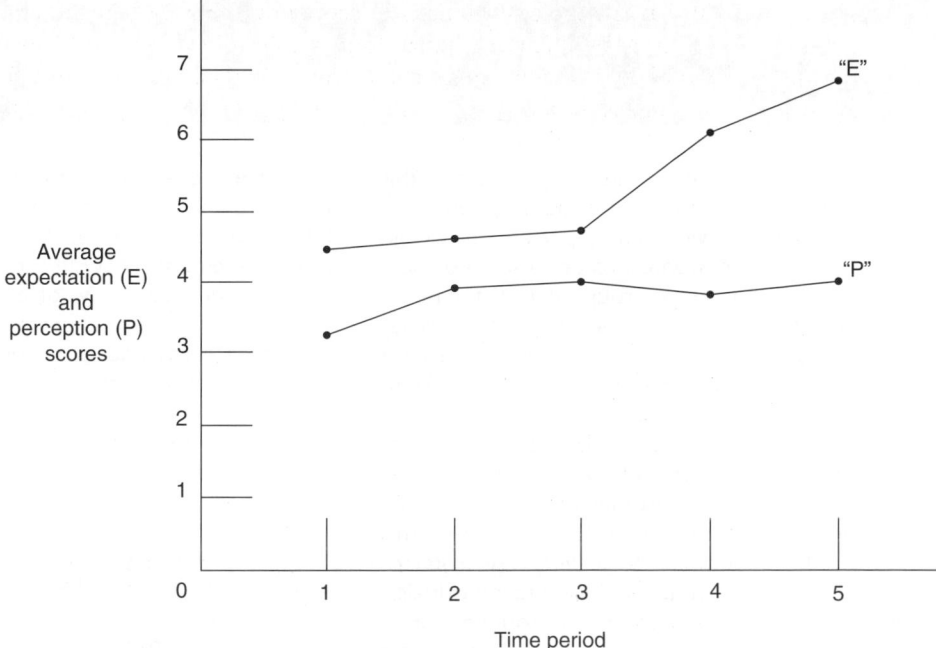

not just current customer expectations but also future expectations—the service features desired in the future. *Future expectations research* is new and includes different types. First, *features research* involves environmental scanning and querying of customers about desirable features of possible services. *Lead user research* brings in customers who are opinion leaders/innovators and asks them what requirements are not currently being met by existing products or services. Another form of this research is the *synectics approach,* which defines lead users more broadly than in standard lead user research.

The question of customer involvement in expectation studies is often debated. Designers and developers claim that consumers do not know what they might want, especially in industries or services that are new and rapidly changing. Consumers and marketing researchers, on the other hand, counter that services developed independent of customer input are likely to be targeted at needs that do not exist. To study this question, researchers assessed the contributions made by users compared with professional developers for end-user telecom services. Three groups were studied: users alone, developers alone, and users with a design expert present to provide information on feasibility. Findings showed that users created more original but less producible ideas. However, inviting users to test and explore possibilities once a prototype has been created can produce positive results.[16]

ANALYZING AND INTERPRETING MARKETING RESEARCH FINDINGS

One of the biggest challenges facing a marketing researcher is converting a complex set of data to a form that can be read and understood quickly by executives, managers, and other employees who will make decisions from the research. For example, database management is being adopted as a strategic initiative by many firms (see the Strategy Insight box), but merely having a sophisticated database does not ensure

Strategy Insight From Greeting Cards to Gambling, Companies Bet on Database Marketing Research

Most of the marketing research approaches in this chapter study patterns of customers in groups. Surveys examine the service quality perceptions of the totality of a firm's customers to get a sense of how they feel as a group. Focus groups identify the needs of important service segments, and lost customer research pinpoints the primary reasons why exiting customers are dissatisfied enough to leave the company. However, an important and powerful form of research—called *database marketing* or *customer relationship management (CRM)*—studies customers one by one to develop profiles on their individual needs, behaviors, and responses to marketing. This approach allows a company to get very close to its customers and to tailor services uniquely to individuals.

Individual customer research is founded on a database that allows a company to tell customers apart and remember them uniquely. You may be most familiar with this form of data collection in grocery store loyalty cards—like VIC for Harris Teeter or MVP for Food Lion—that capture information about your purchases and offer you tailored coupons and specials based on your buying patterns. One of the most familiar examples of using a technology database to remember customers is the Ritz-Carlton's frequent guest registry, which documents preferences of each frequent guest. (Does he like a smoking or nonsmoking room? Feather pillows? Does she read *USA Today* or *The Wall Street Journal?*) Each time a guest visits, new observations about preferences are entered so that the institution itself comes to "know" each guest.

Here are two of the most innovative examples of database marketing and how they are applied to understand and market to individual customers:

HALLMARK GOLD CROWN

Hallmark's database, capable of recognizing customers in all 4,200 Hallmark retail stores, tracks purchases, contacts, and communications so that it learns what each customer individually values about the relationship with the company. This information includes what core product or benefit has the most value to the customer and what differentiates Hallmark from its competition. The mechanism by which the company tracks this information is a Gold Crown Card that customers use to accumulate points for purchases. They receive personalized point statements, newsletters, reward certificates, and individualized news of products and events at local stores. The top 10 percent of customers—who buy more cards and ornaments than others—get special amenities such as longer bonus periods and their own private priority toll-free number, as well as very targeted communication about the specific products they value:

> We are using our data to learn more about our customers and give them what they want. Ornament lovers want to hear all about new products. They want to hear a lot of product info, and they want it as soon as possible. Knowing this, we are able to isolate them and give them just what they want. Other segments represent busy women who want the shortened version—tell me the short notes, the highlights of what I need to know for Valentine's Day, is there a bonus offer, where is my reward certificate? Our whole goal is to respond to what our customers are telling us with their purchases. It really is a dialogue.

Hallmark turns the information it collects into one-on-one marketing communications using three key aspects of consumer shopping behavior: types of products purchased, purchase frequency, and time since last purchase. If the customer has not been in the stores for a period of time, the company sends a special offer to bring her back. If she has been in recently, a thank you message is mailed. When the customers' favorite items are in season—such as ornaments at Christmas—offers and information are mailed to encourage purchase.

Several times a year Hallmark executives sit down with preferred and regular members to hear how they feel about the program, what they would like to see added or changed, and how they react to product offerings. Results of the program have been impressive. The program has more than 17 million permanent cardholders, 10 million who have purchased in the last 6-month period, and over

12 million who have purchased in the last 12 months. Member sales represent 35 percent of total store transactions and 45 percent of total store sales.

HARRAH'S ENTERTAINMENT INC.

The gambling industry has long recognized that certain customers are better than others and that encouraging the "high rollers" to spend time in one's casinos is a worthwhile and profitable strategy. One of the main ways they encourage increased patronage is "comping"—giving free drinks, hotel rooms, limousines, and sometimes chips to top customers. The strategy has been limited in most casinos to customers who could be identified and followed, making the approach spotty and missing many potential repeat patrons. Harrah's Entertainment, which owns and operates 26 gambling casinos in places such as Las Vegas and Atlantic City, found a more systematic way to extend the practice to a wider group of customers. Harrah's developed a customer relationship management system called the Total Rewards program, a loyalty program that tracks the names and addresses of repeat visitors along with what slot machines they play, for how long, and how much money they gamble. The company's approach uses a Total Rewards card that any customer can obtain—often with the incentive of covering their slot losses for half an hour up to $100. To earn points toward drinks, rooms, and other benefits, customers allow their cards to be swiped on the casino floor to monitor the sums gambled and time spent at slot machines and card tables. The company has also considered automating table games such as blackjack by inserting radio frequency transmitters into gaming chips and installing an antenna under the table felt to record the amount of each wager. The reaction of gamblers to this kind of intense scrutiny of their habits is still unknown, but Harrah's is counting on customers wanting the points enough to agree to be tracked.

Although individual players can earn platinum or diamond status based on their gambling levels, the program is designed for mass markets. The average Harrah's customer gambles less than $3,000 annually and comes to Vegas just once or twice a year. This program allows Harrah's to determine how profitable all customers are as individuals and make special offers tailored to their casino behavior to keep them coming back. The newest initiative is to turn the program into immediate rewards. For example, Harrah's data can identify when a customer is losing, thereby providing the winner with an immediate credit toward future gambling. Printers placed at the gaming machines issue customers these real-time credits.

When analysis showed that core customers were slot players, the company recognized that it needed an approach to track a much wider group of visitors than it had considered in the past. The Total Rewards Card was an ideal way to allow everyone to participate and to gather data on all customers. Tracking also showed them that customers with the highest lifetime values were those who regularly stopped by to gamble after work—rather than those who came for a few days—demonstrating that the industry's typical inducements of free hotel stays and steak dinners were not the best way to encourage repeat business.

Database marketing has applications in virtually any service in which customers make repeat purchases. Underlying the approach is the necessity for the company to create customer information files that integrate different data sources on individual customers including demographics, segmentation, usage information, customer satisfaction data, and accounting and financial information. Although the approach raises privacy concerns with some customers, marketing research is enhanced using databases. A company no longer needs to depend on surveys but can instead track actual behavior. It no longer needs to guess which demographics are most related to psychographic segmentation information—the company can run an analysis to provide valid and reliable data on the topic.

Sources: F. Newell, *loyalty.com* (New York: McGraw-Hill, 2000), pp. 232–238; C. T. Heun, "Harrah's Bets on IT to Understand Its Customers," *Informationweek,* December 11, 2000; Gary Loveman, "Diamonds in the Data Mine," *Harvard Business Review,* May 2003, pp 109–112; www.harrahs.com, 2007; www.hallmark.com, 2007; "Getting to Know You," *Chain Store Age,* November 2005, p. 51.

Marketing research practices that are developed in the United States are not always directly transferable to other cultures. Customer satisfaction measurement and CRM (customer relationship management), both created in the United States, have relevance in other countries and geographies but must be adapted to key differences that require a deep understanding of culture. In this box, we discuss how customer research must be adapted in Europe and how CRM must be adapted in Asia.

CUSTOMER SATISFACTION MEASUREMENT IN EUROPE

The industry of customer satisfaction measurement and research started in the United States and spread to Europe and other countries largely when U.S. companies moved their businesses into Europe. Although the need for customer satisfaction measurement may seem universal and the practice of importing effective programs easy, key differences have surfaced between U.S. and European programs.

First, European companies are less likely than U.S. companies to have departments that specialize in or use customer satisfaction measurement as a way to make improvements across organizations. Instead, customer satisfaction is largely a marketing issue—a way to calibrate how effective the marketing mix for a service is—rather than a central issue from which all decisions about services stem. One negative result of this orientation is that nonmarketing problems identified in customer satisfaction research (such as operations and delivery issues) are often left unaddressed, frustrating the customer. Imagine how you would feel providing input about aspects of service that displease you, then having no changes take place! It is probably no surprise that response rates to surveys are also lower in Europe than in the United States; if nothing positive occurs as a result of filling out a survey, why should a customer do it?

Second, few European companies measure employee satisfaction or link employee compensation to customer satisfaction scores. Top management in U.S. companies, who have learned the value of customer service programs and their impact on frontline employees, buy into the idea of motivating employees with monetary incentives. European companies are less inclined to do so, perhaps resulting in the well-documented lower levels of motivation to provide service on the part of frontline personnel. European labor law also protects employees from employers who might penalize them for delivering poor customer service. One of the central causes of the early failure of Disneyland Paris was the unwillingness of French employees to adhere to service standards of dress, friendliness, and responsiveness.

Third, European attitudes toward service quality training are very different from those in the United States. Standardized employee training that results in consistent service delivery is viewed as artificial and uniquely American. European managers see the "one-size-fits-all" style of greeting and dealing with customers as a packaged approach to service delivery. The European approach is more individualistic—perhaps more genuine at times but also less predictable.

Fourth, and very problematic in developing effective customer satisfaction research in Europe, is that customers across countries are very different and respond inconsistently to the same research. Using the same survey across countries is not the most effective technique because respondents of different cultures require customized questions geared to their unique values and attitudes. Language, its structure, and conversational habits also differ, making results difficult to compare. Furthermore, researchers have documented that consumers differ in their levels of response to satisfaction questions. For example, respondents in southern Europe tend to claim that their satisfaction is higher than it is, while those in northern European countries tend to understate it. Comparing scores across countries is therefore very difficult—"a 90 percent satisfaction rate

that the findings will be useful to managers. Many of the people who use marketing research findings have not been trained in statistics and have neither the time nor the expertise to analyze computer printouts and other technical research information. The goal in this stage of the marketing research process is to communicate information clearly to the right people in a timely fashion. Among considerations are the following: Who gets this information? Why do they need it? How will they use it? Does it mean the same thing across cultures? (See the Global Feature box.) When users feel confident that they understand the data, they are far more likely to apply it appropriately. When managers do not understand how to interpret the data, or when they lack confidence in the research, the investment of time, skill, and effort will be lost.

in Italy probably reflects less good performance than an 80 percent satisfaction score in Germany."

Any service company that plans to extend its offerings in Europe or elsewhere should be warned: merely taking U.S. research practices abroad will not gather valid information unless it takes into account these and other potential differences. Other international locations have their idiosyncrasies as well. What is a U.S. researcher to do? One of the best strategies is the same one found to work well in all international business: to involve managers and market research firms from host countries when conducting customer satisfaction studies abroad.

CUSTOMER RELATIONSHIP MANAGEMENT IN ASIA

Don Peppers and Martha Rogers, consultants in CRM and related areas, have noted the Western orientation of CRM and have emphasized that inherent values in the CRM literature do not reconcile with Asian values. Whereas CRM literature in the United States assumes that customers will "unerringly respond [on] the basis of self-interest and self-gratification," Asian values—such as delayed gratification, loyalty to family and clan, and *Guanxi* (networks of obligations and connections)—must be taken into account if CRM is to succeed in Asia. As the consultants point out, customer relationships are different in Asia in these ways:

- Language preferences are more complex in China than in the United States. Chinese/Malaysian customers may speak one Chinese dialect formally, transact business in Bahasa Malay, and complete legal documents in English. Knowing these differences customizes a relationship but very few CRM systems can accommodate this level of customization.

- Customer names are very different in societies that are racially diverse. Some names are very long and do not have surnames. Chinese names start with the last (family) names and then are followed by the first and second given names. As you probably are aware from your Chinese classmates, Chinese people also sometimes give themselves Western names. Recognizing all these differences is very difficult for a CRM system.

- Some Asian customers have more than one marriage, family, and address. Sending information, such as for life insurance or financial services, to the wrong address violates privacy and can create very difficult situations!

- Asians will rarely tell anyone their net worth because of a cultural bias against flaunting wealth. Therefore, it is difficult to find out which customers are most valuable based on their income.

For these and other reasons, CRM has been adopted much more slowly in Asia than in the United States.

An example of a company that has successfully overcome many of these problems is Toys R Us in Hong Kong, Singapore, Taiwan, and Malaysia. Using a loyalty card (which overcomes many of the difficulties relating to tracking individuals only through names in a database), the company enlisted members and obtain their information by having them complete a simple form when they made a one-time purchase totaling $26. After signing on, members got points redeemable for rewards, savings, and member priorities on events and sales. The store sent out reward statements every four months, motivating purchase during nonpeak times, and coordinated store promotions with its website. The program now has close to 500,000 members and generates more than $62 million in increased revenue.

Sources: E. Sivadas, "Europeans Have a Different Take on CS [Customer Satisfaction] Programs," *Marketing News,* October 26, 1998, p. 39; A. Berhad and T. Tyler, "Customer Relationship Management in Asia: A Cross Cultural Case Study Based on Aetna Universal Insurance," Peppers and Rogers Group, 2001; "Puzzles and Protocols of International Market Research," *Communication World,* December 1996/January 1997, pp. 17–20; "How to Turn Customers into Friends," *Media Asia,* August 25, 2006, p. 8.

Depicting marketing research findings graphically is a powerful way to communicate research information. Here are samples of graphic representations of the types of marketing research data we have discussed throughout this chapter.

Tracking of Performance, Gap Scores, and Competition

A simple way of tracking performance is shown in Figure 6.3. Both expectations and perceptions are plotted, and the gap between them shows the service quality shortfall. Although any attribute or dimension of service can be tracked, Figure 6.4 shows the scores for service reliability. Competitor service performance is another frequently tracked service quality measurement. It allows managers to have a better grasp of

FIGURE 6.3
Service Quality
Perceptions
Relative to Zones
of Tolerance by
Dimensions

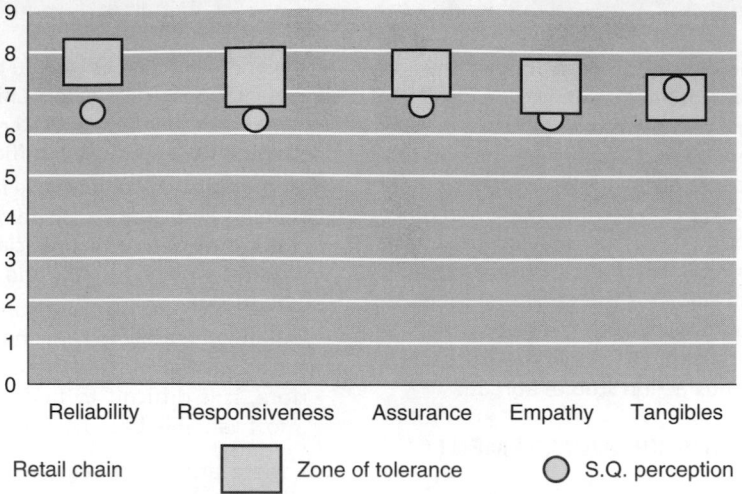

Zones of Tolerance Charts

When companies collect data on the dual expectation levels described in Chapter 4—desired service and adequate service—along with performance data, they can convey the information concisely on zones of tolerance charts. Figure 6.3 above plots customer service quality perceptions relative to customers' zones of tolerance. Perceptions of company performance are indicated by the circles, and the zones of tolerance boxes are bounded on the top by the desired service score and on the bottom by the adequate service score. When the perception scores are within the boxes, as in Figure 6.3, the company is delivering service that is above customers' minimum level of expectations. When the perception scores are below the boxes, the company's service performance is lower than the minimum level, and customers are dissatisfied with the company's service.[18]

Importance/Performance Matrices

One of the most useful forms of analysis in marketing research is the *importance/performance matrix*. This chart combines information about customer perceptions and importance ratings. An example is shown in Figure 6.4. Attribute importance is represented on the vertical axis from high (top) to low (bottom). Performance is shown on the horizontal axis from low (left) to high (right). There are many variations of these matrices: some companies define the horizontal axis as the gap between expectations and perceptions, or as performance relative to competition. The shading on the chart indicates the area of highest leverage for service quality improvements—where importance is high and performance is low. In this quadrant are the attributes that most need to be improved. In the adjacent upper quadrant are attributes to be maintained, ones that a company performs well and that are very important to customers. The lower two quadrants contain attributes that are less important, some of which are performed well and others poorly. Neither of these quadrants merit as much attention in terms of service improvements as the upper quadrants because customers are not as concerned about the attributes that are plotted in them as they are the attributes in the upper quadrants.

FIGURE 6.4
Importance/
Performance Matrix

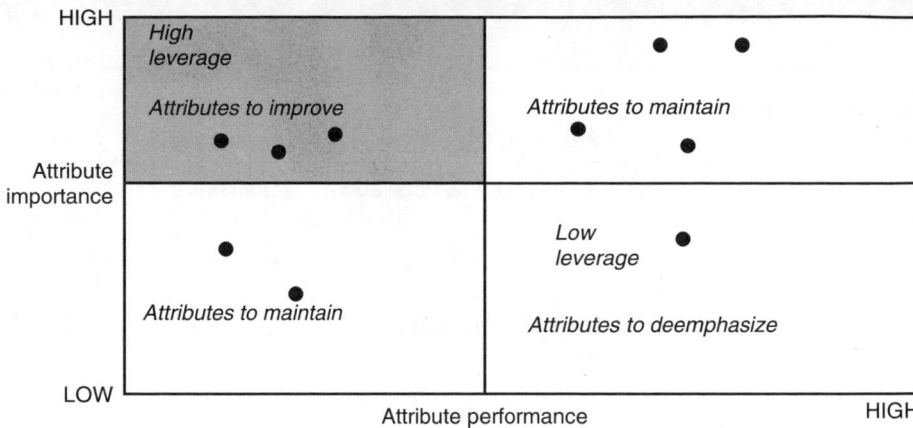

USING MARKETING RESEARCH INFORMATION

Conducting research about customer expectations is only the first part of understanding the customer, even if the research is appropriately designed, executed, and presented. A service firm must also use the research findings in a meaningful way—to drive change or improvement in the way service is delivered. The misuse (or even nonuse) of research data can lead to a large gap in *understanding customer expectations*. When managers do not read research reports because they are too busy dealing with the day-to-day challenges of the business, companies fail to use the resources available to them. And when customers participate in marketing research studies but never see changes in the way the company does business, they feel frustrated and annoyed with the company. Understanding how to make the best use of research—to apply what has been learned to the business—is a key way to close the gap between customer expectations and management perceptions of customer expectations. Managers must learn to turn research information and insights into action, to recognize that the purpose of research is to drive improvement and customer satisfaction.

The research plan should specify the mechanism by which customer data will be used. The research should be actionable: timely, specific, and credible. It can also have a mechanism that allows a company to respond to dissatisfied customers immediately.

A good example of a company that uses its research data for the right purposes is Walt Disney theme parks. When going to the parks, most guests see magic, but the magic is based on solid research discipline. Disney conducts more than 200 different external surveys a year, tracking satisfaction along with demographic profiles of its customers. The company also conducts price sensitivity analysis to determine the tolerance of guests for various levels of pricing. One outcome of this marketing research and price sensitivity analysis was the FastPass, a premium-priced option to the park that allows its purchasers to avoid lines and expedite their access to rides and other attractions. The company also has guests evaluate its different attractions, noting the aspects that are pleasing or troublesome and changing aspects to ensure that the attractions run as smoothly as possible.[19]

UPWARD COMMUNICATION

In some service firms, especially small and localized firms, owners or managers may be in constant contact with customers, thereby gaining firsthand knowledge of customer expectations and perceptions. But in large service organizations, managers do not always get the opportunity to experience firsthand what their customers want.

Exhibit 6.3 Elements in an Effective Program of Upward Communication

Type of Interaction or Research	Research Objective	Qualitative/ Quantitative	Cost of Information		
			Money	**Time**	**Frequency**
Executive visits to customers	To gain firsthand knowledge about customers	Qualitative	Moderate	Moderate	Continuous
Executive listenings	To gain firsthand knowledge about customers	Qualitative	Low	Low	Continuous
Research on intermediate customers	To gain in-depth information on end customers	Quantitative	Moderate	Moderate	Annual
Employee internal satisfaction surveys	To improve internal service quality	Quantitative	Moderate	Moderate	Annual
Employee visits or listenings	To gain firsthand knowledge about employees	Qualitative	Moderate	Moderate	Continuous
Employee suggestions	To obtain ideas for service improvements	Qualitative	Low	Low	Continuous

The larger a company is, the more difficult it will be for managers to interact directly with the customer and the less firsthand information they will have about customer expectations. Even when they read and digest research reports, managers can lose the reality of the customer if they never get the opportunity to experience delivery of the actual service. A theoretical view of how things are supposed to work cannot provide the richness of the service encounter. To truly understand customer needs, management benefits from hands-on knowledge of what really happens in stores, on customer service telephone lines, in service queues, and in face-to-face service encounters. If the listening gap is to be closed, managers in large firms need some form of customer contact.

Objectives for Upward Communication

Exhibit 6.3 shows the major research objectives for improving upward communication in an organization. These objectives include gaining firsthand knowledge about customers, improving internal service quality, gaining firsthand knowledge of employees, and obtaining ideas for service improvement. These objectives can be met by two types of interactive activities in the organization: one designed to improve the type and effectiveness of communications from customers to management, and the other designed to improve communications between employees and management.

Research for Upward Communication

Executive Visits to Customers

This approach is frequently used in business-to-business services marketing. In some visits, executives of the company make sales or service calls with customer contact personnel (salespeople). In other situations, executives of the selling company arrange meetings with executives at a similar level in client companies. When Lou Gerstner became CEO of IBM, one of his first actions was to arrange a meeting with

175 of the company's biggest customers for a discussion of how IBM could better meet their needs. The meeting was viewed as a signal that the new IBM would be more responsive and focused on the customer than it had become in the late 1980s and early 1990s.

Executive or Management Listening to Customers

The marketing director at Milliken, a U.S. textile and chemicals firm, called his experience working the swing shift "naive listening," and he described its benefits as follows:

> Getting close to the customer is a winner!… I worked the second shift (3:00 p.m. to midnight) and actually cleaned carpeting as well as hard-surface floors. I operated all the machinery they used daily, plus handled the same housekeeping problems.… Now I can put together my trade advertising as well as my entire merchandising program based directly upon the needs of my customers as I observed them.… I'm learning—from new-product introduction to maintenance of existing products—exactly what our health care customers require.[20]

As this example illustrates, direct interaction with customers adds clarity and depth to managers' understanding of customer expectations and needs.

Many other companies currently require executives to perform entry-level jobs to promote understanding of their customers. One vice president from a DaVita Inc., the nation's number 2 dialysis-treatment operator, spent three days in spring 2007 helping treat seriously ill patients alongside technicians.[21] A growing number of service companies—including Walt Disney, Continental Airlines, Amazon.com, and Sysco—require that managers spend time on the line, interacting with customers and experiencing service delivery. A formal program for encouraging informal interaction is often the best way to ensure that the contact takes place.

Research on Intermediate Customers

Intermediate customers (such as contact employees, dealers, distributors, agents, and brokers) are people the company serves who serve the end customer. Researching the needs and expectations of these customers *in serving the end customer* can be a useful and efficient way to both improve service to and obtain information about end users. The interaction with intermediate customers provides opportunities for understanding end customers' expectations and problems. It can also help the company learn about and satisfy the service expectations of intermediate customers, a process critical in their providing quality service to end customers.

Research on Internal Customers

Employees who perform services are themselves customers of internal services on which they depend heavily to do their jobs well. As discussed in Chapter 12, there is a strong and direct link between the quality of internal service that employees receive and the quality of service they provide to their own customers. For this reason, it is important to conduct employee research that focuses on the service that internal customers give and receive. In many companies this focus requires adapting existing employee opinion research to focus on service satisfaction. Employee research complements customer research when service quality is the issue being investigated. Customer research provides insight into what is occurring, whereas employee research provides insight into why. The two types of research play unique and equally important roles in improving service quality. Companies that focus service quality research exclusively on external customers are missing a rich and vital source of information.[22]

Executive or Management Listening Approaches to Employees

Employees who actually perform the service have the best possible vantage point for observing the service and identifying impediments to its quality. Customer contact personnel are in regular contact with customers and thereby come to understand a great deal about customer expectations and perceptions.[23] If the information they know can be passed on to top management, top managers' understanding of the customer may improve. In fact, it could be said that in many companies, top management's understanding of the customer depends largely on the extent and types of communication received from customer contact personnel and from noncompany contact personnel (such as independent insurance agents and retailers) who represent the company and its services. When these channels of communication are closed, management may not get feedback about problems encountered in service delivery and about how customer expectations are changing.

Sam Walton, the late founder of the highly successful discount retailer Wal-Mart, once remarked, "Our best ideas come from delivery and stock boys."[24] To stay in touch with the source of new ideas, Walton spent endless hours in stores working the floor, helping clerks, or approving personal checks, even showing up at the loading dock with a bag of doughnuts for a surprised crew of workers.[25] He was well known for having his plane drop him next to a wheat field where he would meet a Wal-Mart truck driver. Giving his pilot instructions to meet him at another landing strip 200 miles down the road, he would make the trip with the Wal-Mart driver, listening to what he had to say about the company.

Upward communication of this sort provides information to upper-level managers about activities and performances throughout the organization. Specific types of communication that may be relevant are formal (such as reports of problems and exceptions in service delivery) and informal (like discussions between contact personnel and upper-level managers). Managers who stay close to their contact people benefit not only by keeping their employees happy but also by learning more about their customers.[26] These companies encourage, appreciate, and reward upward communication from contact people as Exhibit 6.4 shows. Through this important channel, management learns about customer expectations from employees in regular contact with customers and can thereby reduce the size of provider gap 1.

Employee Suggestions

Most companies have some form of employee suggestion program whereby contact personnel can communicate to management their ideas for improving work. Suggestion systems have come a long way from the traditional suggestion box. Effective suggestion systems are ones in which employees are empowered to see their suggestions through, where supervisors can implement proposals immediately, where employees participate for continuous improvement in their jobs, where supervisors respond quickly to ideas, and where coaching is provided in ways to handle suggestions. The National Association of Suggestion Systems (NASS) reports that U.S. companies receive fewer suggestions than do their counterparts in Japan and that the typical financial return for an idea in the United States is much higher than the return in Japan.[27] In today's companies, suggestions from employees are facilitated by self-directed work teams that encourage employees to identify problems and then work to develop solutions to those problems.

About Cabela's

FREE Introductory offer! 5
Postage .... Handling. Cal
Chappell, Nebraska.

Sports Afield
ANNUAL DEER HUNTING ISSUE

1961   1969   1991   1998   2003

WORLD'S FOREMOST OUTFITTER
Cabela's
HUNTING, FISHING AND OUTDOOR GEAR
SINCE 1961

As the
WORLD'S FOREMOST OUTFITTER,
WE PASSIONATELY SERVE PEOPLE WHO ENJOY THE
OUTDOOR LIFESTYLE BY DELIVERING INNOVATION,
QUALITY AND VALUE IN OUR PRODUCTS AND SERVICES.

Core Values
Superior Customer Service • Integrity and Honesty
Quality Products and Services • Respect for Individuals
Excellence in Performance

Unless you fish, hunt, shoot, camp, or cave, you may not know Cabela's, the largest mail order, Internet, and retail outdoor outfitter in the world. Established in 1961 as a specialty cataloguer selling fly fishing lures, the company grew rapidly because of its philosophy that the customer was number 1 and that employees were critical to realizing that philosophy. Because the company was a catalog retailer for the first 30 years of its existence, it relied heavily on employees who were knowledgeable about the outdoors to describe products to consumers.

Its incredibly large (245,000 items) and varied (hunting, archery, shooting, optics, camping, boating, fishing) product mix make Cabela's the ultimate source for outdoor-focused customer needs and wants, but its many items make it difficult to match customers with products. From this challenge was born a novel and creative solution, one that made employees as happy as it made customers. The company decided to loan products to employees so they could learn what the products were like by using them. The extensive loaner program allows employees, who are typically outdoor enthusiasts themselves, to borrow the products for a month and learn to ask the same questions customers would ask. Employees then become experts both on products and on experiences that customers will have using them.

After using the product, the employee returns and teaches everyone else about the product—both by giving a talk to others and by filling out a form about the product's pros and cons. This information becomes part of a giant product database, called "Item notes," that allows easy access to employees, even call center reps, so that customer questions—even the most esoteric ones—can be answered quickly and accurately. The company also invites a small number of knowledgeable customers to borrow products and contribute information as well.

The upward communication extends to the company's cofounder, Jim Cabela, who intercepts and reads all customer comments as they come in before routing them to the appropriate employee. He likes to keep an eye on what customers want to know so that he can be sure his employees are staying informed.

Source: Michael A. Prospero, "Leading Listener Winner: Cabela's," *Fast Company,* October 2005, p. 47.

Summary

This chapter discussed the role of marketing research in understanding customer perceptions and expectations. The chapter began by describing criteria for effective services research that should be incorporated into a services marketing research program. Next, we discussed the elements in an effective services marketing research program and indicated how the approaches satisfied the criteria. In addition to the types and techniques of research (shown in Exhibit 6.1), the boxes in this chapter showed how electronic and other technologies add to the information that managers can collect.

The chapter described key forms of services research including critical incident studies, mystery shopping, service expectation meetings and reviews, process checkpoint evaluations, and database research. Important topics in researching services—including developing research objectives—were also described. Finally, upward communication, ways in which management obtains and uses information from customers and customer contact personnel, was discussed. These topics combine to close the listening gap—the gap between customer expectations and company understanding of customer expectations and the first of four provider gaps in the gaps model of service quality.

Discussion Questions

1. Give five reasons research objectives must be established before marketing research is conducted.

2. Why are both qualitative and quantitative research methods needed in a services marketing research program?

3. Why does the frequency of research differ across the research methods shown in Exhibit 6.1?

4. Compare and contrast the types of research that help a company identify common failure points (see column 2 in Exhibit 6.1). Which of the types do you think produces better information? Why?

5. In what situations does a service company need requirements research?

6. What reasons can you give for companies' lack of use of research information? How might you motivate managers to use the information to a greater extent? How might you motivate frontline workers to use the information?

7. Given a specific marketing research budget, what would be your recommendations for the percentage to be spent on customer research versus upward communication? Why?

8. What kinds of information could be gleaned from research on intermediate customers? What would intermediate customers know that service providers might not?

9. For what types of products and services would research on the Internet be preferable to traditional research?

Exercises

1. Choose a local services organization to interview about marketing research. Find out what the firm's objectives are and the types of marketing research it currently uses. Using the information in this chapter, think about the effectiveness of its marketing research. What are the strengths? Weaknesses?

2. Choose one of the services you consume. If you were in charge of creating a survey for that service, what questions would you ask on the survey? Give several examples. What type of survey (relationship versus transaction based) would be most appropriate for the service? What recommendations would you give to management of the company about making such a survey actionable?

3. If you were the marketing director of your college or university, what types of research (see Exhibit 6.1) would be essential for understanding both external and internal customers? If you could choose only three types of research, which ones would you select? Why?

4. Using the SERVQUAL scale in this chapter, create a questionnaire for a service firm that you use. Give the questionnaire to 10 people, and describe what you learn.

5. To get an idea of the power of the critical incidents technique, try it yourself with reference to restaurant service. Think of a time when, as a customer, you had a particularly satisfying interaction with a restaurant. Follow the instructions here, which are identical to the instructions in an actual study, and observe the insights you obtain about your requirements in restaurant service:

    a. When did the incident happen?

    b. What specific circumstances led up to this situation?

    c. Exactly what did the employee (or firm) say or do?

    d. What resulted that made you feel the interaction was satisfying?

    e. What could or should have been done differently?

Notes

1. J. McGregor, "Customers First: 2004 Fast Company Customers First Awards," *Fast Company,* October 2004, pp. 79–88.

2. Ibid.

3. A. Parasuraman, L. L. Berry, and V. A. Zeithaml, "Guidelines for Conducting Service Quality Research," *Marketing Research: A Magazine of Management and Applications,* December 1990, pp. 34–44.

4. E. Deutskens, K. Ruyter, and M. Wetzels, "An Assessment of Equivalence Between Online and Mail Surveys in Service Research," *Journal of Service Research,* 8 (May 2006), 346–355.

5. This section is based on a comprehensive assessment of the critical incident technique in D. D. Gremler, "The Critical Incident Technique in Service Research," *Journal of Service Research* 7 (August 2004), pp. 65–89.

6. For detailed discussions of the Critical Incident Technique, see J. C. Flanagan, "The Critical Incident Technique," *Psychological Bulletin* 51 (July 1954), pp. 327–358; M. J. Bitner, J. D. Nyquist, and B. H. Booms, "The Critical Incident as a Technique for Analyzing the Service Encounter," in *Services Marketing in a Changing Environment,* ed. T. M. Bloch, G. D. Upah, and V. A. Zeithaml (Chicago: American Marketing Association, 1985), pp. 48–51; S. Wilson-Pessano, "Defining Professional Competence: The Critical Incident Technique 40 Years Later," presentation to the Annual Meeting of the American Educational Research Association, New Orleans, 1988; I. Roos, "Methods of Investigating Critical Incidents," *Journal of Service Research* 4 (February 2002), pp. 193–204; Gremler, "The Critical Incident Technique in Service Research."

7. Ibid.

8. E. E. Lueke and T. W. Suther III, "Market-Driven Quality: A Market Research and Product Requirements Methodology," *IBM Technical Report,* June 1991.

9. J. Carey, J. Buckley, and J. Smith, "Hospital Hospitality," *Newsweek,* February 11, 1985, p. 78.

10. See V. A. Zeithaml and A. Parasuraman, *Service Quality,* MSI Relevant Knowledge Series (Cambridge, MA: Marketing Science Institute, 2004), for a complete review of this research, including the many publications by the original authors of SERVQUAL and the extensions by other authors.

11. E. Day, "Researchers Must Enter Consumer's World," *Marketing News,* August 17, 1998, p. 17.

12. G. Khermouch, "Consumers in the Mist," *BusinessWeek,* February 26, 2001, pp. 92–93.

13. Ibid., p. 92.

14. For examples, see S. J. Grove and R. P. Fiske, "Observational Data Collection Methods for Services Marketing: An Overview," *Journal of the Academy of Marketing Science* 20 (Summer 1992), pp. 117–214.

15. "Knowing What It Takes to Keep (or Lose) Your Best Customers," *Executive Report on Customer Satisfaction* 5 (October 30, 1992).

16. P. R. Magnusson, J. Mathing, and P. Kristensson, "Managing User Involvement in Service Innovation: Experiments with Innovating End Users," *Journal of Service Research* 6 (November 2003), pp. 111–124.

17. V. A. Zeithaml, A. Parasuraman, and L. L. Berry, *Delivering Quality Service: Balancing Customer Perceptions and Expectations* (New York: Free Press, 1990), p. 28.

18. A. Parasuraman, V. A. Zeithaml, and L. L. Berry, "Moving Forward in Service Quality Research," *Marketing Science Institute Report No. 94–114,* September 1994.

19. R. Johnson, "A Strategy for Service—Disney Style," *Journal of Business Strategy,* September–October 1991, pp. 38–43.

20. T. J. Peters and N. Austin, *A Passion for Excellence* (New York: Random House, 1985), p. 16.

21. J. S. Lublin, "Top Brass Try Life in the Trenches," *The Wall Street Journal,* June 25, 2007, p. B1.

22. "Baldridge Winner Co-Convenes Quality Summit," *Executive Report on Customer Satisfaction,* October 30, 1992.

23. M. J. Bitner, B. Booms, and L. Mohr, "Critical Service Encounters: The Employee's Viewpoint," *Journal of Marketing* 58 (October 1994), pp. 95–106.

24. S. Koepp, "Make That Sale, Mr. Sam," *Time,* May 18, 1987.

25. Ibid.

26. Zeithaml, Parasuraman, and Berry, *Delivering Quality Service,* p. 64.

27. "Empowerment Is the Strength of Effective Suggestion Systems," *Total Quality Newsletter,* August 1991.

Chapter Seven

Building Customer Relationships

This chapter's objectives are to

1. Explain relationship marketing, its goals, and the benefits of long-term relationships for firms and customers.
2. Explain why and how to estimate customer relationship value.
3. Introduce the concept of customer profitability segments as a strategy for focusing relationship marketing efforts.
4. Present relationship development strategies—including quality core service, switching barriers, and relationship bonds.
5. Identify challenges in relationship development, including the somewhat controversial idea that "the customer is not always right."

USAA Focuses on Long-Term Relationships

United States Automobile Association (USAA) is a preeminent example of a company focused on building long-term relationships with customers.[1] Customer retention has been a core value of the company since long before customer loyalty became a popular business concept. In business since 1922, USAA provides for the insurance needs of a highly targeted market segment: current and former U.S. military personnel and their families. Headquartered in San Antonio, Texas, USAA owns and manages more than $110 billion in assets. It has been ranked number 1 in a list of "Customer Service Champs" by *BusinessWeek* and consistently appears on *Fortune* magazine's list of the 100 best companies to work for in America. Customer retention figures approach 100 percent;[2] in fact, the most likely reason for a customer to leave the company is death.

The goal of the company is to "think about the events in the life of a career officer and then work out ways to help him get through them." The company is intent on serving its current customer base and growing with them. To do this, USAA relies heavily on extensive customer research through surveys and a member advisory board that meets regularly with executives. The company also focuses on retaining the best employees and rewarding them for customer-oriented objectives such as percentage of customer questions or requests handled on the first call with no need for follow-up. USAA believes so strongly in the importance of customer retention that managers' and executives' bonuses are based on this metric. Such

USAA: *BusinessWeek's* **customer service champs for 2007**

emphasis has been rewarded: independent research firms report that 81 percent of USAA's customers believe the company does what is best for them rather than for the bottom line.[3]

A striking example of how USAA attempts to listen to the customer is illustrated in this excerpt from *BusinessWeek:*

> Many companies give lip service to listening to the "voice of the customer." At USAA, that voice is transformed into what it calls "surround sound"—a comprehensive approach to training its employees to empathize with its customers' unique needs. "We want to cover the light moments, the heart-wrenching moments, what it's like to be bored in the field," says Elizabeth D. Conklyn, USAA's executive vice-president for people services. "We try to develop empathy, not only for our members but also for the family side."[4]

USAA has developed an enhanced military awareness program that requires customer service representatives to engage in tasks that allow them to empathize with their customers. For example, employees may have to strap on a military helmet, 65-pound backpack, and flak vest; consume a "meal ready to eat" (MRE) given to soldiers in the field; and read real letters from troops stationed abroad. It is not uncommon for an employee to read a letter, written by a soldier to his mother, from someone who later died in a war. USAA also archives complete information about its customers in the form of electronic files. These files are accessible to all of its customer service representatives throughout the organization, who can then use the information to personalize and customize each service encounter—often times without having to consult with anyone else in the organization.[5] Although these tactics obviously cost USAA thousands of dollars, actions such as these clearly indicate USAA's commitment to its current members, serving to ensure their loyalty, and strengthen their relationship with the company.

USAA provides a strong example of a company that has focused on keeping its customers and building long-term relationships with them. Unlike the USAA example, however, many companies fail to understand customers accurately because they fail to focus on customer relationships. They tend to fixate on acquiring new customers rather than viewing customers as assets that they need to nurture and retain. By concentrating on new customers, firms can easily fall into the traps of short-term promotions, price discounts, or catchy ads that bring customers in but are not enough to bring them back. By adopting a relationship philosophy, on the other hand, companies begin to understand customers over time and in great depth and are better able to meet their changing needs and expectations.

Marketing strategies for understanding customers over time and building long-term relationships are the subjects of this chapter.

A company interested in a committed relationship with its customers will experience long-term benefits.

RELATIONSHIP MARKETING

There has been a shift from a transactions to a relationship focus in marketing. Customers become partners and the firm must make long-term commitments to maintaining those relationships with quality, service, and innovation.[6]

Relationship marketing essentially represents a paradigm shift within marketing—away from an acquisitions/transaction focus toward a retention/relationship focus.[7] Relationship marketing (or relationship management) is a philosophy of doing business, a strategic orientation, which focuses on *keeping and improving* relationships with current customers rather than on acquiring new customers. This philosophy assumes that many consumers and business customers prefer to have an ongoing relationship with one organization than to switch continually among providers in their search for value. Building on this assumption and another that suggests it is usually much cheaper to keep a current customer than to attract a new one, successful marketers are working on effective strategies for retaining customers. Our opening example shows how USAA has built its business around a relationship philosophy.

It has been suggested that firms frequently focus on attracting customers (the "first act") but then pay little attention to what they should do to keep them (the "second act").[8] Ideas expressed in an interview with James L. Schorr, then executive vice president of marketing at Holiday Inns, illustrate this point.[9] In the interview he referred to the "bucket theory of marketing." By this he meant that marketing can be thought of as a big bucket: it is what the sales, advertising, and promotion programs do that pours business into the top of the bucket. As long as these programs are effective, the bucket stays full. However, "There's only one problem," he said, "there's a hole in the bucket." When the business is running well and the hotel is delivering on its promises, the hole is small and few customers are leaving. As indicated in Figure 7.1, when the operation is weak and customers are not satisfied with what they get—and therefore the relationship is weak—people start falling out of the bucket through the holes faster than they can be poured in through the top.

FIGURE 7.1
There Is a Hole in the Bucket: Why Relationship Development Makes Sense

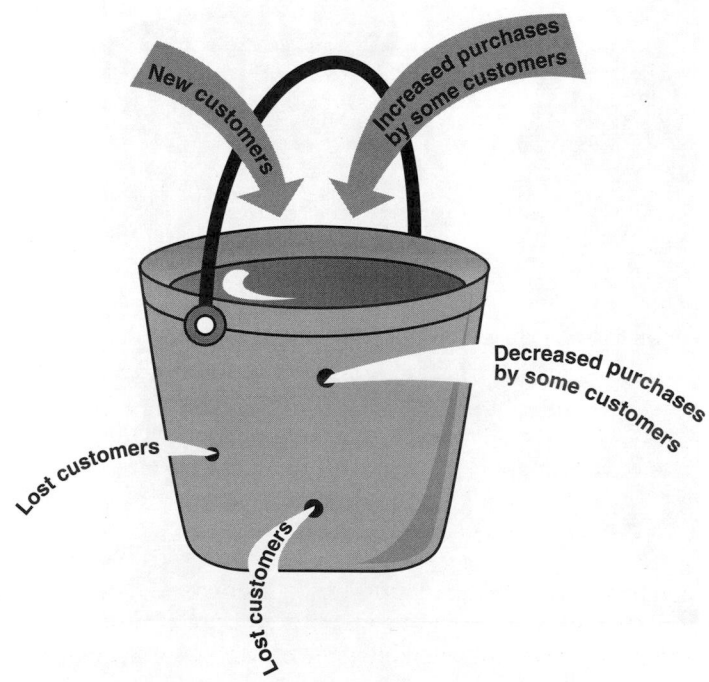

The bucket theory illustrates why a relationship strategy that focuses on plugging the holes in the bucket makes so much sense. Historically, marketers have been more concerned with acquisition of customers, so a shift to a relationship strategy often represents changes in mind-set, organizational culture, and employee reward systems. For example, the sales incentive systems in many organizations are set up to reward bringing in new customers. There are often fewer (or no) rewards for retaining current accounts. Thus, even when people see the logic of customer retention, the existing organizational systems may not support its implementation.

The Evolution of Customer Relationships

Firms' relationships with their customers, like other social relationships, tend to evolve over time. Scholars have suggested that marketing exchange relationships between providers and customers often have the potential to evolve from strangers to acquaintances to friends to partners. Exhibit 7.1 illustrates different issues at each successive level of the relationship.[10]

Customers as Strangers

Strangers are those customers who have not yet had any transactions (interactions) with a firm and may not even be aware of the firm. At the industry level, strangers may be conceptualized as customers who have not yet entered the market; at the firm level, they may include customers of competitors. Clearly the firm has no relationship with the customer at this point. Consequently, the firm's primary goal with these potential customers ("strangers") is to initiate communication with them in order to *attract* them and *acquire* their business. Thus, the primary marketing efforts directed toward such customers deal with familiarizing those potential customers with the firm's offerings and, subsequently, encouraging them to give the firm a try.

Customers as Acquaintances

Once customer awareness and trial are achieved, familiarity is established and the customer and the firm become *acquaintances,* creating the basis for an exchange relationship. A primary goal for the firm at this stage of the relationship is *satisfying* the customer. In the acquaintance stage, firms are generally concerned about providing a value proposition to customers comparable with that of competitors. For a customer, an acquaintanceship is effective as long as the customer is relatively satisfied and what is being received in the exchange is perceived as fair value. With repetitive interactions, the customer gains experience and becomes more familiar with the firm's product offerings. These encounters can help reduce uncertainty about the benefits expected in the exchange and, therefore, increase the attractiveness of the company relative to the competition. Repetitive interactions improve the firm's knowledge of the customer, helping to facilitate marketing, sales, and service efforts. Thus, an acquaintance relationship facilitates transactions primarily through the reduction of the customer's perceived risk and the provider's costs.

In acquaintance relationships, firms generally focus on providing value comparable to the competition, often through the repetitive provision of standardized offerings. As a result, for a firm in such a relationship with a customer, the potential to develop a sustainable competitive advantage through relationship activities is limited. However, firms that have many such relationships with their customers can create value for acquaintances by learning from all their transactions. For example, Amazon.com has created value for its acquaintances through a highly developed order processing system. By processing and organizing historical transaction data from a customer and comparing it with data from other customers demonstrating similar purchase behaviors, the system is able to identify additional products of potential interest to the acquaintance customer and to generate cross-selling opportunities.

Exhibit 7.1 A Typology of Exchange Relationships

Customers as . . .	Strangers	Acquaintances	Friends	Partners
Product offering	Attractive relative to competitive offerings or alternative purchases.	Parity product as a form of industry standard.	Differentiated product adapted to specific market segments.	Customized product and dedicated resources adapted to an individual customer or organization.
Source of competitive advantage	Attractiveness	Satisfaction	Satisfaction + trust	Satisfaction + trust + commitment
Buying activity	Interest, exploration, and trial.	Satisfaction facilitates and reinforces buying activity and reduces need to search for market information.	Trust in firm is needed to continue the buying activity.	Commitment in the form of information sharing and idiosyncratic investments is needed to achieve customized product and to adjust product continuously to changing needs and situations.
Focus of selling activities	Awareness of firm's offerings (encouraging trial) facilitates initial selling.	Familiarity and general knowledge of customer (identification) facilitates selling.	Specific knowledge of customer's need and situation facilitates selling.	Specific knowledge of customer's need and situation and idiosyncratic investments facilitates selling.
Relationship time horizon	*None:* Buyer may have had no previous interactions with or knowledge of the firm.	*Short:* Generally short because the buyer can often switch firms without much effort or cost.	*Medium:* Generally longer than acquaintance relationships because trust in a differentiated position takes a longer time to build and imitate.	*Long:* Generally long because it takes time to build (or replace) interconnected activities and to develop a detailed knowledge of a customer's needs and the unique resources of a supplier to commit resources to the relationship.
Sustainability of competitive advantage	*Low:* Generally low, as firm must continually find ways to be attractive, in terms of the value offered, to induce trial.	*Low:* Generally low, but competitors can vary in how they build unique value into selling and serving even if the product is a form of industry standard.	*Medium:* Generally medium, but depends on ability of competitors to understand heterogeneity of customer needs and situations and the ability to transform this knowledge into meaningful, differentiated products.	*High:* Generally high, but depends on how unique and effective the interconnected activities between customer and supplier are organized.
Primary relationship marketing goal	*Acquire* the customer's business.	*Satisfy* the customer's needs and wants.	*Retain* the customer's business.	*Enhance* the relationship with the customer.

Source: Adapted from M. D. Johnson and F. Seines, "Customer Portfolio Management: Toward a Dynamic Theory of Exchange Relationships," *Journal of Marketing* 68 (April 2004), p. 5. Reprinted by permission of the American Marketing Association.

Customers as Friends

As a customer continues to make purchases from a firm and to receive value in the exchange relationship, the firm begins to acquire specific knowledge of the customer's needs, allowing it to create an offering that directly addresses the customer's situation. The provision of a unique offering, and thus differential value, transforms the relationship from acquaintance to *friendship*. This transition, particularly in service exchange relationships, requires the development of trust.[11] As discussed in an earlier chapter, customers may not be able to assess a service outcome prior to purchase and consumption, and for those services high in credence qualities, customers may not be able to discern service performance even after experiencing it. Therefore, customers must trust the provider to do what is promised. As customers become friends they not only become familiar with the company but also come to trust that it provides superior value.

A primary goal for firms at the friendship stage of the relationship is customer *retention*. Given their likelihood of past satisfying experiences and repeated purchases, these customers ("friends") are more likely to appreciate the firm's product offerings and are, perhaps, more open to other related services. A firm's potential to develop sustainable competitive advantage through friends should be higher than for acquaintances because the offering is more unique (and more difficult for competition to imitate) and the customer comes to trust that uniqueness.[12]

Customers as Partners

As a customer continues to interact with a firm, the level of trust often deepens and the customer may receive more customized product offerings and interactions. The trust developed in the friendship stage is a necessary but not sufficient condition for a customer–firm *partnership* to develop.[13] That is, the creation of trust leads to (ideally) the creation of commitment—and that is the condition necessary for customers to extend the time perspective of a relationship.[14] The deepening of trust and the establishment of commitment reduce the customer's need to solve problems in the traditional sense of "finding a better alternative." Thus, to move the relationship into a partner relationship, a firm must use customer knowledge and information systems to deliver highly personalized and customized offerings.

The key to success in the partnership stage is the firm's ability to organize and use information about individual customers more effectively than competitors. Customers benefit from, and therefore desire to commit to, relationships with firms whose knowledge of their needs enables them to deliver highly personalized and customized offerings.[15] Over time, the customer–firm relationship may evolve through continuous adaptation and commitment, and the parties may become increasingly interdependent. At this point the relationship has advanced from having the purpose of merely meeting the customer's needs to a situation in which both parties sense a deep appreciation of each other. However, to continue to receive such benefits, customers generally must be willing to pay a price premium or to commit themselves to the firm for an extended period of time. For an annual membership fee of $50, Hertz #1 Club Gold customers have personal data and rental preferences stored in their database. Among the many benefits Hertz Gold customers receive are guaranteed availability of a car, separate counters where all they have to do is show their driver's license to receive the car keys, and paperwork that is already completed because their signature is on file.

At the partnership stage, the firm is concerned with *enhancing* the relationship. Customers are more likely to stay in the relationship if they feel that the company understands their changing needs and is willing to invest in the relationship by constantly improving and evolving its product and service mix. By enhancing these relationships, the firm expects such customers to be less likely to be lured away by competitors and more likely to buy additional products and services from the company over time. These loyal customers not

Technology Spotlight Customer Information Systems Help Enhance the Customer Relationship

The potential of today's customer information systems far exceeds any traditional marketing information system that has gone before. These new systems differ from the old in their scale (thousands of bits of information on tens of millions of customers), the depth of information that can be captured on each individual or household, and the ways in which the information can be used. In many cases, access to this type of information about individual customers allows the organization to customize to the individual level what previously would have been undifferentiated services.

HILTON'S OnQ SYSTEM

Hilton Hotels has an integrated technology platform called "OnQ" that provides the basis for its customer relationship management (CRM) system. OnQ centralizes all of the personal profile information that guests provide to Hilton—via hotel or central reservations, their websites, or through membership in the HHonors loyalty program—to create a "Guest Profile Manager." Profiles are created for any guest who is either an HHonors member or simply visits a Hilton hotel at least four times within a year. Such a system requires an extraordinary investment in information technology to capture information from Hilton's almost 3,000 hotels and half a million rooms in six continents and nearly 80 countries worldwide. The information collected via OnQ is combined with the customer's stay history and any prior complaints made during previous visits. The entire packet of information enables many of Hilton's 100,000 employees to recognize and reward guests with appropriate welcome messages, room upgrades, or information related to previous visits.

USING THE INFORMATION TO DEVELOP RELATIONSHIPS WITH CUSTOMERS

OnQ provides a mechanism for Hilton Hotels to learn—and remember—customer interests and preferences. Tim Harvey, Chief Information Officer for Hilton, describes it this way:

It's like when your grandmother comes to your house. You know exactly who she is. You know exactly what she eats for breakfast. You know what kind of pillow she likes. You know whether she can climb the stairs or not so you know what room to put her in. We have the same passion about our hotel business. We want to know who our customers are and we want to take care of those customers every time we have an opportunity to touch them. So the value of OnQ is primarily having that information with that in-depth knowledge about customers.

Collecting information on all of its customers is not an easy task, particularly given the many different hotels in the Hilton family of brands: the company owns, manages, or franchises a hotel portfolio of some of the best known and highly regarded brands, including Hilton, Conrad Hotels & Resorts, Doubletree, Embassy Suites Hotels, Hampton Inn, Hampton Inn & Suites, Hilton Garden Inn, Homewood Suites by Hilton, and the Waldorf-Astoria Collection. OnQ provides a method for capturing and managing information on Hilton customers across a diverse set of properties, differing brands, and various countries with local requirements.

PROVIDING GUESTS WITH OPTIONS

Several customers prefer to initiate contact with Hilton via the Internet; about 20 percent of all rooms, representing about $2.3 billion, are sold in this manner. However, in spite of the lack of face-to-face contact, OnQ has allowed Hilton to create a personal relationship with these customers. Once a customer identifies him- or herself when using the Internet, Hilton knows if the customer is an HHonors member, the customer's preferred room type, and the customer's preferred in-room amenities. OnQ also provides the capability for customers to check into their hotel via the Internet prior to arriving—just like customers do for an airline seat. Customers can view the hotel floor plan, see all of the rooms available, and

only provide a solid base for the organization, they may represent growth potential. This is certainly true for USAA, our opening example in this chapter, whose officer members' needs for insurance increase over their lifetimes as well as the lifetimes of their children. Other examples abound. A bank checking account customer becomes a better customer when she sets up a savings account, takes out a loan, and/or uses the financial advising services of the bank. And a corporate account becomes a better customer when it chooses

then pick the room they want—perhaps on the west side of the building for those how like to sleep in late or one close to the pool or with a view of the mountains. Many Hilton hotels have kiosks, allowing customers not only to check in and out of the hotel without standing in line, but also providing the ability to print airline boarding passes.

Hilton now allows organizers of relatively small groups to book their entire group event or meeting

The Chicago Hilton

from start to finish on the Internet—and receive immediate confirmation of their reservation. Potential customers who represent groups requiring 25 rooms or less—such as family reunions, wedding parties, or those attending a sporting event—can see about room availability across all Hilton brands and locations. Through OnQ amateur event planners, small-business owners, or family representatives can find a hotel that best fits their needs based on price, room types, and proximity to local attractions. Organizers can reserve guest rooms, meeting spaces, food and beverages, audio/visual equipment, and more up to one year in advance without a request for proposal or a waiting period. Additionally, OnQ enables planners to manage their room block, including instant, online access 24/7 to their group reservation details and guest room information. Planners can instantly see who has booked guest rooms for their event or can reserve rooms on behalf of guests, thus keeping track of the total head count at all times.

THE RESULTS

How well has OnQ worked in managing customer relationships? Three of the Hilton brands (Hilton Garden Inn, Embassy Suites Hotels, and Homewood Suites by Hilton) regularly receive the top awards for customer satisfaction in their respective hotel segments by independent research conducted by J. D. Power and Associates. Each of these has received the number one ranking at least five times since 2001, and another brand (Hampton Inn) is generally within the top three. Additionally, Harvey estimates that Hilton's "share of wallet" from its best customers has increased from 40 to 60 percent since OnQ has been fully operational. Hilton's relationship with its many customers has certainly been enhanced through OnQ.

Sources: Tim Harvey, Interview on ZDNet.com, http://video.zdnet.com/CIOSessions/?p=143, accessed August 8, 2007; www.hospitality.net, accessed August 8, 2007; www.hilton.com, accessed August 8, 2007.

to do 75 percent of its business with a particular supplier rather than splitting the business equally among three suppliers. In recent years, in fact, many companies have aspired to be the "exclusive supplier" of a particular product or service for their customers. Over time these enhanced relationships can increase market share and profits for the organization. Our Technology Spotlight features Hilton Hotels and how the company is successfully using information technology to enhance relationships with their customers.

The Goal of Relationship Marketing

The discussion of the evolution of customer relationships demonstrates how a firm's relationship with its customers might be enhanced as customers move further along this relationship continuum. As the relationship value of a customer increases, the provider is more likely to pursue a closer relationship. Thus, the primary goal of relationship marketing is *to build and maintain a base of committed customers who are profitable for the organization.* Figure 7.2 graphically illustrates the goals of relationship marketing. The overriding goal is to move customers up the ladder (i.e., along the relationship continuum) from the point at which they are strangers that need to be attracted through to the point at which they are highly valued, long-term customers whose relationship with the firm has been enhanced. From a customer's problem-solving perspective, the formation of satisfaction, trust, and commitment corresponds to the customer's willingness to more fully engage in an exchange relationship as an acquaintance, friend, and partner, respectively. From a firm's resource-allocation perspective, the delivery of differential, and perhaps customized, value corresponds to the extent of its ability and/or desire to create an acquaintance, friend, or partner relationship with the customer. As customers make the transition from satisfaction-based acquaintanceships to trust-based friendships to commitment-based partnerships, increases are required in both the value received and the level of cooperation.

Benefits for Customers and Firms

Both parties in the customer–firm relationship can benefit from customer retention. That is, it is not only in the best interest of the organization to build and maintain a loyal customer base, but customers themselves also benefit from long-term associations.

Benefits for Customers

Assuming they have a choice, customers will remain loyal to a firm when they receive greater value relative to what they expect from competing firms. *Value* represents a trade-off for the consumer between the "give" and the "get" components. Consumers are more likely to stay in a relationship when the gets (quality, satisfaction, specific

FIGURE 7.2
The goal of relationship marketing is to move customers up the ladder: acquiring customers, satisfying customers, retaining customers, and enhancing customers

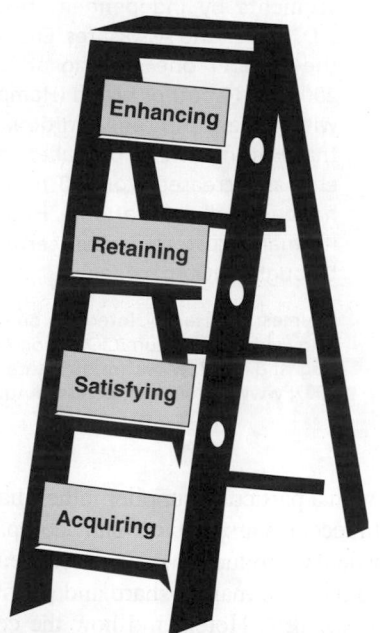

benefits) exceed the gives (monetary and nonmonetary costs). When firms can consistently deliver value from the customer's point of view, clearly the customer benefits and has an incentive to stay in the relationship.

Beyond the specific inherent benefits of receiving service value, customers also benefit in other ways from long-term associations with firms. Sometimes these relationship benefits keep customers loyal to a firm more than the attributes of the core service. Research has uncovered specific types of relational benefits that customers experience in long-term service relationships including confidence benefits, social benefits, and special treatment benefits.[16]

Confidence Benefits   Confidence benefits comprise feelings of trust or confidence in the provider along with a sense of reduced anxiety and comfort in knowing what to expect. One customer described his confidence that resulted from having developed a relationship with a service provider:

> "There is a comfort [in having] a certain level of experience [with the service provider]. In other words, I know that I am going to be treated right because they know me . . . I don't have any anxiety that I will have a less-than-acceptable experience . . . You know it's going to be good in advance, or if something is wrong it will be taken care of."[17]

Across all the services studied in the research just cited, confidence benefits were the most important to customers.

Human nature is such that most consumers would prefer not to change service providers, particularly when there is a considerable investment in the relationship. The costs of switching are frequently high in terms of dollar costs of transferring business and the associated psychological and time-related costs. Most consumers (whether individuals or businesses) have many competing demands for their time and money and are continually searching for ways to balance and simplify decision making to improve the quality of their lives. When they develop confidence in—and can maintain a relationship with—a service provider, they free up time for other concerns and priorities.

Social Benefits   Over time, customers develop a sense of familiarity and even a social relationship with their service providers. These ties make it less likely that they will switch, even if they learn about a competitor that might have better quality or a lower price. This customer's description of her hair stylist in a quote from the research just cited illustrates the concept of social benefits:

> "I like him. . . . He's really funny and always has lots of good jokes. He's kind of like a friend now. . . . It's more fun to deal with somebody that you're used to. You enjoy doing business with them."

In some long-term customer–firm relationships, a service provider may actually become part of the consumer's social support system.[18] Hairdressers, as in the example just cited, often serve as personal confidants. Less common examples include proprietors of local retail stores who become central figures in neighborhood networks, the health club or restaurant manager who knows her customers personally, the private school principal who knows an entire family and its special needs, or the river guide who befriends patrons on a long rafting trip.[19]

These types of personal relationships can develop for business-to-business customers as well as for end consumers of services. The social support benefits resulting from these relationships are important to the consumer's quality of life (personal and/or work life) above and beyond the technical benefits of the service provided. Many times the close personal and professional relationships that develop between service providers and clients are the basis for the customer's loyalty. The flip side of this customer benefit is the risk to the firm of losing customers when a valued employee leaves the firm and takes customers with him or her.[20]

Special Treatment Benefits Special treatment includes getting the benefit of the doubt, being given a special deal or price, or getting preferential treatment as exemplified by the following quotes from the research:

> I think you get special treatment [when you have established a relationship]. My pediatrician allowed me to use the back door to the office so my daughter could avoid contact with other sick children. Other times I have been in a hurry and they take me right back.

> You should get the benefit of the doubt in many situations. For example, I always pay my VISA bill on time, before a service charge is assessed. One time my payment didn't quite arrive on time. When I called them, by looking at my past history, they realized that I always make an early payment. Therefore, they waived the service charge.

Interestingly, the special treatment benefits, while important, are generally found to be less important than the other types of benefits received in service relationships.[21] Although special treatment benefits can clearly be critical for customer loyalty in some industries (think of frequent flyer benefits in the airline industry), they seem to be less important to customers overall.

Benefits for Firms

The benefits to organizations of maintaining and developing a loyal customer base are numerous. In addition to the economic benefits that a firm receives from cultivating close relationships with its customers, a variety of customer behavior benefits and human resource management benefits are also often received.

Economic Benefits Research reveals that over the long run, relationship-oriented service firms achieve *higher overall returns* on their investments than do transaction-oriented firms.[22] These bottom-line benefits come from a variety of sources, including increased revenues over time from the customer, reduced marketing and administrative costs, and the ability to maintain margins without reducing prices. Research also suggests that highly satisfied customers are *willing to pay more* for a provider's services.[23]

One of the most commonly cited economic benefits of customer retention is *increased purchases* over time, as illustrated in Figure 7.3. The figure summarizes results of studies showing that across industries customers generally spent more each year with a particular relationship partner than they did in the preceding period.[24] As customers get to know a firm and are satisfied with the quality of its services relative to that of its competitors, they tend to give more of their business to the firm.

Another economic benefit is *lower costs*. Some estimates suggest that repeat purchases by established customers require as much as 90 percent less marketing expenditure.[25] Many start-up costs are associated with attracting new customers, including advertising and other promotion costs, the operating costs of setting up new accounts, and time costs of getting to know the customers. Sometimes these initial costs can outweigh the revenue expected from the new customers in the short term, so it is to the firm's advantage to cultivate long-term relationships. Even ongoing relationship maintenance costs are likely to drop over time. For example, early in a relationship a customer is likely to have questions and encounter problems as he or she learns to use the service; an experienced customer will likely have fewer problems and questions, and the firm will incur fewer costs in serving the customer. In Chapter 18 we provide more specifics on the financial impact of customer retention.

FIGURE 7.3
**Profit Generated
by a Customer over
Time**

Source: Adapted and
reprinted by permission of
Harvard Business Review. An
exhibit from "Zero Defection:
Quality Comes to Services,"
by F. F. Reichheld and W. E.
Sasser, Jr., *Harvard Business
Review* 68 (September–
October 1990). Copyright ©
1990 by the Harvard Business
School Publishing
Corporation; all rights
reserved.

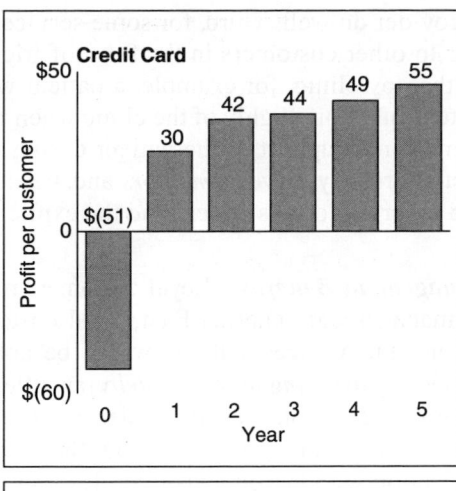

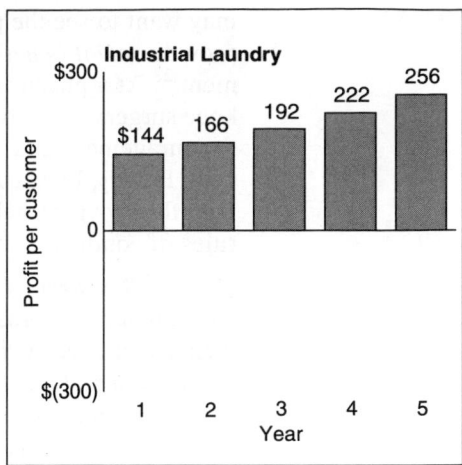

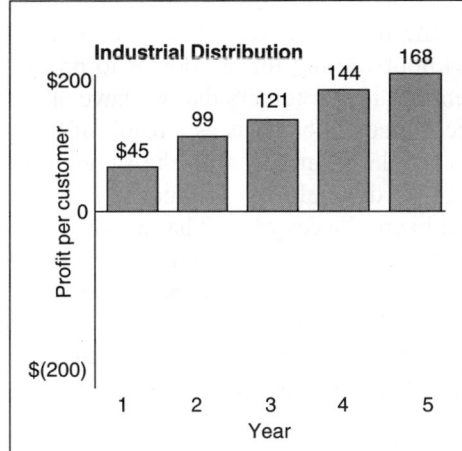

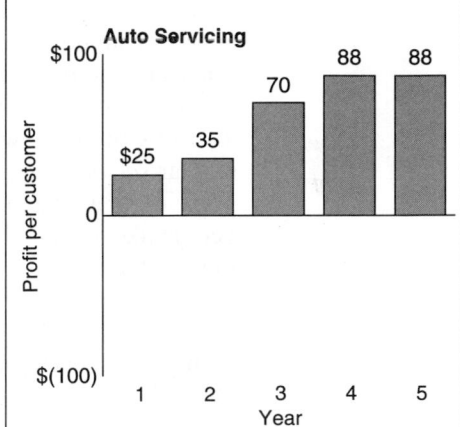

Customer Behavior Benefits The contribution that loyal customers make to a service
business can go well beyond their direct financial impact on the firm.[26] The first,
and maybe the most easily recognized, customer behavior benefit that a firm receives
from long-term customers is the free advertising provided through *word-of-mouth
communication.* When a product is complex and difficult to evaluate and when risk is
involved in the decision to buy it—as is the case with many services—consumers often
look to others for advice on which providers to consider. Satisfied, loyal customers
are likely to provide a firm with strong word-of-mouth endorsements. This form of
advertising can be more effective than any paid advertising that the firm might use,
and it has the added benefit of reducing the costs of attracting new customers. Indeed,
loyal customers often talk a great deal about a company and may generate much new
business over the years.

In addition to word-of-mouth communication, a second consumer behavior
benefit is one that is sometimes labeled *customer voluntary performance;*[27] in a
restaurant, such behavior might include customers busing their own tables, reporting messy restrooms to an employee, or picking up trash in the parking lot. Such
behaviors support the firm's ability to deliver quality services. Although customer
voluntary performance could be engaged in by anyone, those customers who have a
long-term relationship with the firm are perhaps more likely to do so because they

may want to see the provider do well. Third, for some services loyal customers may provide *social benefits* to other customers in the form of friendships or encouragement.[28] At a physical therapy clinic, for example, a patient who is recovering from knee surgery is likely to think more highly of the clinic when fellow patients provide encouragement and emotional support to the patient during the rehabilitation process. Finally, loyal customers may serve as *mentors* and, because of their experience with the provider, help other customers understand the explicitly or implicitly stated rules of conduct.[29]

Human Resource Management Benefits Loyal customers may also provide a firm with human resource management benefits. First, loyal customers may, because of their experience with and knowledge of the provider, be able to contribute to the coproduction of the service by *assisting in service delivery;* often the more experienced customers can make the service employees' job easier. For example, a regular patient of a medical service provider is likely to know how the system works; she would know to bring her medication with her on a visit, to plan on paying by check (having previously learned that the office cannot process credit cards), and to schedule an annual mammogram without waiting for her doctor to prompt her. A second benefit relates to one of the benefits for customers that we have already discussed. We noted that loyal customers receive social benefits as a result of being in a relationship with a firm; employees who regularly interact with the same customers may also receive similar *social benefits*. A third benefit of customer retention is *employee retention*. It is easier for a firm to retain employees when it has a stable base of satisfied customers. People like to work for companies whose customers are happy and loyal. Their jobs are more satisfying, and they are able to spend more of their time fostering relationships than scrambling for new customers. In turn, customers are more satisfied and become even better customers—a positive upward spiral. Because employees stay with the firm longer, service quality improves and costs of turnover are reduced, adding further to profits.

RELATIONSHIP VALUE OF CUSTOMERS

Relationship value of a customer is a concept or calculation that looks at customers from the point of view of their lifetime revenue and/or profitability contributions to a company. This type of calculation is needed when companies start thinking of building long-term relationships with their customers. Just what is the potential financial value of those long-term relationships? And what are the financial implications of *losing* a customer? Here we will first summarize the factors that influence a customer's relationship value, and then show some ways it can be estimated. In Chapter 18 we provide more detail on lifetime value financial calculations.

Factors That Influence Relationship Value

The lifetime or relationship value of a customer is influenced by the length of an average "lifetime," the average revenues generated per relevant time period over the lifetime, sales of additional products and services over time, referrals generated by the customer over time, and costs associated with serving the customer. *Lifetime value* sometimes refers to lifetime revenue stream only; but most often when costs are considered, lifetime value really means *lifetime profitability*. Exhibit 7.2 provides an example of some factors that could be considered when calculating the potential relationship value of a Quicken (personal finance) software customer.

Exhibit 7.2 Calculating the Relationship Value of a Quicken Customer

Intuit Corporation's Quicken Software for personal finance can be purchased for about $50.* However, the relationship value of a Quicken customer to Intuit is potentially much more. How can this be? First, consider the additional products available to Quicken customers. Once a customer gets hooked on using the software, there are several other Quicken products she might find appealing. For example, Quicken provides a bill-paying service for $10 per month. Quicken customers can print their own checks and send them in matching envelopes for about $120 (for a box of 250). For about $45, Quicken customers can purchase Turbo Tax, a software product that can automatically use previously created Quicken data to prepare federal and state income tax returns. For customers who rely heavily on handheld devises or smart phones, Quicken has a Pocket Quicken version of their product for $40 that includes a single-tap data synchronization with a PC. Quicken provides customers with the option to do an automatic backup of the customer's data files on Intuit's website, Quicken. com, for $10 per year. Quicken offers a Medical Expense Manager, which allows customers to access all of their expenses, appointments, and insurance information, for $50 and a Home Inventory Manager for $30. And, for those customers who are parents of young children (ages 5–8), Quicken has a Kids & Money program that helps children discover how to earn, spend, save and share their money wisely for $99 per year. If a customer uses all these services, the revenue generated in just one year would be $454. (Intuit provides several other services, such as small-business accounting software and home mortgages, which might be of interest to Quicken customers. Quicken also offers its customers a credit card;

there is no annual fee, but the card has the potential to generate revenues from interest payments on outstanding balances.) After the first year, a satisfied Quicken customer is likely to continue to purchase annual software updates to acquire the latest product features and tax information. Over the course of five years, the revenue generated from this single customer would be more than $2,200. Finally, Quicken's satisfied customers are likely to refer new customers to Intuit, thus further enhancing the value of the initial customer relationship. Even one new customer referral per year can increase the relationship value potential of the first customer to several thousand dollars in just a few years!

*Figures in this example are based on 2007 prices as listed on http://www.intuit.com.

Estimating Customer Lifetime Value

If companies knew how much it really costs to lose a customer, they would be able to accurately evaluate investments designed to retain customers. One way of documenting the dollar value of loyal customers is to estimate the increased value or profits that accrue for each additional customer who remains loyal to the company rather than defecting to the competition. Bain & Co. has found that when the retention or loyalty rate rises by 5 percentage points total firm profits can increase from 35 to 95 percent.[30]

With sophisticated accounting systems to document actual costs and revenue streams over time, a firm can be quite precise in documenting the dollar value and costs of retaining customers. These systems attempt to estimate the dollar value of *all* the benefits and costs associated with a loyal customer, not just the long-term revenue stream. The value of word-of-mouth advertising, employee retention, and declining account maintenance costs can also enter into the calculation.[31]

For example, Table 7.1 shows how First Data Corporation estimates the lifetime value of an average business customer at its TeleCheck International subsidiary.

TABLE 7.1 **Lifetime Value of an Average Business Customer at Telecheck International**

Source: Reprinted with permission of The Free Press, a Division of Simon & Schuster, Inc., adapted from J. L. Heskett, W. E. Sasser, Jr., and L. A. Schlesinger, *The Service Profit Chain: How Leading Companies Link Profit and Growth to Loyalty* (New York: The Free Press, 1997), p. 201. Copyright © 1997 by J. L. Heskett, W. E. Sasser, and L. A. Schlesinger.

Year 0	Year 1	Year 2	Year 3	Year 4	Year 5
Revenue: [a]					
QuickResponse	—	$33,000	$39,600	$47,520	$57,024	$68,429
FastTrack	—	—	5,500	6,600	7,920	9,504
Costs:					
QuickResponse	$6,600	$24,090	$28,908	$34,690	$41,627	$49,953
FastTrack	—	—	4,152	4,983	5,980	7,175
Lifetime customer value:					
QuickResponse profit	($6,600)	$ 8,910	$10,692	$12,830	$15,397	$18,476
FastTrack profit	—	—	1,348	1,617	1,940	2,329
Reduced overhead allocation [b]	—	—	1,155	1,486	1,663	1,995
Profit from referrals [c]	—	—	1,100	1,650	3,300	6,600
Total profit	($6,600)	$ 8,910	$14,295	$17,583	$22,300	$29,400

Note: Product names and data have been disguised. As a result, profit on these products is overstated.
[a] Assuming revenue increases on both products of 20 percent per year.
[b] Declining at the rate of 15 percent per year in relation to revenue, to reflect lower costs of customer relationship associated with both customer and supplier learning curve effects.
[c] Estimated, based on assumptions concerning (1) the importance of referrals to new customers from old customers, (2) the frequency with which satisfied customers refer new customers, (3) the size of customers referred, and (4) the lifetime value calculations for new customers.

TeleCheck is a large check acceptance company that provides a range of financial services for business customers related to check guarantees, verifications, and collection services. By including estimates over a five-year lifetime of increased revenues from its core product (QuickResponse), declining per-unit service costs, increasing revenues from a new product (FastTrack), and profit from referrals, the company estimated that an annual increase in revenue of 20 percent on its base product would result in a 33 percent annual increase in operating profit over a five-year customer life.[32] Australia Post is another company that uses relationship value metrics to profile and group its top customers. It uses both financial (revenue) and nonfinancial criteria (mail volume, length of contract, and cross-product purchases) to determine who its best customers are—and offers them flexible pricing and personalized messages.[33]

Linking Customer Relationship Value to Firm Value

The emphasis on estimating the relationship value of customers has increased substantially in the past decade. Part of this emphasis has resulted from an increased appreciation of the economic benefits that firms accrue with the retention of loyal customers. Interestingly, recent research suggests that customer retention has a large impact on firm value and that relationship value calculations can also provide a useful proxy for assessing the value of a firm.[34] That is, a firm's market value can be roughly determined by carefully calculating customer lifetime value. The approach is straightforward: estimate the relationship value of a customer, forecast the future growth of the number of customers, and use these figures to determine the value of a company's current and future base. To the extent that the customer base forms a large part of a company's overall value, such a calculation can provide an estimate of a firm's value—a particularly useful figure for young, high-growth firms for which traditional financial methods (e.g., discounted cash flow) do not work well.

CUSTOMER PROFITABILITY SEGMENTS

Companies may want to treat all customers with excellent service, but they generally find that customers differ in their relationship value and that it may be neither practical nor profitable to meet (and certainly not to exceed) *all* customers' expectations.[35] FedEx Corporation, for example, categorized its customers internally as "the good, the bad, and the ugly"—based on their profitability. Rather than treating all its customers the same, the company paid particular attention to enhancing their relationships with the good, tries to move the bad to the good, and discourages the ugly.[36] Other companies also try to identify segments—or, more appropriately, tiers of customers—that differ in current and/or future profitability to a firm. This approach goes beyond usage or volume segmentation because it tracks costs and revenues for segments of customers, thereby capturing their financial worth to companies. After identifying profitability bands, the firm offers services and service levels in line with the identified segments. Building a high-loyalty customer base of the right customers increases profits. At MBNA, a leading financial services firm, a 5 percent jump in retention of the right customers increased the company profits 60 percent by the fifth year.[37]

Profitability Tiers—The Customer Pyramid

Although some people may view the FedEx grouping of customers into "the good, the bad, and the ugly" as negative, descriptive labels of the tiers can be very useful internally. Labels are especially valuable if they help the company keep track of which customers are profitable.

Virtually all firms are aware at some level that their customers differ in profitability; in particular, that a minority of their customers accounts for the highest proportion of sales or profit. This finding has often been called the "80/20 rule"—20 percent of customers produce 80 percent of sales or profit.

In this version of tiering, 20 percent of the customers constitute the top tier, those who can be identified as the most profitable in the company. The rest are indistinguishable from each other but differ from the top tier in profitability. Most companies realize that there are differences among customers within this tier but do not possess the data or capabilities to analyze the distinctions. The 80/20 two-tier scheme assumes that consumers within the two tiers are similar, just as conventional market segmentation schemes typically assume that consumers within segments are similar.

However, more than two tiers are likely and can be used if the company has sufficient data to analyze customer tiers more precisely. Different systems and labels can be helpful. One useful four-tier system, shown in Figure 7.4, includes the following:

1. The *platinum tier* describes the company's most profitable customers, typically those who are heavy users of the product, are not overly price sensitive, are willing to invest in and try new offerings, and are committed customers of the firm.

2. The *gold tier* differs from the platinum tier in that profitability levels are not as high, perhaps because the customers want price discounts that limit margins or are not as loyal. They may be heavy users who minimize risk by working with multiple vendors rather than just the focal company.

3. The *iron tier* contains essential customers who provide the volume needed to utilize the firm's capacity, but their spending levels, loyalty, and profitability are not substantial enough for special treatment.

4. The *lead tier* consists of customers who are costing the company money. They demand more attention than they are due given their spending and profitability and are sometimes problem customers—complaining about the firm to others and tying up the firm's resources.

FIGURE 7.4
The Customer Pyramid

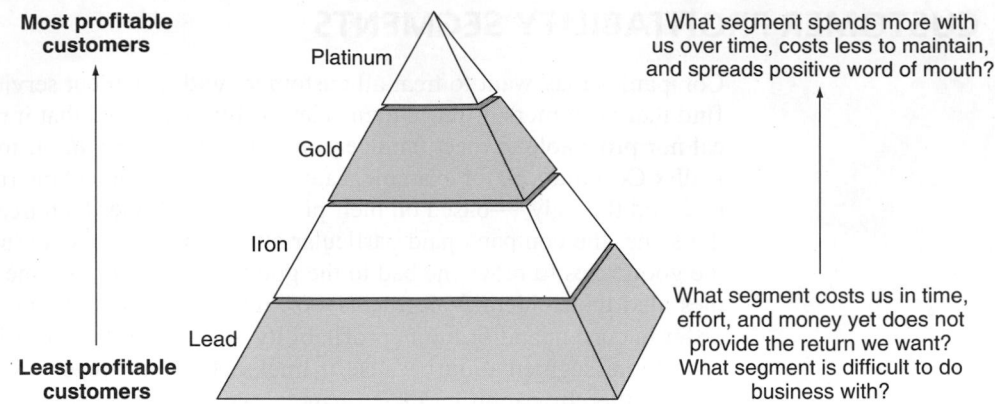

Note that this classification is superficially reminiscent of, but very different from, traditional usage segmentation performed by airlines such as American Airlines. Two differences are obvious. First, in the customer pyramid, profitability rather than usage defines all levels. Second, the lower levels actually articulate classes of customers who require a different sort of attention. The firm must work either to change the customers' behavior—to make them more profitable through increases in revenue—or to change the firm's cost structure to make them more profitable through decreases in costs.

Once a system has been established for categorizing customers, the multiple levels can be identified, motivated, served, and expected to deliver differential levels of profit. Companies improve their opportunities for profit when they increase shares of purchases by customers who either have the greatest need for the services or show the greatest loyalty to a single provider. By strengthening relationships with the loyal customers, increasing sales with existing customers, and increasing the profitability on each sale opportunity, companies thereby increase the potential of each customer.

The Customer's View of Profitability Tiers

Whereas profitability tiers make sense from the company's point of view, customers are not always understanding, nor do they appreciate being categorized into a less desirable segment.[38] For example, at some companies the top clients have their own individual account representative whom they can contact personally. The next tier of clients may be handled by representatives who each have 100 clients. Meanwhile, most clients are served by an 800 number, an automated voice response system, or referral to a website. Customers are often aware of this unequal treatment, and many resist and resent it. It makes perfect sense from a business perspective, but customers are often disappointed in the level of service they receive and give firms poor marks for quality as a result.

Therefore, it is increasingly important that firms communicate with customers so they understand the level of service they can expect and what they would need to do or pay to receive faster or more personalized service. The most significant issues result when customers do not understand why they are receiving a level of service that differs from what other customers are receiving, believe they have been singled out for poor service, or feel that the system is unfair. Although many customers refuse to pay for quality service, they react negatively if they believe it has been taken away from them unfairly.

The ability to segment customers narrowly based on profitability implications also raises questions of privacy for customers. To know who is profitable and who is not, companies must collect large amounts of individualized behavioral and personal data on consumers. Many consumers today resent what they perceive as an intrusion into their lives in this way, especially when it results in differential treatment that they perceive is unfair.

Making Business Decisions Using Profitability Tiers

Prudent business managers are well aware that past customer purchase behavior, although useful in making predictions, can be misleading.[39] What a customer spends today, or has spent in the past, may not necessarily be reflective of what he or she will do (or be worth) in the future. Banks serving college students know this well—a typical college student generally has minimal financial services needs (i.e., a checking account) and tends to not have a high level of deposits. However, within a few years that student may embark on a professional career, start a family, and/or purchase a house, and thus require several financial services and become a potentially very profitable customer to the bank. Generally speaking, a firm would like to keep its consistent big spenders and lose the erratic small spenders. But all too often a firm also has two other groups they must consider: erratic big spenders and consistent small spenders. So, in some situations where consistent cash flow is a concern, it may be helpful to a firm to have a portfolio of customers that includes steady customers, even if they have a history of being less profitable. Some service providers have actually been quite successful in targeting customers who were previously considered to be unworthy of another firm's marketing efforts.[40] Paychex, a payroll processing company, became very successful in serving small businesses that the major companies in this industry did not think were large enough to profitably serve. Similarly, Progressive Insurance became very successful in selling automobile insurance to undesirable customers—young drivers and those with poor driving records—that most of the competition did not feel had a sufficient relationship value. Firms, therefore, need to be cautious in blindly applying customer value calculations without thinking carefully about the implications.

RELATIONSHIP DEVELOPMENT STRATEGIES

To this point in the chapter, we have focused on the rationale for relationship marketing, the benefits (to both firms and customers) of the development of strong exchange relationships, and an understanding of the relationship value of a customer. In this section we examine a variety of factors that influence the development of strong customer relationships, including the customer's overall evaluation of a firm's offering, bonds created with customers by the firm, and barriers that the customer faces in leaving a relationship. These factors, illustrated in Figure 7.5, provide the rationale for specific strategies that firms often use to keep their current customers.

Core Service Provision

Retention strategies will have little long-term success unless the firm has a solid base of service quality and customer satisfaction on which to build. All the retention strategies that we describe in this section are built on the assumption of competitive quality and value being offered. Clearly, a firm needs to begin the relationship development process by providing a good core service delivery that, at a minimum, meets customer expectations; it does no good to design relationship strategies for inferior services.

FIGURE 7.5
**Relationship
Development Model**

Source: Adapted from
D. D. Gremler and
S. W. Brown, "Service
Loyalty: Antecedents,
Components, and Outcomes,"
in *1998 AMA Winter
Educators' Conference:
Marketing Theory and
Applications,* Vol. 9, D.
Grewal and C. Pechmann,
eds. Chicago, IL: American
Marketing Association,
pp. 165–166.

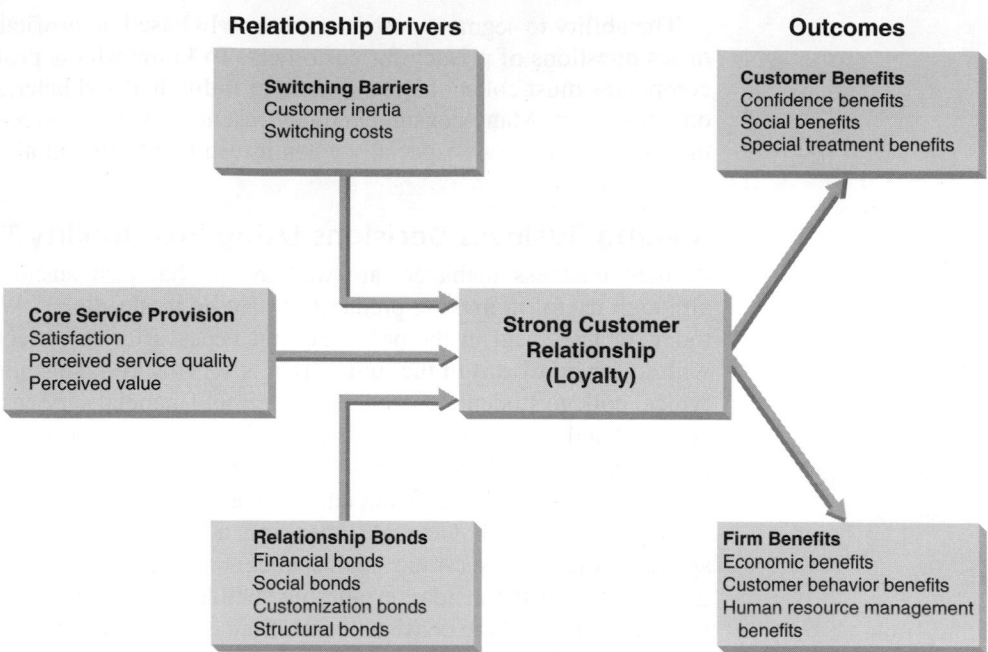

Two earlier examples, Intuit and USAA, provide convincing support for the argument that excellence in the core service or product offered is essential to a successful relationship strategy. Both of these companies have benefited tremendously from their loyal customer base; both offer excellent quality; both use relationship strategies to enhance their success.

Switching Barriers

When considering a switch in service providers, a customer may face a number of barriers that make it difficult to leave one service provider and begin a relationship with another. Literature suggests that these *switching barriers* influence consumers' decisions to exit from relationships with firms and, therefore, help to facilitate customer retention.[41]

Customer Inertia

One reason that customers commit to developing relationships with firms is that a certain amount of effort may be required to change firms. Sometimes consumers simplistically state that "it's just not worth it" to switch providers. *Inertia* may even explain why some dissatisfied customers stay with a provider. In discussing why people remain in relationships (in general) that they no longer find satisfying, scholars suggest that people may stay because breaking the relationship would require them to restructure their life—to develop new habits of living, to refashion old friendships, and to find new ones.[42] In other words, people do not like to change their behavior.

To retain customers, firms might consider increasing the *perceived effort* required on the part of the customer to switch service providers.[43] If a customer believes that a great deal of effort is needed to change companies, the customer is more likely to stay put. For example, automobile repair facilities might keep a complete and detailed maintenance history of a customer's vehicle. These records remove from the customer the burden of having to remember all the services performed on the vehicle and would force the customer to expend considerable effort in providing a complete maintenance history if the vehicle is taken to a new mechanic. Conversely, if a firm is looking to attract a competitor's customers, it might automate the process for switching providers as much as possible to reduce the effort required to switch. Long-distance telephone companies generally make switching providers as simple as saying "yes" on the telephone to a company representative—thereby removing any action required of the customer. Banks are also making it easy for a customer to switch; several banks offer to contact companies and employers on behalf of new customers to help change their direct deposits, automatic payments, and online bill payments from their old account to their new account.[44]

Switching Costs

In many instances, customers develop loyalty to an organization in part because of costs involved in changing to and purchasing from a different firm. These costs, both real and perceived, monetary and nonmonetary, are termed *switching costs*. Switching costs include investments of time, money, or effort—such as setup costs, search costs, learning costs, and contractual costs—that make it challenging for the customer to move to another provider.[45] To illustrate, a patient may incur *setup costs* such as paying for a complete physical when changing doctors or for new X-rays when switching dentists. Because services often have characteristics that make them difficult to evaluate—including intangibility, nonstandardization, and inseparability of production and consumption, as well as high experience and credence qualities—high *search costs* may be required to obtain suitable information about alternative services. *Learning costs* are those costs associated with learning the idiosyncrasies of how to use a product or service; in many situations, a customer who wishes to switch firms may need to accumulate new user skills or customer know-how. *Contractual costs* arise when the customer is required to pay a penalty to switch providers (e.g., prepayment charges for customer-initiated switching of mortgage companies or mobile telephone services), making it financially difficult, if not impossible, for the customer to initiate an early termination of the relationship.

To retain customers, firms might consider increasing their switching costs to make it difficult for customers to exit the relationship (or at least create the perception of difficulty). Indeed, many firms explicitly specify such costs in the contracts that they require their customers to sign (e.g., mobile telephone services, health clubs). To attract new customers, a service provider might consider implementing strategies designed to *lower* the switching costs of customers not currently using the provider. To reduce the setup costs involved when switching, providers could complete the paperwork required from the customer. Some banks, for example, employ "switch kits" that automatically move a customer's online billing information from a competitor's bank; such kits remove the switching costs surrounding one of the biggest barriers preventing customers from changing banks—transferring online bill payments.[46]

Relationship Bonds

Switching barriers tend to serve as constraints that keep customers in relationships with firms because they "have to."[47] However, firms can engage in activities that encourage customers to remain in the relationship because they "want to"—thus creating relationship bonds. Leonard Berry and A. Parasuraman have developed a framework for understanding the types of retention strategies that focus on developing bonds with customers.[48] The framework suggests that relationship marketing can occur at different levels and that each successive level of strategy results in ties that bind the customer

FIGURE 7.6
Levels of
Relationship
Strategies

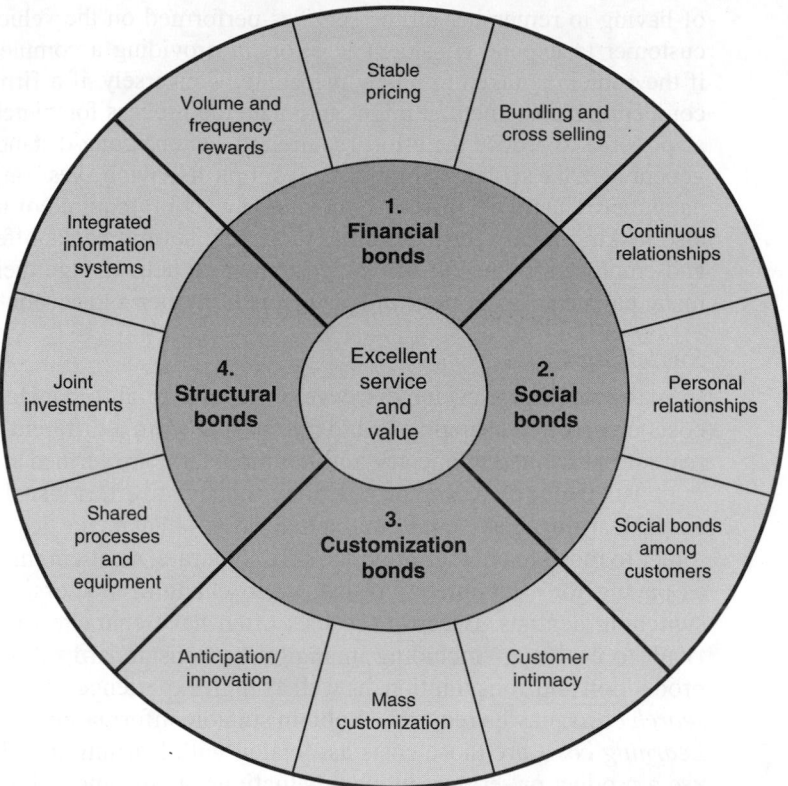

a little closer to the firm—and thus increase the potential for sustained competitive advantage. Building on the levels of the retention strategy idea, Figure 7.6 illustrates four types of retention strategies, which are discussed in the following sections. Recall, however, that the most successful retention strategies will be built on foundations of core service excellence.

Level 1—Financial Bonds

At level 1, the customer is tied to the firm primarily through financial incentives—lower prices for greater volume purchases or lower prices for customers who have been with the firm a long time. Examples of level 1 strategies are not hard to find. Think about the airline industry and related travel service industries like hotels and car rental companies. Frequent flyer programs provide financial incentives and rewards for travelers who bring more of their business to a particular airline. Hotels and car rental companies do the same. One reason these financial incentive programs flourish is that they are not difficult to initiate and frequently result in at least short-term profit gains. Unfortunately, financial incentives do not generally provide long-term advantages to a firm because, unless combined with another relationship strategy, they do not differentiate the firm from its competitors in the long run. Many travelers belong to several frequent flyer programs and do not hesitate to trade off among them. Although price and other financial incentives are important to customers, they are generally not difficult for competitors to imitate because the primary element of the marketing mix being manipulated is price.

Other types of retention strategies that depend primarily on financial rewards are focused on bundling and cross-selling of services. Frequent flyer programs again provide a common example. Many airlines link their reward programs with hotel chains, auto rental, and in some cases, credit card usage. By linking airline mileage points earned to usage of other firms' services, customers can enjoy even greater financial benefits in exchange for their loyalty.

In other cases, firms aim to retain their customers by simply offering their most loyal customers the assurance of stable prices, or at least lower price increases than those paid by new customers. In this way firms reward their loyal customers by sharing with them some of the cost savings and increased revenue that the firm receives through serving them over time.

Although widely and increasingly used as retention tactics, loyalty programs based on financial rewards merit caution.[49] As mentioned earlier, these programs are often easily imitated. Thus, any increased usage or loyalty from customers may be short-lived. Second, these strategies are not likely to be successful unless they are structured to truly lead to repeat or increased usage rather than serving as means to attract new customers and potentially causing endless switching among competitors.

Level 2—Social Bonds

Level 2 strategies bind customers to the firm through more than financial incentives. Although price is still assumed to be important, level 2 strategies seek to build long-term relationships through social and interpersonal as well as financial bonds. Customers are viewed as "clients," not nameless faces, and become individuals whose needs and wants the firm seeks to understand.

Social, interpersonal bonds are common among professional service providers (lawyers, accountants, teachers) and their clients as well as among personal care providers (hairdressers, counselors, health care providers) and their clients.[50] A dentist who takes a few minutes to review her patient's file before coming into the exam room is able to jog her memory on personal facts about the patient (occupation, family details, interests, dental health history). By bringing these personal details into the conversation, the dentist reveals her genuine interest in the patient as an individual and builds social bonds.

Interpersonal bonds are also common in business-to-business relationships in which customers develop relationships with salespeople and/or relationship managers working with their firms.[51] Recognizing the value of continuous relationships in building loyalty, Caterpillar Corporation credits its success to its extensive, stable distribution organization worldwide. Caterpillar is the world's largest manufacturer of mining, construction, and agricultural heavy equipment. Although its engineering and product quality are superior, the company attributes much of its success to its strong dealer network and product support services offered throughout the world. Former CEO David Fites indicated that knowledge of the local market and the close relationships with customers that Caterpillar's dealers provide has been invaluable: "Our dealers tend to be prominent business leaders in their service territories who are deeply involved in community activities and who are committed to living in the area. Their reputations and long-term relationships are important because selling our products is a personal business."[52]

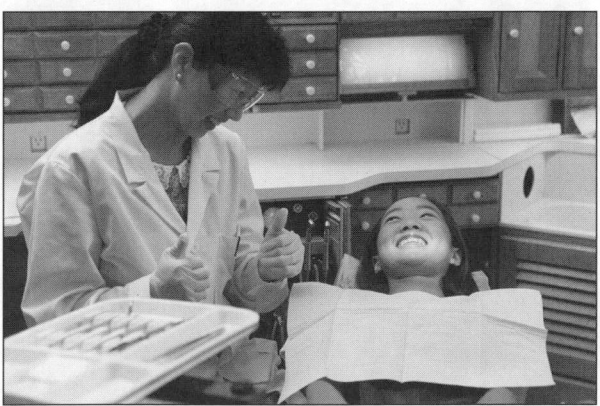

Level 2 strategies create positive social bonds between the client and service provider employees.

Sometimes relationships are formed with the organization because of the social bonds that develop *among customers* rather than between customers and the provider of the service.[53] Such bonds are often formed in health clubs, country clubs, educational settings, and other service environments where customers interact with each other. Over time the social relationships they have with other customers are important factors that keep them from switching to another organization. One company that has built a significant strategy around customer-to-customer bonds is Harley Davidson, with its local Harley Owners Groups, or HOGs. HOGs are involved in local rallies, tours, and parties as well as in national HOG events organized by the company. Through the HOGs, Harley customers come to know each other and develop a sense of community around their common interest—motorcycle riding—as illustrated in the photo below.

Social bonds alone may not tie the customer permanently to the firm, but they are much more difficult for competitors to imitate than are price incentives. In the absence of strong reasons to shift to another provider, interpersonal bonds can encourage customers to stay in a relationship.[54] In combination with financial incentives, social bonding strategies may be very effective.

Level 3—Customization Bonds

Level 3 strategies involve more than social ties and financial incentives, although there are common elements of level 1 and 2 strategies encompassed within a customization strategy and vice versa. Two commonly used terms fit within the customization bonds approach: *mass customization* and *customer intimacy*. Mass customization has been defined as "the use of flexible processes and organizational structures to produce varied and often individually customized products and services at the price of standardized, mass-produced alternatives."[55] Mass customization does not mean providing customers with endless solutions or choices that only make them work harder for what

Harley Davidson riders develop customer-to-customer bonds through Harley Owners Group (HOG) activities.

they want; rather, it means providing them through little effort on their part with tailored services to fit their individual needs. Similarly, customer intimacy is an approach that suggests customer loyalty can be encouraged through intimate knowledge of individual customers and through the development of one-to-one solutions that fit the individual customer's needs.

To illustrate customization bonds, consider Pandora—an Internet-based music discovery service that helps its customers find and enjoy music that they like. Based on a huge database that has categorized songs of more than 10,000 different artists based on unique attributes, it customizes its service offering to play music for customers that has the same characteristics of songs or artists they like. Customers are required to identify favorite songs or artists, and then Pandora's expert system analyses what they like and provides suggestions based on this analysis. To do this Pandora has assembled hundreds of musical attributes or "genes." Taken together these genes capture the unique and musical identity of a song—everything from melody, harmony, and rhythm to instrumentation, orchestration, arrangement, lyrics, singing, and vocal harmony—and uses this information to customize music to each customer's unique tastes and interests. The earlier Technology Spotlight illustrates how Hilton Hotels uses technology to customize services to a large number of individual customers. Our Global Feature illustrates how Boots The Chemists in the United Kingdom has used technology to understand its customers and build the world's largest smart card loyalty scheme.

Level 4—Structural Bonds

Level 4 strategies are the most difficult to imitate; they involve structural as well as financial, social, and customization bonds between the customer and the firm. Structural bonds are created by providing services to the client that are frequently designed right into the service delivery system for that client. Often, structural bonds are created by providing customized services to the client that are technology based and make the customer more productive.

An example of structural bonds can be seen in a business-to-business context with Allegiance Healthcare Corporation. By working closely with its hospital customers, Allegiance (a Cardinal Health company) established ways to improve hospital supply ordering, delivery, and billing that have greatly enhanced its value as a supplier. For example, Allegiance developed "hospital-specific pallet architecture," which meant that all items arriving at a particular hospital were shrink-wrapped with labels visible for easy identification. Separate pallets were assembled to reflect the individual hospital's storage system so that instead of miscellaneous supplies arriving in boxes sorted at the convenience of Allegiance's internal needs, they arrived on client-friendly pallets designed to suit the distribution needs of the individual hospital. By linking the hospital through its ValueLink service into a database ordering system and by providing enhanced value in the actual delivery, Allegiance structurally tied itself to its more than 150 acute care hospitals in the United States. In addition to the enhanced service that ValueLink provides, Allegiance estimates that the system saves its customers an average of $500,000 or more each year.[56]

But there is also a potential downside to this arrangement from the customer's perspective. Customers may fear that tying themselves too closely to one provider will not allow them to take advantage of potential price savings from other providers in the future.

founded in 1887, offers its products through 1,500 retail stores as well as an online store at www.wellbeing.com, and it is deservedly called the "Chemist to the Nation." On its website, the Boots Company states that it intends to become the global leader in well-being products and services and is expanding globally through Boots Healthcare International.

A foundation for Boots's success in recent years is its increased focus on the customer and a desire to develop customer loyalty through a number of retention and relationship strategies. At the heart of the company's loyalty strategy is its Advantage Card, started in 1997. After Boots merged with Alliance in 2006, the Advantage Card became one of the world's largest smart card loyalty schemes, with more than 15 million members. Over 70 percent of Boots's current sales are now linked

Boots The Chemists is one of the best-known and trusted brands in the United Kingdom and is the United Kingdom's leading health and beauty retailer. The company,

RELATIONSHIP CHALLENGES

Given the many benefits of long-term customer relationships, it would seem that a company would not want to refuse to serve or terminate a relationship with any customer. Yet, situations arise in which either the firm, the customer, or both want to end (or have to end) their relationship. This final section of the chapter discusses situations in which the *firm* might actually consider ending the relationship and how that might occur; in the next chapter we discuss situations in which the *customer* might decide to terminate the relationship and switch providers.

The Customer Is *Not* Always Right

The assumption that *all* customers are good customers is very compatible with the belief that "the customer is always right," an almost sacrosanct tenet of business. Yet any service worker can tell you that this statement is *not* always true, and in some cases it may be preferable for the firm and the customer to not continue their relationship. The following discussion presents a view of customer relationships that

to the card. The card offers a number of benefits to customers and has helped the company increase sales, but more than that, it has been the foundation for building greater loyalty among Boots's best customers.

Using the card for purchases, Boots's customers receive four points for every pound spent. These points can be redeemed for selected products, aimed to treat customers to something special rather than simply to offer discounts off purchases. In fact the card is *not* about discounts; rather, it is about treating oneself. Customers can use their points to treat themselves to a simple lunch or to a full day of pampering at a spa. From a financial perspective, the company has seen increasing average transaction values among higher-spending customers. Boots managers say that they have increased loyalty and spending from people who were already good and profitable customers—a clear win for the company.

A number of initiatives are tied to the Advantage Card, taking it beyond a pure points reward program from the customer's perspective. For example, Boots mails a first-class health and beauty magazine to the top-spending 3 million Advantage Card holders. The magazine is Britain's biggest health and beauty magazine; it is not viewed as a "Boots" magazine but rather as a health and beauty magazine sent by Boots. Cardholders also have access to additional benefits and discounts using interactive kiosks in more than 500 stores. The card can be used for purchases at the online store through www.wellbeing.com. Many products offered on the site are not available in Boots stores. In addition, the site provides access to an online magazine, answers to questions, a chat room, and other features and services.

A credit card version of the Advantage Card was launched in 2001, and Boots joined with the Department of Health to enable card holders to register with the National Health Service Organ Donor program.

From the company's perspective as well, the card is much more than a reward program. Data generated through the card are used to understand customers and to anticipate and identify individual needs in health and beauty care products. In fact, the goals with the Advantage Card program back in 1997 were to gain customer insight, build a database that would allow the company to tailor offerings to individual customers' needs, develop incremental sales by building customer loyalty, and use the customer knowledge to develop and introduce new products and services. A great deal of planning and testing went into developing the program, and this planning paid off in customer loyalty. Buy-in from the company's 60,000 staff members at the time also aided in the rapid success of the program. All associates were signed up as members six months before the launch of the card. After experiencing the benefits of the card firsthand, they became enthusiastic advocates, encouraging customers to sign up.

Through the program, Boots has learned that the more broadly customers buy, in more categories over time, the more they increase visits to Boots stores. The result has been customization of product and service offerings and more sales and greater loyalty from its best customers.

Sources: Frederick Newell, *Loyalty.com* (New York: McGraw-Hill, 2000), chap. 24, pp. 239–245; www.boots-the-chemists.co.uk, 2007; www.wellbeing.com, 2007.

suggests that all relationships may not be beneficial and that every customer is not right all the time.

The Wrong Segment

A company cannot target its services to all customers; some segments will be more appropriate than others. It would not be beneficial to either the company or the customer for a company to establish a relationship with a customer whose needs the company cannot meet. For example, a school offering a lock-step, daytime MBA program would not encourage full-time working people to apply for its program nor would a law firm specializing in government issues establish a relationship with individuals seeking advice on trusts and estates. These examples seem obvious. Yet firms frequently do give in to the temptation to make a sale by agreeing to serve a customer who would be better served by someone else.

Similarly, it would not be wise to forge relationships simultaneously with incompatible market segments. In many service businesses (such as restaurants, hotels, tour package operators, entertainment, and education), customers experience the service together and can influence each other's perceptions about value received. Thus, to maximize service to core segments, an organization may choose to turn away marginally profitable segments that would be incompatible. For example, a conference hotel may find that mixing executives in town for a serious educational program with students in town for a regional track meet may not be wise. If the executives are deemed to be key long-term customers, the hotel may choose to pass up the sports group in the interest of retaining the executives.

Not Profitable in the Long Term

In the absence of ethical or legal mandates, organizations will prefer *not* to have long-term relationships with unprofitable customers. Some segments of customers will not be profitable for the company even if their needs can be met by the services offered. Some examples of this situation are when there are not enough customers in the segment to make it profitable to serve, when the segment cannot afford to pay the cost of the service, or when the projected revenue flows from the segment would not cover the costs incurred to originate and maintain their business.

At the individual customer level, it may not be profitable for a firm to engage in a relationship with a particular customer who has bad credit or who is a poor risk for some other reason. Retailers, banks, mortgage companies, and credit card companies routinely refuse to do business with individuals whose credit histories are unreliable. Although the short-term sale may be beneficial, the long-term risk of nonpayment makes the relationship unwise from the company's point of view. Similarly, some car rental companies check into the driving records of customers and reject bad-risk drivers.[57] This practice, while controversial, is logical from the car rental companies' point of view because they can cut back on insurance costs and accident claims (thus reducing rental costs for good drivers) by not doing business with accident-prone drivers.

Beyond the monetary costs associated with serving the wrong customers, there can be substantial time investments in some customers that, if actually computed, would make them unprofitable for the organization. Everyone has had the experience of waiting in a bank, a retail store, or even in an education setting while a particularly demanding customer seems to use more than his share of the service provider's time. The dollar value of the time spent with a specific customer is typically not computed or calculated into the price of the service.

In a business-to-business relationship, the variability in time commitment to customers is even more apparent. Some customers may use considerable resources of the supplier organization through inordinate numbers of phone calls, excessive requests for information, and other time-consuming activities. In the legal profession, clients are billed for every hour of the firm's time that they use in this way because time is essentially the only resource the firm has. Yet in other service businesses, all clients essentially pay the same regardless of the time demands they place on the organization.

Difficult Customers

Managers have repeated the phrase "the customer is always right" so often that you would expect it to be accepted by every employee in every service organization. So why isn't it? Perhaps because it simply is not true. The customer is not always right. No matter how frequently it is said, repeating that mantra does not make it become reality, and service employees know it.

In many situations, firms have service encounters that fail because of *dysfunctional customers*. Dysfunctional customer behavior refers to actions by customers who intentionally, or perhaps unintentionally, act in a manner

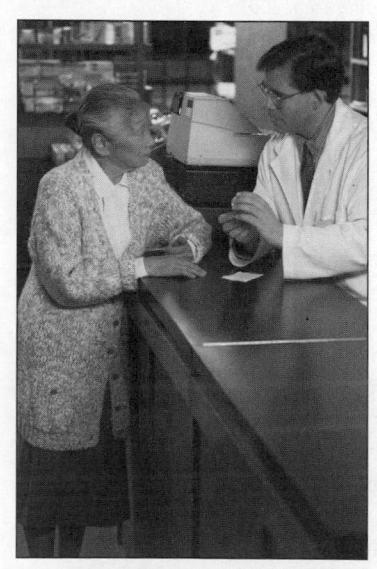

Some customers may be difficult, if not impossible, to serve.

that in some way disrupts otherwise functional service encounters.[58] Such customers have been described as "customers from hell," "problem customers," or "jay customers." One of us was awakened during a hotel stay at 4:00 a.m. by drunk customers who were arguing with each other in a room above; management eventually called the police and asked them to escort the customers off the property. An Enterprise Rent-A-Car customer demanded that she not be charged for any of the two weeks that she had a car because, near the end of the rental period, she found a small stain in the back seat.[59] These customers often have the objective of gaining faster, superior, or perhaps free service, but their behavior is considered dysfunctional from the perspective of the service provider and perhaps fellow customers.

Dysfunctional customer behavior can affect employees, other customers, and the organization. Research suggests that exposure to dysfunctional customer behavior can have psychological, emotional, behavioral, and physical effects on employees.[60] For example, customer-contact employees who are exposed to rude, threatening, obstructive, aggressive, or disruptive behavior by customers often have their mood, motivation, or morale negatively affected. Such customers are difficult to work with and often create stress for employees.[61] (See photo on pg 200 for one example.) Dysfunctional customers can also have an impact on other customers: Such behavior can spoil the service experience for other customers, and the dysfunctional customer behavior may become contagious for other customers witnessing it. Finally, dysfunctional customer behavior can create both direct costs and indirect costs for the organization. Direct costs of such behavior can include the expense of restoring damaged property, increased insurance premiums, property loss by theft, costs incurred in compensating customers affected by the dysfunctional behavior of others, and the costs incurred through illegitimate claims by dysfunctional customers. Additionally, indirect costs might include increased workloads for staff required to deal with dysfunctional behavior as well as increased costs for attracting and retaining appropriate personnel and, perhaps, for absenteeism payments.

Although these difficult customers often will be accommodated and employees can be trained to recognize and deal with them appropriately, at times the best choice may be to not maintain the relationship at all—especially at the business-to-business level, where long-term costs to the firm can be substantial. For example, occasionally advertising agencies find some accounts are so difficult to work with that they simply cannot—or will not—serve them.[62] Difficult clients paralyze an ad agency for a variety of reasons. Some ask that a particular ad campaign work for all their diverse constituencies at the same time, which in some cases may be next to impossible. Others require so much up-front work and ad testing before selecting an agency that the work is essentially done for free by those agencies not selected. Other clients are stingy; call for dozens of storyboards before settling on a concept; or require a lot of direct, frequently disruptive, involvement in the production process. As a result, agencies have become more wary of chasing every client that comes along.

Ending Business Relationships

For the effective management of service relationships, managers should not only know how to establish a relationship but also how to end one. As suggested in the previous section, firms may identify some customers who are not in their targeted segment, who are not profitable in the long run, or who are difficult to work with or dysfunctional. A company may *not* want to continue in a relationship with every customer. However, gracefully exiting a relationship may not be easy. Customers may end up feeling disappointed, confused, or hurt if a firm attempts to terminate the relationship. Our Strategy Insight illustrates how three firms chose to end relationships with their customers.

Strategy Insight "The Customer Is Always Right": Rethinking an Old Tenet

The old tenet, "the customer is always right," has operated as the basic rule in business for so long that it has become entrenched as an "absolute truth." The practical reality, however, is that sometimes the customer is wrong. When taken to the extreme, the issue for the firm becomes what to do about it. Service managers understand that there are situations when employees should be fired. In some situations, this strategy may need to be applied to customers, too.

SPRINT/NEXTEL FIRES 1,000 CUSTOMERS

On June 29, 2007, Sprint/Nextel sent a letter to about 1,000 of its 53 million customers telling them, in effect, they had been fired from the company. In doing so Sprint was attempting to rid itself of customers who frequent its customer service lines by informing them that it was canceling their service at the end of the next month. In these letters the company stated: "While we have worked to resolve your issues and questions to the best of our ability, the number of inquiries you have made to us during this time has led us to determine that we are unable to meet your current wireless needs."

The customers were told their service agreements were being terminated, they would not owe anything on their final bill, and the company would waive its standard early termination fees. They also were told to switch to another wireless provider by July 30 if they wanted to keep their phone number.

A disgruntled Spint/Nextel customer

These 1,000 customers had been calling Sprint's customer service an average of 25 times a month, which is 40 times more frequently than a typical customer. Sprint determined these customers were not generating enough revenue to make up for the high cost of servicing them. The company conducted an internal review, lasting more than six months, to determine what types of problems these customers had and what information they were seeking when they contacted the customer service department. The review found that the subscribers often were calling about the same problems over and over after Sprint officials felt they had resolved the issue. Additionally, some callers were repeatedly asking for information about other customers' accounts, which customer service representatives are not allowed to divulge. Sprint indicated that the amount of time being spent to resolve the same issues again and again was affecting their ability to service other customers.

The Results

Initially Sprint's move made headlines in the business press, stimulated negative word-of-mouth from some portion of these 1,000 customers, and may have cost them some new customers in the short run. But it also improved the customer experience for other customers calling customer service.

ZANE'S CYCLES TELLS CUSTOMER: "GET OUT . . . AND TELL ALL YOUR FRIENDS"

A recent *Business Horizons* article tells the following story of the owner of a bicycle store well known for its dedication to customer service—Zane's Cycles in Branford, Connecticut (for more insights into Zane's Cycles, see our Chapter 5 opener):

> A father was picking up a repaired bicycle for his daughter, who, without telling him, had approved the recommended replacement of both tires (a $40 service). Although the employee patiently and repeatedly explained that the purchase was approved and offered to further verify it, the customer made accusatory remarks and yelled at her angrily, saying at one point, "Either you think I'm stupid or you're stupid. You're trying to rip me

off." At that point, Chris Zane, the store's owner, walked up to the customer and said, "I'm Chris Zane, get out of my store, and tell all your friends!" After the customer wordlessly slapped $40 on the counter and stormed out, the besieged employee looked at Zane and asked "'. . . and tell all your friends'?"

Zane explained to her and other employees who had gravitated to the front of the store that he wanted it to be clear that he valued his employee infinitely more than a rude, belligerent customer. "I also explained that this was the first time I had ever thrown a customer out of the store and that I would not tolerate my employees being mistreated by anyone . . . I believe that my employees need to know that I respect them and expect them to respect our customers. Simply, if I am willing to fire an employee for mistreating a customer (and I have) then I must also be willing to fire a customer for mistreating an employee."

The Results

After returning home and thinking about the service encounter, the fired customer phoned the owner to apologize three hours later. He explained that he had argued with his wife prior to visiting the store and was therefore already in a poor mood. Once the customer returned home and verified the accuracy of the store employee's explanation, he realized he had been unreasonable. The customer asked if he could be allowed to shop in the store again. He also commented that he respected the owner for supporting his employee even if it might mean losing a customer. Mr. Zane thanked him for the call, welcomed him back to the store, and indicated that the apology would be conveyed to the employee.

EVENTS PLANNER TELLS MAJOR CLIENT: "NEVER AGAIN"

Capitol Services Inc.—an event planning company in Washington, DC—spent considerable time and money attempting to secure a major automobile company's potentially very lucrative business. In the midst of the first-ever event for the client at a museum in Washington, DC, the person overseeing the event (who was not an employee of the company but working for a third party) became very demanding, degrading, and disrespectful to the CSI staff. Nearly everything the firm did was, in her opinion, not good enough. The entire team, who was in the midst of delivering an event exactly as promised, was being micromanaged. CSI employees felt they were being abused, and for no good reason. David Hainline, company president, approached the client representative and said that CSI would finish the event but would never conduct business again with her—knowing full well this decision might result in the loss of a client with a very high potential relationship value.

The Results

The event was delivered as promised, but the belligerent staff member was not happy. After the event was completed, she demanded that CSI reduce the amount owed for their services—so CSI reduced the amount by $60,000. Months later Hainline had a meeting with the automobile company and began the meeting with an explanation of the situation that occurred at the Smithsonian. The company understood, and agreed to use CSI to organize future events for them in Washington, DC. And, CSI employees felt valued and supported by the management team.

ENDING A CUSTOMER RELATIONSHIP MAY BE THE RIGHT STRATEGIC DECISION

Service providers are not obligated to serve any and all customers, no matter how much revenue they might generate. Although services marketing strategies intended to develop relationships with customers receive much attention—and rightly so—from managers, occasionally selecting a strategy that results in ending a relationship with a customer may be the most prudent approach to take.

Sources: S. Srivastava, "Sprint Drops Clients over Excessive Inquiries," *The Wall Street Journal,* July 7, 2007, p. A3; L. L. Berry and K. Seiders, "Serving Unfair Customers," *Business Horizons* 51 (January/February 2008), pp. 29–37; D. Hainline, President, Capitol Services Inc., Washington, DC, personal interview, August 15, 2007.

Relationship Endings

Relationships end in different ways—depending on the type of relationship in place.[63] In some situations, a relationship is established for a certain purpose and/or time period and then dissolves when it has served its purpose or the time frame has elapsed. For example, a house painting service may be engaged with the customer for four days while painting the house exterior, but both parties understand that the end of the relationship is predetermined—the end occurs when the house has been painted and the customer has paid for the service. Sometimes a relationship has a natural ending.[64] Piano lessons for children, for example, often cease as the child gets older and develops interests in other musical areas (such as singing or playing the clarinet); in such situations, the need for the relationship has diminished or become obsolete. In other situations, an event may occur that forces the relationship to end; a provider who relocates to the other side of town may force some customers to select a different company. Or an ending may occur because the customer is not fulfilling his or her obligations. For example, a bank may choose to end the relationship with a customer who regularly has insufficient funds in the checking account. Whatever the reason for ending the relationship, firms should clearly communicate their reasons for wanting (or needing) to terminate it so that customers understand what is occurring and why.

Should Firms Fire Their Customers?

A logical conclusion to be drawn from the discussion of the challenges firms face in customer relationships is that perhaps firms should seek to get rid of those customers who are not right for the company. Many companies are making these types of decisions based on the belief that troublesome customers are usually less profitable and less loyal and that it may be counterproductive to attempt to retain their business.[65] Another reason for "firing" a customer is the negative effect that these customers can have on employee quality of life and morale.

One company came to this conclusion when a client, the CEO of an Internet start-up company, paged one of its employees at her home on the West Coast at 4 a.m. and asked her to order a limousine for him in New York City.[66] This incident was enough to push the employee over the edge and cause her boss to agree that the company should fire this client. It did so by directly telling him that the relationship was not working out and to take his business elsewhere.

Another company took reducing its customer base to the extreme. Nypro—a global, employee-owned company specializing in molded plastics applications for such clients as Gillette, Abbott Laboratories, Hewlett-Packard, and other large organizations,[67] reduced its customer base in the 1980s from 800 to approximately 30 clients on the belief that it could better serve those clients and grow more effectively if it focused on fewer relationships. Nypro adopted a customer intimacy strategy and tied itself closely to this much smaller number of clients. Some of these clients have now been with Nypro for more than 40 years. Over time Nypro has selectively added clients to this base, and the company has enjoyed 21 consecutive years of record sales.

Although it may sound like a good idea, firing customers is not that simple and needs to be done in a way that avoids negative publicity or negative word of mouth. Sometimes raising prices or charging for services that previously had been given away for free can move unprofitable customers out of the company. Helping a client find a new provider who can better meet its needs is another way to gracefully exit a nonproductive relationship. If the customer has become too demanding, the relationship may be salvaged by negotiating expectations or finding more efficient ways to serve the client. If not, both parties may need to find an agreeable way to end the relationship.

Summary

In this chapter we focused on the rationale for, benefits of, and strategies for developing long-term relationships with customers. It should be obvious by now that organizations that focus only on acquiring new customers may well fail to understand their current customers; thus, while a company may be bringing customers in through the front door, equal or greater numbers may be exiting. Estimates of lifetime relationship value accentuate the importance of retaining current customers.

The particular strategy that an organization uses to retain its current customers can and should be customized to fit the industry, the culture, and the customer needs of the organization. However, in general, customer relationships are driven by a variety of factors that influence the development of strong customer relationships, including (1) the customer's overall evaluation of the quality of a firm's core service offering, (2) the switching barriers that the customer faces in leaving a relationship, and (3) the relationship bonds developed with that customer by the firm. By developing strong relationships with customers and by focusing on factors that influence customer relationships, the organization will accurately understand customer expectations over time and consequently will narrow service quality gap 1.

The chapter concluded with a discussion of the challenges that firms face in developing relationships with customers. Although long-term customer relationships are critical and can be very profitable, firms should not attempt to build relationships with just any customer. In other words, "the customer is not always right." Indeed, in some situations it may be best for firms to discontinue relationships with some customers—for the sake of the customer, the firm, or both.

Discussion Questions

1. Discuss how relationship marketing or retention marketing is different from the traditional emphasis in marketing.

2. Describe how a firm's relationships with customers may evolve over time. For each level of relationship discussed in the chapter, identify a firm with which you have that level of relationship, and discuss how its marketing efforts differ from other firms.

3. Think about a service organization that retains you as a loyal customer. Why are you loyal to this provider? What are the benefits to you of staying loyal and not switching to another provider? What would it take for you to switch?

4. With regard to the same service organization, what are the benefits to the organization of keeping you as a customer? Calculate your "lifetime value" to the organization.

5. Describe the logic behind "customer profitability segmentation" from the company's point of view. Also discuss what customers may think of the practice.

6. Describe the various switching barriers discussed in the text. What switching barriers might you face in switching banks? Mobile telephone service providers? Universities?

7. Describe the four levels of retention strategies, and give examples of each type. Again, think of a service organization to which you are loyal. Can you describe the reason(s) you are loyal in terms of the different levels? In other words, what ties you to the organization?

8. Have you ever worked as a frontline service employee? Can you remember having to deal with difficult or "problem" customers? Discuss how you handled such situations. As a manager of frontline employees, how would you help your employees deal with difficult customers?

Exercises

1. Interview the manager of a local service organization. Discuss with the manager the target market(s) for the service. Estimate the lifetime value of a customer in one or more of the target segments. To do this estimate, you will need to get as much information from the manager as you can. If the manager cannot answer all of your questions, make some assumptions.

2. In small groups in class, debate the question "Is the customer always right?" In other words, are there times when the customer may be the wrong customer for the organization?

3. Design a customer appreciation program for the organization with whom you currently work. Why would you have such a program, and to whom would it be directed toward?

4. Choose a specific company context (your class project company, the company you work for, or a company in an industry you are familiar with). Calculate the lifetime value of a customer for this company. You will need to make assumptions to do this calculation, so make your assumptions clear. Using ideas and concepts from this chapter, describe a relationship marketing strategy to increase the number of lifetime customers for this firm.

Notes

1. USAA is featured in the following two books, and material in this section is drawn from them: L. L. Berry, *Discovering the Soul of Service* (New York: The Free Press, 1999); F. F. Reichheld, *Loyalty Rules!* (Boston: Harvard Business School Press, 2001).

2. D. Shah, R. T. Rust, A. Parasuraman, R. Staelin, and G. S. Day, "The Path to Customer Centricity," *Journal of Service Research* 9 (November 2006), pp. 113–124.

3. J. McGregor, "Employee Innovator: USAA," *Fast Company,* October 1999, p. 57.

4. J. McGregor, "Customer Service Champs," *BusinessWeek,* March 5, 2007, pp. 52–64.

5. Shah et al., "The Path to Customer Centricity."

6. F. E. Webster Jr., "The Changing Role of Marketing in the Corporation," *Journal of Marketing* 56 (October 1992), pp. 1–17.

7. For discussions of relationship marketing and its influence on the marketing of services, consumer goods, strategic alliances, distribution channels, and buyer–seller interactions, see *Journal of the Academy of Marketing Science,* Special Issue on Relationship Marketing (vol. 23, Fall 1995). Some of the early roots of this paradigm shift can be found in C. Gronroos, *Service Management and Marketing* (New York: Lexington Books, 1990); E. Gummesson, "The New Marketing—Developing Long-Term Interactive Relationships," *Long Range Planning* 20 (1987), pp. 10–20.

For excellent reviews of relationship marketing across a spectrum of topics, see J. N. Sheth, *Handbook of Relationship Marketing* (Thousand Oaks, CA: Sage Publications, 2000).

8. L. L. Berry and A. Parasuraman, *Marketing Services* (New York: Free Press, 1991), chap. 8.

9. G. Knisely, "Comparing Marketing Management in Package Goods and Service Organizations," a series of interviews appearing in *Advertising Age,* January 15, February 19, March 19, and May 14, 1979.

10. This discussion is based on M. D. Johnson and F. Selnes, "Customer Portfolio Management: Toward a Dynamic Theory of Exchange Relationships," *Journal of Marketing* 68 (April 2004), pp. 1–17.

11. R. M. Morgan and S. D. Hunt, "The Commitment-Trust Theory of Relationship Marketing," *Journal of Marketing* 58 (July 1994), pp. 20–38; N. Bendapudi and L. L. Berry, "Customers' Motivations for Maintaining Relationships with Service Providers," *Journal of Retailing* 73 (Spring 1997), pp. 15–37.

12. Johnson and Selnes, "Customer Portfolio Management."

13. Ibid.

14. See also D. Siredeshmukh, J. Singh, and B. Sabol, "Customer Trust, Value, and Loyalty in Relational Exchanges," *Journal of Marketing* 66 (January 2002), pp. 15–37.

15. See C. Huffman and B. Kahn, "Variety for Sale: Mass Customization or Mass Confusion?" *Journal of Retailing* 74 (Winter 1998), pp. 491–513; B. J. Pine and J. H. Gilmore, "Welcome to the Experience Economy," *Harvard Business Review* 76 (July–August 1998), pp. 97–105; B. J. Pine, D. Peppers, and M. Rogers, "Do You Want to Keep Your Customers Forever?" *Harvard Business Review* 73 (March–April 1995), pp. 103–114.

16. The three types of relational benefits discussed in this section are drawn from K. P. Gwinner, D. D. Gremler, and M. J. Bitner, "Relational Benefits in Service Industries: The Customer's Perspective," *Journal of the Academy of Marketing Science* 26 (Spring 1998), pp. 101–114.

17. Ibid, p. 104.

18. See M. B. Adelman, A. Ahuvia, and C. Goodwin, "Beyond Smiling: Social Support and Service Quality," in *Service Quality: New Directions in Theory and Practice,* ed. R. T. Rust and R. L. Oliver (Thousand Oaks, CA: Sage Publications, 1994), pp. 139–172; C. Goodwin, "Private Roles in Public Encounters: Communal Relationships in Service Exchanges," unpublished manuscript, University of Manitoba, 1993.

19. E. J. Arnould and L. L. Price, "River Magic: Extraordinary Experience and the Extended Service Encounter," *Journal of Consumer Research* 20 (June 1993), pp. 24–45.

20. N. Bendapudi and R. P. Leone, "How to Lose Your Star Performer without Losing Customers, Too," *Harvard Business Review 79* (November 2001), pp. 104–115.

21. Gwinner, Gremler, and Bitner, "Relational Benefits in Service Industries"; T. Hennig-Thurau, K. P. Gwinner, and D. D. Gremler, "Understanding Relationship Marketing Outcomes: An Integration of Relational Benefits and Relationship Quality," *Journal of Service Research* 4 (February 2002), pp. 230–247.

22. P. Kumar, "The Impact of Long-Term Client Relationships on the Performance of Business Service Firms," *Journal of Service Research* 2 (August 1999), pp. 4–18.

23. C. Homburg, N. Koschate, and W. D. Hoyer, "Do Satisfied Customers Really Pay More? A Study of the Relationship between Customer Satisfaction and Willingness to Pay," *Journal of Marketing* 69 (April 2005), pp. 84–96.

24. F. F. Reichheld and W. E. Sasser Jr., "Zero Defections: Quality Comes to Services," *Harvard Business Review* 68 (September–October 1990), pp. 105–111; F. F. Reichheld, *The Loyalty Effect* (Boston: Harvard Business School Press, 1996); S. Gupta and V. Zeithaml, "Customer Metrics and Their Impact on Financial Performance," *Marketing Science* 25 (November–December 2006), pp. 718–739.

25. R. Dhar and R. Glazer, "Hedging Customers," *Harvard Business Review* 81 (May 2003), pp. 86–92.

26. D. D. Gremler and S. W. Brown, "The Loyalty Ripple Effect: Appreciating the Full Value of Customers," *International Journal of Service Industry Management* 10, no. 3 (1999), pp. 271–291.

27. L. A. Bettencourt, "Customer Voluntary Performance: Customers as Partners in Service Delivery," *Journal of Retailing* 73 (Fall 1997), pp. 383–406; S. S. Tax, M. Colgate, and D. E. Bowen, "How to Prevent Your Customers from Failing," *Sloan Management Review* 47 (Spring 2006), pp. 30–38.

28. M. S. Rosenbaum and C. A. Massiah, "When Customers Receive Support from Other Customers: Exploring the Influence of Intercustomer Social Support on Customer Voluntary Performance," *Journal of Service Research* 9 (February 2007), pp. 257–270.

29. S. J. Grove and R. P. Fisk, "The Impact of Other Customers on Service Experiences: A Critical Incident Examination of 'Getting Along,'" *Journal of Retailing* 73 (Spring 1997), pp. 63–85.

30. Reichheld and Sasser, "Zero Defections."

31. Additional frameworks for calculating lifetime customer value that include a variety of other variables can be found in W. J. Reinartz and V. Kumar, "The Impact of Customer Relationship Characteristics on Profitable Lifetime Duration," *Journal of Marketing* 67 (January 2003), pp. 77–99; Dhar and Glazer, "Hedging Customers"; H. K. Stahl, K. Matzler, and H. H. Hinterhuber, "Linking Customer Lifetime Value with Shareholder Value," *Industrial Marketing Management* 32, no. 4 (2003), pp. 267–279.

32. This example is cited in J. L. Heskett, W. E. Sasser Jr., and L. A. Schlesinger, *The Service Profit Chain* (New York: The Free Press, 1997), pp. 200–201.

33. http://www.1to1media.com/viewspx?DocID=30371, accessed August 15, 2007.

34. S. Gupta, D. R. Helmann, and J. A. Stuart, "Valuing Customers," *Journal of Marketing Research* 41 (February 2004), pp. 7–18.

35. For more on customer profitability segments and related strategies, see V. A. Zeithaml, R. T. Rust, and K. N. Lemon, "The Customer Pyramid: Creating and Serving Profitable Customers," *California Management Review* 43 (Summer 2001), pp. 118–142.

36. R. Brooks, "Alienating Customers Isn't Always a Bad Idea, Many Firms Discover," *The Wall Street Journal,* January 7, 1999, p. A1.

37. F. Reichheld, "Loyalty-Based Management," *Harvard Business Review* 71 (March–April 1993), pp. 64–74.

38. D. Brady, "Why Service Stinks," *BusinessWeek,* October 23, 2000, pp. 118–128.

39. Dhar and Glazer, "Hedging Customers."

40. D. Rosenblum, D. Tomlinson, and L. Scott, "Bottom-Feeding for Blockbuster Businesses," *Harvard Business Review* 81 (March 2003), pp. 52–59.

41. See T. A. Burnham, J. K. Frels, and V. Mahajan, "Consumer Switching Costs: A Typology, Antecedents, and Consequences," *Journal of the Academy of Marketing Science* 32 (Spring 2003), pp. 109–26; F. Selnes, "An Examination of the Effect of Product Performance on Brand Reputation, Satisfaction, and Loyalty," *European Journal of Marketing* 27, no. 9 (2003), 19–35; P. Klemperer, "The Competitiveness of Markets with Switching Costs," *Rand Journal of Economics* 18 (Spring 1987), pp. 138–50; M. Colgate, V. T.-U. Tong, C. K.-C. Lee, and J. U. Farley, "Back from the Brink: Why Customers Stay," *Journal of Service Research* 9 (February 2007), pp. 211–228.

42. T. L. Huston and R. L. Burgess, "Social Exchange in Developing Relationships: An Overview," in *Social Exchange in Developing Relationships,* ed. R. L. Burgess and T. L. Huston (New York: Academic Press, 1979), pp. 3–28; L. White and V. Yanamandram, "Why Customers Stay: Reasons and Consequences of Inertia in Financial Services," *Managing Service Quality* 14, nos. 2/3 (2004), pp. 183–194.

43. Colgate et al., "Back from the Brink."

44. J. J. Kim, "Banks Push Harder to Get You to Switch—Services Aim to Ease Hassle of Moving Your Accounts," *The Wall Street Journal,* October 12, 2006, p. D1.

45. See J. P. Guiltinan, "A Classification of Switching Costs with Implications for Relationship Marketing," in *Marketing Theory and Practice,* ed. Terry L. Childers et al. (Chicago: American Marketing Association, 1989), pp. 216–220; Klemperer, "The Competitiveness of Markets with Switching Costs"; C. Fornell, "A National Customer Satisfaction Barometer: The Swedish Experience," *Journal of Marketing* 56 (January 1992), pp. 6–21; P. G. Patterson and T. Smith, "A Cross-Cultural Study of Switching Barriers and Propensity to Stay with Service Providers," *Journal of Retailing* 79 (Summer 2003), pp. 107–120.

46. Kim, "Banks Push Harder to Get You to Switch."

47. See Bendapudi and Berry, "Customers' Motivations for Maintaining Relationships with Service Providers"; H. S. Bansal, P. G. Irving, and S. F. Taylor, "A Three-Component Model of Customer Commitment to Service Providers,"*Journal of the Academy of Marketing Science* 32 (Summer 2004), pp. 234–250.

48. Berry and Parasuraman, *Marketing Services,* pp. 136–142.

49. For more information on cautions to be considered in implementing rewards strategies, see L. O'Brien and C. Jones, "Do Rewards Really Create Loyalty?" *Harvard Business Review* 73 (May–June 1995), pp. 75–82; G. R. Dowling and M. Uncles, "Do Customer Loyalty Programs Really Work?" *Sloan Management Review* 38 (Summer 1997), pp. 71–82; H. T. Keh and Y. H. Lee, "Do Reward Programs Build Loyalty for Services? The Moderating Effect of Satisfaction on Type and Timing of Rewards," *Journal of Retailing* 82 (June 2006), pp. 127–136.

50. Colgate et al., "Back from the Brink:"

51. Bendapudi and Leone, "How to Lose Your Star Performer without Losing Customers"; E. Anderson and S. D. Jap, "The Dark Side of Close Relationships," *Sloan Management Review* 46 (Spring 2005), pp. 75–82; R. W. Palmatier, R. P. Dant, D. Grewal, and K. R. Evans, "Factors Influencing the Effectiveness of

Relationship Marketing: A Meta-Analysis," *Journal of Marketing* 70 (October 2006), pp. 136–153.

52. D. V. Fites, "Make Your Dealers Your Partners," *Harvard Business Review* 74 (March–April 1996), pp. 84–95.

53. Rosenbaum and Massiah, "When Customers Receive Support from Other Customers."

54. D. D. Gremler and S. W. Brown, "Service Loyalty: Its Nature, Importance, and Implications," in *Advancing Service Quality: A Global Perspective,* ed. Bo Edvardsson et al. (Jamaica, NY: International Service Quality Association, 1996), pp. 171–180; H. Hansen, K. Sandvik, and F. Selnes, "Direct and Indirect Effects of Commitment to a Service Employee on the Intention to Stay," *Journal of Service Research* 5 (May 2003), pp. 356–368.

55. C. W. Hart, "Made to Order," *Marketing Management* 5 (Summer 1996), pp. 11–23.

56. Arthur Andersen, *Best Practices: Building Your Business with Customer-Focused Solutions* (New York: Simon & Schuster, 1998), pp. 125–127; http://www.cardinal.com/, accessed on August 15, 2007.

57. S. Stellin, "Avoiding Surprises at the Car Rental Counter," *The New York Times,* June 4, 2006.

58. See L. C. Harris and K. L. Reynolds, "The Consequences of Dysfunctional Customer Behavior," *Journal of Service Research* 6 (November 2003), p. 145 for cites; see also, A. A. Grandey, D. N. Dickter, and H. P. Sin, "The Customer Is *Not* Always Right: Customer Aggression and Emotion Regulation of Service Employees," *Journal of Organizational Behavior* 25 (2004), pp. 397–418.

59. K. Ohnezeit, recruiting supervisor for Enterprise Rent-A-Car, personal communication, February 12, 2004.

60. See Harris and Reynolds, "The Consequences of Dysfunctional Customer Behavior."

61. L. L. Berry and K. Seiders, "Serving Unfair Customers," *Business Horizons* 51 (January/February 2008), pp. 29–37.

62. L. Bird, "The Clients That Exasperate Madison Avenue," *The Wall Street Journal,* November 2, 1993, p. B1.

63. For a detailed discussion on relationship ending, see A. Halinen and J. Tähtinen, "A Process Theory of Relationship Ending," *International Journal of Service Industry Management* 13, no. 2 (2002), pp. 163–180.

64. H. Åkerlund, "Fading Customer Relationships in Professional Services," *Managing Service Quality* 15, no. 2 (2005), pp. 156–71.

65. M. Schrage, "Fire Your Customers," *The Wall Street Journal,* March 16, 1992, p. A8.

66. S. Shellenbarger, "More Firms, Siding with Employees, Bid Bad Clients Farewell," *The Wall Street Journal,* February 16, 2000, p. B1.

67. http://www.nypro.com, accessed August 15, 2007.

Chapter **Eight**

Service Recovery

This chapter's objectives are to

1. Illustrate the importance of recovery from service failures in keeping customers and building loyalty.
2. Discuss the nature of consumer complaints and why people do and do not complain.
3. Provide evidence of what customers expect and the kind of responses they want when they do complain.
4. Present strategies for effective service recovery, together with examples of what does and does not work.
5. Discuss service guarantees—what they are, the benefits of guarantees, and when to use them—as a particular type of service recovery strategy.

JetBlue and the 2007 Valentine's Day Ice Storm at JFK

When JetBlue Airways began flying daily in 2000 from New York City to Fort Lauderdale, Florida, and Buffalo, New York, it promised fares that would be as much as 65 percent lower than competitors. At that time JetBlue had 300 employees and provided its customers with comforts like assigned seating, leather upholstery, and satellite TV on individual screens in every seat. The low fares were an immediate hit with passengers, as they found friendly, snappily dressed flight attendants who served animal crackers, Oreo cookies, and blue potato chips on flights very appealing. Indeed, by early 2007 JetBlue had 9,300 employees and 125 jetliners, operating about 575 daily flights to 52 destinations in the United States and the Caribbean. Customers had come to love the airline. It had won many awards for its service and had regularly been ranked near the top of airline satisfaction ratings by J.D. Power and Associates, among others.

JetBlue's reputation for excellent service was challenged on Valentine's Day, February 14, 2007, when a severe storm dumped two inches of ice at New York's JFK Airport. Although the weather created headaches for just about all air carriers in the eastern United States that Wednesday, it was JetBlue who received the most attention. Why? The airline that had developed a reputation for its customer-friendly approach had suffered a startling breakdown. More than 1,000 flights were cancelled over the next six days. Passengers were stuck on planes for up to 10 hours. Delays averaged nearly four hours. It took nearly a week for JetBlue to return operations to normal.

Some JetBlue customers spent as much as nine hours stuck on planes and in terminals.

What actually happened? As discussed in the JetBlue Case in the back of this book, bad weather and poor management decisions led to full gates and a substantial queue of planes waiting for gates. JetBlue's initial responses to the weather disruptions on Valentine's Day were not good. While the storm was occurring, and even immediately afterward, JetBlue failed to cancel flights, leaving some passengers stranded on the tarmac for as long as 10 hours. The policy of initially postponing, but not canceling, flights resulted in snowballing cancellations for nearly a week, with long lines at the airport as customers attempted to get on flights.

Unfortunately for JetBlue, this happened in the media capital of the world—thus its service failures received major attention in the press. Perhaps the most devastating blow of all was delivered by *BusinessWeek;* the magazine described the situation as "one extraordinary stumble" on its March 5 cover touting its first-ever rating of the best firms in customer service. (This cover is depicted in the story about USAA at the beginning of Chapter 7.) Why did JetBlue receive such attention when airlines such as Delta and American had similar problems? Customers had come to expect more from JetBlue than from other airlines.

However, within a week of the debacle, JetBlue introduced a written guarantee to customers. It unveiled a "Customer Bill of Rights" plan and made it retroactive to February 14. In this guarantee the airline pledged to be proactive in canceling flights, to notify customers of flight-scheduling problems or delays, to assist customers in rebooking tickets, and to make financial compensation under certain conditions—delays that were within JetBlue's control. Within a month, plans to upgrade internal processes to allow JetBlue to better cope with major service disruptions were also unveiled. Nonoperational employees were to be cross-trained and given secondary airport responsibilities. The reservations system was to be improved to better support the needs of customers during disruptions and the company website was upgraded so passengers could rebook themselves, using vouchers.

JetBlue had one key issue in its favor: seven years of goodwill. Its customers had largely accepted that the airline cared about them, because it had demonstrated that, flight after flight, for the previous seven years. Customers appeared willing to give JetBlue another chance because it had consistently done right by them before. Compete Inc., a consumer-intelligence firm, conducted a poll of 428 people who had visited JetBlue's website two weeks after the problems occurred. Despite the colossal Valentine's Day meltdown, 43 percent still preferred JetBlue, the most for any airline. And *BusinessWeek,* which admitted that yanking JetBlue from its original number 4 rating in customer service was "a tough call," suggested the potential still existed for JetBlue to become a "Customer Service Champ" in the future.

The preceding two chapters have given you a foundation for understanding customers through research as well as through knowing them as individuals and developing strong relationships with them. These strategies, matched with effective service design, delivery, and communication—treated in other parts of the text—form the foundations for service success. But, in all service contexts—whether customer service, consumer services, or business-to-business services—service failure is inevitable. Failure is inevitable even for the best of firms with the best of intentions, even for those with world-class service systems.

To fully understand and retain their customers, firms must know what customers expect when service failures occur and must implement effective strategies for service recovery. Our chapter-opening vignette illustrates how one firm was able to recover even under the most unexpected and dire circumstances.

THE IMPACT OF SERVICE FAILURE AND RECOVERY

A *service failure* is generally described as service performance that falls below a customer's expectations in such a way that leads to customer dissatisfaction. *Service recovery* refers to the actions taken by an organization in response to a service failure. Failures occur for all kinds of reasons—the service may be unavailable when promised, it may be delivered late or too slowly, the outcome may be incorrect or poorly executed, or employees may be rude or uncaring.[1] These types of failures bring about negative feelings and responses from customers. Research suggests that only a portion (45 percent) of customers who experience a problem with service delivery actually complain to the employees serving them, and a very small number (1 to 5 percent) complain to someone at the company headquarters.[2] This phenomenon, commonly referred to as the "tip of the iceberg" and demonstrated in Figure 8.1, suggests that every complaint management actually receives at company headquarters represents 20 to 100 other customers who experienced the problem and did not complain. Service failures left unfixed can result in customers leaving, telling other customers about their negative experiences, and even challenging the organization through consumer rights organizations or legal channels.

FIGURE 8.1
Complaining Customers: The Tip of the Iceberg

Source: TARP Worldwide Inc., 2007.

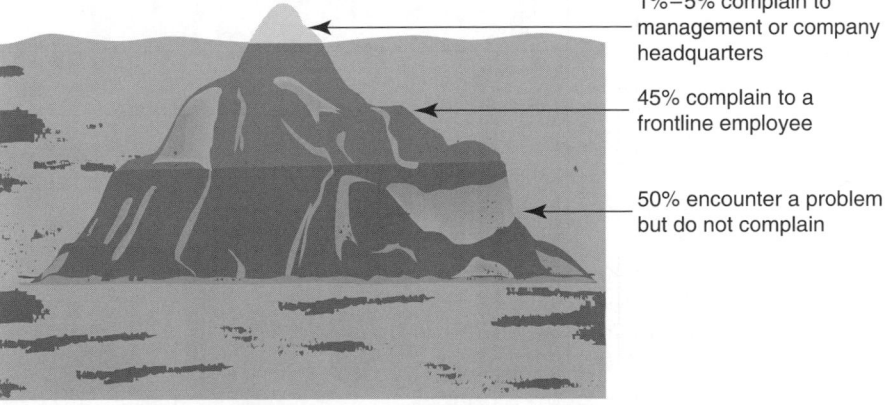

1%–5% complain to management or company headquarters

45% complain to a frontline employee

50% encounter a problem but do not complain

Service Recovery Effects

Research has shown that resolving customer problems effectively has a strong impact on customer satisfaction, loyalty, word-of-mouth communication, and bottom-line performance.[3] That is, customers who experience service failures, but who are ultimately satisfied based on recovery efforts by the firm, will be more loyal than those whose problems are not resolved. That loyalty translates into profitability, as you learned in Chapter 7. Data from TARP Worldwide verifies this relationship, as shown in Figure 8.2.[4] Among customers from service businesses who complain and have their problems satisfactorily resolved, 43 percent indicate they would definitely purchase again from the same provider—illustrating the power of good service recovery. However, this study and other research have found that customers who are dissatisfied with the recovery process after making a complaint are less likely to repurchase than those who do not complain—suggesting the power of poor service recovery![5]

Hampton Inn® Hotels directly realized the benefits of effective service recovery through their service guarantee. They achieved $11 million in additional annual revenue and the highest customer retention rate in their industry after implementing the 100 percent customer satisfaction guarantee shown in Figure 8.3.[6] The guarantee reimburses customers who experience service failures in their hotels—and is part of an overall service recovery and customer retention strategy.

An effective service recovery strategy has multiple potential impacts. It can increase customer satisfaction and loyalty and generate positive word-of-mouth communication. A well-designed, well-documented service recovery strategy also provides information that can be used to improve service as part of a continuous improvement effort. By making adjustments to service processes, systems, and outcomes based on previous service recovery experiences, companies increase the likelihood of "doing it right the first time." In turn, this reduces costs of failures and increases initial customer satisfaction.

Unfortunately, many firms do not employ effective recovery strategies. Studies suggest as much as 60 percent of customers who experience a serious problem receive no response from the firm.[7] There are tremendous downsides to having no service recovery or ineffective service recovery strategies. Poor recovery following a bad service experience can lead to customers who are so dissatisfied that they become

FIGURE 8.2
Unhappy Customers' Repurchase Intentions

Source: TARP Worldwide Inc. Service Industry Data, 2007.

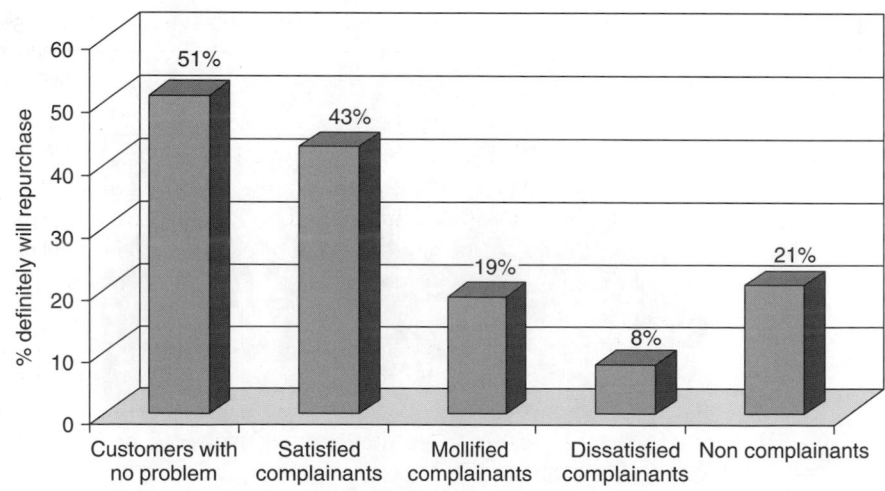

FIGURE 8.3
The 100 Percent Hampton Inn® Hotels Guarantee

Source: Courtesy of Hampton Inn® Hotels.

"terrorists," actively pursuing opportunities to openly criticize the company.[8] When customers experience a service failure, they talk about it to others no matter what the outcome. Research has found that customers who are satisfied with a firm's recovery efforts talk to an average of eight people, whereas those customers who are dissatisfied with the response talk to an average of 18.5 people.[9] With the ability to share such stories on the Internet, the potential reach of such dissatisfied customers is even greater. (See Exhibit 8.1 about the two Doubletree Inn customers who were not happy with the company's service recovery efforts.) Further, repeated service failures without an effective recovery strategy in place can aggravate even the best employees. The reduction in employee morale and even the loss of employees can be huge but often overlooked costs of not having an effective service recovery strategy.

The Service Recovery Paradox

Occasionally some businesses have customers who are initially dissatisfied with a service experience and then experience a high level of excellent service recovery, seemingly leading them to be even more satisfied and more likely to repurchase than if no problem had occurred at all; that is, they appear to be more satisfied after they experience a service failure than they otherwise would have been![10] To illustrate, consider a hotel customer who arrives to check in and finds that no room is available of the size reserved and the price quoted. In an effort to recover, the hotel front desk person immediately upgrades this guest to a better room at the original price. The customer, thrilled with this compensation, reports that she is extremely satisfied with this experience, is even more impressed with the hotel than she was before, and vows to be loyal into the future. Although such extreme instances are relatively rare, this idea—that an initially disappointed customer who has experienced good service recovery might be even more satisfied and loyal as a result—has been labeled the *recovery paradox.*

So, should a firm "screw up" just a little so that it can "fix the problem" superbly? If doing so would actually lead to more satisfied customers, is this strategy worth pursuing? The logical, but not very rational, conclusion is that companies should *plan to disappoint customers* so they can recover well and (hopefully) gain even greater loyalty from them!

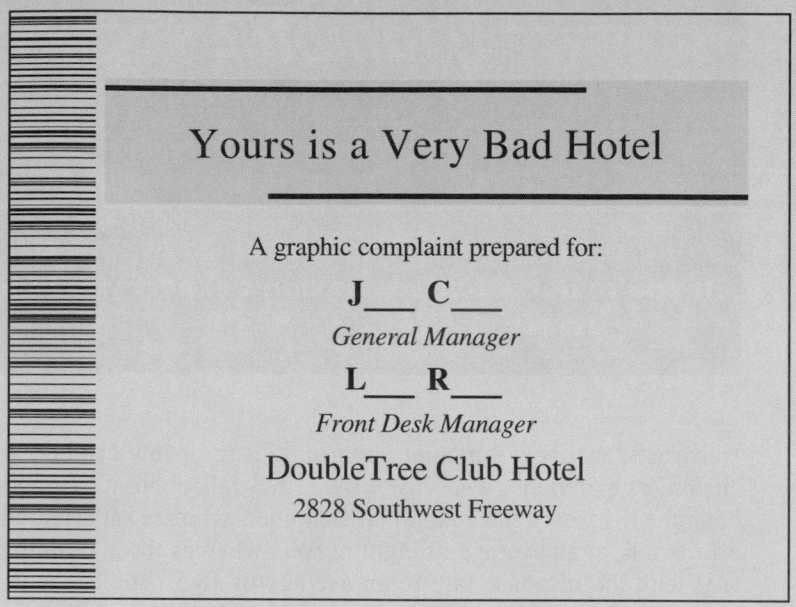

Yours is a Very Bad Hotel

A graphic complaint prepared for:

J___ C___
General Manager

L___ R___
Front Desk Manager

DoubleTree Club Hotel
2828 Southwest Freeway

In November 2001, Tom F. and Shane A. experienced poor service from a hotel in the southwestern United States and decided to create a PowerPoint slide show as a way to vent their frustrations. Their intent was to chronicle the "shabby treatment" they received at a Doubletree Inn while on a business trip. The men sent the PowerPoint presentation to two managers at the hotel, two clients from city where it is located, and Shane's mother-in-law. Within a month this presentation, entitled "Yours is a Very Bad Hotel," had been circulated around the globe. As a result, the Seattle-based web consultants received more than 9,000 e-mail

What are the problems with such an approach?

- As we indicated earlier in this chapter, a vast majority of customers do not complain when they experience a problem. The possibility of a recovery exists only in situations in which the firm is aware of a problem and is able to recover well; if customers do not make the firm aware of the failure—and most do not—dissatisfaction is most likely to be the result.
- It is expensive to fix mistakes; re-creating or reworking a service may be quite costly to a firm.
- It would appear somewhat ludicrous to encourage service failures—after all, reliability ("doing it right the first time") is the most critical determinant of service quality across industries.
- Research suggests that even if a customer's satisfaction with the firm increases as a result of the great service recovery, repurchase intentions and image perceptions of the firm do not increase—that is, customers do not necessarily think more highly of the firm in the long run.[11]
- Although the recovery paradox suggests that a customer *may* end up more satisfied after experiencing excellent recovery, there is certainly *no* guarantee that the customer actually *will* end up more satisfied.

messages from six continents, and their experience was written up in *USA Today.*

The trouble began one early morning that November when the two businessmen, delayed in their arrival at Doubletree (owned by Hilton Hotels) because of a late-arriving plane, stepped up to the front desk at about 2:00 a.m. with a confirmation and credit card guarantee for late arrival. Unfortunately, the hotel was overbooked and their rooms had been given away hours earlier. Although disappointed, they understood. "These things happen, and we didn't expect miracles," recalled Tom. However, as a "card-carrying Hilton HHonors Gold VIP" who had logged 100,000 miles of business travel the previous year, Tom and his traveling companion Shane did expect an apology and a prompt resolution from the employee they would later dub "Night Clerk Mike." Instead, as they noted in the slide show, they received "insolence plus insults" and, eventually, two smokers' rooms in a "dump" of a hotel several miles away (and 15 minutes farther) from the downtown area where they were to have a meeting later that morning.

Once the disappointed travelers returned to Seattle, they detailed their frustrations via bar charts, graphs, and statistical analyses. ("Lifetime chances of dying in a bathtub: 1 in 10,455. Chances of winning the U.K. Lottery: 1 in 13,983,816. Chance of us returning to the Doubletree: Worse than any of those.") After the two had created and e-mailed the PowerPoint file to the hotel managers, they encouraged the three extra people to whom they sent the file to "share it with a few of your friends," anticipating that no more than a few dozen fellow travelers would ever see the PowerPoint slide show. Instead, the response "percolated beyond our wildest dreams," said Tom. At various points in time *The Wall Street Journal, Forbes, MSNBC,* and *Travel Weekly* ran short stories—without any direct input from the travelers—based on a Frequently Asked Questions web page the two businessmen had created in response to inquiries they received about their experience.

Tom and Shane received hundreds of requests from business schools and hospitality companies to use the slide show as an example of "customer service gone horribly wrong." And in addition to the response from supportive well-wishers, the presentation generated an offer of a free two-night stay at any Hilton hotel. The two men declined the offer in lieu of a $1,000 charitable donation to a local charity, Toys for Tots, and encouraged their "fans" to do the same. Hotel management also provided the men with a list of actions taken to improve employee training and overbooking policies. All these changes occurred simply because two men documented their frustrations and made it available to a couple of friends via the Internet!

Source: L. Bly, "Online Complaint about Bad Hotel Service Scores Bull's-eye," *USA Today,* January 4, 2002, p. D6.

The recovery paradox is highly dependent on the context and situation; although one customer may find it easy to forgive a restaurant who provides him with a gift certificate for a later date for having lost his dinner reservation, another customer who had planned to propose marriage to his date over dinner may not be all that happy with the same recovery scenario.

The intrigue stimulated by the recovery paradox has led to empirical research specifically on this issue. Although anecdotal evidence provides limited support for the recovery paradox, research seems to indicate that this phenomenon is not pervasive. In one study, researchers found that only the very highest levels of customers' service recovery ratings resulted in increased satisfaction and loyalty.[12] This research suggests that customers weigh their most recent experiences heavily in their determination of whether to buy again. If the most recent experience is negative, overall feelings about the company will decrease, and repurchase intentions will also diminish significantly. Unless the recovery effort is absolutely superlative, it cannot overcome the negative impression of the initial experience enough to build repurchase intentions beyond the point at which they would be if the service had been provided correctly in the first place. Recent studies suggest the conditions under which a service recovery paradox is most likely to occur is when the failure is not considered by the customer to be severe, the customer has not experienced prior failures with the firm, the cause of the failure is viewed as unstable by the customer, or the customer perceives that the company had little control over the cause of the failure.[13] Apparently conditions must be just right in order for the recovery paradox to be present.

Given the mixed opinions on the extent to which the recovery paradox exists, "doing it right the first time" is still the best and safest strategy in the long run. However, when a failure does occur, then every effort at a superior recovery should be made to mitigate its negative effects. If the failure can be fully overcome, if the failure is less critical, or if the recovery effort is clearly superlative, it may be possible to observe evidence of the recovery paradox.

HOW CUSTOMERS RESPOND TO SERVICE FAILURES

Customers who experience service failures can respond in a variety of ways, as illustrated in Figure 8.4.[14] It is assumed that following a failure, dissatisfaction at some level will occur for the customer. In fact, research suggests that a variety of negative emotions can occur following a service failure, including such feelings as anger, discontent, disappointment, self-pity, anxiety, and regret.[15] These initial negative responses will affect how customers evaluate the service recovery effort and presumably their ultimate decision to return to the provider or not.

Many customers are very passive about their dissatisfaction, simply saying or doing nothing. Whether they take action or not, at some point the customers will decide whether to stay with that provider or switch to a competitor. As we already have pointed out, customers who do not complain are not very likely to return. For companies, customer passivity in the face of dissatisfaction is a threat to future success.

FIGURE 8.4 **Customer Complaint Actions Following Service Failure**

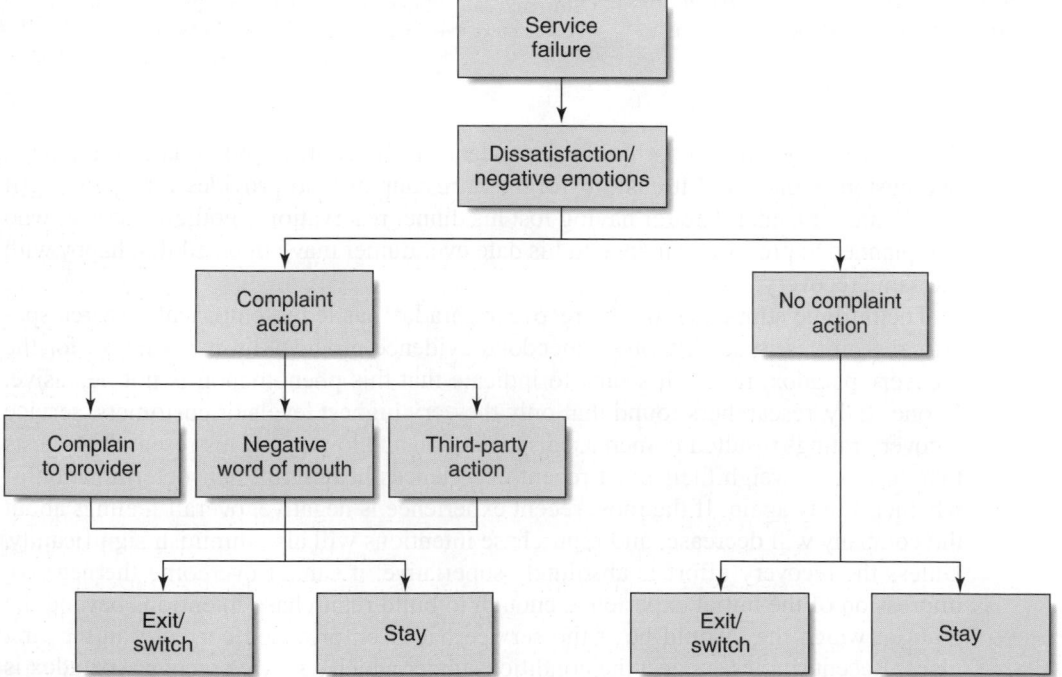

Why People Do (and Do Not) Complain

Some customers are more likely to complain than others for a variety of reasons. These consumers believe that positive consequences may occur and that there are social benefits of complaining, and their personal norms support their complaining behavior. They believe they should and will be provided compensation for the service failure in some form. They believe that fair treatment and good service are their due, and that in cases of service failure, someone should make good. In some cases they feel a social obligation to complain—to help others avoid similar situations or to punish the service provider. A very small number of consumers have "complaining" personalities—they just like to complain or cause trouble.

Consumers who are unlikely to take any action—the majority of customers in most situations, as indicated in Figure 8.1—hold the opposite beliefs. They often see complaining as a waste of their time and effort.[16] They do not believe anything positive will occur for them or others based on their actions. Sometimes they do not know how to complain—they do not understand the process or may not realize that avenues are open to them to voice their complaints. In some cases noncomplainers may engage in "emotion-focused coping" to deal with their negative experiences. This type of coping involves self-blame, denial, and possibly seeking social support.[17] They may feel that the failure was somehow their fault and that they do not deserve redress.

Personal relevance of the failure can also influence whether people complain.[18] If the service failure is really important, if the failure has critical consequences for the consumer, or if the consumer has much ego involvement in the service experience, then he or she is more likely to complain. The situation at Doubletree Inn, which was described in Exhibit 8.1, illustrates a failure for a service that was considered especially important to two customers. Consumers are more likely to complain about services that are expensive, high risk, and ego involving (like vacation packages, airline travel, and medical services) than they are about less expensive, frequently purchased services (fast-food drive-through service, a cab ride, a call to a customer service help line). These latter services are simply not important enough to warrant the time to complain. Unfortunately, even though the experience may not be important to the consumer at the moment, a dissatisfying encounter can still drive him or her to a competitor the next time the service is needed.

Types of Customer Complaint Actions

If customers initiate actions following service failure, the action can be of various types. A dissatisfied customer can choose to complain on the spot to the service provider, giving the company the opportunity to respond immediately. This reaction is often the best-case scenario for the company because it has a second chance right at that moment to satisfy the customer, keep his or her business in the future, and potentially avoid any negative word of mouth. Customers who do not complain immediately may choose to complain later to the provider by phone, in writing, or via the Internet. Again, the company has a chance to recover. Researchers refer to these proactive types of complaining behavior as *voice* responses or *seeking redress*.

Some customers choose not to complain directly to the provider but rather spread negative word of mouth about the company to friends, relatives, and coworkers. This negative word-of-mouth communication can be extremely detrimental because it can reinforce the customer's feelings of negativism and spread that negative impression to others as well. Further, the company has no chance to recover unless the negative word of mouth is accompanied by a complaint directly to the company. In recent years, customers have taken to complaining via the Internet. A variety of websites, including web-based consumer opinion platforms,[19] have been created to facilitate customer complaints and, in doing so, have provided customers with the possibility of spreading negative word-of-mouth communication to a much broader audience. Some customers become so dissatisfied with a product or service failure that they construct websites targeting the firm's current and prospective customers. On these sites,[20] angry customers convey their grievances against the firm in ways designed to convince other consumers of the firm's incompetence and evil.[21]

Finally, customers may choose to complain to third parties such as the Better Business Bureau, to consumer affairs arms of the government, to a licensing authority, to a professional association, or potentially to a private attorney. No matter the action (or inaction), ultimately the customers determine whether to patronize the service provider again or to switch to another provider.

Types of Complainers

Research suggests that people can be grouped into categories based on how they respond to failures. Four categories of response types were identified in a study that focused on grocery stores, automotive repair services, medical care, and banking and financial services: *passives, voicers, irates, and activists.*[22] Although the proportion of the types of complainers is likely to vary across industries and contexts, it is likely that these four types of complainers will be relatively consistent and that each type can be found in all companies and industries.

Passives

This group of customers is least likely to take any action. They are unlikely to say anything to the provider, less likely than others to spread negative word of mouth, and unlikely to complain to a third party. They often doubt the effectiveness of complaining, thinking that the consequences will not merit the time and effort they will expend. Sometimes their personal values or norms argue against complaining. These folks tend to feel less alienated from the marketplace than irates and activists.

Voicers

These customers actively complain to the service provider, but they are less likely to spread negative word of mouth, switch patronage, or go to third parties with their complaints. *These customers should be viewed as the service provider's best friends!* They actively complain and thus give the company a second chance. As with the passives, these customers are less alienated from the marketplace than those in the other two groups. They tend to believe complaining has social benefits and therefore do not hesitate to voice their opinions. They believe that the consequences of complaining to the provider can be very positive, and they believe less in other types of complaining such as spreading negative word of mouth or talking to third parties. Their personal norms are consistent with complaining.

Irates

These consumers are more likely than are others to engage in negative word-of-mouth communication with friends and relatives and to switch providers. They are about average in their propensity to complain to the provider and are unlikely to complain to third parties. These folks tend to feel somewhat alienated from the marketplace. As their label suggests, they are more angry with the provider, although they do believe that complaining to the provider can have social benefits. They are less likely to give the service provider a second chance and instead will switch to a competitor, spreading the word to friends and relatives along the way. Such customers are more likely than the other types to go to the trouble of creating blogs on the Internet to share their frustrations with others.

Activists

These consumers are characterized by above-average propensity to complain on all dimensions: they will complain to the provider, they will tell others, and they are more likely than any other group to complain to third parties. Complaining fits with their personal norms. As with the irates, these consumers are more alienated from the marketplace than the other groups. They have a very optimistic sense of the potential positive consequences of all types of complaining.

CUSTOMERS' RECOVERY EXPECTATIONS

When they take the time and effort to complain, customers generally have high expectations. They not only expect a response, they expect the firm to be accountable. They expect to be helped quickly. They expect to be compensated for their grief and for the hassle of being inconvenienced. And they expect to be treated nicely in the process. Exhibit 8.2 epitomizes this kind of service recovery.

Understanding and Accountability

In many service failure situations, customers are not looking for extreme actions from the firm; however, they are looking to understand what happened and for firms to be accountable for their actions (or inactions).[23] Research by the Customer Care Alliance has identified the eight most common "remedies" that customers seek when they experience a serious problem;[24] three of these remedies are to have the product repaired or service fixed, be reimbursed for the hassle of having experienced a problem, and receive a free product or service in the future. Interestingly, however, the other five remedies—including an explanation by the firm as to what happened, assurance that the problem will not be repeated, a thank you for the customer's business, an apology from the firm, and an opportunity for the customer to vent his or her frustrations to the firm—cost the firm very little to provide.

These five nonmonetary remedies consist primarily of providing employees the opportunity to communicate with customers. Understanding and accountability are very important to many customers after a service failure because, if they perceive an injustice has occurred, someone is to blame. Customers expect an apology when things go wrong, and a company that provides one demonstrates courtesy and respect; customers also want to know what the company is going to do to ensure that the problem does not recur.[25]

Exhibit 8.2   Story of a Service Hero

A good recovery can turn angry, frustrated customers into loyal ones. It can, in fact, create more goodwill than if things had gone smoothly in the first place. A classic story of excellent service recovery comes from Club Med–Cancun, part of the Paris-based Club Mediterranèe; its response to a service nightmare won the loyalty of one group of vacationers and is still being retold two decades later.

The vacationers had nothing but trouble getting from New York to their Mexican destination. The flight took off six hours late, made two unexpected stops, and circled 30 minutes before it could land. Because of all the delays and mishaps, the plane was en route for 10 hours more than planned and ran out of food and drinks. It finally arrived at two o'clock in the morning, with a landing so rough that oxygen masks and luggage dropped from overhead. By the time the plane pulled up to the gate, the soured passengers were faint with hunger and convinced that their vacation was ruined before it had even started. One lawyer on board was already collecting names and addresses for a class-action lawsuit.

Silvio de Bortoli, the general manager of the Cancun resort and a legend throughout the organization for his ability to satisfy customers, got word of the horrendous flight and immediately created an antidote. He took half the staff to the airport, where they laid out a table of snacks and drinks and set up a stereo system to play lively music. As the guests filed through the gate, they received personal greetings, help with their bags, a sympathetic ear, and a chauffeured ride to the resort. Waiting for them at Club Med was a lavish banquet, complete with mariachi band and champagne. Moreover, the staff had rallied other guests to wake up and greet the newcomers, and the partying continued until sunrise. Many guests said it was the most fun they'd had since college.

In the end, the vacationers had a better experience than if their flight from New York had gone like clockwork. Although the company probably couldn't measure it, Club Mediterranèe won market share that night. After all, the battle for market share is won not by analyzing demographic trends, ratings points, and other global measures, but rather by pleasing customers one at a time.

Source: Reprinted by permission of *Harvard Business Review.* An excerpt from C. W. L. Hart, J. L. Heskett, and W. E. Sasser Jr., "The Profitable Art of Service Recovery," *Harvard Business Review* 68 (July–August 1990), pp. 148, 149. Copyright © 1990 by the Harvard Business School Publishing Corporation. All rights reserved.

As the figures in Table 8.1 suggest, customer discontent can be moderated if firms simply communicate well with customers. Customers clearly value such communication, because these nonmonetary remedies are positively related to satisfaction with the complaint process, continued loyalty, and positive word-of-mouth communication.[26]

Fair Treatment

Customers also want justice and fairness in handling their complaints. Service recovery experts Steve Brown and Steve Tax have documented three specific types of justice that customers are looking for following their complaints: *outcome fairness, procedural fairness,* and *interactional fairness.*[27] Outcome fairness concerns the results

TABLE 8.1
Customer Dissatisfaction from Firm Responses to Service Failures

Firm Response	Percentage of Customers Dissatisfied with Action Taken
Do nothing	79%
Explain what happened	20
Provide customer an opportunity to vent frustrations	17
Apologize to customer	10
Thank customer for business	10
Assure customer problem will not recur	6

Source: 2007 National Customer Rage Study conducted by Customer Care Alliance

Exhibit 8.3 Fairness Themes in Service Recovery

	Fair	Unfair
Outcome fairness: the results that customers receive from complaints	*"The waitress agreed that there was a problem. She took the sandwiches back to the kitchen and had them replaced. We were also given a free drink."* *"They were very thorough with my complaint. One week later I received a coupon for a free oil change and an apology from the shop owner."*	*"Their refusal to refund our money or make up for the inconvenience and cold food was inexcusable."* *"If I wanted a refund, I had to go back to the store the next day. It's a 20-minute drive; the refund was barely worth the trouble."* *"All I wanted was for the ticket agent to apologize for doubting my story. I never got the apology."*
Procedural fairness: the policies, rules, and timeliness of the complaint process	*"The hotel manager said that it didn't matter to her who was at fault, she would take responsibility for the problem immediately."* *"The sales manager called me back one week after my complaint to check if the problem was taken care of to my satisfaction."*	*"They should have assisted me with the problem instead of giving me a phone number to call. No one returned my calls, and I never had a chance to speak to a real person."* *"I had to tell my problem to too many people. I had to become irate in order to talk with the manager, who was apparently the only one who could provide a solution."*
Interactional fairness: the interpersonal treatment received during the complaint process	*"The loan officer was very courteous, knowledgeable, and considerate—he kept me informed about the progress of the complaint."* *"The teller explained that they had a power outage that morning so things were delayed. He went through a lot of files [effort] so that I would not have to come back the next day."*	*"The person who handled my complaint about the faulty air conditioner repair wasn't going to do anything about it and didn't seem to care."* *"The receptionist was very rude; she made it seem like the doctor's time was important but mine was not."*

that customers receive from their complaints; procedural fairness refers to the policies, rules, and timeliness of the complaint process; and interactional fairness focuses on the interpersonal treatment received during the complaint process.[28] Exhibit 8.3 shows examples of each type of fairness taken from Brown and Tax's study of consumers who reported on their experiences with complaint resolution.

Outcome Fairness

Customers expect outcomes, or compensation, that match the level of their dissatisfaction. This compensation can take the form of actual monetary compensation, an apology, future free services, reduced charges, repairs, and/or replacements. Customers expect equity in the exchange—that is, they want to feel that the company has "paid" for its mistakes in a manner at least equal to what the customer has suffered. The company's "punishment should fit the crime." Customers expect equality—that is, they want to be compensated in a manner similar to other customers who have experienced the same type of service failure. They also appreciate it when a company gives them choices in terms of compensation. For example, a hotel guest could be offered the choice of a refund or a free upgrade to a better room in compensation for a room not being available on arrival. Outcome fairness is especially important in settings in which customers have particularly negative emotional responses to the service failure; in such situations recovery efforts should focus on improving the outcome from the customer's point of view.[29]

In the Club Med example in Exhibit 8.2, customers were compensated by being met at the airport with snacks and drinks, being chauffeured to the resort, being served a lavish buffet, and being treated to an all-night party that was not part of the package initially. These guests had suffered a lot through the delay of their long-awaited vacation, and the compensation definitely was adequate. Note that in this case the service failure was not even Club Med's fault.

On the other hand, customers can be uncomfortable if they are overly compensated. Early in its experience with service guarantees, Domino's Pizza offered not to charge for the pizza if the driver arrived after the 30-minute guaranteed delivery time. Many customers were not comfortable asking for this level of compensation, especially if the driver was only a few minutes late. In this case "the punishment was greater than the crime." For a while Domino's changed the compensation to a more reasonable $3 off for late deliveries. Later the time guarantee was dropped altogether because of problems it caused with employees who were driving too fast in order to make their deliveries.

Procedural Fairness

In addition to fair compensation, customers expect fairness in terms of policies, rules, and timeliness of the complaint process. They want easy access to the complaint process, and they want things handled quickly, preferably by the first person they contact. They appreciate companies that can be adaptable in their procedures so that the recovery effort can match their individual circumstances. In some cases, particularly in business-to-business services, companies actually ask the customer, "What can we do to compensate you for our failure?" Many times what the customer asks for is actually less than the company might have expected.

Fair procedures are characterized by clarity, speed, and absence of hassles. Unfair procedures are those that customers perceive as slow, prolonged, illogical, and inconvenient. Customers also feel it is unfair if they have to prove their case—when the company's assumption seems to be they are wrong or lying until they can prove otherwise.

In the Club Med case in Exhibit 8.2, the recovery happened as quickly as possible when the passengers landed in Mexico. Even though the problems were not Club Med's fault, the company went out of its way to compensate the delayed guests immediately on arrival. The vacationers had no more hassles once they were on the ground.

Interactional Fairness

Above and beyond their expectations of fair compensation and hassle-free, quick procedures, customers expect to be treated politely, with care and honesty. This form of fairness can dominate the others if customers feel the company and its employees have uncaring attitudes and have done little to try to resolve the problem. This type of behavior on the part of employees may seem strange—why would they treat customers rudely or in an uncaring manner under these circumstances? Often it is due to lack of training and empowerment—a frustrated frontline employee who has no authority to compensate the customer may easily respond in an aloof or uncaring manner, especially if the customer is angry and/or rude.

In the Club Med case in Exhibit 8.2, Silvio de Bortoli and his staff were gracious, caring, and upbeat when they greeted the long-delayed passengers. They personally met them at the airport even though it was late at night. They even involved other guests already staying at the resort to greet the new arrivals and party with them, making them feel welcome and helping to give their vacation a jump start.

SWITCHING VERSUS STAYING FOLLOWING SERVICE RECOVERY

Ultimately, how a service failure is handled and the customer's reaction to the recovery effort can influence future decisions to remain loyal to the service provider or to switch to another provider. In a study of 720 HMO members, researchers found that those who were not satisfied with service recovery were much more likely to switch to a different health care provider than were those who were happy with how their problems were addressed.[30] Whether customers switch to a new provider following service failure will depend in addition on a number of other factors. The magnitude and criticality of the failure will clearly be a factor in future repurchase decisions. The more serious the failure, the more likely the customer is to switch no matter what the recovery effort.[31]

The nature of the customer's relationship with the firm may also influence whether the customer stays or switches providers. Research suggests that customers who have "true relationships" with their service providers are more forgiving of poorly handled service failures and are less likely to switch than are those who have a "pseudo-relationship" or a "first-time encounter" type of relationship.[32] A true relationship is one in which the customer has had repeated contact over time with the same service provider. A first-time encounter relationship is one in which the customer has had only one contact, on a transaction basis, with the provider. And a pseudo-relationship is one in which the customer has interacted many times with the same company, but with different service providers each time.

Other research reveals that a customer's attitude toward switching strongly influences whether he or she ultimately stays with the provider and that this attitude toward switching will be even more influential than basic satisfaction with the service.[33] This research suggests that certain customers will have a greater propensity to switch service providers no matter how their service failure situations are handled. Research in an online service context, for example, shows that demographic factors such as age and income as well as individual factors such as risk aversion influence whether a customer continues to use an online service or switches to another provider.[34] The profile of an "online service switcher" emerged in the research as a person who was influenced to subscribe to the service through positive word-of-mouth communication, who used the service less, who was less satisfied and less involved with the service, who had a lower income and education level, and who also had a lower propensity for taking risks.

Finally, the decision to switch to a different service provider may not occur immediately following service failure or poor service recovery, but may follow an accumulation of events. That is, service switching can be viewed as a process resulting from a series of decisions and critical service encounters over time rather than one

FIGURE 8.5
Causes Behind
Service Switching

Source: Reprinted with
permission of the American
Marketing Association. From
S. Keaveney, "Customer
Switching Behavior in
Service Industries: An
Exploratory Study," *Journal
of Marketing* 59 (April 1995),
pp. 71–82.

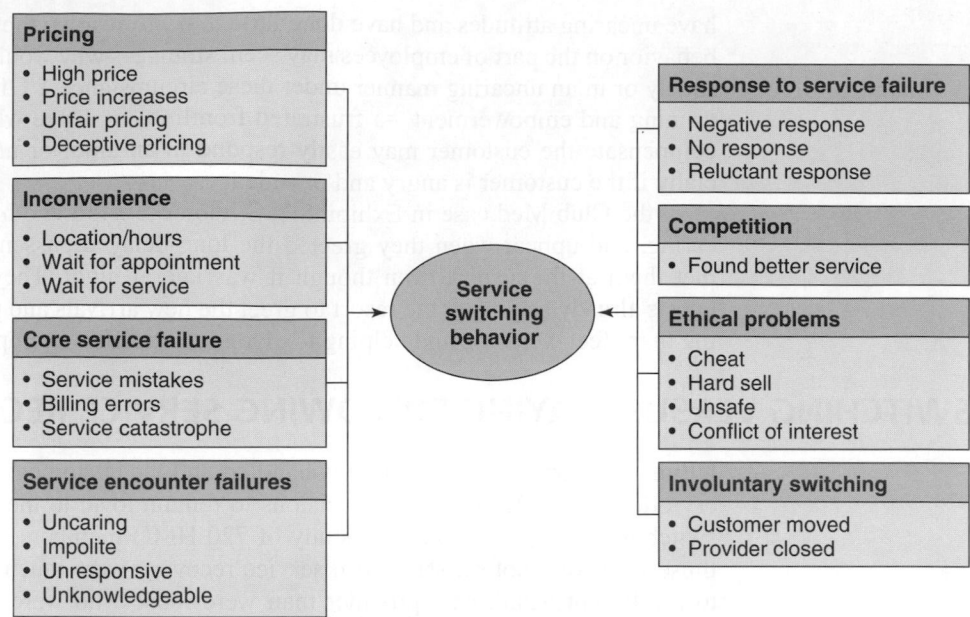

Pricing
- High price
- Price increases
- Unfair pricing
- Deceptive pricing

Inconvenience
- Location/hours
- Wait for appointment
- Wait for service

Core service failure
- Service mistakes
- Billing errors
- Service catastrophe

Service encounter failures
- Uncaring
- Impolite
- Unresponsive
- Unknowledgeable

Service switching behavior

Response to service failure
- Negative response
- No response
- Reluctant response

Competition
- Found better service

Ethical problems
- Cheat
- Hard sell
- Unsafe
- Conflict of interest

Involuntary switching
- Customer moved
- Provider closed

specific moment in time when a decision is made.[35] This process orientation suggests that companies could potentially track customer interactions and predict the likelihood of defection based on a series of events, intervening earlier in the process to head off the customer's decision to switch.

Although customers may decide to switch service providers for a variety of reasons, service failure and poor service recovery are often a cause of such behavior. A study of approximately 500 service-switching incidents identified eight broad themes underlying the decision to defect.[36] These themes (pricing, inconvenience, core service failure, service encounter failure, response to service failure, competition, ethical problems, and involuntary switching) are shown in Figure 8.5. In about 200 of the incidents, a single theme was identified as the cause for switching service providers, and the two largest categories were related to service failure. Core service failure was the cause of switching for 25 percent of the respondents, and service encounter failure was the reason for switching services for an additional 20 percent of the sample. In incidents that listed two themes, 29 percent listed core service failure and 18 percent service encounter failure as contributing to their desire to switch providers; poor response to failure was mentioned by an additional 11 percent of the respondents as the cause for switching. As these findings suggest, service failure can cause customers to switch companies. To minimize the impact of service failure, excellent service recovery is needed. In the next section we discuss several service recovery strategies that attempt to keep dissatisfied customers from defecting.

SERVICE RECOVERY STRATEGIES

Many companies have learned the importance of providing excellent recovery for disappointed customers. In this section we examine their strategies and share examples of benchmark companies and what they are doing. It will become clear that excellent service recovery is really a combination of a variety of strategies, illustrated in Figure 8.6,

FIGURE 8.6
Service Recovery
Strategies

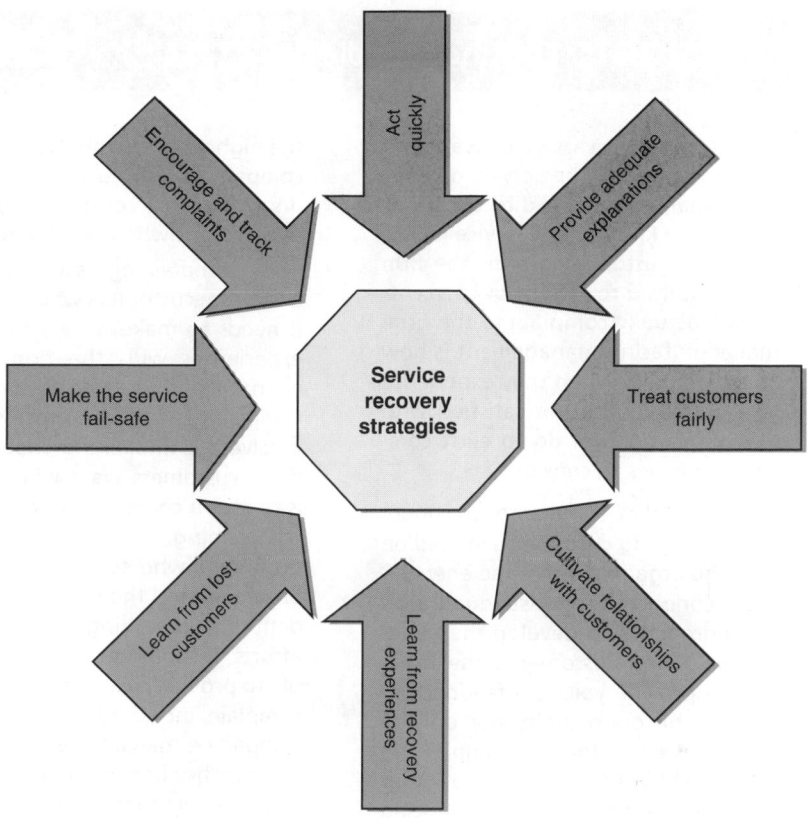

that need to work together. We discuss each of the strategies shown in the figure, starting with the basic "do it right the first time."

Make the Service Fail-Safe—Do It Right the First Time!

The first rule of service quality is to do it right the first time. In this way recovery is unnecessary, customers get what they expect, and the costs of redoing the service and compensating for errors can be avoided. As you have already learned, reliability, or doing it right the first time, is the most important dimension of service quality across industry contexts.[37] Indeed, research suggests that many customers stay in a relationship because they have not experienced a (negative) critical incident.[38]

What specific strategies do firms employ to achieve reliability? Quality practices aimed at "zero defects" are commonly used. However, given the inherent differences between services and manufactured products, these tools typically require considerable adaptation to work well in service contexts. Firms that blindly adopt total quality management (TQM) practices without considering services implications often fail in their efforts.

Dick Chase, noted service operations expert, suggests that services adopt the quality notion of *poka yokes* to improve service reliability.[39] Poka yokes are automatic warnings or controls in place to ensure that mistakes are not made; essentially they are quality control mechanisms, typically used on assembly lines. Chase suggests that poka yokes can be devised in service settings to "mistakeproof" the service, ensure that essential procedures are followed, and ensure that service steps are carried out in

Strategy Insight   Eliciting Complaints

Service failures can occur in a variety of ways and at numerous times throughout the service delivery process. However, in many cases it is difficult, if not impossible, for the firm to know that a service failure has occurred unless the customer informs the firm accordingly. Unfortunately, a relatively low percentage of customers will actually complain to the firm. Thus, a major challenge facing management is how to get customers to complain when they experience a service failure and/or they are not satisfied with service delivery. What can a firm do to elicit complaints? Here are some issues to consider.

- *Develop the mind-set that complaints are good.* Too often the complaining customer is looked on by employees in the organization as the *enemy*—someone to be conquered and subdued. The more prudent approach is to develop the mind-set that the complaining customer is the firm's *friend.* Complaints provide valuable feedback to the firm, giving it the opportunity not only to address the service failure for the complaining customer but also to identify problems that other (less vocal) customers may also be experiencing (the "tip of the iceberg" phenomenon). One scholar suggests that "complainers ought to be treated with the dignity and respect afforded to

the highest-priced analysts and consultants." One company puts all customers who have complained on a VIP list. Accepting complaints is truly reflective of firms who are close to their customers.

- *Make complaining easy.* If the firm truly wants to hear from customers who experience poor service, it needs to make it easy for them to share their experiences with the firm. Sometimes customers have no idea who to speak to if they have a complaint, what the process is, or what will be involved. Complaining should be easy—the last thing customers want when they are dissatisfied is to face a complex, difficult-to-access process for complaining. Customers should know where to go and/or who to talk to when they encounter problems, and they should be made to feel confident that something positive will result from their efforts. Technological advances have made it possible to provide customers with multiple avenues to complain, including toll-free customer call centers, company e-mail addresses, and website feedback forms. The firm should regularly communicate to customers that complaining is easy and that it welcomes and appreciates such feedback.

- *Be an active listener.* Employees should be encouraged and trained to actively listen to customers,

the proper order and in a timely manner. In a hospital setting, numerous poka yokes ensure that procedures are followed to avoid potentially life-threatening mistakes. For example, trays for surgical instruments have indentations for specific instruments, and each instrument is nested in its appropriate spot. In this way surgeons and their staff know that all instruments are in their places prior to closing the patient's incision.[40]

Similarly, poka yokes can be devised to ensure that the tangibles associated with the service are clean and well maintained and that documents are accurate and up-to-date. Poka yokes can also be implemented for employee behaviors (checklists, role-playing and practice, reminder signs) and even for ensuring that customers perform effectively. Many of the strategies we discuss in Parts 4 and 5 of the text ("Aligning Service Design and Standards" and "Delivering and Performing Service") are aimed at ensuring service reliability and can be viewed as applications of the basic fail-safe notion of poka yokes.

Even more fundamentally, it is important for a firm to create a culture of zero defections to ensure doing it right the first time.[41] Within a zero defections culture, everyone understands the importance of reliability. Employees and managers aim to satisfy every customer and look for ways to improve service. Employees in a zero defections culture fully understand and appreciate the "relationship value of a customer" concept

particularly to see if they can pick up on any cues to suggest less-than-ideal service. A restaurant customer might respond "fine" to the waiter's question "How is your meal?" However, the customer's body language and tone of voice, or the amount of food not eaten, might indicate that all is not fine. Some customers may not be assertive in voicing their displeasure, but they may drop clues to suggest that something is amiss. Employees as well as managers should be consistently listening not only to the customer's actual words but also to what he or she may really be trying or wanting to communicate.

- *Ask customers about specific service issues.* A very simple, informal way to find out about any service failure is simply to ask. Managers at one hotel with a high percentage of business travelers make it a point to be at the front desk between 7:45 and 8:45 a.m. every day, because approximately 80 percent of their business travelers check out at that time. During the checkout process, managers avoid questions that can be answered with a simple "yes," "OK," or "fine" (e.g., "How was your stay?") and instead ask questions that force customers to provide specific feedback (e.g., "How could we have improved

the technology accommodations in your room?" or "What needs to be done to improve our recreation center?"). Asking customers very specific questions that cannot be answered with a simple "yes" or "no" may provide customers with an easy way to point out expectations that were not fulfilled.

- *Conduct short, trailer surveys.* A follow-up telephone call to a customer still in the midst of the service experience can help to identify problems in real time and thus enable real-time recovery. Enterprise Rent-A-Car Company, for example, regularly calls customers a day after they have picked up a rental car and asks the customer if everything is okay with the car. Customers who report problems, such as a broken window or a car that smells of smoke, are brought a replacement vehicle that day without any additional questions or hassle. Trailer surveys work especially well in business-to-business services in addressing problems early, before they become major issues.

Sources: S. S. Tax and S. W. Brown, "Recovering and Learning from Service Failure," *Sloan Management Review* 40 (Fall 1998), pp. 75–88; O. Harari, "Thank Heaven for Complainers," *Management Review* 81 (January 1992), p. 59.

that was presented in Chapter 7. Thus they are motivated to provide quality service *every time* and to *every customer.*

Encourage and Track Complaints

Even in a zero defections organization that aims for 100 percent service quality, failures occur. A critical component of a service recovery strategy is thus to encourage and track complaints. Our Strategy Insight describes several ways in which customer complaints can be encouraged.

Firms can utilize a number of ways to encourage and track complaints. Customer research can be designed specifically for this purpose through satisfaction surveys, critical incidents studies, and lost customer research, as discussed in Chapter 6. Toll-free call centers, e-mail, and pagers are now used to facilitate, encourage, and track complaints. Software applications in a number of companies also allow complaints to be analyzed, sorted, responded to, and tracked automatically.[42]

In some cases technology can anticipate problems and complaints before they happen, allowing service employees to diagnose problems before the customer recognizes they exist. At companies such as IBM and Caterpillar, information systems have been implemented to anticipate equipment failures and to send out an electronic alert to the

FIGURE 8.7
Customer Satisfaction with Timeliness of Firm Responses to Service Failures
The numbers across the bottom are the percentage of the total sample whose response (by the firm) was received in that time frame. So, for example, 44 percent of the sample received an immediate response. Of that group, 51 percent were completely satisfied with the response.

Source: TARP Worldwide Inc., Service Industry Data, 2007.

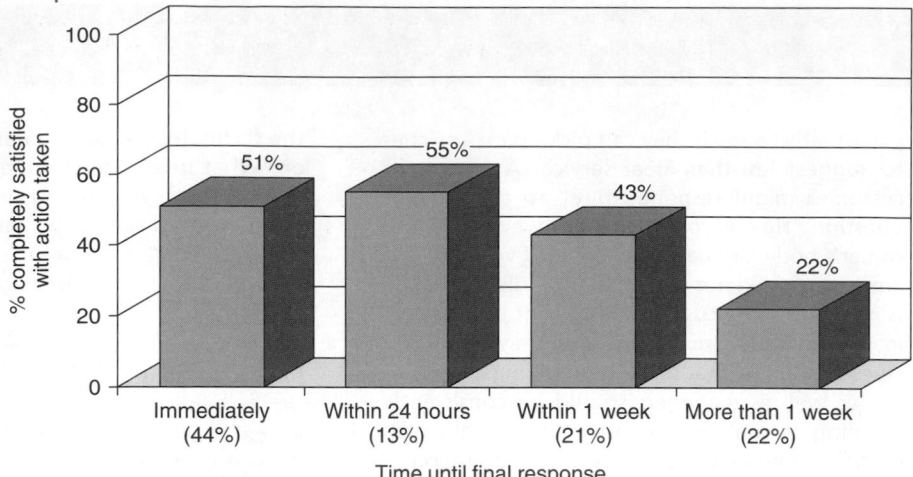

local field technician with the nature of the problem as well as which parts and tools will be needed to make the repair—a repair the customer does not yet know is needed.[43]

Act Quickly

Complaining customers want quick responses.[44] Thus if the company welcomes, even encourages, complaints, it must be prepared to act on them quickly. As indicated in Figure 8.7, research conducted on service customers has found that more than half of all customers who have problems resolved immediately or within 24 hours are "completely satisfied" with the action taken by the company.[45] Unfortunately, many companies require customers to contact multiple employees (a practice often referred to as "ping-ponging") before getting a problem resolved; one recent study found that an average of 4.7 contacts is typically needed to resolve a complaint.[46] Other research suggests that if a problem can be handled by the first contact, customers are satisfied with the firm's response 46 percent of the time; however, once three or more contacts are needed the percentage of customers who are satisfied with the response drops to 21 percent.[47] The lesson here? A quick response to a service failure can go a long way in appeasing a dissatisfied customer. The ability to provide immediate responses requires not only systems and procedures that allow quick action but also empowered employees.

Employees must be trained and empowered to solve problems as they occur. A problem not solved can quickly escalate. As we indicated earlier, customers often experience ping-ponging from employee to employee when service failures occur. Empowerment of employees, a practice discussed in more detail in Chapter 12, can often allow for quick responses and help placate dissatisfied customers. The Ritz-Carlton, for example, insists that the first person to hear a complaint from a customer "owns" that complaint until the employee is sure it is resolved. If a maintenance employee hears a complaint from a customer while the employee is in the middle of fixing a light in the hotel corridor, he owns that complaint and is charged with making sure that the problem is handled appropriately before returning to his work.

Another way that problems or complaints can be handled quickly is by building systems that allow customers to actually solve their own service needs and fix their own problems. Typically this approach is done through technology. Customers directly interface with the company's technology to perform their own customer service, which provides them with instant answers. FedEx uses this strategy for its package tracking services, for example, as does Symantec for its Internet security software products. Our Technology Spotlight features a company that is a master at online customer service—Cisco Systems.

Provide Adequate Explanations

In many service failures, customers look to try to understand why the failure occurred. Explanations can help to diffuse negative reactions and convey respect for the customer.[48] Research suggests that when the firm's ability to provide an adequate outcome is not successful, further dissatisfaction can be reduced if an adequate explanation is

provided to the customer.[49] In order for an explanation to be perceived as adequate, it must possess two primary characteristics. First, the *content* of the explanation must be appropriate; relevant facts and pertinent information arc important in helping the customer understand what occurred. Second, the *style* of the delivery of the explanation, or how the explanation is delivered, can also reduce customer dissatisfaction. Style includes the personal characteristics of the explanation givers, including their credibility and sincerity. Explanations perceived by customers as honest, sincere, and not manipulative are generally the most effective. Part of the frustration of the Doubletree Inn customers mentioned in Exhibit 8.1 was the result of not receiving an adequate explanation from the hotel; they never received an explanation as to why their confirmed, guaranteed reservations were not held, and the night clerk apparently interacted with them in a very apathetic manner.

Treat Customers Fairly

In responding quickly, it is also critical to treat each customer fairly. Customers expect to be treated fairly in terms of the outcome they receive, the process by which the service recovery takes place, and the interpersonal treatment received from employees attempting to address the service failure. Acknowledging a problem has occured, apologizing for the inconvenience, and putting effort into resolving the issue are generally perceived by customers as fair treatment. In the section titled "Customers' Recovery Expectations," we discussed examples, strategies, and results of research that focused on fairness in service recovery. Here we remind you that fair treatment is an essential component of an effective service recovery strategy. Our Global Feature discusses how customers across cultures view fair service recovery.

Cultivate Relationships with Customers

In Chapter 7 we discussed the importance of developing long-term relationships with customers. One additional benefit of relationship marketing is that if the firm fails in service delivery, those customers who have a strong relationship with the firm are often more forgiving of service failures and more open to the firm's service recovery

Technology Spotlight Cisco Systems—Customers Recover for Themselves

One of the challenges of high growth and increasingly diversified product lines is learning how to handle customers' service needs quickly. This was the problem faced by Cisco, a worldwide leader in enabling people to make powerful connections—whether in business, education, philanthropy, or creativity. Cisco hardware, software, and service offerings are used to create the Internet solutions that make networks possible and provide Cisco clients (and their customers) with easy access to information anywhere, at any time. As networks have become mission-critical to its customers and their business, failures in this environment become extremely costly very quickly. Customers want to know that their problems can be solved immediately, and they want control over the situation and its solution.

To address these issues—high growth coupled with the critical and increasingly complex nature of the business—Cisco turned to the Internet to build upon its already world-class suite of customer service offerings. The resulting Cisco Support website provides online documentation and tools to help troubleshoot and resolve technical issues with Cisco products and technologies. This online offering has set Cisco apart in its industry and helped the company build customer loyalty in a highly competitive environment.

Essentially, Cisco has put customers in charge of their own service and support through their corporate website. In most cases, customers now solve their own service problems, with no intervention of Cisco personnel—allowing Cisco staff to focus on complex issues that require hands-on support. Access to information is immediate, and solutions can be highly customized for the individual customer. The "Support" area on Cisco.com includes the following types of services:

- *NetPro Community Discussion forum.* This forum is a gathering place for networking professionals to share questions, suggestions, and information about networking solutions, products, and technologies. This resource allows Cisco customers to collaborate on problem-solving using a community of networking experts, Cisco employees, and others. This community approach also fosters Cisco users identifying solutions working with one another, which helps Cisco engineering resources scale.

- *TAC Case Collection.* The Technical Assistance Center (TAC) Case Collection online knowledge-base helps users interactively identify and troubleshoot common problems themselves involving hardware, configuration, and network performance issues. The TAC Case Collection, provided by Cisco TAC engineers who provide direct support to customers, includes solutions used to resolve actual networking problems; past solutions are reviewed and then published in the TAC Case Collection to benefit other users. This tool saves time for Cisco's customers—they do not have to place a call, wait on the telephone

efforts. Research suggests that strong customer–firm relationships can help shield the firm from the negative effects of failures on customer satisfaction.[50] To illustrate, one study demonstrated that the presence of rapport between customers and employees provided several service recovery benefits, including increased postfailure satisfaction, increased loyalty intentions, and decreased negative word-of-mouth communication.[51] Another study found that customers who expect the relationship to continue also tend to have lower service recovery expectations and may demand less immediate compensation for a failure because they consider the balance of equity across a longer time horizon.[52] Thus, cultivation of strong customer relationships can provide an important buffer to service firms when failures occur.

Learn from Recovery Experiences

"Problem-resolution situations are more than just opportunities to fix flawed services and strengthen ties with customers. They are also a valuable—but frequently ignored or underutilized—source of diagnostic, prescriptive information for improving customer

for an available staff member, and explain their issue or symptoms. The Case Collection is well suited for allowing these customers—many of whom are engineers who operate networks—to handle and solve issues themselves without any help from Cisco staff. Consequently, these customers (1) feel a greater sense of accomplishment if they can tackle an issue unassisted, (2) experience a much greater sense of control, and (3) believe they are making progress in critical situations in which every minute of network error is extremely costly.

- *Software Bug Toolkit.* This is a collection of interactive tools that allows customers to identify, track, and resolve software bugs that may be causing network problems. This online resource is unique in the industry: Cisco was the first high-tech company to release its software defect database to customers. While it seems risky to reveal a collection of defects to customers, Cisco's customers instead responded in an overwhelmingly positive manner. They appreciated that Cisco was willing to provide this level of information in order to increase customer success.

- *"Download Software" Website.* A comprehensive vending machine for Cisco software, the "Download Software" website on Cisco.com is the single point of contact for all customer-initiated software downloads, with more than 19 million files downloaded annually. This website gives customers the power to identify and download Cisco software that will correct a network issue or optimize performance.

- *Service Order Agent.* This parts information, ordering, and tracking system allows customers to conduct transactions online. This system provides fast service for orders and saves on administrative costs for both Cisco and its customers.

- *Service Contract Center.* The system allows customers to view the contents and/or status of their service contracts with Cisco.

Through its continual innovation in providing service to its customers through the Internet, Cisco has recognized tremendous benefits. Currently, 80 percent of customer support problems are handled via the Cisco.com support site, using intellectual property provided by Cisco experts and self-help tools that allow customers to diagnose and solve their own problems. Customer satisfaction and loyalty increased with the introduction of Internet-based customer service, productivity increased at a rate of 200 percent, and the company saves more than $500 million per year. This is truly a win–win situation for Cisco's bottom line, its employees, and its business customers.

Sources: www.cisco.com/support, accessed October 2007; e-mail communication from Barbara Reed, Executive Communications Manager, Cisco Services—Technical Services Division, October 19, 2007.

service."[53] By tracking service recovery efforts and solutions, managers can often learn about systematic problems in the delivery system that need fixing. By conducting root-cause analysis, firms can identify the sources of the problems and modify processes, sometimes almost eliminating the need for recovery. At Ritz-Carlton Hotels, all employees carry service recovery forms called "instant action forms" with them at all times so that they can immediately record service failures and suggest actions to address them. Each individual employee "owns" any complaint that he or she receives and is responsible for seeing that service recovery occurs. In turn, the employees report to management these sources of service failure and the remedies. At Hampton Inn® Hotels, whenever the service guarantee (mentioned earlier in the chapter) is invoked, the reason for the customer's dissatisfaction is recorded as part of the process and the information forwarded on to management. Such information is then entered into a database and analyzed to identify patterns and systemic service issues that need to be fixed. If common themes are observed across a number of failure situations, changes are made to service processes or attributes. In addition, at the Ritz-Carlton the information is entered into

Service failure is inevitable, no matter what the context, country, or culture. Appropriate service recovery procedures, therefore, are needed by all firms. Service firms operating in several countries, as well as those operating in multi-ethnic countries like the United States, United Kingdom, or Australia, need to be sensitive to the cultural diversity and subsequently differing expectations of service and of service recovery.

ATTRIBUTION EXPECTATIONS

When service failures occur, customers spontaneously infer or attribute blame for the unexpected event. Researchers Anna Mattila and Paul Patterson have explored service recovery across cultures and found in Western countries, when the failure is caused by some external factor beyond the control of the service firm, customers will attribute the problem to the context or situation surrounding the service failure—particularly if an explanation is offered by the firm as to what happened. Such action can diminish the blame customers attribute to the firm and its staff, and thus not detract from their perceptions of overall perceived quality. For customers from Eastern cultures, however, a causal explanation has relatively little impact on where the blame for the failure is attributed. These customers prefer other remedies, such as a speedy resolution to the problem and a genuine apology from a manager (rather than a frontline employee) to regain "face" in the eyes of their family and friends. Eastern customers also have a lower tolerance to uncertain and ambiguous situations. Thus when a failure is being remedied, these customers would prefer having a sense of control—the firm can provide this by keeping them informed of exactly what is being done to rectify the situation.

FAIRNESS EXPECTATIONS

Outcome Fairness

Mattila and Patterson also investigated service recovery fairness issues. In their studies they have found Western (i.e., American) customers are more interested in and expect to receive tangible compensation (i.e., a discount) when a service failure occurs than are Eastern (i.e., Thai or Malaysian) customers. Offering compensation is particularly effective in restoring a sense of fairness among American customers; apparently American consumers are particularly concerned with outcome fairness. Indeed, American customers are generally more assertive and more used to asking for reparation than consumers from Eastern cultures. Previous research on service recovery in Western contexts consistently shows that compensation has a positive effect on postrecovery satisfaction and loyalty. Eastern customers, who typically tend to be high on uncertainty avoidance, prefer other types of remedies when service failure occurs. In Eastern cultures there is a tendency to focus on avoidance of losses rather than on individual gains. East Asian customers emphasize the need to fit in with others and to avoid conflict and confrontation.

Interactional Fairness

Mattila and Patterson's research suggests that in Western cultures, offering an explanation for service failure might shift the customer's focus away from thinking that the service provider is incompetent, uncaring, or lazy. Such an explanation tends to cause Western customers to pay more attention to the situation as a cause of the failure. Eastern customers, however, are more likely to be aware of situational constraints, seek to maintain social harmony, and avoid causing a loss of face. For them, interactional fairness appears to be particularly salient. Thus, providing an explanation and treating the offended Eastern customers in a courteous, formal, and empathetic manner is more important than the compensation offered.

Procedural Fairness

For service firms operating in the United States, hassle-free and fast recovery procedures that lead to compensation for any losses or inconveniences triggered by a service failure are preferred by customers. Although compensation is generally the primary driver of American customers' fairness perceptions, speed and convenience in the recovery process also appear to be valued. In Eastern cultures, a genuine apology from a manager (rather than a customer-contact employee) is particularly desirable; such a procedure allows customers to regain "face" in the eyes of their family and friends. Eastern customers would also prefer to have a sense of control, so having management constantly inform them of what is being done to rectify the situation is also appealing to them.

In service recovery, as in any service situation, companies need to be sensitive to the fact that culture and other factors play a role. As these studies suggest, customers in all cultures expect strong service recovery but preferences for the type of recovery or which fairness dimension to emphasize may vary.

Sources: A. S. Mattila and P. G. Patterson, "Service Recovery and Fairness Perceptions in Collectivist and Individualist Contexts," *Journal of Service Research* 6 (May 2004), pp. 336–346; A. S. Mattila and P. G. Patterson, "The Impact of Culture on Consumers' Perceptions of Service Recovery Efforts," *Journal of Retailing* 80 (Fall 2004), pp. 196–206.

the customer's personal data file so when that customer stays at any Ritz-Carlton again (no matter what hotel), employees can be aware of the previous experience, ensuring that it does not happen again for that particular customer.

Learn from Lost Customers

Another key component of an effective service recovery strategy is to learn from the customers who defect or decide to leave. Formal market research to discover the reasons customers have left can assist in preventing failures in the future. This type of research is difficult, even painful for companies, however. No one really likes to examine their failures. Yet such examination is essential for preventing the same mistakes and losing more customers in the future.[54]

As presented in Chapter 6, lost customer research typically involves in-depth probing of customers to determine their true reasons for leaving. This information is most effectively obtained by depth interviews, administered by skilled interviewers who truly understand the business. It may be best to have this type of research done by senior people in the company, particularly in business-to-business contexts in which customers are large and the impact of even one lost customer is great. The type of depth analysis often requires a series of "why" questions or "tell me more about that" questions to get at the actual, core reason for the customer's defection.[55]

In conducting this kind of research, a firm must focus on important or profitable customers who have left—not just everyone who has left the company. An insurance company in Australia once began this type of research to learn about their lost customers, only to find that the customers they were losing tended to be their least profitable customers anyway. They quickly determined that depth research on how to keep these unprofitable customers would not be a good investment!

SERVICE GUARANTEES

A guarantee is a particular type of recovery tool. In a business context, a *guarantee* is a pledge or assurance that a product offered by a firm will perform as promised, and if not then some form of reparation will be undertaken by the firm. Although guarantees are relatively common for manufactured products, they have only recently been used for services. Traditionally, many people believed that services simply could not be guaranteed given their intangible and variable nature. What would be guaranteed? With a tangible product, the customer is guaranteed that it will perform as promised and if not, that it can be returned. With services, it is generally not possible to take returns or to "undo" what has been performed. The skepticism about service guarantees is being dispelled, however, as more and more companies find they can guarantee their services and that there are tremendous benefits for doing so.

Companies are finding that effective service guarantees can complement the company's service recovery strategy—serving as one tool to help accomplish the service recovery strategies depicted in Figure 8.6. The Hampton Inn® Hotels guarantee shown at the beginning of the chapter is an example of such an effective guarantee.

Characteristics of Effective Guarantees

Certain characteristics tend to make some guarantees more effective than others. Christopher Hart has argued that the most effective guarantees tend to have similar characteristics, including being unconditional, meaningful, easy to understand, and easy to invoke.[56]

Unconditional

Hart contends that effective guarantees should be *unconditional*—no strings attached. The Hampton Inn® Hotels guarantee does not impose any conditions. Some guarantees can appear as if they were written by the legal department (and often are), with all kinds of restrictions, proof required, and limitations. These guarantees are generally not effective.

Meaningful

An effective guarantee should be *meaningful*. Guaranteeing what is obvious or expected is not meaningful to customers. For example, a water delivery company offered a guarantee to deliver water on the day promised or a free jug of water would be provided next time. In that industry, delivery on the day scheduled was an expectation nearly always met by every competitor—thus the guarantee was not meaningful to the customer. It was a bit like guaranteeing four wheels on an automobile! The payout, if a problem occurs, should also be meaningful. Customers expect to be reimbursed in a manner that fully compensates them for their dissatisfaction, their time, and even for the hassle involved. One of us has offered university students a guarantee in our Services Markeing classes; compensation for poor service, which includes reimbursement for the cost of the three-credit course, is generally perceived by students as quite meaningful.[57]

Easy to Understand

A firm's guarantee should also be *easy to understand* and communicate to both customers and employees. Sometimes the wording is confusing, the guarantee language is verbose, or the guarantee contains so many restrictions and conditions that neither customers nor employees are certain what is being guaranteed. Bennigan's restaurants guarantees that lunch will be served quickly—within 15 minutes. The promise "It's Fast or It's Free" makes it clear to customers that they will not have to spend a lot of time waiting for lunch; the guarantee also makes it clear to employees that lunches that should take no longer than 15 minutes to get to customers.

Easy to Invoke

Similarly, the guarantee should be *easy to invoke*. British Airways recently offered a guarantee, presented on page 237, to exceed the expectations of its business class customers. To invoke the guarantee, customers merely had to complete an online form and explain why the service at British Airways did not meet or exceed their expectations. Requiring customers to write a detailed letter and/or provide documented proof of service failure are common pitfalls that make invoking a guarantee time-consuming and not worth it to the customer, particularly if the dollar value of the service is relatively low.

Types of Service Guarantees

Service guarantees can be *unconditional satisfaction guarantees* or *service attribute guarantees*. Hampton Inn® Hotels' guarantee is an unconditional satisfaction guarantee. In another context, Bain & Company, a management consulting firm, has offered some clients an unconditional guarantee for its services.[58] If clients are unhappy, they do not pay for the services. Pro Staff offers an unconditional guarantee to any client using its staffing services; if the client organization is unhappy with the person assigned to the client, the client is not billed. Lands' End, a catalog retailer, has abbreviated its guarantee to "Guaranteed. Period."

Advertisement for British Airways Service Guarantee

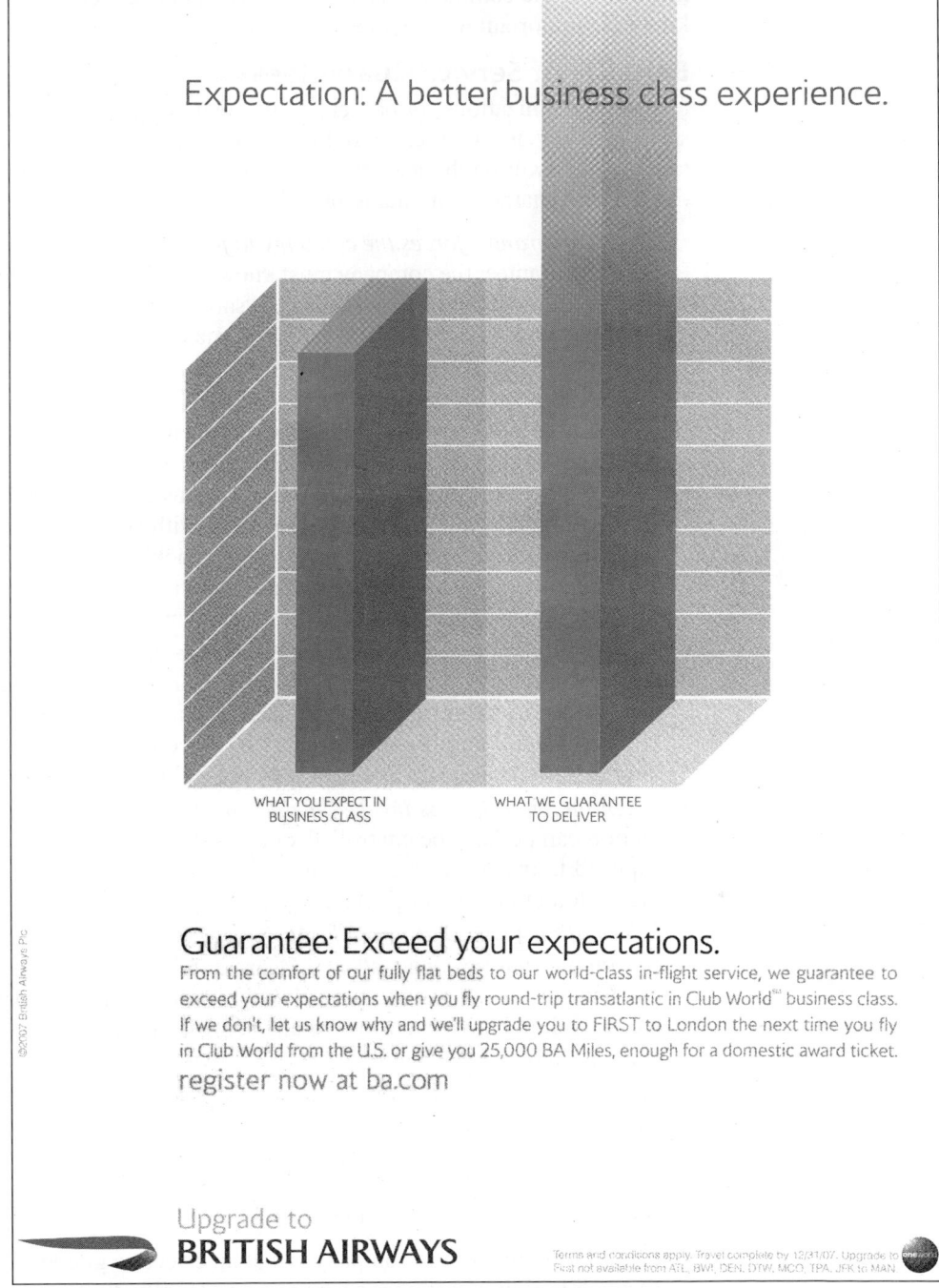

In other cases, firms offer guarantees of particular attributes of the service that are important to customers. FedEx guarantees package delivery by a certain time. In introducing a new seat design in first class, British Airways advertised "Comfort guaranteed or you get 25,000 miles." McDonald's advertised a guarantee that stated "Hot Food; Fast, Friendly Delivery; Double-Check Drive-Thru Accuracy. . . We'll make it right, or your next meal is on us." The Bennigan's guarantee mentioned earlier ensured customers would not have to wait longer than 15 minutes to receive their lunch. In all these cases, the companies have guaranteed specific elements of the service that they know are important to customers.

Benefits of Service Guarantees

"Service organizations, in particular, are beginning to recognize that guarantees can serve not only as a marketing tool but as a means for defining, cultivating, and maintaining quality throughout an organization."[59] The benefits to the company of an effective service guarantee are numerous:[60]

- *A good guarantee forces the company to focus on its customers.* To develop a meaningful guarantee, the company must know what is important to its customers—what they expect and value. In many cases "satisfaction" is guaranteed, but for the guarantee to work effectively, the company must clearly understand what satisfaction means for its customers (what they value and expect).

- *An effective guarantee sets clear standards for the organization.* It prompts the company to clearly define what it expects of its employees and to communicate that expectation to them. The guarantee gives employees service-oriented goals that can quickly align employee behaviors with customer strategies. For example, Pizza Hut's guarantee that "If you're not satisfied with your pizza, let our restaurant know. We'll make it right or give you your money back" lets employees know exactly what they should do if a customer complains. It is also clear to employees that making it right for the customer is an important company goal.

- *A good guarantee generates immediate and relevant feedback from customers.* Having a guarantee can provide an incentive for customers to complain and thereby provides more representative feedback to the company than simply relying on a relatively small number of customers to voice their concerns. The guarantee communicates to customers that they have the right to complain.

- *When the guarantee is invoked there is an instant opportunity to recover.* Dissatisfaction can perhaps be controlled, or at least not allowed to grow, if the customer is exposed to instant recovery. A quick recovery can go a long way toward satisfying the customer and helping retain loyalty.

- *Information generated through the guarantee can be tracked and integrated into continuous improvement efforts.* Guarantees can provide a somewhat structured mechanism for listening to the cusomter, thus helping to close the listening gap. A feedback link between customers and service operations decisions can be strengthened through the guarantee.

- *For customers, the guarantee reduces their sense of risk and builds confidence in the organization.* Because services are intangible and often highly personal or ego-involving, customers seek information and cues that will help reduce their sense of uncertainty. Guarantees have been shown to reduce risk and increase positive evaluation of the service prior to purchase.[61]

The bottom line for the company is that an effective guarantee can affect profitability through building customer awareness and loyalty, through positive word-of-mouth communication, and through reduction in costs as service improvements are made and service recovery expenses are reduced. Indirectly, the guarantee can reduce costs of employee turnover through creating a more positive service culture.

When to Use (or Not Use) a Guarantee

Service guarantees are not appropriate for every company and certainly not in every service situation. Before putting a guarantee strategy in place, a firm needs to address

Exhibit 8.4 Questions to Consider in Implementing a Service Guarantee

DECIDING WHO DECIDES

- Is there a guarantee champion in the company?
- Is senior management committed to a guarantee?
- Is the guarantee design a team effort?
- Are customers providing input?

WHEN DOES A GUARANTEE MAKE SENSE?

- How high are quality standards?
- Can we afford a guarantee?
- How high is customer risk?
- Are competitors offering a guarantee?
- Is the company's culture compatible with a guarantee?

WHAT TYPE OF GUARANTEE SHOULD WE OFFER?

- Should we offer an unconditional guarantee or a specific-outcome one?
- Is our service measurable?
- What should our specific guarantee be about?
- What are the uncontrollables?
- Is the company particularly susceptible to unreasonable triggerings?
- What should the payout be?
- Will a refund send the wrong message?
- Could a full refund make customers feel guilty?
- Is the guarantee easy to invoke?

Source: A. L. Ostrom and C. W. L. Hart, "Service Guarantees: Research and Practice," in *Handbook of Services Marketing and Management,* ed. D. Iacobucci and T. Swartz (Thousand Oaks, CA: Sage Publications, 2000). © 2000 by Sage Publications. Reprinted by permission of Sage Publications.

a number of important questions (see Exhibit 8.4). A guarantee is probably *not* the right strategy when:

- *Existing service quality in the company is poor.* Before instituting a guarantee, the company should fix any significant quality problems. A guarantee will certainly draw attention to failures and to poor service quality, so the costs of implementing the guarantee could easily outweigh any benefits. These costs include actual monetary payouts to customers for poor service as well as costs associated with customer goodwill.

- *A guarantee does not fit the company's image.* If the company already has a reputation for very high quality, and in fact implicitly guarantees its service, then a formal guarantee is most likely unnecessary. For example, if the Four Seasons Hotel were to offer an explicit guarantee, it could potentially confuse customers who already expect the highest of quality, implicitly guaranteed, from this high-end hotel chain. Research suggests that the benefits of offering a guarantee for a high-end hotel like the Four Seasons or the Ritz-Carlton may be significantly less than the benefits that a hotel of lesser quality would offer, and in fact the benefits might not be justified by the costs.[62]

- *Service quality is truly uncontrollable.* Service providers can encounter situations in which service quality is truly uncontrollable. To illustrate it would not be a good practice for a university to guarantee that all MBA students will get the job they want immediately upon graduation—it cannot control what jobs are available in the market place. Similarly, an airline flying out of Chicago in the winter would probably not guarantee on-time departure because of the unpredictability and uncontrollability of the weather.

- *Potential exists for customer abuse of the guarantee.* Fear of opportunistic customer behavior, including customer cheating or fraudulent invocation of service guarantees, is a common reason that firms hesitate to offer guarantees.[63] For example, at one large pizza chain students occasionally "cheated" the company by invoking the service guarantee without cause to receive free food.[64] In those situations in which abuse of the service guarantee can easily occur, firms should carefully consider the consequences of offering a guarantee. A recent study found that guarantees are more likely to be abused when offered in situations in which a large percentage of customers are not regular (repeat) customers.[65] In general, customer abuse of service guarantees is fairly minimal and not at all widespread.[66] Pro Staff reports that it paid out about $300,000 on staffing services sales of $300,000,000 (or about 0.1 percent) on its guarantee in 2006; similarly, each year Hampton Inn® Hotels refunds about 0.5 percent of its total room revenue to dissatisfied customers.[67]

- *Costs of the guarantee outweigh the benefits.* As it would with any quality investment, the company will want to carefully calculate expected costs (payouts for failures and costs of making improvements) against anticipated benefits (customer loyalty, quality improvements, attraction of new customers, word-of-mouth advertising).

- *Customers perceive little risk in the service.* Guarantees are usually most effective when customers are uncertain about the company and/or the quality of its services. The guarantee can allay uncertainties and help reduce risk.[68] If customers perceive little risk, if the service is relatively inexpensive with many potential alternative providers, and if quality is relatively invariable, then a guarantee will likely produce little effectiveness for the company other than perhaps some promotional value.

- *Customers perceive little variability in service quality among competitors.* Some industries exhibit extreme variability in quality among competitors. In these cases a guarantee may be quite effective, particularly for the first company to offer one. Guarantees may also be effective in industries in which quality is perceived to be low overall across competitors. The first firm with a guarantee can often distinguish itself from competitors.

Summary

Part 3 of this text (Chapters 6, 7, and 8) focuses on the critical importance of understanding customer expectations as well as many of the strategies firms use to accomplish this goal. Part of understanding customer expectations is being prepared for and knowing what to do when things go wrong or when the service fails. In this chapter we focused on service recovery, the actions taken by an organization in response to a service failure.

You learned in this chapter the importance of an effective service recovery strategy for retaining customers and increasing positive word-of-mouth communication. Another major benefit of an effective service recovery strategy is that the information it provides can be useful for service improvement. The potential downsides of poor service recovery are tremendous—negative word of mouth, lost customers, and declining business when quality issues are not addressed.

In this chapter you learned how customers respond to service failures and why some complain while others do not. You learned that customers expect to be treated fairly when they complain—not just in terms of the actual outcome or compensation they receive, but also in terms of the procedures that are used and how they are treated interpersonally. We pointed out in this chapter that there is tremendous room for improvement in service recovery effectiveness across firms and industries.

The second half of the chapter focuses on specific strategies that firms are using for service recovery: (1) making the service fail-safe, or doing it right the first time;

(2) encouraging and tracking complaints; (3) acting quickly; (4) providing adequate explanations; (5) treating customers fairly; (6) cultivating relationships with customers; (7) learning from recovery experiences; and (8) learning from lost customers. The chapter ended with a discussion of service guarantees as a tool used by many firms to facilitate service recovery and to listen to customers—thereby helping to close the listening gap. You learned the elements of a good guarantee, the benefits of service guarantees, and the pros and cons of using guarantees under various circumstances.

Discussion Questions

1. Why is it important for a service firm to have a strong recovery strategy? Think of a time when you received less-than-desired service from a particular service organization. Was any effort made to recover? What should/could have been done differently? Do you still buy services from the organization? Why or why not? Did you tell others about your experience?

2. Discuss the benefits to a company of having an effective service recovery strategy. Describe an instance in which you experienced (or delivered as an employee) an effective service recovery. In what ways did the company benefit in this particular situation?

3. Explain the recovery paradox, and discuss its implications for a service firm manager.

4. Discuss the types of actions that customers can take in response to a service failure. What type of complainer are you? Why? As a manager, would you want to encourage your customers to be voicers? If so, how?

5. Review Exhibit 8.1. What would you have done if you were on the management team at Doubletree Inn?

6. Explain the logic behind these two quotes: "a complaint is a gift" and "the customer who complains is your friend."

7. Choose a firm you are familiar with. Describe how you would design an ideal service recovery strategy for that organization.

8. What are the benefits to the company of an effective service guarantee? Should every service organization have one?

9. Describe three service guarantees that are currently offered by companies or organizations in addition to the ones already described in the chapter. (Examples are readily available on the Internet.) Are your examples good guarantees or poor guarantees based on the criteria presented in this chapter?

Exercises

1. Write a letter of complaint (or voice your complaint in person) to a service organization from which you have experienced less-than-desired service. What do you expect the organization to do to recover? (Later, report to the class the results of your complaint, whether you were satisfied with the recovery, what could/should have been done differently, and whether you will continue using the service.)

2. Interview five people about their service recovery experiences. What happened, and what did they expect the firm to do? Were they treated fairly based on the definition of recovery fairness presented in the chapter? Will they return to the company in the future?

3. Interview a manager about service recovery strategies used in his or her firm. Use the strategies shown in Figure 8.6 to frame your questions.

4. Reread the Technology Spotlight in this chapter, featuring Cisco Systems. Visit Cisco System's Support website (www.cisco.com/support). Review what the company is currently doing to help its customers solve their own problems. Compare what Cisco is doing with the self-service efforts of another service provider of your choice.

5. Choose a service you are familiar with. Explain the service offered and develop a good service guarantee for it. Discuss why your guarantee is a good one, and list the benefits to the company of implementing it.

Notes

1. For research that shows different types of service failures, see M. J. Bitner, B. H. Booms, and M. S. Tetreault, "The Service Encounter: Diagnosing Favorable and Unfavorable Incidents," *Journal of Marketing* 54 (January 1990), pp. 71–84; S. M. Keaveney, "Customer Switching Behavior in Service Industries: An Exploratory Study," *Journal of Marketing* 59 (April 1995), pp. 71–82.

2. Information provided by TARP Worldwide Inc., based on data from 10 studies (representing responses from more than 8,000 customers) conducted in 2006 and 2007. Companies from the following industries were included: retail (stores, catalog and online), auto financing, and insurance (property/casualty).

3. For research on important outcomes associated with service recovery, see S. S. Tax, S. W. Brown, and M. Chandrashekaran, "Customer Evaluations of Service Complaint Experiences: Implications for Relationship Marketing," *Journal of Marketing* 62 (April 1998), pp. 60–76; S. S. Tax and S. W. Brown, "Recovering and Learning from Service Failure," *Sloan Management Review* 40 (Fall 1998), pp. 75–88; A. K. Smith and R. N. Bolton, "An Experimental Investigation of Customer Reactions to Service Failure and Recovery Encounters," *Journal of Service Research* 1 (August 1998), pp. 65–81; R. N. Bolton, "A Dynamic Model of the Customer's Relationship with a Continuous Service Provider: The Role of Satisfaction," *Marketing Science* 17, no. 1 (1998), pp. 45–65; A. K. Smith and R. N. Bolton, "The Effect of Customers' Emotional Responses to Service Failures on Their Recovery Effort Evaluations and Satisfaction Judgments," *Journal of the Academy of Marketing Science* 30 (Winter 2002), pp. 5–23; C. M. Voorhees, M. K. Brady, and D. M. Horowitz, "A Voice from the Silent Masses: An Exploratory and Comparative Analysis of Noncomplainers," *Journal of the Academy of Marketing Science* 34 (Fall 2006), pp. 514–527.

4. Information included in Figure 8.1 is based on data from 10 studies conducted in 2006 and 2007, TARP Worldwide Inc.

5. Ibid; Voorhees, Brady, and Horowitz, "A Voice from the Silent Masses."

6. B. Ettorre, "Phenomenal Promises That Mean Business," *Management Review* 83 (March 1994), pp. 18–23.

7. 2007, 2005, and 2004 National Customer Rage Studies conducted by Customer Care Alliance in collaboration with the Center for Services Leadership at Arizona State University's W. P. Carey School of Business.

8. Tax and Brown, "Recovering and Learning from Service Failure."

9. Aggregated results of 2003–2007 National Customer Rage surveys conducted by Customer Care Alliance.

10. See C. W. Hart, J. L. Heskett, and W. E. Sasser Jr., "The Profitable Art of Service Recovery," *Harvard Business Review* 68 (July–August 1990), pp. 148–156; M. A. McCollough and S. G. Bharadwaj, "The Recovery Paradox: An Examination of

Consumer Satisfaction in Relation to Disconfirmation, Service Quality, and Attribution Based Theories," in *Marketing Theory and Applications,* ed. C. T. Allen et al. (Chicago: American Marketing Association, 1992), p. 119.

11. C. A. de Matos, J. L. Henrique, and C. A. V. Rossi, "Service Recovery Paradox: A Meta-Analysis," *Journal of Service Research* 10 (August 2007), pp. 60–77.

12. Smith and Bolton, "An Experimental Investigation of Customer Reactions to Service Failure and Recovery Encounters."

13. V. P. Magnini, J. B. Ford, E. P. Markowski, and E. D. Honeycutt Jr., "The Service Recovery Paradox: Justifiable Theory or Smoldering Myth?" *Journal of Services Marketing* 21, no. 3 (2007), pp. 213–225; J. G. Maxham III and R. G. Netemeyer, "A Longitudinal Study of Complaining Customers' Evaluations of Multiple Service Failures and Recovery Efforts," *Journal of Marketing* 66 (October 2002), pp. 57–71; M. A. McCullough, L. L. Berry, and M. S. Yadav, "An Empirical Investigation of Customer Satisfaction after Service Failure and Recovery," *Journal of Service Research* 3 (November 2000), pp. 121–137.

14. For research foundations on typologies of customer responses to failures, see R. L. Day and E. L. Landon Jr., "Towards a Theory of Consumer Complaining Behavior," in *Consumer and Industrial Buying Behavior,* ed. A. Woodside, J. Sheth, and P. Bennett (Amsterdam: North-Holland Publishing Company, 1977); J. Singh, "Consumer Complaint Intentions and Behavior: Definitional and Taxonomical Issues," *Journal of Marketing* 52 (January 1988), pp. 93–107; J. Singh, "Voice, Exit, and Negative Word-of-Mouth Behaviors: An Investigation across Three Service Categories," *Journal of the Academy of Marketing Science* 18 (Winter 1990), pp. 1–15.

15. Smith and Bolton, "The Effect of Customers' Emotional Responses to Service Failures." M. Zeelenberg and R. Pieters, "Beyond Valence in Customer Dissatisfaction: A Review and New Findings on Behavioral Responses to Regret and Disappointment in Failed Services," *Journal of Business Research* 57 (2004), pp. 445–455.

16. Voorhees, Brady, and Horowitz, "A Voice from the Silent Masses."

17. N. Stephens and K. P. Gwinner, "Why Don't Some People Complain? A Cognitive–Emotive Process Model of Consumer Complaining Behavior," *Journal of the Academy of Marketing Science* 26 (Spring 1998), pp. 172–189.

18. Ibid.

19. T. Hennig-Thurau, K. P. Gwinner, G. Walsh, and D. D. Gremler, "Electronic Word-of-Mouth via Consumer-Opinion Platforms: What Motivates Consumers to Articulate Themselves on the Internet?" *Journal of Interactive Marketing* 18 (Winter 2004), pp. 38–52.

20. Many such websites exist; examples include www.untied.com (for United Airlines experiences), www.starbucked.com (for Starbucks), and www.homedepotsucks.com (for The Home Depot).

21. J. C. Ward and A. L. Ostrom, "Complaining to the Masses: The Role of Protest Framing in Customer-Created Complaint Web Sites," *Journal of Consumer Research* 33 (September 2006), pp. 220–230.

22. J. Singh, "A Typology of Consumer Dissatisfaction Response Styles," *Journal of Retailing* 66 (Spring 1990), pp. 57–99.

23. J. R. McColl-Kennedy and B. A. Sparks, "Application of Fairness Theory to Service Failures and Service Recovery," *Journal of Service Research* 5 (February 2003), pp. 251–266; M. Davidow, "Organizational Responses to Customer

Complaints: What Works and What Doesn't," *Journal of Service Research* 5 (February 2003), pp. 225–250.

24. 2007 National Customer Rage Study conducted by Customer Care Alliance.

25. Davidow, "Organizational Responses to Customer Complaints."

26. 2007 National Customer Rage Study conducted by Customer Care Alliance.

27. See Tax, Brown, and Chandrashekaran, "Customer Evaluations of Service Complaint Experiences"; Tax and Brown, "Recovering and Learning from Service Failure."

28. Tax and Brown, "Recovering and Learning from Service Failure."

29. Smith and Bolton, "The Effect of Customers' Emotional Responses to Service Failures."

30. D. Sarel and H. Marmorstein, "The Role of Service Recovery in HMO Satisfaction," *Marketing Healthcare Services* 19 (Spring 1999), pp. 6–12.

31. McCullough, Berry, and Yadav, "An Empirical Investigation of Customer Satisfaction after Service Failure and Recovery."

32. A. S. Mattila, "The Impact of Relationship Type on Customer Loyalty in a Context of Service Failures," *Journal of Service Research* 4 (November 2001), pp. 91–101; see also R. L. Hess Jr., S. Ganesan, and N. M. Klein, "Service Failure and Recovery: The Impact of Relationship Factors on Customer Satisfaction," *Journal of the Academy of Marketing Science* 31 (Spring 2003), pp. 127–145; R. Priluck, "Relationship Marketing Can Mitigate Product and Service Failures," *Journal of Services Marketing* 17, no. 1 (2003), pp. 37–52.

33. H. S. Bansal and S. F. Taylor, "The Service Provider Switching Model (SPSM)," *Journal of Service Research* 2 (November 1999), pp. 200–218.

34. S. M. Keaveney and M. Parthasarathy, "Customer Switching Behavior in Online Services: An Exploratory Study of the Role of Selected Attitudinal, Behavioral, and Demographic Factors," *Journal of the Academy of Marketing Science* 29 (Fall 2001), pp. 374–390.

35. I. Roos, "Switching Processes in Customer Relationships," *Journal of Service Research* 2 (August 1999), pp. 68–85; I. Roos and A. Gustafsson, "Understanding Frequent Switching Patterns: A Crucial Element in Managing Customer Relationships," *Journal of Service Research* 10 (August 2007), pp. 93–108.

36. Keaveney, "Customer Switching Behavior in Service Industries."

37. A. Parasuraman, V. A. Zeithaml, and L. L. Berry, "SERVQUAL: A Multiple-Item Scale for Measuring Consumer Perceptions of Service Quality," *Journal of Retailing* 64 (Spring 1988), pp. 64–79.

38. M. Colgate, V. T.-U. Tong, C. K.-C. Lee, and J. U. Farley, "Back from the Brink: Why Customers Stay," *Journal of Service Research* 9 (February 2007), pp. 211–228.

39. R. B. Chase and D. M. Stewart, "Make Your Service Fail-Safe," *Sloan Management Review* 35 (Spring 1994), pp. 35–44.

40. Ibid.

41. F. R. Reichheld and W. E. Sasser Jr., "Zero Defections: Quality Comes to Services," *Harvard Business Review* 68 (September–October 1990), pp. 105–107.

42. L. M. Fisher, "Here Comes Front-Office Automation," *Strategy and Business* 13 (Fourth Quarter, 1999), pp. 53–65; R. A. Shaffer, "Handling Customer Service on the Web," *Fortune,* March 1, 1999, pp. 204, 208.

43. S. W. Brown, "Service Recovery through IT," *Marketing Management* 6, (Fall 1997), pp. 25–27.

44. Davidow, "Organizational Responses to Customer Complaints."

45. 2007 study conducted by TARP Worldwide Inc.

46. 2007 National Customer Rage Study conducted by Customer Care Alliance.

47. 2007 study conducted by TARP Worldwide Inc.

48. L. L. Berry and K. Seiders, "Serving Unfair Customers," *Business Horizons* 51 (January/February 2008), pp. 29–37.

49. J. Dunning, A. Pecotich, and A. O'Cass, "What Happens When Things Go Wrong? Retail Sales Explanations and Their Effects," *Psychology and Marketing* 21, no. 7 (2004), pp. 553–572; McColl-Kennedy and Sparks, "Application of Fairness Theory to Service Failures and Service Recovery"; Davidow, "Organizational Responses to Customer Complaints"; Berry and Seiders, "Serving Unfair Customers."

50. Hess, Ganesan, and Klein, "Service Failure and Recovery"; Priluck, "Relationship Marketing Can Mitigate Product and Service Failures."

51. T. DeWitt and M. K. Brady, "Rethinking Service Recovery Strategies: The Effect of Rapport on Consumer Responses to Service Failure," *Journal of Service Research* 6 (November 2003), pp. 193–207.

52. Hess, Ganesan, and Klein, "Service Failure and Recovery."

53. L. L. Berry and A. Parasuraman, *Marketing Services* (New York: Free Press, 1991), p. 52.

54. F. F. Reichheld, "Learning from Customer Defections," *Harvard Business Review* 74 (March–April 1996), pp. 56–69.

55. Ibid.

56. These characteristics are proposed and discussed in C. W. L. Hart, "The Power of Unconditional Guarantees," *Harvard Business Review* 66 (July–August 1988), pp. 54–62; C. W. L. Hart, *Extraordinary Guarantees* (New York: AMACOM, 1993).

57. For more information, see M. A. McCollough and D. D. Gremler, "Guaranteeing Student Satisfaction: An Exercise in Treating Students as Customers," *Journal of Marketing Education* 21 (August 1999), pp. 118–130; D. D. Gremler and M. A. McCollough, "Student Satisfaction Guarantees: An Empirical Examination of Attitudes, Antecedents, and Consequences," *Journal of Marketing Education* 24 (August 2002), pp. 150–160.

58. A. L. Ostrom and C. W. L. Hart, "Service Guarantees: Research and Practice," in *Handbook of Services Marketing and Management,* ed. D. Iacobucci and T. Swartz (Thousand Oaks, CA: Sage Publications, 2000), pp. 299–316.

59. Ibid.

60. See Ibid.; Hart, "The Power of Unconditional Guarantees," Hart, *Extraordinary Guarantees.*

61. A. L. Ostrom and D. Iacobucci, "The Effect of Guarantees on Consumers' Evaluation of Services," *Journal of Services Marketing* 12, no. 5 (1998), pp. 362–378; S. B. Lidén and P. Skålén, "The Effect of Service Guarantees on Service Recovery," *International Journal of Service Industry Management* 14, no. 1 (2003), pp. 36–58.

62. J. Wirtz, D. Kum, and K. S. Lee, "Should a Firm with a Reputation for Outstanding Service Quality Offer a Service Guarantee?" *Journal of Services Marketing* 14, no. 6 (2000), pp. 502–512.

63. J. Wirtz, "Development of a Service Guarantee Model," *Asia Pacific Journal of Management* 15 (April 1998), pp. 51–75.

64. Ibid.

65. J. Wirtz and D. Kum, "Consumer Cheating on Service Guarantees," *Journal of the Academy of Marketing Science* 32 (Spring 2004), pp. 159–175.

66. Wirtz, "Development of a Service Guarantee Model."

67. Candice Winterringer, Pro Staff Vice President of Business Development, personal communication, September 5, 2007; G. Stoller, "Companies Give Front-line Employees More Power," *USA Today,* June 27, 2005, p. A1.

68. Ostrom and Iacobucci, "The Effect of Guarantees."

Aligning Service Design and Standards

Meeting customer expectations of service requires not only understanding what the expectations are, but also taking action on that knowledge. Action takes several forms: designing innovative services and service improvements based on customer requirements, setting service standards to ensure that services are performed as customers expect, and providing physical evidence that creates the appropriate cues and ambience for service. When action does not take place, there is a gap—service design and standards gap—as shown in the accompanying figure. In this section you will learn to identify the causes of gap 2 as well as effective strategies for closing this gap.

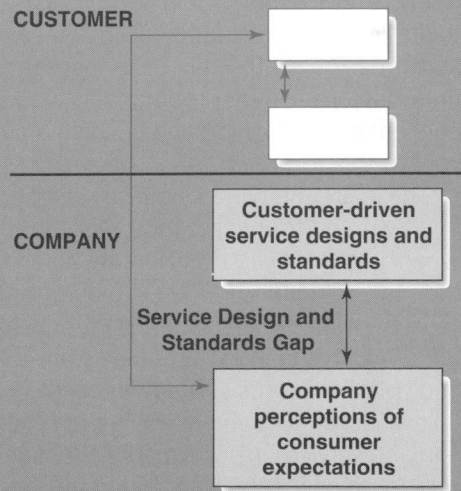

Provider Gap 2

Chapter 9 describes the concepts and tools that are effective for service innovation and design, especially a tool called service blueprinting. Chapter 10 helps you differentiate between company-defined standards and customer-defined standards and to recognize how they can be developed. Chapter 11 explores the strategic importance of physical evidence, the variety of roles it plays, and strategies for effectively designing physical evidence and the servicescape to meet customer expectations.

Chapter Nine

Service Innovation and Design

This chapter's objectives are to

1. Describe the challenges inherent in service innovation and design.
2. Present the stages and unique elements of the service innovation and development process.
3. Demonstrate the value of service blueprinting and how to develop and read service blueprints.
4. Present lessons learned in choosing and implementing high-performance service innovations.

Innovative New Services at Wells Fargo Bank[1]

Have you ever considered starting your own service business? What type of service would it be? What would you do first? Assuming you understood your market and had a good feel for potential customers' needs and expectations, how would you go about designing the service to meet those needs? If you were starting a business to manufacture a new product, you would most likely begin by defining the product concept and designing and building a prototype of your new product. But how could you do this for a service?

These are the types of questions asked by Wells Fargo Bank, fifth largest by assets, and by many counts the most profitable, bank holding company in the United States, when it introduces new services to the marketplace. Wells Fargo is recognized as the industry leader in the United States for alternative delivery strategies of banking services. As such, it constantly introduces new services that allow customers to reach the bank when and where they want to—meeting expectations for speed, flexibility, and accessibility. Its strategy depends on a range of services, from a vast automated teller machine (ATM) system (it even has an ATM in Antarctica) to providing extensive banking services in supermarkets to highly accessible phone banking systems and call centers to online, Internet-based services. Wells was the first U.S. bank to offer online services (in 1989) and Internet banking (1995). Wireless banking was introduced in 2001. Wells has more than 9 million Internet banking retail customers and 950,000 active online small business customers and leads U.S. banks in market share for Internet banking. In 2007, Wells was named the "Best Integrated Consumer Bank Site" in North America by *Global Finance*. To succeed in these pioneering efforts, Wells has had to anticipate its customers' needs, develop effective delivery systems, and be willing to constantly change and innovate with new services.

For example, in the late 1990s Wells introduced WellsTrade, an online discount trading service. This service has evolved into a service line that includes everything from independent online investing to a full-service brokerage account, combining high tech and high touch. The full-service option is designed to combine the convenience of online trading with the guidance of a human financial consultant, while the independent online investing online option is available for those who prefer self-service. To hold onto its position as the top-rated corporate Internet bank, Wells's current efforts revolve around redesigning their corporate online banking services to be even more responsive to customer needs while at the same time enhancing the customer's online experience. In 2000, Wells introduced self-service tools for corporate clients allowing them to access online snapshot data of key banking information through its CEO (Commercial Electronic Office) portals. And in 2007 it became the first major U.S. bank to offer both business and consumer banking through mobile devices. The focus in its innovation efforts is on customized service, speed, and convenience. The bank is also committed to providing accessible services through all its channels to customers with disabilities. Talking ATMs, materials in large print, and accessible online tools are examples of these types of services. Through these improvements and other planned innovations, Wells intends to remain the leader in technology-based and Internet banking.

All these efforts and new service introductions are initiated to support the company's long-standing goal of providing "every channel our customers want, every product our customers need, anytime our customers choose."

So what causes new products and services such as those offered by Wells Fargo to fail or succeed? If you decide to start your own business, what can you do to protect yourself as much as possible from failure? An analysis of more than 60 studies on new product and service success showed that the dominant and most reliable predictors of success for new introductions relate to *product/service characteristics* (product meeting customer needs, product advantage over competing products, technological sophistication), *strategy characteristics* (dedicated human resources to support the initiative, dedicated research and development [R&D] focused on the new product initiative), *process characteristics* (marketing, predevelopment, technological, and launch proficiencies), and *marketplace characteristics* (market potential).[2] Failures, on the other hand, can be traced to a number of causes: no unique benefits offered, insufficient demand, unrealistic goals for the new product/service, poor fit between the new service and others within the organization's portfolio, poor location, insufficient financial backing, or failure to take the necessary time to develop and introduce the product.[3] Frequently a good service idea fails because of development, design, and specification flaws, topics that are emphasized in this chapter. As more firms, across industries, move into services as a growth strategy, the challenges and opportunities of developing and delivering service offerings become even more apparent.

CHALLENGES OF SERVICE INNOVATION AND DESIGN

Because services are largely intangible and process oriented (such as a hospital stay, a golf lesson, an NBA basketball game, or a sophisticated information technology consulting service), they are difficult to describe and communicate. When services

*"Boosting innovation in services is central to improving performance of the service sector. . . .
the sector has traditionally been seen as less innovative than manufacturing
and as playing only a supportive role in the innovation system."*

The above quote from the Organization for Economic Cooperation and Development's 2005 report titled "Promoting Innovation in Services" is sobering. It is even more sobering when the sheer size and growth of the service sector is factored in. For example, in the United States, services represent more than 80 percent of the GDP and labor force, and, although the United States is the highest, similar percentages are found in most advanced economies. Further, it is apparent that services are increasing as an economic force in countries such as China, India, and other fast-growing nations. Yet, despite the economic domination and growth of services, there is relatively little formal focus within companies and governments on service research and innovation compared with the focus on tangible products and technologies. In recent years, companies and countries have begun to awaken to the need for service innovation. Companies are becoming aware that to grow and profit in the future they need to be globally competitive in services—whether they are a pure service business or a manufacturing or high-tech business. Many national governments are also recognizing the need to invest in service innovation, education, and research given the realities of the global service economy.

Here we provide some highlights of service innovation initiatives around the globe.

UNITED STATES

Much of the impetus behind the growing awareness of the need for service innovation can be attributed to the leadership of IBM. The company's foresight is catalyzing a global movement to shape the future of service innovation and a potential new discipline IBM calls "service science, management and engineering" (SSME) to develop skilled professionals for the service economy. IBM's research divisions employ 500 service innovation researchers (up from just 50 in 2004), and their message is being heard by other U.S. global companies such as Oracle, Microsoft, and Xerox. Government agencies are beginning to respond as well. In 2007, the America COMPETES Act was passed by Congress, and a section of the act authorizes a study to determine how the federal government should support service research and education. Also in 2007 the Service Research and Innovation Initiative was launched to foster partnerships for service research among business and academics (www.thesrii.org).

CHINA

The Chinese government has emphasized service growth and service innovation as important goals in its recent

are delivered or cocreated with the customer over a long period—a week's resort vacation, a six-month consulting engagement, 10 weeks on a Weight Watchers program—their complexity increases, and they become even more difficult to define and describe. Further, because services are delivered by employees to customers, they are variable. Rarely are two services alike or experienced in the same way. These fundamental characteristics of service offerings, which we explored in the first chapter of this book, are the heart of the challenge involved in innovating and designing services. Global companies and governments around the world are awakening to these challenges and the recognition that despite the dominance of services in the world's economies, there is relatively little formal focus on service research and innovation.[4] As the importance of service innovation becomes more and more apparent, significant initiatives are beginning to emerge in countries around the world as described in our Global Feature.

Because services cannot be touched, examined, or easily tried out, people have historically resorted to words in their efforts to describe them. Yet, there are a number of risks inherent in attempting to describe services in words alone.[5] The first risk is *oversimplification.* "To say that 'portfolio management' means 'buying and selling stocks' is like describing the space shuttle as 'something that flies.' Some people will picture a

five-year plans. In fact, the GDP of the country grew from 34 percent services to 40 percent services in just over a year's time with a goal of significantly more growth in the near term. The need for service innovation is clear in China and stems from a number of different social and economic developments. First, there is the need for infrastructure services (education, health care, transportation) to serve the masses of people moving from the rural areas into the cities in pursuit of jobs and increased economic well-being. A growing manufacturing sector also demands services to transport, ship, finance, and market the goods produced. There is also recognition that the country cannot become a truly global competitor based solely on manufacturing. These factors have led the government and companies to focus strategically on service innovation and growth.

GERMANY

Germany is a country known for its engineering and manufacturing prowess. But, for many years now, beginning in the early 1990s, the German government has recognized the need to focus on service and has funded projects and research aimed at service innovation. Through its Federal Ministry of Education and Research, it has begun funding service innovation through the "Innovation with Services" program. To quote from the program's brochure, "Germany's overall innovative strength depends on its largest value-added sector [the service sector] becoming a driver in an increasingly globalized market." One of its primary partners in this work is the Fraunhofer Institute (www.fraunhofer.de), an applied research organization funded in large part by industry and government project grants. The Institute employs more than 12,500 scientists, researchers, and engineers. Through its Industrial Engineering arm, Faunhofer is currently conducting more than 200 studies on service development and management. In the last several years, they established "service labs" to experimentally test service innovations.

FINLAND

The Scandinavian countries boast some of the highest ratings in the world for quality of life and progressive economies. Finland is often very high on such lists. With its service sector currently representing about 67 percent of the economy, Finland too recognizes the need to be innovative in services. Through Tekes (www.tekes.fi), the Finnish Funding Agency for Technology and Innovation, Finland has begun to fund research to increase and broaden the services development of Finnish industry and to promote academic research in services related primiarly to technology enabled service innovations.

Sources: M. J. Bitner and S. W. Brown, "The Service Imperative," *Business Horizons 50th Anniversary Issue,* 51 (January–February 2008), pp. 39–46; "Succeeding through Service Innovation," a white paper published by the University of Cambridge Institute for Manufacturing and IBM, October 2007; and Organization for Economic Cooperation and Development, "Promoting Innovation in Services," 2005.

bird, some a helicopter, and some an angel."[6] Words are simply inadequate to describe a complex service system such as financial portfolio management. In our modern-day global economy, service systems have significantly increased in complexity, often involving networks of service firms, customers, and evolution of offerings over time. Within these complex systems, the risks of oversimplification are even more apparent. Take, for example, the retirement planning services provided by Bank of America (see advertisement on the next page). Any attempt to describe this complex service in words alone would surely be oversimplified.

The second risk of using words alone is *incompleteness.* In describing services, people (employees, managers, customers) tend to omit details or elements of the service with which they are not familiar. A person might do a fairly credible job of describing how a discount stock brokerage service takes orders from customers. But would that person be able to describe fully how the monthly statements are created, how the interactive computer system works, and how these two elements of the service are integrated into the order-taking process? The third risk is *subjectivity.* Any one person describing a service in words will be biased by personal experiences and degree of exposure to the service. There is a natural (and mistaken) tendency to assume that because all people have gone to a fast-food restaurant, they all understand what that

Words or a simple photo alone cannot describe the complexity of Bank of America's Retirement Planning Services.

service is. Persons working in different functional areas of the same service organization (a marketing person, an operations person, a finance person) are likely to describe the service very differently as well, biased by their own functional blinders. A final risk of describing services using words alone is *biased interpretation*. No two people will

define "responsive," "quick," or "flexible" in exactly the same way. For example, a supervisor or manager may suggest to a frontline service employee that the employee should try to be more flexible or responsive in providing service to the customer. Unless the term "flexibility" is further defined, the employee is likely to interpret the word differently from the manager.

All these risks and challenges become very apparent in the innovation and service development process, when organizations attempt to design complex services never before experienced by customers or when they attempt to change existing services. In the following sections of this chapter, we present approaches for new service innovation, development, and design to address these challenges.

NEW SERVICE DEVELOPMENT PROCESSES

Research suggests that products designed and introduced via the steps in a structured planning framework have a greater likelihood of ultimate success than those not developed within a framework. Despite the proven value of a structured and analytic approach to innovation, often new services are introduced on the basis of managers' and employees' subjective opinions about what the services should be and whether they will succeed, rather than on objective designs incorporating data about customer perceptions, market needs, and feasibility. A new service design process may be imprecise in defining the nature of the service concept because the people involved believe either that service processes cannot be defined precisely or that "everyone knows what we mean." None of these explanations or defenses for imprecision or lack of planning are justifiable, as we illustrate in this chapter's model for new service innovation and development.[7]

Because services are produced, consumed, and cocreated in real time and often involve interaction between employees and customers, it is critical that innovation and new service development processes involve both employees and customers. Employees frequently *are* the service, or at least they perform or deliver the service, and thus their involvement in choosing which new services to develop and how these services should be designed and implemented can be very beneficial. Contact employees are psychologically and physically close to customers and can be very helpful in identifying customer needs for new services. Involving employees in the design and development process also increases the likelihood of new service success because employees can identify the organizational issues that need to be addressed to support the delivery of the service to customers.[8]

Because customers often actively participate in service delivery and/or cocreation, they too should be involved in the new service development process. Beyond just providing input on their own needs, customers can help design the service concept and the delivery process, particularly in situations in which the customer personally carries out part of the service process. For example, Bank of America was successful with developing new service innovations in branch banking by relying on results of a series of experiments in its Atlanta branches.[9] The experiments were designed to more rigorously test new service innovations, in real time and with real customers, before launching them more broadly throughout the branch system. Similarly, the Mayo Clinic has established its SPARC Innovation lab in Rochester to experiment with new service innovations by testing them with actual patients and doctors in a prototype setting prior to introducing them (see Exhibit 9.2 later in the chapter).

Technology Spotlight   eBay: A Radical Service Innovation

When eBay was founded in 1995 it was not much more than an online flea market for individuals seeking to buy and sell old or unique items to other individuals. The original eBay concept was to provide the online service needed to facilitate these basic, simple trades among buyers and sellers. In the intervening years, the company has grown to a powerhouse of Internet retailing, with approximately 948 million registered users, a global presence in 38 markets, with well over $52 billion in annual trade. Meg Whitman, the company's now-famous CEO, described eBay as a "dynamic self-regulating economy."

Clearly, eBay is a radical service innovation. Nothing like it existed before, and its limits and bounds are yet unknown. From the original basic trading services, the company has evolved to a complex self-regulating system that is highly dependent on its community of members. Services offered by eBay now include PayPal (a safe and secure online payment system), Skype (a free online phone service), education classes for those who want to learn to be successful on eBay, and a developer's program for members who want to create their own software solutions for making eBay transactions more efficient and effective. Going far beyond its original focus on individual members, eBay has introduced important services for small businesses as well. According to an A. C. Nielsen survey, there are approximately 1.3 million sellers around the world whose primary or secondary source of income is their eBay business.

One of the most important aspects of eBay's success is its member community and the support and services they provide to each other. The company encourages open communication among members through chat rooms, discussion groups, and blogs that are actively used. These member-facilitated services and communications can be viewed as new service innovations in their own right. There are even "neighborhood watch" groups that ensure that everyone in the community learns and follows the etiquette and behavior norms that govern the community. The community's fundamental values are prominent on the website:

- *We believe people are basically good.*
- *We believe everyone has something to contribute.*
- *We believe that an honest, open environment can bring out the best in people.*
- *We recognize and respect everyone as a unique individual.*
- *We encourage you to treat others the way you want to be treated.*

Through an ongoing feedback system, members rate each other in terms of reliability and quality;

TYPES OF SERVICE INNOVATIONS

As we describe the service innovation and development process, remember that not all new service innovations are "new" to the same degree. New service options can run the gamut from major innovations to minor style changes:

• *Major or radical innovations* are new services for markets as yet undefined. past examples include the first broadcast television services and Federal Express's introduction of nationwide, overnight small-package delivery. Many innovations now and in the future will evolve from information, computer, and Internet-based technologies. Often these major innovations create brand-new markets.[10] Our Technology Spotlight features eBay, a company that epitomized a radical service innovation that has evolved significantly over the years.

• *Start-up businesses* consist of new services for a market that is already served by existing products that meet the same generic needs. Service examples include the creation of health maintenance organizations to provide an alternative form of health

this system, supported with these values, provides a "self-policing" orientation for the community. Extending the community aspect further, some members even interact with each other offline, going so far as to vacation together and buy special items for one another. One group even spent vacation time doing home repairs for an eBay member in need, and another group planned a Labor Day picnic together. eBay literally has become a part of many people's lives around the world.

Strategically, one of the most important elements of eBay's success has been its unrelenting devotion to its members and its willingness to listen. Being innovative in developing new services depends on listening to customers. One of eBay's most cherished institutions is the Voice of the Customer program. eBay's listening ear encourages constant complaints and suggestions to the company. And unlike many companies, eBay responds. Change is constant on eBay's site and in its service features—almost to a fault, say some users. According to the company's senior vice president of international operations, "Some of the terms you learn in business school— drive, force, commit—don't apply . . . We're over here listening, adapting, enabling."

As eBay's phenomenal growth has slowed (in 2006, gross merchandise sales grew by less than 20 percent, the smallest rate ever), the company is looking to new innovations to continue its success. Probably the most significant move is its newfound focus on buyers rather than sellers. The goal is to bring more active buyers to eBay by focusing on the buyer experience—making it more efficient and fun. eBay has begun by introducing a number of new tools based on buyer needs such as these: eBay Desktop allows users to bid and get streaming price updates without opening a web browser; Bid Assistant automatically places bids for a buyer; eBay Deal Finder helps buyers seek out items that will close soon, but have no bids entered yet; Playground allows buyers to buy things more easily. In addition, the company introduced a social networking feature—"Neighborhoods"—designed to bring old and new users to the site. This feature lets members post photos, discuss topics of interest, and write reviews with the assumption that social connections and networking will translate into increased buyer traffic for eBay.

Sources: R. D. Hof, "The eBay Economy," *BusinessWeek*, August 25, 2003, pp. 124–128; www.ebay.com, 2007; C. Salter, "eBay's Chaos Theory," *Fast Company* (November 2007), p. 100; Y. Yen, "eBay's New Friendly Neighborhood," *Fortune*, October 12, 2007, on CNNMoney.com; and J. Sloane, "With Growth Slowing, eBay Gets Innovative," *Wired*, November 5, 2007, online.

care delivery, online banking for financial transactions, and door-to-door airport shuttle services that compete with traditional taxi and limousine services.

• *New services for the currently served market* represent attempts to offer existing customers of the organization a service not previously available from the company (although it may be available from other companies). Examples include retailers adding a coffee bar or children's play area, a health club offering nutrition classes, and airlines offering phone and Internet services during flights. Sometimes these represent only modest enhancement services as in these examples. Other times the offering may represent a radically new stand-alone service such as PetSmart's PetsHotels, described later in the chapter in the Strategy Insight.

• *Service-line extensions* represent augmentations of the existing service line, such as a restaurant adding new menu items, an airline offering new routes, a law firm offering additional legal services, and a university adding new courses or degrees.

• *Service improvements* represent perhaps the most common type of service innovation. Changes in features of services that are already offered might involve faster execution of an existing service process, extended hours of service, or augmentations such as added amenities in a hotel room (e.g., the addition of wireless Internet connections).

• *Style changes* represent the most modest service innovations, although they are often highly visible and can have significant effects on customer perceptions, emotions, and attitudes. Changing the color scheme of a restaurant, revising the logo for an organization, redesigning a website, or painting aircraft a different color all represent style changes. These innovations do not fundamentally change the service, only its appearance, similar to how packaging changes are used for consumer products.

These types of service innovations are tied to the offerings themselves, suggesting that innovation occurs when a service offering is altered or expanded in some way—either radically on one extreme or stylistically at the other extreme. It is also possible that service innovations may come about when the customer's usage or cocreation role is redefined. For example, assuming the customer plays the role of user, buyer, or payer in a service context, new services can result when the previous role is redefined.[11] Many radical innovations effectively redefine the customer's role in these ways. For example, Netflix totally redefined customer's role for movie rentals. While customers used to visit their local Blockbuster store to rent one or more movies for a predetermined period of time and pay for them on a per-movie basis, NetFlix allows customers to receive movies through the mail, pay for them on a service contract, and return them whenever they are ready to do so. Thus, while movie watching in the home has not changed, the entire service process for renting, receiving, paying for and returning the movies is radically different. (The chapter opener in Chapter 14 provides more detail on Netflix's innovative strategies.)

STAGES IN SERVICE INNOVATION AND DEVELOPMENT

In this section we focus on the actual steps to be followed in service innovation and development. The steps can be applied to any type of new service. Much of what is presented in this section has direct parallels in the new product development process for manufactured goods. Because of the inherent characteristics of services, however, the development process for new services requires adaptations.[12] Figure 9.1 shows the basic principles and steps in new service development. Although these steps may be similar to those for manufactured goods, their implementation is different for services. The challenges typically lie in defining the concept in the early stages of the development process and again at the prototype development stage. Other challenges come about in the design and implementation of the new service because it can involve coordinating human resources, technology, internal processes, and facilities within already-existing systems. Partially because of these challenges, service firms are generally less likely to carry out a structured development process for new innovations than are their manufacturing and consumer-goods counterparts.[13]

An underlying assumption of new product development process models is that new product ideas can be dropped at any stage of the process if they do not satisfy the criteria for success at that particular stage.[14] Figure 9.1 shows the checkpoints (represented by stop signs) that separate critical stages of the development process. The checkpoints specify requirements that a new service must meet before it can proceed to the next stage of development. Despite what Figure 9.1 suggests, however, new service or product development is not always a completely linear process. Many companies are finding that to speed up service innovation, some steps can be worked on simultaneously, and

FIGURE 9.1
Service Innovation and Development Process

Sources: M. J. Bowers, "An Exploration into New Service Development: Organization, Process, and Structure," doctoral dissertation, Texas A&M University, 1985; A. Khurana and S. R. Rosenthal, "Integrating the Fuzzy Front End of New Product Development," *Sloan Management Review* 38 (Winter 1997), pp. 103–120; and R. G. Cooper, *Winning at New Products,* 3rd ed. (Cambridge, MA: Perseus Publishing, 2001).

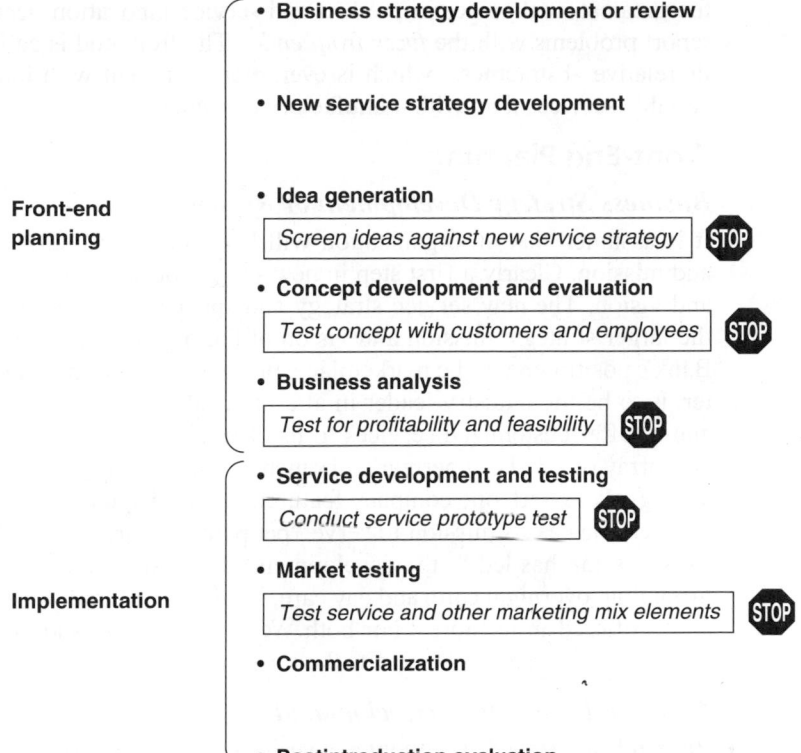

- **Business strategy development or review**

- **New service strategy development**

Front-end planning

- **Idea generation**
  - Screen ideas against new service strategy — STOP
- **Concept development and evaluation**
  - Test concept with customers and employees — STOP
- **Business analysis**
  - Test for profitability and feasibility — STOP

Implementation

- **Service development and testing**
  - Conduct service prototype test — STOP
- **Market testing**
  - Test service and other marketing mix elements — STOP
- **Commercialization**

- **Postintroduction evaluation**

in some instances a step may even be skipped, particularly for simple products and services. The overlapping of steps and simultaneous development of various pieces of the new service/product development process has been referred to as *flexible product development.* This type of flexible, speedy process is particularly important in technology industries, in which products and services evolve extremely quickly. In these environments, computer technology lets companies monitor customer opinions and needs during development and change the final offering right up until it is launched. Often, the next version of the service is in planning stages at the same time that the current version is being launched.[15] Even if the stages are handled simultaneously, however, the important checkpoints noted in Figure 9.1 should be assessed to maximize chances of success.

The process shown in Figure 9.1 is divided into two sections: front-end planning and implementation. The front end determines what service concepts will be developed, whereas the back end executes or implements the service concept. When asked where

FIGURE 9.2
New Service Strategy Matrix for Identifying Growth Opportunities

Source: Adapted from H. I. Ansoff, *Corporate Strategy* (New York: McGraw-Hill, 1965).

Offerings	Markets	
	Current customers	**New customers**
Existing services	Share building	Market development
New services	Service development	Diversification

the greatest weaknesses in product and service innovation occur, managers typically report problems with the *fuzzy front end*.[16] The front end is called "fuzzy" because of its relative abstractness, which is even more apparent with intangible, complex, and variable services than with manufactured products.

Front-End Planning

Business Strategy Development or Review

It is assumed that an organization will have an overall strategic orientation, vision, and mission. Clearly a first step in new service development is to review that mission and vision. The new service strategy and specific new service ideas must fit within the larger strategic mission and vision of the organization. For example, Wells Fargo Bank's positioning in the marketplace, presented in our opening vignette for this chapter, is to be the industry leader in alternative delivery channels for financial services and to offer customized services to its clientele when and where they need them. Its vast array of ATMs, supermarket branches, and Internet banking services support this strategy. PetSmart, one company featured in this chapter's Strategy Insight (later in the chapter), has as its mission to serve "pet parents" through the "lifetime care of pets." This mission has led to the development of a host of new services, such as training, grooming, overnight care, and day care, in addition to traditional food, toys, and accessories offered in its stores. For both Wells Fargo Bank and PetSmart, the company's new services strategy clearly fits the mission of the company.

New Service Strategy Development

Research suggests that without a clear new product or service strategy, a well-planned portfolio of new products and services, and an organizational structure that facilitates product development via ongoing communications and cross-functional sharing of responsibilities, front-end decisions become ineffective.[17] Thus, a product portfolio strategy and a defined organizational structure for new product or service development are critical—and are the foundations—for success.

The types of new services that will be appropriate will depend on the organization's goals, vision, capabilities, and growth plans. By defining a new service innovation strategy (possibly in terms of markets, types of services, time horizon for development, profit criteria, or other relevant factors), the organization will be in a better position to begin generating specific ideas. For example, it may focus its growth on new services at a particular level of the described continuum from major innovations to style changes. Or the organization may define its new service strategy even more specifically in terms of particular markets or market segments or in terms of specific profit generation goals.

One way to begin formulating a new service strategy is to use the framework shown in Figure 9.2 on the previous page for identifying growth opportunities. The framework allows an organization to identify possible directions for growth and can be helpful as a catalyst for creative ideas. The framework may also later serve as an initial idea screen if, for example, the organization chooses to focus its growth efforts on one or two of the four cells in the matrix. The matrix suggests that companies can develop a growth strategy around current customers or new customers and can focus on current offerings or new service offerings. The photo on the next page illustrates how Taco Bell has expanded its existing service to new locations such as universities and airports. Exhibit 9.1 further explains how Taco Bell has pursued growth in all four areas of the matrix.

Idea Generation

The next step in the process is the generation of new ideas that can be passed through the new service strategy screen described in the preceding step. Many methods and avenues are available for searching out new service ideas. Formal brainstorming, solicitation of ideas from employees and customers, lead user research, and learning about competitors' offerings are some of the most common approaches. Some companies are even collaborating with outsiders (e.g., competitors, vendors, alliance partners) or developing licensing agreements and joint ventures in an effort to exploit all possible sources of new ideas.[18]

Taco Bell Grew through Market Development on University Campuses

Observing customers and how they use the firm's products and services can also generate creative ideas for new innovations. Sometimes referred to as *empathic design,* observation is particularly effective in situations in which customers may not be able to recognize or verbalize their needs.[19] In service businesses, contact personnel, who actually deliver the services and interact directly with consumers, can be particularly good sources of ideas for complementary services and ways to improve current offerings. Social media and networks can also be a good source of new service ideas. In its online service group, Wells Fargo Bank uses social networks to dialogue with its customers, partially to generate new service ideas. Other organizations have found that internal networks of employees, across functions and disciplines, can be great sources of innovative ideas; thus, organizational practices that encourage networking and make collaboration easy are also ways to enourage new ideas.[20]

Whether the source of a new idea is inside or outside the organization, some established mechanism should exist for ensuring an ongoing stream of new service possibilities. This mechanism might include a formal service innovation or service R&D department or function with responsibility for generating new ideas, suggestion boxes for employees and customers, new service development teams that meet regularly, surveys and focus groups with customers and employees, or formal competitive analysis to identify new services.

Exhibit 9.1 Taco Bell Expands Markets and Offerings

To illustrate how the matrix shown in Figure 9.2 might function as a catalyst for idea generation, consider growth strategies pursued by Taco Bell, one of the world's fastest growing fast-food chains, specializing in Mexican food.

SHARE BUILDING (CURRENT CUSTOMERS, EXISTING SERVICES)

Share building is another term for market penetration—gaining a greater proportion of sales from existing markets. This strategy is pursued by Taco Bell in the expansion of Taco Bell outlets, resulting in 5,800 restaurants across the United States in 2007. In the late 1990s Taco Bell stepped up its efforts to gain market share among Hispanic consumers, another share-building strategy. Promoting itself as the place for a "fourth meal" (that meal between dinner and breakfast) is another way to sell more to its current market.

MARKET DEVELOPMENT (NEW CUSTOMERS, EXISTING SERVICES)

Taco Bell has expanded by offering its existing services in nontraditional locations, using creative formats to reach new customers. For example, Taco Bells can be found in airports, universities, and schools. Taco Bell has also opened Taco Bell Express units in convenience stores around the United States. Often the outlets in these locations are scaled-back "express" versions with a limited menu and small space requirement. Another form of market development is expansion into international markets, taking existing services to other countries. In 2007, Taco Bell operated more than 280 restaurants outside the United States.

SERVICE DEVELOPMENT (CURRENT CUSTOMERS, NEW SERVICES)

Service growth is possible when current customers are offered additional new services or service improvements. Taco Bell has added new menu items (e.g., its Fresco Style food items), better service delivery, value meals, and lower prices to better serve its current customers.

DIVERSIFICATION (NEW CUSTOMERS, NEW SERVICES)

Diversification, involving new services for consumers not currently served, is frequently the most challenging because it takes the organization into unfamiliar territories on both the product and market dimensions. Taco Bell has pursued this growth option by selling its branded products in grocery stores and by buying significant interests in other restaurant chains.

Source: www.tacobell.com, 2007.

Service Concept Development and Evaluation

Once an idea surfaces that is regarded as a good fit with both the business and the new service strategies, it is ready for initial development. In the case of a tangible product, this next step would mean formulating the basic product definition and then presenting consumers with descriptions and drawings to get their reactions.

The inherent characteristics of services place complex demands on this phase of the process. Drawing pictures and describing an intangible service in concrete terms are difficult, particularly when the service is not standardized and may be cocreated in real time with customers. It is therefore important that agreement be reached at this stage on exactly what the concept is and what customer need it is filling. By involving multiple parties in sharpening the concept definition, it often becomes apparent that individual views of the concept are not the same. For example, in one documented case, the design and development of a new discount brokerage service was initially described by the bank as a way "to buy and sell stocks for customers at low prices."[21] Through the initial concept development phase it became clear that not everyone in the organization had the same idea about how this description would translate into an actual service and that there were a variety of ways the concept could be developed. Only through multiple iterations of the service—and the raising of hundreds of issues, large and small—was an agreement finally reached on the discount brokerage concept.

After clear definition of the concept, it is important to produce a description of the service that represents its specific features and characteristics and then determine initial customer and employee responses to the concept. The service design document would describe the problem addressed by the service, discuss the reasons for offering the new service, itemize the service process and its benefits, and provide a rationale for purchasing the service.[22] The roles of customers and employees in the delivery process would also be described. The new service concept would then be evaluated by asking employees and customers whether they understand the idea of the proposed service, whether they are favorable to the concept, and whether they feel it satisfies an unmet need.

Business Analysis

Assuming that the service concept is favorably evaluated by customers and employees at the concept development stage, the next step is to estimate its economic feasibility and potential profit implications. Demand analysis, revenue projections, cost analyses, and operational feasibility are assessed at this stage. Because the development of service concepts is so closely tied to the operational system of the organization, this stage will involve preliminary assumptions about the costs of personnel hiring and training, delivery system enhancements, facility changes, and any other projected operations costs. The organization will pass the results of the business analysis through its profitability and feasibility screen to determine whether the new service idea meets the minimum requirements.

Implementation

Once the new service concept has passed all the front-end planning hurdles, it is ready for the implementation stages of the process.

Service Prototype Development and Testing

In the development of new tangible products, the development and testing stage involves construction of product prototypes and testing for consumer acceptance. Again, because services are intangible and simultaneously produced, consumed, and frequently cocreated, this step presents unique challenges. To address these challenges, this stage of service development should involve all who have a stake in the new service: customers and contact employees as well as functional representatives from marketing, operations, and human resources. During this phase, the concept is refined to the point at which a detailed service blueprint representing the implementation plan for the service can be produced. The blueprint is likely to evolve over a series of iterations on the basis of input from all involved parties. For example, when Yellow Transportation determined there was a need for a time-definite, guaranteed delivery service in its less-than-truckload market, the company developed detailed blueprints based on marketing, operations, customer service, customer, and employee input to serve as an initial prototype of the new service. The service has since become its most profitable and fastest growing service, even though it is also its most expensive service.[23]

In its service innovation practice, the internationally know design firm, IDEO, makes extensive use of full-scale prototypes and mock-ups to experiment with service concepts, testing both customer reactions and operational aspects of the service. In its work with Marriott's extended stay hotel chain, TownePlace suites, IDEO's smart Space researchers first spent several weeks living in and talking with TownePlace guests to observe and learn how they used the space and what their unmet needs were.[24] The result was a completely redesigned lobby area, including a map wall with notations about local shopping, restaurants, parks, and recreation areas that can be annotated by guests. Another change was a redesigned bedroom that provides the flexibility to be turned into a workspace. To test the design concepts, IDEO built a life-sized lobby

Exhibit 9.2 SPARC: Service Innovation at the Mayo Clinic

The Mayo Clinic in the United States is more than 100 years old and one of the most respected names in health care globally. It is consistently listed among the top hospitals in the United States, and is known for its collaborative health care model, high levels of service, and always being in the forefront of medicine. Following its innovative traditions, and again setting itself apart from other health care organizations, Mayo established its SPARC Innovation Lab in 2003 to focus on testing and evaluating new practices in health care delivery. While medical and technological advances have changed the face of health care dramatically over the past 50 years, the same is not necessarily true of the way health care is delivered to patients. Everything from patient exam rooms to the patient's waiting experience has changed relatively little in comparison to scientific advances in medicine. Mayo recognized this and determined it should again be in the forefront of innovation—this time in the processes and practices of health care delivery.

SPARC stands for "See, Plan, Act, Refine, Communicate," and the lab has become a testing ground for all types of service and delivery innovations at Mayo—innovations that are intended to enhance the patient's experience and that also have potential health benefits. Working with the design firm, IDEO, Mayo designed an experimental lab at its Rochester, Minnesota, facility, where service innovations can be tested with real patients and real Mayo doctors and staff before they are introduced into the clinics. The lab is set up like an actual clinic within the Mayo facility, and experiments are conducted with doctors and patients (of course, with their prior knowledge and consent). The glass walls in the SPARC clinic reveal inner offices and show support staff working and doctors and patients interacting, thus allowing direct observation of experimental services. The space is highly flexible so that exam rooms, common spaces, walls, furniture, and computers can be moved around to test different configurations and services.

SPARC Lab at Mayo Clinic, Rochester

and suite out of white foam core and invited Marriott executives, hotel managers, and guests to provide feedback on the prototype.

The last step is for each area involved in rendering the service to translate the final blueprint and prototypes into specific implementation plans for its part of the service delivery process. Because service development, design, and delivery, and sometimes cocreation activities, are so intricately intertwined, all parties involved in any aspect of the new service must work together at this stage to delineate the details of the new service. If not, seemingly minor operational details can cause an otherwise good new service idea to fail. For example, careful service development and lots of testing are the rules at Expedia.com, the giant travel information and transportation-booking website. Customers who use Expedia's website potentially have a lot to lose—a $1,000 trip may be at stake, or it may be the only week of vacation the person has in a whole year. Before launching any new software onto the site or redesigning the site itself, Expedia

Within the SPARC program, researchers focus on complex and important issues for the health care industry in general, with the overarching principle of "patient-centered design." For example, here are some of the topics they have explored and "re-imagined"—the term they use for service improvement and futuristic innovation:

- What would integrated health care look like from the patient's perspective?
- What is the relationship among communication, understanding, and satisfaction for the patient?
- How could exam rooms be reconfigured for a better patient experience and to improve patient–doctor communication?
- How can the onsite check-in process for appointments be improved?
- How can space within the health care facility be optimized to serve patients and staff?
- What are the unmet education needs of patients, and how can a service be designed to meet those needs?

While innovation in health care delivery practices such as those listed is relatively unique, Mayo's practices within the SPARC lab are particularly unique—combining principles from service, design, and health care. The innovation process begins with a problem or issue that the innovation team takes on as important to the patient experience or service delivery model. For example, the patient check-in process at Mayo Rochester was viewed as particularly problematic for patients, with long lines and frustration on the part of patients who had to stand and wait when all they wanted to do was sit down. The multidisciplinary team began by observing and listening to both patients and staff to start the process of identifying innovative solutions to this challenge. Through this human-centered, participatory approach they developed ideas by telling stories and conveying narratives that morphed into innovations that were tested with prototypes in the lab. In the case of the patient check-in process, the basic innovation idea was to develop an automated self-check-in process. Initial prototypes of the self-service check-in kiosk were quite unsophisticated. For example, the first version was a piece of paper representing a computer screen. Later versions of the prototype, evolved to inactive computer screens to actual touch screens displayed on a kiosk. At each version of the prototype, the team collected feedback from both patients and staff. The results of this experiment led Mayo to invest resources in investigating a roll-out of this innovative solution.

In another case, an innovation studied in the SPARC lab lead to innovative ways to communicate treatment options to diabetic patients who were considering taking statin drugs. A number of patient–doctor communication prototypes were tested to help patients understand their options by conveying information on medical evidence, risk factors, and treatment options via different formats. The prototypes ranged from online information to booklets to a one-page decision aid, and each was tested to determine what was most effective for patient participation, preferences, and adherence to the treatment choice. In this case, the innovation not only improved the patient's experience in the actual interaction with the physician, but the delivery innovation resulted in increased likelihood of the patient following through on the treatment plan—ultimately affecting the health outcome itself.

Sources: http://mayoresearch.mayo.edu/mayo/research/sparc, 2007; and C. Salter, "A Prescription for Innovation," *Fast Company* (April 2006), p. 83.

holds dozens of meetings with the design team to consider customer requirements. It then builds and tests prototypes of the software or website changes, conducts usability tests, and gathers customer feedback on designs. Feedback is reviewed and integrated into the design constantly before, during, and after the launch.[25] Exhibit 9.2 illustrates how Mayo Clinic's SPARC Innovation Lab tests new services and delivery models in its unique experimental setting.

Market Testing

At the market testing stage of the development process, a tangible product might be test marketed in a limited number of trading areas to determine marketplace acceptance of the product as well as other marketing mix variables such as promotion, pricing, and distribution systems. Because new service offerings are often intertwined with the delivery system for existing services, it is difficult to test new services in isolation.

And in some cases, such as a one-site hospital, it may not be possible to introduce the service to an isolated market area because the organization has only one point of delivery. There are alternative ways of testing the response to marketing mix variables, however. The new service might be offered to employees of the organization and their families for a time to assess their responses to variations in the marketing mix. Or the organization might decide to test variations in pricing and promotion in less realistic contexts by presenting customers with hypothetical mixes and getting their responses in terms of intentions to try the service under varying circumstances.

It is also extremely important at this stage in the development process to do a pilot run of the service to be sure that the operational details are functioning smoothly. Frequently this step is overlooked, and the actual market introduction may be the first test of whether the service system functions as planned. By this point, mistakes in design are harder to correct. As one noted service expert says, "There is simply no substitute for a proper rehearsal" when introducing a new service.[26] In the case of the discount brokerage service described earlier, the bank ran a pilot test by offering employees a special price for one month. The offer was marketed internally, allowing the bank to observe the service process in action before it was introduced to the external market.

Commercialization

During the commercialization stage, the service goes live and is introduced to the marketplace. This stage has two primary objectives. The first is to build and maintain acceptance of the new service among large numbers of service delivery personnel who will be responsible day-to-day for service quality. This task is made easier if acceptance has been built in by involving key groups in the design and development process all along. However, it will still be a challenge to maintain enthusiasm and communicate the new service throughout the system; excellent internal marketing will help.

The second objective is to monitor all aspects of the service during introduction and through the complete service cycle. If the customer needs six months to experience the entire service, then careful monitoring must be maintained through at least six months. Every detail of the service should be assessed—phone calls, face-to-face transactions, billing, complaints, and delivery problems. Operating efficiency and costs should also be tracked.

Postintroduction Evaluation

At this point, the information gathered during commercialization of the service can be reviewed and changes made to the delivery process, staffing, or marketing mix variables on the basis of actual market response to the offering. For example, Expedia.com, the travel website, realized that despite prelaunch testing, restrictions on Expedia bargain fares were confusing to customers. A "hot fix" team was called in to repair the problem.[27] Within a day, the project team redesigned the presentation of information so that the fare restrictions would be clear to customers.

No service will ever stay the same. Whether deliberate or unplanned, changes will always occur. Therefore, formalizing the review process to make those changes that enhance service quality from the customer's point of view is critical.

SERVICE BLUEPRINTING

A stumbling block in service innovation and development is the difficulty of describing and depicting the service at the concept development, service development, and market test stages. One of the keys to matching service specifications to customer expectations is the ability to describe critical service process characteristics objectively and to depict them so that employees, customers, and managers alike know what the service is, can see their roles, and can understand all the steps and flows involved in the service process. In this section of the chapter, we look in depth at service blueprinting, a useful technique for designing and specifying intangible service processes.[28]

What Is a Service Blueprint?

The manufacturing and construction industries have a long tradition of engineering and design. Can you imagine a house being built without detailed specifications? Can you imagine a car, a computer, or even a simple product like a child's toy or a shampoo being produced without concrete and detailed plans, written specifications, and engineering drawings? Yet services commonly lack concrete specifications. A service, even a complex one, might be introduced without any formal, objective depiction of the process.

A *service blueprint* is a picture or map that portrays the service system so that the different people involved in providing it can understand and deal with it objectively, regardless of their roles or their individual points of view. Blueprints are particularly useful at the design stage of service development. A service blueprint visually displays the service by simultaneously depicting the process of service delivery, the points of customer contact, the roles of customers and employees, and the visible elements of the service (see Figure 9.3). It provides a way to break a service down into its logical components and to depict the steps or tasks in the process, the means by which the tasks are executed, and the evidence of service as the customer experiences it. Blueprinting has its origins in a variety of fields and techniques, including logistics, industrial engineering, decision theory, computer systems analysis, and software engineering—all of which deal with the definition and explanation of processes.[29] Because services are "experiences" rather than objects or technologies, blueprinting is a particularly useful technique for describing them.

Blueprint Components

The key components of service blueprints are shown in Figure 9.4.[30] They are customer actions, onstage/visible contact employee actions, backstage/invisible contact employee actions, and support processes. The conventions for drawing service blueprints are not rigidly defined, and thus the particular symbols used, the number of horizontal lines in the blueprint, and the particular labels for each part of the blueprint may vary somewhat depending on what you read and the complexity of the blueprint being described. These variations are not a problem as long as you keep in mind the purpose of the blueprint and view it as a useful technique rather than as a set of rigid rules for designing services. In fact, its flexibility—when compared with other process mapping approaches—is one of service blueprinting's major strengths.

The *customer actions* area encompasses the steps, choices, activities, and interactions that the customer performs in the process of purchasing, consuming, and evaluating the service. The total customer experience is apparent in this area of the blueprint. In

FIGURE 9.3   **Service Blueprinting**

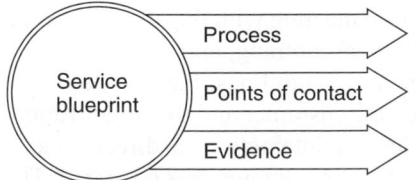

Service blueprinting
A technique for simultaneously depicting the service process, the points of customer contact, and the evidence of service from the customer's point of view.

FIGURE 9.4
Service Blueprint Components

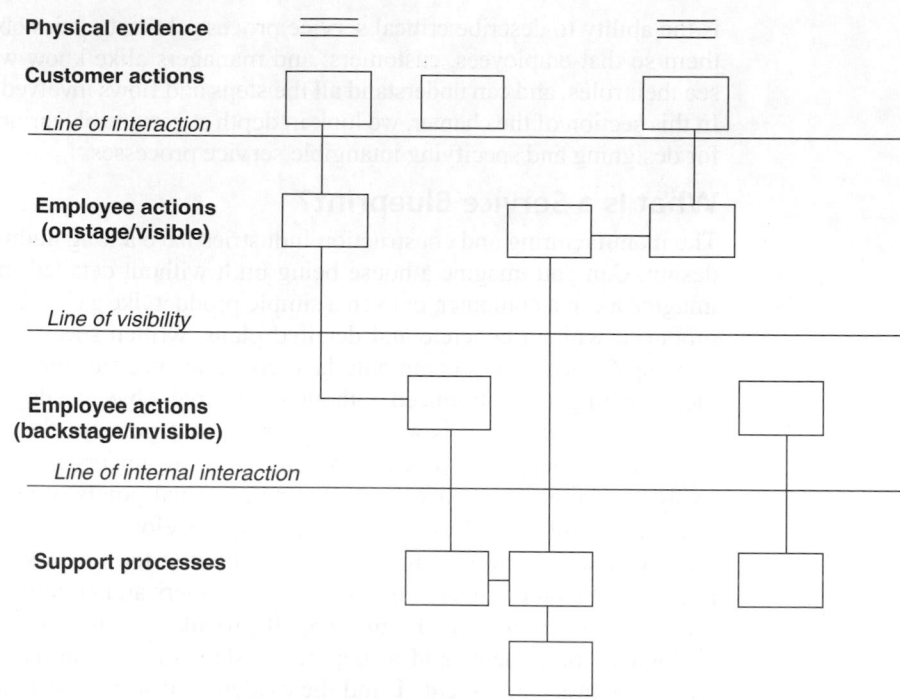

a legal services example, the customer actions might include a decision to contact an attorney, phone calls to the attorney, face-to-face meetings, receipt of documents, and receipt of a bill.

Paralleling the customer actions are two areas of contact employee actions. The steps and activities that the contact employee performs that are visible to the customer are the *onstage/visible contact employee actions.* In the legal services setting, the actions of the attorney (the contact employee) that are visible to the client are, for example, the initial interview, intermediate meetings, and final delivery of legal documents.

Those contact employee actions that occur behind the scenes to support the onstage activities are the *backstage/invisible contact employee actions.* In the example, anything the attorney does behind the scenes to prepare for the meetings or to prepare the final documents will appear in this section of the blueprint, together with phone call contacts the customer has with the attorney or other frontline staff in the firm. All *non-visible* contact employee actions are shown in this area of the blueprint.

The *support processes* section of the blueprint covers the internal services, steps, and interactions that take place to support the contact employees in delivering the service. Again, in our legal example, any service support activities such as legal research by staff, preparation of documents, and secretarial support to set up meetings will be shown in the support processes area of the blueprint.

At the very top of the blueprint you see the *physical evidence* of the service. Typically, above each point of contact the actual physical evidence of the service is listed. In the legal example, the physical evidence of the face-to-face meeting with the attorney would be such items as office decor, written documents, lawyer's clothing, and so forth.

The four key action areas are separated by three horizontal lines. First is the *line of interaction,* representing direct interactions between the customer and the organization. Any time a vertical line crosses the horizontal line of interaction, a direct contact between the customer and the organization, or a service encounter, has occurred. The next horizontal line is the critically important *line of visibility.* This line separates all service activities that are visible to the customer from those that are not visible. In reading blueprints, it is immediately obvious whether the consumer is provided with much visible evidence of the service simply by analyzing how much of the service occurs above the line of visibility versus the activities carried out below the line. This line also separates what the contact employees do onstage from what they do backstage. For example, in a medical examination situation, the doctor would perform the actual exam and answer the patient's questions above the line of visibility, or onstage, whereas she might read the patient's chart in advance and dictate notes following the exam below the line of visibility, or backstage. The third line is the *line of internal interaction,* which separates customer-contact employee activities from those of other service support activities and people. Vertical lines cutting across the line of internal interaction represent internal service encounters.

One of the most significant differences between service blueprints and other process flow diagrams is the primary focus on customers and their views of the service process. In fact, in designing effective service blueprints it is recommended that the diagramming start with the customer's view of the process and then work into the delivery system. The boxes shown within each action area depict steps performed or experienced by the actors at that level.

Service Blueprint Examples

Figures 9.5 and 9.6 show service blueprints for two different services: express mail delivery and an overnight hotel stay.[31] These blueprints are deliberately kept very simple, showing only the most basic steps in the services. Complex diagrams could be

FIGURE 9.5 Blueprint for Express Mail Delivery Service

Source: *Service Quality Handbook* by E. E. Scheuing and W. F. Christopher (eds). Copyright 1993 by AM MGMT ASSN / AMACOM (B). Reproduced with permission of AM MGMT ASSN / AMACOM (B) in the format Textbook via Copyright Clearance Center.

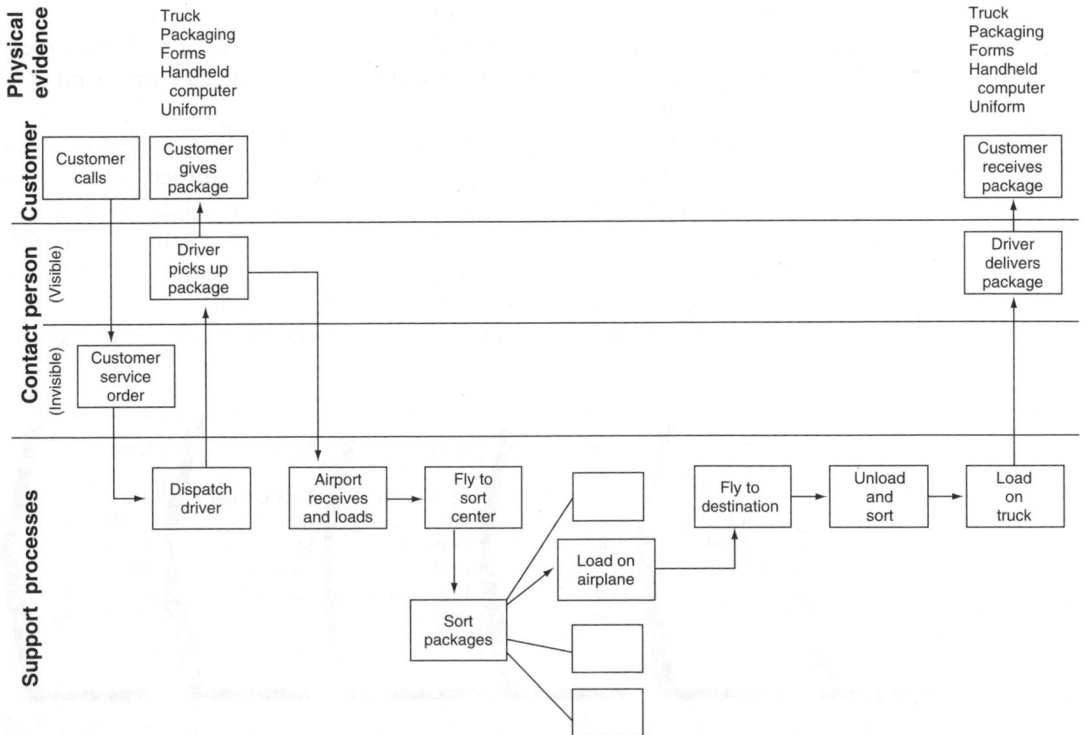

FIGURE 9.6
Blueprint for Overnight Hotel Stay Service

Source: *Service Quality Handbook* by E. E. Scheuing and W. F. Christopher (eds). Copyright 1993 by AM MGMT ASSN / AMACOM (B). Reproduced with permission of AM MGMT ASSN / AMACOM (B) in the format Textbook via Copyright Clearance Center.

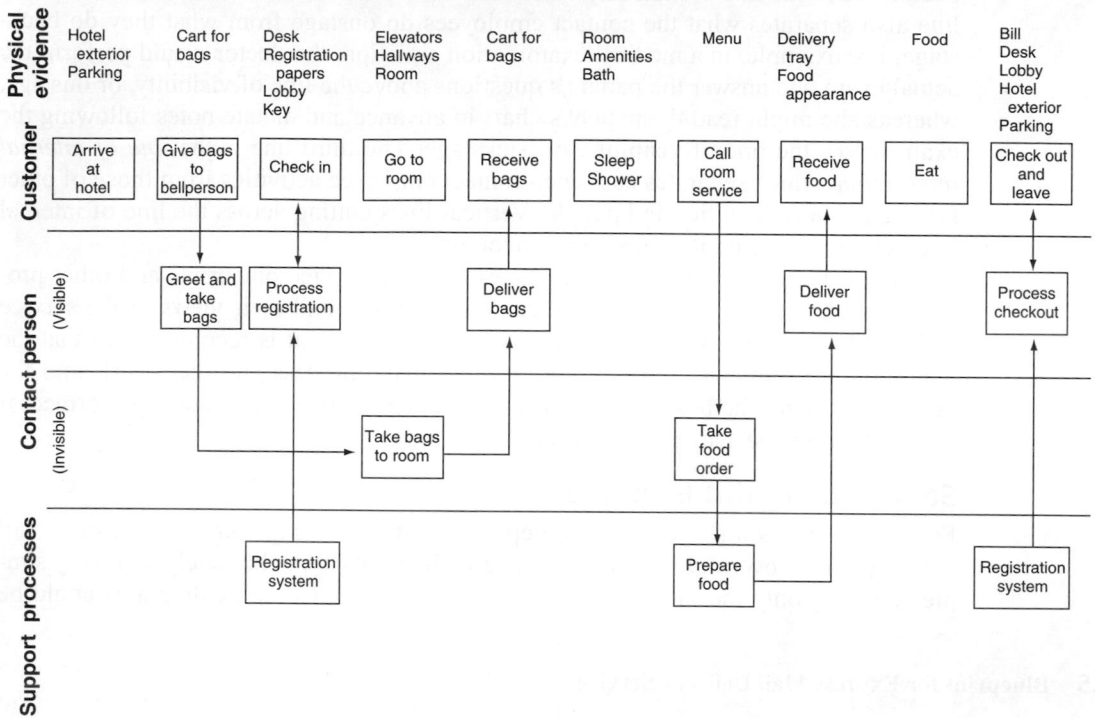

developed for each step, and the internal processes could be much more fully developed. In addition to the four action areas separated by the three horizontal lines, these blueprints also show the physical evidence of the service from the customer's point of view at each step of the process.

Examine the express mail delivery blueprint in Figure 9.5. It is clear that from the customer's point of view there are only three steps in the service process: the phone call, the package pickup, and the package delivery. The process is relatively standardized; the people who perform the service are the phone order-taker and the delivery person; and the physical evidence includes the document package, the transmittal forms, the truck, and the handheld computer. In some cases the customer may also engage the online or phone-based package tracking system. Although critically important for

FIGURE 9.7
Building a Service Blueprint

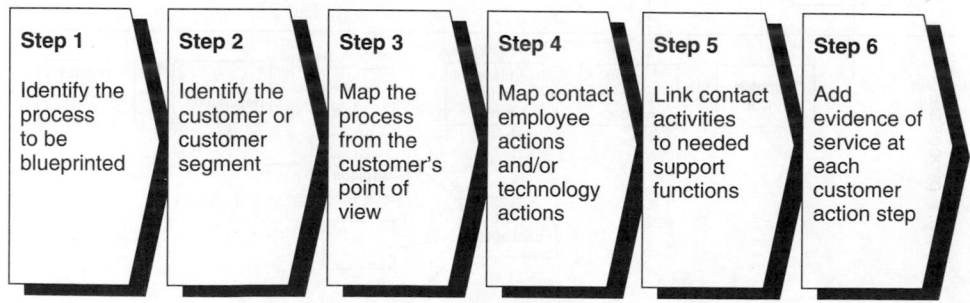

the firm's success, the complex process that occurs behind the line of visibility is of little interest or concern to the customer. However, for the three visible-to-the-customer steps to proceed effectively, invisible internal services are needed. What these steps are and the fact that they support the delivery of the service to the external customer are apparent from the blueprint.

Any of the steps in the blueprint could be exploded into a detailed blueprint if needed for a particular purpose. For example, if the delivery company learned that the "unload and sort" step was taking too long and causing unacceptable delays in delivery, that step could be blueprinted in much greater detail to isolate the problems.

In the case of the overnight hotel stay depicted in Figure 9.6, the customer obviously is more actively involved in the service than he or she is in the express mail service. The guest first checks in, then goes to the hotel room where a variety of steps take place (receiving bags, sleeping, showering, eating breakfast, and so on), and finally checks out. Imagine how much more complex this process could be and how many more interactions might occur if the service blueprint depicted a week-long vacation at the hotel, or even a three-day business conference. The service blueprint also makes clear (by reading across the line of interaction) those employees with whom the guest interacts and thus those employees who provide evidence of the service to the customer. Several interactions occur with a variety of hotel employees, including the bellperson, the front-desk clerk, the food service order-taker, and the food delivery person. Each step in the customer action area is also associated with various forms of physical evidence, from the hotel parking area and hotel exterior and interior to the forms used at guest registration, the lobby, the room, and the food. The hotel facility itself is critical in communicating the image of the hotel company, in providing satisfaction for the guest through the manner in which the hotel room is designed and maintained, and in facilitating the actions and interactions of both the guest and the employees of the hotel. In the hotel case, the process is relatively complex (although again somewhat standardized), the people providing the service are a variety of frontline employees, and the physical evidence includes everything from the guest registration form to the design of the lobby and room to the uniforms worn by frontline employees.

Blueprints for Technology-Delivered Self-Service

To this point all our discussion of service blueprints has related to services that are delivered in person, services in which employees interact directly with customers at some point in the process. But what about technology-delivered services like self-service websites (Expedia's travel information site, Cisco Systems customer self-service site) and interactive kiosks (ATMs, airline self-check-in machines)? Can service blueprinting be used effectively to design these types of services? Certainly it can, but the lines of demarcation will change, and some blueprint labels may need to be adapted.

If no employees are involved in the service (except when there is a problem or the service does not function as planned), the contact person areas of the blueprint are not needed. Instead, the area above the line of visibility can be used to illustrate the interface between the customer and the computer website or the physical interaction with the kiosk. This area can be relabeled *onstage/visible technology*. The backstage contact person actions area would be irrelevant in this case.

If the service involves a combination of human and technology interfaces, as with airline computerized check-in, the onstage area can be cut into two distinct spaces divided by an additional horizontal line. In the airline computerized check-in example, the human contact with the airline employee who takes the bags and checks identification would be shown in one area and the technology interactions with the check-in computer kiosk would be shown in the second area, both above the line of visibility.

Reading and Using Service Blueprints

A service blueprint can be read in a variety of ways, depending on the purpose. If the purpose is to understand the customer's view of the process or the customer experience, the blueprint can be read from left to right, tracking the events in the customer action area. Questions that might be asked include these: How is the service initiated by the customer? What choices does the customer make? Is the customer highly involved in creating the service, or are few actions required of the customer? What is the physical evidence of the service from the customer's point of view? Is the evidence consistent with the organization's strategy and positioning?

If the purpose is to understand contact employees' roles, the blueprint can also be read horizontally but this time focusing on the activities directly above and below the line of visibility. Questions that might be asked include these: How rational, efficient, and effective is the process? Who interacts with customers, when, and how often? Is one person responsible for the customer, or is the customer passed off from one contact employee to another?

If the purpose is to understand the integration of the various elements of the service process, or to identify where particular employees fit into the bigger picture, the blueprint can be analyzed vertically. In this analysis, it becomes clear what tasks and which employees are essential in the delivery of service to the customer. The linkages from internal actions deep within the organization to frontline effects on the customer can also be seen in the blueprint. Questions that might be asked include these: What actions are being performed backstage to support critical customer interaction points? What are the associated support actions? How are handoffs from one employee to another taking place?

If the purpose is service redesign, the blueprint can be looked at as a whole to assess the complexity of the process, how it might be changed, and how changes from the customer's point of view would affect the contact employee and other internal processes, and vice versa. Blueprints can also be used to assess the overall efficiency and productivity of the service system and to evaluate how potential changes will affect the system.[32] The blueprint can also be analyzed to determine likely failure points or bottlenecks in the process. When such points are discovered, a firm can introduce measures to track failures, or that part of the blueprint can be exploded so that the firm can focus in much greater detail on that piece of the system.

Blueprinting applications in a variety of contexts have demonstrated benefits and uses, including:[33]

- Providing a platform for innovation.
- Recognizing roles and interdependencies among functions, people, and organizations.
- Facilitating both strategic and tactical innovations.
- Transferring and storing innovation and service knowledge.
- Designing moments of truth from the customer's point of view.
- Suggesting critical points for measurement and feedback in the service process.
- Clarifying competitive positioning.
- Understanding the ideal customer experience.

Clearly, one of the greatest benefits of blueprinting is education.[34] When people begin to develop a blueprint, it quickly becomes apparent what is actually known about the service. Sometimes the shared knowledge is minimal. Biases and prejudices are made explicit, and agreements and compromises must be reached. The process itself promotes cross-functional integration and understanding. In the attempt to visualize the entire service system, people are forced to consider the service in new and more comprehensive ways. Exhibit 9.3 illustrates a case of blueprinting in action at ARAMARK Parks and Resorts.[35]

Building a Blueprint

Recall that many of the benefits and purposes of building a blueprint evolve from the process of doing it. Thus, the final product is not necessarily the only goal. Through the process of developing the blueprint, many intermediate goals can be achieved: clarification of the concept, development of a shared service vision, recognition of complexities and intricacies of the service that are not initially apparent, and delineation of roles and responsibilities, to name a few. The development of the blueprint needs to involve a variety of functional representatives as well as information from customers. Drawing or building a blueprint is not a task that should be assigned to one person or one functional area. Figure 9.7 on page 268, identifies the basic steps in building a blueprint. Exhibit 9.4 provides answers to frequently asked questions about service blueprints.

Step 1: Identify the Service Process to Be Blueprinted

Blueprints can be developed at a variety of levels, and there needs to be agreement on the starting point. For example, the express mail delivery blueprint shown in Figure 9.5 is at the basic service concept level. Little detail is shown, and variations based on market segment or specific services are not shown. Specific blueprints could be developed for two-day express mail, large accounts, Internet-facilitated services, and/or storefront drop-off centers. Each of these blueprints would share some features with the concept blueprint but would also include unique features. Or if the "sort packages" and "loading" elements of the process were found to be problem areas or bottlenecks that were slowing service to customers, a detailed blueprint of the subprocesses at work in those two steps could be developed. A firm can identify the process to be mapped once it has determined the underlying purpose for building the blueprint.

Step 2: Identify the Customer or Customer Segment Experiencing the Service

A common rationale for market segmentation is that each segment's needs are different and therefore will require variations in the service or product features. Thus, blueprints are most useful when developed for a particular customer or customer segment, assuming that the service process varies across segments. At a very abstract or conceptual level it may be possible to combine customer segments on one blueprint. However, once almost any level of detail is reached, separate blueprints should be developed to avoid confusion and maximize their usefulness.

Step 3: Map the Service Process from the Customer's Point of View

Step 3 involves charting the choices and actions that the customer performs or experiences in purchasing, consuming, and evaluating the service. Identifying the service from the customer's point of view first will help avoid focusing on processes and steps that have no customer impact. This step forces agreement on who the customer is (sometimes no small task) and may involve considerable research and observation to determine exactly how the customer experiences the service. Sometimes the beginning and ending of the service from the customer's point of view may not be obvious. For example, research in a hair-cutting context revealed that customers viewed the

Exhibit 9.3 Blueprinting in Action at Aramark Parks and Resorts

ARAMARK is a global leader in professional services, operating as an outsourcer for everything from food, hospitality, facility management, and uniform services and working with businesses, universities, health care organizations, parks and resorts, convention centers, and other groups. it was ranked first in its industry among *Fortune*'s Most Admired companies; the company has approximately 240,000 employees serving clients in 19 countries. One of its divisions is ARAMARK Parks and Resorts, a group that provides services for 17 major park destinations within the United States, including Denali National Park in Alaska, Shenandoah National Park in Virginia, and Lake Powell Resorts and Marinas in the Glen Canyon National Recreation Area of Arizona to name just a few. Each of the parks has at least three or four service businesses within it that ARAMARK operates on an outsourcing contract.

GOAL: SERVICE IMPROVEMENT AND CUSTOMER RETENTION

A number of years ago, Renee Ryan, then marketing director for ARAMARK Parks and Resorts, confronted a challenge. It was clear that repeat business at ARAMARK's parks was declining overall. This was particularly the case at Lake Powell Resorts and Marinas in Arizona, where the company operated houseboat rentals, a resort, campgrounds, boat tours, and food service operations. Research revealed that many people were not returning to Lake Powell because their first experience there did not match what they expected or were accustomed to based on visits to other resort

destinations. Ryan employed both traditional and visual (photos, videotape) blueprints to help convince the organization that changes were in order and specifically what should be done. The results benefited customers through improvements in service and the company through increased repeat business.

First, Ryan developed a blueprint of a typical, quality hotel/resort experience from a typical customer's point of view. Then she blueprinted the Lake Powell resort experience. The comparison of the two blueprints was revealing in terms of differences in basic services, standards, and processes. This comparison process resulted in the development of new services, facilities upgrades, and modernization of key service elements. Through the visual blueprint in particular, showing all aspects of the service through photos and videotapes, the need for service upgrades became apparent. Another revelation also jumped out of the blueprint. By visually tracking the customer's experience, it was clear that customers were being asked to work extremely hard for their vacations! To experience the luxurious and not-inexpensive houseboat experience they had purchased, customers first had to create extensive grocery lists, shop in crowded stores near the resort, carry all of their food and belongings down a steep embankment, and haul them out to the boat. Once the trip started, more hard labor was required. Anchoring a large houseboat each night is not a trivial matter, and cooking on board can be arduous and time consuming. Navigating the houseboat can also be stressful, especially for inexperienced captains. The run-down resort facilities on

---

process as beginning with the phone call to the salon and setting of the appointment, whereas the hair stylists did not typically view the making of appointments as part of the service process.[36] If the blueprint is being developed for an existing service, it may be helpful at this point in the process to videotape or photograph the service process from the customer's point of view as was done in the ARAMARK case illustrated in Exhibit 9.3. Often managers and others who are not on the front lines do not know what the customers are experiencing and may be quite surprised when they view the actual service experience.

Step 4: Map Contact Employee Actions and/or Technology Actions

First the lines of interaction and visibility are drawn, and then the process from the customer contact person's point of view is mapped, distinguishing visible or onstage activities from invisible backstage activities. For existing services, this step involves questioning or observing frontline operations employees to learn what they do and which activities are performed in full view of the customer versus which activities are carried out behind the scenes.

For technology-delivered services or those that combine technology and human delivery, the required actions of the technology interface will be mapped above the

land, the arduous work required to get on the water, and the stress of navigation all combined to discourage customers from returning after surviving their first Lake Powell vacation. The blueprinting exercise made all of this extremely vivid for top management and resulted

in a suite of new services, renovations of existing facilities, training of staff to perform to new service standards, and new measurement and reward systems. Some of the new services introduced included various levels of concierge services that started with the basic service of taking guests' things to the boat for them and later transporting guests in a cart to the boat dock. Service packages were extended at the high end to include buying groceries for guests and providing executive chefs who would travel with the party and cook on board. Trained captains could also be hired to lessen the stress of navigation. All levels of service in between were also available a la carte.

RESULTS FOR ARAMARK

The result for Lake Powell of all of these service quality improvements and innovative new services was 50 percent fewer complaints. Repeat business increased by 12 percent, and customer satisfaction also increased dramatically. The blueprints in this case were extremely valuable in that they allowed managers to see the service in ways they had never seen it before. The blueprints also provided a focal point for conversations, leading to change and ultimately to new service standards and measures. Using the blueprinting technique helped people within the parks division develop a true customer focus.

Sources: M. J. Bitner, A. L. Ostrom, and F. N. Morgan, "Service Blueprinting: A Practical Technique for Service Innovation," forthcoming *California Management Review,* 2008; Interview with Renee Ryan; and www.aramark.com, 2007.

line of visibility as well. If no employees are involved in the service, the area can be relabeled "onstage technology actions." If both human and technology interactions are involved, an additional horizontal line can separate "visible contact employee actions" from "visible technology actions." Using the additional line will facilitate reading and interpretation of the service blueprint.

Step 5: Link Contact Activities to Needed Support Functions

The line of internal interaction can then be drawn and linkages from contact activities to internal support functions can be identified. In this process, the direct and indirect impact of internal actions on customers becomes apparent. Internal service processes take on added importance when viewed in connection with their link to the customer. Alternatively, certain steps in the process may be viewed as unnecessary if there is no clear link to the customer's experience or to an essential internal support service.

Step 6: Add Evidence of Service at Each Customer Action Step

Finally, the evidence of service can be added to the blueprint to illustrate what the customer sees and receives as tangible evidence of the service at each step in the customer

Exhibit 9.4 Frequently Asked Questions about Service Blueprinting

What process should be blueprinted?

What process to map depends on the team or organization's objectives. If these are not clearly defined, then identifying the process can present a challenge. Questions to ask: Why are we blueprinting the service? What is our objective? Where does the service process begin and end? Are we focusing on the entire service, a component of the service, or a period of time?

Can multiple market segments be included on one blueprint?

Generally the answer to this question is no. Assuming that market segments require different service processes or attributes, the blueprint for one segment may look very different from the blueprint for another. Only at a very high level (sometimes called a *concept blueprint*) might it be relevant to map multiple segments simultaneously.

Who should "draw" the blueprint?

A blueprint is a team effort. It should not be assigned as an individual task, certainly not in the development stages. All relevant parties should be involved or represented in the development effort. The task might include employees across multiple functions in the organization (marketing, operations, human resources, facilities design) as well as customers in some cases.

Should the actual or desired service process be blueprinted?

If a new service is being designed, then clearly it is important to start with the desired service process. However, in cases of service improvement or service redesign, it is very important to map (at least at a conceptual level) the actual service process first. Once the group knows how the service is actually functioning, then the blueprint can be modified or used as a base for changes and improvements.

Should exceptions or recovery processes be incorporated within the blueprint?

It may be possible to map relatively simple, commonly occurring recovery processes onto a blueprint, assuming there are not a lot of these. However, this process can quickly become complex and cause the blueprint to be confusing or unreadable. Often a better strategy is to indicate common fail points on the blueprint and, if needed, develop separate blueprints for the service recovery processes.

What is the appropriate level of detail?

The answer to this question depends again on the objective or purpose for doing the blueprint in the first place. If it is to be used primarily to communicate the general nature of the service, then a concept blueprint with few details is best. If it is being used to focus on diagnosing and improving the service process, then more detail is needed. Because some people are more detail oriented than others, this particular question will always arise and needs to be resolved in any team blueprinting effort.

What symbols should be used?

At this point in time, there is not a lexicon of blueprinting symbols that is commonly used or accepted across companies. What is most important is that the symbols be defined, be kept relatively simple, and be used consistently by the team and across the organization if blueprints are being shared internally.

Should time or dollar costs be included on the blueprint?

Blueprints are very versatile. If reducing the time taken for various parts of the service process is an objective of the blueprinting effort, then time can definitely be included. The same is true for dollar costs or anything else that is relevant as an objective. However, it is not advisable to put such information on the blueprint unless it is of central concern.

experience. A photographic blueprint, including photos, slides, or video of the process, can be very useful at this stage to aid in analyzing the impact of tangible evidence and its consistency with the overall strategy and service positioning.

HIGH-PERFORMANCE SERVICE INNOVATIONS

To this point in the chapter, we have discussed approaches and tools for innovating, developing, and designing services. A dilemma in most companies is that there are too many new ideas from which to choose. New technologies, changing customer needs, deregulation, competitors' actions—these areas result in myriad potential new offerings to consider. The question is which to pursue. How can a company decide which new offerings will likely be major successes and which may be less successful or even fail? How can they decide which are worthy of investment and which are not? Making these kinds of decisions is particularly challenging in manufacturing, technology, and retail industries as they venture into new initiatives to focus on growth through service innovation (see the Strategy Insight). In this section, we summarize some of what has been learned about successful new services in terms of measures of success, key success drivers, and the importance of integrating new services.

Choose the Right Projects

Success with new services is going to be determined by two things: choosing the right projects and doing the projects right.[37] Researchers confirm that following the new service development process discussed earlier in the chapter and illustrated in Figure 9.1 will help with both these goals.[38] The experimental design approaches used in the SPARC lab in the Mayo Clinic (Exhibit 9.2) and tools such as participant observation and service blueprinting will help as well, primarily with the second goal.

Another concept, *portfolio management for new products,* is very useful in helping companies choose the right projects in the first place.[39] Using this approach, companies manage their product portfolio like they manage their financial portfolio. The approach helps companies prioritize projects; choose which ones to accelerate; and determine the best balance between risk versus return, maintenance versus growth, and short-term versus long-term projects. Methods for portfolio management include financial models, scoring models and checklists, mapping approaches, and behavioral approaches.[40]

Integrate New Services

Because of the nature of services—they are processes, typically delivered at least in part by people, consumed, and produced simultaneously—any new service introduction will affect the existing systems and services. Unlike when a manufacturer adds a new product to its production facility, new service introductions are frequently visible to customers and may even require their participation. Explicit recognition of these potential impacts, and planning for the integration of people, processes, and physical evidence, will facilitate success.[41] This recognition will help in both deciding which projects to pursue—sometimes the disruptive effect on existing systems is too great to warrant the investment—and knowing how to proceed with implementation—what elements of existing processes, people, and physical facilities will need to be adjusted, added, or changed.

Consider Multiple Measures of Success

In predicting the success of a new service, multiple performance measures may be considered.[42] First, and most commonly used, is near-term *financial performance,* including revenue growth, profitability, market share, and return on investment (ROI). In other cases, *relationship enhancement* may be a more appropriate measure of success. This measurement might include the new service's effect on customer loyalty, image enhancement, and the effect on the success of other products and services. Or success may be measured in terms of *market development*—the degree to which the new service opens up new markets or new customer segments. Successful projects will lead to increases in one, or perhaps more than one, of these measures.

Strategy Insight Strategic Growth through Services

Firms in many industries are discovering the value of strategically focusing on service innovations to provide value for their customers as well as profits and growth for the firm. Using this strategic approach, services are developed to enhance relationships with customers by providing them total packages of offerings, sometimes referred to as "solutions." By adding services to their traditional offerings, firms can differentiate themselves from their competitors and frequently earn higher profit margins on the new services compared with traditional manufactured or retail product offerings. IBM Global Services is perhaps the best known example of this type of solutions strategy (see opening vignette in Chapter 1). Like IBM, many companies are poised to "grow through services" in business-to-consumer as well as business-to-business markets. As they move in this direction, they quickly recognize the great opportunities as well as the complex challenges of introducing new services. Here we highlight three firms from very diverse industries and their growth-through-services strategies.

PETSMART

The pet products market is booming, and services are a big part of the growth for the leading U.S. pet retailer, PetSmart. With more than 900 pet stores in the United States and Canada, PetSmart's vision is to serve "pet parents" through "total lifetime care" of their pets. Although sales of pet food, toys, and pet accessories are part of this vision, total lifetime care means much more. The company also promotes comprehensive pet training, grooming, day care, and overnight care through its pet hotels. PetSmart PetsHotels not only ensure onsite pet safety and health 24 hours a day, but they also promote professional care and a total "pet experience" through daily "yappy hours" and a "bone booth," where pet parents can call in and speak to their pet. Pet

PetSmart's pet hotel concept

parents are offered a choice of accommodations for their pet, ranging from a glassed-in "atrium room" to a suite including a television tuned to animal channels. Other add-on services include personal training camps for dogs during their stay at the hotel, special snacks, and an exit bath. PetsHotels is a fast-growing and profitable part of the business along with "doggie day camp," grooming, and training services. The company's current success and its future growth projections can be directly traced to the expansion into services.

Maintain Some Flexibility

New service success depends on market-driven, customer-focused new product processes; emphasis on planning for and executing the launch; integration of services within existing processes (including staff training); and strong marketing communications, both external and internal. Yet, firms must be cautioned about being too rigid in their service innovation approach. Steps in the development process should be allowed some flexibility, and there will no doubt be overlapping

ERICSSON

Headquartered in Sweden, Ericsson is a leading global provider of telecommunications equipment and related services and solutions. Since the mid 1990s, it has pursued a growth strategy focused on customers, services, and solutions that enhance and add value to its sophisticated technology products. Among its services, the company lists an array of "solutions" for end users, business operations, and network infrastructure. For example since the 1980s, Ericsson has worked in a partnership with the New Zealand Police force to support its telecommunication needs through products and services. In 2007 Ericsson signed a 21-year exclusive agreement to supply and support a flexible and scalable point-to-point microwave radio network system. The goal for the system is to provide community safety through a customized and secure telecommunications network for the country. As Ericsson continues to move away from its traditional base in manufacturing, the company has reoriented its entire organization toward providing integrated solutions for customers such as the one being developed for the New Zealand Police force.

ROYAL PHILIPS ELECTRONICS

Companies such as Philips Electronics, the European electronics giant, are faced with the realities of price competition from cheaper products produced primarily in Asia. The results for many companies are declining sales and growing losses from their products. Part of the solution for these companies is a venture into services. For Philips this has meant branching out into health care by marrying its expertise in consumer marketing and the knowledge in its professional medical division with an unmet demand for personal health care monitoring. The result is Philips Lifeline service, a medical-alert system that allows elderly patients immediate connection to a call center, where Personal Response Associates, with access to their health profiles, can help them. The immediate access is gained by pushing a button on an electronic bracelet that the patient wears. Other services Philips has in the works include one that allows doctors to monitor patients' vital signs from their homes via the Internet, and an intelligent pill box that can detect when a person has not taken his or her medication. A box with excess pills would automatically alert the system and an operator would call the patient to remind them.

For each of these companies, the move to services represented a significant strategic choice that initially took them into uncharted waters. For PetSmart, a traditional retailer, it meant developing the systems to design, train, and hire employees who could interact effectively with pets and pet parents in intimate service settings. For Ericsson it meant moving away from a manufacturing and technology mind set to one that focuses on customers and solutions. For Philips the move was even more dramatic as it began to understand a whole new industry in health care delivery. Yet the potential rewards are great and customer demands for services and solutions are real. These rewards and demands are what compel more and more firms to pursue the strategic service path..

Sources: A. Davies, T. Brady, and M. Hobday, "Charting a Path toward Integrated Solutions," *Sloan Management Review,* 47 (Spring 2006), pp. 39–48; M. Sawhney, S. Balasubramanian, and V. V. Krishnan, "Creating Growth with Services," *Sloan Management Review* 45 (Winter 2004), pp. 34–43; www.petsmart.com, 2007; C. Dalton, "A Passion for Pets: An Interview with Philip L. Francis, Chairperson and CEO of PetSmart, Inc.," *Business Horizons* 48 (November–December 2005), pp. 469–475; D. Brady and C. Palmeri, "The Pet Economy," *BusinessWeek,* August 6, 2007, p. 44; www.ericsson.com, 2007; www.medical.philips.com/main, 2007; and L. Abboud, "Electronics Giant Seeks a Cure in Health Care," *The Wall Street Journal,* July 11, 2007, p. A1.

processes. Initial service development, for example, can be occurring simultaneously with additional gathering of customer information. Because services, particularly business-to-business services, are often very complex, some creativity and "out of order" decisions will be needed. There must be some elements of improvisation, anarchy, and internal competition in the development of new services. "Consequently, the innovation and adoption of new services must be both a planned process and a happening!"[43]

Summary

Service providers must effectively match customer expectations to new service innovations and actual service process designs. However, because of the very nature of services—specifically, their intangibility, variability, and cocreation elements—the design and development of service offerings are complex and challenging. Many services are only vaguely defined before their introduction to the marketplace. This chapter has outlined some of the challenges involved in innovating and designing services and some strategies for effectively overcoming the challenges.

Through adaptations of the new product development process that is commonplace in goods production and manufacturing companies, service providers can begin to not only make their offerings more explicit but also avoid failures. The new service development process presented in the chapter includes nine stages, beginning with the development of a business and new service strategy and ending with postintroduction evaluation of the new service. Between these initial and ending stages are a number of steps and checkpoints designed to maximize the likelihood of new service success. Carrying out the stages requires the inclusion of customers, contact employees, business partners, and anyone else who will affect or be affected by the new service. Because successful new service introduction is often highly dependent on service employees (often they *are* the service), integration of employees at each stage is critical.

Service blueprinting is a particularly useful technique in the new service development process that is described in detail in this chapter. A blueprint can make a complex service concrete through its visual depiction of all the steps, actors, processes, and physical evidence of the service. The key feature of service blueprints is the focus on the customer—the customer's experience is documented first and is kept fully in view as the other features of the blueprint are developed.

The final section of the chapter summarized some of the factors driving successful new service innovations, including the need for portfolio planning and integration of new services with existing processes and systems. The need to consider multiple measures of success was highlighted as well as the importance of maintaining flexibility in the new service development process.

Discussion Questions

1. Why is it challenging to innovate, design, and develop services?
2. Why is service innovation so critical for firms and countries?
3. What are the risks of attempting to describe services in words alone?
4. Compare and contrast the blueprints in Figures 9.5 and 9.6.
5. How might a service blueprint be used for marketing, human resource, and operations decisions? Focus on one of the blueprint examples shown in the text as a context for your answer.
6. Assume that you are a multiproduct service company that wants to grow through adding new services. Describe a logical process you might use to introduce a new service to the marketplace. What steps in the process might be most difficult and why? How might you incorporate service blueprinting into the process?
7. Discuss Figure 9.2 in terms of the four types of opportunities for growth represented there. Choose a company or service, and explain how it could grow by developing new services in each of the four cells (see the Taco Bell example in Exhibit 9.1).

Exercises

1. Think of a new service you would like to develop if you were an entrepreneur. How would you go about it? Describe what you would do and where you would get your information.

2. Find a new and interesting service in your local area or a service offered on your campus. Document the service process via a service blueprint. To do this exercise, you will probably need to interview one of the service employees. After you have documented the existing service, use blueprinting concepts to redesign the service or change it in some way.

3. Choose a service you are familiar with and document the customer action steps through a photographic blueprint. What is the "evidence of service" from your point of view as a customer?

4. Develop a service blueprint for a technology-delivered service (such as an Internet-based travel service). Compare and contrast this blueprint to one for the same service delivered via more traditional channels (such as a personal travel agent).

5. Compare two services on the Internet. Discuss the design of each in terms of whether it meets your expectations. How could the design or the service process be changed? Which one is most effective, and why?

Notes

1. Wells Fargo website, 2007, www.wellsfargo.com; G. Anders, "Power Partners," *Fast Company,* September 2000, pp. 146–148; "The World's Best Internet Banks 2007," *Global Finance,* July 2007; and B. Condon, "Banking on Brashness," *Forbes,* 174 (August 16, 2004), pp. 91–100.

2. D. H. Henard and D. M. Szymanski, "Why Some New Products Are More Successful than Others," *Journal of Marketing Research* 38 (August 2001), pp. 362–375.

3. R. G. Cooper, *Winning at New Products,* 3rd ed. (Cambridge, MA: Perseus Publishing, 2001); R. G. Cooper and S. J. Edgett, *Product Development for the Service Sector* (Cambridge, MA: Perseus Books, 1999); and C. M. Froehle, A. V. Roth, R. B. Chase, and C. A. Voss, "Antecedents of New Service Development Effectiveness," *Journal of Service Research,* 3 (August 2000), pp. 3–17.

4. M. J. Bitner and S. W. Brown, "The Service Imperative," *Business Horizons* 50th *Anniversary Issue,* 51 (January–February 2008), pp. 39–46.

5. G. L. Shostack, "Understanding Services through Blueprinting," in *Advances in Services Marketing and Management,* vol. 1, ed. T. A. Swartz, D. E. Bowen, and S. W. Brown (Greenwich, CT: JAI Press, 1992), pp. 75–90.

6. Ibid., p. 76.

7. For excellent reviews of research and issues in new services development see *Journal of Operations Management* 20 (2002), Special Issue on New Issues and Opportunities in Service Design Research; A. Johne and C. Story, "New Service Development: A Review of the Literature and Annotated Bibliography," *European Journal of Marketing* 32, no. 3–4 (1998), pp. 184–251; B. Edvardsson, A. Gustafsson, M. D. Johnson, and B. Sanden, *New Service Development and Innovation in the New Economy* (Lund, Sweden: Studentlitteratur AB, 2000); and B. Edvardsson, A. Gustafsson, P. Kristensson, P. Magnusson, and J. Matthing, *Involving Customers in New Service Development,* (London: Imperial College Press, 2006).

8. B. Schneider and D. E. Bowen, "New Services Design, Development and Implementation and the Employee," in *Developing New Services,* ed. W. R. George and C. Marshall (Chicago: America-Marketing Association, 1984), pp. 82–101.

9. S. Thomke, "R&D Comes to Services: Bank of America's Pathbreaking Experiments," *Harvard Business Review* 81 (April 2003), pp. 70–79.

10. L. L. Berry, V. Shankar, J. T. Parish, S. Cadwallader, and T. Dotzel, "Creating New Markets through Service Innovation," *Sloan Management Review* 47 (Winter 2006), pp. 56–63.

11. S. Michel, S. W. Brown and A. S. Gallan, "An Expanded and Strategic View of Discontinuous Innovations: Deploying a Service Dominant Logic," *Journal of the Academy of Marketing Science* 36 (Winter 2008), forthcoming.

12. For a discussion of these adaptations and related research issues, see I. Stuart, "Designing and Executing Memorable Service Experiences: Lights, Camera, Experiment, Integrate, Action!" *Business Horizons* 49 (2006), pp. 149–159; M. V. Tatikonda and V. A. Zeithaml, "Managing the New Service Development Process: Synthesis of Multidisciplinary Literature and Directions for Future Research," in *New Directions in Supply Chain Management: Technology, Strategy, and Implementation,* ed. T. Boone and R. Ganeshan (New York: AMACOM, 2002), pp. 200–236; and B. Edvardsson et al., *New Service Development and Innovation in the New Economy.*

13. See A. Griffin, "PDMA Research on New Product Development Practices: Updating Trends and Benchmarking Best Practices," *Journal of Product Innovation Management* 14 (1997), pp. 429–458; Thomke, "R&D Comes to Services"; Organization for Economic Cooperation and Development, "Promoting Innovation in Services," 2005.

14. R. G. Cooper, "Stage Gate Systems for New Product Success," *Marketing Management* 1, no. 4 (1992), pp. 20–29; J. Hawser, G. J. Tellis and A. Griffin, "Research on Innovations. A Review and Agenda for Marketing Science," *Marketing Science* 25 (63, 2006) pp. 687–717.

15. M. Iansiti and A. MacCormack, "Developing Products on Internet Time," *Harvard Business Review* 75 (September–October 1997), pp. 108–117.

16. A. Khurana and S. R. Rosenthal, "Integrating the Fuzzy Front End of New Product Development," *Sloan Management Review* 38 (Winter 1997), pp. 103–120.

17. Ibid; see also R. G. Cooper, S. J. Edgett, and E. J. Kleinschmidt, *Portfolio Management for New Products* (Cambridge, MA: Perseus Publishing, 2001).

18. D. Rigby and C. Zook, "Open-Market Innovation," *Harvard Business Review* 80 (October 2002), pp. 80–89.

19. D. Leonard and J. F. Rayport, "Spark Innovation through Empathic Design," *Harvard Business Review* 75 (November–December 1997), pp. 103–113.

20. R. Cross, A. Hargadon, S. Parise, and R. J. Thomas, "Together We Innovate," *The Wall Street Journal,* September 15–16, 2007, p. R6.

21. G. L. Shostack, "Service Design in the Operating Environment," in *Developing New Services,* ed. W. R. George and C. Marshall (Chicago: American Marketing Association, 1984), pp. 27–43.

22. E. E. Scheuing and E. M. Johnson, "A Proposed Model for New Service Development," *Journal of Services Marketing* 3, no. 2 (1989), pp. 25–34.

23. M. J. Bitner, A. L. Ostrom, and F. N. Morgan, "Service Blueprinting: A Practical Technique for Service Innovation," forthcoming, *California Management Review,* 2008.

24. L. Chamberlain, "Going Off the Beaten Path for New Design Ideas," *New York Times,* March 12, 2006, Sunday Business Section.

25. D. Maxey, "Testing, Testing, Testing," *The Wall Street Journal,* December 10, 2001, p. R8.

26. Shostack, "Service Design," p. 35; see also, I. Stuart, "Designing and Executing Memorable Service Experiences."

27. Maxey, "Testing, Testing, Testing."

28. The service blueprinting section of the chapter draws from the pioneering works in this area: G. L. Shostack, "Designing Services That Deliver," *Harvard Business Review* 62 (January–February 1984), pp. 133–139; G. L. Shostack, "Service Positioning through Structural Change," *Journal of Marketing* 51 (January 1987), pp. 34–43; and J. Kingman-Brundage, "The ABC's of Service System Blueprinting," in *Designing a Winning Service Strategy,* ed. M. J. Bitner and L. A. Crosby (Chicago: American Marketing Association, 1989), pp. 30–33.

29. Shostack, "Understanding Services through Blueprinting."

30. These key components are drawn from Kingman-Brundage, "The ABC's."

31. The text explaining Figures 9.5 and 9.6 relies on M. J. Bitner, "Managing the Evidence of Service," in *The Service Quality Handbook,* ed. E. E. Scheuing and W. F. Christopher (New York: American Management Association, 1993), pp. 358–370.

32. S. Fliess and M. Kleinaltenkamp, "Blueprinting the Service Company: Managing Service Processes Efficiently," *Journal of Business Research* 57 (2004), pp. 392–404.

33. For coverage of the practical benefits of blueprinting see: E. Gummesson and J. Kingman-Brundage, "Service Design and Quality: Applying Service Blueprinting and Service Mapping to Railroad Services," in *Quality Management in Services,* ed. P. Kunst and J. Lemmink (Assen/Maastricht, Netherlands: Van Gorcum, 1991); and Bitner et al., "Service Blueprinting."

34. Shostack, "Understanding Services through Blueprinting."

35. Bitner, et al., "Service Blueprinting."

36. A. R. Hubbert, A. Garcia Sehorn, and S. W. Brown, "Service Expectations: The Consumer vs. the Provider," *International Journal of Service Industry Management* 6, no. 1 (1995), pp. 6–21.

37. Cooper et al., *Portfolio Management for New Products;* M. Sawhney, S. Balasubramanian, V. V. Krishnan, "Creating Growth with Services;" and B. G. Auguste, E. P. Harmon, and V. Pandit, "The Right Service Strategies for Product Companies," *The McKinsey Quarterly* 1 (2006), pp. 41–51.

38. Froehle et al., "Antecedents of New Service Development Effectiveness"; Henard and Szymanski, "Why Some New Products Are More Successful than Others"; Edvardsson et al., *New Service Development and Innovation in the New Economy;* Hauser, Tellis, and Griffin, "Research on Innovation."

39. Cooper et al., *Portfolio Management for New Products.*

40. See Ibid. for an excellent discussion and coverage of multiple methods for managing product and service portfolios.

41. S. S. Tax and I. Stuart, "Designing and Implementing New Services: The Challenges of Integrating Service Systems," *Journal of Retailing* 73 (Spring 1997), pp. 105–134; and I. Stuart, "Designing and Executing Memorable Service Experiences."

42. R. G. Cooper, C. J. Easingwood, S. Edgett, E. J. Kleinschmidt, and C. Storey, "What Distinguishes the Top Performing New Products in Financial Services," *Journal of Product Innovation Management* 11 (1994), pp. 281–299.

43. Edvardsson, L. Haqlund and J. Mattson, "Analysis, Planning, Improvisation, and Control in the Development of New Services," *International Journal of Service Industry Management,* 6, no. 2, (1995), pp. 24–35.

Chapter Ten

Customer-Defined Service Standards

This chapter's objectives are to

1. Distinguish between company-defined and customer-defined service standards.
2. Differentiate among "hard" and "soft" customer-defined service standards and one-time fixes.
3. Explain the critical role of the service encounter sequence in developing customer-defined standards.
4. Illustrate how to translate customer expectations into behaviors and actions that are definable, repeatable, and actionable.
5. Explain the process of developing customer-defined service standards.
6. Emphasize the importance of service performance indexes in implementing strategy for service delivery.

FedEx Sets Standards through SQI

Marketing research data are not the only numbers that FedEx tracks to run its business. The company drives its operations with the aid of one of the most comprehensive, customer-defined indices of service standards and measures in the world. FedEx's service quality indicator (SQI) was designed as "unforgiving internal performance measurement" to ensure that the company delivered its goal of "100 percent customer satisfaction after every interaction and transaction and 100 percent service performance on every package handled."[1] The development and implementation of SQI led to a Malcolm Baldrige National Quality Award.

What makes this service index different from those of other companies is its foundation in customer feedback. Since the 1980s, FedEx has documented customer complaints and used the information to improve internal processes. The initial composite listing of the 12 most common customer complaints, originally called the "Hierarchy of Horrors," included wrong day deliveries, right day late deliveries, pickup not made, lost packages, customers misinformed by FedEx, billing and paperwork mistakes, employee performance failures, and damaged packages. Although this list was useful, it fell short of giving management the ability to anticipate and eliminate customer complaints before they occurred.

In 1988 the company developed a 12-item statistical SQI to be a more "comprehensive, pro-active, customer-oriented measure of customer satisfaction and service quality."[2] The list of items included in SQI has changed slightly over time, as have the weights assigned to each of the items. Recent versions of SQI consist of the following components and weighting (based on relative importance of each component to customers):[3]

Indicator	Weight
Lost packages	50
Damaged packages	30
Wrong day/late delivery	10
Complaints reopened	10
Invoice adjustments requested	3
Late pick-up stops	3
Traces not resolved	3
Right day/late delivery	1
Missing proofs of delivery	1

Another distinguishing feature of the SQI is its reporting in terms of *numbers* of errors rather than percentages. Management of the company strongly believes that percentages distance the company from the consumer: to report 1 percent of packages late diminishes the reality of 65,000 unhappy customers (1 percent of the approximately 6.5 million packages shipped a day). The SQI report is disseminated weekly to everyone in the company. On receipt of the report, root causes of service failures are investigated. With a senior officer assigned to each component, and with bonuses for everyone in the company tied to performance on the SQI, the company drives continuously closer to its goal of 100 percent satisfaction with every transaction.[4]

As we saw in Chapters 6, 7, and 8, understanding customer requirements is the first step in delivering high service quality. Once managers of service businesses accurately understand what customers expect, they face a second critical challenge: using this knowledge to set service quality standards and goals for the organization. Service companies often experience difficulty in setting standards to match or exceed customer expectations, partly because doing so requires that the marketing and operations departments within a company work together. In most service companies, integrating the work of the marketing function and the operations function (appropriately called *functional integration*) is not a typical approach; more frequently these two functions operate separately—setting and achieving their own internal goals—rather than pursuing a joint goal of developing the operations standards that best meet customer expectations.

Creating service standards that address customer expectations is not a common practice in U.S. firms. Doing so often requires altering the very process by which work is accomplished, which is ingrained in tradition in most companies. Often change requires new equipment or technology. Change also necessitates aligning executives from different parts of the firm to understand collectively the comprehensive view of service quality from the customer's perspective. And almost always, change requires a willingness to be open to different ways of structuring, calibrating, and monitoring the way service is provided.

FACTORS NECESSARY FOR APPROPRIATE SERVICE STANDARDS

Standardization of Service Behaviors and Actions

The translation of customer expectations into specific service quality standards depends on the degree to which tasks and behaviors to be performed can be standardized or routinized. *Standardization* usually implies a nonvarying sequential process—similar to the mass production of goods—in which each step is laid out in order and all outcomes are uniform, whereas *customization* usually refers to some level of adaptation or tailoring of the process to the individual customer.[5] The goal of standardization is for the service firm to produce a consistent service product from one transaction to the next. The goal of customization for the service firm is to develop services that meet each customer's individual needs. Some executives and managers believe that services cannot be standardized—that customization is essential for providing high-quality service. Managers also may feel that standardizing tasks is inconsistent with employee empowerment—that employees will feel controlled by the company if tasks are standardized. Further, they feel that services are too intangible to be measured. This view leads to vague and loose standard setting with little or no measurement or feedback.

The entire FedEx organization is driven by customer-defined service standards.

In reality, many service tasks are routine (such as those needed for opening checking accounts or spraying lawns for weeds), and for these, specific rules and standards can be fairly easily established and effectively executed. Employees may welcome knowing how to perform actions most efficiently: it frees them to use their ingenuity in the more personal and individual aspects of their jobs.

Standardization of service can take three forms: (1) substitution of technology for personal contact and human effort, (2) improvement in work methods, and (3) combinations of these two methods. Examples of technology substitution include automatic teller machines, automatic car washes, and airport X-ray machines. Improvements in work methods are illustrated by restaurant salad bars, home cleaning methods by maid services such as Molly Maid or The Maids, and routinized tax and accounting services developed by firms such as H&R Block.

Technology and work improvement methods facilitate the standardization of service necessary to provide consistent delivery to customers. By breaking tasks down and providing them efficiently, technology also allows the firm to calibrate service standards such as the length of time a transaction takes, the accuracy with which operations are performed, and the number of problems that occur. In developing work improvements, the firm comes to understand completely the process by which the service is delivered. With this understanding, the firm more easily establishes appropriate service standards.

Standardization, whether accomplished by technology or by improvements in work processes, reduces gap 2. Customer-defined standardization ensures that the most critical elements of a service are performed as expected by customers, not just that every action in a service is executed in a uniform manner. Using customer-defined standardization can, in fact, allow for and be compatible with employee empowerment. One example of this compatibility involves the time limits many companies establish for customer service calls. If their customers' highest priorities involve feeling good about the call or resolving problems, then setting a time limit for calls would be company defined and not in customers' best interests. Companies such as American Express and L.L.Bean, in using customer priorities rather than company priorities, have no set standard for the amount of time an employee spends on the telephone with a customer. Instead, they have standards that focus on making the customer satisfied and comfortable, allowing telephone representatives to use their own judgment about the time limits. Standardization of service is not appropriate in some situations. See the Strategy Insight for examples of these situations.

Formal Service Targets and Goals

Companies that have been successful in delivering consistently high service quality are noted for establishing formal standards to guide employees in providing service. These companies have an accurate sense of how well they are performing service that is critical to their customers—how long it takes to conduct transactions, how frequently service fails, how quickly they settle customer complaints—and strive to improve by defining goals that lead them to meet or exceed customer expectations.

One type of formal goal setting that is relevant in service businesses involves specific targets for individual behaviors or actions. As an example, consider the behavior "calls the customer back quickly," an action that signals responsiveness in contact employees. If the service goal for employee behavior is stated in such a general term as "call the customer back quickly," the standard provides little direction for service employees. Different employees will interpret this vague objective in their own ways, leading to inconsistent service: some may call the customer back in 10 minutes, whereas others may wait two to four days. And the firm itself will not be able to determine when or if individual employees meet the goal because its expression is not measurable—virtually any amount of time could be justified as "quickly." On the other hand, if the individual employee's service goal is to call each customer back within four hours, employees have a specific, unambiguous guideline about how quickly they should execute the action (four hours). Whether the goal is met is also unequivocal: if the call occurs within four hours, the company meets the goal; otherwise it does not.

Another type of formal goal setting involves the overall department or company target, most frequently expressed as a percentage, across all executions of the behavior or action. A department might set as its overall goal "to call the customer back within four hours 97 percent of the time" and collect data over a month's or year's time to evaluate the extent to which it meets the target. To illustrate, Puget Sound Energy—a utility company that serves customers in Washington state—has as part of its SQI a goal of answering 75 percent of customer calls within 30 seconds.[6]

Service firms that produce consistently excellent service—firms such as Walt Disney, FedEx, and Merrill Lynch—have very specific, quantified, measurable service goals. Disney calibrates employee performance on myriad behaviors and actions that contribute to guest perceptions of high service quality. Whether they are set and monitored using audits (such as timed actions) or customer perceptions (such as opinions about courtesy), service standards provide a means for formal goal setting.

Customer—Not *Company*—Defined Standards

Virtually all companies possess service standards and measures that are *company defined*—they are established to reach internal company goals for productivity, efficiency, cost, or technical quality. One company-defined standard that often does not meet customer expectations is the common practice of voice-activated

Strategy Insight When Is the Strategy of Customization Better than Standardization?

This chapter focuses on the benefits of customer-defined standards in the context of situations—hotels, retail stores, service outlets—in which it is important to provide the same service to all or most customers. In these situations, standards establish strong guidelines for technology and employees to ensure consistency and reliability. In other services, providing standardization is neither appropriate nor possible, and customization—providing unique types and levels of service to customers—is a deliberate strategy.

In most "expert" services—such as accounting, consulting, engineering, and dentistry, for example—professionals provide customized and individualized services; standardization of the tasks is often perceived as being impersonal, inadequate, and not in the customer's best interests. Because patient and client needs differ, these professionals offer very customized services that address individual requirements. They must adapt their offerings to the particular needs of each customer because each situation is different. Even within a given medical specialty, few patients have the same illness with precisely the same symptoms and the same medical history. Therefore, standardizing the amount of time a doctor spends with a patient is rarely possible—one of the reasons patients usually must wait before receiving medical services even though they have advance appointments. Because professionals such as accountants and lawyers cannot usually standardize what they provide, they often charge by the hour rather than by the job, which allows them to be compensated for the customized periods of time they spend with clients. It is important to recognize, however, that even in highly customized services,

some aspects of service provision can be routinized. Physicians and dentists, for example, can and do standardize recurring and nontechnical aspects such as checking patients in, weighing patients, taking routine measurements, billing patients, and collecting payment. In delegating these routine tasks to assistants, physicians and dentists can spend more of their time on using their expertise in diagnosis or patient care.

Another situation in which customization is the chosen strategy is in business-to-business contexts, particularly with key accounts. When accounts are large and critical to a provider, most aspects of service provision are customized. At a very basic level, this customization takes the form of service contracts—sometimes referred to as service-level agreements—in which the client and the provider agree on issues such as response time when clients have equipment failures or delivery time and fulfillment when retail clients depend on items being in stock in their stores. At a higher level, customization involves creative problem solving and innovative ideas (as in consulting services).

Finally, many consumer services are designed to be (or appear) very customized. These services include spa and upscale hotel visits, rafting trips, exotic vacations such as safaris, and even haircuts from expensive salons. In these situations, the steps taken to ensure the successful delivery of service are often standardized behind the scenes but appear to the customer to be very individualized. Even Disney theme parks use this approach, employing hundreds of standards to ensure the delivery of "magic" to customers in a seemingly unique way across the many service encounters.

telephone support systems that do not allow consumers to speak to humans. Because these systems save companies money (and actually provide faster service to some customers), many organizations have switched from the labor-intensive practice of having customer representatives to these "automated" systems. To close gap 2, standards set by companies must be based on customer requirements and expectations rather than just on internal company goals. In this chapter we make the case that company-defined standards are not typically successful in driving behaviors that close provider gap 2. Instead, a company must set *customer-defined standards*: operational standards based on pivotal customer requirements visible to and measured by customers. These standards are deliberately chosen to match customer expectations and to be calibrated the way the customer views and expresses them. Because these goals are essential to the provision of excellent service, the rest of this chapter focuses on customer-defined standards.

Knowing customer requirements, priorities, and expectation levels can be both effective and efficient. Anchoring service standards on customers can save money by identifying what the customer values, thus eliminating activities and features that the customer either does not notice or will not pay for. One of the key desires of customers visiting a Department of Motor Vehicles office is to not have to wait a long time. In California, Governor Schwarzenegger made it a top priority to improve service at the DMV and get wait-times down—and the results were impressive. Across the entire state, average wait-times in DMV offices were reduced from almost an hour to just under 30 minutes. Among the many changes were the addition of touch-screen kiosks to allow customers to enter information from their registration renewal notices; pay their fees using cash, checks, and credit cards; and within seconds complete their transactions. The government identified what was important to its customers and then implemented processes, hired additional staff, and trained employees to deliver service accordingly.[7]

On the other hand, many firms create standards and policies to suit their own needs that are so counter to the wishes of customers that the companies endanger their customer relationships. In the late 1990s, when the hotel industry was booming, many hotels initiated policies penalizing late arrivals and early departures as well as imposing minimum-stay requirements. The Hilton San Francisco and Towers Hotel began to charge guests $50 when they stayed fewer days than agreed to at check-in. The Peabody Orlando kept guests' one-night deposits unless they canceled at least three days prior to arrival. And a Chicago hotel required a business customer to buy four nights' lodging when all she needed was three, which cost the customer an extra $270.[8] Hotels defend these policies on the basis of self-protection, but they are clearly not customer oriented.

Although customer-defined standards need not conflict with productivity and efficiency, they are not developed for these reasons. Rather, they are anchored in and steered by customer perceptual measures of service quality or satisfaction. The service standards that evolve from a customer perspective are likely to be different from company-defined service standards.

TYPES OF CUSTOMER-DEFINED SERVICE STANDARDS

The types of standards that close provider gap 2 are *customer-defined standards*: operational goals and measures based on pivotal customer requirements visible to and measured by customers rather than on company concerns such as productivity or efficiency. Take a typical operations standard such as inventory control. Most firms control inventory from the company's point of view. However, the highly successful office supply retailer Office Depot captures every single service measurement related to inventory control *from the customer's point of view.* The company began with the question, "What does the customer see?" and answered, "The average number of stockouts per week." Office Depot then designed a customer-focused measurement system based on measures such as the number of complaints and compliments it received about inventory as well as a transaction-based survey with the customer about its performance in this area. These and other customer-defined standards allowed for the translation of customer requirements into goals and guidelines for employee performance. Two major types of customer-defined service standards can be distinguished: "hard" and "soft." These standards will be discussed in the following two sections.

Hard Customer-Defined Standards

All the FedEx standards that comprise its SQI (mentioned in the chapter opener) fall into the category of hard standards and measures: *things that can be counted, timed, or observed* through audits. Many of FedEx's standards relate to on-time delivery and not making mistakes, and for good reason. As we stressed in Chapter 4, customer expectations of reliability—fulfillment of service promises—are high. Recent studies across numerous industries have found that the most frequent customer complaints are associated with poor product performance (29 percent of all complaints) and service mistakes or problems (24 percent of all complaints).[9]

To address the need for reliability, companies can institute a "do it right the first time" and an "honor your promises" value system by establishing reliability standards. An example of a generic reliability standard that would be relevant to virtually any service company is "right first time," which means that the service performed is done correctly the first time according to the customer's assessment. If the service involves delivery of products, "right first time" to the customer might mean that the shipment is accurate—that it contains all that the customer ordered and nothing that the customer did not order. If the service involves installation of equipment, "right first time" would likely mean that the equipment was installed correctly and was able to be used immediately by the customer. Another example of a reliability standard is "right on time," which means that the service is performed at the scheduled time. The company representative arrives when promised, or the delivery is made at the time the customer expects it. In more complex services, such as disaster recovery or systems integration in computer service, "right on time" would likely mean that the service was completed by the promised date.

Reliability is often the single most important concern of service customers. In electronic retailing, on-time and accurate fulfillment of orders is one of the most important aspects of reliability. One of the best examples of customer-defined hard standards in the Internet context is the set of summary metrics that Dell Computer uses for fulfillment.[10] They include:

- *Ship to target (STT)*—the percentage of orders delivered on time with complete accuracy.
- *Initial field incident rate (IFIR)*—the frequency of customer problems.
- *On time first time fix (OTFTF)*—the percentage of problems fixed on the first visit by a service representative arriving at the time promised.

Dell tracks its performance to these standards and rewards employees on the basis of their "met promises" or reliability, which is often greater than 98 percent.

When it comes to providing service across cultures and continents, service providers need to recognize that customer-defined service standards often need to be adapted (see our Global Feature). When dining in the United States we expect wait people to bring the check promptly. In fact, if we do not receive it shortly after the last course, and without our asking for it, we evaluate the service as slow and non-responsive. In Spain, however, customers consider it rude for the wait staff to bring the check to the table without being asked to do so. They feel rushed, a state they dislike during meals. Although bringing the check to the table (whether sooner or later, requested or not) is an activity restaurants need to incorporate as a customer-defined service standard, the parameters of the standard must be adapted to the culture.

How do companies adjust for cultural or local differences in service standards if they recognize that these geographic differences are related to varying customer expectations? Companies with worldwide brands have much to lose if their service standards vary too much across countries, and therefore they must find ways to achieve universally high quality while still allowing for local differences.

SERVICE STANDARDS AT FOUR SEASONS: GLOBAL AND LOCAL NORMS

As one of the world's leading operators of luxury hotels and resorts, the Four Seasons Hotel manages 74 properties in 31 countries, and successfully accomplishes this goal by balancing universal services standards with standards that vary by country. The company, which has received more AAA Five Diamond awards than any other hotel company and is regularly named as the top choice for travelers in the United States in the "Hotels, Resorts, and Spas" category, owes much of its success to its seven "service culture standards" expected of *all* staff *all* over the world at *all* times. The seven standards, which form the acrostic SERVICE, are:

1. **Smile:** employees will actively greet guests, smile, and speak clearly in a friendly manner.
2. **Eye:** employees will make eye contact, even in passing, with an acknowledgment.
3. **Recognition:** all staff will create a sense of recognition by using the guest's name, when known, in a natural and discreet manner.
4. **Voice:** staff will speak to guests in an attentive, natural, and courteous manner, avoiding pretension and in a clear voice.
5. **Informed:** all guest contact staff will be well informed about their hotel, their product, will take ownership of simple requests, and will not refer guests elsewhere.
6. **Clean:** staff will always appear clean, crisp, well-groomed, and well-fitted.
7. **Everyone:** everyone, everywhere, all the time, show their care for our guests.

In addition to these culture standards that are expected of all staff all over the world, the hotel has 270 core standards that apply to different aspects of service provision (examples include "the staff will be aware of arriving vehicles and will move toward them, opening doors within 30 seconds" and "unanswered guest room phones will be picked up within 5 rings, or 20 seconds"). Exceptions to these 270 standards are allowed if they make local or cultural sense. For example, in the United States, coffee pots are left on tables at breakfast; in many parts of Europe, including France, customers perceive this practice as a lack of service and servers personally refill coffee cups as needed. Standards for uniforms and decor differ across cultures, but minimum expectations must be met everywhere.

SERVICE STANDARDS AT TOYOTA IN JAPAN

In 2005 Toyota began selling its luxury car, Lexus, in Japan. Although Lexus was already the best-selling luxury brand in the United States, in Japan it had very little name recognition. The company wanted a way to set Lexus apart from the Toyota brand and decided to focus on emphasizing customer service. Japan has a long history of unique customs and thought that perhaps they could bring that to the Lexus brand. So, Toyota approached an etiquette school—the Ogasawara Ryu Reihou Institute in Tokyo—that specializes in teaching the art of daily behavior, including the correct way to bow, hold chopsticks, and sit on a tatami mat floor, to help develop techniques that they could apply to selling cars.

Although typical clients of the school are well-bred families who want their children to learn good table manners and posture, the institute spent several months studying Lexus and its employees' interactions with customers. The result was the development of new service standards, several patterned after samurai behaviors. For example, salespersons are instructed to:

- Assume the samurai warrior's "waiting position" by leaning 5 to 10 degrees forward when a customer is looking at a car.
- When serving coffee or tea, kneel on the floor with both feet together and both knees on the ground.
- Bow more deeply to a customer who has purchased a car than to a casual window shopper.
- Display the "Lexus Face," a closed-mouth smile intended to put customers at ease.
- Stand with left hand over right, fingers together and thumbs interlocked, as the samurais did to show they were not about to draw their swords.
- Stand about two arms' lengths from customers when they are looking at a car and come in closer when closing a deal.
- Point with all five fingers to a car door's handle, right hand followed by left, then gracefully open the door with both hands.

Toyota understands that these standards would not work well in many of their markets, particularly the United States, but felt the standards were necessary in order for the Lexus brand to compete with the two luxury car market leaders—BMW and Mercedes Benz—in Japan.

SERVICE STANDARDS IN PAKISTAN

Research on service quality in Western countries generally finds reliability to be the most important dimension. Western customers expect firms to be dependable, accurate, and to do what they have promised. Research in Pakistan, however, suggests that customers have different standards of service quality. To illustrate:

- Reliability has been conceptualized as the ability to perform the promised service dependably and accurately. Although Pakistani consumers seem to concur with this conceptualization, they do not expect service delivery to be executed in absolute terms. "Promises are mostly kept" is how reliability would be described. They can apparently tolerate service failure with the content or timing of service as long as an acceptable substitute is provided within an appropriate time frame. It is generally important for them to maintain a long-term relationship with the service provider.
- Pakistani consumers seem to include accessibility as a part of their evaluation of a service provider's reliability. This is especially important in case of health care and other public services. Availability of a service at the time when it is needed is of extreme importance in Pakistan.
- Physical safety is also an important factor when Pakistani consumers evaluate service offerings. In a society that frequently has law-and-order problems, a customer's physical safety becomes important when doing business with a service provider.

Such findings suggest that service firms from Western cultures doing business in Pakistan can probably succeed with service standards that do not call for perfectly reliable service, emphasize service recovery, focus on delivering service when promised and across a wide range of times, or address issues of personal safety.

Sources: R. Hallowell, D. Bowen, and C. Knoop, "Four Seasons Goes to Paris," *Academy of Management Executive* 16, no. 4 (2002), pp. 7–24; A. Chozick, "The Samurai Sell: Lexus Dealers Bow to Move Swank Cars," *The Wall Street Journal,* July 9, 2007, p. A1; and N. Raajpoot, "Reconceptualizing Service Encounter Quality in a Non-Western Context," *Journal of Service Research* 7 (November 2004), pp. 181–201.

Hard service standards for responsiveness are set to ensure the speed or promptness with which companies deliver products (within two working days), handle complaints (by sundown each day), answer questions (within two hours), answer the telephone (see the Technology Spotlight), and arrive for repair calls (within 30 minutes of the estimated time). In addition to settings standards that specify levels of response, companies must have well-staffed customer service departments. Responsiveness perceptions diminish when customers wait to get through to the company by telephone, are put on hold, or are dumped into a telephone mail system.

Exhibit 10.1, on page 295, shows a sampling of the hard standards that have been established by service companies. This list is a small subset of all these standards because we include only those that are customer defined—based on customers' requirements and perspectives. Because FedEx has a relatively simple and standard set of services, it can translate most of its customers' requirements into hard standards and measures. Not all standards, however, are as easily quantifiable as those at FedEx.

Soft Customer-Defined Standards

Not all customer priorities can be counted, timed, or observed through audits. As Albert Einstein once said, "Not everything that counts can be counted, and not everything that can be counted, counts." For example, "understanding and knowing the customer" is a customer priority that cannot be adequately captured by a standard that counts, times, or observes employees. In contrast to hard measures, soft measures are those that must be documented using perceptual data. We call the second category of customer-defined standards *soft standards and measures* because they are opinion-based measures and cannot be directly observed. They must be collected by talking to customers, employees, or others. Soft standards provide direction, guidance, and feedback to employees in ways to achieve customer satisfaction and can be quantified by measuring customer perceptions and beliefs. Soft standards are especially important for person-to-person interactions such as the selling process and the delivery process for professional services. Exhibit 10.2 shows examples of soft customer-defined standards.

The differences between hard and soft standards are illustrated in Exhibit 10.3 using the customer care standards developed at Ford Motor Company. Puget Sound Energy also tracks both hard and soft standards each year to determine how well it is doing in meeting customer-defined service standards. Its customers have identified missed appointments, frequency and duration of power outages, and the amount of time it takes the company to respond to calls as among the most important issues. Figure 10.1 displays how PSE did in 11 key areas, including both hard and soft standards, in 2006.

One-Time Fixes

When customer research is undertaken to find out what aspects of service need to be changed, requirements can sometimes be met using one-time fixes. One-time fixes are *technology, policy, or procedure changes that, when instituted, address customer requirements*. We further define one-time fixes as those company standards that can be met by an outlet (e.g., a franchisee) making a one-time change that does not involve employees and therefore does not require motivation and monitoring to ensure compliance. We include one-time fixes in our discussion of standards because organizations with multiple outlets often must clearly define these standards to ensure consistency.

Technology Spotlight The Power of a Good Telephone Responsiveness Standard

In the 1990s, at the National Performance Review's recommendation, an executive order required all government agencies that dealt directly with the public to survey their customers and establish customer service standards. By 1998 this order resulted in more than 4,000 customer service standards from 570 agencies. One of the most successful came from the Social Security Administration (SSA) and illustrates a customer-defined hard standard relating to a technology issue that all customers face in dealing with public and private companies alike: telephone responsiveness.

The SSA knew that access—getting through to the agency on its 800 number—was the single biggest driver of customer satisfaction and public perception of the agency's competency. Unfortunately, customers more often than not repeatedly encountered busy signals on the 60 million calls they placed to the SSA's high-volume 800 number. The National Performance Review suggested to the agency that its service standard ought to be that everyone who called its 800 number would get through on the first try: 100 percent access! The SSA balked, recognizing that its telephone technology, limited employee resources, and wide fluctuations in demand would prevent the standard from being met.

The agency ultimately settled on a more reasonable standard: 95 percent of all callers would be served within five minutes. This standard became a very clear and focused goal that "everybody knew and everybody was shooting for," according to an SSA manager. Early measurements indicated less-than-stellar performance; in 1995 only 73.5 percent of callers got through in five minutes.

What followed was an impressive effort of technology, people, and measurement. According to an expert, "SSA endured tremendous expense, dislocation, pain—and even failure—to meet its standard." First, SSA officials developed a new phone system with AT&T that involved a sophisticated call-routing approach. Second, the organization trained virtually all technical people who held jobs other than in teleservices in those skills so that they could be shifted during peak hours to help with the volume. Third, the agency restricted leave for teleservice representatives at peak times, increased the use of overtime, and worked with employees to change processes and rules to improve performance.

The low point in performance to the standard was during the transition to the new system. In November 1995, only 57.2 percent of callers got through within five minutes. Even worse was that on the first day back to work in January 1996, the AT&T 800-number system crashed, leading to even more busy signals. By February, after AT&T fixed the system and the organization got used to its changes, performance improved significantly. The five-minute access rate was 92.1 percent in February, 95.9 percent in November, and above 95 percent ever since.

The SSA standard was successful because it was specific, measurable, and meaningful to customers. Because its results were documented and publicized both within and outside the agency, both employees and management were accountable for performance. Unlike many of the vague, meaningless standards that resulted from the National Performance Review's work with government agencies, this one was a winner.

Source: D. Osborne, "Higher Standards," *Government Executive,* July 2000, pp. 63–71.

FIGURE 10.1
Customer Service Report Card for Puget Sound Energy

Source: Puget Sound Energy.

2006 PERFORMANCE

Report Card

Key Measurement	Benchmark	2006 Performance	Achieved
1. Percent of customers satisfied with our performance	90 percent	84 percent	▪
2. Number of complaints to the WUTC per 1,000 customers	Less than 0.5	0.28	✓
3. Length of nonstorm power outages per year	Less than 2 hours, 16 minutes	3 hours, 34 minutes	▪
4. Frequency of nonstorm power outages, per year, per customer	Less than 1.30 outages	1.23 outages	✓
5. Percent of calls answered live within 30 seconds by our Customer Access Center	At least 75 percent	75 percent	✓
6. Percent of customers more than satisfied with our Customer Access Center, based on survey	90 percent	94 percent	✓
7. Time from customer call to arrival of field technicians in response to gas emergencies	No more than 55 minutes	36 minutes	✓
8. Percent of customers more than satisfied with field services, based on survey	At least 90 percent	91 percent	✓
9. Percent of customers disconnected for nonpayment	No more than 3.0 percent	2.4 percent	✓
10. Percent of in-home service appointments kept, as promised	At least 92 percent	98 percent	✓
11. Time from customer call to arrival of field technicians in response to power system emergencies	No more than 55 minutes	49 minutes	✓

As an example, Hampton Inns' "Make It Hampton" program required that all inns institute 60 new product and service standards, many of which were one-time fixes. The fixes implemented in the first phase of the program included providing lap desks in rooms, outdoor planter gardens to hide trash containers, red carpet welcome mats, and new lobby artwork and music.[11] The second phase of the program, labeled the "Cloud Nine Bed Experience," included raising its 150,000 hotel beds to a standard of 28 to 31 inches off the floor—in line with most home bedrooms today, upgrading pillows to jumbo size, and adding comforters, sheets with a greater thread count, and fitted bottom sheets. Performance standards do not typically need to be developed for such fixes because the one-time change in technology, equipment, policy, or procedures accomplishes the desired change.

Examples of successful one-time fixes include Hertz and other rental car companies' express check-in, GM Saturn's one-price policy for automobiles, and Granite Rock's 24-hour express service. In each of these examples, customers expressed a desire to be served in ways different from the past. Hertz's customers had clearly indicated their frustration at waiting in long lines. Saturn customers disliked haggling over car prices in dealer showrooms. And Granite Rock, a Malcolm Baldrige National Quality Award winner with a "commodity" product, had customers who desired 24-hour availability of ground rock from its quarry.

Exhibit 10.1 Examples of Hard Customer-Defined Standards

Company	Customer Priorities	Customer-Defined Standards
FedEx	On-time delivery	• Number of packages right day late • Number of packages wrong day late • Number of missed pickups
Dell Computer	On-time delivery Computer works properly Problems fixed right first time	• Ship to target • Initial field incident rate • Missing, wrong, and damaged rate • Service delivery on time first time fix
Social Security Administration	Telephone access	• 95 percent of calls served within five minutes
Southwest Airlines	Reliability Responsiveness to complaints	• On-time arrival • Two-week reply to letters
Lenscrafters	Quick turnaround on eyeglasses	• Glasses ready in one hour
Fotomat	Quick developing of photographs	• Photographs developed within one hour
Honeywell Home and Building Division	Fast delivery On-time delivery Order accuracy	• Orders entered same day received • Orders delivered when promised • Order 100 percent accurate
Puget Sound Energy	Reliability Responsiveness	• Length of nonstorm power outages per year • Frequency of nonstorm power outages, per year, per customer • Percent of in-home service appointments kept, as promised • Percent of calls answered live within 30 seconds by the Customer Access Center • Time from customer call to arrival of field technicians in response to power system emergencies
Texas Instruments Defense System	Compliance with commitments More personal contact	• On-time delivery • Product compliance to requirements • Increased number of personal visits

Whereas most companies in these industries decided for various reasons not to address these customer requirements, Hertz, Saturn, and Granite Rock each responded with one-time fixes that virtually revolutionized the service quality delivered by their companies. Hertz used technology to create Express Checkout, a one-time fix that also resulted in productivity improvements and cost reductions. The company also pioneered a similar one-time fix for hotel Express Check-In, again in response to customers' expressed desires. Saturn countered industry tradition and offered customers a one-price policy that eliminated the haggling characteristics of automobile dealerships. And Granite Rock created an ATM-like system for 24-hour customer access to rock ground to the 14 most popular consistencies. The company created its own Granite Xpress Card that allowed customers to enter, select, and receive their supplies at any time of the day or night.

Exhibit 10.2 Examples of Soft Customer-Defined Standards

Company	Customer Priorities	Customer-Defined Standards
General Electric	Interpersonal skills of operators: Tone of voice Problem solving Summarizing actions Closing	• Taking ownership of the call; following through with promises made; being courteous and knowledgeable; understanding the customer's question or request
Ritz-Carlton	Being treated with respect	• React quickly to solve any problems immediately • Use proper telephone etiquette • Do not screen calls • Eliminate call transfers when possible
Nationwide Insurance	Responsiveness	• Human voice on the line when customers report problems
L.L.Bean	Calming human voice; minimal customer anxiety	• Tone of voice; other tasks (e.g., arranging gift boxes) not done while on the telephone with customers
Peninsula Regional Medical Center	Respect	• Keep patient information confidential; never discuss patients and their care in public areas; listen to patients with empathy; be courteous and do not use jargon; keep noise to a minimum; never "talk over" a patient
American Express	Resolution of problems	• Resolve problem at first contact (no transfers, other calls, or multiple contacts); communicate and give adequate instructions; take all the time necessary
	Treatment	• Listen; do everything possible to help; be appropriately reassuring (open and honest)
	Courtesy of representative	• Put card member at ease; be patient in explaining billing process; display sincere interest in helping card member; listen attentively; address card member by name; thank card member at end of call

One-time fixes are often accomplished by technology. Technology can simplify and improve customer service, particularly when it frees company personnel by handling routine, repetitive tasks and transactions. Customer service employees can then spend more time on the personal and possibly more essential portions of the job. In recent years some hospital emergency rooms have added check-in kiosks so that patients who are not experiencing a true "emergency" can enter personal information, thus reducing time spent waiting in line to register and explain symptoms.[12] Some technology, in particular computer databases that contain information on individual needs and interests of customers, allows the company to standardize the essential elements of service delivery. These elements include information databases, automated transactions, and scheduling and delivery systems.

One-time fixes also deal with the aspects of service that go beyond human performance: rules and policies, operating hours, product quality, and price. An example of a one-time fix involving a policy change is that of allowing frontline employees to refund money to dissatisfied customers. An example of operating hour changes is scheduling a retail establishment to be open on Sundays.

Exhibit 10.3   Hard and Soft Standards at Ford Motor Company

In this chapter we discuss two types of customer-defined service standards. "Hard" standards and measures are operational measures that can be counted, timed, or observed through audits. The other category, "soft" standards, makes use of opinion-based measures that cannot be obtained by counting or timing but instead must be asked of the customer. Ford Motor Company provides a real example that illustrates the difference between hard and soft standards. Several years ago Ford was looking to develop Customer Care standards for service at their many dealerships. Marketing research involving 2,400 customers asked them about specific expectations for automobile sales and service; Ford used this input to help identify the level of service dealerships would need to provide to receive "Blue Oval Certified" status. The following seven specific service standards were established as most critical to customers in the service department of dealerships.

1. Appointment available within one day of customer's requested service day.
2. Write-up begins within four minutes or less of customer arrival.
3. Service needs are courteously identified, accurately recorded on repair order, and verified with customer.
4. Vehicle serviced right on the first visit.
5. Service status provided within one minute of inquiry.
6. Vehicle ready at agreed-upon time.
7. Thorough explanation given of work done, coverage, and charges.

HARD STANDARDS AND MEASURES

Several of the standards Ford identified fall into the category of hard standards—they can be counted, timed, or observed through audits. Standards 2 and 5, for example, could be timed by an employee in the service establishment. The hard measure could be either the frequency or percentage of times that the standard's time periods are met or the average times themselves (e.g., average time that write-ups begin). Other standards could be counted or audited, such as standards 1, 4, and 6. The service clerk who answers the telephone could record the number of times that appointments were available within one day of the customer's request. The number of repeat visits could be counted to measure standard 4, and the number of vehicles ready at the agreed-upon time could be tallied as customers come in to pick up their cars.

SOFT STANDARDS AND MEASURES

Consider standards 3 and 7 and note how they differ from the ones we have just discussed. These standards represent desired behaviors that are soft and therefore cannot be counted or timed. For example, the courteous behavior included in standard 3 cannot be counted. Likewise, standard 7 requires a different type of measure—the customer's perception or opinion about whether this behavior was performed appropriately. It is not that soft standards cannot be measured; instead, they must be measured in different ways.

Soft standards provide direction, guidance, and feedback to employees in ways to achieve customer satisfaction and can be quantified by measuring customer perceptions and beliefs. Soft standards are especially important for person-to-person interactions such as the selling process and the delivery process for professional services. To be effective, companies must provide feedback to employees about customer perceptions of their performance.

DEVELOPMENT OF CUSTOMER-DEFINED SERVICE STANDARDS

Basing Standards on the Service Encounter Sequence

A customer's overall service quality evaluation is the accumulation of evaluations of multiple service experiences. Service encounters are the component pieces needed to establish service standards in a company. In establishing standards firms are concerned with service encounter quality, because they want to understand for each service encounter the specific requirements and priorities of the customer. When these priorities are known, providers can focus on them as the aspects of service encounters for which standards should be established. Therefore, one of the first steps in establishing customer-defined standards is to delineate the *service encounter sequence*. Identifying the sequence can be done by listing the sequential steps and activities that the customer experiences in receiving the service. Alternatively, service blueprints (see Chapter 9) can be used to identify the sequence by noting all the customers' activities across the top of the blueprint. Vertical lines from customer activities into the lower levels of the blueprint signal the points at which service encounters take place. Standards that meet customer expectations can then be established.

Because many services have multiple encounters, companies and researchers have examined whether some encounters (e.g., the first or the last) are more important than others. The Marriott Corporation identified the encounters that occur in the first 10 minutes of a hotel stay as the most critical, leading the hospitality company to focus on hotel front-desk experiences (such as Express Check-In) when making improvements. Although service management literature has emphasized strong starts, some research indicates that a strong finish in the final event of the encounter has a greater impact on overall satisfaction. Further, the research shows that consistent performance throughout the encounter—widely believed to produce the most favorable evaluations—is not as effective as a pattern of improving performance that culminates in a strong finish.[13] An implication of this research for hotels is that managers should focus on the "back end" of the hotel experience—checkout, parking, bellperson services—to leave a strong final impression. The Ritz-Carlton assumes both the first and last encounter are important, and therefore includes as two of the three "Steps of Service" (part of its famous "Gold Standards") instructions for employees to provide guests with "a warm and sincere greeting" and "a fond farewell [with] a warm goodbye" while using the guests' names.[14]

Expressing Customer Requirements as Specific Behaviors and Actions

Setting a standard in broad conceptual terms, such as "improve skills in the company," is ineffective because the standard is difficult to interpret, measure, and achieve. When a company collects data, it often captures customer requirements in very abstract terms. In general, contact or field people often find such data are not diagnostic, but rather too broad and general. Research neither tells them specifically what is wrong and right in their customer relationships nor helps them understand what activities can be eliminated so that the most important actions can be accomplished. In most cases, field people need help translating the data into specific actions to deliver better customer service.

Effective service standards are defined in very specific ways that enable employees to understand what they are being asked to deliver. At best, these standards are set and measured in terms of specific responses of human behaviors and actions.

Figure 10.2 shows different levels of abstraction/concreteness for standards in a service firm, arrayed from top (most abstract) to bottom (most concrete and specific).

FIGURE 10.2   What Customers Expect: Getting to Actionable Steps

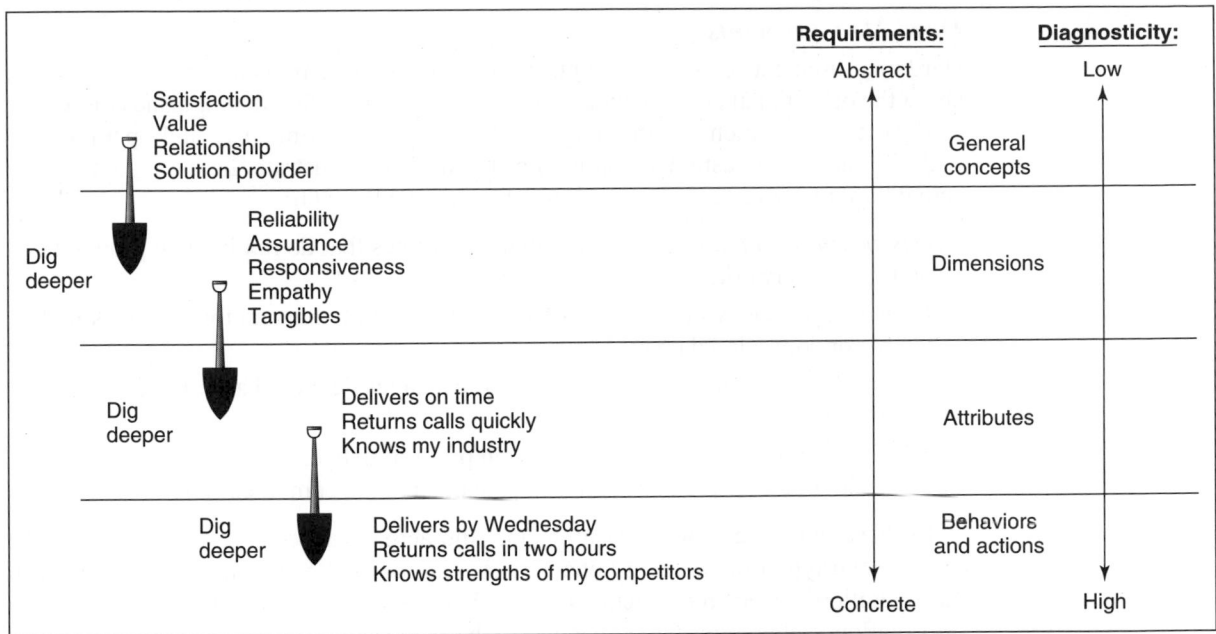

At the very abstract level are customer requirements too general to be useful to employees: customers want satisfaction, value, and relationships. The next level under these very general requirements includes abstract dimensions of service quality already discussed in this text: reliability, responsiveness, empathy, assurance, and tangibles. One level further are attributes more specific in describing requirements. If we dig still deeper beneath the attribute level, we get to specific behaviors and actions at the appropriate level of specificity for setting standards.

A real-world example of the difference in requirements across these levels will illustrate their practical significance. In a traditional measurement system for a major company's training division, only one aspect of the instructor was included in its class evaluation: ability of instructor. During qualitative research relating to the attributes that satisfy students, three somewhat more specific requirements were elicited: (1) instructor's style, (2) instructor's expertise, and (3) instructor's management of class. Although the articulation of the three attributes was more helpful to instructors than the broad "ability of instructor," management found that the attributes were still too broad to help instructors wanting to improve their course delivery. When the company invested in a customer-defined standards project, the resulting measurement system was far more useful in diagnosing student requirements because the research focused on *specific behaviors and actions* of instructors that met student requirements. Instead of a single broad requirement or three general attributes, the requirements of students were articulated in 14 specific behaviors and actions that related to the instructor and 11 specific behaviors and actions that related to the course content. These behaviors and actions were clearly more diagnostic for communicating what was good and bad in the courses. An additional benefit of this approach was that feedback on behaviors and actions was perceived as less personal than feedback on traits or personal characteristics. It was also easier for employees of the company to make changes that related to behaviors rather than to personality traits.

Measuring Behaviors and Actions

Hard Measurements

Hard measurements consist of counts or audits or timed actions that provide feedback about the operational performance of a service standard. What distinguishes these data from soft measurements is that they can be captured continuously and operationally without asking the customer's opinion of them. To demonstrate, here are some of the actual hard measurements for components of the FedEx SQI:

Missing proofs of delivery: the number of invoices that do not include proof-of-delivery paperwork.

Damaged packages: the number of claims for cost of contents for packages with visible or concealed damage.

Wrong day late deliveries: the number of packages delivered after the commitment date.

Traces: the number of package status and proof of delivery requests from customers that cannot be answered through data contained in the computer system.[15]

In these and other hard measurements, the actual gauge involves a count of the number and type of actions or behaviors that are correct or incorrect. Somewhere in the operation system these actions and behaviors are tabulated, frequently through information technology. Other gauges of hard measures include service guarantee lapses (the number of times a service guarantee is invoked because the service did not meet the promise), amounts of time (as in the number of hours or days to respond to a question or complaint or minutes waited in line), and frequencies associated with relevant standards (such as the number of visits made to customers or the number of abandoned telephone inquiries).

Computer information systems are often the basis for setting standards to improve customer service. L.L.Bean, the direct marketer, earned its reputation for outstanding customer service using a computer database that supplies moment-to-moment information about models, colors, and sizes of products in stock. With this system the company can set and achieve high standards of customer service. The database enables L.L.Bean to fill an incredible 99.42 percent of orders accurately.[16]

The appropriate hard measure to deliver to customer requirements is not always intuitive or obvious, and the potential for counting or tracking an irrelevant aspect of operations is high. For this reason, it is desirable to link the measure of operational performance with soft measures (surveys or trailer calls) to be sure that they are strongly correlated.

Soft Measurements

Two types of perceptual measurement that were described in Chapter 6 can document customers' opinions about whether performance met the standards established: trailer calls and relationship surveys. Relationship and SERVQUAL surveys cover all aspects of the customer's relationship with the company, are typically expressed in attributes, and are usually completed once per year. Trailer calls are associated with specific service encounters, are short (approximately six or seven questions), and are administered as close in time to a specific service encounter as possible. Trailer calls can be administered in various ways: company-initiated telephone calls following the interactions, postcards to be mailed, letters requesting feedback, customer-initiated calls to a toll-free number, or online electronic surveys. For requirements that are longer term and at a higher level of abstraction (such as at the attribute level), annual relationship surveys can document customer perceptions on a periodic basis. Trailer calls are administered continuously, whenever a customer experiences a service encounter of the type being considered, and they provide data on a continuous basis. The company must decide on a survey strategy combining relationship surveys and trailer calls to provide soft measurement feedback.

Flexibility in Setting Standards

Although it is common for firms to apply service standards uniformly across the entire organization, some service standards are left to management's discretion once a basic high level of service has been achieved. For example, many hotel brands in the United States have recently changed their standards for breakfast to reflect the dietary preference, speed of service, and varying expectations of consumers.[17] Hampton Inn and Suites revamped its breakfast in phase I of its "Make It Hampton" program, which included more than 60 new product and service standards. As a result, eight different hot menu items were added to its offerings that can be changed periodically; individual Hampton properties can choose menus based on regional preferences of their guests. These changes have proved to be extremely successful, and now 90 percent of Hampton's guests eat breakfast at the hotel. In its "Fit For You" program, Marriott International requires its hotels to include three menu items that fit into diets that are currently popular. Although the company has a standard requirement that all hotels offer three items, each hotel is encouraged to be creative in choosing the particular items and to include seasonal and local variations. One hotel in Wisconsin, for example, offers a Cheesehead Omelet using a Wisconsin cheese. As the vice president of lodging, food, and beverage stated, "We have given them guidelines, and we want the chefs to create something interesting."[18]

Developing Customer-Defined Standards

Figure 10.3 shows the general process for setting customer-defined service standards.

Step 1: Identify Existing or Desired Service Encounter Sequence

The first step involves delineating the service encounter sequence. Some companies will view this sequence like John Robert's Spa, a salon in northeast Ohio, did. They have identified seven typical service encounters that the average customer experiences when coming to the spa, including the initial phone call to schedule a visit, arrival at the spa, consultation with an employee prior to receiving any treatment, delivery of the spa service itself, wrap-up of the treatment, paying and exiting the spa, and postexperience contact. Exhibit 10.4 presents each of these service encounters and the behaviors expected of employees for each. As discussed in Chapter 9, a service blueprint may be used to identify the service encounter sequence. Ideally, the company would be open to discovering customers' desired service encounter sequences, exploring the ways customers want to do business with the firm.

Step 2: Translate Customer Expectations into Behaviors and Actions for Each Service Encounter

The input to step 2 is existing research on customer expectations. In this step, abstract customer requirements and expectations must be translated into concrete, specific behaviors and actions associated with each service encounter. Abstract requirements (like reliability) can call for a different behavior or action in each service encounter,

John Robert's Spa has developed a reputation for extraordinary service as a hair salon. Part of its success stems from its understanding and careful management of the sequence of service encounters customers are subjected to, which it labels the "Customer Experience Cycle." In identifying the various parts of the service process, John Robert's has specified precisely what every client should experience when receiving a haircut at John Robert's. The service standards expected of employees include:

Preexperience: provided by guest care personnel

- Answer the phone enthusiastically, saying, "Thank you for calling John Robert's Mayfield (salon location). This is Kelly. How can I help you?"
- Allow plenty of time to answer all of the client's questions concerning services, the designers' credentials, availability, and so on.
- Give each client an opportunity to book appointments for additional services.
- Use the client's name at least four times during the call.
- Offer directions to the salon.
- Confirm the service, operator, time, and date.
- As the last thing before hanging up, say, "Is there anything else I can do for you?"
- Make a confirmation call to the client 24 hours before the appointment.

Start of the experience: provided by hostess

- Greet the client enthusiastically within 8 to 10 seconds.
- Confirm the client's appointment.
- Ask the client to fill out the information card.
- Immediately notify the operator of the client's arrival.
- Offer to hang up the client's coat and to provide a refreshment.
- Inform the client of any delays.
- Offer a tour of the entire facility.

- Show the client where the changing rooms are.
- Monitor the client's wait, and notify the operator again if the client is not taken within 10 minutes of the scheduled appointment.
- Use the client's name at least four times during the check-in.

Preservice: provided by designer

- Provide consultation every time with every client.
- Show portfolio, analyze client's needs, and discuss client's expectations.
- Provide stress-relieving scalp massage.
- For men, provide a minifacial.
- Provide shampoo and conditioner.
- Use a white cape for new clients.

Service: provided by designer

- Give an excellent haircut.
- Massage hands and arms.
- Clean client's jewelry during massage.
- Keep the conversation on a professional level.
- Give lesson on blow-dry styling.
- Explain products used.

Postservice: provided by designer

- Touch-up makeup for all female clients.
- Make client aware of additional services that salon/spa offers.

  - Give complimentary bang trim.
  - Inform client of complimentary blow-dry lesson in the future, to help the client duplicate it on her own.
  - Offer men complimentary neck and sideburn trimmings between visits.
  - Offer referral incentives: $5 gift certificate for every referral and contest with prizes for the clients who refer the most new clients during the year.

and these differences must be probed. Eliciting these behaviors and actions is likely to require additional qualitative research because, in most service companies, marketing information has not been collected for this purpose.

Information on behaviors and actions must be gathered and interpreted by an objective source such as a research firm or an inside department with no stake in the ultimate decisions. If the information is filtered through company managers or

Conclusion of experience: provided by various staff

- Assistant, operator, and receptionist: give client a friendly and enthusiastic send-off.
- Designer and receptionist: give an opportunity to purchase products used.
- Main operator: give client a business card.
- Receptionist: give client opportunity to schedule next appointment.
- Receptionist: for new clients, give client a new-client package that includes a menu of services, newsletter, business card, magnet, and five-question form. Inform client of 10 percent off next visit if she returns the completed form within six weeks.
- Receptionist: during check-out use client's name at least four times.
- Operator: input personal information (such as name of spouse, children) in computer under client's name for use on future visits.

Postexperience: provided by support staff

- Client receives an enthusiastic phone call within 24 hours.
- Client receives a thank you postcard within 48 hours.
- Client receives a quarterly newsletter.
- Client receives a birthday card.
- If client has a challenge, handle it immediately on the spot. Make it right. Fill out customer challenge sheet and have management follow up.
- If client is not retained after 4 months: send out a reminder card that client is due for an appointment.
- If a client is not retained after 8 months: send out an incentive to return (such as 25 percent off for next visit).
- If a client is not retained after 12 months: survey with a letter or phone call to find out why.

Source: J. R. DiJulius, *Secret Service: Hidden Systems That Deliver Unforgettable Customer Value* (New York: American Management Association, 2001), pp. 8–11.

frontline people with an internal bias, the outcome would be company-defined rather than customer-defined standards.

Research techniques discussed in Chapter 6 that are relevant for eliciting behaviors and actions include in-depth interviewing of customers, focus group interviews, and other forms of research such as partnering. Using such research, John Robert's Spa identified specific employee behaviors for each of the seven service encounters mentioned

FIGURE 10.3 Process for Setting Customer-Defined Standards

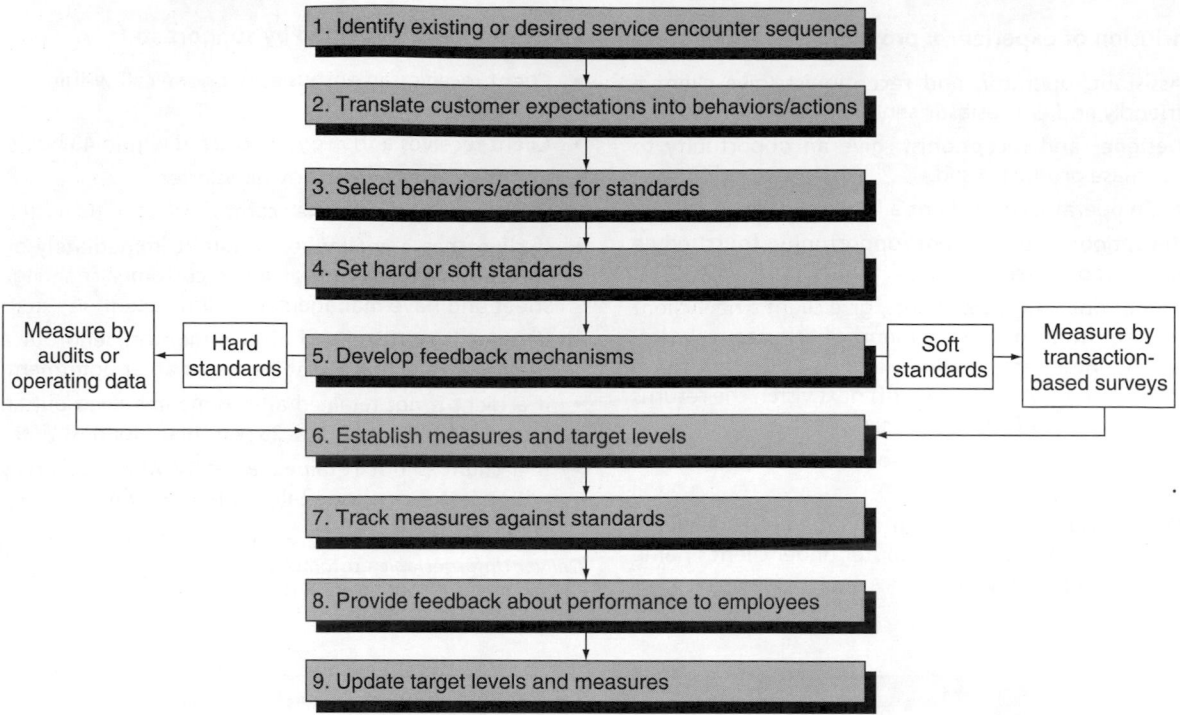

earlier (depicted in Exhibit 10.4). For example, when the client first enters the spa, the hostess is expected to greet the customer enthusiastically within 10 seconds, confirm the appointment, offer to hang up the customer's coat, offer a tour of the facility (if a new customer), and use the customer's name at least four times during the check-in.

Step 3: Select Behaviors and Actions for Standards

This stage involves prioritizing the behaviors and actions, of which there will be many, into those for which customer-defined standards will be established. The following are the most important criteria for creation of the standards.

1. *The standards are based on behaviors and actions that are very important to customers.* Customers have many requirements for the products and services that companies provide. Customer-defined standards need to focus on what is *very important* to customers. Unless very important behaviors/actions are chosen, a company could show improvement in delivering to standards with no impact on overall customer satisfaction or business goals.

2. *The standards cover performance that needs to be improved or maintained.* Customer-defined standards should be established for behaviors that customers feel are important and that need to be improved (or maintained). The company gets the highest leverage or biggest impact from focusing on behaviors and actions that need to be improved. Figure 10.4 shows an importance/performance matrix for a computer manufacturer. It combines the importance and performance criteria and indicates them by the shading in the cell in the matrix where behaviors and actions should be selected to meet those criteria.

3. *The standards cover behaviors and actions employees can improve.* Employees perform according to standards consistently only if they understand, accept, and have

control over the behaviors and actions specified in the standards. Holding customer-contact people to standards they cannot control (such as product quality or time lag in introduction of new products) does not result in improvement. For this reason, service standards should cover controllable aspects of employees' jobs.

4. *The standards are accepted by employees.* Employees will perform to standards consistently only if they understand and accept the standards. Imposing standards on unwilling employees often leads to resistance, resentment, absenteeism, and even turnover. Many companies establish standards for the amount of time it should take (rather than for the time it does take) for each service job and gradually cut back on the time to reduce labor costs. This practice inevitably leads to increasing tensions among employees. In these situations, managers, financial personnel, and union employees can work together to determine new standards for the tasks.

5. *The standards are predictive rather than reactive.* Customer-defined standards should not be established on the basis of complaints or other forms of reactive feedback. Reactive feedback deals with past concerns of customers rather than with current and future customer expectations. Rather than waiting for dissatisfied customers to complain, the company should actively seek both positive and negative perceptions of customers in advance of complaints.

6. *The standards are challenging but realistic.* A large number of studies on goal setting show that highest performance levels are obtained when standards are challenging but realistic. If standards are not challenging, employees get little reinforcement for mastering them. On the other hand, unrealistically high standards leave an employee feeling dissatisfied with performance and frustrated by not being able to attain the goal.

FIGURE 10.4
Selecting Behaviors for Standards Using an Importance/Performance Matrix

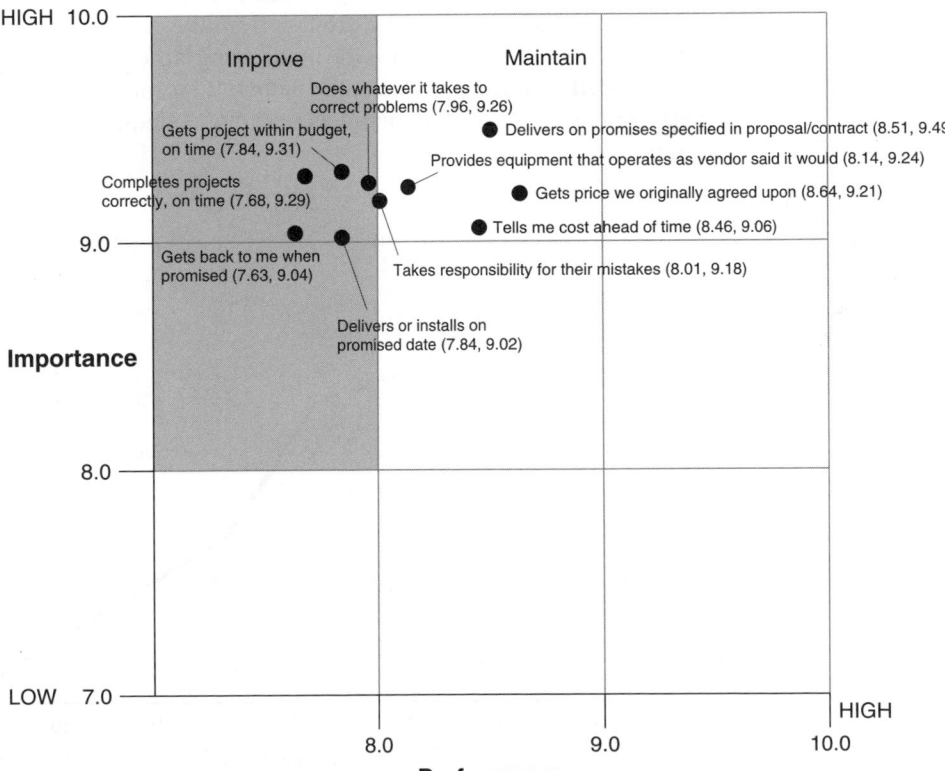

Step 4: Decide Whether Hard or Soft Standards Are Appropriate

The next step involves deciding whether hard or soft standards should be used to capture the behavior and action. One of the biggest mistakes companies make in this step is to choose a hard standard hastily. Companies are accustomed to operational measures and have a bias toward them. However, unless the hard standard adequately captures the expected behavior and action, it is not customer defined. The best way to decide whether a hard standard is appropriate is to first establish a soft standard by means of trailer calls and then determine over time which operational aspect most correlates to this soft measure. Figure 10.5 shows the linkage between speed of complaint handling (a hard measure) and satisfaction (a soft measure); the figure illustrates that satisfaction strongly depends on the number of hours it takes to resolve a complaint.

Step 5: Develop Feedback Mechanisms for Measurement to Standards

Once companies have determined whether hard or soft standards are appropriate and which specific standards best capture customer requirements, they must develop feedback mechanisms that adequately capture the standards. Hard standards typically involve mechanical counts or technology-enabled measurement of time or errors. Soft standards require perceptual measurements through the use of trailer surveys or employee monitoring. Employee monitoring is illustrated by the practice of supervisors listening in on employee telephone interactions with customers. You may have experienced this practice when you called customer service numbers for many organizations and noticed that the voice prompts tell you that calls may be monitored for quality purposes. The purpose of this monitoring is often to provide feedback on employee performance to the standards set by the organization to meet customer needs. One critical aspect of developing feedback mechanisms is ensuring that performance captures the process from the customer's view rather than the company's perspective. A supervisor monitoring an employee's handling of a customer service call, for example, should focus not so much on how quickly the employee gets the customer off the phone as with how adequately she handles the customer's request.

FIGURE 10.5
Linkage between Hard and Soft Measures for Speed of Complaint Handling

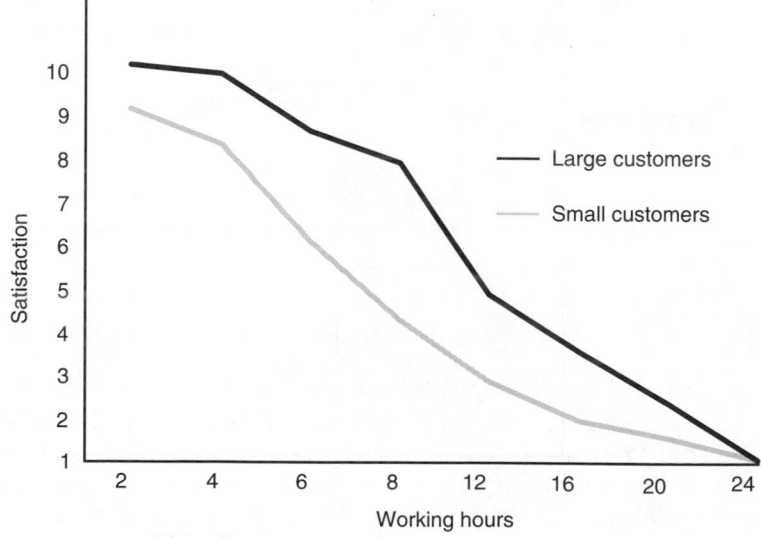

Step 6: Establish Measures and Target Levels

The next step requires that companies establish target levels for the standards. Without this step the company lacks a way to quantify whether the standards are being met. Figure 10.5 provides a good example of an approach that can be used to set standards for timeliness in responding to complaints in a service company. Each time a complaint is made to the company, and each time one is resolved, employees record the times. They can also ask each customer his or her satisfaction with the performance in resolving the complaint. The company can then plot the information from each complaint to determine how well the company is performing as well as where the company would like to be in the future. This technique is but one of several for determining the target level for service standards.

Another technique is a simple perception–action correlation study. When the service consists of repetitive processes, companies can relate levels of customer satisfaction with actual performance of a behavior or task. Consider, for example, a study to determine the standard for customers' wait-time in a line. The information needed includes customer perceptions of their wait in line (soft perceptual measure) and the amount of time they actually stand in line (hard operations measure). The joint collection of these data over many transactions provides evidence of the sensitivity of customers to different wait times.

An airline conducted precisely this study by having a flight attendant intercept customers as they approached the ticket counter. As each customer entered the line, the attendant stamped the entry time on a ticket (using a machine like those in parking lots) and handed the customer the stamped ticket. As the customer exited the line at the end of the transaction, the flight attendant restamped the ticket with the exit time and asked the customer three or four questions about perceptions of the wait in line and satisfaction with the transaction. Aggregating the individual customer data provided a graph that allowed the company to evaluate the impact on perceptions of various levels of line waits.

Step 7: Track Measures against Standards

Roger Milliken, former head of Milliken Industries, is reported to have said, "In God we trust, all others bring data." Successful service businesses, such as FedEx and Disney, have careful and comprehensive fact-based systems about their operations. One company that lives and thrives through management by fact is Granite Rock in Watsonville, California, a family-run business that provides concrete, asphalt, and crushed stone products. Granite Rock, which won a Baldrige Award in the small business category, has systems in place to gather, analyze, and act on information. Statistical process control and other types of charts are everywhere, tracking characteristics of its concrete and crushed stone and processes such as the time it takes customers to fill their trucks. Customer complaints are also tracked through what the company calls "product-service discrepancy reports" and root-cause analysis, and updates are distributed to all plants. The reports show how long it takes to resolve complaints and provide detailed quarterly analyses of trends. Plants can track their trends for four years running. When it comes to product quality and customer service, Granite Rock leaves nothing to chance.

Step 8: Provide Feedback about Performance to Employees

FedEx communicates the performance on its service quality indicator daily so that everyone in the company knows how the company is performing. When problems occur, they can be identified and corrected. The SQI measurement gives everyone in the company immediate feedback on activity that is strongly related to customer perceptions. In a general sense, data and facts need to be analyzed and distributed to support evaluation and decision making at multiple levels within the company. The data also must be deployed quickly enough that the people who need it to make decisions about service or processes can do so. Responsibility for meeting service requirements must also be communicated throughout the organization. All parts of the organization must be measuring their services to internal customers and, ultimately, measuring how that performance relates to external customer requirements.

Step 9: Periodically Update Target Levels and Measures

The final step involves revising the target levels, measures, and even customer requirements regularly enough to keep up with customer expectations. When FedEx originally developed its SQI, it assigned lost packages a weight of 10; over time, FedEx has found that a lost package is much more important to customers than many of the other issues included in the index and now assigns a weight of 50 to such an event.

Developing Service Performance Indexes

One outcome from following the process for developing customer-defined standards is a service performance index. *Service performance indexes* are comprehensive composites of the most critical performance standards. Development of an index begins by identifying the set of customer-defined standards that the company will use to drive behavior. Not all service performance indexes contain customer-defined standards, but the best ones, like FedEx's SQI, are based on them. Most companies build these indexes by understanding the most important requirements of the customer, linking these requirements to tangible and measurable aspects of service provision, and using the feedback from these indexes to identify and improve service problems. The most progressive companies also use the feedback for reward and recognition systems within the company.

Summary

This chapter discussed the discrepancy between company perceptions of customer expectations and the standards they set to deliver to these expectations. Among the major causes for provider gap 2 are inadequate standardization of service behaviors and actions, absence of formal processes for setting service quality goals, and lack of customer-defined standards. These problems were discussed and detailed, along with strategies to close the gap. To close the service design and standards gap, we suggested that standards set by companies must be based on customer requirements and expectations rather than just on internal company goals. That is, we argued that company-defined standards are typically not successful in driving behaviors that close provider gap 2 and that a company must set *customer*-defined standards based on key customer requirements visible to and measured by customers.

In this chapter we describe two types of service standards: hard standards—those that can be counted, timed, or observed through audits, and soft standards—customer perceptions that cannot be directly observed. Customer-defined standards are at the heart of service delivery that customers expect: they are the link between customers' expressed expectations and company actions to deliver to those expectations. Creating these service standards is not a common practice in U.S. firms. Doing so requires that companies' marketing and operations departments work together by using the marketing research as input for operations. Unless the operations standards are defined by customer priorities, they are not likely to have an impact on customer perceptions of service.

Discussion Questions

1. How does the service measurement that we describe in this chapter differ from the service measurement in Chapter 6? Which of the two types do you think is most important? Why?

2. In what types of service industries are standards most difficult to develop? Why? Recommend three standards that might be developed in one of the firms from the industries you specify. How would employees react to these standards? How could you gain buy-in for them?

3. Given the need for customer-defined service standards, do firms need company-defined standards at all? Could all standards in a company be customer defined? Why or why not? What functional departments in a firm would object to having all standards be customer defined?

4. What is the difference between hard and soft standards? Which do you think would be more readily accepted by employees? By management? Why?

5. Consider the university or school you currently attend. What are examples of hard standards, soft standards, and one-time fixes that would address student requirements? Does the school currently use these standards for delivery of service to students? Why or why not? Do you think your reasons would apply to private-sector companies as well? To public or nonprofit companies?

6. Think about a service that you currently use, then map out the service encounter sequence for that service. What is your most important requirement in each interaction? Document these requirements, and make certain that they are expressed at the concrete level of behaviors and actions.

7. Which of the service performance indexes described at the end of this chapter do you think is the most effective? Why? What distinguishes the one you selected from the others? How would you improve each of the others?

Exercises

1. Select a local service firm. Visit the firm and ascertain the service measurements that the company tracks. What hard measures does it monitor? Soft measures? On the basis of what you find, develop a service performance index.

2. Choose one of the peripheral services (such as computer, library, placement) provided by your school. What hard standards would be useful to track to meet student expectations? What soft standards? What one-time fixes would improve service?

3. Think about a service company you have worked for or know about. Using Figure 10.3, write in customer requirements at each of the levels. How far down in the chart can you describe requirements? Is that far enough?

4. Look at three websites from which you can order products (such as amazon.com or llbean.com). What are the companies' delivery promises? What types of standards might they set for these promises? Are these customer- or company-defined standards?

Notes

1. "Taking the Measure of Quality," *Service Savvy,* March 1992, p. 3.
2. Ibid.
3. H.-S. J. Tsao and A. Rizwan, "The Role of Intelligent Transportation Systems (ITS) in Intermodal Air Cargo Operations," Institute of Transportation Studies (2001), University of California at Berkeley.
4. Speech by FedEx Manager in Baltimore, Maryland, June 1993.
5. G. L. Shostack, "Breaking Free from Product Marketing," *Journal of Marketing* 41 (April 1977), pp. 73–80.

6. Puget Sound Energy, "2006 Performance Report," http://www.pse.com/InsidePSE/pdfs/brochure2774dated0307.pdf, accessed September 20, 2007.

7. California Department of Motor Vehicles website, http://www.dmv.ca.gov/pubs/newsrel/archive/2004-12.htm, accessed September 12, 2007.

8. D. Reed, "Hotels Penalize Late Arrivals, Early Departures," *The Wall Street Journal,* August 18, 1998, p. B1.

9. 2005 and 2004 National Customer Rage Studies conducted by Customer Care Alliance in collaboration with the Center for Services Leadership at Arizona State University's W. P. Carey School of Business.

10. F. Reichhold, "e-loyalty," *Harvard Business Review* 78 (July–August 2000), pp. 105–113.

11. J. Weinstein, "Redesigning the Box," *Hotels* 38, no. 3 (2004), p. 7.

12. J. Stengle, "ER Kiosks Let Patients Avoid Long Lines," *Associated Press,* September 13, 2007.

13. D. E. Hansen and P. J. Danaher, "Inconsistent Performance during the Service Encounter: What's a Good Start Worth?" *Journal of Service Research* 1 (February 1999), pp. 227–235.

14. These are two of the "three Steps of Service" included in Ritz-Carlton's Gold Standards, which can be found on the company website at http://corporate.ritzcarlton.com/en/About/GoldStandards.htm, accessed September 20, 2007.

15. Tsao and Rizwan, "The Role of Intelligent Transportation Systems (ITS) in Intermodal Air Cargo Operations."

16. Statistic is provided by Innovative Systems, Inc., on http://www.innovativesystems.com/success/ll_bean.php, accessed September 20, 2007.

17. R. Oliva, "Out with the Old Breakfast," *Hotels* no. 4 (April 2004), p. 46.

18. Ibid., p. 45.

Chapter **Eleven**

Physical Evidence and the Servicescape

This chapter's objectives are to

1. Explain the profound impact of physical evidence, particularly the servicescape, on customer perceptions and experiences.
2. Illustrate differences in types of servicescapes, the roles played by the servicescape, and the implications for strategy.
3. Explain *why* the servicescape affects customer and employee behavior, using a framework based in marketing, organizational behavior, and environmental psychology.
4. Present elements of an effective physical evidence strategy.

Building a Service Brand Using Physical Evidence[1]

Marriott International Inc., the world's largest hotel company, has a brand for every price point, every occasion, and every type of customer. The company is ranked as the most admired company in the lodging industry and one of the best places to work by *Fortune* magazine. Operating in the United States and 68 other countries and territories, Marriott employs more than 150,000 people. From its high-end Ritz-Carlton Hotels to its more budget-oriented Fairfield Inns, the company has been successful at clearly positioning its many brands, distinguishing them from each other, and attracting well-defined market segments for each. According to Michael Jannini, Executive Vice President of Brand Strategy and Innovation for Marriott, building these distinctive hotel brands involves a complex strategy that meshes hotel design, employee training and selection, careful customer segmentation, and specific operational brand standards.

From the customer's perspective, the most visible aspect of Marriott's distinctive brand strategies is the "servicescape" or the physical environment where the service is delivered—the hotel design itself. The luxury design of the Ritz-Carlton brand fits well with its position as the hotel where "ladies and gentlemen serve ladies and gentlemen." On the other hand, the physical presence of a Marriott Courtyard, while still expressing personal comfort and style, is much more efficient and businesslike in its design.

In 2007 Marriott announced two new brand concepts. In both cases the physical, tangible elements of the new brands will be used to distinguish them and position the

Marriott Courtyard, El Segundo, California The lobby has been transformed into a public space where guests can socialize and work.

new concepts apart from existing Marriott brands. The first is a partnership with Nickelodeon to create a group of hotels focused on families, fun, and adventure. Learning from Nickelodeon's experience with one hotel they have operated in Orlando, the partnership between the two companies focuses on developing large hotels—at least 500 rooms—with water slides, live shows, and other family-oriented activities. There will also be places for parents to escape and relax including spas, fitness centers, and adult-oriented "real" food restaurants. Characters tied to Nickeldeon—such as SpongeBob—will reinforce the brand position. The first of these new Nickelodeon hotels is slated to open in San Diego in 2010.

The second new concept is a boutique hotel that will marry unique, destination-inspired hotel design with sophisticated service. For this concept, a partnership with Ian Schrager, a well-known pioneer in the modern boutique-hotel industry, will provide the foundation for Marriott to enter an entirely new market for the company. These types of hotels are generally smaller, upscale properties that emphasize exclusive and unique style for each location. Starwood's W Hotels epitomize this segment of the market. The specific design elements of this new boutique hotel to called "Edition" will be critical to the positioning of the new concept for Marriott.

According to Jannini, as Marriott looks into its future, branding, along with consistent quality service, will remain an important strategic focus across all of its hotels. The company's vision is "to go from being a logical choice to a brand that's loved," according to Jannini. To do that, they aim to connect emotionally with customers across all brands by engaging all of their senses and creating memorable, highly differentiated experiences that are up-to-date and innovative. For example, Marriott has been working with the design firm IDEO and teams of sociologists and anthropologists to identify trends and new innovations for travelers. One series of changes is the introduction of high-tech conveniences for laptops, iPods, and other plug-ins and the latest in TV technology. By introducing the latest technology innovations into the rooms, guests are allowed to experience things they may not even have at home. Another change is the transformation of Courtyard lobbies into "great rooms" for those who prefer social, public places for work rather than their rooms (see photo).

In this chapter we explore the importance of physical evidence for communicating service quality attributes, setting customer expectations, and creating the service experience. In Chapter 1, when we introduced the expanded marketing mix for services, we defined physical evidence as *the environment in which the service is delivered and in which the firm and the customer interact, and any tangible commodities that facilitate performance or communication of the service.* The first part of this definition encompasses the actual physical facility in which the service is performed, delivered, and consumed; throughout this chapter the physical facility is referred to as the *servicescape.*[2] Physical evidence is particularly important for communicating about credence services (such as auto repair and health care), and it is also important for services such as hotels, hospitals, and theme parks that are dominated by experience attributes as described in our opening vignette on Marriott International.

PHYSICAL EVIDENCE

What Is Physical Evidence?

Customers often rely on tangible cues, or physical evidence, to evaluate the service before its purchase and to assess their satisfaction with the service during and after consumption. Effective design of physical, tangible evidence is important for closing provider gap 2. General elements of physical evidence are shown in Table 11.1. They include all aspects of the organization's physical facility (the servicescape) as well as other forms of tangible communication. Elements of the servicescape that affect customers include both exterior attributes (such as signage, parking, and the landscape) and interior attributes (such as design, layout, equipment, and decor). Note that web

TABLE 11.1
Elements of Physical Evidence

Servicescape	Other Tangibles
Facility exterior	Business cards
Exterior design	Stationery
Signage	Billing statements
Parking	Reports
Landscape	Employee dress
Surrounding environment	Uniforms
Facility interior	Brochures
Interior design	Web pages
Equipment	Virtual servicescape
Signage	
Layout	
Air quality/temperature	
Sound/music/scent/lighting	

Technology Spotlight Virtual Servicescapes: Experiencing Services through the Internet

Web pages and virtual service tours allow customers to preview service experiences through the Internet and see tangible evidence of the service without actually being there. This medium offers firms tremendous potential to communicate experiential aspects of their services in ways that were previously very difficult, if not impossible. Here we present several examples, across different industries.

TRAVEL

Travelers can now preview destinations, view hotels and their rooms, tour natural environments, and "experience" entertainment venues before booking their trips or even deciding where to travel. Before booking a trip to Great Britain, travelers can preview websites that show hotels, bed and breakfast inns, and other lodging all over the country. The exterior of the facilities as well as actual rooms can be examined in selecting accommodations. In planning a trip to visit the national parks of the United States, travelers can view full-length videos of the parks and various tours within the parks. For example, at the Yellowstone site (www.yellowstone.net/onlinetours/) video tours are available of driving loops within the park, complete with the sounds of the park's famous geysers. Detailed maps are also included, allowing a traveler to plan a route and choose among the many possible sights prior to even arriving at the park.

SPORTS AND LEISURE

Through sports and leisure websites, fans can now view much of the action and preview upcoming experiences online. For example, fans of the 2008 37th Ryder Cup Golf Match (www.rydercup.com) can view the actual course and other related information online at the Ryder Cup website. The event, a biannual contest between the top U.S. and European golfers, takes place in 2008 at the Valhalla Golf Club in Kentucky. On the website, fans are able to view all 18 holes of the magnificent course by choosing to examine an illustration showing the topography of the hole or a color photo of the hole, or by zooming in on an aerial video that follows the green from the tee to the hole. A graphic of the entire course is also shown on the website. In addition, the site includes video clips of event highlights, details on the players, and a complete history of previous matches. Over a year in advance of the event, the website allowed fans to anticipate and prepare for it while also reviewing video clips of past Ryder Cup highlights. Spending time on the website during the event allows distant fans to more fully enjoy it—almost as if they were there!

UNIQUE RETAIL EXPERIENCES

Many of today's unique retail experiences can be conveyed effectively via the Internet to give customers a preview of what they can expect. A great example is Build-A-Bear Workshop®, where children "from 3 to 103" can create their own teddy bears and other furry friends during their visit to the store. Build-A-Bear Workshop operates more than 370 stores worldwide, including company-owned stores in the U.S., Puerto Rico, Canada, the United Kingdom, Ireland, and France, and franchise stores in Europe, Asia, Australia, and Africa. The interactive retail entertainment experience itself is memorable and fun, and

pages and virtual servicescapes conveyed over the Internet are more recent forms of physical evidence that companies can use to communicate about the service experience, making services more tangible for customers both before and after purchase (see the Technology Spotlight).

Physical evidence examples from different service contexts are given in Table 11.2. It is apparent that some services (such as hospitals, resorts, and child care) rely heavily on physical evidence to communicate and create customer experiences. Others (insurance, express mail) provide limited physical evidence for customers. All the elements of evidence listed for each service communicate something about the service to consumers, facilitate performance of the service, and/or add to the customer's total experience.

the highly visual teddy-bear-themed environment throughout the stores is a big part of the fantasy of this special place. For a preview of how it works and what the stores look like, the website of Build-A-Bear Workshop (www.buildabear.com) includes a step-by-step "virtual visit" that shows the various stations in the store and what happens at each one. In creating a furry friend, consumers go through the following steps: Choose Me; Hear Me; Stuff Me; Stitch Me; Fluff Me; Name Me; Take Me Home®. The virtual visit on the website shows each stage sequentially, detailing the activities at each step and providing a colorful photo that gives a real sense of the store environment and the emotions of its patrons.

HIGHER EDUCATION

One of the most significant decisions that young people and their families make is the decision of what university to attend. For students fortunate enough to have the means and abilities, the choices can be endless. The physical environment of the university—the campus itself as well as specific facilities—can play a major role in students' choices as well as their actual experiences. Some universities now offer virtual tours of their campuses online that allow students to preview the physical environment in advance. The University of Idaho in the United States has a particularly effective tour on their site that allows students to view almost everything on campus, including its recreation centers, student union, library, classroom buildings, administration buildings, and common areas (www.webs.uidaho.edu/vtour/). Selecting one of these options opens a window with a photo, a brief written description, and a panoramic video tour of the chosen place.

Internet technology clearly provides tremendous opportunities for firms to communicate about their services. Images on the Web create expectations for customers that set standards for service delivery, and it is critical that the actual services live up to these expectations. Images and virtual service tours presented on the Internet also need to support the positioning of the service brand and be consistent with other marketing messages.

Although we focus in this chapter primarily on the servicescape and its effects, keep in mind that what is said applies to the other forms of evidence as well.

How Does Physical Evidence Affect the Customer Experience?

Physical evidence, particularly the servicescape, can have a profound effect on the customer experience. This is true whether the experience is mundane (e.g., a bus or subway ride), personally meaningful (e.g., a church wedding experience, or a birthing room at a hospital), or spectacular (e.g., a week-long travel adventure). In all cases, the physical evidence of the service will influence the flow of the experience, the meaning customers attach to it, their satisfaction, and their emotional connections with the company delivering the experience.

TABLE 11.2
Examples of Physical Evidence from the Customer's Point of View

	Physical Evidence	
Service	**Servicescape**	**Other Tangibles**
Insurance	Not applicable	Policy itself
		Billing statements
		Periodic updates
		Company brochure
		Letters/cards
		Claims forms
		Website
Hospital	Building exterior	Uniforms
	Parking	Reports/stationery
	Signs	Billing statements
	Waiting areas	Website
	Admissions office	
	Patient care room	
	Medical equipment	
	Recovery room	
Airline	Airline gate area	Tickets
	Airplane exterior	Food
	Airplane interior (decor, seats, air quality)	Uniforms
	Check-in kiosks	Website
	Security screening area	
Express mail	Free-standing stores	Packaging
	Package drop boxes	Trucks
		Uniforms
		Handheld devices
		Website
Sporting event	Parking	Tickets
	Stadium exterior	Employee uniforms
	Ticketing area	Programs
	Entrance	Team mascot
	Seating	Website
	Restrooms	
	Concession areas	
	Playing field	
	Scoreboard	

As marketers and corporate strategists begin to pay more attention to experiences, they have recognized the impact of physical space and tangibles in creating those experiences. Lewis Carbone, a leading consultant on experience management, has developed an entire lexicon and management process around the basic idea of "experience engineering" through "clue management."[3] *Clue management* refers to the process of clearly identifying and managing *all* the various clues that customers use to form their impressions and feelings about the company. Included in this set of clues are what Carbone refers to as *mechanics clues,* or the physical and tangible clues that we focus on in this chapter. Other writers and consultants who focus on managing customer experiences also zero in on the importance of tangible evidence and physical facilities in shaping those experiences.[4] Throughout this chapter are numerous examples of how physical evidence communicates with customers and shapes their experiences.

TYPES OF SERVICESCAPES

In this chapter we explain the roles played by the servicescape and how it affects employees and customers and their interactions. The chapter relies heavily on ideas and concepts from environmental psychology, a field that encompasses the study of human beings and their relationships with built (man-made), natural, and social environments.[5] The physical setting may be more or less important in achieving the organization's marketing and other goals depending on certain factors. Table 11.3 is a framework for categorizing service organizations on two dimensions that capture some of the key differences that will affect the management of the servicescape. Organizations that share a cell in the matrix tend to face similar issues and decisions regarding their physical spaces.

Servicescape Usage

First, organizations differ in terms of *whom* the servicescape will affect. That is, who actually comes into the service facility and thus is potentially influenced by its design—customers, employees, or both groups? The first column of Table 11.3 suggests three types of service organizations that differ on this dimension. At one extreme is the *self-service* environment, in which the customer performs most of the activities and few if any employees are involved. Examples of self-service environments include ATMs, movie theaters, check-in kiosks at airports, self-service entertainment such as golf and

TABLE 11.3
Typology of Service Organizations Based on Variations in Form and Use of the Servicescape

Source: From M. J. Bitner, "Servicescapes: The Impact of Physical Surroundings on Customers and Employees," *Journal of Marketing* 56 (April 1992), pp. 57–71. Reprinted with permission of the American Marketing Association.

Servicescape Usage	Complexity of the Servicescape	
	Elaborate	**Lean**
Self-service (customer only)	Water park eBay	ATM Car wash Simple Internet services Express mail drop box
Interpersonal services (both customer and employee)	Hotel Restaurant Health clinic Hospital Bank Airline School	Dry cleaner Retail cart Hair salon
Remote service (employee only)	Telecommunications Insurance company Utility Many professional services	Telephone mail-order desk Automated voice-messaging services

theme parks, and online Internet services. In these primarily self-service environments, the organization can plan the servicescape to focus exclusively on marketing goals such as attracting the right market segment, making the facility pleasing and easy to use, and creating the desired service experience.

At the other extreme of the use dimension is the *remote service,* which has little or no customer involvement with the servicescape. Telecommunications, utilities, financial consultants, editorial, and mail-order services are examples of services that can be provided without the customer ever seeing the service facility. In fact, the facility may be in a different state or a different country (see the Global Feature in Chapter 1). In remote services, the facility can be set up to keep employees motivated and to facilitate productivity, teamwork, operational efficiency, or whatever organizational behavior goal is desired without any consideration of customers because they will never see or visit the servicescape. This is the case in the high-technology sector in India today, where Infosys Technologies, a successful information technology company, boasts a showpiece servicescape including an activity center with pool, gyms and bowling, food courts, and a multiplex theater designed to attract and retain in-demand skilled workers.[6]

In Table 11.3, *interpersonal services* are placed between the two extremes and represent situations in which both the customer and the employee are present and active in the servicescape. Examples abound, such as hotels, restaurants, hospitals, educational settings, and banks. In these situations, the servicescape must be planned to attract, satisfy, and facilitate the activities of both customers and employees simultaneously. Special attention must also be given to how the servicescape affects the nature and quality of the social interactions between and among customers and employees. A cruise ship provides a good example of a setting in which the servicescape must support customers and the employees who work there and also facilitate interactions between and within the two groups.

Servicescape Complexity

The horizontal dimension of Table 11.3 suggests another factor that will influence servicescape management. Some service environments are very simple, with few elements, few spaces, and few pieces of equipment. Such environments are termed *lean.* Shopping mall information kiosks and FedEx drop-off kiosks and stores would be considered lean environments because both provide service from one simple structure. For lean servicescapes, design decisions are relatively straightforward, especially in self-service or remote service situations in which there is no interaction among employees and customers.

Other servicescapes are very complicated, with many elements and many forms. They are termed *elaborate* environments. An example is a hospital with its many floors and rooms, sophisticated equipment, and complex variability in functions performed within the physical facility. In such an elaborate environment, the full range of marketing and organizational objectives theoretically can be approached through careful management of the servicescape. For example, a patient's hospital room can be designed to enhance patient comfort and satisfaction while simultaneously facilitating employee productivity. Firms such as hospitals that are located in the elaborate interpersonal service cell face the most complex servicescape decisions. To illustrate, when the Mayo Clinic, probably the best-known name in U.S. health care, opened its hospital in Scottsdale, Arizona, the organization painstakingly considered the interrelated goals, needs, and feelings of its employees, doctors, patients, and visitors in designing its distinctive servicescape (see Exhibit 11.4 later in this chapter).

STRATEGIC ROLES OF THE SERVICESCAPE

Within the cells of the typology, the servicescape can play many strategic roles simultaneously. An examination of the variety of roles and how they interact makes clear how strategically important it is to provide appropriate physical evidence of the service. In fact, the servicescape is frequently one of *the* most important elements used in positioning a service organization (see the Strategy Insight).

Package

Similar to a tangible product's package, the servicescape and other elements of physical evidence essentially "wrap" the service and convey to consumers an external image of what is "inside." Product packages are designed to portray a particular image as well as to evoke a particular sensory or emotional reaction. The physical setting of a service does the same thing through the interaction of many complex stimuli. The servicescape is the outward appearance of the organization and thus can be critical in forming initial impressions or setting up customer expectations—it is a visual metaphor for the intangible service. This packaging role is particularly important in creating expectations for new customers and for newly established service organizations that are trying to build a particular image (see Exhibit 11.1). The physical surroundings offer an organization the opportunity to convey an image in a way not unlike the way an individual chooses to "dress for success." The packaging role extends to the appearance of contact personnel through their uniforms or dress and other elements of their outward appearance.[7] Recognizing the strong link between a service brand and employee appearance, airlines, retailers, and even the U.S. Army are updating uniforms that—in some cases—have not been changed in almost 15 years.[8]

Interestingly, the same care and resource expenditures given to package design in product marketing are often not provided for services, even though the service package serves a variety of important roles. There are many exceptions to this generality, however. Smart companies like Apple Stores (see the Strategy Insight), Starbucks, FedEx, and Marriott spend a lot of time and money relating their servicescape design to their brand, providing their customers with strong visual metaphors and "service packaging" that conveys the brand positioning. FedEx, for example, embarked on a major overhaul of its image by rethinking and redesigning all its tangibles—everything from its drop boxes to its service centers to the bags carried by its couriers.[9] The idea was to convey a consistent look and feel of "things are simple here," and "here, give us your package; we'll take care of everything."

Facilitator

The servicescape can also serve as a facilitator in aiding the performances of persons in the environment. How the setting is designed can enhance or inhibit the efficient flow of activities in the service setting, making it easier or harder for customers and employees to accomplish their goals. A well-designed, functional facility can make the service a pleasure to experience from the customer's point of view and a pleasure to perform from the employee's. On the other hand, poor and inefficient design may frustrate both customers and employees. For example, an international air traveler who

Strategy Insight   Strategic Positioning through Architectural Design

BusinessWeek and *Architectural Record,* both McGraw-Hill publications, together sponsor an annual international competition to identify the best use of architecture that solves strategic business challenges. Company winners clearly demonstrate the impact of design on people—customers, employees, the general public, or all three. Here we present award-winners from several different years to illustrate the ways that architecture and servicescapes execute or reinforce strategic decisions and marketing positioning.

APPLE STORES, NEW YORK

In designing its store in New York's Soho district, Apple Computers brought together architects, graphic designers, product developers, merchandising people, and CEO Steve Jobs to create a retail space that would both convey the company's philosophy and sell computers. The result is a clean, open, and spacious store that displays only a few computers to create the ambience of a museum. The company establishes a modern feel using a central glass staircase, white walls, and a large skylight. A second-floor area encourages children to play with software and offers a large conference room for Apple product demonstrations. As one judge put it, "the store, like Apple, is all about information, interaction, and access." Apple's 5th Avenue store in New York City, its highest volume store, was also an award winner in a later competition. This cube-shaped store is free of structural steel and it relies on a taut glass skin and glass beams to create a sense of a free-floating structure that sits above the actual retail space. Similar to the Soho store, the "cube" is highly effective at drawing customers in, and its cleanly designed interior provides an inviting atmosphere to experiment

with innovative and futuristic Apple products. The store has very high sales per square foot and the space is beautiful, functional and very profitable. (Award Winners in 2003 and 2006)

Apple Store, Soho, NY

finds himself in a poorly designed airport with few signs, poor ventilation, and few places to sit or eat will find the experience quite dissatisfying, and employees who work there will probably be unmotivated as well.

The same international traveler will appreciate seats on the airplane that are conducive to work and sleep. The seating itself, part of the physical surroundings of the service, has been improved over the years to better facilitate airline travelers' needs to sleep. In fact, the competition for better seat and aircraft interior design continues as a major point of contention among the international airline carriers, and the results have translated into greater customer satisfaction for business travelers.[10] Some of the new designs include business class seats that recline into "skybeds," leather ottomans

THE IMAGE FACTORY, OKLAHOMA CITY

Architectural design played a major role in reconceptualizing and rebranding a copy business in Oklahoma City. What was once a small copy firm was repositioned as a large, high-tech scanning and imaging company that attracts upscale clients. Glass walls allow clients to view the company's sophisticated production processes, and a display of old typewriters conveys the history of the company dating back to its days as a typewriter repair business. Other displays show the evolution of reproduction services from typewriters to copying machines to digital scanning. The facility conveys a sense of history, quality, and pride in the work done as well as inventiveness, efficiency, and organization. (Award Winner in 2003)

SEKII LADIES CLINIC, JAPAN

To reposition its childbirth clinic in stark contrast to traditional Japanese hospitals, the Sekii Ladies Clinic relied heavily on a novel servicescape design. The new childbirth delivery and recovery rooms are elegant, warm, and simple, and the building itself is modern, open, and light-filled. Combined with interior gardens, the spaces offer mothers a rich, warm experience for childbirth. Delivery rooms and all areas welcome fathers, a departure from the tradition in Japan in which women typically give birth in large public hospitals without family members present. The clinic brings women's health to the forefront rather than hiding it, another Japanese tradition. (Award Winner in 2003)

DARWIN CENTRE MUSEUM, LONDON

The Darwin Centre Museum needed more room to house its huge collection of 22 million zoological specimens and to provide additional laboratory space for its scientists. To meet these objectives, the museum designed a new building that provided both storage and public access to its collections. An atrium in the building allows visitors to view scientists at work, and open shelves display the specimens. Touch-screen terminals provide another means for exploring the collection. The caterpillar-like roof over the building provides a clue to what is inside! Visits to the museum increased sharply when the new building was opened. (Award Winner in 2003)

HUMANE SOCIETY, SAN ANTONIO

Humane societies house lost, neglected, or unwanted animals and provide a community resource for pet adoption. Typically, the facilities are dark, impersonal, and unpleasant for all involved—the animals, employees, volunteers, and potential adoptive families. Such is not the case in San Antonio, Texas, where a new shelter resembling a retail complex was designed to reverse this pattern. Buildings are now organized around a central courtyard, offering a more communal feel, and the interiors of the buildings are comfortable and inviting. Potential adopters meander through aisles of the building as they would in a retail store. The more desirable animals (typically puppies and kittens) are located in the back of the facility so that visitors will pass by the equally deserving adult animals first. Since the opening of the newly designed facility, adoptions have increased by 95 percent, and three times as many adult animals have been adopted. (Award Winner in 2004)

Source: "The *BusinessWeek/Architectural Record* Awards," Special Report, *BusinessWeek*, November 3, 2003, pp. 57–64; and http://archrecord.construction.com/features/bwarAwards/, accessed September 2007.

in first-class sections, and electronic partition screens between seats in business class. For its "Club World" travelers, British Airways offers a suite of services called the "Sleeper Service" centered on its renowned seat design that allows travelers to get a maximum amount of rest while traveling to their destinations. The service includes preflight supper (so that the travelers will not need to be awakened during the flight to eat), "midnight munchies" available throughout the flight on request, and "breakfast in bed" served closer to landing to allow for longer sleep time.[11]

As hotels began development of new prototype rooms in the early 2000s, they focused on making the rooms more useful to their guests who were spending more time in their hotel rooms. Rooms were designed with colors, fabrics, and textures that

Exhibit 11.1 Using Physical Evidence to Position a New Service

When Speedi-Lube opened its doors in Seattle, Washington, it was one of the first 10-minute oil and lubrication services ever introduced. Now there are thousands of such outlets, but then the concept was totally new. The idea was to offer an alternative to corner gas stations for basic car lubrication service, quickly (within 10 minutes), with no appointment necessary. Because the concept was unknown to consumers at the time, the owners of Speedi-Lube needed to communicate and position the service clearly so that consumers would form accurate expectations. And because car maintenance is highly intangible and consumers often do not understand what is actually done to their cars, the owners relied heavily on tangible physical evidence to communicate the concept before, during, and after the sale.

To communicate an image of fast, efficient service, Speedi-Lube relied on straightforward, to-the-point advertising using clean, crisp letters. For example, a large billboard read in large blue and white letters: SPEEDI-LUBE, 10-MINUTE OIL CHANGE, NO APPOINTMENT, OPEN 7 DAYS, 9 TO 6. The very buildings in which the service was performed communicated the efficiency theme clearly. In fact, the exteriors of some of the first Speedi-Lube facilities had the look of a fast-food restaurant, not inconsistent with the intended image of speed, efficiency, and predictability. Entrance and exit signs were clearly displayed so that customers coming

to Speedi-Lube for the first time would know exactly where to drive their cars.

On driving into the service bay, the customer was greeted with additional physical evidence that clearly differentiated Speedi-Lube from its competitors at that time. The service bay was very neat and brightly painted, with a professional-appearing service counter in the bay, where the customer filled out paperwork to get the service. Service personnel in professional uniforms helped with the paperwork, and the customer was invited to wait in a clean and functional waiting area where coffee and magazines were provided. (Alternatively, customers were welcome to stay in the service area to observe the work on their cars.) On one of the waiting room walls was displayed a large schematic that you see here, showing the underside of an automobile and identifying all the lubrication points and exactly what was being done to the car. This form of evidence informed customers and gave them confidence in what was being done.

On completion, the customer was given a checklist itemizing the lubrication services provided. As a finishing touch, the employee would then lubricate the door locks on the car to indicate that nothing had been overlooked. Three months later Speedi-Lube would send a reminder suggesting that it was time for another oil change.

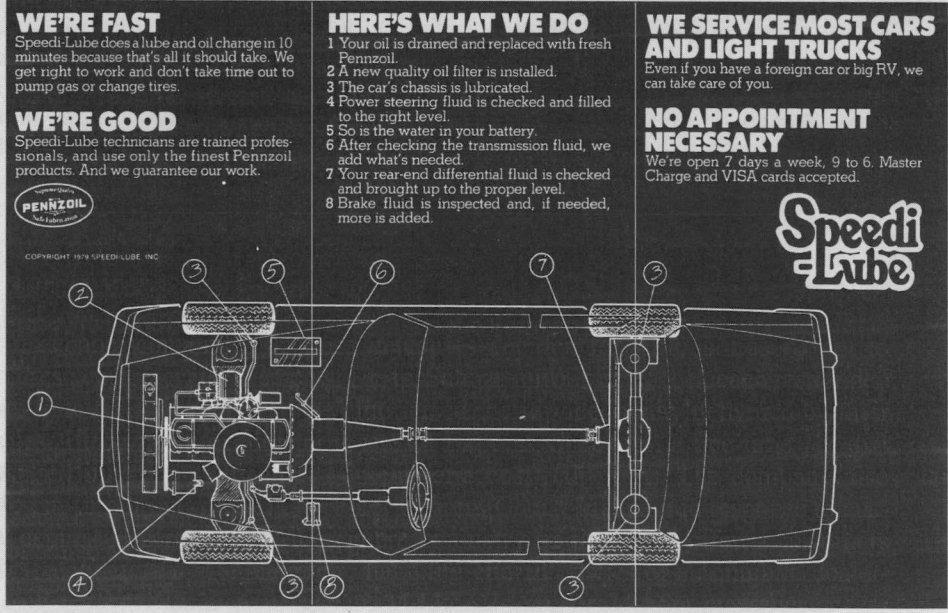

have a homelike look, with bigger desks, more high-speed Internet connections, and larger TVs.[12] All these examples emphasize the facilitator role of the servicescape.

Socializer

The design of the servicescape aids in the socialization of both employees and customers in the sense that it helps convey expected roles, behaviors, and relationships. For example, a new employee in a professional services firm would come to understand her position in the hierarchy partially through noting her office assignment, the quality of her office furnishings, and her location relative to others in the organization.

The design of the facility can also suggest to customers what their role is relative to employees, what parts of the servicescape they are welcome in and which are for employees only, how they should behave while in the environment, and what types of interactions are encouraged. For example, consider a Club Med vacation environment that is set up to facilitate customer–customer interactions as well as customer interactions with Club Med staff. The organization also recognizes the need for privacy, providing areas that encourage solitary activities. To illustrate further, in many Starbucks locations, the company has shifted to more of a traditional coffeehouse environment in which customers spend social time rather than coming in for a quick cup of coffee on the run. To encourage this type of socializing, these Starbucks locations have comfortable lounge chairs and tables set up to encourage customers to interact and to stay longer. The goal is to be the customer's "third place," that is a place where customers think of spending time when not at work or at home (see Exhibit 11.3 later in the chapter for more on third places).

Differentiator

The design of the physical facility can differentiate a firm from its competitors and signal the market segment that the service is intended for. Given its power as a differentiator, changes in the physical environment can be used to reposition a firm and/or to attract new market segments. In shopping malls the signage, colors used in decor and displays, and type of music wafting from a store signal the intended market segment. In the banking industry, Washington Mutual Bank clearly communicates through its servicescape its differentiation as a bank for consumers and families.[13] The bank has an area for children to play as well as a retail store offering financial books, software, and piggy banks, clearly differentiating this bank from those whose focus is commercial accounts or private, upscale banking (see Exhibit 11.2).

In another context, the servicescape has been used as a major point of differentiation for PetSmart in the introduction of its innovative PetsHotel concept.[14] The hotels, which offer overnight care as well as day care for pets, are designed very differently from typical kennels or veterinary facilities. They feature a lobby area, colorful play areas, comfortable sleeping rooms, television, a "bone booth" for calling in, and other amenities that give the facilities a more residential, homelike appeal than traditional kennels have.

The design of a physical setting can also differentiate one area of a service organization from another. For example, in the hotel industry, one large hotel may have several levels of dining possibilities, each signaled by differences in design. Price differentiation is also often partially achieved through variations in physical setting. Bigger rooms with more physical amenities cost more, just as larger seats with more leg room (generally in first class) are more expensive on an airplane.

Exhibit 11.2 Washington Mutual Patents Its Bank Branch Design

Washington Mutual, a large retail bank in the United States, has been particularly effective in differentiating itself as a family-oriented, friendly, inviting retail bank through its innovative branch design, which it has trademarked under the name of "Occasio" (Latin for "favorable opportunity"). Drawing on what it learned from customer research, the bank has transformed the look of more than two-thirds of its branches to the Occasio design. Features range from oval or circular branch layouts to free-standing teller stations. The design offers play areas for kids with toys, television, and child-sized furniture. Bright colors are used for furnishings and walls, and attractive, colorful posters are displayed on the walls. A concierge guides customers to where they need to go—particularly on a first visit. In a somewhat unusual step, the company patented its innovative design. U.S. patent no. 6,681,985 describes the bank as "welcoming and inviting," in contrast to traditional bank branches. The differentiation strategy and resulting branch design reflect the bank's desire to build relationships with its retail customers. Established in 1889, WaMu, as the bank is known, is based in Washington state. The corporation has more than 50,000 employees and operates more than 2,700 banking branches and other types of outlets. It was recognized by *Fortune* magazine as a Most Admired Company, and has also been recognized by *BusinessWeek* as number 14 in its 2007 list of Customer Service Champs. While Washington Mutual pioneered many of the changes in bank

design, many others (Umpqua Bank, Union National Community Bank, Wachovia, and others) are following their lead by introducing children's areas, cafés, new colors and woodtones, Wi-Fi, and other amenties, representing a shift for the retail banking industry.

Washington Mutual Bank Branch

Sources: www.wamu.com, 2007; R. Wiles, "Breaking the Bank—the Mold, That Is," *The Arizona Republic,* July 5, 2004, p. D1; J. J. Kim, "A Latte with Your Loan? Banks Try to Turn Branches into Hangouts with Wi-Fi, Movies, Coffee Bars, and Yoga," *The Wall Street Journal,* May 17, 2006, p. D1; and J. McGregor, "Customer Service Champs," *BusinessWeek,* March 5, 2007, pp. 52–64.

FRAMEWORK FOR UNDERSTANDING SERVICESCAPE EFFECTS ON BEHAVIOR

Although it is useful from a strategic point of view to think about the multiple roles of the servicescape and how they interact, making actual decisions about servicescape design requires an understanding of why the effects occur and how to manage them. The next sections of the chapter present a framework or model of environment and behavior relationships in service settings.

The Underlying Framework

The framework for understanding servicescape effects on behavior follows from basic *stimulus–organism–response* theory. In the framework the multidimensional environment is the *stimulus,* consumers and employees are the *organisms* that respond to the stimuli, and behaviors directed at the environment are the *responses.* The assumptions are that dimensions of the servicescape will affect customers and employees and that they will behave in certain ways depending on their internal reactions to the servicescape.

A specific example will help illustrate the theory in action. Assume there is a cookie cart that is parked outside the student union on campus. The cart is colorful and playful in design, and an aroma of baking cookies wafts from it. The design and the aroma are two elements of the servicescape that will affect customers in some way. Now assume you are a hungry student, just out of class, strolling across campus. The fun design of the cart attracts your attention, and simultaneously you smell baking cookies. The fun design and the delicious smell cause you to feel happy, relaxed, and hungry at the same time. You are attracted to the cart and decide to buy a cookie because you have another class to attend before lunch. The movement toward the cart and the purchase of a cookie are behaviors directed at the servicescape. Depending on how much time you have, you may even choose to converse with the vendor or other customers standing around munching cookies, other forms of behavior directed at the servicescape.

The framework shown in Figure 11.1 is detailed in the next sections. It represents a comprehensive stimulus–organism–response model that recognizes complex

FIGURE 11.1 **A Framework for Understanding Environment–User Relationships in Service Organizations**

Source: Adapted from M. J. Bitner, "Servicescapes: The Impact of Physical Surroundings on Customers and Employees," *Journal of Marketing* 56 (April 1992), pp. 57–71.

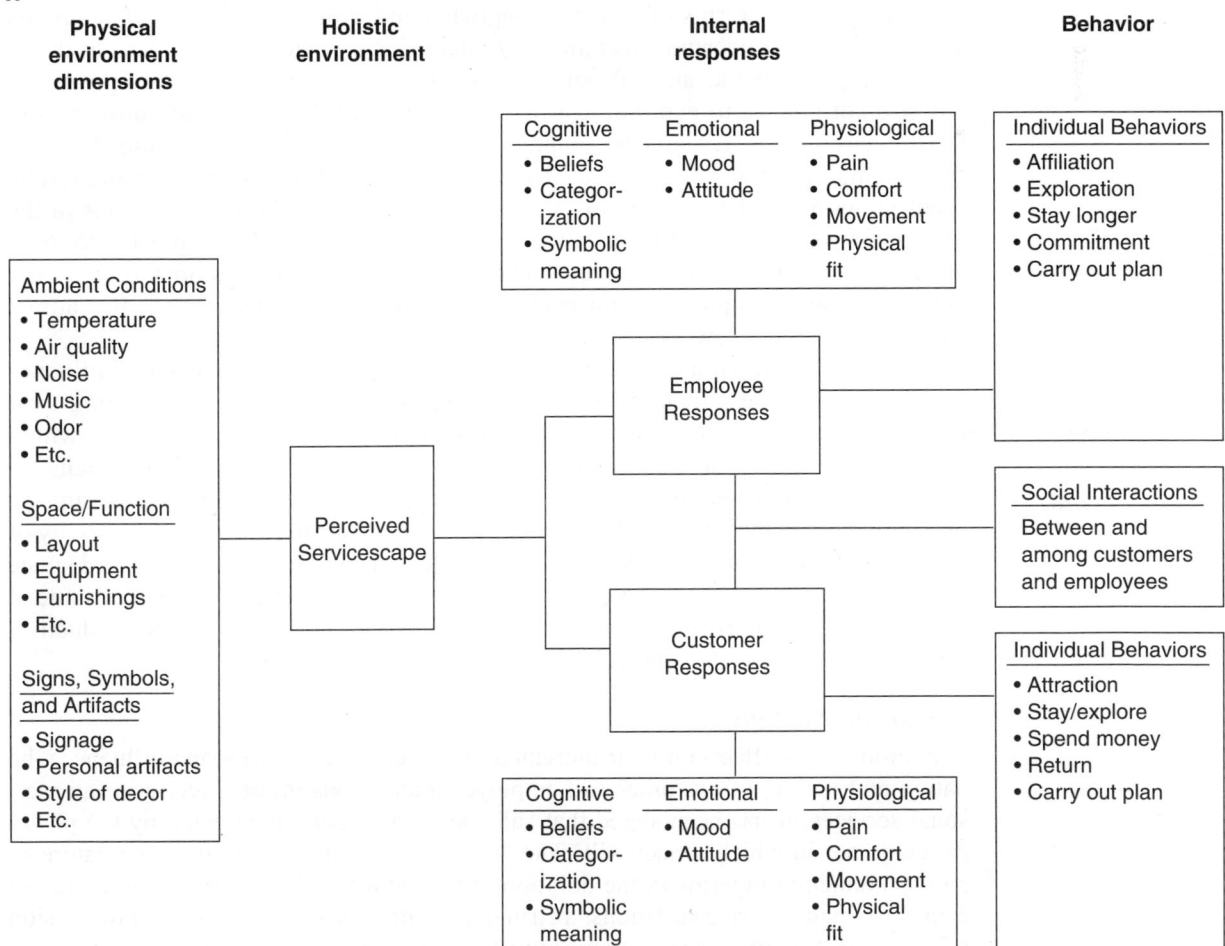

dimensions of the environment, impacts on multiple parties (customers, employees, and their interactions), multiple types of internal responses (cognitive, emotional, and physiological), and a variety of individual and social behaviors that can result.

Our discussion of the framework will begin on the right side of the model with *behaviors*. Next we will explain and develop the *internal responses* portion of the model. Finally we will turn to the dimensions of the *environment* and the holistic perception of the environment.

Behaviors in the Servicescape

That human behavior is influenced by the physical setting in which it occurs is essentially a truism. Interestingly, however, until the 1960s psychologists largely ignored the effects of physical setting in their attempts to predict and explain behavior. Since that time, a large and steadily growing body of literature within the field of environmental psychology has addressed the relationships between human beings and their built environments. Recent marketing focus on the customer experience has also drawn attention to the effects of physical spaces and design on customer behavior.[15]

Individual Behaviors

Environmental psychologists suggest that individuals react to places with two general, and opposite, forms of behavior: approach and avoidance. *Approach behaviors* include all positive behaviors that might be directed at a particular place, such as desire to stay, explore, work, and affiliate.[16] *Avoidance behaviors* reflect the opposite— a desire not to stay, to explore, to work, or to affiliate. In a study of consumers in retail environments, researchers found that approach behaviors (including shopping enjoyment, returning, attraction and friendliness toward others, spending money, time spent browsing, and exploration of the store) were influenced by perceptions of the environment.[17] At one 7-Eleven store, the owners played "elevator music" to drive away the youthful market segment that was detracting from the store's image. And our cookie cart example is reminiscent of cinnamon roll bakeries in malls that attract patrons through the power of smell.

In addition to attracting or deterring entry, the servicescape can actually influence the degree of success that consumers and employees experience in executing their plans once inside. Each individual comes to a particular service organization with a goal or purpose that may be aided or hindered by the setting. NBA basketball fans are aided in their enjoyment of the game by adequate, easy-access parking; clear signage directing them to their seats; efficient food service; and clean restrooms. The ability of employees to do their jobs effectively is also influenced by the servicescape. Adequate space, proper equipment, and comfortable temperature and air quality all contribute to an employee's comfort and job satisfaction, causing him or her to be more productive, stay longer, and affiliate positively with coworkers.

Social Interactions

In addition to its effects on their individual behaviors, the servicescape influences the nature and quality of customer and employee interactions, most directly in interpersonal services. It has been stated that "all social interaction is affected by the physical container in which it occurs."[18] The "physical container" can affect the nature of social interaction in terms of the duration of interaction and the actual progression of events. In many service situations, a firm may want to ensure a particular progression of events (a "standard script") and limit the duration of the service. Environmental variables such as physical proximity, seating arrangements, size, and flexibility can define the possibilities and limits of social episodes such as those occurring between

Social interactions are defined partially by the configuration of the servicescape.

customers and employees, or customers and other customers. The Holland America Cruise Line photo shown here illustrates how the design of the servicescape can help define the social rules, conventions, and expectations in force in a given setting, thus serving to define the nature of social interaction.[19] The close physical proximity of passengers on the sunbathing deck will in and of itself prescribe certain patterns of behavior. This vacation is not designed for a social recluse! Some researchers have implied that recurring social behavior patterns are associated with particular physical settings and that when people encounter typical settings, their social behaviors can be predicted.[20]

Examples of how environments shape social interactions—and how these interactions in turn influence the environment—are abundant.[21] Even casual observation of the retail phenomenon "Nike Town" shows how this form of "entertainment retail" shapes the behaviors of consumers but at the same time allows them to interpret and create their own realities and experiences.[22] In a river-rafting trip, the "wilderness servicescape" profoundly influences the behaviors, interactions, and total experiences of rafting consumers and their guides. In this case the natural, and for the most part uncontrollable, environment is the setting for the service.[23] In some cases, important social bonds and connections are forged within a service place, resulting its becoming a "third place" for the individuals who frequent it (see Exhibit 11.3).[24]

Internal Responses to the Servicescape

Employees and customers respond to dimensions of their physical surroundings cognitively, emotionally, and physiologically, and those responses are what influence their behaviors in the environment (as shown in the middle portion of Figure 11.1). In other words, the perceived servicescape does not directly *cause* people to behave in certain ways. Although the internal responses are discussed independently here, they are clearly interdependent: a person's beliefs about a place, a cognitive response, may well influence the person's emotional response, and vice versa. For example, patients who come into a dentist's office that is designed to calm and sooth their anxieties (emotional responses) may believe as a result that the dentist is caring and competent (cognitive responses).

Environment and Cognition

The perceived servicescape can have an effect on people's beliefs about a place and their beliefs about the people and products found in that place. In a sense, the servicescape can be viewed as a form of nonverbal communication, imparting meaning through what is called "object language."[25] For example, particular environmental cues such as the type of office furniture and decor and the apparel worn by the lawyer may influence a potential client's beliefs about whether the lawyer is successful, expensive, and trustworthy. In a consumer study, variations in descriptions of store atmospheres were found to alter beliefs about a product (perfume) sold in the store.[26] Another study showed that a travel agent's office decor affected customer attributions and beliefs

Exhibit 11.3 Social Support in "Third Places"

The social interactions and attachments among customers and between customers and employees in "third places" can provide companionship and emotional support that results in strong attachments and loyalty to the place itself. A third place is a public or commercial place where people gather regularly and voluntarily outside of work (or school) and home, which are viewed as the first two places in people's lives. Often third places are diners, coffee shops, taverns, pubs, or clubs, but a fitness club, a civic center, or other public gathering place could also be a third place. The "Cheers" bar on the popular television show epitomizes a third place. Think about what types of places might qualify as a third place for you. Do you have a third place?

A study by Mark Rosenbaum and colleagues showed that people can grow attached to a third place to the point where they depend on it above all other alternatives, they are committed to the place and care about it, they personally identify with it, and they structure their lifestyle around it. This type of attachment happens because of the companionship and emotional support they receive from the other customers and employees in the place, not simply because they like the service or feel comfortable in the physical surroundings. These emotional attachments and interactions are particularly strong for people who are lonely or in need of contact with others. The researchers observed and conducted depth interviews with patrons of Sammy's, a casual dining restaurant in the suburbs of a major U.S. metropolitan area that was clearly a third place for many regulars who frequented the restaurant. Through the interviews, they established that patrons who were lonely or who had lost an established form of social support through death, divorce, or illness, found significant companionship and emotional support at Sammy's. The regular patrons who had lost a spouse through death, divorce, or separation had a full 58 percent of their social supportive relationships with people (customers and employees) at Sammy's. These patrons were also extremely attached and loyal to Sammy's.

The research reinforces the idea that servicescapes, while they are defined by their physical elements, can take on a third place character when they become the source of social interactions, bonds, and support for the people who frequent them. The benefits of this type of support go far beyond the benefits intended by the core service. The regulars at Sammy's receive far more than a good meal in pleasant surroundings. Through their interactions with others, their daily lives are enhanced and they are emotionally better off. As the problems associated with loneliness grow in our modern-day society (e.g., the population is aging, more and more people are caring for chronically ill family members or friends, divorce is prevalent, work hours are increasing resulting in less time for friendships), the importance of third places as a form of social support may grow as well. While consumer support networks do not necessarily require a physical presence—for example, online communities can provide social support—physical places are often more accessible and more preferable for nurturing companionship and emotional connections among people.

The Cheers bar epitomized a third place in the well-known television show.

Sources: M. S. Rosenbaum, "Exploring the Social Supportive Role of Third Places in Consumers' Lives," *Journal of Service Research* 9 (August 2006), pp. 59–72; A. Tombs and J. R. McColl-Kennedy, "Social-Servicescape Conceptual Model," *Marketing Theory* 3, no. 4 (2003), pp 447–475; and M. S. Rosenbaum, J. Ward, B. A. Walker, and A. L. Ostrom, "A Cup of Coffee with a Dash of Love: An Investigation of Commercial Social Support and Third-Place Attachment," *Journal of Service Research* 10 (August 2007), pp. 43–59.

about the travel agent's behavior.[27] Travel agents whose facilities were more organized and professional were viewed more positively than were those whose facilities were disorganized and unprofessional.

In other cases, perceptions of the servicescape may simply help people distinguish a firm by influencing how it is categorized. The overall perception of the servicescape enables the consumer or employee to categorize the firm mentally. Research shows that in the restaurant industry a particular configuration of environmental cues suggests "fast food," whereas another configuration suggests "elegant sit-down restaurant."[28] In such situations, environmental cues serve as a shortcut device that enables customers to categorize and distinguish among types of restaurants.

Environment and Emotion

In addition to influencing beliefs, the perceived servicescape can directly elicit emotional responses that, in turn, influence behaviors. Just being in a particular place can make a person feel happy, lighthearted, and relaxed, whereas being in another place may make that person feel sad, depressed, and gloomy. The colors, decor, music, and other elements of the atmosphere can have an unexplainable and sometimes very subconsciousness effect on the moods of people in the place. For some people, certain environmental stimuli (noises, smells) common in a dental office can bring on immediate feelings of fear and anxiety. In very different contexts, the marble interior and grandeur of the Supreme Court buildings in Washington, D.C., call up feelings of pride and awe and respect; lively music and bright decor in a local night spot may cause people to feel excited and happy. In all these examples, the response from the consumer probably does not involve thinking but, rather, is just an unexplained emotional feeling.

REI (Recreational Equipment Inc.) provides another example of emotional connection facilitated through architectural design and the servicescape. At its flagship store in Seattle, the company has created an experience for consumers that includes a climbing mountain, a bicycle track, and walking trails. Its store in Minnesota has a cross-country ski trail around it. REI, through its servicescape design, is simulating the experiences and emotions that customers associate with its products, reinforcing a strong approach response to its stores.

Environmental psychologists have researched people's emotional responses to physical settings.[29] They have concluded that any environment, whether natural or engineered, will elicit emotions that can be captured by two basic dimensions: (1) pleasure/displeasure and (2) degree of arousal (amount of stimulation or excitement). Servicescapes that are both pleasant and arousing would be termed *exciting,* whereas those that are pleasant and nonarousing, or sleepy, would be termed *relaxing.* Unpleasant servicescapes that are arousing would be called *distressing,* whereas unpleasant, sleepy servicescapes would be *gloomy.* These basic emotional responses to environments can be used to begin predicting the expected behaviors of consumers and employees who find themselves in a particular type of place.

Environment and Physiology

The perceived servicescape may also affect people in purely physiological ways. Noise that is too loud may cause physical discomfort, the temperature of a room may cause people to shiver or perspire, the air quality may make it difficult to breathe, and the glare of lighting may decrease ability to see and may cause physical pain. All these physical responses may, in turn, directly influence whether people stay in and enjoy a particular environment. It is well known that the comfort of seating in a restaurant influences how long people stay. The hard seats in a fast-food restaurant cause most people to leave within a predictable period of time, whereas the soft, cozy chairs in some Starbucks coffee shops have the opposite effect, encouraging people to stay. Similarly, environmental design and related physiological responses affect whether employees can perform their job functions well.

A vast amount of research in engineering and design has addressed human physiological responses to ambient conditions as well as physiological responses to equipment design.[30] Such research fits under the rubric of *human factors design* or *ergonomics*. Human factors research systematically applies relevant information about human capabilities and limitations to the design of items and procedures that people use. For example, Choice Hotels targeted empty-nester couples and senior citizens in the redesign of many of the rooms in its Rodeway and EconoLodge brands. A significant percentage of the rooms in these hotels were converted to senior-friendly suites with brighter lighting, larger-button telephones and TV remotes, and grab bars in the showers.[31] Wall switches have lights so they can be found easily at night. To help people with arthritis, doors have lever handles instead of knobs so that every door and every drawer in the room can be opened with a fist rather than requiring hand and wrist dexterity. In these and other ways, Choice Hotels has uniquely adapted its redesign to accommodate older guests.

Variations in Individual Responses

In general, people respond to the environment in the ways just described—cognitively, emotionally, physiologically—and their responses influence how they behave in the environment. However, the response will not be the same for every individual, every time. Personality differences as well as temporary conditions such as moods or the purpose for being there can cause variations in how people respond to the servicescape.[32]

One personality trait that has been shown to affect how people respond to environments is *arousal seeking*. Arousal seekers enjoy and look for high levels of stimulation, whereas arousal avoiders prefer lower levels of stimulation. Thus, an arousal avoider in a loud, bright dance club with flashing lights might show strong dislike for the environment, whereas an arousal seeker would be very happy. In a related vein, it has been suggested that some people are better *screeners* of environmental stimuli than others.[33] Screeners of stimuli would be able to experience a high level of stimulation but not be affected by it. Nonscreeners would be highly affected and might exhibit extreme responses even to low levels of stimulation.

The particular purpose for being in a servicescape can also affect a person's response to it. A person who is on an airplane for a one-hour flight will likely be less affected by the atmosphere on the plane than will the traveler who is embarking on a 14-hour flight from Los Angeles to Shanghai. Similarly, a day-surgery hospital patient will likely be less sensitive and demanding of the hospital environment than would a patient who is spending two weeks in the hospital. And a person who is staying at a resort hotel for a business meeting will respond differently to the environment than will a couple on their honeymoon. Temporary mood states can also cause people to respond differently to environmental stimuli. A person who is feeling frustrated and fatigued after a long day at work is likely to be affected differently by a highly arousing restaurant than the same person would be after a relaxing three-day weekend.

Cultural differences also influence preferences for environmental features and responses to servicescape design. For example, there is a strong cultural preference for the color red in China, whereas Westerners would not share this attraction. And, while Americans and Europeans may prefer to shop in orderly and quiet supermarkets, many Indian shoppers prefer a more jumbled, chaotic environment.[34] This is what India's largest retailer, Pantaloon Retail Ltd, learned when it introduced Western-style supermarkets in India. At first, customers just walked through the wide, pristine aisles and left the store without buying. By studying Indian consumer behavior and focusing on the preferences of Indian shoppers (often the maids, cooks, nannies, and farmers of India, not the elite), Pantaloon redesigned its supermarkets to make them messier, noisier, and more cramped, re-creating in some sense the atmosphere of a public market. This design was appealing to the target market and sales increased far above where they were with the original design.

Environmental Dimensions of the Servicescape

The preceding sections have described customer and employee behaviors in the servicescape and the three primary responses—cognitive, emotional, and physiological—that lead to those behaviors. In this section, we turn to the complex mix of environmental features that influence these responses and behaviors (the left portion of Figure 11.1). Specifically, environmental dimensions of the physical surroundings can include all the objective physical factors that can be controlled by the firm to enhance (or constrain) employee and customer actions. There is an endless list of possibilities: lighting, color, signage, textures, quality of materials, style of furnishings, layout, wall decor, temperature, and so on. In Figure 11.1 and in the discussion that follows here, the hundreds of potential elements have been categorized into three composite dimensions: *ambient conditions; spatial layout and functionality;* and *signs, symbols, and artifacts*. Exhibit 11.4 illustrates how the Mayo Clinic took into consideration all these dimensions in designing its hospital to accommodate patients, doctors, employees, and visitors.

Although we discuss the three dimensions separately, environmental psychology explains that people respond to their environments holistically. That is, although individuals perceive discrete stimuli (e.g., they can perceive noise level, color, and decor as distinct elements), it is the total configuration of stimuli that determines their reactions to a place. Hence, although the dimensions of the environment are defined independently in the following sections, it is important to recognize that they are perceived by employees and customers as a holistic pattern of interdependent stimuli. The holistic response is shown in Figure 11.1 as the "perceived servicescape."

Ambient Conditions

Ambient conditions include background characteristics of the environment such as temperature, lighting, noise, music, scent, and color. As a general rule, ambient conditions affect the five senses. Sometimes such dimensions may be totally imperceptible (gases, chemicals, infrasound) yet have profound effects, particularly on employees who spend long hours in the environment.

All these factors can profoundly affect how people feel, think, and respond to a particular service establishment. For example, a number of studies have documented the effects of music on consumers' perceptions of products, their perceptions of how long they have waited for service, and the amount of money they spend.[35] When there is music, shoppers tend to perceive that they spend less time shopping and in line than when there is no music. Slower music tempos at lower volumes tend to make people shop more leisurely, and in some cases, they spend more. In the Mayo Hospital lobby, piano music serves to reduce stress (see Exhibit 11.4). Shoppers also spend more time when the music "fits" the product or matches their musical tastes. Other studies have similarly shown the effects of scent on consumer responses.[36] Scent in bakeries, coffee shops, and tobacco shops, for example, can be used to draw people in, and pleasant scents can increase lingering time. The presence of a scent can reduce perceptions of time spent and improve store evaluations. The effects of ambient conditions are especially noticeable when they are extreme. For example, people attending a symphony

Exhibit 11.4   Designing the Mayo Clinic Hospital

Mayo Clinic is the best known health care brand in the United States. More than 100 years old, Mayo operates three clinics across the country. Its original and best-known facility is in Rochester, Minnesota, and the two other clinics are in Jacksonville, Florida, and Scottsdale, Arizona. In 1998 Mayo opened the Mayo Clinic Hospital in Arizona, the first hospital planned, designed, and built by Mayo Clinic. Located on a 210-acre site, the hospital houses 178 hospital rooms on five floors. More than 250 physicians; 950 nursing, technical, and support staff; and 300 volunteers work at the facility. The hospital supports inpatient care for 65 medical and surgical specialties and also has a full emergency and urgent care center.

What is unique about this hospital facility is the tremendous care that was taken in its design to serve the needs of patients, doctors, staff, and visitors. The hospital is designed as a "healing environment" focused on patient needs, and focus groups were held with all constituents to determine how the hospital should be designed to facilitate this overall goal. A quotation from the Mayo brothers (founders of the clinic) captures the underlying belief that supported the design of the hospital: "The best interest of the patient is the only interest to be considered." This statement lies at the foundation of all Mayo does, even today, more than 100 years after the Mayo brothers began their practice of medicine. To focus on the best interests of the patient also requires acknowledgment of the needs of the care providers and the patient's family and friend support system. All these interests were clearly considered in the design of the hospital.

A FIVE-STORY ATRIUM LOW-STRESS ENTRY

As patients and others enter the Mayo Hospital, they encounter a five-story enclosed atrium, reminiscent of a luxury hotel lobby. A grand piano sits in the lobby,

and volunteers play beautiful, relaxing music throughout the day. An abundance of plants and glass gives the lobby a natural feel and provides a welcoming atmosphere. On entering, visitors see the elevator bank directly in front of them across the atrium, so there is no stress in figuring out where to go.

ALL PATIENT AND VISITOR SERVICES ARE TOGETHER

All services needed by patients and their families (information desk, cafeteria, chapel, patient admissions, gift shop) are located around the atrium, easily visible and accessible. A sense of peace and quiet permeates the lobby—all by deliberate design to reduce stress and promote caring and wellness. There is no confusion here and very little of the atmosphere of a typical hospital entry.

ROOMS ARE DESIGNED AROUND PATIENT NEEDS AND FEELINGS

On disembarking the elevators to go to patient rooms, people again sense relaxation and peace in the environment. As the doors open, patients and guests face a five-story wall of paned glass with views out to the desert and mountains that surround the hospital site. As people progress left or right down well-marked corridors to the patient rooms, the atmosphere becomes even quieter. Rooms (all of them private) are arranged in 12-bed pods surrounding a nursing station. Nurses are within 20 steps of any patient room. Nurses and other attendants use cell phones—there is no paging system with constant announcements, as in many hospitals.

The rooms themselves have interesting features, some designed by patients. For example, rooms contain a multishelf display area on which patients can put cards, flowers, and other personal items. Fold-out, cushioned bedchairs are in each room so family members

in a hall in which the air conditioning has failed and the air is hot and stuffy will be uncomfortable, and their discomfort will be reflected in how they feel about the concert. If the temperature and air quality were within a comfort tolerance zone, these ambient factors would probably go unnoticed.

Spatial Layout and Functionality

Because service environments generally exist to fulfill specific purposes or needs of customers, spatial layout and functionality of the physical surroundings are particularly important. *Spatial layout* refers to the ways in which machinery, equipment, and furnishings are arranged; the size and shape of those items; and the spatial relationships among them. *Functionality* refers to the ability of the same items to facilitate the accomplishment of customer and employee goals. Previous examples in this chapter illustrate the layout and functionality dimensions of the servicescape (e.g., the cruise ship photo earlier and the design of the Mayo Hospital in Exhibit 11.4).

can nap or even spend the night with their loved ones. Visitors are never told they must leave. The rooms are arranged with consideration to what patients see from the beds, where they spend the most time. For example, special attention is paid to the ceilings, which patients view while flat on their backs; all rooms have windows; and a white board on the wall at the foot of each bed displays important information that patients want to know (like the name of the nurse on duty, the date, the room phone number, and other information).

DEPARTMENTS THAT WORK TOGETHER ARE ADJACENT

Another interesting design feature in this hospital is that departments that work together are housed very close to each other to facilitate communication and to reduce walking time between areas. This important feature allows caregivers to spend more time with patients and also lessens employee fatigue.

MAXIMIZE NURSES' TIME WITH PATIENTS

A critical element in the recovery of patients is the quality of care they are given by nurses. Many of the Mayo Clinic Hospital design features facilitate the quality of nursing care. The pod design puts nurses close to their patients; the white boards in the rooms allow easy communication; the accessible placement of supplies and relevant departments helps maximize the time nurses spend with patients.

It is clear that the design of the Mayo Hospital takes into account the critical importance of the servicescape in facilitating Mayo's primary goal: patient healing. All parties' voices were heard, and the place itself provides an environment that promotes well-being for patients, visitors, doctors, nurses, and other staff.

Mayo Hospital Lobby

Sources: *Teamwork at Mayo: An Experiment in Cooperative Individualism* (Rochester, MN: Mayo Press, 1998); http://www.mayo.edu; author's personal tour of the Mayo Clinic Hospital in Scottsdale; and L. L. Berry and K. D. Seltman, "Building a Strong Services Brand: Lessons from Mayo Clinic," *Business Horizons* 50 (2007), pp. 199–209.

The spatial layout and functionality of the environment are particularly important for customers in self-service environments, where they must perform the service on their own and cannot rely on employees to assist them. Thus, the functionality of an ATM machine and of self-serve restaurants, gasoline pumps, and Internet shopping are critical to success and customer satisfaction.

The importance of facility layout is particularly apparent in retail, hospitality, and leisure settings, where research shows it can influence customer satisfaction, store performance, and consumer search behavior.[37]

Signs, Symbols, and Artifacts

Many items in the physical environment serve as explicit or implicit signals that communicate about the place to its users. *Signs* displayed on the exterior and interior of a structure are examples of explicit communicators. They can be used as labels (name of company, name of department, and so on), for directional purposes (entrances, exits),

People's reactions to elements of the physical environment and design are shaped to a large degree by culture and expectations they have formed through their life experiences, dominated by where they live. Just think of one design element—color—and the variety of uses it has across cultures. Other cultural differences—personal space requirements, social distance preferences, sensitivity to crowding—can affect how consumers experience servicescapes around the world.

McDonald's Corporation recognizes these culturally defined expectations in allowing its franchisees around the world tremendous freedom in designing their servicescapes. In most McDonald's franchises, a large percentage of the ownership is retained locally. Employees are nationals, and marketing strategies reflect local consumers' buying and preference patterns. In all cases, the restaurant is a "community institution," involved in social causes as well as local events. McDonald's strategy is to have its restaurants worldwide reflect the cultures and communities in which they are found—to mirror the communities they serve.

Not only are the servicescapes different, but the delivery options are also different around the globe. In the United States, drive-through windows are prevalent, reflecting the country's automobile culture and relative lack of space constraints. In contrast, many people in cities around the world can now have McDonald's food delivered to them via cars, motor scooters, and bicycles. McDonald's already delivers in more than 25 cities, with more delivery plans in the works. For example, in Egypt deliveries account for more than 27 percent of all McDonald's revenue. The company launched delivery service in Taipei in 2007 with 1,000 drivers and expanded to citywide delivery service in Shanghai the same year. The delivery model works well and is profitable in cities where there is plenty of labor, congested traffic, and little space for stand-alone restaurants. At the same time that it allows this creative energy to flourish in design, delivery, and marketing strategies, McDonald's is extremely tight on its operating procedures and menu standards.

Although the golden arches are always present, a brief tour around the globe shows the wide variation in McDonald's face to the community:

- Bologna, Italy: In Bologna, known as the "City of Arches" for hundreds of years, McDonald's took on the weathered, crafted look of the neighboring historic arches. Even the floor in the restaurant was done by hand, using old-world techniques. The restaurant used local architects and artists to bring the local architectural feel to the golden arches.

- Paris, France: Near the Sorbonne in Paris, the local McDonald's reflects its studious neighbor. The servicescape there has the look of a leather-bound library with books, statues, and heavy wood furniture.

- Salen, Sweden: On the slopes of Lindvallen Resort in Salen, you can find the world's first "ski-thru" restaurant, named McSki, located next to the main ski lift. The building is different from any other McDonald's restaurant, built in a typical mountain style with wood panels and natural stone from the surroundings. Skiers can simply glide to the counter without taking off their skis, or they can be seated indoors or out.

- McCafés in Europe: A common sight in European McDonald's is the "McCafé" section, where upscale coffees and desserts are sold in a separate area of the restaurant. Upgrades to the McCafé sections in several German McDonald's include wooden floors, leather chairs, a fireplace and fresh flowers and candles. The comfortable atmosphere and long hours encourage customers to use McCafés as community and business meeting places, not just places to buy a quick meal or a cup of coffee.

- Beijing, China: McDonald's restaurants here have become a "place to hang out," very different from the truly "fast-food" role they play in the United States. They are part of the community, serving young and old, families and couples. Customers can be seen lingering for long periods of time, relaxing, chatting, reading, enjoying the music, or celebrating birthdays. Teenagers and young couples even find the restaurants to be very romantic environments. The emphasis on a Chinese-style family atmosphere is apparent from the interior walls of local restaurants, which are covered by posters emphasizing family values.

and to communicate rules of behavior (no smoking, children must be accompanied by an adult). Adequate signs have even been shown to reduce perceived crowding and stress.

Other environmental *symbols* and *artifacts* may communicate less directly than signs, giving implicit cues to users about the meaning of the place and norms and expectations for behavior in the place. Quality construction materials, artwork, certificates and photographs, floor coverings, and personal objects displayed in the

- Tokyo, Japan: Although some McDonald's restaurants in Japan are located in prime real-estate districts such as the Ginza in Tokyo, many others are situated near major train stations or other high-traffic locations. The emphasis at these locations is on convenience and speed, not on comfort or socializing. Many of these locations have little frontage space and limited seating. Customers frequently stand while eating, or they may sit on stools at narrow counters. Even the elite Ginza location has few seats. Some locations have a small ordering and service area on the first floor, with limited seating (still primarily stools rather than tables and chairs) on the second floor. Young people—from teenagers to schoolchildren—are a common sight in Japanese McDonald's restaurants.

In 2006, McDonald's began an extensive makeover aimed at modernizing the entire chain's overall look. Many existing restaurants have already invested in extensive upgrades that feature a cleaner and simpler overall design; less plastic; warmer, muted colors (terra cotta instead of bright red); Wi-fi access; and different types of seating sections, including bar stools for customers who eat alone and family areas with booths and fabric-covered seating. Of course, the golden arches will still play an important role in the modernized design.

Sources: *Golden Arches East: McDonald's in East Asia,* ed. J. L. Watson (Stanford, CA: Stanford University Press, 1997); "A Unique Peak," *Franchise Times* 3, no. 4 (1997), p. 46; P. Gogoi, "Mickey D's McMakeover," *BusinessWeek,* May 15, 2006, pp. 42–43; M. Arndt, "Knock Knock, It's Your Big Mac; From Sao Paulo to Shanghai, McDonald's Is Boosting Growth with Speedy Delivery," *BusinessWeek,* July 23, 2007, p. 36; and C. Walkup, "McD Pins Global Growth on Upgrades to Units, Experience," *Nation's Restaurant News,* August 6, 2007, p. 1.

environment can all communicate symbolic meaning and create an overall aesthetic impression. The meanings attached to environmental symbols and artifacts are culturally embedded, as illustrated in this chapter's Global Feature. Restaurant managers in the United States, for example, know that white tablecloths and subdued lighting symbolically convey full service and relatively high prices, whereas counter service, plastic furnishings, and bright lighting symbolize the opposite. In U.S. office environments, certain cues such as desk size and placement symbolize status and may be used to reinforce professional image.[38]

Signs, symbols, and artifacts are particularly important in forming first impressions and for communicating service concepts. When customers are unfamiliar with a particular service establishment, they look for environmental cues to help them categorize the place and form their expectations. A study of dentists' offices found that consumers use the environment, in particular its style of decoration and level of quality, as a cue to the competence and manner of the service provider.[39] Another interesting study explored the roles of ethnicity and sexual orientation on consumers' interpretation of symbols within consumption environments. Specifically, the study found that people of Jewish descent observe particular symbols in places that encourage them to feel at home and approach those places.[40] The same study found that homosexuals were also drawn to environments that included particular symbols and artifacts that they identified with. In the presence of other symbols, these groups felt unwelcome or even discriminated against.

GUIDELINES FOR PHYSICAL EVIDENCE STRATEGY

To this point in the chapter we have presented ideas, frameworks, and psychological models for understanding the effects of physical evidence and most specifically the effects of the physical facility or servicescape. In this section, we suggest some general guidelines for an effective physical evidence strategy.[41]

Recognize the Strategic Impact of Physical Evidence

Physical evidence can play a prominent role in determining service quality expectations and perceptions. For some organizations, just acknowledging the impact of physical evidence is a major first step. After this step, they can take advantage of the potential of physical evidence and plan strategically.

For physical evidence strategy to be effective, it must be linked clearly to the organization's overall goals and vision. Thus planners must know what those goals are and then determine how the physical evidence strategy can support them. At a minimum, the basic service concept must be defined, the target markets (both internal and external) identified, and the firm's broad vision of its future known. Because many evidence decisions are relatively permanent and costly (particularly servicescape decisions), they must be planned and executed deliberately.

Blueprint the Physical Evidence of Service

The next step is to blueprint the service. Everyone in the organization should be able to see the service process and the existing elements of physical evidence. An effective way to depict service evidence is through the service blueprint. (Service blueprinting was presented in detail in Chapter 9.) Although service blueprints clearly have multiple purposes, they can be particularly useful in visually capturing physical evidence opportunities. People, processes, and physical evidence can all be seen in the blueprint. The actions involved in service delivery are visible, as are the complexity of the process, the points of human interaction that provide evidence opportunities, and the tangible representations present at each step. To make the blueprint even more useful, photographs or videotape of the process can be added to develop a photographic blueprint that provides a vivid picture of physical evidence from the customer's point of view.

Clarify Strategic Roles of the Servicescape

Early in the chapter we discussed the varying roles played by the servicescape and how firms could locate themselves in the typology shown in Table 11.3 to begin to identify their roles. For example, a day care center would locate itself in the "elaborate, interpersonal" cell of the matrix and quickly see that its servicescape decisions would be relatively complex and that the servicescape strategy would have to consider the needs of both the children and the service providers and could impact marketing, organizational behavior, and consumer satisfaction goals.

Sometimes the servicescape may have no role in service delivery or marketing from the customer's point of view, such as in telecommunications services or utilities (although in these cases other forms of physical evidence would still be important). Clarifying the roles played by the servicescape in a particular situation will aid in identifying opportunities and deciding who needs to be consulted in making facility design decisions. Clarifying the strategic role of the servicescape also forces recognition of the importance of the servicescape in creating customer experiences.

Assess and Identify Physical Evidence Opportunities

Once the current forms of evidence and the roles of the servicescape are understood, possible changes and improvements can be identified. One question to ask is, are there missed opportunities to provide service evidence? The service blueprint of an insurance or utility service may show that little if any evidence of service is ever provided to the customer. A strategy might then be developed to provide more evidence of service to show customers exactly what they are paying for. This was the case for a large technology services company that provided a "remote repair service" for its customers. Remote repair service means they were able to anticipate and repair certain technology equipment from afar without the customer actually being aware anything had been done. A blueprint of the service revealed that no physical evidence of the service existed at all. Thus, customers did not appreciate the service they had received nor were they anxious to pay for it. Realizing this, the company developed ways to communicate and provide evidence of the service for customers.

Or it may be discovered that the evidence provided is sending messages that do not enhance the firm's image or goals or that do not match customer expectations. For example, a restaurant might find that its high-price menu cues are not consistent with the design of the restaurant, which suggests "family dining" to its intended market segment. Either the pricing or the facility design would need to be changed, depending on the restaurant's overall strategy.

Another set of questions addresses whether the current physical evidence of service suits the needs and preferences of the target market. To begin answering such questions, the framework for understanding environment–user relationships (Figure 11.1) and the research approaches suggested in this chapter could be employed. And finally, does the evidence strategy take into account the needs (sometimes incompatible) of both customers and employees? This question is particularly relevant in making decisions regarding the servicescape.

Be Prepared to Update and Modernize the Evidence

Some aspects of the evidence, particularly the servicescape, require frequent or at least periodic updating and modernizing. Even if the vision, goals, and objectives of the company do not change, time itself takes a toll on physical evidence, necessitating change and modernization. Clearly, an element of fashion is involved, and over time different colors, designs, and styles may come to communicate different messages. Organizations obviously understand this concept when it comes to advertising strategy, but sometimes they overlook other elements of physical evidence.

Work Cross-Functionally

In presenting itself to the consumer, a service firm is concerned with communicating a desired image, with sending consistent and compatible messages through all forms of evidence, and with providing the type of service evidence the target customers want and can understand. Frequently, however, physical evidence decisions are made over time and by various functions within the organization. For example, decisions regarding employee uniforms may be made by the human resources area, servicescape design decisions may be made by the facilities management group, process design decisions are most frequently made by operations managers, and advertising and pricing decisions may be made by the marketing department. Thus, it is not surprising that the physical evidence of service may at times be less than consistent. A multifunction team approach to physical evidence strategy is often necessary, particularly for making decisions about the servicescape. It has been said that "Facility planning and management . . . is a problem-solving activity that lies on the boundaries between architecture, interior space planning and product design, organizational [and consumer] behavior, planning and environmental psychology."[42]

Summary	In this chapter we explored the roles of physical evidence in forming customer and employee perceptions and shaping customer experiences. Because services are intangible and because they are often produced and consumed at the same time, they can be difficult to comprehend or evaluate before their purchase. The physical evidence of the service thus serves as a primary cue for setting customer expectations before purchase. These tangible cues, particularly the servicescape, also influence customers' responses as they experience the service. Because customers and employees often interact in the servicescape, the physical surroundings also influence employees and the nature of employee–customer interactions. The chapter focused primarily on the servicescape—the physical surroundings or the physical facility where the service is produced, delivered, and consumed. We presented a typology of servicescapes that illustrated their range of complexity and usage. General strategic roles of the servicescape were also described. We offered a general framework for understanding servicescape effects on employee and customer behaviors. The servicescape can affect the approach and avoidance behaviors of individual customers and employees as well as their social interactions. These behavioral responses come about because the physical environment influences people's beliefs or cognitions about the service organization, their feelings or emotions in response to the place, and their actual physiological reactions while in the physical facility. Three categories of environmental dimensions capture the complex nature of the servicescape: ambient conditions; spatial layout and functionality; and signs, symbols, and artifacts. These dimensions affect people's beliefs, emotions, and physical responses, causing them to behave in certain ways while in the servicescape. Given the importance of physical evidence and its potentially powerful influence on both customers and employees, it is important for firms to think strategically about the management of the tangible evidence of service. The impact of physical evidence and design decisions needs to be researched and planned as part of the marketing strategy. The chapter concluded with specific guidelines for physical evidence strategy.

Discussion Questions

1. What is physical evidence, and why have we devoted an entire chapter to it in a marketing text?

2. Describe and give an example of how servicescapes play each of the following strategic roles: package, facilitator, socializer, and differentiator.

3. Imagine that you own an independent copying and printing shop (similar to FedEx Kinko's). In which cell would you locate your business in the typology of servicescapes shown in Table 11.3? What are the implications for designing your physical facility?

4. How can an effective physical evidence strategy help close provider gap 2? Explain.

5. Why are both customers and employees included in the framework for understanding servicescape effects on behavior (Figure 11.1)? What types of behaviors are influenced by the servicescape according to the framework? Think of examples.

6. Using your own experiences, give examples of times when you have been affected cognitively, emotionally, and physiologically by elements of the servicescape (in any service context).

7. Why is everyone not affected in exactly the same way by the servicescape?

8. Describe the physical environment of your favorite restaurant in terms of the three categories of servicescape dimensions: ambient conditions; spatial layout and functionality; and signs, symbols, and artifacts.

9. Imagine that you are serving as a consultant to a local health club. How would you advise the health club to begin the process of developing an effective physical evidence strategy?

Exercises

1. Choose two very different firms (different market segments or service levels) in the same industry. Observe both establishments. Describe the service "package" in both cases. How does the package help distinguish the two firms? Do you believe that the package sets accurate expectations for what the firm delivers? Is either firm overpromising through the manner in which its servicescape (or other types of physical evidence) communicates with customers?

2. Think of a particular service organization (it can be a class project company, the company you work for, or some other organization) for which you believe physical evidence is particularly important in communicating with and satisfying customers. Prepare the text of a presentation you would give to the manager of that organization to convince him or her of the importance of physical evidence in the organization's marketing strategy.

3. Create a photographic blueprint for a service of your choice. Analyze the blueprint from the customer's perspective and suggest possible changes that could improve the service design.

4. Choose a service organization and collect all forms of physical evidence that the organization uses to communicate with its customers. If customers see the firm's facility, also take a photo of the servicescape. Analyze the evidence in terms of compatibility, consistency, and whether it overpromises or underpromises what the firm can deliver.

5. Visit the websites of several service providers. Does the physical evidence of the website portray an image consistent with other forms of evidence provided by the organizations?

Notes

1. Michael Jannini, "Building a Service Brand," presentation at the 2006 *Compete Through Service Symposium,* Arizona State University; C. Yang and D. Brady, "Marriott Hip? Well, It's Trying," *BusinessWeek,* September 26, 2005, pp. 70–72; S. Berfield, "Room Service, Send Up Some Slime; Want a Night with Sponge-Bob? Marriott and Nickelodeon Will Accommodate You," *BusinessWeek,* June 11, 2007, pp. 38; and P. Sanders, "Strange Bedfellows: Marriott, Schrager," *The Wall Street Journal,* June 14, 2007, p. B1.

2. The term *servicescape* used throughout this chapter, and much of the content of this chapter, are based, with permission, on M. J. Bitner, "Servicescapes: The Impact of Physical Surroundings on Customers and Employees," *Journal of Marketing* 56 (April 1992), pp. 57–71. For later contributions to this topic, see *Servicescapes: The Concept of Place in Contemporary Markets,* ed. J. F. Sherry Jr. (Chicago: NTC/Contemporary Publishing Company, 1998); and M. J. Bitner, "The Servicescape," in *Handbook of Services Marketing and Management,* ed. T. A. Swartz and D. Iacobucci (Thousand Oaks, CA: Sage Publications, 2000), pp. 37–50.

3. L. P. Carbone, *Clued In: How to Keep Customers Coming Back Again and Again* (Upper Saddle River, NJ: Prentice Hall, 2004). See also L. L. Berry and N. Bendapudi, "Clueing In Customers," *Harvard Business Review,* February 2003, pp. 100–106.

4. J. H. Gilmore and B. J. Pine II, "The Experience Is the Marketing," *Strategic Horizons,* 2002; B. J. Pine II and J. H. Gilmore, *The Experience Economy: Work Is Theater and Every Business Is a Stage* (Boston: Harvard Business School Press, 1999); and B. H. Schmitt, *Experiential Marketing* (New York: The Free Press, 1999).

5. For reviews of environmental psychology, see D. Stokols and I. Altman, *Handbook of Environmental Psychology* (New York: John Wiley, 1987); S. Saegert and G. H. Winkel, "Environmental Psychology," *Annual Review of Psychology* 41 (1990), pp. 441–477; and E. Sundstrom, P. A. Bell, P. L. Busby, and C. Asmus, "Environmental Psychology 1989–1994," *Annual Review of Psychology* 47 (1996), pp. 485–512.

6. P. Engardio, "India's Talent Gets Loads of TLC," *BusinessWeek,* pp. 52–53, in "The Future of Work," *BusinessWeek* cover story, August 20 and 27, 2007.

7. See M. R. Solomon, "Dressing for the Part: The Role of Costume in the Staging of the Servicescape," in Sherry, *Servicescapes;* and A. Rafaeli, "Dress and Behavior of Customer Contact Employees: A Framework for Analysis," in *Advances in Services Marketing and Management,* vol. 2, ed. T. A. Swartz, D. E. Bowen, and S. W. Brown (Greenwich, CT: JAI Press, 1993), pp. 175–212.

8. M. Bauza, "Employment: Trendy Uniforms a Good Fit: Companies are Altering the Look of Their Signature Clothing," *Pittsburgh Post-Gazette,* November 26, 2006.

9. S. Casey, "Federal Expressive," *www.ecompany.com,* May 2001, pp. 45–48.

10. B. Stanley, "Qantas Flaunts Super-Jumbo Perks," *The Wall Street Journal,* July 25, 2007, p. D3; and S. McCartney, "A Bubble Bath and a Glass of Bubbly—at the Airport," *The Wall Street Journal,* July 10, 2007, p. D1.

11. British Airways' website, www.britishairways.com, accessed September 2007.

12. R. Chittum, "New Concepts in Lodging," *The Wall Street Journal,* October 8, 2003, p. B1.

13. E. Gately, "Washington Mutual Banking on Being Different," *Mesa Tribune,* March 25, 2001, p. B1.

14. www.petsmart.com, 2007; C. M. Dalton, "A Passion for Pets: An Interview with Philip L. Francis, Chairperson and CEO of PetSmart, Inc.," *Business Horizons,* November–December 2005, pp. 469–475; and D. Brady and C. Palmeri, "The Pet Economy," *BusinessWeek,* August 6, 2007, pp. 45–54.

15. Carbone, *Clued In;* Berry and Bendapudi, "Clueing In Customers"; Gilmore and Pine, "Experience Is the Marketing"; Pine and Gilmore, *The Experience Economy;* Schmitt, *Experiential Marketing;* and L. L. Berry, E. A. Wall, and L. P. Carbone, "Service Clues and Customer Assessment of the Service Experience: Lessons from Marketing," *Academy of Management Perspectives,* 20 (2), 2006, pp. 43–57.

16. A. Mehrabian and J. A. Russell, *An Approach to Environmental Psychology* (Cambridge, MA: Massachusetts Institute of Technology, 1974).

17. R. Donovan and J. Rossiter, "Store Atmosphere: An Environmental Psychology Approach," *Journal of Retailing* 58 (Spring 1982), pp. 34–57.

18. D. J. Bennett and J. D. Bennett, "Making the Scene," in *Social Psychology through Symbolic Interactionism,* ed. G. Stone and H. Farberman (Waltham, MA: Ginn-Blaisdell, 1970), pp. 190–196.

19. J. P. Forgas, *Social Episodes* (London: Academic Press, 1979).

20. R. G. Barker, *Ecological Psychology* (Stanford, CA: Stanford University Press, 1968).

21. For a number of excellent papers on this topic spanning a range from toy stores to bridal salons to cybermarketspaces to Japanese retail environments and others, see Sherry, *Servicescapes: The Concept of Place in Contemporary Markets.*

22. J. F. Sherry Jr., "The Soul of the Company Store: Nike Town Chicago and the Emplace Brandscape," in Sherry, *Servicescapes,* pp. 81–108.

23. E. J. Arnould, L. L. Price, and P. Tierney, "The Wilderness Servicescape: An Ironic Commercial Landscape," in Sherry, *Servicescapes,* pp. 403–438.

24. Rosenbaum, "Exploring the Social Supportive Role of Third Places in Consumers' Lives, *Journal of Service Research* 9 (August 2006), pp. 59–72; A. Tombs and J. R. McColl-Kennedy, "Social-Servicescape Conceptual Model," *Marketing Theory* 3, no. 4 (2003), pp. 447–475; and M. S. Rosenbaum, J. Ward, B. A. Walker, and A. L. Ostrom, "A Cup of Coffee with a Dash of Love: An Investigation of Commercial Social Support and Third-Place Attachment," *Journal of Service Research* 10 (August 2007), pp. 43–59.

25. A. Rapoport, *The Meaning of the Built Environment* (Beverly Hills, CA: Sage Publications, 1982); and R. G. Golledge, "Environmental Cognition," in Stokols and Altman, *Handbook of Environmental Psychology,* vol. 1, pp. 131–174.

26. M. P. Gardner and G. Siomkos, "Toward a Methodology for Assessing Effects of In-Store Atmospherics," in *Advances in Consumer Research,* vol. 13, ed. R. J. Lutz (Ann Arbor, MI: Association for Consumer Research, 1986), pp. 27–31.

27. M. J. Bitner, "Evaluating Service Encounters: The Effects of Physical Surroundings and Employee Responses," *Journal of Marketing* 54 (April 1990), pp. 69–82.

28. J. C. Ward, M. J. Bitner, and J. Barnes, "Measuring the Prototypicality and Meaning of Retail Environments," *Journal of Retailing* 68 (Summer 1992) pp. 194–220.

29. See, for example, Mehrabian and Russell, *An Approach to Environmental Psychology;* J. A. Russell and U. F. Lanius, "Adaptation Level and the Affective Appraisal

of Environments," *Journal of Environmental Psychology* 4, no. 2 (1984), pp. 199–235; J. A. Russell and G. Pratt, "A Description of the Affective Quality Attributed to Environments," *Journal of Personality and Social Psychology* 38, no. 2 (1980), pp. 311–322; J. A. Russell and J. Snodgrass, "Emotion and the Environment," in Stokols and Altman, *Handbook of Environmental Psychology,* vol. 1, pp. 245–281; and J. A. Russell, L. M. Ward, and G. Pratt, "Affective Quality Attributed to Environments," *Environment and Behavior* 13 (May 1981), pp. 259–288.

30. See, for example, M. S. Sanders and E. J. McCormick, *Human Factors in Engineering and Design,* 7th ed. (New York: McGraw-Hill, 1993); and G. Salvendy (ed), *Handbook of Human Factors and Ergonomics* (Hoboken, NJ: Wiley 2006).

31. "Empty Nests, Full Pockets," *Brandweek,* September 23, 1996, pp. 36ff; and "Lodging Chain to Give Older Guests a Choice," *The Wall Street Journal,* February 19, 1993, p. B1.

32. Mehrabian and Russell, *An Approach to Environmental Psychology;* Russell and Snodgrass, "Emotion and the Environment."

33. A. Mehrabian, "Individual Differences in Stimulus Screening and Arousability," *Journal of Personality* 45, no. 2 (1977), pp. 237–250.

34. E. Bellman, "In India, a Retailer Finds Key to Success Is Clutter," *The Wall Street Journal,* August 8, 2007, p. A1.

35. For research documenting the effects of music on consumers, see J. Baker, D. Grewal, and A. Parasuraman, "The Influence of Store Environment on Quality Inferences and Store Image," *Journal of the Academy of Marketing Science* 22 (Fall 1994), pp. 328–339; J. C. Chebat, C. Gelinas-Chebat, and P. Filliatrault, "Interactive Effects of Musical and Visual Cues on Time Perception: An Application to Waiting Lines in Banks," *Perceptual and Motor Skills* 77 (1993), pp. 995–1020; L. Dube, J. C. Chebat, and S. Morin, "The Effects of Background Music on Consumers' Desire to Affiliate in Buyer–Seller Interactions," *Psychology and Marketing* 12, no. 4 (1995), pp. 305–319; J. D. Herrington and L. M. Capella, "Effects of Music in Service Environments: A Field Study," *Journal of Services Marketing* 10, no. 2 (1996), pp. 26–41; J. D. Herrington and L. M. Capella, "Practical Applications of Music in Service Settings," *Journal of Services Marketing* 8, no. 3 (1994), pp. 50–65; M. K. Hui, L. Dube, and J. C. Chebat, "The Impact of Music on Consumers' Reactions to Waiting for Services," *Journal of Retailing* 73 (Spring 1997), pp. 87–104; A. S. Matila and J. Wirtz, "Congruency of Scent and Music as a Driver of In-Store Evaluations and Behavior," *Journal of Retailing* 77 (Summer 2001), pp. 273–289; L. Dube and S. Morin, "Background Music Pleasure and Store Evaluation: Intensity Effects and Psychological Mechanisms," *Journal of Business Research* 54 (November 2001), pp. 107–113; J. Bakec, A. Parasuraman, D. Grewal, and G. B. Voss, "The Influence of Multiple Store Environment Cues as Perceived Merchandise Value and Patronage Intentions," *Journal of Marketing* 66 (April 2002), pp. 120–141; and S. Morin. L. Dube, and J. Chebat, "The Role of Pleasant Music in Servicescapes: A Test of the Dual Model of Environmental Perception," *Journal of Retailing* 83, no. 1 (2007), pp. 115–130.

36. For research documenting the effects of scent on consumer responses, see D. J. Mitchell, B. E. Kahn, and S. C. Knasko, "There's Something in the Air: Effects of Congruent and Incongruent Ambient Odor on Consumer Decision Making," *Journal of Consumer Research* 22 (September 1995), pp. 229–238; and E. R. Spangenberg, A. E. Crowley, and P. W. Henderson, "Improving the Store

Environment: Do Olfactory Cues Affect Evaluations and Behaviors?" *Journal of Marketing* 60 (April 1996), pp. 67–80.

37. See J. M. Sulek, M. R. Lind, and A. S. Marucheck, "The Impact of a Customer Service Intervention and Facility Design on Firm Performance," *Management Science* 41, no. 11 (1995), pp. 1763–1773; P. A. Titus and P. B. Everett, "Consumer Wayfinding Tasks, Strategies, and Errors: An Exploratory Field Study," *Psychology and Marketing* 13, no. 3 (1996), pp. 265–290; C. Yoo, J. Park, and D. J. MacInnis, "Effects of Store Characteristics and In-Store Emotional Experiences on Store Attitude," *Journal of Business Research* 42 (1998), pp. 253–263; and K. L. Wakefield and J. G. Blodgett, "The Effect of the Servicescape on Customers' Behavioral Intentions in Leisure Service Settings," *Journal of Services Marketing* 10, no. 6 (1996), pp. 45–61.

38. T. R. V. Davis, "The Influence of the Physical Environment in Offices," *Academy of Management Review* 9, no. 2 (1984), pp. 271–283.

39. J. C. Ward and J. P. Eaton, "Service Environments: The Effect of Quality and Decorative Style on Emotions, Expectations, and Attributions," in *Proceedings of the American Marketing Association Summer Educators' Conference,* eds. R. Achrol and A. Mitchell (Chicago: American Marketing Association 1994), pp. 333–334.

40. M. S. Rosenbaum, "The Symbolic Servicescape: Your Kind Is Welcomed Here," *Journal of Consumer Behaviour* 4, no. 4 (2005), pp. 257–267.

41. This section is adapted from M. J. Bitner, "Managing the Evidence of Service," in *The Service Quality Handbook,* ed. E. E. Scheuing and W. F. Christopher (New York: AMACOM, 1993), pp. 358–370.

42. F. D. Becker, *Workspace* (New York: Praeger, 1981).

Part Five

Delivering and Performing Service

In the gaps model of service quality, provider gap 3 (the service performance gap) is the discrepancy between customer-driven service design and standards and actual service delivery (see the accompanying figure). Even when guidelines exist for performing service well and treating customers correctly, high-quality service performance is not a certainty. Part 5 deals with all the ways in which companies ensure that services are performed according to customer-defined designs and standards.

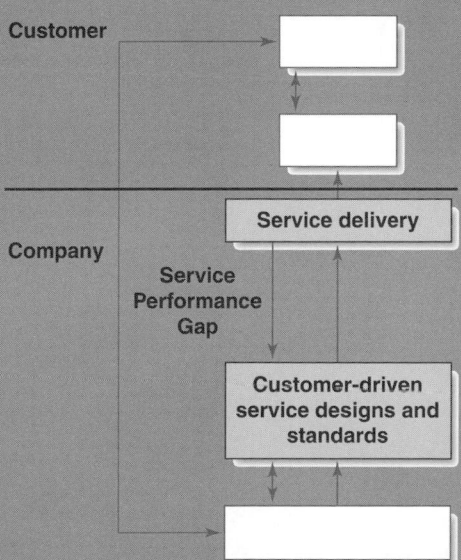

Provider Gap 3

In Chapter 12, we focus on the key roles that employees play in service delivery and strategies that ensure they are effective in their roles. Issues of particular concern include employees who feel in conflict in their position between customers and company management, having the wrong employees, or inadequate technology, inappropriate compensation and recognition, and lack of empowerment and teamwork.

In Chapter 13, we discuss the variability in service performance caused by customers. If customers do not perform appropriately—if they do not follow instructions or if they disturb other customers receiving service at the same time—service quality is jeopardized. Effective service organizations acknowledge the role of customer variability and develop strategies to teach customers to perform their roles appropriately.

Chapter 14 describes service delivery through intermediaries such as retailers, franchisees, agents and brokers, and electronic channels. Although some service companies have control over the delivery channel, many service companies depend on other organizations to provide service to the end customer. For this reason, firms must develop ways to either control or motivate these intermediaries to meet company goals and deliver consistent quality service.

Chapter 15 emphasizes the need to synchronize demand and capacity in service organizations to deliver consistent, high-quality service. Service organizations often face situations of over- or underdemand because they lack inventories to smooth demand. Marketing strategies for managing demand, such as price changes, advertising, promotion, and alternative service offerings, can help this challenge.

Chapter Twelve

Employees' Roles in Service Delivery

This chapter's objectives are to

1. Demonstrate the importance of creating a service culture in which providing excellent service to both internal and external customers is a way of life.
2. Illustrate the pivotal role of service employees in creating customer satisfaction and service quality.
3. Identify the challenges inherent in boundary-spanning roles.
4. Provide examples of strategies for creating customer-oriented service delivery through hiring the right people, developing employees to deliver service quality, providing needed support systems, and retaining the best service employees.

Employees Are the Service and the Brand

Noted service expert Leonard Berry has documented that investments in employees are key drivers of sustained business success in companies as diverse as Charles Schwab, Midwest Express, USAA Insurance, and Chick-fil-A.[1] Why is this true? Why do these companies choose to invest heavily in their employees?

For clues, consider the following true stories:

- On a long overseas Singapore Airlines flight, a restless toddler repeatedly dropped his pacifier. Every time the child would cry, and someone (the mother, another passenger, or a flight attendant) would retrieve the pacifier. Finally, one of the attendants picked up the pacifier, attached it to a ribbon, and sewed it to the child's shirt. The child and mother were happy, and passengers seated nearby gave the attendant a standing ovation.[2]

- A phone associate at Universal Card Services received a call from a customer whose wife, suffering from Alzheimer's disease, had vanished. The man hoped that he could find his wife through tracing her use of her Universal Card. The phone associate placed a hold on the card and arranged to be called personally the moment there was any activity on the card. When it happened, about a week later, the associate contacted the husband, the doctor, and the police, who were then able to assist the missing woman and get her home.[3]

Service employees directly impact customers' satisfaction.

- At the Fairmont Hotel in San Francisco, a computer programmer made a room reservation for a discounted price. On arrival he discovered that all rooms were filled. The front desk clerk responded by sending him to the Sheraton and picking up his room charge, which was more than twice what he would have paid the Fairmont. He also paid for the guest's parking fee at the Fairmont and taxi fare to the new hotel, and threw in a free meal at the Fairmont as well.[4]

These stories illustrate the important roles played by service employees in creating satisfied customers and in building customer relationships. The frontline service providers in each example are enormously important to the success of the organizations they represent. They are responsible for understanding customer needs and for interpreting customer requirements in real time (as suggested by the accompanying photo). Leonard Berry has documented that in case after case, companies that achieve sustained service success all recognize the critical importance of their employees.[5]

In this chapter we focus on service employees and human resource practices that facilitate delivery of quality services. The assumption is that even when customer expectations are well understood (gap 1) and services have been designed and specified to conform to those expectations (gap 2), there may still be discontinuities in service quality when the service is not delivered as specified. These discontinuities are labeled gap 3—the *service performance gap*—in the service quality framework. Because employees frequently deliver or perform the service, human resource issues are a major cause of this gap. By focusing on the critical role of service employees and by developing strategies that lead to effective customer-oriented service, organizations can begin to close the service performance gap.

The failure to deliver services as designed and specified can result from a number of employee and human performance factors: ineffective recruitment of service-oriented employees, role ambiguity and role conflict among contact employees, poor employee-technology-job fit, inappropriate evaluation and compensation systems, and lack of empowerment and teamwork.

SERVICE CULTURE

Before addressing the role of the employee in service delivery, we should look at the bigger picture. The behavior of employees in an organization will be heavily influenced by the culture of that organization, or the pervasive norms and values that shape individual and group behavior. *Corporate culture* has been defined as "the pattern of shared values and beliefs that give the members of an organization meaning, and provide them with the rules for behavior in the organization."[6] *Culture* has been defined more informally as "the way we do things around here."

To understand at a personal level what corporate culture is, think of different places you have worked or organizations you have been a member of, such as churches, fraternities, schools, or associations. Your behavior and the behaviors of others were no doubt influenced by the underlying values, norms, and culture of the organization. Even when you first interview for a new job, you can begin to get a sense of the firm's culture through talking to a number of employees and observing behavior. Once you are on the job, your formal training as well as informal observation of behavior will work together to give you a better picture of the organization's culture.

Experts have suggested that a customer-oriented, service-oriented organization will have at its heart a *service culture,* defined as "a culture where an appreciation for good service exists, and where giving good service to internal as well as ultimate, external customers is considered a natural way of life and one of the most important norms by everyone."[7] This very rich definition has many implications for employee behaviors. First, a service culture exists if there is an "appreciation for good service." This phrase does not mean that the company has an advertising campaign that stresses the importance of service, but people know that good service is appreciated and valued. A second important point in this definition is that good service is given to internal as well as external customers.[8] It is not enough to promise excellent service to final customers; all people within the organization deserve the same kind of service. Finally, in a service culture good service is "a way of life" and it comes naturally because it is an important norm of the organization. Service culture is critical to the creation of a customer-focused organization and has been identified as a source of competitive advantage in companies.[9]

Exhibiting Service Leadership

A strong service culture begins with leaders in the organization who demonstrate a passion for service excellence. Leonard Berry suggests that leaders of successful service firms tend to have similar core values, such as integrity, joy, and respect, and they "infuse those values into the fabric of the organization."[10] Leadership does not consist of bestowing a set of commands from a thick rulebook but, rather, the regular and consistent demonstration of one's values. Employees are more likely to embrace a service culture when they see management living out these values. Espoused values—what managers *say* the values are—tend to have less impact on employees than enacted values—what employees believe the values to be because of what they observe management actually *doing*.[11] That is, culture is what employees perceive that management *really* believes, and employees gain an understanding of what is important in the organization through the daily experiences they have with those people in key roles throughout the organization.

Developing a Service Culture

A service culture cannot be developed overnight, and there is no magic, easy way to sustain a service culture. The human resource and internal marketing practices discussed later in the chapter can help develop a service culture over time. If, however, an organization has a culture rooted in product-, operations-, or government regulation–oriented traditions, no single strategy will magically change it into a service culture. Hundreds of little (but significant) factors, not just one or two big factors, are required to build and sustain a service culture.[12] Successful companies such as Yellow Transportation and IBM Global Services have all found that it takes years of consistent, concerted effort to build a service culture and to shift an organization from its old patterns to new ways of doing business. Even for companies such as FedEx,

Although international markets offer tremendous opportunities for growth, many companies find significant challenges when they attempt to transport their services to other countries. Services depend on people, are often delivered by people, and involve the interaction between employees and customers. Differences in values, norms of behavior, language, and even the definition of service become evident quickly and have implications for training, hiring, and incentives that can ultimately affect the success of the international expansion. Companies with strong service cultures are faced with the question of whether to try to replicate their culture and values in other countries or to adapt significantly. A few examples illustrate different approaches.

McDONALD'S APPROACH

McDonald's has been very successful in its international expansion. In some ways it has remained very "American" in everything it does—people around the world want an American experience when they go to McDonald's. However, the company is sensitive to cultural differences as well. This subtle blending of the "McDonald's" way with adaptations to cultural nuances has resulted in great success. One way that McDonald's maintains its standards is through its Hamburger University, which is required training for *all* McDonald's employees worldwide before they can become managers. Each year approximately 5,000 employees from more than 100 countries enroll and attend the Advanced Operations Course at HU,

located in Oak Brook, Illinois. The curriculum is 80 percent devoted to communications and human relations skills. Because of the international scope of McDonald's, translators and electronic equipment enable professors to teach and communicate in 28 languages at one time. The result is that all managers in all countries have the same "ketchup in their veins," and the restaurant's basic human resources and operating philosophies remain fairly stable from operation to operation. Certain adaptations in decor, menu, and other areas of cultural differences are then allowed (see the Global Feature in Chapter 11 for some specific examples).

UPS'S EXPERIENCE

UPS has a strong culture built on employee productivity, highly standardized service delivery processes, and structured training. Their brown trucks and uniforms are instantly recognizable in the United States. In fact, in 2002 UPS launched the largest and most aggressive television and print advertising campaign in its 100-year history around the tag line, "What Can Brown Do for You?" As it expanded into countries across Europe, UPS was surprised by some of the challenges of managing a global workforce. Here are some of the surprises: indignation in France, when drivers were told they could not have wine with lunch; protests in Britain, when drivers' dogs were banned from delivery trucks; and dismay in Spain, when it was found the brown UPS trucks resembled the local hearses.

Charles Schwab, Disney, and the Ritz-Carlton that started with a strong service and customer focus, sustaining their established service cultures still takes constant attention to hundreds of details.

Transporting a Service Culture

Transporting a service culture through international business expansion is also very challenging. Attempting to "export" a corporate culture to another country creates additional issues. For instance, will the organization's service culture clash with a different *national* culture? If there is a clash, is it over *what* the actual values are, or over *how* they are to be enacted? If the issue is over what the values are, and they are core values critical to the firm's competitive advantage, then perhaps the company cannot be successful in that setting. If the issue is over how the values are enacted, then perhaps some service practices can be modified in the new setting. To illustrate, as discussed in Chapter 10, Four Seasons Hotels has created seven globally uniform "SERVICE" standards that it expects of all its employees throughout the world. The company has also identified several core values that they believe transcend national culture. One such value is to anticipate guests' needs. This value has been enacted in the United States by leaving a coffeepot on the table in the hotel restaurant so that guests can help themselves whenever they like. However, when Four Seasons opened a hotel in Paris, it decided to never leave a coffeepot on restaurant tables; doing so would

DISNEY IN EUROPE

When Disney first expanded into Europe by opening Disneyland Paris, it also faced challenges and surprises. The highly structured, scripted, and customer-oriented approach that Disney used in the United States was not easily duplicated with European employees. In particular, the smiling, friendly, always customer-focused behaviors of Disney's U.S. workforce did not suit the experience and values of young French employees. In attempting to transport the Disney culture and experience to Europe, the company confronted clashing values and norms of behavior in the workplace that made the expansion difficult. Customers also needed to be "trained" in the Disney way—not all cultures are comfortable with waiting in long lines, for example. And not all cultures treat their children the same. For example, in the United States, families will spend lots of money at Disneyland on food, toys, and other things that their children "must" have. Some European cultures view this behavior as highly indulgent, so families will visit the park without buying much beyond the ticket for admission.

A U.S. LAW FIRM GOES TO THE UNITED KINGDOM

The professions such as law and medicine have well-established and quite unique practices across cultures. Pay rates, work styles, and business models can be quite different. So what happens when a law firm seeks to expand its services to another country? Unlike many U.S. law firms that tend to populate their international offices with American lawyers, Weil, Gotshal, and Manges, a New York firm, opened its offices in London by hiring primarily British solicitors who would function as a "firm within a firm." One of the biggest challenges was how to blend the very different American and British legal cultures. First, the U.S. lawyers at Weil, Gotshal, and Manges tend to be workaholics—commonly billing 2,500 hours a year, whereas in London a partner would bill a respectable 1,500 hours. Pay differences were also obvious—$650,000 on average for London partners, $900,000 for Americans. Conflict, rather than synergy, sometimes resulted from the deeply rooted cultural differences. Despite the challenges, the London office has done quite well; the office now has more than 110 lawyers, has become the second largest of the firm's worldwide offices, and received the "U.S. Law Firm of the Year in London" award in 2004.

Sources: www.mcdonalds.com, accessed October 2007; D. Milbank, "Can Europe Deliver?" *The Wall Street Journal*, September 30, 1994, pp. R15, R23; P. M. Barrett, "Joining the Stampede to Europe, Law Firm Suffers a Few Bruises," *The Wall Street Journal*, April 27, 1999, p. A1; and www.weil.com, accessed October 2007.

not be received favorably by French customers, who generally believe one should not have to pour coffee oneself. Four Seasons did not alter other practices; it continued, for example, its employee-of-the-month program as a way to provide recognition for exceptional service, even though such programs are not generally offered in France.[13] These standards and values reflect Four Seasons' attempt to transport its service culture across national borders, but management is keenly aware that they need to carefully consider how these values are enacted in each hotel.

Although tremendous opportunities exist in the global marketplace, the many legal, cultural, and language barriers become particularly evident for services that depend on human interaction. Our Global Feature highlights some of the issues and experiences of several companies as they attempt to transport their service cultures.

THE CRITICAL ROLE OF SERVICE EMPLOYEES

An often-heard quotation about service organizations goes like this: "In a service organization, if you're not serving the customer, you'd better be serving someone who is."[14] People—frontline employees and those supporting them from behind the scenes—are critical to the success of any service organization. The importance of people in the marketing of services is captured in the *people* element of the services marketing mix, which we described in Chapter 1 as *all the human actors who play a part in service delivery and thus influence the buyer's perceptions; namely, the firm's personnel, the customer, and other customers in the service environment.*

The key focus in this chapter is on customer-contact service employees because:

- They *are* the service.
- They *are* the organization in the customer's eyes.
- They *are* the brand.
- They *are* marketers.

In many cases, the contact employee *is the service*—there is nothing else. For example, in most personal and professional services (like haircutting, personal trainers, child care, limousine services, counseling, and legal services) the contact employee provides the entire service singlehandedly. The offering *is* the employee. Thus, investing in the employee to improve the service parallels making a direct investment in the improvement of a manufactured product.

Even if the contact employee does not perform the service entirely, he or she may still *personify the firm in the customer's eyes.* All the employees of a law firm or health clinic—from the professionals who provide the service to the receptionists and office staff—represent the firm to the client, and everything these individuals do or say can influence perceptions of the organization. Even off-duty employees, such as flight attendants or restaurant employees on a break, reflect on the organizations they represent. If they are unprofessional or make rude remarks about or to customers, customers' perceptions of the organization will suffer even though the employee is not on duty. The Disney Corporation insists that its employees maintain "onstage" attitudes and behaviors whenever they are in front of the public; employees may relax these behaviors only when they are truly behind the scenes or "backstage" in underground tunnels where guests cannot see them in their off-duty times.

Service employees *are the brand.* A Merrill Lynch financial advisor, a Nordstrom sales associate, a Southwest Airlines flight attendant—in each case, the primary image that a customer has of the firm is formed by the interactions the customer has with the employees of that firm. A customer sees Merrill Lynch as a good provider of financial services if the employees she interacts with are knowledgeable, understanding, and concerned about her financial situation and goals. Similarly, a customer sees Nordstrom as a professional and empathetic company because of interactions he has with its sales associates. Even in a nonservice setting, Audi, an automobile manufacturer, recognizes the importance of its employees in representing and reinforcing the brand image of the company. As a result, Audi recruits service personnel at all levels whose psychological traits parallel and support the Audi image.[15] For example, Audi looks to hire employees who are not afraid to develop a personal relationship with customers. When looking for a technician, they are not just looking for someone who repairs cars well but also someone who is inclined to spend time interacting with customers and demonstrating empathy—characteristics that they want customers to associate with Audi. At Audi the brand image is not just built and maintained by the cars themselves and the advertising: it is a function of the people who work at Audi. Strategies such as Audi's that recognize the power of employees to create the brand have been referred to as "branded customer service."[16]

Because contact employees represent the organization and can directly influence customer satisfaction, they *perform the role of marketers.* They physically embody the product and are walking billboards from a promotional standpoint. Some service employees may also perform more traditional selling roles. For example, bank tellers are often called on to cross-sell bank products, a departure from the traditional teller role of focusing on operational functions only. Whether acknowledged or not, whether actively selling or not, service employees perform marketing functions. They can perform these functions well, to the organization's advantage, or poorly, to the organization's detriment. In this chapter we examine frameworks, tools, and strategies for ensuring that service employees perform their marketing functions well.

The Services Triangle

Services marketing is about promises—promises made and promises kept to customers. A strategic framework known as the *services triangle* (illustrated in Figure 12.1) visually reinforces the importance of people in the ability of firms to keep their promises and succeed in building customer relationships.[17] The triangle shows the three interlinked groups that work together to develop, promote, and deliver services. These key players are labeled on the points of the triangle: the *company* (or SBU or department or "management"), the *customers,* and the *providers.* Providers can be the firm's employees, subcontractors, or outsourced entities who actually deliver the company's services. Between these three points on the triangle, three types of marketing must be successfully carried out for a service to succeed: external marketing, interactive marketing, and internal marketing.

On the right side of the triangle are the *external marketing* efforts that the firm engages in to develop its customers' expectations and make promises to customers regarding what is to be delivered. Anything or anyone that communicates to the customer before service delivery can be viewed as part of this external marketing function. But external marketing is just the beginning for services marketers: promises made must be kept. On the bottom of the triangle is what has been termed *interactive marketing* or *real-time marketing.* Here is where promises are kept or broken by the firm's employees, subcontractors, or agents. Those people representing the organization are critical at this juncture. If promises are not kept, customers become dissatisfied and eventually leave. The left side of the triangle suggests the critical role played by *internal marketing.* Management engages in these activities to aid the providers in their ability to deliver on the service promise: recruiting, training, motivating,

FIGURE 12.1
**The Services
Marketing Triangle**

Sources: Adapted from
M. J. Bitner, "Building
Service Relationships: It's
All about Promises," *Journal
of the Academy of Marketing
Science* 23 (Fall 1995),
pp. 246–251; C. Gronroos,
*Service Management and
Marketing: A Customer
Relationship Management
Approach,* 2nd ed. (West Sussex,
England: John Wiley and
Sons, Ltd., 2000), p. 55; and
P. Kotler and K. L. Keller,
Marketing Management, 12th
ed. (Upper Saddle River, NJ:
Pearson Prentice Hall, 2006),
p. 412.

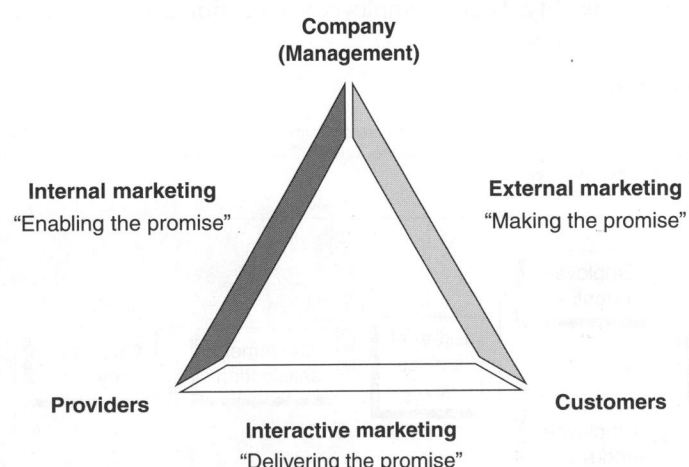

rewarding, and providing equipment and technology. Unless service employees are able and willing to deliver on the promises made, the firm will not be successful, and the services triangle will collapse.

All three sides of the triangle are essential to complete the whole, and the sides of the triangle should be aligned. That is, what is promised through external marketing should be the same as what is delivered; and the enabling activities inside the organization should be aligned with what is expected of service providers. Strategies for aligning the triangle, particularly the strategies associated with internal marketing, are the subject of this chapter.

Employee Satisfaction, Customer Satisfaction, and Profits

Satisfied employees make for satisfied customers (and satisfied customers can, in turn, reinforce employees' sense of satisfaction in their jobs). Some researchers have even gone so far as to suggest that unless service employees are happy in their jobs, customer satisfaction will be difficult to achieve.[18]

Through their research with customers and employees in bank branches, Benjamin Schneider and David Bowen have shown that both a *climate for service* and a *climate for employee well-being* are highly correlated with overall customer perceptions of service quality.[19] That is, both service climate and human resource management experiences that *employees* have within their organizations are reflected in how *customers* experience the service. In a similar vein, Sears found customer satisfaction to be strongly related to employee turnover. In its stores with the highest customer satisfaction, employee turnover was 54 percent, whereas in stores with the lowest customer satisfaction, turnover was 83 percent.[20] Other research suggests that employees who feel they are treated fairly by their organizations will treat customers better, resulting in greater customer satisfaction.[21]

The underlying logic connecting employee satisfaction and loyalty to customer satisfaction and loyalty and ultimately profits is illustrated by the *service profit chain* shown in Figure 12.2.[22] In earlier chapters we focused on customer satisfaction and retention; here we focus on employee issues. The service profit chain suggests that there are critical linkages among internal service quality; employee satisfaction/productivity; the value of services provided to the customer; and ultimately customer satisfaction, retention, and profits.

Service profit chain researchers are careful to point out that the model does not suggest causality. That is, employee satisfaction does not *cause* customer satisfaction;

FIGURE 12.2 **The Service Profit Chain**

Source: Adapted and Reprinted by permission of *Harvard Business Review* an excerpt from J. L. Heskett, T. O. Jones, G. W. Loveman, W. E. Sasser Jr., and L. A. Schlesinger, "Putting the Service-Profit Chain to Work," *Harvard Business Review* 72 (March–April 1994), pp. 164–174. Copyright © 1994 by The Harvard Business School Publishing Corporation; all rights reserved.

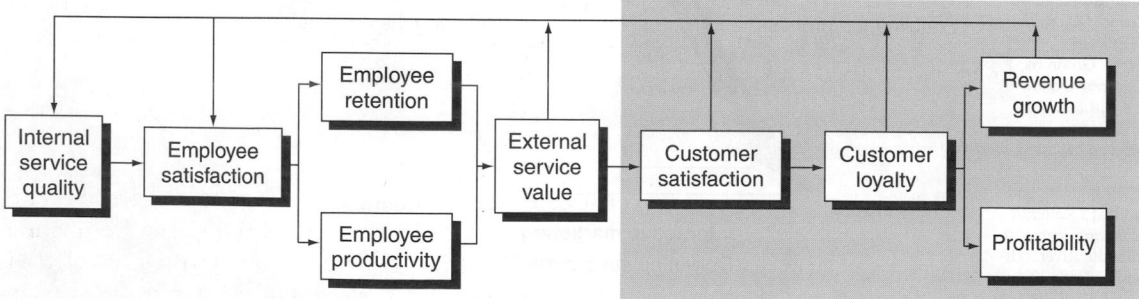

rather the two are interrelated and feed off each other.[23] The model does imply that companies that exhibit high levels of success on the elements of the model will be more successful and profitable than those that do not. This finding is borne out in other research, which reports that companies that manage people right will outperform by 30 to 40 percent companies that do not.[24] Studies have found that *Fortune* magazine's list of the "100 Best Companies to Work For in America" deliver higher average annual returns (more than double over the past decade!) to shareholders than do companies making up the Standard and Poor's 500.[25]

The Effect of Employee Behaviors on Service Quality Dimensions

Customers' perceptions of service quality will be affected by the customer-oriented behaviors of employees.[26] In fact, all five dimensions of service quality (reliability, responsiveness, assurance, empathy, and tangibles) can be influenced directly by service employees.

Delivering the service as promised—*reliability*—is often totally within the control of frontline employees. Even in the case of automated services (such as ATMs, automated ticketing machines, or self-serve and pay gasoline pumps), behind-the-scenes employees are critical for making sure all the systems are working properly. When services fail or errors are made, employees are essential for setting things right and using their judgment to determine the best course of action for service recovery.

Frontline employees directly influence customer perceptions of *responsiveness* through their personal willingness to help and their promptness in serving customers. Consider the range of responses you receive from different retail store clerks when you need help finding a particular item of clothing. One employee may ignore your presence, whereas another offers to help you search and calls other stores to locate the item. One may help you immediately and efficiently, whereas another may move slowly in accommodating even the simplest request.

The *assurance* dimension of service quality is highly dependent on employees' ability to communicate their credibility and to inspire the customer's trust and confidence in the firm. The reputation of the organization will help, but in the end, individual employees with whom the customer interacts confirm and build trust in the organization or detract from its reputation and ultimately destroy trust. For startup or relatively unknown organizations, credibility, trust, and confidence will be tied totally to employee actions.

It is difficult to imagine how an organization would deliver "caring, individualized attention" to customers independent of its employees. *Empathy* implies that employees will pay attention, listen, adapt, and be flexible in delivering what individual customers need.[27] For example, research documents that when employees are customer oriented, have good rapport with customers, and exhibit perceptive and attentive listening skills, customers will evaluate the service more highly and be more likely to return.[28] Employee appearance and dress are important aspects of the *tangibles* dimension of quality, along with many other factors that are independent of service employees (the service facility, decor, brochures, signage, and so on).

BOUNDARY-SPANNING ROLES

Our focus in this chapter is on frontline service employees who interact directly with customers, although much of what is described and recommended can be applied to internal service employees as well. The frontline service employees are referred to as *boundary spanners* because they operate at the organization's boundary. As

FIGURE 12.3
The Critical Roles of Boundary Spanners

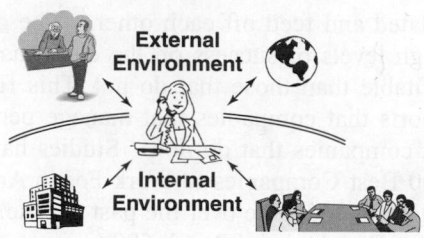

External Environment

Internal Environment

indicated in Figure 12.3, boundary spanners provide a link between the external customer and environment and the internal operations of the organization. They serve a critical function in understanding, filtering, and interpreting information and resources to and from the organization and its external constituencies.

Who are these boundary spanners? What types of people and positions comprise critical boundary-spanning roles? Their skills and experience cover the full spectrum of jobs and careers. In industries such as fast food, hotel, telecommunication, and retail, boundary spanners are generally the least skilled, lowest-paid employees in the organization. They are order-takers, front-desk employees, telephone operators, store clerks, truck drivers, and delivery people. In other industries, boundary spanners are well-paid, highly educated professionals—for example, doctors, lawyers, accountants, consultants, architects, and teachers.

No matter what the level of skill or pay, boundary-spanning positions are often high-stress jobs. In addition to mental and physical skills, these positions require extraordinary levels of emotional labor, frequently demand an ability to handle interpersonal and interorganizational conflict, and call on the employee to make real-time trade-offs between quality and productivity on the job. These stresses and trade-offs can result in failure to deliver services as specified, which widens the service performance gap.

Emotional Labor

The term *emotional labor* was coined by Arlie Hochschild to refer to the labor that goes beyond the physical or mental skills needed to deliver quality service.[29] In general, boundary-spanning service employees are expected to align their displayed emotions with organizationally desired emotions via their use of emotional labor.[30] Such labor includes delivering smiles, making eye contact, showing sincere interest, and engaging in friendly conversation with people who are essentially strangers and who may or may not ever be seen again. Friendliness, courtesy, empathy, and responsiveness directed toward customers all require huge amounts of emotional labor from the frontline employees who shoulder this responsibility for the organization. Emotional labor draws on people's feelings (often requiring them to suppress their true feelings) to be effective in their jobs. A frontline service employee who is having a bad day or is not feeling just right is still expected to put on the face of the organization when dealing with customers. One of the clearest examples of emotional labor is the story (probably apocryphal) of the flight attendant who was approached by a businessman who said, "Let's have a smile." "Okay," she replied, "I'll tell you what, first you smile and then I'll smile, okay?" He smiled. "Good," she said, "Now hold that for 15 hours," and then walked away.[31]

Many of the strategies we will discuss later in the chapter can help organizations and employees deal with the realities of emotional labor on the job. For the organization, such strategies include carefully selecting people who can handle emotional stress, training them in needed skills (like listening and problem solving), and teaching or giving them coping abilities and strategies (via job rotation, scheduled breaks, teamwork, or other techniques).[32] Our Strategy Insight describes additional emotional labor strategies that service firms employ.

Sources of Conflict

Frontline employees often face interpersonal and interorganizational conflicts on the job. Their frustration and confusion can, if left unattended, lead to stress, job dissatisfaction, a diminished ability to serve customers, and burnout.[33] Because they represent the customer to the organization and often need to manage a number of customers simultaneously, frontline employees inevitably have to deal with conflicts, including person/role conflicts, organization/client conflicts, and interclient conflicts, as discussed in the next sections.[34]

Person/Role Conflict

In some situations, boundary spanners feel conflict between what they are asked to do and their own personalities, orientations, or values. In a society such as the United States, where equality and individualism are highly valued, service workers may feel role conflict when they are required to subordinate their feelings or beliefs, as when they are asked to live by the motto "The customer is always right—even when he is wrong." Sometimes there is a conflict between role requirements and the self-image or self-esteem of the employee. An Israeli service expert provides a classic example from that culture:

> In Israel, for instance, most buses are operated by one man, the driver, who is also responsible for selling tickets. No trays are installed in buses for the transferring of bus fare from passenger to driver, and the money is transferred directly. Bus drivers often complain about the humiliating experience of having to stretch out their hands like beggars in order to collect the fare. Another typical case in Israeli buses is when money changes hands and a coin falls down accidentally onto the bus floor. The question, who will bend down to lift the coin, the driver or the passenger, clearly reflects the driver's role conflict.[35]

Whoever stoops to pick up the coin is indicating subservient status.

Person/role conflict also arises when employees are required to wear specific clothing or change some aspect of their appearance to conform to the job requirements. A young lawyer, just out of school, may feel an internal conflict with his new role when his employer requires him to cut his hair and trade his casual clothes for a three-piece suit.

Organization/Client Conflict

A more common type of conflict for frontline service employees is the conflict between their two bosses, the organization and the individual customer. Service employees are typically rewarded for following certain standards, rules, and procedures. Ideally these rules and standards are customer based, as described in Chapter 10. When they are not, or when a customer makes excessive demands, the employee has to choose whether to follow the rules or satisfy the demands. To illustrate, management at an accounting firm may expect an employee to prepare tax returns quickly to maximize revenues during the short tax preparation season. However, the employee's other boss—the customer—may expect personalized attention and a significant amount of her time in preparing the return.[36] The organization/client conflict is greatest when the employee believes the organization is wrong in its policies and must decide whether to

Strategy Insight Strategies for Managing Emotional Labor

Customer contact employees in service positions are often required to display (or, conversely, to withhold display of) a variety of emotions. Such employees are increasingly being required to invest personal identity and expression into their work in many situations. The following description suggests how the experience of the service employee, even in the most routine of occupations, is markedly different from that of the traditional manufacturing worker:

> The assembly-line worker could openly hate his job, despise his supervisor, and even dislike his coworkers, and while this might be an unpleasant state of affairs, if he [completes] his assigned tasks efficiently, his attitude [is] his own problem. For the service worker, inhabiting the job means, at the very least, pretending to like it, and, at most, actually bringing his whole self into the job, liking it, and genuinely caring about the people with whom he interacts.*

Emotional labor occurs more often when the job requires frequent contact and long durations of voice contact or face-to-face contact with customers. These employees often need emotional management to deal with such situations. Later in this chapter we suggest many strategies for organizations to create an environment that helps employees deal with the realities of emotional labor on the job. Here we present some specific strategies some firms use to more directly support employee efforts to manage their emotions in the face of demanding, obnoxious, or unruly customers.

SCREENING FOR EMOTIONAL LABOR ABILITIES

Many firms look to hire employees who are well suited to meet the emotional labor requirements of the job. Dungarvin, an organization that provides a variety of services to people who have mental and physical disabilities, displays a realistic job preview on its website to indicate to prospective employees the emotional labor requirements. In doing so, Dungarvin's intent is to identify applicants who are comfortable with the emotional demands required of employees who must regularly interact with clients with special needs. Call centers often provide job candidates with a realistic job preview, in part, to allow a prospective employee to gauge if he or she is well suited to exert the emotional labor required to interact with customers—often frustrated and unhappy ones—on a continual basis. These simulated customer contact exercises also allow the company to assess the level of friendliness and warmth perspective candidates naturally communicate. Such practices help in identifying employees whose values, background, and personalities match the job's emotional labor requirements.

TEACHING EMOTIONAL MANAGEMENT SKILLS AND APPROPRIATE BEHAVIORS

Most customer contact employees are taught that they need to be courteous to customers. However, customers have no obligation to return empathy or courtesy. In situations in which customers exercise the privilege of "the customer is always right," employees face real challenges in suppressing their true feelings. Seldom do firms provide much training to assist employees in facing these challenges. Arlie Hochschild identifies two forms of emotional labor: *surface acting,* in which employees pretend to feel emotions that are not really present and, in doing so, and could involve both suppression of felt emotions and faking of unfelt emotions; and *deep acting,* in which employees attempt to experience the real feelings they are expected (or required) to express to the customer, including the active invocation of thoughts, images, and memories to induce the associated emotion. Retail store clerks and airline flight attendants are often encouraged to engage in deep-acting strategies such as imagining that the client is a friend or that the passenger is a frightened little child flying for the first time. Companies may also train employees in how to avoid absorbing a customer's bad mood, perhaps by having employees spend hours role-playing to suppress their natural

accommodate the client and risk losing a job, or to follow the policies. These conflicts are especially severe when service employees depend directly on the customer for income. For example, employees who depend on tips or commissions are likely to face greater levels of organization/client conflict because they have even greater incentives to identify with the customer.

reaction to return negative customer emotions with their own negative emotions.

CAREFULLY FASHIONING THE PHYSICAL WORK ENVIRONMENT

As we discussed in Chapter 11, the environment in which the service is delivered can have an impact on employee behaviors and emotions. MedAire, a company that provides telephone consultation to airlines when medical emergencies arise on flights, regularly has employees in the midst of life-threatening situations. To reduce the stress that MedAire employees face on a daily basis, the company designed its Tempe, Arizona, office with an open floor plan so that all employees are able to look through windows to see trees, grass, and cars driving by. Taking this idea one step further, JetBlue Airways allows its reservation agents to work from home rather than requiring them to sit all day in an office call center.

ALLOWING EMPLOYEES TO VENT

Employees who must exert emotional labor often need to have an outlet to let off steam. Allowing employees to vent lets them get rid of their frustrations. If such venting is done in a group setting, it provides emotional support and encouragement, allows employees to see that others are experiencing the same problems, and delivers a message to employees that the company is aware of and acknowledges the emotional contribution that they have made. RitzCarlton, Wal-Mart, and other companies regularly set aside time for such venting. In addition to the cathartic benefit this experience can provide, other employees may reveal coping strategies that they have found useful.

GIVING EMPLOYEES A BREAK

In situations in which employees have extended voice or face-to-face contact with customers, a particularly helpful strategy is to allow them a short break to regroup. Many companies with toll-free call centers rotate employees into different positions throughout the day so that they do not spend the entire time on the telephone with customers. Customer contact employees can be reenergized and refreshed after spending a little time away from demanding or difficult situations, even if they take only a few minutes to finish paperwork or complete some other job responsibility. One call center in Australia has a pool table near the employee work area and plays movies while employees work at their desk to reduce the stress of interacting with customers.

HANDING OFF DEMANDING CUSTOMERS TO MANAGERS

Some customers may be too much for an employee to handle. In such situations, to alleviate pressure on the customer contact employee, firms may shift responsibility for the interaction to managers. Wing Zone, a restaurant chain specializing in chicken wings, understands the stress that angry customers can cause on employees, many of whom are college students. A majority of the company's orders are taken over the phone, and employees—particularly those with little experience—are trained to simply hand off demanding customers to the nearest manager. And a manager who is unsuccessful in handling the situation is encouraged to direct such customers to the corporate office via a toll-free number.

*Quoted from C. L. Macdonald and C. Sirianni, *Working in the Service Society*. (Philadelphia: Temple University Press, 1996), p. 4.

Sources: A. Hochschild, *The Managed Heart: Commercialization of Human Feeling* (Berkeley: University of California Press, 1983); B. F. Ashforth and R. H. Humphrey, "Emotional Labor in Service Roles: The Influence of Identity," *Academy of Management Review* 18 (1993), p. 88–115; S. D. Pugh, "Service with a Smile: Emotional Contagion in the Service Encounter," *Academy of Management Journal* 44, no. 5 (2001), pp. 1018–1027; A. A. Grandey, "When 'The Show Must Go On': Surface Acting and Deep Acting as Determinants of Emotional Exhaustion and Peer-Rated Service Delivery," *Academy of Management Journal* 46, no. 1 (2003), pp. 86–96; and T. Hennig-Thurau, M. Groth, M. Paul, and D. D. Gremler, "Are All Smiles Created Equal? How Employee-Customer Emotional Contagion and Emotional Labor Impact Service Relationships," *Journal of Marketing* 70 (July 2006), pp. 58–73.

Interclient Conflict

Sometimes conflict occurs for boundary spanners when incompatible expectations and requirements arise from two or more customers. This situation occurs most often when the service provider is serving customers in turn (a bank teller, a ticketing agent, a doctor) or is serving many customers simultaneously (teachers, entertainers).

When serving customers in turn, the provider may satisfy one customer by spending additional time, customizing the service, and being very flexible in meeting the customer's needs. Meanwhile, waiting customers may become dissatisfied because their needs are not being met in a timely way. Beyond the timing issue, different clients may prefer different modes of service delivery. Having to serve one client who prefers personal recognition and a degree of familiarity in the presence of another client who is all business and would prefer little interpersonal interaction can also create conflict for the employee.

When serving many customers at the same time, employees often find it difficult or impossible to simultaneously serve the full range of needs of a group of heterogeneous customers. This type of conflict is readily apparent in any college classroom in which the instructor must meet a multitude of student expectations and different preferences for formats and style. It is also apparent in an entertainment venue or any type of group training service.

Quality/Productivity Trade-Offs

Frontline service workers are asked to be both effective and efficient: they are expected to deliver satisfying service to customers and at the same time to be cost-effective and productive in what they do. A physician in an HMO, for example, is expected to deliver caring, quality, individualized service to her patients but at the same time to serve a certain number of patients within a specified time frame. A checker at a grocery store is expected to know his customers and to be polite and courteous, yet also to process the groceries accurately and move people through the line quickly. An architectural draftsperson is expected to create quality drawings, yet to produce a required quantity of drawings in a given period of time. These essential trade-offs between quality and quantity and between maximum effectiveness and efficiency place real-time demands and pressures on service employees.

Jagdip Singh, a noted services researcher, has studied productivity and quality as two types of performance inherent in frontline service jobs.[37] He explains the difficult trade-offs that employees face and has developed ways to measure these two types of performance together with a theoretical model to predict the causes and consequences of these trade-offs. He finds that quality of job performance is particularly susceptible to burnout and job stress. He also finds that internal support from understanding managers and control over the job tasks can help employees in making quality and productivity trade-offs, avoiding burnout, and maintaining their performance. Technology is being used to an ever-greater degree to balance the quality/quantity trade-off to increase productivity of service workers and at the same time free them to provide higher-quality service for the customer (see the Technology Spotlight).

STRATEGIES FOR DELIVERING SERVICE QUALITY THROUGH PEOPLE

A complex combination of strategies is needed to ensure that service employees are willing and able to deliver quality services and that they stay motivated to perform in customer-oriented, service-minded ways. These strategies for enabling service promises are often referred to as *internal marketing,* as shown on the left side of Figure 12.1.[38] The importance of attracting, developing, and retaining good people in knowledge- and service-based industries cannot be overemphasized, as an article in the *Harvard Business Review* suggested:

It's no secret that business success today revolves largely around people, not capital . . .
In most industries, people costs are much higher than capital costs. Even when a

company isn't people intensive overall, a people-based business embedded in the company often drives corporate performance.[39]

By approaching human resource decisions and strategies from the point of view that the primary goal is to motivate and enable employees to deliver customer-oriented promises successfully, an organization will move toward delivering service quality through its people. The strategies presented here are organized around four basic themes. To build a customer-oriented, service-minded workforce, an organization must (1) hire the right people, (2) develop people to deliver service quality, (3) provide the needed support systems, and (4) retain the best people. Within each of these basic strategies are a number of specific substrategies for accomplishing the goal, as shown in Figure 12.4.

Hire the Right People

To effectively deliver service quality, considerable attention should be focused on recruiting and hiring service personnel. Such attention is contrary to traditional practices in many service industries, where service personnel are the lowest on the corporate ladder and work for minimum wage. At the other end of the spectrum, in the professional services, the most important recruiting criteria are typically technical training, certifications, and expertise. However, many organizations are now looking above and beyond the technical qualifications of applicants to assess their customer and service orientation as well. Figure 12.4 shows a number of ways to go about hiring the right people.

FIGURE 12.4
Human Resource Strategies for Delivering Service Quality through People

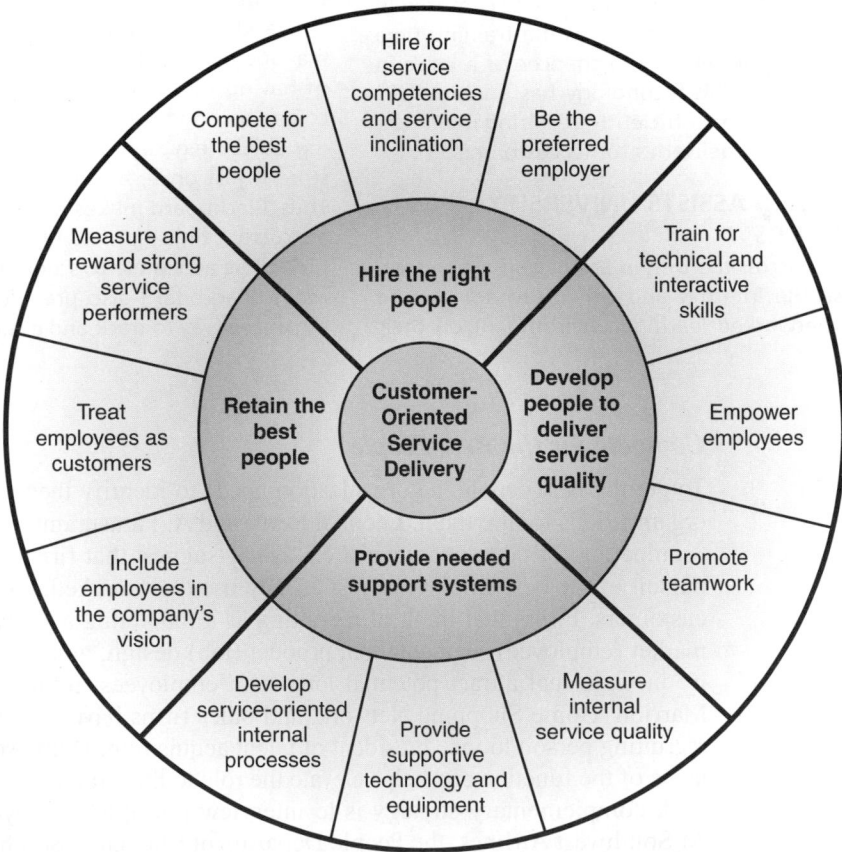

Technology Spotlight How Technology Is Helping Employees Serve Customers More Effectively and Efficiently

OPTIMIZATION TECHNOLOGY HELPS UPS DRIVERS' RELIABILITY EFFORTS

UPS delivers more than 16 million packages every day. Historically, UPS drivers worked off maps, 3 × 5 note cards, and their own memory to figure out the best way to navigate their routes. However, as discussed in the Technology Spotlight in Chapter 2, UPS has implemented a $600 million route optimization system that each evening maps out the next day's schedule for the majority of its more than 56,000 drivers. This software designs each route to minimize the number of left turns, thus reducing the time and gas that drivers waste idling at stoplights. It also reduced a day or more in transit time in nearly 3 million zip code parings. UPS's technology has allowed it to capture institutional knowledge about their customers. Before, when employees retired or quit, the knowledge of package loading techniques or route tips they had accumulated over the years usually went with them. This knowledge is now captured in a centralized system that shortens the training time for new drivers, lessening the chances of a lapse in customer service. This technology has enabled UPS to run its routes more efficiently, resulting in quicker and more reliable deliveries for its customers.

BLACKBOARD ASSISTS UNIVERSITY INSTRUCTORS

Universities across the United States and around the globe use the Internet and other technologies to create a networked learning environment on their campuses. One tool used by universities around the globe, Blackboard, provides an infrastructure that increases instructor effectiveness and efficiency. To illustrate, Blackboard enables instructors by helping them structure a course and organize nearly all teaching-related materials. Among the course management capabilities are electronic storage and controlled access of materials (readings, syllabi, assignments, discussion questions), management of class discussion boards, collection of student assignments, administration of online quizzes and exams, administration of group projects, provision of an online gradebook, and many other capabilities. In effect, most course administration tasks required of instructors can be handled by Blackboard. Students also benefit from having one source for accessing course materials, receiving updated course information, and submitting course assignments—without having to bother instructors with such administrative issues.

Blackboard provides instructors with the ability to manage many different sections of a course. Instead of having to create material for each section of a course being taught, instructors can create a learning object (e.g., a handout or reading supplement), store it just once, and link it to all course sections. Thus, Blackboard makes more effective usage of the instructor's time—providing the instructor with more time to be accessible to students outside of the classroom. Blackboard also provides instructors with an organized way to track and evaluate student learning.

Compete for the Best People

To get the best people, an organization needs to identify them and compete with other organizations to hire them. Leonard Berry and A. Parasuraman refer to this approach as "competing for talent market share."[40] They suggest that firms act as marketers in their pursuit of the best employees, just as they use their marketing expertise to compete for customers. Firms that think of recruiting as a marketing activity will address issues of market (employee) segmentation, product (job) design, and promotion of job availability in ways that attract potential long-term employees. Intuit, Harrah's, U.S. Cellular, Marriott, Home Shopping Network, and other firms have changed the title of the head recruiting person to vice president of talent acquisition. Doing so recognizes the importance of the function and helps elevate the role to the strategic importance it deserves.

A complementary strategy is to interview multiple employees for every position. At Southwest Airlines, the People Department (the name Southwest has given to what

For example, Blackboard provides an e-portfolio option that provides an online repository for storing student work—making it easy for both faculty *and* students to assess a student's progress in a course.

ELECTRONIC MEDICAL RECORDS SUPPORT MAYO CLINIC STAFF

Mayo Clinic has been described as one of the most powerful services brands in the world and is arguably the leading health care brand in the United States. Although there are many reasons for this (as noted in other places in this text), technology plays a key role in its ability to deliver high-quality care for patients with serious medical needs such as cancer treatment, heart surgery, or neurosurgery. At its Jacksonville, Florida, location Mayo Clinic invested $18 million over the past decade in computer system technology, with a large portion of the emphasis on electronic medical records. Like most hospitals, Mayo's inpatient system is very complex and requires that patient care efforts be coordinated across departments and specialists. The many systems required for patient care, including pharmacy systems, laboratory systems, and monitoring systems, need to be interconnected and to function 24/7 without fail.

Mayo Clinic's order-entry system enables hospital physicians to order tests, treatments, and medications. When an entry is made, it automatically launches a series of activities associated with the patient's care. For example, consider a person being admitted to the oncology department for a cancer treatment. A physician might place an order for the patient to receive an anti-nausea medicine 30 minutes before chemotherapy, and then receive three different chemical agents at specific times and in a particular sequence—and might specify that the treatment be repeated every 12 hours. Mayo's order-entry system automatically notifies physicians, pharmacists, and others in the hospital when a particular treatment needs to be performed and monitors dosage amounts and method of administration (e.g., orally or through a vein).

In addition to a savings of nearly $7 million to its Jacksonville clinic, the automated system makes Mayo medical staff more effective and improves patient care. For example, when new test results are reported in a patient's file, they are highlighted so that a nurse or doctor sees them immediately. Thus, the medical staff spends less time waiting or looking for patient files. By transitioning to electronic medical records, Mayo has found staff workflow to be better coordinated in the care of patients suffering from chronic diseases. Thus, electronic medical records have enabled Mayo Clinic staff to be even more efficient and effective in delivering quality health care.

Sources: D. Foust, "How Technology Delivers for UPS," *BusinessWeek* (March 5, 2007), p. 60; 2006 UPS Annual Report; L. L. Berry and K. D. Seltman, "Building a Strong Services Brand: Lessons from Mayo Clinic," *Business Horizons* 50 (May–June 2007), pp. 199–209; and A. M. Virzi, "A Complex Operation," *Baseline* (October 2006), pp. 56–59.

others call the human resources, or personnel, department) is relentless in its pursuit of talented employees. A quote from Southwest's cofounder, Herb Kelleher, illustrates the point: "The People Department came to me one day and said, 'We've interviewed 34 people for this ramp agent's position, and we're getting a little worried about the time and effort and cost that's going into it.' And I said if you have to interview 154 people to get the right person, do it."[41]

Hire for Service Competencies and Service Inclination

Once potential employees have been identified, organizations need to be conscientious in interviewing and screening to identify the best people from the pool of candidates. Service employees need two complementary capacities: service competencies and service inclination.[42]

Service competencies are the skills and knowledge necessary to do the job. In many cases, employees validate competencies by achieving particular degrees and certifications, such as attaining a doctor of law (JD) degree and passing the relevant state bar examination for lawyers. Similar rites of passage are required of doctors, airline pilots, university professors, teachers, and many other job seekers before they are ever interviewed for service jobs in their fields. In other cases, service competencies may not be degree-related but may instead relate to basic intelligence or physical requirements. A retail clerk, for example, must possess basic math skills and the potential to operate a cash register.

Given the multidimensional nature of service quality, service employees should be screened for more than their service competencies. They should also be screened for *service inclination*—their interest in doing service-related work—which is reflected in their attitudes toward service and orientation toward serving customers and others on the job. Self-selection suggests that most service jobs will draw applicants with some level of service inclination and that most employees in service organizations are inclined toward service. However, some employees clearly have a greater service inclination than others. Research has shown that service effectiveness is correlated with service-oriented personality characteristics such as helpfulness, thoughtfulness, and sociability[43] and that the best service companies put a greater emphasis on hiring those with positive attitudes rather than a specific skill set.[44] An ideal selection process for service employees assesses both service competencies and service inclination, resulting in employee hires who are high on both dimensions.

In addition to traditional employment interviews, many firms use innovative approaches to assessing service inclination and other personal characteristics that fit the organization's needs. Southwest Airlines looks for people who are compassionate and who have common sense, a sense of humor, a "can do" attitude, and an egalitarian sense of themselves (they think in terms of "we" rather than "me"). One way the company assesses these service inclinations is by interviewing potential flight attendants in groups to see how they interact with each other. Pilots are also interviewed in groups to assess their teamwork skills, a critical factor above and beyond the essential technical skills they are required to possess.[45]

In many cases a component of the selection process will include a form of work simulation that allows employees to demonstrate how they would actually perform on the job. A simulation may take the form of role-playing or a series of exercises that parallel the demands of the actual job. In addition to being a good way to assess potential employee abilities, simulations can give the potential hire a better view of what the job is actually like. Those candidates who do not like what they experience can back out of the applicant pool before being hired and then finding out the job is not what they had expected.

Be the Preferred Employer

One way to attract the best people is to be known as the preferred employer in a particular industry or in a particular location. UPS regularly conducts a survey among its employees to create an "Employer of Choice Index" and sets, annual goals to remain a preferred employer.[46] Google, the online search service that provides access to information throughout the Internet and is used daily by customers around the world, also enjoys a reputation as a preferred employer. Google states on its website that it "puts employees first when it comes to daily life in all of our offices."[47] Exhibit 12.1 provides some insight into why Google was chosen by *Fortune* as the "Best Company to Work For—2007" and is the preferred employer in its industry.

Other strategies that support a goal of being the preferred employer include extensive training, career and advancement opportunities, excellent internal support, attractive

Exhibit 12.1 Google Quickly Becomes a Preferred Employer in Its Industry

In 1996 Google's founders Larry Page and Sergey Brin developed a new approach to online search that took root in a Stanford University dorm room and quickly spread to information seekers around the globe. They continued to refine their search approaches and in 1998 formed Google—the world's largest search engine—an easy-to-use free service that usually returns results in a fraction of a second. As of 2007, Google was available in 158 domains and more than 100 languages.

In its short history Google has become a preferred employer and was ranked number 1 in *Fortune*'s list of the 100 best companies to work for in America in 2007 (its first year of eligibility). Google has employed a variety of approaches to become an employer of choice for over 11,000 employees worldwide, including:

- *The Googleplex*—The Google world headquarters building is located in Mountain View, California, and helps to attract and retain "Googlers" (employees). Some of the essential elements of the facility, which are presented on its company website, include a lobby with piano, lava lamps, and live projection of current search queries from around the world. In the hallways there are bicycles, large rubber exercise balls are on the floors, press clippings from around the world posted on bulletin boards everywhere. A three-dimensional rotating image of the world toggles between displaying points of light representing real time searches rising from the surface of the globe toward space, color-coded by language and traffic patterns for the entire Internet.

- *Recreation facilities*—Google provides a workout room with weights and rowing machines, locker rooms, washers and dryers, massage room, assorted video games, Foosball, baby grand piano, pool table, and ping pong. Twice a week roller hockey is played in the parking lot.

- *Dining facilities*—Google runs 11 free gourmet cafeterias at its headquarters and offers free meals to all its employees. Its food stations include "Charlie's Grill," "Back to Albuquerque," "East Meets West,"

and "Vegheads." Snack rooms contain bins packed with various cereals, gummy treats, M&Ms, toffee, licorice, cashew nuts, yogurt, carrots, fresh fruit, and other snacks, as well as dozens of different drinks, including fresh juice, soda, and make-your-own cappuccino.

- *Services for employees*—A wide variety of services are provided to Googlers. For example, on-site car washes and oil changes are among the numerous perks Google offers to all its workers. Haircuts are provided on-site. Employees can attend subsidized exercise classes; get a massage; study Mandarin, Japanese, Spanish, or French; and ask a personal concierge to arrange dinner reservations. Other services available to employees include child care, on-site notaries, and five on-site doctors available for employee checkups, all free of charge. And, when traveling to and from the office, Google operates free, Wi-Fi–enabled shuttle buses from five Bay Area locations for its employees.

- *Other benefits*—Several other benefits are also provided to Google employees. Those who buy a hybrid car receive $5,000. A weekly TGIF party takes place, usually with a live band playing, and a "pajama day" is a frequent occurrence. Lactation rooms, complete with breast pumps (so that nursing mothers do not have to haul equipment to work), are provided. All Google engineers are expected to devote 20 percent of their time to pursuing projects they dream up—Gmail, Google News, and the Google Finance site all resulted from such activity.

It is no surprise that Google receives more than 1,300 resumes per day. However, with such benefits Google almost always wins talent wars against Microsoft and Yahoo!. And if these benefits are not enough to encourage employees to talk up the company, Google provides a $2,000 reward for each person hired as the result of a referral.

Sources: A. Lashinsky, "Search and Enjoy," *Fortune* January 29, 2007, pp. 70–82; and www.google.com, 2007.

incentives, and quality goods and services with which employees are proud to be associated. SAS Institute has long been a preferred employer in the statistical software industry. Employees who work for SAS are, for the most part, professional or technical and well paid. A quote from the company's website captures SAS's philosophy about its people: "if you treat employees as if they make a difference to the company, they will make a difference to the company." The company invests heavily in its people: every employee has a private office, a 35-hour schedule is promoted, flexible hours are available, the company provides two top-quality day care centers with very reasonable prices on-site, and employees receive discounts on country club memberships near SAS facilities. For these reasons, the best performers at SAS seldom leave to work for competitors.[48] In a very different industry, dominated by lower-paid workers, Marriott International has a stated company goal of being the "preferred employer" in its industry. Marriott's philosophy concerning its employees, which sounds very similar to that of SAS, has been stated by Bill Marriott: "if the employees are well taken care of, they'll take care of the customer and the customer will come back . . . that's basically the core value of the company."[49] Marriott uses employee stock options, a social services referral network, day care, welfare-to-work training classes, and English and reading classes to be the preferred employer in the highly competitive hospitality industry. If employees have to run errands, go to a doctor's appointment, or handle unexpected events, they can cash in "Flex Coupons," good for a predetermined number of hours off.[50] Both SAS Institute and Marriott International are consistently rated among *Fortune*'s list of the top 100 companies to work for, with rankings of 48 and 89, respectively, as recently as 2007.[51]

Develop People to Deliver Service Quality

To grow and maintain a workforce that is customer oriented and focused on delivering quality, an organization must develop its employees to deliver service quality. That is, once it has hired the right employees, the organization must train and work with these individuals to ensure service performance.

Train for Technical and Interactive Skills

To provide quality service, employees need ongoing training in the necessary technical skills and in interactive skills. Examples of *technical skills* are working with accounting systems in hotels, cash machine procedures in a retail store, underwriting procedures in an insurance company, and any operational rules the company has for running its business. Most service organizations are quite conscious of and relatively effective at training employees in technical skills. These skills may be taught through formal education, as is the case at McDonald's Hamburger University, which trains McDonald's managers from all over the world. Additionally, technical skills are often taught through on-the-job training, as when education students work with experienced teachers in internship programs or when telephone service trainees listen in on the conversations of experienced employees. Companies frequently use information technology to train employees in the technical skills and knowledge needed on the job.

Service employees also need training in *interactive skills* that allow them to provide courteous, caring, responsive, and empathetic service. Research suggests firms can teach employees how to develop rapport with customers—one type of interactive skill—by teaching them in how to engage in pleasant conversation, ask questions, or use humor as they interact with customers.[52] Employees can be taught opening lines or conversation prompts to help identify commonalities with their customers.

Service firms take many approaches to provide interactive training. For example, Imperial Hotel in Toyko provides its employees with "service manners training" that focuses on the etiquette and psychology of guest contact and attitudes of service. Proper etiquette is taught via role-playing and videotaping (to critique appearance, mannerisms, and personal idiosyncrasies). The way the staff should appear to hotel guests is stressed and demonstrated, with emphasis placed on cleanliness, a sense of understated elegance, and good taste. Basic principles of nonverbal communication and body language are discussed. Demonstrations and detailed explanations of appropriate behaviors are given, covering such points as facial expressions, appearance, and posture when standing; pleasing, attractive ways of talking; proper posture; and courtesy when escorting guests within the hotel premises.[53] Outback Steakhouse coaches waiters and waitresses to squat next to or even sit at a customer's table and spend a couple of minutes interacting; such action allows them to establish better eye contact with customers and provides opportunity for engaging interactions. Starbucks has created a board game, *Inside Out,* to be used in training sessions to help its baristas to connect with customers.[54] As part of the game, a barista is presented with a specific scenario—say, a sighing customer doing last-minute Christmas shopping has stopped by for a pick-me-up drink—and is challenged to figure out how to cheer up the customer.

Successful companies invest heavily in training and make sure that the training fits their business goals and strategies. For example, at Midwest Express—the company that takes pride in offering "the best care in the air"—all employees (pilots, baggage handlers, aircraft groomers) take part in a two-day orientation program. The focus revolves around the company values and customer service. In Zagat's regular international airline survey, Midwest Express consistently ranks as one of the top U.S. airlines. At the Ritz-Carlton, all employees go through extensive initial training and are given pocket-sized, laminated credo cards to carry in their wallets. In addition to the credo, the card specifies the three steps of service and Ritz-Carlton's well-known motto "We are Ladies and Gentlemen Serving Ladies and Gentlemen." Further, employees in every hotel attend a brief standing staff meeting each day to review Ritz-Carlton's "Gold Standards" and employee service values so as to continually reinforce earlier training.

Empower Employees

Many organizations have discovered that to be truly responsive to customer needs, frontline providers need to be empowered to accommodate customer requests and to recover on the spot when things go wrong. *Empowerment* means giving employees the authority, skills, tools, and desire to serve the customer. Although the key to empowerment is giving employees authority to make decisions on the customer's behalf, authority alone is not enough. Employees need the knowledge and tools to be able to make these decisions, and they need incentives that encourage them to make the right decisions. Organizations do not succeed in empowering their employees if they simply tell them, "You now have the authority to do whatever it takes to satisfy the customer." First, employees often do not believe this statement, particularly if the organization has functioned hierarchically or bureaucratically in the past. Second, employees often do not know what it means to "do whatever it takes" if they have not received training, guidelines, and the tools needed to make such decisions.

Research suggests positive benefits to empowering frontline service workers. Some of these benefits include reduction in job-related stress, improved job satisfaction, greater adaptability, and better outcomes for customers.[55] But such success does not come easily. In fact, some experts have concluded that few organizations have truly taken advantage of, or properly implemented, successful empowerment strategies.[56] Nor is empowerment the answer for all organizations. Exhibit 12.2 enumerates both the costs and benefits of empowerment as documented by David Bowen and Edward Lawler, experts on this subject.[57] They suggest that organizations well suited to empowerment strategies are ones in which (1) the business strategy is one of differentiation and customization, (2) customers are long-term relationship customers, (3) technology is nonroutine or complex, (4) the business environment is unpredictable, and (5) managers and employees have high growth and social needs and strong interpersonal skills.

Exhibit 12.2 Potential Benefits and Costs of Empowerment

BENEFITS

- *Quicker responses to customer needs during service delivery.* Employees who are allowed to make decisions on behalf of the customer can make decisions more quickly, bypassing what in the past might have meant a long chain of command, or at least a discussion with an immediate supervisor.

- *Quicker responses to dissatisfied customers during service recovery.* When failures occur in the delivery system, customers hope for an immediate recovery effort on the part of the organization. Empowered employees can recover on the spot, and a dissatisfied customer can potentially be turned into a satisfied, even loyal one.

- *Employees feel better about their jobs and themselves.* Giving employees control and authority to make decisions makes them feel responsible and gives them ownership of the customer's satisfaction. Decades of job design research suggest that when employees have a sense of control and of doing meaningful work, they are more satisfied. The result is lower turnover and less absenteeism.

- *Employees will interact with customers with more warmth and enthusiasm.* Employees feel better about themselves and their work, and these attitudes will spill over into their feelings about customers and will be reflected in their interactions.

- *Empowered employees are a great source of service ideas.* When employees are empowered, they feel responsible for the service outcome and they will be excellent sources of ideas about new services or how to improve current offerings.

- *Great word-of-mouth advertising from customers.* Empowered employees do special and unique things that customers will remember and tell their friends, family, and associates about.

COSTS

- *A potentially greater dollar investment in selection and training.* To find employees who will work well in an empowered environment requires creative, potentially more costly selection procedures. Training will also be more expensive in general because employees need more knowledge about the company, its products, and how to work in flexible ways with customers.

- *Higher labor costs.* The organization may not be able to use as many part-time or seasonal employees, and it may need to pay more for asking employees to assume responsibility.

- *Potentially slower or inconsistent service delivery.* If empowered employees spend more time with all, or even some, customers, then service overall may take longer and may annoy customers who are waiting. Empowerment also means that customers will get what they need or request. When decisions regarding customer satisfaction are left to the discretion of employees, there may be inconsistency in the level of service delivered.

- *May violate customers' perceptions of fair play.* Customers may perceive that sticking to procedures with every customer is fair. Thus, if they see that customers are receiving different levels of service or that employees are cutting special deals with some customers, they may believe that the organization is not fair.

- *Employees may "give away the store" or make bad decisions.* Many people fear that empowered employees will make costly decisions that the organization cannot afford. Although this situation can happen, good training and appropriate guidelines will help.

Source: Reprinted from "The Empowerment of Service Workers: What, Why, How, and When," by D. E. Bowen and E. E. Lawler, *Sloan Management Review* 33 (Spring 1992), pp. 31–39, by permission of the publisher. Copyright 1992 by Massachusetts Institute of Technology. All rights reserved.

Promote Teamwork

The nature of many service jobs suggests that customer satisfaction will be enhanced when employees work as teams. Because service jobs are frequently frustrating, demanding, and challenging, a teamwork environment will help alleviate some of the stresses and strains. Employees who feel supported and feel that they have a team backing them up will be better able to maintain their enthusiasm and provide quality service.[58] Such teamwork is the driving force behind the service philosophy at the Mayo Clinic. One of the Mayo's core principles encourages all of those in the organization to "practice medicine as an integrated team of compassionate, multi-disciplinary physicians, scientists and allied health professionals who are focused on the needs of patients."[59] In addition to being an important ingredient for service quality, "an interactive community of coworkers who help each other, commiserate, and achieve together is a powerful antidote to service burnout."[60] Merrill Lynch and Jyske Bank, two of the companies featured in the cases in the back of this book, are both known for developing a team approach to serving clients. By promoting teamwork, an organization can enhance the employees' *abilities* to deliver excellent service while the camaraderie and support enhance their *inclination* to be excellent service providers.

One way of promoting teamwork is to encourage the attitude that "everyone has a customer." That is, even when employees are not directly responsible for or directly interact with the final customer, they need to know whom they serve directly and how the role they play in the total service picture is essential to the final delivery of quality service. If each employee can see how he or she is somehow integral in delivering quality to the final customer and if each employee knows whom to support to make service quality a reality, teamwork will be enhanced. Service blueprints, described in Chapter 9, can serve as useful tools to illustrate for employees their integral roles in delivering service quality to the ultimate customer.

Team goals and rewards also promote teamwork. Harrah's Entertainment is one company that provides incentives and compensation focused on teamwork. The casino hotel company's incentive program is weighted toward team results and a relatively small percentage of compensation (often less than 40 percent) are based on individual goals. Everyone in the organization, from meeting planners to blackjack dealers, are rewarded based on customer service scores. When a firm rewards teams of individuals rather than basing all rewards on individual achievements and performance, team efforts and team spirit are encouraged.

Provide Needed Support Systems

To be efficient and effective in their jobs, service workers require internal support systems that are aligned with their need to be customer focused. This point cannot be overemphasized. In fact, without customer-focused internal support and customer-oriented systems, it is nearly impossible for employees to deliver quality service no matter how much they want to. For example, a bank teller who is rewarded for customer satisfaction as well as for accuracy in bank transactions needs easy access to up-to-date customer records, a well-staffed branch (so that he is not constantly facing a long line of impatient customers), and supportive customer-oriented supervisors and back-office staff. In examining customer service outcomes in Australian call centers, researchers found that internal support from supervisors, teammates, and other departments as well as evaluations of technology used on the job were all strongly related to employee satisfaction and ability to serve customers.[61] The following sections suggest strategies for ensuring customer-oriented internal support.

Measure Internal Service Quality

One way to encourage supportive internal service relationships is to measure and reward internal service. By first acknowledging that everyone in the organization has a customer and then measuring customer perceptions of internal service quality, an organization can begin to develop an internal quality culture.[62] In their quest to provide the best possible service to their patients, the Mayo Clinic formally measures internal service quality between departments annually. An internal customer service audit is one tool that can be used to implement a culture of internal service quality. Through the audit, internal organizations identify their customers, determine their needs, measure how well they are doing, and make improvements. The process

Exhibit 12.3 Steps in Conducting an Internal Customer Service Audit

1. *Define your customer.*

   a. List all the people or departments in the organization who need help from you or your department in any way. This list may include specific departments, particular staff people, the CEO, certain executives, or the board of directors.

   b. Prioritize the names on the list, placing the people or departments that rely on you the most at the top.

2. *Identify your contribution.*

   a. For each of these customers, specify the primary need you think they have to which you can contribute. Talk to your internal customers about what problems they are trying to solve and think about how you can help.

3. *Define service quality.*

   a. What are the critical moments of truth that really define the department–internal customer interface from your customer's point of view? Blueprint the process, and list the moments of truth.

   b. For each major internal customer, design a customer report card (based on customer input) and a set of evaluation criteria for your department's service package, as seen through the eyes of that customer. The criteria might include such dimensions as timeliness, reliability, and cost.

4. *Validate your criteria.*

   a. Talk to your customers. Allow them to revise, as necessary, how you saw their needs and the criteria they used in assessing your performance. This dialogue itself can go a long way toward building internal service teamwork.

5. *Measure service quality.*

   a. Evaluate your service (using internal measures and/or customer surveys) against the quality criteria you established in talking to your customers. See how you score. Identify opportunities for improvement. Set up a process and timetable for following through.

6. *Develop a mission statement based on what you contribute.*

   a. Consider drafting a brief, meaningful service mission statement for your operation. Be certain to frame it in terms of the value you *contribute,* not what you *do.* For example, the mission of the HR department should not be "to deliver training" (the action); it would be "to create competent people" (the contribution).

Source: Reprinted from K. Albrecht, *At America's Service* (Homewood, IL: Dow-Jones-Irwin, 1988), pp. 139–142, as discussed in B. Schneider and D. E. Bowen, *Winning at the Service Game* (Boston: The Harvard Business School Press, 1995), pp. 231–232. © 1988 by Dow-Jones-Irwin. Reprinted by permission of The McGraw-Hill Companies.

parallels market research practices used for external customers. Exhibit 12.3 outlines the steps in an internal service audit.

One risk of measuring and focusing on internal service quality and internal customers is that people can sometimes get so wrapped up in meeting the needs of internal customers that they forget they are in business to serve the ultimate, external customers.[63] In measuring internal service quality, therefore, it is important to constantly draw the linkages between what is being delivered internally and how it supports the delivery of the final service to customers. Service blueprinting, introduced in Chapter 9, can help to illustrate these critical linkages.

Provide Supportive Technology and Equipment

When employees do not have the right equipment or their equipment fails them, they can be easily frustrated in their desire to deliver quality service. To do their jobs effectively and efficiently, service employees need the right equipment and technology. Our Technology Spotlight earlier in this chapter highlights the role of technology in providing support for employees.

Having the right technology and equipment can extend into strategies regarding workplace and workstation design. For example, in designing their corporate headquarters' offices, Scandinavian Airline Systems identified particular service-oriented goals that it wished to achieve, among them teamwork and open, frequent communication among managers. An office environment was designed with open spaces (to encourage meetings) and internal windows in offices (to encourage frequent interactions). In this way the work space facilitated the internal service orientation.

Develop Service-Oriented Internal Processes

To best support service personnel in their delivery of quality service on the front line, an organization's internal processes should be designed with customer value and customer satisfaction in mind. In other words, internal procedures must support quality service performance. In many companies, internal processes are driven by bureaucratic rules, tradition, cost efficiencies, or the needs of employees. Providing service- and customer-oriented internal processes can therefore imply a need for total redesign of systems. This kind of redesign of systems and processes has become known as "process reengineering." Although developing service-oriented internal processes through reengineering sounds sensible, it is probably one of the most difficult strategies to implement, especially in organizations steeped in tradition. Refocusing internal processes and introducing large amounts of new, supportive technology were among the changes made by Yellow Transportation in its transition from a traditional, operations-driven company to a customer-focused one (see Exhibit 12.4).[64]

Retain the Best People

An organization that hires the right people, trains and develops them to deliver service quality, and provides the needed support must also work to retain them. Employee turnover, especially when the best service employees are the ones leaving, can be very detrimental to customer satisfaction, employee morale, and overall service quality. And, just as they do with customers, some firms spend a lot of time attracting employees but then tend to take them for granted (or even worse), causing these good employees to search for job alternatives. Although all the strategies depicted earlier in Figure 12.4 will support the retention of the best employees, here we will focus on some strategies that are particularly aimed at this goal.

Include Employees in the Company's Vision

For employees to remain motivated and interested in sticking with the organization and supporting its goals, they need to share an understanding of the organization's vision. People who deliver service day in and day out need to understand how their work fits into the big picture of the organization and its goals. They will be motivated to some extent by their paychecks and other benefits, but the best employees will be attracted away to other opportunities if they are not committed to the vision of the organization. And they cannot be committed to the vision if that vision is kept secret from them. What this strategy means in practice is that the vision is communicated to employees frequently and that it is communicated by top managers, often by the CEO.[65] Respected CEOs such as Herb Kelleher of Southwest Airlines, Howard Schulz of Starbucks, Fred Smith of FedEx, Bill Marriott of Marriott International, and Charles Schwab of Schwab are known for communicating their visions clearly and often to employees. Bill Zollars, CEO of YRC Worldwide, exemplifies this type of behavior, which was a critical ingredient to his success in turning the company around (see Exhibit 12.4).

Pete Winemiller, Vice President of guest relations for the Seattle SuperSonics of the NBA, has communicated clearly, through words and actions, that his organization's goal is for customer-contact employees to "CLICK With Your Guests," during

Exhibit 12.4 Yellow Reinvents Itself

Yellow Transportation (now part of YRC Worldwide) is one of the largest and oldest transportation companies in the United States. In a little over a decade, Yellow Transportation (Yellow) has been transformed from a traditional, operations-driven trucking company to a service and transportation company with a customer-focused culture and innovative services. The transformation required a new vision for the company, feedback from customers and employees; investments in technology; and hundreds of small, detailed actions. Here is a summary of some of what took place over the past 12 years.

In 1996 Bill Zollars, a respected and experienced executive, was recruited to serve as president of Yellow. At the time, the company was recovering from its worst financial year in its over 70-year history and was still feeling the effects of a long Teamsters strike two years earlier. Zollars's challenge was to help the company start over and turn the negative trends around. His goal was to transform the tradition-bound, formerly regulated company into one that offered multiple services and unprecedented customer service—a customer-centered service business rather than an operations-driven trucking company.

SHARING THE VISION

The first thing Zollars did was share his vision of the new company with all company employees. He did this not through memos or videos but by visiting in person, over about a year and a half, almost every one of the company's U.S. terminals. He talked personally with dockworkers, office people, sales staff, and customers—sharing the same consistent message with each group. The company was going to change, and doing so required the involvement of all employees as well as feedback and ideas from customers.

Top management education was also an integral piece of the transformation. Zollars brought his two dozen top managers—across all functions of the company—to Arizona State University to build their team and to learn cutting-edge concepts of services marketing and management. He attended the program with them, and in future years sent smaller groups of new and continuing executives back for refreshers and continuing team building.

INVESTING IN TECHNOLOGY SUPPORT

To become customer focused, Yellow invested in state-of-the-art technology, not for technology's sake but, rather, to allow every aspect of its business to focus on satisfying customer needs efficiently. Yellow continually invests in infusion of new technologies to influence how orders get processed, how dispatchers assign drivers for pickups and deliveries, and how dockworkers load and unload the trucks. Each dockworker has a wireless mobile data terminal that speeds up the loading and unloading process. Employees who operate the customer service center (1-800-GO-YELLOW) have instant access to customers' account profiles, including customer location, type of loading dock, history of previous shipments, destinations, and delivery signatures. Investments in technology allow customers to interact with the firm in whatever way they please—via phone, fax, e-mail, interactive voice response, or the Internet. The company is now considered a technology leader in its industry.

LISTENING TO CUSTOMERS

By initiating customer feedback processes, the company learned of new service needs of its customers and of service issues it needed to address. A major issue, addressed early on, was reliability. The most

Seattle SuperSonics CLICK! With Your Guests™ Program

their experience. As depicted in the photo here, the "CLICK" acronym translates as: C—Communicate Courteously, L—Listen to Learn, I—Initiate Immediately, C—Create Connections, K—Know Your Stuff. These actions are expected of all of those in the organization who interact with customers—including more than 480 part-time workers (more than 90 percent of the staff). The Sonics Guest Relations department is focused not only on the in-arena fan experience, but also on relationship building with its current season ticket holders. This approach sends a strong message to employees, reinforcing the company vision.[66] When the vision and direction are clear and motivating, employees are more likely to remain with the company through the inevitable rough spots along the path to the vision.

important concern for customers in the freight-handling business is that their shipments get picked up on time and delivered on time and that nothing is damaged. These simple rules of service reliability were ones that Yellow and many of its competitors were not performing well a decade ago. Now Yellow has fixed these basic issues through the infusion of technology and lots of employee communication, training, motivation, and incentive programs. Major investments in service recovery processes were also part of the solution.

Through the customer feedback process, Yellow also identified opportunities for new, innovative services that have taken it way beyond its roots in less-than-truckload freight distribution. One of its most innovative, popular, and profitable forays into the future is Exact Express—an expedited, time-definite, guaranteed service for large shipments. The service allows customers to specify exactly when they want their shipments picked up and delivered, and Yellow is on the mark 98 percent of the time. This new service has resulted in Yellow getting some unique jobs, such as shipping 10,000 pounds of air freshener to Ground Zero after the World Trade Center attack and carrying 40,000 flashlights from Los Angeles to Washington, D.C., for the 2001 presidential inauguration.

VIEWING RESULTS

During the transformation, employees and customers alike have responded with enthusiasm to the changes at Yellow. Financial results have been impressive; even during the downturn in 2001, Yellow continued to grow its newest services and receive recognition and awards. It has won awards for its innovative business practices, for its website, and for quality based on industry

Yellow's success depends on employees being motivated and having the tools to succeed.

surveys. Although much has been accomplished in the past decade, this transformation will surely continue for a long time into the future.

Sources: C. Salter, "On the Road Again," *Fast Company,* January 2002, pp. 50–58; www.yellowcorp.com, 2007; and author's observations.

Treat Employees as Customers

If employees feel valued and their needs are taken care of, they are more likely to stay with the organization. Tom Siebel, for example, saw the CEO's primary job as cultivating a corporate culture that benefits all employees and customers. "If you build a company and a product or service that delivers high levels of customer satisfaction, and if you spend responsibly and manage your human capital assets well, the other external manifestations of success, like market valuation and revenue growth, will follow."[67]

Many companies have adopted the idea that employees are also customers of the organization and that basic marketing strategies can be directed at them.[68] The products that the organization has to offer its employees are a job (with assorted benefits) and quality of work life. To determine whether the job and work-life needs of employees are being met, organizations conduct periodic internal marketing research to assess employee satisfaction and needs. For example, within American Express Travel Related Services, the Travelers Cheque Group (TCG) had a goal of "Becoming the Best Place to Work" by treating employees as customers.[69] On the basis of the research, TCG launched a number of initiatives to benefit employees: an expanded employee assistance program; child care resource and referral service; adoption assistance; health care and dependent care reimbursement plans; family leave; family sick days; flexible returns; sabbaticals; improved part-time employee benefits; flexible benefits; and workplace flexibility initiatives including job-sharing, flexplace, and flextime scheduling. What American Express and many other companies have found is that to ensure employee satisfaction, productivity, and retention, companies must get involved in the private lives and family support of their workers.[70] Employees appreciate such efforts; American Express is regularly included in *Fortune*'s list of "Top 100 Companies to Work For"—making it every year between 2000 and 2007!

In addition to basic internal research, organizations can apply other marketing strategies to their management of employees. For example, segmentation of the employee population is apparent in many of the flexible benefit plans and career path choices now available to employees. Organizations set up to meet the needs of specific segments and to adjust as people proceed through their lives will benefit from increased employee loyalty. Advertising and other forms of communication directed at employees can also increase their sense of value and enhance their commitment to the organization.[71]

Measure and Reward Strong Service Performers

If a company wants the strongest service performers to stay with the organization, it must reward and promote them. This strategy may seem obvious, but often the reward systems in organizations are not set up to reward service excellence. Reward systems may value productivity, sales, or some other dimension that can potentially work *against* providing good service. Even those service workers who are intrinsically motivated to deliver high service quality will become discouraged at some point and start looking elsewhere if their efforts are not recognized and rewarded.

Reward systems need to be linked to the organization's vision and to outcomes that are truly important. For instance, if customer satisfaction and retention are viewed as critical outcomes, service behaviors that increase those outcomes need to be recognized and rewarded. At Harrah's Casinos and Hotels, a portion of employee compensation is linked to customer satisfaction scores as a "Performance Payout," so employees have an investment in achieving excellent service levels. Employees also have a vested interest in the performance of the entire team in serving customers exceptionally well. Beyond monetary incentives, outstanding employees are recognized with special Chairman Awards, and their names published in Harrah's annual report. Management is also awarded incentives based on the positive improvement in customer service, as 25 percent of a manager's annual bonus is tied to achieving customer service goals.[72] Similarly, before Siebel Systems was acquired by Oracle, all employees—the salespeople, the service people, the engineers, the product marketers, and everyone else—received incentive compensation based on the company's customer satisfaction scores. For salespeople the bulk of their incentive compensation was paid only *after* the company knew the level of customer satisfaction—four quarters after the sales contract was signed.[73] At Enterprise Rent-a-Car, branch managers wishing to move up in the organization can do so only if the customer satisfaction scores from their store are in the upper half of all company stores. Such measures, along with all the analyses and service improvement initiatives that are behind them, are intended to align employee behavior around satisfying and retaining customers.

In developing new systems and structures to recognize customer focus and customer satisfaction, organizations have turned to a variety of rewards. Traditional approaches such as higher pay, promotions, and one-time monetary awards or prizes can be linked to service performance. In many organizations employees are encouraged to recognize each other by personally giving a "peer award" to an employee they believe has excelled in providing service to the customer. Other types of rewards include special organizational and team celebrations for achieving improved customer satisfaction or for attaining customer retention goals. In most service organizations it is not only the major accomplishments but the daily perseverance and attention to detail that move the organization forward, so recognition of the "small wins" is also important.

In many situations, a customer's relationship is with a specific employee and may be stronger with the *employee* than with the firm. If this employee leaves the firm and is no longer available to the customer, the firm's relationship with the customer may be jeopardized.[74] Clearly a firm should make great efforts to retain such employees; however, in spite of the firm's best efforts, some good employees are going to leave. If the firm is not successful at retaining a key customer contact employee, what can it do to reduce the impact on the customer? Employees could be rotated occasionally to ensure that the customer has exposure to and is comfortable with more than one employee. Firms might also form teams of employees who are responsible for interacting with each customer. In both cases, the idea is that the customer would have multiple contacts with several employees in the organization, thus reducing the firm's vulnerability to losing the customer should any one employee leave. Emphasis should also be placed on creating a positive firm image in the minds of its customers and in so doing convey that *all* its employees are capable.[75]

CUSTOMER-ORIENTED SERVICE DELIVERY

As indicated by the examples presented in this chapter, specific approaches for hiring and energizing frontline workers take on a different look and feel across companies, based on the organization's values, culture, history, and vision.[76] For example, "developing people to deliver service quality" is accomplished quite differently at Southwest Airlines than at Disney. At Disney the orientation and training process is highly structured, scripted, and standardized. At Southwest, the emphasis is more on developing needed skills and then empowering employees to be spontaneous and nonscripted in their approach to customers. Although the style and culture of the two organizations are different, both pay special attention to all four basic themes shown in Figure 12.4. Both have made significant investments in their people, recognizing the critical roles they play.

Throughout the book we have advocated a strong customer focus. Firms that have a strong service culture clearly put an emphasis on the customer and the customer's experience. To do so, firms must also create an environment that staunchly supports the customer contact employee, because this person in the organization is frequently the most responsible for ensuring that the customer's experience is delivered as designed. Historically, many firms have viewed senior management as the most important people in the firm, and indeed, organizational charts tend to reflect this view in their structure. This approach places management at the top of the structure and (implicitly) the customer at the bottom, with customer contact employees just above them. If the organization's most important people are customers, they should be at the top

FIGURE 12.5 **Customer-Focused Organizational Chart**

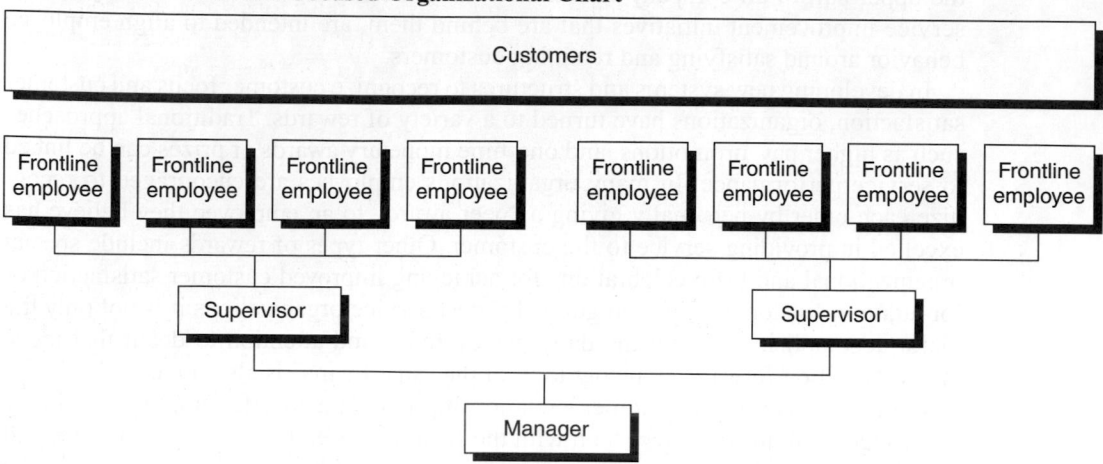

of the chart, followed by those with whom they have contact. Such a view, illustrated in Figure 12.5, is more consistent with a customer-oriented focus. In effect, the role of top-level management changes from that of commanding to that of facilitating and supporting employees in the organization who are closest to the customer. The human resource strategies that we have offered in this chapter are suggested as a means by which management can support the customer contact employee. Indeed, a truly customer-oriented management team might actually "flip" the services marketing triangle presented earlier in the chapter so that the management point of the triangle is at the bottom of the triangle, with customer and employees equally placed at the top—as illustrated in Figure 12.6. A statement by Michel Bon, former CEO of France Telecom, succinctly summarizes the philosophy behind such an approach:

> If you sincerely believe that "the customer is king," the second most important person in this kingdom must be the one who has a direct interaction on a daily basis with the one who is king.[77]

By flipping the services marketing triangle, the two groups that are the most important people to the organization—customers and those who interact with customers—are placed in a position of prominence.

FIGURE 12.6
Inverted Services
Marketing Triangle

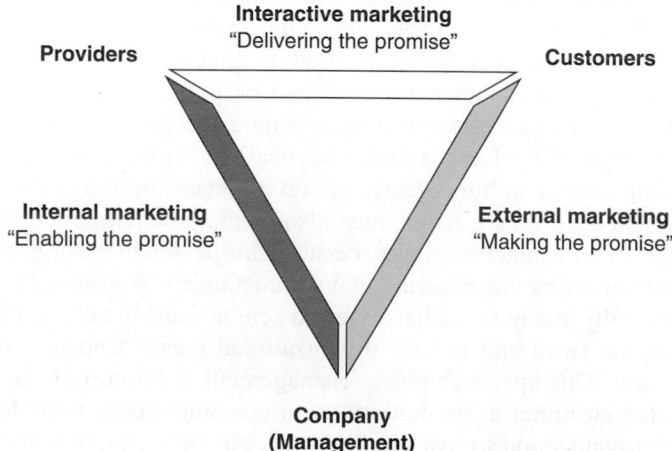

Summary

Because many services are delivered by people in real time, closing the service performance gap is heavily dependent on human resource strategies. The successful execution of such strategies begins with the development and nurturing of a true service culture throughout the organization.

Often, service employees *are* the service, and in all cases they represent the organization in customers' eyes. They affect service quality perceptions to a large degree through their influence on the five dimensions of service quality: reliability, responsiveness, empathy, assurance, and tangibles. It is essential to match what the customer wants and needs with service employees' abilities to deliver.

In this chapter we focused on service employees to provide you with an understanding of the critical nature of their roles and appreciation of the inherent stresses and conflicts they face. You learned that frontline service jobs demand significant investments of emotional labor and that employees confront a variety of on-the-job conflicts. Sometimes service employees are personally uncomfortable with the roles they are asked to play; other times the requirements of the organization may conflict with client expectations, and employees must resolve the dilemma on the spot. Sometimes there are conflicting needs among customers who are being served in turn (such as in a bank teller line) or among customers being served simultaneously (as in a college classroom). At other times a frontline employee may be faced with a decision about whether to satisfy a customer or meet productivity targets (such as an HMO physician who is required to see a certain number of patients in a defined period of time).

Grounded in this understanding of the importance of service employees and the nature of their roles in the organization, you learned strategies for integrating appropriate human resource practices into service firms. The strategies are aimed at allowing employees to effectively satisfy customers as well as be efficient and productive in their jobs. The strategies were organized around four major human resource goals in service organizations: hire the right people, develop people to deliver service quality, provide needed support systems, and retain the best people. A company that works toward implementing these strategies is well on its way to delivering service quality through its people, thereby diminishing gap 3—the service performance gap.

Discussion Questions

1. Define *service culture*. Why is service culture so important? Can a manufacturing firm have a service culture? Why or why not?

2. Why are service employees critical to the success of any service organization? Why do we include an entire chapter on service employees in a marketing course?

3. What is *emotional labor*? How is it different from physical or mental labor?

4. Reflect on your own role as a frontline service provider, whether in a current job or in any full- or part-time service job you have had in the past. Did you experience the kinds of conflicts described in the boundary-spanning roles section of the chapter? Be prepared with some concrete examples for class discussion.

5. Select a service provider (your dentist, doctor, lawyer, hair stylist) with whom you are familiar, and discuss ways this person could positively influence the five dimensions of service quality in the context of delivering his or her services. Do the same for yourself (if you are currently a service provider).

6. Describe the four basic human resource strategy themes and why each plays an important role in building a customer-oriented organization.

7. What is the difference between technical and interactive service skills? Provide examples (preferably from your own work context or from another context with which you are familiar). Why do service employees need training in both?

8. Is empowerment always the best approach for effective service delivery? Why is employee empowerment so controversial?

Exercises

1. Visit the websites of companies with known world-class service cultures (such as Ritz-Carlton, FedEx, or Starbucks). How does the information conveyed on the website reinforce the company's service culture?

2. Review the section of the chapter on boundary-spanning roles. Interview at least two frontline service personnel regarding the stresses they experience in their jobs. How do the examples they provide relate to the sources of conflict and trade-offs described in the text?

3. Assume that you are the manager of a crew of frontline customer-service employees in a credit card company. Assume that these employees work over the phone and that they deal primarily with customer requests, questions, and complaints. In this specific context,

   a. Define what is meant by *boundary-spanning roles,* and discuss the basic purposes or functions performed by participants in these roles.

   b. Discuss two of the potential conflicts that your employees may face on the basis of their roles as boundary spanners.

   c. Discuss how you, as their supervisor, might deal with these conflicts based on what you have learned.

4. Choose one or more of the human resource strategy themes (hire the right people, develop people to deliver service quality, provide needed support systems, retain the best people). Interview a manager in a service organization of your choice regarding his or her current practices within the theme you have chosen. Describe the current practices and recommend any appropriate changes for improving them.

Notes

1. L. L. Berry, *Discovering the Soul of Service* (New York: The Free Press, 1999).

2. Interview with Singapore Airlines senior vice president of marketing services, included in "How May I Help You?" *Fast Company* (March 2000), pp. 93–126.

3. P. Gallagher, "Getting It Right from the Start," *Journal of Retail Banking* 15 (Spring 1993), pp. 39–41.

4. J. S. Hirsch, "Now Hotel Clerks Provide More Than Keys," *The Wall Street Journal,* March 5, 1993, p. B1.

5. Berry, *Discovering the Soul of Service.*

6. S. M. Davis, *Managing Corporate Culture* (Cambridge, MA: Ballinger, 1985).

7. C. Grönroos, *Service Management and Marketing: A Customer Relationship Management Approach,* 2nd ed. (West Sussex, UK: John Wiley and Sons, Ltd., 2000), p. 360.

8. See K. N. Kennedy, F. G. Lassk, and J. R. Goolsby, "Customer Mind-Set of Employees throughout the Organization," *Journal of the Academy of Marketing Science* 30 (Spring 2002), pp. 159–171.

9. R. Hallowell, D. Bowen, and C. Knoop, "Four Seasons Goes to Paris," *Academy of Management Executive* 16, no. 4 (2002), pp. 7–24; J. L. Heskett, L. A. Schlesinger, and E. W. Sasser Jr., *The Service Profit Chain* (New York: The Free Press, 1997); B. Schneider and D. E. Bowen, *Winning the Service Game* (Boston: Harvard Business School Press, 1995); and D. E. Bowen and S. D. Pugh, "Linking Human Resource Management Practices and Customer Outcomes" in *The Routledge Companion to Strategic Human Resource Management,* eds. J. Storey, P. Wright and D. Ulrich (Abingdon, Oxon, UK: Routledge 2008, forthcoming).

10. Berry, *Discovering the Soul of Service,* p. 40.

11. Hallowell, Bowen, and Knoop, "Four Seasons Goes to Paris."

12. For an excellent discussion of the complexities involved in creating and sustaining a service culture, see Schneider and Bowen, *Winning the Service Game,* chap. 9. See also Michael D. Hartline, James G. Maxham III, and Daryl O. McKee, "Corridors of Influence in the Dissemination of Customer-Oriented Strategy to Customer-Contact Service Employees," *Journal of Marketing* 64 (April 2000), pp. 35–50.

13. This discussion is based on Hallowell, Bowen, and Knoop, "Four Seasons Goes to Paris."

14. This quote is most frequently attributed to J. Carlzon of Scandinavian Airline Systems.

15. J. Garrett, "The Human Side of Brand: Why Audi Hires Workers with the Same Traits as Its Luxury Cars," *Gallup Management Journal* 1 (Summer 2001), pp. 4–5.

16. J. Barlow and P. Stewart, *Branded Customer Service* (San Francisco: Barett-Koehler Publishers, 2004).

17. The conceptualization of the services triangle presented in Figure 12.1 and the related text discussion are based on M. J. Bitner, "Building Service Relationships: It's All about Promises," *Journal of the Academy of Marketing Science* 23 (Fall 1995), pp. 246–251; P. Kotler and K. L. Keller, *Marketing Management,* 12th ed. (Upper Saddle River, NJ: Pearson Prentice Hall, 2006); and Grönroos, *Service Management and Marketing.*

18. See, H. Rosenbluth, "Tales from a Nonconformist Company," *Harvard Business Review* 69 (July–August 1991), pp. 26–36; L. A. Schlesinger and J. L. Heskett, "The Service-Driven Service Company," *Harvard Business Review* 69 (September–October 1991), pp. 71–81; and B. Schneider, M. Ehrhart, D. Mayer, J. Saltz, and K. Niles-Jolley, "Understanding Organization-Customer Links in Service Settings," *Academy of Management Journal* 48 (December 2005), pp. 1017–1032.

19. B. Schneider and D. E. Bowen, "The Service Organization: Human Resources Management Is Crucial," *Organizational Dynamics* 21 (Spring 1993), pp. 39–52.

20. Ibid.

21. D. E. Bowen, S. W. Gilliland, and R. Folger, "How Being Fair with Employees Spills Over to Customers," *Organizational Dynamics* 27 (Winter 1999), pp. 7–23; S. Masterson, "The Trickle-Down Model of Organizational Justice: Relating Employees' and Customers' Perceptions of and Reactions to Fairness," *Journal of Applied Psychology* 86 (August 2001), pp. 594–604; J. G. Maxham III and R. G. Netemeyer, "Firms Reap What They Sow: The Effects of Shared Values and Perceived Organizational Justice on Customers' Evaluations of Complaint Handling," *Journal of Marketing* 67 (January 2003), pp. 46–62.

22. See J. L. Heskett, T. O. Jones, G. W. Loveman, W. E. Sasser Jr., and L. A. Schlesinger, "Putting the Service–Profit Chain to Work," *Harvard Business Review* 72 (March– April 1994), pp. 164–174; G. W. Loveman, "Employee Satisfaction, Customer Loyalty, and Financial Performance," *Journal of Service Research* 1 (August 1998), pp. 18–31; A. Rucci, S. P. Kirn, and R. T. Quinn, "The Employee–Customer Profit Chain at Sears," *Harvard Business Review* 76 (January–February 1998), pp. 82–97; and R. Hallowell and L. L. Schlesinger, "The Service–Profit Chain," in *The Handbook for Services Marketing and Management,* ed. T. A. Swartz and D. Iacobucci (Thousand Oaks, CA: Sage Publications, 2000), pp. 203–222.

23. For additional research on the Service-Profit Chain, see: J. L. Heskett, W. E. Sasser Jr., and L. A. Schlesinger, *The Value Profit Chain: Treat Employees Like Customers and Customers Like Employees* (New York: The Free Press, 2003); G. A. Geladel and S. Young, "Test of a Service Profit Chain Model in the Retail Banking Sector," *Journal of Occupational and Organizational Psychology* 78 (March 2005), pp. 1–22; R. D. Anderson, R. D. Mackoy, V. B. Thompson, and G. Harrell, "A Bayesian Network Estimation of the Service-Profit Chain for Transport Service Satisfaction," *Decision Sciences* 35 (Fall 2004), pp. 665–689; W. A. Kamakura, V. Mittal, F. de Rosa, and J. A. Mazzon, "Assessing the Service-Profit Chain," *Marketing Science* 21 (Summer 2002), pp. 294–317; R. Silvestro and S. Cross, "Applying the Service Profit Chain in a Retail Environment: Challenging the "Satisfaction Mirror,' " *International Journal of Service Industry Management* 11, no. 3 (2000), pp. 244–268; and Schneider et al., "Understanding Organization-Customer Links in Service Firms."

24. J. Pfeffer, *The Human Equation* (Boston: Harvard Business School Press, 1998); and A. M. Webber, "Danger: Toxic Company," *Fast Company* 26 (November 1998), pp. 152–162.

25. J. Dickler, "Best Employers, Great Returns," *CNNMoney.com,* January 18, 2007, http://money.cnn.com/2007/01/17/magazines/fortune/bestcompanies_performance/, accessed October 2007.

26. M. K. Brady and J. J. Cronin Jr., "Customer Orientation: Effects on Customer Service Perceptions and Outcome Behaviors," *Journal of Service Research* 3 (February 2001), pp. 241–251.

27. L. A. Bettencourt and K. Gwinner, "Customization of the Service Experience: The Role of the Frontline Employee," *International Journal of Service Industry Management* 7, no. 2 (1996), pp. 3–20.

28. For research on the influence of frontline employee behaviors on customers, see D. D. Gremler and K. P. Gwinner, "Customer–Employee Rapport in Service Relationships," *Journal of Service Research* 3 (August 2000), pp. 82–104; and T. J. Brown, J. C. Mowen, D. T. Donavan, and J. W. Licata, "The Customer Orientation of Service Workers: Personality Trait Effects of Self- and Supervisor Performance Ratings," *Journal of Marketing Research* 39 (February 2002), pp. 110–119.

29. A. Hochschild, *The Managed Heart: Commercialization of Human Feeling* (Berkeley: University of California Press, 1983).

30. T. Hennig-Thurau, M. Groth, M. Paul, and D. D. Gremler, "Are All Smiles Created Equal? How Employee-Customer Emotional Contagion and Emotional Labor Impact Service Relationships," *Journal of Marketing* 70 (July 2006), pp. 58–73.

31. A. Hochschild, "Emotional Labor in the Friendly Skies," *Psychology Today* 16 (June 1982), pp. 13–15.

32. For additional discussion on emotional labor strategies, see R. Leidner, "Emotional Labor in Service Work," *Annals of the American Academy of Political and Social Science* 561, no. 1 (1999), pp. 81–95.

33. M. D. Hartline and O. C. Ferrell, "The Management of Customer-Contact Service Employees: An Empirical Investigation," *Journal of Marketing* 60 (October 1996), pp. 52–70; J. Singh, J. R. Goolsby, and G. K. Rhoads, "Burnout and Customer Service Representatives," *Journal of Marketing Research* 31 (November 1994), pp. 558–69; L. A. Bettencourt and S. W. Brown, "Role Stressors and Customer-Oriented Boundary-Spanning Behaviors in Service Organizations," *Journal of the Academy of Marketing Science* 31 (Fall 2003), pp. 394–408.

34. B. Shamir, "Between Service and Servility: Role Conflict in Subordinate Service Roles," *Human Relations* 33, no. 10 (1980), pp. 741–756.

35. Ibid., pp. 744–45.

36. J. Bowen and R. C. Ford, "Managing Service Organizations: Does Having a 'Thing' Make a Difference?" *Journal of Management* 28 (June 2002), pp. 447–469.

37. J. Singh, "Performance Productivity and Quality of Frontline Employees in Service Organizations," *Journal of Marketing* 64 (April 2000), pp. 15–34.

38. For discussions of internal marketing, see L. L. Berry and A. Parasuraman, "Marketing to Employees," chap. 9 in *Marketing Services* (New York: The Free Press, 1991); C. Grönroos, "Managing Internal Marketing: A Prerequisite for Successful Customer Management," chap. 14 in *Service Management and Marketing: Customer Management in Service Competition,* 3rd ed. (West Sussex, UK: John Wiley and Sons, Ltd., 2007).

39. F. Barber and R. Strack, "The Surprising Economics of a 'People Business,'" *Harvard Business Review* 83 (June 2005), pp. 80–91.

40. Berry and Parasuraman, "Marketing to Employees," p. 153.

41. T. W. Ferguson, "Airline Asks Government for Room to Keep Rising," *The Wall Street Journal,* March 9, 1993, p. A17.

42. This section on hiring for service competencies and service inclination draws from work by B. Schneider and colleagues, specifically, B. Schneider and D. Schechter, "Development of a Personnel Selection System for Service Jobs," in *Service Quality: Multidisciplinary and Multinational Perspectives,* ed. S. W. Brown, E. Gummesson, B. Edvardsson, and B. Gustavsson (Lexington, MA: Lexington Books, 1991), pp. 217–236.

43. J. Hogan, R. Hogan, and C. M. Busch, "How to Measure Service Orientation," *Journal of Applied Psychology* 69, no. 1 (1984), pp. 167–173. See also Brown et al., "The Customer Orientation of Service Workers"; and D. T. Donavan, T. J. Brown, and J. C. Mowen, "Internal Benefits of Service-Worker Customer Orientation: Job Satisfaction, Commitment, and Organizational Citizenship Behaviors," *Journal of Marketing* 68 (January 2004), pp. 128–146.

44. Bowen and Pugh, "Linking Human Resource Management Practices and Customer Outcomes"; and N. Bendapudi and V. Bendapudi, "Creating the Living Brand," *Harvard Business Review* 83 (May 2005), pp. 124–134.

45. For additional information on Southwest Airlines hiring practices, see C. Mitchell, "Selling the Brand Inside," *Harvard Business Review* 80 (January 2002), pp. 99–105.

46. UPS website, www.sustainability.ups.com/social/feedback/choice.html, accessed October 2007.

47. Google website, www.google.com, accessed October 2007.

48. T. D. Schellhardt, "An Idyllic Workplace under a Tycoon's Thumb," *The Wall Street Journal,* November 23, 1998, p. B1; and www.sas.com, accessed October 2007.

49. M. Gunther, "Marriott Family Values," *CNNMoney.com,* May 25, 2007, http://money.cnn.com/2007/05/24/news/companies/pluggedin_gunther_marriott.fortune/index.htm, accessed October 2007.

50. C. Yang, A. T. Palmer, S. Browder, and A. Cuneo, "Low Wage Lessons: How Marriott Keeps Good Help Even at $7.40 an Hour," *BusinessWeek,* November 11, 1996, pp. 108–116; and www.marriott.com, accessed October 2007.

51. R. Levering and M. Moskowitz, "The 100 Best Companies to Work For," *Fortune,* January 29, 2007, pp. 94–114.

52. D. Gremler and K. Gwinner, "Rapport-Building Behaviors Used by Retail Employees," working paper.

53. M. I. Cronin, "Staff Training Delivers Quality Service at Tokyo's Imperial Hotel," in *Service Quality Handbook,* eds. E. E. Schueing and W. F. Christopher (New York: American Management Association, 1993), pp. 312–328.

54. J. Hempel, "Therapy with Your Latte? It's My Job," *BusinessWeek,* October 24, 2005, p. 16.

55. J. C. Chebat and P. Kollias, "The Impact of Empowerment on Customer Contact Employees' Roles in Service Organizations," *Journal of Service Research* 3 (August 2000), pp. 66–81.

56. C. Argyris, "Empowerment: The Emperor's New Clothes," *Harvard Business Review* 76 (May–June 1998), pp. 98–105.

57. D. E. Bowen and E. E. Lawler III, "The Empowerment of Service Workers: What, Why, How, and When," *Sloan Management Review* 33 (Spring 1992), pp. 31–39.

58. J. H. Gittell, "Relationships between Service Providers and Their Impact on Customers," *Journal of Service Research* 4 (May 2002), pp. 299–311.

59. Mayo Clinic website, http://www.mayoclinic.org/about/missionvalues.html, accessed November 2007.

60. Berry and Parasuraman, "Marketing to Employees," p. 162.

61. A. Sergeant and S. Frenkel, "When Do Customer-Contact Employees Satisfy Customers?" *Journal of Service Research* 3 (August 2000), pp. 18–34.

62. J. Reynoso and B. Moores, "Operationalising the Quality on Internal Support Operations in Service Organisations," in *Advances in Services Marketing and Management,* Vol. 6, eds. T. A. Swartz, D. E. Bowen, and S. W. Brown (Greenwich, CT: JAI Press, 1997), pp. 147–170.

63. Schneider and Bowen, *Winning the Service Game,* pp. 230–234.

64. C. Salter, "On the Road Again," *Fast Company* 54 (January 2002), pp. 50–58.

65. O. Gadiesh and J. L. Gilbert, "Transforming Corner-Office Strategy into Frontline Action," *Harvard Business Review* 79 (May 2001), pp. 73–79.

66. B. Fryer, "High Tech the Old Fashioned Way," *Harvard Business Review* 79 (March 2001), pp. 119–125; and C. Hawn, "The Man Who Sees around Corners," *Forbes,* January 21, 2002, pp. 72–78.

67. B. Fryer, "High Tech the Old-Fashioned Way."

68. L. L. Berry, "The Employee as Customer," *Journal of Retail Banking* 3 (March 1981), pp. 33–40.

69. C. Hegge-Kleiser, "American Express Travel-Related Services: A Human Resources Approach to Managing Quality," in *Managing Quality in America's Most Admired Companies,* ed. J. W. Spechler (San Francisco: Berrett-Koehler Publishers, 1993), pp. 205–212.

70. K. Hammonds, "Balancing Work and Family," *BusinessWeek,* September 16, 1996, pp. 74–84.

71. M. C. Gilly and M. Wolfinbarger, "Advertising's Internal Audience," *Journal of Marketing* 62 (January 1998), pp. 69–88.

72. J. Mackey, "Putting the Service Profit Chain to Work: How to Earn Your Customer's Loyalty," *Francising.com,* December 29, 2004, accessed December 2007.

73. B. Fryer, "High Tech the Old-Fashioned Way."

74. N. Bendapudi and R. P. Leone, "Managing Business-to-Business Customer Relationships Following Key Contact Employee Turnover in a Vendor Firm," *Journal of Marketing* 66 (April 2002), pp. 83–101.

75. Ibid.

76. J. R. Katzenbach and J. A. Santamaria, "Firing Up the Front Line," *Harvard Business Review* 77 (May–June 1999), pp. 107–117.

77. Quoted in D. Stauffer, "The Art of Delivering Great Customer Service," *Harvard Management Update* 4, no. 9 (September 1999), pp. 1–3.

Chapter **Thirteen**

Customers' Roles in Service Delivery

This chapter's objectives are to

1. Illustrate the importance of customers in successful service delivery and cocreation of service experiences.
2. Discuss the variety of roles that service customers play: productive resources for the organization, contributors to quality and satisfaction, competitors.
3. Explain strategies for involving service customers effectively to increase satisfaction, quality, and productivity.

iPrint = Self-Service Printing Online

In the world of Internet-based services, customers play new and active roles in producing services for themselves with little or no personal interaction with the service provider. As an example, one company, iPrint, changed the way home-office and small-business customers interact with commercial printers. This change resulted in customers performing services for themselves that traditionally were provided by brick-and-mortar printing companies. iPrint.com is a privately owned, web-based custom printing service, describing itself as a "complete, fully automated, self-service online creation, ordering, and commercial printing environment."[1]

iPrint.com launched in 1996 and was one of the very early companies to offer printing services online. In the intervening years it has earned many industry awards for e-commerce innovation, website design, and customer service as well as a number of recognitions by the Stevie Awards for Women in Business. Much of the company's success can be attributed to its business model, which provides customers an easy, continually accessible way to independently design, create, and order customized print jobs, sometimes at half the cost of traditional commercial printers. A quote from a satisfied customer is indicative: "Always a good experience to do business with iPrint. Top quality work for a reasonable price delivered in record time—and I don't have to go anywhere to order or pick it up!" Customers of iPrint create their own value through participation in the production of customized printing services. Customers with little or no knowledge of graphic design can easily, quickly, and from the convenience of their own homes or offices create their own designs for a wide range of products. iPrint offers business cards, notepads, stationery, various gift items, stamps, calendars, signs, and promotional products.

Although creating graphic designs is a complex process with hundreds of variables to consider, iPrint developed a simple step-by-step process to create personalized products. Customers adapt existing designs to meet their specifications and then view the finished products, selecting from a wide range of options such as paper, font, size, and color as well as art or business logos. Completed designs can be purchased over the Internet and are typically received in a few days. Designs are also automatically saved to allow for easy reordering. Although iPrint notifies customers via e-mail when the order is placed and when it has been printed, customers are also able to actively participate after the order has been placed by tracking it throughout processing, printing, and shipping.

In addition to customer education through detailed step-by-step instructions, iPrint provides easy access to service providers through e-mail or phone. Customers participating in the design of their own products are rewarded with prices significantly lower than what they would normally pay. iPrint also offers a 30-day complete satisfaction guarantee, removing some of the risk customers may feel in ordering customized printed materials online. Through its services iPrint has transformed a people-intensive, manual service business into an electronically automated, self-service function in which its small business customers are empowered to create their own value and satisfaction. Because they do so much of the work, customers essentially become "coproducers" of the service, enhancing iPrint's productivity, which reduces the company's costs. By effectively coproducing the service, customers are rewarded with quality, personalized results, and reduced prices.

In this chapter we examine the unique and varied roles played by customers in service delivery and cocreation. In some cases, service customers are present in the "factory" (the place the service is produced and/or consumed), interacting with employees and with other customers. For example, in a classroom or training situation, students (the customers) are sitting in the factory (the classroom) interacting with the instructor and other students as they consume and cocreate educational services. Because they are present during service production, customers can contribute to or detract from the successful delivery of the service and to their own satisfaction. In a manufacturing context, rarely does the production facility contend with customer presence on the factory floor, nor does it rely on the customer's immediate, real-time input to manufacture the product. As our opening vignette illustrates, service customers can actually produce services themselves and to some extent are responsible for their own satisfaction. Using iPrint's online services, customers cocreate value for themselves and in the process also reduce the prices they pay for printing services.

Because customers are participants in service production and delivery, they can potentially contribute to the widening of gap 3, the service performance gap. That is, customers themselves can influence whether the service meets customer-defined specifications. Sometimes customers contribute to gap 3 because they lack understanding of their roles and exactly what they can or should do in a given situation, particularly if the customer is confronting a service concept for the first time. Customers using the services of iPrint for the first time need detailed, but simple, instructions to help them understand how to use the service effectively and get the greatest value.

At other times customers may understand their roles but be unwilling or unable to perform for some reason. In a health club context, members may understand that to get into good physical shape they must follow the workout guidelines set up by the trainers. If work schedule or illness keeps members from living up to their part

Strategy Insight　Customer Cocreation of Value: The New Strategy Frontier

Consultants, researchers, and strategists are urging companies to think about their customers in new ways. Instead of viewing customers as passive targets and recipients of predesigned goods and services, they encourage a view of customers as active cocreators of value. This perspective goes beyond focusing on customer involvement in generating ideas for new products, and it is more than customer participation in service delivery. Instead, this view suggests that the value customers receive is a *cocreated experience* they build for themselves through interactions with service providers and other customers, and by choosing and combining elements of the company's offerings to create their own "total experience." This feature contains two examples in two very different contexts to help make the cocreation idea more concrete and the strategic possibilities apparent.

JOHN DEERE

John Deere is a century-old global firm that serves the knowledge- and capital-intensive farming industry with sophisticated equipment, services, information, and online peer group dialogue for its farm manager customers. The company is geared toward making the farmer's life easier and more productive. The "experience environment" for their innovations is broadly defined to include anything that will help achieve the farmer's

professional objectives. For example, new technologies available through Deere can help the farmer monitor his equipment remotely to assess location of the equipment and engine condition. This remote monitoring capability is uniquely set up for each farmer and requires the farmer's active involvement with the system to fully take advantage of its value. Another area that Deere is experimenting with is sensor technologies on its equipment that can precisely map soil conditions and thereby prescribe the application of seeds and fertilizers based on the particular soil conditions in an area. Depending on the farmer's land conditions and the specific crops she grows, the information provided by the sensors can be customized to her situation and used to better control her particular crop yields. Productivity tools (online calculators and analysis tools) provided by Deere can also be used by farmers to increase their productivity. Deere has taken cocreated value to even a higher level by helping farmers identify and communicate with other farmers online who have similar problems or challenges. Thematically based dialogues online result in farmers sharing knowledge and increasing the collective expertise of the community by spreading best practices. Deere's annual customer conference, where customers physically get together, is another way the company provides a unique experience

of the guidelines, the service will not be successful because of customer inaction. In a different service situation, customers may choose not to perform the roles defined for them because they are not rewarded in any way for contributing their effort. For example, many grocery store customers choose not to use the automated self-checkout because they see no benefit in terms of speed, price, or convenience. When service customers are enticed through price reductions, greater convenience, or some other tangible benefit, they are more likely to perform their roles willingly, as in the case of our opening vignette about iPrint.

Finally, the service performance gap may be widened not through actions or inactions on the part of the customer, but because of what *other* customers do. Other customers who are in the service factory either receiving the service simultaneously (passengers on an airplane flight) or waiting their turn to receive the service sequentially (bank customers waiting in line, Disneyland customers waiting for one of the rides) can influence whether the service is effectively and efficiently delivered.

This chapter focuses on the roles of customers in service delivery and cocreation of service experiences as well as strategies to effectively manage them.

and face-to-face learning environment for farmers. It is up to each farmer to determine how much to participate in the various services, how to use the information provided, and whether to participate in online peer group discussions or customer conference learning experiences. Deere's strategy and suite of offerings is customer-centric, with the resulting experience being unique to each farmer. Deere has shifted its strategic innovation paradigm to one where value is cocreated through the experience rather than exclusively through product or technology innovation. Value is defined and configured by the customer, not by Deere.

KODAK GALLERY

Kodak Gallery provides a set of services for consumers—all related to photography and experiences associated with photography. Formerly called "Ofoto," the Kodak Gallery is considered one of the best online photo sharing services. It is easy to use, allowing consumers to upload, organize, store, e-mail, and touch-up digital photos. But, Kodak has gone far beyond simply offering a service for organizing and sharing photos by identifying the entire "photography experience space" and offering options, merchandise, and services tied to it. For example, through its website, customers can choose to order prints and pick them up at one of thousands of locations. Or, customers can choose to create photo albums or use a custom framing option for special photos. They can make cards, calendars, brochures, and other gifts with their photos and order merchandise emblazoned with their photos (everything from coasters to mouse pads to clothing and even blankets for pets). Friends and family can view, purchase, and comment on a customer's photos, thus creating a community around the site. While the technology that allows average citizens to easily and economically take hundreds of digital photos was a critical technology innovation, the services and experiences that Kodak and others provide online are what allow consumers to cocreate a truly unique photography experience that can be remembered and relived by them and others. Through these experiences, customers themselves dramatically enhance the value of their cameras and photos.

Sources: S. L. Vargo and R. F. Lusch, "Evolving to a New Dominant Logic for Marketing," *Journal of Marketing* 68 (January 2004), pp. 1–17; C. K. Prahalad and V. Ramaswamy, *The Future of Competition: Co-Creating Unique Value with Customers* (Boston, MA: Harvard Business School Press, 2004); M. Sawhney, S. Balasubramanian, and V. V. Krishnan, "Creating Growth with Services," *Sloan Management Review* 45 (Winter 2004), pp. 34–43; www.kodakgallery.com, 2007; and www.deere.com, 2007.

THE IMPORTANCE OF CUSTOMERS IN SERVICE COCREATION AND DELIVERY

Customer participation at some level is inevitable in all service situations. Services are actions or performances, typically produced and consumed simultaneously. In many situations employees, customers, and even others in the service environment interact to produce the ultimate service outcome. Because they participate, customers are indispensable to the production process of service organizations, and in many situations they can actually control or contribute significantly to their own dis/satisfaction.[2] This view of participatory customers is consistent with the service-dominant logic of marketing that promotes the idea customers are always cocreators of value.[3] Our Strategy Insight illustrates this broadened view and how it can lead to innovative strategies. Recognition of the role of customers is also reflected in the definition of the *people* element of the services marketing mix given in Chapter 1: *all human actors who play a part in service delivery and thus influence the buyer's perceptions; namely, the firm's personnel, the customer, and other customers in the service environment.* Chapter 12 examined the role of the firm's employees in delivering service quality. In this chapter we focus on the customer receiving or cocreating the service and on fellow customers in the service environment.

Customer Receiving the Service

Because the customer participates in the delivery process, he or she can contribute to narrowing or widening gap 3 through behaviors that are appropriate or inappropriate, effective or ineffective, productive or unproductive. The level of customer participation—low, medium, high—varies across services, as shown in Table 13.1. In some cases, all that is required is the customer's physical presence (*low level of participation*), with the employees of the firm doing all the service production work, as in the example of a symphony concert. Symphony-goers must be present to receive the entertainment service, but little else is required once they are seated. In other situations, consumer inputs are required to aid the service organization in creating the service (*moderate level of participation*). Inputs can include *information, effort,* or *physical possessions.* All three of these are required for a certified public accountant (CPA) to prepare a client's tax return effectively: information in the form of tax history, marital status, and number of dependents; effort in putting the information together in a useful fashion; and physical possessions such as receipts and past tax returns. In some situations,

TABLE 13.1 **Levels of Customer Participation across Different Services**

Source: Adapted from A. R. Hubbert, "Customer Co-Creation of Service Outcomes: Effects of Locus of Causality Attributions," doctoral dissertation, Arizona State University, Tempe, Arizona, 1995.

Low: Consumer Presence Required during Service Delivery	Moderate: Consumer Inputs Required for Service Creation	High: Customer Cocreates the Service
Products are standardized.	Client inputs (information, materials) customize a standard service.	Active client participation guides the customized service.
Service is provided regardless of any individual purchase.	Provision of service requires customer purchase.	Service cannot be created apart from the customer's purchase and active participation.
Payment may be the only required customer input.	Customer inputs are necessary for an adequate outcome, but the service firm provides the service.	Customer inputs, choices, and actions cocreate the outcome.
Consumer Examples		
Airline travel	Haircut	Marriage counseling
Motel stay	Annual physical exam	Personal training
Fast-food restaurant	Full-service restaurant	Weight reduction program
		Major illness or surgery
Business-to-Business Customer Examples		
Uniform cleaning service	Agency-created, advertising campaign	Management consulting
Pest control	Payroll service	Executive management seminar
Interior greenery maintenance service	Freight transportation	Installation of computer network

customers are truly cocreators of the service (*high level of participation*). For these services, customers have important participation roles that will affect the nature of the service outcome. For example, in a weight reduction program, the customer, working with a counselor, may actively cocreate a personalized nutritional and exercise program. Then, it is largely up to the customer to carry out the plan and/or enhance it, resulting in value that is unique to that person. Similarly, in a complex or long-term business-to-business consulting engagement, the client can be involved in activities such as identification of issues, shared problem solving, ongoing communication, provision of equipment and work space, and implementation of solutions.[4] Facilitating this type of positive customer participation can help ensure a successful outcome, as described in Exhibit 13.1. Table 13.1 provides several examples of each level of participation for both consumer and business-to-business services. The effectiveness of customer involvement at all the levels will affect organizational productivity and, ultimately, service quality and customer satisfaction.

Fellow Customers

In many service contexts, customers receive and/or cocreate the service simultaneously with other customers or must wait their turn while other customers are being served. In both cases, "fellow customers" are present in the service environment and can affect the nature of the service outcome or process. Fellow customers can *enhance* or *detract* from customer satisfaction and perceptions of quality.[5]

Some of the ways fellow customers can negatively affect the service experience are by exhibiting disruptive behaviors, causing delays, excessively crowding, and manifesting incompatible needs. In restaurants, hotels, airplanes, and other environments in which customers are cheek to jowl as they receive the service, crying babies, smoking patrons, and loud, unruly groups can be disruptive and detract from the experiences of their fellow customers. In college classrooms and other types of education and training environments, customers often complain when fellow customers interrupt and/or detract from the experience of others by using their laptop computers or cell phones in distracting ways. In these cases, the customer is disappointed through no direct fault of the service provider. In other cases, overly demanding customers (even customers with legitimate problems) can cause a delay for others while their needs are met. This occurrence is common in banks, post offices, and customer service counters in retail stores. Excessive crowding or overuse of a service can also affect the nature of the customer's experience. Visiting Sea World in San Diego on the Fourth of July is a very different experience from visiting the same park midweek in February.

Finally, customers who are being served simultaneously but who have incompatible needs can negatively affect each other. This situation can occur in restaurants, college classrooms, hospitals, and any service establishment in which multiple segments are served simultaneously. In a study of critical service encounters occurring in tourist attractions across central Florida, researchers found that customers negatively affected each other when they failed to follow either explicit or implicit "rules of conduct." Customers reported such negative behaviors as pushing, shoving, smoking, drinking alcohol, being verbally abusive, or cutting in line. Other times, dissatisfaction resulted when other customers were impersonal, rude, unfriendly, or even spiteful.[6]

We can offer just as many examples of other customers enhancing satisfaction and quality for their fellow customers as detracting from them. Sometimes the mere presence of other customers enhances the experience, for example, at sporting events, in movie theaters, and in other entertainment venues. The presence of other patrons is essential for true enjoyment of these experiences. In other situations, fellow customers provide

Exhibit 13.1   Client Coproduction in Business-to-Business Services

What do firms like IBM, McKinsey, Accenture, and neoIT have in common? All can be described as knowledge-intensive business services (KIBS), whose value-added activities provide their business clients with highly customized services (e.g., technical engineering, consulting, software development, business process outsourcing). To develop and deliver optimal service solutions, KIBS rely on inputs and cooperation from their clients as integral coproducers of the services. The KIBS provider needs accurate and detailed information from the client, access to people and resources, and cooperation in terms of deadlines and contingencies that inevitably arise.

Depth interviews and research conducted with clients of employees of an IT services provider ("TechCo") identified a number of *client* characteristics that can enhance the quality of the client's participation and the ultimate service outcome in these types of KIBS relationships. The characteristics are listed here with an illustrative quote from or about one of TechCo's clients, using disguised names. Clients who display these types of coproduction behaviors will contribute to the success of their projects and are likely to get better outcomes and be more satisfied.

- **Communication openness.** The client is forthcoming and honest in sharing pertinent information for project success.

  PharmCo actually did the up-front work to understand what it is we have to do, when we have to do it, and how it fits into our overall scheme of things . . . We [spent] the first days doing nothing but teaching

them about what we're trying to accomplish.— TechCo, about PharmCo Client

- **Shared problem solving.** The client takes individual initiative and shared responsibility for developing solutions to problems that arise in the relationship.

  I think, as a customer, I have a responsibility to bring some critical thinking to what they've brought to the table. Not just to accept it . . . [You need to be able to say,] "I don't know if that's going to work for our environment" or technically, "Why did you do that?" So a lot of it's just asking questions and saying, "Why are we doing it that way? Is that the best way to do it?"—GovCo Client

- **Tolerance.** The client responds in an understanding and patient manner in the face of minor project encumbrances.

  That certainly was our goal—not to have roadblocks, not to have problems . . . And even at that, it took us longer than we had hoped. Again, not anybody's fault, it's just one of those things. It's a process, and sometimes those processes take a little longer than you initially had planned for.—EduCo Client

- **Accommodation.** The client demonstrates a willingness to accommodate the desires, approaches, and expert judgment of the service provider.

  [If we saw something that didn't fit with our goals,] we'd call them and ask them . . . If they could do it, they would simply say, "Oh, you bet, no problem" . . . If it was something that we really couldn't monkey with too much, they'd come out and say, "No, you probably don't want to change that because of this

a positive social dimension to the service experience as suggested in the photo on page 392. In some situations, customers may actually help each other achieve service goals and outcomes. The success of the Weight Watchers organization, for example, depends significantly on the camaraderie and support that group members provide each other. And health providers have long recognized the importance of family members (often viewed as customers in this context) in aiding hospital patients in their care and full recovery. Some hospitals have even started encouraging family members to stay and assist with their loved ones who are being cared for in intensive care units (ICUs) in the hospital, turning family members into active members of the health care team.[7]

Academic research also supports the power of other customers to influence service outcomes. In a study done with a franchise of Gold's Gym, it was found that customers who received support from other members of the gym were more likely to participate in positive ways like keeping the gym clean, cooperating with personnel, showing empathy toward other members, and encourageing others to join the gym.[8] The study of central Florida tourist attractions mentioned earlier found that customers increased the satisfaction of others by having friendly conversations while waiting in line, by taking

reason and that reason" and we'd say, "Okay, that's fine" and we'd go on to the next one.—EduCo Client

- **Advocacy.** The client firm provides a vocal advocate and salesperson for the project.

  [The scope of the project] was cumbersome. Had we not had involvement and not had a group of people who had ownership, who really wanted to succeed, we might have been inclined to say . . . "I don't really care how this turns out because the boss told me I need to do it. I don't care if it's ugly because I'm never going to use it." So, I think it was a combination of things. One is having people who have a vested interest in making sure it worked and knew why they were doing it and [second] continuous involvement.—AgCo Client

- **Involvement in project governance.** The client takes an active role in monitoring project progress toward the stated goal.

  We would have our meetings and we'd set these action items. We would say when they're supposed to be done, and we would set the next meeting before we ended that meeting so everybody knew what their expectations were.—DonorCo Client

- **Personal dedication.** The client demonstrates a sense of personal obligation for project success by performing individual responsibilities in a conscientious manner.

  I think that was one of the things that I probably did right—was staying that involved. But it was hard, from my perspective, because it took time away from other things that I had to do. But I think I brought some things to the project that, if I hadn't been as involved, I don't know that we would have had as successful an implementation of the three systems as I think we did.—GovCo Client

The challenge for KIBS firms is to develop processes, systems, and practices that will ensure that clients engage in these ways. The research suggests that these positive coproduction behaviors will be most likely when KIBS provider firms engage in (1) *client selectivity* (carefully screening clients in advance to ensure a good fit between provider and client); (2) *client training, education, and socialization* (making clients feel that they are part of the team by kicking off the relationship with a cooperative spirit, perhaps including events and expectations-setting workshops); and (3) *project leadership and client performance evaluation* (selecting the right project leaders on both sides and evaluating both on their relationship management skills as well as technical capabilities).

This research illustrates the importance of business clients as coproducers of the service and the value to both provider and client that can result from quality coproduction behaviors and associated business practices.

Source: L. A. Bettencourt, A. L. Ostrom, S. W. Brown, and R. I. Roundtree, "Client Co-Production in Knowledge-Intensive Business Services," *California Management Review* 44 (Summer 2002), 100–128; Copyright © 2002, by The Regents of the University of California. Reprinted from the California Management Review, Vol. 44, No. 4. by permission of The Regents.

photos, by assisting with children, and by returning dropped or lost items.[9] And, an ethnographic study that observed hundreds of hours of customer interactions among travelers on the U.K. rail system found that customers often helped each other by (1) providing important service-related information (e.g., schedules, interesting features en route) that can reduce trip-related anxiety; (2) engaging in enjoyable conversation, thus making the trip more pleasant; and (3) serving as someone to complain to when mishaps and service failures occurred.[10]

The influence of fellow customers in helping others is even more apparent in some online service environments such as eBay, Amazon.com, and Craigslist, where customers literally cocreate services together. Customers helping each other is not limited to consumer services as illustrated by John Deere in this chapter's Strategy Insight. Another interesting example occurs at networking giant Cisco. By giving business customers open access to its information and systems through its online self-service, Cisco enables customers to engage in dialogue with each other, helping themselves and other customers who may be experiencing similar challenges. The Technology Spotlight in Chapter 8 discusses in greater detail how Cisco uses these online customer services.

Social interactions with others can influence health club members' satisfaction with the service.

CUSTOMERS' ROLES

The following sections examine in more detail three major roles played by customers in service cocreation and delivery: customers as productive resources, customers as contributors to quality and satisfaction, and customers as competitors.

Customers as Productive Resources

Service customers have been referred to as "partial employees" of the organization—human resources who contribute to the organization's productive capacity.[11] Some management experts have suggested that the organization's boundaries be expanded to consider the customer as part of the service system. In other words, if customers contribute effort, time, or other resources to the service production process, they should be considered as part of the organization. (Later in the chapter we devote a section to defining customers' jobs and strategies for involving them effectively.)

Customer inputs can affect the organization's productivity through both the quality of what they contribute and the resulting quality and quantity of output generated. In a business-to-business services context (see Exhibit 13.1), the contributions of the client can enhance the overall productivity of the firm in both quality and quantity of service.[12] In the hospital ICU example given previously, family members participate in caring for their loved ones in the ICU, thus increasing quality of care and health care outcomes, but also resulting in increased productivity as family members participate as "partial employees" of the hospital.[13] In a very different context, Swedish furniture retailer IKEA depends on customers to perform many critical service roles for themselves including measuring, locating, transporting, and assembling their own furniture, thus acting as productive coproducers and cocreators of value.

Customer participation in service production raises a number of issues for organizations. Because customers can influence both the quality and quantity of production, some experts believe the delivery system should be isolated as much as possible from customer inputs to reduce the uncertainty they can bring into the production process. This view sees customers as a major source of uncertainty—in the timing of their demands and the uncontrollability of their attitudes and actions. The logical conclusion is that any service activities that do not require customer contact or involvement should be performed away from customers: the less direct contact there is between the customer and the service production system, the greater the potential for the system to operate at peak efficiency.[14] Other experts believe that services can be delivered most efficiently if customers are truly viewed as partial employees and their coproduction roles are designed to maximize their contributions to the service creation process. The logic behind this view is that organizational productivity can be increased if customers learn to perform service-related activities they currently are not doing or are educated to perform more effectively the tasks they are already doing.[15]

For example, when self-service gasoline stations first came into being, customers were asked to pump their own gas. With customers performing this task, fewer employees were needed and the overall productivity of gas stations improved. Now most gas stations in the United States offer customers the option of paying for their gas at the pump by popping their credit cards into a slot on the pump or using a wireless device and leaving the station without dealing directly with a cashier. Similarly, the introduction of many automated airline services such as baggage check-in and self-ticketing are intended to speed up the process for customers while freeing employees for other tasks.[16] Organizational productivity is increased by using customers as a resource to perform tasks previously completed by employees. In both business-to-business and business-to-consumer contexts, organizations are turning to automated customer service, either online or via automated voice response systems. One prominent goal with online customer service is to increase organizational productivity by using the customer as a partial employee, performing his or her own service.

There are many, many examples today of organizations seeking to increase productivity through transferring tasks to customers. Although organizations derive obvious cost benefits by involving them as coproducers, customers do not always like or accept their new roles, especially when they perceive the purpose to be bottom-line cost savings for the company. If customers see no clear benefit to being involved in coproduction (e.g., lower prices, quicker access, better quality outcome), then they are likely to resent and resist their coproduction roles, particularly if they feel their own productivity or efficiency is suffering to benefit the company.[17]

Customers as Contributors to Service Quality and Satisfaction

Another role customers can play in service cocreation and delivery is that of contributor to their own satisfaction and the ultimate quality of the services they receive. Customers may care little that they have increased the productivity of the organization through their participation, but they likely care a great deal about whether their needs are fulfilled. Effective customer participation can increase the likelihood that needs are met and that the benefits the customer seeks are actually attained. Think about services such as health care, education, personal fitness, and weight loss in which the service outcome is highly dependent on customer participation. In these services, unless the customers perform their roles effectively, the desired service outcomes are not possible.

Research has shown that in education, active participation by students—as opposed to passive listening—increases learning (a desired service outcome) significantly.[18] The same is true in health care; patient compliance, in terms of taking prescribed medications or changing diet or other habits, can be critical to whether patients regain their health (the desired service outcome).[19] Other research in financial and medical service settings has shown that effective coproduction by customers leads to greater loyalty toward the service provider.[20] In all of these examples, the customers contribute directly to the quality of the outcome and to their own satisfaction with the service. In a business-to-business context, Yellow Transportation and others in the trucking and shipping industries have found that in many situations customers cause their own *dissatisfaction* with the service by failing to pack shipments appropriately, resulting in breakage or delays while items are repacked. Thus, ineffective coproduction can result in negative outcomes and dissatisfaction.

Research suggests that customers who believe they have done their part to be effective in service interactions are more satisfied with the service. In a study of the banking industry, bank customers were asked to rate themselves (on a scale from "strongly agree" to "strongly disagree") on questions related to their contributions to service delivery, as follows:

What They Did—Outcome Quality of Customer Inputs

I clearly explained what I wanted the bank employee to do.

I gave the bank employee proper information.

394 Part Five *Delivering and Performing Service*

I tried to cooperate with the bank employee.

I understand the procedures associated with this service.

How They Did It—Interaction Quality of Customer Inputs

I was friendly to the bank employee.

I have a good relationship with the bank employee.

I was courteous to the bank employee.

Receiving this service was a pleasant experience.

Results of the study indicated that the customers' perceptions of both what they did and how they did it were significantly related to customers' satisfaction with the service they received from the bank.[21] That is, those customers who responded more positively to the questions listed here were also more satisfied with the bank. Research in another context showed that customers' perceptions of service quality increased with greater levels of participation. Specifically, customers (in this case members of a YMCA) who participated more in the club gave the club higher ratings on aspects of service quality than did those who participated less.[22]

Customers contribute to quality service delivery when they ask questions, take responsibility for their own satisfaction, and complain when there is a service failure. Consider the service scenarios shown in Exhibit 13.2.[23] The four scenarios illustrate the wide variations in customer participation that can result in equally wide variations in service quality and customer satisfaction. Customers who take responsibility and providers who encourage their customers to become their partners in identifying and satisfying their own needs will together produce higher levels of service quality. Our Global Feature shows how Sweden's IKEA, the world's largest retailer of home furnishings, has creatively engaged its customers in a new role: "IKEA wants its customers to understand that their role is not to *consume* value but to *create* it."[24]

In addition to contributing to their own satisfaction by improving the quality of service delivered to them, some customers simply enjoy participating in service delivery. These customers find the act of participating to be intrinsically attractive.[25] They enjoy using the Internet to attain airline tickets, or doing all their banking via ATMs and online, pumping their own gas, or shopping at IKEA. Often customers who like self-service in one setting are predisposed to serving themselves in other settings as well.

Interestingly, because service customers must participate in service delivery, they frequently blame themselves (at least partially) when things go wrong. Why did it take so long to reach an accurate diagnosis of my health problem? Why was the service contract for our company's cafeteria food full of errors? Why was the room we reserved for our meeting unavailable when we arrived? If customers believe they are partially (or totally) to blame for the failure, they may be less dissatisfied with the service provider than when they believe the provider is responsible.[26] A series of studies suggests the existence of this "self-serving bias." That is, when services go better than expected, customers who have participated tend to take credit for the outcome and are less satisfied with the firm than are those customers who have not participated. However, when the outcome is worse than expected, customers who have chosen to participate in service production are less dissatisfied with the service than are those who choose not to participate—presumably because the participating customers have taken on some of the blame themselves.[27]

Customers as Competitors

A final role played by service customers is that of potential competitor. If self-service customers can be viewed as resources of the firm, or as "partial employees," they could in some cases partially perform the service or perform the entire service for

Exhibit 13.2 Which Customer (A or B) Will Be Most Satisfied?

For each scenario, ask "Which customer (A or B) will be most satisfied and receive the greatest quality and value, and why?"

SCENARIO 1: A MAJOR INTERNATIONAL HOTEL

Guest A called the desk right after check-in to report that his TV was not working and that the light over the bed was burned out; both problems were fixed immediately. The hotel staff exchanged his TV for one that worked and fixed the light bulb. Later they brought him a fruit plate to make up for the inconvenience. Guest B did not communicate to management until checkout time that his TV did not work and he could not read in his bed. His complaints were overheard by guests checking in, who wondered whether they had chosen the right place to stay.

SCENARIO 2: OFFICE OF A PROFESSIONAL TAX PREPARER

Client A has organized into categories the information necessary to do her taxes and has provided all documents requested by the accountant. Client B has a box full of papers and receipts, many of which are not relevant to her taxes but which she brought along "just in case."

SCENARIO 3: AN AIRLINE FLIGHT FROM LONDON TO NEW YORK

Passenger A arrives for the flight with a DVD player and reading material and wearing warm clothes; passenger A also ordered a special meal in advance. Passenger B, who arrives empty-handed, becomes annoyed when the crew runs out of blankets, complains about the magazine selection and the meal, and starts fidgeting after the inflight movie.

SCENARIO 4: ARCHITECTURAL CONSULTATION FOR REMODELING AN OFFICE BUILDING

Client A has invited the architects to meet with its remodeling and design committee made up of managers, staff, and customers to lay the groundwork for a major remodeling job that will affect everyone who works in the building as well as customers. The committee has already formulated initial ideas and surveyed staff and customers for input. Client B has invited architects in following a decision the previous week to remodel the building; the design committee is two managers who are preoccupied with other, more immediate tasks and have little idea what they need or what customers and staff would prefer in terms of a redesign of the office space.

---

themselves and not need the provider at all. Thus, customers in a sense are competitors of the companies that supply the service. Whether to produce a service for themselves (*internal exchange*)—for example, child care, home maintenance, car repair—or have someone else provide the service for them (*external exchange*) is a common dilemma for consumers.[28] Similar internal versus external exchange decisions are made by organizations. Firms frequently choose to outsource service activities such as payroll, data processing, research, accounting, maintenance, and facilities management. They find that it is advantageous to focus on their core businesses and leave these essential support services to others with greater expertise. Alternatively, a firm may decide to stop purchasing services externally and bring the service production process in-house.

Whether a household or a firm chooses to produce a particular service for itself or contract externally for the service depends on a variety of factors. A proposed model of internal/external exchange suggests that such decisions depend on the following:[29]

- *Expertise capacity.* The likelihood of producing the service internally is increased if the household or firm possesses the specific skills and knowledge needed to produce it. Having the expertise will not necessarily result in internal service production, however, because other factors (available resources and time) will also influence the decision. (For firms, making the decision to outsource is often based on recognizing that although they may have the expertise, someone else can do it better.)

- *Resource capacity.* To decide to produce a service internally, the household or firm must have the needed resources including people, space, money, equipment, and materials. If the resources are not available internally, external exchange is more likely.

IKEA of Sweden has managed to transform itself from a small, mail-order furniture company in the 1950s into the world's largest retailer of home furnishings. In 2007 more than 250 stores in more than 35 countries around the world generated more than 20 billion euros in sales. The company sells simple, functional, yet well-designed furnishings, charging significantly less than its competitors.

THE "DO-IT-YOURSELF" (DIY) CONCEPT

A key to IKEA's success is the company's relationship with its customers. IKEA has drawn the customer into its production system: "if customers agree to take on certain key tasks traditionally done by manufacturers and retailers—the assembly of products and their delivery to customers' homes—then IKEA promises to deliver well-designed products at substantially lower prices." In effect, IKEA's customers become essential contributors to value—they create value for themselves through participating in the selection, transportation, and assembly processes.

IKEA has made being part of the value creation process an easy, fun, and pleasant experience for customers. The company's stores are a pleasure to shop in. The stores are set up with "inspirational displays," including realistic room settings and real-life homes that allow customers to get comfortable with the furnishings, try them out, and visualize the possibilities in their own homes. To make shopping easy, free strollers and supervised child care are provided as well as wheelchairs for those who need them.

When customers enter the store they are given catalogs, tape measures, pens, and notepaper to use as they shop, allowing them to perform functions commonly done by sales and service staff. After payment, customers take their purchases to their cars on carts; if necessary they can rent or buy a roof rack to carry larger purchases. Thus, customers also provide furniture loading and delivery services for themselves. At home, IKEA customers then take on the role of manufacturer in assembling the new furnishings following carefully written, simple, and direct instructions.

GLOBAL ADAPTATIONS

IKEA prints catalogs and provides detailed websites in many different languages, making its products and instructions for their use accessible worldwide. In addition to tailoring its catalogs and websites, another key to IKEA's successful global expansion has been the company's policy of allowing each store to tailor its mix according to the local market needs and budgets. For example, Chinese customers save a high percentage of their income and are extremely price sensitive, so the prices there were initially the lowest in the world to lure the Chinese customers into the stores; $1 place-mats and 12¢ ice cream cones are examples. And, some furniture items were 50 to 60 percent less than similar items in the United States. This low-price strategy was atypical for Western brands in China. The response has been extremely positive, with four IKEA stores now open in China. The Beijing store that opened in 2006 is the largest IKEA store in the world outside of the flagship store in Sweden.

In addition to price variations, the store layout in Chinese stores was also adapted to reflect the design of many Chinese apartments. Because many of the apartments have balconies, the stores have a selection of balcony furnishings and displays. And because Chinese kitchens are generally small, relatively few kitchen items and furnishings are shown. Even IKEA's famous DIY assembly concept has also been adapted to some extent in China. Because fewer people have cars and therefore use public transportation, IKEA has more extensive delivery service in China than in most countries. And because labor is cheaper in China, many customers choose to have their furniture assembled for them rather than doing it themselves. Although IKEA has not abandoned its DIY strategy, it has been somewhat more flexible in China to suit customer realities in that country.

IKEA's success is attributable in part to recognizing that customers can be part of the business system, performing roles they have not performed before. The company's flexible implementation of this idea through clearly defining customers' new roles and making it fun to perform these roles is the genius of its strategy. Through the process, customers around the globe cocreate their own experiences and contribute to their own satisfaction.

Sources: http://www.ikea.com, 2007; R. Normann and R. Ramirez, "From Value Chain to Value Constellation: Designing Interactive Strategy," *Harvard Business Review* 71 (July–August 1993), pp. 65–77; B. Edvardsson and B. Enquist, "The IKEA Saga: How Service Culture Drives Service Strategy," *The Service Industries Journal* 22 (October 2002), pp. 153–186; P. M. Miller, "IKEA with Chinese Characteristics," *The China Business Review* (July/August 2004), pp. 36–38; and M. Fong, "IKEA Hits Home in China," *The Wall Street Journal,* March 3, 2006, pp. B1.

• *Time capacity.* Time is a critical factor in internal/external exchange decisions. Households and firms with adequate time capacity are more likely to produce services internally than are groups with time constraints.

• *Economic rewards.* The economic advantages or disadvantages of a particular exchange decision will be influential in choosing between internal and external options. The actual monetary costs of the two options will sway the decision.

• *Psychic rewards.* Rewards of a noneconomic nature have a potentially strong influence on exchange decisions. Psychic rewards include the degree of satisfaction, enjoyment, gratification, or happiness that is associated with the external or internal exchange.

• *Trust.* In this context, *trust* means the degree of confidence or certainty the household or firm has in the various exchange options. The decision will depend to some extent on the level of self-trust in producing the service versus trust of others.

• *Control.* The household or firm's desire for control over the process and outcome of the exchange will also influence the internal/external choice. Entities that desire and can implement a high degree of control over the task are more likely to engage in internal exchange.

The important thing to remember from this section is that in many service scenarios, customers can and often do choose to fully or partially produce the service themselves. Thus, in addition to recognizing that customers can be productive resources and cocreators of quality and value, organizations also need to recognize the customer's role as a potential competitor.

SELF-SERVICE TECHNOLOGIES—THE ULTIMATE IN CUSTOMER PARTICIPATION

Self-service technologies (SSTs) are services produced entirely by the customer without any direct involvement or interaction with the firm's employees. As such, SSTs represent the ultimate form of customer participation along a continuum from services that are produced entirely by the firm to those that are produced entirely by the customer. This continuum is depicted in Figure 13.1, using the example of retail gasoline service to illustrate the various ways the same service could be delivered along all points on the continuum. At the far right end of the continuum, the gas station attendant does everything from pumping the gas to taking payment. On the other end of the spectrum, the

FIGURE 13.1
Service Production Continuum

Source: Adapted from M. L. Meuter and M. J. Bitner, "Self-Service Technologies: Extending Service Frameworks and Identifying Issues for Research," in *Marketing Theory and Applications,* ed. D. Grewal and C. Pechmann (American Marketing Association Winter Educators' Conference, 1998), pp. 12–19. Reprinted by permission of the American Marketing Association.

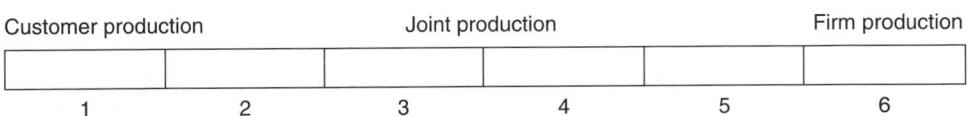

Customer production		Joint production		Firm production	
1	2	3	4	5	6

Gas station illustration
1. Customer pumps gas and pays at the pump with automation.
2. Customer pumps gas and goes inside to pay attendant.
3. Customer pumps gas and attendant takes payment at the pump.
4. Attendant pumps gas and customer pays at the pump with automation.
5. Attendant pumps gas and customer goes inside to pay attendant.
6. Attendant pumps gas and takes payment from customer at the pump.

customer does everything; in between are various forms and levels of customer participation. Many service delivery options, across industries, could be laid out on this type of continuum from total customer production through total firm production.

A Proliferation of New SSTs

Advances in technology, particularly the Internet, have allowed the introduction of a wide range of self-service technologies that occupy the far left end of the customer participation continuum in Figure 13.1. These technologies have proliferated as companies see the potential cost savings and efficiencies that can be achieved, potential sales growth, increased customer satisfaction, and competitive advantage. A partial list of some of the self-service technologies available to consumers includes

- ATMs.
- Pay at the pump.
- Airline check-in.
- Hotel check-in and checkout.
- Automated car rental.
- Automated filing of legal claims.
- Online driver's license testing.
- Automated betting machines.
- Electronic blood pressure machines.
- Various vending services.
- Tax preparation software.
- Self-scanning at retail stores.
- Internet banking.
- Vehicle registration online.
- Online auctions.
- Home and car buying online.
- Automated investment transactions.
- Insurance online.
- Package tracking.
- Internet shopping.
- Internet information search.
- Interactive voice response phone systems.
- Distance education.

The rapid proliferation of new SSTs is occurring for several reasons.[30] Many times firms are tempted by the cost savings that they anticipate by shifting customers to technology-based, automated systems and away from expensive personal service. If cost savings is the only reason for introducing an SST and if customers see no apparent benefits, the SST is likely to fail. Customers quickly see through this strategy and are not likely to adopt the SST if they have alternative options for service. Other times, firms introduce new SSTs based on customer demand. For example, customers now expect to find information, services, and delivery options online. When they do not find what they want from a particular firm online, they are likely to choose a competitor. Thus, customer demand in some industries is forcing firms to develop and offer their services via technology. Other companies are developing SSTs to open up new geographic, socioeconomic, and lifestyle markets that were not available to them through traditional channels.

Customer Usage of SSTs

Some of the SSTs listed earlier—ATMs, online ordering, Internet information search—have been very successful, embraced by customers for the benefits they provide in terms of convenience, accessibility, and ease of use.[31] Benefits to firms, including cost savings and revenue growth, can also result for those SSTs that succeed. Others—airline ticketing kiosks, grocery self-scanning—have been less quickly embraced by customers. With grocery self-scanning systems (as illustrated in the accompanying photo) the early reluctance of customers to adopt them reflected many factors including fear of the technology, looking incompetent in front of other customers, desire for human interaction, and a sense that "scanning and bagging groceries is the store's job, not mine."

Customers help produce the service for themselves through scanning their own groceries.

SST failures result when customers see little personal benefit in the new technology or when they do not have the ability to use it or know what they are supposed to do. Often, adopting a new SST requires customers to change their traditional behaviors significantly, and many are reluctant to make those changes. For example, when the upscale auctioneer, Christie's International, ventured into live online auctions, the response from bidders was slow.[32] The company credited the slow response to clients' needing time to become familiar and grow comfortable with the technology and the new way of bidding as well as to see more clearly how the online approach could benefit them. Christie's initial slow results were consistent with research on SSTs in other contexts. Research looking at customer adoption of SSTs found that "customer readiness" is a major factor in determining whether customers will even try a new self-service option.[33] Customer readiness results from a combination of personal motivation (What is in it for me?), ability (Do I have the ability to use this SST?), and role clarity (Do I understand what I am supposed to do?). In other cases, customers see no value in using the technology when compared to the alternative interpersonal mode of delivery, or the SSTs may be so poorly designed that customers may prefer not to use them.[34]

Success with SSTs

Throughout the text we have highlighted some of the most successful self-service technologies in the marketplace today: Cisco Systems (Chapter 8), Wells Fargo (Chapter 9), Amazon.com (Chapter 5), and iPrint (the opening vignette in this chapter). These companies have been successful because they offer clear benefits to customers, the benefits are well understood and appreciated compared to the alternative delivery modes, and the technology is user-friendly and reliable. In addition, customers understand their roles and have the capability to use the technology.

From a strategic perspective, research suggests that as firms move into SSTs as a mode of delivery, these questions are important to ask:[35]

- What is our strategy? What do we hope to achieve through the SST (cost savings, revenue growth, competitive advantage)?
- What are the benefits to customers of producing the service on their own through the SST? Do they know and understand these benefits?
- How can customers be motivated to try the SST? Do they understand their role? Do they have the capability to perform this role?
- How "technology ready" are our customers?[36] Are some segments of customers more ready to use the technology than others?
- How can customers be involved in the design of the service technology system and processes so that they will be more likely to adopt and use the SST?
- What forms of customer education will be needed to encourage adoption? Will other incentives be needed?
- How will inevitable SST failures be handled to regain customer confidence?

STRATEGIES FOR ENHANCING CUSTOMER PARTICIPATION

The level and the nature of customer participation in the service process are strategic decisions that can impact an organization's productivity, its positioning relative to competitors, its service quality, and its customers' satisfaction. In the following sections we will examine the strategies captured in Figure 13.2 for involving customers

FIGURE 13.2
Strategies for Enhancing Customer Participation

Source: Adapted from M. L. Meuter and M. J. Bitner, "Self Service Technologies: Extending Service Frameworks and Identifying Issues for Research," in *Marketing Theory and Applications,* ed. D. Grewal and C. Pechmann (American Marketing Association Winter Educators' Conference, 1998), pp. 12–19. Reprinted by permission of the American Marketing Association.

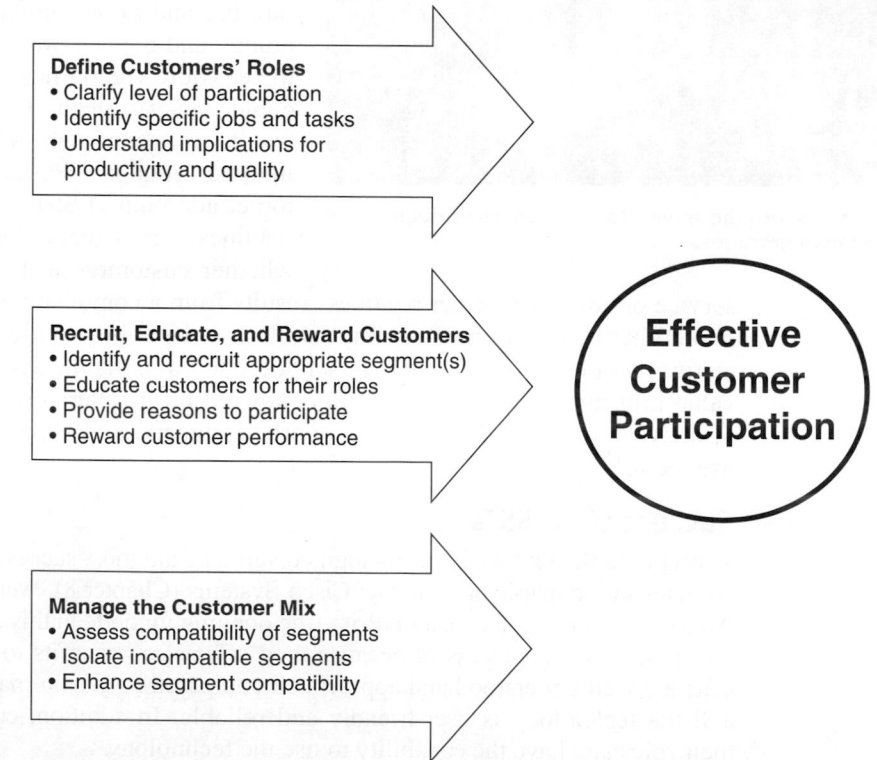

Define Customers' Roles
- Clarify level of participation
- Identify specific jobs and tasks
- Understand implications for productivity and quality

Recruit, Educate, and Reward Customers
- Identify and recruit appropriate segment(s)
- Educate customers for their roles
- Provide reasons to participate
- Reward customer performance

Manage the Customer Mix
- Assess compatibility of segments
- Isolate incompatible segments
- Enhance segment compatibility

Effective Customer Participation

effectively in the service delivery and cocreation process. The overall goals of a customer participation strategy will typically be to increase organizational productivity and customer satisfaction while simultaneously decreasing uncertainty due to unpredictable customer actions

Define Customers' Roles

In developing strategies for addressing customer involvement in service cocreation and delivery, the organization first determines what type of participation is desirable from customers and how the customer wishes to participate. Identifying the current level of customer participation can serve as a starting point. Customers' roles may be partially predetermined by the nature of the service, as suggested in Table 13.1. The service may require only the customer's presence (a concert, airline travel), or it may require moderate levels of input from the customer in the form of effort or information (a haircut, tax preparation), or it may require the customer to actually cocreate the service outcome (fitness training, consulting, self-service offerings). In some cases, the service may be dependent on customers cocreating the service with and for each other as in the case of eBay, Facebook, and many of the social networking services available online.

The organization may decide that it is satisfied with the existing level of participation it requires from customers but wants to make the participation more effective. For example, Charles Schwab has always positioned itself as a company whose customers are highly involved in their personal investment decisions. Over time this position has been implemented in different ways. Advances in technology have allowed Charles Schwab to solidify its position as a leading investment company for independent investors.

Alternatively, the organization may choose to increase the level of customer participation, which may reposition the service in the customers' eyes. Experts have suggested that higher levels of customer participation are strategically advisable when service production and delivery are inseparable; marketing benefits (cross-selling, building loyalty) can be enhanced by on-site contact with the customer; and customers can substitute for the labor and information provided by employees.[37] Higher levels of customer participation may also be advisable when increased participation is desired by customers and when it can enhance their satisfaction and service outcomes. For example, in health care, researchers and providers are working on ways to gain more active customer participation in treatment decisions. The Internet and other technology advances have helped propel customers into this role in taking responsibility for their own health and well-being, as illustrated in our Technology Spotlight.

Finally, the organization may decide it wants to reduce customer participation due to all the uncertainties it causes. In such situations the strategy may be to isolate all but the essential tasks, keeping customers away from the service facility and employees as much as possible.[38] Mail order is an extreme example of this form of service. Customers are in contact with the organization via telephone or the Internet, never see the organization's facility, and have limited employee interactions. The customer's role is thus extremely limited and can interfere very little with the service delivery process.

Once the desired level of participation (from both the customer and firm perspectives) is clear, the organization can define more specifically what the customer's role and tasks entail—in essence the customer's "job description."[39] The job description will vary with the type of service and the organization's desired position within its industry. It might entail helping oneself, helping others, or promoting the company.

Technology Spotlight Technology Facilitates Customer Participation in Health Care

Customer participation is facilitated by technology in many industries. For example, in education, technology allows students to interact with each other and their professors via e-mail, discussion boards, group chat sessions, and course materials provided online. In real estate, technology allows buyers to preview homes and develop lists of places they would like to visit without having to rely totally on a real estate agent to find all available properties. And in high-technology industries, business customers often interact with each other on the Web, helping each other solve problems, answering each other's questions, and so forth. All these examples show how technology—particularly the Internet—has facilitated customer participation and increased customer satisfaction.

Nowhere is this result more apparent than in health care. There is probably no greater, higher-participation service context than health care, where the customer must participate and where the provider and customer clearly cocreate the service. Patient participation is required at multiple levels. To achieve optimal health outcomes, patients must

- Provide accurate information about symptoms and health background.
- Answer detailed questions.
- Help decide on a course of treatment.
- Carry out the prescribed regimen leading to recovery and/or prevention.

Technology is clearly influencing how customers perform these roles and shifting in some senses the power of information into the hands of consumers. Annual studies by the Pew Internet and American Life Project, funded by the Pew Charitable Trusts, illuminate the trends in online health care. This research showed that as of 2006, 80 percent of U.S.

Internet users, or more than 113 million people, had gone online in search of health information. On a typical day in 2006, about 8 million adult Internet users searched for information on a health-related topic online. This is similar to the number of users who are paying bills online, reading blogs, or using the Internet to look up an address or phone number in any given day. They seek information about specific diseases, mental health, nutrition and fitness, drugs and drug interactions, and specific doctors and hospitals. More than 36 percent sought information for themselves and their own medical conditions, and just less than 50 percent sought information on behalf of a friend or family member. People like getting health information this way because of the convenience, the wealth of information that is available, and the fact that research can be done anonymously. Those who seek health information online also report feeling reassured, confident, and relieved or comforted by the information they find. However, significant numbers of online health information seekers still feel overwhelmed, frustrated, confused, or frightened by the information.

Thousands of Internet sites provide some type of health-related information. Some belong to health care providers like Mayo Clinic (www.mayo.edu) or pharmacy benefits providers like CVSCaremark (www.caremark.com). Others are operated totally online—like WebMD (www.webmdhealth.com) or Drugstore.com (www.drugstore.com)—without affiliation to a specific health care provider. Some respected sites are sponsored by governmental entities such as the U.S. Department of Health and Human Services site (www.healthfinder.gov) and a site developed by the National Library of Medicine and the National Institutes of Health (www.medlineplus.gov). Yet other sites provide information for specific health

Helping Oneself

In many cases the organization may decide to increase the level of customer involvement in service delivery through active participation. In such situations, the customer becomes a productive resource, performing aspects of the service previously performed by employees or others. Many of the examples presented in this chapter are illustrations of customers "helping themselves" (IKEA of Sweden, Charles Schwab, the Technology Spotlight). The result may be increased productivity for the firm and/or increased value, quality, and satisfaction for the customer.

conditions such as AIDS, depression, diabetes, breast cancer, and so on. Still others such as Hospital Compare (www.hospitalcompare.hhs.gov) can help patients determine the best hospitals to go to based on various quality and health outcome criteria.

All this readily available medical information is changing the role of the health care consumer to one of active participant in diagnosing illnesses, assessing treatment options, and determining overall well-being. Armed with information, patients gain confidence in asking questions and seeking appropriate diagnoses. In some cases they can e-mail questions to their doctors or other providers or find support in chat groups, bulletin boards, and e-mail lists on the Internet. They are also comforted by what they find online and often make decisions or change their overall approach to maintaining their health based on what they find.

Sources: S. Fox, "Online Health Search 2006," The Pew Internet and American Life Project, October 2006, www.pewinternet.org; and T. Francis, "How to Size Up Your Hospital," *The Wall Street Journal,* July 10, 2007, pp. D1+.

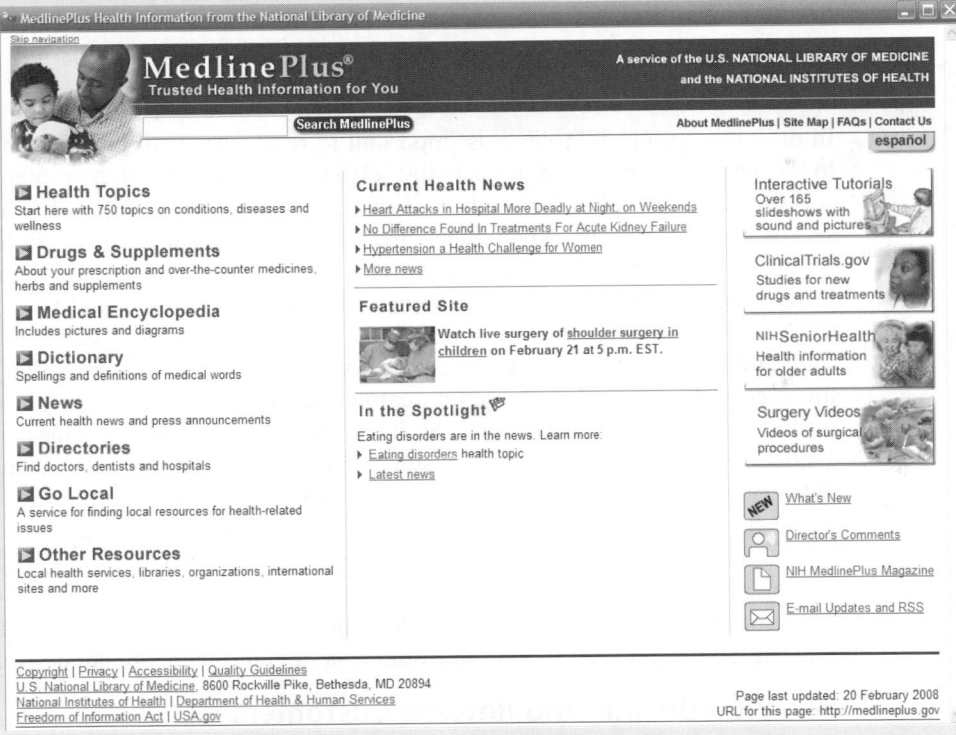

Helping Others

Sometimes the customer may be called on to help others who are experiencing the service. A child at a day care center might be appointed "buddy of the day" to help a new child acclimate into the environment. Long-time residents of retirement communities often assume comparable roles to welcome new residents. Many universities have established mentoring programs in which experienced students with similar backgrounds help newcomers adjust and learn the system. Many membership organizations (like health clubs, churches, and social organizations) also rely heavily, although often informally, on current members to help orient new members and make them feel welcome. In engaging in these types of roles, customers are again performing productive functions for the organization increasing customer satisfaction and retention. Acting as a mentor or facilitator can have very positive effects on the person performing the role and is likely to increase his or her loyalty as well.

Promoting the Company

In some cases the customer's job may include a sales or promotional element. As you know from previous chapters, service customers rely heavily on word-of-mouth endorsements in deciding which providers to try. They are more comfortable getting a recommendation from someone who has actually experienced the service than from advertising alone. A positive recommendation from a friend, relative, colleague, or even an acquaintance can pave the way for a positive service experience. Many service organizations are imaginative in getting their current customers to work as promoters or salespeople. For example, a dental practice encourages referrals by sending flowers, candy, or tickets to a local sports event to its patients whose names appear frequently in their "who referred you?" database. Another example is a nightclub that holds regular drawings (using business cards left by its patrons). Those whose names are drawn get a free party (no entry charge) for as many of their friends as they want to invite.

Individual Differences: Not Everyone Wants to Participate

In defining customers' roles it is important to remember that not everyone will want to participate.[40] Some customers enjoy self-service, whereas others prefer to have the service performed entirely for them. Companies that provide education and training services to organizations know that some customers want to be involved in designing the training and perhaps in delivering it to their employees. Other companies want to hand over the entire training design and delivery to the consulting organization, staying at arms length with little of their own time and energy invested in the service. In health care, it is clear that some patients want lots of information and want to be involved in their own diagnosis and treatment decisions. Others simply want the doctor to tell them what to do. Despite all the customer service and purchase options now available via the Internet, many customers still prefer human, high-contact service delivery rather than self-service. Research has shown, for example, that customers with a high "need for human interaction" are less likely to try new self-service options offered via the Internet and automated phone systems.[41] Because of these differences in preferences, most companies find they need to provide service delivery choices for different market segments. For example, banks typically customize their services by offering both automated self-service options and high-touch, human delivery options.

Recruit, Educate, and Reward Customers

Once the customer's role is clearly defined, the organization can think in terms of facilitating that role. In a sense, the customer becomes a "partial employee" of the organization at some level, and strategies for managing customer behavior in service production and delivery can mimic to some degree the efforts aimed at service employees discussed in Chapter 12. As with employees, customer participation in service production and delivery will be facilitated when (1) customers understand their roles and how they are expected to perform, (2) customers are able to perform as expected, and (3) customers receive valued rewards for performing as expected.[42] Through these means, the organization will also reduce the inherent uncertainty associated with the unpredictable quality and timing of customer participation. Exhibit 13.3 illustrates how the utility

New technologies are allowing utility companies to communicate directly with customers and provide them with innovative tools and information that are shaping energy consumption behavior. The result should benefit all parties by cutting greenhouse emissions from power plants, slowing down rising electricity costs, and saving consumers' money as well. Surveys suggest that U.S. consumers are becoming increasingly open and willing to make the adjustments needed to reduce energy consumption overall and to begin addressing climate change predictions and fears. The new energy saving tools include such things as online calculators, new high-tech meters in homes, visible in-home displays that show energy consumption at different times of day, remote control devices, prepaid electricity, and innovative pricing.

Utilities across the United States are experimenting with different approaches. For example, in northern California, Pacific Gas & Electric has introduced an online tool that shows customers how their personal energy consumption is tied to greenhouse gas emissions. This tool can help individual customers see how changes in their personal behavior can have significant energy and pollution-reducing results. Progress Energy in the Carolinas has introduced many new programs to double its energy conservation over just a few years. One example is a wireless device that measures energy

usage of individual appliances and allows consumers to immediately see the reduction in dollar costs and kilowatt-hour savings when they turn off an appliance. In southern California, customers are volunteering to be part of a plan that allows the utility to turn their air-conditioning units off at predetermined times to save peak demand. And, Florida Power & Light has introduced a program for small-business owners that calculates how much energy different pieces of equipment use, and when energy usage is most costly.

All of these innovative programs depend on customer acceptance, participation, and significant changes in behavior. To be successful, these innovative programs require investments in consumer education and incentives that will encourage them to change their behavior. Through this process, utility customers become "partial employees" of the utility companies by monitoring their own energy consumption and taking actions to reduce it. The result is reduced costs for the energy company, reduced prices for customers, less energy consumption overall, and better air quality in the short and long term.

Sources: R. Smith, "Letting the Power Company Control Your AC," *The Wall Street Journal*, July 10, 2007, p. D1+; and R. Smith, "New Ways to Monitor Your Energy Use," *The Wall Street Journal*, July 19, 2007, p. D1+.

industry is innovating new services that engage customers as partial employees while also rewarding them for their efforts. These initiatives also serve the larger common good by protecting the environment and preserving natural resources.

Recruit the Right Customers

Before the company begins the process of educating and socializing customers for their roles, it must attract the right customers to fill those roles. The expected roles and responsibilities of customers should be clearly communicated in advertising, personal selling, and other company messages. By previewing their roles and what is required of them in the service process, customers can self-select into (or out of) the relationship. Self-selection should result in enhanced perceptions of service quality from the customer's point of view and reduced uncertainty for the organization.

To illustrate, a child care center that requires parent participation on the site at least one-half day per week needs to communicate that expectation before it enrolls any child in its program. For some families, this level of participation will not be possible or desirable, thus precluding them from enrolling in the center. The expected level of participation needs to be communicated clearly to attract customers who are ready and willing to perform their roles. In a sense this situation is similar to a manufacturing firm exercising control over the quality of inputs into the production process.[43]

Exhibit 13.4 Weight Watchers Educates and Orients New Members

When new members first join Weight Watchers, one of the largest and most successful commercial weight loss organizations in the world, they are thoroughly educated regarding the program and their responsibilities. For example, when a new member attends her first meeting at a local chapter of Weight Watchers she receives an orientation to the program as well as step-by-step instructions including a "Getting Started" packet; food-tracking journals; activity calculators; and weekly guides for cooking, eating out, and more. Prior to attending the meeting, a new member can find a great deal of orientation information online that describes the weekly meetings, what happens at the meeting, and what is expected of the customer. Through the orientation, the booklets, and the food and activity forms, the organization clearly defines the member's responsibilities and makes the plan as easy as possible to follow.

Educate and Train Customers to Perform Effectively

Customers need to be educated, or in essence "socialized," so that they can perform their roles effectively. Through the socialization process, service customers gain an appreciation of specific organizational values, develop the abilities necessary to function within a specific context, understand what is expected of them, and acquire the skills and knowledge to interact with employees and other customers.[44] Customer education programs can take the form of formal orientation programs, written literature provided to customers, directional cues and signage in the service environment, and information obtained from employees and other customers.

Many services offer "customer orientation" programs to assist customers in understanding their roles and what to expect from the process before experiencing it. When customers begin the Weight Watchers program, the company website and their first group meeting includes a thorough orientation to the program and their responsibilities, as described in Exhibit 13.4. In another context—mammography screening—research has found that orientation and formal education of customers can relieve customer fears and perceptions of risk and ultimately increase customer satisfaction.[45] Customer education can also be partially accomplished through written literature, online resources, and customer "handbooks." Many hospitals have developed patient materials, very similar in appearance to employee handbooks, to describe what the patient should do in preparation for arrival at the hospital, what will happen when he or she arrives, and policies regarding visiting hours and billing procedures. The information may even describe the roles and responsibilities of family members.

Although formal training and written information are usually provided in advance of the service experience, other strategies can continue customer socialization during the experience itself. On site, customers require two kinds of orientation: *place orientation* (Where am I? How do I get from here to there?) and *function orientation* (How does this organization work? What am I supposed to do?).[46] Signage, the layout of the service facility, and other orientation aids can help customers answer these questions, allowing them to perform their roles more effectively. Orientation aids can also take the form of rules that define customer behavior for safety (airlines, health clubs), appropriate dress (restaurants, entertainment venues), and noise levels (hotels, classrooms, theaters).

Customers may also be socialized to their expected roles through information provided by employees and by observing other customers. It has been said that when McDonald's first went to England, the British customers were not accustomed to busing their own trays. They quickly learned, however, by observing the customers that McDonald's had hired to "demonstrate" appropriate busing behavior. These customers were paid to sit in the restaurants and at predictable intervals carry a dirty tray over to the trash can and dispose of it.

Reward Customers for Their Contributions

Customers are more likely to perform their roles effectively, or to participate actively, if they are rewarded for doing so. Rewards are likely to come in the form of increased control over the delivery process, time savings, monetary savings, and psychological or physical benefits. For instance, some CPA firms require clients to complete extensive forms before they meet with their accountants. If the forms are completed, the CPAs will have less work to do and the clients will be rewarded with fewer billable hours. Those clients who choose not to perform the requested role will pay a higher price for the service. ATM customers who perform banking services for themselves are also rewarded through greater access to the bank, in terms of both locations and times. In health care contexts, patients who perform their roles effectively are likely to be rewarded with better health or quicker recovery. For a long time airlines have offered price discounts for passengers who order tickets online, providing a monetary incentive for customer participation.

Customers may not realize the benefits or rewards of effective participation unless the organization makes the benefits apparent to them. In other words, the organization needs to clarify the performance-contingent benefits that can accrue to customers just as it defines performance-contingent benefits to employees. The organization also should recognize that not all customers are motivated by the same types of rewards. Some may value the increased access and time savings they can gain by performing their service roles effectively. Others may value the monetary savings. Still others may be looking for greater personal control over the service outcome.

Avoid Negative Outcomes of Inappropriate Customer Participation

If customers are not effectively socialized, the organization runs the risk that inappropriate customer behaviors will result in negative outcomes for customers, employees, and the organization itself:[47]

1. Customers who do not understand the service system or the process of delivery may slow down the service process and negatively affect their own as well as other customers' outcomes. In a rental car context, customers who do not understand the reservation process, the information needed from them, insurance coverage issues, and the pickup and drop-off procedures can slow the flow for employees and other customers, lowering both productivity and quality of service.

2. If customers do not perform their roles effectively, it may not be possible for employees to provide the levels of technical and process quality promised by the organization. For example, in a management consulting practice, clients who do not provide the information and cooperation needed by the consultants will likely receive inferior service in terms of both the usefulness of the management report and the timeliness of the delivery.

3. If customers are frustrated because of their own inadequacies and incompetencies, employees are likely to suffer emotionally and be less able to deliver quality service. For example, if customers routinely enter the service delivery process with little knowledge of how the system works and their role in it, they are likely to take out their frustrations on frontline employees. This negative impact on individual employees can take its toll on the organization in the form of turnover and decreased motivation to serve.

Manage the Customer Mix

Because customers frequently interact with each other in the process of service delivery and consumption, another important strategic objective is the effective management of the mix of customers who simultaneously experience the service. If a restaurant chooses to serve two segments during the dinner hour that are incompatible with each other—for example, single college students who want to party and families with small children who want quiet—it may find that the two groups do not merge well. Of course it is possible to manage these segments so that they do not interact with each other by seating them in separate sections or by attracting the two segments at different times of day. Serving incompatible customer segments is also an issue at professional sporting events where families with children may be sitting next to loud (and sometimes drunk and obnoxious) fans. Each of these groups has differing, and incompatible, goals for the experience. Similarly, many university golf courses must often cater to both student customers (who are not knowledgeable of the rules of the game, lack proper equipment and clothing and may be loud and inconsiderate of others) and older, perhaps retired, customers who are very knowledgeable of the rules and follow them religiously, generally have the proper equipment, clothing, and are respectful and serious when playing. Again, the two groups have different goals for the experience and radically different levels of understanding of the sometimes unstated rules.

The process of managing multiple and sometimes conflicting segments is known as *compatibility management,* broadly defined as "a process of first attracting [where possible] homogeneous consumers to the service environment, then actively managing both the physical environment and customer-to-customer encounters in such a way as

TABLE 13.2   Characteristics of Service That Increase the Importance of Compatible Segments

Source: Adapted from C. I. Martin and C. A. Pranter, "Compatibility Management: Customer-to-Customer Relationships in Service Environments," *Journal of Services Marketing* 3, no. 3 (Summer 1989), pp. 5–15. Reprinted with the permission of MCB University Press.

Characteristic	Explanation	Examples
Customers are in close physical proximity to each other.	Customers will more often notice each other and be influenced by each other's behavior when they are in close physical proximity.	Airplane flights Entertainment events Sports events
Verbal interaction takes place among customers.	Conversation (or lack thereof) can be a component of both satisfying and dissatisfying encounters with fellow patrons.	Full-service restaurants Cocktail lounges Educational settings
Customers are engaged in numerous and varied activities.	When a service facility supports varied activities all going on at the same time, the activities themselves may not be compatible.	Universities Health clubs Resort hotels
The service environment attracts a heterogeneous customer mix.	Many service environments, particularly those open to the public, will attract a variety of customer segments.	Public parks Public transportation Open-enrollment colleges
The core service is compatibility.	The core service is to arrange and nurture compatible relationships between customers.	Big Brothers/Big Sisters Weight loss group programs Mental health support groups
Customers must occasionally wait for the service.	Waiting in line for service can be monotonous or anxiety producing. The boredom or stress can be magnified or lessened by other customers, depending on their compatibility.	Medical clinics Tourist attractions Restaurants
Customers are expected to share time, space, or service utensils with each other.	The need to share space, time, and other service factors is common in many services but may become a problem if segments are not comfortable with sharing with each other or if the need to share is intensified because of capacity constraints.	Golf courses Hospitals Retirement communities Airplanes

to enhance satisfying encounters and minimize dissatisfying encounters."[48] Compatibility management will be critically important for some businesses (such as health clubs, public transportation, and hospitals) and less important for others. Table 13.2 lists seven interrelated characteristics of service businesses that will increase the importance of compatibility management.

To manage multiple (and sometimes conflicting) segments, organizations rely on a variety of strategies. Attracting maximally homogeneous groups of customers through careful positioning and segmentation strategies is one approach. This strategy is used by the Ritz-Carlton Hotel, for which upscale travelers are the primary target segment. The Ritz-Carlton is positioned to communicate that message to the marketplace, and customers self-select into the hotel. However, even in that context there are potential conflicts—for example, when the hotel is simultaneously hosting a business convention, an NBA basketball team, and individual leisure travelers.

A second strategy is often used in such cases. Compatible customers are grouped together physically so that the segments are less likely to interact directly with each other. The Ritz-Carlton keeps meetings and large-group events separated from the areas of the hotel used by individual businesspeople. Many amusement parks (such as CedarPoint, Kings Island) that face similar issues will offer a special fee for those who attend after 6:00 p.m. Their target for this special fee is typically price-sensitive teenagers and/or college students. Families with small children tend to come at the beginning of the day and are likely to have exited the park by early evening; thus, the pricing strategy keeps these incompatible segments separated in time.

Other strategies for enhancing customer compatibility include customer "codes of conduct" such as the regulation of smoking behavior and dress codes. Clearly such codes of conduct may vary from one service establishment to another. Finally, training employees to observe customer-to-customer interactions and to be sensitive to potential conflicts is another strategy for increasing compatibility among segments. Employees can also be trained to recognize opportunities to foster positive encounters among customers in certain types of service environments.

Summary

This chapter focused on the role of customers in service cocreation and delivery. The customer receiving the service and fellow customers in the service environment can all potentially cause a widening of gap 3 if they fail to perform their roles effectively. A number of reasons customers may widen the service performance gap were suggested: customers lack understanding of their roles, customers are unwilling or unable to perform their roles, customers are not rewarded for good performance, other customers interfere, or market segments are incompatible.

Managing customers in the process of service delivery is a critical challenge for service firms. Whereas manufacturers are not concerned with customer participation in the manufacturing process, service managers constantly face this issue because their customers are often present and active partners in service production and cocreation. As participants in service creation, production, and delivery, customers can perform three primary roles, discussed and illustrated in the chapter: *productive resources* for the organization, *contributors* to service quality and satisfaction, and *competitors* in performing the service for themselves.

Through understanding the importance of customers in service performance and identifying the roles played by the customer in a particular context, managers can develop strategies to enhance customer participation. Strategies discussed in the text include defining the customers' roles and jobs, recruiting customers who match the customer profile in terms of desired level of participation, educating customers so they can perform their roles effectively, rewarding customers for their contributions, and managing the customer mix to enhance the experiences of all segments. By implementing these strategies, organizations should see a reduction in the service performance gap due to effective, efficient customer contributions to service delivery.

Discussion Questions

1. Using your own personal examples, discuss the general importance of customers in the successful creation and delivery of service experiences.
2. Why might customer actions and attitudes cause the service performance gap to occur? Use your own examples to illustrate your understanding.

3. Using Table 13.1, think of specific services you have experienced that fall within each of the three levels of customer participation: low, medium, high. Describe specifically what you did as a customer in each case. How did your involvement vary across the three types of service situations?

4. Describe a time when your satisfaction in a particular situation was *increased* because of something another customer did. Could (or does) the organization do anything to ensure that this experience happens routinely? What does it do? Should it try to make this situation a routine occurrence?

5. Describe a time when your satisfaction in a particular situation was *decreased* because of something another customer did. Could the organization have done anything to manage this situation more effectively? What?

6. Discuss the customer's role as a *productive resource* for the firm. Describe a time when you played this role. What did you do and how did you feel? Did the firm help you perform your role effectively? How?

7. Discuss the customer's role as a *contributor to service quality and satisfaction.* Describe a time when you played this role. What did you do and how did you feel? Did the firm help you perform your role effectively? How?

8. Discuss the customer's role as a potential *competitor.* Describe a time when you chose to provide a service for yourself rather than pay someone to provide the service for you. Why did you decide to perform the service yourself? What could have changed your mind, causing you to contract with someone else to provide the service?

Exercises

1. Visit a service establishment where customers can influence each other (such as a theme park, entertainment establishment, resort, shopping mall, restaurant, airline, school, or hospital). Observe (or interview) customers and record cases of positive and negative customer influence. Discuss how you would manage the situation to increase overall customer satisfaction.

2. Interview someone regarding his or her decision to outsource a service—for example, legal services, payroll, or maintenance in a company or cleaning, child care, or pet care in a household. Use the criteria for internal versus external exchange described in the text to analyze the decision to outsource.

3. Think of a service in which a high level of customer participation is necessary for the service to be successful (health club, weight loss, educational setting, health care, golf lessons, or the like). Interview a service provider in such an organization to find out what strategies the provider uses to encourage effective customer participation.

4. Visit a service setting in which multiple types of customer segments use the service at the same time (such as a theater, golf course, resort, or theme park). Observe (or interview the manager about) the organization's strategies to manage these segments effectively. Would you do anything differently if you were in charge?

5. Visit iPrint's website (www.iPrint.com). Compare its printing service process to similar onsite services offered by Kinko's. Compare and contrast the customer's role in each situation.

Notes

1. P. B. Seybold, *Customers.com: How to Create a Profitable Business Strategy for the Internet and Beyond* (New York: Random House, 1998), pp. 235–244; and www.iPrint.com, 2007.

2. See B. Schneider and D. E. Bowen, *Winning the Service Game* (Boston: Harvard Business School Press, 1995), chap. 4; L. A. Bettencourt, "Customer Voluntary

Performance: Customers as Partners in Service Delivery, *Journal of Retailing* 73 (Fall 1997), pp. 383–406; P. K. Mills and J. H. Morris, "Clients as 'Partial' Employees: Role Development in Client Participation," *Academy of Management Review* 11, no. 4 (1986), pp. 726–735; C. H. Lovelock and R. F. Young, "Look to Customers to Increase Productivity," *Harvard Business Review* 57 (Summer 1979), pp. 9–20; A. R. Rodie and S. S. Kleine, "Customer Participation in Services Production and Delivery," in *Handbook of Services Marketing and Management,* ed. T. A. Swartz and D. Iacobucci (Thousand Oaks, CA: Sage Publications, 2000), pp. 111–126; C. K. Prahalad and V. Ramaswamy, "Co-opting Customer Competence," *Harvard Business Review* 78 (January–February 2000), p. 7; and N. Bendapudi and R. P. Leone, "Psychological Implications of Customer Participation in Co-Production," *Journal of Marketing* 67 (January 2003), pp. 14–28.

3. S. L. Vargo, and R. F. Lusch, "Evolving to a New Dominant Logic for Marketing," *Journal of Marketing* 68 (January 2004), pp. 1–17; and R. F. Lusch, S. L. Vargo, and M O'Brien, "Competing Through Service: Insights from Service-Dominant Logic," *Journal of Retailing* 83, no. 1 (2007), pp. 5–18.

4. L. A. Bettencourt, S. W. Brown, A. L. Ostrom, and R. I. Roundtree, "Client Co-Production in Knowledge-Intensive Business Services," *California Management Review* 44 (Summer 2002), pp. 100–128.

5. See S. J. Grove and R. P. Fisk, "The Impact of Other Customers on Service Experiences: A Critical Incident Examination of 'Getting Along,' " *Journal of Retailing* 73 (Spring 1997), pp. 63–85; and C. I. Martin and C. A. Pranter, "Compatibility Management: Customer-to-Customer Relationships in Service Environments," *Journal of Services Marketing* 3 (Summer 1989), pp. 5–15.

6. Grove and Fisk, "The Impact of Other Customers on Service Experiences."

7. L. Landro, "ICUs' New Message: Welcome, Families," *The Wall Street Journal,* July 12, 2007, pp. A1+.

8. M. S. Rosenbaum and C. A. Massiah, "When Customers Receive Support from Other Customers," *Journal of Service Research* 9 (February 2007), pp. 257–270.

9. Grove and Fisk, "The Impact of Other Customers on Service Experiences."

10. K. Harris and S. Baron, "Consumer-to-Consumer Conversations in Service Settings," *Journal of Service Research* 6 (February 2004), pp. 287–303.

11. See P. K. Mills, R. B. Chase, and N. Margulies, "Motivating the Client/Employee System as a Service Production Strategy," *Academy of Management Review* 8, no. 2 (1983), pp. 301–310; D. E. Bowen, "Managing Customers as Human Resources in Service Organizations," *Human Resource Management* 25, no. 3 (1986), pp. 371–383; and Mills and Morris, "Clients as 'Partial' Employees."

12. Bettencourt et al., "Client Co-Production in Knowledge-Intensive Business Services."

13. Landro, "ICUs' New Message."

14. R. B. Chase, "Where Does the Customer Fit in a Service Operation?" *Harvard Business Review* 56 (November–December 1978), pp. 137–142.

15. Mills et al., "Motivating the Client/Employee System."

16. Marilyn Adams, "Tech Takes Bigger Role in Air Services," *USA Today,* July 18, 2001, p. 1.

17. M. Xue and P. T. Harker, "Customer Efficiency: Concept and Its Impact on E-Business Management," *Journal of Service Research* 4 (May 2002), pp. 253–267.

18. See D. W. Johnson, R. T. Johnson, and K. A. Smith, *Active Learning: Cooperation in the College Classroom* (Edina, MN: Interaction Book Company, 1991).

19. S. Dellande, M. C. Gilly, and J. L. Graham, "Gaining Compliance and Losing Weight: The Role of the Service Provider in Health Care Services," *Journal of Marketing* 68 (July 2004), pp. 78–91.

20. S. Auh, S. J. Bell, C. S. McLeod, and E. Shih, "Co-Production and Customer Loyalty in Financial Services," *Journal of Retailing* 83, no. 3 (2007), pp. 359–370.

21. S. W. Kelley, S. J. Skinner, and J. H. Donnelly Jr., "Organizational Socialization of Service Customers," *Journal of Business Research* 25 (1992), pp. 197–214.

22. C. Claycomb, C. A. Lengnick-Hall, and L. W. Inks, "The Customer As a Productive Resource: A Pilot Study and Strategic Implications," *Journal of Business Strategies* 18 (Spring 2001), pp. 47–69.

23. Several of the scenarios are adapted from C. Goodwin, "'I Can Do It Myself': Training the Service Consumer to Contribute to Service Productivity," *Journal of Services Marketing* 2 (Fall 1988), pp. 71–78.

24. R. Normann and R. Ramirez, "From Value Chain to Value Constellation: Designing Interactive Strategy," *Harvard Business Review* 71 (July–August 1993), pp. 65–77; and www.ikea.com, 2007.

25. J. E. G. Bateson, "The Self-Service Customer—Empirical Findings," in *Emerging Perspectives in Services Marketing,* eds. L. L. Berry, G. L. Shostack, and G. D. Upah (Chicago: American Marketing Association, 1983), pp. 50–53.

26. V. S. Folkes, "Recent Attribution Research in Consumer Behavior: A Review and New Directions," *Journal of Consumer Research* 14 (March 1988), pp. 548–565; and M. J. Bitner, "Evaluating Service Encounters: The Effects of Physical Surroundings and Employee Responses," *Journal of Marketing* 54 (April 1990), pp. 69–82.

27. Bendapudi and Leone, "Psychological Implications of Customer Participation in Co-Production."

28. R. F. Lusch, S. W. Brown, and G. J. Brunswick, "A General Framework for Explaining Internal vs. External Exchange," *Journal of the Academy of Marketing Science* 10 (Spring 1992), pp. 119–134.

29. Ibid.

30. See M. J. Bitner, A. L. Ostrom, and M. L. Meuter, "Implementing Successful Self-Service Technologies," *Academy of Management Executive* 16 (November 2002), pp. 96–109.

31. See P. Dabholkar, "Consumer Evaluations of New Technology-Based Self-Service Options: An Investigation of Alternative Models of Service Quality," *International Journal of Research in Marketing* 13, no. 1 (1996), pp. 29–51; F. Davis, "User Acceptance of Information Technology: System Characteristics, User Perceptions and Behavioral Impact," *International Journal of Man-Machine Studies* 38 (1993), pp. 475–487; L. M. Bobbitt and P. A. Dabholkar, "Integrating Attitudinal Theories to Understand and Predict Use of Technology-Based Self-Service," *International Journal of Service Industry Management* 12, no. 5 (2001), pp. 423–450; and J. M. Curran, M. L. Meuter, and C. F. Surprenant, "Intentions to Use Self-Service Technologies: A Confluence of Multiple Attitudes," *Journal of Service Research* 5 (February 2003), pp. 209–224.

32. K. Crow, "Online Bids, Christie's Fine-Arts Patrons Are Slow to Click," *The Wall Street Journal,* July 12, 2007, pp. B1+.

33. M. L. Meuter, M. J. Bitner, A. L. Ostrom, and S. W. Brown, "Choosing among Alternative Service Delivery Modes: An Investigation of Customer Trial of Self-Service Technologies," *Journal of Marketing* 69 (April 2005), pp. 61–83.

34. M. L. Meuter, A. L. Ostrom, R. I. Roundtree, and M. J. Bitner, "Self-Service Technologies: Understanding Customer Satisfaction with Technology-Based Service Encounters," *Journal of Marketing* 64 (July 2000), pp. 50–64.

35. Meuter, Bitner et al., "Choosing among Alternative Service Delivery Modes"; see also Y. Moon and F. X. Frei, "Exploding the Self-Service Myth," *Harvard Business Review* 78 (May–June 2000), pp. 26–27; and M. J. Bitner, et al., "Implementing Successful Self-Service Technologies."

36. A. Parasuraman and C. L. Colby, *Techno-Ready Marketing: How and Why Your Customers Adopt Technology* (New York: The Free Press, 2001).

37. Bowen, "Managing Customers as Human Resources."

38. Chase, "Where Does the Customer Fit in a Service Operation?"

39. See Schneider and Bowen, *Winning the Service Game,* chap. 4. The four job descriptions in this section are adapted from M. R. Bowers, C. L. Martin, and A. Luker, "Trading Places, Employees as Customers, Customers as Employees," *Journal of Services Marketing* 4 (Spring 1990), pp. 56–69.

40. Bateson, "The Self-Service Customer."

41. Meuter, Bitner et al., "Choosing among Alternative Service Delivery Modes."

42. Bowen, "Managing Customers as Human Resources"; and Schneider and Bowen, *Winning the Service Game,* chap. 4; Meuter, Bitner, et al., "Choosing among Alternative Service Delivery Modes"; Dellande et al., "Gaining Compliance and Losing Weight."

43. C. Goodwin and R. Radford, "Models of Service Delivery: An Integrative Perspective," in *Advances in Services Marketing and Management,* ed. T. A. Swartz, D. E. Bowen, and S. W. Brown, (Stamford, Ct: Jai Press) pp. 231–252.

44. S. W. Kelley, J. H. Donnelly Jr., and S. J. Skinner, "Customer Participation in Service Production and Delivery," *Journal of Retailing* 66 (Fall 1990), pp. 315–335; and Schneider and Bowen, *Winning the Service Game,* chap. 4.

45. W. T. Faranda, "Customer Participation in Service Production: An Empirical Assessment of the Influence of Realistic Service Previews," doctoral dissertation, Arizona State University, Tempe, Arizona, 1994.

46. Bowen, "Managing Customers as Human Resources."

47. Ibid; see also L. C. Harris and K. L. Reynolds, "The Consequences of Dysfunctional Customer Behavior," *Journal of Service Research* 6 (November 2003), pp. 144–161.

48. Martin and Pranter, "Compatibility Management."

Chapter Fourteen

Delivering Service through Intermediaries and Electronic Channels

This chapter's objectives are to

1. Identify the primary channels through which services are delivered to end customers.
2. Provide examples of each of the key service intermediaries.
3. Discuss the benefits and challenges of each method of service delivery.
4. Outline the strategies that are used to manage service delivery through intermediaries.

Netflix versus Blockbuster: The Battle for Distribution of DVD Rental Service

Videotape and DVD rental was once an in-store service only: customers went to video stores, picked out their movies before going home to watch them, and then returned them to the same stores when due. Consumers were largely satisfied with this approach, with the possible exception of two complaints: movies were not always available when desired, and consumers who returned them late had to pay fees that drove up the cost of the service. The leader in the market, Blockbuster, was a strong competitor with thousands of stores nationwide and a knack for innovation that kept customers satisfied by addressing these and other complaints that arose. To address the complaint of out-of-stock movies, for example, the company offered movies guaranteed to be in stock, and offered them free to customers when they did become available if the promised items were not available when they initially came into the store. It was hard to see how Blockbuster and its approach could be matched or bettered.

Netflix Offers an Online Alternative

In 1999, an upstart dot-com named Netflix invented an entirely new customer value proposition using an innovative DVD delivery system that threatened to beat

Blockbuster's approach. Addressing customers' desires for availability of titles and no late fees, the company created the concept of online video rental. Instead of going to stores to pick out titles, customers went online and chose from 80,000 different titles, five times more than at typical video stores. They made lists of the DVDs in the order they wanted to receive them and could typically keep three at a time for a set monthly fee. After watching the DVDs, they walked only as far as their mailboxes; deposited the viewed DVDs in prepaid mailers; and received new ones, usually within a single business, day by mail. They paid no late fees and had no due dates for the DVDs in their possession.

For a time, no one knew how well the online approach would work. Would customers really change their habits and rent online? Was the market for online rental

merely a niche, or did it have great potential? Were the disadvantages of online rental—particularly that customers did not always have exactly the title they wanted at the time they wanted to watch it—enough to discourage customers? It did not take long to see that customers liked the new service. Customer acceptance, as well as Netflix's ability to create an efficient business model using 40 distribution centers across the country, meant that the company increased revenues and continued to grow and prosper. By 2007, Netflix had 6.3 million subscribers, an increase of 51 percent over 2005. Revenue grew 46 percent to $l billion in 2007. Today, Netflix rents out more than 1.5 million DVDs a day!

Blockbuster Counters with an Online/In-Store Combination

In 2003, when Netflix began to amass a sizable group of customers, Blockbuster countered with a strategy that its competitor could not match. It offered a service that allowed customers to rent online or in its stores with a novel offering called BLOCKBUSTER Total Access.™ With Total Access, customers rented movies online (with delivery by mail) and then chose how to return them: by mail or by taking them to a Blockbuster store where they could exchange them for new movies right away. When customers finished watching movies they rented online, they could go right over to their Blockbuster stores and turn them in for new movies. This way, customers never had to wait (even a day) to have movies to watch and could be spontaneous about choosing something exactly right for their desires at any time. The store mailed back the returned movies, and customers received new items from their lists in another business day. Total Access had all the same benefits as Netflix—free shipping and postage, no late fees, no due dates, large library of DVDs—but also offered two different ways to get videos and actually allowed customers to have more videos at one time than Netflix. Netflix was so concerned about the service that it sued for patent infringement on the online rental process.

Delivery Models of the Future

Analysts believe that plenty of growth potential remains in the online and in-store DVD rental business, predicting an increase as high as 40 percent for 2008. Netflix and Blockbuster each added 2 million subscribers in 2007 alone. Yet Reed Hastings, CEO of Netflix, recently shared his philosophy that the only sustainable way to think about the movie delivery business is to recognize that change is inevitable. He views the business not as DVD rental, but as an online movie service with multiple different delivery models. One of those models being piloted allows subscribers to watch movies directly from the Netflix website, similar to watching on-demand movies in a hotel or on cable. Spending $40 million to put 5,000 titles on the site will offer the company a good idea of whether customers want to watch titles on their computers. And perhaps the most important advancement would be getting movies from its Internet service onto television sets. While Hastings would not confirm that Netflix was in development on its own device to connect to televisions, he did say that they have prototyped multiple possibilities. A device that accomplished this would allow Netflix and Blockbuster to meet and perhaps beat cable, satellite, and other closed systems such as Apple iTunes. None of these technology outlets currently have the breadth and depth of titles that either Netflix or Blockbuster possesses, but neither do the rental firms have the technology capability to get titles to television sets.

What will the distribution of DVD and other entertainment be in the future? We probably cannot envision it today, just like we could not have envisioned Netflix 10 years ago.

Sources: P. Patsuris, "Blockbuster Must Switch Scripts," *Forbes.com,* December 30, 2002; P. Patsuris, "Blockbuster Takes on New Strategy versus Netflix, *Forbes.com,* April 21, 2003; N. Wingfield, "Netflix versus Naysayers," *The Wall Street Journal,* March 27, 2007; "Blockbuster Cuts Online Rental Prices," *USA Today,* June 13, 2007; www.blockbuster.com; www.Netflix.com; and "Blockbuster Settles Clash with Netflix," *USA Today,* June 28, 2007.

As we demonstrate in the chapter-opening vignette, many services are now provided electronically through computers, kiosks, cell phones, televisions, and landline telephones. However, in most services, providers and consumers come into direct contact in service provision. Because of the inseparability of production and consumption in service, providers must either be present themselves when customers receive service or find ways to involve others in distribution. Involving others can be problematic because quality in service occurs in the service encounter between company and customer. Unless the service distributor is willing and able to perform in the service encounter as the service principal would, the value of the offering decreases and the reputation of the original service may be damaged. We all know of situations where nationally known service franchises are disappointing in an individual outlet. Recently, the American Marketing Association's conference of marketing professors was held in the Washington Hilton. While expectations of the professors were high, as the Hilton name conveyed a high level of service, performance at the hotel was low on room availability, responsiveness to requests, tangibles, and empathy.

Chapter 12 pointed out the challenges of controlling encounters within service organizations themselves, but most service (and many manufacturing) companies face an even more formidable task: attaining service excellence and consistency when intermediaries represent them to customers. This chapter discusses both the challenges of delivering service through intermediaries and approaches that engender alignment with the goals of the service provider.

Two distinct services marketers are involved in delivering service through intermediaries: the *service principal,* or originator, and the *service deliverer,* or intermediary. The service principal is the entity that creates the service concept (whose counterpart is the manufacturer of physical goods), and the service deliverer is the entity that interacts with the customer in the actual execution of the service (whose counterpart is the distributor, wholesaler, or retailer of physical goods). In this chapter, we examine the issues surrounding distribution of services from both perspectives.

SERVICE DISTRIBUTION

Direct Delivery of Service

As we have indicated throughout this textbook, services are generally intangible and experiential in nature. Thus, service distribution does not typically involve moving items through a chain of firms that begins with a manufacturer and ends with a consumer, as is the case for goods distribution. In fact, many services are delivered directly from the service producer to the consumer. That is, in contrast to channels for goods, channels for services are often *direct*—with the creator of the service (i.e., the service principal) selling directly to and interacting directly with the customer. Examples include air travel (Southwest Airlines), health care (Mayo Clinic), and consulting services (IBM Global Services). Because services cannot be owned, there are no titles or rights to most services that can be passed along a delivery channel. Because services are intangible and perishable, inventories cannot exist, making warehousing a dispensable function. In general, because services cannot be produced, warehoused, and then retailed, as goods can, many channels available to goods producers are not feasible for service firms. Thus, many of the primary functions that distribution channels serve—inventorying, securing, and taking title to goods—have no meaning in services.

Delivery of Service through Intermediaries

Even though many of the functions that intermediaries provide for goods manufacturers are not relevant for service firms, intermediaries often deliver services and perform several important functions for service principals. First, they may coproduce the service, fulfilling service principals' promises to customers. Franchise services such as haircutting, key making, and dry cleaning are produced by the intermediary (the franchisee) using a process developed by the service principal. Service intermediaries also make services locally available, providing time and place convenience for the customer. Because they represent multiple service principals, such intermediaries as travel and insurance agents provide a retailing function for customers, gathering together in one place a variety of choices. And in many financial or professional services, intermediaries function as the glue between the brand or company name and the customer by building the trusting relationship required in these complex and expert offerings.

The primary types of intermediaries used in service delivery are franchisees, agents, brokers, and electronic channels. *Franchisees* are service outlets licensed by a principal to deliver a unique service concept it has created or popularized. Examples include fast-food chains (McDonald's, Burger King), video stores (Blockbuster), automobile repair services (Jiffy Lube, Midas), and hotels (Holiday Inn, Hampton Inn). *Agents and brokers* are representatives who distribute and sell the services of one or more service suppliers. Examples include insurance (State Farm Insurance), financial services (Oppenheimer mutual funds), and travel services (American Express). *Electronic channels* include all forms of service provision through television, telephone, interactive multimedia, and computers. Many financial and information services are currently distributed through electronic media: banking, bill paying, and education.

We do not include retailers in our short list of service intermediaries because most retailers—from department stores to discount stores—are channels for delivering physical goods rather than services. Retailers that sell only services (movie theaters, film-processing kiosks, restaurants) or retail services that support physical products (automobile dealers, gas stations) can also be described as dealers or franchises. For our purposes in this chapter, such retailers are grouped into the franchise category because they possess the same characteristics, strengths, and weaknesses as franchises.

Goods retailers, by the way, are service organizations themselves; they are intermediaries for goods and perhaps services. Manufacturing companies depend on retailers to represent, explain, and promote their products—all of which are presale services. Manufacturers also need retailers to return, exchange, support, and service products— all of which are postsale services. These roles are increasingly critical as products become more complex, technical, and expensive. For example, camera, lawn mower, and computer firms rely on retailers carrying their products to understand and communicate highly technical information so that customers choose products that fit their needs. A retailer that leads the customer to the wrong product choice or that inadequately instructs the customer on how to use the product creates service problems that strongly influence the manufacturer's reputation.

We also do not include in our list of intermediaries subcontractors that provide services to customers in lieu of the primary company. Many companies hire companies then outsource services such as their call centers (often in India), computer operations (e.g., IBM running all of Philips Electronics' customer service operations, payroll, and billing). Consulting firms like Accenture are hired by companies to develop training and consulting services and then subcontract with other firms to execute the services. While these subcontractors are not typically defined as intermediaries, the issues and challenges they present are very similar to agency and franchise issues.

Service principals depend on their intermediaries to deliver service to their specifications. Service intermediaries determine how the customer evaluates the quality of the company. When a McDonald's franchisee cooks the McNuggets too short a time, the customer's perception of the company—and of other McDonald's franchisees—is tarnished. When one Holiday Inn franchisee has unsanitary conditions, it reflects on all other Holiday Inns and on the Holiday Inn brand itself. Unless service providers ensure that the intermediary's goals, incentives, and motives are consistent with their own, they lose control over the service encounters between the customer and the intermediary. When someone other than the service principal is critical to the fulfillment of quality service, a firm must develop ways to either control or motivate these intermediaries to meet company goals and standards. In the sections that follow, we discuss both direct delivery of service by the service principal and indirect delivery of the service through intermediaries.

DIRECT OR COMPANY-OWNED CHANNELS

Although we call this chapter "Delivering Service through Intermediaries and Electronic Channels," it is important to acknowledge that many services are distributed directly from provider to customer. Some of these are local services—doctors, dry cleaners, and hairstylists—whose area of distribution is limited. Others are national chains with multiple outlets but are considered direct channels because the provider owns all the outlets. Starbucks, the popular chain of coffee shops, is an example of a service provider with all company-owned outlets. Each of its coffee shops in the United States are completely run and managed by the company. Exhibit 14.1, which describes some of the reasons for the success of the chain, illustrates the general benefits of company-owned outlets: control, consistency, and maintenance of image.

Exhibit 14.1   Starbucks: Will Growth Spoil Its Espresso Bar Culture?

One of the biggest services marketing success stories, Starbucks Coffee Company, started out as just a product, coffee. Only when its top executive envisioned coffee not as something to retail in a store but instead as something to experience in a coffeehouse did consumers began to recognize Starbucks as unique. At that point, the Starbucks that "successfully replicates a perfectly creamy café latte in stores from Seattle to St. Paul," was born. Customer connection, committed employees, and consistency of service and product are three of the most important reasons that Starbucks grew to more than 13,500 outlets and that it annually reports profit growth of more than 20 percent a year. Starbucks owns more than 6,000 of the stores and maintains control over all that takes place in those stores, all of it designed to create a special cultural experience that differs in every way from fast-food outlets. Today, however, the company faces a critical crossroads between its long-term service philosophy and an aggressive strategy to grow the company from 13,500 to 40,000 outlets worldwide.

THE PHILOSOPHY: ROMANCE AND THEATER THROUGH CUSTOMER CONNECTION AND COMMITTED EMPLOYEES

On his first visit to Starbucks in 1981, founder and chairman Howard Schulz's philosophy of a coffeehouse was born:

> A heady aroma of coffee reached out and drew me in. I stepped inside and saw what looked like a temple for the worship of coffee . . . It was my Mecca. I had arrived.

The special experience that he created for Starbucks was a place where customers could come and spend time, comfortable in their surroundings. The worship of coffee meant smelling fresh-ground beans and having delicious coffee drinks to languish over. This feeling of being "at home" also depended on the connection between customers and employees, who banter with each other while they order and deliver coffee. Ideally, employees interacted personally with customers, recognizing them and the kind of coffees they liked to drink. To accomplish this, Starbucks treated its employees in special ways. To hire, keep, and motivate the very best employees, Starbucks set three guidelines for on-the-job interpersonal relations: (1) maintain and enhance employee self-esteem, (2) listen to and acknowledge employee issues, and (3) encourage employees to ask for help. These and other human resource practices, including higher-than-average pay, health insurance, and stock options, reduced turnover to 60 percent compared with 140 percent for hourly workers in the fast-food business in general.

All employees are called partners, and those who prepare coffee are called "baristas," the Italian name for one who prepares and serves coffee. As many as 400 to 500 employees per month nationally are carefully trained to "call" ("triple-tall nonfat mocha"), make

Perhaps the major benefit of distributing through company-owned channels is that the company has complete *control* over the outlets. One of the most critical implications of this type of control is that the owner can maintain consistency in service provision. Standards can be established and will be carried out as planned because the company itself monitors and rewards proper execution of the service. Control over hiring, firing, and motivating employees is also a benefit of company-owned channels. As demonstrated in Exhibit 14.1, one of the keys to Starbucks's success is

drinks, clean espresso machines, and deliver quality customer service. Baristas are taught "coffee knowledge"—so that, among other things, they know how everything tastes—and customer service—so that they can explain the Italian drink names to customers.

Both to reward employees and to stretch them to learn more, the company offers an advanced Coffee Master program that teaches them how to discriminate among regional coffee flavors. Patterned after the wine business, graduates earn black aprons and the right to use an insignia on their business cards.

THE THREAT: AGGRESSIVE GROWTH AND PROFIT TARGETS

Given the success of the Starbucks philosophy and execution, one might wonder what strategy could derail Starbucks. Many say that an obsession to grow from the current 13,500 to 40,000 outlets—half of them outside the United States—is the biggest threat to the continuation of the Starbucks success story. Accompanying the growth goals, Starbucks also has aggressive profit targets that can only be achieved by streamlining operations, often in ways that remove the authenticity of the Starbucks experience.

Decisions about streamlining operations have cut costs but also affected the romance and drama of Starbucks's service experience. One of these decisions was to adopt automatic espresso machines rather than having barristas pull shots individually. While this move increased efficiency and speed of service, the new machines blocked the sight line of the drinks being made and eliminated the opportunity for barristas to converse with customers while pulling shots. Another decision involved incorporating drive-in windows, now in one-quarter of the restaurants, which by definition eliminated the need for customers to come into the store altogether. Still another decision ended the practice of scooping fresh coffee from bins in stores and grinding it in front of customers by shipping and using coffee in flavor-locked packaging. This decision alone forever removed the smell of fresh coffee from the outlets. Each of these approaches made operations more efficient but interfered with the service experience.

Despite Howard Schultz's obsession to grow Starbucks, he is concerned that the Starbucks experience may be jeopardized by the time- and cost-saving approaches that might be needed to fuel that growth. In a 2007 memo distributed internally—but leaked externally—he admonished the company for making decisions like those just cited that could commoditize the brand and make it more like a fast-food chain than a coffee house. He commented:

> Many of these decisions were probably right at the time, and on their own merit would not have created the dilution of the experience; but in this case, the sum is much greater and, unfortunately, much more damaging than the individual pieces.

The danger is that the company will become more like fast-food chains (think McDonalds and Dunkin' Donuts, both of which have focused on improving the coffee experience) and less like the casual coffee houses he created in the 1990s. The company knows that customers want their coffee quickly, but Schultz does not want to sacrifice the intensity of customer connection between barristas and customers that makes the firm's services different. "The battle within the company is making sure growth doesn't dilute our culture," Schultz claims. Starbucks, an outstanding example of company-owned channels, faces the same struggle as other highly successful service businesses: growth brings with it efficiency through standardization. In service businesses where personal connections between employees and customers are critical, growth can interfere with the intimacy necessary for the service experience to be real.

Sources: G. Anders, "Starbucks Brews a New Strategy," *Fast Company,* August 2001, pp. 144–146; "Starbucks Keeps Pace," *Beverage Industry,* October 2001, p. 11., www.starbucks.com; M. Lehrer, "Why Did Starbucks Cross the Road?" *The Wall Street Journal,* April 3, 2007, p. B1; J. Adamy, "Starbucks Chairman Says Trouble May Be Brewing," *The Wall Street Journal,* February 24, 2007, p. A4; and B. Helm, "Saving Starbucks' Soul," *BusinessWeek,* April 19, 2007, pp. 56–61.

hiring the right baristas, or coffee makers, something the company is far more likely to do than a franchisee. Using company-owned channels also allows the company to expand or contract sites without being bound by contractual agreements with other entities.

A final benefit of company-owned channels is that the company owns the customer relationship. In service industries in which skilled or professional workers have individual relationships with customers, a major concern is whether the loyalty the customer feels is for the company or for the individual service employee. It is well known, for example, that most people are loyal to individual hairstylists and will follow them from one place of business to another. Therefore, one of the important issues in service delivery is who owns the customer relationship—the store or the employee. With company-owned channels, the company owns both the store and the employee and therefore has control over the customer relationship.

However, several disadvantages exist with company-owned channels. First, and probably the largest impediment to most service chains, the company must bear all the financial risk. When expanding, the firm must find all the capital, sometimes using it for store proliferation rather than for other uses (such as advertising, service quality, or new service development) that would be more profitable. Second, large companies are rarely experts in local markets—they know their businesses but not all markets. When adjustments are needed in business formats for different markets, they may be unaware of what these adjustments should be. This disadvantage is especially evident when companies expand into other cultures and other countries. Partnering or joint venturing is almost always preferred to company-owned channels in these situations.

When two or more service companies want to offer a service and neither has the full financial capability or expertise, they often undertake service partnerships. These partnerships operate very much like company-owned channels except they involve multiple owners. The benefit is that risk and effort are shared, but the disadvantage is that control and returns are also distributed among the partners. Several areas in which partnerships are common are telecommunications, high-technology services, Internet-based services, and entrepreneurial services. Service partnerships also proliferate when companies expand beyond their country boundaries—typically one partner provides the business format and the other provides knowledge of the local market.

FRANCHISING

Franchising is the most common type of distribution in services, with more than 320,000 U.S. franchisers in 75 different industries licensing their brand names, business processes or formats, unique products, services, or reputations in return for fees and royalties.[1] Franchising works well with services that can be standardized and duplicated through the delivery process, service policies, warranties, guarantees, promotion, and branding. Jiffy Lube, H&R Block, Olive Garden, and Red Roof Inns are examples of companies that are ideal for franchise operations. At its best, franchising is a relationship or partnership in which the service provider—the franchiser—develops and optimizes a service format that it licenses for delivery by other parties—the franchisees. There are benefits and disadvantages for both the franchiser and the franchisee in this relationship (see Table 14.1).

The Franchiser's Perspective

A franchiser typically begins by developing a business concept that is unique in some way. Perhaps it is a fast-food concept (such as McDonald's) with unique cooking or delivery processes. Perhaps it is a health and fitness center (such as Gold's Gym) with established formats for marketing to customers, pricing, and hiring employees. Or maybe it is a video store (such as Blockbuster) with unique store environments, employee training, purchasing, and computer systems. A franchiser typically expands business through this method because it expects the benefits described in the following section.

TABLE 14.1
Benefits and Challenges in Franchising

Benefits	Challenges
For Franchisers	
Leveraged business format for greater expansion and revenues	Difficulty in maintaining and motivating franchisees
Consistency in outlets	Highly publicized disputes and conflict
Knowledge of local markets	Inconsistent quality
Shared financial risk and more working capital	Control of customer relationship by intermediary
For Franchisees	
An established business format	Encroachment of other outlets into franchisee territory
National or regional brand marketing	Disappointing profits and revenues
Minimized risk of starting a business	Lack of perceived control over operations
	High fees

Leveraged Business Format for Greater Expansion and Revenues

Most franchisers want wider distribution—and increased revenues, market share, brand name recognition, and economies of scale—for their concepts and practices than they can support in company outlets.

Consistency in Outlets

When franchisers have strong contracts and unique formats, they can require that service be delivered according to their specifications. This chapter's Global Feature, for example, shows how Starbucks is maintaining consistency across cultures and countries through franchising.

Knowledge of Local Markets

National chains are unlikely to understand local markets as well as the businesspeople that live in the geographic areas. With franchising, the company obtains a connection to the local market.

Shared Financial Risk and More Working Capital

Franchisees must contribute their own capital for equipment and personnel, thereby bearing part of the risk of doing business.

Franchising is not without its challenges, however. Most franchisers encounter the following disadvantages.

Difficulty in Maintaining and Motivating Franchisees

Motivating independent operators to price, promote, deliver, and hire according to standards the principal establishes is a difficult job, particularly when business is down.

Highly Publicized Disputes between Franchisees and Franchisers

Franchisees are organizing and hiring lobbyists and lawyers to gain more economic clout. Many states and even the federal government have implemented legislation boosting franchisee rights.

Inconsistent Quality

Although some franchisees deliver the service in the manner in which the franchiser intended, other franchisees do not perform the service as well as desired. This inconsistency can undermine the company's image, reputation, and brand name.

Customer Relationships Controlled by the Franchisee Rather Than the Franchiser

The closer a company is to the customer, the better able it is to listen to that customer's concerns and ideas. When franchisees are involved, a relationship forms between the customer and the franchisee rather than between the customer and the franchiser. All customer information, including demographics, purchase history, and preferences, is in the hands of the intermediary rather than the principal. The Hilton "OnQ" CRM system that is the focus of the Technology Insight in Chapter 7 is a counterexample to this. That is, the customer is still owned by the franchiser (Hilton).

The Franchisee's Perspective

From the perspective of the franchisee, one of the main benefits of franchising is obtaining an established business format on which to base a business, something one expert has defined as an "entrepreneur in a prepackaged box, a super-efficient distributor of services and goods through a decentralized web."[2] A second benefit is receiving national or regional brand marketing. Franchisees obtain advertising and other marketing expertise as well as an established reputation. Finally, franchising minimizes the risks of starting a business. According to the U.S. Small Business Administration, more than 50 percent of small businesses fail in the first year and 95 percent fail within the first five years.[3]

Disadvantages for franchisees also exist. One of the most problematic is *encroachment*—the opening of new units near existing ones without compensation to the existing franchisee. When encroachment occurs, potential revenues are diminished and competition is increased. Another frequent disadvantage involves disappointing profits and revenues: "Most people think of franchising as some kind of bonanza . . . the reality is you get a solid operation, work damn hard, and if you're making $40,000 a year after four years, that's good."[4] Other disadvantages include lack of perceived control over operations and high fees. Many of these problems are due to overpromising by the franchiser, but others are caused by unrealistic expectations about what will be achieved in a franchise agreement.

AGENTS AND BROKERS

An *agent* is an intermediary who acts on behalf of a service principal (such as a real estate agent) or a customer and is authorized to make agreements between the principal and the customer. Some agents, called selling agents, work with the principal and have contractual authority to sell a principal's output (such as travel, insurance, or financial services), usually because the principal lacks the resources or desire to do so. Other agents, called purchasing agents, often have long-term relationships with buyers and help them in evaluating and making purchases. Such agents are frequently hired by companies and individuals to find art, antiques, and rare jewelry. A *broker* is an intermediary who brings buyers and sellers together while assisting in negotiation. Brokers are paid by the party who hired them, rarely become involved

TABLE 14.2
Benefits and Challenges for Companies in Distributing Services through Agents and Brokers

Benefits	Challenges
Reduced selling and distribution costs	Loss of control over pricing
Intermediary's possession of special skills and knowledge	Representation of multiple service principals
Wide representation	
Knowledge of local markets	
Customer choice	

in financing or assuming risk, and are not long-term representatives of buyers or sellers. The most familiar examples are real estate brokers, insurance brokers, and security brokers.

Agents and brokers do not take title to services but instead deliver the rights to them. They have legal authority to market services as well as to perform other marketing functions on behalf of producers. The benefits and challenges in using agents and brokers are summarized in Table 14.2.

Benefits of Agents and Brokers

The travel industry provides an example of both agents and brokers. Three main categories of travel intermediaries exist: tour packagers, retail travel agents, and specialty channelers (including incentive travel firms, meeting and convention planners, hotel representatives, association executives, and corporate travel offices). You are likely to be most familiar with traditional retail travel agents. Industry convention refers to the travel companies as brokers and the individuals who work for them as travel agents or sales associates. We use this industry to illustrate some of the benefits and challenges of delivering service through agents and brokers. This traditional industry is changing rapidly because of electronic channels, and we illustrate these channels and their impact later in the chapter.

Reduced Selling and Distribution Costs

If an airline or resort hotel needed to contact every potential traveler to promote its offerings, costs would be exorbitant. Because most travel services are transactional rather than long term, travelers would need to expend tremendous effort to find services that meet their needs. Travel agents and brokers accomplish the intermediary role by assembling information from travel suppliers and offering it to travelers.

Possession of Special Skills and Knowledge

Agents and brokers have special knowledge and skills in their areas. For example, retail travel agents know the industry well and know how to access the information companies themselves do not possess, often through reference materials and online services. Tour packagers have a more specialized role—they assemble, promote, and price bundles of travel services from travel suppliers, then offer these bundles either to travelers themselves or to retail travel agents. Specialty channelers have even more specialized roles. Some work in corporate travel offices to lend their skills to an entire corporation, others are business meeting and convention planners who act almost as tour packagers for whole companies or associations, and some are incentive travel firms that focus on travel recognition programs in corporations or associations.

Earlier in this chapter we talked about Starbucks coffeehouses as an example of a very successful company-owned service organization with more than 10,000 outlets in the United States. The company now has more than 2,500 outlets abroad in 37 countries outside North America. When the company chose to go international, management realized that its best route was not to own but instead to franchise or form other types of alliances with organizations within each country. This approach would allow Starbucks to understand the individual markets better and limit the capital investment necessary to expand. In an unusual twist, the company began its expansion in Asia rather than in Europe. In each country Starbucks has entered, it has met different scenarios and challenges, as illustrated by its experiences in Japan, China, and Canada.

JAPAN

Joining with Sazaby, a Japanese retailer and restaurateur, Starbucks opened more than a dozen stores in Japan beginning in 1997. The company chose Japan as its first expansion outside North America because it is the third largest coffee-consuming country in the world (6.1 million bags per year compared with 18.1 million bags in the United States). Possibly the most compelling result of the announcement of the entry of Starbucks was intense fear on the part of existing coffee-bar owners in Japan. Even though Starbucks was introducing a mere dozen outlets, the owners of the mega-chains were filled with anxiety. A manager of Doutor Coffee Company, Japan's number one coffee-bar chain (453 shops at the time) exclaimed, "They're a big threat and could take customers away from us." Many coffee bars imitated Starbucks in design and started offering "Seattle coffee." Executives such as the president of Pronto Corporation (with 94 stores at the time), traveled to the United States to gather intelligence from more than 20 Starbucks locations on the West Coast. He, like others, worried that the Japanese outlets lacked the sophistication of Starbucks, the ability to "(package) the store: (mesh) such elements as store design, package design, and other merchandising techniques into a compelling entity." Starbucks had so successfully created and distributed its service in the United States that the Japanese were afraid they could not compete. But as

Starbucks opened more stores (it now has more than 600 in Japan), the Japanese competitors were ready. Rather than entering quietly and gaining a toehold before having to compete, Starbucks was targeted before it opened its first Japanese store.

CHINA

After selling Starbucks coffee to Beijing hotels for four years, the company decided to open franchise outlets there in 1998. Two major challenges faced the company. The biggest was that most of China's 1.3 billion people like tea, not coffee! The second hurdle was the challenge of finding Beijing managers to run coffee shops with the all-important culture of the U.S. Seattle coffee shop. Without those managers, hiring, motivating, and training baristas to deliver the consistent service and coffee drinks that made the chain so successful in the United States would be impossible. Seattle-spirited managers were necessary to uphold the high standards of the company. In 2007, there are nearly 450 outlets in mainland China, and progress on both challenges has been made.

To begin to convert noncoffee customers into coffee drinkers, Starbucks surveyed Chinese consumers and asked them for the top 20 reasons they visit cafés. While coffee drinking was only number six on the list, having a place to gather and be seen was number one. This led to ideas that could build on customers' real

Wide Representation

Because agents and brokers are paid by commission rather than by salary, there is little risk or disadvantage to the service principal in extending the service offerings to a wide geography. Thus companies have representatives in many places, far more than if fixed costs such as buildings, equipment, and salaries were required.

desires: Starbucks outlets now create attention-grabbing experiences for these customers—taste tests, mini-lectures, and contests abound. Workers offer samples—particularly of sweet flavors—and both factual and persuasive information about coffee. Stores also sell green-tea cheesecake and Chinese moon cakes. Chinese customers still find coffee less appealing than tea, but young customers, those with the most disposable income, are willing to experiment. Many of these young people are the product of China's one-child rule and have been pampered by parents and embrace individuality. Coffee is palatable to them if it has a lot of sugar and whipped cream, especially if it can be consumed in an informal gathering place where they want to be seen by others.

The company approached the management issue by targeting young people who had experience in running successful American-style restaurants such as the Hard Rock Café. To help them buy into the corporate passion, they sent these managerial recruits to Seattle for three months to absorb the culture and lifestyle of Starbucks and the West Coast. This immersion helped retain managers because they felt confident in themselves and in the company. Managers in turn recruited baristas through job fairs and ads that emphasize career and personal development and the "cool" factor of being associated with the pop-culture scene in Seattle. Once hired, new employees need to learn what coffee tastes like through education and taste tests.

According to Wang Jinlong, president of Starbucks Greater China, expansion is going well. He claims that a substantial portion of the company's ultimate goal of 2,000 locations outside the United States will be located in China.

CANADA

When Starbucks considered opening stores in Canada, the firm realized that it was dealing with an area unique enough to require firsthand knowledge. Rather than open its own shops, the company decided to license Interaction Restaurants to lead the firm into Montreal. Today, there are more than 200 Starbucks locations in Canada.

Starbucks was concerned about moving the firm into the Montreal culture while maintaining the company identity. Because it wanted to maintain the essence of its image, it was very careful about the company it chose to become its ambassador. Starbucks had dealt with different cultures—such as the U.S. Hispanic community, Japan, and China—but there were important differences in Quebec. One involves the language, which is mandated by government and is a very emotional issue. In 2000, three coffee shops belonging to Second Cup Ltd., a rival of Starbucks, were bombed by an anti-English group because the company retained its English name. To prevent such problems yet remain consistent, Starbucks agreed to be called Café Starbucks Coffee, which combines French and English. Over time, the Starbucks brand became recognizable and accepted in Canada. Today, more than 200 of the Starbucks stores in Canada are known as Starbucks Coffee Canada.

Perhaps a larger issue was that Montreal residents had a firmly entrenched, sophisticated coffee culture with a history of small coffee shops and Van Houtte (the dominant firm in the market) serving dark, rich coffee. Unlike in the United States, where Starbucks popularized the latte and the coffee tradition that went with it, "[t]here already is a café paradigm there, so Starbucks [did not] have quite the free rein to invent café culture in Quebec." Fortunately, Starbucks' darkly roasted taste was consistent with the preferences in Montreal. Even so, the firm created a special blend called Mélange Mon-Royal to recognize the new market and acknowledge that it was special.

The Canadian outlets are also different in that they contain a kitchen for preparing sandwiches and simple meals and an oven for breads and muffins. Freshly prepared food is not typical of Starbucks, and it will be an interesting experiment to see if the outlets can operate the kitchens as efficiently as they do their coffee machines.

Sources: "Business: Coffee with Your Tea? Starbucks in China," *The Economist,* October 6, 2001, p. 62; Z. Olijnyk, "Latte, s'il Vous Plait," *Canadian Business,* September 3, 2001, pp. 50–52; M. Shermer, "Starbucks in the Forbidden City," *Scientific American,* July 2001, pp. 34–35; S. Plog, "Starbucks: More Than a Cup of Coffee," *Cornell Hotel and Restaurant Administration Quarterly,* May 2005, pp. 284–287; A. Chozick, "Tokyo Hearts New York Food," *The Wall Street Journal,* April 21, 2006, p. B1, B5; and J. Adamy, "Eyeing a Billion Tea Drinkers, Starbucks Pours it on in China," *The Wall Street Journal,* November 29, 2006, p. 1.

Knowledge of Local Markets

Another key benefit of agents and brokers is that they become experts in the local markets they serve. They know or learn the unique needs of different markets, including international markets. They understand what their clients' preferences are and how to adapt the principal's services to match the needs of clients. This benefit is particularly needed and appreciated when clients are dispersed internationally. Knowing the culture and taboos of a country is critical for successful selling. Most companies find that obtaining local representation by experts with this knowledge is necessary.

Customer Choice

Travel and insurance agents provide a retailing service for customers—they represent the services of multiple suppliers. If a traveler needed to visit six or eight different travel agencies, or even six or eight different websites and online sources, each of which carried the services of a single supplier, imagine the effort a customer would need to make to plan a trip! This is why even though many travel services are now available online, direct to the customer, there is still a travel agent industry that serves more complex travel needs. Similarly, independent insurance agents have the right to sell a wide variety of insurance, which allows them to offer customers a choice. These types of agents also are able to compare prices across suppliers and get the best prices for their clients.

Challenges of Delivering Service through Agents and Brokers

Loss of Control over Pricing

As representatives of service principals and experts on customer markets, agents and brokers are typically empowered to negotiate price, configure services, and otherwise alter the marketing of a principal's service. This issue could be particularly important—and possibly detrimental—when a service provider depends on a particular (high) price to convey a level of service quality. If the price can be changed, it might drop to a level that undermines the quality image. In addition, the agent often has the flexibility to give different prices to different customers. As long as the customers are geographically dispersed, this variation will not create a problem for the service principal; however, if buyers compare prices and realize they are being given different prices, they may perceive the service principal as unfair or unethical.

Representation of Multiple Service Principals

When independent agents represent multiple suppliers, they can offer customers a wide range of choices. From the perspective of the service principal, however, customer choice means that the agent represents—and in many cases advocates—a competitive service offering. This is the same challenge a manufacturer confronts when distributing products in a retail store. Only in rare cases are its products the only ones in a given category on the retail floor. In a service context, consider the use of independent insurance agents. These agents carry a range of insurance products from different companies, serving as a surrogate service retail store for customers. When they find a customer who needs insurance, they sell from their portfolio the offerings that best match the customer's requirements.

ELECTRONIC CHANNELS

The World Wide Web has "transformed every aspect of our lives—including how we socialize, manage our money, purchase goods and services, and gather information."[5] Electronic channels have vastly expanded the opportunities for goods and services marketers to distribute their officering. They differ from the other types of channels that we have discussed in that they do not require direct human interaction. What they do require is some predesigned service (such as information, education, or entertainment) and an electronic vehicle to deliver it. You are all familiar with telephone, television, and the Internet and may be aware of the other electronic vehicles that are currently under development. The consumer and business services that are made possible through these vehicles include movies on demand; interactive news and music; banking and financial services; multimedia libraries and databases; distance learning; desktop videoconferencing; remote health services; and interactive, network-based games.

The more a service relies on technology and/or equipment for service production and the less it relies on face-to-face contact with service providers, the less the service is characterized by inseparability and nonstandardization. As you will see in the following section, using electronic channels overcomes some of the problems associated with service inseparability and allows a form of standardization not previously possible in most services. Table 14.3 summarizes the benefits and challenges of electronic distribution.

Benefits of Electronic Channels

Consistent Delivery for Standardized Services

Electronic channels such as television and telecommunication do not alter the service, as channels with human interaction tend to do. Unlike delivery from a personal provider, electronic delivery does not interpret the service and execute it according to that interpretation. Its delivery is likely to be the same in all transmissions.

Distribution of television programming from networks through affiliate television and radio stations illustrates standardized electronic distribution. Networks create and finance programming, including shows, news, and sports, and distribute them through local stations in return for fees and advertising dollars. In most cases, the local stations deliver what is fed to them through the networks. Local stations can elect not to carry a particular show because of low ratings or lack of fit with the local market. They can also refuse to carry advertising spots that are judged in bad taste or too controversial. Except for these situations, which are not common, what is distributed through electronic channels is what the service creator sends.

Low Cost

Electronic media offer more efficient means of delivery than do interpersonal distribution. Critics could rightly claim that the personal sales interaction is more powerful and effective, but with interactive media service, advertisers are able to gain some of the credibility benefits of personal interaction (such as being able to answer individual questions or tailor the service for individuals).

TABLE 14.3
Benefits and Challenges for Companies in Electronic Distribution of Services

Benefits	Challenges
Consistent delivery for standardized services	Price competition
Low cost	Inability to customize
Customer convenience	Lack of consistency due to customer involvement
Wide distribution	Changes in consumer behavior
Customer choice and ability to customize	Security concerns
Quick customer feedback	Competition from widening geographies

Online travel has been one of the biggest success stories in electronic channels. The industry expected to have more than $60.7 billion in travel revenues in Europe alone resulting from transactions completed online in 2007.[6] The Internet has been an extremely effective channel for travel for three key reasons:

1. Prices are more competitive than offline prices because of the transparency of pricing—the technology can conjure up literally thousands of providers in an instant.
2. Online travel companies have no inventory costs and therefore low cost of goods sold.
3. Sites obtain significant advertising revenue due to focused clientele, with advertisers knowing that all users are potential buyers of their travel services.

One of the most successful, profitable online travel sites is Travelocity.com. Like other online travel sites, it sells airline tickets, hotel rooms, and car rentals directly to consumers, avoiding travel agents. It has been one of the top online travel sites since its inception in 1996 by Sabre Holdings. The site also offers instantaneous price quotes and the ability to track prices in cities that customers plan to visit. They then alert customers when there are Internet travel sales or reduced prices for travel to places the customer has visited or plans to visit.

Customer Convenience

With electronic channels, customers are able to access a firm's services when and where they want. Just as catalog shopping freed working women from the perceived drudgeries of having to go to the mall—and fattened the purses of forward-thinking companies that recognized an underserved market—e-commerce is changing the way people shop. Many mail-order companies still limit their hours of availability, a real mistake if they are going to match the customer convenience of being able to order online 24 hours a day, seven days a week. For the marketer, electronic channels allow access to a large group of customers who would otherwise be unavailable to them because of busy schedules that do not allow them to shop in other ways.

Wide Distribution

Electronic channels do more than allow the service provider to interact with a large number of consumers. They also allow the service provider to interact (often simultaneously) with a large number of intermediaries. The costs and effort to inform, promote, and motivate consumers to buy through offline channels are higher than the costs to accomplish the same activities with electronic channels. Many franchisers have found that prospecting through the Internet provides better-qualified franchisees than the traditional methods of mainstream advertising and trade shows.

Customer Choice and Ability to Customize

Consider the options available in movies and videos to customers who use video-on-demand services. Just as Dell Computer allows customers to configure entire products to their own particular needs and desires, the Internet allows many companies to design services completely customized to their individual needs. Individuals who want to renovate their kitchen may now go to many Internet sites, specify their requirements, and order what they wish. Whether the supplier is a large retailer such as Home Depot or a small start-up company, customers get exactly what they want. Our Strategy Insight discusses how H&R Block uses the Internet to provide its customers with a wide range of options for receiving tax preparation services.

Quick Customer Feedback

Rapid customer feedback is without doubt one of the major strengths of e-commerce. Companies can find out immediately what customers think of services and can gain far higher participation from customers in surveys. With quick customer feedback, changes can be made rapidly to service assortments, problems can be addressed immediately, and the learning cycles of companies can speed up dramatically.

Challenges in Distributing Services through Electronic Channels

Price Competition

One of the traditional differences between goods and services has been the difficulty of directly comparing features and prices of services with each other. Whereas goods can typically be compared in retail settings, few settings exist that offer services from multiple sources. The Internet has changed all that. Services such as Travelocity.com and Priceline.com make it simple for customers to compare prices for a wide variety of services. Priceline.com allows customers to name their price for a service such as an airline ticket, wait until Priceline.com finds an airline willing to accept it, and then purchase the ticket. Never has the customer had such ability to bid on prices for services.

Inability to Customize

Some of you have learned college basics through distance learning. If you consider what you missed in learning that way compared with learning directly from a professor, you will understand this challenge. In mass sections delivered electronically, you cannot interact directly with the professor, ask questions, raise points for clarification, or experience the connection that you receive in person. In electronic classes—as in videoconferences that are springing up in many businesses—the quality of the service can also be impeded by the way the audience reacts (or does not react) in those situations. People talk among themselves, leave, laugh, and criticize, among other behaviors.

Lack of Consistency Because of Customer Involvement

Although electronic channels are very effective in minimizing the inconsistency from employees or providers of service, customer variability still presents a problem. Many times customers use the technology themselves to produce the service and can lead to errors or frustration unless the technology is highly user-friendly. Maneuvering online can sometimes be overwhelming, and not all websites are easy to use. Furthermore, many customers may not have computers and, even if they do, may be reluctant to use this medium.

Security Concerns One issue confronting marketers using electronic channels is concern about the security of information, particularly health and financial information. Many customers are still hesitant about giving credit-card numbers on the Internet. These problems can undermine consumers' trust in the Internet as a safe place to do business. Companies doing business through the Internet must continually devise ways to protect their systems from penetration, vandalism, eavesdropping, and identity theft.[7] With penetration, intruders steal passwords and exploit unprotected modems and connections, actually taking over the sites. With vandalism, hackers crash corporate and other computers. To combat these problems, firewalls and other software scan for unusual activity. With eavesdropping, hackers snoop on information as it passes through multiple computers to the Internet. The typical solution is encryption software that scrambles electronic mail and other data to make it unintelligible to eavesdroppers.

Strategy Insight Delivering Service through Multiple Channels: H&R Block's Blended Channel Approach

H&R Block, the world's largest tax services company, served nearly 20 million clients in 12,000 offices in the United States as well as 11 other countries in 2006. With so many customers, H&R Block delivers its services through a variety of channels. H&R Block's approach, referred to as a "blended channel" approach, is a multichannel strategy delivered through various types of intermediaries that creates tremendous flexibility for its clients and the means by which they receive services. This approach allows H&R Block to offer what it describes as services with "solutions for every taxpayer." Customers may receive H&R Block's services through retail offices, through the Internet, through software programs, or through some combination of these channels. Each method of service delivery is described in the following sections.

SERVICE DELIVERY VIA COMPANY-OWNED AND FRANCHISED RETAIL OFFICES

H&R Block has approximately 12,000 offices worldwide, including more than 7,000 offices that are company owned. Customers wanting to purchase H&R Block's services through an office have three options. The Face to Face option, in which customers can either call an H&R Block office for an appointment or just walk right in, provides an opportunity for the customer to be interviewed in person and to have the company completely prepare the tax return document. Here customers are paying for an H&R Block representative to spend time with them to understand their unique situation and to do everything possible to help reduce their tax liability. Those customers wanting to use the Office Drop-off option complete a questionnaire that captures key information and informs customers of what forms and documents to bring to the H&R Block office in order to have the company prepare a tax return; the customer is then called when the return has been completed. The third option, Online Drop-off, allows the customer to conduct a tax interview interactively via the Internet or via telephone, fax, or e-mail. Necessary tax data are then provided either via the Internet or fax, and the customer's tax return is prepared by the local H&R Block office.

ONLINE SERVICE DELIVERY

When it comes to preparing tax returns, a relatively large percentage of all taxpayers prefer the "Do It Yourself" method. Traditionally these people have completed their tax returns using pen-and-paper

means. H&R Block offers these customers an alternative means of doing it themselves by providing its services through the Internet by using its website to completely prepare and then electronically file their tax return. Customers who prefer to complete the entire process online can choose from many options. If they are filing the 1040EZ form, they can purchase and file electronically using the Basic option for $14.95. If they want to claim deductions and file just the federal return, the Premium + e-file option is $29.95. The Premium + State + e-file option is $54.95. The new Tango option, costing $70, uses innovative technologies to make tax preparation even easier and provides one-touch customer support throughout the process. Customers choosing this option can store their return information either on their own desktop or on H&R Block's server. For customers with more complex tax issues (such as rental property, home offices, or depreciation), audit alerts (pointing out areas that often trigger government audits), and one free (face-to-face) consultation with a tax advisor, the Signature service option (for $99.95) also includes having a tax advisor check the customer's tax return for errors, correct any problems on the return, and then sign and electronically file the return for the customer. This option also allows the customer year-round access to an H&R Block tax advisor for advice.

SERVICE DELIVERY VIA SOFTWARE

Another alternative for the tax preparation do-it-yourselfer is to purchase H&R Block tax services through its software offering, TaxCut. This program provides most of the same services that are available online but does not require the customer to be connected to the Internet. That is, the TaxCut program also provides a customized tax interview (asking only the questions that pertain to each customer's tax situation), checks for errors that could draw the attention of an auditor, imports financial data from other personal finance programs and/or the previous year's tax data, and electronically files tax returns. Because the software is installed on the customer's personal computer, customers do not have to worry about their financial data being stored somewhere that is accessible to others. Indeed, the software do-it-yourself customer tends to be older, more mature, more affluent, and more concerned with privacy than those who purchase H&R Block's online services. As with the other channels of service delivery, customers can select from three

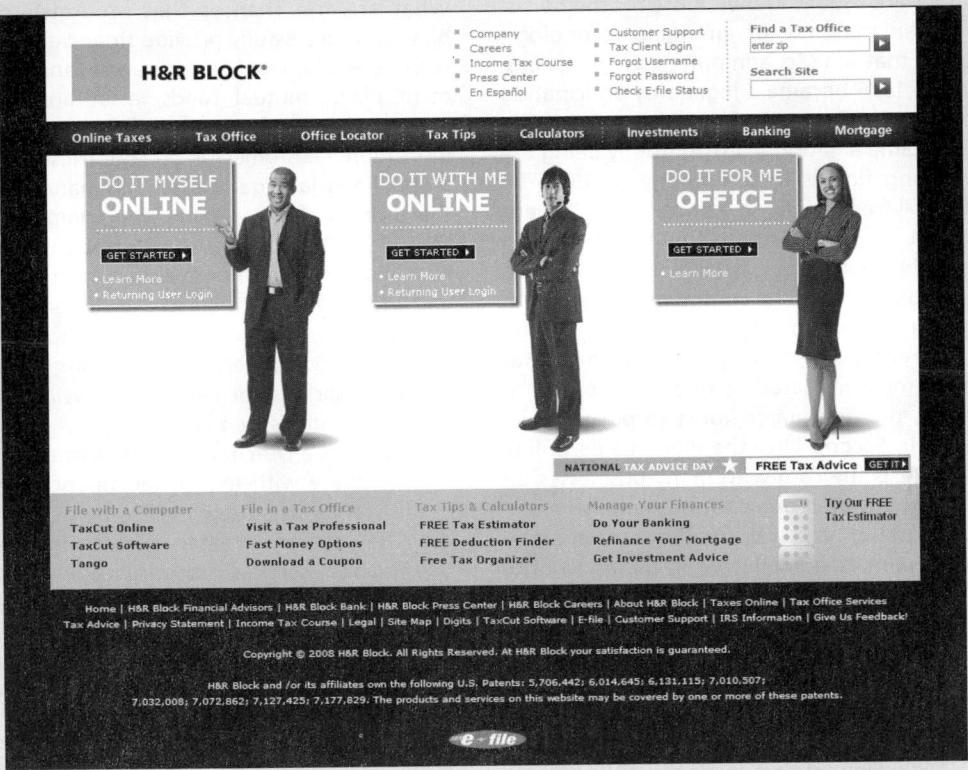

TaxCut options—Standard, Deluxe, or Premium—with differing levels of service provided.

SERVICE DELIVERY VIA THE TELEPHONE

Some customers do not wish to use H&R Block's services to prepare tax returns, but they do have tax questions that they would like answered. H&R Block's Ask a Tax Advisor program allows customers to submit a tax question online and have someone contact them however they wish (via e-mail or phone) within 48 hours. Customers are charged on a per-question basis for this service. H&R Block also provides customer service support for its other products through telephone, e-mail, and live chat vehicles.

H&R Block's blended channel strategy provides clients with many choices as to how they would like their service to be delivered and how much of the work they would like to do themselves. At one extreme, the customer can have the task of tax preparation completed entirely by H&R Block by visiting one of its offices. Alternatively, customers can pursue a do-it-yourself option by purchasing the TaxCut software and completing their tax returns without any assistance from H&R Block. And those customers who would like to coproduce the service by doing some of the work themselves may look to H&R Block for assistance with specific issues or questions. H&R Block provides clients with the ability to choose what method, channel, and products are best for them, at the time that meets their needs, and in the stage of the tax preparation experience that is relevant to them—in effect, allowing customers much flexibility by providing many choices to blend the channels of service delivery in a customized service. Thus, H&R Block has, through its blended channel strategy approach, created value for its customers by providing as much of the service as customers desire and through the channel in which the customer feels the most comfortable.

Source: h&rblock.com.

Technology Spotlight Online Innovators in Service

1-800-FLOWERS.COM: ONLINE FLORIST

Flower shops are usually known more for their artistic talent than their use of emerging technology, but the shop that Jim McCann purchased in Queens, New York, in 1976 became a legend by anticipating new technologies. Instead of remaining local, the company became a national distributor by being the pioneer among florists in technology. In 1987, he bought the toll-free telephone number 1-800-Flowers, allowing him to forge partnerships to sell flowers nationwide 24 hours a day. In 1995, he became the first retailer on AOL, and he continues to forge strategic online relationships with AOL, MSN.com, and Yahoo!. He created a stand-alone website in 1995 at the time Microsoft released its Internet browser. In 2007, he was the first major florist to put a virtual flower shop in Second Life, the video-game online community. As is the case with many businesses on Second Life, purchases are currently virtual. However, he is working on a way to allow customers to order real flowers to be delivered in the real world. Technology helps 1-800-Flowers.com provide a better floral product through its "Fresh from Our Growers" program. Orders are placed directly to growers so that flowers are sent fresh overnight, rather than from another florist who may have had the flowers for several days already.

Today, 1-800-Flowers.com leads the online florist market and has approximately 4.2 million unique visitors a month (compared to ProFlowers, second place with 3.2 unique visitors a month). In 2007, market capitalization was $561 million, and the company had 3,700 employees and $782 million in revenue. What is next for 1-800-Flowers.com? Plans are under way to use social-networking sites like Facebook and MySpace to market the company.

ING DIRECT: ONLINE BANKING

What are the chances that an Amsterdam-based bank can successfully provide financial products and services—including life insurance, annuities, retirement plans, mutual funds, asset and relationship management services—to individual, business, and institutional customers in 50 countries? ING Direct, a global financial organization, has managed to do just that using online banking. The company has more that 115,000 employees in 50 companies worldwide; 60 million private, corporate, and institutional clients; and 14 million customers in the United States alone. Not only that, but ING enjoys top-10 positions in most of its core U.S. business lines, including 401(k), 403(b), and 457 markets for retirement savings, fixed and variable annuities, and life insurance.

How does a Dutch bank build a brand that allows it to compete with the myriad financial institutions in the world? Its strategy varies by geographic market. The company created a name for itself in the U.S. financial services marketplace in a short period of time using strong branding with the color of the Dutch royal house, orange, and a strong campaign called, "Up." The campaign featured a series of ads including "Moving Up," "Saving Up," "Winning Up," and "Looking Up." Because its advertising and promotional materials were strong, and because the Orange Savings Account offered "no fees, no minimums, and no catches," the brand caught on quickly.

ING Direct introduced a new brand promise in the United States in 2006—"Your future. Made easier." The new brand campaign reflects the key findings of the ING Financial Planning and Investment Survey conducted by Roper GfK that found consumers find it difficult dealing with financial services firms. In that survey of more than 1,000 consumers, 73 percent

Finally, with impersonation, criminals steal consumers' identities to buy goods and services. A form of encryption technology is often used to deal with this problem, and special service companies confirm signature holders.[8]

Competition from Widening Geographies Historically, many services were somewhat protected from competition because customers had limited choice among the providers they could physically visit. Banks, for example, supplied all local customers with checking accounts, savings accounts, and mortgages. In fact, it used to be said that because services could not be transported they were limited in their scope. Not any longer—and not with electronic channels. Through the Internet, many services, including financial services, can be purchased from service providers far from the local area. See this chapter's Technology Spotlight for several examples.

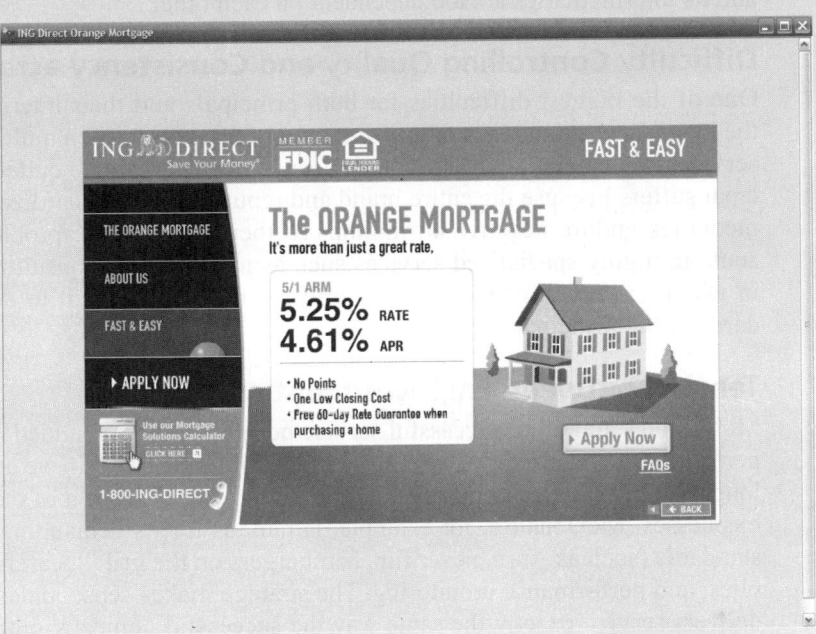

said they would switch to a firm with a reputation for making the financial planning process easier. The company is making changes in everything it does to make working with the firm easier—from creating products that are easier to understand to making continuous improvements in the ways it deals with customers. Another part of the strategy involves explaining to both consumers and financial professionals how to manage money and use ING's services.

ING is truly a successful online service provider. Toby Hoden emphasized that in terms of brand awareness and favorability, ING is now close on the heels of companies that have built their brands over decades:

Five years ago, ING had just begun building its brand in the U.S. . . . Since then, we've seen consumer awareness of ING skyrocket from approximately eight percent to around 80 percent. Because of the tremendously high favorability that ING enjoys among key audiences, the company is extremely well positioned to evolve the brand.

Sources: M. Kessler, "Founder's Bold Moves Deliver 1-800-Flowers.com, *USA TODAY,* June 27, 2007, p. 3B; www.1800flowers.com; Advisors Network & Investment News as of July 2003; and Christina Divigard at christina. divigard@us.ing.com.

COMMON ISSUES INVOLVING INTERMEDIARIES

Key problems with intermediaries include conflict over objectives and performance, difficulty controlling quality and consistency across outlets, tension between empowerment and control, and channel ambiguity.

Channel Conflict over Objectives and Performance

The parties involved in delivering services do not always agree about how the channel should operate. Channel conflict can occur between the service provider and the service intermediary, among intermediaries in a given area, and between different types of channels used by a service provider (such as when a service principal has its own outlets as well as franchised outlets). The conflict most often centers on the parties having different goals, competing roles and rights, and conflicting views of the way the channel is performing. Sometimes the conflict occurs because the service principal and its intermediaries are too dependent on each other.

Difficulty Controlling Quality and Consistency across Outlets

One of the biggest difficulties for both principals and their intermediaries involves the inconsistency and lack of uniform quality that result when multiple outlets deliver services. When shoddy performance occurs, even at a single outlet, the service principal suffers because the entire brand and reputation are jeopardized, and other intermediaries endure negative attributions to their outlets. The problem is particularly acute in highly specialized services such as management consulting or architecture, in which execution of the complex offering may be difficult to deliver to the standards of the principal.

Tension between Empowerment and Control

McDonald's and other successful service businesses were founded on the principle of performance consistency. Both they and their intermediaries have attained profits and longevity because the company controls virtually every aspect of their intermediaries' businesses. McDonald's, for example, is famous for its demanding and rigid service standards (such as "turn, never flip, hamburgers on the grill"), carefully specified supplies, and performance monitoring. The strategy makes sense: unless an intermediary delivers service exactly the same way the successful company outlets provide it, the service may not be as desirable to customers. From the principal's point of view, its name and reputation are on the line in each outlet, making careful control a necessity.

Control, however, can have negative ramifications within intermediaries. Many service franchisees, for example, are entrepreneurial by nature and select service franchising because they can own and operate their own businesses. If they are to deliver according to consistent standards, their independent ideas must be integrated into and often subsumed by the practices and policies of the service principal. In these situations, they often feel like automatons with less freedom than they have anticipated as owners of their own businesses.

Channel Ambiguity

Doubt often exists about the roles of the company and the intermediary. Who will undertake market research to identify customer requirements, the company or an intermediary? Who owns the results and in what way are they to be used? Who determines the standards for service delivery, the franchiser or the franchisee? Who should train a dealer's customer service representatives, the company or the dealer? In these and other situations, the roles of the principal and its intermediaries are unclear, leading to confusion and conflict.

STRATEGIES FOR EFFECTIVE SERVICE DELIVERY THROUGH INTERMEDIARIES

Service principals, of course, want to manage their service intermediaries to improve service performance, solidify their images, and increase profits and revenues. The principal has a variety of choices, which range from strict contractual and measurement control to partnering with intermediaries in a joint effort to improve service to the customer. One of the biggest issues a principal faces is whether to view intermediaries as extensions of its company, as customers, or as partners. We discuss three categories of intermediary management strategies: control strategies, empowerment strategies, and partnering strategies.

Control Strategies

With a *control* strategy, the service principal believes that intermediaries will perform best when it creates standards both for revenues and service performance, measures results, and compensates or rewards on the basis of performance level. To use these strategies the principal must be the most powerful participant in the channel, possessing unique services with strong consumer demand or loyalty, or other forms of economic power.

Measurement

Some franchisers maintain control of the service quality delivered by their franchisees by ongoing measurement programs that feed data back to the principal. Virtually all automobile dealers' sales and service performance is monitored regularly by the manufacturer, which creates the measurement program, administers it, and maintains control of the information. The company surveys customers at key points in the service encounter sequence: after sale, 30 days out, 90 days out, and after a year. The manufacturer designs the survey instruments (some of them with the assistance of dealer councils) and obtains the customer feedback directly. On the basis of this information, the manufacturer rewards and recognizes both individuals and dealerships that perform well and can potentially punish those that perform poorly. The obvious advantage to this approach is that the manufacturer retains control; however, the trust and goodwill between manufacturers and dealers can easily be eroded if dealers feel that the measurement is used to control and punish.

Review

Some franchisers control through terminations, nonrenewals, quotas, and restrictive supplier sources. Another means by which franchisers exert control over franchisees is through quotas and sales goals, typically by offering price breaks after a certain volume is attained.

Empowerment Strategies

Empowerment strategies—in which the service principal allows greater flexibility to intermediaries based on the belief that their talents are best revealed in participation rather than acquiescence—are useful when the service principal is new or lacks sufficient power to govern the channel using control strategies. In empowerment strategies, the principal provides information, research, or processes to help intermediaries perform well in service.

Help the Intermediary Develop Customer-Oriented Service Processes

Individual intermediaries rarely have the funds to sponsor their own customer research studies or training programs. One way for a company to improve intermediary performance is to conduct research or standard-setting studies relating to service performance, then provide the results as a service to intermediaries. As an example, H&R Block amassed its customer information and codified it in a set of 10 "Ultimate Client

Service" standards, which were displayed in each office. The standards, which tend to change over time, have included:

- No client will wait more than 30 minutes in the waiting area.
- Phone calls will be answered by the fourth ring, and no caller will be on hold for more than one minute.
- Every tax preparation client will receive a thorough interview to determine the client's lowest legal tax liability.
- Accurately prepared and checked returns will be delivered in four days or fewer.

Rather than administer this customer program from the home office, which could cause it to be perceived as a measurement "hammer," the company asks each franchisee to devise a way to measure the standards in its own offices, then report this information to H&R Block.

Provide Needed Support Systems

After Ford Motor Company conducted customer research and identified six sales standards and six service standards that address the most important customer expectations, it found that dealers and service centers did not know how to implement, measure, and improve service with these standards. For example, one sales standard specified that customers be approached within the first minute they enter the dealership and be offered help when and if the customer needs it. Although dealers could see that this standard was desirable, they did not immediately know how to make it happen. Ford stepped in and provided the research and process support to help the dealers. As another form of support, the company created national advertising featuring dealers discussing the quality care standards. In airlines and hotels as well as other travel and ticketing services, the service principal's reservation system is an important support system.

Develop Intermediaries to Deliver Service Quality

Service originators can invest in training or other forms of development to improve the skills and knowledge of intermediaries and their employees. Merrill Lynch, a national franchiser of financial brokers, engages in a companywide program of service excellence. To teach sales associates (brokers) about what buyers and sellers expect, the company first conducted focus group interviews with end-customers, and then created training programs to communicate what the research revealed. To teach brokers, the company created a highly successful operations review that examined the operational and financial aspects of the brokers, assessed their levels of effectiveness, then communicated individually with each broker about the specific issues that needed to be addressed and the approaches that would be successful in improving performance.

Change to a Cooperative Management Structure

Companies such as Taco Bell use the technique of empowerment to manage and motivate franchisees. They develop worker teams in their outlets to hire, discipline, and handle financial tasks such as deposits and audits. Taco Bell deliberately reduced levels of management (regional managers used to oversee 5 stores; now they oversee more than 50 stores) and reported improvements in revenue, employee morale, and profits.

Partnering Strategies

The group of strategies with the highest potential for effectiveness involves *partnering* with intermediaries to learn together about end-customers, set specifications, improve delivery, and communicate honestly. This approach capitalizes on the skills and strengths of both principal and intermediary and engenders a sense of trust that improves the relationship.

Alignment of Goals

One of the most successful approaches to partnering involves aligning company and intermediary goals early in the process. Both the service principal and the intermediary have individual goals that they strive to achieve. If channel members can see that they benefit the ultimate consumer of services and in the process optimize their own revenues and profit, they begin the relationship with a target in mind. Sonic Corp, a drive-in hamburger chain, attempts to retain open relationships with its franchisees, continually adapting to changing customer needs and franchisee suggestions.

Consultation and Cooperation

A strategy of consultation and cooperation is not as dramatic as setting joint goals, but it does result in intermediaries participating in decisions. In this approach, which could involve virtually any issue, from compensation to service quality to the service environment, the principal makes a point of consulting intermediaries and asking for their opinions and views before establishing policy. Alpha Graphics, a franchiser of rapid printing services based in Tucson, Arizona, habitually consults its franchisees to hear how they think the operation should be run. For example, when the franchiser found that the outlets needed greater support in promotion, the company began to make customer mailings for franchisees. When the franchiser found that many franchisees were dissatisfied with the one-sided contracts they received, Alpha Graphics revised contracts to make it easier for franchisees to leave the system, changed fees to reflect a sliding scale linked to volume, and allowed franchisees to select the ways they use their royalty fees. This approach makes the franchisees feel that they have some control over the way they do business and also generates a steady stream of improvement ideas. Taco John's, one of the largest Mexican fast-food chains, is known for its cooperative relationships with franchisees.

Summary

This chapter discussed the benefits and challenges of delivering service through intermediaries. Service intermediaries perform many important functions for the service principal—coproducing the service, making services locally available, and functioning as the link between the principal and the customer. The focus in service distribution is on identifying ways to bring the customer and principal or its representatives together.

In contrast to channels for products, channels for services are almost always direct, if not to the customer then to the intermediary that sells to the customer. Many of the primary functions that distribution channels serve—inventorying, securing, and taking title to goods—have no meaning in services. Because services cannot be owned, most have no titles or rights that can be passed along a delivery channel. Because services are intangible and perishable, inventories cannot exist, making warehousing dispensable. In general, because services cannot be produced, warehoused, and then retailed as goods can, many channels available to goods producers are not feasible for service firms.

Four forms of distribution in service were described in the chapter: direct (company-owned) channels, franchisees, agents/brokers, and electronic channels. The benefits and challenges of each type of intermediary were discussed, and examples of firms successful in delivering services through each type were detailed. Discussion centered on strategies that could be used by service principals to improve management of intermediaries.

Discussion Questions

1. In what specific ways does the distribution of services differ from the distribution of goods?

2. Identify other service firms that are company owned and see whether the services they provide are more consistent than ones provided by the franchisees mentioned in this chapter.

3. List five services that are, or could be, distributed on the Internet that are not mentioned in this chapter. Why are these particular services appropriate for electronic distribution? Choose two that you particularly advocate. How would you address the challenges to electronic media discussed in this chapter?

4. List services that are sold through selling agents. Why is the use of agents the chosen method of distribution for these services? Could any be distributed in the other ways described in this chapter?

5. What are the main differences between agents and brokers?

6. What types of services are bought through purchasing agents? What qualifies a purchasing agent to represent a buyer in these transactions? Why do buyers themselves not engage in the purchase, but rather hire someone else to do so?

7. Which of the reasons for channel conflict described in this chapter is the most problematic? Why? Based on the chapter, and in particular the strategies discussed at the end of the chapter, what can be done to address the problem you selected? Rank the possible strategies from most effective to least effective.

8. Which of the three categories of strategies for effective service delivery through intermediaries do you believe is most successful? Why? Why are the other two categories less successful?

Exercises

1. Develop a brief franchising plan for a service concept or idea that you believe could be successful.

2. Visit a franchisee and discuss the pros and cons of the arrangement from his or her perspective. How closely does this list of benefits and challenges fit the one provided in this chapter? What would you add to the chapter's list to reflect the experience of the franchisee you interviewed?

3. Select a service industry with which you are familiar. How do service principals in that industry distribute their services? Develop possible approaches to manage intermediaries using the three categories of strategies in the last section of this chapter. Which approach do you believe would be most effective? Why? Which approaches are currently used by service principals in the industry?

4. On the Internet, locate three services that you believe are interesting. What benefits does buying on the Internet have over buying those services elsewhere?

Notes

1. "Is a Franchise Right for You?" *AARP Newsletter,* www.aarp.org, 2007.

2. A. E. Serwer, "Trouble in Franchise Nation," *Fortune,* March 6, 1995, pp. 115–129.

3. "Are You Ready?" United States Small Business Administration, http://www.sba.gov/smallbusinessplanner/index.html, 2007.

4. Serwer, "Trouble in Franchise Nation," p. 116.

5. R. Woodall, C. Colby, and A. Parasuraman, "'E-volution to Revolution," *Marketing Management,* March/April 2007, pp. 27–38.

6. K. Peterson, "Surge in International Travel Spurs Online Battle," *USA Today,* July 25, 2007, p. D1.

7. D. Clark, "Safety First," *The Wall Street Journal,* December 7, 1998, p. R14.

8. Ibid.

Chapter Fifteen

Managing Demand and Capacity

This chapter's objectives are to

1. Explain the underlying issue for capacity-constrained services: lack of inventory capability.
2. Present the implications of time, labor, equipment, and facilities constraints combined with variations in demand patterns.
3. Lay out strategies for matching supply and demand through (a) shifting demand to match capacity or (b) adjusting capacity to meet demand.
4. Demonstrate the benefits and risks of yield management strategies in forging a balance among capacity utilization, pricing, market segmentation, and financial return.
5. Provide strategies for managing waiting lines for times when capacity and demand cannot be aligned.

How to Fill 281 Rooms 365 Days of the Year

The Ritz-Carlton Hotel in Phoenix, Arizona, is an upscale hotel in the center of a metropolitan area of approximately 3 million people, the fifth largest metropolitan area in the United States. The hotel is frequently cited for its service, and was named the number one business hotel in Arizona by *Travel and Leisure* magazine in 2004.[1] It has 281 luxury rooms, two restaurants, beautiful pools, and spacious meeting and conference facilities. These restaurants and meeting facilities are available to guests 365 days and nights of the year. Yet natural demand for them varies tremendously. During the tourist season from November through mid-April, demand for rooms is high, often exceeding available space. From mid-May through September, however, when temperatures regularly exceed 100 degrees Fahrenheit, the demand for rooms drops considerably. Because the hotel caters to business travelers and business meetings, demand has a weekly cycle in addition to the seasonal fluctuations. Business travelers do not stay over weekends. Thus, demand for rooms from the hotel's primary market segment drops on Friday and Saturday nights.

To smooth the peaks and valleys of demand for its facilities, the Phoenix Ritz-Carlton has employed a number of strategies. Group business (primarily business conferences) is pursued throughout the year to fill the lower demand periods. A variety of special event, sports, wedding, and getaway packages are offered year-round to increase weekend demand for rooms. During the hot summer months, the hotel encourages local Phoenix and nearby Tucson residents to experience the luxury of the hotel. One creative package used in the past included an attractively priced hotel stay combined with a "progressive dinner" at nearby restaurants. The progressive dinner started with a reception in the hotel, a walk to one restaurant for appetizers, followed by dinner at a second restaurant. The evening finished with champagne and dessert in the guests' room. By encouraging local people to use the hotel, the hotel increases its occupancy during slow demand times while residents of the community get a chance to enjoy an experience they may not be able to afford during the high season.

Most downtown hotels in urban areas face the same weekly demand fluctuations that the Phoenix Ritz-Carlton deals with, and many have found a partial solution by catering to families and children on the weekends.[2] For many dual-career couples, weekend getaways are a primary form of relaxation and vacation. The downtown hotels cater to these couples and families by offering discounted room rates, child-oriented activities and amenities, and an environment in which families feel comfortable. For example, the New York Palace Hotel—the closest hotel to American Girl Place—attempts to increase weekend stays by offering an "American Girl Place Package" to families with young daughters. The package, targeted for nonbusiness customers, comes with a complimentary American Girl Futon bed for an American Girl doll that girls can take home with them and includes turndown service for their dolls.

For the Ritz-Carlton Hotel in Phoenix and the other hotels mentioned in this chapter-opening vignette, managing demand and utilizing the hotel's fixed capacity of rooms, restaurants, and meeting facilities can be a seasonal, weekly, and even daily challenge. Although the hotel industry epitomizes the challenges of demand and capacity management, many service providers face similar problems. For example, tax accountants and air-conditioning maintenance services face seasonal demand fluctuations, whereas services such as commuter trains and restaurants face weekly and even hourly variations in customer demand. For some businesses, demand is predictable, as for a tax accountant. For others, such as management or technology consultants, demand may be less predictable, fluctuating based on customer needs and business cycles. Sometimes firms experience too much demand for the existing capacity and sometimes capacity sits idle.

Overuse or underuse of a service can directly contribute to gap 3: failure to deliver what was designed and specified. For example, when demand for services exceeds maximum capacity, the quality of service may drop because staff and facilities are overtaxed. And some customers may be turned away, not receiving the service at all. During periods of slow demand it may be necessary to reduce prices or cut service amenities; however, when firms change the makeup of the clientele and the nature of the service they run the risk of not delivering what customers expect. For example, older travelers or business groups who are in a hotel on a weekend may resent the invasion of families and children because it changes the nature of the service they expected. At the pool, for example, collisions can occur between adults trying to swim laps and children playing water games.

In this chapter we focus on the challenges of matching supply and demand in capacity-constrained services. The service performance gap can occur when organizations fail to smooth the peaks and valleys of demand, overuse their capacities, attract an inappropriate customer mix in their efforts to build demand, or rely too much on price in smoothing demand. The chapter gives you an understanding of these issues and strategies for addressing them. The effective use of capacity is frequently a key success factor for service organizations.

THE UNDERLYING ISSUE: LACK OF INVENTORY CAPABILITY

The fundamental issue underlying supply and demand management in services is the lack of inventory capability. Unlike manufacturing firms, service firms cannot build up inventories during periods of slow demand to use later when demand increases. This lack of inventory capability is due to the perishability of services and their simultaneous production and consumption. An airline seat not sold on a given flight cannot be left in inventory and resold the following day. The productive capacity of that seat on that flight has perished. Similarly, an hour of a lawyer's billable time cannot be saved from one day to the next. Services also cannot be transported from one place to another or transferred from person to person. Thus the Phoenix Ritz-Carlton's services cannot be moved to an alternative location in the summer months—say, to the Pacific Coast where summers are ideal for tourists and demand for hotel rooms is high.

The lack of inventory capability combined with fluctuating demand leads to a variety of potential outcomes, as illustrated in Figure 15.1.[3] The horizontal lines in Figure 15.1 indicate service capacity, and the curved line indicates customer demand for the service. In many services, capacity is fixed; thus capacity can be designated by a flat horizontal line over a certain time period. Demand for service frequently fluctuates, however, as indicated by the curved line. The topmost horizontal line in Figure 15.1 represents maximum capacity. For example, in our opening vignette, the

FIGURE 15.1 **Variations in Demand Relative to Capacity**

Source: Reprinted from C. Lovelock and J. Wirtz, *Services Marketing: People, Technology, Strategy* (Upper Saddle River, NJ: Pearson Prentice Hall, 2007), chap. 9, p. 261. Reprinted by permission of Pearson Prentice Hall.

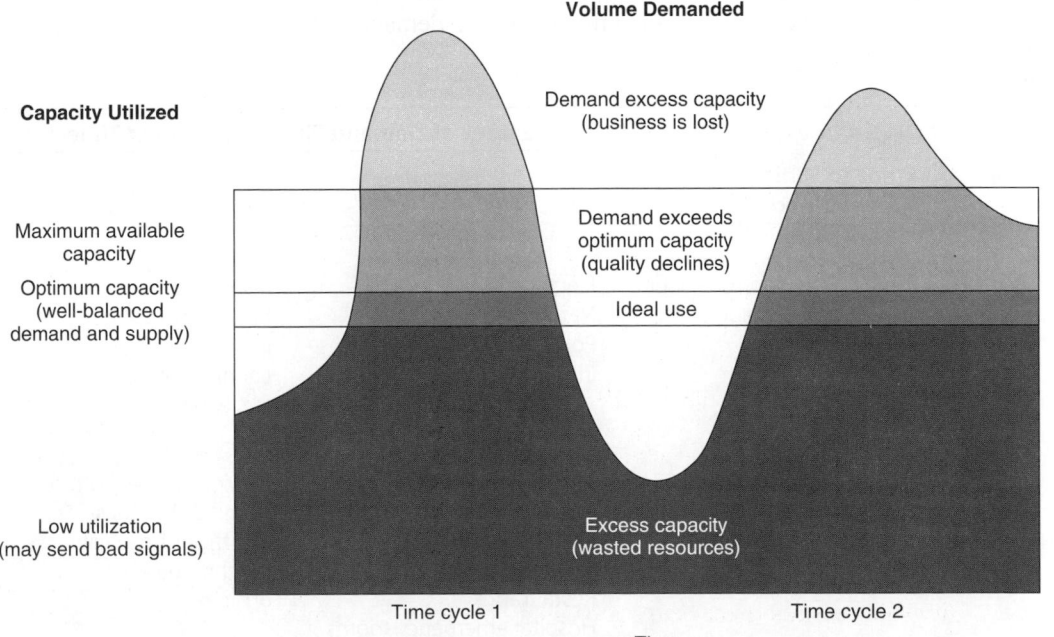

horizontal line would represent the Phoenix Ritz-Carlton's 281 rooms, or it could represent 70,000 seats in a large university football stadium. The rooms and the seats remain constant, but demand for them fluctuates. The band between the second and third horizontal lines represents optimum capacity—the best use of the capacity from the perspective of both customers and the company (the difference between optimal and maximum capacity utilization is discussed later in the chapter). The areas in the middle of Figure 15.1 are labeled to represent four basic scenarios that can result from different combinations of capacity and demand:

1. *Excess demand.* The level of demand exceeds maximum capacity. In this situation some customers will be turned away, resulting in lost business opportunities. For the customers who do receive the service, its quality may not match what was promised because of crowding or overtaxing of staff and facilities.

2. *Demand exceeds optimum capacity.* No one is being turned away, but the quality of service may still suffer because of overuse, crowding, or staff being pushed beyond their abilities to deliver consistent quality.

3. *Demand and supply are balanced at the level of optimum capacity.* Staff and facilities are occupied at an ideal level. No one is overworked, facilities can be maintained, and customers are receiving quality service without undesirable delays.

4. *Excess capacity.* Demand is below optimum capacity. Productive resources in the form of labor, equipment, and facilities are underutilized, resulting in lost productivity and lower profits. Customers may receive excellent quality on an individual level because they have the full use of the facilities, no waiting, and complete attention from the staff. If, however, service quality depends on the presence of other customers, customers may be disappointed or may worry that they have chosen an inferior service provider.

Not all firms will be challenged equally in terms of managing supply and demand. The seriousness of the problem will depend on the *extent of demand fluctuations over time,* and the *extent to which supply is constrained* (Table 15.1).[4] Some types of organizations will experience wide fluctuations in demand (telecommunications, hospitals,

TABLE 15.1
Demand and Capacity for Service Providers

Source: Adapted from C. H. Lovelock, "Classifying Services to Gain Strategic Marketing Insights," *Journal of Marketing* 47 (Summer 1983), p. 17. Reprinted by permission from the American Marketing Association.

Extent to Which Supply Is Constrained	Extent of Demand Fluctuations over Time	
	Wide	**Narrow**
	1	2
Peak demand can usually be met without a major delay.	Electricity Natural gas Police and fire emergencies Internet services	Insurance Legal services Banking Laundry and dry cleaning
	4	3
Peak demand regularly exceeds capacity.	Accounting and tax preparation Passenger transportation Hotels Restaurants Hospital emergency rooms	Services similar to those in cell 2 that have insufficient capacity for their base level of business

transportation, restaurants), whereas others will have narrower fluctuations (insurance, laundry, banking). For some, peak demand can usually be met even when demand fluctuates (electricity, natural gas, Internet services), but for others peak demand may frequently exceed capacity (hospital emergency rooms, restaurants near football stadiums, hotels next to universities). Those firms with wide variations in demand (cells 1 and 4 in Table 15.1), and particularly those with wide fluctuations in demand that regularly exceed capacity (cell 4), will find the issues and strategies in this chapter particularly important to their success. Those firms that find themselves in cell 3 need a "one-time-fix" (as discussed in Chapter 10) to expand their capacity to match regular patterns of excessive demand. The example industries in Table 15.1 are provided to illustrate where *most* firms in those industries would likely be classified. In reality, an individual firm from any industry could find itself in any of the four cells, depending on its immediate circumstances.

To identify effective strategies for managing supply and demand fluctuations, an organization needs a clear understanding of the constraints on its capacity and the underlying demand patterns.

CAPACITY CONSTRAINTS

For many firms, service capacity is fixed. As indicated in Table 15.2, critical fixed-capacity factors can be—depending on the type of service—time, labor, equipment, facilities, or (in many cases) a combination of these.

Time, Labor, Equipment, Facilities

For some service businesses, the primary constraint on service production is *time*. For example, a lawyer, a consultant, a hairdresser, a plumber, and a psychological counselor all primarily sell their time. In such contexts, if the service worker is not available or if her or his time is not used productively, profits are lost. If there is excess demand, additional time cannot be created to satisfy it. From the point of view of the individual service provider, time is the constraint.

From the point of view of a firm that employs a large number of service providers, *labor* or staffing levels can be the primary capacity constraint. A law firm, a university department, a consulting firm, a tax accounting firm, and a repair and maintenance contractor may all face the reality that at certain times demand for their organizations' services cannot be met because the staff is already operating at peak capacity. However, it does not always make sense (nor may it be possible in a competitive labor market) to hire additional service providers if low demand is a reality a large percentage of the time.

In other cases, *equipment* may be the critical constraint. For trucking or air-freight delivery services, the trucks or airplanes needed to service demand may be the capacity limitation. During the Christmas holidays, UPS, FedEx, and other delivery service providers face this issue. Health clubs also deal with this limitation, particularly at certain times of the day (before work, during lunch hours, after work) and in certain months of the year. For network service providers, bandwidth, servers, and switches represent their capacity constraints.

Finally, many firms face restrictions brought about by their limited *facilities*. Hotels have only a certain number of rooms to sell, airlines are limited by the number of seats on their aircraft, educational institutions are constrained by the number of rooms and the number of seats in each classroom, and restaurant capacity is restricted to the number of tables and seats available.

TABLE 15.2
Constraints on Capacity

Nature of the Constraint	Type of Service*
Time	Legal
	Consulting
	Accounting
	Medical
Labor	Law firm
	Accounting firm
	Consulting firm
	Health clinic
Equipment	Delivery services
	Telecommunications
	Network services
	Utilities
	Health club
Facilities	Hotels
	Restaurants
	Hospitals
	Airlines
	Schools
	Theaters
	Churches

* The examples illustrate the most common capacity constraint for each type of service. In reality, any of the service organizations listed can be operating under multiple constraints. For example, a law firm may be operating under constrained labor capacity (too few attorneys) and facilities constraints (not enough office space) at the same time.

Understanding the primary capacity constraint, or the combination of factors that restricts capacity, is a first step in designing strategies to deal with supply and demand issues.

Optimal versus Maximum Use of Capacity

To fully understand capacity issues, it is important to know the difference between *optimal* and *maximum* use of capacity. As suggested in Figure 15.1, optimum and maximum capacity may not be the same. Using capacity at an optimum level means that resources are fully employed but not overused and that customers are receiving quality service in a timely manner. Maximum capacity, on the other hand, represents the absolute limit of service availability. In the case of a sporting event, optimum and maximum capacity may be the same. The entertainment value of the game is enhanced for customers when every single seat is filled, and obviously the profitability for the home team is greatest under these circumstances (see accompanying photo). On the other hand, in a university classroom it is usually not desirable for students or faculty to have every seat filled. In this case, optimal use of capacity is less than the maximum. In some cases, maximum use of capacity may result in excessive waiting by customers, as in a popular restaurant. From the perspective of customer satisfaction, optimum use of the restaurant's capacity will again be less than maximum use.

In the case of equipment or facilities constraints, the maximum capacity at any given time is obvious. There are only a certain number of weight machines in the health club, a certain number of seats in the airplane, and a limited amount of space in a cargo carrier. In the case of a bottling plant, when maximum capacity on the assembly line is exceeded, bottles begin to break and the system shuts down. Thus, it is relatively easy to observe the effects of exceeding maximum equipment capacity.

For sports and other entertainment venues, maximal and optimal capacity are close to the same.

When the limitation is people's time or labor, maximum capacity is harder to specify because people are in a sense more flexible than facilities and equipment. When an individual service provider's maximum capacity has been exceeded, the result is likely to cause decreased service quality, customer dissatisfaction, and employee burnout and turnover, but these outcomes may not be immediately observable even to the employee. While it is relatively easy for firms to identify the maximum capacity for physical constraints like space, it is much more difficult to know what the maximum capacity of a human being is. As a result firms may be able to push employees beyond their optimum capacity for a while, but not learn of the maximum capacity of an employee until the person quits or encounters health problems. Indeed, it is often easy for a consulting firm to take on one more assignment, taxing its employees beyond their maximum capacity, or for an HMO clinic to schedule a few more appointments in a day, stretching its staff and physicians beyond their maximum capacity. Given the potential costs in terms of reduced quality and customer and employee dissatisfaction, it is critical for the firm to understand optimum and maximum human capacity limits.

DEMAND PATTERNS

To manage fluctuating demand in a service business, it is necessary to have a clear understanding of demand patterns, why they vary, and the market segments that comprise demand at different points in time.[5] A number of questions need to be answered regarding the predictability and underlying causes of demand.

The Charting of Demand Patterns

To begin to understand demand patterns, the organization needs to chart the level of demand over relevant time periods. Organizations that have good customer information systems can chart this information very accurately. Others may need to chart demand patterns more informally. Daily, weekly, and monthly demand levels should be tracked, and if seasonality is a suspected problem, graphing should be done for data from at least the past year. In some services, such as restaurants or health care, hourly fluctuations within a day may also be relevant. Sometimes demand patterns are intuitively obvious; in other cases, patterns may not reveal themselves until the data are tracked.

Predictable Cycles

In looking at the graphic representation of demand levels, predictable cycles may be detected, including daily (variations occur by hours), weekly (variations occur by day), monthly (variations occur by day or week), and/or yearly (variations occur according to months or seasons). In some cases, predictable patterns may occur at all periods. For example, in the restaurant industry, especially in seasonal tourist locations, demand can vary predictably by month, by week, by day, and by hour. Similarly, the demand for a bank's services can vary by hour (with lunch time and end of the day with the most demand), by day of the week (with the last day of the week and the first day of the week being the most popular), and by day of the month (with the day that Social Security checks arrive being among the highest in demand).

If a predictable cycle is detected, the underlying causes should be identified. The Ritz-Carlton in Phoenix knows that demand cycles are based on seasonal weather patterns and that weekly variations are based on the work week (business travelers do not stay at the hotel over the weekend). Tax accountants can predict demand based on when taxes are due, quarterly and annually. Services catering to children and families respond to variations in school hours and vacations. Retail and telecommunications services have peak periods at certain holidays and times of the week and day. When predictable patterns exist, generally one or more causes can be determined.

Random Demand Fluctuations

Sometimes the patterns of demand appear to be random—there is no apparent predictable cycle. Yet even in this case, causes can often be identified. For example, day-to-day changes in the weather may affect use of recreational, shopping, or entertainment facilities. Good weather generally increases the demand for the services provided by an amusement park, but it has the opposite effect on movie theaters—people would rather not be inside when the weather is nice. Auto service centers generally find extremely poor weather (either very hot or very cold) increases the demand for their services, whereas mild weather does not seem to have as much of an effect on vehicles. Although the weather cannot be predicted far in advance, it may be possible to anticipate demand a day or two ahead. Health-related events also cannot be predicted. Accidents, heart attacks, and births all increase demand for hospital services, but the level of demand cannot generally be determined in advance. Natural disasters such as floods, fires, and hurricanes can dramatically increase the need for such services as insurance, telecommunications, and health care. Acts of war and terrorism such as that experienced in the United States on September 11, 2001, generate instantaneous need for services that cannot be predicted.

Cox Communications was faced with a sudden increase in demand for services in Baton Rouge, Louisiana, immediately after Hurricane Katrina struck in late August 2005. The Category 5 hurricane, centered in New Orleans, resulted in more than 1,800 deaths and caused more than $80 billion in damages. A disaster of this magnitude increased the demand for Cox's services. Cox's customers needed access to its network, phone services, the Internet, and e-mail to communicate with family members and friends regarding their safety and whereabouts, and then to make arrangements to begin the rebuilding process. In the aftermath of Hurricane Katrina, Baton Rouge's population doubled as people were forced to leave New Orleans. Many of those who took refuge in the city remain today, increasing demand for Cox's services in a way no one could have ever predicted![6]

Our Global Feature illustrates how one company with seemingly random and chaotic demand for its services was able to change its business to serve customers. The feature is also a good example of organizational learning across cultures.

Imagine a business in which customers' orders are unpredictable, where more than half of all customer orders are changed, often repeatedly and at the last minute, and where the product being delivered is never more than 90 minutes from spoiling. Welcome to the concrete delivery business. Cemex, based in Monterrey, Mexico, and founded in 1906, is a highly successful global player in this industry. The company operates in 50 countries across five continents with more than 50,000 employees and annual net sales in excess of $18 billion.

Yet, when two internal consultants examined the business several years ago, they were amazed at the chaos that ruled the industry. Wild weather, unpredictable traffic, spontaneous labor disruptions, and sporadic government inspections of construction sites all combined with ever-changing customer orders to create a sense of chaos and uncontrollability in the business. Add this chaos to 8,000 grades of concrete available through a half-dozen regional mixing plants, and you have an extremely complex system to manage.

Historically, Cemex had attempted to run the business through controlling its customers, requiring them to stick with their orders and imposing fines for changed orders. Efficiency—not customers—ruled in Cemex's effort to conquer the natural randomness of demand and customers' needs to change orders at the last minute.

The company began searching for new ways to do business. It turned to FedEx and to the 911 emergency dispatch center in Houston, Texas, for ideas. What it found were organizations that, instead of trying to control demand for their services, had developed people and technology that could be flexible in meeting customers' seemingly random demand patterns. Instead of penalizing customers for changing their orders, FedEx does not restrict its customers and, in fact, guarantees delivery at a certain time to any and all locations. This ability to serve customers is made possible by sophisticated information systems that track demand and schedule pickups and deliveries, customer-focused frontline employees, and a customer-centric corporate culture that supports it all. From the 911 center in Houston, Cemex learned that even seemingly random occurrences such as emergency health needs and accidents occur in sufficient number to allow patterns of demand to be discerned and planned for. In terms of Figure 15.1, what FedEx and the 911 emergency center did was adjust their capacity to meet the peaks and valleys of customer demand rather than insisting that the customers adjust their demand to fit the company's constrained capacity.

The observations of how both FedEx and the 911 dispatch center handled demand fluctuations were a revelation to Cemex's team. The company went back to Mexico determined to embrace the complexity of its marketplace and to do business on the customers' terms. The company launched a project called Sincronización Dinamica de Operaciones: the dynamic synchronization of operations. It unleashed trucks from previous zone assignments, allowing them to roam the city. It outfitted the trucks with transmitters and receivers connected to a global positioning system (GPS) so that locations, direction, and speed of every vehicle could be tracked. It enrolled its drivers in secondary education classes over a period of two years so they would be more service oriented and able to deal with customers.

Impressed with FedEx's guaranteed service, Cemex worked toward being able to offer "same-day service, with free, unlimited order changes." It instituted a policy for guaranteed delivery: if a load failed to arrive within 20 minutes of its scheduled delivery time, the buyer received back 20 pesos per cubic meter—"guarantia 20 × 20"—amounting to roughly 5 percent of the total cost.

Cemex embraced the chaos of its industry instead of trying to adjust and change it. By using technology, people, and systems, it was able to match its capacity constraints with its customers' wildly fluctuating demands. And the company came out a winner. Cemex could afford to offer its 20 × 20 guarantee because its reliability regularly exceeded 98 percent!

Today, the company's focus on the customer is clearly stated in the slogan across the top of its website: "we produce cement according to customer needs."

Sources: T. Petzinger Jr., "This Promise Is Set in Concrete," *Fast Company,* April 1999, pp. 216–218; see also T. Petzinger Jr., *The New Pioneers* (New York: Simon & Schuster, Inc., 1999), pp. 91–93. Reprinted with the permission of Simon & Schuster, Inc. Copyright © 1999 by Thomas Petzinger Jr.; updated with company information from the Cemex website, www.cemex.com, 2007.

Organizations that predict customer patterns can use that information to anticipate service demands.

Demand Patterns by Market Segment

An organization that has detailed records on customer transactions may be able to disaggregate demand by market segment, revealing patterns within patterns. Or the analysis may reveal that demand from one segment is predictable, whereas demand from another segment is relatively random. For example, for a bank, the visits from its commercial accounts may occur daily at a predictable time, whereas personal account holders may visit the bank at seemingly random intervals. Health clinics often notice that walk-in or "care needed today" patients tend to concentrate their arrivals on Monday, with fewer needing immediate attention on other days of the week. Many auto service centers experience a similar pattern, as more walk-in customers arrive on Monday morning for car servicing and repair than any other day of the week. Knowing that this pattern exists, several health clinics and auto service centers schedule more future appointments (which they can control) for later days of the week, leaving more of Monday available for same-day appointments and walk-ins.

STRATEGIES FOR MATCHING CAPACITY AND DEMAND

When an organization has a clear grasp of its capacity constraints and an understanding of demand patterns, it is in a good position to develop strategies for matching supply and demand. There are two general approaches for accomplishing this match. The first is to smooth the demand fluctuations themselves by shifting demand to match existing capacity. This approach implies that the peaks and valleys of the demand curve (Figure 15.1) will be flattened to match as closely as possible the horizontal optimum capacity line. The second general strategy is to adjust capacity to match fluctuations in demand. This implies moving the horizontal capacity lines shown in Figure 15.1 to match the ups and downs of the demand curve. Each of these two basic strategies is described next with specific examples.

Shifting Demand to Match Capacity

With this strategy an organization seeks to shift customers away from periods in which demand exceeds capacity, perhaps by convincing them to use the service during periods of slow demand. This change may be possible for some customers but not for others. For example, many business travelers are not able to shift their needs for airline, car rental, and hotel services; pleasure travelers, on the other hand, can often shift the timing of their trips. Customers who cannot shift their demand and cannot be accommodated because of insufficient capacity will represent lost business for the firm.

During periods of slow demand, the organization seeks to attract more and/or different customers to increase demand and thus better utilize its productive capacity. A variety of approaches, detailed in the following sections, can be used to shift or increase demand to match capacity. Frequently a firm uses a combination of approaches. Ideas for how to shift demand during both slow and peak periods are shown in Figure 15.2.

FIGURE 15.2   **Strategies for Shifting Demand to Match Capacity**

**DEMAND
TOO HIGH**

SHIFT DEMAND

**DEMAND
TOO LOW**

- Communicate busy days and times to customers.
- Modify timing and location of service delivery.
- Offer incentives for nonpeak usage.
- Set priorities by talking care of loyal or high-need customers first.
- Charge full price for the service—no discounts.

- Stimulate business from current market segments.
- Advertise peak usage times and benefits of nonpeak use.
- Vary how the facility is used.
- Vary the service offering.
- Differentiate on price.

Reduce Demand during Peak Times

One strategic approach to matching capacity and demand for a service provider focuses on *reducing demand* during times when customer demand is at its peak for the service.

Communicate with Customers   One approach for shifting demand is to communicate with customers, letting them know the times of peak demand so they can choose to use the service at alternative times and avoid crowding or delays. For example, signs in banks and post offices that let customers know their busiest hours and busiest days of the week can serve as a warning, allowing customers to shift their demand to another time if possible. Forewarning customers about busy times and possible waits can have added benefits. Many customer service telephone lines provide a similar warning by informing waiting customers about approximately how long it will be until they are served. Those who do not want to wait may choose to call back later when the customer service department is less busy or to visit the company's website for faster service.

Modify Timing and Location of Service Delivery   Some firms adjust their hours and days of service delivery to more directly reflect customer demand. Historically, U.S. banks were open only during "bankers' hours" from 10 a.m. to 3 p.m. every weekday—creating a heavy demand for their services during those hours. However, these hours did not necessarily match the times when most people preferred to do their personal banking. Now U.S. banks open early, stay open until 6 p.m. many days, and are open on Saturdays, better reflecting customer preferences and smoothing demand patterns. Many banks now have branches in hypermarkets such as Wal-Mart and Meijer, and supermarkets such as Albertson's and Kroger, providing customers with multiple choices of both where and when to do their banking. Online banking has also shifted demand from branches to "anytime, anywhere" websites. Movie theaters often augment their primary viewing schedules by offering additional matinees on weekends and holidays when people are free during the day for entertainment.

Offer Incentives for Nonpeak Usage   In an attempt to shift demand away from peak times, some firms will offer incentives to encourage customers to shift their use of the service to other times. In northern Midwest states, swimming pool contractors offer additional amenities (e.g., free diving board, free heater, larger size pool) to customers who are willing to postpone the purchase/use of their services until the end of the swimming season (say September or October). Fitness centers who offer Pilates classes during times of lower demand often tout the advantages of smaller classes and increased instructor interaction with clients and frequently extend the class time by 25 percent or more.

Set Priorities   When demand for the service is high and there is limited capacity, service providers can prioritize who is served by taking care of loyal or high-need customers first. A tax firm might decide to serve its best customers rather than first-time walk-ins just prior to income tax due dates, and emergency centers move the most severe cases to the top of the priority list.

Charge Full Price   Firms generally charge full price for service during those periods of time that they know their services are historically in high demand; no discounts are allowed during such times. One of the busiest periods of the year for airlines are those days just before and just after the Thanksgiving holiday; for this reason, most airlines give priority for seating to those paying full fares and prohibit the use of frequent flyer miles for free seats. Because demand is so high, customers looking for discounted or free tickets find that the days around this holiday have been "blacked out"; to travel, they must purchase tickets at regular fares.

Increase Demand to Match Capacity

Other approaches service providers may consider in matching capacity and demand focus on *increasing demand* for service during times when the service is at less than full capacity.

Stimulate Business from Current Market Segments   Advertising and other forms of promotion can emphasize different service benefits to customers during peak and slow periods. Advertising and sales messages can remind customers about times

The local market can fill the demand gap during the off-peak season.

when demand is low. For example, automobile service centers increase their service advertising during periods when demand is slow by sending out reminders and discounts for oil changes. Similarly, tourist attractions often advertise more to the local market during off-peak times.

Vary How the Facility Is Used   One approach is to change how the service facility is used, depending on the season of the year, day of the week, or time of day. For example, Whistler Mountain, a ski resort in Vancouver, Canada, offers its facilities for executive development and training programs during the summer when snow skiing is not possible. A hospital in the Los Angeles area rents use of its facilities to film production crews who need realistic hospital settings for movies or television shows. Movie theaters are sometimes rented during weekdays by business groups and on Sunday mornings by church groups who have no building of their own. All of these are examples of how varying the use of the service facility can occur during a period of low demand.

Vary the Service Offering   A similar approach entails changing the nature of the service offering. Accounting firms, for example, focus on tax preparation late in the year and until April 15, when federal taxes are due in the United States. During other times of the year, they can focus on audits and general tax consulting activities. During professional basketball games, the demand for food at concession stands increases dramatically during the breaks between quarters—so much so that many customers decide not to make purchases for fear they will miss seeing the game because of long lines. In response to this situation, concessions at many arenas are now offered through menu orders taken by staff roaming through the aisles, and food is delivered right to customers' seats while the game is going on. In larger cities across the globe, McDonald's offers food delivery as a way to increase demand for its service.[7] In these examples, the service offering and associated benefits are changed to smooth customer demand for the organization's resources.

Care should be exercised in implementing strategies to change the service offering because such changes may imply and require alterations in other marketing mix variables—such as promotion, pricing, and staffing—to match the new offering. Unless these additional mix variables are altered effectively to support the offering, the strategy may not work. Even when done well, the downside of such changes can be confusion about the organization's image from the customers' perspective or a loss of strategic focus for the organization and its employees.

Differentiate on Price

A common response during periods of slow demand is to discount the price of the service. This strategy relies on basic economics of supply and demand. To be effective, however, a price differentiation strategy depends on solid understanding of customer price sensitivity and demand curves. For example, business travelers are far less price sensitive than are families traveling for pleasure. For the Ritz-Carlton in Phoenix (our opening vignette), lowering prices during the slow summer months is not likely to increase bookings from business travelers dramatically. However, the lower summer prices attract considerable numbers of families and local guests who want an opportunity to experience a luxury hotel but are not able to afford the rooms during peak season.

The maximum capacity of any hotel, airline, restaurant, or other service establishment can be reached if the price is low enough. But the service provider's goal is usually to ensure the highest level of capacity utilization without sacrificing profits. We explore this complex relationship among price, market segments, capacity utilization, and profitability later in the chapter in the section on yield management.

Heavy use of price differentiation to smooth demand can also be a risky strategy. Overreliance on price can result in price wars in which eventually all competitors in an industry suffer. Price wars are well known in the airline industry, and total industry profits often suffer as a result of many airlines simultaneously trying to attract customers through price discounting. Another risk of relying on price is that customers grow accustomed to the lower price and expect to get the same deal the next time they use the service. If communications with customers are unclear, customers may not understand the reasons for the discounts and will expect to pay the same during peak demand periods. Overuse or exclusive use of price as a strategy for smoothing demand is also risky because of the potential impact on the organization's image, the potential for attracting undesired market segments, and the possibility that those customers paying higher prices may feel they have been treated unfairly.

Adjusting Capacity to Meet Demand

A second strategic approach to matching supply and demand focuses on *adjusting capacity*. The fundamental idea here is to adjust, stretch, and align capacity to match customer demand (rather than working on shifting demand to match capacity, as just described). During periods of peak demand the organization seeks to stretch or expand its capacity as much as possible. During periods of slow demand it tries to shrink

FIGURE 15.3 Strategies for Adjusting Capacity to Match Demand

DEMAND TOO HIGH ← **ADJUST CAPACITY** → **DEMAND TOO LOW**

- Stretch time, labor, facilities, and equipment temporarily.
- Use part-time employees.
- Cross-train employees.
- Hire part-time employees.
- Request overtime work from employees.
- Subcontract or outsource activities.
- Rent or share facilities and equipment.

- Schedule downtime during periods of low demand.
- Perform maintenance, renovations.
- Schedule vacations.
- Schedule employee training.
- Lay off employees.
- Modify or move facilities and equipment.

capacity so as not to waste resources. General strategies for adjusting the four primary service resources (time, people, equipment, and facilities) are discussed throughout the rest of this section. In Figure 15.3, we summarize specific ideas for adjusting capacity during periods of peak and slow demand. Often, a number of different strategies are used simultaneously.

Stretch Existing Capacity

Existing capacity can often be expanded temporarily to match demand. In such cases, no new resources are added; rather, the people, facilities, and equipment are asked to work harder and longer to meet demand.

Stretch Time Temporarily It may be possible to extend the hours of service temporarily to accommodate demand. A health clinic might stay open longer during flu season, retailers are open longer hours during the holiday shopping season, and accountants have extended appointment hours (evenings and Saturdays) in the weeks just before tax deadlines.

Stretch Labor Temporarily In many service organizations, employees are asked to work longer and harder during periods of peak demand. For example, consulting organizations face extensive peaks and valleys with respect to demand for their services. During peak demand, associates are asked to take on additional projects and work longer hours. And frontline service personnel in banks, tourist attractions, restaurants, and telecommunications companies are asked to serve more customers per hour during busy times than during "normal" hours or days.

Stretch Facilities Temporarily Theaters, restaurants, meeting facilities, and classrooms can sometimes be expanded temporarily by the addition of tables, chairs, or other equipment needed by customers. Or, as in the case of a commuter train, a car that holds a fixed number of people seated comfortably can "expand" by accommodating standing passengers.

Stretch Equipment Temporarily Computers, power lines, tour buses, and maintenance equipment can often be stretched beyond what would be considered the maximum capacity for short periods to accommodate peak demand.

In using these types of "stretch" strategies, the organization needs to recognize the wear and tear on resources and the potential for inferior quality of service that may go with extended or sometimes even permanent usage of such strategies. These strategies should thus be used for relatively short periods to allow for refreshment of the people who are asked to exceed their usual capacity and for maintenance of the facilities and equipment. Sometimes it is difficult to know in advance, particularly in the case of human resources, when capacity has been stretched too far.

Align Capacity with Demand Fluctuations

This basic strategy is sometimes known as a "chase demand" strategy. By adjusting service resources creatively, organizations can, in effect, chase the demand curves to match capacity with customer demand patterns. Time, labor, facilities, and equipment are again the focus, this time with an eye toward adjusting the basic mix and use of these resources. Specific actions might include the following.[8]

Use Part-Time Employees   In this situation the organization's labor resource is being aligned with demand. Retailers hire part-time employees during the holiday rush; tax accountants engage temporary help during tax season; tourist resorts bring in extra workers during peak season. Restaurants often ask employees to work split shifts (work the lunch shift, leave for a few hours, and come back for the dinner rush) during peak mealtime hours.

Outsource   Firms that find they have a temporary peak in demand for internal services may choose to outsource the service. For example, in recent years, many firms have found they do not have the capacity to fulfill their own needs for technology support, web design, and software-related services. Rather than try to hire and train additional employees, these companies look to firms that specialize in outsourcing these types of functions as a temporary (or sometimes long-term) solution.

Rent or Share Facilities or Equipment   For some organizations it is best to rent additional equipment or facilities during periods of peak demand. For example, express mail delivery services rent or lease trucks during the peak holiday delivery season. It would not make sense to buy trucks that would sit idle during the rest of the year. Sometimes organizations with complementary demand patterns can share facilities. An example is a church that shares its facilities during the week with a Montessori preschool. The school needs the facilities Monday through Friday during the day; the church needs the facilities in the evenings and on the weekend. Some businesses have been created to satisfy other businesses' fluctuating demand. For example, a firm may offer temporary office suites and clerical support to individuals who do not need such facilities and support on a continuous basis.

Schedule Downtime during Periods of Low Demand   If people, equipment, and facilities are being used at maximum capacity during peak periods, then it is imperative to schedule repair, maintenance, and renovations during off-peak periods. Online banking services, for example, often schedule software upgrades on early Sunday morning (4:00 to 6:00 a.m.) to keep those affected by the disruption of their service to a minimum. Such scheduling attempts to ensure that a provider's resources are in top condition when they are most needed. Vacations and training are also scheduled during slow demand periods.

Cross-Train Employees   If employees are cross-trained, they can shift among tasks, filling in where they are most needed. Cross-training increases the efficiency of the whole system and avoids underutilizing employees in some areas while others are being overtaxed. Many airlines cross-train their employees to move from ticketing to working the gate counter to assisting with baggage if needed. In some fast-food restaurants, employees specialize in one task (like making french fries) during busy

Strategy Insight   Combining Demand (Marketing) and Capacity (Operations) Strategies to Increase Profits

In many situations, firms use multiple demand and capacity management strategies simultaneously to obtain optimal usage and maximize profits. Because each strategy involves costs as well as potential service quality, customer loyalty, and revenue outcomes, determining the appropriate mix can be a complex decision.

Research done for a ski resort illustrates how operations and marketing data can be combined into a sophisticated model to predict the right mix of strategies. The ski industry presents particularly interesting challenges for capacity management because the industry sees typically large fluctuations in demand based on: seasonal, weekly, and even daily usage patterns; unpredictable weather and snowfall; a variety of skiing ability segments that use the resort in different ways; and demographic shifts over time. In addition, most resorts face constraints on their capacity due to environmental regulations that limit acreage and parking as well as the large capital investment required for facility expansion and/or improvement. Furthermore, as ticket prices at ski resorts have continued to escalate, customer expectations have risen.

Powder Valley (PV, a disguised name), a ski resort in northern Utah, had consistently lost market share for five years to its rivals. Lack of facility improvements and increased marketing efforts by its competitors were cited as likely reasons for declining market share. To improve the situation, PV managers had proposed several marketing strategies to increase demand on slow days and increase revenue per customer. Operations strategies that relied on acquisition of new terrain and new, faster ski lifts to improve the skiing experience and reduce waiting during peak demand periods were also proposed. Each of these strategies had its associated costs and less than totally predictable outcomes. Adding to

the complexity of the inherent trade-offs in the various strategies was the fact that the resort offered multiple activities (e.g., restaurants, skiing, shopping) for customers to choose.

The researchers working with PV proposed that the optimal profit strategy would require an integrated set of approaches representing both demand and capacity perspectives. Using data from the resort, they built a sophisticated simulation model to assess the impact on customer usage, waiting times, and profits of several different strategies that were being considered, including:

- *Price variations.* Strategies aimed at leveling demand by charging lower prices for off-peak skiing.
- *Promotions of underutilized services.* Promotions to attract new customer segments or shift existing customers to underutilized services.
- *Information provision on waiting times.* Strategies that provide information about less crowded periods or shorter waiting times to move customers temporarily to underutilized services.
- *Capacity expansion.* Investments in additional fixed capacity for skiing such as adding new terrain or expanding the number of lifts.
- *Capacity upgrades.* Improving or replacing existing lifts to carry more skiers and/or run faster.

As input to their model, the researchers used historic data on daily demand, demand smoothing and capacity expansion options, service times for each lift, flow patterns across various lifts within the resort, travel time between lifts, customer perceptions, and customer choice data. By combining these marketing and operations data, the researchers showed that retaining the current customer mix, installing two new chairs, and providing waiting

hours, and the team of specialists may number 10 people. During slow hours the team may shrink to three, with each of the remaining persons performing a variety of other functions. Grocery stores also use this strategy, with most employees able to move as needed from cashiering to stocking shelves to bagging groceries.

Modify or Move Facilities and Equipment   Sometimes it is possible to adjust, move, or creatively modify existing capacity to meet demand fluctuations. Hotels utilize this strategy by reconfiguring rooms—two rooms with a locked door between can be rented to two different parties in high demand times or turned into a suite during

time information would maximize profits for the resort. Adding new chair lifts with higher speeds and doubled seating capacity within the existing terrain was a more profitable approach than expanding to new terrain. The simulation model showed that contrary to management predictions, smoothing demand across the day through differential pricing would actually decrease profits significantly. The model results were also useful in suggesting a priority order for the investments. The wait time signage investment was the least expensive and offered the largest single improvement for customers as well as the largest single profit impact. Upgrading at least one chair lift was the next priority.

Balancing demand and capacity can involve a complex set of decisions, and sometimes the outcomes are not obvious, especially when strategies seem to have contradictory objectives. For example in the PV simulation, a marketing objective of increased revenues through attracting more customers was contradicted by an operations objective of providing optimal wait times for lifts. As illustrated in the ski resort research, firms can combine marketing and operations data into one overall model and run simulated experiments to determine the best set of combined strategies. One company, ProModel, has developed simulations similar to the one described here that have been successfully used by such service providers as American Express, the American Red Cross, Disneyland, Chase Bank, Delta Air Lines, JetBlue, the Mayo Clinic, and UPS. The Salt Lake Organizing Committee for the 2002 Winter Olympics also used a similar simulation to evaluate and successfully optimize spectator flow, emergency planning, and transportation systems. Of course, the quality of the decisions based on simulation models is highly dependent on the accuracy of the assumptions in the model and the quality of the input data.

Managing demand and capacity in ski resorts can be very challenging.

Sources: M. E. Pullman and G. Thompson, "Strategies for Integrating Capacity with Demand in Service Networks," *Journal of Service Research* 5 (February 2003), pp. 169–183; and ProModel Corporation (www.promodel.com).

slow demand. The airline industry offers another example of this strategy. Using an approach known as "demand-driven dispatch," airlines often assign airplanes to flight schedules on the basis of fluctuating market needs.[9] The method depends on accurate knowledge of demand and the ability to quickly move airplanes with different seating capacities to flight assignments that match their capacity. The Boeing 777 aircraft is so flexible that it can be reconfigured within hours to vary the number of seats allocated to one, two, or three classes.[10] The plane can thus be quickly modified to match demand from different market segments, essentially molding capacity to fit demand. Another strategy may involve moving the service to a new location to meet customer demand or even bringing the service to customers. Mobile training facilities, pet grooming vans, and flu shot and blood donation facilities are examples of services that physically follow customers.

Combining Demand and Capacity Strategies

Many firms use multiple strategies, combining marketing-driven demand management approaches with operations-driven capacity management strategies. Figuring out which is the best set of strategies for maximizing capacity utilization, customer satisfaction, and profitability can be challenging, particularly when the service represents a constellation of offerings within one service setting. Examples of such services include theme parks with rides, restaurants, and shopping; hotel vacation villages with hotels, shopping, spas, pools, and restaurants; or ski resorts with ski slopes, spas, restaurants, and entertainment. Firms face complex problems in trying to balance demand across all the different offerings with an eye to quality and profitability. Our Strategy Insight describes a ski resort simulation that was created to use operations and marketing variables to determine the optimal combination of demand and capacity management strategies across the resort's various offerings and activities.

YIELD MANAGEMENT: BALANCING CAPACITY UTILIZATION, PRICING, MARKET SEGMENTATION, AND FINANCIAL RETURN

Yield management is a term that has become attached to a variety of methods, some very sophisticated, employed to match demand and supply in capacity-constrained services. Using yield management models, organizations find the best balance at a particular point in time among the prices charged, the segments sold to, and the capacity used. The goal of yield management is to produce the best possible financial return from a limited available capacity. Specifically, yield management—also referred to as *revenue management*—attempts to allocate the fixed capacity of a service provider (e.g., seats on a flight, rooms in a hotel, rental cars) to match the potential demand in various market segments (e.g., business traveler, tourist) so as to maximize revenue or yield.[11]

Although the implementation of yield management can involve complex mathematical models and computer programs, the underlying effectiveness measure is the ratio of actual revenue to potential revenue for a particular measurement period:

$$\text{Yield} = \frac{\text{Actual revenue}}{\text{Potential revenue}}$$

where

$$\text{Actual revenue} = \text{Actual capacity used} \times \text{Average actual price}$$
$$\text{Potential revenue} = \text{Total capacity} \times \text{Maximum price}$$

The equations indicate that yield is a function of price and capacity used. Recall that capacity constraints can be in the form of time, labor, equipment, or facilities. Yield is essentially a measure of the extent to which an organization's resources (or capacities) are achieving their full revenue-generating potential. Assuming that total capacity and maximum price cannot be changed, yield approaches a value of 1 as actual capacity utilization increases or when a higher actual price can be charged for a given capacity

Basic yield calculations can be done for any capacity constrained service assuming the actual capacity, average price charged for different market segments, and maximum price that could be charged are known. Ideally, yield will approach the number 1, or 100 percent, where:

Yield = Actual revenue/Potential revenue

In this box we describe yield calculations for two simple examples—a 200-room hotel and a lawyer with a 40-hour work week—under different assumed pricing and usage situations. Although companies use much more complex mathematical models to determine yield, the underlying ideas are the same. The goal is to maximize the revenue-generating capability of the organization's capacity.

200-ROOM HOTEL WITH MAXIMUM ROOM RATE OF $100 PER ROOM PER NIGHT

Potential revenue = $200 × 200 rooms
= $40,000 per night

1. Assume: the hotel rents all its rooms at a discounted rate of $100 per night.

Yield = $100 × 200 rooms / $40,000 = 50%

At this rate, the hotel is maximizing capacity utilization, but not getting a very good price.

2. Assume: the hotel charges its full rate, but can only rent 40 percent of its rooms at that price, due to price sensitivity.

Yield = $200 × 80 rooms / $40,000 = 40%

In this situation the hotel has maximized the per-room price, but the yield is even lower than in the first situation because so few rooms are rented at that relatively high rate.

3. Assume: the hotel charges its full rate of $200 for 40 percent of its rooms and then gives a discount of $100 for the remaining 120 rooms.

Yield = [($200 × 80) + ($100 × 120)] / $40,000
= $28,000 / $40,000 = 70%

Clearly, the final alternative, which takes into account price sensitivity and charges different prices for different rooms or market segments, results in the highest yield among these three alternatives.

40 HOURS OF A LAWYER'S TIME ACROSS A TYPICAL WORK WEEK AT $200 PER HOUR MAXIMUM (PRIVATE CLIENT RATE)

Potential revenue = 40 hours × $200 per hour
= $8,000 per week

1. Assume: the lawyer is able to bill out 30 percent of her billable time at $200 per hour.

Yield = $200 × 12 hours / $8,000 = 30%

In this case the lawyer has maximized her hourly rate, but has only enough work to occupy 12 billable hours.

2. Assume: the lawyer decides to charge $100 for nonprofit or government clients and is able to bill out all 40 hours at this rate for these types of clients.

Yield = $100 × 40 hours / $8,000 = 50%

In this case, although she has worked a full week, yield is still not very good given the relatively low rate per hour.

3. Assume: the lawyer uses a combined strategy in which she works 12 hours for private clients and fills the rest of her time with nonprofit clients at $100 per hour.

Yield = [($200 × 12) + ($100 × 28)] / $8,000
= $5,200 / $8,000 = 65%

Again, catering to two different market segments with different price sensitivities is the best overall strategy in terms of maximizing revenue-generating capacity of the lawyer's time.

used. For example, in an airline context, a manager could focus on increasing yield by finding ways to bring in more passengers to fill the capacity or by finding higher-paying passengers to fill a more limited capacity. In reality, expert yield managers work on capacity and pricing issues simultaneously to maximize revenue across different customer segments. Exhibit 15.1 shows simple yield calculations and the inherent trade-offs for two types of services: hotel and legal.

Technology Spotlight Information and Technology Drive Yield Management Systems

Yield management is not a new concept. In fact, the basic idea behind yield management—achieving maximum profits through the most effective use of capacity—has been around forever. It is easy to find examples of capacity-constrained businesses using price to shift demand: theaters that charge different prices for matinees versus evening performances, intercity trains with different prices on weekdays than on weekends, ski resorts with cheaper prices for night skiing, and restaurants with "twilight" dinner specials. All these strategies illustrate attempts to smooth the peaks and valleys of demand using price as the primary motivator.

The difference in these basic pricing strategies and more sophisticated yield management approaches currently in use by airlines, car rental companies, hotels, shippers, and others is the reliance of these latter strategies on massive databases, sophisticated mathematical algorithms, and complex analyses. These forms of yield management consider not only price but also market segments, price sensitivity among segments, timing of demand, and potential profitability of customer segments—all simultaneously. What makes new forms of yield management possible are the technology and systems underlying them. Here we provide a few examples of what some companies and industries have done.

AMERICAN AIRLINES

American Airlines is the original pioneer and still the king of yield management. Beginning with Super Saver Fares in the mid-1970s, American depends on systems developed by Sabre (the oldest and leading provider of technology for the travel industry) to support an exceedingly complex system of fares.

Using a system of models containing algorithms that optimize prices, manage wait lists, and handle traffic management, American allocates seats on every one of its flights. The number of seats sold on each of American's flights is continuously compared with a sales forecast for that flight. Blocks of seats are moved from higher to lower fares if sales are below projections. If sales are at or above the forecast, no changes are made. American's stated objective was, and still is, to "sell the right seats to the right customers at the right price."

AIR BERLIN

Air Berlin, Germany's second largest airline, provides relatively low-cost services to popular European holiday destinations, as well as to major cities in Europe, from more than 20 German airports and uses yield management in an effort to maximize passenger revenue. Its yield management process begins six to nine months prior to a flight's scheduled departure date. Air Berlin often sells initial blocks of seats at what it terms "headline prices" to price sensitive customers and to tour operators; any seats not initially sold are then managed through Air Berlin's yield management technology. Its yield management system requires massive amounts of data that take into account the season when the flight takes place, general popularity of the route, local holiday schedules and upcoming events, and the exact time of departure. Similar to other airlines, Air Berlin adjusts its fares frequently, sometimes several times a day as the flight's departure date nears, to reflect customer demand and the time remaining until the departure date. However, because Air Berlin's focus is on relatively short routes, it offers only a single class of

Implementing a Yield Management System

Our Technology Spotlight illustrates several examples of how information technology supports effective yield management applications. To implement a yield management system, an organization needs detailed data on past demand patterns by market segment as well as methods of projecting current market demand. The data can be combined through mathematical programming models, threshold analysis, or use of expert systems to project the best allocation of limited capacity at a particular point in time.[12] Allocations of capacity for specific market segments can then be communicated to sales representatives or reservations staff as targets for selling rooms, seats, time, or service on all of its flights and each flight is available on a one-way ticket basis. This practice means that each flight is subject to its own price management, enabling Air Berlin to charge passengers different fares on outbound flights and return flights. By developing profiles for each flight, Air Berlin's yield management technology helps it to maximize passenger revenue by flight and by regions while maintaining high passenger load factors.

MARRIOTT HOTELS

The hotel industry has also embraced the concepts of yield management, and Marriott Hotels has been a leader. The systems at Marriott, for example, maximize profits for a hotel across full weeks rather than by day. In their hotels that target business travelers, Marriott has peak days during the middle of the week. Rather than simply sell the hotel out on those nights on a first-come, first-served basis with no discounts, the revenue management system (which is reviewed and revised daily) projects guest demand both by price and length of stay, providing discounts in some cases to guests who will stay longer, even on a peak demand night. One early test of the system was at the Munich Marriott during Oktoberfest. Typically, no discounts would be offered during this peak period. However, the yield management system recommended that the hotel offer some rooms at a discount, but only for those guests who stayed an extended period before or after the peak days. Although the average daily rate went down 11.7 percent for the period, occupancy went up more than 20 percent, and overall revenues went up 12.3 percent. Using yield management practices, Marriott Hotels estimates it generates an additional $400 million per year in revenue.

YELLOW TRANSPORTATION

Pricing in the freight industry still seems to be stuck in a regulated mind-set in which costs dominate and discounts from class rates are determined by complex formulas. However, companies such as Yellow Transportation (part of YRC Worldwide) have moved to market-driven models that price services consistent with the value as perceived by the customer. These pricing structures recognize the customers' and freight providers' desires for simplification while combining this with sophisticated use of yield management models that take into account the most profitable use of resources. Yield management systems encourage more rational scheduling of trucks and drivers by considering such subtle factors as equipment type and the skills of a particular driver. The systems can match hundreds of drivers with loads in fractions of seconds to make the best dispatch and driver decisions. By analyzing its services, prices, and demand patterns in this way, Yellow Transportation was able to project the success of its time-definite delivery service—Exact Express. This service targets a particular segment of customers who are willing to pay a premium for guaranteed, time-definite delivery.

Sources: The primary source for this Technology Spotlight is R. G. Cross, *Revenue Management* (New York: Broadway Books, 1997). Other sources include "Dynamic Pricing at American Airlines," *Business Quarterly* 61 (Autumn 1996), p. 45; Air Berlin's 2006 Company Prospectus and website (www.airberlin.com); N. Templin, "Your Room Costs $250 . . . No! $200 . . . No," *The Wall Street Journal*, May 5, 1999, p. B1; H. Richardson, "Simplify! Simplify! Simplify!," *Transportation and Distribution* 39 (October 1998), pp. 111–117; and C. Salter "On the Road Again," *Fast Company,* January 2002, pp. 50–58.

other limited resources. Sometimes the allocations, once determined, remain fixed. At other times allocations change weekly, or even daily or hourly, in response to new information.

Research indicates that traditional yield management approaches are most appropriate for service firms when:

1. They have relatively fixed capacity.

2. They have perishable inventory.

3. They have different market segments or customers, who arrive or make their reservations at different times.

4. They have low marginal sales costs and high marginal capacity change costs.

5. The product is sold in advance.

6. There is fluctuating demand.

7. Customers who arrive or reserve early are more price sensitive than those who arrive or reserve late.[13]

When these conditions are present, yield management approaches can generally be employed to identify the best mix of service offerings to produce and sell in the period, and at what prices, to generate the highest expected revenue. These criteria exactly fit the situation for airlines, car rental agencies, and many hotels—industries that have effectively and extensively used yield management techniques to allocate capacity. In other services (entertainment, sports, fashion), those customers willing to pay the higher prices are the ones who buy early rather than late. People who really want to see a particular performance reserve their seats at the earliest possible moment. Discounting for early purchases would reduce profits. In these situations, the price generally starts out high and is reduced later to fill capacity if needed.

Interestingly, some airlines now use both these strategies effectively. They start with discounted seats for customers who are willing to buy early, usually leisure and discretionary travelers. They charge a higher fare for those who want a seat at the last minute, typically the less-price-sensitive business travelers whose destinations and schedules are inflexible. However, in some cases a bargain fare can be found at the last minute as well, commonly via Internet sales, to fill seats that would otherwise go unoccupied. Online auctions and services offered by companies like Priceline.com serve a purpose in filling capacity at the last minute, often charging much lower fares. (See the Technology Spotlight in Chapter 17 for examples of dynamic pricing via the Internet.)

Challenges and Risks in Using Yield Management

Yield management programs can significantly improve revenues. However, although yield management may appear to be an ideal solution to the problem of matching supply and demand, it is not without risks. By becoming focused on maximizing financial returns through differential capacity allocation and pricing, an organization may encounter these problems:[14]

• *Loss of competitive focus.* Yield management may cause a firm to overfocus on profit maximization and inadvertently neglect aspects of the service that provide long-term competitive success.

• *Customer alienation.* If customers learn that they are paying a higher price for service than someone else, they may perceive the pricing as unfair, particularly if they do not understand the reasons. However, a study done in the restaurant industry found that when customers were informed of different prices being charged by time of day, week, or table location, they generally felt the practice was fair, particularly if the price difference was framed as a discount for less desirable times rather than a premium for peak times or table locations.[15] Customer education is thus essential in an effective yield management program.

• *Overbooking.* Customers can be further alienated if they fall victim (and are not compensated adequately) to the overbooking practices often necessary to make yield management systems work effectively. Recent research suggests that customers who experience negative consequences of revenue management (i.e., denied service or downgrades), particularly high-value customers, subsequently reduce their number of transactions with the firm.[16]

- *Employee morale problems.* Yield management systems take much guesswork and judgment in setting prices away from sales and reservations people. Although some employees may appreciate the guidance, others may resent the rules and restrictions on their own discretion.

- *Incompatible incentive and reward systems.* Employees may resent yield management systems that do not match incentive structures. For example, many managers are rewarded on the basis of capacity utilization *or* average rate charged, whereas yield management balances the two factors.

- *Lack of employee training.* Extensive training is required to make a yield management system work. Employees need to understand its purpose, how it works, how they should make decisions, and how the system will affect their jobs.

- *Inappropriate organization of the yield management function.* To be most effective with yield management, an organization must have centralized reservations. Although airlines and some large hotel chains and shipping companies do have such centralization, smaller organizations may have decentralized reservations systems and thus find it difficult to operate a yield management system effectively.

WAITING LINE STRATEGIES: WHEN DEMAND AND CAPACITY CANNOT BE MATCHED

Sometimes it is not possible to manage capacity to match demand, or vice versa. It may be too costly—for example, most health clinics would not find it economically feasible to add additional facilities or physicians to handle peaks in demand during the winter flu season; patients usually simply have to wait to be seen. Or demand may be very unpredictable and the service capacity very inflexible (it cannot be easily stretched to match unpredictable peaks in demand). Sometimes waits may occur when demand backs up because of the variability in length of time for service. For example, even though patients are scheduled by appointments in a physician's office, frequently there is a wait because some patients take longer to serve than the time allotted to them. According to many sources, the misalignment in capacity and demand has reached crisis proportions in the emergency health care context, as is described in Exhibit 15.2.

For most service organizations, waiting customers are a fact of life at some point (see the accompanying photo). Waiting can occur on the telephone (customers put on hold when they call in to ask for information, order something, or make a complaint) and in person (customers waiting in line at the bank, post office, Disneyland, or a physician's office). Waiting can occur even with service transactions through the mail—delays in mail-order delivery—or backlogs of correspondence on a manager's desk.

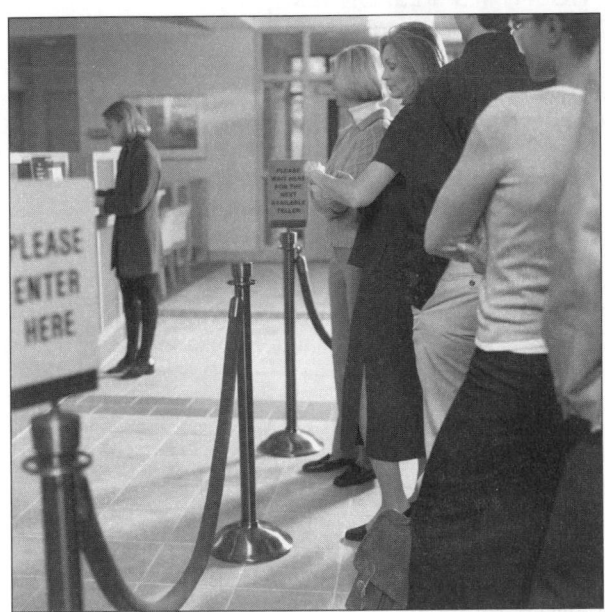

Customer satisfaction is heavily dependent upon the amount time customers spend waiting for a service.

Nowhere is there a more vivid example of demand and capacity issues than in the nearly 5,000 emergency departments (EDs) in hospitals across the United States (*emergency department* is the preferred term within the medical community for what has traditionally been called the ER). In a typical ED, rooms are filled, the corridors may be clogged with waiting patients, wait time may be anywhere from 15 minutes to 8 or 10 hours, and ambulances are routinely turned away to seek other hospitals on what is called "reroute" or "diversion." Many experts have referred to these issues as a national crisis in health care. The emergency department is the front door of hospitals and is also the treatment of last resort for many. Why has this overcrowding issue reached national proportions? Many factors come into play, including increased demand and severe capacity constraints.

INCREASED DEMAND FOR SERVICES

Emergency departments are to some extent victims of their own success. Decades of public health campaigns urging people to call 911 in case of medical emergency have been successful in educating people to do just that—and they end up in the ED. Many do indeed have life-threatening emergencies that belong in the ED. Others waiting in the ED are uninsured; as of 2006, more than 47 million people in the United States were uninsured. The ED is their only option, and legally the ED must care for them. But it is not only the uninsured and those with life-threatening emergencies who crowd the ED. It is also insured patients who cannot get appointments with their doctors in a timely manner or who learn that it may be their fastest entry into a hospital bed. Patients and their doctors are becoming aware that they can get sophisticated care in the ED relatively quickly. Thus, the demand for ED services has increased.

CAPACITY CONSTRAINTS

It is not just an increase in demand that is causing the overcrowding. It is also a shrinkage or unavailability of critical capacity at the same time. Doctors are overbooked

in private practices, so patients who do not want to wait turn to the ED. Also, a shortage of specialists who are willing to take patients on call from the ED results in increased waiting times because these patients waiting for specialized care occupy beds in the ED longer than necessary. Another very critical capacity constraint is the number of beds in hospitals. Over the years, many hospitals across the country have closed for financial reasons, reducing the number of beds available. So ED patients often cannot get beds right away even if they need one, again increasing waiting time for themselves and others. There is a critical shortage of nurses as well, and a hospital bed requires a nurse to attend it before it can be occupied. In the 1990s enrollment in nursing programs slumped as people turned to more lucrative careers, and in 2006 the average age of a registered nurse was 47. Many hospitals have 20 percent of their nursing slots empty. Staffing shortages in housekeeping also play a role. A bed may be empty, but until it is cleaned and remade, it is not available for a waiting patient. In some communities, patients may find that ED facilities are simply not available. Some hospitals have actually closed their emergency departments after determining that it is unprofitable to run them at current reimbursement rates. In other areas, population growth is outpacing hospital and ED construction.

HOSPITALS' RESPONSES

To address this complex set of issues, a few changes are being made or considered.

Technology and Systems Improvements

A partial solution is to turn to technology to smooth the process of admitting patients into the ED and to track the availability of hospital beds. Some web-based systems are used to reroute ambulances to hospitals that have capacity. Other systems help EDs track the availability of rooms in their own hospitals in terms of knowing exactly when a bed is vacant and when it has been cleaned and is available—similar to what hotels

In today's fast-paced society, waiting is not something most people tolerate well. As people work longer hours, as individuals have less leisure, and as families have fewer hours together, the pressure on people's time is greater than ever. In this environment, customers are looking for efficient, quick service with no wait. Organizations that make customers wait take the chance that they will lose business or at the very least that customers will be dissatisfied.[17] Research suggests that waiting time satisfaction is nearly as important as service delivery satisfaction with respect to

have done for decades. Wireless systems for registering patients at bedside and "radar screens" that track everything going on in the ED are other partial solutions. These screens can track patients, staff, carts, and equipment, making the service delivery process more efficient and quicker.

Other hospitals have segmented their patients and have developed parallel "fast track" processes for dealing with minor emergency patients that can account for 30 to 50 percent of total visits. This process can be separated from the major-emergency situations that may require more time and special equipment. Quicker admitting processes are also being implemented. Kiosks have been installed in some hospitals to allow emergency patients to check themselves in and describe their symptoms to help speed up the admission process. Patients who are not experiencing true emergencies (true emergencies being gunshot victims or car accident victims with serious injuries) use touch screens to enter their name, age, and other personal information. Such kiosks display a list of ailments to choose from, like "pain" or "fever and/or chills," and a list of body parts to indicate where the discomfort is occurring. Once a patient's problem is entered into the system, it pops up on a screen accessible to nurses; those with chest pains, stroke symptoms, or other potentially serious issues take priority.

Yet another innovation is to have staff administer routine tests while the patient is waiting so that the doctor who finally sees the patient has information at hand. This solution also satisfies the patient's need for "something to happen" during the waiting time. Giving patients pagers so they can do something else while waiting is another way that EDs are helping patients cope with the long waits.

Increasing Capacity
Another set of partial solutions relates directly to hospital and staff capacity issues. Some hospitals have already begun adding rooms and other facilities. More urgent care centers are being built to take some of the pressure off EDs. For patients who need to be admitted to the hospital, however, increasing capacity is not a total solution. The nursing shortage, one of the most critical problems, is very difficult to solve. Individual hospital systems have gotten creative in their efforts to steal nurses away from other hospitals, even recruiting heavily overseas. However, in the long term the solution rests more in making the occupation attractive in salaries and working conditions, thus increasing the number of people entering nursing programs.

Insuring the Uninsured
A major political and social issue is how to handle the growing numbers of uninsured in the United States. Finding a way to provide coverage to these millions of Americans—many of whom are employed, but whose employers do not provide health insurance—has been a focus of political debate for decades.

It is obvious that this classic dilemma of matching supply and demand in a service context has multiple, deeply rooted causes when examined in the context of emergency care. The solutions to the issues are also multifaceted—some can be undertaken by individual hospitals, whereas others need to be addressed by the entire health care industry. Some, however, are societal issues with only long-term solutions. Yet all these issues play out daily in the very immediate environment of hospital emergency departments.

Sources: L. Landro, "ERs Now Turn to Technology to Help Deal with Overcapacity," *The Wall Street Journal,* July 13, 2001, p. B1; J. Snyder, "Curing the ER," *The Arizona Republic,* December 9, 2001, pp. D1+; N. Shute and M. B. Marcus, CODE BLUE "Crisis in the ER," *US News & World Report,* September 10, 2001 pp. 54–61; U.S. Census Bureau; 2006 National Survey of Registered Nurses; and J. Stengle, "ER Kiosks Let Patients Avoid Long Lines," *Associated Press,* September 13, 2007.

customer loyalty.[18] To deal effectively with the inevitability of waits, organizations can utilize a variety of strategies; four general strategies are described next.

Employ Operational Logic
If customer waits are common, a first step is to analyze the operational processes to remove any inefficiencies. It may be possible to redesign the system to move customers along more quickly. Modifications in the operational system were part of the

solution employed by the First National Bank of Chicago in one of the earliest efforts to reduce customer waiting and improve service. The bank developed a computer-based customer information system to allow tellers to answer questions more quickly, implemented an electronic queuing system, hired "peak-time" tellers, expanded its hours, and provided customers with alternative delivery channels. Collectively these efforts reduced customer wait time, increased productivity, and improved customer satisfaction.[19]

In introducing its express check-in, Marriott Hotels used an operations-based modification to eliminate much of the waiting previously experienced by its guests. Guests who use a credit card and preregister can avoid waiting in line at the hotel front desk altogether. The guest can make it from the curb outside the hotel to his or her room in as little as three minutes when escorted by a "guest service associate," who checks the guest into the hotel, picks up keys and paperwork from a rack in the lobby, and then escorts the guest directly to the room.[20] The U.S. Department of Transportation Security Administration (TSA) offers similar preferential treatment for selected frequent travelers through its "Registered Traveler Program."[21] Only U.S. citizens or permanent legal residents who meet certain flying criteria may apply. After registering with the system and clearing an extensive background check, travelers who qualify for this program are allowed to bypass the usual security checkpoint in their designated airport and instead be screened through a security system that reads either their fingerprints or irises in their eyes. They must still go through a metal detector and their bags are still passed through an X-ray scanner, but they get their own special line and are not randomly selected for additional screening.

Waiting is common in many service industries.

When queues are inevitable, the organization faces the operational decision of what kind of queuing system to use or how to configure the queue. Queue configuration refers to the number of queues, their locations, their spatial requirement, and their effect on customer behavior.[22] Several possibilities exist, as shown in Figure 15.4. In the multiple-queue alternative, the customer arrives at the service facility and must decide which queue

FIGURE 15.4
Waiting Line Configurations

Source: J. A. Fitzsimmons and M. J. Fitzsimmons, *Service Management,* 5th ed. (New York: Irwin/McGraw-Hill, 2006), chap. 13, p. 403. © 2006 by The McGraw-Hill Companies, Inc. Reprinted by permission of The McGraw-Hill Companies.

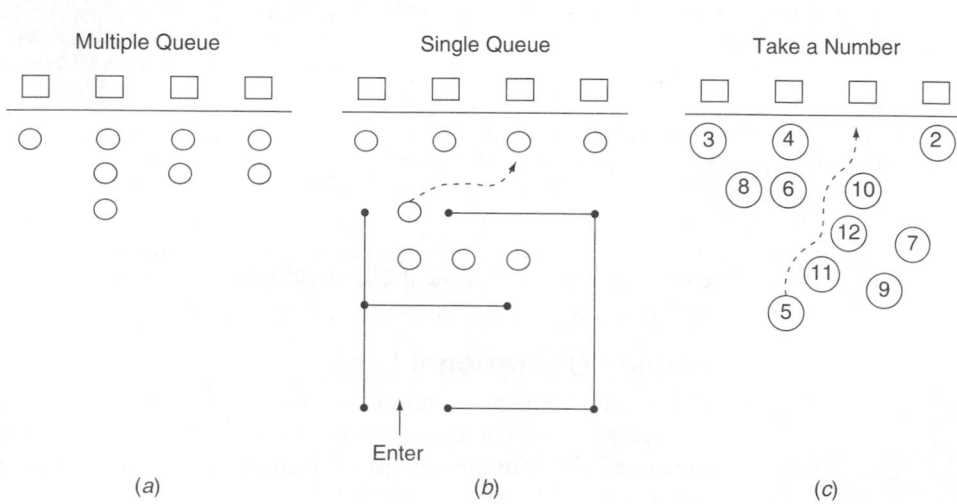

to join and whether to switch later if the wait appears to be shorter in another line. In the single-queue alternative, fairness of waiting time is ensured in that the first-come, first-served rule applies to everyone; the system can also reduce the average time customers spend waiting overall. However, customers may leave if they perceive that the line is too long or if they have no opportunity to select a particular service provider. The last option shown in Figure 15.4 is the take-a-number option in which arriving customers take a number to indicate line position. Advantages are similar to the single-queue alternative with the additional benefit that customers are able to mill about, browse, and talk to each other. The disadvantage is that customers must be on the alert to hear their numbers when they are called. Research suggests that length of the queue and perceived cost of waiting are not the only influences on customers' likelihood of staying in line. In a series of experiments and field tests, researchers showed that the larger the number of customers waiting in line *behind* a consumer, the more likely that consumer is to stay in line and wait for the service.[23]

Many service businesses have become experts at handling queues effectively in terms of minimizing customer dissatisfaction. Some of the benchmarks include Disney, Marriott, and FedEx. In fact, in its effort to plan and implement an effective, efficient, service-oriented security process at U.S. airports, the U.S. government consulted these benchmark companies for advice.[24]

Establish a Reservation Process

When waiting cannot be avoided, a reservation system can help to spread demand. Restaurants, transportation companies, theaters, physicians, and many other service providers use reservation systems to alleviate long waits. The California Department of Motor Vehicles allows customers to make appointments via the Internet to help reduce the time they must spending waiting at its offices. The idea behind a reservation system is to guarantee that the service will be available when the customer arrives. Beyond simply reducing waiting time, a reservation system has the added benefit of potentially shifting demand to less desirable time periods. A challenge inherent in reservation systems, however, is what to do about "no shows." Inevitably there will be customers who reserve a time but do not show up. Some organizations deal with this problem by overbooking their service capacity on the basis of past records of no-show percentages. If the predictions are accurate, overbooking is a good solution. When predictions are inaccurate, however, customers may still have to wait and sometimes may not be served at all, as when airlines overbook the number of seats available on a flight. Victims of overbooking may be compensated for their inconvenience in such cases. To minimize the no-show problem, some organizations (such as hotels, airlines, conferences/training programs, and theaters) charge customers who fail to show up or cancel their reservations within a certain time frame.

Differentiate Waiting Customers

Not all customers necessarily need to wait the same length of time for service. On the basis of need or customer priority, some organizations differentiate among customers, allowing some to experience shorter waits for service than others. Known as "queue discipline," such differentiation reflects management policies regarding whom to select next for service.[25] The most popular discipline is first-come, first-served. However, other rules may apply. Differentiation can be based on factors such as[26]

  • *Importance of the customer.* Frequent customers or customers who spend large amounts with the organization can be given priority in service by providing them with a special waiting area or segregated lines.

- *Urgency of the job.* Those customers with the most urgent need may be served first. This strategy is used in emergency health care. It is also used by maintenance services such as air-conditioning repair that give priority to customers whose air conditioning is not functioning over those who call for routine maintenance.

- *Duration of the service transaction.* In many situations, shorter service jobs get priority through "express lanes." At other times, when a service provider sees that a transaction is going to require extra time, the customer is referred to a designated provider who deals only with these special-needs customers.

- *Payment of a premium price.* Customers who pay extra (e.g., first class on an airline) are often given priority via separate check-in lines or express systems. At several Six Flags amusement parks, groups of up to six customers can purchase the use of Flashpass for about $15 for a palm-sized device and $15 per person (in addition to park entrance fees) to use the device, which is inserted at signs near the popular rides throughout the park, to keep their place in line virtually. The device sends a signal 10 minutes before it is time to come back and get on the ride (through a separate entrance), allowing customers to visit other attractions in the park without having to spend as much time in line. A "Gold" Flashpass can also be purchased, for $25 per person and $25 for the device, to move customers up in the queue so that they experience very little or even no wait.[27]

Make Waiting Pleasurable, or at Least Tolerable

Even when they have to wait, customers can be more or less satisfied, depending on how the wait is handled by the organization. Of course the actual length of the wait will affect how customers feel about their service experience. But it is not just the actual time spent waiting that has an impact on customer satisfaction—it is how customers feel about the wait and their perceptions during it. The type of wait (e.g., a standard queue versus a wait due to a delay of service) can also influence how customers will react.[28] In a classic article entitled "The Psychology of Waiting Lines," David Maister proposes several principles about waiting, each of which has implications for how organizations can make waiting more pleasurable or at least tolerable.[29]

Unoccupied Time Feels Longer Than Occupied Time

When customers are unoccupied they will likely be bored and will notice the passage of time more than when they have something to do. Providing something for waiting customers to do, particularly if the activity offers a benefit in and of itself or is related in some way to the service, can improve the customer's experience and may benefit the organization as well.[30] Examples include giving customers menus to look at while waiting in a restaurant, providing interesting information to read in a dentist's office, or playing entertaining programs over the phone while customers are on hold.

Preprocess Waits Feel Longer Than In-Process Waits

If wait time is occupied with activities that relate to the upcoming service, customers may perceive that the service has started and they are no longer actually waiting. This in-process activity will make the length of the wait seem shorter and will also benefit the service provider by making the customer better prepared when the service actually does begin. Filling out medical information while waiting to see the physician, reading a menu while waiting to be seated in a restaurant, and watching a videotape of the upcoming service event are all activities that can both educate the customer and reduce perceptions of waiting.

Research in a restaurant context has found that customers react more negatively to preprocess waits than to either in-process or postprocess waits; that is, preprocess waits are relatively more important in determining customers' overall satisfaction.[31] Other researchers have found that if a wait is due to routine slowness of the process, then preprocess waits produce the most negative impact. However, if the wait is due to a service failure, then the in-process wait is viewed more negatively than the preprocess wait.[32] Thus, how customers perceive preprocess, in-process, and postprocess waits may depend to some extent on the cause of the wait.

Anxiety Makes Waits Seem Longer

When customers fear that they have been forgotten or do not know how long they will have to wait, they become anxious, and this anxiety can increase the negative impact of waiting. Anxiety also results when customers are forced to choose in a multiple-line situation and they discover they have chosen the "wrong line." To combat waiting line anxiety, organizations can provide information on the length of the wait. At its theme parks, Disney uses signs at intervals along the line that let customers know how long the wait will be from that point on. Using a single line also alleviates customer anxiety over having chosen the wrong line. Explanations and reassurances that no one has forgotten them alleviate customer anxiety by taking away their cause for worry.

Uncertain Waits Are Longer Than Known, Finite Waits

Anxiety is intensified when customers do not know how long they will have to wait. Health care providers combat this problem by letting customers know when they check in how far behind the physician is that day. Some patients resolve this uncertainty themselves by calling ahead to ask. Maister provides an interesting example of the role of uncertainty, which he terms the "appointment syndrome."[33] Customers who arrive early for an appointment will wait patiently until the scheduled time, even if they arrive very early. However, once the expected appointment time has passed, customers grow increasingly anxious. Before the appointment time the wait time is known; after that, the length of the wait is not known.

Research in an airline context has suggested that as uncertainty about the wait increases, customers become angrier, and their anger in turn results in greater dissatisfaction.[34] Research also shows that giving customers information on the length of the anticipated wait and/or their relative position in the queue can result in more positive feelings and acceptance of the wait and ultimately more positive evaluation of the service.[35]

Unexplained Waits Are Longer Than Explained Waits

When people understand the causes for waiting, they frequently have greater patience and are less anxious, particularly when the wait is justifiable. An explanation can reduce customer uncertainty and may help customers estimate how long they will be delayed. One of us, when waiting once with our children to see a pediatrician, was told that the doctor was delayed because another child had arrived with possible life-threatening injuries and he chose to focus his attention on that child. As a parent who would want the same treatment for our children, the amount of extra wait time was acceptable—much more so than if there was no explanation at all and we were left to think that perhaps the doctor had not yet arrived from his early morning trip to the golf course. Customers who do not know the reason for a wait begin to feel powerless and irritated.

Unfair Waits Are Longer Than Equitable Waits

When customers perceive that they are waiting while others who arrived after them have already been served, the apparent inequity will make the wait seem even longer. This situation can easily occur when there is no apparent order in the waiting area and many customers are trying to be served. Queuing systems that work on a first-come, first-served rule are best at combating perceived unfairness. However, other approaches may be required to determine who will be served next. For example, in an emergency medical care situation, the most seriously ill or injured patients would be seen first. When customers understand the priorities and the rules are clearly communicated and enforced, fairness of waiting time should not be an issue.

The More Valuable the Service, the Longer the Customer Will Wait

Customers who have substantial purchases or who are waiting for a high-value service will be more tolerant of long wait times and may even expect to wait longer. For example, customers waiting to see a lawyer might consider a 15-minute wait to be acceptable, whereas the same wait at a convenience store might be considered completely unacceptable. In a supermarket, customers who have a full cart of groceries will generally wait longer than customers who have only a few items and expect to be checked through quickly. And diners expect to wait longer for service in an expensive restaurant than they do when eating at a "greasy spoon."

Solo Waits Feel Longer Than Group Waits

People are more accepting of a longer wait when they are in a group than when they are alone because of the distractions provided by other members of the group. People also feel comfort in waiting with a group rather than alone.[36] In some group waiting situations, such as at Disneyland or when patrons are waiting in long lines to purchase concert tickets, customers who are strangers begin to talk to each other and the waiting experience can actually become a fun part of the total service experience.

Summary

Because service organizations lack the ability to inventory their products, the effective use of capacity can be critical to success. Idle capacity in the form of unused time, labor, facilities, or equipment represents a direct drain on bottom-line profitability. When the capacity represents a major investment (e.g., airplanes, expensive medical imaging equipment, or lawyers and physicians paid on a salary), the losses associated with underuse of capacity are even more accentuated. Overused capacity can also be a problem. People, facilities, and equipment can become worn out over time when used beyond optimum capacity. People can quit, facilities can become run down, and equipment can break. From the customer's perspective, service quality also deteriorates. Organizations focused on delivering quality service, therefore, have a natural drive to balance capacity utilization and demand at an optimum level in order to meet customer expectations.

Based on grounding in the fundamental issues, the chapter presented a variety of strategies for matching supply and demand. The basic strategies fall under two headings: *demand strategies* (shifting demand to match capacity) and *capacity strategies* (adjusting capacity to meet demand). Demand strategies seek to flatten the peaks and valleys of demand to match the flat capacity constraint, whereas capacity strategies seek to align, flex, or stretch capacity to match the peaks and valleys of demand. Organizations frequently employ several strategies simultaneously to solve the complex problem of balancing supply and demand.

Yield management was presented as a sophisticated form of supply and demand management that balances capacity utilization, pricing, market segmentation, and financial return. Long practiced by the passenger airline industry, this strategy is growing in use by hotel, shipping, car rental, and other capacity-constrained industries in which bookings are made in advance. Essentially, yield management allows organizations to decide on a monthly, weekly, daily, or even hourly basis to whom they want to sell their service capacity at what price.

In the last section of the chapter, we discussed situations in which it is not possible to align supply and demand. In these unresolved capacity utilization situations, the inevitable result is customer waiting. We described strategies for effectively managing waiting lines, such as employing operational logic, establishing a reservation process, differentiating waiting customers, and making waiting fun or at least tolerable.

Discussion Questions

1. Why do service organizations lack the capability to inventory their services? Compare a car repair and maintenance service with an automobile manufacturer/dealer in terms of inventory capability.

2. Discuss the four scenarios illustrated in Figure 15.1 and presented in the text (excess demand, demand exceeds optimum capacity, demand and supply are balanced, excess capacity) in the context of a professional basketball team selling seats for its games. What are the challenges for management under each scenario?

3. Discuss the four common types of constraints (time, labor, equipment, facilities) facing service businesses, and give an example of each (real or hypothetical).

4. How does optimal capacity utilization differ from maximum capacity utilization? Give an example of a situation in which the two might be the same and one in which they are different.

5. Choose a local restaurant or some other type of service with fluctuating demand. What is the likely underlying pattern of demand? What causes the pattern? Is it predictable or random?

6. Describe the two basic strategies for matching supply and demand, and give at least two specific examples of each.

7. What is yield management? Discuss the risks in adopting a yield management strategy.

8. How might yield management apply in the management of the following: a Broadway theater? a consulting firm? a commuter train?

9. Describe the four basic waiting line strategies, and give an example of each one, preferably based on your own experiences as a consumer.

Exercises

1. Choose a local service organization that is challenged by fixed capacity and fluctuating demand. Interview the marketing manager (or other knowledgeable person) to learn (*a*) in what ways capacity is constrained, (*b*) the basic patterns of demand, and (*c*) strategies the organization has used to align supply and demand. Write up the answers to these questions, and make your own recommendations regarding other strategies the organization might use.

2. Assume you manage a winter ski resort in Colorado or Banff, Canada. (*a*) Explain the underlying pattern of demand fluctuation likely to occur at your resort and the challenges it would present to you as a manager. Is the pattern of demand

predictable or random? (*b*) Explain and give examples of how you might use both demand-oriented and capacity-oriented strategies to smooth the peaks and valleys of demand during peak and slow periods.

3. Choose a local organization in which people have to wait in line for service. Design a waiting line strategy for the organization.

4. Visit the website of Wells Fargo Bank (www.wellsfargo.com), a leader in online banking. What online services does the bank currently offer? How do these online services help Wells Fargo manage the peaks and valleys of customer demand? How do its strategies to use more ATMs, in-store bank branches, and other alternative delivery strategies complement the online strategies?

Notes

1. www.ritzcarlton.com, 2004.

2. J. S. Hirsch, "Vacationing Families Head Downtown to Welcoming Arms of Business Hotels," *The Wall Street Journal,* June 13, 1994, p. B1.

3. C. Lovelock, "Getting the Most Out of Your Productive Capacity," in *Product Plus* (Boston: McGraw-Hill, 1994), chap. 16.

4. C. H. Lovelock, "Classifying Services to Gain Strategic Marketing Insights," *Journal of Marketing* 47 (Summer 1983), pp. 9–20.

5. Portions of this section are based on C. H. Lovelock, "Strategies for Managing Capacity-Constrained Service Organizations," in *Managing Services: Marketing, Operations, and Human Resources,* 2nd ed. (Englewood Cliffs, NJ: Prentice Hall, 1992), pp. 154–168.

6. "Cable Company Provides Emergency Services Following Hurricane Katrina" case study on Cisco website, http://www.cisco.com/en/US/netsol/ns522/networking_solutions_customer_profile0900aecd8049247c.html, accessed October 2007.

7. M. Arndt, "Knock Knock, It's Your Big Mac," *BusinessWeek,* July 23, 2007, p. 36.

8. Lovelock, "Getting the Most Out of Your Productive Capacity."

9. J. M. Feldman, "Matching Planes to Demand," *Air Transport World* 39 (December 2002), pp. 31–33; and J. M. Feldman, "IT Systems Start to Converge," *Air Transport World* 37 (September 2000), pp. 78–81.

10. Boeing website, http://www.boeing.com, accessed September 27, 2007.

11. See J. A. Fitzsimmons and M. J. Fitzsimmons, *Service Management: Operations, Strategy, and Information Technology,* 5th ed. (Boston, MA: McGraw-Hill, 2006), pp. 364–370; S. E. Kimes, "Yield Management: A Tool for Capacity-Constrained Service Firms," *Journal of Operations Management* 8 (October 1989), pp. 348–363; S. E. Kimes and R. B. Chase, "The Strategic Levers of Yield Management," *Journal of Service Research* 1 (November 1998), pp. 156–166; and S. E. Kimes, "Revenue Management: A Retrospective," *Cornell Hotel and Restaurant Administration Quarterly* 44, no. 5/6 (2003), pp. 131–138.

12. Kimes, "Yield Management."

13. R. Desiraji and S. M. Shugan, "Strategic Service Pricing and Yield Management," *Journal of Marketing* 63 (January 1999), pp. 44–56; and Fitzsimmons and Fitzsimmons, *Service Management,* chap. 13, p. 403.

14. Kimes, "Yield Management."

15. S. E. Kimes and J. Wirtz, "Has Revenue Management Become Acceptable? Findings from an International Study on the Perceived Fairness of Rate Fences," *Journal of Service Research* 6 (November 2003), pp. 125–135.

16. F. v. Wangenheim and T. Bayón, "Behavioral Consequences of Overbooking Service Capacity," *Journal of Marketing* 71 (October 2007), pp. 36–47.

17. For research supporting the relationship between longer waits and decreased satisfaction, quality evaluations, and patronage intentions see E. C. Clemmer and B. Schneider, "Toward Understanding and Controlling Customer Dissatisfaction with Waiting During Peak Demand Times," in *Designing a Winning Service Strategy,* ed. M. J. Bitner and L. A. Crosby (Chicago: American Marketing Association, 1989), pp. 87–91; A. Th. H. Pruyn and A. Smidts, "Customer Evaluation of Queues: Three Exploratory Studies," *European Advances in Consumer Research* 1 (1993), pp. 371–382; S. Taylor, "Waiting for Service: The Relationship between Delays and Evaluations of Service," *Journal of Marketing* 58 (April 1994), pp. 56–69; K. L. Katz, B. M. Larson, and R. C. Larson, "Prescription for the Waiting-in-Line Blues: Entertain, Enlighten, and Engage," *Sloan Management Review* 33 (Winter 1991), pp. 44–53; S. Taylor and J. D. Claxton, "Delays and the Dynamics of Service Evaluations," *Journal of the Academy of Marketing Science* 22 (Summer 1994), pp. 254–264; and D. Grewal, J. Baker, M. Levy, and G. B. Voss, "The Effects of Wait Expectations and Store Atmosphere on Patronage Intentions in Service-Intensive Retail Stores," *Journal of Retailing* 79 (Winter 2003), pp. 259–268.

18. F. Bielen and N. Demoulin, "Waiting Time Influence on the Satisfaction-Loyalty Relationship in Services," *Managing Service Quality* 17, no. 2 (2007), pp. 174–193.

19. L. L. Berry and L. R. Cooper, "Competing with Time-Saving Service," *Business,* April–June 1990, pp. 3–7.

20. R. Henkoff, "Finding, Training, and Keeping the Best Service Workers," *Fortune,* October 3, 1994, pp. 110–122.

21. E. Anderson, "Registered Traveler Land Opens Tomorrow at Airport," *Albany Times Union,* August 1, 2007, accessed via http://blogs.timesunion.com/business/?p=1870 on October 16, 2007.

22. Fitzsimmons and Fitzsimmons, *Service Management,* chap. 13.

23. R. Zhou and D. Soman, "Looking Back: Exploring the Psychology of Queuing and the Effect of the Number of People Behind," *Journal of Consumer Research* 29 (March 2003), pp. 517–530.

24. S. Power, "Mickey Mouse, Nike Give Advice on Air Security," *The Wall Street Journal,* January 24, 2002, p. B1.

25. Fitzsimmons and Fitzsimmons, *Service Management,* chap. 13.

26. Lovelock, "Getting the Most Out of Your Productive Capacity."

27. Lo-Q website, http://www.lo-qusa.com, accessed October 1, 2007.

28. For an excellent review of the literature on customer perceptions of and reactions to various aspects of waiting time, see S. Taylor and G. Fullerton, "Waiting for Services: Perceptions Management of the Wait Experience," in *Handbook of Services Marketing and Management,* ed. T. A. Swartz and D. Iacobucci (Thousands Oaks, CA: Sage Publications), 2000, pp. 171–189.

29. D. A. Maister, "The Psychology of Waiting Lines," in *The Service Encounter,* ed. J. A. Czepiel, M. R. Solomon, and C. F. Surprenant (Lexington, MA: Lexington Books, 1985), pp. 113–123.

30. S. Taylor, "The Effects of Filled Waiting Time and Service Provider Control over the Delay on Evaluations of Service," *Journal of the Academy of Marketing Science* 23 (Summer 1995), pp. 38–48.

31. R. L. Hensley and J. Sulek, "Customer Satisfaction with Waits in Multi-stage Services," *Managing Service Quality* 17, no. 2 (2007), pp. 152–173.

32. M. K. Hui, M. V. Thakor, and R. Gill, "The Effect of Delay Type and Service Stage on Consumers' Reactions to Waiting," *Journal of Consumer Research* 24 (March 1998), pp. 469–479.

33. Maister, "The Psychology of Waiting Lines."

34. Taylor and Fullerton, "Waiting for Services."

35. M. K. Hui and D. K. Tse, "What to Tell Consumers in Waits of Different Lengths: An Integrative Model of Service Evaluation," *Journal of Marketing* 60 (April 1996), pp. 81–90.

36. J. Baker and M. Cameron, "The Effects of the Service Environment on Affect and Consumer Perception of Waiting Time: An Integrative Review and Research Propositions," *Journal of the Academy of Marketing Science* 24 (Fall 1996), pp. 338–349.

Managing Service Promises

The fourth provider gap, shown in the accompanying figure, illustrates the difference between service delivery and the service provider's external communications. Promises made by a service company through its media advertising, sales force, and other communications may potentially raise customer expectations that serve as the standard against which customers assess service quality. Broken promises can occur for many reasons: ineffective marketing communications, overpromising in advertising or personal selling, inadequate coordination between operations and marketing, and differences in policies and procedures across service outlets.

In service companies, a fit between communications about service and actual service delivery is necessary. Chapter 16 is devoted to the topic of integrated services

Provider Gap 4:
The Communication Gap

Customer

Company

Service Delivery

Gap 4: The
Communication
Gap

External
Communications
to Customers

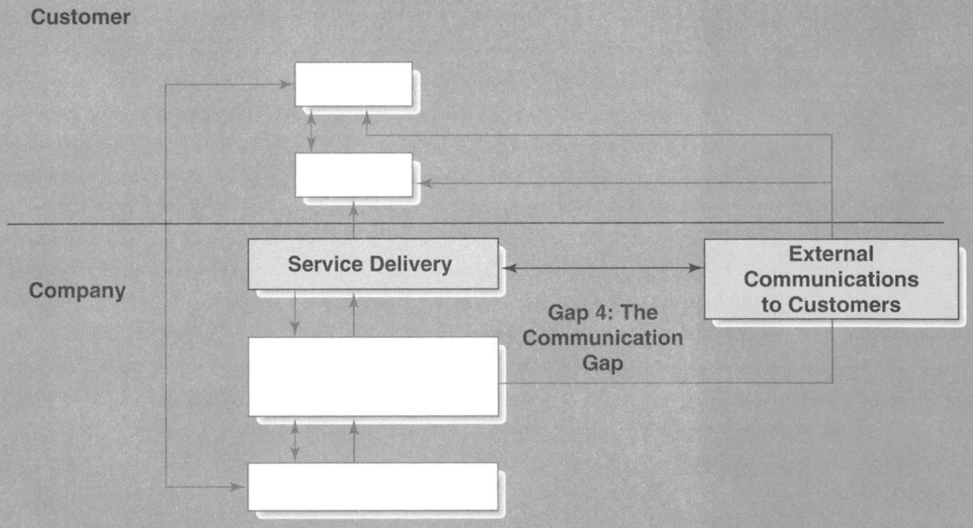

marketing communications—careful integration and organization of all of a service marketing organization's external and interactive communications channels. The chapter describes why this communication is necessary and how companies can do it well. Successful company communications are the responsibility of both marketing and operations: marketing must accurately but beguilingly reflect what happens in actual service encounters, and operations must deliver what is promised in marketing communication. If communications set up unrealistic expectations for customers, the actual encounter will disappoint the customer.

Chapter 17 deals with another issue related to managing promises, the pricing of services. In packaged goods (and even in durable goods), many customers possess enough price knowledge before purchase to be able to judge whether a price is fair or in line with competition. With services, customers often have no internal reference point for prices before purchase and consumption. Techniques for developing prices for services are more complicated than those for pricing tangible goods, and all the approaches for setting prices must be adapted for the special characteristics of services.

In summary, external communications—whether from marketing communications or pricing—can create a larger customer gap by raising expectations about service delivery. In addition to improving service delivery, companies must also manage all communications to customers so that inflated promises do not lead to higher expectations. Companies must also manage the messages conveyed by pricing so that customer expectations are in line with what they perceive that they receive.

Integrated Services Marketing Communications

This chapter's objectives are to

1. Discuss the key service communication challenges.
2. Introduce the concept of integrated service marketing communications.
3. Discuss ways to integrate marketing communications in service organizations.
4. Present specific strategies for addressing service intangibility, managing promises, managing customer expectations, educating customers, and managing internal communications.

GEICO Insurance Is "So Easy a Caveman Could Do It"

Being memorable in the category of automobile insurance is not easy. Insurance is a service that few people want to think about, much less spend money to buy. Yet GEICO Insurance has managed to create an unforgettable and highly successful integrated marketing communications campaign over the past few years. The campaign works in part because it generates buzz in a boring category and also because it makes its point: that GEICO is an easy company to do business with.

The campaign began with television commercials. The first commercial featured a GEICO spokesman explaining that using geico.com is "so easy a caveman could do it." In all subsequent commercials, the theme involves cavemen (that apparently still exist in modern society) being offended by the commercials. The cavemen are unexpectedly sophisticated and demonstrate the attack on their dignity in humorous, indignant ways.

In one commercial, for example, the GEICO spokesman tries to apologize to two cavemen in a restaurant. One of the cavemen is too insulted to be hungry, but the other urbanely orders "roast duck with the mango salsa." Another commercial features a caveman on a moving sidewalk at an airport when he spots a billboard for GEICO featuring a picture of a caveman along with the insulting phrase. He strikes a pose that would wither the parents of most cranky teenagers. A follow-up advertisement shows the same caveman talking on a cell phone about the billboard in a displeased manner. The situation gets so bad that the caveman sees a therapist about the offensive GEICO commercials, only to be told by the therapist in a condescending manner that "it's just a commercial." Other ads show the cavemen complaining at a party, appearing on a television talk show to counter the tagline, and being supported by a sticker superimposed on top of the ad saying "Cavemen are people too."

To extend the campaign across other media, GEICO's internal communications and marketing departments launched two websites, the first called Caveman's Crib. The site followed up on an intriguing commercial of the same name that invited viewers to a penthouse party at a caveman's apartment. When the user gets to the site, she finds the caveman not fully dressed and the party not yet started. Before the perturbed caveman goes into the back of the apartment to get ready, he urges the visitor to help get things ready. Site users then feel free to nose around the apartment, look through bookshelves and closets, and even follow one of them back into the bathroom and up to a steam-filled shower. Naturally, negative references to GEICO are occasionally visible in the apartment. Later, when the party is taking place, one caveman sells out and becomes a GEICO customer.

The company created another website supposedly run by the cavemen themselves, called UpwithCavemen.com, where cavemen urge support in their crusade against prejudice. The website, shown here, contains marketing communication for GEICO

UPWITHCAVEMEN
Cavemen are people too.℠

To see GEICO's newest offensive ad click here.

▶ **Home**

Cavemen are:

Intelligent
"I graduated summa cum laude."

Thoughtful
"I write haikus."

Powerful
"I manage a hedge fund."

Cognitive
"I research subatomic particles."

Ambitious
"I'm an executive of a Hollywood studio."

Social
"I'm a party-planner in the Hamptons."

About Us

Mission Statement:

As America's oldest and largest caveman civil rights organization, Up With Cavemen works with a unified voice to ensure that cavemen everywhere, no matter their physical appearance, can live open, honest lives.

We support:

The effective lobbying of governments and companies to stop their discriminatory practices and biased imagery. Additionally, we support educating the general community on the historical pedigree and cultural mind of cavemen, and funding public research on pre-recorded historical anthropology.

Past campaigns:

Cavemen are beautiful: A campaign designed to instill the caveman community with a message of pride and reduce the number of cavemen who feel the need to alter their appearance with plastic surgery or hair-removal.

Cavemen are history: A campaign designed to educate the scientific community about the negative effects that prehistoric studies have on young caveman self-esteem. Up With Cavemen organized petitions and sit-ins to change the vernacular prehistoric, which literally means pre-history, with the more appropriate pre-recorded history.

and opportunities to request rate quotes couched in a clever message from the cavemen about GEICO's insensitivity.

Other communication elements have contributed to the success of the campaign. Fansites, blogs, publicity, and interviews have extended the spend on advertising.

When communications campaigns are as attention-getting and persuasive as Geico's, they often raise service expectations. As this chapter explains, a company must be certain that it can deliver to the promises made, even to the expectations inadvertently raised by such messages.

Sources: "GEICO Caveman," Wikipedia; geico.com; cavemanscrib.com; upwithcavemen.com.

A major cause of poorly perceived service is the difference between what a firm promises about a service and what it actually delivers. Customer expectations are shaped by both uncontrollable and company-controlled factors. Word-of-mouth communication, social media, publicity, customer-generated media, customer experiences with other service providers, and customer needs are key factors that influence customer expectations and are rarely controllable by the firm. Controllable factors such as company advertising, personal selling, and promises made by service personnel also influence customer expectations. In this chapter, we discuss both types of communication but focus more heavily on the controllable factors because these factors can be influenced by the company. Accurate, coordinated, and appropriate company communication—advertising, personal selling, and online and other messages that do not overpromise or misrepresent— is essential to delivering services that customers perceive as high in quality.

Because company communications about services promise what *people* do and because people's behavior cannot be standardized like physical goods produced by machines, the potential for a mismatch between what is communicated and perceptions of actual service delivery (provider gap 4, the communications gap) is high. By coordinating communication within and outside the organization, companies can minimize the size of this gap.

THE NEED FOR COORDINATION IN MARKETING COMMUNICATION

Marketing communication is more complex today than it used to be. In the past, customers received marketing information about goods and services from a limited number of sources, usually mass communication sources such as network television and newspapers. With a limited number of sources, marketers could easily convey a uniform brand image and coordinate promises. However, today's consumers of both goods and services receive communications from a far richer variety of marketing vehicles—websites, direct mail, movie theater advertising, e-mail solicitation, targeted magazines, and a host of sales promotions. Communications innovations in the past five years are now being added to the communications mix in ways that change everything. Buzz and viral marketing, blogs, virtual communities (e.g., MySpace, YouTube, and iVillage), cell phone advertising, and gaming are but a few examples of these new tools. Consumers of services receive additional communication from servicescapes, customer service departments, and everyday service encounters with employees. These service interactions add to the variety, volume, and complexity of information that a customer receives. While a company cannot control outside sources, ensuring that messages from all company sources are consistent is a major challenge for marketers of services.

FIGURE 16.1
**Communications
and the Services
Marketing Triangle**

Source: Adapted from
M. J. Bitner, "Building
Service Relationships: It's
All about Promises," *Journal
of the Academy of Marketing
Science* 23, no. 4 (1995);
and C. Gronroos, *Services
Management and Marketing*
(Lexington, MA: Lexington
Books, 1990).

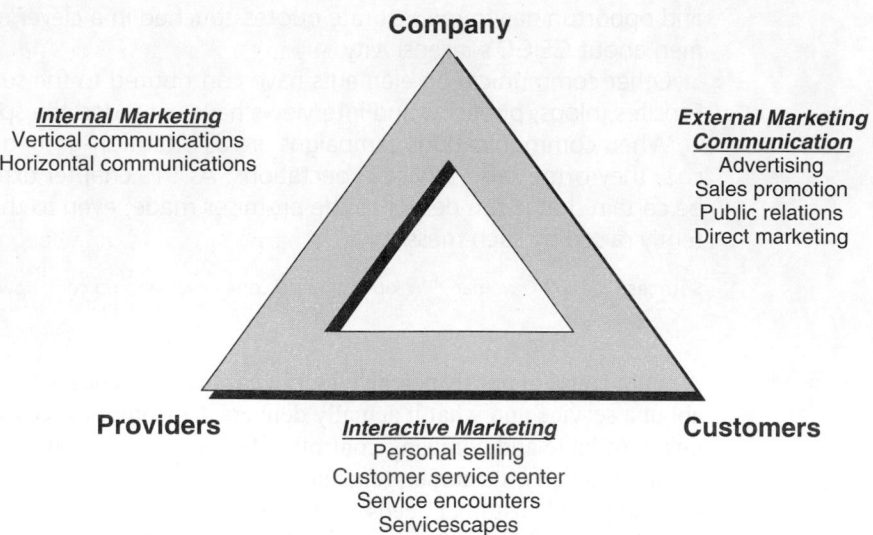

Company

Internal Marketing
Vertical communications
Horizontal communications

***External Marketing
Communication***
Advertising
Sales promotion
Public relations
Direct marketing

Providers

Interactive Marketing
Personal selling
Customer service center
Service encounters
Servicescapes

Customers

Any company that disseminates information through multiple channels needs to be certain that customers receive unified messages and promises. These channels include not only marketing communication messages that flow directly from the company but also personal messages that employees send to customers. Figure 16.1 shows an enhanced version of the services marketing triangle that we presented in Chapter 12, emphasizing that the customer of services is the target of two types of communication. First, external marketing communication includes traditional channels such as sales promotion, advertising, and public relations. Second, interactive marketing communication involves the messages that employees give to customers through such channels as personal selling, customer service interactions, service encounter interactions, and servicescapes (discussed in Chapter 11). A service company must be sure that these interactive messages are consistent both among themselves and with those sent through external communications. To do so, the third side of the triangle, internal marketing communications, must be managed so that information from the company to employees is accurate, complete, and consistent with what customers are hearing or seeing.

The need for integrated marketing campaigns is evident in both business-to-business situations and business-to-consumer instances. In business-to-business situations, the problem often comes because multiple parts of a service organization deal with a client and do not communicate well internally. For example, consider a large business customer of IBM who buys hardware, software, and services. If the client deals with someone different in each part of the organization, the company needs to—but may not—coordinate internally to ensure that they are sending the customer the same messages. Not only that, but each of these internal organizations may have its own promotional campaign with different promises and messages. An example from your own experience may illustrate what happens when services marketing communications are not integrated. Have you ever seen an advertisement for a service, such as a special sandwich from Subway, then gone to your local Subway and not found it available? Did the employee behind the counter offer a reason the sandwich was not available? Did he or she even realize that it was advertised and for sale elsewhere? One of us consulted for a bank on the West Coast in which both customers and employees constantly faced this situation. Bank marketing communication was changed frequently and quickly to meet competitive offerings, but the bank tellers' training in the new offerings did not keep pace with the changes in advertising. As a result, customers came in expecting new accounts and rates to be available, and employees were embarrassed because they had not been informed.

This example demonstrates one of the main reasons integrated marketing communications have not been the norm in many companies. All too often, various parts of the company are responsible for different aspects of communication. The sales department develops and executes sales communication. The marketing department prepares and disseminates advertising. A public relations firm is responsible for publicity. Functional specialists handle sales promotions, direct marketing, and company websites. The human resources department trains frontline employees for service interactions, and still another area is responsible for the customer service department. Rarely is one person responsible for the overall communications strategy in a company, and all too often people responsible for the different communication components do not coordinate their efforts.

Today, however, more companies are adopting the concept of *integrated marketing communications (IMC),* where the company carefully integrates and organizes all of its external communications channels. Exhibit 16.1 illustrates an excellent example of integrated marketing communications. As a marketing executive explained it,

> Integrated marketing communications build a strong brand identity in the marketplace by tying together and reinforcing all your images and messages. IMC means that all your corporate messages, positioning and images, and identity are coordinated across all venues. It means that your PR materials say the same things as your direct mail campaign, and your advertising has the same "look and feel" as your website.[1]

In this chapter we propose that a more complex type of integrated marketing communication is needed for services than for goods. External communications channels must be coordinated, as with physical goods, but both external communications and interactive communication channels must be integrated to create consistent service promises. To do that, internal marketing communications channels must be managed so that employees and the company are in agreement about what is communicated to the customer. We call this more complicated version of IMC *integrated services marketing communications (ISMC).* ISMC requires that everyone involved with communication clearly understand both the company's marketing strategy and its promises to consumers.

KEY SERVICE COMMUNICATION CHALLENGES

Discrepancies between what is communicated about a service and what a customer receives—or perceives that she receives—can powerfully affect consumer evaluations of service quality. The factors that contribute to these communication challenges include (1) service intangibility, (2) management of service promises, (3) management of customer expectations, (4) customer education, and (5) internal marketing communication. In this chapter, we first describe the challenges stemming from these factors and then detail strategies firms have found useful in dealing with them.

Service Intangibility

Because services are performances rather than objects, their essence and benefits are difficult to communicate to customers. Intangibility makes marketing communication

For decades, industry giants Federal Express and United Parcel Service together owned 70 percent of the U.S. market for express and package delivery services. DHL, the 34-year-old acknowledged leader in the global market, serving over 225 countries and territories, was little known to U.S. customers; it had only a 6 percent market share in 2003. When DHL acquired Airborne that year, the company knew it needed an all-out effort

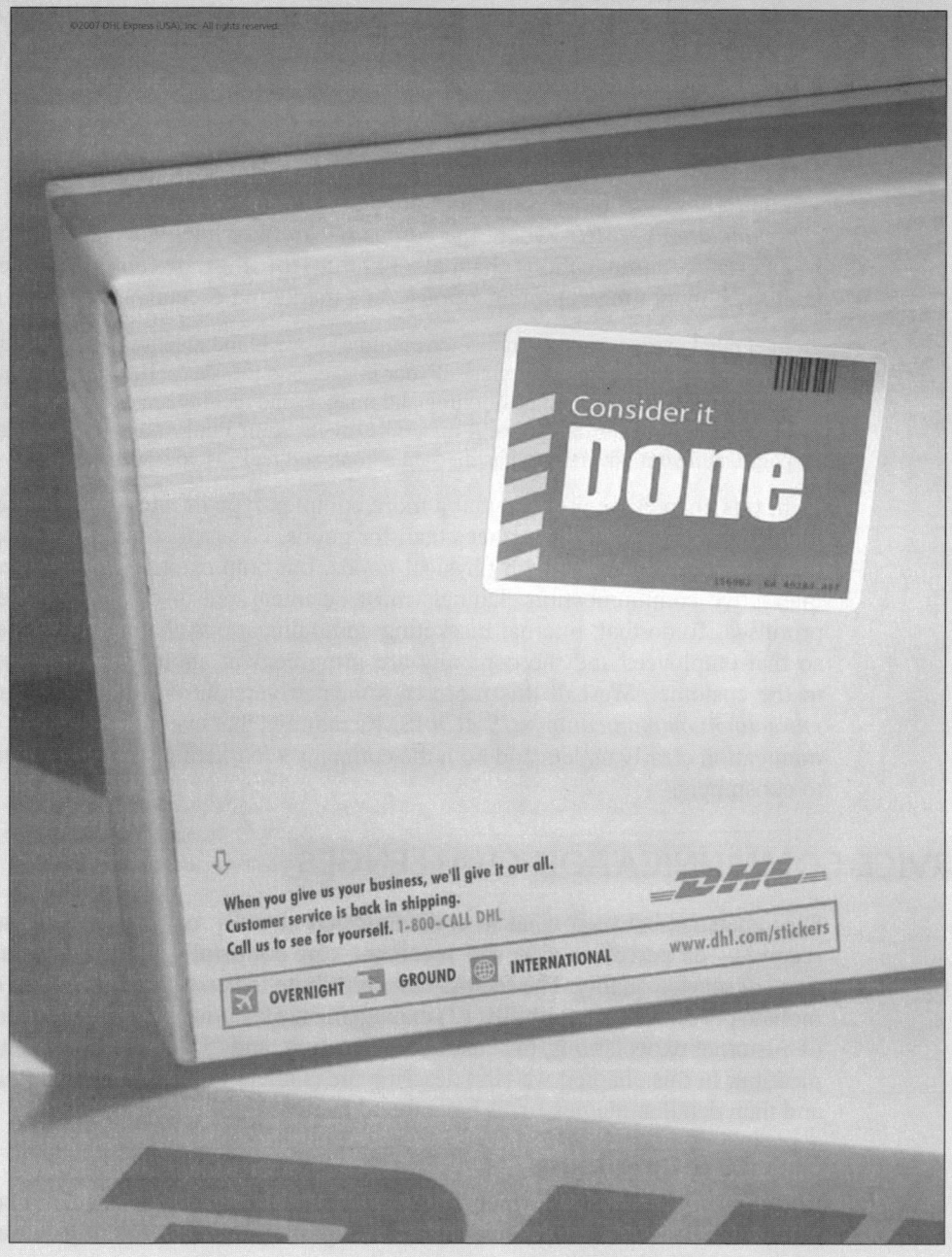

to compete head-on with the domestic behemoths. The company budgeted $1.2 billion for new initiatives to boost its presence in the U.S. market, starting with the addition of seven regional sorting centers to increase delivery capacity by 60 percent. In 2004, to support its ambitious goal of becoming another key choice in the U.S. parcel-delivery market, the company created an innovative new yellow and red logo and spent $150 million on an integrated six-month marketing communications campaign—including broadcast, print, interactive, and outdoor advertising as well as sponsorships, public relations, and a new website—that focused on brand awareness and brand value. As DHL Americas executive vice president of marketing explained, "Using a full 360 degree arsenal of marketing channels, we are showcasing the DHL brand's value message to current and potential customers across all points of contact."

The DHL marketing campaign, in 2004, developed by advertising agency Ogilvy and Mather New York, opened with a June 2004 television ad showing drivers for FedEx and UPS watching in wonder as a freight train rolls by carrying brand-new yellow trucks with the yellow and red DHL logo. High impact print and magazines supported the broadcast advertising with the headline, "The merger with Airborne in 2003 has made DHL strong in the following areas" followed by two full pages of ZIP codes. In 2004, billboards trumpeted: "Competition. Bad for them. Great for You." In 2005, impossible-to-ignore outdoor advertising spanning the full height of the Reuters building in New York's Times Square presented five different, fully animated video messages carrying the same theme and colors. Not only did the company completely renovate its own website (see http://www.dhl-usa.com), but it also placed full-motion interactive advertising on other websites. In 2004, the company's website allowed customers to download all its television, interactive, print, and outdoor advertising, as well as a computer screensaver with DHL trucks continuously streaming across a red background and interspersed with the campaign's catchy headlines. A public relations campaign by Ogilvy PR Worldwide, created in 2005 that was aimed at key target audiences and opinion leaders complemented the paid advertising. They launched the customer service campaign in Times Square with free hot dogs and Wall Street Journals, DHL branded rickshaws, flip flops, and water bottles among other items. And the company's tangibles became an integral part of the marketing communications plan, with the new yellow and red logo and bright yellow background on every DHL building, vehicle, courier uniform, packaging unit, and drop box in North America.

DHL used sponsorship as a key element of the campaign, highlighted by its role as the "Official Express Delivery and Logistics Provider of the 2004 U.S. Olympics Team." According to *B to B* magazine, DHL "grabbed the gold" among business-to-business companies that advertised during the televised Olympics coverage. Fifteen-second television spots included one with two Olympic cyclists spinning their wheels on the ramp of a DHL truck while the driver tossed water bottles, another with a long jumper soaring into a landing pit of packing peanuts as DHL employees prepared to rake more packing peanuts into the pit, and a third with a pole vaulter landing on a bed of bubble wrap as DHL employees stood by to ensure that everything went smoothly. The narrator announced, "DHL is proud to support the U.S. Olympic team any way we can." According to *B to B* magazine, "No other b-to-b advertiser came close to DHL's Olympic work."

Targeting small- and medium-sized businesses DHL created one of the most coordinated services marketing communication campaigns in history. In 2004, the advertising agency achieved integration through color (yellow and red), theme (choice, competition, and innovation), tagline ("Competition. Bad for them. Great for You."), and design. The executive vice president of marketing claimed at the beginning of the campaign, "As our red and bright yellow trucks begin rolling through the streets, advertising increases and customers see our expanded product offering, the realization will set in that DHL is an even more powerful force in the American marketplace."

DHL's 2007 campaign, called the "Capabilities Campaign," is also an example of a 360° integrated marketing campaign. The campaign was strongly unified visually by having all TV, print, and online messages delivered in the same way—with a yellow background, a yellow DHL package, and the consistent use of DHL stickers and icons. The messages were simple: "Your Way," "Sleep Well," "Consider it Done," "Si" and highlights DHL's express capabilities of overnight, international, and ground. They could be read quickly on outdoor signs or on trucks, but they varied enough that they retained customer interest.

Sources: Robin Londner, "Ads Will Tell What's Yellow, Red, and Brings Packages," *South Florida Business Journal,* June 18, 2004, p. A13; "Going for Gold in B-to-B Marketing," *B to B,* September 13, 2004, p. 38; Matthew Creamer, "DHL Bets on Flexibility as It Moves on FedEx, UPS in U.S.," *Advertising Age,* September 6, 2004, p. 8; www.dhl.com 2007.

for services more challenging for both marketers and consumers. The intangible nature of services creates problems for consumers both before and after purchase. Before buying services, consumers have difficulty understanding what they will be buying and evoking names and types of services to consider.[2] During purchase, consumers often cannot clearly see the differences among services. After purchase, consumers have trouble evaluating their service experiences.

Banwari Mittal described the difficulties associated with intangibility by dividing it into five properties, each of which has implications for services marketing communication. In his view, intangibility involves incorporeal existence, abstractness, generality, nonsearchability, and mental impalpability:[3]

- *Incorporeal existence.* The service product is neither made out of physical matter nor occupies physical space. Although the delivery mechanism (such as a Jiffy Lube outlet) may occupy space, the service itself (car servicing and oil change) does not. The implication is that showing the service is difficult, if not impossible.

- *Abstractness.* Service benefits such as financial security, fun, or health do not correspond directly with objects, making them difficult to visualize and understand. When businesses need consulting, for example, they often do not know where to begin because the concept is so vague that they do not understand the specific goals, processes, or deliverables that they are seeking.

- *Generality. Generality* refers to a class of things, persons, events, or properties, whereas *specificity* refers to particular objects, people, or events. Many services and service promises are described in generalities (wonderful experience, superior education, completely satisfied customers), making them difficult to differentiate from those of competitors.

- *Nonsearchability.* Because service is a performance, it often cannot be previewed or inspected in advance of purchase. If we are interested in finding a doctor, an air-conditioning repair firm, a personal trainer, or virtually any service, we cannot search the options as easily as we can search the shelves in a grocery store. Considerably more effort must be expended, and what we find may not be useful. For example, if a customer needs a plumber, the information contained in a source such as the Yellow Pages does not adequately discriminate among the choices. As we discussed in Chapter 3, nonsearchability is particularly true of services that are classified as either experience or credence services.

- *Mental impalpability.* Services are often complex, multidimensional, and difficult to grasp mentally. When customers have not had prior exposure, familiarity, or knowledge services are difficult to interpret. You may have experienced this when buying automobile insurance for the first time.

These five aspects of service intangibility make customers feel more uncertain about their purchases, and evidence indicates that the greater the risk that customers perceive in purchasing services, the more actively they will seek and rely on word-of-mouth communications to guide their choices.[4] Word of mouth can be a very convincing source of information about services for consumers, but it is not under the control of the service provider.

Management of Service Promises

A serious problem occurs when companies fail to manage service marketing communications—the vows made by salespeople, advertising, and service personnel— and service falls short of what is promised. This sometimes occurs because the part of the company making the promise lacks the information necessary to make accurate statements. For example, business-to-business salespeople often sell services, particularly new business services such as software, before their actual availability and without having an exact date of when they will be ready for market. Demand and supply variations make service provision possible at some times, improbable at others, and difficult to predict. The traditional functional structure in many companies (often called silos) also makes communication about promises and delivery difficult internally.

Management of Customer Expectations

Appropriate and accurate communication about services is the responsibility of both marketing and operations. Marketing must accurately (and compellingly) reflect what happens in actual service encounters; operations must deliver what is promised in communications. For example, when a management consulting firm introduces a new offering, the marketing and sales departments must make the offering appealing enough to be viewed as superior to competing services. In promoting and differentiating the service, however, the company cannot afford to raise expectations above the level at which its consultants can consistently perform. If advertising, personal selling, or any other external communication sets up unrealistic expectations, actual encounters will disappoint customers.

Because of increasing deregulation and intensifying competition in the services sector, many service firms feel pressure to acquire new business and to meet or beat competition. To accomplish these ends, service firms often overpromise in selling, advertising, and other company communications. In the telecommunications and airline industries, advertising is a constant battlefield of competing offers and price reductions to gain the patronage of customers. The greater the extent to which a service firm feels pressured to generate new customers, and perceives that the industry norm is to overpromise ("everyone else in our industry overpromises"), the greater is the firm's propensity to overpromise.

Many product and service companies also find themselves in the position of having to actively manage customer expectations downward—to tell customers that service previously provided will be discontinued or available only at a higher price. Airlines cancel flights that are not full and charge for food. Credit card companies that offer multiple value-added services when interest rates are high withdraw these services when interest rates drop. Health care insurers cut back on service while raising prices, and hospital patients experience far shorter stays and fewer diagnostic procedures. Patients requiring psychotherapy are limited to six visits unless their doctors can substantiate in writing the need for more. Alcohol treatment is handled on an outpatient rather than inpatient basis. In these situations—perhaps more than any others—the need to manage customer expectations is critical.

Customer Education

Service companies must educate their customers. If customers are unclear about how service will be provided, what their role in delivery involves, and how to evaluate services they have never used before, they will be disappointed. When disappointed, they will often hold the service company, not themselves, responsible. These errors or problems in service—even when they are "caused" by the customer—still lead customers to defect. For this reason the firm must assume responsibility for educating customers.

For services high in credence properties—expert services that are difficult for customers to evaluate even after they have received the services—many customers do not know the criteria by which they should judge the service. For high-involvement services, such as long-term medical treatment or purchase of a first home, customers are also unlikely to comprehend and anticipate the service process. First-time home buyers rarely understand the complex set of services (inspection, title services, insurance) and processes (securing a mortgage, offers and counteroffers, escrow) that will be involved in their purchases. Professionals and other providers of high-involvement services often forget that customers who are novices must be educated about each step in the process. They assume that an overview at the beginning of the service, or a manual or set of instructions, will equip the customer. Unfortunately, these steps are rarely sufficient, and customers defect because they can neither understand the process nor appreciate the value received from the service.

A final condition under which customer education can be beneficial involves services in which demand and supply are not synchronized, as discussed in Chapter 15. If the customer is not informed about peaks and valleys in demand, service overloads and failures, not to mention underutilized capacity, are likely to result.

Internal Marketing Communication

Multiple functions in the organization, such as marketing and operations, must be coordinated to achieve the goal of service provision. Because service advertising and personal selling promise what *people* do, frequent and effective communication across functions—horizontal communication—is critical. If internal communication is poor, perceived service quality is at risk. If company marketing communication and other promises are developed without input from operations, contact personnel may not be able to deliver service that matches the image portrayed in marketing efforts.

Not all service organizations advertise, but all need coordination or integration across departments or functions to deliver quality service. All need internal communication between the sales force and service providers. Horizontal communication also must occur between the human resource and marketing departments. To deliver excellent customer service, firms must be certain to inform and motivate employees to deliver what their customers expect. If marketing and sales personnel who understand customer expectations do not communicate this information to contact employees, the lack of knowledge for these employees will affect the quality of service that they deliver.

A final form of internal coordination central to providing service excellence is consistency in policies and procedures across departments and branches. If a service organization operates many outlets under the same name, whether franchised or company owned, customers expect similar performance across those outlets. If managers of individual branches or outlets have significant autonomy in procedures and policies, customers may not receive the same level of service quality across the branches.

FIVE CATEGORIES OF STRATEGIES TO MATCH SERVICE PROMISES WITH DELIVERY

Figure 16.2 shows the major approaches to overcome the service communication challenges that we just described. The goal is to deliver service that is greater than or equal to promises made, and all three sides of the triangle must be addressed to do so.

Address Service Intangibility

Approaches to address service intangibility include advertising and other communication strategies that clearly communicate service attributes and benefits to consumers, and strategies designed to encourage word-of-mouth communication.

FIGURE 16.2
Five Major Approaches to overcome Service Communication Channels

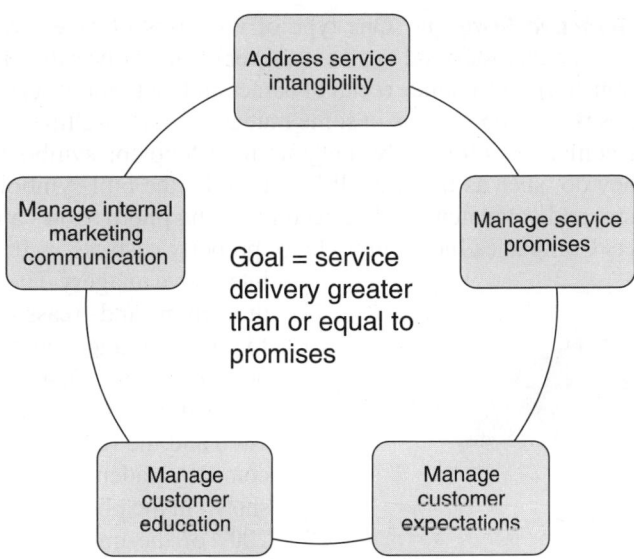

If service companies recognize the challenges they face due to intangibility, they can use selected strategies to compensate. In one way or another, each of the individual strategies we discuss here focuses on ways to make the message dramatic and memorable.

Use Narrative to Demonstrate the Service Experience Many services are experiential, and a uniquely effective approach to communicating them involves story-based appeals. Showing consumers having realistic and positive experiences with services is generally more effective than describing service attributes, particularly because the attributes themselves are often intangible. Research has concluded that consumers with relatively low familiarity with a service category prefer appeals based on stories to appeals based on lists of service attributes. Furthermore, the relative advantage of the story is intensified when the novice consumer is in a happy mood rather than a sad one.[5] For example, young consumers needing their first home mortgage will react more positively to an ad that shows a couple in their situation finding a house they love and then having a banker quickly find them a mortgage than to a discussion about rates and terms. This research finding is likely at the root of most insurance advertising, which limits specifics but instead shows narrative problem–solution situations in which the insurance company helps the customer out of difficult situations.

Present Vivid Information Effective service marketing communication creates a strong or clear impression on the senses and produces a distinct mental picture. One way to use vivid information is to evoke a strong emotion such as fear. Advertising that shows the harmful effects of smoking or the dangers of not wearing seat belts are typically very vivid. Vividness can also be achieved by concrete language and dramatization. One of the most effective examples of vividness was an Ad Council advertisement called "I am an American," created after the September 11, 2001, attacks. The spot featured people of different races and cultures who were all American citizens. The ad was simple and powerful, and TV stations picked it up immediately. Using vivid information cues is particularly desirable when services are highly intangible and complex. A print example of vividness is shown in an ad for the United Negro College Fund. The abstract themes of "limitless potential" and "chance to achieve" are made vivid by a photograph of a mind filled with books.

Use Interactive Imagery   One type of vividness involves what is called *interactive imagery*.[6] Imagery (defined as a mental event that involves the visualization of a concept or relationship) can enhance recall of names and facts about service. Interactive imagery integrates two or more items in some mutual action, resulting in improved recall. Some service companies effectively integrate their logos or symbols with an expression of what they do, such as the Merrill Lynch bull—the bull symbolizes "growth, strength, optimism, and competence.[7] The accompanying photo shows an advertisement for The Travelers Companies Inc., a provider of property casualty insurance, that demonstrates interactive imagery. The red umbrella represents protection and reassurance, an apt symbol for an insurance company. The umbrella is believed to have first appeared as an illustration of insurance protection in a Travelers ad in 1870 and the red umbrella, became the official company trademark in 1959. The advertisement shown in the photo refers to the reacquisition in 2007 of the trademark from Citigroup, which also used an umbrella as part of its logo.

Focus on the Tangibles.[8]   Another way that advertisers can increase the effectiveness of services communications is to feature the tangibles associated with the service, such as showing a bank's marble columns or gold credit card. Showing the tangibles provides clues about the nature and quality of the service. The photo on page 493, which is an advertisement for the Sierra Club, features the tangible benefits of the club in saving the gray wolf from extinction. Showing the wolf itself communicates the benefits of the organization emphatically, far more clearly than if words alone were used.

Use Brand Icons to Make the Service Tangible   How does an advertiser of services gain in competitive differentiation and strong brand awareness in a highly competitive market? In the fast-food and insurance industries, one answer is to create a recognizable brand icon that represents the company and generates brand visibility. One of the most enduring service brand icons is Ronald McDonald, the red-and-yellow clown that represents McDonald's and its children's charity, the Ronald McDonald House. McDonald's competitor, Jack in the Box, has its own mascot named Jack, a ball-shaped head with a pointed hat. In television advertising, he appears as the "founder" of the chain—part clown and part businessman in a suit with the head of the icon. He is always part fun and part serious. Advertising icons are even more critical in industries in which the service is complex and difficult to understand. Insurance is an example. American Family Life Insurance Company, or Aflac, a company that sells supplemental insurance on a voluntary basis in U.S. and Japanese worksites, faced a difficult challenge: getting potential customers to ask for its service by name. Enter the Aflac duck, an insistent and vocal character who screams "Aflac!" in commercials in which actors are

Quick, name an insurance company.

The 33,000 people of Travelers proudly welcome back their classic icon. Complete with a brand-new stock symbol (TRV) and a new official name: The Travelers Companies, Inc.

TRAVELERS

Interactive imagery is demonstrated by the Travelers umbrella.

trying to solve their insurance problems. The comic Gilbert Gottfried is responsible for the waterfowl's unrelenting honk. The duck, introduced in 2000, has generated such visibility that he has been featured on CNBC, *The Tonight Show with Jay Leno,* and *Saturday Night Live.* GEICO, the automobile insurance company that we featured in the chapter opener, has a wise-cracking gecko that is constantly forced to correct unfortunates who confuse the words *gecko* and *GEICO.* The mascot, shown in the photo on this page, helps customers remember the company's difficult brand name and provides a tangible that unifies the company's humorous advertising.[9]

Use Association, Physical Representation, Documentation, and Visualization
Leonard Berry and Terry Clark propose four strategies of tangibilization: association, physical representation, documentation, and visualization.[10] *Association* means linking the service to a tangible person, place, or object, such as "being in good hands with Allstate." *Physical representation* means showing tangibles that are directly or indirectly part of the service, such as employees, buildings, or equipment. *Documentation* means featuring objective data and factual information. *Visualization* is a vivid mental picture of a service's benefits or qualities, such as showing people on vacation having fun. Our Strategy Insight shows how marketing communication icons can be used as tangibles.

Feature Service Employees in Communication Customer contact personnel are tangible representations of the service and are also an important second audience for services advertising.[11] Featuring actual employees doing their jobs or explaining their services in advertising is effective for both the primary audience (customers) and the secondary audience (employees) because it communicates to employees that they are important. Furthermore, when employees who perform a service well are featured in marketing communication, they become standards for other employees' behaviors.

Earlier in this chapter, we discussed five aspects of intangibility that make service marketing communication challenging. In Exhibit 16.2, Mittal describes strategies that can be used in service advertising to overcome these properties. Through careful planning and execution, the abstract can be made concrete, the general can be made specific, the nonsearchable can be made searchable, and the mentally impalpable can be made palpable.

Recommendations and opinions from other customers are virtually always more credible than firm communications. In situations in which consumers have little information prior to purchase—something that occurs far more often in services than in goods because services are high in experience and credence properties—people turn to others for information rather than to traditional marketing

The GEICO Gecko is an advertising icon

Strategy Insight Google's Strategy Dominates Web Advertising and Communication

Search engine Google is one of the most successful services marketing stories of the past two decades. Google's strategic vision is "to organize the world's information and make it universally accessible and useful." The company has achieved that vision, as you no doubt are aware, by becoming such a universally accessible and useful search engine that it draws nearly 60 percent of all consumer searches. You may not be aware, however, of how Google has built a toolbox of advertising approaches and in the process become the most important new advertising medium in the world. In 2006, advertisers spent $10.6 billion (31 percent of online advertising revenue) on search advertising, sponsored links, and on Google content networks. Banner ads will also soon be available through Google's recent acquisition of Double Click, the biggest ad-serving company on the Internet.

Our Technology Spotlight, found later in this chapter, describes the most popular type of Internet advertising today: search-based or paid search advertising. In this form of advertising, which currently represents the largest share of online spending (40 percent) among all online ad formats, companies can either pay for small display ads to the right of listings or pay for listings themselves. The display ads, short messages to the right of the top-ranked searches that are relevant to the company, are called Google AdWords. When a consumer searches Google using one of those keywords, the advertiser's URL, along with its name and description, appears in a colored box beside the search results. The next time you call something up on Google, click on one or two of these boxes and you will see that they are advertisements. Companies can also pay for placement, which means that they buy rankings in the search results. When you call up a search on Google, some of the links in the column of search results have actually been purchased by advertisers. Google shades these paid listings to show consumers that these rankings are sponsored.

Google also provides business-to-business service by acting as a go-between for advertisers and websites through two other forms of advertising. In one, involving site-targeted ads, advertisers ask Google either to find specific websites or website content (such as ice hockey or figure skating) that is relevant to what they offer. Advertisers choose their target audiences both by size and interests, then give Google a list of keywords that describe the site. Google AdWords matches terms and creates a list of available content network sites where the company can advertise. Google AdSense is an advertising service targeted to website publishers. AdSense automatically crawls the content of a company's pages and delivers text or image ads that are relevant and high performing. Google then provides the ads to the sites for the companies. These two services actually work together—one is the source of advertisements and the other is the placement for the ads.

channels. Services advertising and types of promotion can generate word-of-mouth communication that extends the investment in paid communication and improves the credibility of the messages.

Use Buzz or Viral Marketing   Buzz marketing, also called viral marketing, involves the use of real consumers to spread the word about products without (or without the appearance of) being paid by the company. Sometimes buzz marketing occurs simply because customers are avid fans of the service, and sometimes the company seeds customers with services or products. Chipotle Mexican Grill, a Denver-based company with nearly 600 outlets, avoids advertising and instead depends almost completely on the word-of-mouth communication its customers spread about its unique and tasty food. Chipotle's founder, M. Steven Ells, makes giving away samples of its food (as well as satisfying customers) the basis for its strategy. For example, when the chain opened a midtown Manhattan outlet in 2006, it gave burritos away to

DoubleClick is a company that develops and provides the technology and services that place advertisements on websites, an approach called *ad serving*. Companies like DoubleClick provide software to websites and advertisers to place ads, count them, select the ads that will make the website or advertiser most money, and track progress of different advertising campaigns. For advertisers, Double-Click chooses the websites with the best potential to sell products and services. For sites themselves, DoubleClick chooses advertisers offering products and services that best fit with the sites and also brings in advertising revenues. For agencies, the company manages online inventory and reports and manages online activity. With the purchase of DoubleClick, Google gains a powerful advertising tool on its own but also will be able to offer advertisers the ability to create integrated search-and-display campaign.

Upon purchasing YouTube, Google immediately began posting video images in Google's Video search index so that users could be taken to YouTube.com to experience the videos. Google promises that over time, Google Video will become even more comprehensive as it evolves into a service through which users can search for the world's online video content wherever it is hosted. A Google representative stated, "Ultimately, we envision most user-generated and premium video content being hosted on YouTube so that it can further enhance the YouTube experience. We also envision YouTube benefiting from future

Google Video innovations—especially those involving video search, monetization and distribution."

Google's 2007 acquisition of YouTube will bring advertising to YouTube, but likely in unique forms. After testing many approaches, Google introduced its first advertising effort on YouTube in August 2007: ad "overlays." In this approach, advertising sponsors develop "overlays" that look like the messages that appear at the bottom of TV screens 15 seconds into a video. Users can ignore the message, close it, or click on the ad, which causes the clip to pause and the ad to be shown in the video window. Only a select number and type of sponsors—typically those that can provide information or interest to YouTube viewers—will be allowed to participate. One of the first sponsors, for example, was New York fashion agency Ford Models. In the words of Eileen Naughton, Google's director for media platforms, "We want our users to be able to accept and choose what type of advertising they engage in."

Sources: G. Stricker, "A Look Ahead at Google Video and YouTube," www.google.com, January 25, 2007; A. Klaassen, "Sorry Yahoo, MSN. Google Just Got Bigger," *Advertising Age,* April 16, 2007, pp. 3+; R. D. Hof, "Is Google Too Powerful?" *BusinessWeek,* April 9, 2007, pp. 46–55; R. Farzad and B. Elgin, "Googling for Gold," *BusinessWeek,* December 5, 2005, pp. 60–70; www.google.com 2007; J. Graham, "Google Plans Ad 'Overlays' for Some YouTube Videos," *USA Today,* August 22, 2007, p. 2A; and M. Helft, "Google Aims to Make YouTube Profitable with Ads," *New York Times,* August 22, 2007, p. C1.

6,000 people. Even though this cost the company $35,000, the strategy created 6,000 satisfied spokespeople.[12]

Leverage Social Media   Social media—interactive communication among customers on the Internet through such sites as MySpace, YouTube, and FaceBook—are becoming avenues for consumers to exchange information. More than half (55 percent) of teens online have a personal profile on a social networking site, and nearly half incorporate social networking into their daily lives.[13] Some of this activity is directly related to decisions about products and services. More than half of respondents to a consumer study claimed that they used customer-generated media (CGM) to make or narrow decisions: 23 percent to confirm decisions and 15 percent to make a top choice.[14] In the category of travel, a full 71 percent of consumers are influenced by CGM, and two-thirds of travelers prefer consumer reviews over company advertising.[15] Evidence also indicates that 66 percent of the fastest-growing companies in corporate America claim

Property of Intangibility	Advertising Strategy	Description
Incorporeal existence	Physical representation	Show physical components of service that are unique, indicate high quality, and create the right association.
Generality	System documentation	Objectively document physical system capacity by showing facts and figures.
	Performance documentation	Document and cite past positive performance statistics.
	Service performance episode	Present a vivid story of an actual service delivery incident that relates to an important service attribute.
Abstractness	Service consumption episode	Capture and display typical customers benefiting from the service, evoking particular incidents.
Nonsearchability	Performance documentation	Cite independently audited performance.
	Consumption documentation	Obtain and present customer testimonials.
Impalpability	Service process episode	Present a vivid documentary on the step-by-step service process.
	Case history episode	Present an actual case history of what the firm did for a specific client

Source: Adapted from B. Mittal, "The Advertising of Services: Meeting the Challenge of Intangibility," *Journal of Service Research* 2, no. 1. (August 1999), pp. 98–116.

that CGM is either "very important" or "important" and that increasing percentages are using messages to encourage social media: 33 percent are using message/bulletin boards; 27 percent are using online video; 19 percent blogging; 17 percent wikis, and 11 percent podcasting.[16] While social media are not controllable by the firm, the company can monitor the media and understand what consumers are saying and recommending. Formal methods and sophisticated technologies are being developed to track, monitor, and analyze online communication for brands. Nielsen BuzzMetrics, the innovator of this approach, gathers brand information online by trolling millions of lines of Internet communication to find out how customers feel about brands, how many are talking online, what issues they are discussing, how marketing is being viewed, and how efforts to affect word-of-mouth communications are being received. The service provides industry norms and benchmarks to the companies who buy their service as well as real-time alerts about issues.[17]

Aim Messages to Influencers   Improved technologies are now allowing companies to identify online influencers—those individuals with more connections than others and therefore more ability to influence others about services. Both researchers and research companies are developing technologies similar to the BuzzMetric approach described earlier that can identify those people in a viral community who are most critical to receive brand messages. When identified, these individuals can be "seeded"—given services or service information, invited to participate in special events, and otherwise encouraged to know and communicate about a service.

BACK BY POPULAR DEMAND.

It took a public outcry and an act of Congress to save the gray wolf from literally vanishing off the face of the earth. But we did it. Today, a lot of other creatures face similar extinction. And unless we step up our efforts to protect their habitats, they may not be so lucky. At the Sierra Club, we've mounted a major campaign to defend the Endangered Species Act and preserve threatened habitats before their inhabitants are gone forever. Please, contact us to find out how you can help protect threatened and endangered animals. Because no amount of popular demand can bring an extinct species back to life.

SIERRA CLUB
FOUNDED 1892

Protect America's Environment: For Our Families, For Our Future.

85 Second Street, San Francisco, CA 94105 • (415) 977-5653
Or visit our website at: www.sierraclub.org
Email us at: information@sierraclub.org

This advertisement for the Sierra Club features the gray wolf as a way to communicate the organization's efforts in a tangible and concrete way.

Create Advertising That Generates Talk Because It Is Humorous, Compelling, or Unique   Sprint's advertisement for system reliability with the tagline, "Can you hear me now?" became part of many consumers' speech for more than a year after the ad ran, providing a large bump in awareness for the advertisement. A humorous commercial that generated talk and was highly popular first aired on the 2007 Super Bowl and featured Kevin Federline, Brittany Spears' ex-husband. In the beginning of the commercial, "K-fed" is shown in a series of high-profile situations reflecting affluence, only to find himself at the end of the ad working in a fast-food restaurant. The Nationwide commercial under the tagline, "Life Comes at you Fast," played upon his ex-wife's fame and his fall from privilege. The advertisement was so memorable that it ran for months after the Super Bowl.

Feature Satisfied Customers in the Communication   Advertising testimonials featuring actual service customers simulate personal communications between people and are thereby a credible way to communicate the benefits of service. A successful 2004 advertising campaign for Blue Cross/Blue Shield of North Carolina featured real customers whose family members suffered medical crises that were handled successfully by the health insurance company. The testimonials were powerful and believable, particularly one featuring two parents and their cancer-surviving son, Davis. The campaign helped restore faith in the health insurance and generated positive word of mouth.

Generate Word-of-Mouth through Employee Relationships   Research shows that customer satisfaction with a service experience alone is not sufficient to stimulate word-of-mouth activity. However, when customers gained trust in a specific employee, positive word of mouth would result. In this research, trust was shown to be a consequence of three aspects of the employee–customer relationship: a personal connection between employees and customers, care displayed by employees, and employee familiarity with customers.[18] Companies can strengthen the interpersonal bonds that lead to trust using strategies that focus on service design, support systems, employees, and customers.[19] Examples include designing the service environment so that opportunities for interactions between customers and employees are plentiful, using support systems (such as customer relationship management software) to help employees remember customer characteristics, and empowering employees to correct problems fully and quickly.

A related approach involves using existing employees to recruit customers for the company. Upon recognizing that word-of-mouth communication was the best source of recruiting volunteers, the Army National Guard developed a program to use part-time soldiers who live and work full-time in their own communities to attract new soldiers. The Guard Recruiter Assistant Program (GRAP) began in 2006 by recruiting more than 100,000 "recruiter assistants" and brought in more than 35,000 new recruits in its first year. The recruiter assistants are paid commissions for the referrals they bring in and are highly credible, largely because they are viewed as talking about their own experiences rather than selling. The program has been so successful that the regular Army and Reserves have adopted it under the name, "Every Soldier a Recruiter."[20]

Manage Service Promises

In manufacturing physical goods, the departments that make promises and those that deliver them can operate independently. Goods can be fully designed and produced and then turned over to marketing for promotion and sale. In services, however, the sales and marketing departments make promises about what other employees in the organization will fulfill. Because what employees do cannot be standardized like physical goods produced mechanically, greater coordination and management of promises are required. This coordination can be accomplished by creating a strong service brand and by coordinating all of the company's marketing communications.

Create a Strong Service Brand

Leonard Berry, an expert in *service branding,* emphasizes that branding plays a special role in service companies:

> Strong brands enable customers to better visualize and understand intangible products. They reduce customers' perceived monetary, social, or safety risk in buying services, which are difficult to evaluate prior to purchase. Strong brands are the surrogates when the company offers no fabric to touch, no trousers to try on, no watermelons or apples to scrutinize, no automobile to test drive.[21]

In contrast to branding in goods situations, where each individual product has its own brand, the primary brand in service is the company itself. The focus of brand creation is on awareness, meaning, and equity of the company. For example, companies like Federal Express, Disney World, Starbucks, and NBC all focus communication and information on their companies rather than individual services that the company offers. Therefore, the brand becomes the company's method of integrating marketing communication.

Figure 16.3 is a service branding model developed by Berry that shows the relationships among the main elements in creating a strong service brand.[22] The *presented brand* is the part of the brand image that the company controls and disseminates through all personal and impersonal channels. Advertising, the brand name itself, websites, employees, facilities, and all other types of information dissemination must be coordinated and controlled. These messages lead to *brand awareness,* the customer's recall and recognition of the brand. The higher and more positive the brand awareness, the stronger the brand image and the more differentiation—or *brand equity*—the service company has. *Customer experience with the company*—the actual interactions with company employees and other firm manifestations—is another element that shapes the brand and is likely to be more powerful than any marketing messages. No matter how effective and unified advertising is for a service, actual experiences disproportionately provide meaning to customers.

The Mayo Clinic, one of the strongest service brands in the world, carefully cultivates its brand through patient experience rather than media promotion, of which it

FIGURE 16.3
A Services Branding Model

Source: Leonard L. Berry, "Cultivating Service Brand Equity," *Journal of the Academy of Marketing Science* 28 (Winter 2000), pp. 128–137.

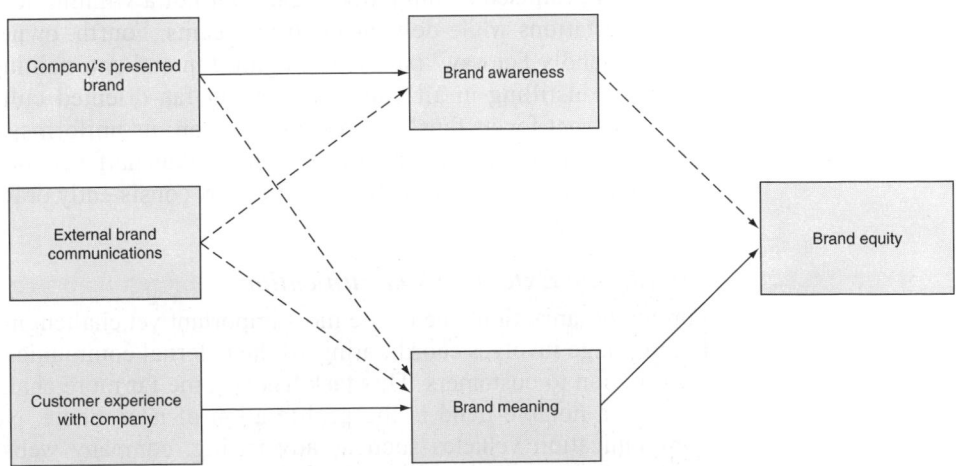

uses little. Strong core values, teamwork, physician responsibility, patient care, high quality staff, and facilities all contribute to the Mayo Clinic Model of Care, which ensures that patient experience is strong enough to perpetuate the Clinic's brand strength. Notably, the brand awareness of the Mayo Clinic is strong even though it does not use media promotion. In a study conducted in 2003 in which primary decision makers in the United States were asked what health care institutions in the United States they would choose if they could go anywhere for a serious medical problem, almost 27 percent of respondents named Mayo Clinic, far more than the second choice, which was named about 9 percent of the time.[23] Other research indicates that 95 percent of Mayo Clinic patients voluntarily say positive things about the Clinic to others, a testament to the Mayo brand and to the positive experiences they have there.[24]

Figure 16.3 shows two other factors that shape the service brand. First, *noncontrollable external brand communications* involve information—such as word-of-mouth communication and publicity—that the company does not have in its power. These sources of communication are potent because they are perceived by customers to be credible and unbiased but can have either positive or negative effects on the service brand. In another section of this chapter, we describe ways to influence word-of-mouth communication in positive ways. Second, *brand meaning* is the collection of customer's associations with the brand. Brand meaning largely emanates from customer experience but is also shaped by the company's presented brand and external communications.

An example of a successful service brand based firmly in brand meaning is the Boston Red Sox baseball team. The team, which until 2004 had not won a World Series since 1918, has built a fan base with messianic loyalty through deliberate management and marketing strategies that have been highly successful.[25] Virtually all elements of the strategy involve giving fans a meaningful personal and community experience. First, owners created a community of fans around the team by deliberately building the stadium right in the middle of the city's neighborhoods and taverns. They knew that locating the field in the center of the city would encourage fans to come to multiple games. Second, rather than focus on superstar players, they emphasized Fenway Park itself, avoiding the loss of allegiance when star players left. As part of this approach, the builders created the "Green Monster," the unique left-field wall that became part of the Boston region's folklore. Third, owners and managers promised a competitive team but not a winning team, credibly managing fan expectations while delivering strong teams. Fourth, owners vowed to make the park "Friendly Fenway," partly by staging fun and entertaining events at games and partly by instilling in all vendors a strong fan-oriented culture. Finally, the team shows respect for its fans' desires for tradition: its uniforms, logo, and focus on the game itself have remained the same for more than half a century. One indicator of the success of these strategies is that the Red Sox consistently draw a 90 percent capacity crowd at home.[26]

Coordinate External Communication

For any organization, one of the most important yet challenging aspects of managing brand image involves coordinating all the external communication vehicles that send information to customers. This task has become far more challenging in recent years because a notable trend is the proliferation of new media. Not only are traditional communication vehicles such as advertising, company websites, sales promotion, public relations, direct marketing, and personal selling proliferating, but many forms of new media are now available to marketers. Cell phones, digital signage, blogs, digital assistants, many forms of Internet advertising, and increasing usage of product placement in movies and television all complicate the goal of coordinating messages. Our Global Feature shows an international campaign for Virgin Atlantic Airways that uses many elements of the *marketing communication mix.*

Advertising is any paid form of nonpersonal presentation and promotion of a company's offerings by an identified sponsor. Dominant advertising vehicles include television, radio, newspapers, magazines, outdoor signage, and the Internet. Because advertising is paid, marketers control the creative appeals, placement, and timing. Internet advertising is becoming a more important and larger portion of companies' advertising budgets (see the Technology Spotlight) and should be synchronized with traditional advertising vehicles. MasterCard's highly successful "Priceless" advertising campaign, which launched in 1997, lists three or four tangible items and their prices followed by a key customer benefit that is "priceless." The campaign is an example of solid synchronization because it is "extraordinarily flexible, and carries a brand message that is not only relevant globally but also adapts well to different media, different payment channels, different markets."[27] The campaign, now seen in 96 countries and 47 languages, has generated strong brand recall and has received the advertising industry's prestigious Gold Effie, Addy, and Cresta awards.

Websites are the company's own online communication to customers. Often a disconnect exists between the look, feel, and content of a company's website and its advertising, usually because different parts of the company (or different advertising vendors) are responsible for creating these vehicles. When websites are coordinated in theme, content, and promises—as they are in the DHL advertising described in this chapter—a company is better able to match service delivery with promises because the promises themselves are consistent. A useful strategy to link websites and advertising is to send customers to company websites directly from an advertisement, often for more information or details. Television advertising for entertainment programs, such as USA Network series *Monk,* includes in its TV promotions an urge to go to the website to read the diaries of lead characters, see reprises of the episodes, and otherwise become more engaged with the shows. A 2007 campaign for the Army, called "Army Strong," focused on the soldiers themselves, claiming, "There's strong. And then there's Army Strong. It's more than physical strength. It's emotional strength. It's not just strength in numbers. It's strength in brothers." The tagline, "There's nothing stronger than the U.S. Army because there's nothing stronger than a U.S. Army Soldier," was then extended to video profiles of 10 soldiers and their personal stories on the Army website, goarmy.com/strong. An interactive MySpace.com profile also contains videos that show real overseas soldiers.[28]

Sales promotion includes short-term incentives such as coupons, premiums, discounts, and other activities that stimulate customer purchases and stretch media spending. The fast-food industry, including McDonald's, Burger King, and Wendy's, offers premiums such as action figures that link the chains' offerings to current movies and television shows. A particularly successful version of joint promotions between service advertisers and entertainment was created by CKE Restaurants' Carl's Jr. The restaurant incorporated footage of television season premieres, finales, and other television shows into the company's advertising, "[deliver] ing upwards of 30% of an increase in the impact of media spending."[29]

Public relations include activities that build a favorable company image with a firm's publics through publicity, relations with the news media, and community events. Richard Branson, founder of Virgin Atlantic Airways (see the Global Feature) is a

"A brand name that is known internationally for innovation, quality and a sense of fun—this is what we have always aspired to with Virgin." Richard Branson

Richard Branson, first known for Virgin Records, the legendary record label that signed the Rolling Stones, Janet Jackson, and The Human League, surprised the world in 1984 when he launched an upstart airline called Virgin Atlantic Airways. His vision was to create a high-quality, value-for-the-money airline to challenge the United Kingdom's market leader, British Airways. Twenty-five years later, Virgin Atlantic is the third-largest European carrier over the North Atlantic and includes destinations in the United States, Caribbean, Far East, India, China, Hong Kong, and Africa.

Parent company Virgin Group, with combined sales exceeding $20 billion, is known worldwide as an innovative global brand with megastore music retailing, book and software publishing, film and video editing facilities, clubs, trains, and financial advising through more than 200 branded companies in 29 countries. Virgin Atlantic Airways' brand and marketing campaign epitomizes successful global communication, with universal marketing components that are integrated in theme and design across the world as well as individual advertisements that adapt to geographies.

Virgin Atlantic Airways' common global marketing elements include its brand values, logo, and distinctive airplanes. The airlines' brand values—"caring, honest, value, fun, innovative"—are executed in all communications and strategies. Virgin focuses on customer service and low cost while also being the first to offer up unique services. For example, Virgin was the first airline to install television screens in every seat, offer massages and beauty services in first class, and mount a gambling casino right in the plane! The red and white logo, in the shape of an airline tail fin, appears in all worldwide marketing communication media including television, press, magazines, price promotions, outdoor posters, and taxi sides. Another common image is the company's Flying Lady, a Vargas painting of a red-headed, scantily-dressed woman holding a scarf. Distinctive airplanes feature the Flying Lady on the fuselage and Union Jacks on their wings in three core colors of red, purple and silver

metallic. Even the paint technology—based on mica, a hard mineral that produces a pearl-like shine—is unique. When the iridescent gleam combines with the plane's vibrant colors, the aircraft stirs up memories of the 1930s, when flying was glamorous and romantic.

As shown in the accompanying international advertisement, Virgin Atlantic Airways manages to translate its brand themes in culturally specific ways while retaining its global image. The Caribbean ad draws in readers with its bananas. Although the text and appeal change to suit the culture, all international advertisements contain the same Virgin Atlantic Airways logo and the same company colors.

Source: www.virgin-atlantic.com

master at obtaining publicity for his airline. When launching the airline, he claimed, "I knew that the only way of competing with British Airways and the others was to get out there and use myself to promote it."[30] In the years since the airline's launch, his publicity-winning stunts included recording the fastest time across the Atlantic Ocean in a speedboat, flying a hot-air balloon across the Atlantic Ocean and from Japan to

Canada, dressing up in everything from a stewardess's uniform to a bikini on Virgin flights, and being photographed in his bath.

Direct marketing involves the use of mail, telephone, fax, e-mail, and other tools to communicate directly with specific consumers to obtain a direct response. American Express is a service company that uses direct marketing extensively and ensures that it integrates well with all other messages, including interactive messages from employees. As the executive vice president of global advertising at American Express clearly states,

> Service brands are not created solely in advertising. In fact, much of a brand's equity stems from the direct consumer experiences with the brand. We partner with [a relationship marketing company] to help us manage consumer experiences with our brand across all products and services—Card, Travel, Financial Services, and Relationship Services—via all direct channels, including phone, Internet, and mail.[31]

Personal selling is face-to-face presentation by a representative from the firm to make sales and build customer relationships. One way that personal selling and advertising are integrated in business-to-business companies is through the development of advertising materials that salespeople distribute to customers. This approach not only creates an integrated message to customers but also keeps salespeople fully informed of the promises the company is making.

Managing Customer Expectations

Accurately promising when and how service will be delivered is one of the most important ways to close the communication gap. Among the most effective strategies to manage customer expectations are to make realistic promises; to offer service guarantees, options, and tiered-value offerings; and to communicate criteria customer can use to assess service.

Make Realistic Promises

The expectations that customers bring to the service affect their evaluations of its quality: the higher the expectation, the higher the delivered service must be to be perceived as high quality. Therefore, making promises about any aspect of service delivery is appropriate only when these aspects are actually delivered. It is essential for a firm's marketing or sales department to understand the actual levels of service delivery (percentage of times the service is provided correctly, or percentage and number of problems that arise) before making promises. To be appropriate and effective, communications about service quality must accurately reflect what customers will actually receive in service encounters.

Probably the simplest and most important point to remember is to promise what is possible.[32] Many companies hope to create the perception that they have high quality service by claiming it in marketing communication, but this strategy can backfire when the actual service does not live up to the promises in advertising. In line with the strategies we discuss in the next section, all service communications should promise only what is possible and not attempt to make services more attractive than they actually are.

Offer Service Guarantees

As discussed in Chapter 8, service guarantees are formal promises made to customers about aspects of the service they will receive. Although many services carry implicit service satisfaction guarantees, the true benefits from them—an increase in the likelihood of a customer choosing or remaining with the company—come only when the customer knows that guarantees exist and trusts that the company will stand behind them.

Technology Spotlight Internet Advertising Continues to Surge

Since 1994, when the first Internet banner ad went online, advertisers have spent billions of dollars to catch the attention of online users. The digital market research firm eMarketer reported Web ads were a $16.9 billion per year business in 2006, with Internet advertising spending growing at the highest rate of increase ever at 35 percent. The increase in online advertising is due in large part to consumers' changing preferences in media. Although television and newspapers used to be the media of choice, consumers in all age groups up to age 54 currently select the Internet as their top medium. A full 70 percent use the Internet for entertainment, and 67 percent of the high-spending 25- to 34-year-old and 35- to 54-year-old groups said content on the Internet provides them with useful information about products and services. Recent research also shows that broadband users spend 48 percent of their spare time (1 hour and 40 minutes) online in a typical weekday. That same study shows that 48 percent of younger users say they learn about new entertainment through community, review, and video sharing sites and blogs. In another study, a media-buying organization found that the Internet is indispensable to consumers. When 28 people received $150 each to stay off the Internet for two weeks, they were lost in figuring out how to pay bills, make vacation plans, take breaks from work, keep up with the news, and stay in touch with friends. With the Internet so pervasive in people's lives, advertisers recognize that reaching consumers through this vehicle is worth more now than ever.

Another major factor contributing to the success of Internet advertising is the availability of advertising approaches that are more popular than the banner ad, which dominated the medium for years.

BANNER BLINDNESS

Banner ads still account for 21 percent or $3.4 billion of spending on Internet ads, but their effectiveness as a marketing tool is being seriously questioned. Click-through rates, the most common measure of effectiveness, have dropped to between 0.1 and 0.025 percent. Scientists who track eye movements measuring where consumers look on websites have found an explanation for why they ignore banners even though they include relevant information. Apparently, people look at web sites in an F-shaped pattern, merely scanning the top before focusing in on the middle of the page where content is usually featured. The phenomenon has been documented as so strong that even nonadvertising material at the top of the site is ignored.

Analysts also suggest the following reasons for the drop in effectiveness of banner ads:

- *Banner clutter.* As spending increased, so did the number of ads, which reduced the novelty and created sites filled with banners that often led to no value. Just as with other advertising clutter, users learned to stop paying attention.
- *Boring banners.* Although the potential to create fun and interactive banner ads existed, many advertisers simply created me-too banners that were low on content and creativity.
- *Built-in banners.* Once advertisers started using animation and other colorful attention-getting devices, the ads became intrusive, interfering with the users' surfing stream and with the time they spent on sites. Some ads took so long to download that they delayed and derailed users' interactions on the Web.

Advertisers have continued to develop ways to improve the click-through rates of banner ads. One technique currently producing click-through rates of 0.4 to 0.74 percent involved live online videos, wherein streaming videos are placed in the banners to grab viewer attention. General Electric, for

Offer Choices

One way to reset expectations is to give customers options for aspects of service that are meaningful, such as time and cost. A clinical psychologist charging $100 per hour, for example, might offer clients the choice between a price increase of $10 per hour or a reduction in the number of minutes comprising the hour (such as 50 minutes). With the choice, clients can select the aspect of the trade-off (time or money) that is most meaningful to them. Making the choice solidifies the client's expectations of service.

example, ran a live video of CEO Jeff Immelt and California Governor Arnold Schwarzenegger discussing energy issues at a news conference. More than 95,000 consumers watched the ad.

SEARCH ADVERTISING

Improved advertising approaches have been developed for the Internet, with the most significant being search-based or paid search advertising. In this form of advertising, which currently represents the largest share of online spending (40 percent) among all online ad formats, advertisers have several different options. In one option, illustrated by Google AdWords, companies can pay for short messages to the right of the top-ranked searches that are relevant to the company. When a consumer searches Google using one of those keywords, the advertiser's URL, along with its name and description, appears in a colored box beside the search results. The advertiser pays only when a user clicks on the ad, and the going rate is as little as 5 cents per click. Companies can also pay for placement, which means that they buy rankings in the search results. Google shades these paid listings to show consumers that these rankings are sponsored.

RICH MEDIA AND FLASH ANIMATIONS

Rich media—the use of flash animations and streaming video—are predicted to grow faster than search marketing. Rich media can easily be coordinated with television advertising because they can contain moving images. Rich media ads stand out more than banner ads, and innovations are constantly being developed. Point Roll is a promising approach that enables advertisers to simultaneously deliver multiple ad messages within a single banner ad when users point and roll their mouse across the banner. Liquid-Image ads allow a user to reveal hidden layers of editorial content, streaming audio and video, advertising information, and e-commerce capabilities.

WIDGETS

While a 2007 study of attitudes about online advertising in preteens and teenagers showed that they did not like banner ads and other interruptions from marketers, it also suggested that they do enjoy playing with certain features on their personal web pages if they feel that they control them. "Widgets"—small, easy-to-download computer programs that allow web pages to be more interactive with graphics, videos, music, and chats—are one way to get this group of users to spread marketing messages on social networking sites such as Facebook. Using widgets, 20 percent of the users in a study conducted by Alloy Media + Marketing posted logos or promotions from advertisers when given incentives (e.g., coupons, games, or videos). For example, promoters of the film called *The Golden Compass* let users create a virtual demon from the film to share with friends. More than 200,000 people created the demons, and 4 million people in their networks interacted with them. Widgets, and other novel techniques to involve users, are sure to be a larger part of advertising as social media is used increasingly in the future.

Sources: K. Oser, "More Marketing Budgets Shift Money Online: Advertising Week Buzzes about Growing Impact of Internet," AdAge.com, September 27, 2004, QwikFIND ID: AAP99T; Kris Oser, "Ad Spending Returns to Good Old Days: 2004 Total Will Top Pre-Dot-Com-Crash High by $1 Billion," AdAge.com, August 10, 2004, QwikFIND ID: AAP87R; Karen J. Bannan, "Seven Ways to Make Online Advertising Work for You," *Advertising Age,* October 11, 2004, p. 11; "Americans Spend Half of Their Spare Time Online," Research Brief from the Center for Media Research, May 23, 2007, www.centerformediaresearch.com; E. Steel, "Young Surfers Spurn Banner Ads, Embrace 'Widgets,'" *The Wall Street Journal,* July 2, 2007; and E. Steel, "Neglected Banner Ads Get a Second Life," *The Wall Street Journal,* June 20, 2007, p. B4.

This strategy is effective in business-to-business situations, particularly in terms of speed versus quality. Customers who are time conscious often want reports, proposals, or other written documents quickly. When asked to provide a 10-page proposal for a project within three days, an architectural firm responded that it could provide either a 2-page proposal in three days or a 10-page proposal in a week. Its customer selected the latter option, recognizing that the deadline could be extended. In most business-to-business services, speed is often essential but threatens performance. If customers understand the trade-off and are asked to make a choice, they are likely to be more satisfied because their service expectations for each *option become more realistic.*

Create Tiered-Value Service Offerings

Product companies are accustomed to offering different versions of their products with prices commensurate with the value customers perceive. Automobiles with different configurations of features carry price tags that match not their cost but instead their perceived value to the customer. This same type of formal bundling and pricing can be accomplished in services, with the extra benefit of managing expectations.

Credit card companies offer tiered-value offerings. American Express has multiple levels of credit card services based on the type of service provided: the traditional green card offers basic service features, the gold card additional benefits, and the platinum card still more. Two advantages of tiered offerings are as follows:

1. The practice puts the burden of choosing the service level on the customer, thereby familiarizing the customer with specific service expectations.
2. The company can identify which customers are willing to pay higher prices for higher service levels.

The opportunity to set expectations accurately is present when the customer makes the decision at the time of purchase when customers can be reminded of the terms of the agreement if they request support that is above the level in the contract.

Communicate the Criteria and Levels of Service Effectiveness

At times companies can establish the criteria by which customers assess service. Consider a business customer who is purchasing market research services for the first time. Because market research is an expert service, it is high in credence properties that are hard for customers to judge. Moreover, the effectiveness of this type of service differs depending on the objectives the client brings to the service. In this situation, a service provider can teach the customer the criteria by which to evaluate the service. The provider that teaches the customer in a credible manner will have an advantage in shaping the evaluation process.

As an example, consider research company A, which communicates the following criteria to the customer: (1) a low price signals low quality, (2) reputation of the firm is critical, and (3) person-to-person interviews are the only type of customer feedback that will provide accurate information. A customer who accepts these criteria will evaluate all other suppliers using them. If research company B had talked to the customer first, consider these (very different!) criteria and their impact on the buyer: (1) market research companies with good reputations are charging for their reputation, not their skill; (2) telephone interviews have been found to work as well as person-to-person interviews; and (3) price does not indicate quality level.

The same approach can be used with service *levels* rather than evaluative criteria. If research company B provides four-day turnaround on the results of the data analysis, the company has just set the customer's expectation level for all other suppliers.

Manage Customer Education

As discussed in Chapter 13, customers must perform their roles properly for many services to be effective. If customers forget to perform their roles, or perform them improperly, disappointment may result. For this reason, communication to customers can take the form of customer education. Figure 16.3 showed several types of customer education approaches that can help match promises with delivery.

Prepare Customers for the Service Process

One of us, on a return trip from Singapore on Singapore Airlines, neglected to heed the airline's warning that return flights to the United States must be confirmed 24 hours in advance. Upon arrival at the airport to return home, my seat had been given to another customer who had conformed to the airline's request for confirmation. Depending on the perspective taken, you could argue that either the company or the customer was right in this situation. Whose responsibility is it to make sure that customers perform their roles properly?

Companies can avoid such situations by preparing customers for the service process. And companies may need to prepare the customer often, even every step of the way, for the subsequent actions the customer needs to take. A business-to-business example will help illustrate this strategy.

Customers of management consulting services purchase intangible benefits: marketing effectiveness, motivated workforces, culture change. The very fact that companies purchase these services usually indicates that they do not know how to perform them alone. Many clients will also not know what to look for along the way to judge progress. In management consulting and other complex service situations, the effective provider prepares the customer for the service process and creates structure for the customer. At the beginning of the engagement, the management consulting firm establishes checkpoints throughout the process, at which times progress will be evaluated, and also leads the customer to establish objectives for project completion. Because customers do not know what that progress will look like, the consulting firm takes the lead in setting goals or criteria to be examined at those times.

A similar approach is effective with individual service customers. Do you remember registration at the beginning of your first college semester or quarter? How aware were you of the steps in the process and where to go after each step? It is unlikely that directions, even in great detail, made you feel confident and competent in the new service experience. You may have required step-by-step—"next call this telephone number or go to page B"—guidance.

As these examples show, any time a customer is inexperienced or a service process is new or unique, education about what to expect is essential.

Confirm Performance to Standards and Expectations

Service providers sometimes provide service, even explicitly requested service, yet fail to communicate to the customer what has been accomplished. These providers stop short of getting credit for their actions when they do not reinforce actions with communication about their fulfillment of the request. This situation may happen under one or more of the following conditions:

- The customer cannot evaluate the effectiveness of a service.
- The decision maker in the service purchase is a person different from the users of the service.
- The service is invisible.

When customers cannot evaluate service effectiveness, usually because they are inexperienced or the service is technical, the provider may fail to communicate specific actions that address client concerns because the actions seem too complex for the customer to comprehend. In this situation, the service provider can improve perceptions by translating the actions into customer-friendly terms. A personal injury lawyer who aids a client with the medical and financial implications of an accident needs to be able to tell the client in language the client can understand that the lawyer has performed the necessary actions.

When the decision maker in service purchases is different from the users of the service, a wide discrepancy in satisfaction may exist between decision makers and users. An example is in the purchase of information technology products and services in a company. The decision maker—the manager of information technology or someone in a similar position—makes the purchase decisions and understands the service promises. If users are not involved in the purchase process, they may not know what has been promised and may be dissatisfied.

Customers are not always aware of everything done behind the scenes to serve them well. Most services have invisible support processes. For instance, physicians frequently request diagnostic tests to rule out possible causes for illness. When these tests come back negative, doctors may neglect to inform patients. Many hairstyling firms have guarantees that ensure customer satisfaction with haircuts, permanents, and color treatments. However, only a few of them actively communicate these guarantees in marketing communication because they assume customers know about them. The firm that explicitly communicates the guarantee may be selected over others by a customer who is uncertain about the quality of the service. Making customers aware of standards or efforts to improve service that are not readily apparent can improve service quality perceptions.

Clarify Expectations after the Sale

When service involves a hand-off between sales and operations, clarifying expectations with customers helps the operations arm of the company align delivery with customer expectations. Salespeople are motivated and compensated to raise customer expectations—at least to the point of making the sale—rather than to communicate realistically what the company can provide. In these situations, service providers can avoid future disappointment by clarifying to customers what was promised as soon as the hand-off is made from sales to operations.

Teach Customers to Avoid Peak Demand Periods and Seek Slow Demand Periods

Few customers want to face lines or delays in receiving services. In the words of two researchers, "At best, waiting takes their time, and at worst, they may experience a range of unpleasant reactions—feeling trapped, tired, bored, angry, or demeaned."[33] In a bank setting, researchers tested three strategies for dealing with customer waits: (1) giving customers prior notice of busy times, (2) having employees apologize for the delays, and (3) assigning all visible employees to serving customers. Only the first strategy focuses on educating customers; the other two involve managing employees. Researchers expected—and confirmed—that customers warned of a wait in line tended to minimize the negative effects of waiting to justify their decision to seek service at peak times. In general, customers given a card listing the branch's busiest and slowest times were more satisfied with the banking service. The other two strategies, apology and all-tellers-serving, showed no effects on satisfaction.[34] Educating customers to avoid peak times benefits both customers (through faster service) and companies (by easing the problem of overdemand).

Manage Internal Marketing Communication

The fifth major category of strategies necessary to match service delivery with promises involves managing internal marketing communications. Internal marketing communications can be both vertical and horizontal. *Vertical communications* are either downward, from management to employees, or upward, from employees to management. *Horizontal communications* are those across functional boundaries in an organization. A third strategy is *internal branding,* which consists of various strategies to sell the brand inside the company.

Create Effective Vertical Communications

Companies that give customer contact employees adequate information, tools, and skills allow them to perform successful interactive marketing. Some of these skills come through training and other human resource efforts discussed in Chapter 12, but some are provided through *downward communication.* Among the most important forms of downward communication are company newsletters and magazines, corporate television networks, e-mail, briefings, videotapes and internal promotional campaigns, and recognition programs. One of the keys to successful downward communication is keeping employees informed of everything that is being conveyed to customers through external marketing. Employees should see company marketing communication before it is aired or published and should be familiar with the website, mailings, and direct-selling approaches used. If these vertical communications are not present, both customers and employees suffer—customers will not receive the same messages from employees that they hear in company external marketing, and employees will feel uninformed and not be aware of what their company is doing. Customers come to them asking for services that have been marketed externally but not internally, making the employees feel uninformed, left out, and helpless.[35]

Sell the Brand Inside the Company[36]

Having knowledge about what the company is doing in marketing communications is one aspect of internal marketing communication, but it is not enough. Consultant Colin Mitchell emphasizes the importance of marketing the company's brand and brand message to employees so that they can make powerful connections with customers. He recommends three principles for bringing the brand alive: choosing the right moment to teach and inspire employees, linking internal and external marketing, and bringing the brand alive for employees.

Choosing the right moment is essential because employees are not capable of or willing to accept too many change initiatives, and therefore the company has to be selective in identifying opportunities when it can create enthusiasm for the brand. When British Petroleum merged with both Amoco and then ARCO, it rebranded itself as BP and launched a campaign to both customers and employees declaring that it was going "beyond petroleum."[37] Had the company rebranded itself after Amoco and before ARCO, employees would have had less energy to support the rebranding and carry out the message to customers.

Linking internal and external marketing means that employees need to hear the same thing from management that customers hear. If customers hear that serving them is most important and employees are told that cost savings matter more, employees will be confused and unable to live the message. One of the best ways to link the two types of communication is to create advertising that targets both customers and employees. When IBM launched its highly successful e-business campaign in 1997, it took out a large advertisement in *The Wall Street Journal* to show its intent to both target audiences, and then followed up with support for both audiences throughout the campaign.[38]

Bringing the brand alive to employees involves creating a strong emotional connection between employees and the company. Employees at Southwest Airlines are encouraged to live the Southwest brand by dressing informally (although still in uniform), ad-libbing when giving instructions both on the ground and in the plane, and decorating the check-in counters on holidays. Employees at Singapore Airlines, on the other hand, connect with its employees through the company's emphasis on grace, formal dress, quiet tone, and Asian food.

Create Effective Upward Communication

Upward communication is also necessary in closing the gap between service promises and service delivery. Employees are at the front line of service, and they know—more than anyone else in the organization—what can and cannot be delivered. They know when service breakdowns are occurring and, very often, why they are happening. Having open communication channels from employees to management can prevent service problems before they occur and minimize them when they do take place.

Create Effective Horizontal Communications

Horizontal communication—communication across functional boundaries in an organization—facilitates coordinated efforts for service delivery. This task is difficult because functions typically differ in goals, philosophies, outlooks, and views of the customer—but the payoff is high. Coordination between marketing and operations can result in communication that accurately reflects service delivery, thus reducing the gap between customer expectations and actual service delivery. Integration of effort between marketing and human resources can improve the ability of each employee to become a better marketer. Coordination between finance and marketing can create prices that accurately reflect the customer's evaluation of a service. In service firms, all these functions need to be integrated to produce consistent messages and to narrow the service gaps.

One important strategy for effective horizontal communications is to open channels of communication between the marketing department and operations personnel. For example, when a company creates advertising that depicts the service encounter, it is essential that the advertising accurately reflect what customers will experience in actual service encounters. Puffery or exaggeration puts service quality perceptions at risk, especially when the firm is consistently unable to deliver to the level of service portrayed in the marketing communication. Coordination and communication between advertising and service providers are pivotal in delivering service that meets expectations.

Featuring actual employees doing their jobs or explaining the services they provide, a strategy we mentioned earlier in this chapter, is one way to coordinate advertising portrayals and the reality of the service encounter. To create this type of advertising, the advertising department or agency interacts directly with service employees, facilitating horizontal communications. Similar benefits can be achieved if employees are included in the advertising process in other ways, such as by being shown advertising in its pretest forms.

Another important strategy for horizontal communications involves opening channels of communication between sales and operations. Mechanisms for achieving this goal can be formal or informal and can include annual planning meetings, retreats, team meetings, or workshops in which departments clarify service issues. In these sessions, the departments can interact to understand the goals, capabilities, and constraints of the other. Some companies hold "gap workshops" at which employees from both functions meet for a day or two to try to understand the difficulties in matching promises made through selling with delivery accomplished by operations personnel.[39]

Involving the operations staff in face-to-face meetings with external customers is also a strategy that allows operations personnel to more readily understand the salesperson's role and the needs and desires of customers. Rather than filtering customers' needs through the sales force, operations employees can witness firsthand the pressures and demands of customers. A frequent and desirable result is better service to the internal customer—the salesperson—from the operations staff as they become aware of their own roles in satisfying both external and internal customers.

Align Back-Office and Support Personnel with External Customers through Interaction or Measurement

As companies become increasingly customer focused, frontline personnel develop improved skills in discerning what customers require. As they become more knowledgeable about and empathetic toward external customers, they also experience intrinsic rewards for satisfying customers. Back-office or support personnel, who typically do not interact directly with external customers, miss out on this bonding and, as a consequence, fail to gain the skills and rewards associated with it.

Interaction   Companies are creating ways to facilitate the interaction between back-office and support personnel and external customers. Weyerhaeuser, for example, sends hourly employees to customers' plants to better understand their needs. When actual interaction is difficult or impossible, some companies videotape customers in their service facilities during the purchase and consumption process to vividly portray needs and requirements of customers and to show personnel the support that frontline people need to deliver to those expectations.

Measurement   When company measurement systems are established, employees are sometimes judged on the basis of how they perform for the next internal customer in the chain. Although this approach provides feedback in terms of how well the employees are serving the internal customer, it lacks the motivation and reward that come from seeing their efforts affect the end customer. Federal Express has aligned internal personnel with the external customer using measurement. As we discussed in Chapter 10, FedEx's service quality indicator (SQI) computes daily the number of companywide service failures. To clearly communicate customer fail points to internal employees, the company created linking measures to trace the causes to each internal department. For example, the company's information technology department affects 8 of the 12 SQI measurements and therefore has submeasures that provide feedback on how the department's work is affecting the SQI.

Create Cross-Functional Teams

Another approach to improving horizontal communications to better serve customers is to involve employees in cross-functional teams to align their jobs with end customer requirements. For example, if a team of telecommunications service representatives is working to improve interaction with customers, back-office people such as computer technicians or training personnel can become part of the team. The team then learns requirements and sets goals for achieving them together, an approach that directly creates communications across the functions.

The cross-functional team approach can best be explained by the examples of an advertising agency. The individual in an advertising agency who typically interacts directly with the client is the account executive (often called a "suit" by the creative staff). In the traditional agency, the account executive visits the client, elicits client expectations, and then interacts with the various departments in the agency (art, copywriting, production, traffic, and media buying) that will perform the work. All functions are specialized and, in extreme cases, get direction for their portion of the work right from the account executive. A cross-functional team approach has representatives from all the areas meet with the account executive, even the client, and collectively discuss the account and approaches to address client needs. Each team member brings his or her function's perspectives and opens communication. All members can then understand the constraints and schedules of the other groups.

Summary

Discrepancies between service delivery and external communications have a strong impact on customer perceptions of service quality. In this chapter we discussed the role of and need for integrated services marketing communications in minimizing these discrepancies. We described external and interactive communications using the service triangle and emphasized the need to coordinate all communication to deliver service that meets customer expectations. We emphasized the difficulties and possibilities associated with new media. We also discussed the factors that lead to challenges in services marketing communications, including service intangibility; management of service promises; and management of customer expectations, customer education, and internal marketing communication. We then offered strategies to address each of these services communications problems. To address service intangibility, we described specific strategies such as the use of vivid imagery and tangible icons in communications, as well as ways to maximize the use of word-of-mouth communication. To manage service promises, we delineated the need for a strong service brand, coordination of service promises, realistic promises, and service guarantees. To manage customer expectations, we suggested that allowing customers to choose among options, creating tiered-value options, communicating service effectiveness criteria, and negotiating unrealistic expectations can be effective. To improve customer education, we described the need to prepare customers for the service process, confirm performance to standards and expectations, clarify expectations after the sale, and teach customers to choose the best times to seek service. Finally, to manage internal communication, we discussed effective vertical communication, horizontal communication, and internal branding.

Discussion Questions

1. Think of another services company that provides integrated services marketing communications. Go to the services company's website and find the section where it posts its advertising and communication. Is the company's campaign as comprehensive and as integrated as GEICO's or DHL's campaign, as described in the opening vignette and Exhibit 16.1? Why or why not? What should be added, changed, or deleted to improve the campaign?

2. Which of the key reasons for the communication gap (provider gap 4) discussed in the beginning of this chapter is the easiest to address in a company? Which is the hardest to address? Why?

3. Review the five general strategies for achieving integrated services marketing communications. Would all these strategies be relevant in goods firms? Which would be most critical in goods firms? Which would be most critical in services firms? Are there any differences between those most critical in goods firms and those most critical in services firms?

4. What are the most effective Internet advertisements you have seen? Why are they effective?

5. Using the section on managing customer expectations, put yourself in the position of your professor, who must reduce the amount of "service" provided to the students in your class. Give an example of each strategy in this context. Which of the strategies would work best with you (the student) in managing your expectations? Why?

6. Why are social marketing media like MySpace and YouTube so important in service firms? Are they important in product firms?

7. What other strategies can you suggest for leveraging consumer-generated media?

8. What other strategies can you add to the four offered in the section on customer education? What types of education do you expect from service firms? Give an example of a firm from which you have received adequate education. What firm has not provided you with adequate education?

Exercises

1. Go to the Google website and select the tab called "Business Solutions." This is the section of the site that describes the types of advertising that Google offers. Do the same thing for YouTube (you must go to "Company Information" and then to "Advertising"). Review these types of advertising, and describe the benefits and disadvantages of each. If you were an advertiser, which of these types of ads would you want to use? Why?

2. Find five effective service advertisements in newspapers and magazines. According to the criteria given in this chapter, identify why they are effective. Critique them using the list of criteria, and discuss ways they could be improved.

Notes

1. P. G. Lindell, "You Need Integrated Attitude to Develop IMC," *Marketing News,* May 26, 1997, p. 5.

2. D. Legg and J. Baker, "Advertising Strategies for Service Firms," in *Add Value to Your Service,* ed. C. Suprenant (Chicago: American Marketing Association, 1987), pp. 163–168.

3. B. Mittal, "The Advertising of Services: Meeting the Challenge of Intangibility," *Journal of Service Research* 2 (August 1999), pp. 98–116.

4. H. S. Bansal and P. A. Voyer, "Word-of-Mouth Processes within a Services Purchase Decision Context," *Journal of Service Research* 3 (November 2000), pp. 166–177.

5. A. S. Mattila, "The Role of Narratives in the Advertising of Experiential Services," *Journal of Service Research* 3 (August 2000), pp. 35–45.

6. K. L. Alesandri, "Strategies That Influence Memory for Advertising Communications," in *Information Processing Research in Advertising,* ed. R. J. Harris (Hillsdale, NJ: Erlbaum, 1983).

7. www.merrilllynch.com, accessed September 2007.

8. L. L. Berry and T. Clark, "Four Ways to Make Services More Tangible," *Business,* October–December 1986, pp. 53–54.

9. www.geico.com; www.Aflac.com; and "Who's Your Favorite Advertising Icon?" advertising insert, *New York Times,* Monday, September 20, 2004, p. 6.

10. Berry and Clark, "Four ways to Make Service More Tangible."

11. W. R. George and L. L. Berry, "Guidelines for the Advertising of Services," *Business Horizons,* May–June 1981, pp. 52–56.

12. M. Arndt, "Burrito Buzz—and So Few Ads," *BusinessWeek,* March 12, 2007, pp. 84–85.

13. "48% of Teens Visit Social Networking Sites Daily," *WOM Research,* www.womma.org, February 16, 2007.

14. "Consumer-generated Media: Influencing Over Half of Us," *WOM Research,* www.womma.org, January 26, 2007.

15. Ibid.

16. "66% of Fastest-Growing Companies Value Social Media," *WOM Research,* www.womma.org, February 16, 2007.

17. "VNU Brings Together BuzzMetrics, Intelliseek to Create Nielsen BuzzMetrics Service," www.prnewswire.com. September 25, 2006.

18. D. D. Gremler, K. P. Gwinner, and S. W. Brown, "Generating Positive Word-of-Mouth Communications through Customer-Employee Relationships," *International Journal of Service Industry Management,* January 2001, pp. 44–59.

19. Ibid, pp. 54–56.

20. O. Dorell, "Word of Mouth Helps Guard Gain," *USA Today,* July 5, 2007, p. 3A.

21. Leonard L. Berry, "Cultivating Service Brand Equity," *Journal of the Academy of Marketing Science* 28 (Winter 2000), pp. 128–137.

22. The figure and definitions contained in this section are all from Berry, "Cultivating Service Brand Equity."

23. L. L. Berry and K. D. Seltman, " Building a Strong Brand: Lessons from Mayo Clinic," *Business Horizons* 50 (2007), 199–209.

24. Ibid., p. 201.

25. G. Rifkin, "How the Red Sox Touch All the Branding Bases," strategy + business .com, downloaded April 2007.

26. Ibid, page 2.

27. www.mastercardinternational.com

28. L. Petrecca, "Strong Response to Tough Task, " *USA Today,* January 29, 2007.

29. Alice Z. Cuneo, "Sue Johenning," *Advertising Age,* September 27, 2004.

30. P. Denoyelle and J. Larreche, "Virgin Atlantic Airways—Ten Years Later," INSEAD Case, 1995.

31. D. E. Bell and D. M. Leavitt, "Bronner Slosberg Humphrey," *Harvard Business School Case 9-598-136,* 1998, p. 5.

32. Ibid.

33. E. C. Clemmer and B. Schneider, "Managing Customer Dissatisfaction with Waiting: Applying Social-Psychological Theory in a Service Setting," in *Advances in Services Marketing and Management,* vol. 2, ed. T. Schwartz, D. E. Bowen, and S. W. Brown (Greenwich, CT: JAI Press, 1993), pp. 213–229.

34. Ibid.

35. L. L. Berry, V. A. Zeithaml, and A. Parasuraman, "Quality Counts in Services, Too," *Business Horizons,* May–June 1985, pp. 44–52.

36. C. Mitchell, "Selling the Brand Inside," *Harvard Business Review* 80 (January 2002), pp. 5–11.

37. Ibid., p. 6.

38. Ibid., p. 9.

39. V. A. Zeithaml, A. Parasuraman, and L. L. Berry, *Delivering Quality Service: Balancing Customer Perceptions and Expectations* (New York: The Free Press, 1990), p. 120.

Chapter **Seventeen**

Pricing of Services

This chapter's objectives are to

1. Discuss three major ways that service prices are perceived differently from goods prices by customers.
2. Articulate the key ways that pricing of services differs from pricing of goods from a company's perspective.
3. Demonstrate what value means to customers and the role that price plays in value.
4. Describe strategies that companies use to price services.
5. Give examples of pricing strategy in action.

Fly Ryanair—Only €9.50 per Bag, €3.40 per Bottle of Water, and €3 for Online Check-In

Ryanair, Dublin's discount airline, has an average fare ($53) that is almost half that of Southwest Airlines ($93), but many passengers would call the prices for its "extra" services—such as baggage and online check-in—far from cheap. The airline has one of the most unusual pricing policies in the world. Depending on your perspective, it could be called penny-pinching (water costs almost as much as beer on U.S. flights) or pay-for-service (even reserving online requires payment). While the fares are low, everything else costs money. In fact, at one time the airline charged $34 for the use of a wheelchair! Customers aren't the only ones who have to pay: staff buy their own uniforms and provide their own pens. Michael O'Leary, CEO of the holding company, clearly states his philosophy: "You want luxury? Go somewhere else."

Inspired by Southwest Airlines, O'Leary revolutionized the strategy for running a low-cost airline. He took Southwest's basic approach and improved on it. First, he cut costs in as many places as possible—selling virtually all tickets online, removing seatback pockets and window shades to save staff between-flight maintenance, and using nonreclining seats to pack in more passengers. Second, he based his pricing strategy on factors that were not directly comparable to other airlines, insulating the airline from head-to-head price competition. When larger airlines dropped fares, making them more competitive with Southwest and JetBlue, the discounters had to add amenities and/or eliminate cost-saving practices to compete. O'Leary kept fares low but charged for everything else to keep profits up. Kerry Capell of *BusinessWeek* likens this to strategy used with cell phones:

> He thinks like a retailer and charges for absolutely every little thing, except the seat itself. Imagine the seat as akin to a cell phone: it comes free, or nearly free, but its owner winds up spending on all sorts of services. Last year, Ryanair gave away 25% of its seats, a figure O'Leary thinks he can double within five years. In the not-too distant future, he wants all seats to go for free.

Among the other on-airplane, money-making approaches O'Leary uses are advertising, sales of products such as cameras, and services such as bus and train tickets. The bus and train tickets are particularly useful to passengers as the airline serves small outlying airports, as does Southwest, that are not in major cities. Online, the company promotes and sells such services as hotels, rental cars, travel insurance, and gambling, from which it receives commissions. Planned in-flight, mobile phone service will soon allow gaming on the planes themselves.

The pricing strategy is highly effective, making Ryanair Europe's most profitable airline. The airline's profits for the first half of 2006 were $422 million, up 39 percent, on sales of $1.6 billion. Net margins were 18 percent during that time, compared with 7 percent at Southwest.

Sources: K. Capell, "Wal-Mart with Wings," *BusinessWeek,* November 16, 2006; and www.ryanair.com, 2007.

According to one of the leading experts on pricing, most service organizations use a "naive and unsophisticated approach to pricing without regard to underlying shifts in demand, the rate that supply can be expanded, prices of available substitutes, consideration of the price–volume relationship, or the availability of future substitutes."[1] What makes the pricing of services more difficult than pricing of goods? What approaches work well in the context of services?

This chapter builds on three key differences between customer evaluation of pricing for services and goods:

1. Customers often have inaccurate or limited reference prices for services.
2. Price is a key signal of quality in services.
3. Monetary price is not the only price relevant to service customers.

As we demonstrate, these three differences can have profound impact on the strategies companies use to set and administer prices for services.

The chapter also discusses common pricing structures including (1) cost-based, (2) competition-based, and (3) demand-based pricing. One of the most important aspects of demand-based pricing is perceived value, which must be understood by service providers so that they price in line with offerings and customer expectations. For that reason, we also describe how customers define value and discuss pricing strategies in the context of value.

THREE KEY WAYS THAT SERVICE PRICES ARE DIFFERENT FOR CONSUMERS

What role does price play in consumer decisions about services? How important is price to potential buyers compared with other factors and service features? Service companies must understand how pricing works, but first they must understand how customers perceive prices and price changes. The three sections that follow describe what we know about the ways that customers perceive services, and each is central to effective pricing.

Customer Knowledge of Service Prices

To what extent do customers use price as a criterion in selecting services? How much do consumers know about the costs of services? Before you answer these questions,

Exhibit 17.1 What Do You Know about the Prices of Services?

1. What do the following services cost in your hometown?

Dental checkup   _____

General medical checkup   _____

Legal help with a DWI (driving while
intoxicated) charge   _____

Dental braces   _____

Rental of a video or DVD for one night   _____

One hour of housecleaning   _____

Room at the Hilton   _____

Haircut   _____

Oil change and lube   _____

2. Which of the following would you select if you
needed a filling replaced in a tooth?

a. Dentist A—cost is $50, located 15 miles from your
home, wait is three weeks for an appointment and
1.5 hours in waiting room

b. Dentist B—cost is $75, located 15 miles from your
home, wait is one week for appointment and 0.5
hour in waiting room

c. Dentist C—cost is $125, located 3 miles from your
job, wait is one week for appointment and no time
in waiting room

d. Dentist D—cost is $175, located 3 miles from your
job, wait is one week for appointment and no time
in waiting room; nitrous oxide used so no pain is
involved

take the services pricing quiz in Exhibit 17.1. Were you able to fill in a price for each of the services listed? If you were able to answer the questions on the basis of memory, you have internal *reference prices* for the services. A reference price is *a price point in memory for a good or a service* and can consist of the price last paid, the price most frequently paid, or the average of all prices customers have paid for similar offerings.[2]

To see how accurate your reference prices for services are, you can compare them with the actual price of these services from the providers in your hometown. If you are like many consumers, you feel quite uncertain about your knowledge of the prices of services, and the reference prices you hold in memory for services are not generally as accurate as those you hold for goods. There are many reasons for this difference.

Service Variability Limits Knowledge

Because services are not created on a factory assembly line, service firms have great flexibility in the configurations of services they offer. Firms can conceivably offer an infinite variety of combinations and permutations, leading to complex and complicated pricing structures. As an example, consider how difficult it is to get comparable price quotes when buying life insurance. With the multitude of types (such as whole life versus term), features (different deductibles), and variations associated with customers (age, health risk, smoking or nonsmoking), few insurance companies offer exactly the same features and the same prices. Only an expert customer, one who knows enough about insurance to completely specify the options across providers, is likely to find prices that are directly comparable.

How did you answer the questions about prices for a medical checkup? If you are like most consumers, you probably wanted more information before you offered a reference price. You probably wanted to know what type of checkup the physician is providing. Does it include X-rays and other diagnostic tests? What types of tests? How long does the checkup take? What is its purpose? If the checkup is undertaken simply to get a signature on a health form or a marriage certificate, the doctor may take a brief medical history, listen for a heartbeat, and measure blood pressure. If, however, the checkup is to monitor a chronic ailment such as diabetes or high blood pressure, the doctor may be more thorough. The point we want to illustrate here is that a high degree of variability often exists across providers of services. Not every physician defines a checkup the same way.

Providers Are Unwilling to Estimate Prices

Another reason customers lack accurate reference prices for services is that many providers are unable or unwilling to estimate price in advance. For example, legal and medical service providers are rarely willing—or even able—to estimate a price in advance. The fundamental reason is that they do not know themselves what the services will involve until they have fully examined the patient or the client's situation or until the process of service delivery (such as an operation in a hospital or a trial) unfolds. Most hospitals contend that their fee schedules, called chargemasters, should not be made available to patients beforehand, and have fought to keep them private.[3] In a business-to-business context, companies will obtain bids or estimates for complex services such as consulting or construction, but this type of price estimation is typically not undertaken with end consumers; therefore, they often buy without advance knowledge about the final price of the service.

Individual Customer Needs Vary

Another factor that results in the inaccuracy of reference prices is that individual customer needs vary. Some hairstylists' service prices vary across customers on the basis of length of hair, type of haircut, and whether a conditioning treatment and style are included. Therefore, if you were to ask a friend what a cut costs from a particular stylist, chances are that your cut from the same stylist may be a different price. In a similar vein, a service as simple as a hotel room will have prices that vary greatly: by size of room, time of year, type of room availability, and individual versus group rate. These two examples are for very simple services. Now consider a service purchase as idiosyncratic as braces from a dentist or help from a lawyer. In these and many other services, customer differences in need will play a strong role in the price of the service.

Collection of Price Information Is Overwhelming in Services

Still another reason customers lack accurate reference prices for services is that customers feel overwhelmed with the information they need to gather. With most goods, retail stores display the products by category to allow customers to compare and contrast the prices of different brands and sizes. Rarely is there a similar display of services in a single outlet. If customers want to compare prices (such as for dry cleaning), they must drive to or call individual outlets. This can be an overwhelming task for consumers, even for the most basic services, as we illustrated in our price quiz.

When services are more specialized, finding out what they cost is even more difficult, See if you have reference prices for the these providers: wedding adviser, pet chiropractor, baby-proofing expert, and executive coach. We expect that your reference prices—if you can even come up with some—are even more uncertain and less accurate than for the services in the price quiz in Exhibit 17.1. Here are estimates from actual consultants: $5,500 for a wedding adviser's attention to all details, $70 to $140 a visit for chiropractic adjustment for pets, $300 to $450 to protect a house for and from a baby, and $1,300 for four hours of executive coaching.[4]

Here's one final test about reference prices. Suppose you were having a birthday party and wanted a celebrity—say, Chris Rock or Rod Stewart—to perform. Do you know what celebrities charge for a performance? *Us Weekly* reports these going rates for private performances or appearances:[5]

Mariah Carey private performance	$1,000,000
Usher private performance	$1,000,000
Dr. Phil speech	$750,000 – $1,000,000
Nicole Kidman party appearance	$500,000 + jet
Jessica Simpson private performance	$400,000
Scarlett Johansson party appearance	$200,000
Demi Moore party appearance	$200,000
Nick Lachey party appearance	$100,000 (negotiable)
Pam Anderson party appearance	$75,000 – $250,000
Adrian Grenier private performance with band	$35,000
Tara Reid party appearance	$10,000 – $50,000

The fact that consumers often possess inaccurate reference prices for services has several important managerial implications. Promotional pricing (as in couponing or special pricing) may be less meaningful for services, for which price anchors typically do not exist. Perhaps that is why price is not featured in service advertising as much as it is featured in advertising for goods. Promotional pricing may also create problems if the promotional price (such as a $50 permanent wave special from a salon) is the only one customers see in advertising: it could become the customer's anchor price, making the regular price of $75 for a future purchase seem high by comparison.

The absence of accurate reference prices also suggests that advertising actual prices for services the customer is not used to purchasing may reduce uncertainty and overcome a customer's inflated price expectations for some services. For example, a marketing research firm's advertisements citing the price for a simple study (such as $10,000) would be informative to business customers who are not familiar with the costs of research studies and therefore would be guessing at the cost. By featuring price in advertising, the company overcomes the fear of high cost by giving readers a price anchor.

Prices Are Not Visible

One requirement for the existence of customer reference prices is *price visibility*—the price cannot be hidden or implicit. In many services, particularly financial services, most customers know about only the rate of return and not the costs they pay in the form of fund and insurance fees. In securities and term life insurance, customers are made aware of fees. However, price is invisible in certificates, whole-life insurance, and annuities (which have rear-load charges), and customers rarely know how they are charged or what they pay. Credit card fees are assessed on the basis of what consumers spend, and while customers may know their interest rates they are often shocked at what they are spending in fees to the financial institutions. Compounding and other financial practices—such as compressed periods to pay and dramatic increases in interest rates due to late payments—do not affect their costs until after they have made purchases.

For all the reasons discussed here, many customers do not see the price at all until *after* they receive certain services. Of course in situations of urgency, such as in accident or illness, customers must make the decision to purchase without respect to cost.

And if cost is not known to the customer before purchase, it cannot be used as a key criterion for purchase, as it often is for goods.

The Role of Nonmonetary Costs

Economists have long recognized that monetary price is not the only sacrifice consumers make to obtain products and services. Demand, therefore, is not just a function of monetary price but is influenced by other costs as well. Nonmonetary costs represent other sources of sacrifice perceived by consumers when buying and using a service. Time costs, search costs, and psychological costs often enter into the evaluation of whether to buy or rebuy a service and may at times be more important concerns than monetary price. Customers will trade money for these other costs.

Time Costs

Most services require direct participation of the consumer and thus consume real time: time waiting as well as time when the customer interacts with the service provider. Consider the investment you make to exercise, see a physician, or get through the crowds to watch a concert or baseball game. Not only are you paying money to receive these services, but you are also expending time. Time becomes a sacrifice made to receive service in multiple ways. First, because service providers cannot completely control the number of customers or the length of time it will take for each customer to be served, customers are likely to expend time waiting to receive the service. The average waiting time in physicians' offices is 20.2 minutes, according to the American Medical Association.[6] Waiting time for a service is frequently longer and less predictable than waiting time to buy goods. Second, customers often wait for an available appointment from a service provider (in the price quiz, dentist A required a three-week wait, whereas dentist D required only one week). Virtually everyone has expended waiting time to receive services.

Customers will trade money for time savings. Customers who purchase lawn care, housekeeping, and other services often do so because the value of their time is higher than the value of money.

Search Costs

Search costs—the effort invested to identify and select among services you desire—are often higher for services than for physical goods. Prices for services are rarely displayed on shelves of service establishments for customers to examine as they shop, so these prices are often known only when a customer has decided to experience the service. As an example, how well did you estimate the costs of an hour of housecleaning in the price quiz? As a student, it is unlikely that you regularly purchase housecleaning, and you probably have not seen the price of an hour of cleaning displayed in any retail store. Another factor that increases search costs is that each service establishment typically offers only one "brand" of a service (with the exception of brokers in insurance or financial services), so a customer must initiate contact with several different companies to get information across sellers. Price comparisons for many services (e.g., travel and hotels) are now facilitated through the Internet, reducing search costs. Orbitz and Travelocity, for example, offer customers a search of most airlines (with the notable exception of Southwest, which does not participate in reservation services), many hotels, and rental car companies.

Convenience Costs

There are also convenience (or, perhaps more accurately, inconvenience) costs of services. If customers have to travel to receive a service, they incur a cost, and the cost becomes greater when travel is difficult, as it is for elderly persons. Further, if a service provider's hours do not coincide with customers' available time, they must arrange their schedules to correspond to the company's schedule. And if consumers have to expend effort and time to prepare to receive a service (such as removing all food from kitchen cabinets in preparation for an exterminator's spraying), they make additional sacrifices.

Psychological Costs

Often the most painful nonmonetary costs are the psychological costs incurred in receiving some services. Fear of not understanding (insurance), fear of rejection (bank loans), and fear of outcomes (medical treatment or surgery), for example, all constitute psychological costs that customers experience as sacrifices when purchasing and using services. New services, even those that create positive change, bring about psychological costs that consumers factor into the purchase of services. When banks first introduced ATMs, customer resistance was significant, particularly to the idea of putting money into a machine: customers felt uncomfortable with the idea of letting go of their checks and bank cards. Direct deposit, a clear improvement in banking service for the elderly with limited mobility, was viewed with suspicion until the level of comfort improved. And most customers rejected voice mail when it was first developed.

Reducing Nonmonetary Costs

The managerial implications of these other sources of sacrifice are compelling. First, a firm may be able to increase monetary price by reducing time and other costs. For example, a services marketer can reduce the perceptions of time and convenience costs when use of the service is embedded in other activities (such as when a convenience store cashes checks, sells stamps, and serves coffee along with selling products). Second, customers may be willing to pay to avoid the other costs. Many customers willingly pay extra to have items delivered to their home—including restaurant meals or bedroom furniture—rather than transporting the services and products themselves.

Some customers also pay a premium for fast check-in and checkout (as in joining the Hertz #1 club), for reduced waiting time in a professional's office (as in so-called executive appointments where, for a premium price, a busy executive comes early in the morning and does not have to wait), and to avoid doing the work themselves (such as paying one and one-half times the price per gallon to avoid having to put gas in a rental car before returning it). If time or other costs are pivotal for a given service, the company's advertising can emphasize these savings rather than monetary savings.

Many other services save time, thus actually allowing the customer to "buy" time. Household cleaning services, lawn care, babysitting, personal shopper service, online banking, home delivery of groceries, house painting, and carpet cleaning—all these services represent net gains in the discretionary time of consumers and can be marketed that way. Services that allow the customer to buy time are likely to have monetary value for busy consumers.

Price as an Indicator of Service Quality

One of the intriguing aspects of pricing is that buyers are likely to use price as an indicator of both service costs and service quality—price is at once an attraction variable and a repellent.[7] Customers' use of price as an indicator of quality depends on several factors, one of which is the other information available to them. When service cues to quality are readily accessible, when brand names provide evidence of a company's reputation, or when the level of advertising communicates the company's belief in the brand, customers may prefer to use those cues instead of price. In other situations, however, such as when quality is hard to detect or when quality or price varies a great deal within a class of services, consumers may believe that price is the best indicator of quality. Many of these conditions typify situations that face consumers when purchasing services.[8] Another factor that increases the dependence on price as a quality indicator is the risk associated with the service purchase. In high-risk situations, many of which involve credence services such as medical treatment or management consulting, the customer will look to price as a surrogate for quality.

Because customers depend on price as a cue to quality and because price sets expectations of quality, service prices must be determined carefully. In addition to being chosen to cover costs or match competitors, prices must be selected to convey the appropriate quality signal. Pricing too low can lead to inaccurate inferences about the quality of the service. Pricing too high can set expectations that may be difficult to match in service delivery.

APPROACHES TO PRICING SERVICES

Rather than repeat what you learned about pricing in your marketing principles class, we want to emphasize in this chapter the way that services prices and pricing differ from both the customer's and the company's perspective. We discuss these differences in the context of the three pricing structures typically used to set prices: (1) cost-based, (2) competition-based, and (3) demand-based pricing. These categories, as shown in Figure 17.1, are the same bases on which goods prices are set, but adaptations must be made in services. The figure shows the three structures interrelating because companies need to consider each of the three to some extent in setting prices. In the following sections, we describe in general each basis for pricing and discuss challenges that occur when the approach is used in services pricing. Figure 17.1 summarizes those challenges.

FIGURE 17.1
Three Basic Marketing Price Structures and Challenges Associated with Their Use for Services

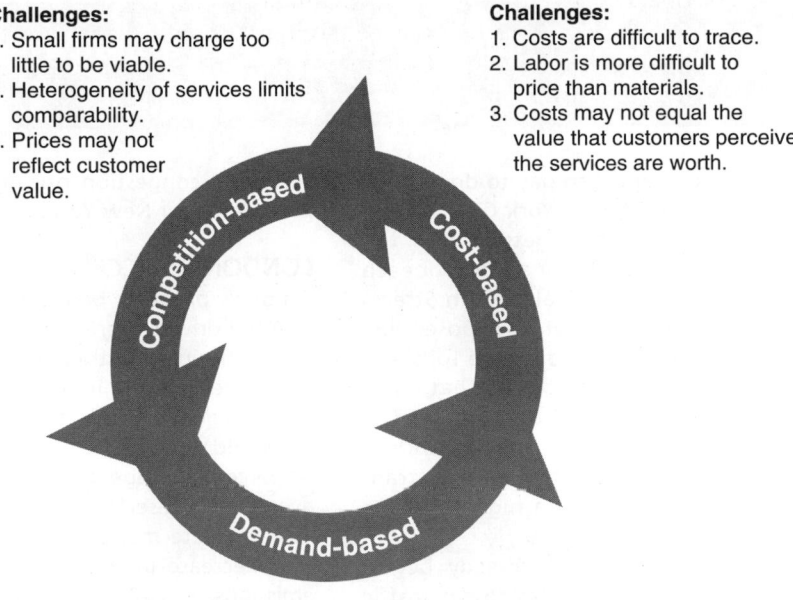

Challenges:
1. Small firms may charge too little to be viable.
2. Heterogeneity of services limits comparability.
3. Prices may not reflect customer value.

Challenges:
1. Costs are difficult to trace.
2. Labor is more difficult to price than materials.
3. Costs may not equal the value that customers perceive the services are worth.

Challenges:
1. Monetary price must be adjusted to reflect the value of nonmonetary costs.
2. Information on service costs is less available to customers; hence, price may not be a central factor.

Cost-Based Pricing

In cost-based pricing, a company determines expenses from raw materials and labor, adds amounts or percentages for overhead and profit, and thereby arrives at the price. This method is widely used by industries such as utilities, contracting, wholesaling, and advertising. The basic formula for cost-based pricing is

$$\text{Price} = \text{Direct costs} + \text{Overhead costs} + \text{Profit margin}$$

Direct costs involve materials and labor that are associated with delivering the service, overhead costs are a share of fixed costs, and the profit margin is a percentage of full costs (Direct + Overhead).

Special Challenges in Cost-Based Pricing for Services

What is unique about services when using cost-based approaches to pricing? First, costs are difficult to trace or calculate in services businesses, particularly where multiple services are provided by the firm.[9] Consider how difficult it must be for a bank to allocate teller time accurately across its checking, savings, and money market accounts to decide what to charge for the services. Second, a major component of cost is employee time rather than materials, and the value of people's time, particularly nonprofessional time, is not easy to calculate or estimate. One of the major difficulties in cost-based pricing involves defining the units in which a service is purchased. Thus the *price per unit*—a well-understood concept in pricing of manufactured goods—is a vague entity. For this reason many services are sold in terms of input units rather than units of measured output. For example, most professional services (such as consulting, engineering, architecture, psychotherapy, and tutoring) are sold by the hour.

Strategy Insight   "Congestion Pricing" as a Strategy to Change Driving Behavior in Big Cities

How much would you expect to pay to drive a car or truck into the center of New York City? If New York's Mayor Michael Bloomberg gets his wish, the fees will be $8 for a car and $21 for a truck for each weekday trip into the "zone" (below 86th Street) in Manhattan. These fees will not be imposed just to raise money, as most road and bridge tolls are, but instead to limit the number of cars that enter the city and thereby to reduce congestion. The purpose of congestion pricing is to signal to drivers when they should consider taking mass transit, reschedule their trip, or pay a higher fee for driving.

Cities around the world have already begun to use congestion pricing strategies to cut traffic in their urban centers and along heavily used corridors. Cities like London, with dense central business districts, charge motorists when they enter the cities' centers and induce them, through fees, to avoid driving into the city during peak times or to use alternative transportation. London, Singapore, Stockholm, and Norway have all implemented successful congestion pricing strategies and offer precedents for New York.

LONDON'S SUCCESS

London's program began in 2003 when they first charged drivers a premium to enter the city's gridlocked business district. While policymakers knew the strategy would improve economic competitiveness and quality of life, they were less sure that drivers would respond. Results, however, were dramatic: 30 percent average drop in congestion, 37 percent average increase in traffic speed, 12 percent drop in particulate matter and nitrogen oxides, 20 percent decrease in fossil fuel consumption and CO_2 emissions, and 20 percent increase in use of public transportation. Besides reducing congestion, London raised hundreds of millions of dollars in new revenue that it invested in better transit. Perhaps even more encouraging is that 78 percent of drivers who pay to enter the cordon area are satisfied with the system, and the system was reinstated in August 2007.

An added difficulty is that actual service costs may underrepresent the value of the service to the customer. A local tailor charges $10 for taking in a seam on a $350 ladies' suit jacket and an equal $10 for taking in a seam on a pair of $14 sweat shorts. The tailor's rationale is that both jobs require the same amount of time. What she neglects to see is that the customer would pay a higher price—and might even be happier about the alterations—for the expensive suit jacket, and that $10 is too high a price for the sweat shorts.

Examples of Cost-Based Pricing Strategies Used in Services

Cost-plus pricing is a commonly used approach in which component costs are calculated and a markup added. In product pricing, this approach is quite simple; in service industries, however, it is complicated because the tracking and identification of costs are difficult. The approach is typically used in industries in which cost must be estimated in advance, such as construction, engineering, and advertising. In construction or engineering, bids are solicited by clients on the basis of the description of the service desired. Using their knowledge of the costs of the components of the service (including the raw materials such as masonry and lumber), labor (including both professional and unskilled), and margin, the company estimates and presents to the client a price for the finished service. A contingency amount—to cover the possibility that costs may be higher than estimated—is also stated because, in large projects, specifications can change as the service is provided.

Fee for service is the pricing strategy used by professionals; it represents the cost of the time involved in providing the service. Consultants, psychologists, accountants,

STOCKHOLM'S TRIAL LEADS TO CUSTOMER ACCEPTANCE

Stockholm, Sweden, tried the pricing approach, which it called "cordon pricing," for the first half of 2006. The impact on public opinion as a result of the trail is impressive. Before the trial, only 31 percent of residents were in favor of the strategy. After a 15 percent reduction in traffic and a 10 to 14 percent drop in CO_2 emissions, however, voters were far more favorable, and they passed a referendum to reinstate the charge. A recent poll says 67 percent of respondents now agree that it is good that the government introduced the system.

NEW YORK'S PLAN

The New York City pricing plan would charge $8 daily on cars entering or leaving Manhattan below 86th Street ("the zone") between 6 a.m. and 6 p.m., Monday through Friday; trucks would pay $21 per day. There would be no charge on weekends, and no charge to drive in downtown parts of the city outside the zone. Taxis, vehicles with handicapped plates, buses, and emergency vehicles would not pay the fees. Bridge or tunnel tolls would be subtracted from the daily total. The federal government, which recently awarded the city a $350 million grant to help the city reduce traffic congestion, has made the congestion pricing mechanism a condition that must be met by a specified deadline. The three-year pilot program is projected to raise $400 million each year, which would be dedicated to regional transportation investments. Proposed benefits of the plan include the same benefits realized by plans in other big cities—improving the health of New Yorkers due to reduced emissions, reducing street noise, increasing ridership on public transportation, and improving productivity.

Sources: "Congestion Pricing: A Smart Solution for Reducing Traffic in Urban Centers and Busy Corridors," www.environmentaldefense.org, 2007; Drum Major Institute for Public Policy, "Congestion Pricing: Good Policy for New York's Middle Class," *DMI Report 2007*, www.drummajorinstitute.org; "A Bonus for Congestion Pricing," *New York Times Digest*, August 15, 2007, p. 7; and E. Thornton and M. Arndt, "Fees! Fees! Fees!" *BusinessWeek*, September 29, 2003.

and lawyers, among other professionals, charge for their services on an hourly basis. Virtually all psychologists and social workers have a set hourly rate they charge to their clients, and most structure their time in increments of an hour.

In the early 1900s, lawyers typically billed clients a certain fee for services rendered regardless of the amount of time they spent delivering them. Then in the 1970s, law firms began to bill on an hourly rate, in part because this approach offered accountability to clients and an internal budgeting system for the firm. One of the most difficult aspects of this approach is that recordkeeping is tedious for professionals. Lawyers and accountants must keep track of the time they spend for a given client, often down to 10-minute increments. For this reason the method has been criticized because it does not promote efficiency and sometimes ignores the expertise of the lawyers (those who are very experienced can accomplish much more than novices in a given time period, yet billings do not always reflect this). Clients also feared padding of their legal bills and began to audit them. Despite these concerns, the hourly bill dominates the industry, with the majority of revenues billed this way.[10]

Competition-Based Pricing

The competition-based pricing approach focuses on the prices charged by other firms in the same industry or market. Competition-based pricing does not always imply charging the identical rate others charge but rather using others' prices as an anchor for the firm's price. This approach is used predominantly in two situations: (1) when services are standard across providers, such as in the dry cleaning industry, and (2) in oligopolies with a few large service providers, such as in the airline or rental car

Global Feature   Unique Pricing around the World

TIPPING

A Cornell University study revealed an interesting fact about tipping: The custom of tipping is more prevalent in countries where citizens value status and prestige than in countries where they do not. Michael Lynn found that the number of service professionals tipped is relatively small in countries where citizens value recognition and esteem less. "Tipping is really a form of conspicuous consumption. We tip more people in this country because we value status. Americans value recognition and esteem, and we receive that when we tip these service professionals."

One measure of the differences in tipping is the number of service professionals who are given tips in different countries. The United States leads the list with about 35 different professions. Other countries that place a high value on recognition and esteem also tip a large number of professionals. These include Spain (29), Canada (25), India (25), and Italy (24). In contrast, in Denmark and Sweden, the number of tipped professionals is less than 10, reflecting the lower value placed on recognition and esteem in these countries. Tipping is not practiced at all in 11 countries: Brunei, Malaysia, Japan, Oman, New Zealand, Samoa, Singapore, South Korea, Thailand, United Arab Emirates, and Vietnam.

Magellan's, the company that sells travel supplies from two retail stores and a website, provides the following general regional tipping "tips" in a guide:

- In *Asia and the Pacific,* tipping could be considered insulting, and it is best not to tip.
- In *Europe,* many hotels and restaurants add a service charge to the bill, making an additional tip unnecessary.
- In the *Middle East and Africa,* tips will not be seen as insulting but are unnecessary.
- In *Central and South America,* most restaurants and hotels add a service charge, making an additional tip unnecessary.

Magellan's guide details tipping standards for 70 countries, excerpts of which are presented here.

Country	Waiter/Waitress	Porter	Taxi Driver
Australia	10% in fine restaurants only	$2 per bag	Round up to next unit of local currency
Costa Rico	None	$1 per bag	None
Denmark	None	$1 per bag	Round up
Greece	5 to 10% plus service charge	$1 per bag	Round up
Japan	None	None	None
Romania	Round up bill	$1 per bag	Roup up
Venezuala	10%	75 ¢ per bag	10%
Spain	7 to 10% plus service charge	$1 per bag	10%

industry. Difficulties involved in provision of services sometimes make competition-based pricing less simple than it is in goods industries.

Special Challenges in Competition-Based Pricing for Services

Competition-based pricing, commonly practiced in good firms, can be difficult for service firms. Small firms may find it difficult to charge the same prices that larger service firms charge and make margins high enough to remain in business. Many mom-and-pop service establishments—dry cleaning, retail, and tax accounting, among others—cannot deliver services at the low prices charged by chain operations.

Further, the heterogeneity of services across and within providers makes this approach complicated. As an example, banks offer many different types of accounts and services that differ from each other. To try to determine how a competitive bank prices for individual accounts and may differ in features and costs—and whether those prices give sufficient margins and profits—can be difficult. Only in very standardized

PRICELESS

Several restaurants in different parts of the world have a extraordinary approach to pricing which might best be called voluntary pricing. These restaurants allow customers to pay whatever they think the meal is worth. A London restaurant called Just Around the Corner has found the policy to be extremely successful since it was started in 1986, with most customers paying more for their meals than the restaurant would charge if it set the prices. Customers average £25 ($41) for a three-course dinner, but some are especially careful to pay enough. "One night, four American government officials handed over nearly $1,000 for a meal worth less than $200. They asked if they had left enough." The owner, Michael Vasos, claims, "I make more money from this restaurant than from any of my other [four] establishments." He thinks his customers' generosity accounts for the success of the restaurant and its pricing policies, although others state that the fear of embarrassment common to the English prevents patrons from paying too little.

"Eat as you want, give as you feel," is the concept on which Annalakshmt, a group of restaurants in Singapore, Kuala Lumpur, Penang, Chennair, Coimbatore, and Perth. "We believe in you, we trust you." The restaurant contends. Its principal motive is service, rather than profit, and it is run by volunteers who choose to cook, clean, serve, and wash dishes because they "find joy in the underlying philosophy of serve, love, and give." The restaurant asks customers to eat first, then pay whatever comes to mind. As they claim, "There is no right or wrong amount for the meal you had in Annalaksmi. We gratefully accept whatever it is."

PAY BY THE MINUTE IN TOKYO

Some restaurants in Japan are charging for dinner according to how quickly customers eat. At Dai-ichi Hotel Tokyo Seafort, diners punch a time clock when they start their meals, then pay 25 cents per minute until they clock out. Fast diners—like two young girls who gulped down platefuls of cake in 10 minutes and paid only $3—can get bargain meals. Perhaps that is why the restaurant is popular among college students! Other franchise restaurants throughout Japan put time limits on their all-you-can-eat buffets. Prices range from $10 an hour to $100 for 90 minutes. During that time, diners can consume unlimited quantities of top-quality sushi or shabu shabu, a Japanese specialty consisting of thin slices of beef cooked in boiling broth. At one restaurant, Mo Mo Paradise in Tokyo, for example, diners can pay $13.50 to eat for 90 minutes or $30 to eat as much as they want for as long as they want.

Sources: Andrea Sachs, "Eat All You Want; Pay by the Minute," *Washington Post*, September 26, 1999, p. H3; © 1999, *The Washington Post*, Reprinted with permission. "Study Examines Tipping," *Hotel and Motel Management*, March 17, 1997, p. 14; B. Ortega, "Priceless," *People*, February 15, 1999, p. 114; I. Wall, "It May Be a Dog-Eat-Dog World, But This Restaurant Won't Prove It," *The Wall Street Journal*, December 11, 1998, p. B1; www.londonrestaurantreview.com, July 23, 2007; G. Stoller, "Tipping Can Trip Up Any Globe Trotter," *USA Today*, September 11, 2007; and www.Magellan.com., accessed September 2007.

services that a bank provides, such at ATM surcharges, can banks benefit from competitive prices. In 2007, Bank of America made headlines by raising ATM withdrawal charges for noncustomers to $3 per withdrawal. Other banks like Citi, Chase, Wachovia, and Wells Fargo did not immediately match the increase, but did comment that they review what their competitors do in setting prices.[11]

Examples of Competition-Based Pricing in Services Industries

Price signaling occurs in markets with a high concentration of sellers. In this type of market, any price offered by one company will be matched by competitors to avoid giving a low-cost seller a distinct advantage. The airline industry exemplifies price signaling in services. When any competitor drops the price of routes, others match the lowered price almost immediately.

Going-rate pricing involves charging the most prevalent price in the market. Rental car pricing is an illustration of this technique (and also an illustration of price signaling, because the rental car market is dominated by a small number of large companies). For years, the prices set by one company (Hertz) have been followed by the other companies. When Hertz instituted a new pricing plan that involved "no mileage charges, ever," other rental car companies imitated the policy. They then had to raise other factors such as base rates, size and type of car, daily or weekly rates, and drop-off charges to continue to make profits. Prices in different geographic markets, even cities, depend on the going rate in that location, and customers often pay different rates in contiguous cities in the same state. The Global Feature in this chapter illustrates some of the practices in pricing that differ across countries.

Demand-Based Pricing

The two approaches to pricing just described are based on the company and its competitors rather than on customers. Neither approach takes into consideration that customers may lack reference prices, may be sensitive to nonmonetary prices, and may judge quality on the basis of price. All these factors can be accounted for in a company's pricing decisions. The third major approach to pricing, *demand-based pricing,* involves setting prices consistent with customer perceptions of value: prices are based on what customers will pay for the services provided.

Special Challenges in Demand-Based Pricing for Services

One of the major ways that pricing of services differs from pricing of goods in demand-based pricing is that nonmonetary costs and benefits must be factored into the calculation of perceived value to the customer. When services require time, inconvenience, psychological and search costs, the monetary price must be adjusted to compensate. And when services save time, inconvenience psychological and search costs, the customer is willing to pay a higher monetary price. The challenge is to determine the value to customers of each of the nonmonetary aspects involved.

Another way services and goods differ with respect to this form of pricing is that information on service costs may be less available to customers, making monetary price not as salient a factor in initial service selection as it is in goods purchasing.

Four Meanings of Perceived Value

One of the most appropriate ways that companies price their services is basing the price on the perceived value of the service to customers. Among the questions a services marketer needs to ask are the following: What do consumers mean by *value?* How can we quantify perceived value in dollars so that we can set appropriate prices for our services? Is the meaning of value similar across consumers and services? How can value perceptions be influenced? To understand demand-based pricing approaches, we must fully understand what value means to customers.

This is not a simple task. When consumers discuss value, they use the term in many different ways and talk about myriad attributes or components. What constitutes value, even in a single service category, appears to be highly personal and idiosyncratic. Customers define value in four ways

1. Value is low price.
2. Value is whatever I want in a product or service.
3. Value is the quality I get for the price I pay.
4. Value is what I get for what I give (Figure 17.2).[12]

Let us take a look at each of these definitions more carefully.

FIGURE 17.2
Four Customer
Definitions of Value

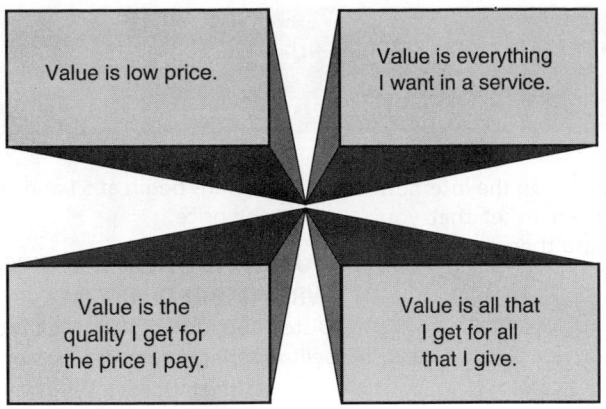

Value is low price.

Value is everything
I want in a service.

Value is the
quality I get for
the price I pay.

Value is all that
I get for all
that I give.

Value Is Low Price   Some consumers equate value with low price, indicating that what they have to give up in terms of money is most salient in their perceptions of value, as typified in these representative comments from customers:

For dry cleaning: "Value means the lowest price."

For carpet steam cleaning: "Value is price—which one is on sale."

For a fast-food restaurant: "When I can use coupons, I feel that the service is a value."

For airline travel: "Value is when airline tickets are discounted."[13]

Value Is Whatever I Want in a Product or Service   Rather than focusing on the money given up, some consumers emphasize the benefits they receive from a service or product as the most important component of value. In this value definition, price is far less important than the quality or features that match what the consumer wants. In the telecommunications industry, for example, business customers strongly value the reliability of the systems and are willing to pay for the safety and confidentiality of the connections. Service customers describe this definition of value as follows:

For an MBA degree: "Value is the very best education I can get."

For medical services: "Value is high quality."

For a social club: "Value is what makes me look good to my friends and family."

For a rock or country music concert: "Value is the best performance."

For a hotel room for a honeymoon: "Value is a luxurious room with a hot tub."

Value Is the Quality I Get for the Price I Pay   Other consumers see value as a trade-off between the money they give up and the quality they receive.

For a hotel for vacation: "Value is price first and quality second."

For a hotel for business travel: "Value is the lowest price for a quality brand."

For a computer services contract: "Value is the same as quality. No—value is affordable quality."

Value Is What I Get for What I Give   Finally, some consumers consider all the benefits they receive as well as all sacrifice components (money, time, effort) when describing value.

For a housekeeping service: "Value is how many rooms I can get cleaned for what the price is."

Technology Spotlight Dynamic Pricing on the Internet Allows Price Adjustments Based on Supply and Demand

When shopping for an airline ticket on the Internet, have you ever found a low-priced ticket that you did not purchase immediately, and then returned to the site four hours later to find the same ticket had increased $100 in price? This experience is *dynamic pricing* in action—the buying and selling of goods in markets in which prices move quickly in response to supply and demand fluctuations. In the case of your airline ticket, chances are that other travelers had purchased tickets at the original low price, reducing the airlines' inventory and allowing the airline to gamble on getting customers to buy the remaining seats at higher prices.

Dynamic pricing is estimated to account for more than 40 percent of total online transactions. The approach—often incorporating auctions and other forms of online bidding—is typically used at the end of the supply chain to eliminate surplus inventory or perishable service capacity, as with airline seats. Dynamic pricing has allowed companies to generate significant revenue from excess supply or discontinued products, which they previously turned over to intermediaries. In the past, liquidators would receive unsold services, getting five cents on the dollar in liquidation fees in addition to whatever they could get from reselling the products. Not only did the firm not receive revenue from the sale of the services, but it would also have to pay for liquidation services.

AUCTIONS: EBAY AND 1,500 RIVALS

Online auctions represent dynamic pricing because customers pay what they are willing and they compete with each other on the goods they desire. In 1995, eBay pioneered the Internet auction, but more than 3,000 websites now offer person-to-person online trading. Market leader eBay offers thousands of new items for auction each day and reported net income of $1.25 billion in 2006. Whereas eBay focuses on consumer-to-consumer transactions, uBid.com acts as a consignment house for manufacturers selling directly to customers. Founded in 1997, uBid offers leading manufacturers' merchandise to consumers and businesses at prices lower than wholesale. Most uBid auctions begin at $1 and allow market dynamics to set the price.

DUTCH AUCTIONS: KLIK-KLOK.COM, WRHAMBRECHT.COM

Dutch auctions, which originated in Netherlands for selling services such as insurance or perishable items such as tulips, reverse the typical auction in that the prices go down as the auction progresses. Also unlike typical auctions, in which one of a particular type of product is sold at a given time, in Dutch auctions multiple—albeit limited—quantities of the same services are sold at the same time. The duration of the auction is very short, and the price drops rapidly over this time. At any given time (or price point), a bidder can stop the clock by bidding at the instantaneous price. The bid with time, price, and quantity is then recorded. This bidding continues until all bids have been received. At that point all winning bidders pay the same price, which is the lowest "successful" bid. The catch here is that there is a limited supply of each product. As the clock progresses and the remaining available inventory decreases, the nonbidders (those waiting for the lowest selling price) risk not getting their desired quantities.

REVERSE AUCTIONS: HOTWIRE.COM AND PRICELINE.COM

Reverse auctions are used on the buy-side, allowing buyers to see the lowest bid, but they do not identify the buyer or the seller. The brand or identity of the seller is revealed only if the seller decides to accept the bid offered by the buyer. An advantage for buyers is that they do not need to guess at the price and can receive the same products and services offered elsewhere with static prices at significant discounts. A disadvantage is that although buyers see a rating of the seller, they cannot be sure who the seller is and what the service outcome will be. The brand is eliminated as a signal of quality. Furthermore, the buyer has to sacrifice controls over some aspects of the service that is being consumed. For instance, on Priceline.com, the buyer does not have full control over time of the flights.

GROUP BUYING: ONLINECHOICE.COM, HAPPYMANY.COM

Group buying sites such as OnlineChoice.com in the United States and HappyMany.com in other parts of the world, aggregate demand for sellers. The sites offer group rates on long distance and cell phone service, automobile and term life insurance, and mortgages. The concept behind this form of dynamic pricing is that the greater the number of people who want to buy products, the lower the price will be for everyone. Sellers generally bucket the prices of the product being sold based on the number of buyers. For example, for 0 to 10 buyers, the price for each buyer is $100; for 10 to 20 buyers, the price for each buyer is $95, and so on. Word of mouth is critical, because interested buyers are encouraged to enlist their friends and relatives to get a cheaper price for the whole group. Sellers motivate this action by placing an "Invite Your Friend" icon right next to the service or price information. Advantages of this form of dynamic pricing are that the price decreases as a greater number of people bid, and the exact service and its specifications are known to buyers when bidding.

FINDING THE LOWEST PRICE ACROSS INTERNET SITES: BUY.COM

Buy.com's slogan is "lowest prices on Earth." The Internet allows consumers to do quick price comparisons, and Buy.com wants to make sure its services and products end up being the lowest prices in everyone's search. To deliver on its promises, Buy.com uses software to monitor price changes for products on competing sites. When these price changes occur, the software then recommends price adjustments to Buy.com. The process is automated, but the decision to change prices is made by a manager, usually once a day rather than moment to moment. Buy.com relies on this strategy in highly competitive online categories such as computer software. The software makes recommendations throughout the day, and decisions are made the next morning. Prices tend to fall more often than they go up.

DINING WITH DYNAMIC PRICING

Flexible, or dynamic, pricing in the restaurant industry involves changing menu prices by hour or time of day to attract diners in nonpeak hours, such as afternoons between 2 p.m. and 6 p.m. or late evenings. Restaurants may use discounts, such as 15 to 30 percent off the total check, to build traffic during off-hours. Typically, the restaurants use a "dining aggregator," a site that collects and coordinates information about all restaurants in an area that want to offer dynamic pricing. For example, www.DinnerBroker.com, a novel dynamic-pricing website, represents 1,000 restaurants in more than 50 metropolitan areas that use off-peak discount programs to gain incremental business and new customers. DinnerBroker.com has an easy-to-use graphic matrix that allows users to see on one page all participating restaurants and the discounts they offer. The site also enables customers to make online reservations and offers access to prime-time tables. To participate in these services, DinnerBroker.com requires restaurants to pay a subscription of $49 a month and $1 for every off-hour reservation booked and fulfilled by the service.

Another discount diner aggregator, iDine Rewards Network of Miami, reported a 45 percent increase in dining sales, to $255 million, generated through its consumer rewards program. Its website, www.idine.com, promotes discounts that run as high as 20 percent for particular times of day at thousands of participating restaurants.

Sources: Michael Bazeley, "eBay has Strong Earnings in Quarter," *Knight Ridder Tribune Business News,* October 21, 2004, p. 1; Georgia Perakis, "Third Informs Revenue Management and Pricing Conference," *Journal of Revenue and Pricing Management,* January 2004, p. 388; Vaidyanathan Jayaraman and Tim Baker, "The Internet as an Enabler for Dynamic Pricing of Goods," *IEEE Transactions on Engineering Management,* November 2003, p. 470; Alan J. Liddle, "Using Web for Discounting Clicks with Digital Diners," *Nation's Restaurant News,* May 19, 2003, p. 172; Christopher T. Heun, "Dynamic Pricing Boosts Bottom Line," *Informationweek,* October 29, 2001; Michael Vizard, "With So Very Few Internet Players, Is Dynamic Pricing Good for Our Economy?" *InfoWorld,* March 26, 2001; Michael Vizard, Ed Scannel, and Dan Neel, "Suppliers Toy with Dynamic Pricing," *InfoWorld,* May 14, 2001; and www.idine.com, 2007.

For a hairstylist: "Value is what I pay in cost and time for the look I get."
For executive education: "Value is getting a good educational experience in the shortest time possible."

The four consumer expressions of value can be captured in one overall definition consistent with the concept of utility in economics: *Perceived value is the consumer's overall assessment of the utility of a service based on perceptions of what is received and what is given.* Although what is received varies across consumers (some may want volume, others high quality, still others convenience), as does what is given (some are concerned only with money expended, others with time and effort), value represents a trade-off of the give-and-get components. Customers will make a purchase decision on the basis of perceived value, not solely to minimize the price paid. These definitions are the first step in identifying the elements that must be quantified in setting prices for services.

Incorporating Perceived Value into Service Pricing

The buyer's perception of total value prompts the willingness to pay a particular price for a service. To translate the customer's value perceptions into an appropriate price for a specific service offering, the marketer must answer a number of questions: What benefits does the service provide? How important is each of these benefits? How much is it worth to the customer to receive a particular benefit from a service? At what price will the service be economically acceptable to potential buyers? In what context is the customer purchasing the service?

The most important thing a company must do—and often a difficult thing—is to estimate the value to customers of the company's services.[14] Value may be perceived differently by consumers because of idiosyncratic tastes, knowledge about the service, buying power, and ability to pay. In this type of pricing, what the consumers value—not what they pay—forms the basis for pricing. Therefore, its effectiveness rests solely on accurately determining what the market perceives the service to be worth.

When the services are for the retail consumers, service providers can rarely afford to give each individual exactly the bundle of attributes valued. They will, however, attempt to find one or more bundles that address segments of the market. When individual customers are large (e.g., business-to-business customers or very large and profitable retail customers), the company may find it worthwhile to provide individual bundles to each customer.

An interesting manifestation of demand-oriented pricing is shown in the Technology Spotlight.

One of the most complex and difficult tasks of services marketers is setting prices internationally. If services marketers price on the basis of perceived value and if perceived value and willingness to pay differ across countries (which they often do), then service firms may provide essentially the same service but charge different prices in different countries.

PRICING STRATEGIES THAT LINK TO THE FOUR VALUE DEFINITIONS

In this section we describe the approaches to services pricing that are particularly suited to each of the four value definitions. Exhibit 17.2 presents research approaches to setting prices.

FIGURE 17.3
**Pricing Strategies
When the Customer
Defines Value as
Low Price**

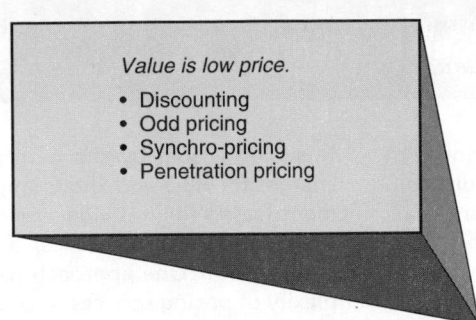

Value is low price.

- Discounting
- Odd pricing
- Synchro-pricing
- Penetration pricing

Pricing Strategies When the Customer Means "Value Is Low Price"

When monetary price is the most important determinant of value to a customer, the company focuses mainly on price. This focus does not mean that the quality level and intrinsic attributes are always irrelevant, just that monetary price dominates in importance. To establish a service price in this definition of value, the marketer must understand to what extent customers know the objective prices of services in this category, how they interpret various prices, and how much is too much of a perceived sacrifice. These factors are best understood when the service provider also knows the relative dollar size of the purchase, the frequency of past price changes, and the range of acceptable prices for the service. Some of the specific pricing approaches appropriate when customers define value as low price include discounting, odd pricing, synchro-pricing, and penetration pricing (Figure 17.3).

Discounting

Service providers offer discounts or price cuts to communicate to price-sensitive buyers that they are receiving value. Colleges are now providing many forms of discounting to attract students. Discount pricing has become a creative art at other educational institutions. The University of Rochester offered a $5,000 grant to all New York State residents enrolling as freshmen. Miami University of Ohio now lists only one tuition for *all* students (both in-state and out-of-state), but offers a discount to in-state students. The end result is that each group of students pays the same as before, but the perception is that in-state students get a discount.

Odd Pricing

Odd pricing is the practice of pricing services just below the exact dollar amount to make buyers perceive that they are getting a lower price. Dry cleaners charge $2.98 for a shirt rather than $3.00, health clubs have dues priced at $33.90 per month rather than $34, and haircuts are $9.50 rather than $10.00. Odd prices suggest discounting and bargains and are appealing to customers for whom value means low price.

Synchro-Pricing

Synchro-pricing is the use of price to manage demand for a service by capitalizing on customer sensitivity to prices. Certain services, such as tax preparation, passenger transportation, long-distance telephone, hotels, and theaters, have demand that fluctuates over time as well as constrained supply at peak times. For companies in these and other industries, setting a price that provides a profit over time can be difficult. Pricing can, however, play a role in smoothing demand and synchronizing demand and supply.

As described in this chapter, pricing a service in line with what customers perceive it is worth is often difficult. Two approaches that have gained favor in recent years are modular service pricing and service tiering.

MODULAR SERVICE PRICING

One of the reasons pricing of services is more difficult than pricing of goods is that service units are more variable and difficult to identify than units of goods. Units of goods—automobiles, jeans, gallons of milk, and microwaves—are easy to define. Units of service are more difficult, in part because they are sold by a variety of units. Information services, for example, are sold by the minute, the web page, the file (as in buying online music), or the search (as in finding and purchasing magazine articles). The services of your doctor are sold by the length and type of the visit, the test performed, the shot given, and the X rays taken. Cable television is sold by the month (basic fees, premium charges for HBO and Showtime), by the type of equipment leased (digital video recorders or DVRs, remote controls, digital cable boxes), and by the unit (pay-per-view movies). One approach to dealing with the complexity of pricing services is to develop modular service bundles.

Modular service pricing involves first identifying the basic and value-added services of a provider as components or building blocks for pricing. To create modules, the company first defines the full range of services both that could meet customer needs and for which customers will pay. In the airlines, for example, the base price is set for a seat, but customers will also pay for excess baggage, special ticketing, class of seats, animals, alcoholic beverages, and food (many airlines now offer meals on flights at different prices). Ryanair, which we discussed in our chapter opener, is perhaps the best

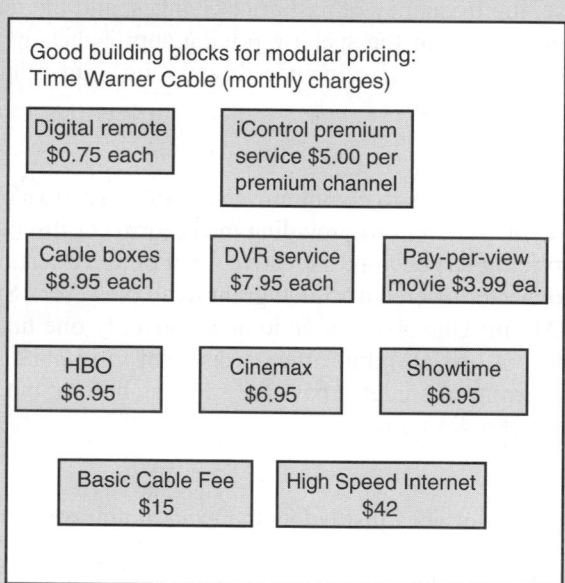

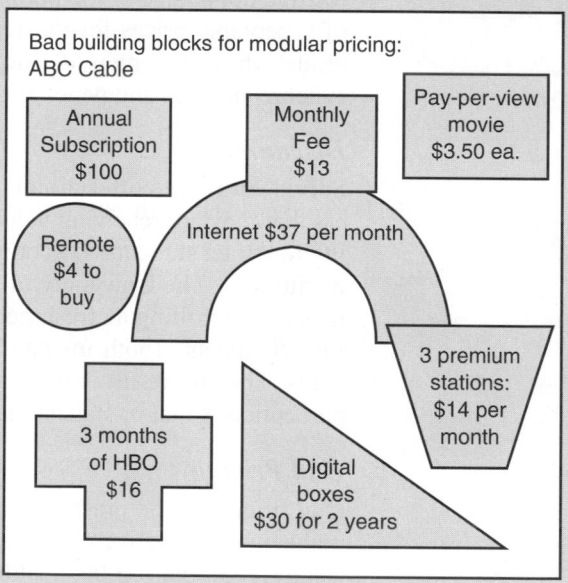

Time, place, quantity, and incentive differentials have all been used effectively by service firms, as discussed in Chapter 15.

Place differentials are used for services in which customers have a sensitivity to location. The front row at concerts, the 50-yard line in football, center court in tennis or basketball, ocean-side rooms in resort hotels—all these represent place differentials that are meaningful to customers and that therefore command higher prices.

Time differentials involve price variations that depend on when the service is consumed. Telephone service after 11 p.m., hospital rooms on weekends, and health spas

example of modular pricing in the airlines. Customers of rental car companies pay by the day but also buy additional services such as liability insurance, collision insurance, drop-off services, and refueling services. To create modular pricing, firms need:

1. Available price for each different service.
2. The ability to combine prices and services using easy rules.
3. Minimum overlap among the service elements so that customers do not pay twice or more for the same service.

Graphically, good modular pricing looks like the left side of the accompanying figure, which approximates the pricing for Time Warner's cable services. Each component has a price that is in line with customers' perceptions of the worth of that service, and the components can be selected individually by customers or combined in bundles. The right side of the figure shows poor building blocks for modular pricing—the components are in different units that are hard to combine and there appears to be overlap among them (e.g., the annual subscription and the monthly fee seem to be covering the same service, and three months of HBO and the monthly charge for three premium stations also overlap). With good modular pricing such as Time Warner's, the customers can mix or match the services and get exactly what they desire.

SERVICE TIERING

Sometimes even good modular pricing can become too complex, and simpler ways to present the company's prices are needed. *Service tiering,* usually called *versioning* when applied to the pricing of goods, involves creating a set of prices that corresponds to the price points and value bundles of different customer segments. For example, Time Warner Cable offers service tiers that correspond to service components that are typically desired together. Notice that when customers buy the bundles, they receive discounts from what the services would cost individually.

DIGIPiC 1000 (includes Basic, Standard and choice of 1 digital programming tier) $64.75
DIGIPiC 1500 (includes all services in DIGIPiC 1000 plus 1 premium channel) $75.75
DIGIPiC 2000 (includes all services in DIGIPiC 1000 plus 2 premium channels and corresponding premiums on demand) $83.75
DIGIPiC 3000 (includes all services in DIGIPiC 1000 plus 3 premium channels and corresponding premiums on demand) $91.75
DIGIPiC 4000 (includes all services in DIGIPiC 1000 plus all premiums and corresponding premiums on demand) $99.75

In general, service tiers allow customers to quickly and simply match their desires and the price they are willing to pay with an offering from the company. The customer perceives a benefit in choosing one of the tiers because each tier provides a discount over individual services. The company enjoys a benefit because customers typically buy more services when they are sold in tiers than when they are offered individually. The customer can also easily add components—for example, digital video recorders or cable boxes—to the packages, which then provides additional profit to the firm.

Modular pricing and service tiering allow the company to maximize sales from all parts of a service that the customer desires without having to create unique service bundles for each different customer.

Sources: R. Docters, M. Reopel, J. Sun, and S. Tanny, "Capturing the Unique Value of Services: Why Pricing of Services Is Different," *The Journal of Business Strategy* 25, no. 2 (2004), pp. 23–28; and Time Warner Cable price list, Durham, North Carolina, 2007.

in the off-season are time differentials that reflect slow periods of service. By offering lower prices for underused time periods, a service company can smooth demand and also gain incremental revenue.

Quantity differentials are usually price decreases given for volume purchasing. This pricing structure allows a service company to predict future demand for its services. Customers who buy a booklet of coupons for a tanning salon or facial, a quantity of tokens for public bridges, or packages of advertising spots on radio or television are all responding to price incentives achieved by committing to future services. Corporate discounts for airlines, hotels, and rental cars exemplify quantity discounts in the business context; by offering lower prices, the service provider locks in future business.

*Differentials as incentives a*re lower prices for new or existing clients in the hope of encouraging them to be regular users or more frequent users. Some professionals—lawyers, dentists, electrologists, and even some physicians—offer free consultations at the front end, usually to overcome fear and uncertainty about high service prices. Other companies stimulate use by offering regular customers discounts or premiums during slow periods. Sports teams are now using differential prices as incentives to attract customers who would otherwise not be able to afford the high cost of attending sports events. The Phoenix Suns, in claiming that "You should have pricing for every pocketbook," revamped its ticket pricing by raising premium seats by 26 percent, decreasing arena seats by 31 percent, and adding 500 $10 tickets. The net result was a 6 percent increase in the average ticket price (paid for by the premium seat holders), but more attendance at the games because more fans in different segments could afford the seats.[15]

Penetration Pricing

Penetration pricing is a strategy in which new services are introduced at low prices to stimulate trial and widespread use. The strategy is appropriate when (1) sales volume of the service is very sensitive to price, even in the early stages of introduction; (2) it is possible to achieve economies in unit costs by operating at large volumes; (3) a service faces threats of strong potential competition very soon after introduction; and (4) there is no class of buyers willing to pay a higher price to obtain the service.[16] Penetration pricing can lead to problems when companies then select a "regular" increased price. Care must be taken not to penetrate with so low a price that customers feel the regular price is outside the range of acceptable prices.

Pricing Strategies When the Customer Means "Value Is Everything I Want in a Service"

When the customer is concerned principally with the "get" components of a service, monetary price is not of primary concern. The more desirable intrinsic attributes a given service possesses, the more highly valued the service is likely to be and the higher the price the marketer can set. Figure 17.4 shows appropriate pricing strategies.

Prestige Pricing

Prestige pricing is a special form of demand-based pricing by service marketers who offer high-quality or status services. For certain services—restaurants, health clubs, airlines, and hotels—a higher price is charged for the luxury end of the business. For

FIGURE 17.4
Pricing Strategies When the Customer Defines Value as Everything Wanted in a Service

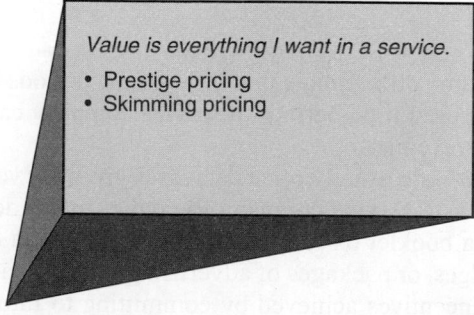

Value is everything I want in a service.
- Prestige pricing
- Skimming pricing

example, for hotel guests who crave pampering, many chains are offering club floors that add high-end amenities into their offerings for large price increases. Some of Sheraton's club floors provide a Microsoft Surface tabletop computer that lets guests order songs or download photos, as well as self-service refrigerators to help themselves to drinks and yogurt. Hyatt has cappuccino machines on club floors and is testing marble-topped tables to make it easier to work on laptops and hold meetings. Ritz-Carlton offers free lunch foods such as sandwiches and salads.[17] Some customers of service companies who use this approach may actually value the high price because it represents prestige or a quality image. Others prefer purchasing at the high end because they are given preference in seating or accommodations and are entitled to other special benefits. In prestige pricing, demand may actually increase as price increases because the costlier service has more value in reflecting quality or prestige.

Skimming Pricing

Skimming, a strategy in which new services are introduced at high prices, is an effective approach when services are major improvements over past services. In this situation, customers are more concerned about obtaining the service than about the cost of the service, allowing service providers to skim the customers most willing to pay the highest prices. Services that are related to anti-aging, such as Botox injections and new forms of laser liposuction, often are introduced at high prices, thereby attracting customers who are willing to pay more to obtain the services in the short term rather than wait until a later time when the prices might be reduced.

Pricing Strategies When the Customer Means "Value Is the Quality I Get for the Price I Pay"

Some customers primarily consider both quality and monetary price. The task of the marketer is to understand what *quality* means to the customer (or segments of customers) and then to match quality level with price level. Specific strategies are shown in Figure 17.5.

Value Pricing

The widely used term *value pricing* has come to mean "giving more for less." In current usage, it involves assembling a bundle of services that are desirable to a wide group of customers and then pricing them lower than they would cost alone. Taco Bell pioneered value pricing with a $0.59 Value Menu. After sales at the chain rose 50 percent in two years to $2.4 billion, McDonald's and Burger King adopted the value pricing practice. The menu at Taco Bell has since been reconfigured to emphasize plain tacos and burritos (which are easier and faster for the chain to make) for less than

FIGURE 17.5
Pricing Strategies When the Customer Defines Value as Quality for the Price Paid

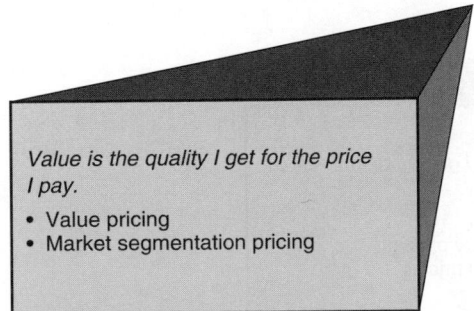

Value is the quality I get for the price I pay.
- Value pricing
- Market segmentation pricing

a dollar. Southwest Airlines also offers value pricing in its airline service: a low cost for a bundle of desirable service attributes such as frequent departures, friendly and funny employees, and on-time arrival. The airline offers consistently low fares with bare-bones service.

Market Segmentation Pricing

With *market segmentation pricing,* a service marketer charges different prices to groups of customers for what are perceived to be different quality levels of service, even though there may not be corresponding differences in the costs of providing the service to each of these groups. This form of pricing is based on the premise that segments show different price elasticities of demand and desire different quality levels.

Services marketers often price by *client category,* based on the recognition that some groups find it difficult to pay a recommended price. Health clubs located in college communities will typically offer student memberships, recognizing that this segment of customers has limited ability to pay full price. In addition to the lower price, student memberships may also carry with them reduced hours of use, particularly in peak times. The same line of reasoning leads to memberships for "seniors," who are less able to pay full price but are willing to patronize the clubs during daytime hours when most full-price members are working.

Companies also use market segmentation by *service version,* recognizing that not all segments want the basic level of service at the lowest price. When they can identify a bundle of attributes that are desirable enough for another segment of customers, they can charge a higher price for that bundle. Companies can configure service bundles that reflect price and service points appealing to different groups in the market. Hotels, for example, offer standard rooms at a basic rate but then combine amenities and tangibles related to the room to attract customers willing to pay more for the concierge level, jacuzzis, additional beds, and sitting areas.

Pricing Strategies When the Customer Means "Value Is All That I Get for All That I Give"

Some customers define value as including not just the benefits they receive but also the time, money, and effort they put into a service. Figure 17.6 illustrates the pricing strategies described in this definition of value.

Price Framing

Because many customers do not possess accurate reference prices for services, services marketers are more likely than goods marketers to organize price information for customers so they know how to view it. Customers naturally look for price anchors as well as familiar services against which to judge focal services. If they accept the

FIGURE 17.6
Pricing Strategies When the Customer Defines Value as All That Is Received for All That Is Given

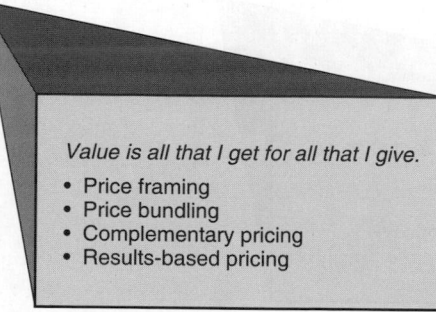

Value is all that I get for all that I give.
- Price framing
- Price bundling
- Complementary pricing
- Results-based pricing

anchors, they view the price and service package favorably. Gerald Smith, a professor at Boston College, provided an enlightening example of the way price framing could have improved sales of the 1994 Olympic TripleCast, minute-by-minute coverage of different Olympic arenas that was a well-documented failure because customers were not willing to pay the price of $130. He suggested that if CBS had segmented the market, isolated meaningful packages of sports, and framed them in a way that was familiar to customers, the service might have been successful. He proposed a boxing package for $24.95, a skating package for $24.95, and equestrian and wrestling packages for $19.95. In each case the service could be framed in an appropriate price context. For example, boxing at $24.95 is priced somewhere between attending a boxing match and watching it on pay-per-view. Boxing aficionados would recognize that the price for the full package of matches was a value.[18]

Price Bundling

Some services are consumed more effectively in conjunction with other services; other services accompany the products they support (such as extended service warranties, training, and expedited delivery). When customers find value in a package of services that are interrelated, price bundling is an appropriate strategy. Bundling, which means pricing and selling services as a group rather than individually, has benefits to both customers and service companies. Customers find that bundling simplifies their purchase and payment, and companies find that the approach stimulates demand for the firm's service line, thereby achieving cost economies for the operations as a whole while increasing net contributions.[19] Bundling also allows the customer to pay less than when purchasing each of the services individually, which contributes to perceptions of value.

The effectiveness of price bundling depends on how well the service firm understands the bundles of value that customers or segments perceive and on the complementarity of demand for these services. Effectiveness also depends on the right choice of services from the firm's point of view. Because the firm's objective is to increase overall sales, the services selected for bundling should be those with a relatively small sales volume without the bundling to minimize revenue loss from discounting a service that already has a high sales volume. See Exhibit 17.2 for examples.

Approaches to bundling include mixed bundling, mixed-leader bundling, and mixed-joint bundling.[20] In *mixed bundling,* the customer can purchase the services individually or as a package, but a price incentive is offered for purchasing the package. As an example, a health club customer may be able to contract for aerobics classes at $10 per month, weight machines at $15, and pool privileges at $15—or the group of three services for $27 (a price incentive of $13 per month).[21] In *mixed-leader bundling,* the price of one service is discounted if the first service is purchased at full price. For example, if customers buy one premium cable channel at full price, they can acquire a second premium channel at a reduced monthly rate. The objective is to reduce the price of the higher-volume service to generate an increase in its volume that "pulls" an increase in demand for a lower-volume but higher-contribution margin service. In *mixed-joint bundling,* a single price is formed for the combined set of services to increase demand for multiple services by packaging them together. For example, when Time Warner Cable introduced digital telephone service, the company offered a special price of $29.95 per month for cable, digital phone, and high-speed online service.

Complementary Pricing

Services that are highly interrelated can be leveraged by using *complementary pricing.* This pricing includes three related strategies—captive pricing, two-part pricing, and loss leadership.[22] In *captive pricing,* the firm offers a base service or product and then provides the supplies or peripheral services needed to continue using the service. In this situation the company could off-load some part of the price for the basic service to the peripherals. For example, cable services often drop the price for installation to a very low level, then compensate by charging enough for the peripheral services to make up for the loss in revenue. With service firms, this strategy is often called *two-part pricing* because the service price is broken into a fixed fee plus variable usage fees (also found in telephone services, health clubs, and commercial services such as rentals). *Loss leadership* is the term typically used in retail stores when providers place a familiar service on special largely to draw the customer to the store and then reveal other levels of service available at higher prices. Cleaners, for example, will offer a special low price to launder men's shirts to draw customers in to pay the higher regular prices for other items.

Results-Based Pricing

In service industries in which outcome is very important but uncertainty is high, the most relevant aspect of value is the *result* of the service. In personal injury lawsuits, for example, clients value the settlement they receive at the conclusion of the service. From tax accountants, clients value cost savings. From trade schools, students most value getting a job upon graduation. From Hollywood stars, production companies value high grosses. In these and other situations, an appropriate value-based pricing strategy is to price on the basis of results or outcome of the service.

The most commonly known form of results-based pricing is a practice called *contingency pricing* used by lawyers. Contingency pricing is the major way that personal injury and certain consumer cases are billed. In this approach, lawyers do not receive fees or payment until the case is settled, when they are paid a percentage of the money that the client receives. Therefore, only an outcome in the client's favor is compensated. From the client's point of view, the pricing makes sense in part because most clients in these cases are unfamiliar with and possibly intimidated by law firms. Their biggest fears are high fees for a case that may take years to settle. By using contingency pricing, clients are ensured that they pay no fees until they receive a settlement.

In these and other instances of contingency pricing, the economic value of the service is hard to determine before the service, and providers develop a price that allows them to share the risks and rewards of delivering value to the buyer. Partial contingency pricing, now being used in commercial law cases, is a version in which the client pays a lower fee than usual but offers a bonus if the settlement exceeds a certain level. Real estate agents are another example of service providers who earn their fees based on a percentage of the selling price of the properties they offer.

Results-based pricing is demonstrated clealy in the online "pay-per-click" advertising industry today. Rather than buying media with estimated audiences, companies that buy advertisements on Google and Yahoo! pay only for users who actually respond to their ads. In 2001, before Google adopted pay-per-click pricing, it had $86 million in revenue; in the 12 months ending September 30, 2002, sales hit $2.7 billion.[23] Some public relations firms are also moving from charging fixed fees for obtaining media exposure for their clients to a results-based approach. PayPerClip, for example, a division of a traditional public relations firm, bases its fees on very specific results—$750, for example, for a mention in a small-market newspaper.

The commission approach to services pricing is compelling in that agents are compensated most when they find the highest rates and fares. It would seem that agents have an underlying motivation to avoid the lowest fares and rates for their clients.

FIGURE 17.7
Summary of Service Pricing Strategies for Four Customer Definitions of Value

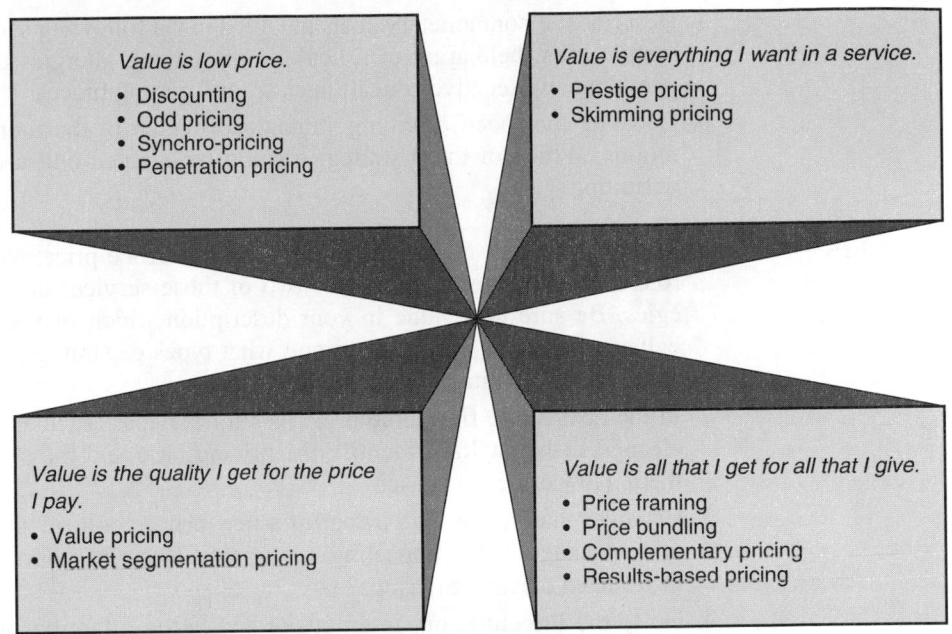

Value is low price.
- Discounting
- Odd pricing
- Synchro-pricing
- Penetration pricing

Value is everything I want in a service.
- Prestige pricing
- Skimming pricing

Value is the quality I get for the price I pay.
- Value pricing
- Market segmentation pricing

Value is all that I get for all that I give.
- Price framing
- Price bundling
- Complementary pricing
- Results-based pricing

Summary

This chapter began with three key differences between customer evaluation of pricing for services and goods: (1) customers often have inaccurate or limited reference prices for services, (2) price is a key signal of quality in services, and (3) monetary price is not the only relevant price to service customers. These three differences can have profound effects on the strategies that companies use to set and administer prices for services. The chapter next discussed common pricing structures, including (1) cost-based, (2) competition-based, and (3) demand-based pricing. Central to the discussion were the specific challenges in each of these structures and the services pricing techniques that have emerged in practice.

Finally, the chapter defined customer perceptions of value and suggested appropriate pricing strategies that match each customer definition. Figure 17.7 summarizes these definitions and strategies. The four value definitions include (1) value is low price, (2) value is whatever I want in a product or service, (3) value is the quality I get for the price I pay, and (4) value is all that I get for all that I give.

Discussion Questions

1. Which approach to pricing (cost-based, competition-based, or demand-based) is the most fair to customers? Why?
2. Is it possible to use all three approaches simultaneously when pricing services? If you answer yes, describe a service that is priced this way.
3. For what consumer services do you have reference prices? What makes these services different from others for which you lack reference prices?
4. Name three services you purchase in which price is a signal to quality. Do you believe that there are true differences across services that are priced high and those that are priced low? Why or why not?

5. Describe the nonmonetary costs involved in the following services: getting an automobile loan, belonging to a health club, having allergies diagnosed and treated, attending an executive education class, and getting braces.

6. Consider the specific pricing strategies for each of the four customer value definitions. Which of these strategies could be adapted and used with another value definition?

Exercises

1. List five services for which you have no reference price. Now put yourself in the role of the service providers for two of those services and develop pricing strategies. Be sure to include in your description which of the value definitions you believe customers will possess and what types of strategies would be appropriate given those definitions.

2. In the next week, find three price lists for services (such as from a restaurant, dry cleaner, or hairstylist). Identify the pricing base and the strategy used in each of them. How effective is each?

3. Consider that you are the owner of a new private college and can prepare a value/price package that is appealing to students. Describe your approach. How does it differ from existing offerings?

4. Go to the Priceline.com Internet site and become familiar with the way it works. Next, go to Orbitz and Travelocity and compare the way they operate. What are the benefits and tradeoffs in using Priceline over Orbitz and Travelocity?

Notes

1. K. Monroe, "The Pricing of Services," *Handbook of Services Marketing,* ed. C. A. Congram and M. L. Friedman (New York: AMACOM, 1989), pp. 20–31.

2. Ibid.

3. W. Woellert, "How Much Is That Brain Scan?" *BusinessWeek,* November 8, 2004, p. 94.

4. V. M. Mallozzi and J. Gettleman, "Taming the Runaway Wedding Planner," *New York Times,* June 24, 2007; Pet Body Builders website, www.petbodybuilders .com/services.html accessed August 30, 2007; Child Safety Specialists website, www.safe4mychild.com/about-us.html, accessed August 28, 2007; and Evaluating Your Business website www.elevatingyourbusiness.com/servicesandprograms .html, accessed August 30, 2007.

5. "How Much Do Stars Cost?" *Us Weekly,* November 13, 2006, p. 10.

6. American Medical Association's 2003 Physician Socioeconomic Statistics, reported at http://www.amaassn.org/amednews/2003/08/18/prl20818.htm, accessed August 28, 2007.

7. Monroe, "The Pricing of Services."

8. V. A. Zeithaml, "The Acquisition, Meaning, and Use of Price Information by Consumers of Professional Services," in *Marketing Theory: Philosophy of Science Perspectives,* ed. R. Bush and S. Hunt (Chicago: American Marketing Association, 1982), pp. 237–241.

9. C. H. Lovelock, "Understanding Costs and Developing Pricing Strategies," *Services Marketing* (New York: Prentice Hall, 1991), pp. 236–246.

10. A. Stevens, "Firms Try More Lucrative Ways of Charging for Legal Services," *The Wall Street Journal,* November 25, 1994, pp. B1ff.

11. K. Chu, "Bank of America Raises ATM Surcharge," *USA Today* September 13, 2007, 2A.

12. V. A. Zeithaml, "Consumer Perceptions of Price, Quality, and Value: A Means-End Model and Synthesis of Evidence," *Journal of Marketing* 52 (July 1988), pp. 2–22.

13. All comments from these four sections are based on those from Zeithaml, "Consumer Perceptions," pp. 13–14.

14. B. Donan, "Set Price Metrics Parallel to Value Proposition," *Marketing News,* April 1, 2007, p. 6.

15. G. Boeck, "Teams Woo Fans with Cheaper Seats," *USA Today,* August 31, 2004, p. 3C.

16. Monroe, "The Pricing of Services."

17. B. DeLollis, "Hotels Take Pampering to Next Level on Club Floors," *USA Today,* June 19, 2007, p. 3B.

18. G. E. Smith, "Framing and Customers' Perceptions of Price and Value in Service-Oriented Businesses," presentation at the Effective Pricing Strategies for Service Providers Conference, Institute for International Research, Boston, MA, October 1994.

19. Monroe, "The Pricing of Services."

20. Ibid.

21. J. P. Guiltinan, "The Price Bundling of Services: A Normative Framework," *Journal of Marketing* 51 (April 1987), pp. 74–85.

22. G. J. Tellis, "Beyond the Many Faces of Price: An Integration of Pricing Strategies," *Journal of Marketing* 50 (October 1986), pp. 146–160.

23. G. Mannes, "The Urge to Unbundle," *Fast Company,* February 2005, p. 23.

Part Seven

Service and the Bottom Line

Chapter 18: The Financial and Economic Impact of Service

In this final section of the text, we discuss one of the most important questions about service that managers have been debating over the past 25 years: is excellent service profitable to an organization? We pull together research and company experience, virtually all of it from the past decade, to answer this question. We present our own model of how the relationship works and offer examples of the relationship in companies. Our model shows how service quality has offensive effects (gaining new customers) and defensive effects (retaining customers).

   We also discuss several important performance models in this chapter. Return on service quality (ROSQ) is a modeling approach that allows a company to gauge the return on investments in different service activities. Customer equity is an extension of the ROSQ approach that compares investments in service with expenditures on other marketing activities. The balanced performance scorecard is an approach that includes multiple company factors including financial, customer, operational, and innovative measures. The balanced performance scorecard allows a company to measure performance from the customer's perspective (Chapter 10), from the employee's perspective (Chapter 12), and from an innovation and new service perspective (Chapter 9). Thus, in Chapter 18, we synthesize the measurement issues that underlie the provision of service and offer a way for companies to demonstrate that service is accountable financially. These models help companies understand more accurately their benefits from investments in service excellence.

Chapter **Eighteen**

The Financial and Economic Impact of Service

This chapter's objectives are to

1. Examine the direct effects of service on profits.
2. Consider the effect of service in getting new customers.
3. Evaluate the role of service in keeping customers.
4. Discuss what is known about the key service drivers of overall service quality, customer retention, and profitability.
5. Discuss the balanced performance scorecard that allows for strategic focus on measurements other than financials.

"What return can I expect on service quality improvements?"

—*A typical CEO*

All authors of this text work with companies to improve their service quality and better meet their customers' expectations. The two most frequent questions asked by executives of these companies are

"How do I know that service quality improvements will be a good investment?"
"Where in the company do I invest money to achieve the highest return?"

For example, a restaurant chain, after conducting consumer research, found that service quality perceptions averaged 85 percent across the chain. The specific items receiving the lowest scores on the survey were appearance of the restaurant's exterior (70 percent), wait time for service (78 percent), and limited menu (76 percent). The company's CEO wanted to know, first of all, whether making improvements in overall service quality or to any of the specific areas would result in revenues that exceeded their costs. Moreover, he wanted guidance as to which of the service aspects to tackle. He could determine how much each of the initiatives would cost to change, but that was as far as his financial estimates would take him. Clearly, the restaurant's exterior was most in need of change because it was rated lowest; but would it not also be by far the most expensive to change? What could he expect in return for improvements in each service area? Would adjustments in the other two factors be better investments? Which of the three service initiatives would generate noticeable improvements to raise the overall customer perceptions of the restaurant?

Ten years ago, these questions had to be answered on the basis of executive intuition. Today, fortunately, more analytical and rigorous approaches exist to help managers make these decisions about service quality investments. The best known and most widely respected approach is called return on service quality (ROSQ) and was developed by Roland Rust, Anthony Zahorik, and Tim Keiningham, a team of researchers and consultants. The ROSQ approach is based on the following assumptions:

1. Service quality is an investment.
2. Service quality efforts must be financially accountable.
3. It is possible to spend too much on service quality.
4. Not all service quality expenditures are equally valid.

Their approach looks at investments in services as a chain of effects of the following form:

1. A service improvement effort will produce an increased level of customer satisfaction at the process or attribute level. For example, expending money to refurbish the exterior of the restaurants will likely increase customers' satisfaction level from the current low rating of 70 percent.
2. Increased customer satisfaction at the process or attribute level will lead to increased overall customer satisfaction. If satisfaction with the restaurant's exterior goes from 70 to 80 percent, overall service quality ratings may increase from 85 to 90 percent. (Both these percentage changes could be accurately measured the next time surveys are conducted and could even be projected in advance using the ROSQ model.)
3. Higher overall service quality or customer satisfaction will lead to increased behavioral intentions, such as greater repurchase intention and intention to increase usage. Customers who have not yet eaten at the restaurant will be drawn to do so, and many who currently eat there once a month will consider increasing their patronage.
4. Increased behavioral intentions will lead to behavioral impact, including repurchase or customer retention, positive word of mouth, and increased usage. Intentions about patronizing the restaurant will become reality, resulting in higher revenues and more positive word-of-mouth communications.
5. Behavioral effects will then lead to improved profitability and other financial outcomes. Higher revenues will lead to higher profits for the restaurant, assuming that the original investment in refurbishing the exterior is covered.

The ROSQ methodology can help distinguish among all the company strategies, processes, approaches, and tactics that can be altered. The ROSQ approach is informative because it can be applied in companies to direct their individual strategies. Software has been developed to accompany the approach, and consulting firms work with companies to apply it. No longer do firms like the restaurant discussed here have to depend on intuition alone to guide them in their service quality investments.

Sources: R. T. Rust, A. J. Zahorik, and T. L. Keiningham, *Return on Quality* (Chicago: Probus, 1994); and Roland T. Rust, C. Moorman and P. R. Dickson, "Getting a Return on Quality: Revenue Expansion, Cost Reduction, or Both," *Journal of Marketing,* October 2002, pp. 7–24.

Virtually all companies hunger for evidence and tools to ascertain and monitor the payoff and payback of new investments in service. Many managers still see service and service quality as costs rather than as contributors to profits, partly because of the difficulty involved in tracing the link between service and financial returns. Determining the financial impact of service parallels the age-old search for the connection between advertising and sales. Service quality's results—like advertising's results—are cumulative, and therefore evidence of the link may not come immediately or even quickly after investments. And, like advertising, service quality is one of many variables—among them pricing, advertising, efficiency, and image—that simultaneously influence profits. Furthermore, spending on service per se does not guarantee results because strategy and execution must both also be considered.

In recent years, however, researchers and company executives have sought to understand the relationship between service and profits and have found strong evidence to support the relationship. For example, one study examined the comparative benefits of revenue expansion and cost reduction on return on quality. The research addressed a common strategic dilemma faced by executives: whether to reduce costs through the use of quality programs, such as Six Sigma, that focus on efficiencies and cost cutting or to build revenues through improvements to customer service, customer satisfaction, and customer retention.[1] Using managers' reports as well as secondary data on firm profitability and stock returns, the study investigated whether the highest return on quality was generated from cost cutting, revenue expansion, or a combination of the two approaches. The results suggest that firms that adopt primarily a revenue expansion emphasis perform better and have higher return on quality than firms that emphasize either cost reduction or both revenue expansion and cost reduction together.[2]

Executives are also realizing that the link between service and profits is neither straightforward nor simple. Service quality affects many economic factors in a company, some of them leading to profits through variables not traditionally in the domain of marketing. For example, the traditional total quality management approach expresses the financial impact of service quality in lowered costs or increased productivity. These relationships involve operational issues that concern marketing only in the sense that marketing research is used to identify service improvements that customers notice and value.

More recently, other types of evidence have become available with which to examine the relationship between service and profitability. The overall goal of this chapter is to synthesize that evidence and to identify relationships between service and profits. This chapter is divided into five sections, paralleling the chapter's objectives. In each section we assess the evidence and identify what is currently known about the topics. The chapter is organized using a conceptual framework linking all the variables in the topics.

SERVICE AND PROFITABILITY: THE DIRECT RELATIONSHIP

Figure 18.1 shows the underlying question at the heart of this chapter. Managers were first interested in this question in the late 1980s when service quality emerged as a pivotal competitive strategy. The executives of leading service companies such as FedEx and Disney were willing to trust their intuition that better service would lead to improved financial success. Without formal documentation of the financial payoff, they committed resources to improving service and were richly rewarded for their leaps of faith. In the 1990s, the strategy of using service for competitive advantage and profits was embraced by forward-thinking manufacturing and information technology

FIGURE 18.1
The Direct Relationship between Service and Profits

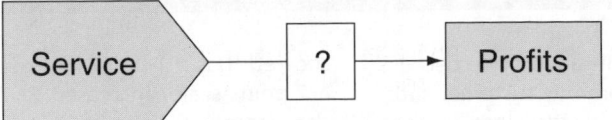

companies such as General Electric and IBM. However, executives in other companies withheld judgment about investing in service, waiting for solid evidence of its financial soundness.

Early evidence came from the U.S. General Accounting Office (GAO), which sought grounds for belief in the financial impact of quality in companies that had been finalists or winners of the Malcolm Baldrige National Quality Award. The GAO found that these elite quality firms had benefited in terms of market share, sales per employee, return on sales, and return on assets. Based on responses from 22 companies who won or were finalists, the GAO found that 34 of 40 financial variables showed positive performance improvements while only 6 measurements were negative or neutral.[3]

In later years, evidence from more rigorous research showed the positive impact of service. One study showed the favorable financial impact of complaint recovery systems.[4] Another found a significant and positive relationship between patient satisfaction and hospital profitability. In this study, specific dimensions of hospital service quality, such as billing and discharge processes, explained 17 to 27 percent of hospital earnings, net revenues, and return on assets.[5] Extending the definition of financial performance to include stock returns, another study found a significant positive link between changes in customer quality perceptions and stock return while holding constant the effects of advertising expenditures and return on investment.[6] Executives and researchers at Sears, describing the transformation of the company during the period 1994–1995, developed a model to identify relationships between employee attitude, customer satisfaction, and revenue growth. Results indicated that a 5-point improvement in employee attitude led to a 1.3-point improvement in customer satisfaction, which in turn led to a 0.5 percent improvement in revenue growth. They further estimated that 4 percent improvement in customer satisfaction would translate to more than $200 million in additional 12-month revenues. These extra revenues would increase Sears's market capitalization by nearly $250 million.[7]

Exhibit 18.1 reviews the studies that have examined links among customer satisfaction, service quality, and financial performance. This information is enlightening because it validates that improving customer satisfaction and service quality generate financial returns.

While general questions such as the overall relationships among service quality, customer satisfaction, and company performance are relevant at a broad level, individual companies and researchers also have more focused questions about particular elements of the relationship. For example, what role does service quality have in getting customers? How does service quality contribute to keeping the customers a firm already has?

OFFENSIVE MARKETING EFFECTS OF SERVICE: ATTRACTING MORE AND BETTER CUSTOMERS

Service quality can help companies attract more and better customers to the business through *offensive marketing*.[8] Offensive effects (shown in Figure 18.2) involve market share, reputation, and price premiums. When service is good, a company gains a positive reputation and through that reputation a higher market share and

Exhibit 18.1 Customer Satisfaction, Service Quality, and Firm Performance

A recent review by Gupta and Zeithaml of two decades of studies examining the links among customer satisfaction, service quality, and firm performance resulted in several important recurring findings across studies. Some studies explicitly consider the impact of service quality on financial performance while others subsume service quality as a driver of customer satisfaction and therefore focus on the impact of overall customer satisfaction on financial performance. As discussed in Chapter 5, customer satisfaction is a broader concept than service quality, but service quality is almost always an important driver of customer satisfaction across all types of industries. Therefore, the results of the review of both concepts are relevant in this chapter. Because so many studies were examined in the review, only a subset are mentioned in this exhibit, but the complete list of sources can be found in the published review itself.

Studies that were reviewed used a variety of metrics for financial performance: profit, stock price, Tobin's q (ratio of market value of a firm to the replacement cost of its tangible assets), return on assets (ROA), return on investment (ROI), abnormal earnings, and cash flows. Here is what the authors concluded:

Generalization 1: Improvement in customer satisfaction has a significant and positive impact on firms' financial performance.

Many studies have shown a strong link between customer satisfaction and firm profitability. For example, one comprehensive study by Anderson, Fornell, and Mazvancheryl using 200 of the *Fortune* 500 firms across 40 industries showed that a 1 percent change in ACSI (as measured by the American Customer Satisfaction Index on a 0–100 scale) is associated with 1.016 percent change in shareholder value as measured by Tobin's q. This implies that a 1 percent improvement in satisfaction for these firms will lead to an increase in firm's value of approximately $275 million. Supporting this finding, a similar study by Gruca and Rego found that a 1-point increase in ACSI results in an increase of $55 million in a firm's net operational cash flow next year and a decrease of 4 percent in cash flow variability.

In a service-industry study using data from almost 8,000 customers of a national hotel chain, researchers found that return on investment in service quality (e.g., cleanliness) was almost 45 percent. Another study

showed that a 1-point improvement in satisfaction (on a 7-point scale) increased ROA by 0.59 percent. With data from 106 firms in 68 industries during the period 1981–1991, still another study found that news reports about increases in customer service led to average cumulative abnormal earnings of about 0.46 percent, or $17 million in market value.

Collectively, these studies show a strong and positive impact of customer satisfaction on firm performance. They further provide a rough benchmark about the size of the impact: a 1 percent change in ACSI can lead to a $240 to $275 million improvement in firm value. In sum, these results provide a strong guideline to firms about how much they should spend on improving customer satisfaction.

Generalization 2: The link between satisfaction and firm performance is asymmetric.

An *asymmetric relationship* means that increases in customer satisfaction do not always have the same impact on firm performance as decreases in customer satisfaction. For example, a study by Anderson and Mittal found that a 1 percent increase in satisfaction led to 2.37 percent increase in ROI, whereas a 1 percent drop in satisfaction reduced ROI by 5.08 percent (see the accompanying figure). Another study by Nayyar found that positive news about customer service led to an increase in compounded annualized rate (CAR) of about 0.46 percent, whereas reports of reductions in customer service were met with declines in CAR of about half or 0.22 percent. Still another study by Anderson and Mittal found that a drop in satisfaction produced twice the impact on ROI than an increase in satisfaction. In contrast, another study found negative news of customer service had only half the impact on CAR than the positive news.

Generalization 3: The strength of the satisfaction-profitability link varies across industries as well as across firms within an industry.

The strength of the relationships among customer satisfaction, service quality, and profitability are not consistent across industries. In a study by Ittner ad Larcker, the impact was found to be stronger in service industries than in durable and nondurable manufacturing firms. In that study, the ACSI had a positive but insignificant impact on market value of durable and

the ability to charge more than its competitors for services. These benefits were documented in a classic multiyear, multicompany study called PIMS (profit impact of marketing strategy). The PIMS research shows that companies offering superior service achieve higher-than-normal market share growth and that service quality influences profits through increased market share and premium prices as well as

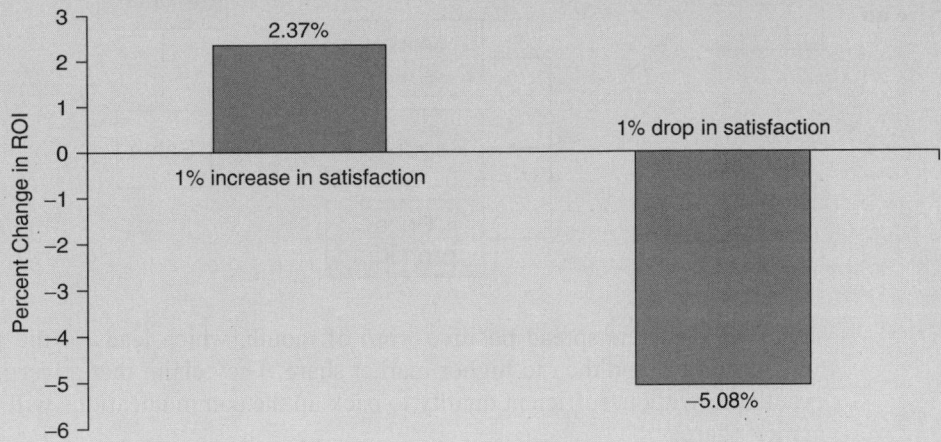

The Asymmetric Relationship between Satisfaction and ROI (Based on 125 Swedish Firms)

Source: E. Anderson and V. Mittal, "Strengthening the Satisfaction-Profit Chain," *Journal of Service Research* 3 (2000), pp. 107–20.

nondurable manufacturing firms and a positive and significant impact on the market value of transportation, utility and communication firms. The effect was strongly negative for retailers. Another study by Anderson found that trade-offs between customer satisfaction and productivity (e.g., labor productivity) were more likely for services than for goods. Specifically, a simultaneous 1 percent increase in both customer satisfaction and productivity is likely to increase ROI by 0.365 percent for goods, but only 0.22 percent for services.

In addition to the differences found in the studies cited, Anderson et al.'s recent study found that while a 1 percent change in satisfaction had an *average* impact of 1.016 percent on shareholder value (Tobin's q), the impact ranged from 2.8 percent for department stores to –0.3 percent for discount stores. Anderson and Mittal's study again found that industry characteristics explain 35 percent of the variance in cash flow growth and 54 percent of the variance in cash flow variability. They also found that the influence of customer satisfaction on cash flow growth is greatest for low-involvement, routinized, and frequently purchased products (e.g., beer and fast food).

While this summary represents a considerable improvement over what we knew in the past, companies

are very eager to learn more. This general information about the relationships among customer satisfaction, service quality, and financial performance will help them understand that investing in customer satisfaction and service quality is beneficial. Thus, indications are that the investments are worthwhile and that not investing can be harmful to firms. Later in the chapter, we will describe other, more specific information that firms want to understand about these relationships.

Sources: S. Gupta and V. Zeithaml, "Customer Metrics and Their Impact on Financial Performance, *"Marketing Science* 25 (November–December 2006), pp. 718–739; E. Anderson, C. Fornell, and S. Mazvancheryl, "Customer Satisfaction and Shareholder Value," *Journal of Marketing* 68 (2004), pp. 172–185; C. Ittner and D. Larcker, "Are Non-Financial Measures Leading Indicators of Financial Performance? An Analysis of Customer Satisfaction," *Journal of Accounting Research,* 36 (3) (1998), pp. 1–35; R. Rust, A. Zahorik, and T. Keiningham, "Return on Quality (ROQ): Making Service Quality Financially Accountable," *Journal of Marketing* 59 (1995) pp. 58–70; T. S.Gruca and L. L. Rego, "Customer Satisfaction, Cash Flow and Shareholder Value," *Journal of Marketing* 69 (2005), pp. 115–130; E. Anderson and V. Mittal, "Strengthening the Satisfaction-Profit Chain," *Journal of Service Research* 3 (2000), pp. 107–120; and P. Nayyar, "Stock Market Reactions to Customer Service Changes," *Strategic Management Journal* 16, no. 1 (1995), pp. 39–53.

lowered costs and less rework.[9] The study found that businesses rated in the top fifth of competitors on relative service quality average an 8 percent price premium over their competitors.[10]

To document the impact of service on market share, a group of researchers described their version of the path between quality and market share, claiming that

FIGURE 18.2
Offensive Marketing Effects of Service on Profits

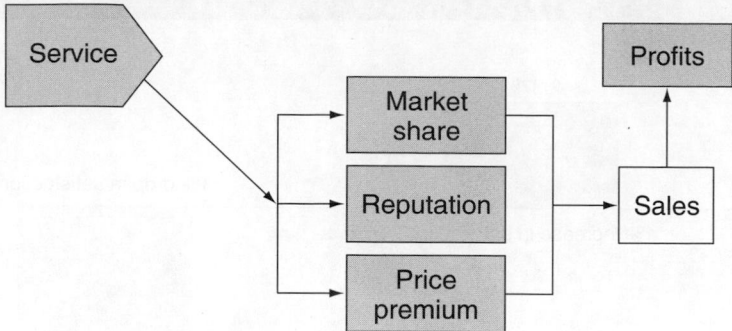

satisfied customers spread positive word of mouth, which leads to the attraction of new customers and then to higher market share. They claim that advertising service excellence without sufficient quality to back up the communications will not increase market share.[11]

DEFENSIVE MARKETING EFFECTS OF SERVICE: CUSTOMER RETENTION

When it comes to keeping the customers a firm already has—an approach called *defensive marketing*[12]—researchers and consulting firms have in the past 20 years documented and quantified the financial impact of existing customers. In Chapter 7 we explained that customer defection, or "customer churn," is widespread in service businesses. Customer defection is costly to companies because new customers must replace lost customers, and replacement comes at a high cost. Getting new customers is expensive; it involves advertising, promotion, and sales costs as well as start-up operating expenses. New customers are often unprofitable for a period of time after acquisition. In the insurance industry, for example, the insurer does not typically recover selling costs until the third or fourth year of the relationship. Capturing customers from other companies is also an expensive proposition: a greater degree of service improvement is necessary to make a customer switch from a competitor than to retain a current customer.

In general, the longer a customer remains with the company, the more profitable the relationship is for the organization:

> Served correctly, customers generate increasingly more profits each year they stay with a company. Across a wide range of businesses, the pattern is the same: the longer a company keeps a customer, the more money it stands to make.[13]

The money a company makes from retention comes from four sources (shown in Figure 18.3): costs, volume of purchases, price premium, and word-of-mouth communication. This section provides research evidence for many of the sources.

Lower Costs

Attracting a new customer is five times as costly as retaining an existing one. Consultants who have focused on these relationships assert that customer defections have a stronger effect on a company's profits than market share, scale, unit costs, and many other factors usually associated with competitive advantage.[14] They also claim that, depending on the industry, companies can increase profits from 25 to 85 percent by retaining just 5 percent more of their customers. The GAO study of semifinalists in the Malcolm Baldrige competition (described earlier in this chapter) found that

FIGURE 18.3
Defensive Marketing Effects of Service on Profits

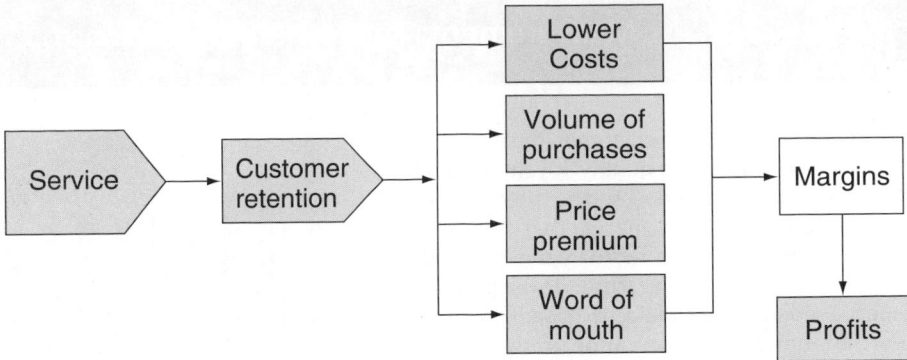

quality reduced costs: order-processing time decreased on average by 12 percent per year, errors and defects fell by 10 percent per year, and cost of quality declined by 9 percent per year.

Consider the following facts about the role of service quality in lowering costs:

- "Our highest quality day was our lowest cost of operations day" (Fred Smith, founder and chairman of FedEx).
- "Our costs of not doing things right the first time were from 25 to 30 percent of our revenue" (David F. Colicchio, regional quality manager, Hewlett-Packard Company).[15]
- Bain and Company, a consulting organization specializing in retention research, estimates that in the life insurance business, a 5 percent annual increase in customer retention lowers a company's costs per policy by 18 percent.

Volume of Purchases

Customers who are satisfied with a company's services are likely to increase the amount of money they spend with that company or the types of services offered. A customer satisfied with a broker's services, for example, will likely invest more money when it becomes available. Similarly, a customer satisfied with a bank's checking services is likely to open a savings account with the same bank and to use the bank's loan services as well.

Price Premium

Evidence suggests that a customer who notices and values the services provided by a company will pay a price premium for those services. Granite Rock, a winner of the Baldrige Award, has been able to command prices up to 30 percent higher than competitors for its rock (a product that many would claim is a commodity!) because it offers off-hour delivery and 24-hour self-service. In fact, most of the service quality leaders in industry command higher prices than their competitors: FedEx collects more for overnight delivery than the U.S. Postal Service, Hertz rental cars cost more than Avis cars, and staying at the Ritz-Carlton is a more expensive undertaking than staying at the Hyatt.

Word-of-Mouth Communication

In Chapter 3, we described the valuable role of word-of-mouth communications in service purchase decisions. Because word-of-mouth communication is considered more credible than other sources of information, the best type of promotion for a service may

Many different methods of customer measurement—customer satisfaction, service quality, loyalty, and retention for example—have been used to predict a firm's financial performance. One metric that has become popular, yet controversial, in recent years is called the Net Promoter Score (NPS). The score, developed by loyalty expert Frederick Reichheld, is based on the idea that word-of-mouth communication, rather than any of the other metrics, is the best predictor of growth and therefore financial performance.

The score is based on just one survey question: would you recommend us to a friend or colleague? To get the NPS, a company simply asks consumers the likelihood (out of 10) that they would recommend the company, and then subtracts the proportion of "detractors" (who rate the company lower than 6) from the proportion of "promoters" (who rate the company at 9 or 10).

Executives of many of the world's most prestigious firms seem to agree with Reichheld that the NPS is the "single most reliable indicator of a company's ability to grow." General Electric, American Express, Microsoft, Intuit, and the Progressive Corporation are but a few companies that have wholeheartedly adopted the approach. The popularity of the NPS comes in part because the approach is simple. To top management, long confused by the growing complexity of customer measurement and how to apply it, the idea of having just one number on which to focus is very appealing. And the measure is intuitive—if customers like the firm or its service enough to talk about it to others, it signals a stronger bond than merely being satisfied. The Net Promoter Score became, in essence, a "magic number" for companies.

HOW DO COMPANIES MEASURE UP ON THE NET PROMOTER SCORE?

In many firms, promoters barely outnumber detractors giving them NPS scores of only 5 to 10 percent. Worse

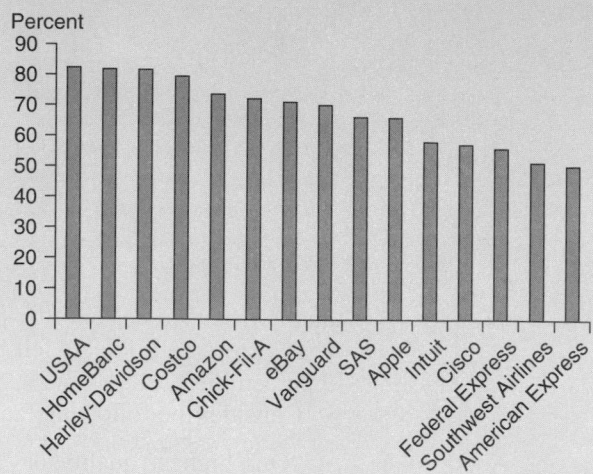

Net Promoter Score Stars

Source: www.netpromoter.com. All NPS statistics are based on Bain or Satmetrix surveys with the exceptions of Intuit, Chick-fil-A, and HomeBanc. For these firms, they used data provided by the companies in a reasonable (but not perfectly equivalent) fashion.

yet, many firms and industries have negative NPSs, which means that they are constantly creating detractors. During the summer of 2007, the airline industry was one of the net negative industries. Some firms shine, however, and the accompanying figure shows some of the stars.

CONTROVERSY: IS THE NET PROMOTER INDEX SUPERIOR, APPROPRIATE, OR COMPLETE?

While executives are embracing the Net Promoter Score, researchers and loyalty experts question the superiority, appropriateness, and completeness of the metric. For example, one researcher questioned, convincingly, whether word of mouth would be a better driver of

well come from other customers who advocate the services provided by the company. Word-of-mouth communication brings new customers to the firm, and the financial value of this form of advocacy can be calibrated by the company in terms of the promotional costs it saves as well as the streams of revenues from new customers. In fact, researchers have developed models of customer lifetime value in which they can quantify the monetary worth of word-of-mouth communications, called *referral values,* for different segments of consumers.[16] As discussed in Exhibit 18.2, many companies are now using the extent of word of mouth as their main measure of customer loyalty.

growth than other factors like reducing customer loss or increasing current customers' volume through cross-sales and share of category purchase. More dramatically, would actions driven to increase word of mouth create stronger growth than actions to acquire profitable new customers?

Another key concern is the extent to which word of mouth is a relevant goal for all products and services in all contexts. Consumers feel strongly about some products and services, and these feelings drive word of mouth. Services (such as restaurants, vacations, and entertainment), fashions, and new electronic products are referral-worthy products. However, the majority of products and services are unlikely to be interesting enough for customers to talk about them. *BusinessWeek* writer Steven Nicks also points out that the NPS ignores what he calls *experiential demographics.* Customers at different points in their life or buying cycles with products and services and in different contexts may be stronger or weaker promoters. New customers may be stronger promoters, as would be ones who just experienced a positive interaction with the company.

From a practical standpoint, a major problem is that while the single number provides a sign of health, as a thermometer would do in signalling body temperature, it neither diagnoses firm problems nor describes how to treat them. To be actionable, metrics must also contain other questions (such as those we described in Chapter 6) to identify what customers expect and perceive about the company. In the drive to simplicity in using NPS, many companies never follow up on the NPS with other metrics, research, or programs. Recently, Reichheld's findings have been put to the test by other researchers. In a recent major study, a team of loyalty experts matched the way that NPS was calculated using two to three years' worth of data from 21 companies and 15,500 interviews. While they expected that the findings would replicate what Reichheld had found, they did not. Furthermore, when comparing the results to the American Customer Satisfaction Index, this team also found that NPS had no clear superiority to other measures. The only other independent study on the subject does confirm a strong correlation between word of mouth and growth, but it cannot confirm causality. Only when more research has been conducted to examine NPS more closely will we know whether it is a valid predictor.

THE BOTTOM LINE

Loyalty expert Timothy Keiningham dismisses the quest for NPS or any other magic number:

> Even the best ideas aren't universal. If they were, everybody would do them and they would already be known. You need to know what is the number one demonstration of loyalty from your customers, then model back from that—what causes that to happen and what causes that to break? And once you start thinking about it that way, you realize there isn't going to be a magic number because [loyalty] is driven by different things depending on what industry you are in.

Sources: F. Reichheld, "The One Number You Need to Grow," *Harvard Business Review* 81 (December 2003), pp. 46–54; F. Reichheld, *The Ultimate Question. Driving Good Profits and True Growth,* Harvard Business School Press, 2006; www .netpromoter.com, accessed September 2007; P. Marsden, "Net Promoter—the Ultimate Debate on Customer Loyalty," www.MyCustomer.com, accessed September 2007; D. Grisaffe, "Guru Misses the Mark with 'One Number' Fallacy," www .creatingloyalty.com/story.cfm?article_id=656, accessed September 2007; N. Davey, "Can a Magic Number Really Guide Your Business?" www.MyCustomer.com, accessed September 2007; and T. Keiningham, B. Cooil, T. Andreassen, and L. Aksoy, "A Longitudinal Examination of Net Promoter and Firm Revenue Growth," *Journal of Marketing* 71 (July 2007), pp. 39–51.

Word-of-mouth communications are especially important for services high in experience qualities (where the customer must experience the service to determine its quality) and credence qualities (where the customer may not be able to determine the quality of the service even after it is delivered).[17]

Many questions remain about defensive marketing, among them the ones shown in Exhibit 18.3. Although research has come a long way in the last decade, researchers and companies must continue working on these questions for a more complete understanding of the impact of service on defensive marketing.

Managers are only beginning to understand the topics discussed in this chapter. For each of the sections on the service quality/profitability relationship in this chapter, Exhibit 18.4 (on page 555) lists an inventory of questions that managers and researchers most want to know. To give you an idea of the specific questions that managers are asking, we elaborate here on the topic of defensive marketing.

1. *What is a loyal customer?* Customer loyalty can be viewed as the way customers feel or as the way they act. A simple definition is possible with some products and services: Customers are loyal as long as they continue to use a good or service. For washing machines or long-distance telephone service, customers are deemed loyal if they continue to use the machine or telephone service. Defining customer loyalty for other products and services is more problematic. What is the definition of loyalty to a restaurant: always eat there, eat there more times than at other restaurants, or eat there at least once during a given period? These questions highlight the growing popularity of the concept of "share of wallet" that company managers are very interested in. *Share of wallet* refers to the percentage of spending in a particular category that is given to a particular service provider. The other way to define loyalty is in terms of the customer's sense of belonging or commitment to the product. Some companies have been noted for their "apostles," customers who care so much about the company that they stay in contact to provide suggestions for improvement and constantly preach to others the benefits of the company. Is this the best way to define loyalty?

2. *What is the role of service in defensive marketing?* Quality products at appropriate prices are important elements in the retention equation, but both these marketing variables can be imitated. Service plays a critical role—if not *the* critical role—in retaining customers. Providing consistently good service is not as easy to duplicate and therefore is likely to be the cementing force in customer relationships. Exactly how important is service in defensive marketing? How does service compare in effectiveness with other retention strategies such as price? To date, no studies have incorporated all or most factors to examine their relative importance in keeping customers. Many companies actually have survey data that could answer this question but either have not analyzed the data for this purpose or have not reported their findings.

3. *What levels of service provision are needed to retain customers?* How much spending on service quality is enough to retain customers? Initial investigations into this question have been argued but have not been confirmed. One consultant, for example, proposed that when satisfaction rose above a certain threshold, repurchase loyalty would climb rapidly. When satisfaction fell below a different threshold, customer loyalty would decline equally rapidly. Between these thresholds, he believed that loyalty was relatively flat. The material discussed in Chapter 4 offered a different prediction. The zone of tolerance in that chapter captured the range within which a company is meeting expectations. This framework suggests that firms operating within the zone of tolerance should continue to improve service, even to the point of reaching the desired service level. This hypothesis implies an upward-sloping (rather than flat) relationship between the zone of tolerance and retaining customers.

4. *What specific aspects of service are most important for customer retention?* Most companies realize that service is multifaceted and want to identify the specific aspects of service provision that will lead to keeping customers.

5. *How can defection-prone customers be identified?* Companies find it difficult to create and execute strategies responsive enough to detect customer defections. Systems must be developed to isolate potential defecting customers, evaluate them, and retain them if it is in the best interest of the company. One author and consultant advises that companies focus on three groups of customers who may be candidates for defection: (a) customers who close their accounts and shift business to a competitor, (b) customers who shift some of their business to another firm, and (c) customers who actually buy more but whose purchases represent a smaller share of their total expenditures. The first of these groups is easiest to identify, and the third group is the most difficult. Among the other customers who would be vulnerable are any customer with a negative service experience, new customers, and customers of companies in very competitive markets. Developing early warning systems of such customers is a pivotal requirement for companies.

Source: Reprinted with permission from V. A. Zeithaml, "Service Quality, Profitability and the Economic Worth of Customers," *Journal of the Academy of Marketing Science,* January 2000, © 2000 by the Academy of Marketing Science.

CUSTOMER PERCEPTIONS OF SERVICE QUALITY AND PURCHASE INTENTIONS

In Chapter 5 we highlighted the links among customer satisfaction, service quality, and increased purchases. Here we provide more research and empirical evidence supporting these relationships. For example, researchers at Xerox offered a compelling insight about the relationship between satisfaction and purchase intentions during the company's early years of customer satisfaction research. Initially, the company focused on satisfied customers, which they identified as those checking either a "4" or a "5" on a 5-point satisfaction scale. Careful analysis of the data showed that customers giving Xerox 5s were six times more likely to indicate that they would repurchase Xerox equipment than those giving 4s. This relationship encouraged the company to focus on increasing the 5s rather than the 4s *and* 5s because of the strong sales and profitability implications.[18] A recent and more encompassing update of the importance of scoring in the "top box" of customer satisfaction is shown in Figure 18.4. TARP Worldwide Inc. found similar results across 10 studies incorporating 8,000 customers worldwide. A full 96 percent of customers who report being "very satisfied" (i.e., they are in the *top box* in satisfaction) say they will "definitely repurchase" from the same company. When they are only "somewhat satisfied," the number drops to only 52 percent, and only 7 percent of customers who are "neutral or very dissatisfied" will definitely repurchase.[19]

Evidence also shows that customer satisfaction and service quality perceptions affect consumer intentions to behave in many positive ways—praising the firm, preferring the company over others, increasing volume of purchases, or agreeably paying a price premium. Figure 18.5 shows these other relationships. Most of the early evidence looked only at overall benefits in terms of repurchase intention rather than extending past that relationship and examining specific types of behavioral intentions. One study, for example, found a significant association between overall patient satisfaction and intent to choose a hospital again.[20] Another, using information from a Swedish customer satisfaction barometer, found that stated repurchase intention is strongly related to stated satisfaction across virtually all product categories.[21]

Studies have found relationships between service quality and more specific behavioral intentions. One study involving university students found strong links between

FIGURE 18.4
Top-Box Scores, Repurchase Intentions, and Referral Intentions

Source: Information Courtesy of TARP Worldwide, 2007

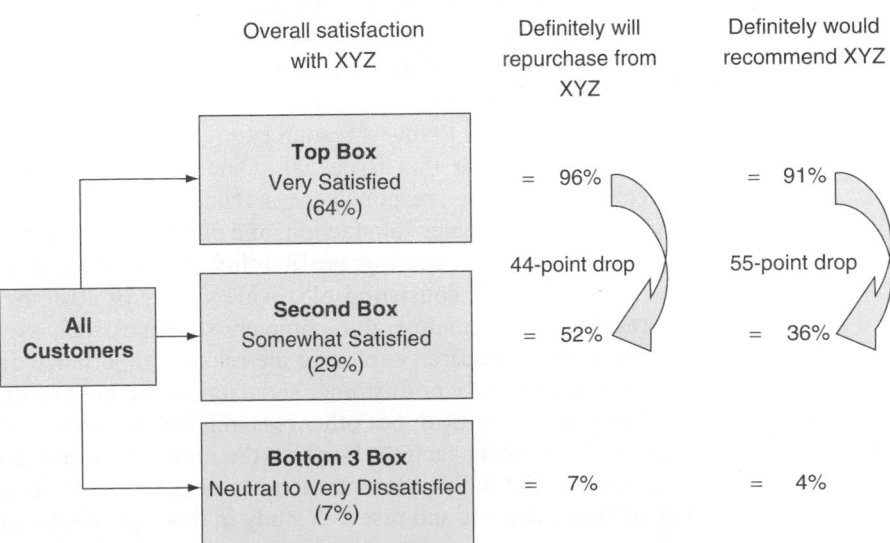

FIGURE 18.5
**The Effects
of Service on
Behavioral
Intentions
and Behavior**

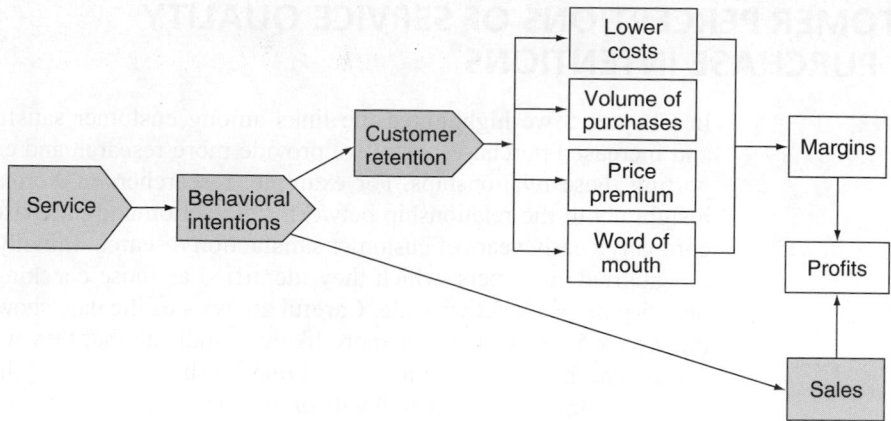

service quality and other behavioral intentions of strategic importance to a university, including behavior such as saying positive things about the school, planning to contribute money to the class pledge on graduation, and planning to recommend the school to employers as a place from which to recruit.[22] Another comprehensive study examined a battery comprised of 13 specific behavioral intentions (such as saying positive things about the company, remaining loyal to the company, spending more with the company) likely to result from perceived service quality. The overall measure was significantly correlated with customer perceptions of service quality.[23] Individual companies have also monitored the impact of service quality on selected behavioral intentions. Toyota found that intent to repurchase a Toyota automobile increased from a base of 37 to 45 percent with a positive sales experience, from 37 to 79 percent with a positive service experience, and from 37 to 91 percent with both positive sales and service experiences.[24]

Exhibit 18.4 shows a list of the questions that businesses still need to know more about on this topic and the others in this chapter.

THE KEY DRIVERS OF SERVICE QUALITY, CUSTOMER RETENTION, AND PROFITS

Understanding the relationship between overall service quality and profitability is important, but it is perhaps more useful to managers to identify specific drivers of service quality that most relate to profitability (shown in Figure 18.6). Doing so will help firms understand what aspects of service quality to change to influence the relationship and, therefore, where to invest resources.

Most evidence for this issue has come from examining the effects of specific aspects of service (e.g., responsiveness, reliability, assurance, and tangibles) on overall service quality, customer satisfaction, and purchase intentions rather than on financial outcomes such as retention or profitability. As you have discovered in this text, service is multifaceted, consisting of a wide variety of customer-perceived dimensions and resulting from innumerable company strategies such as technology and process improvement. In research exploring the relative importance of service dimensions on overall service quality or customer satisfaction, the bulk of the support confirms that reliability is most critical; but other research has demonstrated the importance of customization and other factors. Because the dimensions and attributes are delivered in many cases with totally different internal strategies, resources must be allocated where they are most needed, and research study in this topic could provide direction.

Exhibit 18.4 Service Quality and the Economic Worth of Customers: Businesses Still Need to Know More

Topic	Key Research Questions
Service quality and profitability: the direct relationship	1. What methodologies need to be developed to allow companies to capture the effect of service quality on profit within individual companies? 2. What measures are necessary to examine the relationship in a consistent, valid, and reliable manner? 3. How and why does the relationship between service quality and profitability vary by industry, country, category of business, or other variable? What does this imply for investment in service quality? 4. What are the moderating factors of the relationship between service quality and profitability? 5. What is the optimal spending level on service in order to affect profitability?
Offensive effects of service quality	1. What is the optimal amount of spending on service quality to obtain offensive effects? 2. To obtain offensive effects, are expenditures on advertising or service quality itself more effective? 3. In what ways can companies signal high service quality to customers to obtain offensive effects?
Defensive effects of service quality	1. What is a loyal customer? 2. What is the role of service in defensive marketing? 3. How does service compare in effectiveness to other retention strategies such as price? 4. What levels of service provision are needed to retain customers? 5. How can the effects of word-of-mouth communication from retained customers be quantified? 6. What aspects of service are most important for customer retention? 7. How can defection-prone customers be identified and then retained?
Perceptions of service quality	1. What is the relationship between customer purchase intentions and initial purchase behavior in services? 2. What is the relationship between behavioral intentions and repurchase in services? 3. Does the degree of association between service quality and behavior change at different quality levels?
Identifying the key drivers of service quality, customer retention, and profits	1. Which service encounters are most responsible for perceptions of service quality? 2. What are the key drivers of service quality, customer retention, and profits in each service encounter? 3. Where should investments be made to affect service quality, purchase, retention, and profits? 4. Are key drivers of service quality the same as key drivers of behavioral intentions, customer retention, and profits?

Some companies and researchers have viewed the effect of specific service encounters on overall service quality or customer satisfaction and the effect of specific behaviors within service encounters. Marriott Hotels conducted extensive customer research to determine what service elements contribute most to customer loyalty. They found that four of the top five factors came into play in the first 10 minutes of the guest's stay—those that involved the early encounters of arriving, checking in, and entering

Strategy Insight Customer Equity and Return on Marketing: Metrics to Match a Strategic Customer-Centered View of the Firm

Although the marketing concept has articulated a customer-centered viewpoint since the 1960s, marketing theory and practice have become incrementally customer-centered over the past 40 years. For example, marketing has only recently decreased its emphasis on short-term transactions and increased its focus on long-term customer relationships. Much of this refocus stems from the changing nature of the world's leading economies, which have undergone a century-long shift from the goods sector to the service sector.

Because service often tends to be more relationship based, this structural shift in the economy has resulted in more attention to relationships and therefore more attention to customers. This customer-centered viewpoint is starting to be reflected in the concepts and metrics that drive marketing management, including such metrics as customer value and voice of the customer. For example, the concept of brand equity, a fundamentally product-centered concept, is now being challenged by the customer-centered concept of *customer equity*, deferred as the total of the discounted lifetime values summed over all the firm's customers.

In other words, customer equity is obtained by summing up the customer lifetime values of the firm's customers. In fast-moving and dynamic industries that involve customer relationships, products come and go but customers remain. Customers and customer equity may be more central to many firms than brands and brand equity, although current management practices and metrics do not yet fully reflect this shift. The shift from product-centered thinking to customer-centered thinking implies the need for an accompanying shift from product-based metrics to customer-based metrics.

USING CUSTOMER EQUITY IN A STRATEGIC FRAMEWORK

Consider the issues facing a typical marketing manager or marketing-oriented CEO: How do I manage my brand? How will my customers react to changes in service and service quality? Should I raise price? What is the best way to enhance the relationships with my current customers? Where should I focus my efforts? Determining customer lifetime value, or customer equity, is the first step, but the more important step is to evaluate and test ideas and strategies using lifetime value as the measuring stick. At a very basic level, strategies for building customer relationships can affect five basic factors: retention rate, referrals, increased sales, reduced direct costs, and reduced marketing costs.

Researchers Roland Rust, Valarie Zeithaml, and Kay Lemon have developed an approach based on customer equity that can help business executives answer their questions. The model that represents this approach is shown in the accompanying figure. In this context, customer equity is an approach to marketing and corporate strategy that finally puts the customer—and, more importantly, strategies that grow the value of the customer—at the heart of the organization. The researchers identify the drivers of customer equity—value equity, brand equity, and relationship equity—and explain how these drivers work, independently and together, to grow customer equity. Service strategies are prominent in both value equity and relationship equity. Within each of these drivers are specific, incisive actions ("levers") that the firm can take to enhance the firm's overall customer equity.

WHY IS CUSTOMER EQUITY IMPORTANT?

For most firms, customer equity—the total of the discounted lifetime values of all the firm's customers—is certain to be the most important determinant of the long-term value of the firm. Although customer equity will not be responsible for the entire value of the firm (consider, e.g., physical assets, intellectual property, research and development competencies), the firm's current customers provide the most reliable source of future revenues and profits—and provide a focal point for marketing strategy.

the hotel rooms. Other companies have found that mistakes or problems that occur in early service encounters are particularly critical, because a failure at early points results in greater risk for dissatisfaction in each ensuing encounter. IBM found that the sales encounter was the most critical of all, in large part because salespeople establish expectations for the remaining service encounters.

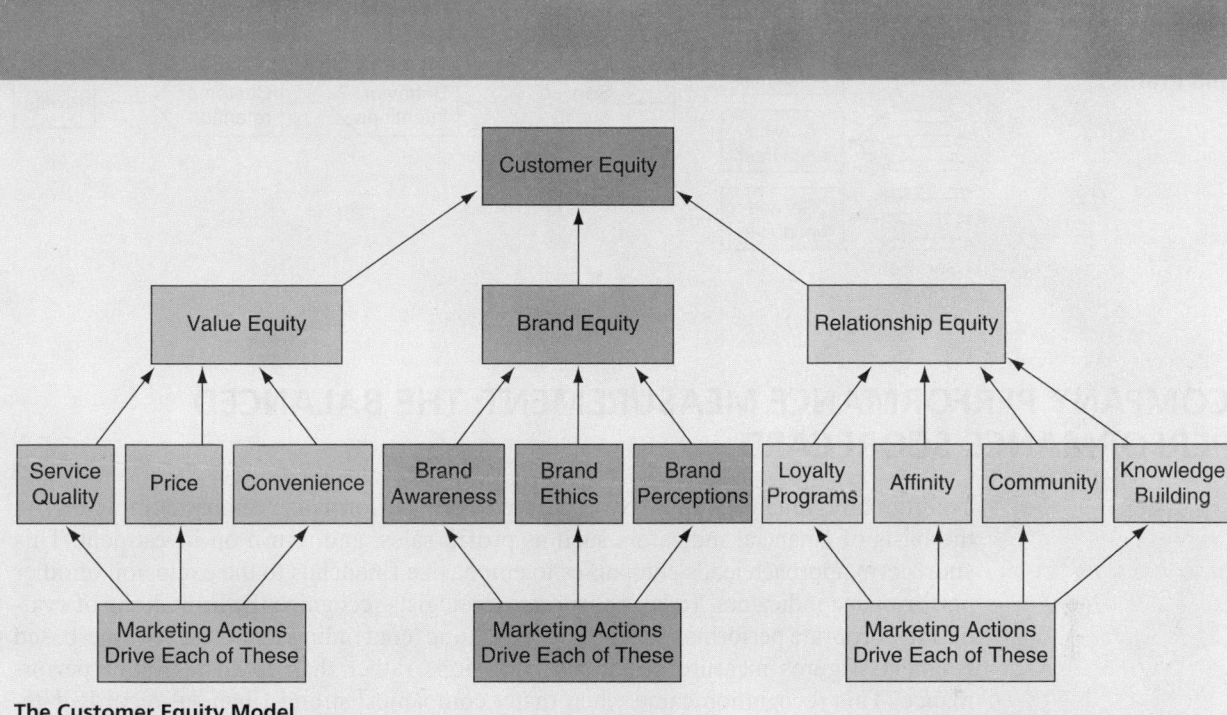

The Customer Equity Model

Although it may seem obvious that customer equity is key to long-term success, understanding how to grow and manage customer equity is much more complex. Growing customer equity is of utmost importance, and doing it well can lead to significant competitive advantage.

CALCULATING RETURN ON MARKETING USING CUSTOMER EQUITY

At the beginning of this chapter, we told you about an approach called return on quality that was developed to help companies understand where they could get the biggest impact from quality investments. A more general form of that approach is called *return on marketing,* which enables companies to look at all competing marketing strategy options and trade them off on the basis of projected financial return. This approach allows companies to not just examine the impact of service on financial return but

also compare the impact of service with the impact of branding, price changes, and all other marketing strategies. Using the customer equity model, firms can analyze the drivers that have the greatest impact, compare the drivers' performance with that of competitors' drivers, and project return on investment from improvements in the drivers. The framework enables what-if evaluation of marketing return on investment, which can include such criteria as return on quality, return on advertising, return on loyalty programs, and even return on corporate citizenship, given a particular shift in customer perceptions. This approach enables firms to focus marketing efforts on strategic initiatives that generate the greatest return.

Sources: R. T. Rust, K. N. Lemon, and V. A. Zeithaml, "Return on Marketing: Using Customer Equity to Focus Marketing Strategy," *Journal of Marketing* 68 (January 2004), pp. 109; and R. Rust, V. Zeithaml, and K. Lemon, *Driving Customer Equity* (New York: The Free Press, 2000).

Another way of looking at the problem, based largely in the operations and management literature, involves investigating the effect of service programs and managerial approaches within an organization on financial measures such as profitability. A customer-focused approach to metrics is described in the Strategy Insight.

FIGURE 18.6
The Key Drivers of Service Quality, Customer Retention, and Profits

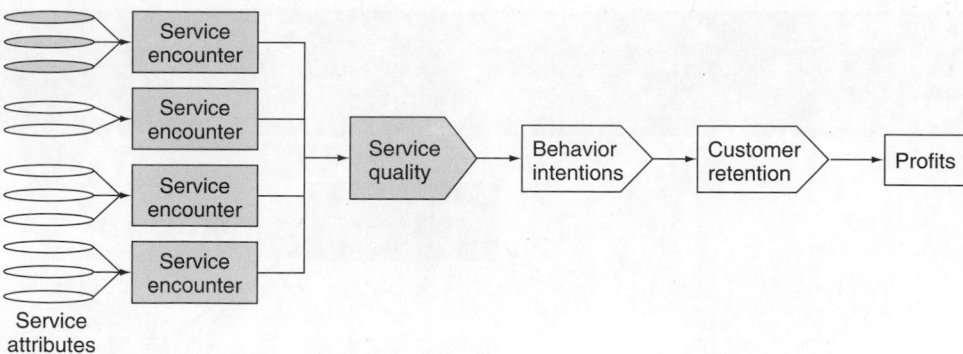

Service attributes

COMPANY PERFORMANCE MEASUREMENT: THE BALANCED PERFORMANCE SCORECARD

Traditionally, organizations have measured their performance almost completely on the basis of financial indicators such as profit, sales, and return on investment. This short-term approach leads companies to emphasize financials to the exclusion of other performance indicators. Today's corporate strategists recognize the limitations of evaluating corporate performance on financials alone, contending that these income-based financial figures measure yesterday's decisions rather than indicate future performance. This recognition came when many companies' strong financial records deteriorated because of unnoticed declines in operational processes, quality, or customer satisfaction.[25] In the words of one observer of corporate strategy:

> Financial measures emphasize profitability of inert assets over any other mission of the company. They do not recognize the emerging leverage of the soft stuff—skilled people and employment of information—as the new keys to high performance and near-perfect customer satisfaction. . . . If the only mission a measurement system conveys is financial discipline, an organization is directionless.[26]

For this reason, companies began to recognize that *balanced performance scorecards*—strategic measurement systems that captured other areas of performance—were needed. The developers of balanced performance scorecards defined them as follows:

> . . . a set of measures that gives top managers a fast but comprehensive view of the business . . . [that] complements the financial measures with operational measures of customer satisfaction, internal processes, and the organization's innovation and improvement activities—operational measures that are the drivers of future financial performance.[27]

Having a firm handle on what had been viewed as "soft" measures became the way to help organizations identify customer problems, improve processes, and achieve company objectives.

As shown in Figure 18.7, the balanced performance scorecard captures three perspectives in addition to the financial perspective: customer, operational, and learning. The balanced scorecard brings together, in a single management report, many of the previously separated elements of a company's competitive agenda and forces senior managers to consider all the important measures together. The scorecard has been facilitated by recent developments in enterprise-wide software (discussed in

FIGURE 18.7 **Sample Measurements for the Balanced Scorecard**

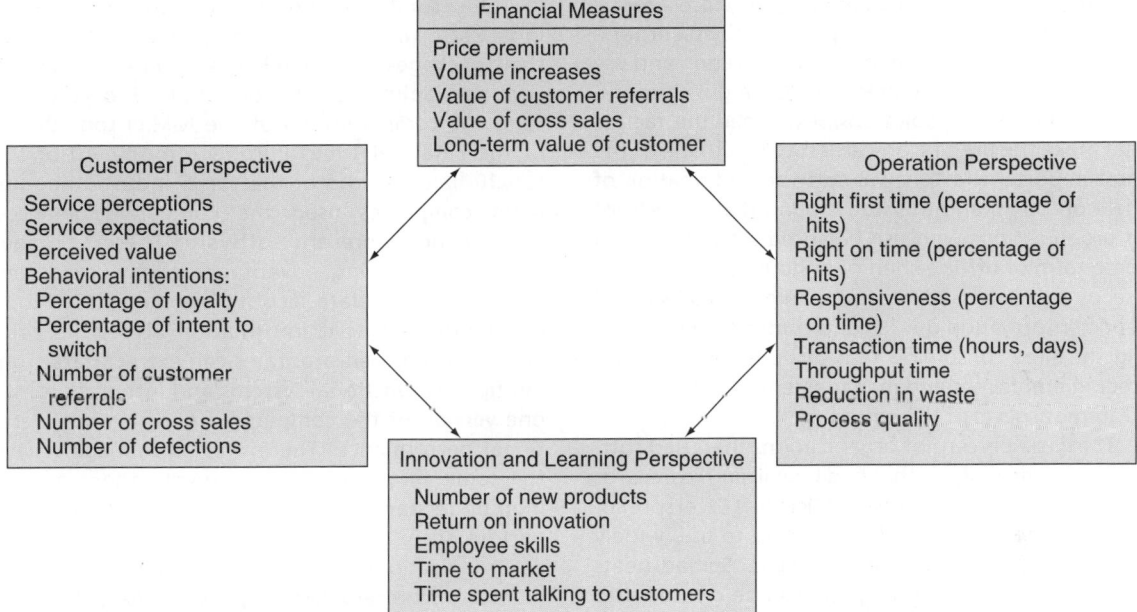

the Technology Spotlight) that allow companies to create, automate, and integrate measurements from all parts of the company.

Methods for measuring financial performance are the most developed and established in corporations, having been created more than 400 years ago. In contrast, efforts to measure market share, quality, innovation, human resources, and customer satisfaction have only recently been created. Companies can improve their performance by developing this discipline in their measurement of all four categories.

Changes to Financial Measurement

One way that service leaders are changing financial measurement is to calibrate the defensive effect of retaining and losing customers. The monetary value of retaining customers can be projected through the use of average revenues over the lifetimes of customers. The number of customer defections can then be translated into lost revenue to the firm and become a critical company performance standard:

> Ultimately, defections should be a key performance measure for senior management and a fundamental component of incentive systems. Managers should know the company's defection rate, what happens to profits when the rate moves up or down and why defections occur.[28]

Companies can also measure actual increases or decreases in revenue from retention or defection of customers by capturing the value of a loyal customer, including expected cash flows over a customer's lifetime or lifetime customer value (as described in Chapter 7). Other possible financial measures (as shown in Figure 18.7) include the value of price premiums, volume increases, customer referrals, and cross-sales.

Technology Spotlight Automating the Balanced Scorecard

A major study of the usage of balanced scorecards by North American companies, sponsored by six organizations that are involved in their preparation and use (AICPA, CAM-I, CMA Canada, IQPC, Targus Corporation, and Hyperion Solutions), examined the factors that make the use of scorecards successful. One of the most important factors was software automation of the scorecards, and the study found that 70 percent of organizations who use balanced scorecards used some form of off-the-shelf or in-house software. The use of software allowed companies to collect and report information quickly and continuously, removing the time-consuming task of updating data and freeing employees and management to focus on the strategic aspects of the scorecard.

Thirty-six percent of organizations that used software, and virtually all that had been using scorecards for more than five years, used Microsoft Excel spreadsheets, largely because they are easy to use, widely available, inexpensive, and flexible. Spreadsheets are flexible because a template can be created into which multiple parts of the organization can enter data. Organizations also tend to add, eliminate, or change measures, and spreadsheets offer the flexibility of adapting. However, users have found that spreadsheets make benchmarking scorecards across performance units difficult because departments can interpret measures differently and can engage in gamesmanship. Spreadsheets are also difficult to maintain because the data are not collected electronically and must be updated by area.

The second most popular software was Hyperion's Performance Scorecard, one of the off-the-shelf packages developed by software companies. Hyperion Solutions reported that 88 of the *Fortune* 100 companies, 66 of the Nikkei top 100, 53 of the Financial Times Europe Top 100, 10 of the top 10 banks, and 5 of the top 5 industrial equipment companies used the company's balanced performance scorecard software. These packages have the following advantages over spreadsheet software: better data security, a more focused tool, and more consistent information across the firm. These off-the-shelf programs can extract data from multiple transactional systems and integrate it into one version of the company's financial and operational performance. Therefore, all managers have the same facts and metrics, giving them a common understanding of the factors affecting overall performance.

Organizations use five different ways to communicate scorecard results: paper, e-mail, the Web, local area networks (LANs), and wide area networks (WANs). The method used by a company tends to be related to organizational size and the use of software. The smallest organizations (fewer than 100 employees) typically used paper-based reporting. Medium-sized companies used e-mail and the Web to report the results of spreadsheet software, and companies that used the Web were the most likely to report success. The largest organizations used technologically sophisticated techniques like the

Customer Perceptual Measures

Customer perceptual measures are leading indicators of financial performance. As we discussed in this chapter, customers who are not happy with the company will defect and will tell others about their dissatisfaction. As we also discussed, perceptual measures reflect customer beliefs and feelings about the company and its products and services and can predict how the customer will behave in the future. Overall forms of the measurements we discussed in Chapters 5 and 6 (shown in the customer perspective box of Figure 18.7) are measures that can be included in this category. Among the measures that are valuable to track are overall service perceptions and expectations, customer satisfaction, perceptual measures of value, and behavioral intention measures such as loyalty and intent to switch. A company that notices a decline in these numbers should be concerned that the decline will translate into lost dollars for the company.

Operational Measures

Operational measures involve the translation of customer perceptual measures into the standards or actions that must be set internally to meet customers' expectations.

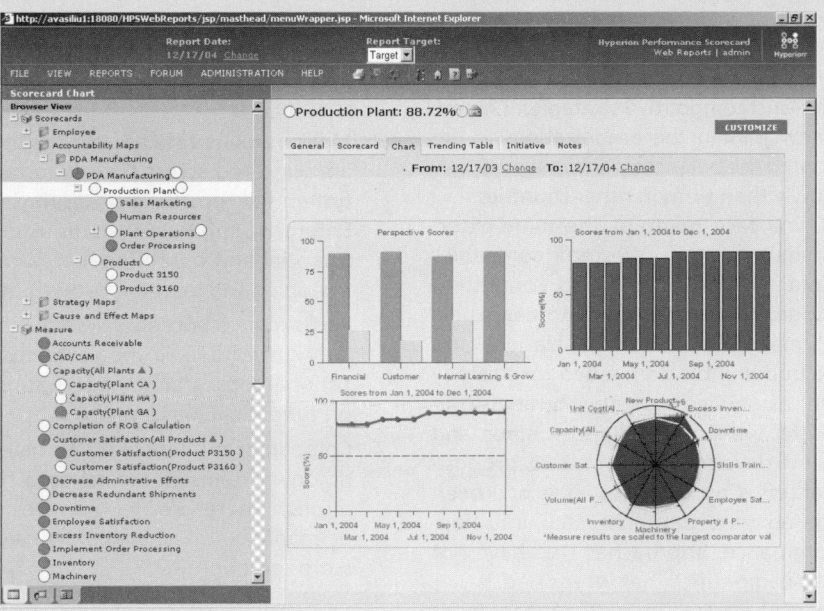

Web and LANs, which were easy to use in combination with off-the-shelf software.

The survey showed that the most important feature related to success in using software for balanced scorecards was the ability to provide web-based reporting. This feature was followed by the ability to drill down to root data, the ability to customize reports, and the ability to link scorecards and roll them up. The system also needed to be able to access data from multiple legacy systems and other data sources and be flexible enough to easily accommodate future changes to the scorecarding system.

Sources: R. Lawson, W. Stratton, and T. Hatch, "Automating the Balanced Scorecard," *CMA Management* 77, no. 9 (2004), pp. 39–44; and www.Hyperion.com.

Although virtually all companies count or calculate operational measures in some form, the balanced scorecard requires that these measures stem from the business processes that have the greatest effect on customer satisfaction. In other words, these measures are not independent of customer perceptual measures but instead are intricately linked with them. In Chapter 10 we called these customer-linked operational measures *customer-defined standards*—operational standards determined through customer expectations and calibrated the way the customer views and expresses them.

Innovation and Learning

The final area of measurement involves a company's ability to innovate, improve, and learn—by launching new products, creating more value for customers, and improving operating efficiencies. This measurement area is most difficult to capture quantitatively but can be accomplished using performance-to-goal percentages. For example, a company can set a goal of launching 10 new products a year, then measure what percentage of that goal it achieves in a year. If four new products are launched, its percentage for the year is 40 percent, which can then be compared with subsequent years.

As China continues to develop into a world economic power, its organizations are recognizing the value of strategic management concepts to help them formulate and execute effective and competitive strategies. Chinese organizations are now joining the organizations in the world that have adopted the balanced performance scorecard, albeit more slowly than firms in other countries.

Companies in China face many of the same external and internal challenges as Western companies face, including rapidly changing business conditions, increasing competition, and increasing customer expectations. However, many Chinese organizations are unfamiliar with the building blocks needed for strategy development—such as analysis of the business life cycle, SWOT (strengths, weaknesses, opportunities, and threats) analysis, and development of value propositions for target markets. Chinese companies had been successful largely based on entrepreneurship, intuition, or prior market dominance, approaches that have not been as successful as competition has intensified.

In a recent study of the adoption of 25 management accounting practices in China—among them cost allocation, activity-based costing, target costing, and capital budgeting—researchers found that the balanced scorecard had one of the lowest average levels of implementation. Companies in manufacturing had higher levels of adoption than services firms, and large firms had higher levels of adoption than small firms.

Consultants and companies that have implemented balanced scorecards in China recognize special challenges in the adoption of this tool:

1. Goal-setting processes are not flexible enough to allow companies to adapt quickly, largely because companies lack the ability to track, analyze, and change goals.

2. Measurement data are either not readily available or are scattered across the organization, with no single system for recording or displaying the information. Enterprise software systems usually have data in the financial and operational areas but lack data in the customer and learning/growth perspectives.

3. Performance appraisal systems in China are particularly susceptible to the problems created by organizational silos, and managers are compensated based on functional performance.

4. Companies are less likely to have information technology systems to record data for employee evaluations. Therefore, human resource professionals or managers must manually calculate performance scores and bonuses.

Irv Beiman and Yong-Ling Sun of e-Gate Consulting Shanghai, consultants who have applied the balanced performance scorecard to workplaces in China, identify six critical success factors in implementing the scorecard methodology in workplaces: (1) committing and involving top management; (2) overcoming implementation hurdles; (3) overcoming functional silos; (4) establishing linkages to competency development and variable pay; (5) developing infrastructure to communicate the strategy, track performance, and make adjustments based on results; and (6) elevating human resources to the

The Balanced Scorecard in Practice

The balanced scorecard has been implemented not only in corporations but also in government and nonprofit organizations as well. In 2001 the University of Virginia Library (UVL), a system of 11 different libraries with holdings of 4 million volumes, became the first library in North America to begin using a balanced scorecard to improve its performance.[29] The Global Feature shows that implementation of the balanced performance scorecard can vary by culture.

Lynda White, associate director of management information services at UVL, says that the scorecard is used as a management tool to assess the health of the organization, to indicate areas in which it is doing well and other areas that need attention, and to assemble information in a meaningful way. The organization began development of the scorecard by prioritizing the many numbers in the statistics and data that it had collected over the years.

status of a strategic partner to line management. All these criteria are important for a firm in any country to have a successful balanced scorecard, but the challenges in China are harder to overcome, particularly in the area of human resources.

One of the biggest human resource issues is the way that executives, directors, and managers are paid. Variable pay, which creates incentives to aim for common goals, is infrequently used, and compensation is almost always based on individual departments' sales and revenue goals. For example, Chinese sales personnel are almost always paid exclusively for sales volume or revenue. Because of the way they are paid, they do not cooperate with other departments, which results in conflict and tension, particularly with production departments. Consider the experience of a private entrepreneurial company in China. Each department in the firm had developed its own way of approaching work, without coordinating with other departments. Compensation was based on each department's performance rather than common performance. When faced with increasing pressure from international competition in their domestic markets, the firm recognized that it needed to revise its strategy and focus on external customer needs. The company adopted the balanced scorecard methodology and initially found that managers constantly complained about employees in other departments, placing the blame on them. After implementation of the scorecard, managers began working more cooperatively with each other by sharing objectives across departments, improving cross-functional business processes, and fostering teamwork. Measurable improvements in company performance resulted.

Another group of human resource issues include performance appraisal, performance management, and job descriptions, which do not always exist in Chinese firms. When they do exist, they are created in each individual department, meaning that each department knows only a piece of the work done by the organization. As a result, training across departments is not connected with a focus on the customer or the firm's overall strategy. In situations in which the balanced performance scorecard approach has been used effectively, the human resource function assumes the responsibility for job descriptions, performance appraisals, variable compensation, and other policies that support strategy execution.

If China is to continue to be competitive with other nations, these issues will need to be resolved. Given Chinese companies' progress in adopting lower-level management accounting practices in the last three years, as reported in recent research, the trend toward adoption of more strategic tools like the balanced performance scorecard is likely.

Sources: I. Beiman and Y. L. Sun, "Using the Balanced Scorecard for Strategy Execution in China," *China Staff* 9, no. 8 (2003), pp. 10–14; I. Beiman and Y. Sun, "Implementing a Balanced Scorecard in China: Steps for Success," *China Staff* 9, no. 9 (2003), pp. 11–15. Used with permission; and J. Xiao, C. Chow, R. Duh, and L. Zhao, "Management Accounting in China," *Financial Management* Vol. 35 (December–January 2006/2007), pp. 32–36.

The library's scorecard uses four categories of measures: the user perspective, the internal processes perspective, the financial perspective, and the learning and growth perspective. Each of the four perspectives has four to six measures that tell the organization how well the library is doing in each area. The first two categories, focusing on users and internal processes, were easy for the library to understand and measure. The metrics for user perspective helped the library improve customer service, as White describes:

> We measure how well we do in customer service, what faculty and students think of services and collections, what students think of user instruction, how much special collections is used, how much patrons use new books and electronic resources, how quickly we turn around requests (for searches, recalls, library electronic ordering [LEO] document delivery, interlibrary loan, scanning for e-reserves, new books), how fast and accurately we re-shelve, Web-site usability, renovation of public-service areas, increasing access to digital materials. And of course, measuring the unit cost of various services affects them as taxpayers or donors. It addresses whether we are using their money wisely and efficiently.[30]

According to Jim Self, director of management information services at the library, the other two categories were more difficult. Because UVL, like most libraries, is nonprofit, the financial perspective was the most challenging. In determining what to measure, the scorecard gave the library an opportunity to look at the financial aspects of its operation that had not been emphasized before, such as processing costs incurred in cataloging and acquisitions and transaction costs in reference, circulation, and interlibrary loan.

The organization realized the value of the scorecard when it compared its actual performance to its assumed performance. It found out, for example, that turnaround times for ordering books requested by users were much slower than its promises. It had been promising users that it could get new books for them in one week, but it found that only 17 percent of new books it ordered on request were ready in seven days. Through this comparison and others, the balanced scorecard helped the library look at its priorities, goals, and vision statements, align them with each other, and simplify its priority list. The library's special website (www.lib.virginia.edu/bsc) describes the history, measures, and implementation of the scorecard.

Effective Nonfinancial Performance Measurements

According to field research conducted in 60 companies and survey responses from 297 senior executives, many companies do not identify and act on the correct non-financial measures.[31] One example involves a bank that only surveyed the satisfaction of customers who physically entered the branches (rather than all customers, including those who banked by phone or ATM), a policy that caused some branch managers to offer free food and drinks in order to increase their scores. According to the authors of the study, companies make four major mistakes:

1. *Not linking measures to strategy.* Companies can easily identify hundreds of nonfinancial measures to track, but they also need to use analysis that identifies the most important drivers of their strategy. Successful organizations use value driver maps, tools that lay out the cause-and-effect relationships between drivers and strategic success. Figure 18.8 shows the causal model developed by a successful fast-food chain to understand the key drivers of shareholder value. The factors on the right were identified as most important in leading to the concepts on the left, and the sequence of concepts from top to bottom show the relationships among company strategies (such as selection and staffing) and intermediate results (such as employee and customer satisfaction) that result in financial results (such as sustained profitability and share-holder value). The study found that fewer than 30 percent of the firms surveyed used this causal modeling approach.

2. *Not validating the links.* Only 21 percent of companies in the study verify that the nonfinancial measures lead to financial performance. Instead, many firms decide what they are going to measure in each category and never link the categories. Many managers believed that the relationships were self-evident instead of conducting analysis to validate the linkages. This chapter's Strategy Insight showed one way that companies can create this type of linkage. In general, it is critical that companies pull together all their data and examine the relationships among the categories.

3. *Not setting the right performance targets.* Companies sometimes aim too high in setting improvement targets. Trying to make all customers 100 percent satisfied might seem to be a desirable goal, but many companies expend far too many resources to gain too little improvement in satisfaction. The study's authors found that a telecommunications company aiming for customers who were completely satisfied was

FIGURE 18.8
**The Measures That Matter Most:
A causal model for a fast-food company shows the critical drivers of performance and the concepts that lead to shareholder value.**

Source: Christopher D. Ittner and David F. Larcker, "Coming Up Short on Nonfinancial Performance Measurement," *Harvard Business Review* 81 (November 2003), pp. 88–95.

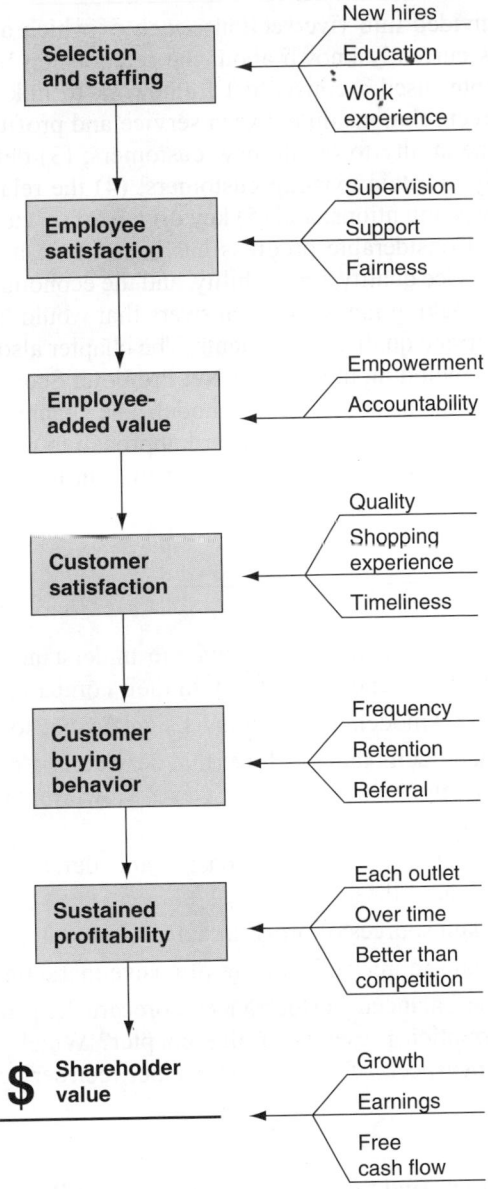

wasting resources because these customers spent no more money than those who were 80 percent satisfied.[32]

4. *Measuring incorrectly.* Companies need to use metrics with statistical validity and reliability. Organizations cannot measure complex phenomenon with one or two simple measures, nor can they use inconsistent methodologies to measure the same concept, such as customer satisfaction. Another problem that companies may encounter is trying to use quantitative metrics to capture qualitative results for important factors such as leadership and innovation.

Creating a balanced scorecard in and of itself does not improve performance. Companies will not reap the benefits of techniques such as the balanced scorecard unless they address these four issues.

Summary

This chapter is divided into five sections, each of which assesses the evidence and identifies what is currently known about the relationship between service and profitability. The chapter used a conceptual framework to link all the variables in these topics: (1) the direct relationship between service and profits; (2) offensive effects of service quality, the ability to obtain new customers; (3) defensive effects of service quality, the ability to retain existing customers; (4) the relationship between service quality and purchase intentions; and (5) key drivers of service quality, customer retention, and profits. Considerable progress has been made in the past 15 years in the investigation of service quality, profitability, and the economic worth of customers, but managers are still lacking many of the answers that would help them make informed decisions about service quality investments. The chapter also discussed approaches to measuring loyalty, including the popular Net Promoter Score, and to measuring return on marketing using the customer equity model. The chapter concluded with a discussion of the balanced performance scorecard approach to measuring corporate performance, which offers a strategic approach for measuring all aspects of a company's performance.

Discussion Questions

1. Why has it been difficult for executives to understand the relationship between service improvements and profitability in their companies?
2. What is the ROSQ model, and what is its significance to corporate America?
3. To this day, many companies believe that service is a cost rather than a revenue producer. Why might they hold this view? How would you argue the opposite view?
4. What is the difference between offensive and defensive marketing? How does service affect each of these?
5. What are the main sources of profit in defensive marketing?
6. What are the main sources of profit in offensive marketing?
7. How would the balanced performance scorecard help us understand and document the information presented in this chapter? Which of the five sections that discuss different aspects of the relationship between service quality and profits can it illuminate?

Exercises

1. Using the Internet, find the official site for the Net Promoter Score. Use the links in the site to locate other researchers' opinions of the measure, and make a list of the benefits and disadvantages discussed in those articles. If you were a CEO, would you use this measure as the "only number you need" to predict growth? Why or why not?
2. Interview a local firm and see what it knows about its key drivers of financial performance. What are the key service drivers of the firm? Does the company know whether these service drivers relate to profit?
3. Select a service industry (such as fast food) or a company (such as McDonald's) that you are familiar with, either as a customer or employee, and create a balanced scorecard. Describe the operational, customer, financial, and learning measures that could be used to capture performance.

Notes

1. R. T. Rust, C. Moorman, and P. R. Dickson, "Getting Return on Quality: Revenue Expansion, Cost Reduction, or Both?" *Journal of Marketing* 66 (October 2002), pp. 7–24.

2. Ibid.

3. *Management Practice, U.S. Companies Improve Performance through Quality Efforts,* Report No. GAO/NSIAD-91-190 (Washington, DC: U.S. General Accounting Office, 1992).

4. R. Rust, B. Subramanian, and M. Wells, "Making Complaints a Management Tool," *Marketing Management* 3 (1993), pp. 40–45.

5. E. Nelson, R. T. Rust, A. Zahorik, R. L. Rose, P. Batalden, and B. Siemanski, "Do Patient Perceptions of Quality Relate to Hospital Financial Performance?" *Journal of Healthcare Marketing* 12 (December 1992), pp. 1–13.

6. D. A. Aaker and R. Jacobson, "The Financial Information Content of Perceived Quality," *Journal of Marketing* 58 (May 1994), pp. 191–201.

7. A. Rucci, S. Kirn, and R. Quinn (1998), "The Employee – Customer – Profit Chain at Sears," *Harvard Business Review* 76 (January–February 1998), pp. 83–97.

8. C. Fornell and B. Wernerfelt, "Defensive Marketing Strategy by Customer Complaint Management: A Theoretical Analysis," *Journal of Marketing Research* 24 (November 1987), pp. 337–46; see also C. Fornell and B. Wernerfelt, "A Model for Customer Complaint Management," *Marketing Science* 7 (Summer 1988), pp. 271–286.

9. B. Gale, "Monitoring Customer Satisfaction and Market-Perceived Quality," *American Marketing Association Worth Repeating Series,* no. 922CS01 (Chicago: American Marketing Association, 1992).

10. Ibid.

11. R. E. Kordupleski, R. T. Rust, and A. J. Zahorik, "Why Improving Quality Doesn't Improve Quality (or Whatever Happened to Marketing?)," *California Management Review* 35 (1993), pp. 82–95.

12. Fornell and Wernerfelt, "Defensive Marketing Strategy by Customer Complaint Management"; also Fornell and Wernerfelt, "A Model for Customer Complaint Management."

13. F. Reichheld and E. Sasser, "Zero Defections: Quality Comes to Services," *Harvard Business Review* 68 (September–October 1990), p. 106.

14. Ibid., p. 105.

15. D. F. Colicchio, regional quality manager, Hewlett-Packard Company, personal communication.

16. V. Kumar, J. A. Petersen and R. P. Leone, "How Valuable Is Word of Mouth?" *Harvard Business Review,* October 207, pp. 2–8.

17. R. Hallowell, "Word-of-Mouth Referral," *Harvard Business School Module Note,* 2002.

18. J. L. Heskett, W. E. Sasser Jr., and L. A. Schlesinger, *The Service Profit Chain* (New York: The Free Press, 1997).

19. Information provided by TARP Worldwide Inc., August 2007.

20. A. Woodside, L. Frey, and R. Daly, "Linking Service Quality, Customer Satisfaction and Behavioral Intentions," *Journal of Health Care Marketing* 9 (December 1989), pp. 5–17.

21. E. W. Anderson and M. Sullivan, "The Antecedents and Consequences of Customer Satisfaction for Firms," *Marketing Science* 12 (Spring 1992), pp. 125–143.

22. W. Boulding, R. Staelin, A. Kalra, and V. A. Zeithaml, "Conceptualizing and Testing a Dynamic Process Model of Service Quality," report no. 92-121, Marketing Science Institute, 1992.

23. V. A. Zeithaml, L. L. Berry, and A. Parasuraman, "The Behavioral Consequences of Service Quality," *Journal of Marketing* 60 (April 1996), pp. 31–46.

24. J. P. McLaughlin, "Ensuring Customer Satisfaction Is a Strategic Issue, Not Just an Operational One," presentation at the AIC Customer Satisfaction Measurement Conference, Chicago, December 6–7, 1993.

25. R. S. Kaplan and D. P. Norton, "The Balanced Scorecard—Measures That Drive Performance," *Harvard Business Review* 70 (January–February 1992), pp. 71–79.

26. Ibid.

27. S. Silk, "Automating the Balance Scorecard," *Management Accounting,* May 1998, pp. 38–42.

28. Reichheld and Sasser, "Zero Defections," p. 111.

29. A. Willis, "Using the Balanced Scorecard at the University of Virginia Library: An Interview with Jim Self and Lynda White," *Library Administration and Management* 18, (2004), pp. 64–67.

30. Ibid., p. 66.

31. The material in this section comes from C. D. Ittner and D. F. Larcker, "Coming Up Short on Nonfinancial Performance Measurement," *Harvard Business Review* 81 (November 2003), pp. 88–95.

32. Ibid., p. 92.

Case 1
People, Service, and Profit at Jyske Bank

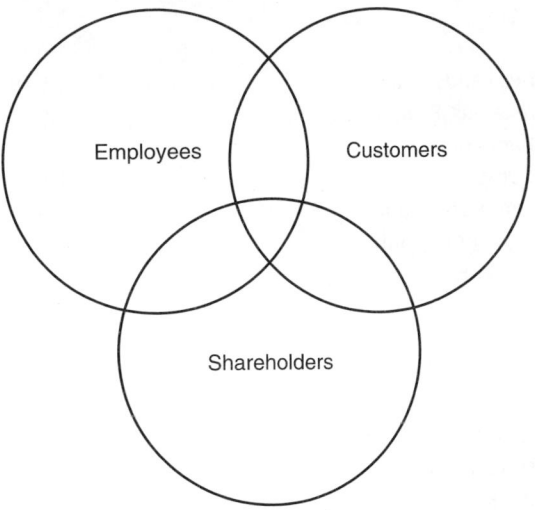

The Jyske Bank Group is managed and operated as a business. At the same time, we attach great importance to treating our three groups of stakeholders—shareholders, customers and employees—with equal respect. This is illustrated by three equally big overlapping circles which must remain in perfect balance. If the balance shifts in favor of one or two of the groups, this will be to the long-term detriment of all the groups.

—Jyske Bank Management Philosophy

In 2003, Jyske Bank Group's primary operations consisted of Jyske Bank, which was the third largest bank in Denmark after Den Danske Bank and Nordea's Danish operations (see **Exhibit 1**). Jyske Bank was created in 1967 through the merger of four Danish banks having their operations in Jutland, Jyske being Danish for "Jutland-ish." Jutland was the large portion of Denmark attached to the European mainland to the north of Germany. Until the late 1990s, Jyske Bank was characterized as a typical Danish bank: prudent, conservative, well-managed, generally unremarkable, and largely undifferentiated.

Beginning in the mid-1990s, Jyske Bank embarked on a change process that led to its no longer being characterized as either unremarkable or undifferentiated. By 2003 its unique "flavor" of service made it a leader in customer satisfaction among Danish banks (see **Exhibit 2**). At the heart of these changes was the bank's determination to be, in the words of one executive, "the most customer-oriented bank in Denmark." The bank achieved its goal by focusing on what it called *Jyske Forskelle,* or Jyske Differences.

This case was prepared under the auspices of the Scandinavian International Management Institute. It was written by Roger Hallowell. It is intended to be used as a basis for class discussion rather than to illustrate either effective or ineffective handling of an administrative situation.
© 2003 SIMI, Scandinavian International Management Institute.

EXHIBIT 1
Danish Banks
Shareholders' Equity
at January 1, 2002

Source: Jyske Bank.

Bank	Shareholders' Equity
1. DDB	57.091
2.* Jyske Bank	6.174
3. Sydbank	3.435
4. Nykredit Bank	2.708
5. Spar Nord	1.692
6. Arbejdernes Landsbank	1.518
7. Amtssparekassen Fyn	994
8. Amargerbanken	956
9. Sparbank Vest	841
10. Sparekassen, Kornjylland	816
11. Ringkøbing Landbobank	794
12. Alm. Brand Bank	749
13. Forstædernes Bank	706
14. Loskilde Bank	698
15. Lån Lan& Spar Bank	589
16. Nørresundby Bank	583
17. Sparekassen Sjælland	582
18. Sparekassen Lolland	559
19. Nordvestbank	545

*Note: Nordea is not shown as it was a Swedish bank with operations in Denmark, having acquired Unibank.

DENMARK

At the onset of the twenty-first century Denmark had a population of approximately five million. A member of the European Union retaining its own currency (the Danish Kronor, DKK[1]), Denmark was the southernmost of the Scandinavian countries. Denmark had been a wealthy country for hundreds of years. This was originally due to its strategic location in the Baltic Sea (see **Exhibit 3**) enabling it to extract tolls from merchants who were forced to sail within cannon range of its shores. More recently, much of Denmark's wealth came from high-value-added goods such as agricultural products, pharmaceuticals, machinery, instruments, and medical equipment, in addition to a highly-developed service sector including shipping.

Following the Second World War, Denmark adopted a social welfare system its government described as follows:

> The basic principle of the Danish welfare system, often referred to as the Scandinavian welfare model, is that all citizens have equal rights to social security. Within the Danish welfare system, a number of services are available to citizens, free of charge. . . . The Danish welfare model is subsidized by the state, and as a result Denmark has one of the highest taxation levels in the world.[2]

JUTLAND

Jutland was physically separated from Denmark's capital, Copenhagen (see **Exhibit 3** for a map). Copenhagen, with a population comprising almost one-quarter of all Danes, was located on the island of Zealand (*Sjaelland*). Jutland's isolation from the capital prior to modern transportation led to its people being characterized differently

[1]Euro bought approximately DKK 7.4 and U.S. $1 bought approximately DKK 6.3 as of June 10, 2003.
[2]See www.denmark.dk

EXHIBIT 2   **Danish Banks' Quality of Service Metrics**

Source: survey of 1,750 small companies conducted by the Danish newspaper *Erhvervs Bladet,* 22 March 2002, p. 2.

				Part I: Analysis of Bank Image			
	Total Image	Willingness to Take Risk	Management	They Are a Strategic Coach for Me	Service and Customer Treatment	Expert in Advice and Competence	Chose This Bank If We Want to Change Banks
Jyske Bank	1	1	1	1	1	1	1
Sydbank	2	2	3	2	2	2	2
Spar Nord Bank	3	4	4	3	3	5	5
Midtbank/ Handeslbank	4	6	7	4	6	4	7
Amagerbanken	5	3	5	6	4	8	6
Amtssparekassen Fyn	6	5	6	5	5	7	8
Nordea	7	7	8	8	7	6	3
Danske Bank	8	8	2	7	8	3	4
BG Bank	9	9	9	9	9	9	9

Part II: (A) Consumer Satisfaction Survey; Very Satisfied

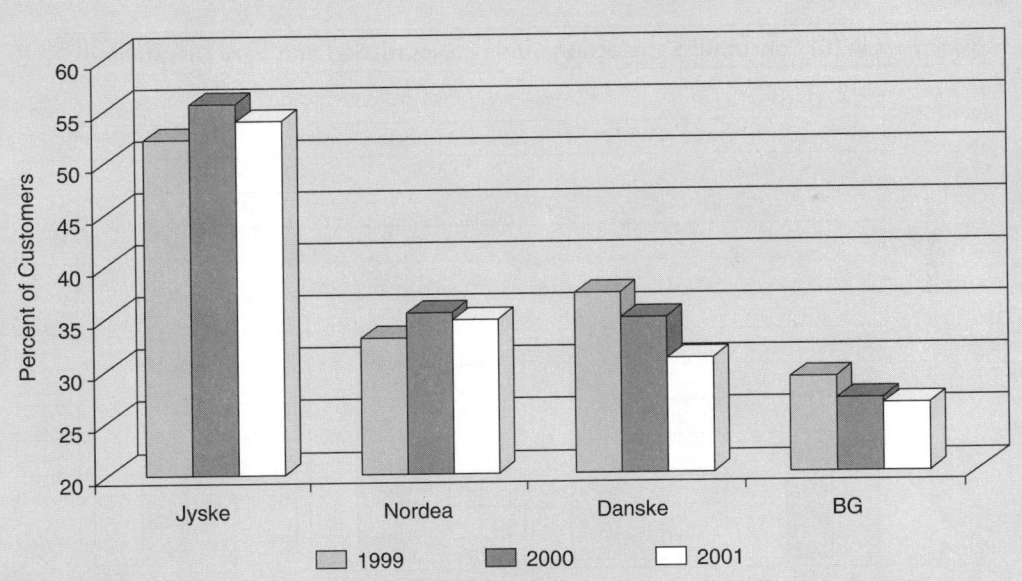

continued

EXHIBIT 2   Danish Banks' Quality of Service Metrics—continued

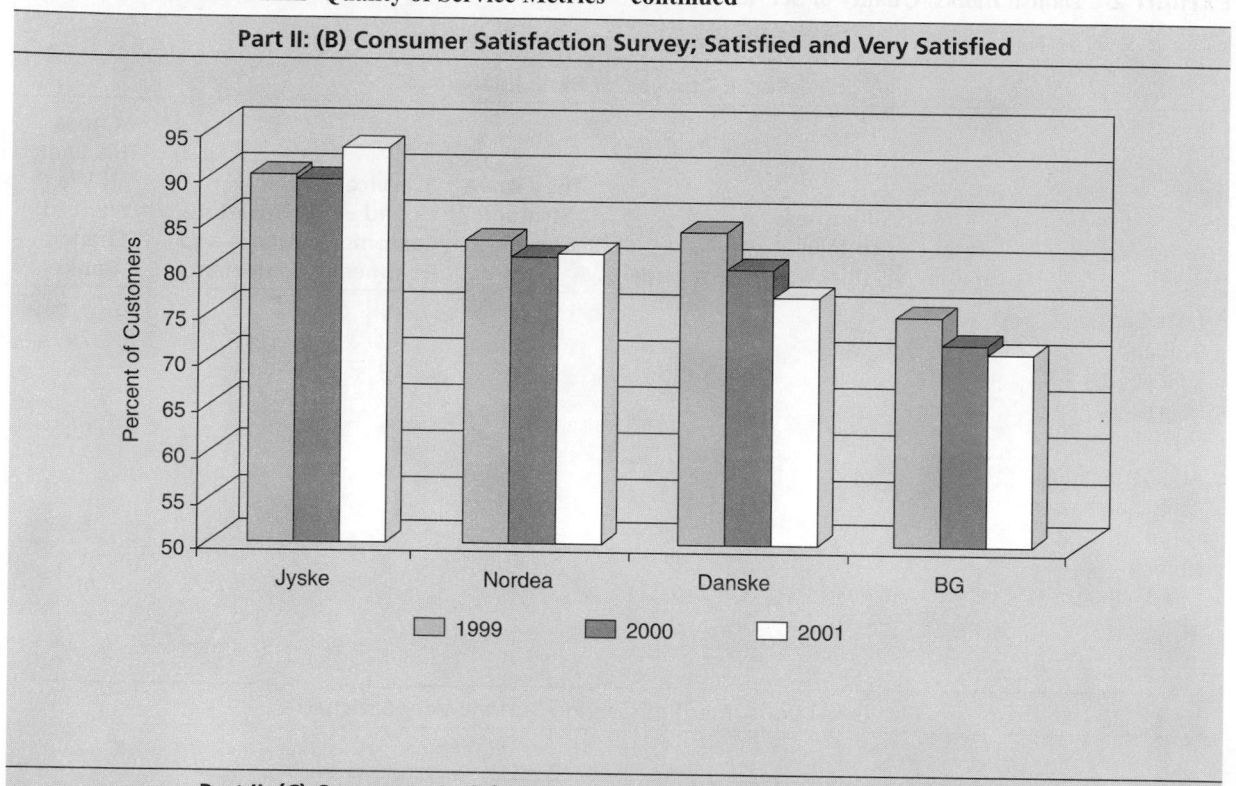

Part II: (B) Consumer Satisfaction Survey; Satisfied and Very Satisfied

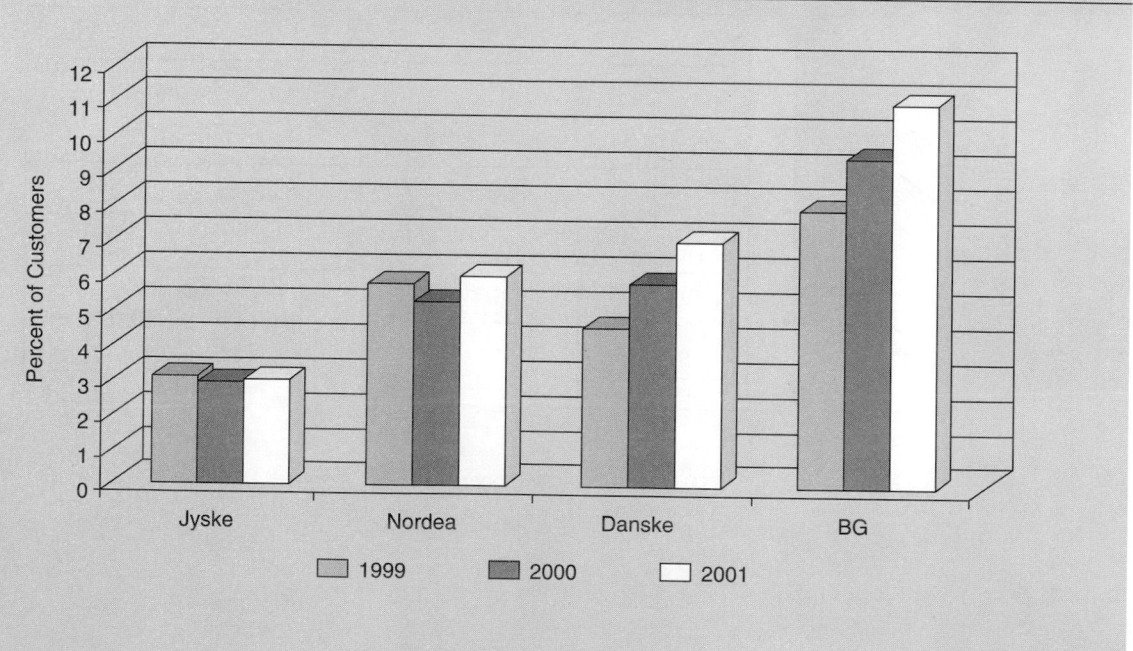

Part II: (C) Consumer Satisfaction Survey; Dissatisfied and Very Dissatisfied

EXHIBIT 3
Denmark

Source: CIA World Factbook

from their Zealander neighbors: Jutlanders were supposed to be honest, unpretentious, egalitarian, open and direct in their communication style (candid), commonsensical, frugal, sober-minded, and relatively unsophisticated, at least in contrast to those, as one Jutlander put it, "slippery people from Copenhagen."

JYSKE DIFFERENCES

Jyske Differences stemmed from Jyske Bank's core values. These stood as central tenets, guiding virtually all aspects of the organization's life. As one manager pointed out, the values were consistent with the bank's Jyske heritage: "Really, when we started talking about our core values, and their Jyskeness, we just became overt about values we had long held." Jyske Bank's core values, published for employees, customers, and shareholders, were that the bank should (1) have common sense; (2) be open and honest; (3) be different and unpretentious; (4) have genuine interest and equal respect for people; and (5) be efficient and persevering. See **Exhibit 4** for a more detailed description.

The core values led management to reevaluate how the bank did business with its customers. Managers determined that if the bank were to be true to its values, it would have to deliver service differently from both how it had in the past, and how other banks delivered service. Jyske Differences were thus operationalized as specific practices that distinguished Jyske Bank.

Competitive Positioning

Managers looked to Jyske values and differences for the bank's competitive positioning. This process was aided by a Dutch consultant, whose market research indicated that Jyske bank's core target market of Danish families and small-to-medium sized Danish companies (earnings were 40% commercial, 60% retail) generally liked the idea of a bank that was Jyske. Additional research suggested that what managers described as the "hard factors" of price, product, and location had become *sine qua non* in the eyes of customers. In contrast, "soft factors" relating to an individual customer's relationship with her service providers served as the basis for differentiation, specifically, "being nice," "making time for the customer," and "caring about the customer and his family."

EXHIBIT 4 Jyske Bank's Core Values

Common Sense

>>With both feet placed firmly on the ground, we think before we act<<

That means that we:

- consider common sense our best guide
- apply common sense when solving problems and meeting daily challenges
- allow common sense to override awkward customs and routines
- take action whenever we encounter examples of bureaucratic procedures
- observe existing rules and regulations
- accept that control measures are necessary to a certain degree
- generate satisfactory short- and long-term financial results by pursuing sound business practices
- apply common sense whenever we incur group expenses

Open and Honest

>>We are open and honest in both word and action<<

That means that we:

- keep each other up-to-date on relevant matters, and do not misuse information obtained in the course of our work
- restrict the degree of openness only by business considerations or by consideration for other stakeholders
- respect agreements entered into and do not betray the Bank's confidence
- strive towards making important decisions concerning individual employees on the basis of a constructive dialogue
- communicate openly about the mistakes we make and the problems we encounter
- accept that mistakes are made, that they are corrected, and that focus is then on learning from the process
- listen openly to new ideas and constructive criticism

Different and Unpretentious

>>We think and act differently and are generally unpretentious<<

That means that we:

- encourage creativity and initiative by being untraditional
- are full of initiative, and are committed and proactive
- encourage relaxed and straightforward communication—both internally and externally

Managers felt that the "genuine interest" component of the bank's values dictated a shift from traditional product focused selling to a customer-solution approach. They characterized the new approach by contrasting the statement, "Let me tell you about our demand-deposit account," with the question, "What do you need?"

Although the bank's core financial products remained essentially similar to those of other Danish banks,[3] the way they were delivered changed. This required significant changes in the branches, both tangible and intangible, and how they were supported. Tools were developed to support solution-based service delivery. For example, new IT systems helped employees take customers through processes to determine their needs and find appropriate solutions. In one, the customer and her banker filled out an on-line investor profile to determine what style of investment products were most

---

[3]Typical core financial products included house, car, and personal loans as well as cash management and investment services for individuals, as well as loans, cash management, and investment services for small-to-medium sized companies. Jyske Bank did not offer credit cards.

Genuine Interest and Equal Respect

>>*We demonstrate insight and respect for other people*<<

That means that we:

- recognize that no two people are alike
- seek lasting relations with shareholders, customers, and employees
- offer qualified advice matching the financial needs and requirements of each customer
- have job security based on mutual obligations and that we pay attention to individual and personal needs
- allow the highest possible degree of personal influence on assignments, working hours, and place of work

Efficient and Persevering

>>*We work consistently and with determination to reach our goals*<<

That means that we:

- use JB 2005 (the bank's core values) as a guide in our daily work
- are not blown off course because of external circumstances—but take a bearing and plot a new course when this is deemed appropriate
- adopt an organization which promotes efficiency
- consider security important to efficiency
- are convinced that efficiency increases with the level of personal responsibility
- allow employees to assume personal responsibility for day-to-day decisions—even when the basis for decision making may not be 100% perfect
- acquire the level of skills required through personal and professional development
- act on the basis of competence rather than organizational charge
- support our decisions by well-founded arguments

appropriate for her based on risk aversion, time frame, and return goals, among other factors. A manager commented that, "The tools themselves aren't proprietary. We've seen other financial services with similar programs—it's how our people use them that makes the difference." Another stated, "Our tools are designed either to enhance our ability to deliver solutions, or to reduce administrative tasks and increase the amount of time our people can spend with customers—delivering solutions."

Finally, being overtly Jyske meant that the bank would no longer be a good place for any customer meeting its demographic criteria for two reasons. First, delivering this type of service was expensive. As a result, the bank charged a slight premium, and targeted only those customers who were less likely to represent a credit risk. Second, the bank would have a personality. According to one manager, "The danger in having a personality is, someone, inevitably, won't like you." Senior management considered this the price of being candid, and welcomed the effect it had on some customers. For example, Jyske Bank's cash/debit card had a picture of a black grouse on it, black grouses being found in Jutland's rural countryside. When a few customers complained that the bird didn't seem very business-like, or wasn't hip (one was "embarrassed to pull it out at the disco") managers were happy to invite them to open accounts at competitor institutions. A manager noted:

> Actually, if no one reacts to our materials, they're not strong enough. Some people should dislike us. After all, we're only about 6% of the market. I don't want everyone to like us—we're not for everyone and don't want to be.

Tangible Differences

Account Teams

Delivering on the bank's competitive positioning required a number of tangible changes in its service delivery system. These began with assigning each customer a branch employee to serve as primary point of contact. Over time, managers discovered that this created problems, because customers often arrived at a branch when their service provider was busy with other customers or otherwise unavailable. Nevertheless, managers were committed to providing individualized service. According to one, "How can we be honest in saying we care about customers as individuals if we don't get to know them as individuals? And without knowing them, we can't identify and solve their problems." The solution was found in account teams: each customer was assigned to a small team of branch bankers. These employees worked together to know and serve their customers, sitting in close physical proximity within the branch.

Branch Design

Jyske Bank planned to spend approximately DKK 750 million to physically redesign its branches (most of this had been spent by 2003). Danish observers described the new branches as looking "like an advertising agency" or "a smart hotel." These effects were accomplished through the use of modern, up-scale materials such as light wood, warm colors, and original art. Branch redesign also included changes in the way customers interacted with their bankers, made possible by architectural and design changes. For example, customers waiting for their banker could help themselves to fresh coffee in a small part of the branch resembling a café. A customer commented on the café, "It means more than you initially think—it makes you feel welcome, it says they're really interested in me." Fruit juice was available for children, who could amuse themselves with toys in the play center. Bankers' desks were now round tables, signifying equality. A team of three or four bankers sat at a single large round table, with customers making themselves comfortable between the bankers' work stations. Customers could see bankers' computer screens, reinforcing openness. Customers' ability to view the screens also facilitated the use of IT programs designed to structure interactions between account team members and customers. As equals, bankers and customers sat in the same type of chairs, and bankers no longer sat on a raised dais, the origins of which went back to feudal times when the heads of certain people were supposed to be higher than those of others. If a conversation required more discretion, specially designed meeting rooms giving the feeling of "home" were available. **Exhibit 5** contains pictures of a remodeled branch.

Details

Jyskeness was infused into the bank wherever possible, a formal policy requiring Jyske differences to be considered in all product and IT development. No detail was too small: for example, although employees' business cards had their pictures on them,

EXHIBIT 5   Pictures of a Remodeled Branch

Source: Jyske Bank

(A)

(B)

(C)

(D)

as one manager put it, "They were bad pictures, really gray. They weren't warm—the people in them looked stiff and uncaring." To make them more Jyske, the bank hired a professional photographer who worked with each employee to "get the genuine interest in that employee's eye to come to life." Each picture was then tinted slightly yellow to make it resemble "an old family photo."

Intangible Differences

Delivering the bank's new competitive positioning also required numerous intangible changes and other changes not immediately visible to the customer. Managers stated that the most important of these involved training and empowering those employees closest to the customer to serve the customer.

Training

Before a branch was remodeled, all staff took part in special training sessions. These included teambuilding and customer service, drawing on best practices from the "traditional" retail sector.

Empowering the Branches

Jyske Bank leadership examined its organizational structure, asking, "Where is value created?" and "Where should decisions be made in order to create the most value?" The answer to both questions was "in the branches."

Previously, almost all lending decisions of any consequence required approval at the branch, regional, and headquarters levels. Specifically, a customer would approach an employee for a loan. The request would be communicated to the branch manager. The branch manager would then make out the formal application, which if the loan was for more than DKK 3 million, was sent to a regional office with the branch manager's comments. The regional office would then comment on the application, and if the loan were for more than DKK 15 million, send it to headquarters for approval, where additional comments were added to the application. Loans of more than DKK 30 million also required approval from the head of credit for the bank as a whole. In examining this process, managers discovered that most of the debate and communication were among individuals in the middle, rather than between the employee closest to the customer (who presumably had the most information about the customer) and the ultimate decision maker.

After reviewing the situation, the bank's leadership stated, "If we are to be true to our value of using common sense, we shouldn't need so many people, and so many layers, reviewing loans." First, the process was changed so that the employee receiving the request for the loan completed the formal application. This empowered that employee by giving him ownership of the loan, which he was trained in how to handle. He was also put in charge of pricing the loan, as long as his suggested pricing was within a set range of where the final approval authority felt it should be. Most loans received final approval from the branch manager, who was either selected in part based on her credit skills or given additional training in credit. A few loans required approval at the regional level because of their size. In these instances, the employee completing the application sent it directly to the regional head of credit. 98% of loans were handled at the branch or regional levels, where loans of up to DKK 90 million were approved. The credit department at headquarters was disbanded, leaving only the bank's head of credit who reviewed loans of more than DKK 90 million. This additional review was retained for loans of this size because exposure to the customer would be so great that default could significantly affect the bank's capital.

The changes implemented were originally designed to affect internal processes. However, they also improved customers' experiences. For example, managers believed that because the employee in direct contact with the customer made the application, the quality of information in applications increased; as a result, more borrowers worthy of credit received it, and the quality of loans in the bank's portfolio improved. In addition, the time to reach a decision for the largest loans declined from a maximum of three weeks to ten days. Smaller loans able to be approved within the branch could be made almost instantly. Finally, customers' expectations regarding price and terms were more often included in the application. This helped the approving authority to see whether the loan, in a form acceptable to the bank, was likely to be accepted by the customer, saving time and effort when customers' expectations were inconsistent with the bank's requirements.

The streamlined approval process did not pose a credit risk, according to managers, because of the combination of: (1) improved branch credit skills, (2) lack of incentive to make poor loans (branch managers had no incentives immediately related to loan volume or quality), and (3) a robust internal auditing function that monitored credit quality.

At the same time that the credit process was redesigned, the bank consolidated from five regions to three, and increased spans of control so that between 35 and 45 branches reported to each business unit director, who had a staff of marketing, credit, human resources, and control professionals at the regional level (many of whom had previously been at headquarters).

A senior manager commented on the roles of headquarters, the regions, and the branches:

> Headquarters is where we transform our values and strategy into products, processes, and information technology. The three regions are where we make sure that what comes from headquarters is translated for the local marketplace, and where we ensure that Jyske Differences are being acted upon—that customers experience them. The 119 branches are where we serve customers and thus where value is really created. 20% of what we do is development at headquarters, and 80% is implementation in the field, supported by the regions. Given the small size of our branches we need the regional level to ensure that implementation is done right.

Empowerment throughout the Bank

Empowerment was not limited to the branches. Throughout the bank, employees were encouraged to make decisions of all sorts if they felt comfortable doing so. In general, employees were encouraged to ask themselves, "Does it make sense to ask for help or permission? Is there a business reason for asking? Is this something you've never done before? Is this a 'big' decision (big being relative)? Is it debatable, or is it a new principle?" In general, employees were told, "When in doubt, ask. However, if there is no doubt, go ahead." Managers were expected to set an example.

Examples of this policy in action included working hours and vacation time. One employee noted, "If your job makes it possible, you set your hours, you just have to agree with your colleagues, you don't need approval from your boss. You do the same with holidays." A manager noted, "The union[4] at headquarters didn't have a problem with this, but the union in Copenhagen worried that employees might misuse the flexibility."

---

[4]As was typical in Scandinavia, most employees and managers were members of a union.

Another example involved the amount employees were able to spend on meals and entertainment while traveling or entertaining customers. Previously, there had been a set amount, DKK 125, and bills consistently came to DKK 125. Consistent with its value of common sense, the bank changed the policy to be (paraphrased) "Spend what you need to spend." This resulted in what an executive stated was a "substantial decline in travel and entertainment expenses." When asked, "How do you get a system like this to work?" he replied:

First, you tell people what's expected.

Second, you check on their behavior. If they are buying expensive wine, you ask, "Why?" You explain what makes sense, and why. You do it in a way that tells them you honestly want to help them improve.

Third, if there are continued problems, this person may not be right for the bank.

The real challenge is when we hire someone from another bank. We expect them to be up to speed quickly because of their background, but they aren't used to making these kinds of decisions—they have to be taught how.

Management Style

A senior manager commented:

You can train and educate all day long, but unless your managers and employees are committed to Jyske Differences, they just won't happen. Getting them committed required a great deal of my effort.

When we started this process there were times when it was hard—really hard. The branch managers didn't think strategically—they sat in their offices and focused on their day-to- day work. I wanted the branch manager to get up on a hill and look around, to get a bigger picture. To get them to change I asked them questions: What's the market? Where—and who—are your competitors? What are your strengths and weaknesses, how do they tie to Jyske Differences? Now, contrast what you need with what you have. Are the teams in your branch living up to the demands? What do you need to do to ensure that that they will? There will be resistance; understand where it is coming from. One way to deal with it is to make agreements with individuals on how they will develop new skills. If there is a complete mismatch you may need new team members, but for the most part, you can coach your people through this kind of change—you can lead them.

According to another executive:

The branch managers have to be able to motivate employees to work a little harder, and differently. The most successful give their employees a lot of latitude for decision making. They do a lot of training, 80% of which is on the job. When it isn't, it's mostly role playing. There aren't any high-powered incentives to offer, but there are really good tools coming out of IT. It's more *how the branch managers do it* than *what they do.* They constantly link the tools, training, and behaviors to our Jyske values. They get their employees to share the values and act on them.

A third noted:

When I have a difficult situation I look for what I call a "culture carrier." I try to put that person into the middle of it, because they live our values. What I usually see is that the other employees who are on the fence about the values start to come over—they see the example and they like what they see. This leaves the few people who really don't want to be Jyske on the outside, and they tend not to last long. Most people are willing to change, but they've got to be supported in the process.

Human Resources

Legal aspects of human resources, record keeping, and training were centralized at headquarters. In contrast, advice on how to deal with human issues was provided by human resource professionals located in the field (at the regional level). They delivered this advice to general managers in the field such as branch managers. The branches had to pay for this service, and they could choose to either buy the service or do without if they preferred.

Selection   An executive discussed employee selection at the bank:

> It's very important. For most of the jobs, we're not only looking for banking skills, we're looking for social abilities—service mindedness and compatibility with our Jyske values: openness, genuine interest in other people. You can smell it when you speak with someone. We don't have a systematic approach to this, although when we're hiring someone from another bank we ask why they want to work for us and listen for answers consistent with Jyske values. We can train most banking skills, but we can't train these attitudes. Maybe our biggest challenge is hiring people with them, and getting a few of our established employees to adopt them.

Some departments of the bank asked potential hires to write about themselves. A manager noted, "We're looking to see whether they're engaged in what they do, or if they're promoting themselves."

Training   A manager in human resources commented:

> We have told every employee that his or her development is his or her responsibility. We believe development is incredibly important. While my peers at other Danish banks are cutting staff and saving every way possible, our goal is to get employees and managers to invest in more development. But it's up to the individual to decide what to invest in. We're outsourcing a lot of development activities, but we keep anything related to Jyske values in house.

Incentives   Managers pointed out that the bank had few monetary incentives. The few in place consisted of three types, stock, one-time payments, and annual raises.

> Stock incentives: if the bank's annual performance was above the average of the top ten Danish banks', a stock option grant valued at DKK 8.000 was made available to all employees and managers. In addition, any employee could use up to DKK 13.200 to buy company stock annually at a 20% discount. If the bank's annual performance was among the top three Danish banks', the discount rose to 40%.
> One-time payments: for truly exceptional work, employees could be awarded one-time payments. Fewer than 1% of individuals at the bank received this type of payment.
> Raise incentives: employees and managers received annual salary increases based on their manager's evaluation of their work. The highest raise practicably possible was 10%, although an employee or manager in the top 15% of performers (the highest level) typically received a raise of approximately 7%. Salary raises were eventually limited as total salary had to remain within the bands established for a particular position. Once an increase was granted it became a permanent part of the employee's salary.

Commitment   An employee commented on what it was like to work for Jyske Bank: "I'm not restricted. I don't have to leave my head at home—I can take it with me to work and I'm supposed to." Another commented:

> You're treated as a human being here. At other banks you have to be really careful what you say. Here, you can be open and honest—I can approach anyone—even the CEO.

> Jyske Bank is a way of life. You come in at 8:00 and you leave when you collect your pension. I pay a premium for this, I could earn more at another bank, but it's worth it for me. At some banks, bankers have prostituted themselves for higher pay, stuffing products down the throats of customers those customers may not need. We don't.

Anders Dam, Jyske Bank's CEO, stated:

> If you can create an environment in which people aren't talking about money, but where they gain value in their relationships with their colleagues and their customers, where the bank will take care of those who work hard even if they get sick, then people will be committed to the bank.

Metrics and Financial Results

Bank managers frequently referred to the importance of measuring performance, in both quantitative and qualitative ways, and at a variety of locations in the bank. Traditional financial measures were considered important, but not all-important. In addition to traditional measures, Jyske Bank implemented an information technology system to measure account profitability on a risk-adjusted basis (risk adjusted return on capital, or RAROC). This had been a considerable effort and was just coming on-line in 2003.

Customer and employee measures were also considered important. Managers reported that employee satisfaction was higher at Jyske Bank than at any of its major competitors based on data collected by independent third parties. Several sources of data indicated that Jyske Bank customer satisfaction was also the highest among the bank's major competitors (see **Exhibit 2**). Customer satisfaction could be tracked to the regional level. Plans were in place to be able to measure and report it at the branch, and eventually the individual customer, levels.

Financial and selected operating results are presented in **Exhibit 6**. Jyske Bank took a conservative approach to earnings, writing off its entire investment in remodeling branches, building a new headquarters, and new information technology systems in the years in which spending occurred. This amounted to DKK 302 million in 2002, DKK 253 million in 2001, DKK 194 million in 2000, and DKK 212 million in 1999. Results for 2002 also reflected an extraordinary tax payment of DKK 222 million, which was described as "a potential liability in light of discussions with the Danish tax authorities."[5]

Jyske Bank's statement of core values and principles included the following:

> . . . the aim is for Jyske Bank every year to be one of the top performing Danish banks
> . . . Jyske Bank is thus an excellent choice for shareholders who want to make a long-term investment and who do not attach great importance to decisions which generate only short-term price increases.

Communication

Management believed that most employees liked working for the bank and appreciated Jyske Differences as they affected their jobs. Sustaining Jyske Differences required the bank to remain independent, not an easy task in the Scandinavian banking market, which had consolidated considerably during the 1990s and early twenty-first century. Executives believed that they had taken the right steps to remain independent by investing in employees, systems, and infrastructure that would enable the bank to deliver superior value to its targeted customers, and thus achieve superior financial returns. This economic model was built on the bank's value chain (see **Exhibit 7**).

[5]According to an executive, "If we are right [and we eventually reverse the charge] we have an upside. If we are wrong it won't impact future results. All in all the tax issue is not related to the 2002 result and it would be more correct to judge the result before tax."

EXHIBIT 6   Jyske Bank Group Financial and Selected Operating Results

Source: Jyske Bank

Five-Year Summary of Financial Results					
Summary of Profit and Loss Account (DKKm)	**2002**	**2001**	**2000**	**1999**	**1998**
Net interest income	**2,826**	2,623	2,350	2,078	2,133
Dividend on capital holdings	**64**	98	69	52	34
Net fee and commission income	**758**	668	759	646	594
Net interest and fee income	**3,648**	3,389	3,178	2,776	2,761
Revaluations	**386**	129	379	631	−361
Other ordinary income	**203**	213	162	175	219
Operating expenses and depreciation	**2,598**	2,443	2,142	2,014	1,764
Losses and provisions for bad debts	**408**	286	318	248	197
Revaluation of capital interests	**−148**	−112	−4	−44	52
Profit/loss on ordinary activities before tax	**1,083**	890	1,255	1,276	710
Tax	**572**	267	172	379	199
Profit/loss for the year	**511**	623	1,083	897	511
Summary of Balance Sheet (DKKm)	**2002**	**2001**	**2000**	**1999**	**1998**
Advances	**95,302**	82,537	75,362	49,790	39,762
Deposits	**58,963**	54,393	52,267	49,813	43,816
Issued bonds	**43,362**	36,964	26,902	192	623
Total assets	**153,169**	133,156	127,359	92,557	76,938
Shareholders' funds	**6,658**	6,174	5,887	5,391	5,108
Supplementary capital	**2,000**	2,663	2,110	1,395	434
Key Figures	**2002**	**2001**	**2000**	**1999**	**1998**
Per Jyske Bank share					
Core earnings	**23.17**	25.39	22.07	14.68	19.89
Profit/loss on ordinary activities before tax	**29.32**	24.11	31.86	29.58	15.77
Net profit/loss for the year	**13.84**	16.77	27.51	20.83	11.22
Dividend	**0.00**	0.00	0.00	3.20	2.80
Price at year-end	**192**	177	161	149	123
Book value	**178**	170	157	131	114
Price/book value	**1.08**	1.04	1.03	1.14	1.08
Price/earnings	**13.8**	10.5	5.9	7.2	10.9
The Jyske Bank Group					
Solvency ratio	**11.3**	11.4	11.0	10.5	10.4
Core capital ratio	**8.2**	7.9	8.0	8.2	9.5
Income on every krone of expenditure	**1.36**	1.33	1.51	1.56	1.36
Total provisions as % of total loans	**1.8**	1.9	2.0	2.7	3.0
Losses and provisions for the year as % of total loans	**0.4**	0.3	0.4	0.4	0.4

continued

EXHIBIT 6 Jyske Bank Group Financial and Selected Operating Results—continued

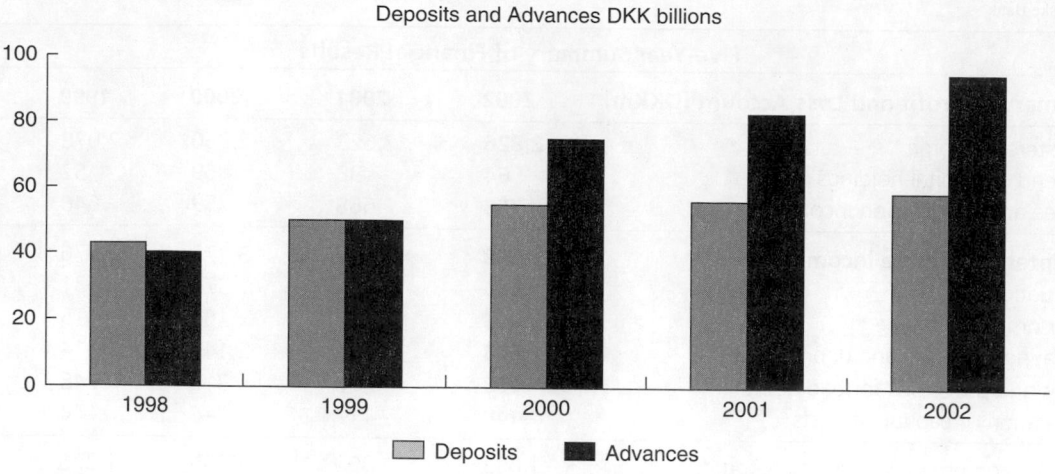

Deposits and Advances DKK billions

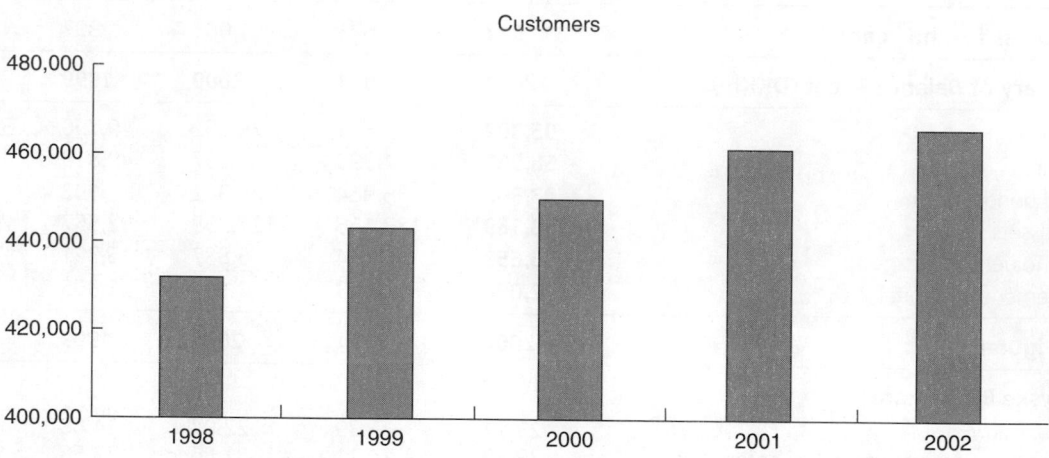

Customers

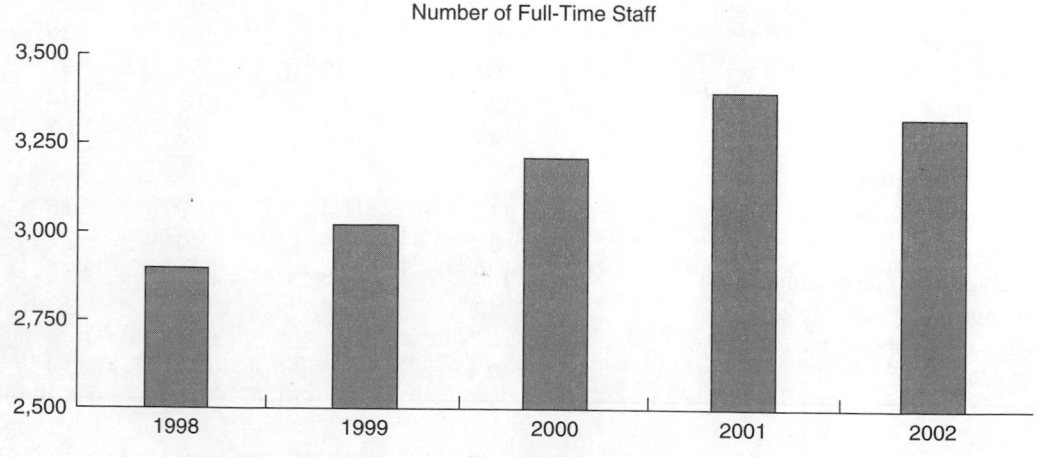

Number of Full-Time Staff

EXHIBIT 7
The Jyske Bank
Value Chain

Source: Jyske Bank's
adaptation of Heskett, Sasser,
and Schlesinger's Service
Profit Chain, see Heskett
et al., 1997.

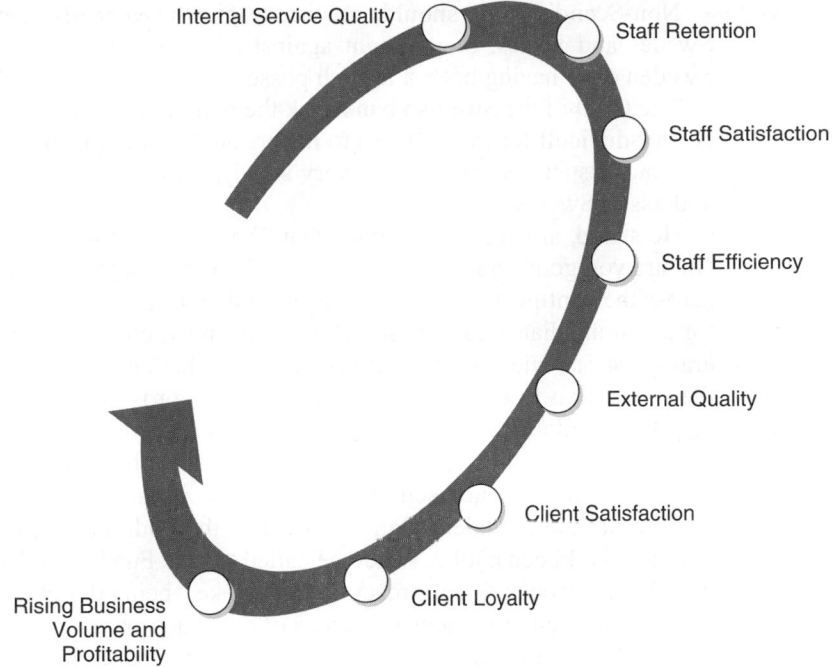

Internal Service Quality

Staff Retention

Staff Satisfaction

Staff Efficiency

External Quality

Client Satisfaction

Client Loyalty

Rising Business
Volume and
Profitability

Delivering that value required considerable change. One manager stated a point that several alluded to:

> If you want employees to behave differently, you have to be sure they know what that means—how they should behave going forward, and why they should change. We can't ask people to change without communicating this kind of information to them—it's not fair.

Bank leadership believed that communication should be, in the words of an executive, "a car wash, not a waterfall—communication must come from all directions at once, not just cascade down from above." In that spirit, in 1997 communication reinforced Jyske values and differences when the bank produced a video tape on Jyske Differences made available to all employees. This was designed to look like a television talk show. The host was a prominent Danish television personality and the guests were Anders Dam and Danish experts on business. Each was interviewed and they discussed what Jyske Differences were, how they were being implemented, and what they meant to employees and customers, supported by video clips of employees and customers in the branches.

Communication efforts continued in 1999, executives planning a surprise for the bank's strategic meeting, to which all employees were invited every third year.

The Battle at Vejle   The 1999 strategic meeting took place in Vejle, the closest city to the bank's headquarters with an auditorium large enough for the 82% of the bank's 3,107 employees who chose to attend. The meeting opened with a panel of senior executives, some of whom were from Jyske Bank, and others who were strangers. A grim-faced Anders Dam got up, and introduced one of the strangers as "the CEO of a large, very large, Swedish bank." Dam then continued, explaining that the Swedish bank had offered to buy Jyske Bank for almost twice its current stock market valuation, a premium of 2.3 times what other Danish banks had recently been acquired for. A fax was to be sent to the Copenhagen stock exchange, suspending trading in Jyske Bank shares immediately after the meeting. As he spoke, a sense of foreboding rose in the audience.

Non-Scandinavians should note that despite the currently cozy relationship between Swedes and Danes, they fought against one another for many centuries, Southern Sweden once having been a Danish possession.

The CEO of the Swedish bank took the podium and announced (in Swedish, which is very difficult for most Danes to understand) that his Danish was very poor, so that he would "speak Scandinavian, very slowly," after which he continued to deliver his address in Swedish.

He stated, among other things, that "You—Jyske Bank, you are good, very good. But are you good enough? For tomorrow? For the future? For a world without borders across the continent?" After his speech Anders Dam took the podium again and asked for an "immediate and honest response" from the employees. Over the course of several questions and responses it became clear that although the takeover was friendly, the integration would be anything but. In the words of the Swedish CEO, "A merger has certain administrative advantages, which will require an adjustment in staffing." Eventually, a manager got up and said, "Do something for the environment. Put the Swedes on the ferry and send them back!" His suggestion received wild applause.

After a pause, Anders Dam returned to the podium and, now smiling, explained that it had all been a joke, which he called "Jyske Fun." He added that he was "proud, proud as a peacock of your reaction to the joke," being delighted that the vast majority of the audience flatly rejected the idea of being acquired. One questioner put it bluntly, stating that (paraphrased) "Jyske Bank couldn't live Jyske Differences, couldn't do the things for employees and customers they had been working so hard on, if it were to be acquired." Dam finished his speech by pointing out that if Jyske Bank were to remain independent in the increasingly-competitive environment Danish banks now faced, everyone would have to contribute.

Part of that contribution was an effort to diversify the bank's type of shareholders and increase their number in order to ensure that they shared its long-term perspective on financial performance. Employees encouraged customers to consider purchasing Jyske Bank Group shares. Between the "Battle at Vejle" and 2003, the number of shareholders increased from 150.000 to more than 210.000.

Managers and employees agreed that the message of the "Battle at Vejle" was heard throughout the organization and that Jyske Fun was a good idea. Subsequent examples of it included the only national advertising campaign the bank had engaged in during the past decade, which was effectively a dog beauty contest with entry requiring a visit to a local branch. When asked why advertising was so limited, an executive replied:

> Two reasons. First, we rely on word of mouth, so we don't need to advertise that much— our advertising cost as a percentage of revenue is half what banks of similar size spend. Second, we have to be absolutely sure we can consistently deliver Jyske Differences before we advertise them.

Later in 1999, communication efforts continued when managers created a video tape illustrating Jyske Differences in an unusual way. The tape introduces Max Performa, an ex-KGB agent hired by a mysterious and beautiful senior manager of a competitor bank. Performa is assigned to find out if Jyske Differences are actually being delivered at Jyske Bank's branches. He checks off each Jyske Difference as he experiences it, pretending to be a Jutlandish farmer wanting a loan (speaking Danish with a thick Russian accent). In the course of applying for the loan he discovers that Jyske Differences are being delivered, among them that the employee opening his account has the authority necessary to meet his needs (*common sense*), that the bank will go to great lengths to show *genuine interest* in him (he and the branch manager drink an entire bottle of vodka one afternoon), and that Jyske Bank *is different* and isn't for everyone: when he complains about the black grouse on his debit card he is politely told he might be happier banking with a competitor. At the end of the tape the viewer learns that the mysterious senior manager who hired Performa actually works for Jyske Bank.

Executives believed that they needed to constantly reinforce the message that remaining independent required every employee to work a little harder, and to behave in a manner consistent with Jyske Differences. To deliver that constant reinforcement, they printed the bank's values and Jyske Differences in materials that managers were asked to discuss with their employees. On one occasion, branch employees were asked to come in on a Saturday, without pay, to discuss the values and differences and their implications for day to-day behavior. 80% chose to come in.

In 2002, communication efforts included the bank's strategic employee meeting, called "Return to Vejle." The meeting, complete with live, high-energy music (a locally popular drum duo) and entertainment, celebrated the bank's accomplishments and served as a reminder of what still needed to be done.

Finally, in 2002 the bank introduced what it called a "tool box" for communicating value chain information to and from the branches. The tool box enabled each branch to select elements on the bank's value chain (see **Exhibit 7**) and measure the branch's performance against goals related to that element. The tool box delivered regularly updated information including guides such as green or red lights describing the branch's performance on the selected value chain elements. An executive described the tool box as "a way to operationalize the value chain so that everyone in the organization understands how they need to behave on a day-to-day basis in order to optimize it."

CONCLUSION

The bank's leadership believed that Jyske values and differences, and the bank's value chain, provided ways to achieve the balance they wanted among their three stakeholders: employees, customers, and shareholders. Several leaders commented that with the large capital investments behind them as of 2003, net income would increase considerably in the coming years, assuming the recession of 2001 and 2002 was over. Shareholders had received a 17.8% annual return on their investment for the ten years prior to year-end 2002. Anders Dam's 2002–2003 goal for shareholders was to increase the bank's stock multiple approximately 40% to the level of Danske Bank's, the largest and most richly-priced bank in Denmark. This was achieved in July 2003.[6] While the bank's leadership was pleased with the bank's success, they were more interested in determining how the bank would remain in a position of leadership while still keeping the interests of its key stakeholders in balance.

QUESTIONS TO THE JYSKE BANK CASE

1. As of the mid-1990s, what was Jyske Bank's competitive positioning, that is, what did it do for customers relative to its competitors?
2. As of 2003, what was Jyske Bank's competitive positioning?
3. What did Jyske Bank change to enable it to deliver its new competitive positioning?
4. How did Jyske Bank implement those changes?

[6]Managers attributed the increase in the bank's stock price multiple to recognition among stock analysts that investments in Jyske Differences made in the previous five years and expensed immediately were bearing fruit.

Case 2
Merrill Lynch: *Supernova*

Rogelio Oliva

There's a good chance that Supernova is the right thing at the right time. But I need to be sure before I recommend total adoption. Even if I do decide to back it, how do we roll it out? How can we get this organization, top, middle, and front-line, to buy into it—and change their behavior accordingly? Does everyone need to buy in, or will it be enough to have a "critical mass?" What would a critical mass look like?

> — *Jim Walker, managing director and chief administrative officer,*
> *Merrill Lynch Client Relationship Group*

Founded in 1907, Merrill Lynch grew rapidly under its founders' strategy to "Bring Wall Street to Main Street." In the 1970s, the firm became a powerful force in investment banking in addition to retail brokerage. By 2000, Merrill described itself as "the preeminent financial management and advisory company—serving governments, institutions, and investors throughout the world." In 2003, Merrill Lynch was one of the leading financial-services firms in the world, and was the largest of the "broker dealer" firms on Wall Street, employing more financial advisors (individuals who managed relationships with retail clients) than any of its competitors (see **Exhibit 1**).

Jim Walker was a member of Merrill's Client Relationship Group, part of Merrill's Private Client Group, which was responsible for financial-advisory services for

Professor Rogelio Oliva, Roger Hallowell (MBA '89, DBA '97) of the Center for Executive Development, and MIT Sloan Nippon Telephone and Telegraph Professor of Management Science Gabriel R. Bitran prepared this case. It is based, in part, on research conducted by Bassim Halaby, Qunmei Li, Hugo Barra, Luca Donà, Geyza Salgado, Muhammad Farid, and Mary Schaefer of MIT Sloan. HBS cases are developed solely as the basis for class discussion. Cases are not intended to serve as endorsements, sources of primary data, or illustrations of effective or ineffective management.

EXHIBIT 1 **Stockbrokerages and Stockbrokers/Financial Advisors**

Source: Adapted from *Securities Industry Yearbook,* Securities Industry Association, Inc.: Washington, D.C., 2002.

Firm	Stockbrokers/FAs (Registered reps)	Rank
Merrill Lynch & Co., Inc.	15,753	1
Salomon Smith Barney Holdings, Inc.	13,826	2
Morgan Stanley	13,690	3
UBS PaineWebber Inc.	8,801	4
Edward Jones	8,595	5

EXHIBIT 2
Market Share for Traditional (full-line) Brokers and Discounters

Source: Created using data from Securities Industries Association DATABANK.

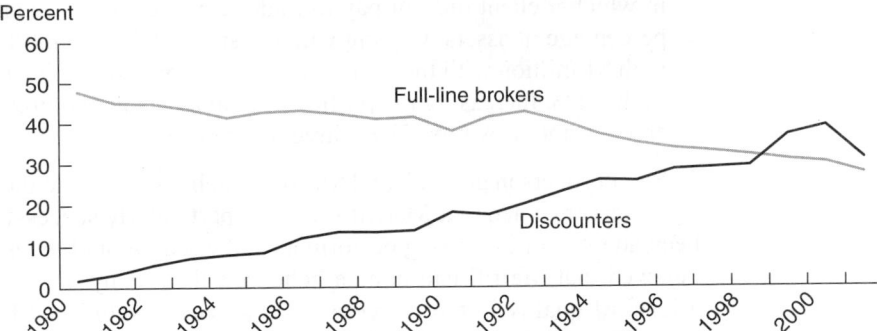

Market Share of NYSE Commissions

Note: Post-1997, this chart may not reflect all full-line broker revenues as many full-line brokerages began to encourage their brokers/FAs to convert their accounts from commission generating (traditional) to fee-based (annuitized).

individuals (retail brokerage). The retail-brokerage environment had begun to change in the 1970s with the partial deregulation of stock brokering. Under deregulation, new firms entered the market with different service offerings. For example, Charles Schwab offered discounted trading directed by the investor, in contrast to the traditional brokerage model in which investors received advice from their stockbroker, and or placed orders through him or her. **Exhibit 2** illustrates market share of traditional brokers and discounters. Mutual-fund distribution was also deregulated in the 1970s, enabling firms such as Fidelity Investments to compete with stock brokerages indirectly by selling shares in their mutual funds to the public directly.[1]

FINANCIAL ADVISORS

Retail brokerages such as Merrill Lynch delivered their services to individual clients through stockbrokers, or "financial advisors" (FAs) as they were called at Merrill. Typically, an FA would bring clients to the firm through his or her relationships, networking, professional alliances, industry affiliations, and by "cold calling"[2] individuals thought to be good prospects.

Once an account was opened, the experience of an individual client varied considerably depending on his or her financial advisor. Some FAs routinely contacted clients to check on the client, offer advice on existing investments with the firm, and solicit additional business. Others rarely contacted their clients except to offer them new investment products the firm wanted to sell. For these FAs, contact with clients more often occurred when the client called to initiate a trade, or report a problem. According to a senior Merrill manager, "Unfortunately, a lot of our FAs fall into this category. The problem is, we've always charged for good service, and everyone has wanted to deliver it, but some of our people haven't followed through."

FA compensation, like that of most stockbrokers, was purely variable, based on the quantity of business they brought to the firm. Compensation was a combination of:

1. A percentage of the revenue generated from commission for buying and selling financial products in a client's account ("trades"). For example, if a client were charged $120 to trade 1,000 shares of stock, the FA might keep 40%.

[1] Prior to the 1970s, mutual-fund shares had to be sold through financial intermediaries such as stockbrokers. In 2003 Fidelity Investments was the largest mutual-fund company in the world.

[2] "Cold calling" meant contacting potential clients with no prior introduction, often by telephone or direct mail.

2. A percentage of the revenue generated from "annuitized," or fee-based accounts, in which a client did not pay to trade securities, but was annually charged a small percentage of assets, varying with the size of the account. For example, a customer with $1 million with the firm might pay 1% of assets.[3] The FA would keep a portion of that 1%. Increasing the portion of total assets in annuitized accounts was considered a priority by most Wall Street brokerages.

Stockbrokers in general, and Merrill Lynch FAs in particular, were well paid. Industry observers noted that Merrill FAs were particularly successful because the firm had been adept at hiring strong performers and weeding out the less successful. Some also believed that Merrill had done a better job than many of its competitors of ensuring a level of quality in the delivery of its service. Established brokers typically earned several hundred thousand dollars annually, with the most successful earning more than a million dollars each year.

FAs enjoyed the autonomy their jobs provided. According to one: "What *I* bring in, is *mine*. I work for Merrill Lynch, but I have my own clients. As long as I keep within the letter of the law I can serve them as I like and sell them any of Merrill's products. I'm in competition with every other FA in this office. If Merrill wants me to be a "we" person, they can pay me a salary—they don't."

Good FAs, like all good stockbrokers, were in demand among the various retail-brokerage firms, and could earn additional income by changing firms, when the acquiring firm would pay a substantial bonus to the new broker based on his or her "production" or historical revenue volume. The bonus was designed to compensate the stockbroker for the portion of clients who remained with the old firm rather than moving with the broker. However, the bonus more than compensated for the loss. In fact, many firms viewed the "signing bonus" as a way to acquire both brokers and clients. Historically, the relationship between the stockbroker and the client was considered to be stronger than the relationship between the client and the firm, or the firm and the stockbroker. Some brokers changed firms frequently.

Stockbroker acquisition was the job of the head of a local office. These individuals were often highly talented brokers who split their time between their own clients and managing the other brokers in the office. Many found the acquisition of new brokers a thrill, not unlike the acquisition of new clients.

FAs, like all stockbrokers, came from a variety of backgrounds. They typically had college educations, and all U.S. brokers were required to pass examinations such as the National Association of Securities Dealers' Series 7. All successful stockbrokers were gifted salespeople. Many used sporting terms to describe the acquisition of new clients, an activity (when successful) they uniformly enjoyed.

The acquisition of new clients resulted in what many brokers called their "book." This was a broker's list of clients having an account at the firm. Many firms, including Merrill Lynch, had encouraged their brokers to increase the size of their books, paying them incentives to open new accounts. According to one Merrill FA, "In the 1990s, Merrill ran what it called 'The Masters' program—you got a trip to Hawaii if you opened enough new accounts. Everyone was opening any account they could. Service, customer retention, and profitability didn't matter—it was all about new accounts." As a result, the size of their book came to be important to many FAs. Another noted: "I know I'm going to be OK, even in a downturn, if I've got a big book. All those names really make you feel secure, and that's important in a business

---

[3]The percentage varied considerably based on whether or not the client used third-party investment advice.

EXHIBIT 3
Merrill Lynch
Private Client Group
Field Organization
Structure

Source: Merrill Lynch.

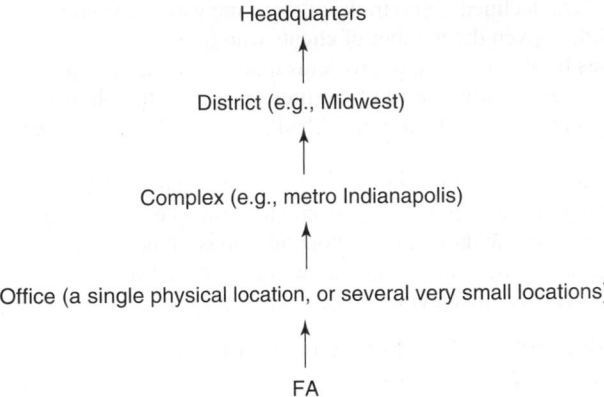

like this where you can only rely on yourself and you have to keep producing if you want to eat."

Merrill Lynch's FAs were thought to be among the best on Wall Street. The firm enjoyed a reputation for being an attractive place to work, based on (1) the support provided for brokers in the form of a strong brand and good financial products, and (2) the freedom brokers were given to effectively run their own businesses as long as they generated enough business, used Merrill Lynch financial products, and met basic ethical standards. An executive of another brokerage commented on Merrill Lynch and its FAs: "They're the best—they do what we do, what everyone does, but they do it better. How they 'out execute' us I'm not exactly sure, but they do it—again and again."

SUPERNOVA

Supernova was the name given to a new way to manage client relationships that originated in one of Merrill Lynch's Indianapolis offices (**Exhibit 3** illustrates Merrill's field organization structure). Unlike a strategic initiative from headquarters, it came up through the ranks as a strategy for implementation, in response to conceptual strategy set at the top.

The "father" of Supernova was Rob Knapp, who ran Merrill Lynch's Mid-West district. In 1995, Knapp had had a good year in revenue terms, but was concerned about future revenues because his district ranked last in client satisfaction among the 32 districts in the country. Eighteen months later, following the implementation of a Supernova predecessor, Knapp's office ranked fourth.

Client Service before Supernova

Merrill's research led management to believe that three aspects of a relationship were critical to client satisfaction:

1. The frequency and quality of contact
2. Rapid response to problems
3. Attention to details

An FA commented on the ability to deliver these prior to Supernova:

> Most of us didn't pay any attention to frequency of contact—if a client called, we spoke to them. We didn't have time to make calls to clients because we were busy dealing with clients calling us—wanting us to fix problems they were having, hold their hands when

the markets declined, or do trades. Extra time was spent prospecting—and we had to do a lot of that given the number of clients who quit.

It was hard to respond to problems quickly. We used to get overwhelmed—my assistant was spending most of her time answering the phones—she didn't have time to deal with problems, which meant I had to deal with them, except I was supposed to be dealing with clients.

Attention to detail means things like being aware of life events for a client—an impending birth, retirement, the desire to refinance a mortgage. These are really important because they represent opportunities to meet a client's needs by selling them something they need and want. But we didn't have time to listen for these kinds of details—we were just trying to keep our heads above water.

According to Knapp: "The objective of Supernova is to create the 'ultimate' client experience. We asked ourselves, 'What would the ultimate client experience look like?' That was when we came up with 12-4-2."

12-4-2

12-4-2 was the Supernova description of what clients' minimum annual contact with their financial advisor should be: 12 monthly contacts (to stay in touch and ask for updates on financial goals or changes in needs), of which 4 were portfolio reviews, and 2 were face-to-face meetings. Some clients needed more contact, but 12-4-2 was the minimum.

12-4-2 was based on studies conducted within and outside of Merrill on client desires. According to one FA, 12-4-2 enforced discipline: "I'm just not that organized—I'm a people person. 12-4-2 forces me to make the contacts I know I should make, but I've always found excuses not to."

12-4-2 was predicated upon the completion of a financial plan for the client at the beginning of the relationship. Although Merrill had been encouraging all of its FAs to develop financial plans for their clients, according to several FAs, "More often than not, it wasn't happening."

While 12-4-2 was a breakthrough from the clients' perspective, it posed a dilemma for the FAs who wanted to implement it: there were too few hours in the day to deliver even a fraction of 12-4-2 because the average Merrill FA had 550 clients. As a result, the way FAs planning to adopt 12-4-2 conducted their business had to change. The changes ultimately becoming a part of Supernova, in addition to 12-4-2 and financial planning, were described as *segmentation, organization,* and *acquisition.*

Segmentation

Knapp used an analogy to suits to discuss the principle of client segmentation:

Let's say you really like the process of buying suits. Over the years, you develop a really big collection of suits. The problem is, you don't have the space to keep them all in good condition. Your closet's only big enough for 20. So you clean out your closet, and you send all but your 20 best suits to a relative. During the next year, you buy a few more suits—good ones. Remember, you *like* buying suits. At the end of the year, you clean out your closet again—and you force yourself to keep only the 20 best suits. Now, you have 20 really beautiful suits. You're happy, the suits have enough space in the closet, and you always look great.

It's no different with clients. The typical FA has 550. She can't give them all good service— there's not enough room in the closet. Most of them aren't capable of being very profitable— most aren't really good suits. Only by segmenting clients and only keeping the best can an FA have time to give them the service they need—that will make them loyal.

EXHIBIT 4 12-4-2 and the Need to Segment

Source: Merrill Lynch.

4A. **Number of Primary Client: 550**		
12-4-2 Contacts per Week: 22 semi-annual, 22 quarterly, and 88 monthly calls		
	Assumptions	**Minutes Consumed**
Weeks per Year =	50	
Minutes Required for:		
Face-to-Face Meeting	90	1,980
Quarterly Phone Review	45	990
Monthly Phone Contact	15	1,320
Minutes Consumed per Week (in hours)		72
Time Available for Acquisition and Administration		0

4B. **Number of Primary Client: 200**		
12-4-2 Contacts per Week: 8 semi-annual, 8 quarterly and 32 monthly calls		
	Assumptions	**Minutes Consumed**
Weeks per Year =	50	
Minutes Required for:		
Face-to-Face Meeting	90	720
Quarterly Phone Review	45	360
Monthly Phone Contact	15	480
Minutes Consumed per Week (in hours)		26
Time Available for Acquisition and Administration (in hours)		14

Note: Excludes nonprimary clients.

Knapp believed that the appropriate number of clients was 200 based on an analysis he conducted, which is illustrated in **Exhibits 4 (A)** and **(B)**. One Merrill office in which every FA adopted Supernova set a goal per FA of 200 clients, each having at least $1 million in annuitized assets at Merrill, or $10,000 in annual production (fees from trading).

The decision to keep or forgo a client was complex. Fortunately, an FA developed a spreadsheet model to help other FAs in the process. Developing the model took 11 months, however, once the model was completed an FA could conduct the analysis in approximately 30 minutes.

The FA who developed the model recognized that in order to deliver the high level of service he wanted all of his clients to receive he would have to reduce their number. He initially decided to keep only his top 100 clients. While that decision was easy, determining which clients made up his top 100 proved difficult.

Initially, he ranked his clients by revenue generation. Then, he ranked them by assets. He discovered that the two rankings were very different. Third, he ranked his clients by those he and his assistant liked doing business with. Again, the ranking was different from the earlier two. In all, he produced 11 rankings based on different criteria for keeping clients. He then decided to see which clients were on all 11 lists. Thirty-three clients appeared on every list. Those 33 generated 89% of his income during the previous year. In addition, his assistant noted that only 3 of the 53 clients she had helped with problems over the past five weeks were among the 33. Ultimately, the FA kept only those 33 clients, stating, "With those 33 I had 89% of my income and a lot fewer hassles—I've been able to spend my time giving them *really* great service and acquiring more *really* good clients. My income—and my life—has never been so good."

Most Supernova FAs decided to reduce their book to (1) 200 primary clients, (2) important family or business associates of those clients (whom FAs kept to avoid endangering the primary client relationship), and (3) those clients described as "necessary to keep if you want to get into heaven." The ratio of primary clients to important family or business associates was targeted at 3:1.

Clients whom an FA decided not to keep were given to another FA or were sent to the Financial Advisory Center, Merrill's centralized facility for smaller accounts, if their assets with Merrill totaled less than $100,000 and were unlikely to increase in the foreseeable future. The center served these accounts through a toll-free telephone number and proactively called them at least four times a year to ensure that their needs were being met. Many clients did not object to this new style of service; the center's client-retention rate was actually higher than that of the average FA's. FAs received payments from corporate for those clients sent to the center. Several FAs noted that once transferred, their clients increased the business they did with Merrill, and as a result, they earned considerably more on them than they had previously. FAs noted, however, that rumors about corporate ending the payments were rampant. Clients given to another FA were generally given away with no remuneration. According to one FA, "This way you're totally focused on the clients you're keeping—there's no looking over your shoulder."

Organization

Historically, each FA organized his or her practice in whatever way he or she thought best. Supernova did not require an FA to adopt a particular organization scheme, but it did provide tools that many Supernova FAs found useful. Merrill studies of FA desires indicated that what they wanted most was "more administrative support," followed closely by "help getting organized."

One of the biggest organizational problems FAs encountered involved using their time effectively. Day-to-day, this meant delegating routine, administrative tasks to their administrative assistants, called client associates. An FA using Supernova commented:

> In the past, clients wanted to speak with their FA whenever they had a problem or needed something. I can't blame them, otherwise they rarely spoke to their FA. Under Supernova, clients know they'll speak to their FA at least monthly, in fact, they know exactly when the conversation is scheduled for. As a result, if they have a problem or need a small, administrative change, the client associate can usually handle it.

Another FA added: "Clients used to feel it was OK to call and interrupt me whenever. Now, I'm more of a professional to them. Think about it—would you call your dentist and expect to speak with him immediately?"

In effect, under Supernova client associates "triaged" client telephone calls, only involving the FA when necessary.[4] Supernova client associates also prepared FAs' daily "folders." Each folder contained a client's most recent financial plan, amendments to it, and information on the client's family and business that the FA believed was germane to the relationship. This included mortgage and tax rates, real estate, insurance policies, hobbies, immediate family and important relatives/associates, and

---

[4]Note that for legal reasons, transactions involving buying or selling were conducted by FAs or registered client associates.

financial holdings not at Merrill. According to one Supernova FA: "I never want to be speaking with a client and not have the information I need to do my job—which is to take care of that client's total financial-service needs."

The folder supported the "folder system," which enforced discipline on the FA in the following way: client associates set up telephone or in-person meetings between the FA and clients, consistent with 12-4-2. These meetings were placed on the FA's calendar, with FA's dedicating between six and eight hours each day to these meetings (the time dedicated to meetings corresponded to the number of clients an FA could have under Supernova). Each morning, the FA would be given the folders for clients with whom he or she was meeting that day. These practices accomplished four things:

First, they forced the FA to make good on 12-4-2 without increasing his or her administrative burden.

Second, they ensured that he or she would have the most up-to-date information available for the meeting.

Third, they induced "folder guilt." If an FA didn't contact all the clients on the list for that day, her client associate would have wasted time preparing the folders. Because FAs tended to work closely with their client associates, folder guilt was often strong enough to get the FA to meet her contact obligations, something numerous "contact systems" had failed to do.

Finally, the folder system helped to ensure that the financial plan the client and the FA agreed to was implemented, an occasional failure in the past according to several FAs.

Client associates generally preferred to work under Supernova. According to one Supernova FA:

> The first three months on Supernova are hell for a client associate because the transition isn't easy—they're doing both the traditional work and the Supernova work. But once everyone settles into the Supernova routine, it's great. The client associate's day is much more predictable—prepare folders for the next day, set up meetings, and deal with a few problems. Because there are fewer clients—and happier clients—there are fewer problems, and everyone is happier.

Some FAs experimented with offering bonuses to their client associates to help them through the transition. At one office, client associates getting their FAs fully segmented and organized under Supernova received $1,000 directly from the FAs.

The Supernova Service Promise

Commitment to developing a financial plan for every client and 12-4-2, coupled with (1) segmentation and (2) organization, enabled Supernova FAs to make the following service promise to their clients:

You are guaranteed three things.

1. You will have a multi-generation financial plan in place.
2. You will be contacted by your FA at least 12 times every year.
3. You will receive rapid response to any problem you may have, hearing from us within 1 hour, and having resolution within 24.

Acquisition

The final part of Supernova was called "acquisition." As suggested by Knapp's suit analogy, each year a Supernova FA would acquire some new, high-quality clients, handing the least promising clients displaced by the new clients to another FA, or the Financial Advisory Center.

The time dedicated to 12-4-2 left between two and four hours each day for client acquisition, which the FAs found more than adequate. As one commented:

> At first, I was skeptical that this would be enough time. What I've found is that it's more than enough, for two reasons. First, since I segmented my book, gave up all but my top 200, and committed to 12-4-2, my client turnover has decreased dramatically. It used to be that I had to do a lot of selling just to stay even. In fact, for every new client I got, I usually lost a client—I had to run just to stay in place.
>
> Second, I've found that the best way to get new clients is through my existing clients. I've got a lot of clients who have been so impressed with the way I handle them, they've recommended me to their friends and relatives. I'm pretty obvious about wanting referrals, so they know I'm hungry for new business. But it doesn't seem to bother them, as long as I'm delivering on the service promise.

Many FAs found that referrals were their best source of new business. A number used their spare time to specialize in financial products of interest to their clients and potential clients. In one case, an FA lived in an area where many people with company retirement assets were about to retire. She developed expertise in individual retirement accounts (IRAs), becoming a local expert. Another FA had a prominent anesthesiologist as a client. In order to understand him better, he subscribed to anesthesiology journals and attended professional association meetings. As a result, he received four referrals that led to four new relationships, each of which brought in more than $1 million.

Supernova FAs found that their greatest problem was to force themselves to become actively involved in client acquisition once the initial disruption caused by converting to Supernova was over. According to one: "Under the Supernova way of doing things, you aren't constantly putting out fires or worrying about the fact that you're losing so many clients—because there aren't so many fires and your clients don't leave. To be honest, you have to light a fire under yourself to get more business instead of just taking it easy. I call this the 'golf problem'."

Some senior managers believed that the "golf problem" was serious because while FAs adopting Supernova very effectively experienced an immediate increase in compensation, the average new Supernova adopter saw an initial small reduction in pay. The senior managers attributed this loss to local management's failure to coach the average new adopters to begin their acquiring as early as possible in the transition process.

Transaction and Annuitized FAs

FAs adopting Supernova were both transactional FAs, who were paid by charging fees per trade, and annuitized FAs. Some were a combination of the two. According to one fully annuitized FA: "The soft underbelly of annuitized business is that unless you commit to providing a certain level of service, once you're being paid whether or not you do anything, there is less incentive to contact your client. Supernova solves that problem."

A transactional FA added: Once you call your client a few times having no intention of selling anything, it's a lot easier to sell the next time you call. Supernova also helps because it increases my knowledge of the client—when you know someone better, you can figure out what their needs are— and sell them what they want."

THE PROCESS OF ADOPTING SUPERNOVA

Supernova had been spread though road-show presentations made by users who were enthusiastic about what the program had done for them, their client associates, and their clients. Knapp often used a two-part pitch to "sell" Supernova to potential adopters. First, he described how good it felt to be delivering, "The Ultimate Client Experience." Second, he described Supernova as "Plan, Process, and Discipline," noting, "You're going from chaos to plan, process, and discipline— that gives you control of your time. Once you really move from chaos to control, you can't go back."

A Supernova office head noted:

> All of my FAs use Supernova—they have no choice. When I'm hiring, I look for people who are service-oriented, as opposed to transaction-oriented. Lots of people can sell a mother diapers. But can you make her feel good about them when they're dirty?
>
> I didn't force my experienced FAs to adopt the program. My immediate team adopted it, and the others liked what they saw: the phone doesn't ring very often; we meet with the people who pay us, and get rid of the rest; we do very little cold calling—we get new clients almost exclusively through referrals. Every FA in the office chose to join.

Support for FAs Adopting Supernova

The first step in Supernova adoption was called, "FA buy-in." Road shows alone did not ensure buy-in. Skeptical FAs, or those who did not attend road shows, could only be persuaded by a manager sitting down with them and making a compelling argument in favor of the program. Some managers asked the FA how much he or she would like to be earning in a few years. Inevitably, given that FA's current business, there was no way the number could be reached. Once the FA realized the implications of the current situation, the manager could illustrate how the income goal could be reached by adopting Supernova.

The second step in Supernova adoption was segmentation. After that was accomplished, financial planning, 12-4-2, organization, and acquisition were introduced. However, segmentation was often the most difficult to implement. According to an early Supernova adopter:

> Initially, most FAs don't cut their books deep enough, maybe to 300. It's really hard to cut—for years we've been told to get more names. After all, who knows if someone will win the lottery—and some of those clients have been with you for years. The problem is, you just can't give 12-4-2 service to 300 clients—you'll kill yourself trying. If the leadership isn't on top of it, these FAs usually fall off the wagon. A lot of the leadership is made up of the best transactional people we have—it's hardest for them to adopt a relationship perspective. Hunter-gatherers just don't turn into farmers overnight.

Adoption ranged from what one manager described as "They say their doing Supernova, but they haven't even segmented their book" to "Supernova evangelists."

Merrill Lynch assigned one employee to devote herself exclusively to the program. She spent her time organizing and participating in road-show presentations on Supernova and developing new segmentation and organization software to support the program. She stated:

> There's so much more I'd like to be doing. I need to be helping the FAs over hurdles. With Supernova, FAs have to fundamentally change. In some locations, the office head provides a lot of coaching and personal support. But in other offices, there's no one there to help. After we conduct our two-day kickoff road-show meeting, we try to find an FA in the office who's admired by his peers and is ahead of the pack on Supernova. We make that person the local resource for the other FAs. But they don't get anything for doing it, and they may or may not succeed at Supernova themselves.
>
> There's a lot we could be doing, like how to run the segmentation software, and how to set up a folder system. These things aren't brain surgery, but when you haven't done it before it's tough. We review these at the road shows, but people tend to forget over time. Most of it can be done over the phone—the average office only needs two hours a week of in-person assistance during those critical three months after a group of FAs decide to adopt Supernova. They usually need help segmenting, transitioning clients they are giving up, getting organized, and changing their day-to-day behaviors.

KNOWN CHALLENGES TO IMPLEMENTATION

Jim Walker had to decide whether or not to recommend the national roll out of Supernova. As part of his decision making, he reviewed data on Supernova results to date and projections for the future (see **Exhibit 5**). In addition, he identified the challenges he would encounter if he decided to go forward. Among Walker's concerns were the following:

Economic Backdrop

In 2003, times were not good for retail brokerages; stock prices were down, and trading volumes were depressed (see **Exhibit 6**). These conditions made people in the industry tense and directed the attention of Merrill's top managers to immediate issues such as meeting earnings projections. Conversely, some believed that a downturn was the best time to drive change through a brokerage firm since firms tended to poach each other's brokers less often while production was down.

Politics and Recognition

Supernova was seen as the child of its founders. Those in the firm who liked its founders tended to like it. Those with mixed feelings about its founders tended to be less positive. Professional jealousy may also have played a role in negative reactions. Recognition of, and or rewards for Supernova's founders might exacerbate this situation.

EXHIBIT 5   **Selected Supernova Results and Projections**

Source: Merrill Lynch.

Results

Merrill Lynch's Management Science Group studied a sample of 75 Supernova FAs and arrived at the following conclusions:

> Average number of clients: 208 with average assets of $333,000.

> Upon joining Supernova transferred 14 clients to another FA (average assets $153,000), and 67 clients to the centralized facility (average assets $30,000).

> Supernova FA production (revenue) increased 1% while production from a control group of non-Supernova FAs designed to mirror the demographics of the Supernova group decreased 6%. Total FA population production declined 12% (the markets were down during the period of the study).

> Market errors (mistakes in processing transactions due to FA or client associate errors Merrill was responsible for) declined 54%.

> The following client satisfaction measures improved:

>> – Satisfaction with client associate service

>> – Percentage of clients feeling they need more FA contact (declined)

>> – Percentage of clients feeling their FA exceeds in "looking out for their best interests"

>> – Satisfaction with FA (however, not by a statistically significant amount)

Projections

> Based on the above study, Merrill Lynch's Management Science group made the following projections, assuming Supernova were adopted by 200 FAs per district (approximately 20% of FAs):

>> – $130 million annual increase in FA production (with 90% confidence)

>> – $6.6 million annual reduction in market errors (with 90% confidence)

>> – Total: $58 million in annual pre-tax profit, requiring "some investment" to develop a supporting infrastructure (note that this projection may exclude most benefits from customer retention and word-of-mouth referral)

EXHIBIT 6   Merrill Lynch Financial Statements

Source: Merrill Lynch.

	Year Ended Last Friday in December		
	2002	**2001**	**2000**
Net Revenues			
Commissions	$ 4,657	$ 5,266	$ 6,977
Principal transactions	2,340	3,930	5,964
Investment banking			
Underwriting	1,710	2,438	2,699
Strategic advisory	703	1,101	1,381
Asset management and portfolio service fees	4,914	5,351	5,688
Other	751	528	967
	15,075	18,614	23,676
Interest and dividend revenues	13,178	20,143	21,176
Less interest expenses	9,645	16,877	18,086
Net interest profit	3,533	3,266	3,090
Total Net Revenues	18,608	21,880	26,766
Non-Interest Expenses			
Compensation and benefits	9,426	11,269	13,730
Communications and technology	1,741	2,232	2,320
Occupancy and related depreciation	909	1,077	1,006
Brokerage, clearing, and exchange fees	727	895	893
Advertising and market development	540	703	939
Professional fees	552	545	637
Office supplies and postage	258	349	404
Goodwill amortization	—	207	217
Other	611	902	903
Research and other settlement-related expenses	291	—	—
(Recoveries)/expenses related to September 11	(212)	131	—
Restructuring and other charges	8	2,193	—
Total Non-Interest Expenses	14,851	20,503	21,049
Earnings Before Income Taxes and Dividends on Preferred Securities Issued by Subsidiaries	3,757	1,377	5,717
Income Tax Expense	1,053	609	1,738
Dividends on Preferred Securities Issued by Subsidiaries	191	195	195
Net Earnings	$ 2,513	$ 573	$ 3,784
Net Earnings Applicable to Common Stockholders	$ 2,475	$ 535	$ 3,745
Earnings Per Common Share			
Basic	$ 2.87	$ 0.64	$ 4.69
Diluted	$ 2.63	$ 0.57	$ 4.11

(Continued)

Organizational Leverage Points

Achieving change in any Merrill Lynch office required buy-in from the head of that office. That person could be thought of as an "organizational leverage point." However, according to one FA, "A lot of office managers were trained that you manage by hoping things will get better, and when they don't, by yelling at people, firing them, and hiring

EXHIBIT 6 Merrill Lynch Financial Statements Continued

Consolidated Balance Sheets (dollars in millions, except per share amounts)	December 27, 2002	December 28, 2001
Assets		
Cash and cash equivalents	$ 10,211	$ 11,070
Cash and securities segregated for regulatory purposes or deposited with clearing organizations	7,375	4,467
Securities financing transactions		
Receivables under resale agreements	75,292	69,707
Receivables under securities borrowed transactions	45,543	54,930
	120,835	124,637
Trading assets, at fair value *(includes securities pledged as collateral of $11,344 in 2002 and $12,084 in 2001)*		
Contractual agreements	38,728	31,040
Corporate debt and preferred stock	18,569	19,147
Mortgages, mortgage-backed, and asset-backed securities	14,987	11,526
Equities and convertible debentures	13,530	18,487
U.S. Government and agencies	10,116	12,999
Non-U.S. governments and agencies	10,095	6,207
Municipals and money markets	5,535	5,561
	111,560	104,967
Investment securities	81,787	87,672
Other receivables	2,020	3,234
Customers *(net of allowance for doubtful accounts of $79 in 2002 and $81 in 2001)*	35,317	39,856
Brokers and dealers	8,485	6,868
Interest and other	10,581	8,221
	54,383	54,945
Loans, notes, and mortgages *(net of allowance for loan losses of $265 in 2002 and $201 in 2001)*	34,735	19,313
Separate account assets	13,042	15,965
Equipment and Facilities *(net of accumulated depreciation and amortization of $4,671 in 2002 and $4,910 in 2001)*	3,080	2,873
Goodwill *(net of accumulated amortization of $984 in 2002 and $924 in 2001)*	4,446	4,071
Other assets	4,454	2,478
Total Assets	**$ 447,928**	**$ 435,692**

new ones." A Supernova office head continued: "Remember that lots of office heads are both managers and FAs. As a result, they're competing with the people they're supposed to be managing—competing for space and resources in the office, and to a lesser degree, for clients. Every time I walk into an FA's office I know he's asking, 'Is what my manager's saying best for me—or for him?"

EXHIBIT 6 Merrill Lynch Financial Statements   Concluded

Consolidated Balance Sheets (dollars in millions, except per share amounts)	December 27, 2002	December 28, 2001
Liabilities		
Securities financing transactions		
Payables under repurchase agreements	$ 85,378	$ 74,903
Payables under securities loaned transactions	7,640	12,291
	93,018	87,194
Commercial paper and other short-term borrowings	5,353	5,141
Deposits	81,842	85,819
Trading liabilities, at fair value		
Contractual agreements	45,202	36,679
U.S. Government and agencies	14,678	18,674
Non-U.S. governments and agencies	7,952	5,857
Corporate debt, municipals and preferred stock	6,500	4,796
Equities and convertible debentures	4,864	9,911
	79,196	75,917
Obligation to return securities received as collateral	2,020	3,234
Other payables		
Customers	28,569	28,704
Brokers and dealers	16,541	11,932
Interest and other	20,724	18,773
	65,834	59,409
Liabilities of insurance subsidiaries	3,566	3,738
Separate accounts liabilities	13,042	15,965
Long-term borrowings	78,524	76,572
Total Liabilities	422,395	412,989
Preferred Securities Issued by Subsidiaries	2,658	2,695
Stockholders' Equity		
Preferred Stockholders' Equity *(42,500 shares issued and outstanding, liquidation preference $10,000 per share)*	425	425
Common Stockholders' Equity		
Shares exchangeable into common stock	58	62
Common stock *(par value $1.33 1/3 per share; authorized: 3,000,000,000 shares; issued: 2002—983,502,078 shares and 2001— 962,533,498 shares)*	1,311	1,283
Paid-in capital	5,315	4,209
Accumulated other comprehensive loss *(net for tax)*	(570)	(368)
Retained earnings	18,072	16,150
	24,186	21,336
Less: Treasury stock, at cost *(2002—116,211,158 shares; 2001—119,059,651 shares)*	961	977
Unamortized employee stock grants	775	776
Total Common Stockholders' Equity	22,450	19,583
Total Stockholders' Equity	22,875	20,008
Total Liabilities, Preferred Securities Issued by Subsidiaries, and Stockholders' Equity	$ 447,928	$ 435,692

Heads of offices who had adopted Supernova and encouraged their FAs to do the same believed that Merrill's FAs could be broken down into three groups. Twenty percent would buy into Supernova quickly and adopt it with few problems. Another 20% were unlikely to ever buy into it. The remaining 60% would need 60 hours of coaching over two years. Coaching often involved asking questions such as:

1. What's your financial planning process?
2. What's your investment process?
3. What's your service delivery process?
4. What's your new business—your marketing—process?

Follow Up/Support

To date, Supernova had been spread through road shows and other presentations. While many FAs attended those road shows, only 2,000 had completely adopted Supernova. Another 4,000 had partially adopted Supernova. These FAs posed several risks. First, they jeopardized the Supernova "brand" in that their clients would not be as satisfied as those of complete adopters. Second, Supernova advocates agreed that a failure to fully adopt the program meant that its benefits for FAs, such as improved compensation and quality of work life, would not be enjoyed.

Client Expectations

Many Supernova FAs believed that after clients became accustomed to Supernova, their expectations for service rose dramatically. In the words of one, "We designed Supernova to spoil them—and it does." This situation created a problem in measuring customer satisfaction when comparing non-Supernova clients with Supernova clients. It also created a problem when service promises were made to clients by FAs who intended to fully adopt Supernova, but never completely implemented the program.

Changing Role of Some FAs

Historically, the individual FA often made recommendations on what investments a client should make. However, many FAs in general, and most Supernova FAs, saw their role as asset gathering and allocation, leaving asset management to professional asset advisors. Supernova FAs noted that they preferred this new role because it enabled them to provide consultative service, examining risk relative to reward, as opposed to selling a product. Many traditional FAs, who wanted to continue recommending investments, associated the new approach (gathering and allocation) with Supernova.

Misinterpretation

Walker often received calls from FAs interested in Supernova in which they asked him for the "Supernova software," believing that if they loaded it on their computers they would be "Supernova compliant." Walker felt that these FAs saw Supernova as an exercise in implementing technology. He noted, "We've got great new CRM software, the best out there. It will make good Supernova FAs even better. But it's only one piece of a complex solution."

Metrics

Both Supernova FAs and managers believed there was a problem with metrics, one noting: "We don't get paid as well for a lot of the new things we're selling under Supernova, like mortgages and insurance, despite their better profitability for the firm."

FA Nature

FAs valued their independence. According to a senior manager, "They don't want to walk in lock step. They like autonomy. Anything that looks like a requirement from a centralized authority is usually rejected out of hand, or at least fought vigorously."

Inclusion of Client Associates

Even though client associates were essential to Supernova's working effectively, most FAs made the decision to adopt it, or not, without involving their administrative assistants.

Exhibit 7 presents excerpts from an FA's presentation on Supernova. **Exhibit 8** illustrates portions of the contents of a folder.

EXHIBIT 7 **Excerpts from FA's Presentation on Supernova**

Source: Company documents.

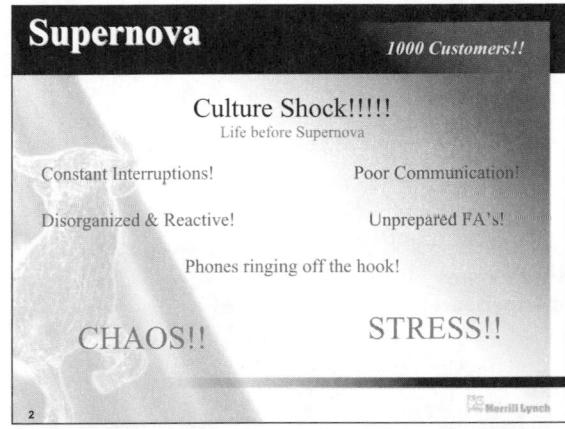

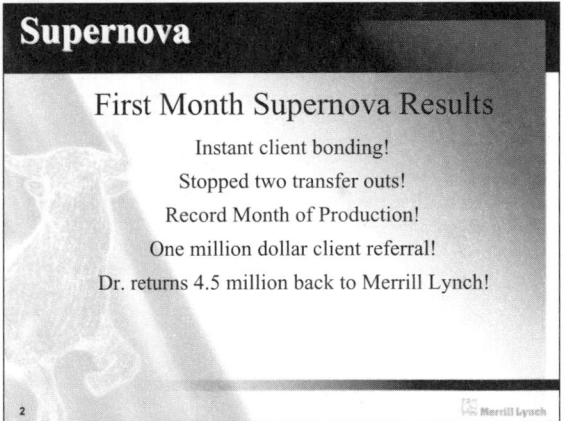

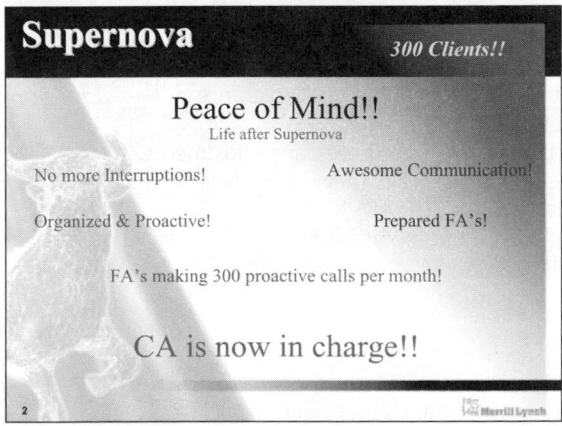

EXHIBIT 8 **Portions of a Folder's Contents**

Source: Company documents.

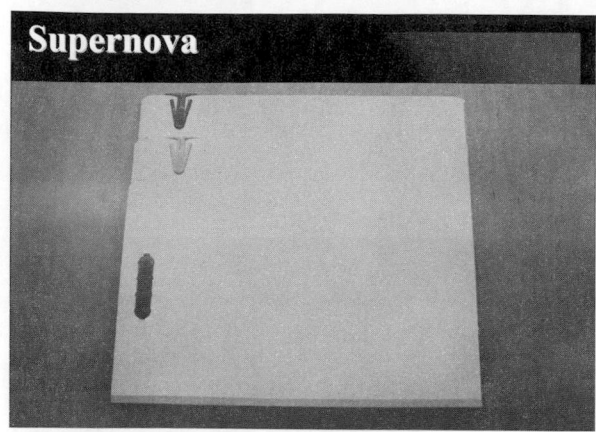

PROJECT SUPERNOVA
(12-4-2 The Ultimate Client Experience)

1.) 8 Outgoing Calls:

JG	___ ___ ___ ___ ___ ___ ___	Outgoing call to client was placed.
JG	___ ___ ___ ___ ___ ___ ___	Action Plan Proposal Report was reviewed and updated.
JG	___ ___ ___ ___ ___ ___ ___	Client portfolio was checked and reviewed.
JG	___ ___ ___ ___ ___ ___ ___	Client Performance was checked and reviewed.

2.) 2 Quarterly Phone Reviews:

___	___	Quarterly review call was placed.
___	___	Action Plan Proposal Report was reviewed and updated.
___	___	Market overview given to client.
___	___	Client Portfolio was checked and reviewed.
___	___	Client Performance was checked and reviewed.

3.) 2 Face to Face Reviews:

JG	___	Financial Foundation & IFF completed and updated.
JG	___	Reconfirm Financial goals and risk tolerance.
JG	___	Review Client performance vs. Goals.
JG	___	Review client portfolio for necessary adjustments.
JG	___	Introduce client to services they do not have.
JG	___	Smart Market (ASK FOR ADVICE.)
JG	___	Complete service questionnaire & schedule next appointment.

EXHIBIT 8   **Portions of a Folder's Contents   Continued**

CLIENT ACTION PLAN

Client Name: _____

Performance Need: _____	**Risk Tolerance:** _____	**Time Horizon:** _____
Performance Want: _____	**Profile Score:** _____	**Allocation Type:** _____

BOSAR

Investment Assets:

Cash Flow Control:	**Discussed**	**Who**	**Done**
CMA Account	_____	____	____
Visa Signature Card	_____	____	____
Merrill Lynch Online	_____	____	____
MLUA	_____	____	____

Stocks/Equities:	**Discussed**	**Who**	**Done**
Consults	_____	____	____
Strategy Power	_____	____	____
MFA	_____	____	____
Annuities	_____	____	____

Bonds/Fixed Income:	**Discussed**	**Who**	**Done**
Municipal Bonds	_____	____	____
Taxable Bonds	_____	____	____
CD's	_____	____	____

Asset Allocation:	**Discussed**	**Who**	**Done**
Reviewed Asset Allocation	_____	____	____
Portfolio Re-balanced	_____	____	____

Retirement: _____ ____ ____

IRA's:	**Discussed**	**Who**	**Done**
Client #1 IRA Contribution	_____	____	____
Client #2 IRA Contribution	_____	____	____

(Continued)

EXHIBIT 8 **Portions of a Folder's Contents** **Continued**

401K's:			Discussed	Who	Done
Client #1 Contribution Reviewed			_____	____	_____
Client #1 Portfolio Allocation Reviewed			_____	____	_____
Client #2 Contribution Reviewed			_____	____	_____
Client #2 Portfolio allocation Reviewed			_____	____	_____
Rollover from Job Transition			_____	____	_____

Net Worth:

Liability Management:	Client Rate	Our Rate	Discussed	Who	Done
Omega	_____	_____	_____	____	_____
Mortgage	_____	_____	_____	____	_____
Home Equity	_____	_____	_____	____	_____
Commercial Loan	_____	_____	_____	____	_____
Consumer Debt	_____	_____	_____	____	_____

Tax Planning:

Tax Reduction Strategies:	Client Tax Rate	Discussed	Who	Done
Client Tax Information	_____	_____	____	_____
Taxable Equivalent Yield	____ = ____	_____	____	_____
Year End Tax Wash Selling		_____	____	_____

Education Planning:

Education Planning Strategies:	Discussed	Who	Done
UGMA/UTMA Accounts	_____	____	_____
529 Account Funding	_____	____	_____

EXHIBIT 8   Portions of a Folder's Contents   Continued

<u>**Survivor Protection:**</u>

Life Insurance Established:	**Discussed**	**Who**	**Done**
Client #1 Insured vs. Needs	_____	____	_____
Client #2 Insured vs. Needs	_____	____	_____

<u>**Income & Asset Protection:**</u>

Income Protection:

Client #1 Disability Insurance in Place	_____	____	_____
Client #2 Disability Insurance in Place	_____	____	_____

Asset Protection:

Long Term Care Insurance	_____	____	_____
Personal Excess Liability Insurance in Place	_____	____	_____
Home Owners Insurance Reviewed	_____	____	_____

<u>**Estate Planning:**</u>

Estate Planning issues:

Wills Updated and Reviewed	_____	_____	_____
Living Trust Established	_____	_____	_____
Assets and Accounts Re-titled for Trust	_____	_____	_____
Beneficiaries Reviewed	_____	_____	_____
Transfer On Death Completed	_____	_____	_____

Providing for each Other:

Appoint Guardian for Minor Children	_____	_____	_____
Durable Power of Attorney Appointed	_____	_____	_____
Health Care Provider Appointed	_____	_____	_____
Business Buy-Sell Agreement in Place	_____	_____	_____

Wealth Replacement:

Wealth Replacement Trust	_____	____	_____
Wealth Replacement Insurance	_____	____	_____

(Continued)

EXHIBIT 8 Portions of a Folder's Contents   Concluded

BE HUMAN!

I.) Client 1's Career:

Client 2's Career:

II. Client 1's Hobbies:

Cliennt 2's Hobbies:

III. Client 1's Passions:

Client 2's Passions:

CONCLUSION

A Supernova FA commented: "Historically, when we sold a *product* to a client, Merrill Lynch made money and the FA made money. Supernova helps to solve the dilemma that created. Supernova enables us to earn our money for handholding, and to do it really well. It provides a business process—not a product. We've never had that before."

Case 3

JetBlue: *High-Flying Airline Melts Down in Ice Storm*

Joe Brennan, Ph.D., University at Buffalo, The State University of New York
Felicia Morgan, Ph.D., University of West Florida

INTRODUCTION

On Wednesday, February 14, 2007, JetBlue Airways Corp. (NYSE:JBLU) suffered the most severe service disruption in its seven-year history. A winter storm snarled operations at the regional carrier's JFK International Airport in New York, its main East Coast hub, forcing the airline to cancel more than half of its flights. Ten planes sat unable to move on icy runways in New York, trapping passengers inside for up to 10 hours. JetBlue's ordeal continued for nearly a week. The airline had trouble resuming normal operations when additional storms struck, leaving planes and crews out of position. The carrier ultimately cancelled nearly 1,900 flights, affecting 130,000 travelers, before it was able to restore normal operations on February 20. The unprecedented service failure would force the airline to grant $26 million in passenger refunds and vouchers and to spend another $4 million on employee overtime and other storm-related costs.[1]

Although the massive Valentine's Day storm affected every airline flying East Coast routes, the news media focused their attention on JetBlue's problems. Commentators wondered if the company that had once promised to "bring humanity back to air travel" had abandoned its commitment to stellar customer service and become yet another uncaring airline. Stranded passengers wasted no time publicizing their complaints on blogs and in the media, and skittish investors began unloading JBLU stock. This was the worst crisis in the young company's history. JetBlue's management had to act quickly to regain customer loyalty, reverse a barrage of hostile press coverage, and reconfigure operations to prevent a similar disaster from recurring.

"MAKING FLYING HAPPIER AND EASIER FOR EVERYONE"

The airline was founded in 1998 by 38-year-old David Neeleman, who saw himself as "bringing humanity back to air travel and making the experience of flying happier and easier for everyone."[2]

A former Mormon missionary, Neeleman started his first company, a travel business, while a student at the University of Utah. He went on to establish a regional carrier, Morris Air, and in 1992 sold it to Southwest, where he became executive vice president. The entrepreneurial Neeleman lasted for six months at Southwest, where his fast-paced style did not suit the more cautious corporate culture. As one of his colleagues there later said, "He didn't understand the nuance of the organization. He needed to walk, not run."[3] Still in his 30s, Neeleman moved on to co-found WestJet, a Canadian regional airline, and after making it profitable, he helped develop Open Skies, an electronic ticketing system later acquired by Hewlett Packard.

NOTE: This case is based entirely on published sources and has been prepared for teaching purposes.

In 1998, Neeleman gathered a team of investors and seasoned airline industry executives and founded "New Air Corporation." The firm changed its name to JetBlue in July 1999, when it announced that it would offer low-cost, high-quality service to and from New York City, as "New York's hometown airline." At that time, the CEO promised that JetBlue would be a "new kind of low fare airline," offering the types of amenities reserved for pricier carriers, including wider seats, more legroom and storage space, and 24 channels of inflight television. The company's press release promised innovations like touch-screen check-in and "fares 65 percent less than other airlines on identical routes." JetBlue began flying in February 2000, offering non-stop service between New York and Fort Lauderdale, Florida.

The traveling public responded favorably to Neeleman's offer of excellent customer service, upscale amenities, and low fares. Thanks to its younger fleet and newer staff, the firm enjoyed lower maintenance and labor costs than its old-school competitors. It was also well-capitalized; the combination of lower costs and a strong balance sheet helped JetBlue avoid the major losses its competitors incurred after September 11, 2001, and positioned it to take market share away from them. Neeleman took the company public in April 2002. By the end of 2004, JetBlue was flying high. Its revenues had quadrupled—and the company had made a profit every year. It had climbed to 11th place in revenue passenger miles generated, and had done so with fewer planes than many of its bigger competitors.[4] Exhibits A, B, C, and D provide data about the airline's growth and performance.

FLYING HIGH IN A TURBULENT INDUSTRY

By 2005, Neeleman was leading one of the few successful start-ups in the highly competitive U.S. airline business. More than 100 airlines had been launched since the industry was deregulated in 1978, but only a handful had survived the tremendous competitive pressures in this mature industry.[5] The events of September 11, 2001, had a significant impact on the U.S. economy in general and on the airlines in particular. In 2000, the industry generated total sales of $120 billion; over the next two years, revenues plummeted to $105 billion, and it would be five years before sales recovered (see Exhibit E on page 614). The airlines also faced strongly rising fuel prices, heavy debt loads, and increasing pension liabilities related to their aging workforces.[6] By September, 2005, four major carriers (United, US Airways, Delta, and Northwest), representing 40 percent of the industry's total capacity, were operating under Chapter 11 protection.[7,8]

During this period, JetBlue had effectively established a powerful brand and carved out a distinct and profitable position as a low-cost airline offering a high level of service. The firm strove to provide every customer with "the JetBlue Experience," which combined value, service, and style. Passengers enjoyed free co-branded amenities, including brand name snacks, Dunkin Donuts coffee, XM satellite radio, DIRECTV satellite television, and Bliss Spa comfort kits. Passengers could watch live television, listen to satellite radio, purchase 20th Century Fox inflight movies, and sip wines chosen by "low fare sommelier" Josh Wesson of Best Cellars, a value-oriented chain of retail wine shops. The JetBlue Experience also included innovation. From its inception, all JetBlue travel had been ticketless, all fares one-way, and all seats assigned. It was the first airline to deploy the new Embraer 190 regional jet and the first to offer free live television; in 2002 it acquired inflight television provider Live TV and began marketing the service to other airlines.

EXHIBIT A Jet Blue Financial Data

Source: Standard & Poor's Net Advantage Company Profiles, 3/10/07

Revenues (Million $) for Fiscal Year Ending Dec.

	2006	2005	2004	2003	2002	2001
1Q	490	374.2	289	217.1	133.4	63.85
2Q	612	429.1	319.7	244.7	149.3	78.4
3Q	628	452.9	323.2	273.6	165.3	82.61
4Q	633	446	334	262.9	187.3	95.56
Year	2,363	1,701	1,266	998.4	635.2	320.4

Earnings Per Share ($) for Fiscal Year Ending Dec.

	2007	2006	2005	2004	2003	2002
1Q	E−0.15	−0.18	0.04	0.09	0.11	0.1
2Q	E0.22	0.08	0.08	0.13	0.24	0.1
3Q	E0.20	NI	0.01	0.05	0.17	0.08
4Q	E0.16	0.1	−0.25	0.01	0.11	0.1
Year	E0.43	NI	−0.13	0.29	0.65	0.37

Income Statement (Million $).

	2006	2005	2004	2003	2002	2001
Net Inc.	−1	−20	47.5	104	54.9	38.5
Depr.	154	117	77.4	50.4	26.9	10.4
Int. Exp.	146	91	44.6	23.7	15.7	6.1
Eff. Tax Rate	NM	NM	38%	41%	42%	8.10%
Pretax Inc.	9	−24	76.8	175	95	41.9
Oper. Inc.	281	165	190	219	132	37.2
Revs.	2,363	1,701	1,266	998	635	320

Other Financial Data (Million $).

	2006	2005	2004	2003	2002	2001
Cash	10	6	410	571	247	263
Curr. Liab.	854	676	486	370	270	0
LT Debt	2,626	2,103	1,396	1,012	639	291
% Ret. on Equity	NM	NM	6.7	19.1	25.6	
Total Cap.	3,714	3,130	2,275	1,782	1,093	615
Total Assets	4,843	3,892	2,799	2,186	1,379	820
% Net Inc.of Revs.	NM	NM	3.7	10.4	8.6	12
% LT Debt of Cap.	70.7	67.2	61.4	56.8	58.5	47.3
Curr. Assets	927	635	515	646	283	0
Curr. Ratio	1.1	0.9	1.1	1.7	1	0
Cash Flow	153	97	125	154	75.9	32
Cap. Exp.	996	941	617	573	544	0
% Ret. on Assets	NM	NM	1.9	5.8	5.3	0
Common Equity	952	911	756	671	415	324

Data as originally reported; before results of discontinued operations and/or specific items.
Per share data adjusted for stock dividends as of ex-dividend date.
E—Estimated. N/A—Not Available. NM—Not Meaningful. NR—Not Ranked.
JetBlue Airways Corp. Nasdaq:JBLU

EXHIBIT B **JetBlue's Growth**

Sources: Jet Blue 10K reports, Air Transport Association of America, Standard & Poor's.

	Revenue Passengers (000s)	Revenue Passenger Miles (millions)	Operating Revenues (million $)	Employees (full- and part-time)	Operating Aircraft	Destinations
2000	1,144	1,005	320.4	1,174	10	12
2001	3,117	3,282	320.4	2,361	21	18
2002	5,752	6,836	635.2	4,011	37	20
2003	9,012	11,527	998.4	5,433	53	21
2004	11,783	15,730	1,266	7,211	69	30
2005	14,729	20,200	1,701	9,021	93	33
2006	18,565	23,320	2,363	10,377	119	49

"Revenue passengers" represents the total number of paying passengers on all flight segments flown.
"Revenue passenger miles" represents the number of miles flown by revenue passengers.
Employee count does not include LiveTV employees.

SERVICE EXCELLENCE

JetBlue has sought to provide what it calls "the best customer service in the business," and has won dozens of top awards for its performance.[9] In 2007, it was named the #3 most admired airline by *Fortune* and best in customer satisfaction by *Market Metrix.* In 2006, it was picked as the best domestic airline by both *Conde Nast Traveler* and *Travel + Leisure,* the best low cost/no frills airline by OAG, and the best U.S. airline in the annual quality ranking survey conducted by the University of Nebraska–Omaha and Wichita State University. In 2006, JetBlue enjoyed the second-lowest rate of customer complaints among the 10 largest U.S. airlines (see Exhibit F on page 614).

Neeleman's vision of a new category of airline, one that would make flying more fun and more civilized, was as compelling for employees as it was for passengers. A former missionary to Brazil, Neeleman had an extraordinary ability to connect with people and to inspire them, like the pilot who told *Fast Company,* "I would walk through fire for him."[10] He traveled frequently on JetBlue flights, working alongside employees, talking with pilots in the cockpit, visiting with customers about their experiences, and asking how the airline could better serve them. Neeleman and his executive team placed a high value on involving employees in all aspects of the business

EXHIBIT C

Passengers per Employee

Source: authors' calculations

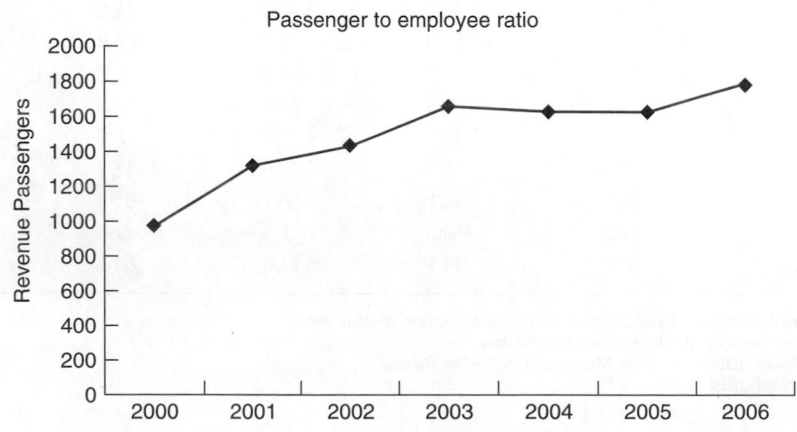

Passenger to employee ratio

EXHIBIT D   Top 25 U.S. Airlines, 2003

Source: Air Transport Association of America Annual Report, 2004.
Note: Airlines listed in **bold** are members of the Air Transport Association of America.

#	Revenue Passengers Enplaned[1] (Thousands)		Revenue Passenger Miles[1] (Millions)		Cargo Revenue Ton Miles[2] (Millions)		Operating Revenues[2] (Millions)	
1	American	88,151	American	120,004	FedEx	9,487	American	$17,403
2	Delta	84,076	United	103,857	UPS	4,624	FedEx	16,807
3	Southwest	74,719	Delta	89,154	Atlas	3,006	Delta	14,203
4	United	66,018	Northwest	68,459	Northwest	2,184	United	13,398
5	Northwest	51,865	Continental	56,886	American	2,012	Northwest	9,184
6	US Airways	41,250	Southwest	47,940	United	1,888	Continental	7,333
7	Continental	38,474	US Airways	37,727	Delta	1,349	US Airways	6,762
8	America West	20,031	America West	21,266	Polar	1,115	Southwest	5,937
9	Alaska	15,046	Alaska	14,557	Continental	865	UPS	3,046
10	**American Eagle**	12,474	**ATA**	11,840	Gemini	732	**America West**	2,223
11	AirTran	11,651	**JetBlue**	10,442	**ABX**	700	Alaska	2,019
12	Continental Express	11,227	AirTran	7,159	Evergreen Int'l	677	**ATA**	1,398
13	Comair	10,935	Continental Express	5,769	Kalitta	660	Continental Express	1,311
14	Skywest	10,719	**Hawaiian**	5,560	**US Airways**	361	**ABX**	1,161
15	**ATA**	9,386	Comair	5,227	ASTAR	348	American Eagle	1,128
16	Atlantic Southeast	9,205	Frontier	4,666	World	301	Comair	1,032
17	**JetBlue**	8,949	Spirit	4,578	Air Transport Int'l	203	**JetBlue**	998
18	Atlantic Coast	8,390	Skywest	4,232	Florida West	197	AirTran	918
19	Air Wisconsin	5,865	American Eagle	4,135	Express.Net	165	Atlantic Coast	876
20	Mesaba	5,702	Atlantic Southeast	4,008	Tradewinds	164	Atlantic Southeast	837
21	**Hawaiian**	5,597	Atlantic Coast	3,320	**Southwest**	141	**Hawaiian**	706
22	Frontier	5,061	Continental Micronesia	2,286	Kitty Hawk	122	Frontier	590
23	Horizon	4,934	Air Wisconsin	2,212	Ryan Int'l	118	Air Wisconsin	527
24	**Aloha**	4,119	**Midwest**	1,969	Centurion	118	World	475
25	Spirit	4,105	**Aloha**	1,968	Southern	106	Horizon	464

[1] Scheduled service only   [2] All services   ■ ATA member

613

EXHIBIT E
Total Revenues,
U.S. Airlines

Source: Datamonitor Industry
Profiles, 2005, 2006

Year	$ billion	% Growth
2000	120.0	
2001	111.9	−6.8%
2002	105.0	−6.1%
2003	110.2	4.9%
2004	116.3	5.6%
2005	125.0	7.5%

and cultivating a sense of team work. All employees are called "crewmembers," and supervisors attend "Jet Blue University" for a course in the company's principles of leadership taught by Neeleman and chief operating officer Dave Barger. Al Spain, senior vice president of operations, said, "There is no 'they' here. It's 'we' and 'us.' We succeed together or we fail together."[11]

Even after the ice storm, employees defended the airline. On February 19, someone who identified him- or herself as a JetBlue employee posted a response to a blogger who had been critical of the company's handling of the situation:

Had you booked a ticket on Delta or American, your flight would have been cancelled and you wouldn't have gotten a refund. You would have had to fly at another time, but you wouldn't have been compensated for your delay—at all . . . in no way. In fact, they wouldn't have apologized . . . at all . . . EVER!

What happened to all of you (including my fellow pilots and flight attendants that were stuck right along with you—and just as miserable as you were) was awful, not cool, uncomfortable, a huge pain in the ass and a really, really, really bad day.

That's about it though. See, when you travel it's like buying a lottery ticket: if you get to your destination hassle free—you win! If you have issues along the way . . . that's life! But if you get a refund for your troubles . . . that's amazing! . . .

I'm sorry you went through what you went through on Valentine's Day, and I want you to come back to jetBlue so I can give you the jetBlue Experience you've grown accustomed to and we do our best to deliver every day.[12]

WARNING LIGHTS IN THE COCKPIT

In May 2004, *Fast Company* profiled the young CEO, praising his hands-on approach and warning that it would be increasingly hard to maintain as JetBlue got bigger:

Much that's distinctive about this airline—from the enthusiasm of its employees to its relentless customer focus to its hip, slightly countercultural image—is precisely the

EXHIBIT F
Customer
Complaint Rates for
the 10 Largest U.S.
Airlines (2006)

Source: U.S. Department of
Transportation Air Travel
Consumer Report, Feb. 2007;
Wall Street Journal,
March 27, 2007.

Airline	Complaints per 1 Million Passenger Emplanements
United Airlines	13.60
US Airways	13.59
American Airlines	10.87
Delta	10.35
Northwest Airlines	8.84
Continental Airlines	8.83
AirTran Airways	6.24
Alaska Airlines	5.24
JetBlue Airways	3.98
Southwest Airlines	1.82
Average of all airlines	**8.67**

sort of thing you can pull off when you're small, and that becomes far tougher the bigger you get. Can JetBlue maintain those qualities as it morphs from nimble startup into the bureaucracy that's required to manage a vastly more complex operation?

It's a question that applies to many truly innovative companies these days. Call them postmodern corporations, perhaps. If they pull off this transition, they become big, but remain in important ways the antithesis of bigness-think Starbucks, Dell, and Amazon. Like JetBlue, they depend on flexibility, speed, and a sense of intimacy with employees and customers alike. Put another-way, the challenge JetBlue now faces is this: Is small scalable?[13]

Neeleman began flying into turbulence in 2005. At the same time as *Fast Company* was pondering his ability to save his company from the fate of People Express, a similar concept which failed in the 1980s, rivals Delta and United were launching Song and Ted, low-cost/high-frills offerings meant to directly compete with JetBlue. Labor and maintenance expenses began to creep up as JetBlue's people and planes got older and the company experienced problems with the introduction of a brand-new aircraft type, the Embraer 190. As is often the case when an airline brings a new type of aircraft into its fleet, JetBlue experienced unexpected glitches. Not only did the new Embraer 190s arrive behind schedule, installing the in-flight entertainment system so integral to the JetBlue passenger experience took longer than expected. Also, pilots and mechanics used to doing things a certain way on the existing fleet experienced significant learning curves in operating the new aircraft. On-time performance eroded and flights were canceled.[14] In addition, Florida and the Gulf Coast, important markets for JetBlue, were ravaged by Hurricanes Rita, Wilma, and Katrina in the summer of 2005. The demand for air travel to the affected regions fell, petroleum refineries were closed, and JetBlue's fuel costs soared 52 percent. At the end of 2005, the company reported its first-ever operating loss, $20 million.[15]

Neeleman and Barger discussed these challenges in the company's 2005 Annual Report and offered a plan for recovery. They planned to grow revenues by raising average fares, using capacity more efficiently and adding service to small and medium-sized cities where a relative lack of competition would allow JetBlue to command a price premium. They also reiterated the airline's commitment to reliable service, which meant "operating flights even with a delay rather than canceling the flight for the schedule's convenience." To manage costs, they promised to improve workforce productivity through better training, smarter business processes, and more extensive use of automation, and they said they would control the risk of rising fuel prices through financial hedging strategies. The executive team also refused bonuses, and Neeleman delayed the delivery of 36 new aircraft.[16]

By the end of 2006, Neeleman and Barger's plan to grow their way out of trouble seemed to be working. Revenues rose 39 percent in 2006, to $2.36 billion. The firm enjoyed three successive profitable quarters, ending the year just $1 million in the red. In January 2007, David Neeleman told investors, "I'm tremendously proud of the efforts our crewmembers have made in advancing our plan to institutionalize low-cost carrier spending habits and improve revenue overall." Dave Barger said that the airline's performance in 2006 "positions us well for 2007, a year in which we plan to grow capacity 11 to 14 percent, while continuing to enhance the JetBlue Experience." Investors appeared to share management's confidence. Towards the end of 2006, analysts began to upgrade their recommendations, and by mid-January, the stock price had soared to a new 52-week high. No one knew the turbulence that lay just ahead.

STORMY WEATHER

On its seventh anniversary, February 11, 2007, JetBlue was operating some 500 flights a day to 50 cities in the U.S., Mexico, and the Caribbean. David Neeleman had built one of the very few successful major new airlines since the industry was deregulated nearly 30 years before. The company's prospects seemed bright. And then, three days later, JetBlue was hit with the worst crisis in its history.

February 14 began as a normal day at JetBlue's Forest Hills, New York headquarters, near John F. Kennedy International Airport. The company had issued a routine news release shortly after 9 a.m., announcing that it had formed a partnership with Cape Air to offer service to four communities on Cape Cod. The day before, a front had moved into the New York City region from the west, dropping one-tenth of an inch of snow. Heavy snow was in the forecast for upstate, but it appeared that the city would be spared the brunt of the storm. At the airport's weather station, the barometer started falling at midnight. By dawn, what had been light snow in the early morning hours had become ice pellets and light freezing rain, with temperatures hovering in the upper 20s. No one seemed to know that by lunchtime, barometric pressure would drop nearly an inch and a full blown nor'easter would be raking the airport with winds gusting up to 40 miles per hour, coating planes and runways with ice. Early that morning, in keeping with the airline's desire to avoid cancellations, JetBlue gate agents loaded passengers onto six planes, in hopes that they could get out during a break in the weather. These planes remained stuck at the gate; while over the course of the morning, four more JetBlue aircraft arrived and remained on the tarmac, unable to reach the terminal because all gates were occupied, and ground equipment used to tow planes was frozen in place.

As the hours crept by for the passengers and crewmembers stuck onboard the 10 airliners, JetBlue's operations appeared to have become paralyzed. The problems at JFK, its East Coast hub, rippled throughout JetBlue's system. Its 800 number, staffed by home-based workers in Utah, was overwhelmed by the crush of calls from customers seeking information or trying to rebook delayed flights. Its New York-based 20-person crew services department, which handles the scheduling of crewmembers, was also overwhelmed.

The storm showed signs of relenting by early afternoon, as freezing snow changed into light snow, and JetBlue officials kept the loaded planes in place, apparently still hoping to salvage some of the flights. By 3 p.m., however, they had admitted defeat and asked the Port Authority of New York and New Jersey for help in rescuing stranded passengers. The last passengers entered the terminal after 7 p.m., having sat onboard for six to 10½ hours.

Television news crews were waiting for the passengers in the terminal. WABC-TV interviewed some of the 134 passengers on Flight 751, which had been bound for Cancun, Mexico. "There was no power and it was hot. There was no air. They kept having to open the actual plane doors so we could breathe," said one passenger.

"Nobody gave us any answers. They kept telling us we know as much as you do. And I said, I don't work here, you work here, give me answers," another passenger said.

"Everybody is incredibly tired and frustrated and we didn't expect to be in New York tonight, so it's ridiculous. Just sitting there and sitting there and them saying they were going to pull us into the gate and they never did. There was very little food. It was just a nightmare," a third passenger was quoted as saying.[17]

JetBlue's problems quickly became national headline news. Yossi Glieberman, a 41-year-old Brooklyn man who came in on a flight from Nashville that could not make it to the gate, told *Newsday* that the pilots provided frequent updates and flight attendants distributed snacks liberally, allowed passengers to recharge cell phones and let children help push the service carts.[18] "It could have been worse," he said of the nine-hour ordeal. Other fliers were less complimentary. An unnamed man told ABC World News, "My vacation is canceled. No flights out. I can't go anywhere. They can't get me out on vacation. My kids are home in four-degree weather when we're supposed to be on a beach with 90-degree weather."[19] Cheryl Chesner, a bride who had to cancel her honeymoon trip to Aruba, told the *San Francisco Chronicle,* "It was the worst. It was horrific."[20]

One customer, a New York resident who was angry about missing a much-anticipated Valentine's Day trip home to Los Angeles with her new boyfriend, started a blog called www.jetbluehostage.com.[21] Using the screen name "Gen Starchild," she wrote, "Nothing says 'I love you' like being held hostage on a frozen plane with the man you love, 99 strangers, 4 other people you happen to know, 4 screaming babies and 3 rambunctious kids running about, nothing but chips and soda for sustenance, faulty power, unreliable direct TV, and an overfilled sewage system for 11 hours."

The blog became well-known and led to an interview for Gen and her boyfriend on CNN. JetBlue's public relations department asked her to meet with David Neeleman. She recapped the March 5 meeting on her blog:

It went a lot like this.

Canned answer
Canned answer
We're sorry
It'll never happen again
I don't have the answer, this is who you need to talk to.
I'm sorry.
Etc.

Then he hit a wall and I could actually see the change in him. From the beginning of the meeting, he was playing these passive aggressive "you're not important" games, by taking FOUR PHONE CALLS, on his mobile at that. Not from JetBlue employees concerned about the weather cancellations. Calls from his wife. Calls from his neighbor. I'm the queen of mind games, you can't pull that on me.

Gen Starchild and her fellow "hostages" were not the only travelers inconvenienced by the events of February 14, though they may have been the most visible. And JetBlue was not the only carrier grounded by the storm. Between February 13 and 15, American cancelled 914 flights, or 13.4 percent of its schedule; United grounded 865 flights (17.1 percent); US Airways 728 (19.6 percent); and Contintental 119 (3.7 percent). By comparison, JetBlue's 634 cancelled flights represented 39.6 percent of its schedule.[22]

In all, some 250 flights, nearly half of JetBlue's entire schedule, were cancelled on Valentine's Day. The following days were also plagued by problems, because the ice storm had left airplanes and crews out of position and additional winter weather created more headaches. Internal communications and coordination between airline staff seemed to be a problem. A woman who took a JetBlue flight from California to New York on February 17 posted this report on jetbluehostage.com: "JetBlue's system was completely overloaded. The staff at Burbank had no clue what was going on—the lack of pilots was a total shock to them—and there were so few staff actually at JFK that no passengers could get answers. A man with a bullhorn finally came out (because the baggage carousel board was completely inaccurate) to tell people which flights were coming out on which carousels."

In an effort to restore order, the airline cancelled some of its flights on February 15 and 16, but problems persisted, so managers took the unprecedented step of preemptively cancelling ("precancelling") 23 percent of all flights over the next two days in order to reposition planes and allow pilots and crews to rest. This action demonstrated a significant shift in thinking on the part of JetBlue managers, who had always tried to take a "wait-and-see approach" with the weather.[23] Announcing the move on February 17, spokeswoman Jenny Dervin told *The New York Times:* "Sometime in the afternoon, it just fell apart. The folks running the operation are just exhausted. We said, 'Let's stop the madness.'"[24] "We ran into an operational death spiral," Dervin told *Newsweek.*[25] The pre-cancellations, which fell over the President's Day long weekend, worked, and by Monday, February 20 JetBlue was back to normal.

JETBLUE WORKS TO REBUILD PUBLIC TRUST

As the airline's executives struggled to climb out of the operational death spiral, its public relations staff got busy trying to repair the firm's damaged image. On the evening of February 14, JetBlue issued a public apology and announced that it would give a full refund and a free roundtrip ticket to any passenger detained onboard for more than three hours; it would also give refunds to any passenger whose flight was cancelled. Over the next few days, the airline announced that it was relaxing its policies about rebooking so that customers who were affected by the storm would not be penalized for re-booking new flights. Throughout the ordeal, top executives practiced their commitment to "visible leadership." Dave Barger went to JFK on the 14th to oversee the operational response and speak with passengers and crewmembers. David Neeleman became the company's public face, granting dozens of media interviews, in which he accepted responsibility, expressed remorse, and pledged to prevent this kind of problem from happening again. In a front-page *New York Times* story on Sunday, February 19, Neeleman said he was "humiliated and mortified" and promised that JetBlue would pay penalties to customers if they were the victims of mistakes by the airline.[26]

One week after the Valentine's Day ice storm, the operations were finally back to normal. Neeleman had issued a personal apology, which appeared in his blog and in full-page ads in major newspapers (see Exhibit G). The airline also published a Customer's Bill of Rights, specifying how and when it would compensate passengers for delays and other problems (see Exhibit H). Reactions to Neeleman's apology and the Bill of Rights were generally positive. On February 21, *USA Today* published an editorial calling JetBlue's service failure "inexcusable" but praising its response. The paper contrasted JetBlue's handling of the Valentine's Day snafu to similar, smaller-scale strandings by American and United in December and wrote that it hoped this would touch off "a round of competition over customer-service guarantees, instead of the usual cost-cutting."[27]

The business press, however, was far less kind. In a stinging rebuke, *BusinessWeek* struck JetBlue from its list of "customer service champs." The magazine's March 5 cover (see Exhibit I) was headlined "Our first-ever ranking of companies where the consumer is king. Here's the magnificent 25—and one extraordinary stumble." The cover graphic was a numbered list of the top four companies, with a squiggly blue line drawn through JetBlue's name. The editors said kicking the airline off the list was a "tough call." Despite Neeleman's candid, public apologies, "the road to recovery isn't paved with TV appearances," the magazine cautioned.

> What matters most is execution—doing the deep, hard organizational work to ensure the crisis never happens again. While JetBlue recognizes that fact, it still has plenty to prove . . . JetBlue has piled up service accolades faster than most airlines collect

EXHIBIT G   David Neeleman's Apology

Dear JetBlue Customers,

We are sorry and embarrassed. But most of all, we are deeply sorry. Last week was the worst operational week in JetBlue's seven year history. Many of you were either stranded, delayed or had flights cancelled following the severe winter ice storm in the Northeast. The storm disrupted the movement of aircraft, and, more importantly, disrupted the movement of JetBlue's pilot and inflight crewmembers who were depending on those planes to get them to the airports where they were scheduled to serve you. With the busy President's Day weekend upon us, rebooking opportunities were scarce and hold times at 1-800-JETBLUE were unusually long or not even available, further hindering our recovery efforts.

Words cannot express how truly sorry we are for the anxiety, frustration and inconvenience that you, your family, friends and colleagues experienced. This is especially saddening because JetBlue was founded on the promise of bringing humanity back to air travel, and making the experience of flying happier and easier for everyone who chooses to fly with us. We know we failed to deliver on this promise last week.

We are committed to you, our valued customers, and are taking immediate corrective steps to regain your confidence in us. We have begun putting a comprehensive plan in place to provide better and more timely information to you, more tools and resources for our crewmembers and improved procedures for handling operational difficulties. Most importantly, we have published the JetBlue Airways Customer Bill of Rights—our official commitment to you of how we will handle operational interruptions going forward—including details of compensation. We invite you to learn more at jetblue.com/promise.

You deserved better—a lot better—from us last week and we let you down. Nothing is more important than regaining your trust and all of us here hope you will give us the opportunity to once again welcome you onboard and provide you the positive JetBlue Experience you have come to expect from us.

Sincerely,

David Neeleman
Founder and CEO

complaints . . . plus JetBlue's trumpeting of its own customer-friendly approach, means its passengers' expectations are inevitably higher. Other airlines, after all, had long waits at JFK . . . but interminable delays, cancellations and service snafus, says UNC Kenan-Flagler Business School professor Valarie Zeithaml, can be "more detrimental [to JetBlue] than to a larger airline. It runs totally counter to who they are coming out and saying they are and what they live."[28]

Other observers raised questions about Neeleman's leadership. On February 20, Larry Kudlow, host of CNBC's Kudlow and Co., said:

The guy's a great entrepreneur. He created and built and grew this company. OK, no question about it. But how many times in the past do we know that entrepreneurial CEOs are not necessarily the ones that take these companies to the next stage where management and administration are really the keys? He clearly struck out on management, information, communications, where's this equipment, where were the pilots, how to get in touch with one another, where are the flight attendants? And I know he's made a lot of mea culpas, and I appreciate his character in doing that, but the fact remains: Can he manage a large airline company?

Earlier that day, the embattled CEO held a news conference at which said he had no intention of stepping down from his post. "I'm the founder of the company, I'm the CEO, and I think I'm uniquely qualified to deal with these issues."[29]

The incident also spurred calls by passenger advocates for tougher oversight by the federal government. The Coalition for Airline Passengers' Bill of Rights, a newly formed group, used JetBlue's woes to again demand relief. The coalition was formed

EXHIBIT H JetBlue Customer Bill of Rights

JetBlue Airways Customer Bill of Rights

JetBlue Airways exists to provide superior service in every aspect of our customer's air travel experience. In order to reaffirm this commitment, we set forth this Bill of Rights for our customers. These Rights will always be subject to the highest level of safety and security for our customers and crewmembers.

INFORMATION

JetBlue will notify customers of the following:
- Delays prior to scheduled departure
- Cancellations and their cause
- Diversions and their cause

CANCELLATIONS

All customers whose flight is cancelled by JetBlue will, at the customer's option, receive a full refund or re-accommodation on a future JetBlue flight at no additional charge or fare. If JetBlue cancels a flight within 12 hours of scheduled departure and the cancellation is due to a Controllable Irregularity, JetBlue will also provide the customer with a Voucher valid for future travel on JetBlue in the amount paid to JetBlue for the customer's roundtrip.

DEPARTURE DELAYS

1. Customers whose flight is delayed prior to scheduled departure for 1-1:59 hours due to a Controllable Irregularity are entitled to a $25 Voucher good for future travel on JetBlue.
2. Customers whose flight is delayed prior to scheduled departure for 2-3:59 hours due to a Controllable Irregularity are entitled to a $50 Voucher good for future travel on JetBlue.
3. Customers whose flight is delayed prior to scheduled departure for 4-5:59 hours due to a Controllable Irregularity are entitled to a Voucher good for future travel on JetBlue in the amount paid by the customer for the one way trip.
4. Customers whose flight is delayed prior to scheduled departure for 6 or more hours due to a Controllable Irregularity are entitled to a Voucher good for future travel on JetBlue in the amount paid by the customer for the roundtrip.

OVERBOOKINGS (As defined in JetBlue's Contract of Carriage)

Customers who are involuntarily denied boarding shall receive $1,000.

GROUND DELAYS

For customers who experience a Ground Delay for more than 5 hours, JetBlue will take necessary action so that customers may deplane. JetBlue will also provide customers experiencing a Ground Delay with food and drink, access to restrooms and, as necessary, medical treatment.

Arrivals:
1. Customers who experience a Ground Delay on Arrival for 30-59 minutes after scheduled arrival time are entitled to a $25 Voucher good for future travel on JetBlue.
2. Customers who experience a Ground Delay on Arrival for 1-1:59 hours after scheduled arrival time are entitled to a $100 Voucher good for future travel on JetBlue.
3. Customers who experience a Ground Delay on Arrival for 2-2:59 hours after scheduled arrival time are entitled to a Voucher good for future travel on JetBlue in the amount paid by the customer for the oneway trip.
4. Customers who experience a Ground Delay on Arrival for 3 or more hours after scheduled arrival time are entitled to a Voucher good for future travel on JetBlue in the amount paid by the customer for the roundtrip.

Departures:
1. Customers who experience a Ground Delay on Departure for 3-3:59 hours are entitled to a $100 Voucher good for future travel on JetBlue.
2. Customers who experience a Ground Delay on Departure for 4 or more hours are entitled to a Voucher good for future travel on JetBlue in the amount paid by the customer for the roundtrip.

JetBlue Airways
Forest Hills Support Center
118-29 Queens Blvd
Forest Hills, NY 11375

1-800-JETBLUE   1-800-538-2583   jetblue.com

*These Rights are subject to JetBlue's Contract of Carriage and, as applicable, the operational control of the flight crew.
This document is representative of what JetBlue intends to incorporate into its Contract of Carriage, the legal binding document between JetBlue and its customers.

EXHIBIT I
Cover of
BusinessWeek,
March 5, 2005

by Tim and Kate Hanni, a Napa, California couple who were trapped on the ground for nine hours in Austin, Texas by American Airlines in late December 2006. The Hannis described their experience in a February 4 letter to the *Mobile (Ala.) Press-Register.*[30] These angry, frustrated travelers demanded that Congress pass new laws to force airlines to refund 150 percent of the ticket price to passengers stranded more than three hours and inform passengers about what's going on within 10 minutes of a prolonged delay. They launched a web site, strandedpassengers.blogspot.com, and within its first month reportedly collected 4,200 signatures on a petition.[31]

A similar incident in 1999, when Northwest Airlines detained passengers for seven hours on a snow-covered runway in Detroit, had sparked calls for action by Congress. The airline industry staved off new regulations then by promising to take care of the problem. Now, in the wake of the Hannis' experience and the JetBlue debacle, it appeared that federal lawmakers were ready to act. Over the President's Day weekend, before JetBlue issued its own Bill of Rights, U.S. Senators Barbara Boxer (D–Calif.) and Olympia Snow (R–Maine) proposed a new law to prevent airlines from holding passengers onboard for more than three hours and to require them to provide food, water, and clean toilets. Congressman Mike Thompson, a Democrat who represented the Hannis' district, promised to introduce a similar bill in the House. Sen. Boxer told National Public Radio:

> We have to protect the people of the United States of America. We have to protect their families. We have to protect our children. And now, post-9/11, it's very difficult for

passengers to complain about anything because of the seriousness of what happened on 9/11. Passengers who cause any trouble at all can get themselves in a lot of trouble. So when you're on an aircraft, you're pretty much—have to comply with everything. And here you're in a situation where you're in a lock-down, almost a hostage situation. It's just unacceptable. This is a very simple thing we're talking about. It's common sense. The airlines, I think, will benefit from it, and I hope we can get it done. I'm not naive about it. Every single time there's a regulation we propose, there's an outcry. The automobile industry didn't want to do seatbelts. They didn't want to do airbags. Now they take credit for it. So, you know, there is a role for the government, since we are really responsible for licensing these airlines.[32]

Aviation experts warned that the proposed new regulations could actually make things worse for passengers by depriving the airlines of flexibility. Daryl Jenkins, a consultant who teaches airline management, told *USA Today* that the proposal was "totally impractical . . . What if a plane is ordered after three hours to go back to the terminal when they are second in line to take off? That doesn't make sense." John Cox, a former airline pilot, said that it would reduce the reliability of the system because airlines need to keep flights ready to take off as soon as the weather permits. Returning them to the terminal could increase delays.[33]

WHAT LIES AHEAD FOR JETBLUE?

Three weeks after the crisis, Neeleman was still communicating with customers about the company's response. It appeared that some customers were confused by the conditions for when the company would and would not offer compensation for delays. Neeleman explained the differences between "controllable" and "uncontrollable" delays on his blog, "David's Flight Log."[34]

On March 8, the company announced that John Owen, executive vice president–supply chain and information technology, had resigned but would remain with the company as a "senior advisor" through the end of 2008, and that Russell Chew had been hired to serve as chief operating officer. Chew, a veteran of American Airlines and the Federal Aviation Agency, "brings a big-airline perspective to JetBlue . . . Russ will be in charge of making sure our operations run on time and as scheduled, so that you don't have to rely on our Bill of Rights for compensation," Neeleman told customers. "Because let's face it—getting a $25 voucher or more is nice, but it's better to arrive or depart on time." Chew will report to Dave Barger, who would remain with the company as "President and Founding Crew Member."

The press continued to raise questions about JetBlue's long term viability, however. On March 12, *BusinessWeek* cited unnamed "industry sources" as saying that, as part of its 2006 cost cutting moves, the company had sacrificed needed upgrades to its reservations, call center, and crew scheduling systems. It also warned that the market may be tapped out, quoting a consultant who said, "there aren't too many markets you can throw 150-seat airplanes into," and raised the specter of a unionization drive among pilots who have watched the value of their stock options fall.[35]

The market appeared to have lost confidence in the once high-flying company. By March 14, JetBlue's stock price had fallen to $11.75, 11 percent below its February 14 closing price of $13.23.

One month after the ice storm, JetBlue's management team was still digging out.

CHALLENGES

JetBlue was confronted with some serious issues as it continued to try to recover from its Valentine's Day meltdown. Although operations had returned to "normal," the company had spent millions of dollars on passenger refunds and vouchers, employee overtime, and other storm-related costs. JetBlue executives had spent countless hours practicing "visible leadership" and David Neeleman, the public face of the airline, had accepted responsibility, expressed remorse repeatedly, and promised that this type of problem would never happen again. But, could JetBlue depend on Neeleman to lead the company out of trouble? Did the executives at JetBlue learn enough from their service failure to fix what was wrong and prevent it from happening again? If not, what further action should be taken? What, if any, strategic and operational changes should be made to ensure the company's full recovery?

SOURCES

1. Wong, Grace. "JetBlue fiasco: $30M price tag: CEO Neeleman pledges reforms, vows to keep job after cancellation leaves passengers stranded; airline back to full schedule." CNNMoney.com, February 20, 2007.

2. Neeleman, David. "Dear JetBlue Customers." David's Flight Log, http://www.jetblue.com/about/ourcompany/flightlog/, February 22, 2007.

3. Salter, Chuck. "And Now the Hard Part." Fast Company 82, May 2004.

4. Air Transport Association. 2004 Economic Report. www.airlines.org, accessed March 10, 2007.

5. Salter, op. cit.

6. Weber, Harry R. and Joshua Freed. "Delta, Northwest file for Chapter 11 bankruptcy protection." Associated Press, September 14, 2005.

7. Ibid.

8. Carpenter, Dave. "Leaner United might be bankruptcy model for Delta, Northwest." Associated Press, September 18, 2005.

9. JetBlue Airways Corporation. (http://www.jetblue.com/about/ourcompany/history/about_ourhistory.html).

10. Salter, op. cit.

11. Ibid.

12. JetBlue Hostage website. http://www.jetbluehostage.com.

13. Salter, op. cit.

14. Reed, Dan. "Loss Shifts JetBlue's Focus to Climbing Back Into Black." USA Today, February 21, 2006.

15. JetBlue Airways Corporation. Annual Report 2005. http://investor.jetblue.com/phoenix.zhtml?c=131045&p=irol-reportsAnnual

16. Foust, Dean. "Is JetBlue the Next People Express?" BusinessWeek, March 12, 2007.

17. Lipoff, Phil. "A Nightmare for JetBlue: Planes ran out of food and water as they sat for over 8 hours." WABC-TV, New York, February 14, 2007.

18. Strickler, Andrew. "Stormy Weather: Waiting til they're blue; Jet Blue passengers stranded on planes for hours amid icy snarl at JFK gates." Newsday, February 15, 2007.

19. Gibson, Charles. "JetBlue's Airline Meltdown." ABC World News Now, February 19, 2007.

20. Armstrong, David. "Beleaguered air passengers want new laws." San Francisco Chronicle, February 16, 2007.

21. JetBlue Hostage website, op. cit.

22. Carey, Susan and Andrew Pasztor. "Behind Travel Mess: New Rules for Sleet." The Wall Street Journal, March 23, 2007.

23. Lyons, Patrick. "A Snowshocked JetBlue Hits the Cancel Button." The Lede, March 16, 2007. http://theledeblogs.nytimes.com/2007/03/16/a-showshocked-jetblue-hits-the-cancel-button/

24. Bailey, Jeff. "JetBlue Cancels More Flights in Storm's Wake." The New York Times, February 18, 2007.

25. Sloan, Allan and Temma Ehrenfeld. "Skies Were Cloudy Before Jet Blew It." Newsweek 149:10, March 5, 2007.

26. Bailey, op. cit.

27. USA Today. "Crisis Management Says a Lot About an Airline." February 21, 2007.

28. McGregor, Jena. "An Extraordinary Stumble at JetBlue." BusinessWeek, March 5, 2007.

29. Wong, op. cit.

30. Hanni, Tim and Kate Hanni. "Family Endures 57-hour Journey from San Francisco to Mobile." Mobile Press-Register, February 4, 2007.

31. Martinez, Michael. "Boxer to Introduce Airline Passengers' Bill of Rights: Crusade picks up steam after this week's JetBlue delays." San Jose Mercury News, February 15, 2007.

32. Block, Melissa. "Air Passengers Rights Bill Introduced in Senate." National Public Radio, February 20, 2007.

33. Levin, Alan. "Bill of Rights for Fliers Questioned." USA Today, February 22, 2007.

34. Neeleman, David. David's Flight Log. http://www.jetblue.com/about/ourcompany/flightlog/

35. Foust, op. cit.

Case 4

Giordano: *Positioning for International Expansion*

Jochen Wirtz

To make people "feel good" and "look great."

—Giordano's Corporate mission

As it looks to the future, a successful Asian retailer of casual apparel must decide whether to maintain its existing positioning strategy. Management wonders what factors will be critical to success and whether the firm's competitive strengths in merchandise selection and service are readily transferable to new international markets.

In early 2006, Giordano, a Hong Kong-based retailer of casual clothes targeted at men, women and children through its four company brands, Giordano, Giordano Ladies, Giordano Junior and Blue Star Exchange, was operating over 1,600 retail stores and counters in some 31 markets in the Asia-Pacific and Middle-East region. Its main markets were Mainland China, Hong Kong, Japan, Korea, Singapore, and Taiwan. Other countries in which it had a presence were Australia, Indonesia, Malaysia and the Middle East. In its main markets there were 1478 Giordano and Giordano Junior stores, 27 Giordano Ladies stores, and 132 Blue Star Exchange stores. Sales had grown to HK$4,003 million (US$517 million) by 2004 (see **Exhibit 1**). Giordano stores were located in retail shopping districts with good foot traffic. Views of a typical storefront and store interior are shown in **Exhibit 2**. In most geographic markets serviced by Giordano, the retail clothing business was deemed to be extremely competitive.

The board and top management team were eager to maintain Giordano's success in existing markets and to enter new markets in Asia and beyond. Several issues were under discussion. First, in what ways, if at all, should Giordano change its current positioning in the market-place? Second, would the factors that had contributed to Giordano's success in the past remain equally critical over the coming years or were new key success factors emerging? Finally, as Giordano sought to enter new markets around the world, were its competitive strengths readily transferable to other markets?

COMPANY BACKGROUND

Giordano was founded in Hong Kong in 1980 by Jimmy Lai. In 1981, it opened its first retail store in Hong Kong and also began to expand its market by distributing Giordano merchandise in Taiwan through a joint venture. In 1985, it opened its first retail outlet in Singapore.

Responding to slow sales, Giordano changed its positioning strategy in 1987. Until 1987, it had sold exclusively men's casual apparel. When Lai and his colleagues realized that an increasing number of female customers were attracted to its stores, he repositioned the chain as a retailer of value-for-money merchandise, selling discounted casual unisex apparel, with the goal of maximizing unit sales instead of margins. This

© 2007 Jochen Wirtz.

This case is based on published information and quotes from a wide array of sources. The generous help and feedback provided by Alison Law, former Assistant to Chairman, Giordano International Ltd, to earlier versions of this case are gratefully acknowledged. The author thanks Zhaohui Chen for his excellent research assistance.

EXHIBIT 1   Giordano Financial Highlights

Source: Annual Report 2004, Giordano International.

	2004	2003	2002	2001	2000	1999	1998	1997	1996	1995	1994
Turnover (million HK$)	4,003	3,389	3,588	3,479	3,431	3,092	2,609	3,014	3,522	3,482	2,864
Turnover increase (percent)	18.1	(5.5)	3.1	1.4	11.0	18.5	(13.4)	(14.4)	1.1	21.5	22.7
Profit after tax and minority interests (million HK$)	393	266	328	377	416	360	76	68	261	250	195
Profit after tax and minority interests increase over previous year (percent)	47.7	(18.9)	(13.0)	(9.4)	15.3	373.7	11.8	(73.9)	4.4	28.2	41.9
Shareholders' fund (million HK$)	1,954	1,799	1,794	1,695	1,558	1,449	1,135	1,069	1,220	976	593
Working capital (million HK$)	1,004	961	861	798	1,014	960	725	655	752	560	410
Total debt to equity ratio	0.35	0.4	0.3	0.4	0.3	0.3	0.3	0.3	0.4	0.7	0.9
Inventory turnover on sales (days)	30	24	26	30	32	28	44	48	58	55	53
Return on total assets (percent)	14.9	10.7	13.7	16.8	20.7	21.5	5.3	4.5	16.8	19.5	20.9
Return on average equity (percent)	20.9	14.8	18.8	23.2	27.7	27.9	6.9	5.9	23.8	31.8	35.8
Return on sales (percent)	9.8	7.8	9.1	10.8	12.1	11.6	2.9	2.3	7.4	7.2	6.8
Earning per share (cents)	27.20	18.50	22.80	26.30	29.30	25.65	5.40	4.80	18.45	19.40	15.45
Cash dividend per share (cents)	23.00	21.00	19.00	14.00	15.25	17.25	2.25	2.50	8.00	6.75	5.50

shift in strategy was successful, leading to a substantial increase in turnover. In 1994, Peter Lau Kwok Kuen succeeded Lai and became Chairman.

Management Values and Style

A willingness to try new and unconventional ways of doing business and to learn from past errors was part of Lai's management philosophy and soon became an integral part of Giordano's culture. Lai saw the occasional failure as a current limitation that indirectly pointed management to the right decision in the future. To demonstrate his commitment to this philosophy, Lai took the lead by being a role model for his employees, adding, ". . . Like in a meeting, I say, look, I have made this mistake. I'm sorry for that. I hope everybody learns from this. If I can make mistakes, who . . . do you think you are that you can't make mistakes?" He also believed strongly that empowerment would minimize mistakes—that if everyone was allowed to contribute and participate, mistakes could be minimized.

Another factor that contributed to the firm's success was its dedicated, ever-smiling sales staff of over 8000. Giordano considered front-line workers to be its

EXHIBIT 2   **Typical Giordano Storefront**

customer-service heroes. Charles Fung, executive director and chief operations officer (Southeast Asia), remarked:

> Even the most sophisticated training program won't guarantee the best customer service. People are the key. They make exceptional service possible. Training is merely a skeleton of a customer service program. It's the people who deliver that give it form and meaning.

Giordano had instituted stringent selection procedures to make sure that the candidates selected matched the desired employee profile. Selection continued into its training workshops, which tested the service orientation and character of a new employee.

Giordano's philosophy of quality service could be observed not only in Hong Kong but also in its overseas outlets. The company had been honored by numerous service awards over the years (see **Exhibit 3**). Fung described its obsession with providing excellent customer service in the following terms:

> The only way to keep abreast with stiff competition in the retail market is to know the customers' needs and serve them well. Customers pay our pay checks; they are our bosses. . . . Giordano considers service to be a very important element [in trying to draw customers]; . . . service is in the blood of every member of our staff.

Giordano believed and invested heavily in employee training and had been recognized for its commitment to training and developing its staff by such awards as the Hong Kong Management Association Certificate of Merit for Excellence in Training and the People Developer Award from Singapore, among others.

> Training is important. However, what is more important is the transfer of learning to the store. When there is a transfer of learning, each dollar invested in training yields a high

EXHIBIT 3 Selected Awards Giordano Received over the Years

Award	Awarding Organization	Category	Year(s)
American Service Excellence Award	American Express	Fashion/Apparel	1995
Ear Award	Radio Corporation of Singapore	Listeners' Choice & Creative Merits	1996
Excellent Service Award	Singapore Productivity Award and Standards Board	—	1996, 1997, 1998
People Developer Award	Singapore Productivity and Standards Board	—	1998
HKRMA Customer Service Award	Hong Kong Retail Management Association	—	1999
The Fourth Hong Kong Awards for Services	Hong Kong Trade Development Council	Export Marketing & Customer Service	2000
Grand Award (Giordano International)	Hong Kong Trade Development Council	Export Marketing	2002
Grand Award (Giordano Ladies)	Hong Kong Retail Management Association	—	2002
Business-to-Consumer Service Supplier Award	Middle East Economic Digest (MEED)	—	2002
Dubai Services Excellence Scheme Award	Dubai Department of Economic Development Customer Service	Customer Service	2003
Hong Kong Superbrands$^{(TM)}$ Award	Hong Kong Superbrands Council	—	2004
Top Service Award	Next Magazine	Chain Stores of Fashion & Accessories	2004

return. We try to encourage this [transfer of learning] by cultivating a culture and by providing positive reinforcement, rewarding those who practice what they learned.

Giordano offered what Fung claimed was "an attractive package in an industry where employee turnover is high." Giordano motivated its people through a base salary that probably was below market average, but added attractive performance-related bonuses. These initiatives and Giordano's emphasis on training had resulted in a lower staff turnover rate.

Managing its vital human resources (HR) became a challenge to Giordano when it decided to expand into global markets. To replicate its high-service-quality positioning, Giordano needed to consider the HR issues involved in setting up retail outlets in unfamiliar territory. For example, the recruitment, selection and training of local employees could require modifications to its formula for success in its current markets, owing to differences in the culture, education and technology of the new countries. Labor regulations could also affect such HR policies as compensation and welfare benefits. Finally, management needed to consider expatriate policies for staff members who had been seconded to help run Giordano outside their home countries, as well as the management practices themselves in those countries.

Focusing Giordano's Organizational Structure on Simplicity and Speed

Giordano maintained a flat organizational structure. The company's decentralized management style empowered line managers, and at the same time encouraged fast and close communication and coordination. For example, top management and staff had desks located next to each other, separated only by shoulder panels. This closeness allowed easy communication, efficient project management and speedy decision making, which were all seen as critical ingredients to success amid fast-changing consumer tastes and fashion trends. This kept Giordano's product development cycle short. The firm made similar demands on its suppliers.

Service

Giordano's commitment to service began with its major Customer Service Campaign in 1989. In that campaign, yellow badges bearing the words "Giordano Means Service" were worn by every Giordano employee, and its service philosophy had three tenets: "We welcome unlimited try-ons; we exchange—no questions asked; and we serve with a smile." As a result, the firm started receiving its numerous service-related awards over the years. It had also been ranked number one for eight consecutive years by the *Far Eastern Economic Review* for being innovative in responding to customers' needs.

Management had launched several creative, customer-focused campaigns and promotions to extend its service orientation. For instance, in Singapore, Giordano asked its customers what they thought would be the fairest price to charge for a pair of jeans and charged each customer the price that they were willing to pay. This one-month campaign was immensely successful, with some 3,000 pairs of jeans sold every day during the promotion. In another service-related campaign, over 10,000 free T-shirts were given to customers for giving feedback and criticizing Giordano's services.

To ensure customer service excellence, performance evaluations were conducted frequently at the store level, as well as for individual employees. Internal competitions were designed to motivate employees and store teams to do their best in serving customers. Every month, Giordano awarded the "Service Star" to individual employees, based on nominations provided by shoppers. In addition, every Giordano store was evaluated every month by mystery shoppers. Based on the combined results of these evaluations, the "Best Service Shop" award was given to the top store. Customer feedback cards were available at all stores, and were collected and posted at the office for further action. Increasingly, customers were providing feedback via the firm's corporate Web site.

Value for Money

Lai explained the rationale for Giordano's value-for-money policy.

> Consumers are learning a lot better about what value is. So we always ask ourselves how can we sell it cheaper, make it more convenient for the consumer to buy and deliver faster today than [we did] yesterday. That is all value, because convenience is value for the consumer. Time is value for the customer.

Giordano was able to sell value-for-money merchandise consistently through careful selection of suppliers, strict cost control and by resisting the temptation to increase retail prices unnecessarily. For instance, to provide greater shopping convenience to customers, Giordano started to open kiosks in subway and train stations in 2003 aimed at providing their customers with a "grab and go" service.

Inventory Control

In order to maximize use of store space for sales opportunities, a central distribution center replaced the function of a back storeroom in its outlets. Information technology (IT) was used to facilitate inventory management and demand forecasting. When an item was sold, the barcode information—identifying size, color, style and price—was recorded by the point-of-sale cash register and transmitted to the company's main computer. At the end of each day, the information was compiled at the store level and sent to the sales department and the distribution center. The compiled sales information became the store's order for the following day. Orders were filled during the night and were ready for delivery by early morning, ensuring that before a Giordano store opened for business, new inventory was already on the shelves.

Another advantage of its IT system was that information was disseminated to production facilities in real time. Such information allowed customers' purchase patterns to be understood, and this provided valuable input to its manufacturing operations, resulting in less problems and costs related to slow-moving inventory. The use of IT also afforded more efficient inventory holding. Giordano's inventory turnover on sales was reduced from 58 days in 1996 to merely 30 days in 2004. Its excellent inventory management reduced costs and allowed reasonable margins, while still allowing Giordano to reinforce its value-for-money philosophy. All in all, despite the relatively lower margins as compared to its peers, Giordano was still able to post healthy profits. Such efficiency became a crucial factor when periodic price wars were encountered.

PRODUCT POSITIONING

Fung recognized the importance of limiting the firm's expansion and focusing on one specific area. Simplicity and focus were reflected in the way Giordano merchandised its goods. Its stores featured no more than 100 variants of 17 core items, whereas competing retailers might feature 200 to 300 items. He believed that merchandising a wide range of products made it difficult to react quickly to market changes.

Giordano's willingness to experiment with new ideas and its perseverance despite past failures could also be seen in its introduction of new product lines. It ventured into mid-priced women's fashion with the label "Gio Ladies"—featuring a line of smart blouses, dress pants and skirts—targeted at executive women. Reflecting retailer practices for such clothing, Giordano enjoyed higher margins on upscale women's clothing—typically 50 to 60 percent of selling price as compared to 40 percent for casual wear.

Here, however, Giordano ran into some difficulties as it found itself competing with more than a dozen seasoned players in the retail clothing business, including Theme and Esprit. Initially, the firm failed to differentiate its new Giordano Ladies line from its mainstream product line, and even sold both through the same outlets. In 1999, however, Giordano took advantage of the financial troubles facing rivals such as Theme, as well as the boom that followed the Asian currency crisis in many parts of Asia, to aggressively re-launch its "Giordano Ladies" line, which subsequently met with great success. As of January 2006, the reinforced "Giordano Ladies" focused on a select segment, with 27 "Giordano Ladies" shops in Hong Kong, Taiwan, Singapore and China, offering personalized service. Among other things, the staff were trained to memorize names of regular customers and recall their past purchases.

Differentiation and Repositioning

During the late 1990s, Giordano had begun to reposition its brand, by emphasizing differentiated, functionally value-added products clothes and broadening its appeal by improving on visual merchandising and apparel. A typical storefront and store layout are shown in **Exhibit 2** and **Exhibit 4**. Giordano's relatively mid-priced positioning worked well—inexpensive, yet contemporary-looking outfits appealed to Asia's frugal customers, especially during a period of economic slowdown. However, over time, this

EXHIBIT 4 **A Typical Store Layout**

positioning became inconsistent with the brand image that Giordano had tried hard to build over the years. As one senior executive remarked, "The feeling went from 'this is nice and good value' to 'this is cheap.'"

Giordano gradually remarketed its core brand in ways that sort to create the image of a trendier label. To continue meeting the needs of customers who favored its value-for-money positioning, Giordano launched several promotions. Among its successes was the "Simply Khakis" promotion, launched in April 1999, which emphasized basic, street-culture style that "mixed and matched," and thus fitted all occasions. Within days of its launch in Singapore, the new line sold out and had to be re-launched two weeks later. By October 1999, over a million pairs of khaki trousers and shorts had been sold. The firm's skills in executing innovative and effective promotional strategies helped the retailer to reduce the impact of the Asian crisis on its sales and to take advantage of the slight recovery seen in early 1999.

In 1999, the firm launched a new brand of casual clothing, Blue Star Exchange (BSE), following successful prototyping in Hong Kong and Taiwan. In 2002, the first Blue Star Exchange store was set up in Southern China. The strong market response to this new brand led the company to expand the number of stores branded as Blue Star Exchange to 132 by 2005. The Group was also evaluating the possibility of launching the Blue Star chain in its other markets.

In June 2003, right after the SARS (severe acute respiratory syndrome) health crisis, which discouraged shopping and consumer spending, Giordano launched the "Yoga Collection" which used a moisture-managed fabric, Dry-Tech™. It was an instant big hit, allowing Giordano to recover nicely from the SARS crisis in Hong Kong and enabling its new brand to stand out from competing offerings.

EXHIBIT 5   **Market Positioning of Giordano and Principal Competitors**

Firms	Positioning	Target Market
Giordano (www.giordano.com.hk)	Value for money Mid-priced but trendy fashion	Unisex casual wear for all ages (under different brands)
The Gap (www.gap.com)	Value for money Mid-priced but trendy fashion	Unisex casual wear for all ages (under different brands)
Esprit (www.esprit-intl.com)	More up-market than Giordano Stylish, trendy	Ladies' casual, but also other specialized lines for children and men
Bossini (www.bossini.com)	Value for money (comparable to Giordano)	Unisex, casual wear, both young and old (above 30s)
Baleno (www.baleno.com.hk)	Value for money Trendy, young age casual wear	Unisex appeal, young adults
Hang Ten (www.hangten.com)	Value for money Sporty lifestyle	Casual wear and sports wear, teens and young adults

Giordano's Competitors

To beat the intense competition prevalent in Asia—especially in Hong Kong—founder Jimmy Lai believed that Giordano had to develop a distinctive competitive advantage. So he benchmarked Giordano against best-practice organizations in four key areas: (1) computerization (from The Limited), (2) a tightly controlled menu (from McDonald's), (3) frugality (from Wal-Mart), and (4) value pricing (as implemented at the British retail chain Marks & Spencer). The emphasis on service and the value-for-money concept had proven to be successful.

Giordano's main competitors in the value-for-money segment had been Hang Ten, Bossini, and Baleno, and at the higher end, Esprit. **Exhibit 5** shows the relative positioning of Giordano and its competitors: The Gap, Bossini, Hang Ten, Baleno, and Esprit.

Hang Ten and Bossini were generally positioned as low-price retailers offering reasonable quality and service. The clothes emphasized versatility and simplicity. But while Hang Ten and Baleno were more popular among teenagers and young adults, Bossini had a more general appeal. Their distribution strategies were somewhat similar, but they focused on different markets. For instance, while Hang Ten was mainly strong in Taiwan, Baleno increasingly penetrated Mainland China and Taiwan. On the other hand, Bossini was very strong in Hong Kong and relatively strong in China. The company planned to make its business in China into the group's largest turnover and profit contributor. The geographic areas in which Giordano, The Gap, Espirit, Bossini, Baleno, and Hang Ten operate are shown in **Exhibit 6**.

Esprit was an international fashion lifestyle brand. Esprit promoted a "lifestyle" image and its products were strategically positioned as good quality and value for money—a position that Giordano was occupying. By 2005, Esprit had a distribution network of over 10,000 stores and outlets in 40 countries in Europe, Asia, America, Middle East and Australia. The main markets were in Europe, which accounted for approximately 65 percent sales. The Esprit brand products were principally sold via directly managed retail outlets, wholesale customers (including department stores, specialty stores and franchisees), and by licensees for products manufactured under license, principally through the licensees' own distribution networks.

EXHIBIT 6   Geographic Presence of Giordano and Its Principal Competitors

Sources: *Annual Report 2004,* Giordano International; *Gap Inc.,* retrieved June 23, 2004, from http://www.gapinc.com/ about/realestate/storecount.htm; Annual Report 2004/5, *Esprit; Financial Report 2004/5,* Bossini International Holdings Limited; *Baleno,* Retrieved December 12, 2005, from http://www.baleno.com. hk/EN/stores_list.asp?area=cn; Hang Ten, retrieved December 12, 2005, from http://www.hangten.com.

Country	Giordano	The Gap	Esprit	Bossini	Baleno	Hang Ten
Asia						
Hong Kong/Macau	X	—	X	X	X	X
Singapore	X	—	X	X	X	X
South Korea	X	—	X	—	—	X
Taiwan	X	—	X	X	X	X
China	X	—	X	X	X	X
Malaysia	X	—	X	—	X	—
Indonesia	X	—	X	X	—	—
Philippines	X	—	X	X	—	X
Thailand	X	—	X	X	—	—
World						
U.S. and Canada	—	X	X	X	—	X
Europe	—	X	X	—	—	X
Japan	X	X	—	—	—	X
Australia	X	—	X	—	—	X
Total	1,585	3,117	9,751	827	1,160	NA

Note: "X" indicates presence in the country/region; "—" indicates no presence.

Theme International Holdings Limited was founded in Hong Kong in 1986 by Chairman and CEO Kenneth Lai. He identified a niche in the local market, for high-quality, fashionable ladies' businesswear, although the firm subsequently expanded into casual wear. The Theme label and chain were in direct competition with "Giordano Ladies." From the first store in 1986 to a chain comprising over 130 outlets in Hong Kong, Mainland China, Macau, Taiwan, Singapore, Malaysia, Indonesia, the Philippines, the phenomenal growth of Theme was built on a vertically integrated corporate structure and advanced management system. However, its ambitious expansion proved to be costly. In 1999, the company announced a HK$106.1 million net loss for the six months up to September 30, 1998, and was subsequently acquired by High Fashion International, a Hong Kong-based fashion retailer specializing in up-market, trendy apparel. Theme was then focusing on expansion in China, after having fortified its image as a sophisticated and high-end smart-causal fashion for career women.

Although each of these firms had slightly different positioning strategies, they competed in a number of areas. For example, all firms heavily emphasized advertising and sales promotion—selling fashionable clothes at attractive prices. Almost all stores were also located primarily in good ground-floor areas, drawing high-volume traffic and facilitating shopping, browsing and impulse buying. However, none had been able to match the great customer value offered by Giordano.

A threat from U.S.-based The Gap was also looming. The Gap had already entered Japan. After 2005, when garment quotas were largely abolished, imports into the region had become more cost effective for this U.S. competitor.

Financial data for Giordano, Esprit, The Gap, Bossini, and Theme are shown in **Exhibit 7**.

EXHIBIT 7   Competitive Financial Data for Giordano, The Gap, Esprit, Bossini and Theme

Sources: *Annual Report 2004,* Giordano International; *Annual Report 2004,* The Gap; *Financial Highlights 2004/5,* Esprit International; *Financial Report 2004/5,* Bossini International Holdings Limited; *Annual Report 2004,* Theme Holdings; Reuters, Retrieved December 12, 2005, from www.knowledge.reuters.com.

	Giordano	The Gap	Esprit	Bossini	Theme
Turnover (US$ million)	517	16,267	2,662	260	26
Profit after tax and minority interests (US$ million)	51	1,150	431	23	(1)
Return on total assets (percent)	14.9	11.1	36.2	24.9	(7.3)
Return on average equity (percent)	20.9	24	53.6	36.2	NA
Return on sales (percent)	9.8	7.1	20.6	13.5	(3.2)
Number of employees	9,000	152,000	7,720	3,963	2,500
Sales per employee (US$ '000)	57.44	107.02	344.82	65.61	10.4

Note: The Gap reports its earnings in US$. All reported figures have been converted into US$ at the following exchange rate (as of January 2006): US$1 = HK$7.75.

GIORDANO'S GROWTH STRATEGY

Early in its existence, Giordano's management had realized that regional expansion was required to achieve substantial growth and economies of scale. By 2006, Giordano had over 1,600 stores in 31 markets. **Exhibit 8** shows the growth achieved across a number of dimensions from 1994 to 2004.

Driven in part by its desire for growth and in part by the need to reduce its dependence on Asia in the wake of the 1998 economic meltdown, Giordano set its sights

EXHIBIT 8   Operational Highlights for Giordano's Retail and Distribution Division

Source: *Annual Report 2004,* Giordano International.

	2004	2003	2002	2001	2000	1999	1998	1997	1996	1995	1994
Number of retail outlets											
Managed directly by the group	811	550	473	456	367	317	308	324	294	280	283
Franchised	774	813	783	703	553	423	370	316	221	171	77
Total number of retail outlets	1,585	1,363	1,256	1,159	920	740	678	640	515	451	360
Retail floor area managed directly by the group (in '000 sq. ft.)	846	650	599	597	465	301	358	313	295	286	282
Sales per square foot (HK$)	4,300	4,200	4,500	5,100	7,400	8,400	6,800	8,000	9,900	10,500	10,600
Number of employees	9,000	7,900	8,000	8,287	7,166	6,237	6,319	8,175	10,004	10,348	6,863
Comparable store sales: increase/(decrease) (percent)	7	(9)	(2)	(4)	4	21	(13)	(11)	(6)	8	(9)
Number of sales associates	NA	3,200	2,900	2,603	2,417	2,026	1,681	1,929	1,958	2,069	1,928

EXHIBIT 9   Giordano's Flagship Store in Shanghai

on markets outside Asia. Australia was an early target and the number of retail outlets increased from four in 1999 to 46 in 2006. In Japan, Giordano opened 21 outlets from 2001 to 2006. Although the Asian financial crisis had caused Giordano to rethink its regional strategy, it was still determined to enter and further penetrate new Asian markets. This determination led to successful expansion in Mainland China (see **Exhibit 9**), where the number of retail outlets grew from 253 in 1999 to 644 by 2006. Giordano's management foresaw both challenges and opportunities arising from the People's Republic of China's accession to the World Trade Organization.

Giordano opened more stores in Indonesia, bringing its total in that country to 39 stores. In Malaysia, Giordano planned to refurnish its outlets and intensify its local promotional campaigns to consolidate its leadership position in the Malaysian market. To improve store profitability, Giordano had already converted some of its franchised Malaysian stores into company-owned stores.

The senior management team knew that Giordano's future success in such markets would depend on a detailed understanding of consumer tastes and preferences for fabrics, colors and advertising. In the past, the firm had relied on maintaining a consistent strategy across different countries, including such elements as positioning, service levels, information systems, logistics, and human resource policies. However, implementation of such tactical elements as promotional campaigns was usually left mostly to local managers. A country's overall performance in terms of sales, contribution, service levels and customer feedback was monitored by regional headquarters (for instance, Singapore for Southeast Asia) and the head office in Hong Kong. Weekly performance reports were distributed to all managers.

As the organization expanded beyond Asia, it was becoming clear that different strategies had to be developed for different regions or countries. For instance, to enhance profitability in Mainland China, the company recognized that better sourcing was needed to enhance price competitiveness. Turning around the Taiwan operation required refocusing on basic designs, streamlining product portfolio, and implementing their micromarketing strategy more aggressively. The company was continuing to explore the market in Japan and planned to open a few more stores in the second half of 2006. In Europe, it was investigating a variety of distribution channels, including a wholesale-based business model.

Decisions Facing the Senior Management Team

Although Giordano had been extremely successful, it faced a number of challenges. A key issue was how the Giordano brand should be positioned against the competition in both new and existing markets. Was a repositioning required in existing markets and would it be necessary to follow different positioning strategies for different markets (e.g., Hong Kong versus Southeast Asia)?

A second issue was the sustainability of Giordano's key success factors. Giordano had to carefully explore how its core competencies and the pillars of its success were likely to develop over the coming years. Which of its competitive advantages were likely to be sustainable and which ones were likely to be eroded?

A third issue was Giordano's growth strategy in Asia as well as across continents. Would Giordano's competitive strengths be readily transferable to other markets? Would strategic adaptations to its strategy and marketing mix be required, or would tactical moves suffice?

STUDY QUESTIONS

1. Describe and evaluate Giordano's product, business and corporate strategies.
2. Describe and evaluate Giordano's current positioning strategy. Should Giordano reposition itself against its competitors in its current and new markets, and should it have different positioning strategies for different geographic markets?
3. What are Giordano's key success factors and sources of competitive advantage? Are its competitive advantages sustainable, and how would they develop in the future?
4. Could Giordano transfer its key success factors to new markets as it expands both in Asia and in other parts of the world?
5. How do you think Giordano had/would have to adapt its marketing and operations strategies and tactics when entering and penetrating your country?
6. What general lessons can major clothing retailers in your country learn from Giordano?

Case 5
Shouldice Hospital Limited (Abridged)

Two shadowy figures, enrobed and in slippers, walked slowly down the semi-darkened hall of the Shouldice Hospital. They didn't notice Alan O'Dell, the hospital's managing director, and his guest. Once they were out of earshot, O'Dell remarked good naturedly, "By the way they act, you'd think our patients own this place. And while they're here, in a way they do." Following a visit to the five operating rooms, O'Dell and his visitor once again encountered the same pair of patients still engrossed in discussing their hernia operations, which had been performed the previous morning.

HISTORY

An attractive brochure that was recently printed, although neither dated nor distributed to prospective patients, described Dr. Earle Shouldice, the founder of the hospital:

> Dr Shouldice's interest in early ambulation stemmed, in part, from an operation he performed in 1932 to remove the appendix from a seven-year-old girl and the girl's subsequent refusal to stay quietly in bed. In spite of her activity, no harm was done, and the experience recalled to the doctor the postoperative actions of animals upon which he had performed surgery. They had all moved about freely with no ill effects.

By 1940, Shouldice had given extensive thought to several factors that contributed to early ambulation following surgery. Among them were the use of a local anesthetic, the nature of the surgical procedure itself, the design of a facility to encourage movement without unnecessarily causing discomfort and the postoperative regimen. With these things in mind, he began to develop a surgical technique for repairing hernias[1] that was superior to others; word of his early success generated demand.

Dr. Shouldice's medical license permitted him to operate anywhere, even on a kitchen table. However, as more and more patients requested operations, Dr. Shouldice created new facilities by buying a rambling 130-acre estate with a 17,000-square foot main house in the Toronto suburb of Thornhill. After some years of planning, a large wing was added to provide a total capacity of 89 beds.

Dr. Shouldice died in 1965. At that time, Shouldice Hospital Limited was formed to operate both the hospital and clinical facilities under the surgical direction of Dr. Nicholas Obney. In 1999, Dr. Casim Degani, an internationally-recognized authority, became surgeon-in-chief. By 2004, 7,600 operations were performed per year.

---

[1]Most hernias, known as external abdominal hernias, are protrusions of some part of the abdominal contents through a hole or slit in the muscular layers of the abdominal wall which is supposed to contain them. Well over 90% of these hernias occur in the groin area. Of these, by far the most common are inguinal hernias, many of which are caused by a slight weakness in the muscle layers brought about by the passage of the testicles in male babies through the groin area shortly before birth. Aging also contributes to the development of inguinal hernias. Because of the cause of the affliction, 85% of all hernias occur in males.

Professor James Heskett prepared the original version of this case, "Shouldice Hospital Limited," HBS No. 683-068. This version was prepared jointly by Professor James Heskett and Roger Hallowell (MBA 1989, DBA 1997). HBS cases are developed solely as the basis for class discussion. Cases are not intended to serve as endorsements, sources of primary data, or illustrations of effective or ineffective management.

THE SHOULDICE METHOD

Only external (vs. internal) abdominal hernias were repaired at Shouldice Hospital. Thus most first-time repairs, "primaries," were straightforward operations requiring about 45 minutes. The remaining procedures involved patients suffering recurrences of hernias previously repaired elsewhere.[2] Many of the recurrences and very difficult hernia repairs required 90 minutes or more.

In the Shouldice method, the muscles of the abdominal wall were arranged in three distinct layers, and the opening was repaired—each layer in turn—by overlapping its margins as the edges of a coat might be overlapped when buttoned. The end result reinforced the muscular wall of the abdomen with six rows of sutures (stitches) under the skin cover, which was then closed with clamps that were later removed. (Other methods might not separate muscle layers, often involved fewer rows of sutures, and sometimes involved the insertion of screens or meshes under the skin.)

A typical first-time repair could be completed with the use of preoperative sedation (sleeping pill) and analgesic (pain killer) plus a local anesthetic, an injection of Novocain in the region of the incision. This allowed immediate post-operative patient ambulation and facilitated rapid recovery.

THE PATIENTS' EXPERIENCE

Most potential Shouldice patients learned about the hospital from previous Shouldice patients. Although thousands of doctors had referred patients, doctors were less likely to recommend Shouldice because of the generally regarded simplicity of the surgery, often considered a "bread and butter" operation. Typically, many patients had their problem diagnosed by a personal physician and then contacted Shouldice directly. Many more made this diagnosis themselves.

The process experienced by Shouldice patients depended on whether or not they lived close enough to the hospital to visit the facility to obtain a diagnosis. Approximately 10% of Shouldice patients came from outside the province of Ontario, most of these from the United States. Another 60% of patients lived beyond the Toronto area. These out-of-town patients often were diagnosed by mail using the Medical Information Questionnaire shown in **Exhibit 1.** Based on information in the questionnaire, a Shouldice surgeon would determine the type of hernia the respondent had and whether there were signs that some risk might be associated with surgery (for example, an overweight or heart condition, or a patient who had suffered a heart attack or a stroke in the past six months to a year, or whether a general or local anesthetic was required). At this point, a patient was given a operating date and sent a brochure describing the hospital and the Shouldice method. If necessary, a sheet outlining a weight-loss program prior to surgery was also sent. A small proportion was refused treatment, either because they were overweight, represented an undue medical risk, or because it was determined that they did not have a hernia.

Arriving at the clinic between 1:00 p.m. and 3:00 p.m. the day before the operation, a patient joined other patients in the waiting room. He or she was soon examined in one of six examination rooms staffed by surgeons who had completed their operating schedules for the day. This examination required no more than 20 minutes, unless the patient needed reassurance. (Patients typically exhibited a moderate level of anxiety

[2]Based on tracking of patients over more than 30 years, the gross recurrence rate for all operations performed at Shouldice was 0.8%. Recurrence rates reported in the literature for these types of hernia varied greatly. However, one text stated, "In the United States the gross rate of recurrence for groin hernias approaches 10%."

until their operation was completed.) At this point it occasionally was discovered that a patient had not corrected his or her weight problem; others might be found not to have a hernia at all. In either case, the patient was sent home.

After checking administrative details, about an hour after arriving at the hospital, a patient was directed to the room number shown on his or her wrist band. Throughout the process, patients were asked to keep their luggage (usually light) with them.

All patient rooms at the hospital were semiprivate, containing two beds. Patients with similar jobs, backgrounds, or interests were assigned to the same room to the extent possible. Upon reaching their rooms, patients busied themselves unpacking, getting acquainted with roommates, shaving themselves in the area of the operation, and changing into pajamas.

At 4:30 p.m., a nurse's orientation provided the group of incoming patients with information about what to expect, including the need for exercise after the operation and the daily routine. According to Alan O'Dell, "Half are so nervous they don't remember much." Dinner was then served, followed by further recreation and tea and cookies at 9:00 p.m. Nurses emphasized the importance of attendance at that time because it provided an opportunity for preoperative patients to talk with those whose operations had been completed earlier that same day.

EXHIBIT 1   Medical Information Questionnaire

FAMILY NAME (Last Name)		FIRST NAME		MIDDLE NAME	

| STREET & NUMBER (or Rural Route or P.O. Box) | | Town/City | | Province/State | |

County	Township	Zip or Postal Code	Birthdate: Month Day Year	

SHOULDICE HOSPITAL

7750 Bayview Avenue
Box 370, Thornhill, Ontario L3T 4A3 Canada
Phone (418) 889-1125

(Thornhill - One Mile North Metro Toronto)

Telephone
Home .... If none, give
Work .... neighbour's number ....

Married or Single | Religion

NEXT OF KIN: Name | Address | Telephone #

INSURANCE INFORMATION: Please give name of Insurance Company and Numbers. | Date form completed

MEDICAL

INFORMATION

HOSPITAL INSURANCE: (Please bring hospital certificates) | OTHER HOSPITAL INSURANCE
O.H.I.P.   BLUE CROSS | Company Name _____
Number _____ Number _____ | Policy Number _____

SURGICAL INSURANCE: (Please bring insurance certificates) | OTHER SURGICAL INSURANCE
O.H.I.P.   BLUE SHIELD | Company Name _____
Number _____ Number _____ | Policy Number _____

Patients who live at a distance often prefer their examination, admission and operation to be arranged all on a single visit – to save making two lengthy journeys. The whole purpose of this questionnarie is to make such arrangements possible, although, of course, it cannot replace the examination in any way. Its completion and return will not put you under any obligation.

WORKMEN'S COMPENSATION BOARD | Approved | Social Insurance (Security) Number
Claim No. | Yes   No |

Occupation   Name of Business | Are you the owner? If Retired – Former Occupation
                                     Yes   No

How did you hear about Shouldice Hospital? If referred by a doctor, give name & address)

Please be sure to fill in both sides.

Are you a former patient of Shouldice Hospital?   Yes   No | Do you smoke?   Yes   No

Have you ever written to Shouldice Hospital in the past?   Yes   No

What is your preferred admission date? (Please give as much advance notice as possible)
No admissions Friday, Saturday or Sunday.

FOR OFFICE USE ONLY

Date Received | Type of Hemia | Weight Loss
                                lbs.

Consent to Operate ☐ | Special Instructions | Approved
Heart Report ☐

This information will be treated as confidential.

Referring Doctor Notified | Operation Date | *(continued on next page)*

EXHIBIT 1 Medical Information Questionnaire—continued

THIS CHART IS FOR EXPLANATION ONLY

Ordinary hernias are mostly either at the navel ("belly-button") - or just above it

or down in the groin area on either side

An "inclsional hernia" is one that bulges through the scar of any other surgical operation that has failed to hold - wherever it may be.

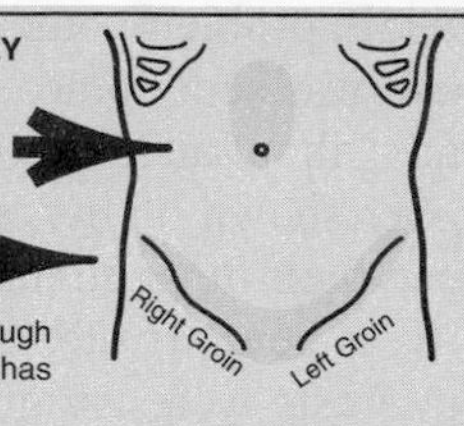

THIS IS YOUR CHART – PLEASE MARK IT!

(MARK THE POSITION OF EACH HERNIA YOU WANT REPAIRED WITH AN "X")

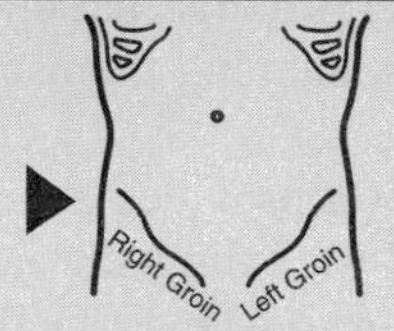

APPROXIMATE SIZE . . .
Walnut (or less) ☐ ☐
Hen's Egg or Lemon ☐ ☐
Grapefruit (or more) ☐ ☐

ESSENTIAL EXTRA INFORMATION

Use only the sections that apply to your hernias and put a √ in each box that seems appropriate.

NAVEL AREA (AND JUST ABOVE NAVEL) ONLY Yes No
Is this navel (bellybutton) hernia your FIRST one? ☐ ☐

If it's NOT your first, how many repair attempts so far? ☐

GROIN HERNIAS ONLY

	RIGHT GROIN		LEFT GROIN	
	Yes	No	Yes	No
Is this your FIRST GROIN HERNIA ON THIS SIDE?	☐	☐	☐	☐

How many hernia operations in this groin already? Right ☐ Left ☐

DATE OF LAST OPERATION ☐

INCISIONAL HERNIAS ONLY (the ones bulging through previous operation scars)
Was the original operation for your Appendix? ☐ . or Gallbladder? ☐ .
or Stomach? ☐ . or Prostate? ☐ . or Hysterectomy? ☐ . or Other? . . . .
. . . .
How many attempts to repair the hernia have been made so far? ☐

PLEASE BE ACCURATE: Misleading figures, when checked on a adminsion day, could mean postponement of your operation till your weight is suitable.

HEIGHT . . . . ft . . . . ins. WEIGHT . . . . lbs. Nude or just pyjamas Recent gain? . . . . lbs. Recent loss? . . . . lbs.

Waist (muscles relaxed) . . . . ins. Chest (not expanded) . . . . ins.

GENERAL HEALTH

Age . . . . years Is your health now GOOD ☐ . FAIR ☐ . or POOR ☐

Please mention briefly any severe past illness — such as a "heart attack" or a "stroke", for example, from which you have now recovered (and its approximate date) . . . .
. . . .

We need to know about other present conditions, even though your admission is NOT likely to be refused because of them.

Please tick ☑ any condition for which you are having regular treatment:		Name of any prescribed pills, tablets or capsules you take regularly: –
Blood Pressure	☐	
Excess body fluids	☐	
Chest pain ("angina")	☐	
Irregular Heartbeat	☐	
Diabetes	☐	
Asthma & Bronchitis	☐	
Ulcers	☐	
Anticoagulants (to delay blood-clotting or to "thin the blood")	☐	
Other		

Did you remember to MARK AN "X" on your body chart to show us where each of your hernias is located?

Patients to be operated on early were awakened at 5:30 a.m. to be given preop sedation. An attempt was made to schedule operations for roommates at approximately the same time. Patients were taken to the preoperating room where the circulating nurse administered Demerol, an analgesic, 45 minutes before surgery. A few minutes prior to the first operation at 7:30 a.m., the surgeon assigned to each patient administered Novocain, a local anesthetic, in the operating room. This was in contrast to the typical hospital procedure in which patients were sedated in their rooms prior to being taken to the operating rooms.

Upon the completion of their operation, during which a few patients were "chatty" and fully aware of what was going on, patients were invited to get off the operating table and walk to the post-operating room with the help of their surgeons. According to the director of nursing:

> Ninety-nine percent accept the surgeon's invitation. While we use wheelchairs to return them to their rooms, the walk from the operating table is for psychological as well as physiological [blood pressure, respiratory] reasons. Patients prove to themselves that they can do it, and they start their all-important exercise immediately.

Throughout the day after their operation, patients were encouraged to exercise by nurses and housekeepers alike. By 9:00 p.m. on the day of their operations, all patients were ready and able to walk down to the dining room for tea and cookies, even if it meant climbing stairs, to help indoctrinate the new "class" admitted that day. On the fourth morning, patients were ready for discharge.

During their stay, patients were encouraged to take advantage of the opportunity to explore the premises and make new friends. Some members of the staff felt that the patients and their attitudes were the most important element of the Shouldice program. According to Dr. Byrnes Shouldice, son of the founder, a surgeon on the staff, and a 50% owner of the hospital:

> Patients sometimes ask to stay an extra day. Why? Well, think about it. They are basically well to begin with. But they arrive with a problem and a certain amount of nervousness, tension, and anxiety about their surgery. Their first morning here they're operated on and experience a sense of relief from something that's been bothering them for a long time. They are immediately able to get around, and they've got a three-day holiday ahead of them with a perfectly good reason to be away from work with no sense of guilt. They share experiences with other patients, make friends easily, and have the run of the hospital. In summer, the most common after-effect from the surgery is sunburn.

THE NURSES' EXPERIENCE

34 full-time-equivalent nurses staffed Shouldice each 24 hour period. However, during non-operating hours, only six full-time-equivalent nurses were on the premises at any given time. While the Canadian acute-care hospital average ratio of nurses to patients was 1:4, at Shouldice the ratio was 1:15. Shouldice nurses spent an unusually large proportion of their time in counseling activities. As one supervisor commented, "We don't use bedpans." According to a manager, "Shouldice has a waiting list of nurses wanting to be hired, while other hospitals in Toronto are short-staffed and perpetually recruiting."

THE DOCTORS' EXPERIENCE

The hospital employed 10 full-time surgeons and 8 part-time assistant surgeons. Two anesthetists were also on site. The anesthetists floated among cases except when general anesthesia was in use. Each operating team required a surgeon, an assistant surgeon, a scrub nurse, and a circulating nurse. The operating load varied from 30 to 36 operations per day. As a result, each surgeon typically performed three or four operations each day.

A typical surgeon's day started with a *scrubbing* shortly before the first scheduled operation at 7:30 a.m. If the first operation was routine, it usually was completed by 8:15 a.m. At its conclusion, the surgical team helped the patient walk from the room and summoned the next patient. After scrubbing, the surgeon could be ready to operate again at 8:30 a.m. Surgeons were advised to take a coffee break after their second or third operation. Even so, a surgeon could complete three routine operations and a fourth involving a recurrence and still be finished in time for a 12:30 p.m. lunch in the staff dining room.

Upon finishing lunch, surgeons not scheduled to operate in the afternoon examined incoming patients. A surgeon's day ended by 4:00 p.m. In addition, a surgeon could expect to be on call one weekday night in ten and one weekend in ten. Alan O'Dell commented that the position appealed to doctors who "want to watch their children grow up. A doctor on call is rarely called to the hospital and has regular hours." According to Dr. Obney:

> When I interview prospective surgeons, I look for experience and a good education. I try to gain some insight into their domestic situation and personal interests and habits.

I also try to find out why a surgeon wants to switch positions. And I try to determine if he's willing to perform the repair exactly as he's told. This is no place for prima donnas.

Dr. Shouldice added:

> Traditionally a hernia is often the first operation that a junior resident in surgery performs. Hernia repair is regarded as a relatively simple operation compared to other major operations. This is quite wrong, as is borne out by the resulting high recurrence rate. It is a tricky anatomical area and occasionally very complicated, especially to the novice or those doing very few hernia repairs each year. But at Shouldice Hospital a surgeon learns the Shouldice technique over a period of several months. He learns when he can go fast and when he must go slow. He develops a pace and a touch. If he encounters something unusual, he is encouraged to consult immediately with other surgeons. We teach each other and try to encourage a group effort. And he learns not to take risks to achieve absolute perfection. Excellence is the enemy of good.

Chief Surgeon Degani assigned surgeons to an operating room on a daily basis by noon of the preceding day. This allowed surgeons to examine the specific patients that they were to operate on. Surgeons and assistants were rotated every few days. Cases were assigned to give doctors a non-routine operation (often involving a recurrence) several times a week. More complex procedures were assigned to more senior and experienced members of the staff. Dr Obney commented:

> If something goes wrong, we want to make sure that we have an experienced surgeon in charge. Experience is most important. The typical general surgeon may perform 25 to 50 hernia operations per year. Ours perform 750 or more.

The 10 full-time surgeons were paid a straight salary, typically $144,000.[3] In addition, bonuses to doctors were distributed monthly. These depended on profit, individual productivity, and performance. The total bonus pool paid to the surgeons in a recent year was approximately $400,000. Total surgeon compensation (including benefits) was approximately 15% more than the average income for a surgeon in Ontario.

Training in the Shouldice technique was important because the procedure could not be varied. It was accomplished through direct supervision by one or more of the senior surgeons. The rotation of teams and frequent consultations allowed for an ongoing opportunity to appraise performance and take corrective action. Where possible, former Shouldice patients suffering recurrences were assigned to the doctor who performed the first operation "to allow the doctor to learn from his mistake." Dr. Obney commented on being a Shouldice surgeon:

> A doctor must decide after several years whether he wants to do this for the rest of his life because, just as in other specialties—for example, radiology—he loses touch with other medical disciplines. If he stays for five years, he doesn't leave. Even among younger doctors, few elect to leave.

THE FACILITY

The Shouldice Hospital contained two facilities in one building—the hospital and the clinic. On its first level, the hospital contained the kitchen and dining rooms. The second level contained a large, open lounge area, the admissions offices, patient rooms, and a spacious glass-covered Florida room. The third level had additional patient rooms and recreational areas. Patients could be seen visiting in each others' rooms, walking

---

[3]All monetary references in the case are to Canadian dollars. $1 US equaled $1.33 Canadian on February 23, 2004.

up and down hallways, lounging in the sunroom, and making use of light recreational facilities ranging from a pool table to an exercycle. Alan O'Dell pointed out some of the features of the hospital:

> The rooms contain no telephone or television sets. If a patient needs to make a call or wants to watch television, he or she has to take a walk. The steps are designed specially with a small rise to allow patients recently operated on to negotiate the stairs without undue discomfort. Every square foot of the hospital is carpeted to reduce the hospital feeling and the possibility of a fall. Carpeting also gives the place a smell other than that of disinfectant.
>
> This facility was designed by an architect with input from Dr. Byrnes Shouldice and Mrs. W. H. Urquhart (the daughter of the founder). The facility was discussed for years and many changes in the plans were made before the first concrete was poured. A number of unique policies were also instituted. For example, parents accompanying children here for an operation stay free. You may wonder why we can do it, but we learned that we save more in nursing costs than we spend for the parent's room and board.

Patients and staff were served food prepared in the same kitchen, and staff members picked up food from a cafeteria line placed in the very center of the kitchen. This provided an opportunity for everyone to chat with the kitchen staff several times a day, and the hospital staff to eat together. According to O'Dell, "We use all fresh ingredients and prepare the food from scratch in the kitchen."

The director of housekeeping pointed out:

> I have only three on my housekeeping staff for the entire facility. One of the reasons for so few housekeepers is that we don't need to change linens during a patient's four-day stay. Also, the medical staff doesn't want the patients in bed all day. They want the nurses to encourage the patients to be up socializing, comparing notes [for confidence], encouraging each other, and walking around, getting exercise. Of course, we're in the rooms straightening up throughout the day. This gives the housekeepers a chance to josh with the patients and to encourage them to exercise.

The clinic housed five operating rooms, a laboratory, and the patient-recovery room. In total, the estimated cost to furnish an operating room was $30,000. This was considerably less than for other hospitals requiring a bank of equipment with which to administer anesthetics for each room. At Shouldice, two mobile units were used by the anesthetists when needed. In addition, the complex had one "crash cart" per floor for use if a patient should suffer a heart attack or stroke.

ADMINISTRATION

Alan O'Dell described his job:

> We try to meet people's needs and make this as good a place to work as possible. There is a strong concern for employees here. Nobody is fired. [This was later reinforced by Dr. Shouldice, who described a situation involving two employees who confessed to theft in the hospital. They agreed to seek psychiatric help and were allowed to remain on the job.] As a result, turnover is low.
>
> Our administrative and support staff are non-union, but we try to maintain a pay scale higher than the union scale for comparable jobs in the area. We have a profit-sharing plan that is separate from the doctors.' Last year the administrative and support staff divided up $60,000.
>
> If work needs to be done, people pitch in to help each other. A unique aspect of our administration is that I insist that each secretary is trained to do another's work and in an emergency is able to switch to another function immediately. We don't have an

organization chart. A chart tends to make people think they're boxed in jobs.[4] I try to stay one night a week, having dinner and listening to the patients, to find out how things are really going around here.

Operating Costs

The 2004 budgets for the hospital and clinic were close to $8.5 million,[5] and $3.5 million, respectively.[6]

THE MARKET

Hernia operations were among the most common performed on males. In 2000 an estimated 1,000,000 such operations were performed in the United States alone. According to Dr. Shouldice:

> When our backlog of scheduled operations gets too large, we wonder how many people decide instead to have their local doctor perform the operation. Every time we've expanded our capacity, the backlog has declined briefly, only to climb once again. Right now, at 2,400, it is larger than it has ever been and is growing by 100 every six months.

The hospital relied entirely on word-of-mouth advertising, the importance of which was suggested by the results of a poll carried out by students of DePaul University as part of a project (**Exhibit 3** shows a portion of these results). Although little systematic data about patients had been collected, Alan O'Dell remarked that "if we had to rely on wealthy patients only, our practice would be much smaller."

Patients were attracted to the hospital, in part, by its reasonable rates. Charges for a typical operation were four days of hospital stay at $320 per day, and a $650 surgical fee for a primary inguinal (the most common hernia). An additional fee of $300 was assessed if general anesthesia was required (in about 20% of cases). These charges compared to an average charge of $5,240 for operations performed elsewhere.

Round-trip fares for travel to Toronto from various major cities on the North American continent ranged from roughly $200 to $600.

The hospital also provided annual checkups to alumni, free of charge. Many occurred at the time of the patient reunion. The most recent reunion, featuring dinner and a floor show, was held at a first-class hotel in downtown Toronto and was attended by 1,000 former patients, many from outside Canada.

PROBLEMS AND PLANS

When asked about major questions confronting the management of the hospital, Dr. Shouldice cited a desire to seek ways of increasing the hospital's capacity while at the same time maintaining control over the quality of service delivered, the future role of government in the operations of the hospital, and the use of the Shouldice name by potential competitors. As Dr Shouldice put it:

> I'm a doctor first and an entrepreneur second. For example, we could refuse permission to other doctors who want to visit the hospital. They may copy our technique and misapply it or misinform their patients about the use of it. This results in failure, and we are concerned that the technique will be blamed. But we're doctors, and it is our obligation to help other surgeons learn. On the other hand, it's quite clear that others are trying to emulate us. Look at this ad. [The advertisement is shown in **Exhibit 4.**]

[4]The chart in **Exhibit 2** was prepared by the casewriter, based on conversations with hospital personnel.
[5]This figure included a provincially mandated return on investment.
[6]The latter figure included the bonus pool for doctors.

EXHIBIT 2 Organization Chart

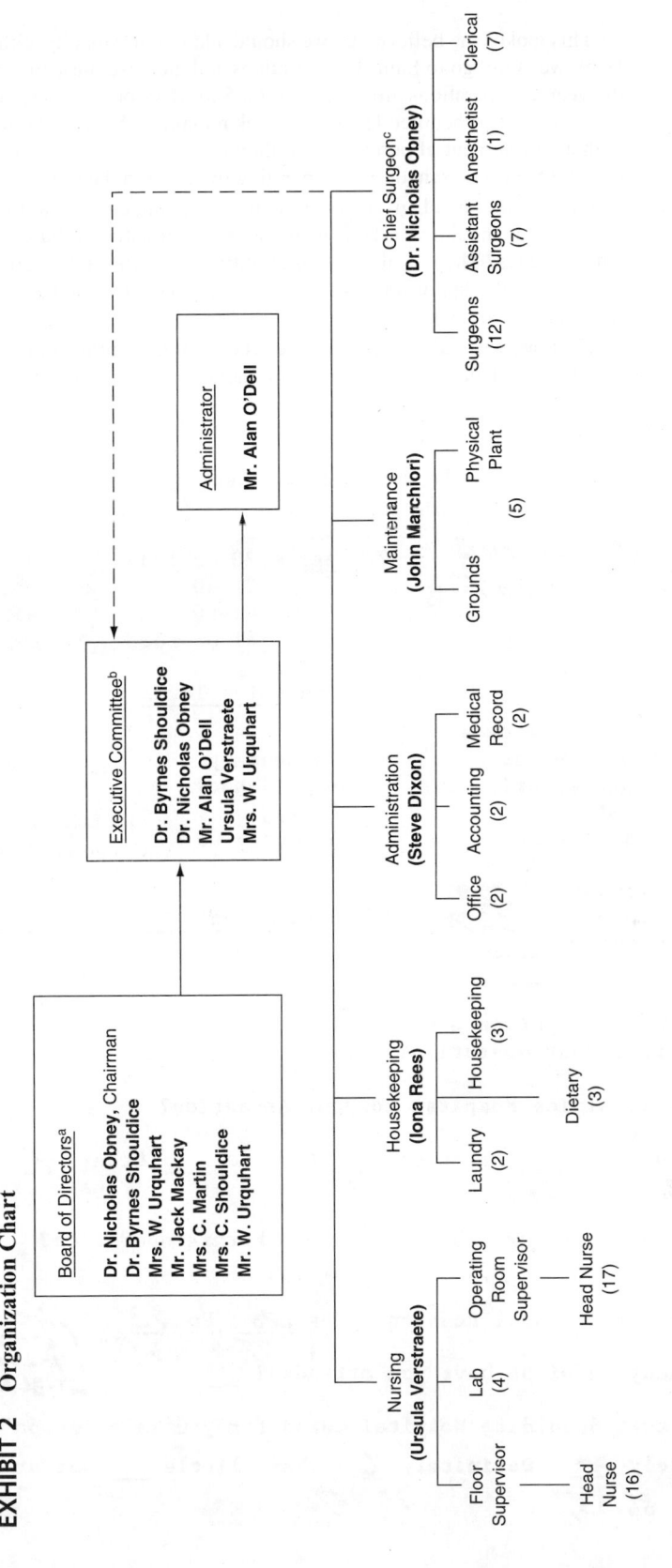

Board of Directors[a]

Dr. Nicholas Obney, Chairman
Dr. Byrnes Shouldice
Mrs. W. Urquhart
Mr. Jack Mackay
Mrs. C. Martin
Mrs. C. Shouldice
Mr. W. Urquhart

Executive Committee[b]

Dr. Byrnes Shouldice
Dr. Nicholas Obney
Mr. Alan O'Dell
Ursula Verstraete
Mrs. W. Urquhart

Administrator
Mr. Alan O'Dell

Chief Surgeon[c]
(Dr. Nicholas Obney)

Surgeons (12)
Assistant Surgeons (7)
Anesthetist (1)
Clerical (7)

Maintenance
(John Marchiori)

Grounds
Physical Plant (5)

Administration
(Steve Dixon)

Office (2)
Accounting (2)
Medical Record (2)

Housekeeping
(Iona Rees)

Laundry (2)
Housekeeping (3)
Dietary (3)

Nursing
(Ursula Verstraete)

Floor Supervisor
Lab (4)
Operating Room Supervisor

Head Nurse (16)
Head Nurse (17)

[a]Meets three times a year or as needed.
[b]Meet as needed (usually twice a month).
[c]Informally reports to Executive Committee.

645

This makes me believe that we should add to our capacity, either here or elsewhere. Here, we could go to Saturday operations and increase our capacity by 20%. Throughout the year, no operations are scheduled for Saturdays or Sundays, although patients whose operations are scheduled late in the week remain in the hospital over the weekend. Or, with an investment of perhaps $4 million in new space, we could expand our number of beds by 50%, and schedule the operating rooms more heavily.

On the other hand, given government regulation, do we want to invest more in Toronto? Or should we establish another hospital with similar design, perhaps in the United States? There is also the possibility that we could diversify into other specialties offering similar opportunities such as eye surgery, varicose veins, or diagnostic services (e.g. colonoscopies).

For now, we're also beginning the process of grooming someone to succeed Dr. Degani when he retires. He's in his early 60s, but at some point we'll have to

EXHIBIT 3 **Shouldice Hospital Annual Patient Reunion Data**

Direction: For each question, please place a check mark as it applies to you.

1. **Sex**   Male _41_ 95.34%
             Female _2_ 4.65%

2. **Age**   20 or less ____
             21-40 _4_ 9.30%
             41-60 _17_ 39.54%
             61 or more _22_ 51.16%

3. **Nationality**

   Directions: Please place a check mark in nation you represent and please write in your province, state or country where it applies.

   Canada _38_ Province _88.37%_
   America _5_ State _11.63%_
   Europe ____ Country ____
   Other ____ ____

4. **Education level**

   Elementary _5_ 11.63%
   High School _18_ 41.86%
   College _13?_ 30.23%
   Graduate work _7_ 16.28%

5. **Occupation** _____

6. Have you been overnight in a hospital other than Shouldice before your operation?   Yes _31_   No _12_

7. What brought Shouldice Hospital to your attention?

   Friend _23_ Doctor _9_ Relative _7_ Article ____ Other _4_
   53.49%   20.93%   16.28%   (Please explain) 9.30%

8. Did you have a single _25_ or double _18_ hernia operation?
                         54.14%   41.86%

9. Is this your first Annual Reunion? Yes _20_ No _23_ (2-5 reunions - 11 47.83%
                                     46.51%   53.49%   (6-10 reunions - 5 21.73%
   If no, how many reunions have you attended? ____ (11-20 reunions - 4 12.39%
                                                      21-36 reunions - 3 13.05%

10. Do you feel that Shouldice Hospital cared for you as a person?

    Most definitely _37_ Definitely _6_ Very little ____ Not at all ____
                    86.05%   13.95%

EXHIBIT 3 Shouldice Hospital Annual Patient Reunion Data—continued

11. What impressed you the most about your stay at Shouldice? Please
     check one answer for each of the following.

A. Fees charged for operation and hospital stay
    Very   Somewhat   Not
    Important _10_   Important _3_   Important _6_   Important _24_

B. Operation Procedure
    Very   Somewhat   Not
    Important _33_   Important _9_   Important _1_   Important ____
       76.74%   20.93%   2.33%

C. Physician's Care
    Very   Somewhat   Not
    Important _31_   Important _12_   Important _—_   Important _—_
       72.10%   27.90%

D. Nursing Care
    Very   Somewhat   Not
    Important _28_   Important _14_   Important _1_   Important ____
       65.12%   32.56%   2.33%

E. Food Service
    Very   Somewhat   Not
    Important _23_   Important _11_   Important _7_   Important _2_
       53.48%   25.59%   16.28%   4.65%

F. Shortness of Hospital Stay
    Very   Somewhat   Not
    Important _17_   Important _15_   Important _8_   Important _3_
       39.53%   34.88%   18.60%   6.98%

G. Exercise; Recreational Activities
    Very   Somewhat   Not
    Important _17_   Important _14_   Important _12_   Important _—_
       39.53%   32.56%   27.91%

H. Friendships with Patients
    Very   Somewhat   Not
    Important _25_   Important _10_   Important _5_   Important _3_
       58.15%   23.25%   11.63%   6.98%

I. "Shouldice Hospital hardly seemed like a hospital at all."
    Very   Somewhat   Not
    Important _25_   Important _13_   Important _5_   Important ____
       58.14%   30.23%   11.63%

12. In a few words, give the MAIN REASON why you returned for this annual
     reunion.

address this issue. And for good reason, he's resisted changing certain successful procedures that I think we could improve on. We had quite a time changing the schedule for the administration of Demerol to patients to increase their comfort level during the operation. Dr Degani has opposed a Saturday operating program on the premise that he won't be here and won't be able to maintain proper control.

Alan O'Dell added his own concerns:

> How should we be marketing our services? Right now, we don't advertise directly to patients. We're even afraid to send out this new brochure we've put together, unless a potential patient specifically requests it, for fear it will generate too much demand. Our records show that just under 1% of our patients are medical doctors, a significantly high percentage. How should we capitalize on that? I'm also concerned about this talk of Saturday operations. We are already getting good utilization of this facility. And if we expand further, it will be very difficult to maintain the same kind of working relationships and attitudes. Already there are rumors floating around among the staff about it. And the staff is not pleased.

The matter of Saturday operations had been a topic of conversation among the doctors as well. Four of the older doctors were opposed to it. While most of the younger doctors were indifferent or supportive, at least two who had been at the hospital for some time were particularly concerned about the possibility that the issue would drive a wedge between the two groups. As one put it, "I'd hate to see the practice split over the issue."

Case 6

Hong Kong Disneyland

September 12, 2006, marked the one-year anniversary of the opening of Hong Kong Disneyland (HKD). Amid the hoopla and celebrations, media experts were reflecting on the high points and low points of HKD's first year of operations, including several controversies that had generated some negative publicity.

At a press conference and interview to discuss the first year of operations, Bill Ernest, HKD's executive vice-president, acknowledged that the park had learnt a lot from its experiences and that the problems had made it stronger. Ernest also announced that HKD attendance for the year had been "well over" five million visitors. Still, this figure was short of the 5.6 million visitors that had earlier been projected by park officials. Ernest stated that the park was on sound financial footing but would not release the details.[1] He also announced the appointment of two non-executive directors; Payson Cha Mou-sing, managing director of HKR International, and Philip Chen Nan-lok of Cathay Pacific would be joining the board of directors in a move calculated to counter charges of a lack of transparency. The criticisms were, in part, coming from members of the Hong Kong Legislative Council as HKD was 57 percent owned by the Hong Kong Government, which had invested HK$23 billion.[2]

Since plans for the high-profile HKD project were first announced, there had been criticisms of a lack of transparency from Hong Kong government officials, the Consumer Council and members of the public. The dissatisfaction was reflected in a survey conducted by Hong Kong Polytechnic University in March 2006.[3] Although 56 percent of the 524 respondents believed the government's HK$13.6 billion (about US$1.74 billion) investment to be of a "fair" value, 70 percent of respondents had a negative impression of the public investment in HKD. This response was a considerably more pessimistic result than previous surveys. It was in the interests of HKD to turn this situation around.

HKD was the third park that Disney had opened outside of the United States, following the Tokyo Disney Resort and Disneyland Resort Paris. The Tokyo Disney Resort was the most successful of all of the Disney parks worldwide, and indeed one of the most successful theme parks in the world; the Disneyland Paris Resort was much less

---

[1]Linda Choy and Dennis Eng, "5 Million Visit Disney Park, Short of Target," *South China Morning Post*, electronic edition, September 5, 2006, available at http://scmp.com, accessed December 3, 2006.

[2]In 2006, the Hong Kong dollar was pegged to the U.S. dollar at approximately US$1 = HK$7.80.

[3]May Chan, "Disneyland's Image Has Soured Since Its Opening." *South China Morning Post*, p. CITY3.

Michael N. Young and Donald Liu wrote this case solely to provide material for class discussion. The authors do not intend to illustrate either effective or ineffective handling of a managerial situation. The authors may have disguised certain names and other identifying information to protect confidentiality.

Ivey Management Services prohibits any form of reproduction, storage or transmittal without its written permission. Reproduction of this material is not covered under authorization by any reproduction rights organization. To order copies or request permission to reproduce materials, contact Ivey Publishing, Ivey Management Services, c/o Richard Ivey School of Business, The University of Western Ontario, London, Ontario, Canada, N6A 3K7; phone (519) 661-3208; fax (519) 661-3882; e-mail cases@ivey.uwo.ca.

Copyright © 2007, Ivey Management Services   *Version: (A) 2007-08-27*

The initial research and a first draft of this case were completed by Edwina H. S. Chan, Lutricia S. M. Kwot, John C. M. Lee, Jacky W. Y. Shing and Sally P. M. Tsui as an assignment under the direction of Professor Michael Young.

successful.[4] Pundits had begun to wonder whether the outcome of HKD would more closely resemble that of its successful Far Eastern Japanese cousin or whether it would more closely resemble that of the French park. That outcome depended in part on how well Disney would be able to translate its strategic assets, such as its products, practices and ideologies, to the Chinese context.

COMPANY BACKGROUND

The Walt Disney Company (Disney) was founded in 1923, and was committed to delivering quality entertainment experiences for people of all ages. As a global entertainment empire, the company leveraged its amazing heritage of creativity, fantasy and imagination established by its founder, Walt Disney. By 2006, Disney's business portfolio consisted of four major segments: Studio Entertainment, Parks and Resorts, Consumer Products and Media Networks. **Exhibit 1** summarizes the details of the company's holdings and their respective financial performance in 2005.

Other Disney Parks and Resorts

Disney opened the first Disneyland, Disneyland Resort, at Anaheim, California, in July 1955. The company's second theme park, Walt Disney World Resort, was opened at Lake Buena Vista, Florida, in 1971. After the establishment of these two large theme parks in the United States, Disney sought to expand internationally. Disney's international expansion strategy was straightforward, consisting of "bringing the original Disneyland model to a new territory, and then, if feasible, adding a specialty theme park."[5] Tokyo Disney Resort was Disney's first attempt at executing this strategy.

Tokyo Disney Resort

Disney opened its first non-U.S. park in Tokyo, Japan, in 1983. The scope and thematic foundation of the Tokyo park was modeled after the Disney parks in California and Florida. The US$1.4 billion cost to develop Tokyo Disney Resort was financed solely by Oriental Land Co., a land-reclamation company formed under a joint-venture agreement between Mitsui Real Estate Development Co. and Keisei Electric Railway Co.[6]

---

[4]Mary Yoko Brannen, "When Mickey Loses Face: Recontextualization, Semantic Fit, and the Semiotics of Foreignness," *Academy of Management Review,* October 2004, pp. 593–616.

[5]Sara Bakhshian, "The Offspring," *Amusement Business,* May 2005, pp. 20–21.

[6]Eva Liu and Elyssa Wong, "Information Note: Tokyo Disneyland: Some Basic Facts," Research and Library Services Division of the Legislative Council Secretariat, Hong Kong, 1999, retrieved March 10, 2006 from

---

EXHIBIT 1   Current Holdings of the Walt Disney Company

Source: Annual Report 2005, The Walt Disney Company.

Business Segments	Performance (2005)
Studio Entertainment	This segment had the greatest decrease of 69%, which the company attributed to the overall decline in unit sales in worldwide home entertainment and at Miramax.
Consumer Products	This division reported decrease in operating income of 3% due to lower revenue generated from the sales of Disney goods and merchandise.
Media Networks	The higher rates paid by cable operators for ESPN and the Disney Channels and higher advertising revenue at ESPN and ABC were the primary factors driving the 27% growth in revenue at the media network unit.
Parks & Resorts	The Parks and Resorts division also enjoyed a 5% increase in revenue, largely due to the higher occupancy at the resorts, theme park attendance, and guest expenditure.

Disney did not assume any ownership of Tokyo Disney Resort to minimize risks. The contract signed in 1979 spelled out Oriental Land as the owner and licensee, whereas Disney was designated as the designer and licensor. Although Disney received a US$100 million royalty every year, this amount was less than would have been the case if Disney were the sole owner or even a co-owner of Tokyo Disney Resort. By 2006, the 23-year-old Tokyo Disney Resort, along with the addition of Tokyo DisneySea, at an additional cost of US$3 billion in 2000[7] was a huge success, with a combined annual attendance of more than 25 million visitors and an operating income of ¥ 28,957 million (about US$245.47 million) generated in 2005 alone.[8]

Tokyo Disney Resort was well received by the Japanese, owing in part to the Japanese interest in Western cultures and the Asian love of fantasy and costume. The secret underlying this success was to provide the visitors with "a slice of unadulterated Disney-style Americana," proclaimed Toshio Kagami, president of Oriental Land Co. Tokyo Disney Resort had attracted wide support from the local Japanese, who accounted for more than 95 percent of the annual attendance. Moreover, around 15 percent of the total visitors had visited the park 30 times or more, making Tokyo Disney Resort one of the world's most popular theme parks in terms of annual attendance.[9] The Tokyo Disney Resort also had the highest sales of souvenirs of all the Disney land resorts, in part, because it was the only Disney property to give special admission just for the purpose of purchasing souvenirs.

Disneyland Resort Paris

France was the largest consumer of Disney products outside the United States, particularly in the area of publications, such as comic books.[10] However, this status did not provide much help to Disneyland Resort Paris (formerly named Euro Disney), Disney's second attempt at international expansion. Disneyland Resort Paris came into operation in 1992, after two-and-a-half years of negotiations with the French Government. Disney was determined to avoid the mistake of forgoing majority ownership and profits as had been the case with Tokyo Disney Resort. Thus, Disney became one of the partners in this project. Under the initial financial arrangement, Disney had a 49 percent stake in the project. The French Government provided cash and loans of US$770 million at interest rates below the market rates, and financed the majority of the US$400 million infrastructure.

However, cost overruns pushed overall construction costs to US$5 billion—five times the previous estimate of US$1 billion. This increase was due to alterations in design and construction plans. This higher cost, coupled with the theme park's mediocre performance during its initial years of operation and other factors, caused the park severe difficulties between 1992 and 1994. The park did not report a profit until 1995, which was largely due to a reduction of interest costs from US$265 million to US$93 million and the rigorous financial re-engineering efforts in late 1994.[11]

---

www.legco.gov.hk/yr990/english/sec/library/990in02.pdf.

[7]Ibid.

[8]Oriental Land Co., *2005 Annual Report,* retrieved March 10, 2006 from http://olc.netir-wsp.com/medias/1656486483_OLCAR2005final.pdf.

[9]James Zoltak, "Lots of Walks in the Past Parks the Past Year," *Amusement Business,* December 2004, pp. 6–7.

[10]Mary Yoko Brannen, "When Mickey Loses Face: Recontextualization, Semantic Fit, and the Semiotics of Foreignness," *Academy of Management Review,* October 2004, pp. 593–616.

[11]James B. Stewart, *Disney War,* Simon & Schuster, New York, 2005.

Despite poor results between 1995 and 2001, Disney added a new park, Walt Disney Studios, which brought Hollywood-themed attractions to the French park. At its opening in 2004, the second park attracted only 2.2 million visitors, 5.8 million short of its original projections. At the end of the fiscal year on September 30, 2004, Disneyland Resort Paris announced a loss of €145.2 million (about US$190 million).[12]

Part of the problem with the Paris resort was the resistance by the French to what they considered American cultural imperialism. French cultural critics claimed that Disney would be a "cultural Chernobyl," and some stated publicly a desire for the park's failure. For example, critic Stephen Bayley wrote:

> The Old World is presented with all the confident big ticket flimflam of painstaking fakery that this bizarre campaign of reverse-engineered cultural imperialism represents. I like to think that by the turn of the century Euro Disney will have become a deserted city, similar to Angkor Wat [in Cambodia].[13]

Disney had to assure the French government that French would be the primary language spoken within the park. Even the French president, Francois Mitterand, joined in the fray, declining to attend the opening-day ceremony, dismissing the expensive new investment with Gallic indifference as "pas ma tasse de thé" ("just not my cup of tea").[14]

Robert Fitzpatrick, the first chairman of the Disneyland Resort Paris, was a French-speaking American who knew Europe quite well, in part because of his French wife. Fitzpatrick did not, however, realize that Disney could not approach France in the same way as it had approached Florida when setting up its second theme park. For example, the recruitment process and training programs for its staff were initially not well-adapted to the French business culture. The 13-page manual specifying the dress code within the theme park was apparently unacceptable to the French; the court had even ruled that imposing such a dress code was against the labour laws.

The miscalculations of cultural differences were found in other operational aspects as well. For instance, Disney's policy of banning the serving of alcoholic beverages in its parks, including in California, Florida and Tokyo, was unsurprisingly extended to France. This restriction outraged the French for whom enjoying wine during lunch and dinner was part of their daily custom. In May 1993, Disney yielded to the external pressure, and altered its policy to permit the serving of wines and beers in the theme park. With the renaming and the retooling of the entire theme park complex to better appeal to European taste, Disneyland Resort Paris finally began to profit in 1995.

Why Such Different Outcomes for Tokyo and Paris?

Why was Disney so successful in Tokyo but largely a failure in Paris? Professor Mary Yoko Brannen maintains that it may in part have been due to the way that Disney's strategic assets—such as products, practices and ideologies—were translated to and interpreted in the Japanese and French contexts.[15] According to Brannen, the

---

[12]Jo Wrighton and Bruce Orwall, "Mutual Attractions: Despite Losses and Bailouts, France Stays Devoted to Disney," *Wall Street Journal,* January 26, 2005, p. A1.

[13]James B. Stewart, *Disney War,* Simon & Schuster, New York, 2006, p. 128.

[14]Ibid.

[15]Mary Yoko Brannen, "When Mickey Loses Face: Recontextualization, Semantic Fit and the Semiotics of Foreignness," *Academy of Management Review,* October 2004, pp. 593–616.

"Americana" represented by Disney was an asset in Japan, where a trip to Disney was seen as an exotic, foreign-like experience. However, this association with the pure form of all things American was a liability in France, where it was seen as a form of reverse cultural imperialism. The result was a "lost-in-translation" effect for many of Disney's most valued icons and established business practices. For example, Mickey Mouse was seen as a squeaky-clean all-American boy in the United States, and he was viewed as conservative and reliable enough to sell money market accounts in Japan. However, in France, he was seen as a street-smart detective because of the popularity of a comic book series *Le Journal Mickey.*

Likewise, Disney's service training, human resource management (HRM) practices and training required to achieve the "happiest place on earth" were quite easy to implement in Japan, where such practices represented the cultural norm. In France, however, the same training practices were perceived as invasive and totalitarian. **Exhibit 2** summarizes how other strategic assets of Disney were recontextualized to the Japanese and French environments.

In 2006, it remained to be seen how Disney's strategic assets would translate to, and be interpreted in, the Chinese culture of Hong Kong, the topic to which we turn next.

EXHIBIT 2   **How Disney's Assets and Practices Recontextualize to Japan and France**

Source: Mary Yoko Brannen, "When Mickey Loses Face: Recontextualization, Semantic Fit and the Semiotics of Foreignness," *Academy of Management Review*, October 2004, p. 593.

	United States	Japan	France
Products			
Mickey Mouse	Squeaky-clean, all-American boy representing wholesome American values	Safe and reliable (used to sell money market accounts)	Cunning, street-smart detective epitomized in *Le Journal Mickey*—squeaky clean version is boring
Cowboy	Rugged, self-reliant individualist	Quintessential team player	Carefree, somewhat dim-witted anti-establishment individual
Souvenirs	Fun, part of the experience	Legitimating mementos that fit into the formalized system of gift giving, known as sembetsu	Tacky, waste of money
Practices			
Service Orientation	Hypernormal	Cultural norm	Abnormal
Personnel Management	Hypernormal	Cultural norm	Invasive/illegal
Training	Hypernormal	Cultural norm	Totalitarian
Ideologies			
Disneyland	Modernist theme—fun, clean, wholesome entertainment	Translated modernist theme—fun, clean, safe foreign vacation	Postmodernist theme—resistance to Disney's meta narrative
Foreignness	• Fantasized European roots • Marginalized native and minority others	• Keeping the U.S. exotic • Marginalizing the Asian other	• Politicized repatriation • Schizophrenic relationship with the U.S.

Mickey Mouse Goes to China

We know we have an addressable market just crying out for Disney products.

—*Andy Bird, Walt Disney International president, discussing China's potential*[16]

The Chinese "have heard so much about the parks around the world, and they want to experience the same thing," said Don Robinson, the former managing director of HKD. Chinese consumers wanted to connect with the global popular culture and distance themselves from their previous collective poverty and communist dictate. Kevin Wong, a tourism economist at the Hong Kong Polytechnic University, remarked that the Chinese "want to come to Disney because it is American. The foreignness is part of the appeal." The Chinese needed Disney, and Disney needed China. For example, Ted Parrish, co-manager of the Henssler Equity Fund, an investment fund house, said, "If Disney wants to maintain earnings growth in the high teens going forward, China will be a big source of that."[17]

Because the Chinese economy was booming, Disney thought it would be a good time to set up a new theme park there. China's infrastructure was still substandard by world standards. In addition, the Chinese currency, the renminbi, was not fully convertible. These and other factors increased the attractiveness of Hong Kong—a Special Administrative Region of China since the handover of sovereignty from the United Kingdom in 1997. Hong Kong had world-class infrastructure and a reputation as an international financial center. Most importantly, Hong Kong had always been a gateway to China. These factors gave Hong Kong an edge as a location for Disney's third international theme park.

THE HONG KONG TOURISM INDUSTRY

Hong Kong, with its unusual blend of East and West, of Chinese roots and British colonial heritage, of ultramodern sophistication and ancient traditions, is one of the most diverse and exciting cities in the world. It is an international city brimming with energy and dynamism, yet also a place where peace and tranquility are easily found.[18]

Tourism was one of the major pillars of the Hong Kong economy. In 2005, the total number of visitors was more than 23 million, a new record and approximately a 7.1 percent increase over 2004 (see **Exhibit 3**). Visitors came from all over the world, including Taiwan, America, Africa, the Middle East and Macao (see **Exhibit 4**). Mainland China was the biggest source of visitors, accounting for 53.7 percent of the total in 2005.[19] The dominance of this group was, in part, supported by the Individual Travel Scheme[20] introduced in 2003.

[16]Jeffrey Ressner and Michael Schuman, "Disney's Great Leap into China," *Time*, July 11, 2005, pp. 52–54.

[17]Paul R. La Monica, "For Disney, It's a Small World after All," CNNmoney.com, September 12, 2005, retrieved March 10, 2006 from http://money.cnn.com/2005/09/12/news/fortune500/hongkongdisney/.

[18]Hong Kong Tourism Board, www.discoverhongkong.com, accessed August 17, 2007.

[19]Hong Kong Census & Statistics Department, "Hong Kong Monthly Digest of Statistics," Department, Hong Kong, March 2006.

[20]The Individual Travel Scheme was a policy that permitted urban residents from selected cities in Mainland China to apply for visas from the Public Security Department to visit Hong Kong. In 2006, the Scheme covered 38 mainland cities. Until the implementation of this policy, mainlanders could only visit Hong Kong through business or travel groups.

EXHIBIT 3
Annual Visitor Arrivals in Hong Kong

Source: Hong Kong Tourism Board (2006).

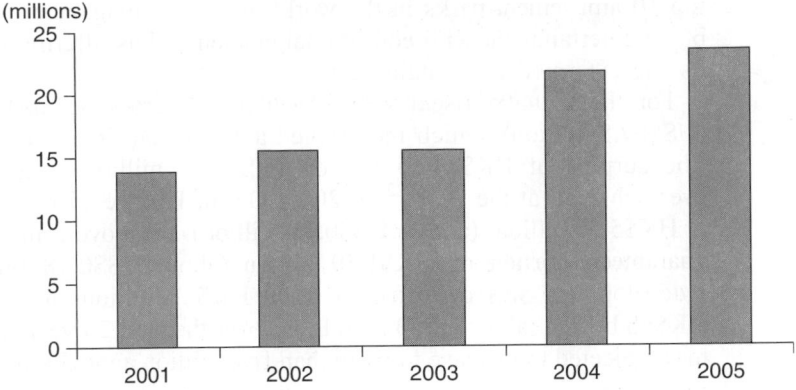

Local Attractions

Popular tourist attractions in Hong Kong included, but were not limited to, Victoria Peak, Repulse Bay, open-air markets and Ocean Park. Hong Kong's colonial heritage provided several attractions, such as Cenotaph, Statue Square and the Government House. Traditional Chinese festivals, such as Tin Hau Festival, Cheung Chau Bun Festival and Temple Fair, added local flavor. Visitors often took part in the celebration of these annual festive events during their stay. The Hong Kong Tourism Board had designated 2006 as "Discover Hong Kong Year" to attract more travelers and encourage them to extend their stay. Furthermore, the AsiaWorld-Expo opened in early 2006, and it was expected to attract more business travelers. Other initiatives included a sky rail to the world's largest sitting Buddha statue and Hong Kong Wetland Park. In addition, the Dr. Sun Yat-sen Museum was being renovated and was scheduled to reopen in early 2007.

Ocean Park

Ocean Park was another prime attraction in Hong Kong and was well-recognized worldwide. Prior to Disney's entry, Ocean Park occupied a quasi-monopoly position as the only local theme park. Founded in 1977, Ocean Park was located near Hong Kong's Central district, the heart of the bustling city. Ocean Park had an annual attendance of more than four million visitors and had been ranked recently as one of the

EXHIBIT 4
Visitor Arrivals by Country/Territory of Residence

Source: Hong Kong Monthly Digest of Statistics (March 2006).

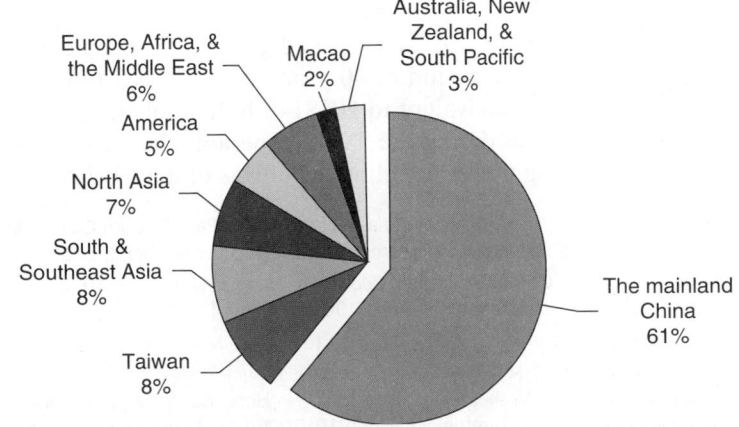

top 10 amusement parks in the world by *Forbes* magazine.[21] Ocean Park sought to blend entertainment with educational elements, thus offering the dual experience for its guests termed as "edutainment."

For the 2004/05 fiscal year, Ocean Park's gross revenue was HK$684 million (US$87.8 million), which represented a 12 percent increase over the previous year. The surplus of HK$119.5 million (US$15.3 million) was the best performance ever achieved at the Park.[22] In 2006, Ocean Park received necessary financing for a HK$5.55 billion (about US$0.71 billion) makeover, including a government-guaranteed portion of HK$1.39 billion (about US$0.18 billion).[23] Ocean Park's redevelopment was expected to bring HK$23 billion (about US$2.95 billion) to HK$28 billion (about US$3.59 billion) over the first 20 years of operation, with visitors projected to increase to more than five million annually by 2011.

HONG KONG'S VERY OWN DISNEYLAND

Hong Kong Disneyland will be the flagship for the Disney brand in this huge and growing country and play a pivotal role in helping to bring entertainment to this . . . part of the world. . . . It is our first destination opening in a market where [there] isn't a very deep knowledge of Disney culture and stories.

—*Jay Rasulo, chairman of Walt Disney Parks and Resorts*[24]

Disney initiated a conversation with the Hong Kong Special Administrative Region (SAR) government in August 1998 about the possibility of setting up a Disney theme park. To avoid a situation like the one encountered by Disneyland Resort Paris, Disney initially planned to simply run the park on a management fee and licensing contract basis. After extended talks and negotiations, however, Disney agreed to take an ownership stake as well.

HKD was expected to bring a number of economic benefits to Hong Kong. First, approximately 18,400 jobs would be created directly or indirectly at HKD's opening, and this number was expected to increase to 35,800 in 20 years. Plus, 3.4 million visitors, mainly from Hong Kong and Mainland China, would be attracted to the park, and attendance was projected to increase to 7.3 million after 15 years. The additional spending by tourists would amount to HK$8.3 billion (about US$1.1 million) in Year 1, rising to HK$16.8 billion (about US$2.2 billion) annually by Year 20 and beyond. There would be "soft" benefits as well, such as with the acquisition of first-class technological innovations and facilities and gaining hands-on experience with quality service training. Over a period of 40 years, it was forecast that HKD would generate an economic benefit equivalent to HK$148 billion (about US$19 billion). This forecast sounded promising during the 1998/99 period when negotiations were taking place, when Hong Kong was still feeling the effects of the 1997 Asian financial crisis.

[21]Norma Connolly, "Top 10 Accolade a Boost to Ocean Park," *South China Morning Post*, electronic edition, June 3, 2006, http://www.scmp.com, accessed December 3, 2006.

[22]The Walt Disney Company, *Annual Report*, 2005, retrieved March 10, 2006 from http://corporate.disney.go.com/investors/annual_reports/2005/index.html.

[23]Charis Yau, "Ocean Park Eyes $4.1B Loan to Finance Makeover," *South China Morning Post*, April 13, 2006, p. BIZ1, retrieved May 3, 2006 from WiseNews Database.

[24]Greg Hernandez, "Mickey Gains Recognition in Hong Kong," *Knight Ridder/Tribune Business News*, September 8, 2005, p. 1, retrieved March 10, 2006 from Lexis-Nexis Academic Universe Database.

The Concluded Deal

This is a happy marriage between a world-class tourism attraction and a world-class tourist destination. We hope that Hong Kong Disneyland will not just bring us more tourists, but also wholesome quality entertainment for local families as well.[25]

After a year of negotiations, the final contract was signed in December of 1999. The theme park and hotels would cost US$1.8 billion to construct over six years. In addition, US$1.7 billion would be spent for land reclamation as no other suitable location was available in the densely populated territory. The park would be situated on Penny's Bay of Lantau Island, the largest of Hong Kong's outlying islands. The Hong Kong Government and Disney would invest US$416 million and US$314 million, respectively. In return, Disney held a 43 percent stake in HKD, and the government held the remaining 57 percent, which could later be increased to 73 percent by converting subordinate shares. A further US$1.1 billion was put up in the form of government and commercial loans.

Hong Kong International Theme Park Limited (HKITP), the joint venture formed between Disney and the Hong Kong Government in December 1999, oversaw the construction and running of HKD. While the government developed the infrastructure, Disney provided master planning, real estate development, attraction and show design, engineering support, production support, project management and other development services. Disney also set up a wholly owned subsidiary, Hong Kong Disneyland Management Limited, to manage HKD on behalf of HKITP.

A Rocky Start

There was a palpable excitement when the new Disneyland theme opened, but the skeptics and critics were not so easily impressed. Press reports described the first few months as a "rocky start." Some locals called the park's management policies "absurd."[26]

Four weeks prior to the official opening, HKD invited 30,000 selected individuals per day to visit the park to test the rides and other attractions. During the trial period, a thick haze hovered over the whole park, a result of the air pollutants passing down from Mainland China. This problem was well-recognized by Hong Kong authorities and was particularly acute during low wind periods, which trapped all of Hong Kong in smog.[27] Smog virtually engulfed Sleeping Beauty's Castle.

The first problem noticed was that the capacity limit of 30,000 visitors may have been too high. For example, on September 4, 2005, approximately 29,000 local visitors went to the park. The average queuing time was 45 minutes at the restaurants and more than two hours for the rides. The park faced pressure to lower the daily capacity limit. Instead, the park proposed other measures, such as extending the opening time by an hour and encouraging visits during weekdays by offering discounts, as opposed to reducing the actual limit.[28]

[25]Stephen Ip, Hong Kong secretary for Economic Services, press release from Hong Kong government, "Hong Kong Disneyland Final Agreement Signed," www.info.gov.hk/gia/general/99912/10/1210286.htm, accessed August 17, 2007.

[26]"Mousekeeping," *South China Morning Post*, December 28, 2005, features section, page 12.

[27]Bruce Einhorn, "Disney's Not-so-magic New Kingdom," *BusinessWeek Online*, September 13, 2005, retrieved March 10, 2006 from http://www.businessweek.com/bwdaily/dnflash/sep2005/nf20050913_9145_db046.htm?chan=search.

[28]"HK Disneyland Considers Longer Opening Hours to Beat Long Lines," *The Associated Press*, retrieved March 10, 2006, from http://english.sina.com/taiwan_hk/p/1/2005/0906/44951.html.

The park faced another problem when inspectors from the Hygiene Department were asked to remove their badges and caps prior to carrying out an official investigation of a food-poisoning case. Park officials later apologized and pledged to operate in compliance with all local regulations and customs. But problems continued. The police could not get into the park—even when deemed necessary—unless pre-arranged with the park's security unit.[29]

OPERATIONS

Product Offerings

HKD, like its counterparts in the United States, Japan and France, symbolized happiness, fantasy and dreams, and sought to offer an unparalleled experience to its visitors. The admission price was initially set at HK$295 (US$38) during the weekdays and HK$350 (US$45) on weekends and peak days, the lowest pricing among the five Disney theme parks. A day pass for a child was HK$250 (US$32), while it was HK$200 (US$27) for seniors aged 65 and above. Tickets were sold primarily via the company's website (http://www.hongkongdisneyland.com), which allowed three-month advance bookings. Tickets were sold through travel agencies. These two measures aimed to control the daily number of visitors and avoiding long queues at the entrance. Only a small portion of tickets were available for walk-in customers.

HKD, like other Disney theme parks, was divided into four parts, including Main Street, U.S.A.; Fantasyland; Adventureland and Tomorrowland. Disney's classic attractions, such as Space Mountain, Mad Hatter Tea Cups and Dumbo, were included in the park. In Main Street, U.S.A., guests could ride a steam train to tour the park. A large part of Fantasyland was the Sleeping Beauty Castle, which included Dumbo and Winnie the Pooh. Guests could find Mickey, Minnie and other popular Disney characters available for photos in the Fantasy Garden, which was unique to HKD. Adventureland was home to Tarzan's tree house, the jungle river cruise and the Festival of the Lion King show. Tomorrowland featured science fiction and space adventures.

To cater to the time-pressed Hong Kong residents, HKD offered a Fastpass ticketing system, which provided a one-hour window to bypass queues for favored rides. Guests preferring an extended stay could check in to one of the two hotels, HKD Hotel and Disney's Hollywood Hotel, which offered on-site lodging services.

Marketing

HKD collaborated with the Hong Kong Government to jointly promote the theme park. It was estimated that one-third of the visitors would come from Hong Kong, one-third would come from Mainland China and the remaining third would come from Southeast Asian countries.[30] The free-to-air TV program, *The Magical World of Disneyland,* was broadcast in Hong Kong, and could be received in various regions across Southern China. In each episode, famous pop stars from the region (for example, Jacky Cheung, who was also the official ambassador of HKD) would introduce some behind-the-scene stories about HKD, such as interviews with rides designers. Disney believed that the widespread popularity of Jacky Cheung would connect well with the audience

---

[29]Jonathan Hill and Richard Welford, "A Case Study of Disney in Hong Kong," *Corporate Social Responsibility Asia Weekly,* November 16, 2005, retrieved March 10, 2006 from http://www.csr-asia.com/index.php?p=5318.

[30]Suchat Sritama, "HK Disneyland to Boost Thai Visitor Numbers," *The Nation,* September 13, 2005, retrieved March 10, 2006 from http://www.nationmultimedia.com/2005/09/13/business/index.php?news=business_18587589.html.

in Asia. HKD also launched a special TV channel on local cable TV. This channel included background stories on founder Walt Disney, information about The Walt Disney Company and its evolution, interesting facts about the company's state-of-the-art animated films, and regular updates on the construction progress of the park.

The theme park also introduced a line of Disney-themed apparel at Giordano, a Hong Kong-based clothing retailer with more than 1,500 outlets in Asia, Australia and the Middle East.[31] Giordano featured low-price fashionable clothes similar to The Gap in the United States. The Disney line featured adult and children's T-shirts and sweatshirts with popular Disney cartoon characters, such as Mickey Mouse and Nemo. The T-shirts were about HK$80 (US$10) at Giordano, much less expensive than comparable items at HKD for HK$380 (US$49).

HKD outsourced part of its marketing effort to *Colour Life,* a Guangzhou-based magazine. In September 2005, 100,000 extra copies were printed, featuring the grand opening of HKD that month. It was hoped the extra publicity would increase awareness of the theme park among the residents of Guangzhou, the major metropolitan area of southern China, just north of Hong Kong. The company also donated 200 HKD umbrellas to key newsstands in Guangzhou to provide even more publicity. In addition, HKD partnered with the Communist Youth League of China to run special events for children, such as Mickey Mouse drawing contests.

Human Resource Management

The magical experience of a HKD visit depended upon the quality of service. HKD treated human resource management (HRM) as one of the cornerstones of its competitive advantage. To fill the remaining positions at the park, in April 2005, HKD launched one of the city's largest recruitment events ever. The park screened job candidates according to qualities such as service orientation, language capabilities, passion for excellence and friendliness. Employees were referred to as cast members because "they are always on stage when interacting with guests, and therefore represent a very important element of the show," said Greg Wann, vice-president for HRM at HKD.[32]

In January 2005, HKD sent the first cohort of 500 cultural representatives to Walt Disney World in Orlando for a six-month training program. The cast members would learn about the magical Disney culture and would have a platform to share their Chinese cultural experience with other cast members at Walt Disney World. During their stay at Orlando, the Hong Kong crew was trained according to standards set by The Walt Disney Company worldwide. They also had the opportunity to work in other divisions, including merchandising, food and beverage operations, park operations, custodial services and hotel operations. In addition to training, HKD provided handbooks to each cast member, which literally detailed the regulations from head to toe. For example, male cast members could not have goatees or beards, and female cast members were not allowed to have fingernails longer than six centimetres.

Local Cultural Responsiveness

Given the cultural *faux pas* that occurred with Disneyland Resort Paris, Disney paid special attention to cultural issues pertaining to HKD. Because the prime target

---

[31] "Hong Kong Disneyland Rolls out Fashions: Hong Kong Disneyland Takes Publicity Blitz to Masses with Fashion Line," *The Associated Press,* retrieved March 10, 2006 from http://abcnews.go.com/Business/wire Story?id=963083&CMP=OTC-RSSFeeds0312, archived at http://news.ewoss.com/articles/D8BFNL1O0.aspx.

[32] Based on: Steven Knipp, "The Magic Kingdom Comes to the Middle Kingdom: What It Took for Hong Kong Disneyland to Finally Open in 2005," *Fun World,* February 2005, retrieved March 10, 2006 from http://www.funworldmagazine.com/2005/february05/features/magic_kingdom/magickingdom.html.

customer segment was the growing group of affluent Mainland Chinese tourists, *feng shui*[33] masters were consulted for advice on the park layout and design. New constructions often began with a traditional good-luck ceremony featuring a carved suckling pig.[34] One of the main ballrooms was constructed to be 888 square meters since eight was an auspicious number in Chinese culture, signifying good fortune. The hotels deliberately skipped the fourth floor because the Chinese associated four with bad luck. Other finer details were incorporated throughout the park to better fit the local culture. For example, the theme park sold mooncakes during the Chinese Mid-Autumn Festival. Phyllis Wong, the merchandising director, stated that green hats were not sold at the park because they were a symbol of a wife's infidelity in Chinese culture.[35]

Cast members at HKD were expected to converse proficiently in English, Cantonese and Mandarin, and signs in the park were written in both Chinese and English. Another local adaptation was the squat toilets, which were popular throughout China. "These toilets benefit those Mainland Chinese who prefer squatting and those who don't want to see muddy footprints on toilet seats," commented a Hong Kong visitor.[36]

Restaurants offered a wide variety of food, ranging from American-style burgers and French fries to Chinese dim sum and sweet and sour pork. Although some animal activists groups initially protested, shark fin soup was on the menu as "it is what the locals see as appropriate," said Esther Wong, a spokeswoman of HKD.[37]

NEGATIVE PUBLICITY

The Lunar New Year Holiday Fiasco

The park faced several public relations problems during its first year of operations, none bigger than that which occurred during the popular Chinese Lunar New Year holiday period. HKD had introduced a new, discounted, one-day ticket that could be used at any time during a given six-month period. These tickets could not be used on "special days" when the park anticipated an influx of visitors. The first period of special days was the Lunar New Year holidays.[38] In Hong Kong, the 2006 Lunar New Year period started on January 28 (Saturday) and ended on January 31 (Tuesday). However, HKD failed to take into account that the following two days (i.e. February 1 and 2) were still public holidays in Mainland China. Mainland tour agencies had purchased large batches of the discounted tickets and escorted large groups of Mainland tourists to HKD during those two days.

This influx created a major problem for HKD as thousands of mainland tourists clinching their tickets swarmed the front gates of the park. The park could not

---

[33]Feng shui is the Chinese art and practice of positioning objects in accordance to the patterns of yin and yang, and in flow with chi, the energy source that resides in all matter.

[34]Jeffrey Ressner and Michael Schuman, "Disney's Great Leap into China," *Time,* July 11, 2005, pp. 52–54.

[35]"Disney Uses Feng Shui to Build Mickey's New Kingdom in Hong Kong," *The Associated Press,* retrieved March 10, 2006 from http://english.sina.com/taiwan_hk/1/2005/0907/45097.html.

[36]"Disneyland with Chinese Characteristics," *Letters from China: China and Independent Travel,* July 22, 2005, retrieved March 10, 2006 from http://voyage.typepad.com/china/2005/07/disneyland_with.html.

[37]"HK Disneyland Draws Fire over Soup," *Chinadaily.com.cn* May 24, 2005, retrieved March 10, 2006 from http://www.chinadaily.com.cn/english/doc/2005-05/24/content_445139.htm.

[38]The Lunar New year Holiday, or Chinese New Year, was one of the most important traditional Chinese festivals. A series of celebrations usually took place during the period, starting from the first day of the first month on the Chinese calendar.

accommodate the additional guests, and the steel gates were locked shut. Many of these Mainland Chinese tourists had saved all year for this trip and had accompanied their extended families to Hong Kong to experience the Disney magic. Needless to say, they were understandably upset. The crowd turned into an angry mob, and, brandishing their tickets, started shouting profanities and hurling objects at the police and security guards. Some tourists even tried to climb over the gates, which were topped with sharp spikes. The front page of the local paper the next morning showed a Mainland tourist throwing a young child over the closed gates to his parents who had managed to get inside the park. As one disgruntled customer commented from that fateful day, "I won't come again, even if I am paid to."[39]

To China observers, the behavior was not entirely surprising, given that Mainland Chinese consumers can be very vocal when they are dissatisfied with a product or service. For example, in 2001, the dissatisfied owner of a Mercedes Benz SLK230 had his car towed to the center of town by a pair of oxen, where workers with sledgehammers demolished the car in front of media crews, creating a publicity nightmare for DaimlerChrysler.[40]

There was plenty of finger-pointing for the fiasco. Fengtan Peiling, the commissioner of the Hong Kong Consumer Council, claimed that Disney had failed to learn about the cultural traditions and consumption habits of Chinese people. Wang Shuxin, from the Shenzhen Tourism Tour Group Centre, blamed HKD of falsely accusing the travel agents for the predicament. His center, which oversaw Mainland tourists traveling to Hong Kong, had more than 300 claims for compensation through travel agencies. Some agencies wanted to sue HKD for a possible breach of contractual terms.[41] Soon afterwards, the Hong Kong government released a statement requesting the park to improve its ticketing and guest-entry procedures. Bill Ernest, HKD's executive vice-president, later apologized, stating "every market has unique dynamics that must be taken into consideration and must be learned over time," and that Disney was still learning.[42]

Customer Complaints

Customers also complained that the park was too small and that it had too few Hong Kong-themed attractions. HKD had only 22 attractions, 18 fewer than the other Disney theme parks. Other guests claimed that they were mistreated during their stay at the park. Some guests even planned to take legal action against HKD. For example, a park visitor from Singapore alleged negligence and discrimination of Disney's staff because they refused to call an ambulance for her mother who later died of heart failure at an HKD hotel. A spokesperson for HKD denied the allegations, saying that the staff handled the case in the "most appropriate" manner.[43] In another case, a guest and his daughter were in a bakery shop on Main Street, U.S.A. when they were hit by falling debris. The guest stated "the park does not seem to regard customers' safety as

[39]Helen Wu, "Queues Take the Magic out of a Crowded Kingdom," *South China Morning Post,* February 4, 2006, p. CITY1.

[40]"Luxury Car Under Hammer," *Herald Sun,* December 28, 2001, retrieved May 3, 2006 from Lexi-Nexis Academic Universe Database.

[41]"Meng Chu, "Disneyland Suffers Crowd Problems in Hong Kong," *Voice,* February 10, 2006, retrieved March 10, 2006 from http://bjtoday.ynet.com/article.jsp?oid=7653476.

[42]"HK Disneyland Underestimates Lunar New Year Holiday Potential," *Asia Pulse,* February 6, 2006, retrieved March 10, 2006 from Lexis-Nexis Academic Universe Database.

[43]Patsy Moy and Ravina Shamdasani, "Call for Inquest into Disney Visitor's Death," *South China Morning Post,* February 20, 2006, p. CITY1.

its priority" and threatened to take legal action against HKD, adding that they tried to placate him with a Winnie the Pooh for his daughter.[44]

Working Conditions

The character performers at HKD complained that they were overworked and underpaid. The spokesperson of the staff union stated that workdays of more than 12 hours and inadequate rest breaks had overwhelmed many workers, causing work-related injuries, such as joint and muscle strain. In response, Lauren Jordan, the theme park's vice-president of entertainment, claimed that "there are a few cast members who have found this work to be less rewarding than others and perhaps more physically challenging than they anticipated."

In addition the character performers, who performed in the daily parade and met visitors, were petitioning for the same salaries as stage performers. The entry salaries for parade performers averaged about HK$9,000 per month (US$1,153) per month compared to about HK$11,000 (US$1,409) for stage performers.[45] In response to the staff's concerns, management announced extended breaks of 40 minutes for every 20-minute session with guests during the hot and humid summer season. Cooling vests, designed for the character performers, were also being tested.

Complaints were not limited to the line staff; there was also turnover among the executive staff. As one disgruntled executive complained:

> The Americans make all the key decisions and often the wrong ones. Finance is also king here, and when things go wrong, they look for local scapegoats. The mood and morale is very low here. I know a lot of us are actively looking for jobs [and many of us] are totally disillusioned.[46]

HKD'S RESPONSE

To combat problems highlighted through the media, such as low park attendance, limited attractions, long queues, disgruntled employees and guests' accounts of rude treatment, HKD implemented several recovery strategies.

New Promotion

To boost attendance, HKD adjusted its pricing strategy. In November 2005, the park offered ticket discounts in which the price for local residents was reduced by HK$50 (US$6.41). Moreover, HKD promoted a ticket express package: guests could purchase a one-day rail pass for an extra HK$6.4 over the admission price. This pass gave unlimited rides to and from the park plus a souvenir showcase of the popular Disney characters. Many believed that these new policies were intended to boost attendance but park spokespersons dismissed such a claim.

In mid-2006, 50,000 taxi drivers were invited to HKD free of charge. Every taxi driver who took up the offer was given free admission to the park between May 15 and June 11, 2006. In addition, a 50 percent discount was provided to up to three family members or friends who accompanied each driver. The aim of this promotion was to give taxi drivers a personal experience of the park that they could share with others.

---

[44]May Chan, "Disney's Pooh Unable to Mollify Irate Father," *South China Morning Post,* December 8, 2005, p. CITY4.

[45]Dennis Eng, "Mickey and Friends Call for a Better Work Environment," *South China Morning Post,* April 10, 2006, p. CITY3.

[46]Dennis Eng, "Two More Executives Quit Disney Park," *South China Morning Post,* p. CITY1.

The Urban Taxi Drivers Association Joint Committee welcomed this scheme but it was not clear whether it was successful.

HKD also introduced a "one-day trip guide" in Chinese during November of 2005.[47] This initiative was intended to explain HKD to local travel guides. Furthermore, special VIP treatment was extended to local celebrities in the form of a Dining with Disney program. Local TV commercials also featured testimonials of previous guests and enticing scenes from inside HKD.

External Liaison with Mainland Travel Agents

Since Mainland visitors were a primary target of HKD, more proactive and collaborative moves were made with Chinese travel agencies, some of which were reluctant to sell HKD tickets in view of their slim profitability and extensive hassles: "when there are problems, [travel agencies] have to eat the cost and other troubles." To overcome this resistance, HKD offered Chinese travel agents a 50 percent discount on visits to the park and hotels. Incentives of approximately US$2.50 per adult ticket were also given to tour operators who incorporated an HKD visit into their package tours. HKD also changed the sales packages to open-ended tickets, from just fixed-date tickets, which offered greater flexibility for visitors and minimized the number of returned tickets.[48]

SETTING THE COURSE FOR EVENTUAL SUCCESS

The performance of HKD during its first year of operation had not turned out as good as had been hoped with some potentially devastating mistakes. Tour operators further complained that HKD was not big enough to keep the guests occupied for a whole day. Worse still, HKD had faced much negative publicity: from overcrowding, to customer lawsuits, to chaotic incidents during the Chinese Lunar New Year that were front page news in Hong Kong. Further, a survey of current visitors to HKD revealed that 30 percent of guests opted not to revisit the park, which did not bode well for HKD's future.[49]

Disney had experience in operating parks internationally in both good and bad conditions. Inevitably comparisons had begun being made between HKD and Disneyland Resort Paris in France, which attracted a mere 1.5 million visitors by the end of its second month of operation and nowhere could it match Disney management's original projection of 15 million in the first year. However, some academics believed that it might take another five years to determine whether HKD could be judged as an economic success or failure.

Although maintaining an optimistic public face, the management team at HKD was facing pressures to turn things around. How could HKD steer through the cultural minefield to ensure Hong Kong Disneyland's success? How well had Disney achieved its goal of translating its strategic assets to the Chinese cultural context? What could HKD do to ensure a successful outcome along the lines of Tokyo Disney and avoid the type of embarrassment experienced with Disneyland Paris? What could the company do to rescue the park from the onslaught of continuing negative publicity? The park's management certainly had its challenges cut out for it.

[47] Geoffrey A. Fowler and Merissa Marr, "Hong Kong Disneyland Gets Lost in Translation," *The Wall Street Journal Asia,* February 9, 2006, p. 26.
[48] Ibid.
[49] "Feature: Concerns Growing over HK Disneyland's Future," *Knight Ridder/Tribune Business News,* October 20, 2005, p. 1. retrieved March 10, 2006 from Lexis-Nexis Academic Universe Database.

Case 7
Virgin Mobile USA: *Pricing for the Very First Time*

GAIL MCGOVERN

> When Richard Branson called me to discuss the CEO position at Virgin Mobile USA, I quickly considered the opportunity: a chance to be the chief executive of a newly formed start-up in an overcrowded, increasingly mature, capital-intensive, highly competitive industry. Oh yeah, I should also mention that this is not an industry known for its customer service and we'd be entering with a brand that had little U.S. name recognition except for possibly as an airline. But then I thought, "It's these kinds of opportunities where a team can define itself, and if this could be pulled off, it would be unbelievable."
>
> — *Dan Schulman, CEO, Virgin Mobile USA*

Schulman accepted the challenge in the summer of 2001 and began to assemble a team to develop the new Virgin-branded service with a launch date of July 2002. Schulman had 18 years of telecommunications experience with AT&T and had most recently been CEO of Priceline.com. He would need to draw on his experiences from both firms to create an appealing offer that would take off in a saturated market. His goal was to achieve a run rate in which Virgin Mobile would have 1 million total subscribers by the end of the first year, and 3 million by year four.[1]

One of the key decisions for Virgin Mobile USA was the selection of a pricing strategy that would attract and retain subscribers.

COMPANY BACKGROUND

Virgin, a U.K.-based company led by Sir Richard Branson, was one of the top three most recognized brands in Britain. The company had a history of brand extensions—more than any other major firm in the past 20 years—resulting in a vast portfolio consisting of more than 200 different corporate entities involved in everything from planes and trains to beverages and cosmetics. What tied all of these businesses together were the values of the Virgin brand:

> We believe in making a difference. In our customers' eyes, Virgin stands for value for money, quality, innovation, fun and a sense of competitive challenge. . . . We look for

[1]Numbers in this case are disguised for competitive reasons and utilize primary data from industry analysts.

Professor Gail McGovern prepared this case. HBS cases are developed solely as the basis for class discussion. Certain details have been disguised. Cases are not intended to serve as endorsements, sources of primary data, or illustrations of effective or ineffective management.

opportunities where we can offer something better, fresher and more valuable, and we seize them. We often move into areas where the customer has traditionally received a poor deal, and where the competition is complacent. . . . We are pro-active and quick to act, often leaving bigger and more cumbersome organizations in our wake.[2]

Many of the company's ventures, such as Virgin Music Group, had proven to be phenomenally successful; others, such as Virgin Cola, had resulted in failure. Virgin's cellular operations in the U.K. had been among the company's success stories—Virgin had signed up approximately 2.5 million customers in just three years. The venture had broken new ground by being the country's first mobile virtual network operator (MVNO), which meant that rather than investing in and running a network in-house, the company leased network space from another firm, Deutsche Telekom.

In Singapore, however, the story had been different. There, the company's cellular service—a joint venture with Singapore Telecommunications—had run into difficulties, attracting fewer than 30,000 subscribers after its launch in October 2001. The Singapore MVNO had recently shut its doors, and although both partners had agreed that the market had been too saturated to sustain a new entrant, some analysts had offered another explanation for the failure: Virgin's hip and trendy positioning had failed to strike a chord in the Singapore market.

Despite this setback, Virgin had forged ahead with its plans to launch a wireless phone service in the U.S. Utilizing the MVNO model once again, the company had entered into a 50-50 joint venture with Sprint in which Virgin Mobile USA's services would be hosted on Sprint's PCS network. (Sprint was in the process of updating its network and increasing its capacity, so that it had ample capacity to allow for additional users.) Under the agreement, Virgin Mobile would purchase minutes from Sprint on an as-used basis.

"The nice thing about this model is that we don't have to worry about huge fixed costs or the physical infrastructure," said Schulman. "We can focus on what we do best—understanding and meeting customer needs."

THE CROWDED CELLULAR MARKET: IDENTIFYING A NICHE

The team leading Virgin Mobile USA was acutely aware of the overcrowded nature of the mobile communications industry in the United States. At the end of 2001, the U.S. had six national carriers and a number of regional and affiliate providers. Industry penetration was close to 50% with about 130 million subscribers, and the market was considered to have reached maturity. (Please see **Exhibit 1** for subscribers by carrier.)

Among consumers aged 15 to 29, however, penetration was significantly lower, and the growth rate among this demographic was projected to be robust for the next five years.[3] (Please see **Exhibit 2** for growth rates.)

Still, as Schulman observed, "The big players haven't targeted this segment." One reason was that young consumers often had poor credit quality. "These are people who don't necessarily have credit cards and often don't pass the credit checks that the cellular contracts require," Schulman noted.

In addition, in an industry in which the average cost to acquire a customer was roughly $370, many carriers did not believe it was worth acquiring consumers who

[2]Source: Company Web site.
[3]Source: Strategis Group.

EXHIBIT 1
Wireless Subscribers in the United States, by Carrier (Q4 2001, in millions)

Source: Adapted from The Yankee Group.

Carrier	Subscribers
AT&T (affiliates)	20.5
Cingular	21.7
Verizon	29.5
VoiceStream	6.5
Alltel	6.7
Sprint	14.5
U.S. Cellular	3.5
Leap	1.1
Other Carriers	26.1
Total	130.0

might not use their cell phones on a frequent basis. "The assumption is that if you're not using the phone for business or if you don't already subscribe to a cell phone service, then you're probably not going to be someone who uses their cell phone a lot," explained Schulman. In fact, the average monthly cell phone bill for the national carriers was $52, representing about 417 minutes of use. Because the cost to serve a customer was roughly $30 a month, the carriers tended to be wary of acquiring low-value subscribers.

Despite these challenges, the Virgin Mobile team decided that this segment represented the greatest opportunity. "This is a market that has been underserved by the existing carriers," explained Schulman. "They have specific needs that haven't been met." He continued:

> A lot of the consumers in this age group are in flux in their lives. They're either in college, they're just leaving their home, or they may be getting their first cell phone. Their usage is probably inconsistent. One month, they may not use the phone at all, and another month, they may use it quite a bit, depending on whether they're on vacation or in school.
>
> Their calling patterns are different from the typical businessperson. They're more open to new things, like text messaging and downloading information using their phones. And they're more likely to use ring tones, faceplates, and graphics. In fact, some of them need to go to "ring tone anonymous," that's how addicted they are. Phones are more than a tool for these young people; they're a fashion accessory and a personal statement.

EXHIBIT 2
Mobile Penetration by Age Group

Source: Adapted from IDC, Salomon Smith Barney.

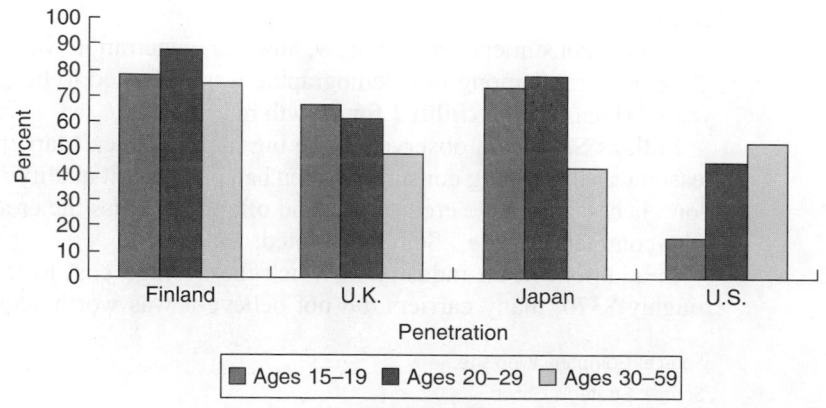

VIRGINXTRAS

The rock in our slingshot in this battle of David versus many Goliaths is focus. By focusing exclusively on the youth market from the ground up, we're putting ourselves in a position to serve these customers in a way that they've never been served before.

— Dan Schulman

The Virgin Mobile USA team quickly began to seek ways to develop a value proposition that would appeal to the youth market. Because revenue for mobile entertainment was projected to increase steadily over the next few years (see **Exhibit 3**), the team decided that a key part of the Virgin Mobile service would involve the delivery of content, features, and entertainment, which they called "VirginXtras." To this end, the company signed an exclusive, multiyear content and marketing agreement with MTV networks to deliver music, games, and other MTV-, VH1-, and Nickelodeon-based content to Virgin Mobile subscribers. (See **Exhibit 4** for screenshots.) The deal ensured that subscribers would have access to MTV-branded accessories and phones, as well as branded content such as graphics, ring tones, text alerts, and voice mail. The company would also receive promotional airtime on MTV's channels and Web site. And under the agreement, Virgin Mobile subscribers would be able to use their phones to vote for their favorite videos on shows like MTV's "Total Request Live." As Schulman put it:

> We're taking cell phone content to a whole new level. It's a great match: MTV Networks is home to some of the most recognized youth brands in the country; it has unparalleled reach for the under-30 market. The Virgin brand is all about fun, honesty, and great value for money, which is what our target market wants. You put the two together, and you've got some of the most exciting cell phone features in the market. It's a powerful relationship for us.

In addition to the MTV-branded content, the Virgin Mobile service would also include the following VirginXtras:

- **Text Messaging.** Schulman believed text messaging was a key selling point for youth: "The number of text messages tends to skyrocket during school hours. Kids discreetly text message while they're in class. Part of the reason why they

EXHIBIT 3
Revenue from Mobile Entertainment Services

Source: Adapted from The Yankee Group.

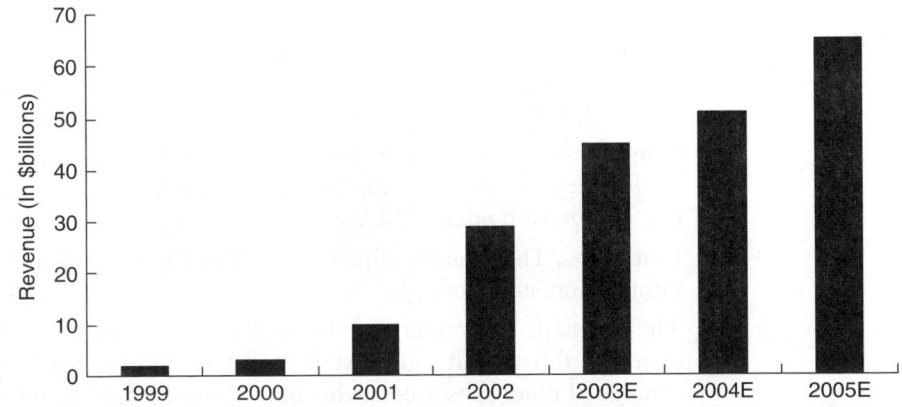

Note: Revenues include video, audio, graphics, and game [E—estimated.]

EXHIBIT 4
Screenshots of
Virgin Mobile USA
Content

Source: Company Web site.

communicate like this is so their parents don't see who they call. It's a very private form of communication for them."

- **Online Real-Time Billing.** For additional privacy from their parents, kids would not have call detail on monthly bills. Virgin Mobile would provide a Web site with a record of individual calls on a real-time basis.

- **Rescue Ring.** Virgin Mobile subscribers would be able to schedule a "rescue ring," which would call them at a prearranged time to provide them with an "escape" in case a date was not going well. If the date was going well, they could always tell the "caller" that they would get back to them tomorrow.

- **Wake-Up Call.** For those who needed a little help getting out of bed in the morning, Virgin Mobile USA would offer its customers the chance to wake up to original messages from a variety of cheeky celebrity personalities.

- **Ring Tones.** A large selection of tunes would be available for subscribers to download if they wanted to customize their ring tones, ranging from hip hop to rock to the Sponge Bob Square Pants anthem.

- **Fun Clips.** These audio clips would consist of news tidbits, jokes, gossip, sports information, and more.

- **The Hit List.** Subscribers would be able to use their handsets to listen to and vote on a top 10 list of hit songs. After voting, customers would be able to hear the percentage of other subscribers who either "loved it" or "hated it."

- **Music Messenger.** This service would let subscribers tap into a top 10 song list and then would shoot a message to a friend allowing them to check out a hot new track.
- **Movies.** This service would provide movie descriptions, show times, and allow subscribers to buy tickets in advance using their phones.

The Virgin team believed that these features would appeal to the youth market, generate additional usage, and create loyalty. Schulman elaborated: "Our market research indicates that VirginXtras will attract and retain the youth segment. Not only will these features be appealing, but we also believe they will be addictive and will bond our customers to their cell phones."

PURCHASING THE SERVICE

Most cellular providers sold their services in their own proprietary retail outlets, kiosks in malls, high-end electronic stores (e.g., Radio Shack), specialty stores, and so on. Because these retail outlets typically employed high-touch salespeople, most providers paid high sales commissions to ensure hands-on service.

In contrast, the Virgin Mobile team had already decided to adopt a different channel strategy that was more closely aligned to its target-market selection. Schulman explained:

> We've decided to distribute in channels where youth shop. This means places like Target, Sam Goody music stores, and Best Buy. In these stores, kids are used to buying consumer electronics products. They're used to buying a CD player or an MP3 player. So we've decided to package our products in consumer electronics packaging. Instead of being in a box locked behind some counter, we've created a clamshell, clear, see-through package where consumers can pick up the phone without a salesperson helping them and purchase it like they would any other consumer electronics product.

Cellular carriers historically purchased handsets from cell phone manufacturers such as Nokia, Motorola, Samsung, and Lucky Goldstar. Although the cost per handset generally ranged from $150 to $300, carriers typically charged end users between $60 and $90.[4] This handset subsidy was an accepted part of the carrier's acquisition costs.

Virgin had a contract with handset manufacturer Kyocera by which it would buy phones for anywhere from $60 to $100 depending on the features and functions of the phones.[5] The first two basic models would be named the "Party Animal" (a Kyocera 2119) and the "Super Model" (a Kyocera 2255). Both would come bundled with interchangeable faceplates that would be decorated with eye-catching colors and patterns (see **Exhibit 5** for sample phones) and would be nestled inside one of Virgin Mobile's bright red clamshell-style Starter Packs (see **Exhibit 6** for pictures of packaging).

The Starter Packs would be easily visible on large point-of-sale displays (see **Exhibit 7**) that the company would make available to its retailers. The company had entered into distribution agreements with Target and Best Buy, both of which charged lower commissions than traditional industry channels—$30 per phone, versus an industry average of $100.[6] The Starter Packs would also be available at retailers such as Sam Goody, Circuit City, Media Play, and Virgin Megastores. In total, the company

[4]Source: Morgan Stanley research.
[5]Numbers are disguised for competitive reasons.
[6]Numbers are disguised for competitive reasons.

EXHIBIT 5
Virgin Mobile USA
Handset Models

Source: Company Web site.

Note: Phones in second row show various faceplates for a single model.

expected its phones to be available at more than 3,000 U.S. retail outlets by the time the service launched in July.

ADVERTISING

Unless you're between 14 and 24, you're probably never going to see our ads. If you ever see us on "60 Minutes," then you know we've gone astray. Think WB, MTV, and Comedy Central [three youth-oriented networks].

— *Dan Schulman*

The U.S. cellular industry was projected to spend about $1.8 billion in advertising in 2002. Most national carriers had huge ad budgets; for example, Verizon Wireless alone was expected to spend more than $650 million advertising in major media in 2002.[7]

[7]Source: TNS Media Intelligence/CMR. For the national carriers, advertising spending typically ranged from $75 to $105 per customer acquired.

EXHIBIT 6
Virgin Mobile USA: The Super Model Starter Pack (clamshell packaging)

Source: Company Web site.

Virgin Mobile USA's advertising budget was miniscule by comparison: approximately $60 million.

Still, Schulman was determined to make the most of the limited budget. "By definition, the big players need to be all things to all people. They are throwing huge amounts of money into messages that are largely undifferentiated," he said. "Our goal is different; we want to break through the clutter. Our advantage is that we've got a much tighter focus on a much narrower target market; this means we have to be able to get our message out more efficiently than our competitors."

The team had already decided on an advertising campaign that it believed was quirky, offbeat, and completely different from competitive ad treatments. The ads would feature teens and would make use of strange, often-indecipherable metaphors. As Howard Handler, Virgin Mobile's Chief Marketing Officer, put it, "We need to stand out from the rest of the crowd, which means that we need to deliver ads that are not run-of-the-mill. They need to be more entertaining and more unique in their creative execution." In addition, the company was working with youth magazine editors of publications such as *The Complex, Vibe,* and *XXL* to publish "advertorials," pieces extolling Virgin Mobile to their readers. "These are the opinion-leading magazines," Handler said. "Getting their buy-in is important for us."

Virgin Mobile was also planning a number of high-profile street marketing events. These events would feature paid performers—dancers and gymnasts dressed in red from head to toe—who would engage in various stunts.

Finally, the team was in the process of planning a highly unusual event to kick off the launch of the Virgin Mobile USA service. The plan called for the cast of *The Full Monty,* a Broadway show, to appear with Sir Richard Branson, dangling from a building in New York City's Time Square, wearing nothing but a large, strategically placed cell phone. (See **Exhibit 8** for pictures from the launch.)

EXHIBIT 7
Virgin Mobile
USA Point-of-Sale
Displays

Source: Company Web site.

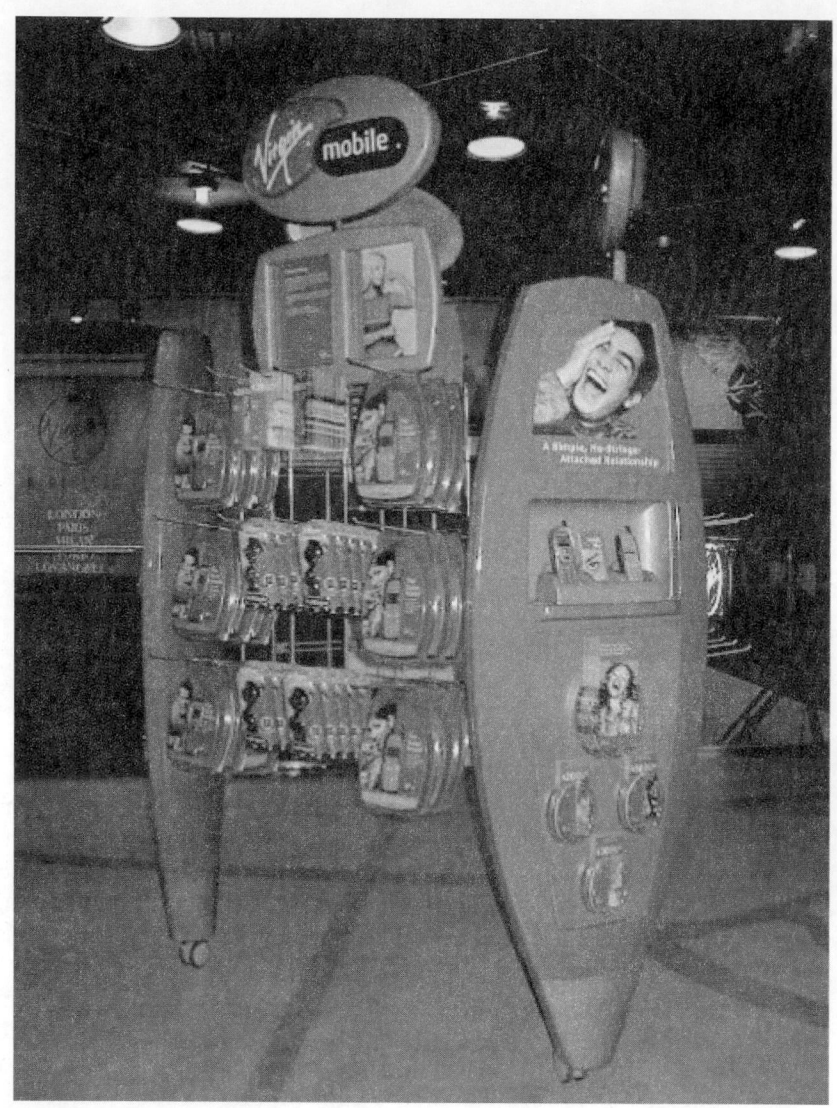

THE PRICING DECISION

We knew that we couldn't afford to get pricing wrong when we designed our offer. It can make or break your success. Consequently, we did a tremendous amount of market research among our target segment, and one thing became clear: Our audience did not trust the industry pricing plans. They all advertise "free this" and "free that," but young people know that there are a lot of hidden charges, and they resent this. These are savvy consumers, and they hate feeling like they're being conned. So we've got an opportunity to use pricing as a way to differentiate ourselves from the competition.

— *Dan Schulman*

EXHIBIT 8
Picture of Branson
at Launch

Source: *Forbes* Magazine,
October 7, 2002.

© Lawrence Lucier/Getty Images

Over 90% of all subscribers in the U.S. had contractual agreements with their cellular providers. The contracts were generally for a period of one to two years, and they required a rigorous credit check. Many plans had established "buckets" of minutes. Customers could sign up for a bucket of 300 minutes, for example. However, if they actually used more than 300 minutes, they were penalized with extremely high rates (e.g., 40 cents/minute) for the overage. If they used fewer than 300 minutes, they were still charged the fixed monthly fee, which then drove up their price per minute.

The carriers typically charged less for off-peak than on-peak minutes, but the off-peak period had shrunk over time. Originally, off-peak had begun at 6:00 p.m.; the starting time had since shifted to 7:00 p.m., then 8:00 p.m., and finally 9:00 p.m. Some carriers such as Cingular charged a monthly fee (about $7) to move the peak time back one hour. Schulman noted:

> The industry is making money from customer confusion. As a customer, you need to use minutes within the tight range that you signed up for in order to get a good rate. Your on-peak and off-peak minutes have to be in the right mix too. If all customers actually signed up for the optimal plan for their usage, the carriers would be making far less money than they are today.

In fact, the industry's pricing plans were quite rational if customers would always select the right plan for their usage patterns. (Please refer to **Exhibit 9a**.) However, customers usually could not predict their usage. Virgin Mobile studied hundreds of customers and found that the prices they actually paid varied widely. (Please refer to **Exhibit 9b**.) Schulman continued:

> Often customers *think* that they use more minutes than they *actually* use. For example, in our target segment, the majority of young people actually use from 100 to

EXHIBIT 9A
Calling Plans—Industry Prices

Source: Adapted from company data, Morgan Stanley research.

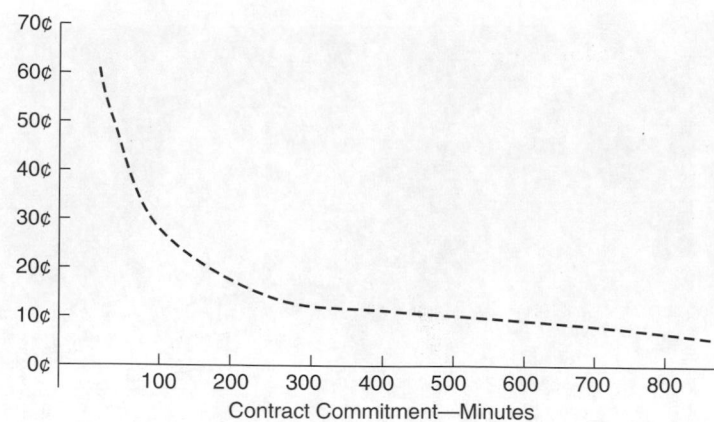

300 minutes per month. However, if you ask them to predict their usage, they'll often come up with a much higher number. Other people will try to pick lower bucket plans to avoid high monthly fees. Then they'll get a $100 bill because they didn't realize that it would cost them 40 cents for every minute above the bucket.

Adding to consumer resentment was the fact that most carriers slapped on additional fees to add to the monthly bill. Schulman explained: "The carriers will only tell you about the monthly bucket fee; they won't mention the taxes you'll have to pay or the universal services charge that you'll have to pay. There are a bunch of one-time costs that are loaded on top of the bill that they don't advertise. So even if you end up being exactly right in your bucket, a $29 plan ends up being a $35 plan."

Schulman and his team carefully considered various pricing strategies. Although the pricing possibilities were endless, the team believed that there were realistically three viable options. Schulman said: "We're trying to be as open-minded as possible. We have the luxury of starting from scratch, so this is an opportunity to fix some of the problems that are endemic in this industry. Our only constraints are that (1) we want to make sure our prices are competitive, (2) we want to make sure we can make money, and (3) we don't want to trigger off competitive reactions."

EXHIBIT 9B
Actual Prices Paid by Customers

Source: Adapted from company data, Morgan Stanley research.

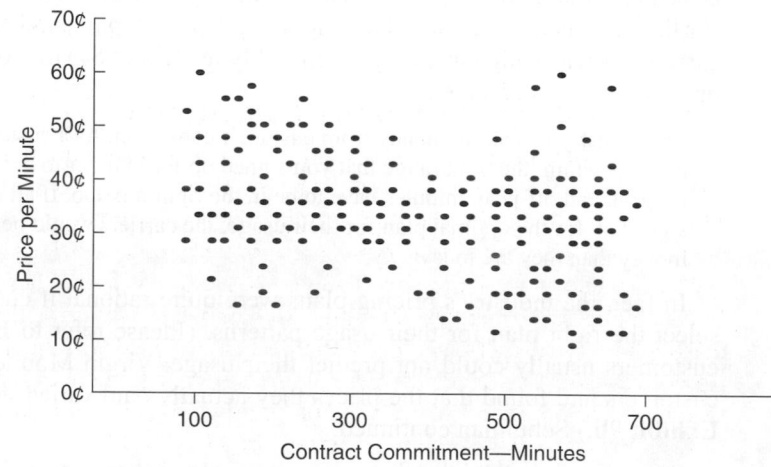

EXHIBIT 10A
Option 1 Pricing Structure

Source: Adapted from company data, Morgan Stanley research.

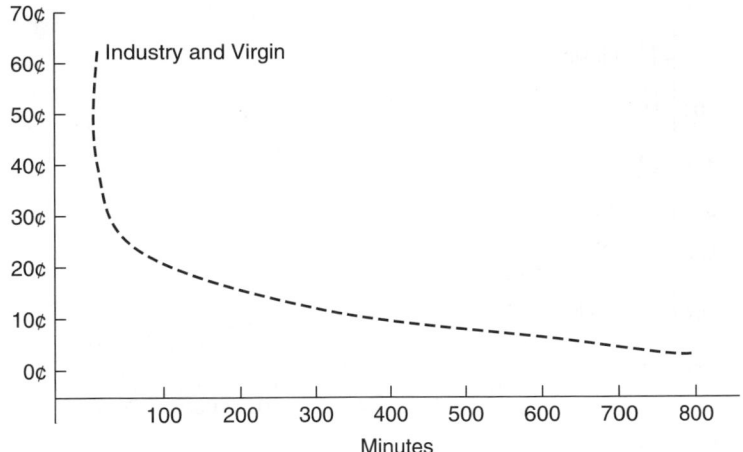

Option 1—"Clone the Industry Prices"

The first option was to merely "clone" the existing industry price structure. (See **Exhibit 10a** for Option 1 pricing.) All of the major carriers paid high commissions to salespeople to explain their complicated pricing structures and to perform credit checks. (In fact, 30% of prospective customers failed to pass these credit checks.) Given Virgin Mobile's nontraditional channel strategy, its pricing message would have to be relatively simple. Schulman said, "With this first option, we would simply be telling consumers that we're priced competitively with everyone else, but with a few key advantages like differentiated applications [MTV] and superior customer service."

In addition, Virgin Mobile could attempt to differentiate from the competition by offering better off-peak hours and fewer hidden fees. "We know that consumers are sick of hidden fees and they hate off-peak deals that start at 9 p.m., so we'd be address-ing a real sore spot among young people," said Schulman.

He added, "The nice thing about this idea is that it's easy to promote. People may not like the pricing plans, but given all the money the industry spends to promote them, the customers are used to 'buckets' and peak/off-peak distinctions. Given our limited advertising budget, it may be a stretch for us to break through with anything different. We could also put it on our packaging so that even without the help of a salesperson, consumers would get the message."

Option 2—"Price Below the Competition"

The second option was to adopt a similar pricing *structure* as that of the rest of the industry, with *actual* prices slightly below those of the competition. That is, Virgin Mobile would maintain the buckets and volume discounts, but its price per minute would be set below the industry average for certain key buckets (see **Exhibit 10b**).

"This option would allow us to tell consumers that we're cheaper, plain and simple. Because our target market generally uses between 100 and 300 minutes per month, that's where consumers would get the best price," said Schulman. "Under this option, we could also offer better off-peak hours and fewer hidden fees, but I don't know if that would be necessary if our price per minute was clearly below the competition. We wouldn't want to leave too much money on the table."

EXHIBIT 10B
Option 2 Pricing Structure

Source: Adapted from company data, Morgan Stanley research.

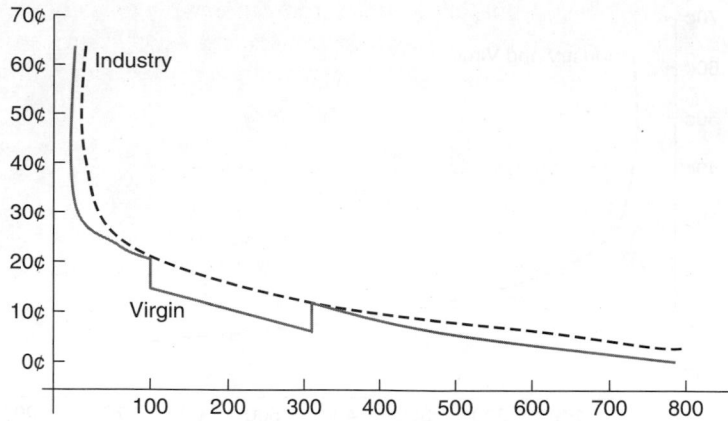

Note: Prices are for a blend of on- and off-peak minutes, with off-peak beginning at 9:00 p.m. Each additional off-peak hour reduces average price per minute by approximately 1.5 cents.

Option 3—"A Whole New Plan"

The third option was the most radical. The idea was to start from scratch and come up with an entirely different pricing structure, one that was significantly different from anything offered by the competition. The pricing variables that Schulman was toying with included:

- **The role of contracts.** Did it make sense to shorten the term of the subscription contracts, or perhaps even eliminate the contracts altogether? Contracts provided carriers with a hedge against churn and a guaranteed annuity stream; yet even with the contracts, cellular providers struggled with an industry churn rate that averaged 2% per month. If Virgin Mobile were to shorten or eliminate such contracts, the risk would be that its churn rate would skyrocket. In fact it was estimated that churn would climb to 6% each month.[8]

Schulman added:

From a marketing perspective, there's no question that it would be great if we could announce to the world that we've eliminated contracts. Keep in mind that, if you're under 18, you can't even enter into a contract with a cellular provider. Your parents need to do it for you. So eliminating contracts would be a big advantage for us from a customer-acquisition standpoint. Of course, in terms of retention, contracts are a safety net. So the question is, does it make sense for us to try to fly without a safety net?

- **Prepaid versus post-paid.** The vast majority (92%) of current cell phone subscribers in the U.S. had post-paid plans, which meant that they were billed monthly on the basis of their contract. Prepaid arrangements, in which consumers purchased a number of minutes in advance, were unusual because of prohibitive pricing (generally, between 35 and 50 cents per minute, and as high as 75 cents per minute). Most prepaid customers used their phones on an occasional basis as a safety device: "They just keep them in their glove compartment," as Schulman put it. Many of these customers had poor credit; in fact, the reason prepaid plans appealed to them was that such plans required no credit checks. Customers

[8]Source: Morgan Stanley research.

therefore thought that prepaid arrangements were a stigma, and the prepaid offers tended to attract low-usage customers. Still, in countries such as Finland and the U.K., prepaid arrangements were commonplace, accounting for the majority of new gross adds.

Schulman knew that the risks of adopting a prepaid pricing structure were significant. U.S. carriers were extremely wary of prepaying consumers because of their high churn rates; prepaying consumers tended to exhibit no loyalty to a provider once they had used up all of their prepaid minutes. If Virgin Mobile were to adopt a prepaid pricing structure, the danger was that the company would never be able to recoup its customer acquisition costs. In fact, industry analysts estimate that total acquisition costs would have to be at or below $100 per new gross add for prepaid to be viable.[9]

In addition, there were a number of related issues to consider. A prepaid pricing structure would require some mechanism—perhaps via the Web or through physical phone cards—whereby consumers could easily add minutes to their phone.

- **Handset subsidies.** Most carriers purchased handsets from cell phone manufacturers such as Nokia, Motorola, and Samsung at a cost per handset ranging from $150 to $300 for the industry. The carriers then subsidized the cost of the handset to end users. This subsidy—which was typically about $100 to $200—was part of the customer acquisition cost.

"We're debating all of our options here," said Schulman, "everything from increasing the subsidy so that our phones are cheaper than the competition, to lowering the subsidy as a way of getting consumers to feel more invested and loyal towards our service."

- **Hidden fees and off-peak hours.** "One of our goals is to offer a service that is priced so simply that consumers don't need a math degree to figure it out," noted Schulman. "One way to do this would be to eliminate *all* hidden fees, including taxes, universal service charges, *everything*. It would literally be 'what you see is what you get.' However, this would mean rolling all of those hidden costs into our pricing structure in such a way that our pricing feels competitive to our target market, and yet we still make money."

As for off-peak hours, "We need to think about what makes sense for our target customer," said Schulman. "These kids don't lead the same kind of lifestyle as the typical business-person, so our service should define off-peak with that in mind."

As Schulman reviewed the various options for pricing, he realized the importance of laying the foundation for future profitability. "There's this assumption that you can't target young people and make money," he said. "Our goal is to prove otherwise. Ideally, every customer we acquire will have positive lifetime value (LTV) for us." (See **Exhibit 11** for LTV details.)

"That's why this pricing decision is so critical," he continued. "If we can figure out a way to create value so that we can successfully enter a very competitive and saturated market, and also create profitability with this target segment, then we will have truly-accomplished something big."

[9]Source: Morgan Stanley research.

EXHIBIT 11 Calculating Lifetime Value (LTV) for Cellular Subscribers

In general, lifetime value (LTV) for a customer is calculated as follows:

$$LTV = \sum_{a=1}^{N} \frac{(M_a)r^{(a-1)}}{(1+i)^a} - AC$$

where
N = the number of years over which the relationship is calculated
M_a = the margin the customer generates in year a
r = the retention rate ($r^{(a-1)}$ is the survival rate for year a)
i = the interest rate
AC = the acquisition cost

Source: Adapted from "Customer Profitability and Lifetime Value," HBS Note 503-019.

In the cellular industry, margin is relatively fixed across periods. Therefore, one can simplify the above expression by assuming an infinite economic life (i.e., letting $N \rightarrow \infty$), which leads to:

$$LTV = \frac{M}{1-r+i} - AC$$

Monthly Margin = average revenue per unit per month (ARPU) – monthly cost to serve (CCPU, or cash cost per user)

The components of AC were advertising per gross add, the sales commission paid per subscriber, and the handset subsidy provided to the subscriber.

CCPU consisted of customer-care costs, network costs (the cost of using Sprint's network), IT costs, and overhead. Industry analysts estimated that Virgin Mobile's CCPU would be constant at 45% of revenues during its first year of operations, since most of Virgin's costs were variable. Monthly churn was estimated to be 2% for customers under contract and 6% for prepaid customers.[a]

Interest rates were 5%.

[a]Numbers disguised for competitive reasons.

Case 8

Using Services Marketing to Develop and Deliver Integrated Solutions at Caterpillar in Latin America

Holger Pietzsch, Caterpillar, Inc.
Valarie A. Zeithaml, University of North Carolina

'Any industrial manufacturer that has not awakened to the fact that it must become a service business is in serious peril today.'[1]

Jose "Pepe" Brousset, Marketing and Operations Director of the Latin America Commercial Division (LACD) of Caterpillar, Inc., called the division's Dealer Advisory Panel to order in the spring of 2006 with the message that the company's five-year growth targets could not be met unless the organization moved from a product focus to an integrated customer focus. His plan was that LACD would pilot the development and deployment of a plan for services that could be sold with Caterpillar's heavy equipment in the form of customer service agreements (CSAs). The initiative was a direct consequence of Caterpillar's enterprise strategy known as Vision 2020. This strategy stipulated that growth of the distribution system of the company would be a critical success factor for the future: Specifically, Vision 2020 specified that "[Caterpillar's] distribution system will be the global benchmark in delivering *integrated business solutions* [our emphasis] to customers." A key performance metric of this strategy was the volume of service business generated through CSAs. CSAs had been offered by Caterpillar dealers in the past but the many difficulties encountered had led to doubts about the ability of the company to make money with CSAs. These difficulties included the lack of consistency across Latin American counties, inability to deliver, and inability to calculate costs and benefits of the CSAs.

Caterpillar, like many highly successful product companies, embraces what might best be termed a product focus. The company, dealers, and suppliers work as a team to provide what they believe is the most extraordinary product support system in the world. Their formula for success can be stated briefly:

> Find out what products customers want. Design and build them. Keep'em running.
> When they wear out, rebuild or recycle. Do it better than anybody else.

Services were a different story. Except for the company's very large mining customers, and other large users with whom dealers had strong relationships that involved many types of services that created integrated solutions, the company had not consistently adopted a customer focus with service.

Pepe Brousset's goal was to develop, deploy, and pilot a plan using the best practices in the service industry to redefine the CSA value proposition and to grow customer

---

[1]G. Allmendinger and R. Lombreglia, "Four Strategies for the Age of Smart Services," *Harvard Business Review,* October 2005.

service agreements at an average 30% per year between 2006 and 2010. While service did not have to be limited to CSAs in achieving this goal, he strongly believed that learning how to deliver service through these agreements was the best approach to making both the company and its dealerships ready for the challenges involved in delivering service. His immediate goal was to convince the members of the Dealer Advisory Panel that this plan was also in their best interests.

CATERPILLAR: THE COMPANY

On November 24, 1904, Benjamin Holt tested the first track-type tractor. Shortly after, the first Caterpillar trademark was copyrighted. In April 1925, C.L. Best Tractor Co. and The Holt Manufacturing Company merged to form the Caterpillar Tractor Company. By the 1930's the East Peoria, Illinois, plant had become one of America's major industrial complexes and by 1951 the company opened its first overseas manufacturing facility in the United Kingdom.

Figure 2, on page 682, shows the history of Caterpillar from that point on. Some of the highlights, as shown in the exhibit, include (1) the addition of Caterpillar to the Dow Jones Industrial Average, replacing Navistar, in 1991; (2) the naming of Caterpillar as one of Fortune Magazine's most admired companies in 1997; (3) and Caterpillar becoming the world's largest producer of diesel engines in 1999.

By the year 2000 Caterpillar manufactured more than 300 different models including engines and turbines from five horsepower to over 22,000 horsepower in 88 manufacturing locations. Seventy five percent of products were made in the U.S., while 50% of sales were outside the U.S. In 2006, total sales of Caterpillar products exceeded 41 billion dollars.

Caterpillar Products

Caterpillar provides a wide range of products that are used in many different industries. The majority of machine applications address earth-moving needs including excavation, loading, and carrying of material. Skid steer loaders, backhoe loaders, wheeled excavators, and compact wheel loaders (see Figure 1) perform the work in urban and general construction. Articulated trucks, hydraulic excavators, scrapers, motor graders, and track-type tractors are used in larger earth-moving projects such as road, airport, or heavy construction tasks. Wheel dozers and material handlers operate in demolition and waste applications. Mining operations are more complicated and require a multitude of equipment including off-highway trucks and underground mining equipment. Wheel loaders are key machines in the material-handling process of quarries or industrial applications. Caterpillar diesel engines are used in highway trucks, boats, locomotives, or oil platforms. Finally, a large range of power generations sets provides electricity in a variety of applications.

Caterpillar Services

Despite the fact that Caterpillar is largely a product firm, the company offers several services that complement its products. Largely, these services consist of services that refurbish used machine and engine components into "like-new" condition, financing and insurance services for equipment owners, equipment rental, and logistics services.

CATERPILLAR: THE DEALERS

Caterpillar prides itself on enduring and close relationship with its dealers. In 2006, over 180 independent dealers around the world represented the company's products, managing customer relationships, servicing the equipment, and providing parts

FIGURE 1   **Examples of Caterpillar Products**

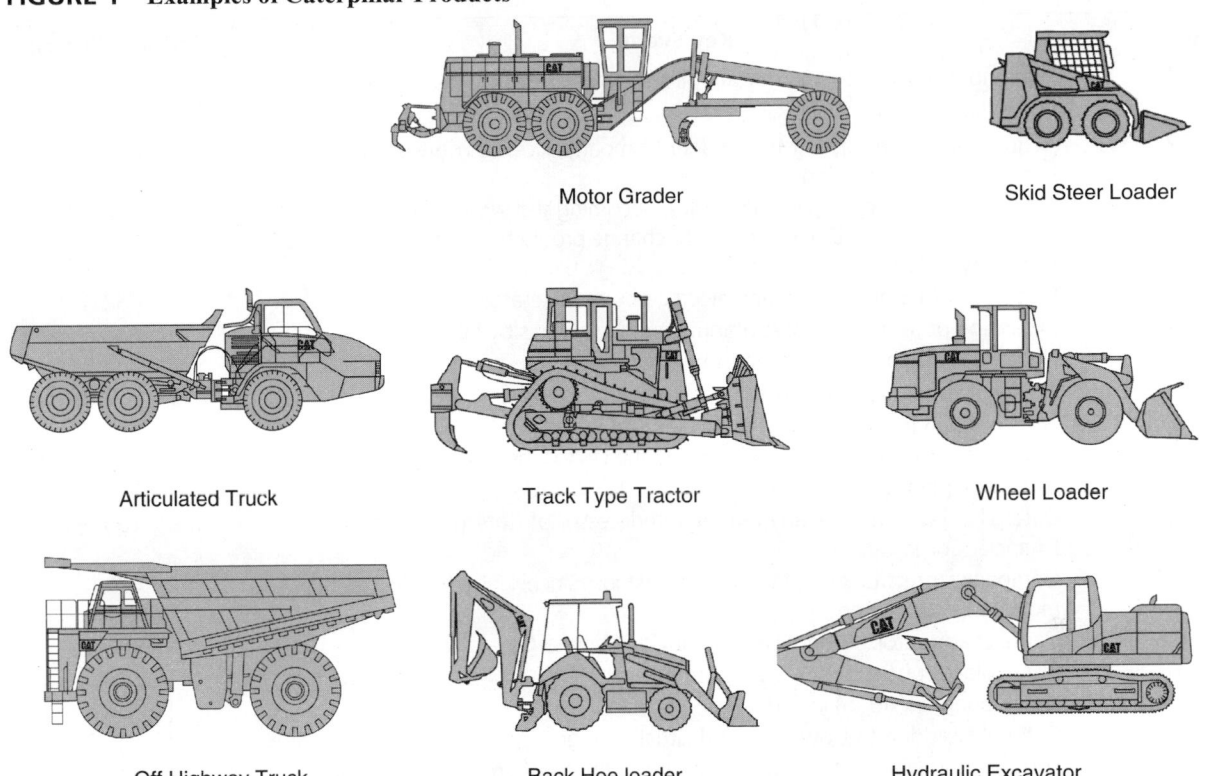

Motor Grader

Skid Steer Loader

Articulated Truck

Track Type Tractor

Wheel Loader

Off Highway Truck

Back Hoe loader

Hydraulic Excavator

throughout the lifetime of the equipment. Dealers invested millions of dollars in parts inventories, warehouses, service shops, tools, information technology, and rental fleets. Collectively, the dealerships employed more people than Caterpillar itself. Many dealers were family-owned businesses but some were much larger—with revenues exceeding a billion dollars. For example, one Caterpillar dealer, Finning International, operated in Canada, South America, and Europe and provided work for more than 12,000 employees.

Caterpillar dealers form a distribution channel unmatched in the industry, and the dealer network is one of Caterpillar's principal competitive advantages. No other heavy equipment manufacturer offers comparable coverage in terms of quantity and quality of customer contact points. Many dealerships have represented the Caterpillar brand for more than half a century and have established long lasting relationships with their customer bases—sometimes over generations.

COMPETITIVE LANDSCAPE

Besides the goal of increasing revenues, the most important reason for the Vision 2020 objective to move into services was that competition was heating up and the company saw the potential for competitors to capture the growth and profits that Caterpillar assumed it would achieve. Competition came from a number of different places. Third party service providers that allowed customers to outsource their entire fleet management for both Caterpillar and non-Caterpillar equipment were emerging. Compared to Caterpillar's nationally-organized dealer network, these service companies operated internationally, allowing customers to work on construction projects all over Latin

FIGURE 2 The History of Caterpillar

Year	Key Event	Sales (in millions)
1925	Holt and Best merge to form Caterpillar Tractor Company headquartered in Peoria, Illinois	13.8
1928	Acquisition of the Russel Motorgrader Company accelerating the entry into the rod construction	35.1
1931	Caterpillar starts to use Diesel engines, becoming the world's largest diesel manufacturer, Decison made to change product color from grey to High-way Yellow	24.1
1939	First line of Marine engines and electric power generators	58.4
1946	Expansion program increases manufacturing facilities by 50%	128.4
1951	First overseas plant opens in the United Kingdom	394.3
1955	Australia subsidiary announced	533.0
1966	Sales in USSR resume after three decades of hiatus	1,524.0
1970	Sales outside the US exceed sales inside the US for the first time	2,127.8
1976	Piracicaba plant opens in Brazil	5,043.2
1981	Caterpillar Leasing company formed (predecessor of Caterpillar Financial Corporation)	9,160.0
1982	Company suffers loss of $180 Million, first loss since 1932. Employment reduced by 29 percent.	6,472.0
1986	Name change from Caterpillar Tractor Company to Caterpillar Inc.	7,380.0
1987	Caterpillar Logistics Services Inc. formed	8,294.0
1988	New trademark (logo) introduced	10,435.0
1991	Caterpillar added to Dow Jones industrial average, replacing Navistar	10,182.0
1997	Fortune magazine names Caterpillar one of the most admired companies in the world	18,925.0
1999	Caterpillar becomes world's largest producer of diesel engines	19,702.0
2006	Total sales exceed 41 Billion dollars	41,517.0

America without having to engage with multiple Caterpillar and non-Caterpillar service providers. While their service offerings and competencies were generally less sophisticated than those of Caterpillar dealers, they were developing successful customer relationships within certain market segments. Fluor, a Fortune 500 company, through one of its subsidiaries—Ameco provides total service solutions, and has successfully grown its fleet management business in Latin America.

Other competitors, aftermarket suppliers and distributors, were commercializing "will-fit" parts that, though inferior in quality and durability, were sold at significantly lower price points. While offering no services, these companies held about 30% to 50% of the aftermarket in parts.

Thousands of small local workshops also offered repair services ranging from simple repairs to complex ones. Many of them had been established by former Caterpillar dealer mechanics and enjoyed high customer acceptance, but none had the financial reserves to invest in large outlets or market coverage. Many customers also had their own mechanics, which they used for both maintenance and repair activities. Small workshops and customer mechanics had difficulty keeping up with the increasingly sophisticated technology built into new machines, which required both specialized tools as well as expertise. Consequently many of them focused on servicing older machines.

Finally, competitive manufacturers like Komatsu, John Deere, and Volvo had established their own dealer networks in Latin America. While largely focusing on their own machines rather than Caterpillar equipment, they often had the same customers because owners had equipment from different manufacturers. Owners of mixed fleets carefully considered the performance of the product support organizations before purchasing new equipment, making service capability a key factor in new purchases.

THE CATERPILLAR–DEALER RELATIONSHIP

As a company, Caterpillar for a significant portion of its business interacts with end users through its independent dealers. They are responsible for initiating and supporting customer relationships and the types of services provided. Product and service offerings could vary significantly between dealers.

As a corporation, Caterpillar's headquarters and factories rely on regional marketing profit centers (MPCs) to work with the dealer network for product commercialization and distribution (see Figure 3). The main MPC for Latin America (LACD) is situated in Miami, a regional hub to serve Mexico, the Caribbean, and Central and South America. Several smaller commercial teams in district offices are also located

FIGURE 3
**The Caterpillar–
Dealer Relationship**

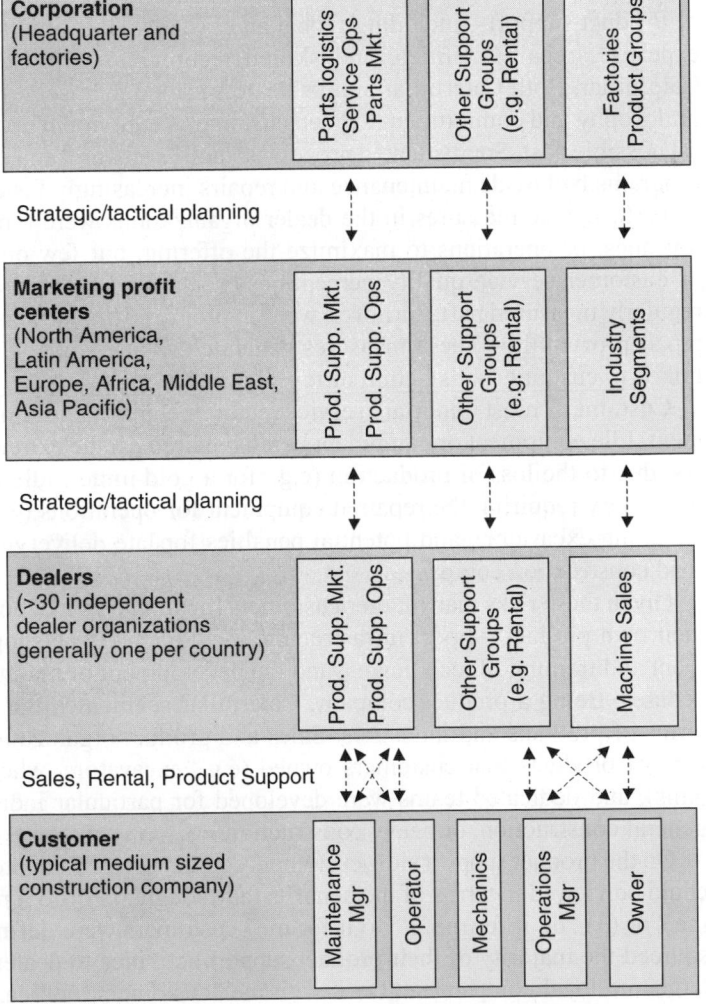

in the dealer's territories for ongoing support. LACD's marketing profit center has employees in both product divisions and product support divisions. These employees work as liaisons between headquarters and the dealers, offering the skills and knowledge of Caterpillar to their functional counterparts in the dealer organizations for strategic and operational issues. LACD's region includes over twenty different dealers (generally one per country) whose organizations themselves are usually divided into equipment sales, parts sales, and equipment service. Depending on customer needs, all three parts of the dealerships may interact individually with the customer. Figure 3 shows the relationship among Caterpillar, the MPCs, and the dealers.

This organizational division both in the MPCs and in the dealerships themselves fostered expertise and consistency within divisions, but over time has created functional silos that had different priorities and performance goals. For example, while the product support organization was responsible for increasing the sales of CSA, they were not the department responsible for machine sales, where the primary sales contract was set up. The machine sales people were not required to include CSAs in offers to customers and, in fact, were not inclined to do so because in many cases they were not fully informed about CSAs (including information about what the dealership was capable of promising) and were not awarded incentives for selling them.

Product support—including global and fast availability of spare parts, local dealer expertise, repair facilities, and skilled technicians—were key differentiators for Caterpillar. Both Caterpillar and its dealers prided themselves on their "built-to-last" philosophy and commitment to keep customers' equipment up and running at the lowest possible cost. Sophisticated processes, tools, software, and component replacement programs had made maintenance and repairs increasingly faster and more effective.

Performance measures in the dealer organizations were typically focused on cost, revenues, or operations to maximize the offering, but few on customer profitability or customer service quality perceptions. For example, both Caterpillar and dealers regularly measured parts turnover, work in progress, time utilization of mechanics, and repair profitability. These measures generated savings in cost and time, but were not linked to customer satisfaction or revenue increases.

Customers' most important service requirement is maximum up-time of their equipment. Idle equipment or equipment being repaired can be extremely costly for customers, due to the loss of production (e.g., for a gold mine), idle time of other pieces of machinery requiring the repaired equipment for operations (e.g. trucks in absence of a loading excavator), and potential penalties for late delivery of the project (e.g., for road construction companies).

Given these risks many larger customers (owning five machines or more) developed their own product support infrastructure including service shops, the hiring, employment and training of technicians, and the development of maintenance and repair procedures. Being a product company, Caterpillar segmented the marketplace simply in terms of products and industries. Sales and product organizations were set up by the type of products that customers owned (e.g., excavators, wheel loaders, power systems), and dedicated teams were developed for particular industries such as mining, general construction, or heavy construction.

On the product support side, customers could be classified into three segments which could be viewed in terms of the benefits they sought: (1) "do it myself," (2) "work with me," or (3) "do it for me." "Do it for me" customers were defined as owners that outsourced the majority of their product support activities to dealers. Many of them were large and loyal companies. "Do it with me" customers took care of their own day-to-day product support but used dealer services for more complex repair needs. Many medium-sized, traditional construction customers fell into this category. "Do it myself" customers generally used internal or competitive resources to satisfy their product support needs. Most small and/or general construction customers fell into this segment.

Identification of customers that fell into these segments was possible but complex and required multiple assumptions concerning the customer's total repair needs. Some customers could also fall into more than one segment, preferring dealer services for their newer machines but performing their own repairs on older equipment.

GENERAL CONSTRUCTION CUSTOMERS

Because Caterpillar's product line was so diverse, its customers varied greatly in size and requirements. For its very largest customers—typically those who purchased mining and construction equipment—dealers provided customized and full service. The most important considerations for these customers included productivity and up-time—having equipment in working condition 100% of the time. Customers paid for CSA and repair services to achieve these goals and were typically very satisfied.

This group of customers, however, was not the segment from which further growth of market share was expected in the future. For this reason, the LACD division chose to focus on the general construction customer.

General and urban construction companies and subcontractors of major construction projects used Caterpillar type of equipment for its versatility rather than its productivity. These smaller customers also had to manage short-term affordability and cash flow limitations, contributing to a situation where they postponed preventive and small repairs as long as possible. Lack of emphasis in these areas some times resulted in costly repairs and these unplanned downtimes were disruptive to customer operations. However, because these customers considered machine up-time as less important for their business, they were less willing to pay for premium parts and parts availability, and often migrated to a patchwork of internal or external lower-priced suppliers for product repair and support needs.

CUSTOMER SUPPORT AGREEMENTS (CSAs)

Over the years, Caterpillar dealers had packaged services into customer service agreements (CSAs)—flexible contracts that could include virtually any services that customers wanted and that dealers could provide. These customer services agreements could be highly customized in content, length, and cost—many involving total maintenance and repair contracts where customers outsourced the entire machine product support of all of their equipment. The agreements were sold separately from the machines at purchase and were delivered through the dealer product support organizations. CSA for larger customers had demonstrated significant benefits regarding the risks and costs of unplanned machine downtime and resulted in high levels of customer loyalty. The current degree of customization and complexity, however, limited the CSA marketability and the dealer's operational efficiency to serve the growing number of customers in the general construction market.

The smaller and simple contracts, called preventive maintenance agreements (PM CSAs), were purchased by many small customers. Preventive maintenance contracts basically involved the provision of superior Caterpillar oils and filters at predetermined service intervals and were delivered through dealer field technician who traveled to customer sites. Some technician activities, such as visual machine inspection, monitoring of the condition of the machine, and feedback discussions with the customer, were not built explicitly into the contracts. They were extra services but were not neceserally offered and executed consistently. Many of these extra services, and the preventive maintenance intervals themselves, went unnoticed by business owners because field technicians interacted with operators and machines and did not always come into contact with those who purchased the contracts. Consequently, many decision makers and purchasers of the equipment did not recognize the benefits of the agreements and did not renew the CSAs once expired. Some dealers, however, had turned PM CSA contracts into a dedicated business. They had dedicated PM technicians, specialized PM service trucks, and proactive processes that provided regular feedback to customers on the condition of their machine, potential issues, and recommended solutions.

CSAs were typically sold by either the machine or product support sales reps and delivered by the service organization. Given unprecedented construction growth in the mid 2000s, the industry was suffering from technician shortage resulting in capacity bottlenecks in fulfilling CSA promises. Facing this situation, the sales organizations were sometimes reluctant to sell CSAs if they were concerned that the service organization would not deliver on the promise. In addition to these concerns, the dealer sales force was generally more comfortable selling solutions based upon tangible product differentiation than advocating intangible services that are harder to explain, sell, and differentiate.

CSA customers generally demonstrated higher loyalty and repeat business than non-CSA customers. A key driver of their loyalty seemed to be the quality of service provided in the field by technicians (e.g., accessing the machine at regular intervals for preventive maintenance tasks such as changing oil and filters as well as some diagnostic services called "condition monitoring"). Dealers had different philosophies regarding the degree to which field technicians were trained and empowered to act upon recommended repairs that they identified as a result of their preventive maintenance work. Most dealers used entry-level technicians for the basic work on preventive maintenance contracts; they were then responsible to relay the machine condition information to the product support sales organization for follow-up and quoting on additional work that could be done to improve the condition of the machine. Other dealers had decided to empower their technicians for a larger portion of the process. Generally customers appreciated both the speed of service as well as the quality of the resulting machine condition advice.

THE SERVICES MARKETING INTERVENTION

The recent and consistent growth of the Latin American economies had attracted an increasing number of competitive equipment distributors—all of them selling at lower price points than Caterpillar. Most of them had a limited product support infrastructure at their disposal. As a consequence LACD management team decided to leverage Caterpillar's product support strength as a differentiator in all customer decisions—before, during, and after the machine purchase. Recognizing that Caterpillar excelled in making products but had limited experience in designing and delivering solution services, Pepe Brousset in 2006 invited an expert in the services marketing field to attend the dealer advisory panel. He had taken a services marketing course in his graduate program and recognized that many different concepts and tools were available that could help the company and believed that having an expert spend a day describing what services industries know about services marketing and service quality would open their eyes.

Especially useful to the group was the *gaps model of service quality*.[2] The model explains the nature and impact of each gap on the customer experience, brand

---

[2]The Gaps model of service quality and most other elements of Services Marketing mentioned in this paper have been developed or described by Valarie Zeithaml, Professor at UNC Chapel Hill. She is also the Co–author of *Services Marketing*, McGraw-Hill; the most extensive work that the team has found on the topic.

FIGURE 4
The Customer Gap

Zeithaml, Parasuraman, and Berry, *Delivering Quality Service: Balancing Customer Perceptions and Expectations.*

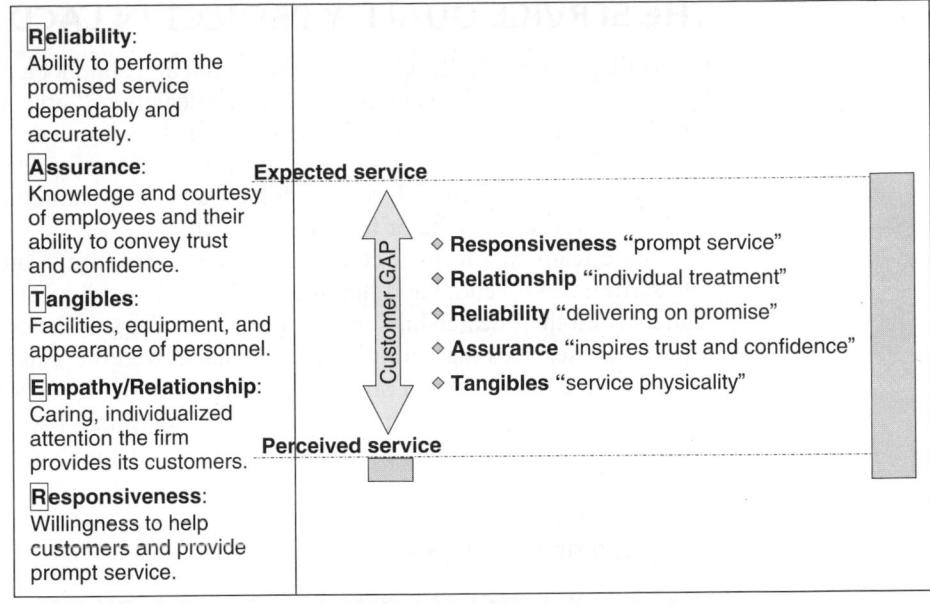

positioning, and service differentiation. Services marketing comprises a collection of tools and methodologies to assess and address the critical service capabilities required to close those gaps. Other concepts covered were service blueprinting, customer-defined service standards, and integrated services marketing communication.

The dealer advisory panel embraced the concept of services marketing, and decided to adapt the concepts to Caterpillar to grow its services business. Figures 4 and 5 show the gaps model concepts.

FIGURE 5
The Service Quality Gaps Model

Zeithaml, Parasuraman, and Berry, *Delivering Quality Service: Balancing Customer Perceptions and Expectations.*

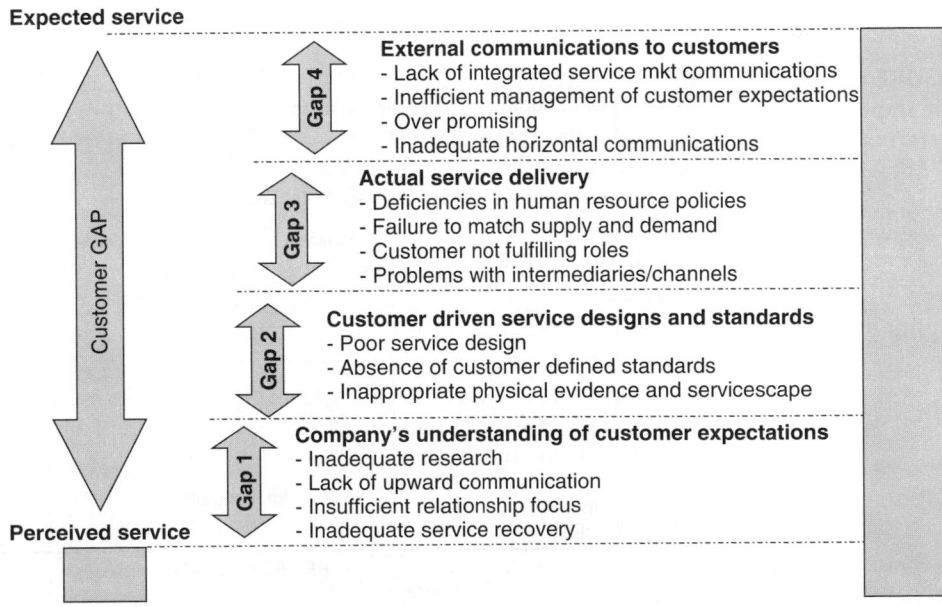

THE SERVICE QUALITY PROJECT IN LACD

Caterpillar and the dealer advisory panel decided to conduct a pilot program for CSAs by working through the gaps model in three dealers in Latin America. These dealers were chosen because they were responsible for key countries or territories in LACD and had shown promising customer and services focus in previous initiatives. Their combined sales exceeded 1 billion dollars and their strategic plans had identified CSAs as a key success factor for future growth.

A core team was formed consisting of members from Caterpillar LACD, corporate staffers from Peoria, and the pilot dealerships. Each pilot dealer assigned project leaders from their dealerships that served as members of the core project team. Initial training on services marketing and its elements were held at LACD headquarters in Miami on the key steps and processes and then follow-up occurred within the dealerships with district support from Caterpillar. Caterpillar LACD core team members were responsible for action items in the individual functions they represented such as product support, marketing, and communication. LACD also assumed the overall coordination of the implementation plan and managed the relationship with the consultant and strategic advisor.

GAPS ASSESSMENT WITH THREE PILOT DEALERSHIPS

After learning about the gaps model, members of the core team conducted a general assessment of each service gap based on feedback from the dealer advisory panel and other sources such as marketing research conducted both by Caterpillar itself and the dealers. They identified the following key issues in each of the four provider gaps.

The Listening Gap (Gap 1)

Using existing surveys conducted by Caterpillar called "customer value surveys," the team grouped survey items by the service quality dimension shown in Figure 5. Each dimension was then mapped on an importance/performance matrix shown in Figure 6.

FIGURE 6
The Importance/
Performance Matrix

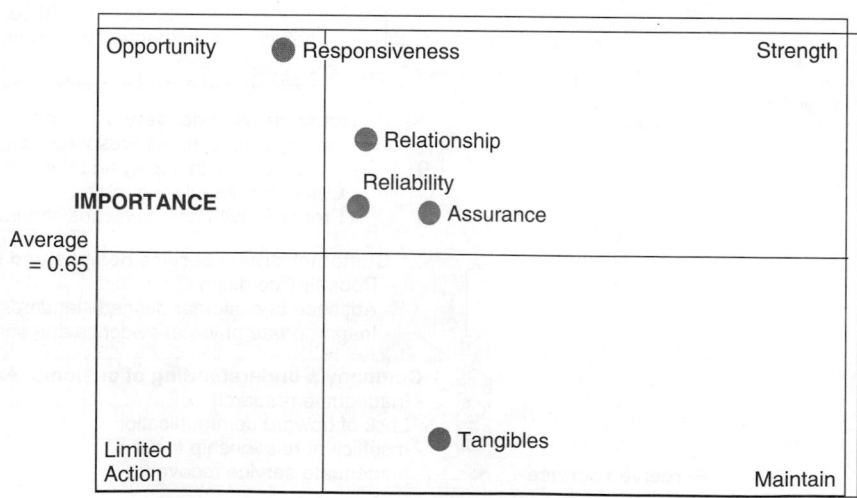

The research provided several key findings:

- **Responsiveness** was the most influential factor on customer loyalty and underperformed as compared to other factors. This dimension required urgent attention.
- **Empathy (Relationship), Reliability,** and **Assurance** tracked above average in perception and importance. They provided competitive differentiation but none of them were positioned as a dominant element of the value proposition. All of them show significant potential for improvement.
- Customer performance perception of **tangibles** was high but had relatively low impact on the overall customer loyalty.

To address these issues, the team concluded that (1) service reliability, responsiveness, and relationship needed improvement; (2) product differentiation and quality could not offset these issues; and (3) dealer product support operations and marketing capabilities played an equally important role in addressing these critical customer requirements. The team also recognized that customer surveys were sporadically performed and only partially designed for the purpose of service quality feedback. In support of Caterpillar's services strategy, the LACD service operation manager recognized that the customer value survey measures were inadequate for capturing and addressing customer satisfaction with individual interactions. The customer value surveys fell into the category of "relationship surveys" and were conducted annually. Post-interaction customer surveys, which captured customer reactions immediately after service calls, were thought to be necessary to prioritize operational improvement projects in the areas that were truly valued by the customer. Also, dealers and Caterpillar employees in the regions lacked the tools to interpret the results of surveys and to translate them into specific strategies.

Segmentation was also a key issue. The team estimated that accelerated growth could be best achieved by developing and communicating attractive service packages to small customers. Analysis of various factors identified characteristics of certain groups of small customers that were good targets. Overall satisfaction and loyalty indicators of some customers were significantly better and CSA renewal rates were notably higher. At the same time, these dealers had a higher share of wallet with these CSA customers, and the continuous experience and constant customer contact allowed dealers to identify, quote, and win many repeat repair opportunities. These customers would be ideal to focus on as the pilot project unfolded.

The Service Designs and Standards Gap (Gap 2)

The project identified a number of important issues in the standards and measures gap. First, currently very few CSAs were created, branded, positioned, and marketed based upon the timing, piece of mind, risk reduction, relationship, or convenience they provided to customers. CSAs were created in an ad hoc manner; they varied across dealerships and often across customers within dealerships. With this variability, it was never quite clear what had been promised to customers and expectations often were not met. Second, while machine salespeople felt very comfortable selling the attributes and benefits of the heavy equipment, they were unsure about what to offer and promise in the CSAs, largely because salespeople were not the employees who delivered on the CSAs. Further, CSA selling materials did not exist for them to understand what was possible and what options could be offered. Third, performance standards were typically operationally focused and not customer driven.

Dealers had different opinions on what customers expected and measurement to standards was not captured except on an ad-hoc basis. One difficulty in making promises involved the fact that customers were often located far from dealers, meaning that travel time complicated the process of setting standards. Among other things, the absence of standards and measures made it difficult to know what to promise customers when problems occurred. Dealerships were organized in silos—sales, product support, parts—and interacted inconsistently with each other and rarely planned together. Finally, each of the Latin American countries was different in structure, cultures, and laws, making the sharing of practices less than ideal.

Provider Gap 3: The Service Performance Gap

There were a number of major issues identified in Gap 3. First, there was an inadequate supply of qualified mechanics and few sources to find new ones. Technicians were also selected, trained, and rewarded for their technical performance. Attention was not given to their interaction or communication skills, which could become very important in describing issues to customers and in suggesting additional work that should be done on machines.

The lack of teamwork and communication among parts, service, and sales departments made the provision of service difficult. Formal ways to communicate about what should be done, what had been accomplished, and how well it had been performed did not exist. Dealers did not have a reliable system for keeping track of which customer machines had reached their service intervals, the contractual time for service. The scheduling process for field technicians was complex and based on cumbersome systems, which further complicated timely and responsive technician appointments.

Customers contributed to the difficulties in this gap. When they called for service, they often did not tell the dealers where their machines were physically located on the customer's property. Many customers actually forgot to inform the dealer that their machines had reached the service interval and were due for service.

Supply and demand often did not match, as most customers wanted machines maintained and inspected with little advance notice or after business hours. During peak construction session (e.g., in spring and early summer) the industry frequently suffered from technician shortages. Equally of concern were slow times when few customers needed or wanted repairs.

Finally the actual inspection and recommendation reports provided as part of the CSAs (and eagerly consulted and stored by customers) were functional but unattractively presented.

Provider Gap 4: The Communication Gap

Caterpillar promotion material almost exclusively focused on product features and benefits. At the time the project began, there were no brochures or advertisements describing CSAs, which limited the ability to sell CSAs both externally and internally. Externally, customers could not be certain that Caterpillar could deliver something for which there were no tangibles representations or written descriptions. Customers could not compare different options or packages and evaluate those against alternative services. Different types of CSAs were named and described the same way and carried no specific slogans or descriptions that easily explained the difference in value.

Internally, these materials would have helped employees understand what the service offerings were and how they differed. The absence of clearly defined service features occasionally led to over-customization or over-promising. The lack of written communication also confused the verbal communication. The sales force had no consistent selling process or message that explained and differentiated the individual CSA offerings. This created an unclear competitive positioning.

DECISIONS AND IMPLEMENTATION AS THE PILOT BEGAN IN 2007

Now that the team had learned the basics about service quality delivery and assessed the state of each service quality gap for the three pilot dealers, they were ready to develop a plan for developing, designing, and delivering CSAs in the three dealerships. They knew that they had a great deal of ground to cover and that they faced many challenges. They also knew that LACD's successful development and deployment of CSAs was essential. As they met to plan their next steps, they laid out some of the issues most on their minds.

What else did they need to learn in Gap 1 about customer needs and expectations? They had general information from the customer value surveys, but this information did not tell them what features customers expected in the CSAs. What were they and how could they find out? In particular, how could they find out what they needed to know to established standards in Gap 2?

Should they offer different CSAs to the different segments of general construction? What would that imply for research, standards, and implementation?

What standards and measures should be set in Gap 2 to deliver to customer expectations? How formal should they be? How should they create and design the new CSAs? How should they get everyone in the dealerships to learn about them and get on board to deliver them?

How should the dealerships overcome all the Gap 3 issues that they faced in order to insure consistent delivery?

What internal and external materials were necessary to communicate the CSAs to salespeople and customers? What else would be needed?

Credits

Page 273, ©Tom Bean/DRK Photo.

Page 276, Courtesy of PETsMart.

Chapter 10

Page 285, Courtesy FedEx Corporation.

Page 290, Courtesy Four Seasons; Photographer: Frank Herholdt. Del.

Page 293, Royalty-Free/CORBIS.

Page 297, Benelux Press/Taxi/Getty Images.

Page 303, Courtesy John Robert's Spa.

Chapter 11

Page 312, Courtesy Marriott International, Inc.

Page 315, Courtesy Build-A-Bear Workshop.

Page 320, Mario Tama/Getty Images.

Page 322, *No credit.*

Page 324, AP Photo/Ralph Radford.

Page 327, Courtesy Holland America.

Page 328, Courtesy Cheers Boston.

Page 333, Photo Courtesy of Mayo Clinic Scottsdale.

Page 335, Courtesy McDonald's USA, LLC.

Chapter 12

Page 348, John A. Rizzo/Getty Images.Digital Vision/ Getty Images.

Page 373, Courtesy of Yellow Roadway Corporation.

Chapter 13

Page 392, David Madison/Stone/Getty Images.

Page 399, NCR FastLane™ Self Checkout from NCR Corporation.

Page 403, Courtesy of the National Library of Medicine.

Page 406, ©2008 Weight Watchers International, Inc. Reprinted courtesy of Weight Watchers.com.

Page 410, AP Photo/Peter Cosgrove.

Chapter 14

Page 416, Photo by Andrew H. Walker/Getty Images.

Page 420, Reprinted with permission of Starbuck's Coffee Company.

Page 426, ©Keren Su/CORBIS.

Page 433, Courtesy H&R Block.

Page 435, Courtesy ING North America Insurance Company.

Chapter 15

Page 447, Photodisc/Getty Images.

Page 449, Courtesy Cemex.

Page 450, Ryan McVay/Getty Images.

Page 452, Steve Mason/Getty Images.

Page 457, Getty Images.

Page 463, Ryan McVay/Getty Images.

Page 466, Doug Menuez/Getty Images.

Chapter 16

Page 478, Courtesy GEICO.

Page 482, Courtesy DHL Express; Agency: OgilvyOne Worldwide.

Page 488, Courtesy of Travelers and Fallon Worldwide.

Page 489, Courtesy GEICO.

Page 493, Courtesy of the Sierra Club.

Page 498 top, Courtesy Virgin Atlantic Airway.

Page 498 bottom, Red Advertising & Marketing/ Barbados W.I.; Courtesy Virgin Atlantic Airway.

Chapter 17

Page 516, AP Photo/The Patriot-News, John C. Whitehead.

Index